# ASP.NET: The Complete Reference

# ASP.NET: The Complete Reference

Matthew MacDonald



**McGraw-Hill**/Osborne

New York Chicago San Francisco Lisbon
London Madrid Mexico City Milan New Delhi
San Juan Seoul Singapore Sydney Toronto

**McGraw-Hill**/Osborne
2600 Tenth Street
Berkeley, California 94710
U.S.A.

To arrange bulk purchase discounts for sales promotions, premiums, or fund-raisers, please contact **McGraw-Hill/**Osborne at the above address. For information on translations or book distributors outside the U.S.A., please see the International Contact Information page immediately following the index of this book.

**ASP.NET: The Complete Reference**



1234567890 DOC DOC 01987654321

ISBN 0-07-219513-4

**Publisher**
Brandon A. Nordin

**Vice President & Associate Publisher**
Scott Rogers

**Acquisitions Editor**
Jane Brownlow

**Acquisitions Coordinator**
Emma Acker

**Project Manager**
Jenn Tust

**Freelance Project Manager**
Laurie Stewart

**Technical Editor**
Tim Verycruysse

**Copy Editor**
Lunaea Weatherstone

**Proofreaders**
Sarah Kaminker
Kelly Marshall

**Indexer**
Jack Lewis

**Computer Designer**
Kate Kaminski,
Happenstance Type-O-Rama

**Illustrator**
Jeffrey Wilson,
Happenstance Type-O-Rama

**Series Design**
Peter Hancik

This book was composed with QuarkXPress 4.11 on a Macintosh G4.

**For**
**Faria**

## About the Author

**Matthew MacDonald** is an author, educator, and MCSD developer in all things Visual Basic and .NET. He's worked with Visual Basic and ASP since their initial versions and watched with amazement as they've evolved into modern object-oriented programming tools. Matthew is a regular contributor to developer journals such as *ASPToday*, *C#Today*, and *Inside Visual Basic*, a contributor to several books about programming, and the author of *The Book of VB .NET*. Email him with criticism, adulation, and everything in between at CompleteReference@prosetech.com.

# Contents at a Glance

## Part III Working with Data



## Part IV Web Services



## Part V Advanced ASP.NET



## Part VI ASP.NET Reference

# Contents

## Part IV

## Web Services

# Acknowledgments

This book could never have been completed without the tireless work of many others. At McGraw-Hill, Emma Acker and Jane Brownlow were instrumental in seeing the project through its many stages and occasional growing pains. Tim Verycruysse provided valuable feedback on each and every chapter, and numerous others have worked behind the scenes to ensure that indexing, figures, and copy editing worked out as planned. I owe them all heartfelt thanks.

I also can't overestimate the importance of the .NET development community, which is alive and well—sharing tips and undocumented secrets in periodicals, newsgroups, and countless web sites. I hope that all the readers of this book will add their voices to this world.

Lastly, I should thank my parents (all four of them) for all the things that parents do, and my wife, who is endlessly supportive and as dedicated to my dreams as I am.

# Introduction

ASP (Active Server Pages) is a relatively new technology that has already leapt through several stages of evolution. It was introduced about five years ago as an easy way to add dynamic content to ordinary web pages. Since then, it's quickly transformed into something entirely different: a platform for creating advanced web applications, including e-commerce shops, data-driven portal sites, and just about anything else you can find on the Internet.

As a result of this transformation, ASP developers have become experts in compromise. They've created innovative solutions using custom components, include files, and other tricks in order to manage the tangle of scripting code and provide advanced features. With a little work, it's possible—but not easy—to work with transactions, databases, and remote components. In other words, what began as a simple solution for creating interactive web pages has become a complicated discipline that requires knowledge in several fields and some painful experience.

The .NET platform promises to change all that. The drawback is the fairly serious learning curve involved in mastering a whole new framework. The good news is that this framework is designed for web applications from the ground up. It's well planned, well organized, and easier to learn than traditional ASP. It's also stuffed full of prebuilt functionality that can make many common tasks effortless.

## What this Book Covers

This book explores ASP.NET, which is a core part of Microsoft's new .NET framework. The .NET framework is actually a collection of different technologies. In order to master ASP.NET, you need to learn how to write code in the VB .NET language (the successor to Visual Basic), how to master the .NET class library (which provides tools for everything from sending email to managing disconnected data), and how to program the new event-driven web form model.

This book covers these new topics comprehensively, moving from basics to advanced concepts. As a side effect, you'll find that you learn about many topics that would interest any .NET developer, even a desktop application programmer. For example, you'll learn about component-based programming, structured exception handling, and how to access files, XML, and relational databases. You'll also learn about the key topics that are required to master web applications, such as state management, web controls, and Web Services.

## Who Should Read this Book

This book is aimed at experienced developers who have programmed in ASP or Visual Basic before. However, .NET is an entirely new programming framework, which means even experienced developers will feel a little like beginners. For that reason, this book begins with the fundamentals: VB .NET and C# syntax, the basics of object-oriented programming, and the philosophy of the .NET framework. After that, we'll build up from ASP.NET basics to advanced examples that show the techniques you'll use in real-world web applications.

### What You Need to Read this Book

If you are just starting with ASP.NET, you should check that you have all the necessary ingredients to create, test, and host web applications:

- To develop on the .NET framework and host a web site, your computer requires Windows 2000 Professional or Windows XP (with the optional Internet Information Services component installed).
- The only software you need to create ASP.NET applications is the .NET framework. You can download the redistributable installation files (provided you have a fast Internet connection) from http://www.asp.net/ or http://www.gotdotnet.com/.
- For the best results, you should purchase the full Visual Studio. NET package. This product includes the .NET framework and the Visual Studio .NET code editor, which comes complete with countless productivity enhancements and timesavers. You don't need Visual Studio .NET to read this book and create ASP.NET applications, but you will find that it simplifies your life a great deal. Everything you need to know about Visual Studio .NET is described in Chapter 8.

## The Online Samples

To master ASP.NET, you need to experiment with it. One of the best ways for you to do this is to try out the code samples for this book, examine them, and dive in with your own modifications. To obtain the sample code, go to the companion web page at http://www.prosetech.com/CompleteReference/. You'll also find some links to additional resources, and any updates or errata that affect the book.

In addition, you can send your comments about this work to CompleteReference@prosetech.com. I won't be able to answer ASP.NET questions or critique your web pages, but I will be interested to read criticism, praise, or any other feedback about this work and the material it covered.

> **VB or C#?**
>
> ASP.NET applications can be designed with any .NET language, including Visual Basic .NET, C#, or even a third-party offering. This book describes the syntax for the two most common choices—VB .NET and C#—but for reasons of space, the examples in the book can't be provided in both languages. For that reason, I've standardized on VB .NET, which will be the natural migration path for current ASP developers who are familiar with VBScript. As you'll discover in the first couple of chapters, all .NET languages are created equal, and VB .NET and C# match features blow-for-blow, with only a few minor discrepancies.

## Overview

This book is divided into six separate parts. Unless you've already had experience with the .NET framework, the most productive way to read this book is in order from start to finish. Chapters later in the book sometimes incorporate features that were introduced earlier in order to create more well-rounded and realistic examples.

### Part I: ASP.NET Introduction

You could start coding in ASP.NET right away by following the examples in the second part of this book. But to really master ASP.NET, you need to understand a few fundamental concepts about the .NET framework.

Chapter 1 sorts through Microsoft's newest field of jargon, and explains what the .NET framework really does, and why we need it. Chapter 2 introduces you to VB .NET and C# with a comprehensive language reference, and Chapter 3 explains the basics of modern object-oriented programming. Chapter 4 gets you started with ASP.NET, leading you through the steps needed to create virtual directories, and plan a migration path for existing ASP sites.

## Part II: Developing ASP.NET Applications

The second part of this book delves into the heart of ASP.NET programming, introducing the new server-control model. You'll learn how to program a web page's user interface through its object layer. You'll also see some of ASP.NET's remarkable new web controls, such as the full-featured Calendar and the automatic validation controls.

This part also covers some key topics for web applications. Chapters 5 through 7 explain how to organize multiple web forms into an ASP.NET application. Chapter 8 introduces the Visual Studio .NET design environment. Chapter 10 describes different strategies for state management, and Chapter 11 presents different techniques for handling errors. Taken together, these chapters represent all the fundamentals you need to design web pages and create a basic ASP.NET web site.

## Part III: Working with Data

Almost all business software needs to work with data, and web applications are no exception. The majority of this part focuses on ADO.NET, Microsoft's new technology for retrieving and managing disconnected data. In Chapters 12 and 13 you'll learn how to create web sites that interact with relational databases. Chapters 14 and 15 explain how to use ASP.NET's built-in data-binding features and advanced data controls to create web pages that integrate attractive, customizable data displays with automatic support for paging, sorting, and editing.

Chapter 16 moves out of the database world and considers common file and email access tasks. Chapter 17 broadens the picture even further, and describes how ASP.NET applications can use the XML-support built into the .NET framework.

## Part IV: Web Services

Web Services are an entirely new addition to web programming and one of Microsoft's most heavily promoted new technologies. Using Web Services, you can create code routines and access them from other applications or other computers just as easily as you could use local, native code. Best of all, the whole process works with open standards such as SOAP and XML, ensuring that even applications on other platforms can access your services.

This part begins with an overview of Web Service technology in Chapter 18 and a description of the basic StockQuote Web Service. Chapter 19 shows how to enhance this service with state, caching, data objects, and transactions, while Chapter 20 shows how to consume it in another application, and presents a full sample client that interacts with Microsoft's TerraService over the Internet.

## Part V: Advanced ASP.NET

This part includes several additional topics that are useful for advanced web projects. Chapters 21 and 22 consider how you can create reusable components and web controls for ASP.NET applications. In Chapter 23, you'll learn how a careful use of caching can boost the performance of any web application. In Chapter 24, you'll learn how to use different security models to safeguard your site or provide subscription services.

Chapter 25 shifts focus to the IBuySpy case studies. Microsoft provides these sample sites to demonstrate the best way to design an e-commerce application or web portal. While they are incredibly useful examples, they are also hard to sort out at first glance and provide little developer documentation. This chapter dissects the samples, and shows you how they use the concepts and features demonstrated throughout this book.

## Part VI: ASP.NET Reference

The last part of this book provides a dense reference that lists web controls in Chapters 26 and 27, each with an illustration, control tag, and list of properties. Chapter 28 rounds out our coverage with an in-depth look at ASP.NET configuration files. You can turn to these chapters once you've learned the ASP.NET basics for quick, comprehensive information.

The Complete Reference

# Part I

## ASP.NET Introduction

The Complete Reference

# Chapter 1

## The .NET Framework

Once again, Microsoft is doing what it does best: creating innovative new technologies and wrapping them in marketing terms that cause widespread confusion. Most developers have finally started to sort out buzzwords like ActiveX and Windows DNA, and are now faced with a whole new set of jargon revolving around .NET and the CLR. So exactly what does it all mean?

This chapter examines the technologies that underlie .NET. I'll present a high-level overview that gives you your first taste of some of the radical changes that will affect ASP.NET applications, and some of the long-awaited improvements that are finally in place. I'll also explain the philosophy that led to the creation of the .NET platform, and show how it fits into the wider world of development—and Microsoft's long-term plans.

## The .NET Programming Framework

The starting point for any analysis of the .NET framework is the understanding that .NET is really a cluster of different technologies. It includes:

- **The .NET languages**, which include C# and Visual Basic .NET, the object-oriented and modernized successor to Visual Basic 6.0.
- **The Common Language Runtime (CLR)**, the .NET runtime engine that executes all .NET programs, and provides modern services such as automatic memory management, security, optimization, and garbage collection.
- **The .NET class library**, which collects thousands of pieces of prebuilt functionality that you can snap in to your applications. These are sometimes organized into technology sets, such as ADO.NET (the technology for creating database applications) and Windows Forms (the technology for creating desktop user interfaces).
- **ASP.NET**, the platform services that allow you to program web applications and Web Services in any .NET language, with almost any feature from the .NET class library.
- **Visual Studio .NET**, an optional development tool that contains a rich set of productivity and debugging features.

The division between these components is not sharp. For example, ASP.NET is sometimes used in a very narrow sense to refer to the portion of the .NET class library used to design web forms. On the other hand, ASP.NET is also used to refer to the whole topic of .NET web applications, which includes language and editor issues, and many fundamental pieces of the class library that are not web-specific. That's generally the way that the term is used in this book. Our exhaustive examination of ASP.NET includes .NET basics, the VB .NET language, and topics that any .NET developer could use, such as component-based programming and ADO.NET data access. The .NET class library and Common Language Runtime—the two fundamental parts of .NET—are shown in Figure 1-1.

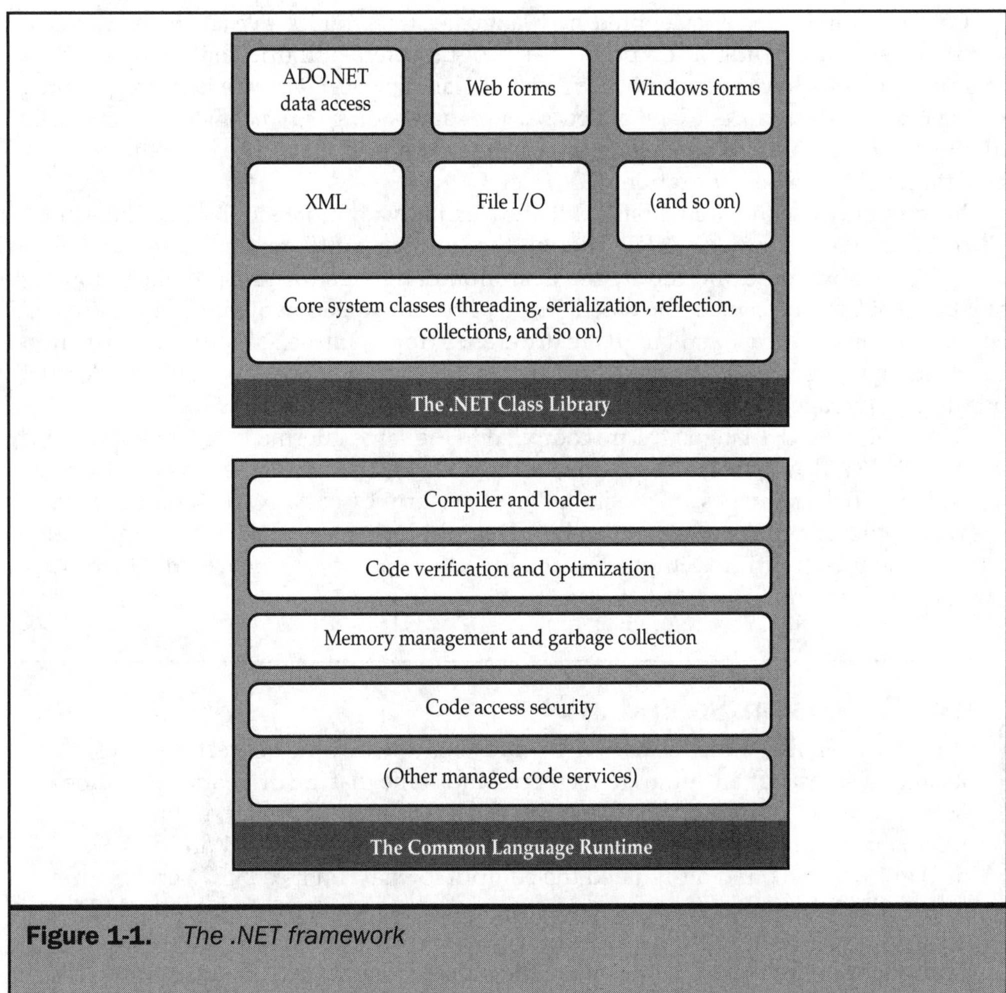


**Figure 1-1.** *The .NET framework*

## VB .NET, C#, and the .NET Languages

Visual Basic .NET (sometimes called VB .NET) is a redesigned language that improves on traditional Visual Basic, and even breaks compatibility with existing VB programs. Migrating to Visual Basic .NET is a stretch—and a process of discovery for most seasoned VB developers. The change is even more dramatic if you are an ASP developer used to the scaled-down capabilities of VBScript.

C#, on the other hand, is an entirely new language. It resembles Java and C++ in syntax, but there is no direct migration path. C++ programmers will find that many of the frustrating tangles have been removed from their language in C#, while Java programmers will find that C# introduces a host of new features and coding enhancements. In short, C#, like Visual Basic .NET, is an elegant, modern language ideal for creating the next generation of business applications.

Interestingly, C# and Visual Basic .NET are actually far more similar than Java and C# or Visual Basic 6 and VB .NET. Though the syntax is different, both use the .NET class library and are supported by the Common Language Runtime. In fact, almost any block of C# code can be translated, line by line, into an equivalent block of VB .NET code. There is the occasional language difference (for example, C# supports operator overloading while VB .NET does not), but for the most part, a developer who has learned one .NET language can move quickly and efficiently to another.

In fact, all the .NET languages are compiled to the same intermediate language, which is known as MSIL, or just IL. The CLR only runs IL code, which is the reason why the C# and VB .NET languages are so similar (and perform essentially the same). Figure 1-2 shows the compilation process, with a bit of simplification—in an ASP.NET application, a final machine-specific executable is cached on the web server to provide the best possible performance.

## The Confusion Behind .NET

As with most marketing terms, .NET represents a wide range of technologies, including some that are minor refinements and some that are dramatic revolutions. Many of these ".NET technologies" are not distributed together. In fact, Microsoft has already named the new server-targeted version of Windows XP as Windows .NET and designated the computers that run it as .NET servers. In traditional Microsoft style, new marketing terms are created infrequently and reused for a variety of products. As time goes on, more and more products will be brought under the .NET name, and the name will gradually mean less and less. We may even see an Office .NET or SQL Server .NET before the madness subsides.

Some developers have hesitated to embrace .NET because they believe they will be forced to subscribe to Microsoft's .NET My Services (formerly codenamed Hailstorm). These services, which are built on the .NET Web Service foundation, allow developers to use centralized user authentication, information, and notification services—for a cost. The debate over the validity of .NET My Services is heated, but it really has little to do with ASP.NET development. You certainly won't need to use (or even understand) any part of the .NET My Services product to create full-featured web sites.

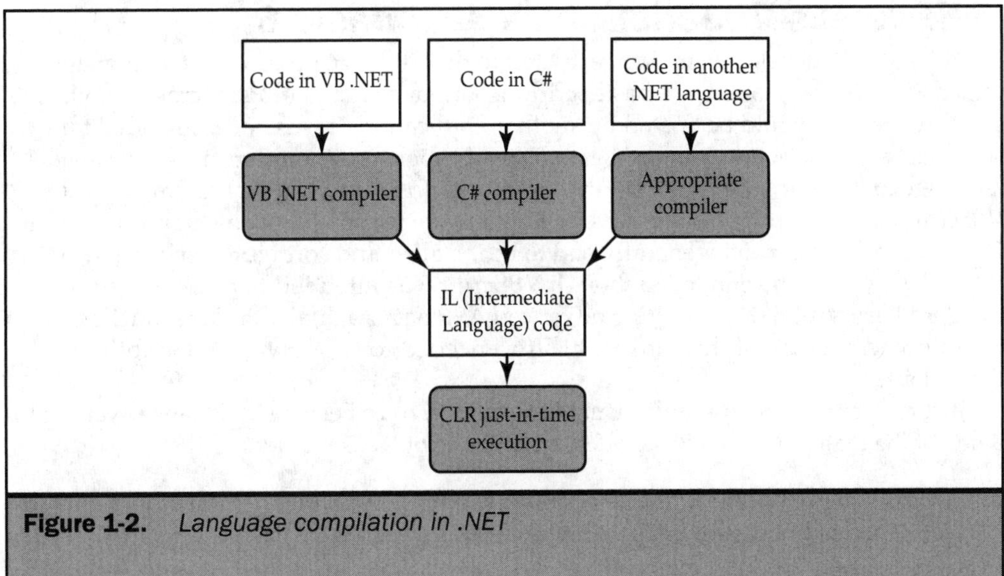


**Figure 1-2.** *Language compilation in .NET*

Chapter 2 provides a comprehensive summary of C# and VB .NET syntax. Unfortunately, a book of this size does not have the space to list examples in both languages. VB .NET, because it allows easier migration from existing VBScript pages, is used as a standard in all discussions and examples.

## Other .NET Languages

C# and VB .NET are not the only choices for ASP.NET development. When creating a .NET web application, you can use any .NET language, including JScript .NET or the Java-clone J# .NET (currently available as a separate download). You can even use a .NET language provided by a third-party developer, such as a .NET version of Eiffel or Perl. This increasing range of language choices is possible because Microsoft has released a set of guidelines called the CLS (Common Language Specifications) that define basic requirements and standards that allow other companies to write languages that run under the CLR (Common Language Runtime).

In this book, I'll only consider the two most popular and common language choices: C# and VB .NET. Once you understand the fundamentals of the .NET framework, you're free to explore other languages, although some (such as JScript .NET) may only support a limited set of the full range of possible features.

## VB .NET versus VBScript and Visual Basic 6

Traditional ASP development was restricted to the VBScript programming language, which was first developed as a basic scripting language for writing macros and other simple code that would be hosted by another application. It was never intended for sophisticated, interactive web applications, and expert programmers had to strain the language to its limit to create first-rate ASP pages. To get around many limitations in VBScript, advanced pages that used data access or transactions needed to rely on separate COM components, which generally had to be installed and configured separately on the web server. In the end, even though VBScript was intended to be easier to use than ordinary Visual Basic, writing advanced ASP pages actually became much more complicated because of the additional effort needed to circumvent VBScript's limitations.

Just replacing VBScript with Visual Basic would have been a significant advantage. Some of the features Visual Basic offers that VBScript lacks include:

**Access to the Win32 API and platform services** VBScript, on the other hand, is automatically isolated by the scripting host and has many security-related restrictions.

**Typed programming** VBScript doesn't allow you strict control over data types, and works with special "variant" variables instead, which are supposed to be easier to use. Unfortunately, they also introduce data type conversion problems and difficult-to-detect errors.

**Event-driven programming** Unlike Visual Basic, VBScript is notoriously disorganized, with little flexibility to group or organize code so it can be easily debugged and reused.

**Support for objects** Visual Basic doesn't have perfect object-oriented features, but they are still light years over what VBScript can accomplish, making it impossible to design a modern multi-layered application.

However, ASP.NET has completely skipped over this stage in evolution and moved directly to the advanced capabilities of Visual Basic .NET. This latest version of Visual Basic is a complete redesign that answers years of unmet complaints and extends the VB language into new territory. Some of the new features include:

**True object-oriented programming** Inheritance, interfaces, polymorphism, constructors, shared members and abstract classes… the list goes on, and Visual Basic .NET has them all closely integrated into the language.

**Language refinements** Every aspect of the VB language has been tweaked and refined. You can now overload functions, declare and assign variables on the same line, and use shortened assignment syntax. Many of these enhancements mean that existing VB (and VBScript) code won't compile.

**Structured error handling** The end of the aggravating On Error Goto has finally arrived. VB .NET introduces .NET's new standard: clean, concise structure exception handling.

**Strong typing** VBScript used variants, but even Visual Basic 6 could perform some automatic variable conversions that would cause unusual bugs. VB .NET allows you to rein in your program and prevent possible errors with strict type checking.

These are only some of the changes, but they are enough to show you that VB .NET is separated from VBScript by two major evolutionary leaps. All of these features are available in other .NET languages such as C#, but Visual Basic and VBScript developers will have to deal with some of the greatest changes from what they know.

### Learning About Visual Basic .NET and Objects

These dramatic changes present some challenges to even the most experienced of developers. In the next two chapters, we'll sort through the new syntax of Visual Basic .NET, and I'll introduce the basics of object-oriented programming. By learning the fundamentals before you start creating simple web pages, you'll face less confusion and move more rapidly to advanced topics like database access and web services.

## The Common Language Runtime

The Common Language Runtime (CLR) is the engine that supports all the .NET languages. Most modern languages use runtimes, such as msvbvm60.dll for Visual Basic 6 applications and mscrt40.dll for C++ applications. These runtimes may provide libraries used by the language, or they may have the additional responsibility of executing the code (as with Java).

Runtimes are nothing new, but the CLR represents a radical departure from Microsoft's previous strategy. To start, the CLR and .NET framework are much larger and more ambitious. The CLR also provides a whole set of related services such as code verification, optimization, and garbage collection, and can run the code from any .NET language.

The CLR is the reason that some developers have accused .NET of being a Java clone. As with Java, .NET applications run inside a special managed environment with garbage collection and an intermediate language, and acquire features from a rich class library. (The claim is fairly silly. It's true that .NET is quite similar to Java in key respects, but it's also true that every programming language "steals" and improves from previous programming languages. This includes Java, which adopted parts of the C/C++ language and syntax. Of course, in many other aspects .NET differs just as radically from Java as it does from VBScript code.)

The implications of the CLR are wide-ranging:

**Deep language integration** C# and VB .NET, like all .NET languages, compile to a special Intermediate Language called MSIL (or just IL). In other words, the CLR makes no distinction between different languages—in fact, it has no way of knowing what language was used to create an executable. This is far more than just language compatibility; it's really language integration.

**No more "DLL hell"** IL programs store extra information about their classes and the components they require (called metadata). The CLR examines this information and automatically prevents an application from using the wrong version of a component.

**Side-by-side execution** The CLR also has the ability to load more than one version of a component at a time. In other words, you can update a component many times, and the correct version will be loaded and used for each application. As a side effect, multiple versions of the .NET framework can be installed, meaning that you will be able to upgrade to new versions of ASP.NET without replacing the current version or needing to rewrite your applications.

**Fewer errors** Whole categories of errors are impossible with the CLR. For example, the CLR monitors memory, automatically removes objects that aren't being used with its garbage collection, and prevents the wide variety of memory mistakes that are possible with pointers and C++. For Visual Basic programmers, many of these advantages are nothing new—they are similar to features of the traditional VB framework.

Along with these truly revolutionary benefits, there are some other potential drawbacks, and some issues that haven't yet been answered:

**Performance** A typical ASP application will gain considerably in performance because of various improvements, including automatic caching and precompiling. However, .NET components or other applications probably won't match the blinding speed of well-written C++, because the CLR imposes many other safety checks and additional overhead. Generally, this will be a factor only in a few performance-critical high-workload applications (like real-time games). With high-volume web applications, the potential bottlenecks are rarely processor-related, but usually tied to the speed of an external resource such as a database or the server's file system. ASP.NET caching and well-written database code can ensure excellent performance for a web application.

**Code transparency** The IL language is much easier to disassemble, meaning that if you distribute a compiled component, other programmers may have an easier time determining how your code works. This also isn't much of an issue for ASP.NET applications, which aren't distributed, but are hosted on a secure web server.

**Cross-platform?** No one is entirely sure whether .NET is destined for use on other operating systems and platforms. Currently, .NET programs will make the switch to upcoming 64-bit versions of Windows without a problem. Other rumors persist, including suggestions that we will see an ASP.NET service that runs on Apache, or a limited .NET framework that allows users to develop Unix applications. This is just speculation, however, and .NET will probably never have the wide reach of a language like Java because it incorporates too many different platform-specific and operating-system–specific technologies and features.

## The .NET Class Library

The .NET class library is a giant repository of classes that provide prefabricated functionality for everything from reading an XML file to sending an email message. If you've had any exposure to Java, you may already be familiar with the idea of a class library. However, the .NET class library is more ambitious and comprehensive than just about any other programming framework. Any .NET language can use its features, by interacting with a consistent set of objects. This helps encourage consistency among different .NET languages, and removes the need to install numerous separate components and SDKs.

Some parts of the class library include features you'll never need to use (such as the classes used to create desktop applications with the Windows interface). Other parts of the class library are targeted directly at web development, enabling Web Services, web form user interface, and countless other utility classes. Still more classes can be used in a number of different programming scenarios, and aren't specific to web or Windows development. These include the base set of classes that define common variable types, and the classes for file I/O, data access, and XML information, to name just a few.

Other characteristics of the .NET framework include:

**Open standards** Microsoft currently provides programming tools that allow you to work with many open standards, such as XML and SOAP. In .NET, however, many of these standards are baked in to the framework. For example, ADO.NET (Microsoft's data access technology) uses XML natively, behind the scenes. Similarly, Web Services work automatically through XML and HTTP. This deep integration of open standards makes cross-platform work much easier.

**Disconnected model** The .NET framework inherits many of the principles of Microsoft's DNA programming model. This includes an emphasis on distributed and Internet applications. Technologies like ADO.NET are designed from the ground up for disconnected, scalable access, and don't need any special code to be used in an ASP.NET application.

**Emphasis on infrastructure** Microsoft's philosophy is that they will provide the tedious infrastructure so that application developers only need to write business-specific code. For example, the .NET framework automatically handles files, message queues, databases, and remote method calls (through Web Services). You just add the logic needed for your organization.

## ASP.NET

ASP.NET is a part of the .NET framework. As a programmer, you interact with it by using the appropriate types in the class library to write programs and design web forms. When a client requests a page, the ASP.NET service runs (inside the CLR environment), executes your code, and creates a final HTML page to send to the client.

To understand ASP.NET's features, it helps to understand ASP's limitations. In other words, before you can understand the .NET solution, you need to understand the problems developers are struggling with today.

**Scripting limitations** ASP applications rely on VBScript, which suffers from a number of limitations. To overcome these problems, developers usually need to add separately developed components, which add a new layer of complexity. In ASP.NET, web pages are designed in a modern .NET language, not a scripting language.

**Headaches with deployment and configuration** Because of the way COM and ASP work, you can't easily update the components your web site uses. Often, you need to manually stop and restart the server, which just isn't practical on a live web server. Changing configuration options can be just as ugly. ASP.NET introduces a slew of new features to allow web sites to be dynamically updated and reconfigured.

**No application structure** ASP code is inserted directly into a web page along with HTML markup. The resulting tangle has nothing in common with today's modern, object-oriented languages. As a result, web form code can rarely be reused or modified without hours of effort.

**State limitations** One of ASP's strongest features is its integrated session state facility. However, session state is useless in scenarios where a web site is hosted by several separate web servers. In this scenario, a client might access server B while its session information is trapped on server A and essentially abandoned. ASP.NET corrects this problem by allowing state to be stored in a central repository: either a separate process or a database that all servers can access.

## Visual Studio .NET

The last part of .NET is the optional Visual Studio .NET editor, which provides a rich environment where you can rapidly create advanced applications. Some of its features include:

**Automatic error detection** You could save hours of work when Visual Studio .NET detects and reports an error before you try to run your application. Potential problems are underlined, just like the "spell-as-you-go" feature found in many word processors.

**Debugging tools** Visual Studio .NET retains its legendary debugging tools that allow you to watch your code in action and track the contents of variables.

**Page design** You can create an attractive page with drag-and-drop ease using Visual Studio .NET's integrated web form designer.

**IntelliSense** Visual Studio .NET provides statement completion for recognized objects, and automatically lists information such as function parameters in helpful ToolTips.

### Does this Book Use Visual Studio .NET?

I recommend Visual Studio .NET highly. However, in this book you will start with the basics of ASP.NET, code behind, and web control development using Notepad. This is the best way to get a real sense of what is happening behind the scenes. Once you understand how ASP.NET works, you can quickly master Visual Studio .NET, which I introduce in Chapter 8. I hope you'll use Visual Studio .NET for all the remaining examples, but if you prefer Notepad or a third-party tool, you can use that instead—with a little more typing required.

The Complete Reference

# Chapter 2

## Learning the .NET Languages

In order to create an ASP.NET application, you need to choose a .NET language to program it. If you're an ASP or Visual Basic developer, the natural choice is VB .NET. If you are a long-time Java programmer or old-hand C++ coder, C# will probably suit you best. VBScript isn't an option—as discussed in Chapter 1, it just doesn't have the range, flexibility, and elegance a modern language demands.

In this chapter, you'll learn about the basic features of all .NET languages. This includes the common set of data types, types of variable operations, and use of functions, events, enumerations, and attributes. These ingredients are built into the Common Language Runtime. They are available (and work almost exactly the same) in any .NET language.

While you learn about these elements, you'll also learn the corresponding VB .NET or C# syntax you need to use them. This syntax is really just the top layer of .NET, which sits like a thin skin over a common engine (the CLR). The more you learn about .NET, the more you'll realize that all .NET languages share the same concepts and require the same understanding.

## The .NET Languages

The .NET framework ships with three code languages: Visual Basic, C#, and JScript. These languages are, for the most part, functionally equivalent. Microsoft has worked hard to eliminate language conflicts in the .NET framework. These battles (while entertaining) slow down adoption, distract from the core framework features, and make it difficult for the developer community to solve problems together and share solutions. If you believe Microsoft, choosing VB .NET instead of C# is just a lifestyle choice and won't affect the performance, interoperability, feature set, or development time of your applications. Surprisingly, this ambitious claim is essentially true.

.NET also allows other third-party developers to release languages that are just as feature rich as VB .NET or C#. These languages (which already include Eiffel, Perl, Python, and even COBOL) "snap in" to the .NET framework effortlessly. The secret is the special machine.config configuration file that is installed with the .NET framework. In one of its sections, it lists the language compilers that are currently installed.

```
<!-- Other configuration settings omitted. >
<compilers>
  <compiler language="c#;cs;csharp" extension=".cs"
            type="Microsoft.CSharp.CSharpCodeProvider, System,
            Version=1.0.2411.0 />
  <compiler language="vb;visualbasic;vbscript" extension=".vb"
            type="Microsoft.VisualBasic.VBCodeProvider, System,
            Version=1.0.2411.0 />
  <compiler language="js;jscript;javascript" extension=".js"
            type="Microsoft.JScript.JScriptCodeProvider,
```

```
Microsoft.JScript" />
</compilers>
```

To install another .NET language, all you need to do is copy the compiler to your computer and add a line to the machine.config file. (Typically, a setup program will perform these steps for you automatically.) The new compiler will then transform your code creations into a sequence of Intermediate Language (IL) instructions.

IL is the only "language" that the Common Language Runtime recognizes. When you create the code for an ASP.NET web form, it is changed into IL using the VB .NET compiler (vbc.exe), the C# compiler (csc.exe), or the JScript compiler (jsc.exe). You can perform the compilation manually or let ASP.NET handle it automatically when a web page is requested. We'll discuss the difference between these two techniques in Chapter 5.

## Learning the Language Basics

This chapter presents a fairly dense language overview. It assumes you are already familiar with programming basics such as variables, data types, and functions. It won't teach you how to program, but it will give you a good, detailed review of the changes that have been implemented in the .NET languages.

You may find it easiest to browse through this chapter to get a basic idea about language syntax, without reading every section. You can then return to this chapter later as a reference when needed. As I hinted before, you can program an ASP.NET application without mastering the fundamentals, but this knowledge is often what separates the casual programmer from the legendary programming guru.

### This Chapter Uses Code Snippets

In .NET, every piece of code is located inside a namespace and some sort of class. The examples in this chapter show individual lines and code snippets that show the syntax of important code constructs. You won't actually be able to use these in an application until you've read through the next chapter, and learned about objects and .NET types.

## Basic Differences Between C# and VB .NET

As you learn more about C# and VB .NET, you'll start to understand how similar they really are. Almost any line in one of these languages can be converted into an equivalent line in the other. Often, these lines look virtually identical. That said, there are some minor but important differences that can frustrate a user trying to switch between C# and VB .NET.

## Case Sensitivity

C# is case-sensitive, while VB .NET is not. This isn't much of a problem for a C# programmer writing VB code, but it can frustrate a VB programmer who doesn't realize that keywords, variables, and functions must be typed with the exact case. Remember, in C# the variables "name" and "Name" are not equivalent!

## Commenting

C# provides two types of comments. C# comments usually start with two slashes and continue for the entire current line. Optionally, C# programmers can also comment out multiple lines using the /* and */ comment brackets.

VB .NET comments always start with an apostrophe and continue for the entire current line.

#### VB .NET

```
' A VB comment.
```

#### C#

```
// C# comment.
/* A multi-line
   C# comment. */
```

## Line Termination

C# uses a semicolon (;) as a line-termination character. Every line of C# code must end with this semicolon, except when you are defining a block structure such as a procedure, a conditional statement, or a looping construct. By omitting this semicolon, you can easily split a line of code over multiple physical lines.

In Visual Basic, there is no line-termination character. To break a code statement over multiple lines, you need to insert a space followed by the line-continuation character, which is an underscore.

#### VB .NET

```
' A code statement split over several lines in VB.
MyValue = MyValue1 + MyValue2 + _
          MyValue3
```

**C#**

```
// A code statement split over several lines in C#.
myValue = myValue1 + myValue2 +
          myValue3;
```

## Conciseness

C# is more concise. In C# programming, it's common to define a variable on the same line that you use it with the new keyword. You'll also see that loops, conditional code, and functions are preceded by a declaration, and wrapped in curly { } braces.

Visual Basic, on the other hand, uses a closing statement (such as Next, End Loop, End If, or End Sub).

**VB .NET**

```
' A VB If block.
If Condition = True Then
    ' Do something here.
End If
```

**C#**

```
' A C# if block.
if (condition == true)
{
    // Do Something here.
}
```

## Strings and Escaped Characters

C# treats strings a little differently than VB .NET. It interprets any embedded slash as a special character. For example, \n means add a new line (carriage return). In order to specify the actual slash character (for example, in a directory name), two slashes are required.

**VB .NET**

```
' A VB variable holding a path.
Path = "c:\MyApp\MyFiles"
```

**C#**

```
// A C# variable holding a path.
path = "c:\\MyApp\\MyFiles";
```

## Data Types

Every .NET language uses the same variable data types. Different languages may provide slightly different names (for example, a VB .NET Integer is the same as a C# int), but the CLR makes no distinction. This allows the deep language integration that was discussed in Chapter 1. Because languages share the same data types, you can easily use classes from one .NET language in a client written in another .NET language. Variables can be exchanged natively, and no conversion is required.

In order to create this system, Microsoft needed to iron out many of the inconsistencies that existed between VBScript, Visual Basic 6, C++, and other languages. Their solution was to create a set of basic data types, which are provided in the .NET class library. These data types are shown in Table 2-1.

| Class Library Name | VB .NET Name | C# Name | Contains |
|---|---|---|---|
| Byte | Byte | byte | An integer from 0 to 255. |
| Int16 | Short | short | An integer from –32768 to 32767. |
| Int32 | Integer | int | An integer from –2,147,483,648 to 2,147,483,647. |
| Int64 | Long | long | An integer from about –9.2e18 to 9.2e18. |
| Single | Single | float | A single-precision floating point number from approximately –3.4e38 to 3.4e38. |
| Double | Double | double | A double-precision floating point number from approximately –1.8e308 to 1.8e308. |

**Table 2-1.** *Common Data Types*

| Class Library Name | VB .NET Name | C# Name | Contains |
|---|---|---|---|
| Decimal | Decimal | decimal | A 128-bit fixed-point fractional number that supports up to 28 significant digits. |
| Char | Char | char | A single 16-bit Unicode character. |
| String | String | string | A variable-length series of Unicode characters. |
| Boolean | Boolean | bool | A True or False value (or lowercase true or false in C#). |
| DateTime | Date | N/A* | Represents any date and time from 12:00:00 AM, January 1 of the year 1 in the Gregorian calendar to 11:59:59 PM, December 31, year 9999. Time values can resolve values to 100 nanosecond increments. Internally, this data type is stored as a 64-bit integer. |
| TimeSpan | N/A* | N/A* | Represents a period of time, as in 10 seconds or 3 days. The smallest possible interval is 1 "tick" (100 nanoseconds). |
| Object | Object | object | The ultimate base class of all .NET types. Can contain any data type or object. |

* If the language does not provide an alias for a given type, you can use the .NET class name.

**Table 2-1.** *Common Data Types (continued)*

### Data Type Changes from Visual Basic 6

Luckily for VB developers, the list of data types in .NET is quite similar to the data types from earlier versions. Some changes, however, were unavoidable:

- Visual Basic defined an Integer as a 16-bit number with a maximum value of 32,767. VB .NET, on the other hand, defines an Integer as a 32-bit number. Long now refers to a 64-bit integer, while Short refers to a 16-bit integer.
- The Currency data type has been replaced by Decimal, which supports more decimal places (and thus greater accuracy).
- Fixed-length strings are no longer supported.
- Variants are no longer supported and have been replaced with the generic Object type, which can hold any object or data type.
- The Date data type has increased range and precision and works slightly differently. Depending on your code, you may need to rewrite date manipulation code.

## Declaring Variables

To create a variable, you need to identify a data type and a variable name. In VB .NET, the name comes first, after a special Dim keyword. In C#, the data type starts the line.

#### VB .NET

```
Dim ErrorCode As Integer
Dim MyName As String
```

#### C#

```
int errorCode;
string myName;
```

In C#, the convention is to begin variable names with a lowercase letter, unless you are creating a public variable that can be seen from other classes. Public variables or properties should always use an initial capital.

You can also create a variable by using the type from the .NET class library. This approach produces identical variables. It's also a requirement if you need to create a variable to hold an object or a type of data that doesn't have an alias built into the language.

**VB .NET**

```
Dim ErrorCode As System.Int32
Dim MyName As System.String
```

**C#**

```
System.Int32 errorCode;
System.String myName;
```

These examples use fully qualified type names that indicate that the Int32 type is found in the System namespace (along with all the fundamental types). In Chapter 3, we'll discuss types and namespaces in more detail.

### What's in a Name: Data Types

You'll notice that the preceding examples don't use variable prefixes. Most Visual Basic and C++ programmers are in the habit of adding a few characters to the start of a variable name to indicate its data type. In .NET, this practice is de-emphasized because data types can be used in more flexible ways without any problem, and most variables hold references to full objects anyway. In this book, variable prefixes are not used, except for web controls, where it helps to distinguish lists, text boxes, buttons, and other common user interface elements. In your own programs, you should follow a consistent (typically company-wide) standard that may or may not adopt a system of variable prefixes.

## Initializers

You can also assign a value to a variable in the same line that you create it. This feature is common to C++ programmers, but a new addition to VB .NET.

**VB .NET**

```
Dim ErrorCode As Integer = 10
Dim MyName As String = "Matthew"
```

**C#**

```
int errorCode = 10;
string myName = "Matthew";
```

In Visual Basic, you can use a simple data variable without initializing it. Numbers will be automatically initialized to 0, and strings to an empty string (""). In C#, however, you must assign a value to a variable before you attempt to read from it. For example, the following statement will succeed in VB .NET, but would fail in C# if the Number variable had not been initialized to a value.

```
Number = Number + 1
```

## Arrays

Visual Basic programmers will find that arrays are one of the most profoundly changed language elements. In order to harmonize .NET languages, Microsoft decided that all arrays must start at a fixed lower bound of 0. There are no exceptions.

Arrays still have a few subtle differences in C# and in VB .NET, though. For example, when you create an array in VB .NET, you specify the upper bound, while in C# you specify the number of elements. This change is bound to go unnoticed by many programmers until it leads to inevitable errors.

**VB .NET**

```
' Create an array with 10 strings (from index 0 to index 9).
Dim StringArray(9) As String
```

**C#**

```
// Create an array with 9 strings (from index 0 to index 8).
// Unlike in VB .NET, you need to initialize the array with empty
// values in order to use it.
string[] stringArray = new string[9];
```

You can also fill an array with data at the same time that you create it. In this case, you don't need to explicitly specify the number of elements because .NET can determine it automatically.

**VB .NET**

```
Dim MyArray() As String = {"1", "2", "3", "4"}
```

**C#**

```
string[] myArray = {"1", "2", "3", "4"};
```

The same technique works for multi-dimensional arrays, except two sets of curly brackets are required:

**VB .NET**

```
Dim MyArray() As Integer = {{1, 1}, {2, 2}, {3, 3}, {4, 4}}
```

**C#**

```
int[] myArray = {{1, 1}, {2, 2}, {3, 3}, {4, 4}};
```

To access an array, you specify the index number. In Visual Basic, you use ordinary brackets, while in C# you use square brackets.

**VB .NET**

```
Dim Element As Integer
Element = MyArray(1, 2)
```

**C#**

```
int element;
element = myArray[1, 2];
```

Arrays can include any data type, including objects. They also automatically support read-only iteration. This means you can use a For Each syntax to loop through all the elements in an array. This is a common trick that is often used with collections, but .NET allows you to use it with arrays as well.

**VB .NET**

```
Dim StringArray() As String = {"one", "two", "three"}
Dim Element As String

For Each Element In MyStringArray
    ' This code loops three times, with the Element variable set to
    ' "one", then "two", and then "three".
Next
```

**C#**

```
string[] stringArray = {"one", "two", "three"};

// Note that you don't need to define the element variable first in C#.
// Instead, you define it "inside" the foreach brackets.
foreach (string element in myStringArray)
{
    // This code loops three times, with the element variable set to
    // "one", then "two", and then "three".
}
```

In a multi-dimensional array, the For Each iteration would move over each column in a single row first, and then move to the next row.

One nice feature that VB .NET offers but C# lacks is array redimensioning. In VB .NET, all arrays start with an initial size, and any array can be resized. To resize an array, you use the ReDim keyword.

```
Dim MyArray(10, 10) As Integer
ReDim MyArray(20, 20)
```

In this example, all the contents in the array will be erased when it is resized. To preserve the contents, you can use the optional Preserve keyword when redimensioning the array. However, if you are using a multi-dimensional array you will only be able to change the last dimension, or a runtime error will occur.

```
Dim MyArray(10, 10) As Integer
'Allowed, and the contents will remain.
ReDim Preserve MyArray(10, 20)
' Not allowed. A runtime error will occur.
ReDim Preserve MyArray(20, 20)
```

To achieve the same effect in C#, you need to write manual array copying code, or just use a collection class such as the ArrayList, which always allows a dynamic size.

### Collections Replace Arrays in Many Scenarios

In many cases, it's easier to use a full-fledged collection rather than an array. Collections are generally better suited to modern object-oriented programming and are used extensively in ASP.NET. The .NET class library provides many types of collection classes, including simple collections, sorted lists, key-indexed lists (dictionaries), and queues.

## Enumerations

An enumeration is group of related constants. In reality, every enumerated value just corresponds to a preset integer. In your program, however, you refer to an enumerated value by name, which makes your code clearer and helps to prevent errors.

Enumerations cannot be declared inside a procedure. Instead, they are declared at the class or module level using a special block structure.

**VB .NET**

```
' Define an enumeration called UserType with three possible values.
Enum UserType
    Admin
    Guest
    Invalid
End Enum
```

**C#**

```
// Define an enumeration called UserType with three possible values.
enum UserType
{
    Admin,
    Guest,
    Invalid
}
```

Now you can use the UserType enumeration as a special data type that is restricted to one of three possible values. You set or compare the enumerated value using a special dot syntax.

**VB .NET**

```
Dim NewUserType As UserType = UserType.Admin
```

**C#**

```
UserType newUserType = UserType.Admin;
```

Internally, enumerations are maintained as numbers. In the preceding example, 0 is automatically assigned to Admin, 1 to Guest, and 2 to Invalid. You can set a number directly into an enumeration, although this can lead to an undetected error if you use a number that doesn't correspond to a named value.

In some cases, however, you want to control what numbers are set for various enumerations. This technique is typically used when the number corresponds to something else (for example, an error code returned by a legacy piece of code).

**VB .NET**

```
Enum ErrorCode
    NoResponse = 166
    TooBusy = 167
    Pass = 0
End Enum
```

**C#**

```
enum ErrorCode
{
    NoResponse = 166,
    TooBusy = 167,
    Pass = 0
}
```

You could then use this ErrorCode enumeration with a function that returns an integer.

**VB .NET**

```
Dim Err As ErrorCode
Err = DoSomething()
If Err = ErrorCode.Pass
    ' Operation succeeded.
End If
```

**C#**

```
ErrorCode err = DoSomething()
if (err == ErrorCode.Pass)
{
    // Operation succeeded.
}
```

### Enumerations Are Widely Used in .NET

You may not need to create your own enumerations to use in ASP.NET applications, unless you are designing your own components. However, the concept of enumerated values is extremely important, because the .NET class library uses it extensively. For example, you set colors, border styles, alignment, and various other web control styles using enumerations provided in the .NET class library.

## Scope and Accessibility

The variable declaration examples shown so far are ideal for creating variables inside a code procedure (for example, a variable for a temporary counter). You can also create a variable outside a procedure that belongs to an entire class or module. In Visual Basic 6, this was often known as a form-level variable.

In this case, you can still create the variable in the same way, or you can explicitly set the access level by adding a keyword.

**VB .NET**

```
' A public class-level or module-level variable.
Public ErrorCode As Integer
```

**C#**

```
// A public class-level variable.
public int errorCode;
```

Generally, in a simple ASP.NET application most of your variables will be Private because the majority of your code will be self-contained in a single web page class. As you start creating separate components to reuse functionality, however, accessibility becomes much more important. Table 2-2 explains the different access levels you can use.

| VB .NET Keyword | C# Keyword | Accessibility |
|---|---|---|
| Public | public | Can be accessed by any other class. |
| Private | private | Can only be accessed by code procedures inside the current class. This is the default if you don't specify an accessibility keyword. |
| Friend | internal | Can be accessed by code procedures in any of the classes in the current assembly. |
| Protected | protected | Can be accessed by code procedures in the current class, or any class that inherits from this class. |
| Protected Friend | protected internal | Can be accessed by code procedures in the current application, or any class that inherits from this class. |

**Table 2-2.** *Accessibility Keywords*

Accessibility is defined on a class-by-class basis. For the purposes of this discussion, a class is just a container for related code routines and variables. Chapter 3 will go into much more detail. If you are new to class-based programming, don't worry about understanding all of these different options. The full list is included for completeness only, or as a reference when you start to design your own custom classes and components.

You can use initializers with class variables in the same way that you use them with procedure-level variables. These variables will be automatically created and initialized when the class is first created.

### Scope Changes from Visual Basic 6

In traditional Visual Basic, there were only two types of scope for a variable: form level and procedure level. VB .NET tightens these rules a notch by introducing block scope. Block scope means that any variables created inside a block structure (such as a conditional If … End If or a For … Next or a Do … Loop) are only accessible inside that block of code.

```
For i = 0 To 10
    Dim TempVariable As Integer
    ' (Do some calculation with TempVariable.)
Next
' You cannot access TempVariable here.
```

This change won't affect many programs. It's really designed to catch a few more accidental errors.

## Variable Operations

You can use the standard type of variable operations in both languages, including math symbols (+, -, /, *, and ^ for exponents), and string concatenation (+ or & in VB .NET). In addition, Visual Basic .NET now provides special shorthand assignment operators to match C#. A few examples are shown below.

#### VB .NET

```
' Add 10 to MyValue (the same as MyValue = MyValue + 10).
MyValue += 10

' Multiple MyValue by 3 (the same as MyValue = MyValue * 3).
MyValue *= 3

' Divide MyValue by 12 (the same as MyValue = MyValue / 12).
MyValue /= 12
```

#### C#

```
// Add 10 to myValue (the same as myValue = myValue + 10;)
myValue += 10;

// Multiple myValue by 3 (the same as myValue = myValue * 3;)
```

```
myValue *= 3;

// Divide myValue by 12 (the same as myValue = myValue / 12;)
myValue /= 12;
```

Only C# supports the special increment and decrement operators, which can automatically add 1 to a counter variable.

```
// Add 1 to myValue (the same as myValue = myValue + 1;)
myValue++
```

String operations are unchanged in VB .NET, and essentially the same in C#. The only difference is that C# does not use the ampersand (&) operator.

**VB .NET**

```
Join two strings together. Could also use the + operator.
MyName = FirstName & " " & LastName
```

**C#**

```
// Join two strings together.
myName = firstName + " " + lastName;
```

## Advanced Math Operations

In the past, every language has had its own set of keywords for common math operations such as rounding. In .NET languages, many of these keywords remain. However, you can also use a centralized class from the .NET framework. This has the pleasant side effect of ensuring that the code you use to perform mathematical operations can easily be translated into equivalent statements in any .NET language with a minimum of fuss.

To use these math operations, you invoke the methods of the System.Math class. These methods are shared (or static, to use C# terminology), which essentially means that they are always available and ready to use without any extra steps involved. (We'll define shared and instance members in more detail in Chapter 3.)

**VB .NET**

```
Dim MyValue As Integer
MyValue = Math.Sqrt(81)            ' MyValue = 8
MyValue = Math.Round(42.889, 2)    ' MyValue = 42.89
```

```
MyValue = Math.Abs(-10)              ' MyValue = 10
MyValue = Math.Log(24.212)           ' MyValue = 1.38.. (and so on)
MyValue = Math.PI                    ' MyValue = 3.14159265358979323846
```

**C#**

```
int myValue;
myValue = Math.Sqrt(81);             // myValue = 8
myValue = Math.Round(42.889, 2);     // myValue = 42.89
myValue = Math.Abs(-10);             // myValue = 10
myValue = Math.Log(24.212);          // myValue = 1.38.. (and so on)
myValue = Math.PI;                   // myValue = 3.14159265358979323846
```

The features of the Math class are too numerous to list here in their entirety. The preceding examples show some common numeric operations. For more information about the trigonometric and logarithmic functions it provides, refer to the MSDN reference for the Math class.

## Type Conversions

Visual Basic .NET's rules for type conversion are more relaxed than C#. It will automatically convert numbers into strings, for example, while C# will generate an error if you try to assign a number to a string variable. It is possible to tighten up Visual Basic's type conversion habits by adding Option Strict to the beginning of your code files. In this case, it will behave exactly like C# and not allow any automatic conversion. This can potentially catch some mysterious errors.

```
Option Strict On
```

To perform a variable conversion, you can use VB .NET's CType function. This function takes two arguments. The first specifies the variable, and the second specifies the type of variable you are converting it to.

```
Dim Count As Integer
Dim CountString As String = "10"

Count = CType(CountString, Integer)
```

You can also use the standard Visual Basic keywords such as Val, Str, CInt, CBool, and so on. However, the CType function is a nice generic solution that works for all scenarios. The examples in this book do not require Option Strict, but they do use explicit conversion with the CType function. This kind of controlled conversion is a more disciplined approach that protects against unexpected errors.

C# uses an elegant method of type conversion. You simply need to specify the type in brackets before the expression you are converting.

```
int count;
string countString = "10";

count = (int)CountString;
```

Just because you convert a value explicitly does not mean that your conversion will succeed. Conversions are essentially of two types: narrowing and widening. Widening conversions always succeed. For example, you can always convert a number into a string, or a 16-bit Short into a 32-bit Integer. On the other hand, narrowing conversions may or may not succeed, depending on the data. If you are converting a 32-bit number to a 16-bit number, you could have a value that is too large to be converted. Or you might have a string that can't be interpreted as a number. These scenarios will cause an error to occur, which you should catch using good error-handling techniques as described in Chapter 11. Some exceptions apply—for example, Visual Basic's Val function just returns a zero if it fails to convert a string to a number.

## Object-Based Manipulation

Every one of the basic data types is also a complete object that provides some built-in smarts to handle basic operations. This is interesting, because it means that C# and VB .NET can manipulate strings, dates, and numbers in the exact same way, rather than relying on special keywords in the respective language. The overall effect is also more satisfying, because the functionality you use to manipulate the variable originates from the variable itself.

For example, every type in the .NET class library includes a ToString method. The default implementation of this method returns the class name. In simple variables, a more useful result is returned: the string representation of the given variable.

**VB .NET**

```
Dim MyString As String
Dim MyInteger As Integer = 100

' Convert a number to a string (MyString will have the contents "100").
MyString = MyInteger.ToString()
```

**C#**

```
string myString;
int myInteger = 100;

// Convert a number to a string (MyString will have the contents "100").
myString = myInteger.ToString();
```

## The String Object

Probably the best example of how object members are replacing built-in functions is found with strings. You are probably familiar with the standard Visual Basic string functions such as Len, Left, Right, and Instr. These functions are still available in VB .NET, but a preferred solution is to use the methods of the String object, which provide greater consistency between .NET languages.

The next example shows several ways to manipulate a string using its object nature.

**VB .NET**

```
Dim MyString As String = "This is a test string      "
MyString = MyString.Trim()                   ' = "This is a test string"
MyString = MyString.Substring(0, 4)          ' = "This"
MyString = MyString.ToUpper()                ' = "THIS"
MyString = MyString.Replace("IS", "AT")      ' = "THAT"
```

**C#**

```
string myString = "This is a test string      ";
myString = myString.Trim();                   // = "This is a test string"
myString = myString.Substring(0, 4);          // = "This"
myString = myString.ToUpper();                // = "THIS"
myString = myString.Replace("IS", "AT");      // = "THAT"
```

Each of these statements replaces MyString with a new string object. Note that the Substring method requires a starting offset and a character length. String characters are counted starting at zero for the first letter, unlike the traditional Visual Basic functions. This change to zero-based counting is found throughout the .NET framework for the sake of consistency.

You can even use these methods in succession in a single (rather ugly) line:

```
MyString = MyString.Trim.SubString(0, 4).ToUpper().Replace("IS", "AT")
```

The C# code for this example is identical, with the addition of a semicolon at the end. Table 2-3 lists some useful members of the System.String class.

| Member | Description |
|---|---|
| Length | Returns the number of characters in the string (as an integer). |
| ToUpper() and ToLower() | Changes the string to contain all uppercase or all lowercase characters. |
| Trim(), TrimEnd(), and TrimStart() | Removes spaces or some other characters from either (or both) ends of a string. |
| PadLeft() and PadRight() | Adds the specified character to either side of a string, the number of times you indicate. (For example, PadLeft(3, " ") adds three spaces to the left side.) |
| Insert() | Puts another string inside a string at a specified (zero-based) index position. (For example, Insert(1, "pre") adds the string "pre" after the first character of the current string.) |
| Remove() | Removes a specified number of strings from a specified position. (For example, Remove(0, 1) removes the first character.) |
| Replace() | Replaces a specified substring with another string. (For example, Replace("a", "b") changes all "a" characters in a string into "b" characters.) |
| Substring() | Extracts a portion of a string at the specified location and of the specified length. (For example, Substring(0, 2) retrieves the first two characters.) |
| StartsWith() and EndsWith() | Determines whether a string ends or starts with a specified substring. (For example, StartsWith("pre") will return either True or False, depending on whether the string begins with the letters "pre" in lowercase.) |
| IndexOf() and LastIndexOf() | Finds the zero-based position of a substring in a string. This returns only the first match, and can start at the end or beginning. You can also use overloaded versions of these methods that accept a parameter specifying the position to start the search. |

**Table 2-3.** *Useful String Members*

| Member | Description |
|---|---|
| Split() | Divides a string into an array of substrings delimited by a specific substring. (For example, with Split(".") you could chop a paragraph into an array of sentence strings.) |
| Join() | Joins an array of strings together. You can also specify a separator that will be inserted between each element. |

**Table 2-3.** *Useful String Members (continued)*

## The DateTime and TimeSpan Objects

The DateTime and TimeSpan data types have built-in methods and properties that provide three useful functions:

- Extract a part of a DateTime (for example, just the year), or convert a TimeSpan to a specific representation (such as the total number of days or minutes).
- Perform date calculations.
- Determine the current date and time, and other information (such as the day of the week or the presence of a leap year).

For example, the following block of code creates a DateTime object, sets it to the current date and time, and adds a number of days. It then creates a string that indicates the year that the new date falls in (for example, "2003").

**VB .NET**

```
Dim MyDate As DateTime = DateTime.Now
MyDate = MyDate.AddDays(365)
Dim DateString As String = MyDate.Year.ToString()
```

**C#**

```
DateTime myDate = DateTime.Now;
myDate = myDate.AddDays(365);
string dateString = MyDate.Year.ToString();
```

The next example shows how you can use a TimeSpan object to find the total number of minutes between two DateTime objects.

**VB .NET**

```
Dim MyDate1 As DateTime = DateTime.Now
Dim MyDate2 As DateTime = DateTime.Now.AddHours(3000)

Dim Difference As TimeSpan
Difference = MyDate2.Subtract(MyDate1)

Dim NumberOfMinutes As Double
NumberOfMinutes = Difference.TotalMinutes
```

**C#**

```
DateTime myDate1 = DateTime.Now;
DateTime myDate2 = DateTime.Now.AddHours(3000);

TimeSpan difference;
difference = myDate2.Subtract(myDate1);

double numberOfMinutes;
numberOfMinutes = difference.TotalMinutes;
```

These examples give you an idea of the flexibility .NET provides for manipulating date and time data. Tables 2-4 and 2-5 list some of the more useful built-in features of the DateTime and TimeSpan objects.

| Member | Description |
|---|---|
| Now | Gets the current date and time. |
| Today | Gets the current date, and leaves time set to 00:00:00. |
| Year, Date, Day, Hour, Minute, Second, Millisecond | Returns one part of the DateTime object as an integer. (For example, Month will return 12 for any day in December.) |

**Table 2-4.** *Useful DateTime Members*

| Member | Description |
|---|---|
| DayOfWeek | Returns an enumerated value that indicates the day of the week for this DateTime, using the DayOfWeek enumeration. (For example, if the date falls on Sunday, this will return DayOfWeek.Sunday.) |
| Add() and Subtract() | Adds or subtracts a TimeSpan from the DateTime. |
| AddYears(), AddMonths(), AddDays(), AddHours(), AddMinutes(), AddSeconds(), AddMilliseconds() | Adds an integer that represents a number of years, months, and so on, and returns a new DateTime. You can use a negative integer to perform a date subtraction. |
| DaysInMonth() | Returns the number of days in the month represented by the current DateTime. |
| IsLeapYear() | Returns True or False depending on whether the current DateTime is in a leap year. |
| ToString() | Changes the current DateTime to its string representation. You can also use an overloaded version of this method that allows you to specify a parameter with a format string. |

**Table 2-4.** *Useful DateTime Members (continued)*

| Member | Description |
|---|---|
| Days, Hours, Minutes, Seconds, Milliseconds | Returns one component of the current TimeSpan. (For example, the Hours property can return an integer from 0 to 23.) |

**Table 2-5.** *Useful TimeSpan Members*

| Member | Description |
|---|---|
| TotalDays, TotalHours, TotalMinutes, TotalSeconds, TotalMilliseconds | Returns the total value of the current TimeSpan, indicated as a number of days, hours, minutes, and so on. (For example, the TotalDays property might return a number like 234.342.) |
| Add() and Subtract() | Combines TimeSpan objects together. |
| FromDays(), FromHours(), FromMinutes(), FromSeconds(), FromMilliseconds() | Allows you to quickly specify a new TimeSpan. (For example, you can use TimeSpan.FromHours(24) to define a TimeSpan object exactly 24 hours long.) |
| ToString() | Changes the current TimeSpan to its string representation. You can also use an overloaded version of this method that allows you to specify a parameter with a format string. |

**Table 2-5.** *Useful TimeSpan Members (continued)*

## The Array Object

Arrays also behave like objects in the new world of .NET. For example, instead of using the standard Visual Basic UBound built-in function, you can use the GetUpperBound method.

**VB .NET**

```
Dim MyArray() As Integer = {1, 2, 3, 4, 5}
Dim Bound As Integer

' Zero represent the first dimension of an array.
Bound = MyArray.GetUpperBound(0)     ' Bound = 4
```

**C#**

```
int[] myArray = {1, 2, 3, 4, 5};
int bound;
```

```
// Zero represent the first dimension of an array.
bound = myArray.GetUpperBound(0);    // bound = 4
```

Arrays also provide a few other useful methods that allow you to sort, reverse, and search them for a specified element. Table 2-6 lists some useful members of the System.Array class.

| Member | Description |
|---|---|
| Length | Returns an integer that represents the total number of elements in all dimensions of an array. For example, a 3 x 3 array has a length of 9. |
| GetLowerBound() and GetUpperBound() | Determines the dimensions of an array. As with just about everything in .NET, you start counting at zero (which represents the first dimension). |
| Clear() | Empties an array's contents. |
| IndexOf() and LastIndexOf() | Searches a one-dimensional array for a specified value, and returns the index number. You cannot use this with multi-dimensional arrays. |
| Sort() | Sorts a one-dimensional array made up of simple comparable types such as strings and numbers. |
| Reverse() | Reverses a one-dimensional array so that its elements are backwards, from last to first. |

**Table 2-6.** *Useful Array Members*

## Conditional Structures

Both C# and VB .NET use an equivalent syntax for evaluating conditions. The if block in C# is slightly less verbose, and uses brackets to identify the expression and curly braces to group the conditional code. The comparison operators (>, <, and =) are the same, with the exception that C# uses two equal signs to indicate comparison. This prevents it from being confused with a statement that assigns a value to a variable.

**VB .NET**

```
If MyNumber > 10 Then
    ' Do something.
ElseIf MyString = "hello" Then
    ' Do something.
Else
    ' Do something.
End If
```

**C#**

```
if (myNumber > 10)
{
    // Do something.
}
elseif (myString == "hello")
{
    // Do something.
}
else
{
    // Do something.
}
```

Both languages also provide a Select Case structure that you can use to evaluate a single variable or expression for multiple possible values. In this case, the C# syntax is slightly more awkward because it inherits the convention of C/C++ programming, which requires that every conditional block of code is ended by a special break keyword.

**VB .NET**

```
Select Case MyNumber
    Case 1
        ' Do something.
    Case 2
        ' Do something.
    Case Else
        ' Do something.
End Select
```

**C#**

```
switch (MyNumber)
{
    case 1:
        // Do something.
        break;
    case 2:
        // Do something.
        break;
    default:
        // Do something.
        break;
}
```

## Loop Structures

One of the most basic ingredients in many programs is the For … Next loop, which allows you to repeat a given block of code a set number of times. In Visual Basic, you specify a starting value, an ending value, and the amount to increment with each pass.

```
Dim i As Integer
For i = 1 To 10 Step 1
    ' This code executes 10 times.
Next
```

The "Step 1" clause specifies that i will be increased by 1 for each new loop. You can omit this part of the code, as 1 is the default increment.

In C#, the for loop has a similar syntax, with a few differences. First of all, you don't need to define the counter variable first; it is usually created in the actual loop definition. You'll also notice that you explicitly specify the condition that is tested to decide whether the loop should continue. In Visual Basic code, this condition is implicit—the code always checks if the counter variable has reached or exceeded the specified target.

```
for (int i = 0; i < 10; i++)
{
    // This code executes 10 times.
}
```

As you've already seen with the array example, both languages also provide a For Each block that allows you to loop through the items in a collection.

Visual Basic also supports a Do … Loop structure that tests a specific condition using the While or Until keyword. These two keywords are opposites: While means "as long as this is true," and Until means "as long as this is not true." C# dispenses with this duplication, and only supports a while condition.

```
Dim i As Integer = 1
Do
    i += 1
    ' This code executes 10 times.
Loop While i < 10
```

You can also place the condition at the beginning of the loop. In this case, the condition is tested before the loop is started. This code is equivalent, unless the condition you are testing is False to begin with. In that case, none of the code in the loop will execute. If the condition is evaluated at the end of the loop, the code will always be executed at least once.

```
Dim i As Integer = 1
Do While i < 10
    i += 1
    ' This code executes 10 times.
Loop
```

In C#, these two types of loops (with the condition at the beginning and the condition at the end) are treated differently. The while loop, which places the condition at the beginning, is the most common.

```
int i = 1;
while (i < 10)
{
    i += 1;
    // This code executes 10 times.
}
```

The do … while block allows you to evaluate the condition at the end.

```
int i = 1;
do
{
```

```
    i += 1;
    // This code executes 10 times.
}
while (i < 10);
```

Sometimes you need to exit a loop in a hurry. In C#, you can use the break statement to exit any type of loop. In Visual Basic, you need to use the corresponding Exit statement (such as Exit For, or Exit Do). C# provides an additional statement that Visual Basic does not. The continue keyword automatically skips the rest of the code in the loop and continues from the start with a new iteration.

## Functions and Subroutines

Visual Basic distinguished between two types of procedures: ordinary subroutines and functions, which return a value. As in past versions of Visual Basic, you can set the return value by assigning a value to the function name. VB .NET also introduces the useful Return keyword, which allows you to exit a function and return a result in one quick, clear step.

```
Private Sub MySub()
    ' Code goes here.
End Sub

Private Function MyFunc() As Integer
    ' As an example, return the number 10.
    Return 10
End Function
```

C# uses an inverted syntax that places the return value first, followed by the procedure name. The procedure name must always be followed by parentheses, even if it does not accept parameters, in order to identify it as a procedure. Subroutines are differentiated by functions in that they specify the keyword void to indicate that no information is returned.

```
void MySub()
{
    // Code goes here.
}

int MyFunc()
{
```

```
    // As an example, return the number 10.
    return 10;
}
```

In this case, the C# examples omit the Private keyword. This is just a C# convention; you could include it if you want (or you could omit the Private keyword from the Visual Basic code). As in Visual Basic, all procedures are private by default. Alternatively, you can also specify any of the access keywords described in Table 2-2 to change the accessibility of a procedure.

## Parameters

Procedures can also accept additional information through parameters. Parameters are defined in a similar way to variables. By convention, parameters always begin with a lowercase first letter in any language.

**VB .NET**

```
Private Function AddNumbers(number1 As Integer, number2 As Integer)
As Integer
    Return (number1 + number2)
End Sub
```

**C#**

```
int AddNumbers(int number1, int number2)
{
    return (number1 + number2);
}
```

When calling a procedure, you specify any required parameters in parentheses, or use an empty set of parentheses if no parameters are required.

**VB .NET**

```
' Call a subroutine with no parameters.
MySub()

' Call a subroutine with two Integer parameters.
MySub(10, 20)
```

```
' Call a function with two Integer parameters and an Integer return
value.
Dim ReturnValue As Integer = AddNumbers(10, 10)
```

**C#**

```
// Call a subroutine with no parameters.
MySub();

// Call a subroutine with two Integer parameters.
MySub(10, 20);

// Call a function with two int parameters and an int return value.
int ReturnValue = AddNumbers(10, 10);
```

### Parameter Changes from Visual Basic 6

Visual Basic now requires parentheses around the parameters for any procedure call, regardless of whether the procedure returns a value. This new syntax is clearer than before, when parentheses were only used when receiving a return value from a function. Visual Basic also now defaults to ByVal for all parameters, ensuring a greater level of protection and clarity. (Although for the sake of clarity, many of the code examples in this book omit the extra ByVal keywords for parameters.)

Finally, VB .NET now requires that optional parameters have a default value specified.

```
Private Sub DoSomething(Optional taskNumber As Integer = 20)
```

As a side effect, the IsMissing function is no longer supported.

## By Reference and By Value Parameters

You can create two types of procedure parameters. The standard (known as ByVal in Visual Basic) ensures that any changes do not propagate back to the calling code and modify the original variable. In other words, a copy of the variable's value is submitted to the procedure. Another option is ByRef (known as ref in C#), which allows you to modify the original variable.

**VB .NET**

```
Private Sub ProcessNumber(ByRef number As Integer)
    number *= 2
End Sub
```

**C#**

```
void ProcessNumber(ref int number)
{
    number *= 2;
}
```

With ByRef, the calling code must submit a variable, not a literal value. In C# code, the ref value must also be specified in the function call, which indicates that the calling code is aware the parameter value could be changed.

**VB .NET**

```
Dim Num As Integer = 10
ProcessNumber(Num)
```

**C#**

```
int num = 10;
ProcessNumber(ref num);
```

## C# Also Supports an out Parameter

The out keyword works just like the ref keyword, but it allows the calling code to use an uninitialized variable as a parameter, which is otherwise forbidden in C#. This wouldn't be appropriate for the ProcessNumber procedure, because it reads the submitted parameter value (and then doubles it). If, on the other hand, the variable is not used at all by the procedure except to return information, you can use the out keyword. In this case, C# won't try to submit the value of the parameter to the procedure, but it will return the value that was set in the procedure. As with the ref keyword, out must be specified before the parameter in the procedure declaration *and* in the procedure call.

Note that Visual Basic .NET does not require this keyword, because Visual Basic always initializes new variables.

## Procedure Overloading

C# and VB .NET both support overloading, which allows you to create more than one function and subroutine with the same name, but that accepts a different list of parameters (or a similar parameter list with different data types). The CLR will automatically choose the correct procedure for a given call by examining the list of parameters the calling code uses.

This is old hat to C programmers, but a valuable new introduction to the Visual Basic world. It allows you to collect different versions of several functions together. For example, you might allow a database search that returns an author name. Rather than create three functions with different names depending on the criteria (such as GetNameFromID, GetNameFromSSN, GetNameFromBookTile), you could create three versions of the GetCustomerName function.

To overload a procedure, you use the Overloads keyword in VB .NET. No additional keyword is required in C#.

**VB .NET**

```
Private Overloads Function GetCustomerName(ID As Integer) As String
    ' Code here.
End Function

Private Overloads Function GetCustomerName(bookTitle As String) _
  As String
    ' Code here.
End Function

' And so on...
```

**C#**

```
string GetCustomerName(int ID)
{
    // Code here.
}

string GetCustomerName(string bookTitle)
{
    // Code here.
}

// And so on...
```

You cannot overload a function with versions that have the same signature (number of parameters and data types), as the CLR will not be able to distinguish them from each other. When you call an overloaded function, the version that matches the parameter list you supply is used. (If no version matches, an error occurs.)

### Overloaded Methods Are Used Extensively in .NET

.NET uses overloaded methods in most of its classes, allowing you to use a range of different parameters, but centralizing functionality under common names. Even the methods we've looked at so far (like the String methods for padding or replacing text) have multiple versions that provide similar features with various options. .NET classes never use optional parameters.

## Delegates

Delegates are a new feature of .NET languages. They allow you to create a variable that refers to a procedure. You can use this variable at any time to invoke the procedure.

The first step when using a delegate is to define its signature. Delegate variables can only point to functions or procedures that match its specific, defined signature (list of parameters). This allows a level of type safety that isn't found with traditional function pointers in languages like C++.

#### VB .NET

```
' Define a delegate that can represent any function that accepts
' a single string parameter and returns a string.
Private Delegate Function StringFunction(In As String) As String
```

#### C#

```
// Define a delegate that can represent any function that accepts
// a single string parameter and returns a string.
delegate string StringFunction(string In);
```

Once you have defined a type of delegate, you can create and assign a delegate variable. For example, assume your program has the next function.

**VB .NET**

```
Private Function TransalteEnglishToFrench(english As String) As String
    ' Code goes here.
End Function
```

**C#**

```
string TransalteEnglishToFrench(string english)
{
    // Code goes here.
}
```

This function matches the delegate definition because it requires one string and returns a string. That means you can create a variable of type StringFunction, and use it to store a reference to this function.

**VB .NET**

```
' Create a delegate variable.
Dim FunctionReference As StringFunction

' Store a reference to a matching procedure.
FunctionReference = AddressOf TranslateEnglishToFrench
```

**C#**

```
// Create a delegate variable.
StringFunction functionReference;

// Store a reference to a matching procedure.
functionReference = TranslateEnglishToFrench()
```

This code is equivalent, but the C# statement does not require the special AddressOf keyword. If you try the same syntax with VB .NET, your program will run the function, return a value, and attempt to apply that value to the delegate variable, which will generate an error.

Once you have a delegate variable that references a function, you can invoke the function through the delegate. To do this, you just use the delegate name as though it were the function name:

**VB .NET**

```
Dim FrenchString As String
FrenchString = FunctionReference("Hello")
```

**C#**

```
string frenchString;
frenchString = functionreference("Hello");
```

In the code example above, the procedure that the FunctionReference delegate points to will be invoked with the parameter "Hello" and the return value will be stored in the FrenchString variable.

### Delegates Are the Basis of Events

Wouldn't it be nice to have a delegate that could refer to more than one function at once, and invoke them simultaneously? That would allow the client application to have multiple "listeners," and notify them all at once when something happens. In fact, delegates do have this functionality, but you are more likely to see it in use with .NET events. Events, which are described in Chapter 3, are based on delegates, but work at a slightly higher level and provide a few automatic niceties. In a typical ASP.NET program, you'll use events extensively, but probably never work directly with delegates.

# Chapter 3

## Types, Objects, and Namespaces

Object-oriented programming has been a popular buzzword over the last several years. In fact, one of the few places that object-oriented programming *wasn't* emphasized was in ordinary ASP pages. With .NET, the story changes considerably. Not only does .NET allow you to use objects, it demands it. Almost every ingredient you'll need to use to create a web application is, on some level, really a kind of object.

So how much do you need to know about object-oriented programming to write .NET pages? It depends whether you want to follow existing examples and cut-and-paste code samples, or have a deeper understanding of the way .NET works and gain a finer grain of control. This book assumes that if you are willing to pick up a thousand-page book, you are the latter type of programmer—one who excels by understanding how things work, and why they work the way that they do. It also assumes that you are interested in some of the advance ASP.NET programming that *will* require class-based design, like designing custom controls (see Chapter 22) and creating your own components (see Chapter 21).

This chapter explains objects from the point of view of the .NET framework. I won't rehash the typical object-oriented theory, because there are already countless excellent programming books on the subject. Instead, I'll show you the types of objects .NET allows, how they are constructed, and how they fit into the larger framework of namespaces and assemblies.

## The Basics About Classes

As a developer, you've probably already created classes, or at least heard about them. Classes are the definitions for objects. The nice thing about a class is that you can use it to create as many objects as you need. For example, you might have a class tha represents an XML file, which can be used to read some data. If you want to access multiple XML files at once, you can create several instances of your class. These instances are called objects.

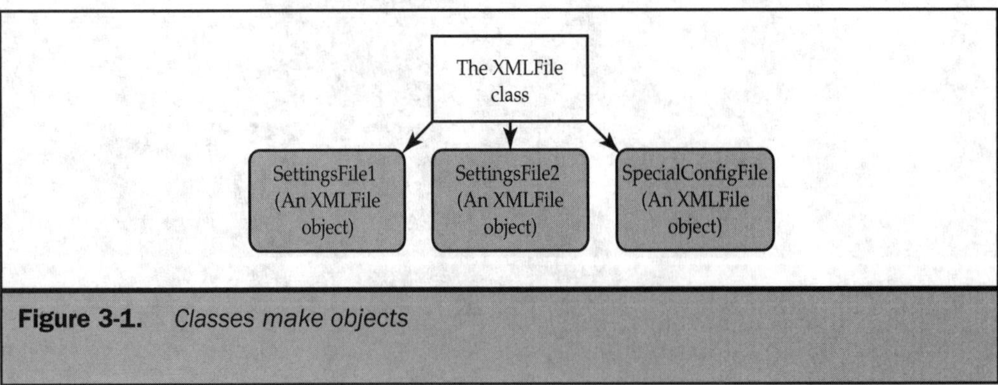


**Figure 3-1.** *Classes make objects*

Every class is made up of exactly three things:

**Properties** These store information about an object. Some properties may be read-only (so they cannot be modified), while others can be changed by the code that is using the object. For example, ASP pages provide a built-in Request object that you can use to retrieve information about the current client request. One property of this object, Cookies, provides a collection of cookies that were sent with the request.

**Methods** These allow you to perform an action with an object. (You can also interact with an object by setting properties, but methods are used for compound actions that perform a distinct task or may change the object's state significantly.) For example, ASP pages provide a built-in Server object that provides a CreateObject method you can use to run a COM component on the server.

**Events** These provide notification from the control that something has happened. In traditional ASP programming, you saw events only in the global.asa file, and they were not clearly tied to any specific object. If you've programmed ordinary Visual Basic programs, you have seen how controls fire events to notify your code about mouse clicks and data changes. ASP.NET controls provide a similar (although reduced) set of events.

In addition, classes contain their own code and internal set of private data. Classes behave like black boxes, which means that when you use one, you shouldn't waste any time wondering about what low-level information it's retaining. When using a class, you only need to worry about its public interface, which is the set of properties, methods, and events you have to work with. Together, these elements are called class members.

In ASP.NET, you will create your own custom classes to represent individual web pages. In addition, you will create custom classes if you design any special components (as you'll see in Chapter 21). For the most part, however, you'll be using prebuilt classes from the .NET class library, rather than programming your own.

## Shared Members

One of the tricks about .NET classes is that there are really two ways to use them. Some class members can be used without creating an object first. These are called shared members, and they are accessed by class name. For example, you can use the shared property DateTime.Now to retrieve a DateTime object that represents the current date and time. You don't need to create a DateTime instance first.

On the other hand, the majority of the DateTime members require a valid instance. For example, you can't use the AddDays method or the Hour property without a valid object instance. These members have no meaning without a live object and some valid data to draw on.

```
' Get the current date using a shared method.
' Note that you need to use the class name: DateTime.
```

```
Dim MyDate As DateTime = DateTime.Now

' Use an instance method to add a day.
' Note that you need to use the object name: MyDate.
MyDate = MyDate.AddDays(1)

' The following code makes no sense.
' It tries to use the instance method AddDays
' with the class name DateTime!
MyDate = DateTime.AddDays(1)
```

Both properties and methods can be designated as shared (C# programmers use the word *static* instead). Shared methods are a major part of the .NET framework, and you will make frequent use of them in this book. Remember, some classes may consist entirely of shared members, and some may use only instance members. Other classes, like DateTime, can provide a combination of the two.

In the next example, which introduces a basic class, we'll use only instance members. This is the default and a good starting point.

## A Simple Class

In the next example, we'll build up a simple .NET class bit by bit. First of all, we start by defining the class itself using a special block structure.

**VB .NET**

```
Public Class MyClass
    ' Class code goes here.
End Class
```

**C#**

```
public class MyClass
{
    // Class code goes here.
}
```

You can define as many classes as you need in the same file (which is a departure from Visual Basic 6, which required a separate file for each class).

Classes exist in many forms. They may represent an actual *thing* in the real world (as they do in most programming textbooks), they may represent some programming abstraction (such as a rectangle structure), or they may just be a convenient way to group together related functionality. In this example, our class represents a single product in a company database.

In order to give it some basic functionality, define three private variables that store data about the product: namely, its name, price, and a URL to an image file.

**VB .NET**

```
Public Class Product
    Private Name As String
    Private Price As Decimal
    Private ImageUrl As String
End Class
```

**C#**

```
public class Product
{
    string name;
    decimal price;
    string imageUrl;
}
```

The client can create an object out of this class quite easily. From the client's point of view, the only difference in creating an object variable instead of a class variable is that the New keyword must be specified in order to actually instantiate the class. Otherwise, when you try to use the class you will receive a "null reference" error, because it doesn't actually exist yet.

On the other hand, sometimes you will create an object variable without actually using the New keyword. For example, you might want to assign the variable to an instance that already exists, or you might receive a live object as a return value from a function, and just need a variable to refer to it. In these cases—when you aren't actually creating the class—you shouldn't use the New keyword.

**VB .NET**

```
Dim SaleProduct As New Product()

' Optionally you could do this in two steps:
' Dim SaleProduct As Product
' SaleProduct = New Product()
```

```
' Now release the class from memory.
SaleProduct = Nothing
```

**C#**

```
Product saleProduct = new Product();

// Optionally you could do this in two steps:
// Product saleProduct;
// saleProduct = new Product();

// Now release the class from memory.
saleProduct = null;
```

### Class Creation Changes from Visual Basic 6

In Visual Basic 6, it was a bad idea to define an object with the New keyword in the definition. This would not actually create the class, but cause it to be automatically created the first time you refer to it in a code statement. The problem was that you could release the object, try to use the variable again, and end up with a new blank copy of the object automatically recreated. This bizarre behavior has been stamped out in VB .NET. You'll also notice that the Set keyword is no longer needed. VB .NET can distinguish between variables and objects automatically, and does not need your help.

## Adding Properties

The simple Product class is essentially useless because there's no way your code can manipulate it. All its information is private and internal. You could make the member variables public, but that could lead to problems because it would allow the client code free access to change any variables, even applying invalid or inconsistent data. Instead, you need to add a "control panel" through which your code can manipulate Product objects. You do this by adding property procedures.

Property procedures have two parts: one procedure that allows the class user to retrieve data, and another part that allows the class user to set data. Property procedures are similar to any other type of procedure in that you can write as much code as you need. For example, you could raise an error to alert the client code of invalid data and prevent the change from being applied. Or you could change multiple internal variables to match the public property. In the Product class example, the property procedures just provide straight access to the internal variables.

To prevent confusion between the internal variables and the property names, the internal variables have been renamed to start with an underscore in the VB .NET code. This is a common convention, but it doesn't represent the only possible approach. In the C# code, the names are differentiated by case.

**VB .NET**

```
Public Class Product
    Private _Name As String
    Private _Price As Decimal
    Private _ImageUrl As String

    Public Property Name() As String
        Get
            Return _Name
        End Get
        Set(Value As String)
            _Name = Value
        End Set
    End Property

    Public Property Price() As Decimal
        Get
            Return _Price
        End Get
        Set(Value As Decimal)
            _Price = Value
        End Set
    End Property

    Public Property ImageUrl() As String
        Get
            Return _ImageUrl
        End Get
        Set(Value As String)
            _ImageUrl = Value
        End Set
    End Property

End Class
```

**C#**

```
public class Product
{
    string name;
    decimal price;
    string imageUrl;

    public string Name
    {
        get
        { return name; }
        set
        { name = value; }
    }

    public decimal Price
    {
        get
        { return price; }
        set
        { price = value; }
    }
    public string ImageUrl
    {
        get
        { return imageUrl; }
        set
        { imageUrl = value; }
    }
}
```

The client can now create and configure the class by using its properties and the familiar dot syntax.

**VB .NET**

```
Dim SaleProduct As New Product()
SaleProduct.Name = "Kitchen Garbage"
SaleProduct.Price = 49.99
SaleProduct.ImageUrl = "http://mysite/garbage.png"
```

**C#**

```
Product saleProduct = new Product();
saleProduct.Name = "Kitchen Garbage";
saleProduct.Price = 49.99;
saleProduct.ImageUrl = "http://mysite/garbage.png";
```

# A Basic Method

You can easily add a method to a class—all you need to do is add a public function or subroutine to the class. The class user can then call this method.

For example, the Product class could have a special GetHtml method that returns a string representing a formatted block of HTML. This HTML can be placed on a web page to represent the product.

**VB .NET**

```
Public Class Product
    ' (Variables and property procedures omitted for clarity.)

    Public Function GetHtml() As String
        Dim HtmlString As String
        HtmlString = "<h1>" & _Name & "</h1><br>"
        HtmlString &= "<h3>Costs: " & _Price.ToString() & "</h3><br>"
        HtmlString &= "<img src=" & _ImageUrl & ">"
        Return HtmlString
    End Function

End Class
```

**C#**

```
public class Product
{
    // (Variables and property procedures omitted for clarity.)

    string GetHtml()
    {
        string htmlString;
        htmlString = "<h1>" & _Name & "</h1><br>";
```

```
        htmlString += "<h3>Costs: " & _Price.ToString() & "</h3><br>";
        htmlString += "<img src=" & _ImageUrl & ">";
        return HtmlString;
    }

}
```

All the GetHtml method does is read the internal data, and format it in some attractive way. This really targets our class as a user interface class rather than a pure data class or "business object." Your code can use this method to create a dynamic web page in ASP style, using Response.Write. A web page created in this way is shown in Figure 3-2.

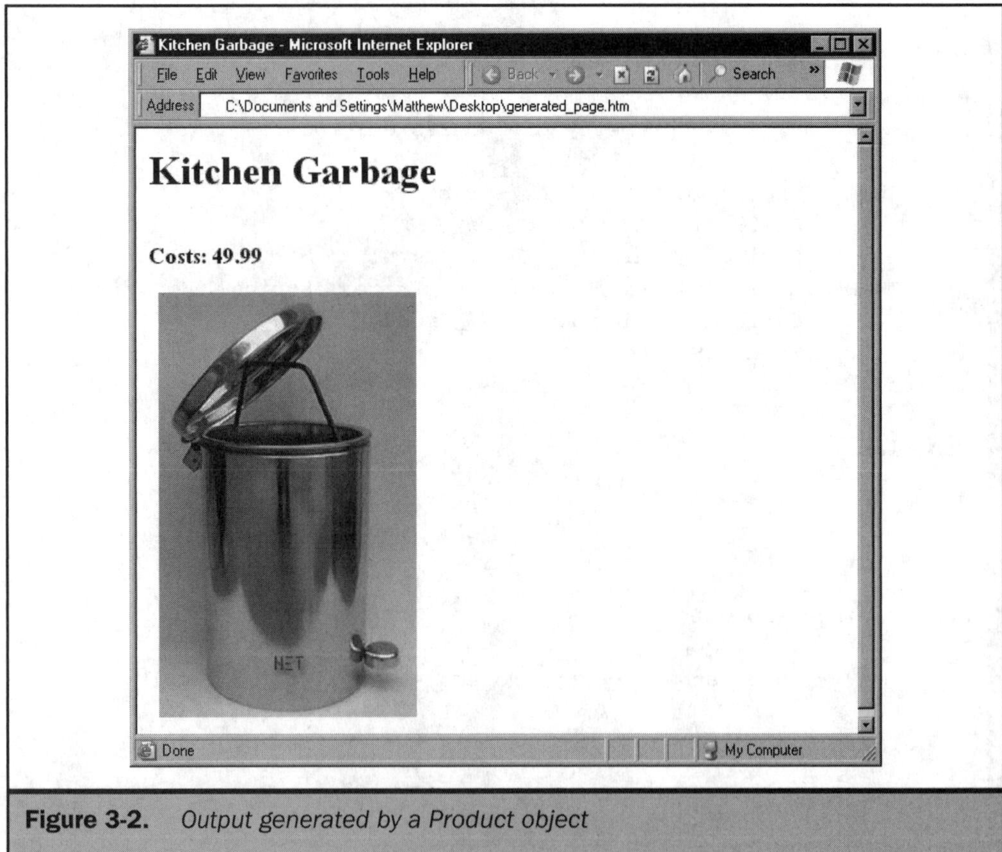


**Figure 3-2.** *Output generated by a Product object*

**VB .NET**

```
Dim SaleProduct As New Product()
SaleProduct.Name = "Kitchen Garbage"
SaleProduct.Price = 49.99
SaleProduct.ImageUrl = "http://mysite/garbage.png"
Response.Write(SaleProduct.GetHtml())
```

**C#**

```
Product saleProduct = new Product();
saleProduct.Name = "Kitchen Garbage";
saleProduct.Price = 49.99;
saleProduct.ImageUrl = "http://mysite/garbage.png";
Response.Write(saleProduct.GetHtml());
```

The interesting thing about the GetHtml method is that it is similar to how an ASP.NET web control works (on a much cruder level). To use an ASP.NET control, you create an object (explicitly or implicitly), and configure some properties. Then ASP.NET automatically creates a web page by examining all these objects and requesting their associated HTML (by calling a hidden GetHtml method, or something conceptually similar). It then sends the completed page to the user.

When using a web control, you only see the public interface made up of properties, methods, and events. However, understanding how class code actually works will help you master advanced development. Incidentally, the .NET class library is written using C#, although you can use its classes in any .NET language with equal ease.

## A Basic Event

Classes can also use events to notify your code. ASP.NET uses a new event-driven programming model, and you'll soon become very used to writing code that reacts to events. Unless you are creating your own components, however, you won't need to fire your own custom events.

As an illustration, the Product class example has been enhanced with a NameChanged event that occurs whenever the Name is modified through the property procedure. (Note that this event won't fire if code inside the class changes the underlying private name variable without going through the property procedure.)

**VB .NET**

```
Public Class Product
    ' (Additional class code omitted for clarity.)
```

```
    ' Define the event.
    Public Event NameChanged()

    Public Property Name() As String
        Get
            Return _Name
        End Get
        Set(Value As String)
            _Name = Value
            ' Fire the event to all listeners.
            RaiseEvent NameChanged()
        End Set
    End Property

End Class
```

**C#**

```
public class Product
{
    // (Additional class code omitted for clarity.)

    // Define the delegate that represents the event.
    public delegate void NameChangedEventHandler();
    // Define the event.
    public event NameChangedEventHandler NameChanged;

    public string Name
    {
        get
        { return name; }
        set
        {
            name = value;
            // Fire the event to all listeners.
            NameChanged();
        }
    }
}
```

The C# and VB .NET syntax differ slightly. Visual Basic allows you to define the event and any arguments it might have using the special Event keyword, and then fire it with the RaiseEvent statement. C#, on the other hand, requires that you first create a delegate that represents the type of event you are going to use (and its parameters). Then you can define an event. When you fire an event in C#, you just use it by name, you do not need any special function.

VB .NET and C# event handling also differs slightly. Both languages allow you to connect an event to an event handler dynamically, but the syntax differs. Consider the example for our Product class:

**VB .NET**

```
Dim SaleProduct As New Product()

' This connects the saleProduct.NameChanged event to an event handling
' procedure called ChangeDetected.
AddHandler SaleProduct.NameChanged AddressOf(ChangeDetected)

' Now the event will occur in response to this code:
SaleProduct.Name = "Kitchen Garbage"
```

**C#**

```
Product saleProduct = new Product();

// This connects the saleProduct.NameChanged event to an event handling
// procedure called ChangeDetected.
// Note that ChangedDetected needs to match the
// NameChangedEventHandler delegate.
saleProduct.NameChanged += new NameChangedEventHandler(ChangeDetected);

// Now the event will occur in response to this code:
saleProduct.Name = "Kitchen Garbage";
```

The event handler is just a simple procedure called ChangeDetected:

**VB .NET**

```
Public Sub ChangeDetected()
    ' This code executes in response to the NameChanged event.
End Sub
```

**C#**

```
public void ChangeDetected()
{
    // This code executes in response to the NameChanged event.
}
```

If you're using C#, that's essentially the end of the story. If you are a VB .NET programmer, you have an additional option. You don't need to connect events dynamically, instead you can connect them declaratively with the WithEvents keyword and the Handles clause. You'll see this technique in our web form examples when we introduce server control events in next few chapters.

### Event Handling Changes from Visual Basic 6

In traditional Visual Basic programming, events were connected to event handlers based on the procedure name. In .NET, this clumsy system is abandoned. Your event handler can have any name you want, and it can even be used to handle more than one event, provided they pass the same type of information in their parameters.

## Constructors

Currently, the Product class has a problem. Ideally, classes should ensure that they are always in a valid state. However, unless you explicitly set all the appropriate properties, the Product object won't correspond to a valid product. This could cause an error if you tried to use a method that relied on some of the data that hasn't been supplied. In the past, this was a major limitation of classes in Visual Basic programming. Today, .NET brings VB up to the level of other modern languages by introducing constructors.

A constructor is just a special method that automatically runs when the class is first created. In C#, this method always has the same name as the name of the class, by convention. In VB .NET, the constructor always has the name New.

If you don't create a constructor, .NET supplies a default constructor that does nothing. If, however, you create a constructor, the client code must use it. This restriction is useful because you can create constructors that require specific parameters. If the calling code tries to create an object without specifying valid values for all these parameters, you can raise an error and refuse to create the object.

As a quick example, consider the new version of the Product class shown next. It adds a constructor that requires the product price and name as arguments.

**VB .NET**

```
Public Class Product
    ' (Additional class code omitted for clarity.)

    Public Sub New(name As String, price As Decimal)
        ' These parameters have the same name as the property
        ' procedures, but that doesn't cause a problem.
        ' The local variables have priority.
        _Name = name
        _Price = price
    End Sub

End Class
```

**C#**

```
public class Product
{
    // (Additional class code omitted for clarity.)

    public void Product(string name, decimal price)
    {
        // These parameters have the same name as the
        // internal variables. The "this" keyword is used to refer
        // to the class variables. "this" is the same as "Me" in VB:
        // it refers to the current class.
        this.name = name;
        this.price = price;
    }
}
```

To create a Product object, you need to supply information for these parameters, ensuring it will start its life with valid information.

**VB .NET**

```
Dim SaleProduct As New Product("Kitchen Garbage", 49.99)
```

**C#**

```
Product saleProduct = new Product("Kitchen Garbage", 49.99);
```

Most of the classes you use will have special constructors. As with any other method, constructors can be overloaded with multiple versions, each providing a different set of parameters. You can choose the one that suits you best based on the information you have. The .NET framework classes use this technique extensively.

**VB .NET Constructors Don't Use the Overloads Keyword**

When creating multiple constructors in VB .NET, you don't use the Overloads keyword that was introduced in Chapter 2. There's no technical reason for this discrepancy; it's just a harmless quirk.

## Value Types and Reference Types

In Chapter 2, you learned how simple data types such as strings and integers are actually objects created from the class library. This allows some impressive tricks, like built-in string handling and date calculation. However, simple data types differ from more complex objects in one important way: they work like value types, while objects behave like reference types.

What this means is that a variable for a simple data type contains the actual information you put in it (such as the number 7, or the text "hello"). On the other hand, object variables actually store a reference that points to a location in memory where the full object is stored. (To use C++ parlance, object variables are pointers.) However, .NET masks you from this underlying reality, and in most cases you won't notice any difference in the way you work with object variables and the way you manipulate simple data variables.

There are two cases when you will notice that object variables act a little differently than ordinary data types: in assignment operations and comparison operations.

### Assignment Operations

When you assign a simple data variable to another simple data variable, the contents of the variable are copied.

```
IntegerA = IntegerB
' IntegerA now has a copy of the contents of IntegerB.
' There are two duplicate integers in memory.
```

Objects work a little differently. Copying the entire contents of an object could slow down an application, particularly if you were performing multiple assignments. With objects, the default is to just copy the reference in an assignment operation.

```
ObjectA = ObjectB
' ObjectA and ObjectB now both point to the same thing.
' There is one object, and two ways to access it.
```

In the preceding example, if you modify ObjectB by setting a property, ObjectA will be automatically affected. In fact, ObjectA *is* ObjectB. To override this behavior, you would need to manually create a new object and initialize its information to match the existing object. Some objects (like the DataSet used when retrieving information from a database) provide a Clone method that allows you to easily copy the object. You'll see this trick in action later in the book.

## Equality Testing

A similar distinction is made when you compare two variables. When you compare simple variables, you are comparing the contents.

```
If IntegerA = IntegerB Then
    ' This is True as long as the integers have the same content.
End If
```

When you compare object variables you are actually testing whether they are the same instance. You are testing if they are pointing to the same object in memory, not if their contents match. VB .NET uses slightly different syntax (the Is keyword) to emphasize this difference.

### VB .NET

```
If ObjectA Is ObjectB Then
    ' This is True if both ObjectA and ObjectB point to the same thing.
    ' This is False if they are separate, yet identical objects.
End If
```

### C#

```
if (objectA == objectB)
{
    // This is true if both objectA and objectB point to the same thing.
```

```
    // This is false if they are separate, yet identical objects.
}
```

## What Types Are Really Objects?

Occasionally, a class can override this behavior. For example, the String type is a full-featured class, not a simple data type. (This is a requirement to make strings efficient, because they can contain a variable amount of data.) However, the String type overrides its equality and assignment operations to work like a simple value type, because this is the way that most programmers expect to use strings. Arrays, on the other hand, are classes through and through. If you assign one array variable to another, you copy the reference, not the array (although the Array class also provides a Clone method that returns a duplicate array to allow true copying).

Table 3-1 sets the record straight and explains exactly what data types are value types, and what data types are really reference types.

| Data Type | Nature | Behavior |
|---|---|---|
| Integer, Decimal, Single, Double, and all other basic numeric types | Value Type | Equality and assignment operations work with the variable contents, not a reference. |
| DateTime, TimeSpan | Value Type | Equality and assignment operations work with the variable contents, not a reference. |
| Char, Byte, and Boolean | Value Type | Equality and assignment operations work with the variable contents, not a reference. |
| String | Reference Type | Equality and assignment operations are overridden; they work with the variable contents, not a reference. |
| Array | Reference Type | Equality and assignment operations work with the reference, not the contents. |
| Object | Reference Type | Equality and assignment operations work with the reference, not the contents. |

**Table 3-1.** *Common Reference and Value Types*

### Reviewing .NET Types

So far the discussion has focused on simple data types and classes. The .NET class library is actually composed of *types*, which is a catch-all term that includes several object-like relatives:

- **Classes**, which we explored in this chapter. Strings and arrays are two examples of .NET classes.
- **Structures**, which are generally simpler, and use value type equality and assignment semantics. Integers, dates, and chars are all structures.
- **Enumerations**, which are basic sets of constants. Enumerations were introduced in the last chapter.
- **Delegates**, which define a method signature and allow you to create function pointers. Delegates are the foundation for .NET event handling, and were introduced in the last chapter.
- **Interfaces**, which define a class contract. Interfaces are an advanced technique of object-oriented programming, and aren't discussed in this book.

## Advanced Class Programming

Part of the art of object-oriented programming is determining class relations. For example, you could create a Product class that contains a Pricing class, or a Car class that contains four Wheel classes. To create this sort of class relationship, all you need to do is define the appropriate object variable in the class (along with the corresponding property procedures if you want to allow the calling code to change the sub-object). This type of relationship is called containment.

In ASP and ASP.NET programming, you'll find special classes called collections that have no purpose other than to group together various objects and label each one with a key name. You'll learn more about collection objects in Chapter 10.

In addition, classes can have a different type of relationship known as inheritance.

### Inheritance

Inheritance allows one class to acquire and extend the functionality of another class. For example, you could create a class called TaxableProduct that inherits from Product. It automatically has all the same methods and properties (aside from the constructor), and you can add additional members that relate to taxation.

**VB .NET**

```
Public Class TaxableProduct
    Inherits Product

    Private _TaxRate As Decimal = 1.15

    Public ReadOnly Property TotalPrice() As Decimal
        Get
            ' The code can access the Price property because it is
            ' a public part of the base class Product.
            ' The code cannot access the private _Price variable.
            Return (Price * _TaxRate)
        End Get
    End Property

End Class
```

**C#**

```
public class TaxableProduct : Product
{
    decimal taxRate = 1.15;

    public decimal TotalPrice
    {
        get
        {
            // The code can access the Price property because it is
            // a public part of the base class Product.
            // The code cannot access the private price variable.
            return (Price * taxRate);
        }
    }
}
```

This technique appears much more useful than it really is. In an ordinary application, most classes use containment and other relationships instead of inheritance, which can complicate life needlessly without delivering many benefits.

### Inheritance in ASP.NET

There is one place that you will see inheritance at work in ASP.NET. Inheritance allows you to create a custom class that inherits the features of a class in the .NET class library. For example, when you create a custom web form, you actually inherit from a basic Page class to gain the standard set of features (such as accessing the Response and Request objects). Similarly, when you create a custom Web Service, you inherit from the WebService class. You'll see this type of inheritance throughout the book.

## Shared Members

The beginning of this chapter introduced the idea of shared properties and methods, which can be used without a live object. Shared members are often used to provide useful functionality related to an object. The .NET class library uses this technique heavily. For example, the System.Math class is entirely composed of shared methods for performing mathematical operations. You never need to specifically create a Math object.

```
' Math is the class name, not an instance object!
MyVal = Math.Sin(AngleInRadians)
```

Shared members have a wide variety of possible uses. Sometimes they provide basic conversions and utility functions that support a class. To create a shared properties or method, you just need to use the shared (or static in C#) keyword, right after the public/private access keyword.

**VB .NET**

```
Public Class TaxableProduct
    Inherits Product

    ' (Other class code omitted for clarity.)

    Public Shared ReadOnly Property TaxRate() As Decimal
        Get
            ' Now you can call TaxableProduct.TaxRate,
            ' even without an object.
```

```
            Return _TaxRate
        End Get
    End Property

End Class
```

**C#**

```
public class TaxableProduct : Product
{

    // (Other class code omitted for clarity.)

    public static decimal TaxRate
    {
        get
        {
            // Now you can call TaxableProduct.TaxRate,
            // even without an object.
            return taxRate;
        }
    }
}
```

A shared member can't access an instance member. In order to access a non-shared member, it needs an actual instance of your object—in which case it must also be an instance member.

## Casting

Classes can be converted using the same syntax you used with simple data types. However, a class can only be converted into three things: itself, an interface that it supports, or a base class that it inherits from. You can't convert a class into a string or an integer. Instead, you will need to call a supported method such as ToString.

For example, you could convert a TaxableProduct variable into a Product variable. You wouldn't actually lose any information, but you would no longer be able to access the TotalPrice property, unless you converted the reference back to a TaxableProduct variable. Similarly, every class can be converted to the base System.Object type, because all .NET classes implicitly inherit from it.

The following code example creates a TaxableProduct, assigns it to a Product variable, and then checks if the object can be safely transformed into a TaxableProduct (it can).

**VB .NET**

```
' Create two empty variables (don't use the New keyword).
Dim TheProduct As Product
Dim TheTaxableProduct As TaxableProduct

' This works, because TaxableProduct derives from Product.
TheProduct = New TaxableProduct()

' This will be True.
If TypeOf TheProduct Is TaxableProduct Then
    ' Convert the object and assign to the other variable.
    TheTaxableProduct = CType(TheProduct, TaxableProduct)
End If

Dim TotalPrice As Decimal

' This works.
TotalPrice = TheTaxableProduct.TotalPrice

' This won't work, even though TheTaxableProduct and TheProduct are
' the same object.
' The Product class does not provide a TotalPrice property.
TotalPrice = TheProduct.TotalPrice
```

**C#**

```
// Create two empty variables (don't use the New keyword).
Product theProduct;
TaxableProduct theTaxableProduct;

// This works, because TaxableProduct derives from Product.
theProduct = new TaxableProduct();

// This will be true.
if (theProduct == TaxableProduct)
{
    // Convert the object and assign to the other variable.
    theTaxableProduct = (TaxableProduct)theProduct;
}

decimal totalPrice;
```

```
// This works.
totalPrice = theTaxableProduct.TotalPrice;

// This won't work, even though theTaxableProduct and theProduct
// are the same object.
// The Product class does not provide a TotalPrice property.
totalPrice = theProduct.TotalPrice;
```

There are many more subtleties of class-based programming with inheritance. For example, you can override parts of a base class, prevent classes from being inherited, or create a class that must be used for inheritance and can't be directly created. These topics aren't covered in this book, and they don't affect most ASP.NET programmers.

## Understanding Namespaces and Assemblies

Whether you realize it at first or not, every piece of code in .NET exists inside a class. In turn, every class exists inside a namespace. Figure 3-3 shows this arrangement for your own code and the DataTime object. Keep in mind that this is an extreme simplification—the System namespace alone is stocked with several hundred classes.

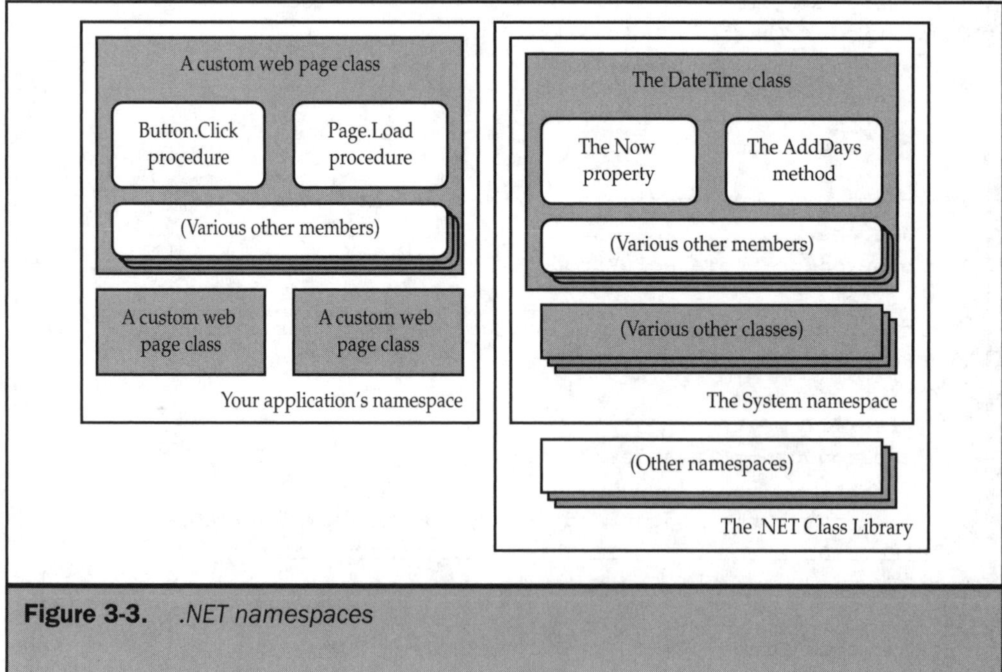


**Figure 3-3.** *.NET namespaces*

Namespaces represent the single organizing principle used to group all the different types in the class library. Without namespaces, these types would all be grouped into a single long and messy list, much like the disorganized Windows API. This type of organization is practical for a small set of information, but it would be useless for the thousands of types included with .NET.

Many of the chapters in this book introduce you to one of .NET's namespaces. For example, in the chapters on web controls, you'll learn how to use the objects in the System.Web.UI namespace. In the chapters about Web Services, you'll study the types in the System.Web.Services namespace. For databases, you'll turn to the System.Data namespace. In fact, you've already learned a little about one namespace: the basic System namespace that contains all the simple data types explained in the previous chapter. To continue your exploration after you've finished the book, you'll need to turn to the MSDN reference, which painstakingly documents the properties, methods, and events of every class in every namespace (see Figure 3-4).

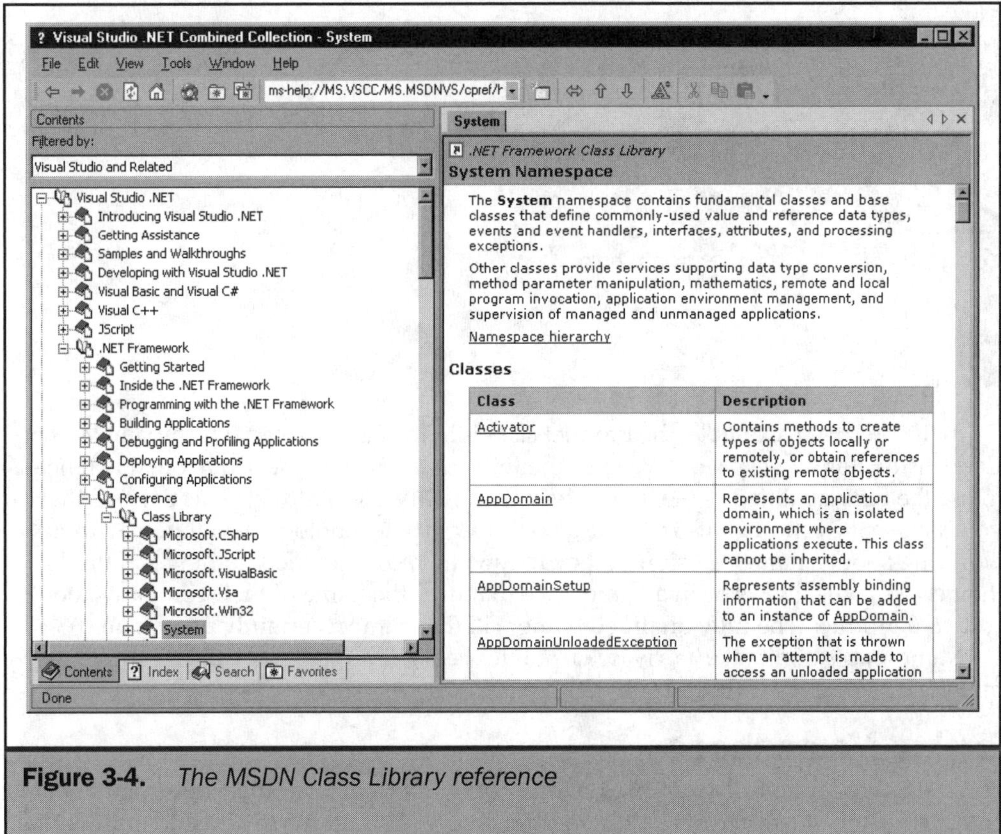


**Figure 3-4.** *The MSDN Class Library reference*

Often when you write ASP.NET code, you will just use the default namespace. If, however, you want to create a more specific namespace, you can do so using a simple block structure:

**VB .NET**

```
Namespace MyCompany
    Namespace MyApp
        Public Class Product
            ' Code goes here.
        End Class
    End Namespace
End Namespace
```

**C#**

```
namespace MyCompany
{
    namespace MyApp
    {
        public class Product
        {
            // Code goes here.
        }
    }
}
```

In the preceding example, the Product class is in the namespace MyCompany.MyApp. Code inside this namespace can access the Product class by name. Code outside it needs to use the fully qualified name, as in MyCompany.MyApp.Product. This ensures that you can use the components from various third-party technology developers without worrying about a name collision. If they follow the recommended naming standards, their classes will always be in a namespace that uses the name of their company and software product. The fully qualified name will then almost certainly be unique.

Namespaces don't take a private or public access keyword, and can be stacked as many layers deep as you need.

## Importing Namespaces

Having to type long fully qualified names is certain to tire out the fingers and create overly verbose code. To tighten things up, it's standard practice to import the namespaces you want to use. When you import a namespace, you don't need to type the fully qualified name. Instead, you can use the object as though it is defined locally.

To import a namespace, you use the Imports statement in VB .NET, or the using statement in C#. These statements must appear as the first lines in your code file, outside of any namespaces or block structures.

**VB .NET**

```
Imports MyCompany.MyApp
```

**C#**

```
using MyCompany.MyApp;
```

Consider the situation without importing a namespace:

**VB .NET**

```
Dim salesProduct As New MyCompany.MyApp.Product()
```

**C#**

```
MyCompany.MyApp.Product salesProduct = new MyCompany.MyApp.Product();
```

It's much more manageable when you import the MyCompany.MyApp namespace:

**VB .NET**

```
Dim salesProduct As New Product()
```

**C#**

```
Product salesProduct = new Product();
```

## Assemblies

You might wonder what gives you the ability to use the class library namespaces in a .NET program. Are they hard-wired directly into the language? The truth is that all

.NET classes are contained in assemblies, which is the .NET equivalent of traditional .exe and .dll files. There are two ways you can use an assembly:

- By placing it in the same directory or in a subdirectory of your application. The CLR will automatically examine all these assemblies and make their classes available to your application. No additional steps or registration are required.
- By placing it in the Global Assembly Cache (GAC), which is a systemwide store of shared assemblies. You won't take this option for your own components unless you are a component vendor. All the .NET classes, however, are a part of the GAC, because it wouldn't make sense to install them separately in every application directory. You'll learn more about assemblies in Chapter 21.

### Assemblies and the .NET Classes

The .NET classes are actually contained in a number of different assemblies. For example, the basic types in the System namespace come from the mscorlib.dll assembly. Many ASP.NET types are found in the System.Web.dll assembly. If you are precompiling your ASP.NET pages, you will need to explicitly reference these assemblies. This topic is covered in Chapter 5.

# The Complete Reference

# Chapter 4

## Setting Up ASP.NET and IIS

The last few chapters have presented a close-up, intensive look at the .NET languages. Before you start to apply some of this information to creating ASP.NET pages and applications, you need to make sure that you have the correct environment on your computer.

In other words, it's time to take a break from all the theory and new concepts, and handle a few simpler tasks. In this chapter, I'll walk you through the process of installing ASP.NET, using IIS Manager, and creating virtual directories. These tasks are supported by wizards or graphical tools, so they don't require the same level of expertise as actual ASP.NET programming. (If you are a seasoned ASP developer, you may already be familiar with IIS and the process of setting up a web server, in which case you'll make short work of this chapter.) The chapter ends with a few thoughts on how you can start to plan your migration strategy for existing ASP sites.

## Web Servers and You

Web servers run special software (namely, the built-in Internet Information Services, or IIS) to support mail exchange, FTP and HTTP access, and everything else clients expect in order to access web content. In most cases, you won't be developing on the same computer that you use for actual web hosting. If you were, you would hamper the performance of your web server by tying it up with development work. You might also frustrate clients when buggy testing leads to crashes and renders the web site unavailable, or when you accidentally overwrite the real deployed web site with a work in progress. Generally, you will perfect your web application on another computer, and then just copy all the files to the web server.

However, in order to use ASP.NET, your computer needs to act like a web server. In fact, while you are testing an ASP.NET application your development computer will work in exactly the same way as it would over an Internet connection to a remote client. When you test a page, you will actually access the page through IIS (which runs the ASP.NET service), and retrieve the final HTML through an HTTP transfer. The only difference between the way your computer works and the way a web server behaves is that your computer won't be visible and accessible to remote clients on the Internet.

This setup ensures that you can perfect security and perform realistic testing on your development computer. It also requires you to have the IIS software on your computer in order to use ASP.NET. IIS is included with Windows 2000, Windows XP, and Windows NT, but it is included as an optional component and is not installed by default. To create ASP.NET programs successfully, you need to make sure IIS is installed, preferably before you install the .NET framework or Visual Studio .NET.

### Installing IIS

Installing IIS is easy:

1. Click Start, and select Settings | Control Panel.
2. Choose Add Or Remove Programs.

3. Click Add/Remove Windows Components.
4. If Internet Information Services is checked (see Figure 4-1), you already have this component installed. Otherwise, click it and click Next to install the required IIS files.

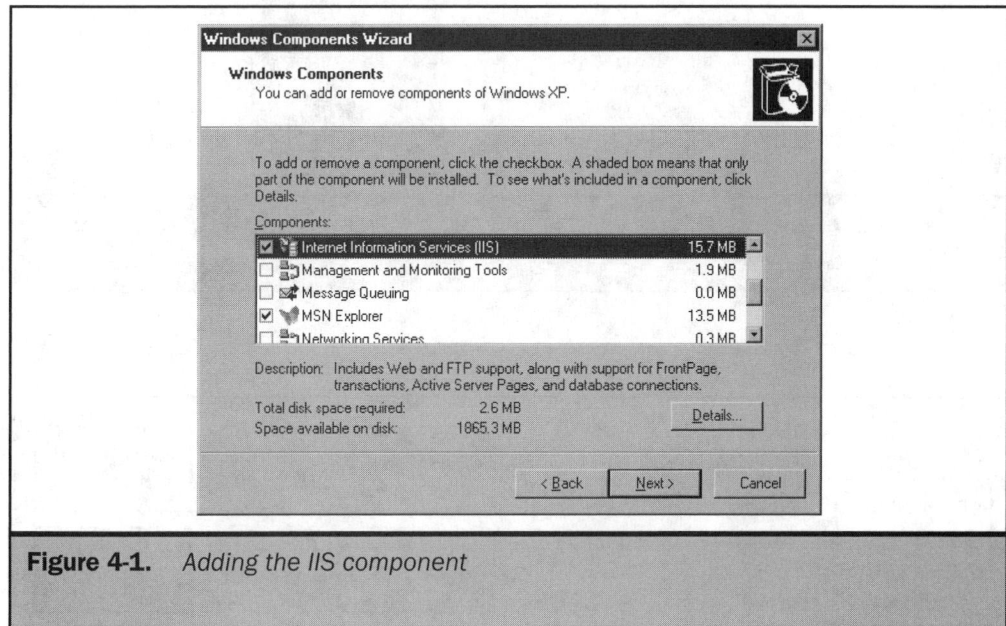


**Figure 4-1.** *Adding the IIS component*

When IIS is installed, it automatically creates a directory that represents your web site. This is the directory c:\Inetpub\wwwroot. Any files in this directory will appear as though they are in the root of your web server.

To test that IIS is installed correctly and running, browse to the c:\Inetpub\wwwroot directory, and verify that it contains a file called localstart.asp. This is a simple ASP (not ASP.NET) file that is automatically installed with IIS. If you try to double-click on this file to run it from the local directory, you'll receive an error message informing you that your computer doesn't know how to handle direct requests for ASP files (see Figure 4-2), or another program such as Microsoft FrontPage will try to open it for editing.

This limitation exists because of the way that ASP and ASP.NET files are processed. In a typical web scenario, IIS receives a request for a file. It then looks at the file extension, and uses that to determine if the file should be allowed, and what program (if any) is required to handle it. Ordinary HTML files will be sent directly to your browser. ASP files, however, will be processed by the ASP service (which IIS starts and invokes automatically). The ASP service creates an HTML stream with the final result of its processing, and IIS sends this file to the client. The whole process, which is diagrammed in Figure 4-3, is quite similar to how ASP.NET files are processed, as you'll see later.

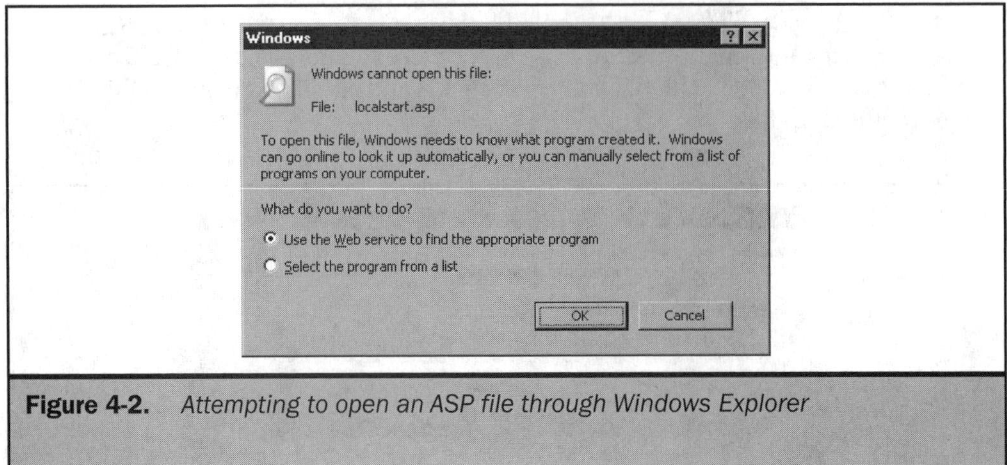


**Figure 4-2.** *Attempting to open an ASP file through Windows Explorer*

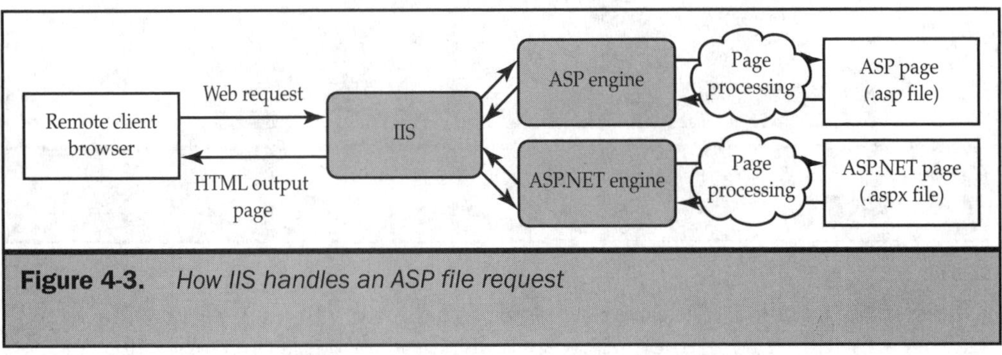


**Figure 4-3.** *How IIS handles an ASP file request*

So in order to test that IIS is working correctly, you need to request the localstart.asp file through IIS (and over the standard HTTP channel). To do this, open an Internet browser, and type a request for the file using the name of your computer. For example, if your computer name is devtest, you would type http://devtest/localstart.asp. IIS will receive your request, ASP will process the file, and you'll receive a generic introductory page in your browser (see Figure 4-4).

If you don't know the name of your computer, you can always find it out in IIS Manager. You can also use one of two presets that automatically refer to the local computer, whatever its name. These are the "loopback" address 127.0.0.1, and the alias localhost. That means you can try http://localhost/localstart.asp and http://127.0.0.1/localstart.asp.

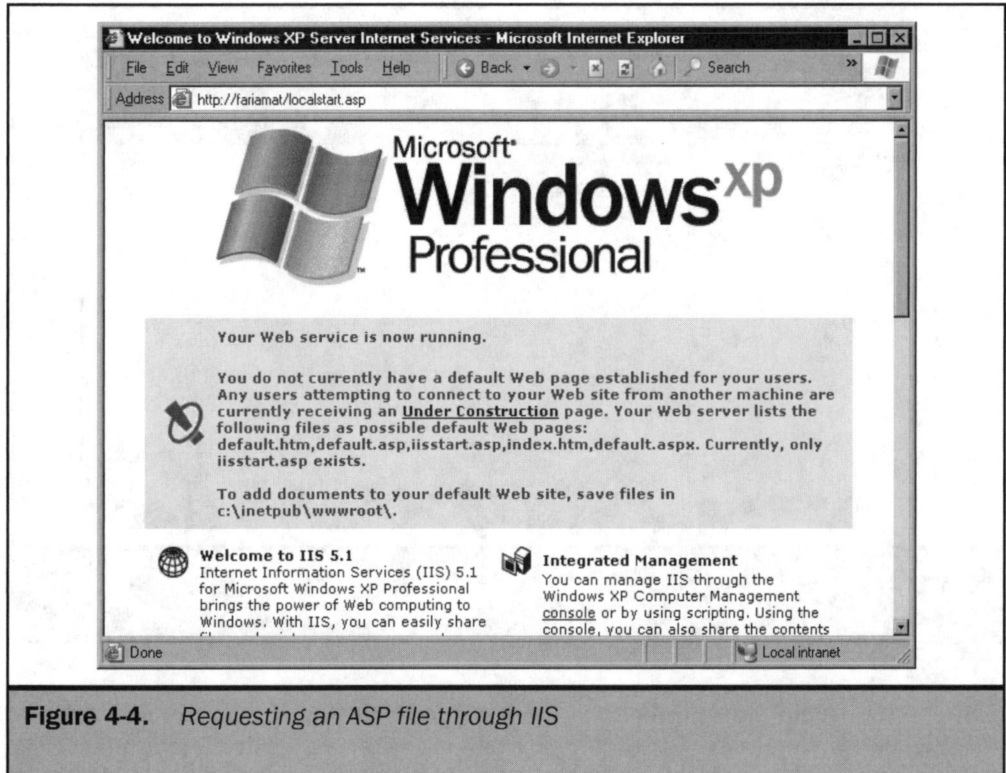


**Figure 4-4.** *Requesting an ASP file through IIS*

## What If I Can't Connect?

If you try the preceding steps, but receive an "unable to connect" message, you may need to investigate a little deeper. First of all, make sure you have the correct name for your computer. To verify it, start IIS Manager (select Settings | Control Panel | Administrative Tools | Internet Services Manager from the taskbar), and check what computer name appears in the tree.

Then expand the items under your computer, and click on the Web Sites folder. In the list on the right, it should indicate that your computer's default web site is running, as shown in Figure 4-5. If not, try right-clicking on the icon that represents your computer and choose to restart IIS.

Finally, you may need to tweak your Internet settings. For this task, choose Settings | Control Panel | Internet Options from the taskbar. Then choose the Connections tab.

If you are working on a local network and have special proxy server settings applied, verify that they do not conflict with your computer by clicking the LAN Settings button.

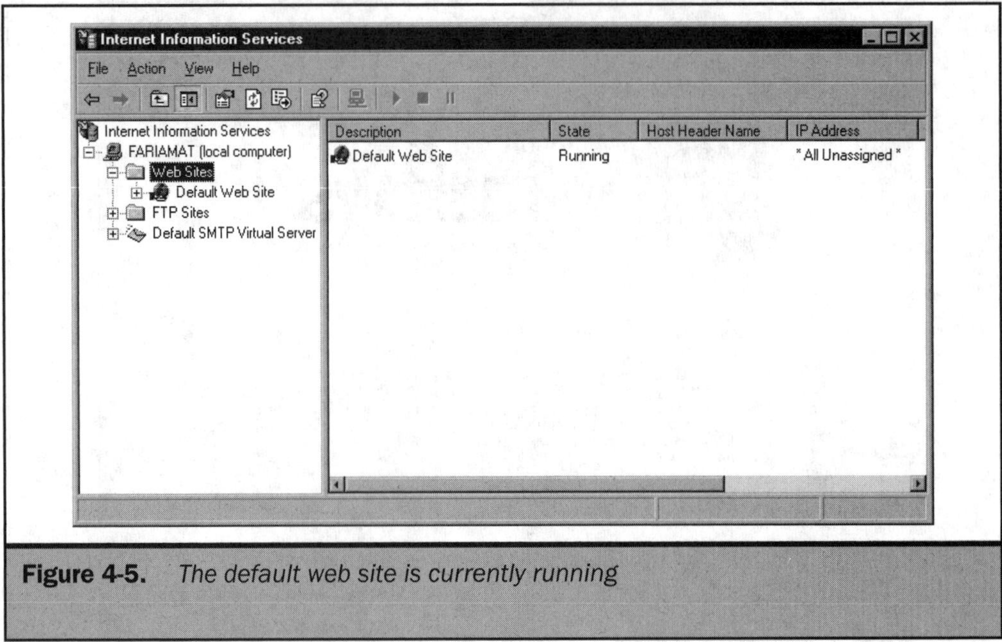


**Figure 4-5.** *The default web site is currently running*

If you connect to the Internet using a connection that is not always present (for example, using a modem to connect over a telephone line periodically), you may receive an error message that informs you that a local page cannot be loaded because you are currently working offline. In this case, just click Connect, and the page will appear successfully without you needing to actually connect to the Internet, as shown here:

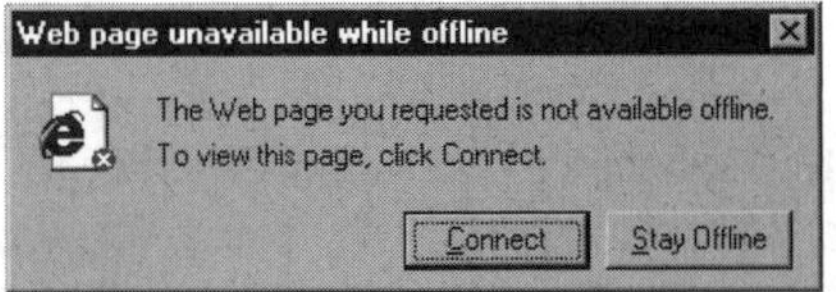


To prevent this message from appearing, you can select Never Dial A Connection from the Connections tab, although this will not always stop the problem from reoccurring. If you are prevented from performing another operation (such as creating a web project in Visual Studio .NET) because the operating system believes you are offline, simply request the http://localhost/localstart.asp file and click Connect when you are prompted to go online.

# IIS Manager

To add more ASP pages to your web server, you can copy the corresponding files into the c:\Intetpub\wwroot directory. You can even create subdirectories to group together related resources. However, this makes for poor organization. To properly use ASP or ASP.NET, you need to make your own custom virtual directory for each application you are designing. With a virtual directory, you can expose any physical directory (on any drive on your computer) on your web server, as though it were located in the c:\Inetpup\wwwroot directory.

To create virtual directories, you need to use the administrative IIS Manager program. To start it, select Settings | Control Panel | Administrative Tools | Internet Services Manager from the Start menu on the taskbar.

## Creating a Virtual Directory

To create a new virtual directory for an existing physical directory, right-click on the Default Web Site item (under your computer in the tree), and choose New | Virtual Directory from the context menu. A wizard will start, as shown in Figure 4-6.

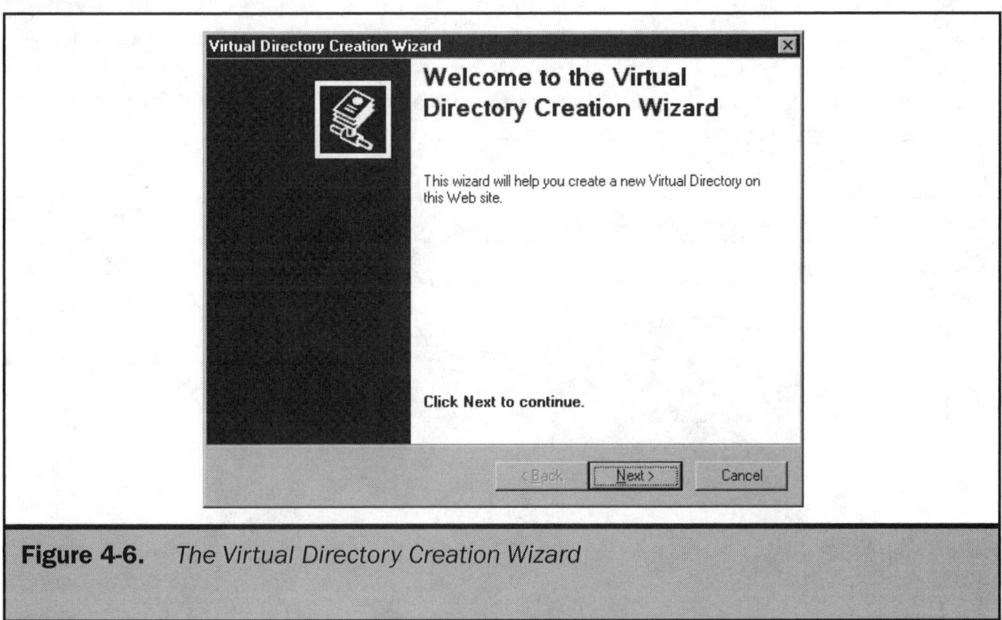


**Figure 4-6.** *The Virtual Directory Creation Wizard*

As you step through the wizard, you will need to provide several pieces of information.

## Alias

The alias is the name a client will use to access the files in this virtual directory. For example, if your alias is MyApp and your computer is MyServer, the user will request pages like http://MyServer/MyApp/MyPage.aspx.

## Directory

The directory is the physical source on your hard drive that is exposed as a virtual directory. For example, c:\Intetpub\wwwroot is the physical directory that is used for the root virtual directory of your web server. IIS will provide access to all the allowed file types in this directory. Generally, when starting a web application you will create a new physical directory to use, and then map it to a suitable virtual directory name.

## Permissions

Finally, you're asked to set Permissions for your virtual directory (Figure 4-7). There are several options:

- **Read** is the most basic permission—it's required in order for IIS to provide any requested files to the user. If this is disabled, the client will not be able to access ASP or ASP.NET pages, or static files like HTML and images. Note that even when you enable read permission, there are several other layers of possible security in IIS. For example, some file types (such as those that correspond to ASP.NET configuration files) are automatically restricted, even if they are in a directory that has read permission.

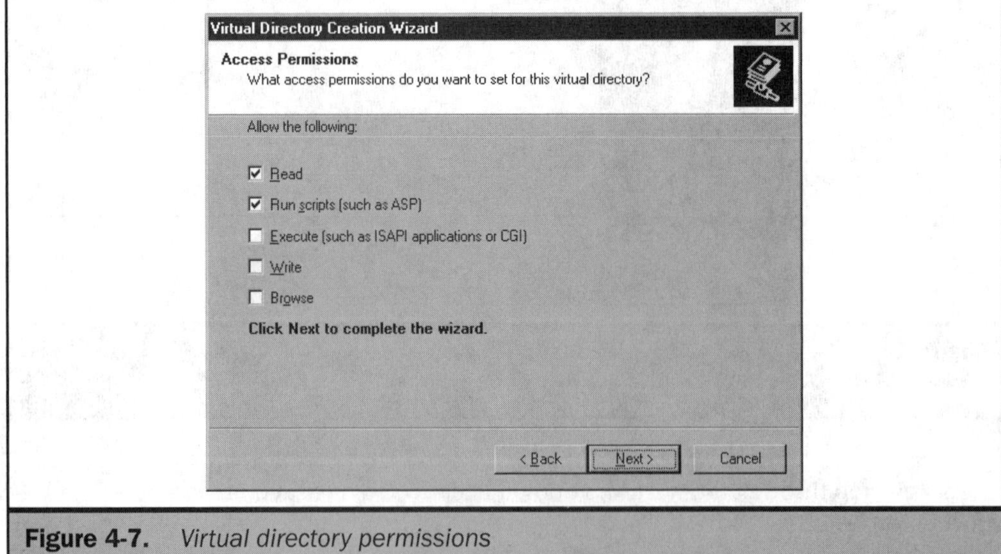


**Figure 4-7.** *Virtual directory permissions*

- **Run scripts** allows the user to request an ASP or ASP.NET page. If you enable read, but don't allow script permission, the user will be restricted to static file types such as HTML documents. ASP and ASP.NET pages require a higher permission because they could conceivable perform operations that would damage the web server or compromise security.
- **Execute** allows the user to run an ordinary executable file or CGI application. This is a possible security risk as well, and shouldn't be enabled unless you require it (which you won't for ordinary ASP or ASP.NET applications).
- **Write** allows the user to add, modify, or delete files on the web server. This permission should never be granted, because it could easily allow the computer to upload and then execute a dangerous script file (or at the least, use up all your available disk space). Instead, use an FTP site, or create an ASP.NET application that allows the user to upload specific types of information or files.
- **Browse** allows the user to look at all the files in the virtual directory, even if the contents of those files are restricted (as in the case of a special ASP.NET configuration file). Browse is generally disabled, because it allows users to discover additional information about your web site and its structure, and exploit possible security holes. On the other hand, it is quite useful for testing on a development computer.

You only need to enable the first two checkboxes, although you can allow more on a development computer that will never act as a live web server (keep in mind, however, this could allow other users on a local network to access and modify your files in the virtual directory). You can also change these settings after you have created the virtual directory.

## Virtual Directories and Applications

You can manage all the virtual directories on your computer in IIS manager by expanding the list under Default Web Site. You'll notice that items in the tree have three different types of icons (see Figure 4-8).

**Ordinary folder** This represents a subdirectory inside another virtual directory. For example, if you create a virtual directory and then add a subdirectory to the physical directory, it will be displayed here.

**Folders with a globe** This represents a distinct virtual directory.

**Package folders** This represents a virtual directory that is also a web application. By default, when you use the wizard to create a virtual directory, it is also configured as a web application. This means that it will share a common set of resources and run in its own separate application domain. The topic of web applications is examined in more detail in Chapter 5.

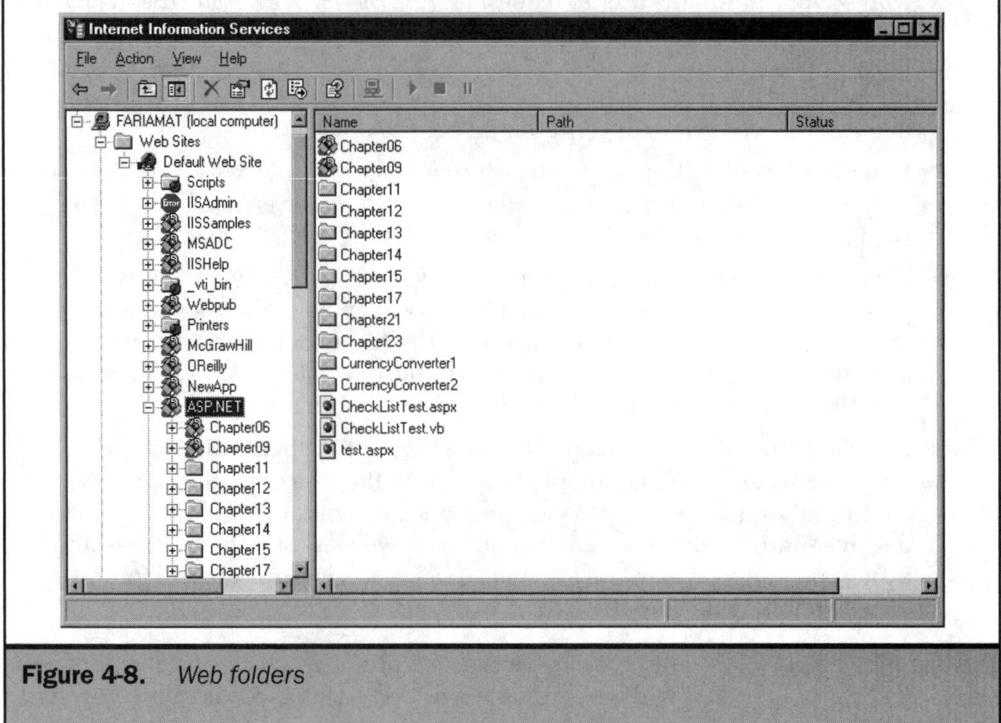


**Figure 4-8.** *Web folders*

## Virtual Directories Allow Access to Subdirectories

Imagine you create a virtual directory called MyApp on a computer called MyServer. The virtual directory corresponds to the physical directory c:\MyApp. If you add the subdirectory c:\MyApp\MoreFiles, this directory will automatically be included in the IIS Manager list as an ordinary folder. Clients will be able to access files in this folder by specifying the folder name, as in http://MyServer/MyApp/MoreFiles/.

By default, the subdirectory will inherit all the permissions of the virtual directory. However, you can change these settings in IIS Manager. This is a common technique used to break a single application into different parts (for example, if some pages require heightened security settings).

## Folder Settings

Permissions are managed on a directory-by-directory basis, which means that all the files in a directory need to share the same set of permissions. (Of course, not all file types are treated equally, as you'll see in the next chapter.) To apply different settings, you would typically create a virtual directory with more than one subdirectory, and set different options for each subdirectory.

To configure the options for a directory, right-click on it and choose Properties. The Properties window will appear, as shown in Figure 4-9.

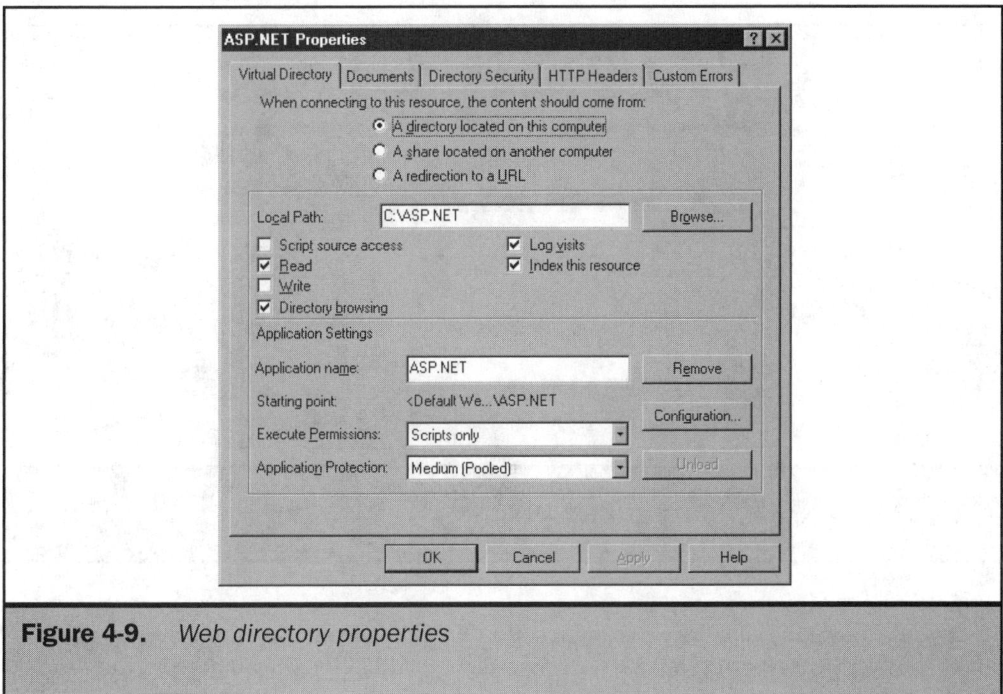


**Figure 4-9.** *Web directory properties*

The Virtual Directory tab contains the most important settings. These include options that allow you to change whatever permissions you set in the wizard. You are also provided with the local path that this directory corresponds to. If it's a virtual directory, you can change it to correspond to a different physical directory, but if it is an ordinary subdirectory inside a virtual directory, this field will be read-only.

Remember, when you create a virtual directory with the wizard, it is also configured as a web application. You can change this by clicking the Remove button next to the application name. Similarly, you can click the Create button to transform an ordinary virtual directory into a full-fledged application. Usually you won't need to perform these tasks, but it's nice to know they are available if you need to make a change.

Changes that you make are automatically propagated down to all subdirectories. If you want to make a change that will affect all applications, you can do it from the root directory (by right-clicking on the Default Web Site item and choosing Properties). If you have set custom settings in any other application or subdirectory, you will be warned. IIS will then present a list of directories that will be affected, as shown in Figure 4-10, and give you the chance to specify exactly which ones you want to change and which ones you want to leave as is.

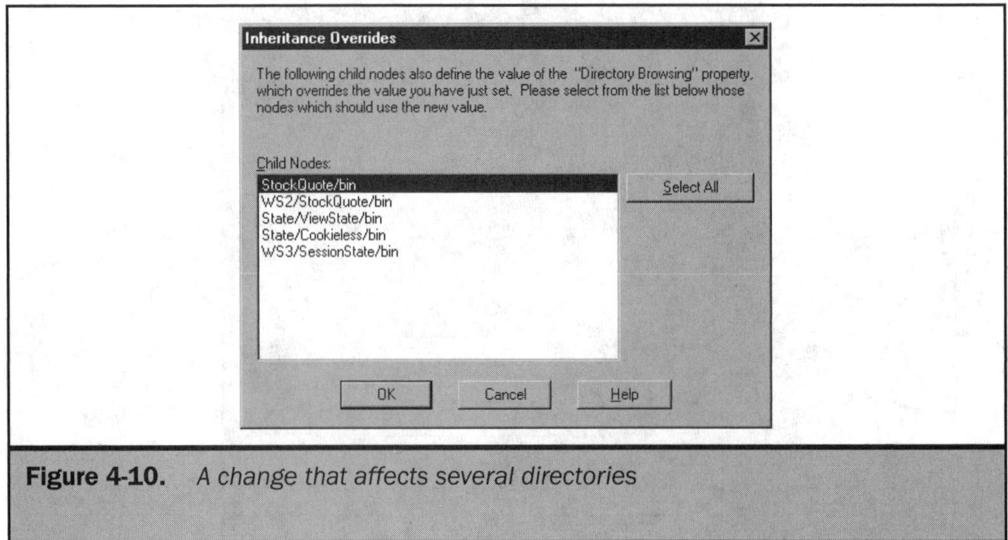


**Figure 4-10.** *A change that affects several directories*

If you explore the directory properties, you'll discover several other settings that affect ASP applications but don't have any effect on ASP.NET sites. These include the Application Protection (memory isolation) setting, and the options for session state, script timeout, and default language. These settings are all replaced by ASP.NET's new configuration file system, which you'll learn about in the next chapter. Some other settings are designed for security, and these are examined in Chapter 24.

There are only a few other settings worth noting.

## Custom Errors

This tab (see Figure 4-11) allows you to specify an error page that will displayed for specific types of HTTP errors. As you'll discover in Chapter 11, you can use various ASP.NET features to replace web or application errors with custom messages. However, these techniques won't work if the web request never makes it to the ASP.NET service (for example, if the user requests an HTML file that doesn't exist). In this case, you may want to supplement custom ASP.NET error handling with the appropriate IIS error pages for other error generic conditions.

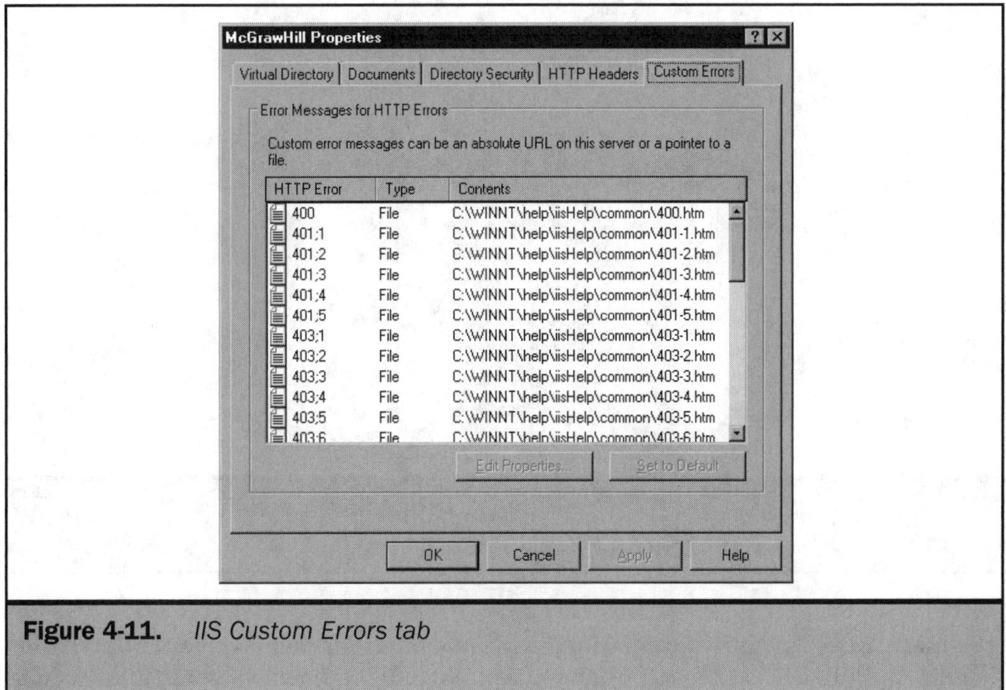


**Figure 4-11.** *IIS Custom Errors tab*

## File Mappings

As explained earlier in this chapter, IIS hands off requests for ASP.NET pages to the ASP.NET service, which is a specific DLL installed on your computer. However, both ASP and ASP.NET support a variety of file types. How does IIS know which files belong to ASP.NET and which ones belong to ASP?

The answer is found in the application file mappings. To view file mappings, click the Configuration button on the Virtual Directory tab (see Figure 4-12).

You'll notice that ASP files are mapped differently than ASP.NET files. For example, .asp requests are handled by C:\WINNT\System32\inetsrv\asp.dll, while .aspx requests are handled by C:\WINNT\Microsoft.NET\Framework\[version]\aspnet_isapi.dll. In other words, ASP.NET does not replace ASP. Instead, it runs alongside it, allowing ASP requests to be handled by the existing asp.dll, and providing a new aspnet_isapi.dll for ASP.NET page requests. This allows both types of applications to be hosted on the same web server with no potential conflict (and little possible integration).

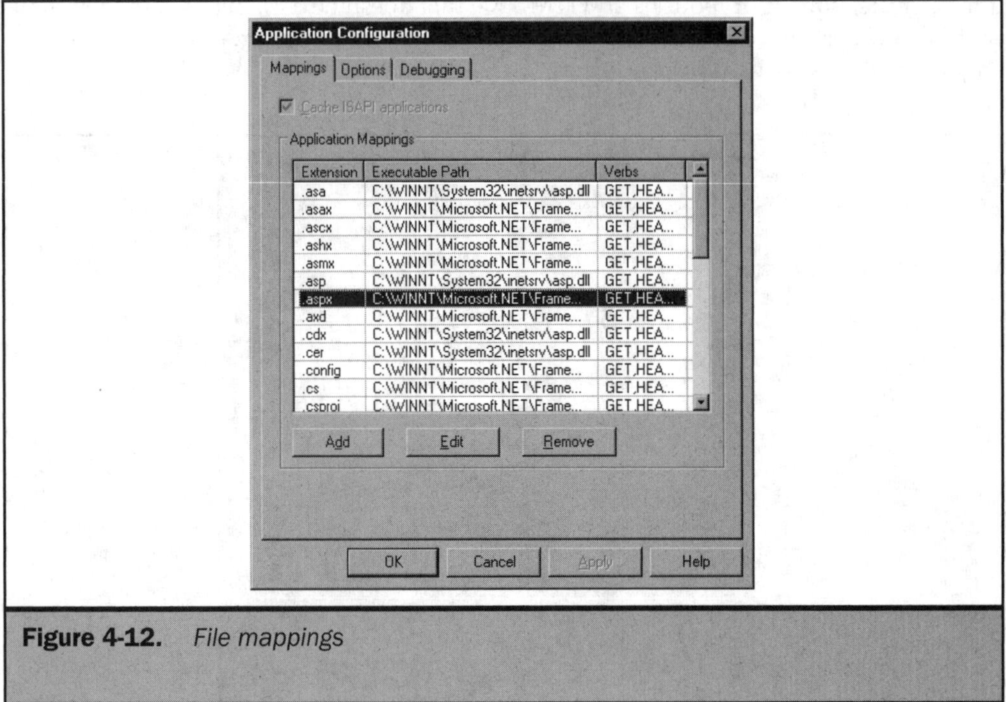


**Figure 4-12.** *File mappings*

In some cases, you might want to add a file mapping. For example, you could specify that the ASP.NET DLL will handle any requests for .GIF files, which would allow you to use ASP.NET security services to determine whether or not to allow the file, and ASP.NET events to log the request. (Note that this sort of change can slow down performance for GIF requests, which now need to trickle through more layers on the server.) ASP.NET uses this technique for configuration files. It is registered to handle all .config requests so that it can explicitly deny them, regardless of the IIS security settings.

Alternatively, you might want to remove a file mapping you don't need or a mapping that could be a security risk. In most cases, however, you won't need to worry about file mapping.

## File Mappings Are Configured Globally

When you modify a file mapping, it automatically applies to all virtual directories. All the other directory settings act on a single directory. For example, if you modify the custom error pages for an application, this change will not affect other applications.

## Adding a Virtual Directory to Your Neighborhood

Working with a web application can sometimes be a little inflexible. If you use Windows Explorer and look at the physical directory for the web site, you can see the full list of files, but you can't execute any of them directly. On the other hand, if you use your browser and go through the virtual directory, you can run any page, but there's no way to browse through a directory listing because virtual directories almost always have directory browsing permission disabled.

While you're developing an application you may want to circumvent this limitation. That way you can examine exactly what comprises your web application, and run several different pages easily, without needing to constantly type a full filename or dart back and forth between Internet Explorer and Windows Explorer. All you need to do is enable directory browsing for your virtual directory in IIS Manager. (You can easily enable or disable this setting from the directory properties window.)

Next, to make life even easier, you can add the virtual directory to the network neighborhood in Windows Explorer. First, open Windows Explorer. Then click on Network, and double-click on Add Network Place from the file list, as shown in Figure 4-13.

The Add Network Place Wizard will appear. This wizard allows you to create a network folder in Windows Explorer that represents your virtual directory (see Figure 4-14). The only important piece of information you need to specify is the address for your virtual directory (such as http://MyServer/MyFolder). Don't use the physical directory path.

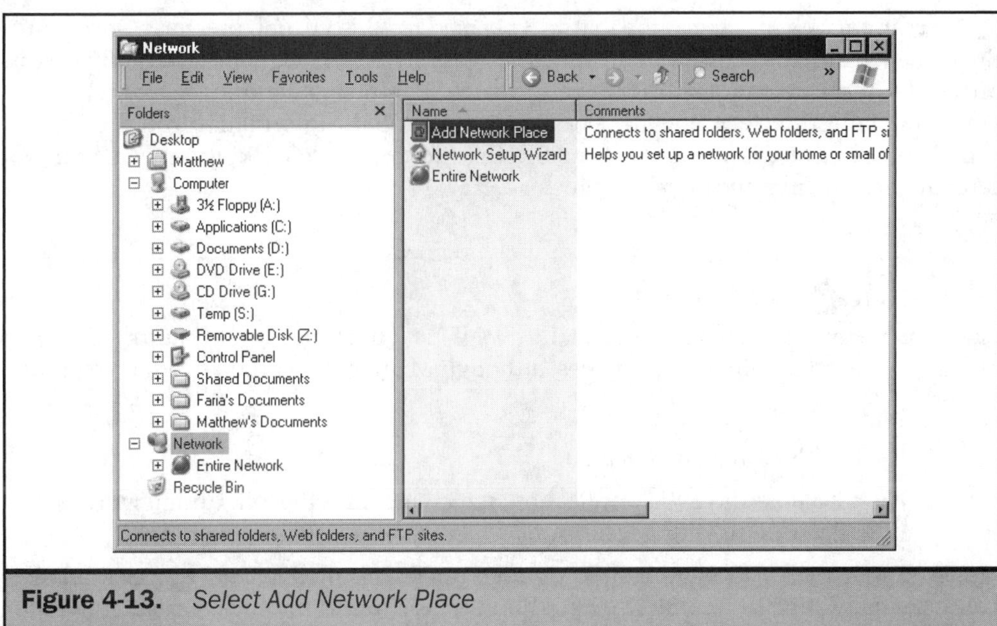


**Figure 4-13.** *Select Add Network Place*

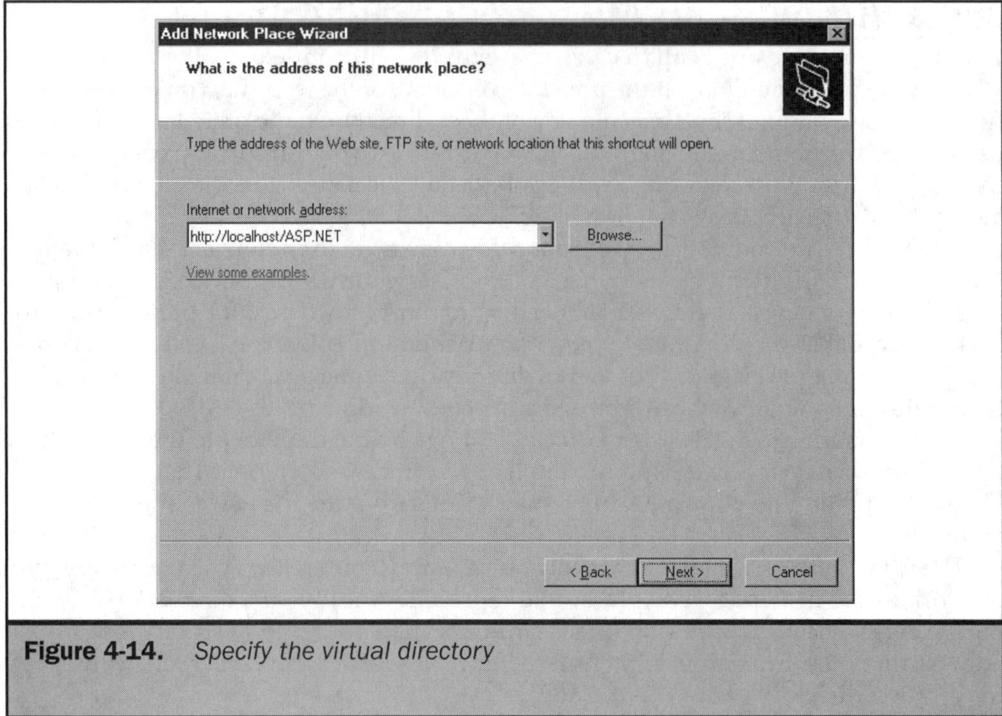


**Figure 4-14.** *Specify the virtual directory*

You can then choose the name that will be used for this virtual directory. Once you finish the wizard, the directory will appear in your network neighborhood, and you can browse through the remote files (see Figure 4-15). The interesting thing is that when you browse this directory, you are actually receiving all the information you need over HTTP. You can also execute an ASP or ASP.NET file by double-clicking—which you can't do directly from the physical directory.

## Installing ASP.NET

Once you've installed IIS, you can install ASP.NET. At the time of publication ASP.NET was available in two different packages, although Microsoft is certain to add even more options.

- The free .NET redistributable.
- The Visual Studio .NET application, which includes the .NET framework and an IDE to design your applications.
- The ASP.NET Premium edition, which can be installed instead of the standard redistributable, or after it. This edition adds support for output caching, web farm session state, and more than four CPUs in the web server.

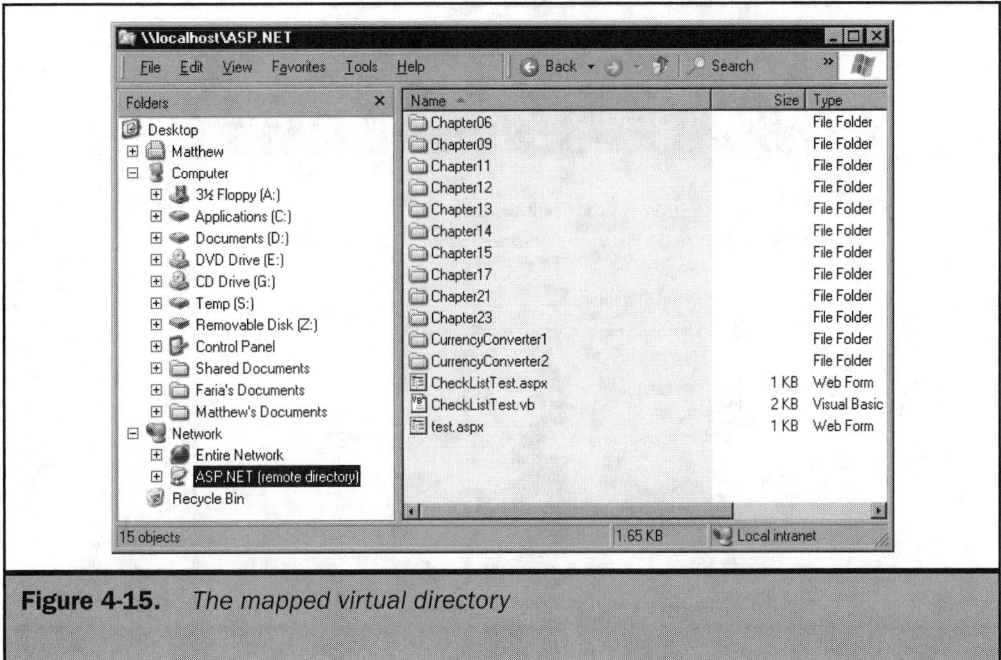


**Figure 4-15.** *The mapped virtual directory*

Like most Microsoft setups, the process is quite straightforward. A graphical wizard takes you through every step of the extremely long process (see Figure 4-16).

Depending on the version of the setup that you are using, the Microsoft Data Access Components 2.7 may not be automatically installed. If this is the case, you will receive a warning message when you start the install that asks if you want to continue. Before going any further, you should install these components. You can find them on the Internet at http://www.microsoft.com/data/.

## Getting the Samples

This book includes a wide range of code examples that are available online at http://www.prosetech.com/CompleteReference. These samples are downloadable as a single .ZIP file, which you can extract onto your computer using a utility like WinZip. In order to run the files, you'll need to place them into a virtual directory of your choice.

Along with the sample files are the additional project and solution files that Visual Studio .NET creates automatically for web applications. In order to open these projects in Visual Studio .NET without any problem, you need to use the exact same directory structure that I have used (which incorporates a C:\ASP.NET root directory). Generally, this directory structure will be created automatically when you unzip the file, but you will need to make sure you use the same drive (C:) to match what Visual Studio .NET expects. The exact installation instructions are described on the web site.

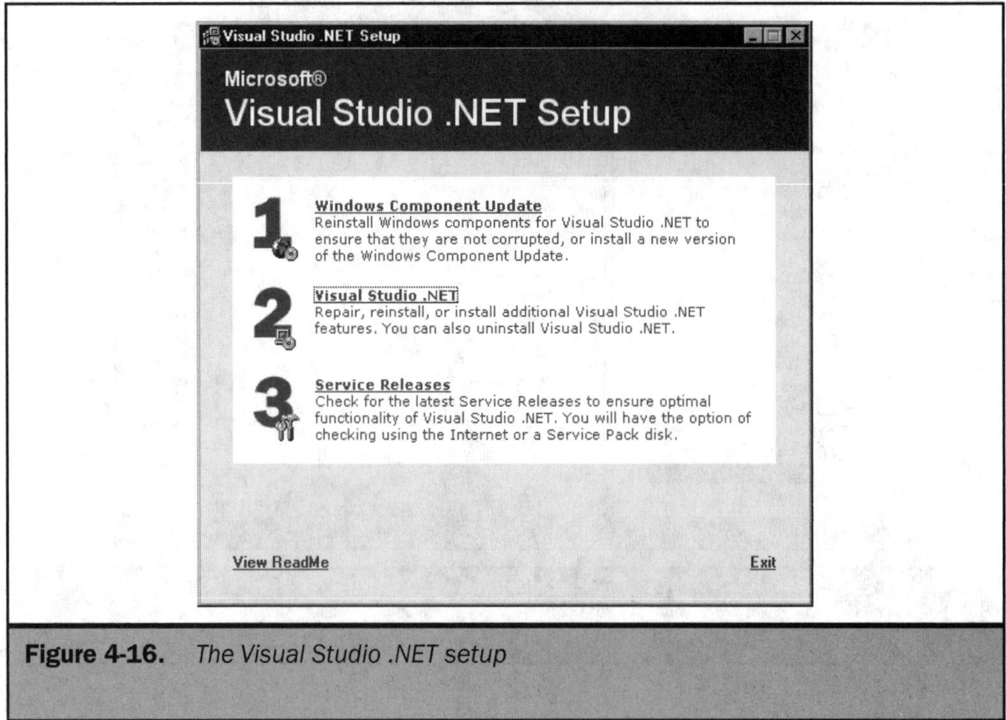


**Figure 4-16.** *The Visual Studio .NET setup*

## Migrating from ASP

Before continuing to the second part of this book, where we dive into ASP.NET coding, it makes sense to consider what will happen to the legacy ASP sites that exist today. If you're an ASP developer, you've probably created numerous web sites already. You may be interested in turning these ASP sites into full-featured ASP.NET applications so you can gain some of the benefits discussed in this book. Unfortunately, migration is often a tricky issue, and ASP.NET does not represent a minor upgrade. If you have a complex application that relies on COM components, client-side scripting, and Response.Write commands to create a sophisticated interface, you may have a substantial migration task on your hand. This section gives you a preview of the difficulties and changes that lie ahead. I won't try to hide the painful truth—migrating any application to .NET properly is not a quick task.

Fortunately, migration isn't always necessary. The .NET framework is designed with interoperability in mind, because Microsoft recognizes that it just isn't possible to abandon the last several years of development effort. With ASP.NET, you have three options:

- Run ASP applications alongside ASP.NET

- Replace ASP pages with similar ASP.NET pages
- Replace ASP pages with completely redesigned ASP.NET pages

## Run ASP Applications Alongside ASP.NET

ASP.NET does not replace ASP. In fact, even the file extensions used for ASP and ASP.NET web pages are different, which allows you to easily host ASP.NET and ASP web sites on the same server. Given time, you can start to replace some ASP pages with ASP.NET pages, and upgrade your application bit by bit. This approach has the advantage of allowing you to learn about ASP.NET as you develop, without forcing you to rush into extra work or commit to an abrupt upgrade that could replace your current, tested site with new bug-ridden software.

The main drawback to mingling ASP and ASP.NET pages in the same application is the fact that you cannot share state information. For example, if you add an object to Application state in an ASP page, you cannot retrieve it in an ASP.NET page, because the ASP.NET page uses an entirely different memory space and set of data on the server. Similarly, session information won't be shared (see Chapter 10 for a discussion about state management). Even worse, if you set information into the Session collection in an ASP page, and redirect the user to a series of ASP.NET pages, the current ASP session could actually time out because IIS will not detect any new requests to the ASP application. Mingling ASP with ASP.NET is generally easiest when you have a content-driven site that does not use much state management (or works directly with an underlying database or data store).

## Replace ASP Pages with Similar ASP.NET Pages

This approach tries to minimize development time by creating ASP.NET pages that resemble ASP pages. In many cases, this solution may work, because ASP.NET supports most of the syntax and features that were used in previous versions. However, this solution loses many of the advantages that ASP.NET offers, and also provides poor performance with apartment-threaded COM components.

In this case, it's worth asking whether it makes any sense to transfer an application to a different platform without cleaning up the mess traditional ASP code imposed. If you need a specific advanced feature that's offered in ASP.NET—for example, you need to enable web farm session state support—and you aren't interested in much else, this solution may make good sense. But in any other case, you will be wasting time tweaking your code and ironing out new inconsistencies when you really should be redesigning parts of your application.

## Replace ASP Pages with Redesigned ASP.NET Pages

This, of course, is the ideal solution. In this case, you will benefit from all of ASP.NET's new features, and create an application that is easier to debug, modify, and enhance. This approach also has a very significant drawback: it is by far the most time consuming.

If your ASP application works fine the way it is, there may not be much of a business case for replacing it with a new and improved version.

The actual difficulty required to move an application to ASP.NET depends on its sophistication, and how many custom workarounds or unusual solutions you are already using in ASP. Pages that make heavy use of Response.Write to create dynamic interfaces will need to be completely redesigned with the new event-driven server control model (see Chapters 6 and 7). Custom authentication routines may be replaced with ASP.NET's new forms-based security (see Chapter 24). COM components should be removed, and replaced with similar .NET assemblies (see Chapter 21). Database code must be rewritten from scratch using the new disconnected model and ADO.NET (see Chapters 12 and 13). If you have created a sophisticate e-commerce web site with a well thought-out and componentized design, it may be easier to start a new application from scratch than to attempt a migration—but it won't be quick.

The Complete Reference

# Part II

## Developing ASP.NET Applications

The Complete Reference

# Chapter 5

## ASP.NET Applications

The last few chapters gave a sweeping introduction to the .NET framework, including its languages, architecture, and underlying philosophy. They also examined how to set up your computer with the software and virtual directories you need to make ASP.NET applications. In this chapter, we dive into real ASP.NET programming with our first .aspx page.

As we introduce ASP.NET applications, you'll learn some of the core topics that every ASP.NET developer must master. We'll examine what makes up an ASP.NET site, and what file types you can use. Even more importantly, you'll learn how an ASP.NET application works behind the scenes, how to configure it, and how to use code-behind development to separate your web page user interface from its business logic. These concepts are the starting point for any ASP.NET programming project.

## ASP.NET Applications

It's sometimes difficult to define exactly what a web application is. Unlike a traditional desktop program (which is usually contained in a single .exe file), ASP.NET applications are divided into multiple web pages. This division means that a user can often enter an ASP.NET application at several different points, and follow a link out of your application to another part of your web site or another web server. So does it make sense to consider a web site as an application?

In ASP.NET, the answer is yes. Every individual ASP.NET application shares a common set of resources and configuration options. Web pages from other ASP.NET applications, even if they are on the same server, do not share these resources. Technically speaking, every ASP.NET application is executed inside a separate application domain, which is roughly similar to a Windows "process" in ordinary unmanaged code. Application domains are isolated in memory, meaning that if one web application causes a fatal error it won't affect any other applications that are currently running. Similarly, it also means that the web pages in one application can't access the in-memory information from another application. Each application has its own set of caching, application, and session state data.

The standard definition of an ASP.NET application describes it as a combination of files, pages, handlers, modules, and executable code that can be invoked from a virtual directory (and, optionally, its subdirectories) on a web server (see Figure 5-1). In other words, the virtual directory is the basic grouping structure that delimits an application.

In Chapter 4, you saw how you could create a virtual directory. The next step is to examine what this directory can contain.

### ASP.NET File Types

Applications in ASP.NET are a little more sophisticated than their ASP counterparts, and support several different types of files. Table 5-1 describes these file types.

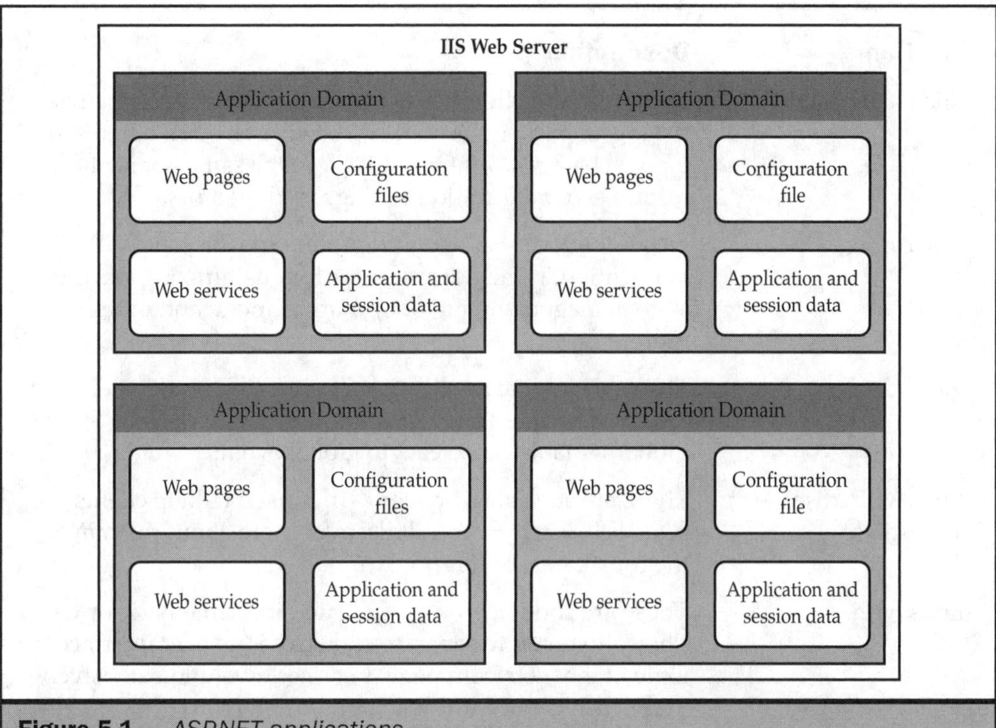


**Figure 5-1.** *ASP.NET applications*



| File Name | Description |
|---|---|
| Ends with .aspx | These are ASP.NET web pages (the .NET equivalent for the .asp file). They contain the user interface and some or all of the underlying code. Users request or navigate directly to one of these pages to start your web application. |
| Ends with .ascx | These are ASP.NET user controls. They are very similar to web pages, except that they must be hosted inside an .aspx file. User controls allow you to develop an important piece of user interface and reuse it in as many web forms as you want without repetitive code. |

**Table 5-1.** *ASP.NET File Types*

| File Name | Description |
|---|---|
| Ends with .asmx | These are ASP.NET Web Services, which are described in the fourth part of this book. Web Services work differently than web pages, but they still share the same application resources, configuration settings, and memory. |
| web.config | This is the XML-based configuration file for your ASP.NET application. It includes settings for customizing security, state management, memory management, and much more. |
| global.asax | This is the global application file (the .NET equivalent for the global.asa file). You use this file to define global variables and react to global events. |
| Ends with .disco or .vsdisco | These are special "discovery" files used to help clients find Web Services. You'll discover more about them in the fourth part of this book. |
| Ends with .vb or .cs | These are code-behind files created in Visual Basic or C#. They allow you to separate code from the user interface logic in the web form page. I use code-behind extensively in this book, and introduce it in this chapter. |
| Ends with .resx | These files may exist if you are using Visual Studio .NET. They are used to store information that you add at design time. |
| Ends with .sln, .suo, and .vbproj, csproj | These files are used by Visual Studio .NET to group together projects (a collection of files in a web application) and solutions (a collection of projects that you are developing or testing at once). They store a list of related files and some options for the Visual Studio .NET IDE. These files are only used during development and should not be deployed to a web server. However, even if they are the default, ASP.NET security setting will prevent a user from viewing them. |

**Table 5-1.** *ASP.NET File Types (continued)*

In addition, your directory can contain other resources that aren't special ASP.NET files. For example, it could hold image files, HTML files, or cascading style sheets (CSS files). Visual Studio .NET even adds a Styles.css file to your projects automatically for you to define styles that you want to use with controls. Its use is completely optional, and it has more to do with straight HTML than ASP.NET programming.

All of these files types are optional. You can create a legitimate ASP.NET application with a single web form (.aspx file) or Web Service (.asmx file).

### What About ASP Files?

None of the basic ASP files (such as .asp pages and the global.asa file) are used in ASP.NET. If you have a directory with .aspx and .asp files, you really have two applications. In fact, the process that manages and renders ASP files, and the .NET service that compiles and serves .aspx files, are two separate programs that don't share any information. That has a couple of important results:

- You can't share state information between ASP and ASP.NET applications. The Session and Application collections, for example, are completely separate.
- You specify ASP and ASP.NET settings in different ways. If you specify an ASP setting, it won't apply to ASP.NET, and vice versa.

Generally, you should keep ASP and ASP.NET files separate to avoid confusion. However, if you are migrating a large web site, you can safely use (and transfer the user between) both types of files, as long as they don't try to share resources.



## The bin Directory

In addition, every web application directory can have a special subdirectory called \bin. This directory holds the .NET assemblies used by your application. For example, you can develop a special database component in any .NET language, compile it to a DLL file, and place it in this directory. ASP.NET will automatically detect it and allow any page in that application to use it. This is far easier than traditional COM-based component development, which requires a component to be registered before it can be used (and often re-registered when it changes). Component-based development is explored in Chapter 21.

The \bin directory is also used with Visual Studio .NET to hold a compiled version of your code. This topic, which is a common source of confusion for new ASP.NET developers, is explained in detail a little later in this chapter.

## Application Updates

One of the most useful features of ASP.NET has nothing to do with new controls or enhanced functionality. Instead, it's the so-called "zero-touch" deployment and application updating that means you can modify your ASP.NET application easily and painlessly without needing to restart the server.

## Page Updates

If you modify a code file or web form, ASP.NET automatically recompiles an updated version with the next client request. This means that new client requests always use the most recent version of the page, as in ASP. The only difference is that ASP.NET uses automatic compilation to native machine code and caching to improve performance.

## Component Updates

You can replace any assembly in the \bin directory with a new version, even if it is currently in use. The file will never be locked. You can also add or delete assembly files without any problem. ASP.NET continuously monitors the \bin directory for changes. When a change is detected, it creates a new application domain and uses it to handle any new requests. Existing requests are completed using the old application domain, which contains a cached copy of all the old versions of the components. When all the existing requests are completed, this application domain is destroyed.

This automatic rollover feature, sometimes called shadow copy, allows you to painlessly update a web site that needs to be continuously active. If you favor the modern style of programming and design sites with reusable objects, ASP.NET's effortless updating will be a welcome change.

## Configuration Changes

In the somewhat painful days of ASP programming, configuring a web application was no easy task. You needed to either create a script that modified the IIS metabase or use the IIS Manager. Once a change was made, you would usually need to stop and start the IIS web service (again by using IIS Manager or the iisreset utility). Sometimes you would even need to reboot the server before the modification would take effect!

Fortunately, these tasks are no longer required for ASP.NET, which manages its own configuration independently from IIS. The configuration for a web application is defined using a web.config file, which is described at the end of this chapter. The web.config file stores information in a plain text XML format, so you can easily edit it with a tool like Notepad. If you change a web.config setting, the same automatic rollover happens that occurs for component updates. Existing requests complete with the original settings, and new requests are served by a new application domain that uses the new web.config settings. Once again, it's surprisingly easy (and relieving).

### Some IIS Settings Still Apply

There are still a few settings that need to be made at the IIS level and not just the web.config file. One example is with security—because IIS processes the request before ASP.NET, both IIS *and* ASP.NET security settings come into play. These minor exceptions are noted in this book, wherever they apply.

## A Simple Application from Start to Finish

Now that you know all the essential ingredients of a web application—files in a virtual directory—it's a good time to walk through the process from start to finish. In this case, we won't be using ASP.NET's new code-behind feature. We'll also steer away from Visual Studio .NET, and rely entirely on Notepad.

1. First, create the virtual directory for your application. In this case, I created C:\ASP.NET\TestWeb for this purpose in Windows Explorer.
2. The next step is to turn this folder into a virtual directory and web application, a process described in detail in Chapter 4. Essentially, you start the IIS Manager (Start | Programs | Administrative Tools | Internet Services Manager), right-click on Default Web Site, and select New Virtual Directory. IIS Manager is shown in Figure 5-2.

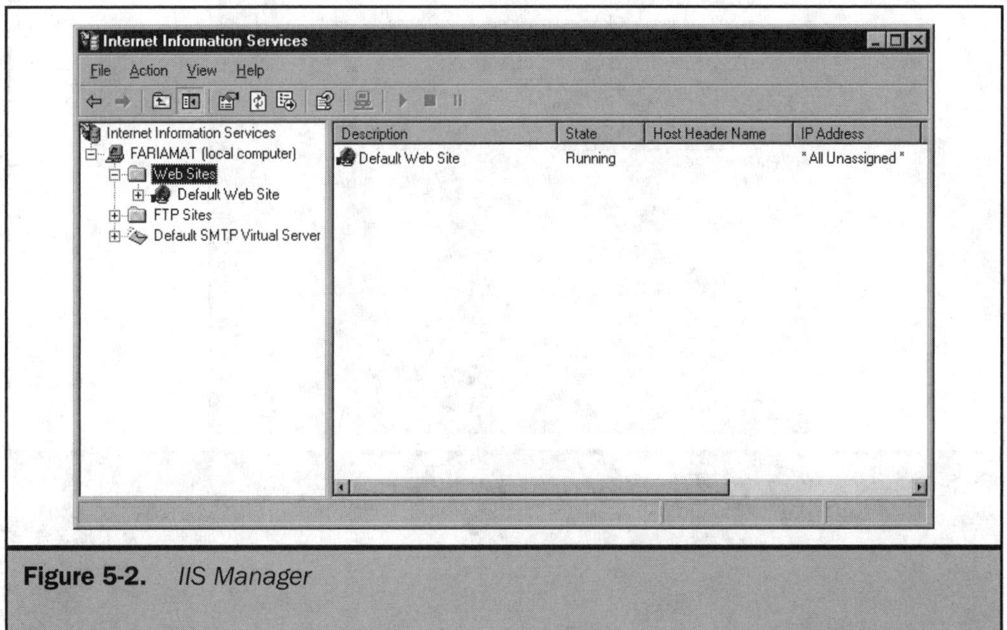


**Figure 5-2.** *IIS Manager*

3. Follow the wizard, choosing MyFirstWebApp for the virtual folder name (see Figure 5-3), and using the default settings.
4. Now, return to the C:\ASP.NET\TestWeb directory, and create a new text file called HelloWorld.aspx. Using Notepad, you can create the simple web page shown here. (We'll analyze this page a just a moment.)

```
<html>
<script language="VB" runat="server">
    Public Sub Page_Load()
```

```
        lblTest.Text = "Hello, the Page_Load event occurred."
    End Sub
</script>

<body>
<form id="Form" runat="server">
    <asp:Label id="lblTest" runat="server" />
</form>

</body>
</html>
```

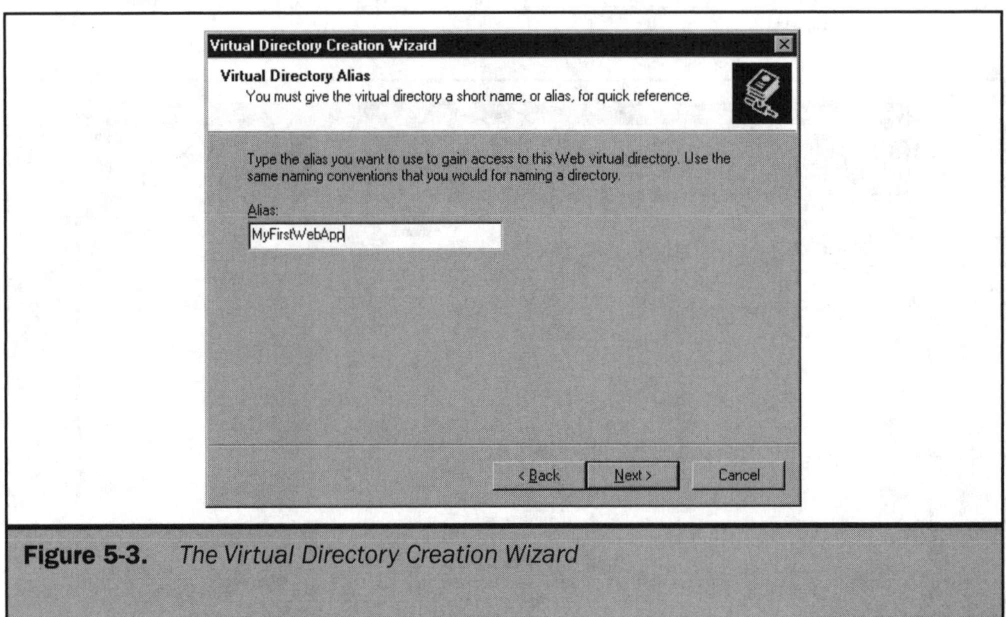


**Figure 5-3.** *The Virtual Directory Creation Wizard*

5. Save this file, open your browser, and request the web page. Remember, when you request the web page you need to specify the virtual directory name, which is not necessarily the same as the real directory name. You also need to know your computer name. For example, I set C:\ASP.NET\TestWeb to be a virtual directory called MyFirstWebApp, and my computer is called fariamat. That means I need to request http://fariamat/MyFirstWebApp/HelloWorld.aspx. The output for the HelloWorld.aspx page is shown in Figure 5-4.

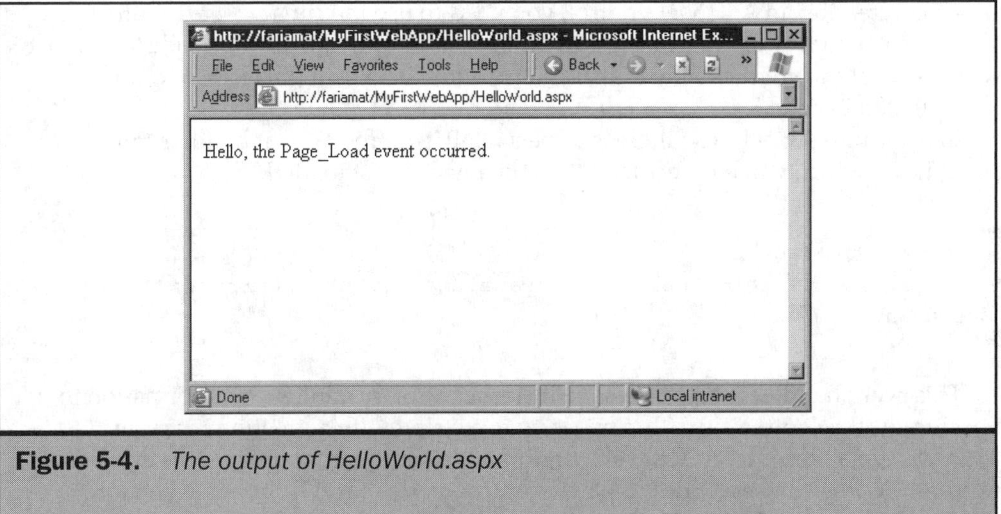


**Figure 5-4.** *The output of HelloWorld.aspx*



### What If I Don't Know the Computer Name?

You should always be able to determine your computer name by opening up Windows Explorer and looking at the network section. Alternatively, you can try the special TCP/IP "loop back" address 127.0.0.1, or the special computer name localhost, both of which are configured to always access the local server. The web address would then become http://127.0.0.1/MyFirstWebApp/HelloWorld.aspx or http://localhost/MyFirstWebApp/HelloWorld.aspx.

## Line by Line with HelloWorld.aspx

The HelloWorld.aspx web page has two parts: a script block that contains VB .NET code, and a form tag that holds all the ASP.NET server controls used on the page. We'll start backwards, by examining the controls first. In this case, there is only one, a special Label control (the <asp:Label> tag), which is a part of the ASP.NET framework. The Label control outputs plain text in a browser.

```
<form id="Form" runat="server">
    <asp:Label id="lblTest" runat="server" />
</form>
```

When creating an ASP.NET control, you need to use the runat="server" attribute. This specifies that your control is based on the server and allows your code to interact with it directly. A unique name is also assigned to the control (lblTest) so it can be manipulated in code.

In the actual script block, there is a special .NET-defined event handler called Page_Load, which will be executed when the page is first loaded.

```
Public Sub Page_Load()
    lblTest.Text = "Hello, the Page.Load event occurred."
End Sub
```

This event handler manipulates the lblTest control, putting some information in it. Specifically, the code sets the Text property to a string with a greeting message.

If you are a seasoned ASP developer, this code snippet probably seems extremely unusual, because it uses ASP.NET's new control model. (You'll probably be more familiar with this type of interaction if you are a traditional Visual Basic developer.) Chapter 6 explains this new model—and its many advantages—in detail.

## Behind the Scenes with HelloWorld.aspx

So what really happens when ASP.NET receives a request for the HelloWorld.aspx file? The process actually unfolds over several steps.

1. First of all, IIS determines that the .aspx file extension belongs to ASP.NET and passes it along to the ASP.NET worker process. If the file extension belonged to another service (as it would for .asp or .bmp files), ASP.NET would never get involved.

2. If this is the first time a page in this application has been requested, ASP.NET automatically creates the application domain and a special application object (technically, an instance derived from the .NET class System.Web.Http-Application). If there are any global.asax variables that need to be created or events that need to be run, ASP.NET performs those tasks now. ASP.NET applications are only created once and are shared by all clients. Once the application is running, it will never shut down unless you reboot the computer or terminate the process manually.

3. ASP.NET now considers the specific .aspx file. If it has never been executed, ASP.NET compiles and caches an executable version (compiled to native machine code) for optimum performance. If this task has already been performed (for example, someone else has already requested this page) and the file has not been changed, ASP.NET will use the precompiled version.

4. The compiled HelloWorld.aspx acts like a miniature program. It starts and runs all its code (in this case the Page_Load event). At this stage, everything is working together as a set of in-memory .NET objects.

5. When the code is finished, ASP.NET asks every control in the web page to render itself. For example, the label control takes its text property and transforms it into the standard HTML that is required. (In fact, ASP.NET performs a little sleight of hand, and may customize the output with additional client-side JavaScript or DHTML if it detects that the client browser supports it. In the case of HelloWorld.aspx, the output of the label control is too simple to require this type of automatic tweaking.)
6. The final page is sent to the user, and the application ends.

The description is lengthy, but it's important to start off with a good understanding of the fundamentals. Figure 5-5 illustrates the stages in a web page request.



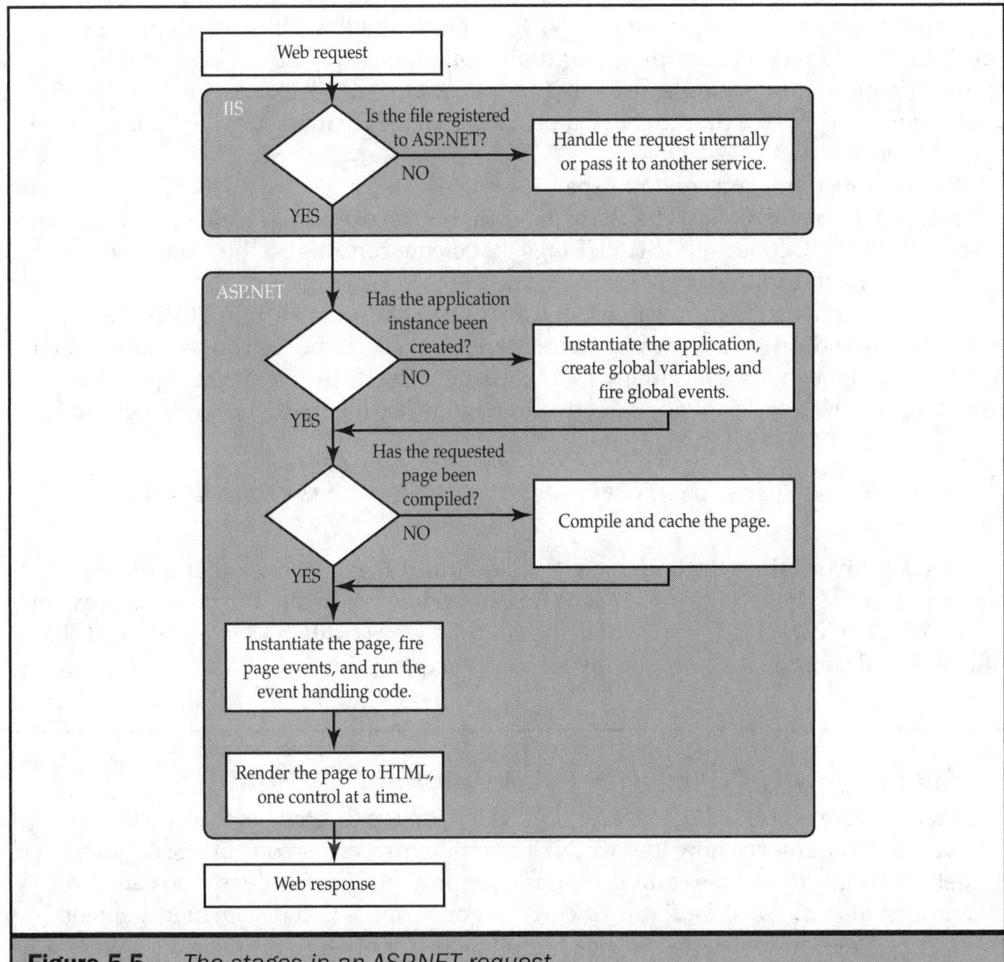


**Figure 5-5.** *The stages in an ASP.NET request*

The most important detail is the fact that your code works with objects. The final step is to transform these objects into the appropriate HTML output. A similar conversion from objects to output happens with a Windows program in Visual Basic 6 or VB .NET, but it's so automatic that programmers rarely give it much thought. Also, in those environments the code is always being run locally. In an ASP.NET application, the code runs in a protected environment on the server. The client only sees the results once the web page processing has ended and the program has been released from memory.

## Code-Behind

Before we can finish our transformation from traditional ASP development to the object-oriented .NET world, we need to consider the technique of code-behind programming. This innovation is so important to ASP.NET development that I believe all professional ASP.NET developers will adopt it eventually. Microsoft-sponsored best-of-breed platform samples (for example, the IBuySpy case studies we'll explore in Chapter 25) use it extensively. Visual Studio .NET, a premier tool for creating ASP.NET sites, uses it natively and exclusively.

With code-behind, you create a separate code file (a .vb file for VB .NET or .cs file for C#) to match every .aspx file. The .aspx file contains the user interface logic, which is the series of HTML code and ASP.NET tags that create controls on the page. The .vb or .cs file contains code only.

To create the .aspx file, you can use the advanced features of any HTML editor, or you can drag-and-drop your way to success with Visual Studio .NET's own integrated web form designer, which has many more indispensable features. At the top of the .aspx file, you use a special Page directive that identifies the matching code-behind file.

```
<%@ Page Language="VB" Inherits="MyPageClass" Src="MyPage.vb" %>
```

This directive defines the language (VB), identifies the page class that contains all the page code (MyPageClass), and identifies the source file where the page class can be found (MyPage.vb). Like the .aspx file, the source code is contained in a plain text file. ASP.NET will compile it automatically for a web request.

### The Page Directive Sets Pre-processor Options

Directives are processed before any ASP.NET code is executed, and set various options that influence how the ASP.NET compiler processes your file. Setting the default language and the code-behind file are only two possibilities. You can also add attributes that will configure tracing, language options, and state management settings. These attributes are explained throughout this book, in the related chapters.

The MyPage.vb file needs to have a page class, which is defined like any other .NET class. In Visual Basic, you use a Class/End Class block.

```
Public Class MyPageClass
  Inherits System.Web.UI.Page
    ' (Code goes here.)
End Class
```

The only trick is that this page inherits from a special generic Page class. If you remember the .NET primer in Chapter 3, you'll recognize that the Page class is in the namespace System.Web.UI, which contains all sorts of types used for ASP.NET user interface.

You can now add code inside the page class. For example, you could rewrite HelloWorld2.aspx with code-behind as two files:

**HelloWorld2.aspx**

```
<%@ Page Language="VB" Inherits="HelloWorldClass"
Src="HelloWorld2.vb" %>
<html>
<body>
<form id="Form" runat="server">
    <asp:Label id="lblTest" runat="server" />
</form>

</body>
</html>
```

**HelloWorld2.vb**

```
Public Class HelloWorldClass
  Inherits System.Web.UI.Page
    Protected lblTest As System.Web.UI.WebControls.Label

    Public Sub Page_Load()
        lblTest.Text = "Hello, the Page_Load event occurred."
    End Sub

End Class
```

In the HelloWorld2.vb code-behind file, you need to add an additional line to define the Label control. All ASP.NET controls must be defined using the Protected keyword.

```
Protected lblTest As System.Web.UI.WebControls.Label
```

You should make sure that the control name matches the id attribute in the <asp:Label> tag exactly. This allows ASP.NET to connect the controls in your .aspx template file to the controls that you manipulate in your code. It also allows code editors like Visual Studio .NET to check for syntax errors, such as an attempt to use an undeclared variable or a property that the label control doesn't support. You'll learn more about how Visual Studio .NET automates some of the chores associated with ASP.NET development in Chapter 8.

In the case of HelloWorld.aspx, the code is so simple that you don't receive much of a benefit from code-behind development. However, the advantage increases dramatically as you begin to add more complex ASP.NET controls and code routines.

## Web Form Inheritance Explained

One potentially confusing aspect in the preceding example is the fact that the word "Inherits" is used twice: once in the .aspx template file, and once in the code file. You might be wondering who is inheriting from what, and why?

There are actually three stages involved, as shown in Figure 5-6.

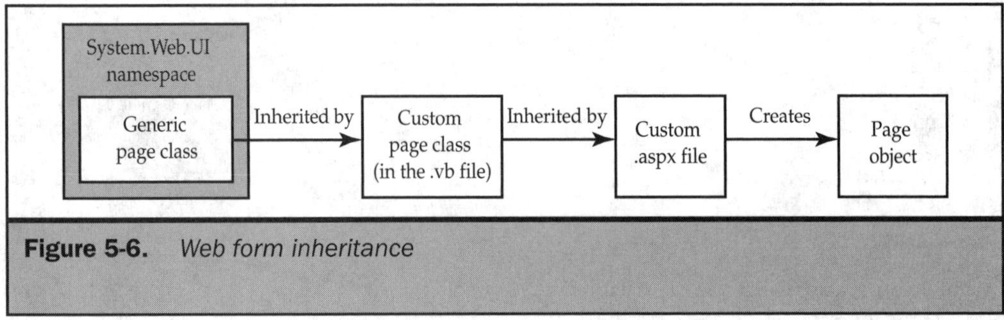


**Figure 5-6.** *Web form inheritance*

1. First, there is the Page class from the .NET class library. This class defines the basic functionality that allows a web page to host other controls, render itself to HTML, and provide access to the traditional ASP objects such as Request, Response, and Session.
2. Second, there is your code-behind class (for example, HelloWorldPage). This class inherits from the Page class to acquire the basic set of ASP.NET web page functionality. (And believe me, you wouldn't want to code that yourself.)

3. Finally, the .aspx page (for example, HelloWorld.aspx) inherits the code from the custom form class you created. This allows it to combine the user interface with the code that supports it.

### The Page Class Is Not Just a Code-Behind Feature

Even if you aren't using code-behind development, the System.Web.UI.Page class is still being used. Every time an .aspx file is requested, ASP.NET derives a special custom class from the generic Page class to represent the page. That means you can use all the properties and features of the Page class in your code, even if you write your code routines in a script block inside the .aspx file.

The only difference is the syntax. In code-behind development, you *explicitly* inherit from the Page class. This technique provides you with increased clarity, and an extra layer of flexibility. For example, you could create your own template class that inherits from Page and defines some additional features. Then you could inherit from this class in your code-behind files to create several different web pages in your site. This technique might not be used by most programmers, but it's a key to .NET's expandable, object-oriented design. It also becomes much more important when you start to design custom controls like those described in Chapter 22.



## Compiled Code-Behind Files

There is another way to use code-behind files: as precompiled assemblies. This technique is important because Visual Studio .NET uses it automatically. It's also a point of confusion that confounds many new ASP.NET programmers.

Essentially, you can precompile your code-behind file into a .NET assembly. (An assembly is just a logical container for compiled code. It's usually provided in a DLL or EXE file.) When compiling a code-behind file, you create a DLL assembly. You can then create an .aspx file that uses the compiled code-behind assembly. The end result is the same, but the actual syntax is a little different.

First, you create a code-behind file as normal. Then you compile it using the command-line compiler. For Visual Basic, you use the vbc.exe utility included with the .NET framework and found in the C:\WINNT\Microsoft.NET\Framework\[version]\ directory. Typically, you would open a Command Prompt window and type something like the following:

```
vbc /t:library /r:System.dll /r:System.Web.dll HelloWorld.vb
```

The /t:library parameter indicates that you want to create a DLL assembly instead of an EXE assembly. The compiled assembly will have the name HelloWorld.dll. Additionally, you use the /r parameter to specify any dependent assemblies that you use. In the case of HelloWorld, we use the standard system and web classes, which are contained in two namespaces: System.dll and System.Web.dll. Figure 5-7 shows a successful command-line compilation. A DLL file has been created, but no feedback is provided.

Figure 5-8 shows the problem caused by leaving out a required namespace—an unrecognized class is found and the code is not compiled.

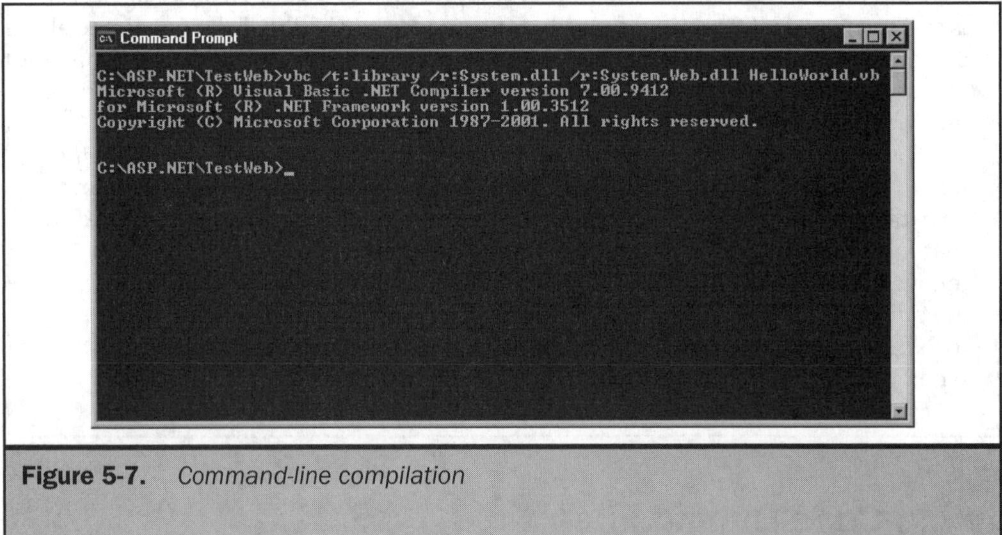


**Figure 5-7.** *Command-line compilation*

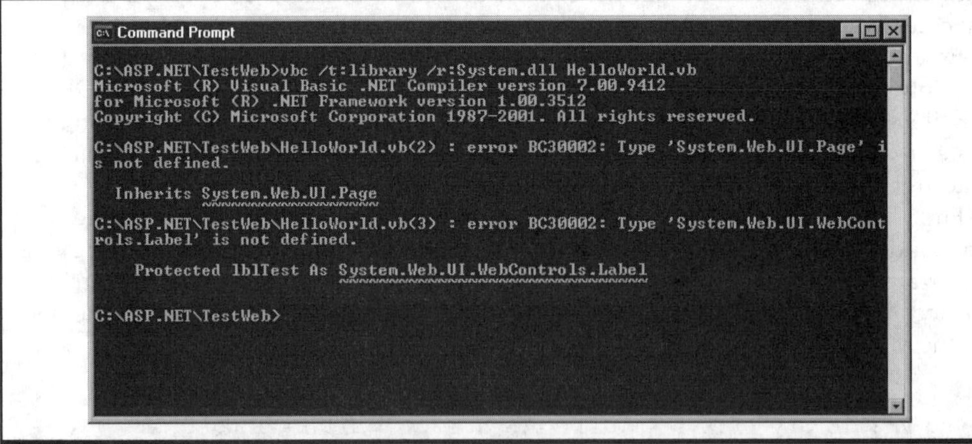


**Figure 5-8.** *A failed compilation attempt*

The next statement shows the equivalent for a C# file. It uses the csc.exe compiler.

```
csc /t:library /r:System.dll /r:System.Web.dll HelloWorld.cs
```

Once the file is compiled, you must copy it to the ASP.NET application's \bin directory. Now you can reference it in your .aspx file by class name.

```
<%@ Page Language="VB" Inherits="HelloWorldClass" %>
```



You don't need to specify a source file, because ASP.NET automatically registers and recognizes every class name in every assembly in your web application's \bin directory. If you specify a class that ASP.NET can't find, you'll receive an error page like the one shown in Figure 5-9.

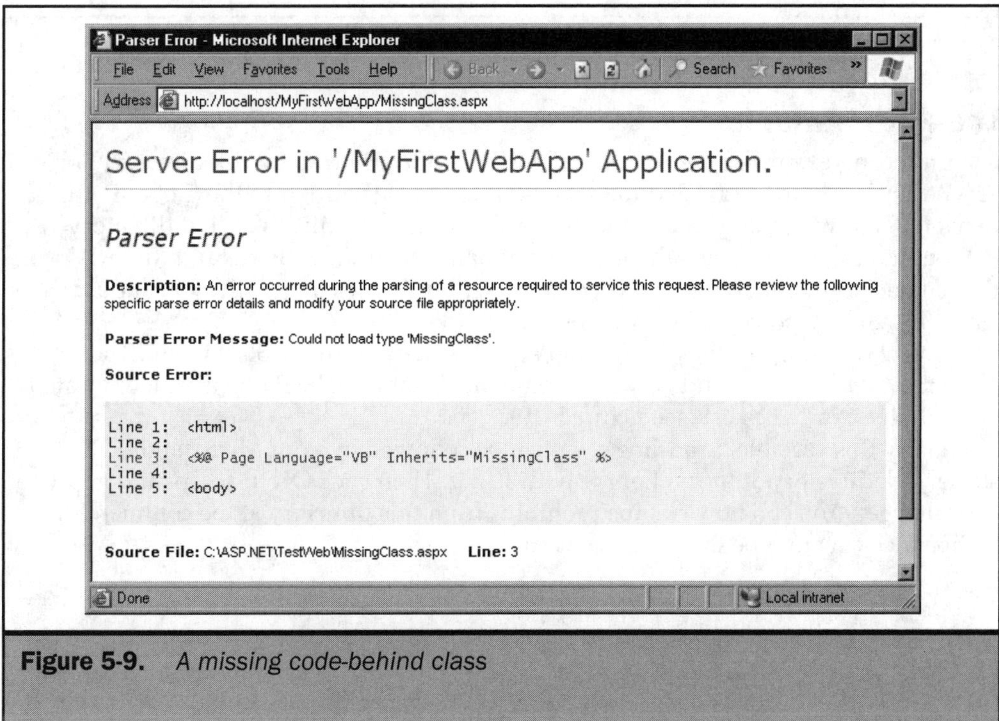


**Figure 5-9.** *A missing code-behind class*

That's all there is to it. The samples for this chapter include a set of three files—CompiledHelloWorld.aspx, CompiledHelloWorld.vb, and CompiledHelloWorld.dll—that allow you to test the compiled code-behind option. Remember, you don't need to perform this extra step, as ASP.NET will compile your source files for you automatically the first time they are requested by a client.

### Compiling a Code-Behind File Improves Security

Code-behind compilation is not necessary. Either way, your web application functions the same. However, precompiling can help if you don't want to leave source code files on the server. This way, your application can be deployed in a compiled form, ensuring that it can never be tampered with or easily inspected. Even better, if you understand the basics of compiling a code-behind file, you know most of what you need to understand to create a .NET component.

## The Path Variable

The preceding examples assume that the Microsoft.NET framework directory (C:\WINNT\Microsoft.NET\Framework\[version]) is added to the global Path variable. That way, you can run the vbc.exe and csc.exe utilities in that directory without having to type the whole directory name each time. By default, this convenience is not enabled, and if you often compile files manually, you should make this change so you can save a few keystrokes.

Start by selecting Settings | Control Panel | System from the Start menu. Then select the Advanced tab, and click Environment Variables. The Path variable is located in the System Variables list (see Figure 5-10).

Modify this variable by adding a semicolon followed by your Microsoft.NET framework directory at the end of the path string. Then click OK to accept and apply your changes. You can now run the programs from this directory at the command line without needing to type the directory name.

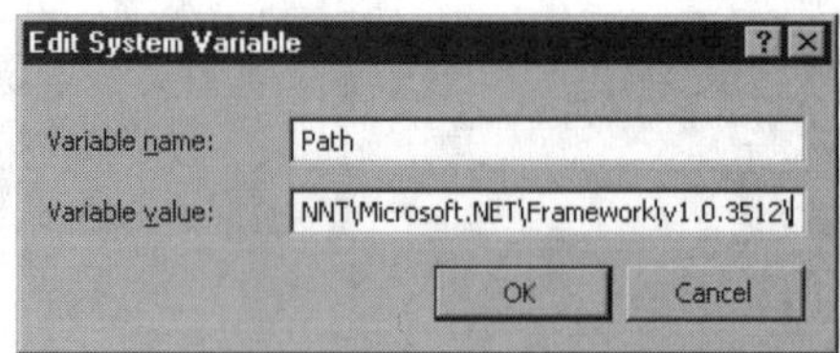

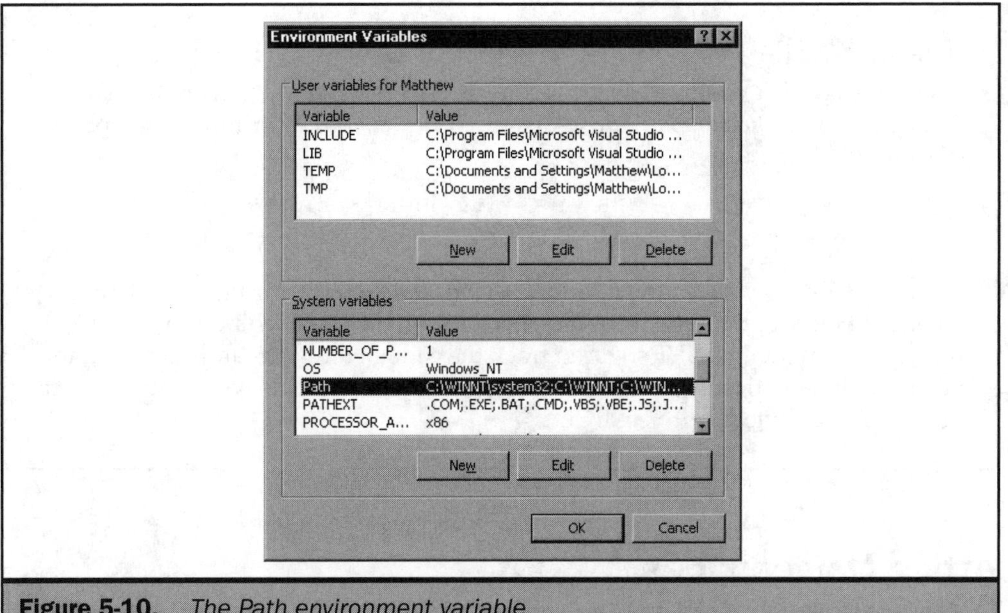


**Figure 5-10.** *The Path environment variable*



## Compiling Multiple Files into One Assembly

When compiling a code-behind file, you don't need to create a separate DLL for each page. Instead, you can compile all your web page classes into one assembly, provided each web page class has a different name (or is located in a different namespace).

```
vbc /out:MyWebApp.dll /t:library /r:System.dll /r:System.Web.dll
 HelloWorld.vb GoodbyeCruelWorld.vb MainPage.vb
```

This example (split over two lines) combines three VB files into one assembly, named MyWebApp.dll. The .aspx web pages would then inherit from the appropriate class as before.

You can also use a wildcard to automatically compile a selection of files.

```
vbc /out:MyWebApp.dll /t:library /r:System.dll /r:System.Web.dll *.vb
```

### Visual Studio .NET Uses Multi-File Compilation

Visual Studio .NET compiles all the web page classes in your project into one DLL file. In addition, each .aspx file uses a special Codebehind attribute in the page directive.

```
<%@ Page Language="VB" Inherits="HelloWorldPage"
Codebehind="HelloWorld.vb" %>
```

ASP.NET does *not* pay any attention to the Codebehind attribute. It will not attempt to retrieve the class from this file. Instead, the Codebehind attribute is used by Visual Studio .NET so it can track the code-behind file, and provide it to you for editing in the design environment. Changes in this file will not take effect until you recompile the project DLL.

## Importing Namespaces

There is one additional nicety that our code-behind file has left out. To make it easier to work with a namespace, you can use the Imports statement, which was introduced in Chapter 3.

The following is a revised code-behind example for the HelloWorld page (the changed lines are highlighted in bold). Note that the Page and Label class can be used without fully qualified names, because the relevant namespaces have been imported.

```
Imports System.Web.UI
Imports System.Web.UI.WebControls

 Public Class MyPageClass
  Inherits Page
    Protected lblTest As Label

    Public Sub Page_Load()
        lblTest.Text = "Hello, the Page_Load event occurred."
    End Sub

End Class
```

You can also import namespaces into an .aspx file using a directive. This is a technique you would probably use if you were *not* using code-behind development. It allows your script blocks to use class names instead of the long, fully qualified name.

```
<%@ Import Namespace="System.Web.UI" %>
<%@ Import Namespace="System.Web.UI.WebControls" %>
```

Generally, every code file imports a common set of basic namespaces for standard types, web controls, web utility classes, and Visual Basic compatibility. To make life a little easier, you might want to get into the habit of copying this block of code into the beginning of every code-behind file:

```
Imports Microsoft.VisualBasic
Imports System
Imports System.Web
Imports System.Web.UI
Imports System.Web.UI.WebControls
Imports System.Web.UI.HtmlControls
```



## Assessing Code-Behind

Code-behind represents a major change in philosophy that brings ASP.NET in line with modern programming practices. The advantages don't all appear until you begin to develop complex, multi-layered applications. Some of the reasons you might want to use code-behind include:

**Better organization** ASP pages are infamous for their tangle of script commands and HTML formatting tags. This confusion often results in a spaghetti-like mess that is difficult to debug, impossible to reuse, and even harder for other programmers to work with. With code-behind, your code is encapsulated in a neat class. It's easier to read, and it's easier to isolate and reuse pieces of useful functionality. The only way you could do this with ASP was to create separate COM components.

**Separation of the user interface** One of the most well-known problems with traditional ASP development is that it mingles formatting and content (the information displayed to the user) with programming logic. This means that programmers are often the only ones able to perform the graphic design for an

ASP web site. If professional web designers get involved, you need to give them the source code files, raising the possibility that sensitive information will leak out or some code will be inadvertently broken. With code-behind, the .aspx file can be manipulated, polished, and perfected by any other user, as long as the control names remain the same. It can even be designed in a third-party designer like Microsoft FrontPage or Macromedia Dreamweaver.

**The ability to use advanced code editors** Embracing code-behind programming allows you to benefit from indispensable tools—namely Visual Studio .NET. Visual Studio .NET can automatically verify the syntax of your code-behind files, provide IntelliSense statement completion, and allow you to design the corresponding .aspx web form. Even if you are an unredeemed Notepad user, I heartily encourage you to try out Visual Studio .NET. It's light years ahead of past ASP editors like Visual Interdev, which were generally more trouble than they were worth.

This book uses code-behind for all its examples. That said, you don't need to use code-behind programming to use ASP.NET or follow the examples in this book. You can just take the code out of its page class and paste it into a script block in a normal .aspx file.

### This Book Focuses on Code, Not HTML

The focus in this book is on programming ASP.NET pages. That means most examples only show you the code, not the control tags from the .aspx page layout. When a new control is introduced, I'll show you the ASP.NET tag and how to use it. In some cases, we'll dive right into the .aspx file to create control templates and other user interface code. However, for the most part I assume you'll learn more from a code example that focuses on objects and code statements rather than repeating the standard control tags.

To see the .aspx template files for examples in this book, you should refer to the online samples. You can also find a comprehensive control tag reference in Chapters 26 and 27. However, in an ideal world you should think, like .NET does, in terms of objects, and use Visual Studio .NET to draw your controls and configure their properties.

## Three Ways to Code Web Forms

To summarize, there are three different ways that you can program web forms, as outlined in Table 5-2.

| Development Type | You Create | You Deploy (to the Web Server) |
|---|---|---|
| Traditional inline code | .aspx files that contain code and user interface layout | .aspx files |
| Code-behind | .aspx files with user interface and .vb files with code | .aspx and .vb files |
| Compiled code-behind | .aspx files with user interface and .vb files with code | .aspx files and the compiled .dll files (which go in the \bin directory) |

**Table 5-2.** *Development Types*



## The Global.asax Application File

The global.asax file allows you to write global application code. The global.asax file looks similar to a normal .aspx file, except for the fact that it can't contain any HTML or ASP.NET tags. Instead, it contains event-handling code that reacts to application or session events.

For example, the following global.asax file reacts to the Application_OnEndRequest event, which happens just before the page is sent to the user.

```
<script runat="server">
    Public Sub Application_OnEndRequest()
        Response.Write("<hr>This page was served at " & _
          DateTime.Now.ToString())
    End Sub
</script>
```

This event handler writes a footer at the bottom of the page with the date and time that the page was created.

Each ASP.NET application can have one global.asax file. Once you place it in the appropriate virtual directory, ASP.NET recognizes it and uses it automatically. For example, if you place it in the TestWeb directory, the HelloWorld.aspx file will be affected, as shown in Figure 5-11.

Adding an automatic footer is generally not a useful function for a professional web site. A more typical use might be writing an entry to a database log. That way, usage information would be tracked automatically.

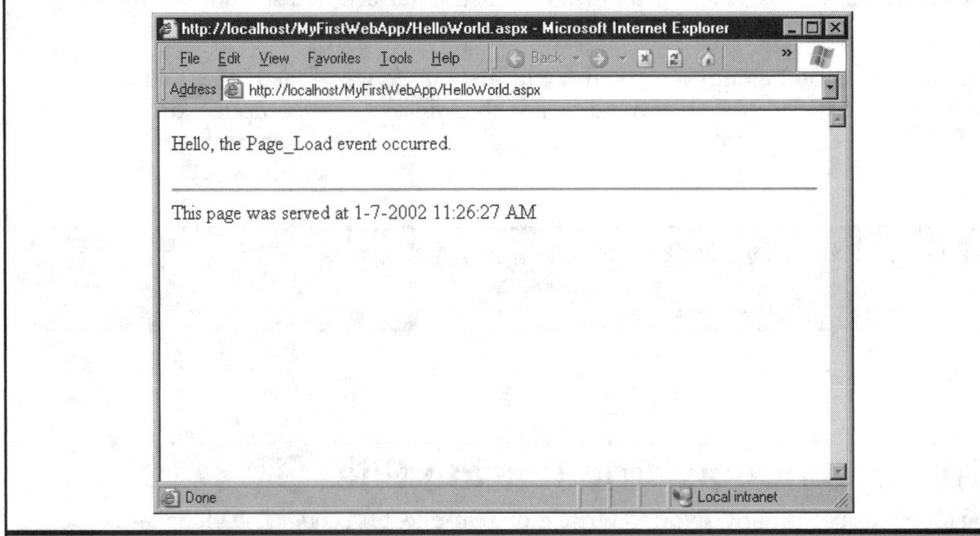


**Figure 5-11.** *HelloWorld.aspx with an automatic footer*

## What Is DateTime.Now?

Your ASP.NET code can use the full range of features from the .NET class library. In the preceding example, we use the special System.DateTime class, which allows us to store and manipulate date information. The DateTime class provides a special shared property, Now, which can be called at any time to retrieve a DateTime object that represents the current date and time. (You might remember from Chapter 3 that shared properties can always be accessed, even without creating an instance of the class.)

The DateTime object is then converted to its string representation, using the ToString method that every .NET object supports. The string representation is created based on the web server's current regional settings. In traditional ASP development, you would need to use a built-in language function instead of an object method to accomplish the same task.

## Global.asax Code-Behind

The global.asax file also supports code-behind development. In this case, however, the code-behind class does not inherit from the Page class, because the global.asax file does not represent a page. Instead, it inherits from the special System.Web.HttpApplication class. Similarly, the global.asax uses an Application directive instead of a Page directive.

The next example rewrites our global.asax file using code-behind programming.

**global.asax**

```
<%@ Application Codebehind="Global.vb" Inherits="GlobalApp" %>
```

**global.vb**

```
Public Class Global
  Inherits System.Web.HttpApplication

    Public Sub Application_OnEndRequest()
        Response.Write("This page was served at " & _
          DateTime.Now.ToString())
    End Sub

End Class
```

Once again, ASP.NET always create a custom HttpApplication class to represent your application when you first run it, as described in the "Behind the Scenes with HelloWorld.aspx" list of steps earlier in this chapter. The difference with code-behind development is that you need to understand and specify that detail explicitly.

## Application Events

Application_OnEndRequest is only one of more than a dozen events you can respond to in your code. To create a different event handler, just create a subroutine with the defined name. Table 5-3 shows some of the most commonly used events.

| Event Name | Description |
|---|---|
| Application_OnStart | Occurs when the application starts, which is the first time it receives a request from any user. It does not occur on subsequent requests. This event is commonly used to create or cache some initial information that will be reused later. |

**Table 5-3.** *Basic Events*

| Event Name | Description |
|---|---|
| Application_OnEnd | Occurs when the application is shutting down, generally because the web server is being restarted. You can create cleanup code here. |
| Application_OnBeginRequest | Occurs with each request the application receives, just before the page code is executed. |
| Application_OnEndRequest | Occurs with each request the application receives, just after the page code is executed. |
| Session_OnStart | Occurs whenever a new user request is received and a session is started. Sessions are described in Chapter 10. |
| Session_OnEnd | Occurs when a session times out or is programmatically ended. |
| Application_OnError | Occurs when an unhandled error occurs. You can find more information about error handling in Chapter 11. |

**Table 5-3.** *Basic Events (continued)*

## Understanding ASP.NET Classes

Once you understand that all web pages are instances of the Page class and all global.asax files are instances of the HttpApplication class, many mysteries are cleared up.

For example, consider this line from the global.asax (or global.vb) file:

```
Response.Write("This page was served at " & DateTime.Now.ToString())
```

You might wonder what gives you the ability to use the Response object. In previous versions of ASP, Response was just a special object built into ASP programming. ASP.NET, however, uses a more consistent object-oriented approach. In ASP.NET, the Response object is available because it's a part of the HttpApplication class.

When you inherit from HttpApplication (either explicitly in a code-behind file or automatically), your class acquires all the features of the HttpApplication class. These include properties such as Request, Response, Session, Application, and Server. In turn, each of these properties holds an instance of a special ASP.NET object. For example, HttpApplication.Response holds a reference to the HttpResponse object, which provides a method called Write.

Similarly, when you create an .aspx page, you are creating a class that inherits from ASP.NET's Page class. This class also provides properties such as Request, Response, Session, and Application, along with a number of additional user-interface related members.



### The Built-In ASP Objects Are Still Available

ASP.NET provides the traditional built-in objects through properties in basic classes such as Page and Application. For backward compatibility, these objects still support almost all the ASP syntax, and they add some new properties. However, the major change between ASP and ASP.NET is that these built-in objects are used much less often. For example, dynamic pages are usually created by setting control properties rather than using the Reponse.Write command. These controls are introduced in Chapter 6.

## The MSDN Reference

Understanding the underlying object model is probably the best way to become an ASP.NET guru and distinguish yourself from other, less experienced ASP.NET programmers. It allows you to use the MSDN to find out the full set of capabilities available to you. For example, now that you understand all global.asax files are custom HttpApplication instances, you can refer to the documentation for the HttpApplication class (see Figure 5-12). You can use any of the HttpApplication properties inside your global.asax or global.vb file. Similarly, you can write event handlers for any of its events.

If you also understand that the Response property is an instance of the HttpResponse class, you can find out more information about the ways you can use the Response object.

The basic set of ASP.NET objects is described in the next chapter. However, knowing the classes that these objects are based on allows you to get a better understanding of ASP.NET development.

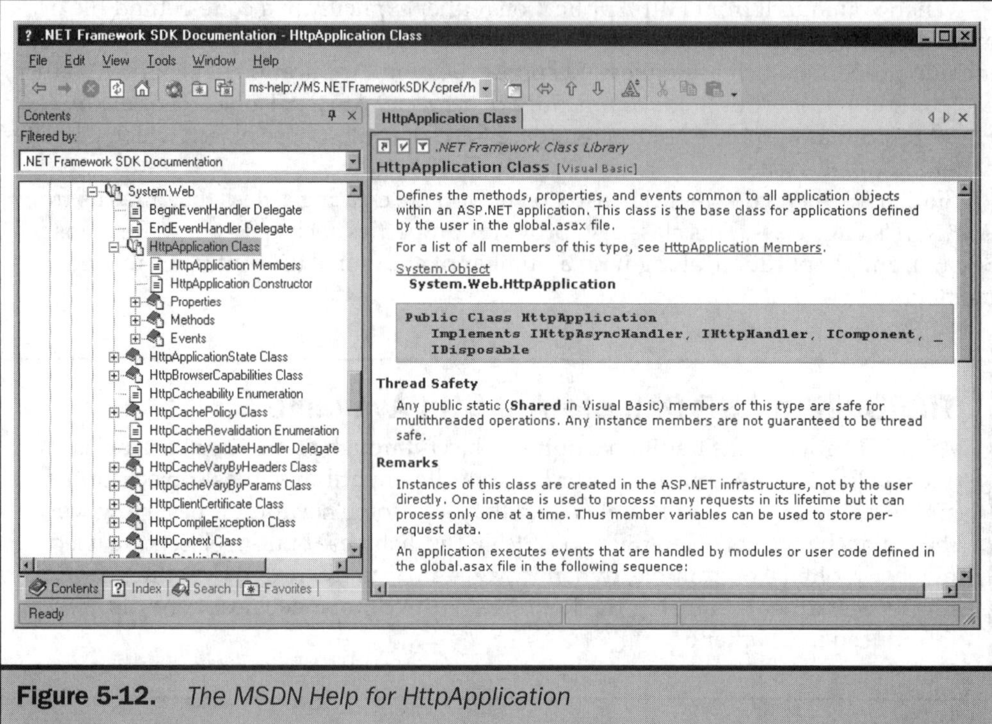


**Figure 5-12.** *The MSDN Help for HttpApplication*

# ASP.NET Configuration

The last topic we'll consider in this chapter is the web.config configuration file. In the MyFirstWebApp application, there is currently no web.config file. That means that the default settings are used from the server's machine.config file.

Every web server has a single machine.config file that defines the default options. Typically, this file is found in the directory C:\WINNT\Microsoft.NET\Framework\[version]\CONFIG, where [version] is the version number of the .NET framework. Generally, you won't edit this file manually. It contains a complex mess of computer-specific settings. Instead, you can create a web.config file for your application that contains all the special settings.

The web.config files has several advantages over traditional ASP configuration:

**It's never locked.** As described in the beginning of this chapter, you can update web.config settings at any point, and ASP.NET will smoothly transition to a new application domain.

**It's easily accessed and replicated.** With the appropriate rights, you can change a web.config file from a remote computer. You can also copy the web.config file and use it to apply identical settings to another application, or another web server that runs the same application in a web farm scenario.

**It's easy to edit and understand.** The settings in the web.config file are human-readable. In the future, it's likely that Microsoft will provide a graphical tool that automates web.config changes. Even without it, you can easily add or modify settings using a text editor like Notepad.



### IIS Manager Is Still Required for Some Tasks

With ASP.NET, you don't need to worry about the metabase. However, there are still a few tasks that you can't perform with a web.config file. For example, you can't create or remove a virtual directory. Similarly, you can't change file mappings. If you want the ASP.NET service to process requests for additional file types (such as .html, or a custom file type you define such as .mycompany), you must use IIS Manager, as described in Chapter 4.

## The Web.config File

The web.config file uses a special XML format. Everything is nested in a root <configuration> element, which contains a <system.web> element. Inside the <system.web> element are separate elements for each aspect of configuration.

```
<?xml version="1.0" encoding="utf-8" ?>
<configuration>
  <system.web>
    <!-- Configuration sections go here. -->
  </system.web>
</configuration>
```

You can include as few or as many configuration sections as you want. For example, if you need to specify special error settings, you could add just the <customError> group. If you create an ASP.NET application in Visual Studio .NET, a web.config file is created for you with a basic skeleton showing you all the important sections. Additional comments are added to each section, describing the purpose of various options.

```
<!-- This is the format for an XML comment. -->
```

The following example shows a web.config file with its most important sections (and no settings). Note that the web.config file is case-sensitive, and uses a standard where the first word is always lowercase. That means you cannot write <CustomErrors> instead of <customErrors>.

```
<?xml version="1.0" encoding="utf-8" ?>
<configuration>
  <system.web>
    <httpRuntime />
    <pages />
    <compilation />
    <customErrors />
    <authentication />
    <authorization />
    <identity />
    <trace />
    <sessionState />
    <httpHandlers />
    <httpModules />
    <globalization />
    <compilation />

  </system.web>
</configuration>
```

If you want to learn about all the settings that are available in the web.config file, you have two options:

- In this book, each section discusses any appropriate web.config settings. For example, in Chapter 10, the settings in the <sessionState> group are described.
- In Chapter 28, you can find a detailed list of configuration settings.

## Nested Configuration

ASP.NET uses a multi-layered configuration system that allows you to use different settings for different parts of your application. To use this technique, you need to create additional subdirectories inside your virtual directory. These subdirectories can contain their own web.config files with additional settings.

Subdirectories also inherit web.config settings from the parent directory. For example, consider the web request http://localhost/MyFirstWebApp/Special/SpecialHelloWorld.aspx, which accesses a file in Special, which is a subdirectory of the application virtual directory MyFirstWebApp. The corresponding physical directory is C:\TestWeb.

The web request for SpecialHelloWorld.aspx can acquire settings from three different files, as shown in Figure 5-13.

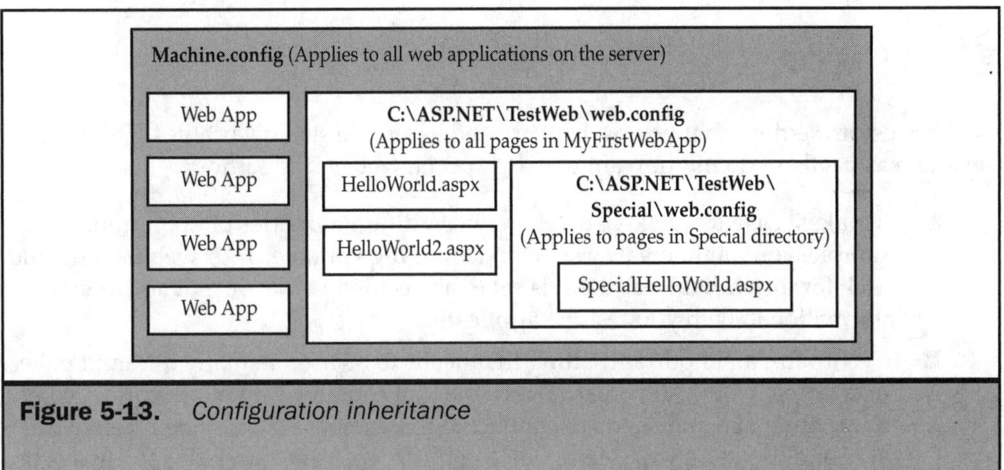


**Figure 5-13.** *Configuration inheritance*



Any machine.config or TestWeb\web.config settings that are not explicitly overridden in the TestWeb\Special\web.config file will still apply to the SpecialHelloWorld.aspx page. In this way, subdirectories can specify just a small set of settings that differ from the rest of the web application. One reason you might want to use multiple directories in an application is to apply different security settings. Files that need to be secured would then be placed in a special directory with a web.config file that defines more stringent security settings.

# Storing Custom Settings in the Web.config File

Before rounding up our discussion of configuration, it's worth examining how you can add some of your own settings to the web.config file, and use them with the simple HelloWorld.aspx page.

You add custom settings to a special element called <appSettings>. Note that this is nested in the root <configuration> element, not the <system.web> element, which contains the other groups of predefined settings.

```
<?xml version="1.0" encoding="utf-8" ?>
<configuration>

  <appSettings>
    <!-- Special application settings go here. -->
  </appSettings>
```

```
  <system.web>
    <!-- Configuration sections go here. -->
  </system.web>

</configuration>
```

The custom settings that you add are created as simple string variables. There are several reasons that you might want to use a special web.config setting:

- To make it easy to quickly switch between different modes of operation. For example, you might create a special debugging variable. Your web pages could check for this variable, and if it is set to a specified value, output additional information to help you test the application.
- To centralize an important setting that needs to be used in many different pages. For example, you could create a variable that contains a database connection string. Any page that needs to connect to the database could then retrieve this value and use it. As you'll learn later in this book, it's a good idea to always use the exact same database connection string in all your pages, as this ensures that SQL Server can reuse connections for different clients. The technical term for this time-saving feature is connection pooling.
- To set some initial values. Depending on the operation, the user might be able to modify these values, but the web.config file could supply the default selection.

Custom settings are entered using an <add> element that identifies a unique variable name (key) and the variable contents (value). The following example adds two special variables, one that contains a database connection string, and one that defines a suitable SQL statement for retrieving sales records.

```
<?xml version="1.0" encoding="utf-8" ?>
<configuration>

  <appSettings>
    <add key="ConnectionString"
         value="Data Source=localhost;Initial
         Catalog=Pubs;User ID=sa" />
    <add key="SelectSales" value="SELECT * FROM Sales" />
  </appSettings>
```

```
  <system.web>
    <!-- Configuration sections go here. -->
  </system.web>

</configuration>
```

You can create a simple ShowSettings.vb (or ShowSettings.aspx) file to query this information and display the results. You access these settings by key name, using the System.Configuration.ConfigurationSettings class. This class provides a shared property called AppSettings.



```
Imports System.Web.UI
Imports System.Web.UI.WebControls
Imports System.Configuration

Public Class ShowSettings
  Inherits Page
    Protected lblTest As Label

    Public Sub Page_Load()
        lblTest.Text = "This app will connect with the connection
        lblTest.Text &= "string:<br><b>"& _
          ConfigurationSettings.AppSettings("ConnectionString")
        lblTest.Text &= "</b><br><br>"
        lblTest.Text &= "And will execute the SQL Statement:"
        lblTest.Text &= "<br><b>" & _
          ConfigurationSettings.AppSettings("SelectSales")
        lblTest.Text &= "</b>"
    End Sub

End Class
```

## Ineresting Facts About this Code

- The System.Configuration namespace is imported to make it easier to access the ConfigurationSettings class.
- The &= operator is used to quickly add information to the label. This is equivalent to writing lblTest.Text = lblText.Text & "<extra content>".

- A few HTML tags are added to the label, including bold tags (<b>) to emphasize certain words, and a line break (<br>) to split the output over multiple lines.

Later, in the third part of this book, you'll learn how to use connection strings and SQL statements with a database. For now, our simple application just displays the custom web.config settings, as shown in Figure 5-14.

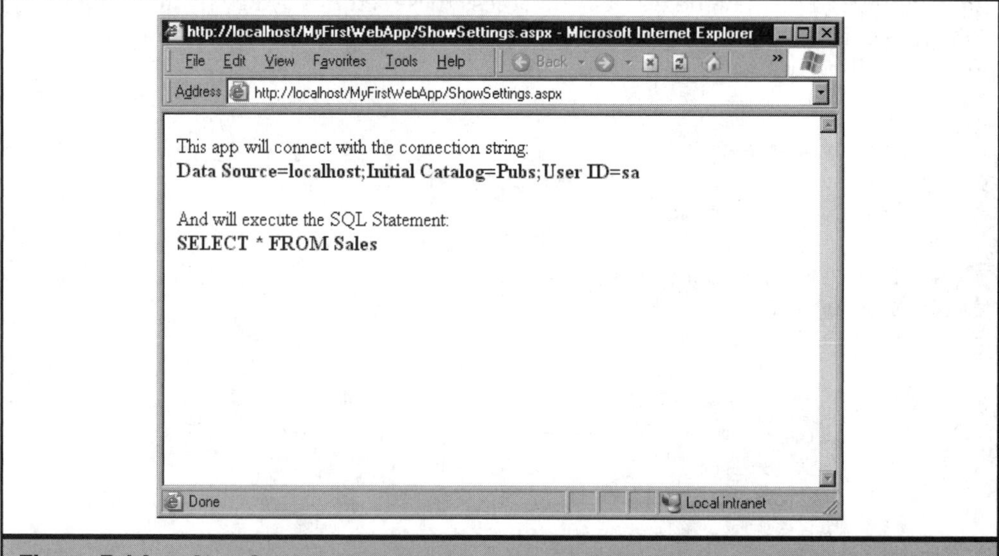


**Figure 5-14.** *ShowSettings.aspx displays the custom application settings*

### Isn't This a Security Risk?

Unlike code files, the web.config can't be deployed in a compiled form. For that reason, it might seem like a potential security risk to store information such as a database access password in plain text. Indeed, in some cases you might want to use precompiled code-behind files or other measures to make sure information like this is harder to reach. However, ASP.NET is configured, by default, to deny any requests for .config files. That means a remote user will not be able to access the file through IIS. Instead, they'll receive the error message shown in Figure 5-15.

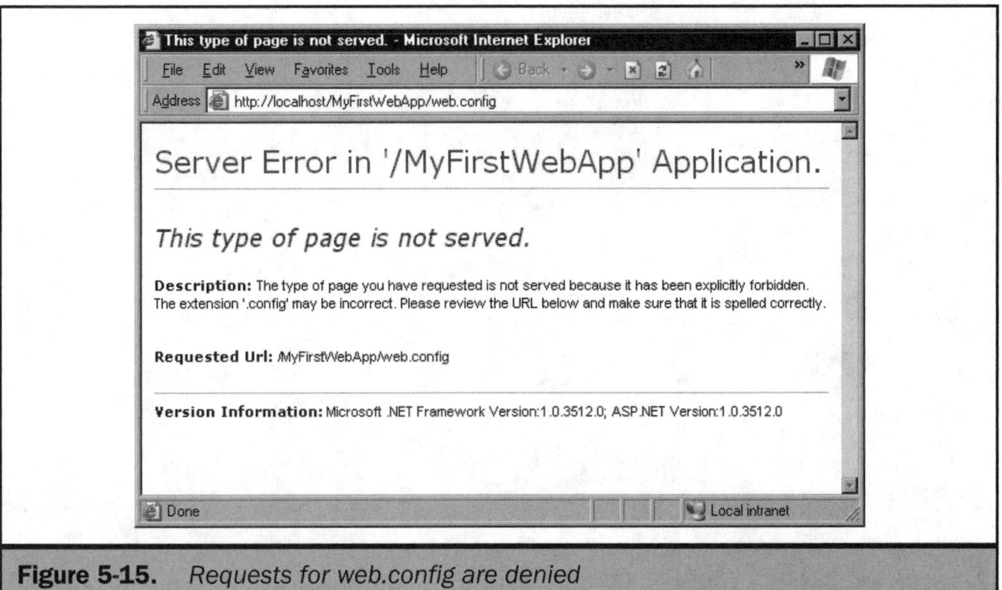


**Figure 5-15.** *Requests for web.config are denied*

The Complete Reference

# Chapter 6

## Web Form Fundamentals

ASP.NET introduces a remarkable new model for creating web pages. In traditional ASP development, programmers had to master the quirks and details of HTML markup before being able to design dynamic web pages. Pages had to be carefully tailored to a specific task, and additional content could only be generated by writing raw HTML tags. Worst of all, ASP.NET programs usually required extensive code changes whenever a site's user interface was updated with a new look.

In ASP.NET, you can use a higher-level model of server-side web controls. These controls are created and configured as objects, and automatically provide their own HTML output. Even better, ASP.NET allows web controls to behave like their Windows counterparts: maintaining state, and even raising events that you can react to in code.

This chapter explains the basics of the server controls. You'll learn how to handle events, interact with control objects, and understand the object hierarchy of HTML server controls. These topics are entirely different from traditional ASP programming, and represent an innovative new way to program the Web.

## A Simple Page Applet

We'll start our exploration with a simple example of how server-based controls work with a single-page applet. This type of program, which combines user input and the program output on the same page, is used to provide popular tools on many sites. Some examples include calculators for mortgages, taxes, health or weight indices, and retirement savings plans, single-phrase translators, and stock tracking utilities.

Our example is a simple page that allows the user to convert a number of U.S. dollars to the equivalent amount of Euros (see Figure 6-1).

The HTML for this page is shown next. To make it as clear as possible, the style attribute of the <div> tag used for the border has been omitted. There are two <input> tags: one for the text box, and one for the submit button. These elements are enclosed in a <form> tag, so they can be submitted back to the server when the button is clicked. The rest of the page is static text.

```
<HTML><body>
  <form method="post" >
    <div>

      Convert:  
      <input type="text">  US dollars to Euros.<br><br>
      <input type="submit" value="OK">

    </div>
  </form>
</body></HTML>
```

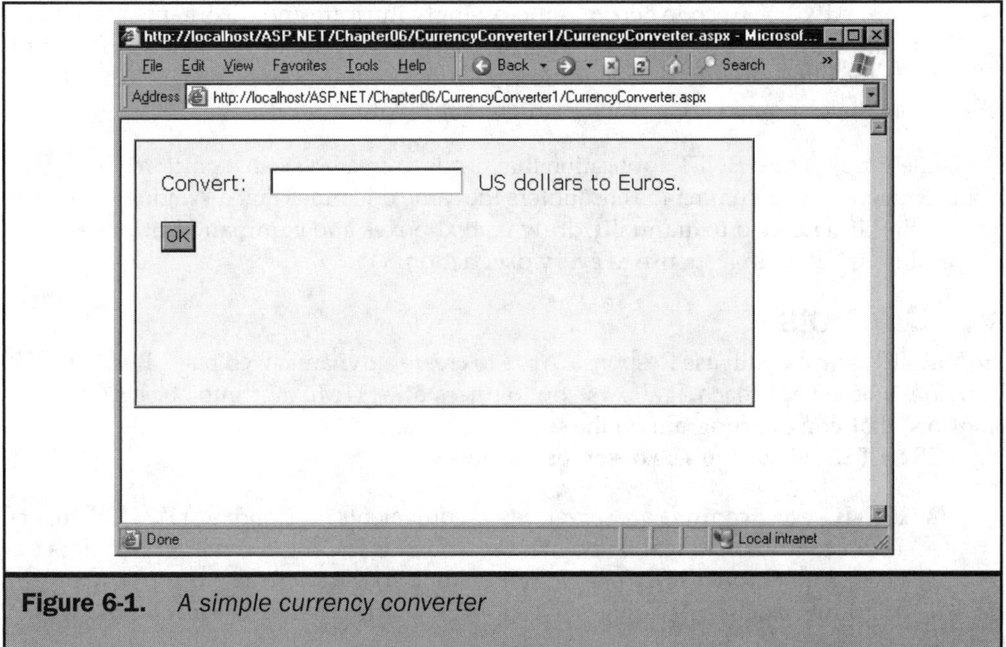


**Figure 6-1.** *A simple currency converter*

# The Problem with Response.Write

In a traditional ASP program, you would add the currency conversion functionality to this page by examining the posted form values and manually writing the result to the end of the page with the Response.Write command. This approach works well for a simple page, but it encounters a number of difficulties as the program becomes more sophisticated:

**"Spaghetti" code** The order of the Response.Write statements determines the output. If you want to tailor different parts of the output based on a condition, you will need to reevaluate that condition at several different places in your code.

**Lack of flexibility** Once you have perfected your output, it's very difficult to change it. If you decide to modify the page several months later, you have to read through the code, follow the logic, and try to sort out numerous details.

**Confusing content and formatting** Depending on the complexity of your user interface, your Response.Write may need to add new HTML tags and style attributes. This encourages programs to tangle formatting and content details together, making it difficult to change just one or the other at a later date.

**Complexity** Your code becomes increasingly intricate and disorganized as you add different types of functionality. For example, it could be extremely difficult to track the effects of different conditions and different Response.Write blocks if you created a combined tax-mortgage-interest calculator.

Quite simply, an ASP.NET application that needs to create a sizable portion of interface using Response.Write commands encounters the same dilemmas that a Windows program would find if it needed to manually draw its text boxes and command buttons on an application window in response to every user action.

## Server Controls

In ASP.NET, you can still use Response.Write to create a dynamic web page. But ASP.NET provides a better approach. It allows you to turn static HTML tags into objects (called controls) that you can program on the server.

ASP.NET provides two sets of server controls:

- **HTML server controls** are server-based equivalents for standard HTML elements. These controls are ideal if you are a seasoned web programmer who prefers to work with familiar HTML tags (at least at first). They are also useful when migrating existing ASP pages to ASP.NET, as they require the fewest changes.
- **Web controls** are similar to the HTML server controls, but provide a richer object model with a variety of properties for style and formatting details, more events, and a closer parallel to Windows development. Web controls also feature some user interface elements that have no HTML equivalent, such as the DataGrid and validation controls. We examine web controls in the next chapter.

## HTML Server Controls

HTML server controls provide an object interface for standard HTML elements. They provide three key features:

**They generate their own interface.** You set properties in code, and the underlying HTML tag is updated automatically when the page is rendered and sent to the client.

**They retain their state.** You can write your program the same way you would write a traditional Windows program. There's no need to recreate a web page from scratch each time you send it to the user.

**They fire events.** Your code can respond to these events, just like ordinary controls in a Windows application. In ASP code, everything is grouped into one block that executes from start to finish. With event-based programming, you can easily respond to individual user actions and create more structured code.

To convert the currency converter to an ASP.NET page that uses server controls, all you need to do is add the special attribute runat="server" to each tag that you want to transform into a server control. You should also add an id attribute to each control that you need to interact with in code. The id attribute assigns the unique name that you will use to refer to the control in code.

In the currency converter application, the input text box and submit button can be changed into server controls. In addition, the <form> element must also be processed as a server control to allow ASP.NET to access the controls it contains.

```
<HTML><body>
  <form method="post" runat="server">
    <div>

      Convert:  
      <input type="text" id="US" runat="server">  US dollars to
      Euros.
      <br><br>
      <input type="submit" value="OK" id="Convert" runat="server">

    </div>
  </form>
</body></HTML>
```



## Viewstate

If you look at the HTML that is sent to you when you request the page, you'll see it is slightly different than the information in the .aspx file. First of all, the runat="server" attributes are stripped out (as they have no meaning to the client browser, which can't interpret them). More importantly, an additional hidden field has been added to the form.

```
<HTML><body>
  <form method="post" runat="server">
  <input type="hidden" name="__VIEWSTATE"
  value="dDw3NDg2NTI5MDg7Oz4=" />
    <div>

      Convert:  
      <input type="text" id="US" runat="server">  US dollars to
      Euros.
      <br><br>
      <input type="submit" value="OK" id="Convert" runat="server">

    </div>
  </form>
</body></HTML>
```

This hidden field stores information about the state of every control in the page in a compressed and lightly encrypted form. It allows you to manipulate control properties in code and have the changes automatically persisted. This is a key part of the web forms programming model, which allows you to forget about the stateless nature of the Internet, and treat your page like a continuously running application.

### ASP.NET Controls Maintain State Automatically

Even though the currency converter program does not yet include any code, you will already notice one change. If you enter information in the text box, and click the submit button to post the page, the refreshed page will still contain the value you entered in the text box. (In the original example that uses ordinary HTML elements, the value will be cleared every time the page is posted back.)

## The HTML Control Classes

Before you can continue any further with the currency calculator, you need to know about the control objects you have created. All the HTML server controls are defined in the System.Web.UI.HtmlControls namespace. There is a separate class for each kind of control. Table 6-1 describes the basic HTML server controls.

So far, the currency converter defines three controls, which are instances of the HtmlForm, HtmlInputText, and HtmlInputButton classes, respectively. It's important that you know the class names, because you need to define each control class in the code-behind file if you want to interact with it. (Visual Studio .NET simplifies this task: whenever you add a control using its web designer, the appropriate tag is added to the .aspx file and the appropriate variables are defined in the code-behind class.)

| Class Name | HTML Tag Represented |
|---|---|
| HtmlAnchor | <a> |
| HtmlButton | <button> |
| HtmlForm | <form> |
| HtmlImage | <img> |

**Table 6-1.** *The HTML Server Control Classes*

| Class Name | HTML Tag Represented |
|---|---|
| HtmlInputButton | <input type="button">, <input type="submit">, and <input type="reset"> |
| HtmlInputCheckBox | <input type="checkbox"> |
| HtmlInputControl | <input type="text">, <input type="submit">, and <input type="file"> |
| HtmlInputFile | <input type="file"> |
| HtmlInputHidden | <input type="hidden"> |
| HtmlInputImage | <input type="image"> |
| HtmlInputRadioButton | <input type="radio"> |
| HtmlInputText | <input type="text"> and <input type="password"> |
| HtmlSelect | <select> |
| HtmlTable, HtmlTableRow, and HtmlTableCell | <table>, <tr>, <th> and <td> |
| HtmlTextArea | <textarea> |
| HtmlGenericControl | Any other HTML element |

**Table 6-1.** *The HTML Server Control Classes (continued)*



## The HTML Server Control Reference

This chapter introduces many new server controls. As we work our way through the examples, I'll explain many of the corresponding properties and events, and the class hierarchy. However, for single-stop shopping, you are encouraged to refer to Chapter 26, which provides a complete HTML server control reference. Each control is featured separately, with a picture, example tag, and a list of properties, events, and methods. In the meantime, Table 6-2 gives a quick overview of some important properties.

| Control | Most Important Properties |
|---|---|
| HtmlAnchor | Href, Target, Title |
| HtmlImage and HtmlInputImage | Src, Alt, Width, and Height |
| HtmlInputCheckBox and HtmlInputRadioButton | Checked |
| HtmlInputText | Value |
| HtmlSelect | Items (collection) |
| HtmlTextArea | Value |
| HtmlGenericControl | InnerText |

**Table 6-2.** *Important Properties*

## Events

To actually add some functionality to the currency converter, you need to add some ASP.NET code. Web forms are event-driven, which means that every piece of code acts in response to a specific event. In the simple currency converter page case, the event is when the user clicks the submit button (named Convert). The HtmlInputButton class provides this as the ServerClick event.

Before continuing, it makes sense to add another control that can be used to display the result of the calculation (named Result). The example now has four server controls:

- A form (HtmlForm object). This is the only control you do not need to use in your code-behind class.
- An input text box named US (HtmlInputText object).
- A submit button named Convert (HtmlInputButton object).
- A div tag named Result (HtmlGenericControl object).

**CurrencyConverter.aspx**

```
<%@ Page Language="VB" Inherits="CurrencyConverter"
    Src="CurrencyConverter.vb"
    AutoEventWireup="False" %>
```

```
<HTML><body>
  <form method="post" runat="server">
    <div>

      Convert:  
      <input type="text" id="US" runat="server">  US dollars to
      Euros.
      <br><br>
      <input type="submit" value="OK" id="Convert" runat="server">
      <div style="FONT-WEIGHT: bold" id="Result" runat="server"></div>

    </div>
  </form>
</body></HTML>
```



**CurrencyConverter.vb**

```
Imports Microsoft.VisualBasic
Imports System
Imports System.Web
Imports System.Web.UI
Imports System.Web.UI.WebControls
Imports System.Web.UI.HtmlControls

Public Class CurrencyConverter
  Inherits Page

    Protected Result As HtmlGenericControl
    Protected WithEvents Convert As HtmlInputButton
    Protected US As HtmlInputText

    Private Sub Convert_ServerClick(sender As Object, e As EventArgs) _
     Handles Convert.ServerClick

        Dim USAmount As Decimal = Val(US.Value)
        Dim EuroAmount As Decimal = USAmount * 1.12
        Result.InnerText = USAmount.ToString() & " US dollars = "
        Result.InnerText &= EuroAmount.ToString() & " Euros."

    End Sub

End Class
```

The code-behind class is a typical example of an ASP.NET page:

**It uses the Imports statement.** These statements provide access to all the important namespaces. This is a typical first step in any code-behind file. You'll notice that the namespace Microsoft.VisualBasic is included. This allows you to use the traditional Visual Basic Val method to convert the text box entry into a number. Otherwise, you would need to use the static Parse method of one of the number types to accomplish the same thing.

```
' This line is equivalent to the traditional Val function.
Dim Amount As Decimal = Decimal.Parse(US.Value)
```

**It defines a custom Page class and control variables.** This is also the standard format of all code-behind files. You'll notice that the variable names match the id attribute set in each control tag. The WithEvents keyword is used for the HtmlInputButton control so the page can receive its ServerClick event. You could define all controls using the WithEvents keyword, but in this case it's not needed.

**It defines a single event handler.** This event handler retrieves the value from the text box, multiplies it by a preset conversion ratio (which would typically be stored in another file or a database), and sets the text of the div tag.

The complete program works seamlessly. When the button is clicked, the page is resubmitted, the event handling code is triggered, and the page is resent (see Figure 6-2). Note that the ToString method, which converts the numbers into strings before they are displayed, isn't strictly necessary. In most cases, Visual Basic .NET will perform this conversion automatically. However, it's always a good practice to handle conversions explicitly.

## Event Handling Changes

The currency converter adds a few refinements that weren't found in the previous chapter's "hello world" page. The most important differences are found in the event handler definition. (Note that the underscore is used to split this code over two lines. In your programs, you can include this on a single line without the underscore.)

```
Private Sub Convert_ServerClick(sender As Object, e As EventArgs) _
  Handles Convert.ServerClick
```

First, the event handler now accepts two parameters (source and e). This is the recommended .NET standard for events, and it allows your code to identify the control that sent the event and retrieve any other information that may be required. We'll examine examples of these advanced techniques later in the next chapter.

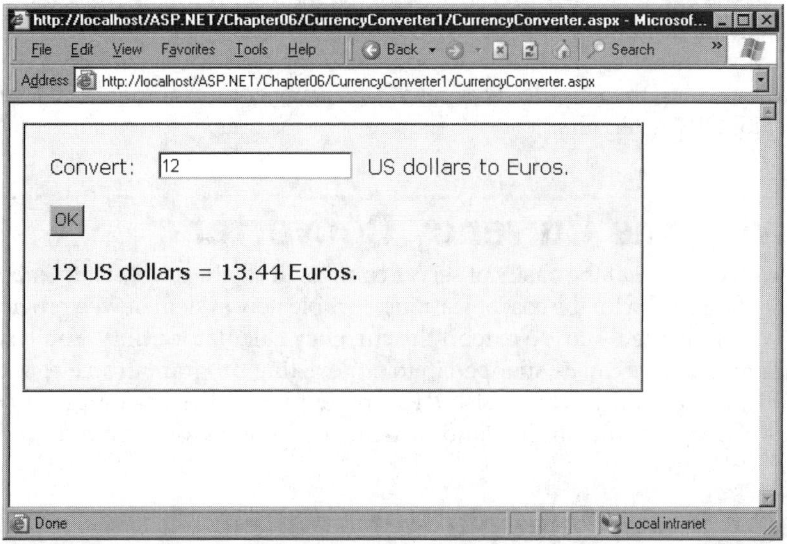

**Figure 6-2.** *The ASP.NET currency converter*

Second, the event handler explicitly connects itself to the appropriate event using the Handles clause. This allows the event handler subroutine to take any name, and ensures that an error will be raised if the event or control is not found. We also add the AutoEventWireup="False" attribute to the Page directive of the .aspx file.

```
<%@ Page Language="VB" Inherits="CurrencyConverter"
    Src="CurrencyConverter.vb"
    AutoEventWireup="False" %>
```

When AutoEventWireup is set to False, ASP.NET will always rely on the Handles keyword to connect events to event handlers. Alternatively, you can leave out the AutoEventWireup attribute (it defaults to True), and specify the name of the event handler in the control tag. For example, the button shown below sends its ServerClick event to the subroutine named Convert_ServerClick.

```
<input type="submit" value="OK" id="Convert"
       OnServerClick="Convert_ServerClick"
       runat="server">
```

Note that the event name is preceded with On in the control tag (for example, the ServerClick event becomes the OnServerClick attribute).

Both techniques are equivalent. This book uses the first option, which connects event handlers using the Handles keyword. This brings our examples into line with Visual Studio .NET's defaults.

# Improving the Currency Converter

Now that we've looked at the basics of server controls, it might seem that their benefits are fairly minor compared with the cost of learning a whole new system of web programming. In this next section, we'll start to extend the currency calculator utility. You'll see how additional functionality can be snapped in to our existing program in an elegant, modular way. As our program grows, the ASP.NET framework handles its complexity easily, steering us away from the tangled and intricate code that would be required in a traditional ASP application.

## Adding Support for Multiple Currencies

First, we'll add a <select> element (named Currency) that allows the user to choose the destination currency. To reduce the amount of HTML programming, no actual <option> entries are added to the drop-down list in the .aspx file.

```
<%@ Page Language="VB" Inherits="CurrencyConverter"
    Src="CurrencyConverter.vb"
    AutoEventWireup="False" %>

<HTML><body>
  <form method="post" runat="server">

    <!-- div tag used for formatting. -->
      Convert:  
      <input type="text" id="US" runat="server">  US dollars to
      Euros.
      <select style="WIDTH: 155px" id="Currency"
              runat="server"></select><br><br>
      <input type="submit" value="OK" id="Convert"
      runat="server"><br><br>
      <div style="FONT-WEIGHT: bold" id="Result" runat="server"></div>
    </div>

  </form>
</body></HTML>
```

Then we add the corresponding control variable to the CurrencyConverter class.

```
Protected Currency As HtmlSelect
```

The currency list is filled through code at runtime. In this case, the ideal event is the Page.Load event. This is the first event that occurs when the page is executed.

```
Private Sub Page_Load(sender As Object, e As EventArgs) _
  Handles MyBase.Load

    If Me.IsPostBack = False
        Currency.Items.Add("Euro")
        Currency.Items.Add("Japanese Yen")
        Currency.Items.Add("Canadian Dollars")
    End If

End Sub
```



## Interesting Facts About this Code

**Specify MyBase to handle a Page event.** This keyword identifies the class that your page inherited from (in this case, the Page class).

**Use the Items property with a list control.** This allows you to append, insert, and remove <option> elements. Remember, when generating dynamic content with a server control, you set the properties, and the control creates the appropriate HTML tags.

**Check for postbacks.** Before adding any items to this list, we need to make sure that this is the first time the page is being served. Otherwise, we will continuously add more items to the list or inadvertently overwrite the user's selection. The Me keyword points to the current instance of our page class. In other words, IsPostback is a property of the CurrencyConverter class, which CurrencyConverter inherited from the generic Page class.

Of course, if you are a veteran HTML coder, you know that a select list also provides a value attribute that you can use to store additional information. As our currency converter uses a short list of hard-coded values, this would be an ideal place to store the conversion rate.

To set the value tag, you need to create a ListItem object, and add that to the HtmlInputSelect control. The ListItem class provides a constructor that allows us to specify the text and value at the same time that we create it, allowing condensed code like this:

```
Private Sub Page_Load(sender As Object, e As EventArgs) _
  Handles MyBase.Load

    If Me.IsPostBack = False
        ' The HtmlInputSelect control accepts text or ListItem objects.
        Currency.Items.Add(New ListItem("Euro", "1.12"))
        Currency.Items.Add(New ListItem("Japanese Yen", "122.33"))
        Currency.Items.Add(New ListItem("Canadian Dollar", "1.58"))
    End If

End Sub
```

To complete our example, the calculation code must be rewritten.

```
Private Sub Convert_ServerClick(sender As Object, e As EventArgs) _
  Handles convert.ServerClick
    Dim Amount As Decimal = Val(US.Value)

    ' Retrieve the select ListItem object by its index number.
    ' Each ListItem object provides a Text and Value property.
    Dim Item As ListItem
    Item = Currency.Items(Currency.SelectedIndex)

    Dim NewAmount As Decimal = Amount * Val(Item.Value)
    Result.InnerText = Amount.ToString() & " US dollars = "
    Result.InnerText &= NewAmount.ToString() & " " & Item.Text
End Sub
```

Figure 6-3 shows you what the converter will now look like.

## Adding Linked Images

Adding a different set of functionality to our currency converter is just as easy as adding a new button. For example, it might be useful for our utility to display a currency conversion rate graph. To provide this feature, the program would need an additional button and image control.

```
<%@ Page Language="VB" Inherits="CurrencyConverter"
        Src="CurrencyConverter.vb" AutoEventWireup="False" %>
```

```
<HTML><body>
  <form method="post" runat="server">

    <!-- div tag used for formatting. -->
      Convert:  
      <input type="text" id="US" runat="server">  US dollars to
       Euros.
      <select style="WIDTH: 155px" id="Currency"
              runat="server"></select><br><br>
      <input type="submit" value="OK" id="Convert" runat="server">
      <input type="submit" value="Show Graph" id="ShowGraph"
       runat="server"><br><br>
      <img id="Graph" runat="server"><br><br>
      <div style="FONT-WEIGHT: bold" id="Result"
       runat="server"></div>
    </div>

  </form>
</body></HTML>
```

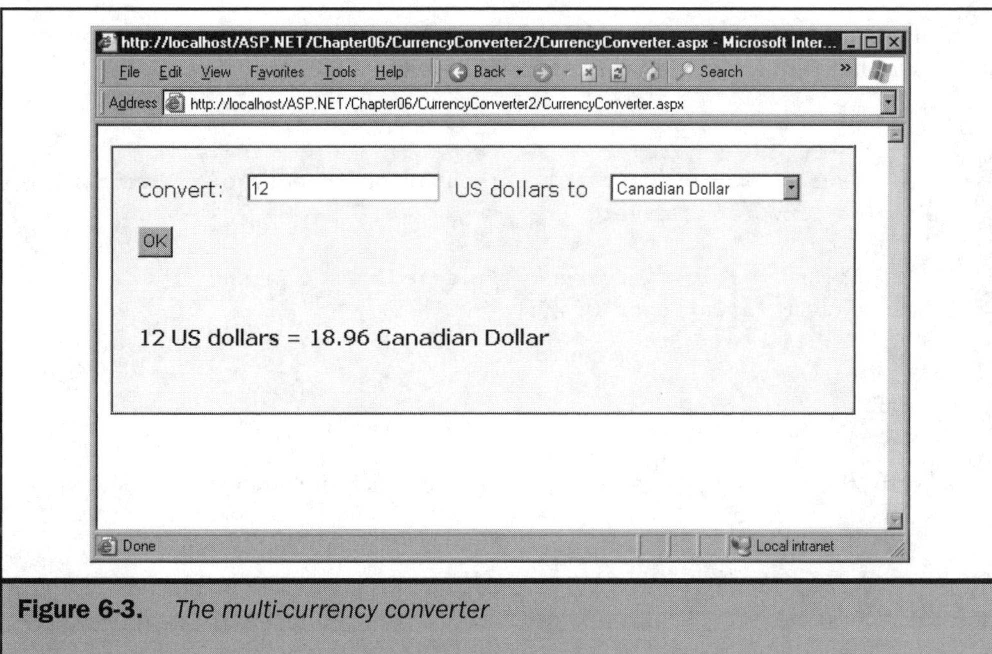


**Figure 6-3.** *The multi-currency converter*

They are also defined in the code-behind file.

```
Protected Graph As HtmlImage
Protected WithEvents ShowGraph As HtmlInputButton
```

This image does not yet refer to a picture. For that reason, it's useful to hide it when the page is first processed. Interestingly, when a server control is hidden, ASP.NET leaves it out of the final HTML page.

```
Private Sub Page_Load(sender As Object, e As EventArgs) _
  Handles MyBase.Load

    If Me.IsPostBack = False
        Currency.Items.Add(New ListItem("Euro", "1.12"))
        Currency.Items.Add(New ListItem("Japanese Yen", "122.33"))
        Currency.Items.Add(New ListItem("Canadian Dollar", "1.58"))
    End If
    Graph.Visible = False

End Sub
```

You can handle the click event of the new button to display the appropriate picture. In the currency converter, there are three possible picture files: pic0.png, pic1.png, and pic2.png.

```
Private Sub ShowGraph_ServerClick(sender As Object, e As EventArgs) _
  Handles ShowGraph.ServerClick

    Graph.Src = "Pic" & Currency.SelectedIndex & ".png"
    Graph.Alt = "Currency Graph"
    Graph.Visible = True

End Sub
```

Already, the currency calculator is beginning to look more interesting, as shown in Figure 6-4.

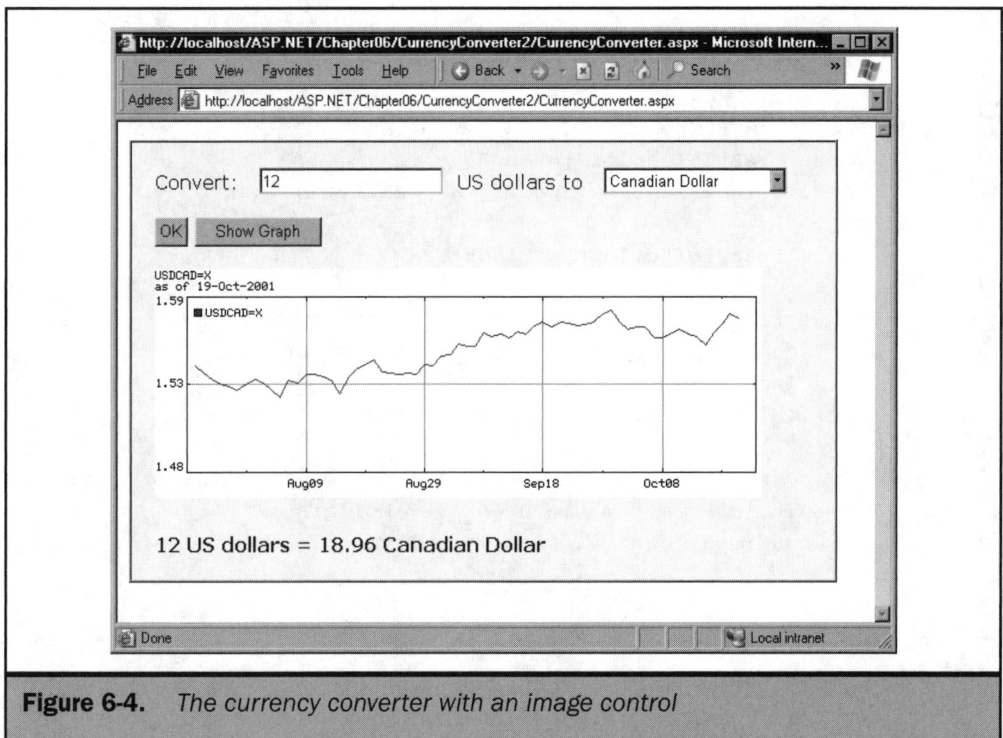


**Figure 6-4.** *The currency converter with an image control*



## Setting Styles

In addition to a limited set of properties, each HTML control also provides access to the CSS style attributes through a collection in the Style property. To use this collection, you need to specify the name of the CSS style attribute.

```
ControlName.Style("AttributeName") = "AttributeValue"
```

For example, you could use this technique to emphasize an invalid entry in the currency converter with the color red. In this case, you will also need to reset the color to its original value for valid input, as the control uses viewstate to remember all its settings, including its style properties.

```
Private Sub Convert_ServerClick(sender As Object, e As EventArgs) _
  Handles convert.ServerClick
```

```
    Dim Amount As Decimal = Val(US.Value)

    If Amount <= 0 Then
        Result.Style("color")="Red"
        Result.InnerText = "Specify a positive number"
    Else
        Result.Style("color")="Black"

        ' Retrieve the select ListItem object by its index number.
        ' Each ListItem object provides a Text and Value property.
        Dim Item As ListItem
        Item = Currency.Items(Currency.SelectedIndex)

        Dim ConvertedAmount As Decimal = Amount * Val(Item.Value)
        Result.InnerText = Amount & " US dollars = " & _
          ConvertedAmount & " " & Item.Text
    End If

End Sub
```

### Use Styles for HTML Controls, Not Web Controls

The Style collection is used to set the style attribute in the HTML tag with a list of formatting options such as font family, size, and color. If you aren't familiar with CSS styles, there's no need to learn them now. Instead, you should use the web control equivalents, which provide higher-level properties that allow you to configure their appearance and automatically create the appropriate style attributes. You'll learn about web controls in the next chapter.

## A Deeper Look at HTML Control Classes

Related classes in the .NET framework use inheritance to share functionality. For example, every HTML control inherits from the base class HtmlControl, which provides some essential features every HTML server control uses. The inheritance diagram is shown in Figure 6-5.

The next few sections aim to shed some light on the ASP.NET classes used for controls. For the specific details about each HTML control class, refer to Chapter 26.

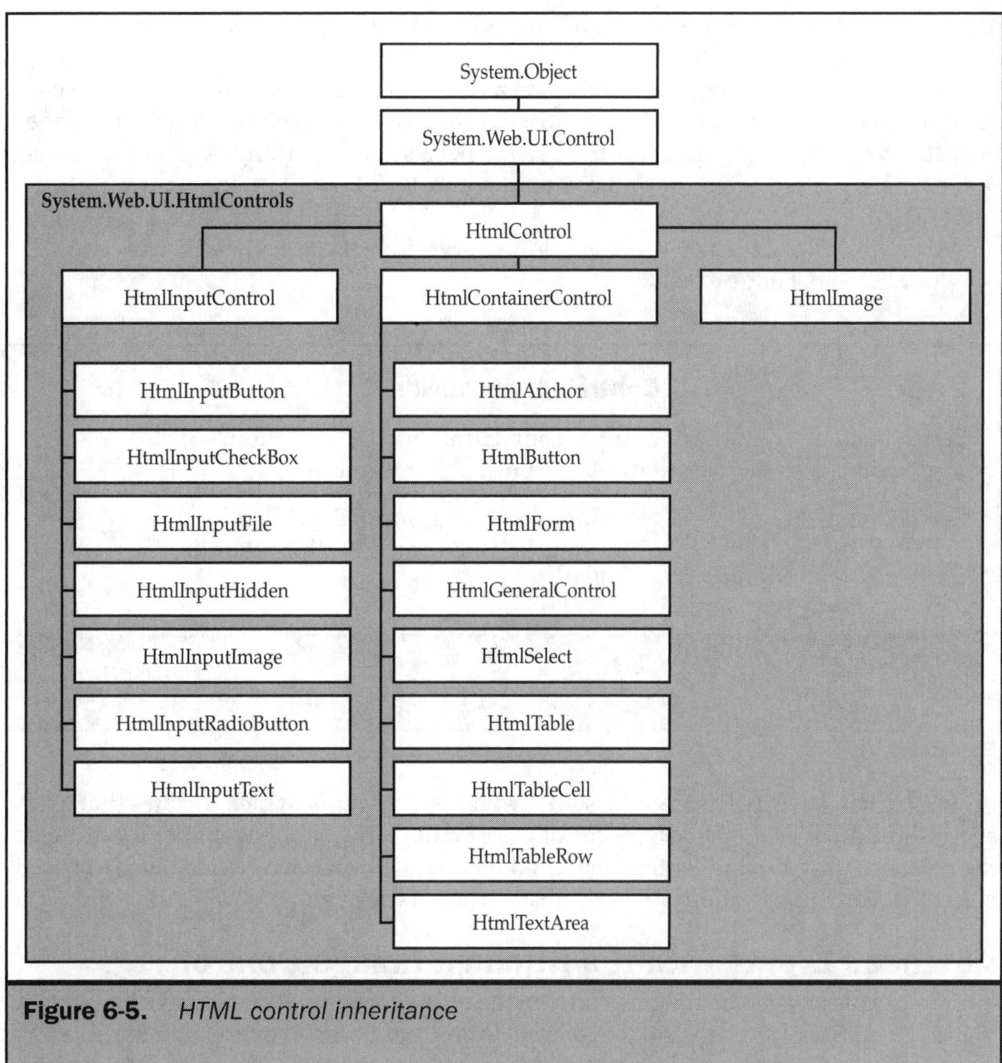


**Figure 6-5.** *HTML control inheritance*

HTML server controls generally provide properties that closely match their tag attributes (for example, the HtmlImage class provides Align, Alt, Border, Src, Height, and Width properties) and one of two possible events: ServerClick or ServerChange.

## HTML Control Events

The ServerClick is simply a click that is processed on the server side. It's provided by most button controls, and it allows your code to take immediate action. This action might override the expected behavior. For example, if you intercept the click event of an anchor control, the user won't be redirected to a new page unless you provide extra code to forward the request.

The ServerChange event responds when a change has been made to a text or selection control. This event is not as useful as it appears because it doesn't occur until the page is posted back (for example, after the user clicks a submit button). At this point, the ServerChange event occurs for all changed controls, followed by the appropriate ServerClick.

Table 6-3 shows which controls provide a ServerClick event, and which ones provide a ServerChange event.

| Event | Controls that Provide It |
|---|---|
| ServerClick | HtmlAnchor, HtmlForm, HtmlButton, HtmlInputButton, HtmlInputImage |
| ServerChange | HtmlInputText, HtmlInputCheckBox, HtmlInputRadioButton, HtmlInputHidden, HtmlSelect, HtmlTextArea |

**Table 6-3.** *HTML Control Events*

In Chapter 3, we introduced the standard for .NET events, which dictates that every event should pass exactly two pieces of information. The first parameter identifies the object (in this case, the control) that fired the event. The second parameter is a special object that can include additional information about the event.

## Advanced Events with the HtmlInputImage Control

In the examples we've looked at so far, the second parameter (e) has always been used to pass an empty System.EventArgs object. This object doesn't contain any additional information—it's just a glorified placeholder.

```
Private Sub Convert_ServerClick(sender As Object, e As EventArgs) _
  Handles convert.ServerClick
```

In fact, there is only one HTML server control that sends additional information: the HtmlInputImage control. It sends a special ImageClickEventArgs object (from the System.Web.UI namespace) that provides X and Y properties representing the location where the image was clicked.

```
Private Sub ImgButton_ServerClick(sender As Object, _
  e As ImageClickEventArgs) Handles ImgButton.ServerClick
```

This makes for an exceptionally easy way to replace multiple button controls and image maps when you need a sophisticated graphical user interface. The sample ImageTest.aspx page shown in Figure 6-6 puts this feature to work with a simple graphical button. Depending on whether the user clicks on the button border or on the button surface, a different message is displayed.



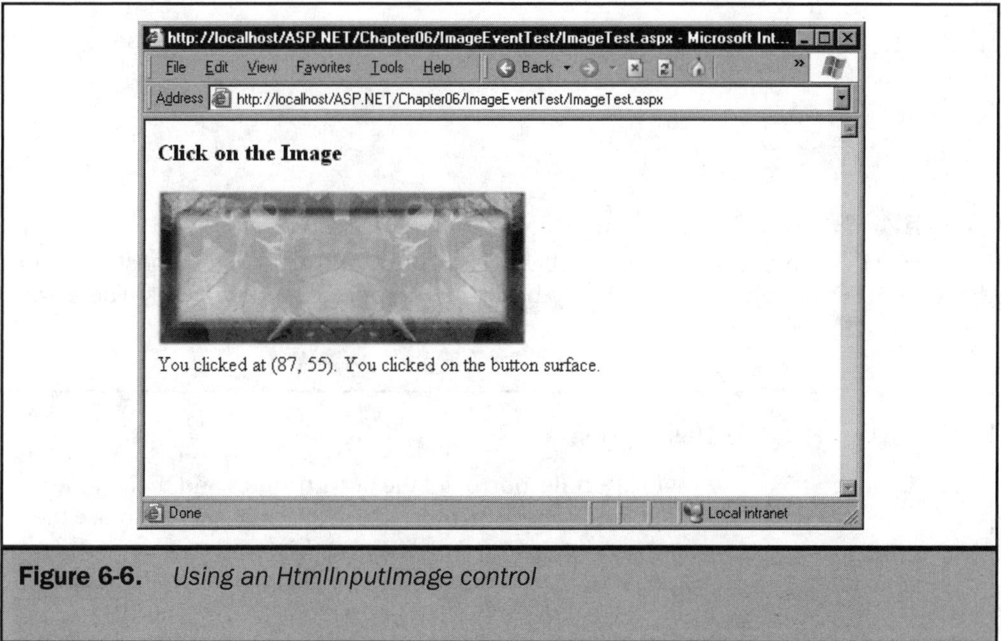


**Figure 6-6.** *Using an HtmlInputImage control*

The page code examines the click coordinates provided by the HtmlInputImage. ServerClick event.

```
Public Class ImageTest
  Inherits Page

    Protected Result As HtmlGenericControl
    Protected WithEvents ImgButton As HtmlInputImage
```

```
    Private Sub ImgButton_ServerClick(sender As Object, _
      e As ImageClickEventArgs) Handles ImgButton.ServerClick

        Result.InnerText = "You clicked at (" & e.X.ToString() & _
                           ", " & e.Y.ToString() & "). "

        If e.Y < 100 And e.Y > 20 And e.X > 20 and e.X < 275 Then
            Result.InnerText &= "You clicked on the button surface."
        Else
            Result.InnerText &= "You clicked the button border."
        End If
    End Sub

End Class
```

## The HtmlControl Base Class

Every HTML control inherits from the base class HtmlControl. This relationship means that every HTML control will support a basic set of properties and features. These are shown in Table 6-4.

| Property | Description |
|---|---|
| Attributes | Provides a collection of all the tag attributes and their values. Rather than setting an attribute directly, it's better to use the corresponding property. However, this collection is useful if you need to add or configure a custom attribute or an attribute that doesn't have a corresponding property. |
| Controls | Provides a collection of all the controls contained inside the current control. (For example, a <div> server control could contain an <input> server control.) Each object is provided as a generic System.Web.UI.Control object, so you may need to cast the reference with the CType function to access control-specific properties. |

**Table 6-4.** *HtmlControl Properties*

| Property | Description |
|---|---|
| Disabled | Set this to True to disable the control, ensuring that the user cannot interact with it and its events will not be fired. |
| EnableViewState | Set this to False to disable the automatic state management for this control. In this case, the control will be reset to the properties and formatting specified in the control tag every time the page is posted back. If this is set to True (the default), the control uses the hidden input field to store information about its properties, ensuring that any changes you make in code are remembered. |
| Page | Provides a reference to the web page that contains this control as a System.Web.UI.Page object. |
| Parent | Provides a reference to the control that contains this control. If the control is placed directly on the page (rather than inside another control), it will return a reference to the page object. |
| Style | Provides a collection of CSS style properties that can be used to format the control. |
| TagName | Indicates the name of the underlying HTML element (for example, "img" or "div"). |
| Visible | When set to False, the control will be hidden and will not be rendered to the final HTML page that is sent to the client. |

**Table 6-4.** *HtmlControl Properties (continued)*

The HtmlControl class also provides built-in support for data binding, which we examine in Chapter 14.

## The HtmlContainerControl Class

Any HTML control that requires a closing tag also inherits from the HtmlContainer control. For example, elements such as <a>, <form>, and <div> always use a closing tag, while <img> and <input> can be used as single tags. Thus, the HtmlAnchor, HtmlForm, and HtmlGenericControl classes inherit from HtmlContainerControl, while HtmlImage and HtmlInput do not.

## Properties Can Be Set in Code or in the Tag

To set the initial value of a property, you can configure the control in the Page.Load event handler, or you can adjust the control tag by adding special attributes. Note that the Page.Load event occurs after the page is initialized with the default values and the tag settings. That means that your code can override the properties set in the tag (but not vice versa).

The following HtmlImage control is an example that sets properties through attributes in the control tag. The control is automatically disabled and will not have its viewstate information stored.

```
<img EnableViewState="False" Disabled="True" id="Graph"
runat="server">
```

The only disadvantage with using control tag attributes is that errors will not necessarily be detected. An invalid property assignment in the code-behind, on the other hand, will almost always generate a friendly runtime error informing you about the problem.

The HtmlContainerControl adds two properties, described in Table 6-5.

| Property | Description |
|---|---|
| InnerHtml | The HTML content between the opening and closing tags of the control. Special characters that are set through this property will *not* be converted to the equivalent HTML entities. This means you can use this property to apply formatting with nested tags like <b>, <i>, and <h1>. |
| InnerText | The text content between the opening and closing tags of the control. Special characters will be automatically converted to HTML entities and displayed like text (for example, the less than character (<) will be converted to < and will be displayed as < in the web page). That means that you can't use HTML tags to apply additional formatting with this property. The simple currency converter page used the InnerText property to enter results into a <div> tag. |

**Table 6-5.** *HtmlContainerControl Properties*

## The HtmlInputControl Class

This control defines some properties (shown in Table 6-6) that are common to all the HTML controls based on the <input> tag, including the <input type="text">, <input type="submit">, and <input type="file"> elements.

| Property | Description |
|---|---|
| Type | Provides the type of input control. For example, a control based on <input type="file"> would return "file" for the type property. |
| Value | Returns the contents of the control as a string. In the simple currency converter, this property allowed the code to retrieve the information entered in the text input control. |

**Table 6-6.** *HtmlInputControl Properties*

# The Page Class

One control we haven't discussed in detail is the Page object. As explained in the previous chapter, every web page is a custom class that inherits from the System.Web.UI.Page control. By inheriting from this class, your page class acquires a number of properties that your code can use. These include properties for enabling caching, validation, and tracing, which are discussed in various chapters of this book.

Some of the more fundamental properties are described in Table 6-7, including the traditional built-in objects that you probably used in ASP programming, such as Response, Request, and Session.

| Property | Description |
|---|---|
| Application and Session | These collections are used to hold state information on the server. Chapter 10 discusses this topic. |
| Cache | This collection allows you to store objects for reuse in other pages or for other clients. Caching is described in Chapter 23. |

**Table 6-7.** *Basic Page Properties*

| Property | Description |
|---|---|
| Controls | Provides a collection of all the controls contained on the web page. You can also use the methods of this collection to add new controls dynamically. |
| EnableViewState | When set to False, this overrides the EnableViewState property of the contained controls, ensuring that no controls will maintain state information. |
| IsPostBack | This Boolean property indicates whether this is the first time the page is being run (False), or whether the page is being resubmitted in response to a control event, typically with stored viewstate information (True). This property is often used in the Page.Load event handler, ensuring that basic setup is only performed once for controls that maintain viewstate. |
| Request | Refers to an HttpRequest object that contains information about the current web request, including client certificates, cookies, and values submitted through HTML form elements. It supports the same features as the built-in ASP Request object. |
| Response | Refers to an HttpResponse object that allows you to set the web response or redirect the user to another web page. It supports the same features as the built-in ASP Response object, although it's used much less in .NET development. |
| Server | Refers to an HttpServerUtility object that allows you to perform some miscellaneous tasks, such as URL and HTML encoding. It supports the same features as the built-in ASP Server object. |
| User | If the user has been authenticated, this property will be initialized with user information. This property is described in more detail when we examine security in Chapter 24. |

**Table 6-7.** *Basic Page Properties (continued)*

## The Controls Collection

The Page.Controls collection includes all the controls on the current web form. You can loop through this collection and access each control. For example, the following code writes out the name of every control on the current page to a server control called Result.

```
Result.InnerText = "List of controls: "
Dim ctrl As Control
For Each ctrl In Me.Controls
    Result.InnerText &= " " & ctrl.ID
Next
```

You can also use the Controls collection to add a dynamic control. The following code creates a new button with the caption "Dynamic Button" and adds it to the bottom of the page.

```
Dim ctrl As New HtmlButton()
ctrl.InnerText = "Dynamic Button"
Me.Controls.Add(ctrl)
```

This dynamically added button won't be stored in viewstate, so you will need to keep track of it and recreate it after postbacks if you want it to remain.

## The HttpRequest Class

The HttpRequest class encapsulates all the information related to a client request for a web page (see Table 6-8). Most of this information corresponds to low-level details such as posted-back form values, server variables, the response encoding, and so on. If you are using the ASP.NET framework to its fullest, you'll almost never dive down to that level. Other properties are generally useful for retrieving information, particularly about the capabilities of the client browser. Some of the security-related properties will return in our discussion in Chapter 24.

| Property | Description |
|---|---|
| ApplicationPath and PhysicalPath | ApplicationPath gets the ASP.NET application's virtual directory (URL), while PhysicalPath gets the "real" directory. |

**Table 6-8.** *HttpRequest Properties*

| Property | Description |
|---|---|
| Browser | Provides a link to an HttpBrowserCapabilities object which contains properties describing various browser features, such as support for ActiveX controls, cookies, VBScript, and frames. This replaces the BrowserCapabilities component that was sometimes used in ASP development. |
| ClientCertificate | An HttpClientCertificate object that gets the security certificate for the current request, if there is one. |
| Cookies | Gets the collection cookies sent with this request. Cookies are discussed in more detail in Chapter 10. |
| Headers and ServerVariables | Provides a name/value collection of HTTP headers and server variables. You can get the low-level information you need if you know the corresponding header or variable name. |
| IsAuthenticated and IsSecureConnection | Returns True if the user has been successfully authenticated and if the user is connected over secure sockets (also known as SSL or HTTPS). |
| QueryString | Provides the parameters that were passed along with the query string. Chapter 10 discusses how you can use the query string to transfer information between pages. |
| Url and UrlReferrer | Provides a Uri object that represents the current address for the page, and the page where the user is coming from (the previous page that linked to this page). |
| UserAgent | A string representing the browser type. Internet Explorer provides the value "MSIE" for this property. |
| UserHostAddress and UserHostName | Gets the IP address and the DNS name of the remote client. You could also access this information through the ServerVariables collection. |
| UserLanguages | Provides a sorted string array that lists the client's language preferences. This can be useful if you need to create multilingual pages. |

**Table 6-8.** *HttpRequest Properties (continued)*

## The HttpResponse Class

The HttpResponse class allows you to send information directly to the client. In traditional ASP development, the Response object was used heavily to create dynamic pages. Now, with the introduction of the new server-based control model, these relatively crude methods are no longer needed.

The HttpResponse does still provide some important functionality: namely caching support, cookie features, and the Redirect method that allows you to transfer the user to another page. A list of HttpResponse members is provided in Table 6-9.



```
' You can redirect to a file in the current directory.
Response.Redirect("newpage.aspx")

' You can redirect to another website.
Response.Redirect("http://www.prosetech.com")
```

| Member | Description |
|---|---|
| BufferOutput | When set to True (the default), the page is not sent to the client until it is completely rendered and ready to send, rather than piecemeal. |
| Cache | References an HttpCachePolicy object that allows you to configure how this page will be cached. Caching is discussed in Chapter 23. |
| Cookies | The collection of cookies sent with the response. You can use this property to add additional cookies, as described in Chapter 10. |
| Write(), BinaryWrite(), and WriteFile() | These methods allow you to write text or binary content directly to the response stream. You can even write the contents of a file. These methods are de-emphasized in ASP.NET, and shouldn't be used in conjunction with server controls. |
| Redirect() | This method transfers the user to another page in your application or a different web site. |

**Table 6-9.** *HttpResponse Members*

## The ServerUtility Class

The ServerUtility class provides some miscellaneous helper methods, as listed in Table 6-10. The most commonly used are UrlEncode/UrlDecode and HtmlEncode/HtmlDecode. These functions change a string into a representation that can safely be used as part of a URL or displayed in a web page.

| Method | Description |
|---|---|
| CreateObject | Creates an instance of the COM object that is identified by its programmatic ID (progID). This is included for backward compatibility, as it will generally be easier to interact with COM objects using the .NET framework services. |
| HtmlEncode and HtmlDecode | Changes an ordinary string into a string with legal HTML characters and back again. |
| UrlEncode and UrlDecode | Changes an ordinary string into a string with legal URL characters and back again. |
| MapPath | Returns the physical file path that corresponds to a specified virtual file path on the web server. |
| Transfer | Transfers execution to another web page in the current application. This is similar to the Response.Redirect method, but slightly faster. It cannot be used to transfer the user to a site on another web server. |

**Table 6-10.** *ServerUtility Methods*

For example, imagine you want to display this text on a web page:

```
Enter a word <here>
```

If you try to write this information to a page or place it inside a control, you may end up with this instead:

```
Enter a word
```

In this case, the browser has tried to interpret the text "<here>" as an HTML tag. A similar problem occurs if you actually use valid HTML tags. For example, consider this text:

```
To bold text use the <b> tag.
```

Not only will the text "<b>" not appear, the browser will interpret it as an instruction to make the following text bold. To circumvent this automatic behavior, you need to convert potential problematic values to their special HTML equivalents. For example < becomes < in your final HTML page, which the browser displays as the < character.



You can perform this transformation on your own, or you can circumvent the problem by using the InnerText property. When you set the contents of a control using InnerText, any illegal characters are automatically converted into their HTML equivalents. However, this won't help if you want to set a tag that contains a mix of embedded HTML tags and encoded characters. It also won't be of any use for controls that don't provide an InnerText property, such as the Label web control we'll examine in the next chapter.

In these cases, you can use the HtmlEncode method to replace the special characters.

```
' Will output as "Enter a word &lt;here&gt;" in the HTML file, but the
' browser will display it as "Enter a word <here>".
ctrl.InnerHtml = Server.HtmlEncode("Enter a word <here>")
```

Or consider this example, which mingles real HTML tags with text that needs to be encoded.

```
ctrl.InnerHtml = "To <b>bold</b> text use the "
ctrl.InnerHtml &= Server.HtmlEncode("<b>") & " tag."
```

Figure 6-7 shows the results of successfully and incorrectly encoding special HTML characters. You can try out this sample as the HtmlEncodeTest.aspx page included with the examples for this chapter.

The HtmlEncode method is particularly useful if you are retrieving values from a database, where you aren't sure if the text is HTML-legal. You can use the HtmlDecode method to revert the text to its normal form if you need to perform additional operations or comparisons with it in your code.

Similarly, the UrlEncode method changes text into a form that can be used in a URL. Generally, this allows information to work as a query string variable, even if it contains spaces and other characters that aren't URL-legal.

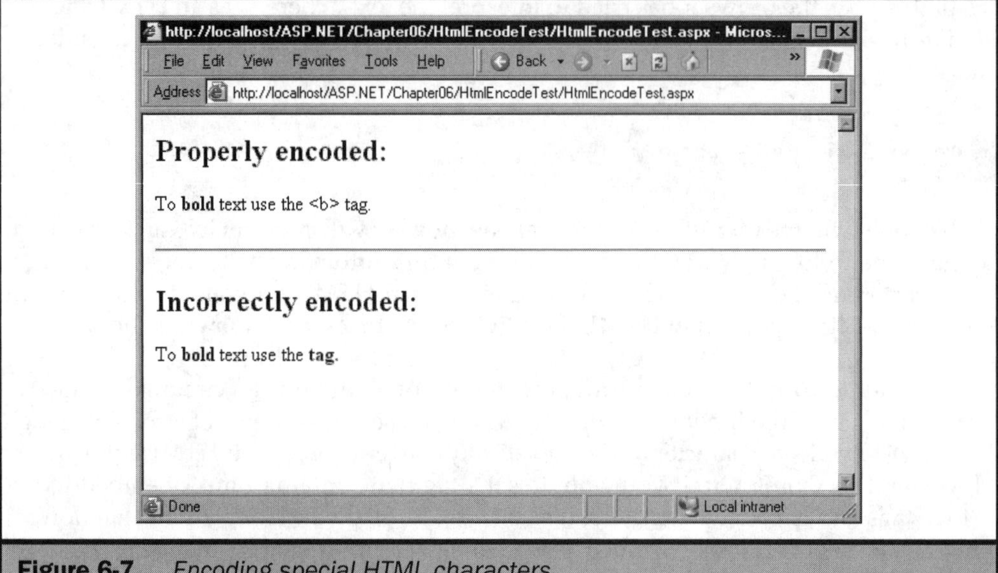


**Figure 6-7.** *Encoding special HTML characters*

## Assessing HTML Server Controls

HTML controls are a compromise between web controls and traditional ASP.NET programming. They use the familiar HTML elements, but provide a limited object-oriented interface. Essentially, HTML controls are designed to be straightforward, predictable, and automatically compatible with existing programs. With HTML controls, the final HTML page that is sent to the client closely resembles the original .aspx page.

In the next chapter, we introduce web controls, which provide a more sophisticated object interface that abstracts away the underlying HTML. If you are starting a new project, or need to add some of ASP.NET's most powerful controls, web controls are the best option.

# Chapter 7

## Web Controls

The last chapter introduced one of ASP.NET's most surprising revolutions: the change to event-driven and control-based programming. This change allows you to create programs for the Internet following the same structured, modern style you would use for a Windows application.

However, HTML server controls really only show a glimpse of what is possible with ASP.NET's new control model. To see some of the real advantages provided by this shift, you need to explore web controls, which provide a rich, extensible set of control objects. In this chapter, we'll examine the basic web controls and their class hierarchy. We'll also delve deeper into ASP.NET's event handling, and examine the web page lifecycle.

## Stepping Up to Web Controls

Now that you've seen the new model of server controls, you might wonder why we need additional web controls. But in fact, HTML controls are still more limited than server controls need to be. For example, every HTML control corresponds directly to an HTML tag, meaning that you are bound by the limitations and abilities of the HTML language. Web controls, on the other hand, emphasize the future of web design:

**They provide rich user interface.** A web control is programmed as an object, but doesn't necessarily correspond to a single tag in the final HTML page. For example, you might create a single Calendar or DataGrid control, which will be rendered as dozens of HTML elements in the final page. When using ASP.NET programs, you don't need to know anything about HTML. The control creates the required HTML tags for you.

**They provide a consistent object model.** The HTML language is full of quirks and idiosyncrasies. For example, a simple text box can appear as one of three elements, including <textarea>, <input type="text">, and <input type="password">. With web controls, these three elements are consolidated as a single TextBox control. Depending on the properties you set, the underlying HTML element that ASP.NET renders may differ. Similarly, the names of properties don't follow the HTML attribute names. Controls that display text, whether it is a caption or a user-editable text box, expose a Text property.

**They tailor their output automatically.** ASP.NET server controls can detect the type of browser, and automatically adjust the HTML code they write to take advantage of features such as support for DHTML. You don't need to know about the client because ASP.NET handles that layer and automatically uses the best possible set of features.

**They provide high-level features.** You'll see that web controls allow you to access additional events, properties, and methods that don't correspond directly to typical HTML controls. ASP.NET implements these features by using a combination of tricks.

> **The Examples in this Book Use Web Controls**
>
> Throughout this book, I'll show examples that use the full set of web controls. In order to master ASP.NET development, you need to become comfortable with these user interface ingredients and understand all their abilities. HTML server controls, on the other hand, are less important for web development, unless you need to have a fine-grained control over the HTML code that will be generated and sent to the client. They are de-emphasized.



## Basic Web Control Classes

If you have created Windows applications before, you are probably familiar with the basic set of standard controls, including labels, buttons, and text boxes. ASP.NET provides web controls for all these standbys. (If you've created .NET Windows applications, you'll notice that the class names and properties have many striking similarities, which are designed to make it easy to transfer the experience you acquire in one framework to another.)

Table 7-1 lists the basic control classes, and the HTML elements they generate. Note that some controls, such as Button and TextBox, can be rendered as different HTML elements. ASP.NET uses the element that matches the properties you have set. Also, some controls have no single HTML equivalent. For example, the CheckBoxList and RadioButtonList controls output as a <table> that contains multiple HTML checkboxes or radio buttons. ASP.NET wraps them into a single object on the server side for convenient programming, illustrating one of the primary strengths of web controls.

| Control Class | Underlying HTML Element |
|---|---|
| Label | <span> |
| Button | <input type="submit"> or <input type="button"> |
| TextBox | <input type="text">, <input type="password">, or <textarea> |
| CheckBox | <input type="checkbox"> |
| RadioButton | <input type="radio"> |

**Table 7-1.** *Basic Web Controls*

| Control Class | Underlying HTML Element |
|---|---|
| Hyperlink | <a> |
| LinkButton | <a> with a contained <img> tag |
| ImageButton | <input type="image"> |
| Image | <img> |
| ListBox | <select size="X"> where X is the number of rows that are visible at once |
| DropDownList | <select> |
| CheckBoxList | A list or <table> with multiple <input type="checkbox"> tags |
| RadioButtonList | A list or <table> with multiple <input type="radio"> tags |
| Panel | <div> |
| Table, TableRow, and TableCell | <table>, <tr>, and <td> or <th> |

**Table 7-1.** *Basic Web Controls (continued)*

This table omits some of the more specialized rich controls, which we'll see in Chapter 9, and the advanced data controls, which we'll see in Chapter 15.

## The Web Control Tags

ASP.NET tags have a special format. They always begin with the prefix asp: followed by the class name. If there is no closing tag, the tag must end with />. Any attributes in the tag correspond to a control property, aside from the runat="server" attribute, which declares that the control will be processed on the server.

The following, for example, is an ASP.NET TextBox.

```
<asp:TextBox id="txt" runat="server" />
```

When a client requests this .aspx page, the following HTML is returned. The name is a special attribute that ASP.NET uses to track the control.

```
<input type="text" name="ctrl0" />
```

Alternatively, you could place some text in the TextBox, set its size, make it read-only, and change the background color. All these actions have defined properties. For example, TextBox.TextMode property allows you to specify SingleLine (the default), MultiLine (for a text area type of control), or Password (for an input control that displays all asterisks when the user types in a value).

```
<asp:TextBox id="txt" BackColor="Yellow" Text="Hello World"
 ReadOnly="True" TextMode="MultiLine" Rows="5" runat="server" />
```

The resulting HTML uses the text area element and sets all the required style attributes.

```
<textarea name="txt" rows="5" readonly="readonly" id="txt"
 style="background-color:Yellow;">Hello World</textarea>
```

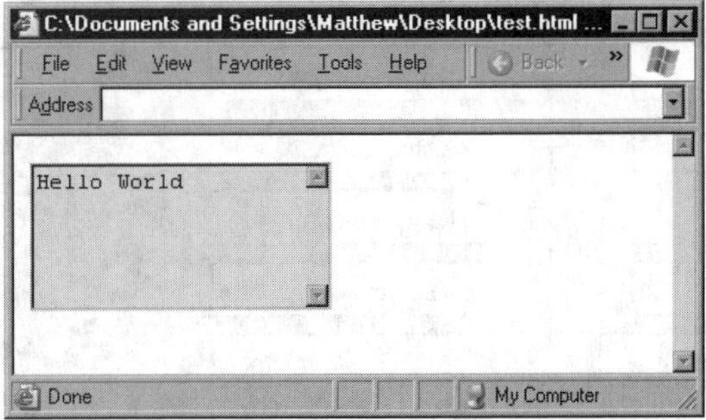


Clearly, it's easy to create a web control tag. However, you need to understand the control class and the properties that are available to you.

## Web Control Classes

Web control classes are defined in the System.Web.UI.WebControls namespace. They follow a slightly more tangled object hierarchy than HTML server controls, as shown in Figure 7-1.

This inheritance diagram includes some controls that we won't examine in this chapter, including the data controls such as the Repeater, DataList, and DataGrid, and the validation controls.

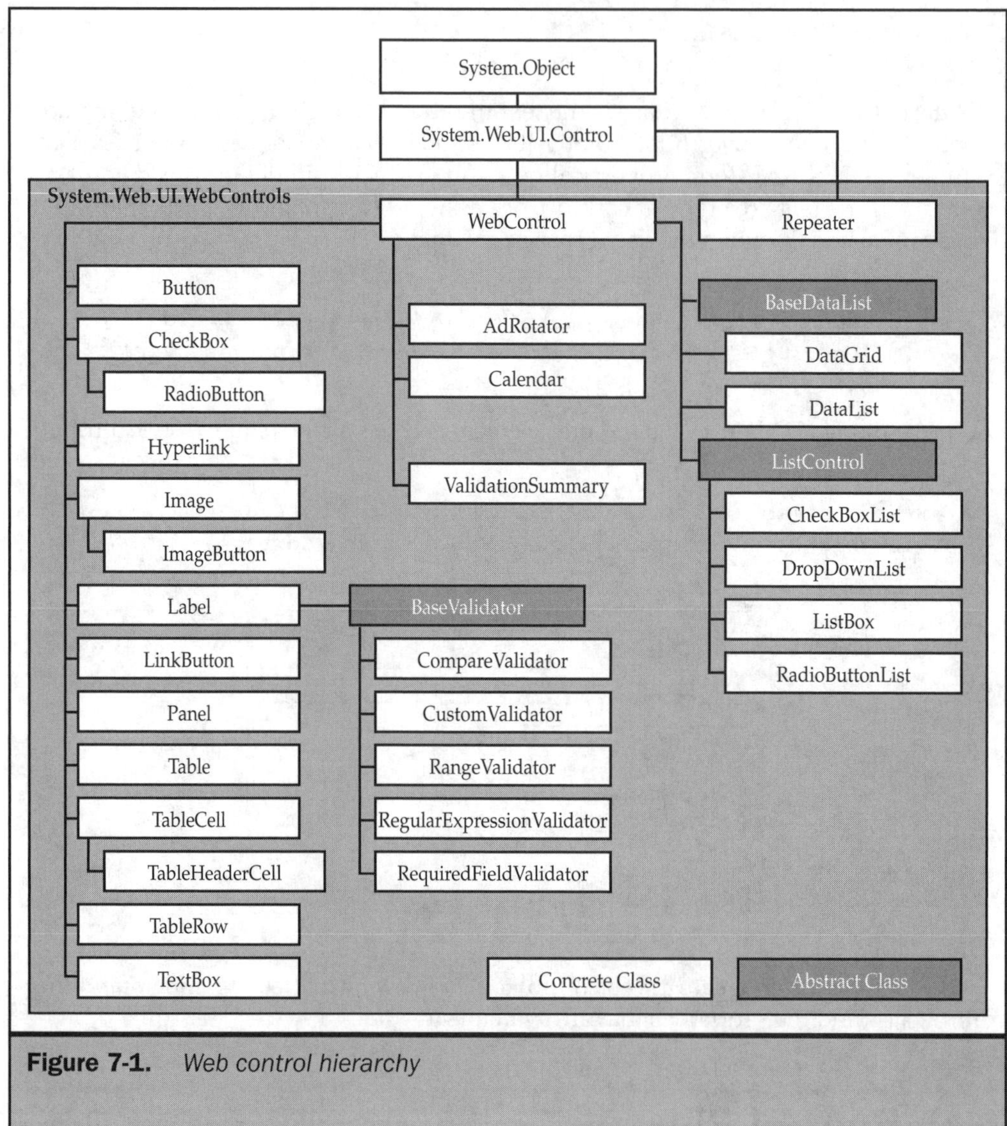


**Figure 7-1.** *Web control hierarchy*

## The WebControl Base Class

All web controls begin by inheriting from the WebControl base class. This class defines essential functionality for tasks such as data binding, and includes some basic properties that you can use with any control (see Table 7-2).

| Property | Description |
| --- | --- |
| AccessKey | Specifies the keyboard shortcut as one letter. For example, if you set this to "Y", the ALT-Y keyboard combination will automatically change focus to this web control. This feature is only supported on Internet Explorer 4.0 and higher. |
| BackColor, BorderColor and ForeColor | Sets the colors used for the background, foreground, and border of the control. Usually, the foreground color is used for text. |
| BorderWidth | Specifies the size of the control border. |
| BorderStyle | One of the values from the BorderStyle enumeration, including Dashed, Dotted, Double, Groove, Ridge, Inset, Outset, Solid, and None. |
| Controls | Provides a collection of all the controls contained inside the current control. Each object is provided as a generic System.Web.UI.Control object, so you may need to cast the reference with the CType function to access control-specific properties. |
| Enabled | When set to False, the control will be visible, but will not be able to receive user input or focus. |
| EnableViewState | Set this to False to disable the automatic state management for this control. In this case, the control will be reset to the properties and formatting specified in the control tag every time the page is posted back. If this is set to True (the default), the control uses the hidden input field to store information about its properties, ensuring that any changes you make in code are remembered. |
| Font | Specifies the font used to render any text in the control as a special System.Drawing.Font object. |
| Height and Width | Specifies the width and height of the control. For some controls, these properties will be ignored when used with older browsers. |

**Table 7-2.** *WebControl Properties*

| Property | Description |
|---|---|
| Page | Provides a reference to the web page that contains this control as a System.Web.UI.Page object. |
| Parent | Provides a reference to the control that contains this control. If the control is placed directly on the page (rather than inside another control), it will return a reference to the page object. |
| TabIndex | A number that allows you to control the tab order. The control with a TabIndex of 0 has the focus when the page first loads. Pressing TAB moves the user to the control with the next lowest TabIndex, provided it is enabled. This property is only supported in Internet Explorer 4.0 and higher. |
| ToolTip | Displays a text message when the user hovers the mouse above the control. Many older browsers do not support this property. |
| Visible | When set to False, the control will be hidden and will not be rendered to the final HTML page that is sent to the client. |

**Table 7-2.** *WebControl Properties (continued)*

## Units

All the properties that use measurements, including BorderWidth, Height, and Width, use the special Unit structure. When setting a unit in a control tag, make sure you add append px (pixel) or % (for percentage) to the number to indicate the type of unit.

```
<asp:Panel Height="300px" Width="50%" id="pnl" runat="server" />
```

If you are assigning one of these values at runtime, you need to use one of the shared properties of the Unit type.

```
' Convert the number 300 to a Unit object
' representing pixels, and assign it.
pnl.Height = Unit.Pixel(300)
```

```
' Convert the number 50 to a Unit object
' representing percent, and assign it.
pnl.Width = Unit.Percentage(50)
```

You could also manually create a Unit object and initialize it using one of the supplied constructors and the UnitType enumeration. This requires a few more steps, but allows you to easily assign the same unit to several controls.

```
' Create a Unit object
Dim MyUnit as New Unit(300, UnitType.Pixel)

' Assign the Unit object to several controls or properties.
pnl.Height = MyUnit
pnl.Width = MyUnit
```



## Enumerated Values

Enumerations are used heavily in the .NET class library to group together a set of related constants. For example, when you set a control's BorderStyle property, you can choose one of several predefined values from the BorderStyle enumeration. In code, you set an enumeration using the dot syntax.

```
ctrl.BorderStyle = BorderStyle.Dashed
```

In the .aspx file, you set an enumeration by specifying one of the allowed values as a string. You don't include the name of the enumeration type, which is assumed automatically.

```
<asp:TextBox BorderStyle="Dashed" Text="Border Test" id="txt"
runat="server" />
```

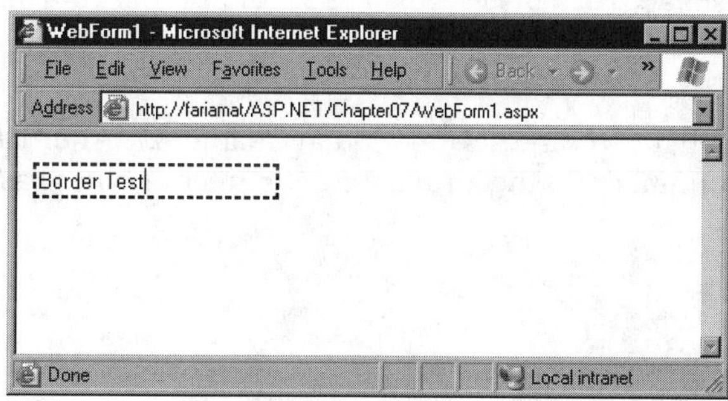

## Colors

The Color property refers to a Color object from the System.Drawing namespace. Color objects can be created in several different ways:

**Using an ARGB (alpha, red, green, blue) color value.** You specify each value as an integer.

**Using a predefined .NET color name.** You choose the correspondingly named read-only property from the Color class. These properties include all the HTML colors.

**Using an HTML color name.** You specify this value as a string using the ColorTranslator class.

To use these techniques, you must import the System.Drawing namespace.

```
Import System.Drawing
```

The following code shows several ways to specify a color in code.

```
' Create a color from an ARGB value
Dim Alpha As Integer = 255, Red As Integer = 0
Dim Green As Integer = 255, Blue As Integer = 0
ctrl.ForeColor = Color.FromARGB(alpha, red, green, blue)

' Create a color using a .NET name
ctrl.ForeColor = Color.Crimson

' Create a color from an HTML code
ctrl.ForeColor = ColorTranslator.FromHtml("Blue")
```

When defining a color in the .aspx file, you can use any one of the known color names.

```
<asp:TextBox ForeColor="Red" Text="Border Test" id="txt"
runat="server" />
```

The color names that you can use are listed in Chapter 27. Alternatively, you can use a hexadecimal color number (in the format #<red><green><blue>) as shown next.

```
<asp:TextBox ForeColor="#ff50ff" Text="Border Test"
     id="txt" runat="server" />
```

# Fonts

The Font property actually references a full FontInfo object (which is defined in the System.Drawing namespace). Every FontInfo object has several properties that define its name, size, and style (see Table 7-3).

| Property | Description |
|---|---|
| Name | A string indicating the font name (such as "Verdana"). |
| Size | The size of the font as a FontUnit object. This can represent an absolute or relative size. |
| Bold, Italic, Strikeout, Underline, and Overline | Boolean properties that either apply the given style attribute or ignore it. |

**Table 7-3.** *FontInfo Properties*

In code, you can assign to the various font properties using the familiar dot syntax.

```
ctrl.Font.Name = "Verdana"
ctrl.Font.Bold = "True"
```

You can set the size using the FontUnit type.

```
' Specifies a relative size.
ctrl.Font.Size = FontUnit.Small

' Specifies an absolute size of 14 pixels.
ctrl.Font.Size = FontUnit.Point(14)
```

In the .aspx file, you need to use a special "object walker" syntax to specify object properties such as font. The object walker syntax uses a hyphen (-) to separate properties.

For example, you could set a control with a specific font (Tahoma) and font size (40 point) like this:

```
<asp:TextBox Font-Name="Tahoma" Font-Size="40" Text="Size Test"
 id="txt" runat="server" />
```

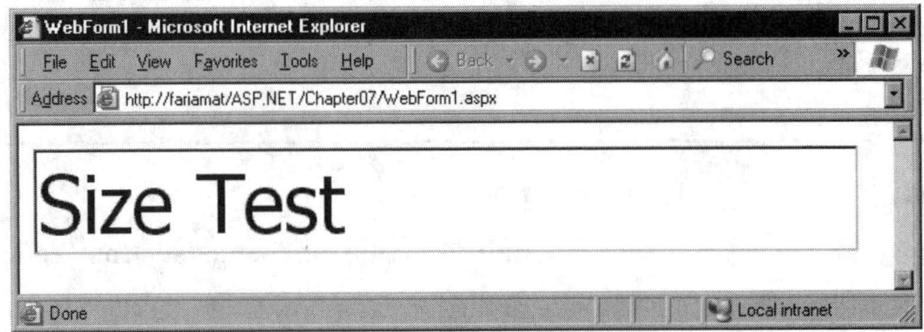


Or with a relative size:

```
<asp:TextBox Font-Name="Tahoma" Font-Size="Large" Text="Size Test"
 id="txt" runat="server" />
```

## List Controls

The simple list controls (ListBox, DropDownList, CheckBoxList, and RadioButtonList) are extremely easy to use. Like the HtmlSelect control described in the previous chapter, they provide a SelectedIndex property that indicates the selected row as a zero-based index. (For example, if the first item in the list is selected, ctrl.SelectedIndex will be 0.) List controls also provide an additional SelectedItem property, which allows your code to retrieve the ListItem object that represents the selected item. The ListItem object provides three important properties: Text (the displayed content), Value (the hidden value in the HTML code), and Selected (True or False depending on whether the item is selected).

In the last chapter, we used code like this to retrieve the selected ListItem object from an HtmlSelect control called Currency.

```
Dim Item As ListItem
Item = Currency.Items(Currency.SelectedIndex)
```

With a web control, this can be simplified with a clearer syntax.

```
Dim Item As ListItem
Item = Currency.SelectedItem
```

## Multiple-Select List Controls

Some list controls can allow multiple selections. This isn't possible for DropDownList or RadioButtonList, but it is possible for a ListBox if you have set the SelectionMode property to the enumerated value ListSelectionMode.Multiple. With the CheckBoxList, multiple selections are always possible. To find all the selected items, you need to iterate through the Items collection of the list control, and check the ListItem.Selected property of each item.

Figure 7-2 shows a simple web page example. It provides a list of computer languages and indicates which selections the user made when the OK button is clicked.



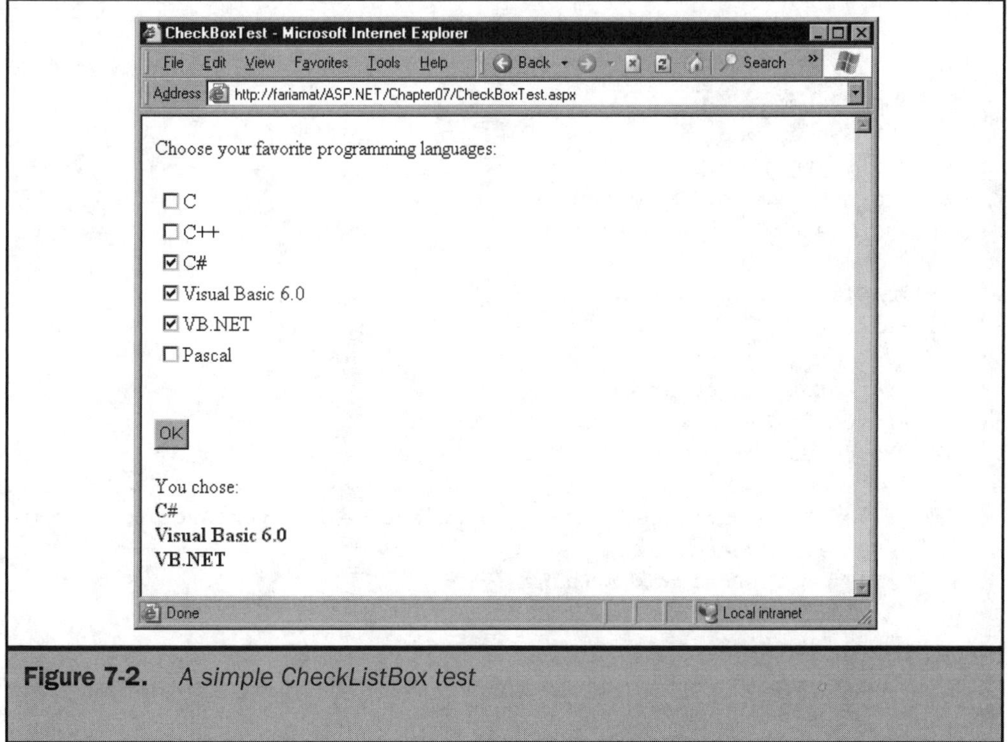


**Figure 7-2.** *A simple CheckListBox test*

The .aspx file defines CheckListBox, Button, and Label controls.

```
<%@ Page Language="VB" Inherits="CheckListTest" Src="CheckListTest.vb"
    AutoEventWireup="False" %>

<HTML><body>
  <form method="post" runat="server">

  Choose your favorite programming languages:<br><br>
  <asp:CheckBoxList id="chklst" runat="server" /><br><br>
  <asp:Button id="cmdOK" Text="OK" runat="server" /><br><br>
  <asp:Label id="lblResult" runat="server" />

  </form>
</body></HTML>
```

The code adds items to the CheckListBox at startup, and iterates through the collection when the button is clicked.

```
Imports System
Imports System.Web
Imports System.Web.UI
Imports system.Web.UI.WebControls
Imports System.Web.UI.HtmlControls

Public Class CheckListTest
  Inherits Page

    Protected chklst as CheckBoxList
    Protected WithEvents cmdOK As Button
    Protected lblResult as Label

    Private Sub Page_Load(sender As Object, e As EventArgs) _
      Handles MyBase.Load
        If Me.IsPostBack = False
            chklst.Items.Add("C")
            chklst.Items.Add("C++")
            chklst.Items.Add("C#")
            chklst.Items.Add("Visual Basic 6.0")
            chklst.Items.Add("VB.NET")
            chklst.Items.Add("Pascal")
        End If
    End Sub
```

```
    Private Sub cmdOK_Click(sender As Object, e As EventArgs) _
      Handles cmdOK.Click

        lblResult.Text = "You chose:<b>"

        Dim lstItem As ListItem
        For Each lstItem In chklst.Items
            If lstItem.Selected = True Then
                ' Add text to label.
                lblResult.Text &= "<br>" & lstItem.Text
            End If
        Next

        lblResult.Text &= "</b>"

    End Sub

End Class
```



## Control Prefixes

When working with web controls, it's often useful to use a three-letter lowercase prefix to identify the type of control. The preceding example (and those in the rest of this book) follow this convention to make user interface code as clear as possible. Some recommended control prefixes are as follows:

- Button: cmd
- CheckBox: chk
- Image: img
- Label: lbl
- List control: lst
- Panel: pnl
- RadioButton: opt
- TextBox: txt

If you're a veteran VB programmer, you'll also notice that this book doesn't use prefixes to identify data types. This is in keeping with the new philosophy of .NET, which recognizes that data types can often change freely and without consequence, and where variables often point to full featured objects instead of simple data variables.

## Table Controls

Essentially, the Table object contains a hierarchy of objects. Each Table object contains one or more TableRow objects. Each TableRow object contains one or more TableCell object, and each TableCell object contains other ASP.NET controls that display information. If you're familiar with the HTML table tags, this relationship (shown in Figure 7-3) will seem fairly logical.

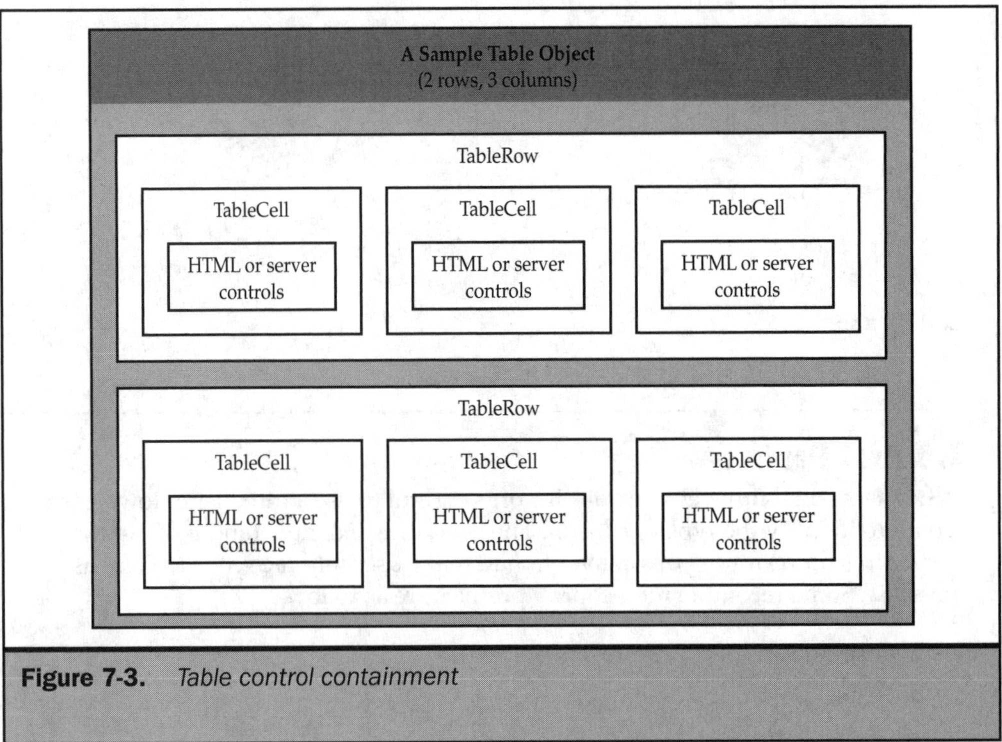


**Figure 7-3.** *Table control containment*

To create a table dynamically, you follow the same philosophy as you would for any other web control. First, you create and configure the necessary ASP.NET objects. Then ASP.NET converts these objects to their final HTML representation before the page is sent to the client.

Consider the example shown in Figure 7-4. It allows the user to specify a number of rows and columns, and an option that specifies whether cells should have borders.

When the user clicks the generate button, the table is filled dynamically with sample data according to the selected options, as shown in Figure 7-5.

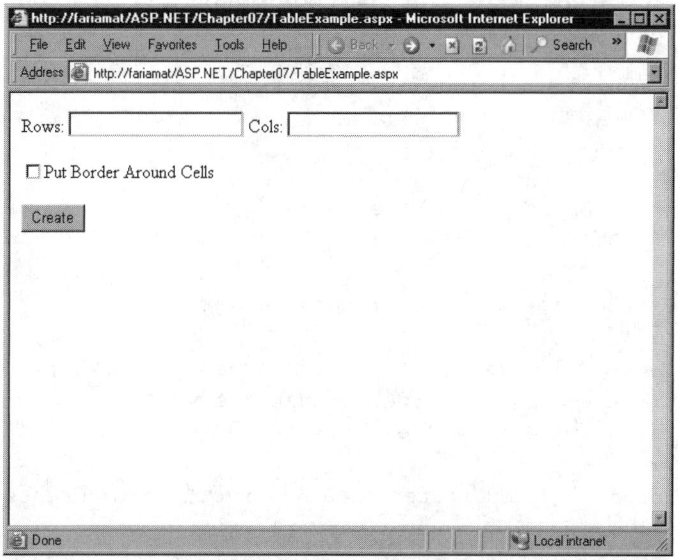

**Figure 7-4.** *The table test options*

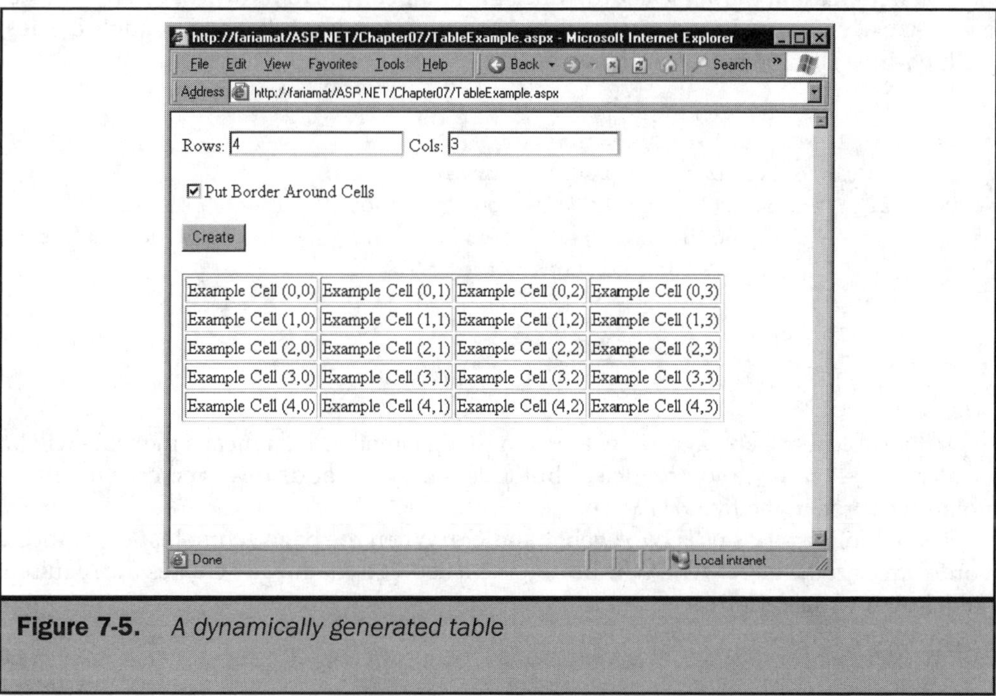


**Figure 7-5.** *A dynamically generated table*

The .aspx code creates the TextBox, CheckBox, Button, and Table controls.

```
<%@ Page Language="VB" Inherits="TableTest" Src="TableTest.vb"
    AutoEventWireup="False" %>

<HTML><body>
  <form method="post" runat="server">

    Rows:
    <asp:TextBox id="txtRows" runat="server" /> 
    Cols:
    <asp:TextBox id="txtCols" runat="server" /><br><br>
    <asp:CheckBox id="chkBorder" runat="server"
         Text="Put Border Around Cells" />
    <br><br>
    <asp:Button id="cmdCreate" runat="server" Text="Create" /><br><br>
    <asp:Table id="tbl" runat="server" />

  </form>
</body></HTML>
```

You'll notice that the Table control doesn't contain any actual rows or cells. To make a valid table, you would need to nest several layers of tags. The following example creates a table with a single cell that contains the text "A Test Row."

```
<asp:Table id="tbl" runat="server">
  <asp:TableRow id="row" runat="server">
    <asp:TableCell Text="A Test Row" id="cell" runat="server">
      <!-- Instead of using the Text property, you could add other
           ASP.NET control tags here. -->
    </asp:TableCell>
  </asp:TableRow>
</asp:Table>
```

In the table test web page, there are no nested elements. That means the table will be created as a server-side control object, but unless the code adds rows and cells it will not be rendered in the final HTML page.

The TablePage class uses two event handlers. When the page is first loaded, it adds a border around the table. When the button is clicked, it dynamically creates the required TableRow and TableCell objects in a loop.

```
Public Class TableTest
  Inherits Page

    Protected txtRows As TextBox
    Protected txtCols As TextBox
    Protected tbl As Table
    Protected chkBorder As CheckBox
    Protected WithEvents cmdCreate As Button

    Private Sub Page_Load(sender As Object, e As EventArgs) _
      Handles MyBase.Load
        ' Configure the table's appearance.
        ' This could also be performed in the .aspx file,
        ' or in the cmdCreate_Click event handler.
        tbl.BorderStyle = BorderStyle.Inset
        tbl.BorderWidth = Unit.Pixel(1)
    End Sub

    Private Sub cmdCreate_Click(sender As Object, e As EventArgs) _
      Handles cmdCreate.Click

        ' Remove all the current rows and cells.
        ' This would not be necessary if you set
        ' EnableViewState = False.
        tbl.Controls.Clear()

        Dim i, j As Integer
        For i = 0 To Val(txtRows.Text)

            ' Create a new TableRow object.
            Dim rowNew As New TableRow()

            ' Put the TableRow in the Table.
            tbl.Controls.Add(rowNew)

            For j = 0 To Val(txtCols.Text)

                ' Create a new TableCell object.
                Dim cellNew As New TableCell()
                cellNew.Text = "Example Cell (" & i.ToString() & ","
                cellNew.Text &= j.ToString & ")"

                If chkBorder.Checked = True Then
```

```
                cellNew.BorderStyle = BorderStyle.Inset
                cellNew.BorderWidth = Unit.Pixel(1)
            End If
            ' Put the TableCell in the TableRow.
            rowNew.Controls.Add(cellNew)

        Next
    Next

End Sub

End Class
```

This code uses the Controls collection to add child controls. Every container control provides this property. You could also use the TableCell.Controls collection to add special web controls to each TableCell. For example, you could place an Image control and a Label control in each cell. In this case, you can't set the TableCell.Text property. The following code example uses this technique (see Figure 7-6).

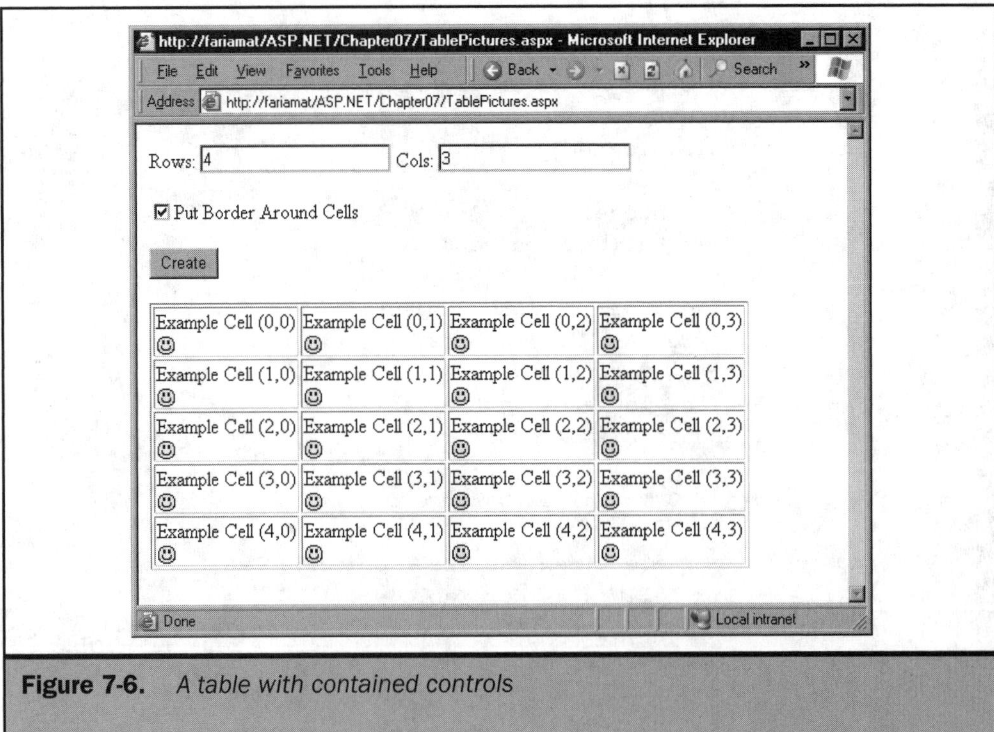


**Figure 7-6.** *A table with contained controls*

```
' Create a new TableCell object.
Dim cellNew As New TableCell()

' Create a new Label object.
Dim lblNew As New Label()
lblNew.Text = "Example Cell (" & i.ToString()
lblNew.Text &= "," & j.ToString() & ")<br>"

Dim imgNew As New System.Web.UI.WebControls.Image()
imgNew.ImageUrl = "cellpic.png"

' Put the label and picture in the cell.
cellNew.Controls.Add(lblNew)
cellNew.Controls.Add(imgNew)

' Put the TableCell in the TableRow.
rowNew.Controls.Add(cellNew)
```



The real flexibility of the table test page is the fact the each TableRow and TableCell are full-featured objects. If you wanted, you could give each cell a different border style, border color, and text color. The full list of TableRow and TableCell properties is described in Chapter 27.

## AutoPostBack and Web Control Events

The previous chapter explained that one of the main limitations of HTML server controls is their limited set of useful events—exactly two. HTML controls that trigger a postback, such as buttons, raise a ServerClick event. Input controls provide a ServerChange event that won't be detected until the page is posted back.

Server controls are really an ingenious illusion. You'll recall that the code in an ASP.NET page is processed on the server. It's then sent to the user as ordinary HTML (see Figure 7-7).

This is the same in ASP.NET as it was in traditional ASP programming. The question is, how can you write server code that will react to an event that occurs on the client? The answer is a new innovation called the automatic postback.

Automatic postback submits a page back to the server when it detects a specific user action. This gives your code the chance to run again and create a new, updated page. Controls that support automatic postbacks include almost all input controls. A basic list of web controls and their events is provided in Table 7-4.

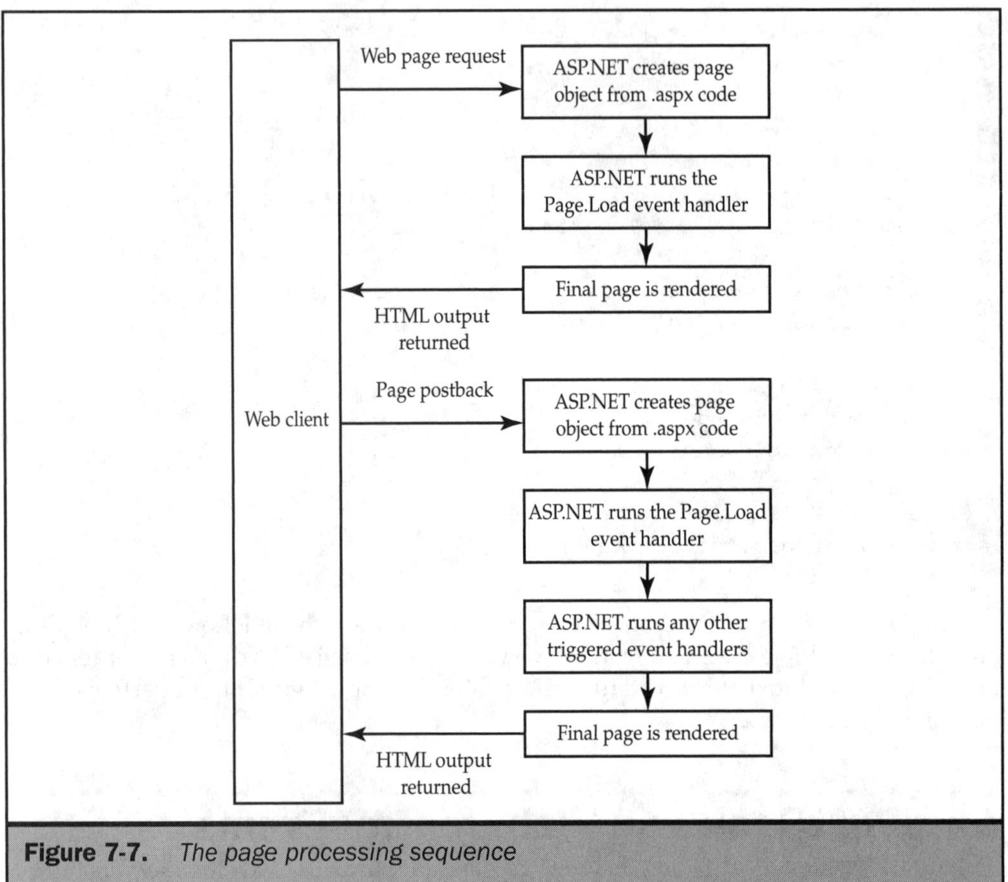


**Figure 7-7.** *The page processing sequence*

| Event | Web Controls that Provide It |
|---|---|
| Click | Button, ImageButton |
| TextChange | TextBox (only fires after the user changes the focus to another control) |
| CheckChanged | CheckBox, RadioButton |
| SelectedIndexChanged | DropDownList, ListBox, CheckBoxList, RadioButtonList |

**Table 7-4.** *Web Control Events*

If you want to capture a change event for a web control, you need to set its AutoPostBack property to True. That means that when the user clicks a radio button or checkbox, the page will be resubmitted to the server. The server examines the page, loads all the current information, and then allows your code to perform some extra processing before returning the page back to the user.

In other words, every time you need to update the web page, it is actually being sent to the server and recreated (see Figure 7-8). However, ASP.NET makes this process so transparent that your code can treat your web page like a continuously running program that fires events.



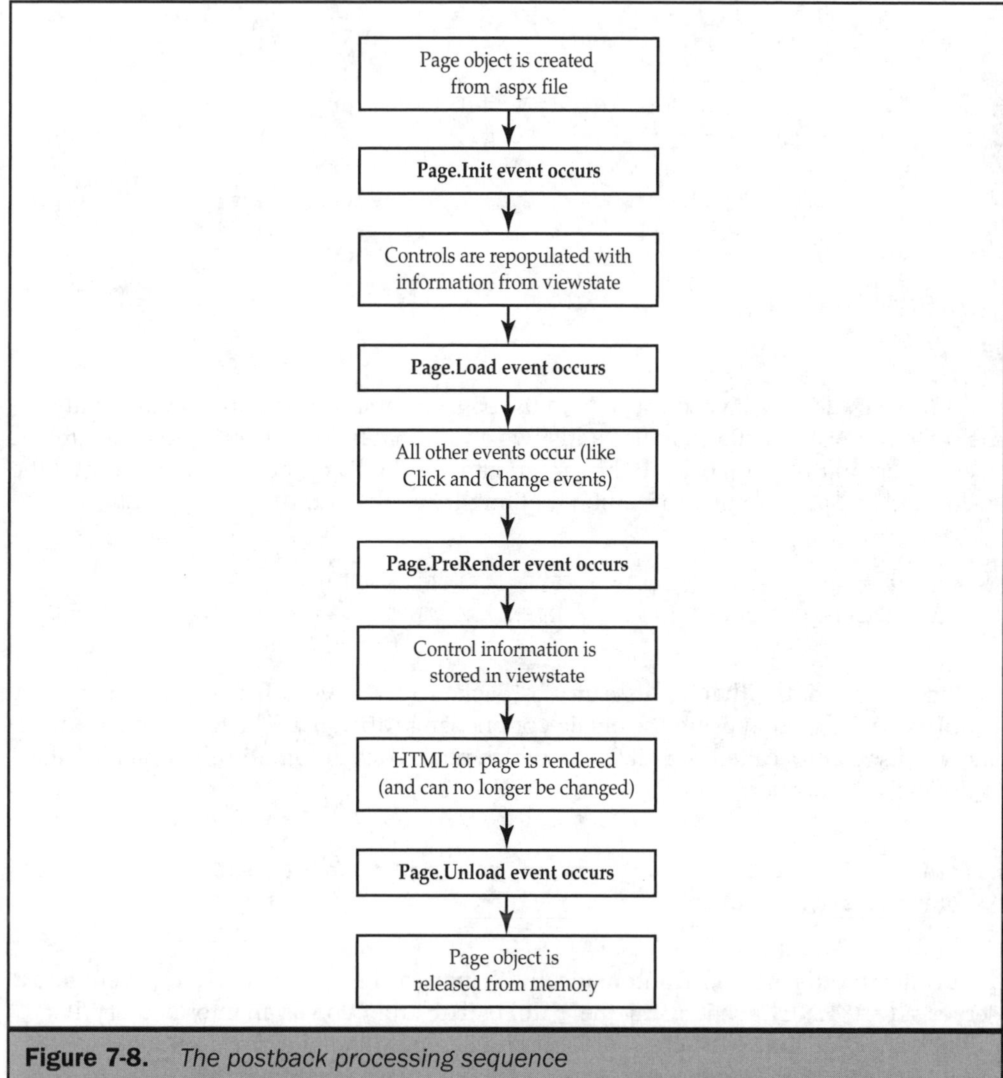


**Figure 7-8.** *The postback processing sequence*

This postback system is not ideal for all events. For example, some events that you may be familiar with from Windows programs, such as mouse movement events or key press events, are not practical in an ASP.NET application. Resubmitting the page every time a key is pressed or the mouse is moved would make the application unbearably slow and unresponsive.

## How Postback Events Work

The AutoPostBack feature uses a couple of interesting tricks and a well-placed JavaScript function named __doPostBack.

```
<script language="javascript">
<!--
    function __doPostBack(eventTarget, eventArgument) {
        var theform = document.Form1;
        theform.__EVENTTARGET.value = eventTarget;
        theform.__EVENTARGUMENT.value = eventArgument;
        theform.submit();
    }
// -->
</script>
```

ASP.NET adds the JavaScript code to the page automatically if any of your controls are set to use AutoPostBack. It also adds two additional hidden input fields that are used to pass information back to the server: namely, the ID of the control that raised the event, and any additional information that might be relevant.

```
<input type="hidden" name="__EVENTTARGET" value="" />
<input type="hidden" name="__EVENTARGUMENT" value="" />
```

Finally, the control that has its AutoPostBack property set to True is connected to the __doPostBack function using the onclick or onchange attribute. The following example shows a list control called lstBackColor, which posts back automatically by calling the __doPostBack function.

```
<select id="lstBackColor" onchange="__doPostBack('lstBackColor','')"
 language="javascript">
```

In other words, ASP.NET automatically changes a client-side JavaScript event into a server-side ASP.NET event, using the __doPostBack function as an intermediary. It's possible that you may have created a solution like this manually for traditional ASP programs. The ASP.NET framework handles these details for you automatically, simplifying life a great deal.

## The Page Lifecycle

To understand how web control events work, you need to have a solid understanding of the page lifecycle. Consider what happens when a user changes a control that has the AutoPostBack property set to True.

1. On the client side, the JavaScript __doPostBack event is invoked, and the page is resubmitted to the server.
2. ASP.NET recreates the page object using the .aspx file.
3. ASP.NET retrieves state information from the hidden viewstate field, and updates the controls accordingly.
4. The Page.Load event is fired.
5. The appropriate change event is fired for the control.
6. The Page.Unload event fires and the page is rendered (transformed from a set of objects to an HTML page).
7. The new page is sent to the client.

To watch these events in action, it helps to create a simple event tracker application (see Figure 7-9). All this application does is write a new entry to a list control every time one of the events it's monitoring occurs. This allows you to see the order of events.



**EventTracker.aspx**

```
<%@ Page Language="VB" Src="EventTracker.vb" Inherits="EventTracker"
    AutoEventWireup="False"%>

<HTML><body>
  <form method="post" runat="server">
    <h3>Controls being monitored for change events:</h3>
    <asp:TextBox id=txt runat="server" AutoPostBack="True" /><br><br>
    <asp:CheckBox id=chk runat="server" AutoPostBack="True" /><br><br>
    <asp:RadioButton id=opt1 runat="server" GroupName="Sample"
         AutoPostBack="True" />
    <asp:RadioButton id=opt2 runat="server" GroupName="Sample"
         AutoPostBack="True" /><br><br><br>
    <h3>List of events:</h3>
    <asp:ListBox id=lstEvents runat="server" Width="355px"
         Height="505px" /><br>
  </form>
</body></HTML>
```

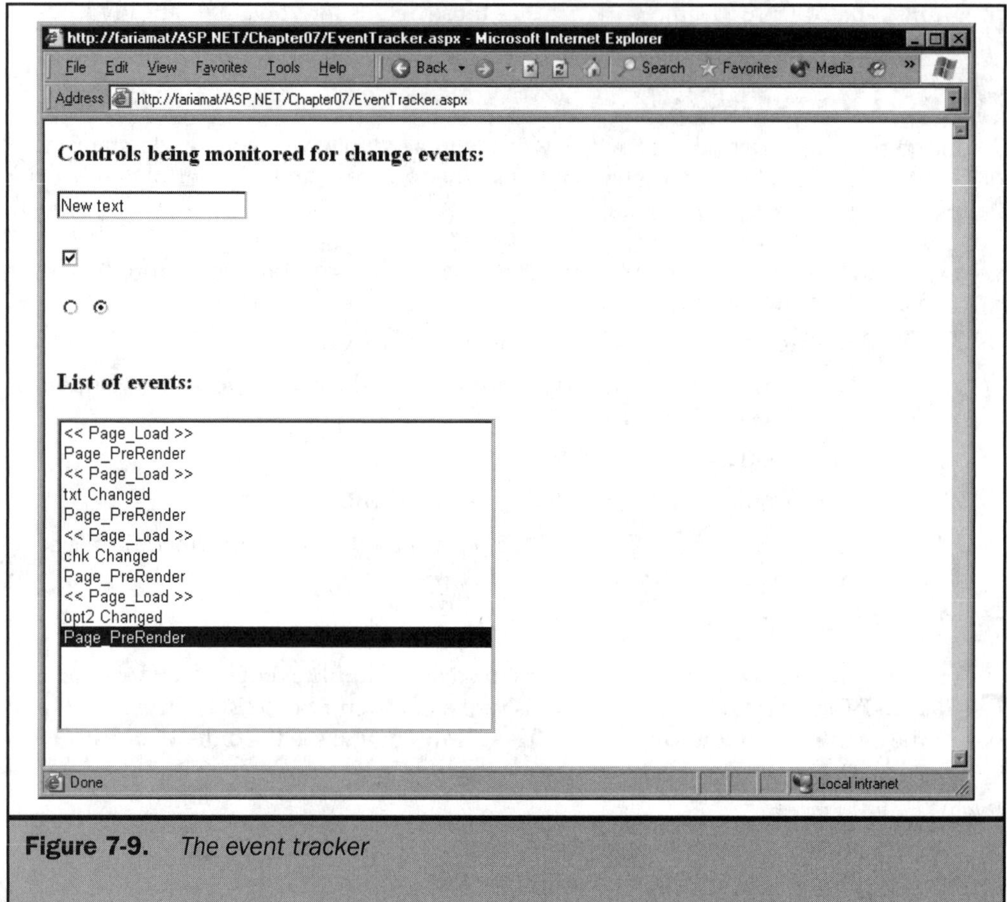


**Figure 7-9.** *The event tracker*

### EvenTracker.vb

```
Public Class EventTracker
  Inherits System.Web.UI.Page

    Protected WithEvents lstEvents As ListBox
    Protected WithEvents chk As CheckBox
    Protected WithEvents txt As TextBox
    Protected WithEvents opt1 As RadioButton
    Protected WithEvents opt2 As RadioButton
```

```
    Private Sub Page_Load(sender As Object, e As EventArgs) _
      Handles MyBase.Load
        Log("<< Page_Load >>")
    End Sub

    Private Sub Page_PreRender(sender As Object, e As EventArgs) _
      Handles MyBase.PreRender
        ' When the Page.UnLoad event occurs it is too late
        ' to change the list.
        Log("Page_PreRender")
    End Sub

    Private Sub CtrlChanged(sender As Object, e As System.EventArgs) _
      Handles chk.CheckedChanged, opt1.CheckedChanged, _
      opt2.CheckedChanged, txt.TextChanged
        ' Find the control ID of the sender.
        ' This requires converting the Object type into a Control.
        Dim ctrlName As String = CType(sender, Control).ID
        Log(ctrlName & " Changed")
    End Sub

    Private Sub Log(entry As String)
        lstEvents.Items.Add(entry)

        ' Select the last item to scroll the list so the most recent
        ' entries are visible.
        lstEvents.SelectedIndex = lstEvents.Items.Count - 1
    End Sub

End Class
```

## Interesting Facts About this Code

- The code encapsulates the ListBox logging in a Log subroutine, which automatically scrolls to the bottom of the list each time a new entry is added.
- All the change events are handled by the same subroutine, CtrlChanged. The event handling code uses the source parameter to find out what control sent the event and incorporate that in the log string.
- All the controls that use automatic postback have to be defined WithEvents in the Page class, or the Handles clause will not work.

# A Simple Web Page Applet

Now that you've had a whirlwind tour of the basic web control model, it's time to put it to work with our second single-page utility. In this case, it's a simple example for a dynamic e-card generator (see Figure 7-10). You could extend this sample (for example, allowing users to store e-cards to a database, or using the techniques in Chapter 16 to mail notification to card recipients), but on its own it represents a good example of basic control manipulation.

The page is divided into two regions. On the left is an ordinary <div> tag containing a set of web controls for specifying card options. On the right is a Panel control (named pnlCard), which contains two other controls (lblGreeting and imgDefault) that are used to display user-configurable text and a picture.

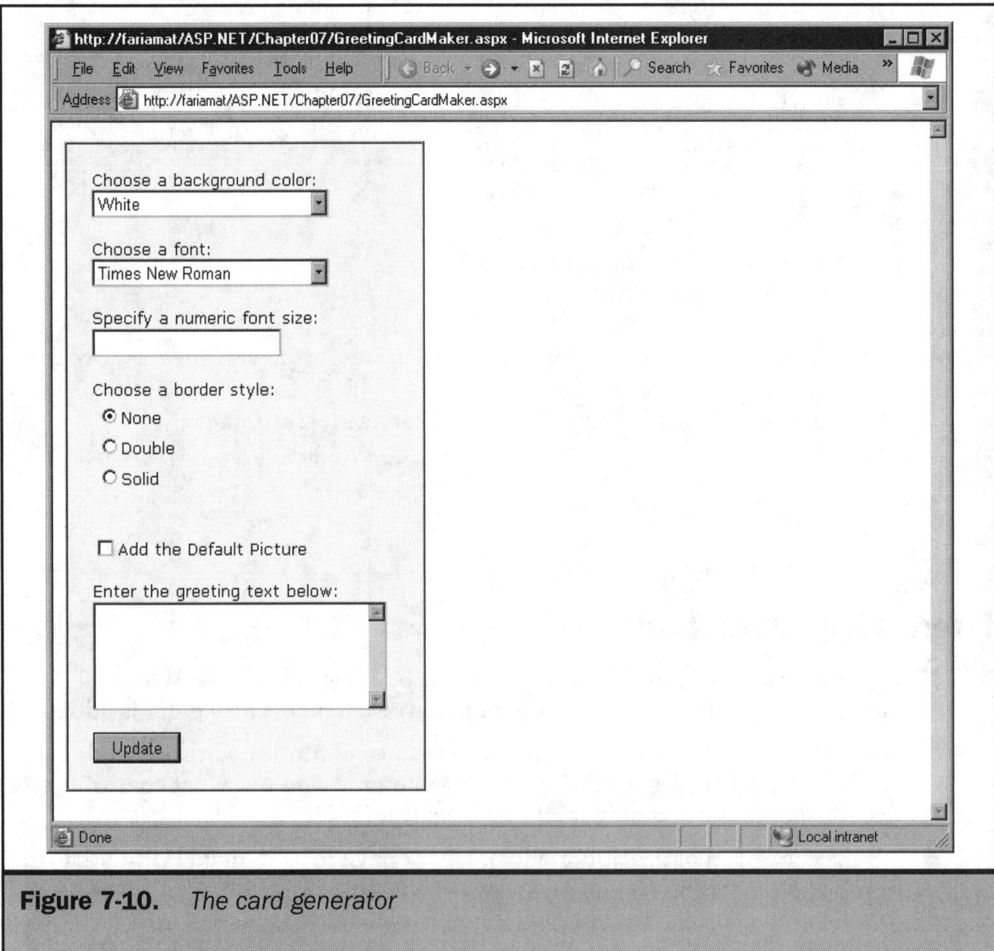


**Figure 7-10.** *The card generator*

Whenever the user clicks the OK button, the page is posted back, and the "card" is updated (see Figure 7-11).

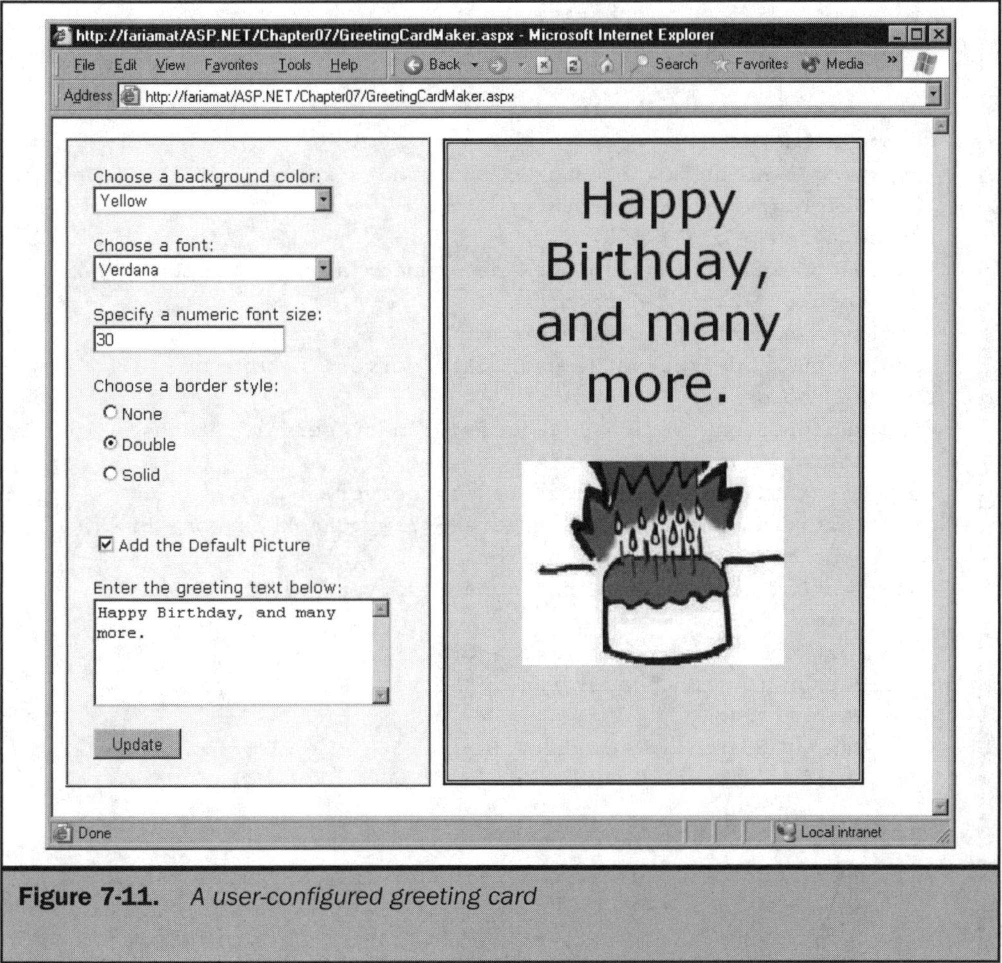


**Figure 7-11.** *A user-configured greeting card*

The .aspx layout code is very straightforward. Of course, the sheer length of it makes it difficult to work with efficiently. This is an ideal point to start considering Visual Studio .NET, which will handle the .aspx details for you automatically, and not require you to painstakingly format and organize the user interface markup tags.

```
<%@ Page Language="VB" Src="GreetingCardMaker.vb"
    Inherits="GreetingCardMaker"
```

```
    AutoEventWireup="False"%>

<HTML><body>
  <form method="post" runat="server">
  <!-- div formatting tag left out for clarity. -->

  <!-- Here are the controls: -->
  Choose a background color:<br>
  <asp:DropDownList id="lstBackColor" runat="server" Width="194px"
       Height="22px"/><br><br>
  Choose a font:<br>
  <asp:DropDownList id="lstFontName" runat="server" Width="194px"
       Height="22px" /><br><br>
  Specify a numeric font size:<br>
  <asp:TextBox id="txtFontSize" runat="server" /><br><br>
  Choose a border style:<br>
  <asp:RadioButtonList id="lstBorder" runat="server" Width="177px"
       Height="59px" /><br><br>
  <asp:CheckBox id="chkPicture" runat="server"
       Text="Add the Default Picture"></asp:CheckBox><br><br>
  Enter the greeting text below:<br>
  <asp:TextBox id="txtGreeting" runat="server" Width="240px"
       Height="85px"
       TextMode="MultiLine" /><br><br>
  <asp:Button id="cmdUpdate" runat="server" Width="71px"
       Height="24px"
       Text="Update" />
  </div>

  <!-- Here is the card: -->
  <asp:Panel id="pnlCard" style="Z-INDEX: 101; LEFT: 313px; POSITION:
       absolute;
       TOP: 16px" runat="server" Width="339px" Height="481px"
       HorizontalAlign="Center"><br> 
  <asp:Label id="lblGreeting" runat="server" Width="256px"
       Height="150px" /><br><br><br>
  <asp:Image id="imgDefault" runat="server" Width="212px"
       Height="160px" />
  </asp:Panel>

  </form>
</body></HTML>
```

The code follows the familiar pattern with an emphasis on two events: the Page.Load event, where initial values are set, and the Button.Click event, where the card is generated. I've left out the Imports statements in the following listing, as the basic set of required namespaces should be familiar by now.

```
Public Class GreetingCardMaker
  Inherits Page
    Protected lstBackColor As DropDownList
    Protected lstFontName As DropDownList
    Protected txtFontSize As TextBox
    Protected chkPicture As CheckBox
    Protected txtGreeting As TextBox
    Protected pnlCard As Panel
    Protected lblGreeting As Label
    Protected lstBorder As RadioButtonList
    Protected imgDefault As Image
    Protected WithEvents cmdUpdate As Button

    Private Sub Page_Load(sender As Object, e As EventArgs) _
      Handles MyBase.Load
        If Me.IsPostBack = False Then

            ' Set color options.
            lstBackColor.Items.Add("White")
            lstBackColor.Items.Add("Red")
            lstBackColor.Items.Add("Green")
            lstBackColor.Items.Add("Blue")
            lstBackColor.Items.Add("Yellow")

            ' Set font options.
            lstFontName.Items.Add("Times New Roman")
            lstFontName.Items.Add("Arial")
            lstFontName.Items.Add("Verdana")
            lstFontName.Items.Add("Tahoma")

            ' Set border style options by adding a series of
            ' ListItem objects.
            ' Each item indicates the name of the option,
            ' and contains the corresponding integer
            ' in the Value property.
            lstBorder.Items.Add(New _
              ListItem(BorderStyle.None.ToString(), BorderStyle.None))
```

```
            lstBorder.Items.Add(New _
                ListItem(BorderStyle.Double.ToString(), _
                BorderStyle.Double))
            lstBorder.Items.Add(New _
                ListItem(BorderStyle.Solid.ToString, _
                BorderStyle.Solid))

            ' Select the first border option.
            lstBorder.SelectedIndex = 0

            ' Set the picture.
            imgDefault.ImageUrl = "defaultpic.png"
        End If
    End Sub

    Private Sub cmdUpdate_Click(sender As Object, e As EventArgs) _
      Handles cmdUpdate.Click

        ' Update the color.
        pnlCard.BackColor = Color.FromName( _
                            lstBackColor.SelectedItem.Text)

        ' Update the font.
        lblGreeting.Font.Name = lstFontName.SelectedItem.Text

        If Val(txtFontSize.Text) > 0 Then
        lblGreeting.Font.Size = FontUnit.Point( _
                                Val(txtFontSize.Text))
        End If

        ' Update the border style.
        pnlCard.BorderStyle = Val(lstBorder.SelectedItem.Value)

        ' Update the picture.
        If chkPicture.Checked = True Then
            imgDefault.Visible = True
        Else
            imgDefault.Visible = False
        End If

        ' Set the text.
        lblGreeting.Text = txtGreeting.Text
```

```
    End Sub

End Class
```

As you can see, this example limits the user to a few preset font and color choices. The code for the BorderStyle option is particularly interesting. The lstBorder control has a list that displays the text name of one of the BoderStyle enumerated values. You'll remember from the introductory chapters that every enumerated value is really an integer with a name assigned to it. The lstBorder also secretly stores the corresponding number, so that it can set the enumeration easily in the cmdUpdate_Click event handler.



## Improving the Greeting Card Applet

ASP.NET pages have access to the full .NET class library. With a little exploration, you'll find classes that might help the greeting card maker, such as tools that let you retrieve all the known color names and all the fonts installed on the web server.

For example, you can fill the lstFontName control with a list of fonts using the special System.Drawing.Text.InstalledFontCollection class.

```
' Get the list of available fonts, and add them to the font list.
Dim Family As FontFamily
Dim Fonts As New System.Drawing.Text.InstalledFontCollection()
For Each Family In Fonts.Families
    lstFontName.Items.Add(Family.Name)
Next
```

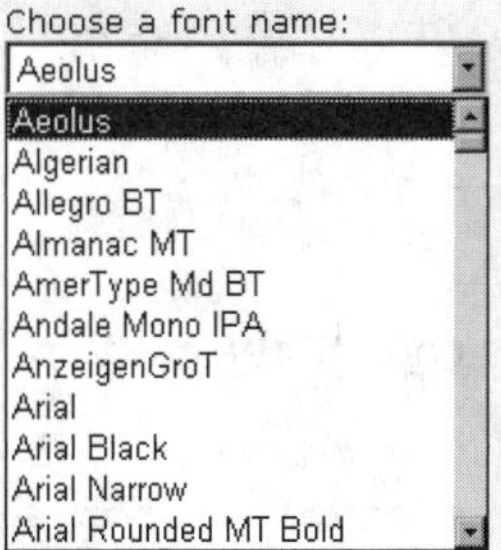


You can also get a list of color names from the System.Drawing.KnownColor enumeration. In order to do this, you use one of basic enumeration features: the shared Enum.GetNames method, which inspects an enumeration and provides an array of strings, with one string for each value in the enumeration. A minor problem with this approach is that it includes system environment colors (for example "Active Border") in the list.

```
' Get the list of colors.
Dim ColorArray As String() = System.Enum.GetNames( _
                              GetType(System.Drawing.KnownColor))
lstBackColor.DataSource = ColorArray
lstBackColor.DataBind()
```

This example uses data binding to automatically fill the list control with information from the ColorArray. We'll explore this topic in detail in Chapter 14.

A similar technique can be used to fill in BorderStyle options.

```
' Set border style options.
Dim BorderStyleArray As String()
BorderStyleArray = System.Enum.GetNames(GetType(BorderStyle))
lstBorder.DataSource = BorderStyleArray
lstBorder.DataBind()
```

However, in this case there is no easy way to change the user's selection back into an enumeration. There are a few different ways to handle this problem (earlier, you saw an example where the enumeration integer was stored as a value in the list control). In this case, the most direct approach involves using an advanced feature called a TypeConverter. A TypeConverter is a special class that is able to convert from a specialized type (in this case, the BorderStyle enumeration) to a simpler type (such as a string).

To access this class, you need to import the System.ComponentModel namespace.

```
Imports System.ComponentModel
```

You can then add the following code to the cmdUpdate_Click event handler.

```
' Find the appropriate TypeConverter for the BorderStyle enumeration.
Dim cnvrt As TypeConverter
cnvrt = TypeDescriptor.GetConverter(GetType(BorderStyle))

' Update the border style using the value from the converter.
pnlCard.BorderStyle = _
  cnvrt.ConvertFromString(lstBorder.SelectedItem.Text)
```

Don't worry if this example introduces a few features that look entirely alien! These features are more advanced (and they aren't tied specifically to ASP.NET), but they show you some of the flavor the full .NET class library can provide to a mature application.

## Generating the Cards Automatically

The last step is to use ASP.NET's automatic postback events to make the card update dynamically every time an option is changed. The OK button could now be used to submit the final, perfected greeting card.

To accomplish this, simply add the AutoPostBack="True" attribute to each user input control. An example is shown here:

```
Choose a background color:<br>
 <asp:DropDownList id="lstBackColor" AutoPostBack="True"
  runat="server" Width="194px" Height="22px"/>
  <br><br>
```

Next, you need to make sure the control variables are defined in your class with the WithEvents keyword, enabling your code to access their events.

```
Protected WithEvents lstBackColor As DropDownList
```

Finally, you need to create an event handler for each control's change event. To save a few steps, you can use the same event handler for all the controls. All this event handler needs to do is call the update routine. (You'll notice that the improved greeting card applet adds a list box for the fore color as well as the background color.)

```
Private Sub ControlChanged(sender As System.Object, _
  e As System.EventArgs) Handles _
  lstBackColor.SelectedIndexChanged, _
  chkPicture.CheckedChanged, txtFontSize.TextChanged, _
  lstBackColor.SelectedIndexChanged, _
  lstBorder.SelectedIndexChanged, _
  lstFontName.SelectedIndexChanged, _
  lstForeColor.SelectedIndexChanged

    ' Call the button event handler to refresh the window.
    cmdUpdate_Click(Nothing, Nothing)

End Sub
```

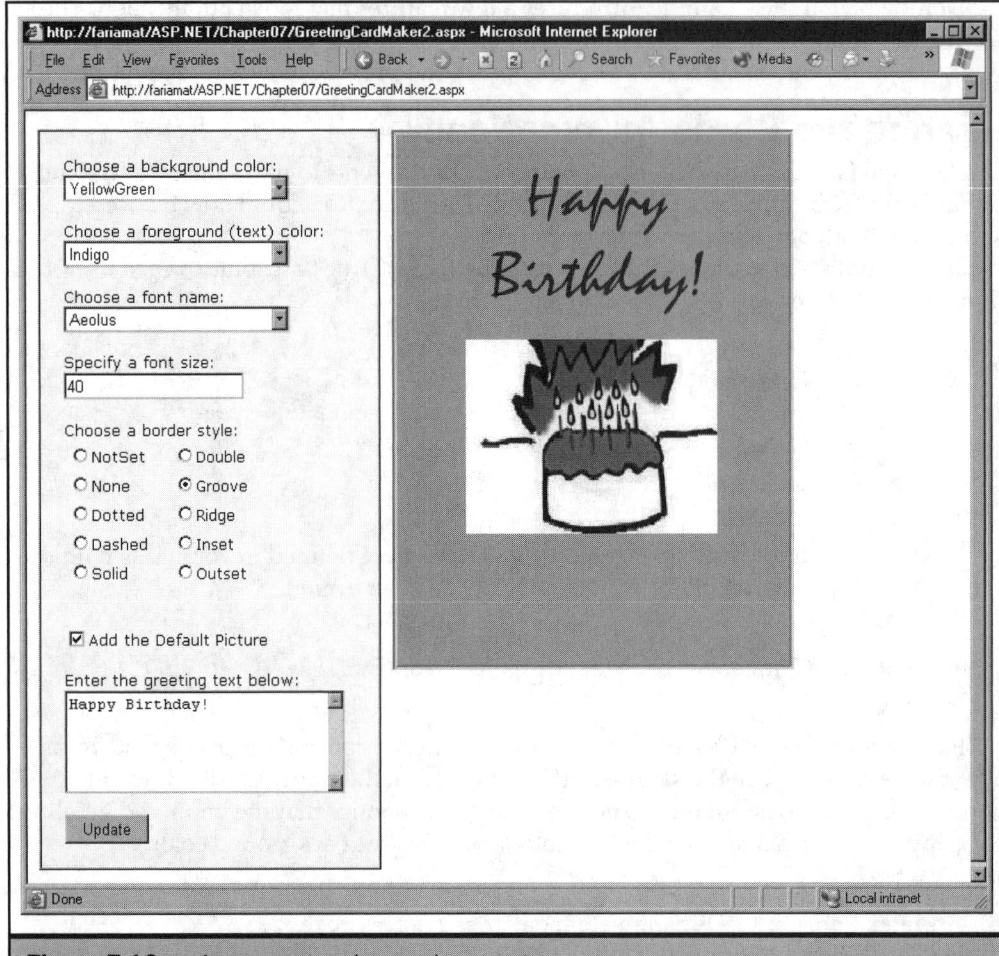


**Figure 7-12.** *A more extensive card generator*

## Automatic Postback Is Not Always Best

Sometimes an automatic postback can annoy a user, especially when working over a slow connection, or when the server needs to perform a time-consuming option. For that reason, it's sometimes best to use an explicit submit button and not enable AutoPostBack for most input controls.

Using these features, it's easy to perfect a more extensive card-generating program (see Figure 7-12). The full code for this application is provided with the online samples.

## Assessing Web Controls

This chapter has introduced you to web controls and their object interface. Our exploration continues in chapters throughout this book:

- In Chapter 9, you'll learn about advanced controls such as the AdRotator, the Calendar, and the validation controls. You'll also learn about third-party controls, like the advanced Internet Explorer web controls.
- In Chapter 15, you'll learn about the DataGrid, DataList, and Repeater—high-level web controls that let you manipulate a complex table of data from any data source.
- In Chapter 22, you'll learn how you can use .NET inheritance to create your own customized web controls.

For a good reference that lists the important properties for each web control, refer to Chapter 27.

### A Word About Conventions

The examples from this point adopt a few conventions designed to make code examples more clear, concise, and readable:

- The .aspx layout file is rarely shown with an example, unless it requires special coding (such as the creation of a template or data binding syntax, two topics we'll explore in the third part of this book). The .aspx files are really nothing more than an ordering of standard control tags.
- The Imports directives in the code-behind file are left out, unless they reference an unusual namespace that hasn't been identified. Generally, you will reuse the same standard block of Imports statements for each code-behind file.
- The control variables in the page class are sometimes omitted and replaced with a comment. The control variable declarations are also standard boilerplate code.

These changes won't affect you at all if you're using an IDE such as Visual Studio .NET, which generates the .aspx file, control variables, and most Imports statements automatically.

The Complete Reference

# Chapter 8

## Using Visual Studio .NET

In the past, ASP developers have overwhelmingly favored simple text editors like Notepad for programming web pages. Other choices were possible, but each one suffered from its own quirks and limitations. Tools like Visual Interdev and Visual Basic web classes were useful for rapid development, but often made deployment more difficult or obscured some important features. In short, the standard was a plain, gloves-off approach of raw HTML text with blocks of code inserted wherever necessary.

Visual Studio .NET provides the first design tool that can change that. First of all, it's extensible, and can even work in tandem with other straight HTML editors like FrontPage or Dreamweaver. It also inherits the best features from editors like Visual Interdev, Visual Basic 6.0, and the Visual Studio IDE for C++ 6.0, including a matchless set of productivity enhancements.

This chapter provides a lightning tour that shows how to create a web application in the Visual Studio .NET environment. You'll also learn how IntelliSense can dramatically reduce the number of errors you'll make, and how to use the renowned single-step debugger that lets you peer under the hood and "watch" your program in action.

## The Promise of Visual Studio .NET

All .NET programs are created with text source files. For example, C# programs are stored in .cs files and VB programs in .vb files, regardless of whether they are targeted for the Windows platform, ASP.NET, or the simple command prompt window. Despite this fact, you'll rarely find VB or C# developers creating Windows applications by hand in a text editor. Not only is the process tiring, it also opens the door to a host of possible errors that could be easily caught at design time.

Visual Studio .NET is an indispensable tool for the developers of any platform. It provides impressive benefits:

**Integrated error checking** Visual Studio .NET can detect a wide range of problems, such as data type conversion errors, missing namespaces or classes, and undefined variables. Errors are detected as you type, then underlined and added to an error list for quick reference.

**Web form designer** To add ASP.NET controls, you simply drag them to the appropriate location, resize them by hand, and configure their properties. Visual Studio .NET does the heavy lifting: it automatically creates the underlying .aspx template file for you with the appropriate tags and attributes, and adds the control variables to your code-behind file.

**Productivity enhancements** Visual Studio .NET makes coding quick and efficient, with a collapsible code display, automatic statement completion, and color-coded syntax. You can even create sophisticated macro programs that automate repetitive tasks.

**Easy deployment** When you start an ASP.NET project in Visual Studio .NET, all the files you need are generated automatically, including a sample web.config file.

When you compile the application, all your page classes are compiled into one DLL for easy deployment.

**Complete extensibility** You can add your own custom add-ins, controls, and dynamic help plug-ins to Visual Studio .NET, and customize almost every aspect of its appearance and behavior.

**Fine-grained debugging** Visual Studio .NET's integrated debugger allows you to witness code execution, pause your program at any point, and trace variable contents. These debugging tools can save endless headaches when writing complex code routines.



# Starting a Visual Studio .NET Project

You start Visual Studio .NET from the Start menu by selecting Programs | Microsoft Visual Studio .NET 7.0 | Visual Studio .NET 7.0. The IDE will load up with a special start page (see Figure 8-1).

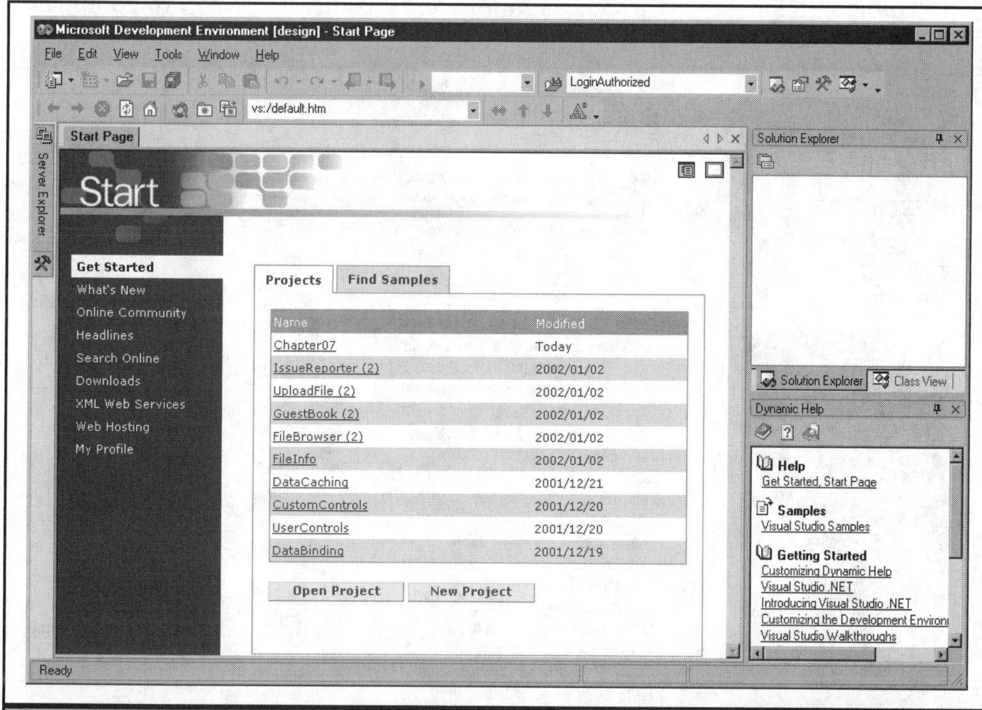


**Figure 8-1.** *The Visual Studio .NET start page*

The start page provides some interesting options. Its primary purpose is to provide a list of recent projects that you can open with a single mouse click (these projects are also available through the File | Recent Projects submenu). Each project is identified with a last modified date.

On the left of the start page are some additional options that allow you to configure Visual Studio .NET, connect to the developer community, and find important MSDN documentation.

- **Get Started** is the default page with a list of projects. At the bottom of the page are two buttons that allow you to open a project (by browsing) or create a new one.
- **What's New** takes you to some of the MSDN documentation installed with Visual Studio .NET. It explains (in a brief overview) some of the fundamental differences between Visual Basic .NET and its earlier versions.
- **Online Community** provides a list of Visual Studio .NET newsgroups hosted by Microsoft on the Internet (see Figure 8-2). When you click on a newsgroup, your default news reader (typically Microsoft Outlook) will open to allow you to read and browse postings. Newsgroups are an excellent place to ask programming questions and communicate with other ASP.NET programmers.

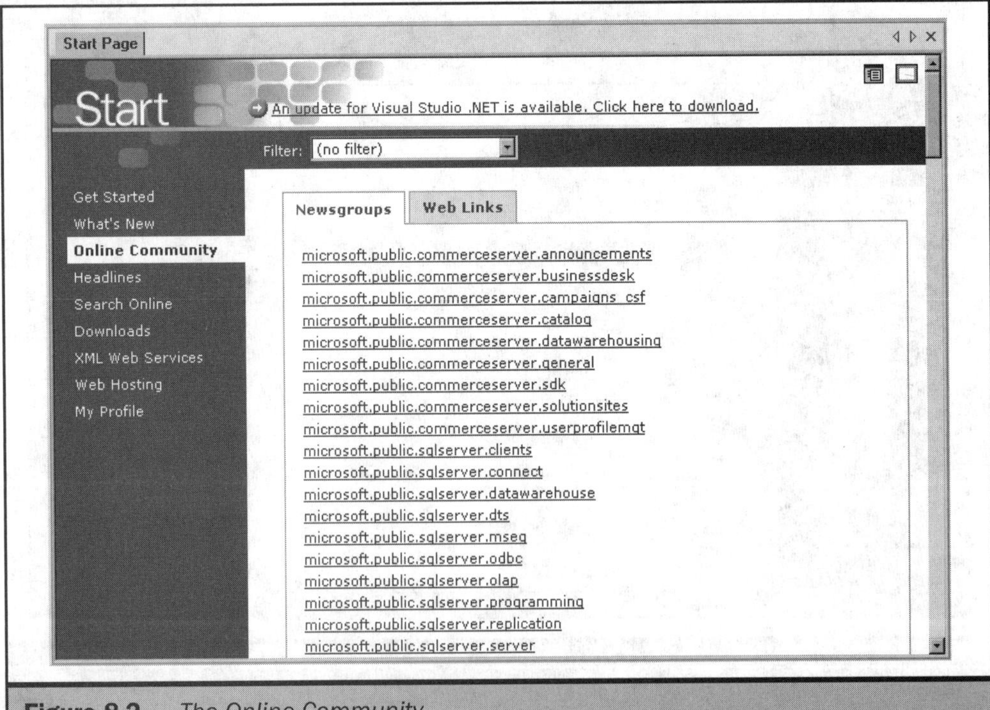


**Figure 8-2.** *The Online Community*

- **Headlines** includes a wealth of information from Microsoft's MSDN developer site. You can use this section to read recent articles from the knowledge base (answers to technical problems or fixes and workarounds for known bugs), technical articles, and news releases. When you click on a link, the related web page will open inside Visual Studio .NET. If you want more comfortable browsing using your default Internet browser, just right-click on the link and choose External Window.
- **Search Online** allows you to search the MSDN online library (see Figure 8-3). This search option is available through the MSDN site (http://msdn.microsoft.com), but Visual Studio .NET makes it easy to search for information without needing to browse to a page or use an Internet user interface. This is an example of how you might want to use Web Services to integrate Internet features into desktop programs. For more information, refer to the fourth part of this book.
- **Downloads** provides access to source code, service packs, and other updates. You'll also find add-ons beyond just program updates. For example, you might find tools for programming with Office applications or mobile (embedded) browsers.



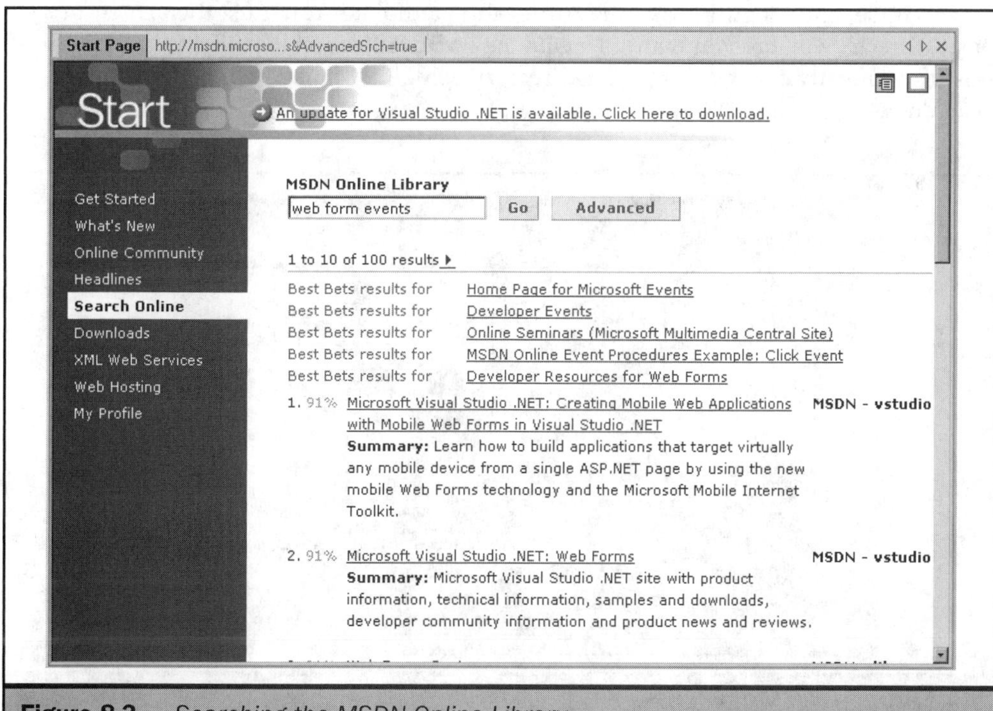


**Figure 8-3.** *Searching the MSDN Online Library*

- **XML Web Services** allows you to search for Web Services or register your own using the UDDI registry. Web Services are detailed in the fourth part of this book.
- **Web Hosting** is a special feature that lets you find companies that host ASP.NET sites and, in many cases, directly upload your ASP.NET pages from Visual Studio .NET to the remote site.
- **My Profile** provides configuration options that let you set the default language and help options, as well as the window layout and action on startup. Many more configuration options are provided in the Options window (select Tools | Options from the menu). You can also configure toolbars, menus, and create keyboard shortcuts from the Customize window (select Tools | Customize from the menu).

## Creating a New Application

To start your first Visual Studio .NET application, click the New Project button on the start page or select File | New | Project.

The New Project window (shown in Figure 8-4) allows you to choose the type of project and the location where it will be created. You should choose the Visual Basic Projects node, and the ASP.NET Web Application template. You must then enter the virtual directory where you want to create the web application. For this to work, you must have already created the virtual directory using IIS Manager. The project will be created when you click OK.

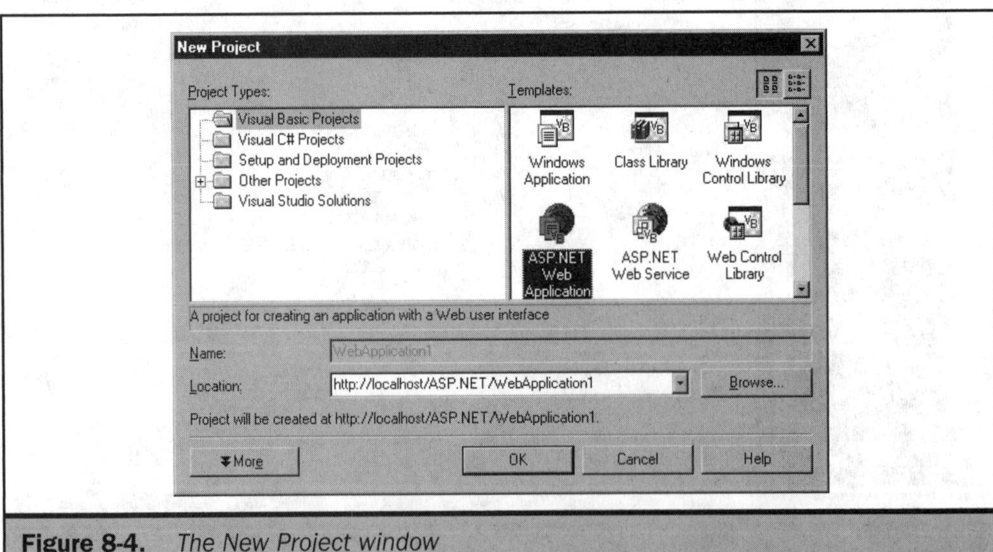


**Figure 8-4.** *The New Project window*

Interestingly, Visual Studio .NET can automatically create a project subdirectory in the virtual directory you chose. For example, if your computer has the virtual directory http://WebApps, you can create the application http://WebApps/Ecommerce in Visual Studio .NET. The project subdirectory (in this case Ecommerce) will automatically be configured as an application directory, which means the web pages will execute in a separate memory space from all other web applications.

## Project Files

When you create a web application, Visual Studio .NET will add a collection of files. You can see all the files that your project contains in the Solution Explorer window (see Figure 8-5).



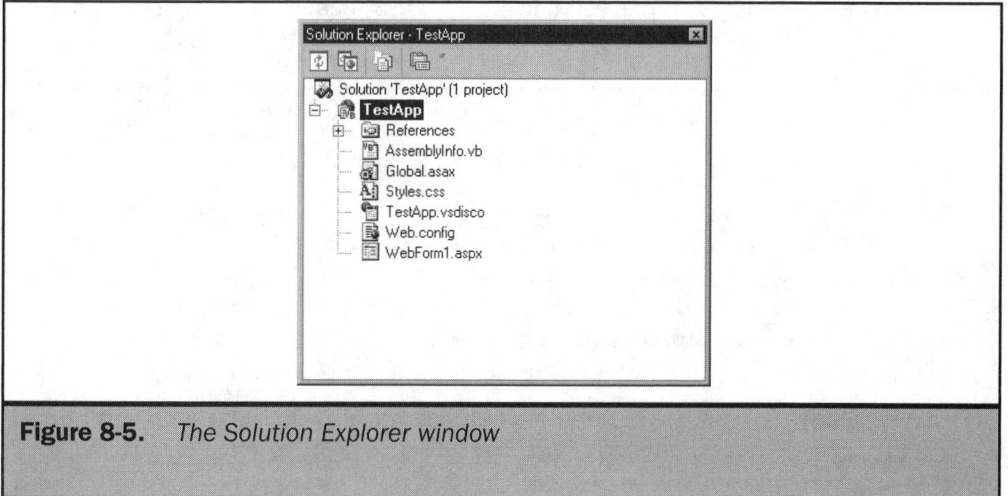


**Figure 8-5.** *The Solution Explorer window*

The Solution Explorer also shows all the references configured for your project. These are the .NET assemblies that your code-behind files link to automatically. If you want to use additional features, you may need to import more assemblies.

When creating files outside of Visual Studio .NET, you don't need to manually specify these references because they are resolved dynamically at runtime. However, if you want to precompile a code-behind file, you need to list all the referenced namespaces as parameters on the vbc.exe command line. Because Visual Studio .NET compiles all code-behind files, it needs to explicitly reference them.

The Solution Explorer also contains a file called AssemblyInfo.vb, which defines information that will be added to the compiled DLL file for your web application. This includes information such as the web application version number, company name, and so on. This information doesn't affect the performance of your web application, but it does make it easier to track multiple versions.

### Assemblies Can Contain Multiple Namespaces

Once you create a reference to an assembly, you can use the types defined in that assembly. Assemblies can contain more than one namespace. For example, the System.Web.dll assembly includes classes in the System.Web namespace and the System.Web.UI namespace.

Adding a reference is not the same as using the Imports statement. The Imports statement creates an alias to a namespace in an available assembly. If you haven't added the reference, the namespace won't be available for importing. (For example, if you haven't imported the System.Web.dll, you won't be able to import the System.Web.UI namespace or use any of its classes.) Similarly, if you add a reference but don't import a namespace, you will have to use fully qualified names for classes in that namespace (for example, you'll need to write System.Web.UI.Page instead of just Page).

A sample AssemblyInfo.vb file is shown here:

```
<Assembly: AssemblyTitle("MyWebApp")>
<Assembly: AssemblyDescription("ProseTech Inc. E-Commerce Site.")>
<Assembly: AssemblyCompany("ProseTech")>
<Assembly: AssemblyCopyright("Copyright 2001")>
<Assembly: AssemblyTrademark("ProseTech™")>
```

Your project also includes a global.asax global application file, a web.config configuration file, a .vsdisco file used with Web Services, a Styles.css file you can use to create CSS styles, and all the .aspx files in your application.

Visual Studio .NET also creates a single .vbproj project file that references all these files. In addition, you can optionally combine more than one project into a .sln file. This technique is useful if you want to test a component with a web site, or Web Service project with a Windows application. It's described in Chapter 20.

The relationships of Visual Studio .NET project files are shown in Figure 8-6.

## Configuring a File

To get information about a file, click on it once in the Solution Explorer. You can then read various pieces of information in the Properties window (see Figure 8-7). For example, the Build Action property describes what will happen when you run the application in Visual Studio .NET (typically, it will compile the file). The File Name property allows you to rename files without leaving the IDE.

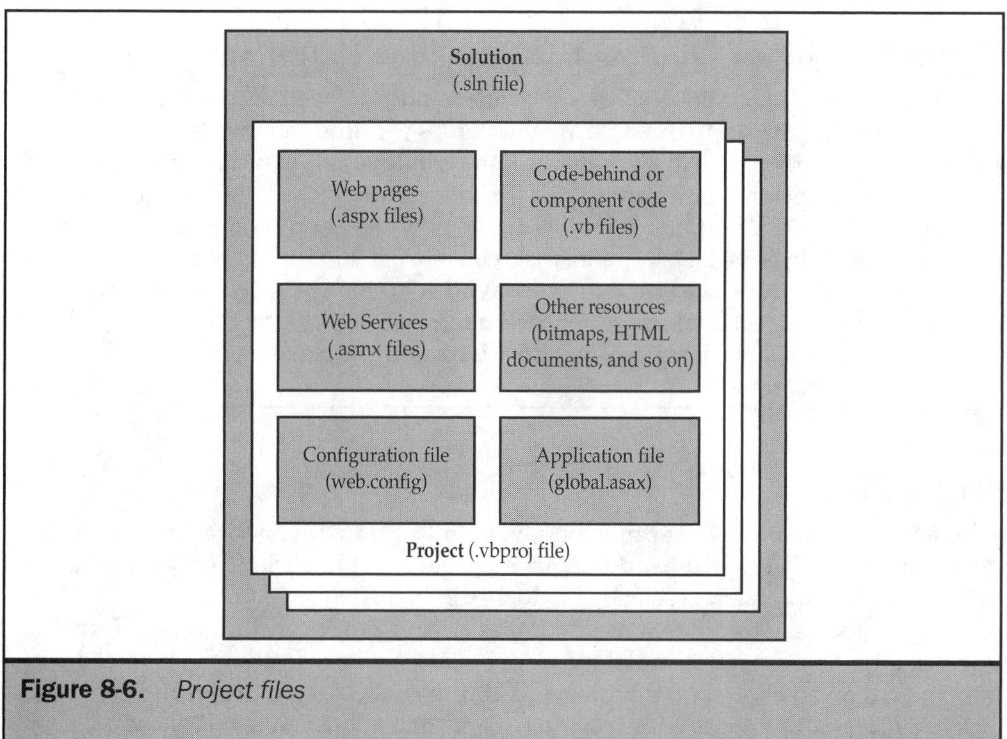


**Figure 8-6.** *Project files*

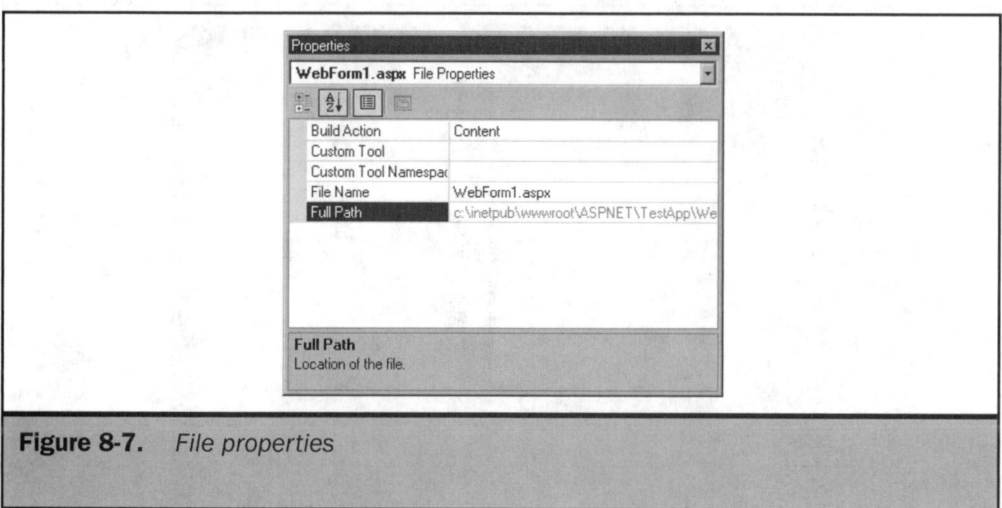


**Figure 8-7.** *File properties*

### The Properties Window Is Grouped with Dynamic Help

By default, Visual Studio .NET groups some windows together in special tabs to save on-screen space. For example, the Properties window and the Dynamic Help window are both placed at the bottom of the window, and you can switch back and forth by clicking the appropriate tab. You can also close the Dynamic Help window entirely if you find it is slowing your computer down, or drag it and dock it to a different screen location. Just remember, if you end up with windows strewn all over the place and no easy way to get them back to their original configuration, select Tools | Options from the menu, go to the Environment | General settings, and click Reset Window Layout to return to normal.

## Adding a File

When you first create a web application, you will begin with one web page called WebForm1.aspx. You can add additional web pages by right-clicking on your project in the Solution Explorer, and selecting Add | Add New Item.

You can add various different types of files to your project, including web forms (the default), Web Services, standalone components, resources you want to track like bitmaps and text files, and even ordinary HTML and XML files (see Figure 8-8). Visual Studio .NET event provides some basic designers that allow you to edit these types of files directly in the IDE.

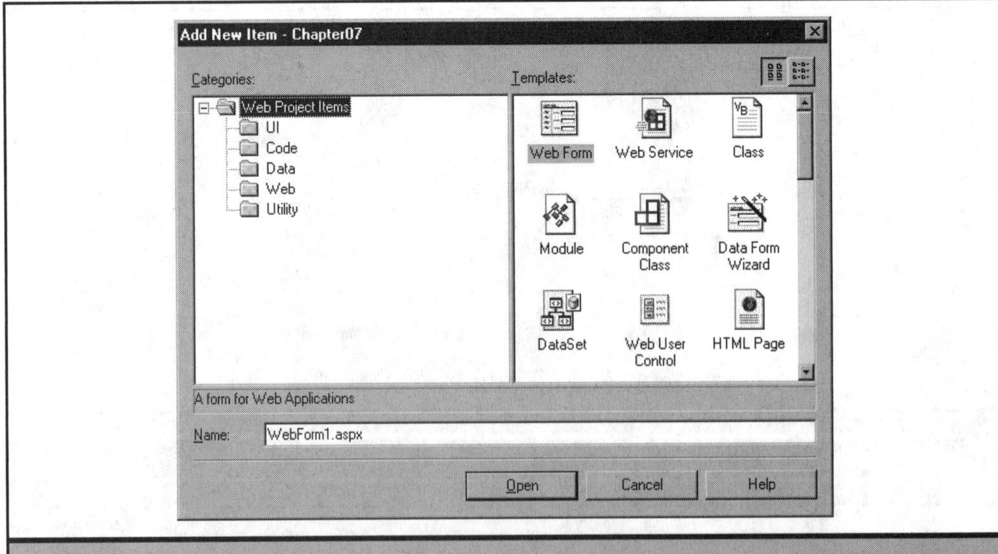


**Figure 8-8.** *File types*

## The Web Form Designer

Now that you understand the basic organization of Visual Studio .NET, you can begin designing a simple web page. To start, double-click on the web page you want to design (start with WebPage1.aspx if you haven't added any additional pages). A special blank designer page will appear.

Before you begin, you may want to switch to grid layout, which gives you complete freedom to place controls wherever you want on the page. Select DOCUMENT in the Properties window (or just click on the blank web form once), and find the pageLayout property.

- In a FlowLayout page, elements are positioned line by line, like in a word processor document. To add a control, you need to drag and drop it to an appropriate place. You also need to add spaces and hard returns to position elements the way you want them.
- In a GridLayout page, elements can be positioned with absolute coordinates. You can draw controls directly onto the web form surface. The disadvantage is that if a control becomes much larger (for example, you place more text in a label at runtime) it could overwrite another adjacent control.

To add controls, choose the control type from the toolbox on the right. By default, the toolbox is enabled to automatically hide itself when your mouse moves away from it, somewhat like the AutoHide feature for the Windows taskbar. This behavior is often annoying, so you may want to click the pushpin in the top-right corner of the toolbox to make it stop in its fully expanded position.



### You Can Combine Layout Modes

Although you must choose GridLayout or FlowLayout for the page, you can place controls inside special Grid Layout or Flow Layout panels. This allows you to align some controls relative to one another, but place them at a specific location on the page. (It also allows you to do the converse: align controls absolutely in a Grid Layout box, but have this box change position to accommodate the content on the rest of a FlowLayout page.)

You'll find the Grid Layout Panel and Flow Layout Panel in the HTML tab on the toolbox. These controls look like boxes. You can configure the border and background of a panel by right-clicking on it and choosing Build Style. These controls are actually just <div> tags that use a special attribute to tell Visual Studio .NET how to treat them:

```
<div ms_positioning="FlowLayout">[HTML and controls go
here.]</div>
```

In the online examples, you'll find many cases that use this control.

There are two types of controls that you can add to web pages from the toolbox. Click on the Web Forms tab to add a web control. Click on the HTML tag to add an HTML element, which can be either a static tag or a server control. Once you have chosen the type of control, you can place it on your web form and resize it to the right dimensions (see Figure 8-9).

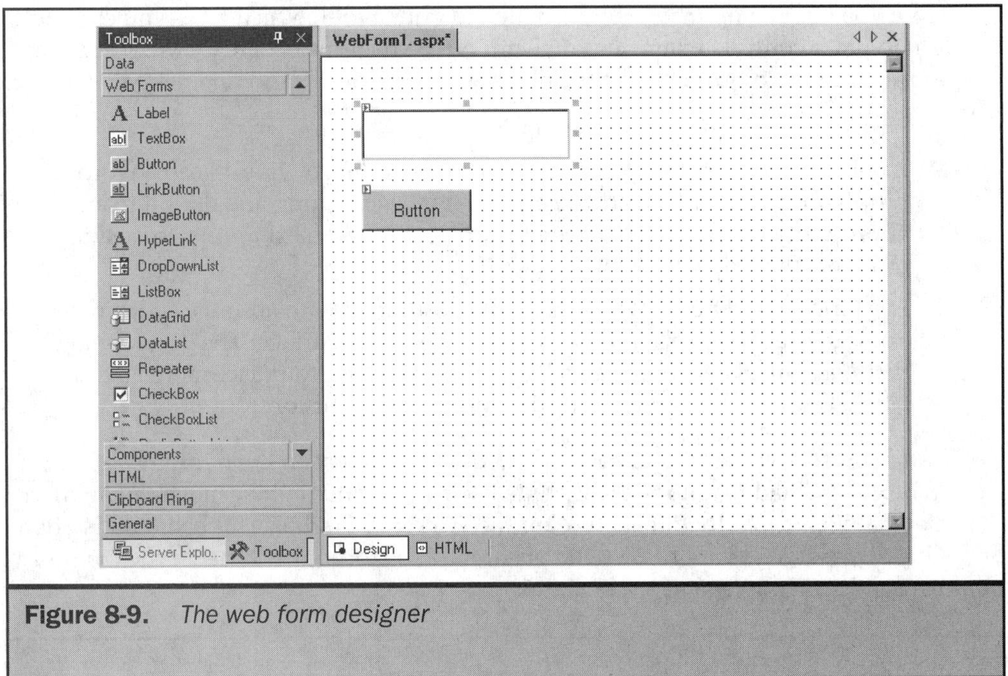


**Figure 8-9.** *The web form designer*

Every time you add a web control, Visual Studio automatically adds the corresponding tag to your .aspx file. You can even look at the .aspx code, or add server control tags and HTML elements manually by typing them in. To switch your view, click the HTML button at the bottom of the web designer. You can click Design to revert back to the graphical web form designer.

Figure 8-10 shows the HTML view of what you might see after you add a TextBox control to a web page.

You can manually add attributes or rearrange controls. In fact, Visual Studio .NET even provides limited IntelliSense features that automatically complete opening tags and alert you if you use an invalid tag. Generally, however, you won't need to use the HTML view in Visual Studio .NET. Instead, you can switch back to the design view, and configure controls using the Properties window.

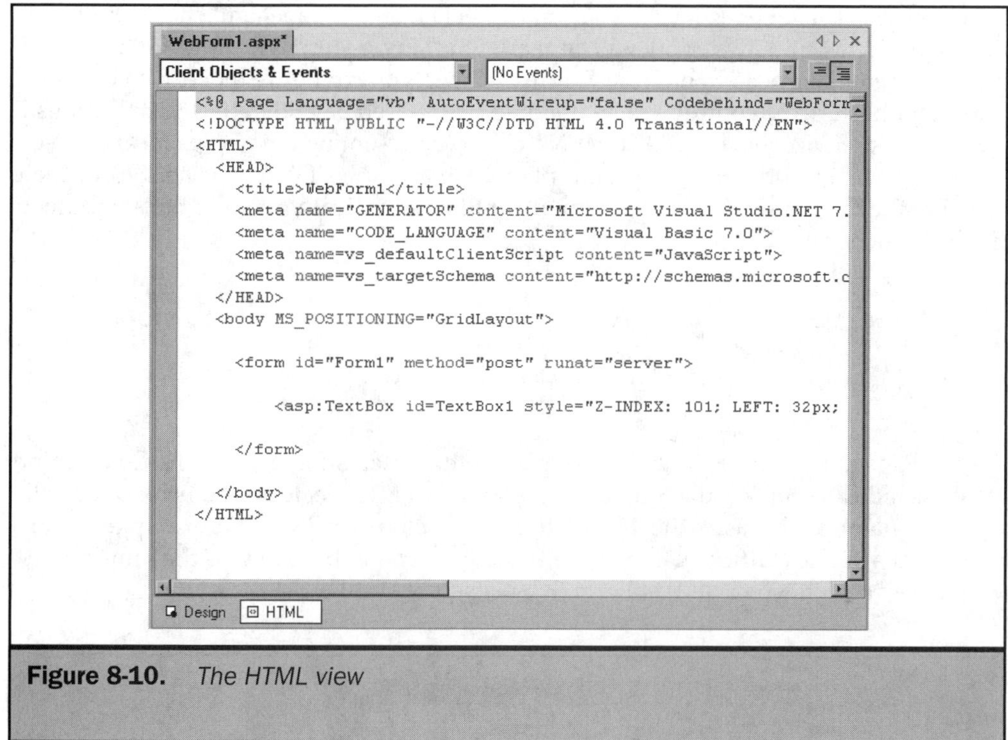


**Figure 8-10.** *The HTML view*

To configure a control, click once to select it (or choose it by name in the drop-down list at the top of the Properties window). Then modify the appropriate properties in the window, such as Text, ID, and ForeColor. These settings are automatically translated to the corresponding ASP.NET control tag attributes and define the initial appearance of your control. Visual Studio .NET even provides special "choosers" that allow you to select extended properties. For example, you can set a color from a drop-down list that shows you the color (see Figure 8-11), and you can configure the font from a standard font selection dialog box.

If you try to configure an HTML control, you'll realize that the properties you are given correspond to the static HTML element, not the server control. Before you can use an HTML element as a server control, you need to right-click on it in the web page, and select Run As Server Control. This adds the required runat="server" attribute. (Alternatively, you could switch to design view and type this in on your own.)

Of course, not all HTML elements need to be server controls. For example, you might want to create a simple <div> tag (provided as the Grid Layout panel or Flow Layout panel). Visual Studio .NET still provides you with some indispensable tools to create this basic tag. For example, you can right-click on the panel and choose Build Style. The Style Builder window will appear with "single-stop shopping" for all the style attributes you need to use (see Figure 8-12). As you configure the text, color, and border properties, the control will be updated on the web page to reflect your settings.

You'll also notice that the DOCUMENT object (representing the web page) allows you to configure many additional web page options. For example, if you set enableSessionState to False, the Page directive in the .aspx file will automatically include the attribute EnableSessionState=False.

```
<%@ Page Language="vb" AutoEventWireup="false"
    Codebehind="WebForm1.aspx.vb"
    Inherits="TestProject.WebForm1"%>
```

The Page directive also hints at a couple of other interesting points. The Codebehind attribute indicates that Visual Studio .NET's standard is to create a code-behind file with the same name as the .aspx file, but with the extension .aspx.vb. Our examples so far have used a slightly different convention, and given code-behind files the same name with the extension .vb (as in WebForm1.vb instead of WebForm1.aspx.vb).

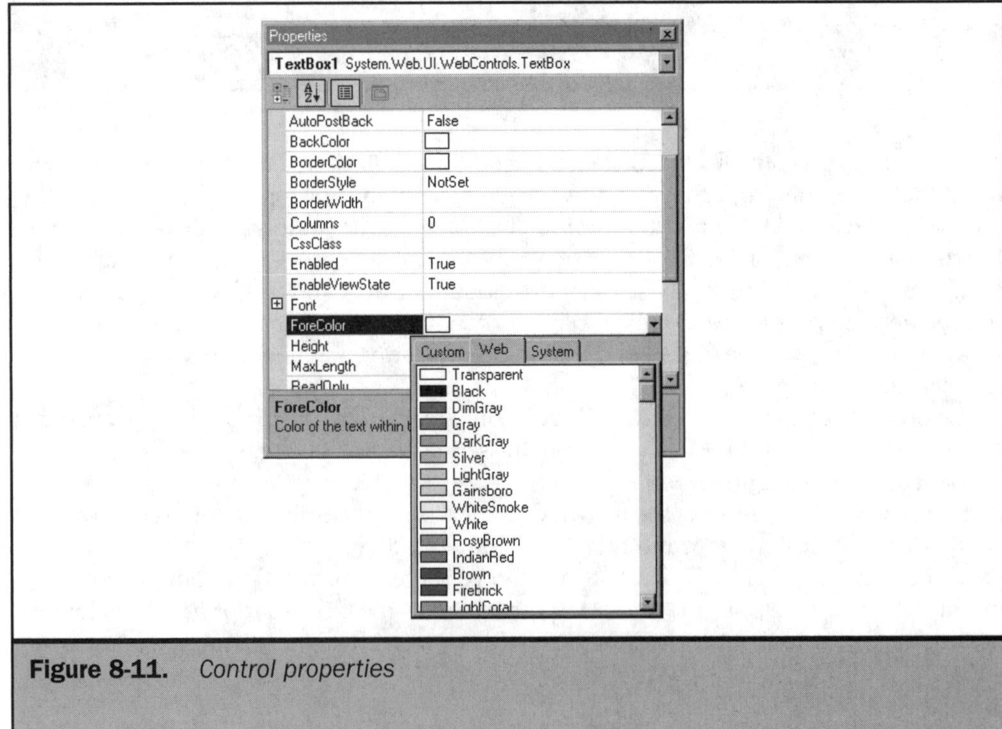


**Figure 8-11.** *Control properties*

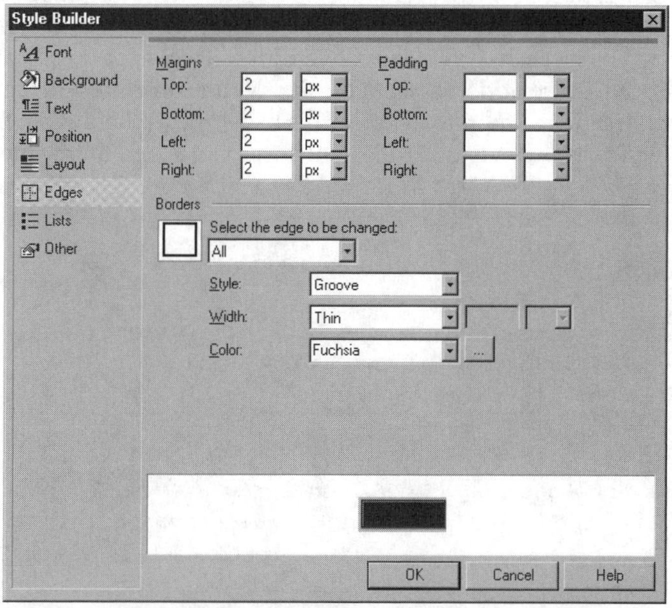

**Figure 8-12.** *Building HTML styles*

You'll also notice that the Inherits directive references a class with the same name in a namespace defined by your project. In other words, when you create a project called Test and a web page class called TestPage, it will be provided as Test.TestPage. This default namespace can be configured using the project options, as you'll see later in this chapter.

## Writing Code

Some of Visual Studio .NET's most welcome enhancements appear when you start to write the code that supports your user interface. To start coding, you need to switch to the code-behind view. To switch back and forth, you can use two buttons that are placed just above the Solution Explorer window as shown in the following illustration. The ToolTips read View Code and View Designer. The "code" in question is the VB code, not the .aspx markup.

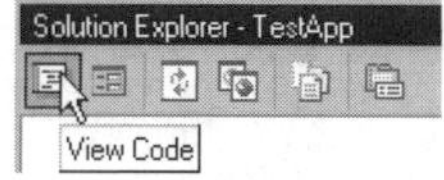

When you switch to code view, you'll see that Visual Basic automatically creates a Page class for you as you design it. It also adds the appropriate member variable, with the appropriate name, for each control you have added. This saves many extra keystrokes.

Visual Studio .NET also adds a special block of extra code into a collapsible region titled Web Form Designer Generated Code. This code, shown below, simply initializes the page so it will work with Visual Studio .NET in the design environment, and can safely be ignored.

```
#Region " Web Form Designer Generated Code "

    'This call is required by the Web Form Designer.
    <System.Diagnostics.DebuggerStepThrough()>_
    Private Sub InitializeComponent()
    End Sub

    Private Sub Page_Init(ByVal sender As System.Object, _
      ByVal e As System.EventArgs) Handles MyBase.Init
        'CODEGEN: This method call is required by the Web Form Designer
        'Do not modify it using the code editor.
        InitializeComponent()
    End Sub

#End Region
```

### Where Are the Code-Behind Files?

You may have noticed that the code-behind files don't appear in the project list. In fact, they are there, but they are hidden by default to present a simpler programming model to new users. This gives the illusion that the .aspx file and the .vb file are combined in one entity.

To see a code-behind file, select Project | Show All Files. Now the Solution Explorer will show an .aspx.vb code-behind file under each .aspx page.

## Adding an Event

There are three ways to add an event to your code:

**Type it in manually** You must specify the appropriate parameters and the Handles clause, just like when we created the files by hand in the previous two chapters.

**Double-click on a control in the design view** Visual Studio .NET will create an event handler for that control's "default event." For example, if you double-click on the page, it will create a Page.Load event handler. If you double-click on a button or input control, it will create the required click or change event handler.

**Choose the event from the drop-down list** At the top of the code view, there are two drop-down lists. To add an event handler, choose the control in the list on the left, and the event you want to react to in the list on the right (see Figure 8-13). To add an event for the page, choose MyBase for the control name.



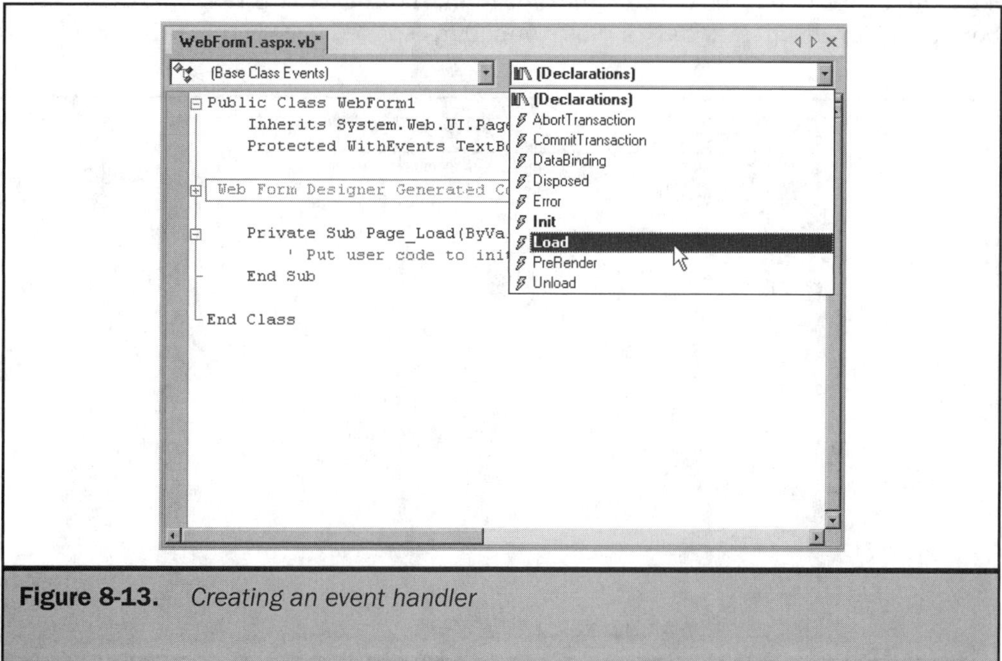


**Figure 8-13.** *Creating an event handler*

When Visual Studio .NET creates an event handler for you, it automatically adds the required Handles clause. It also adds ByVal before each parameter. This indicates that you receive a copy of the parameter, and that any modifications you make will not affect the calling code (in this case, the .NET framework). This keyword is purely optional—in fact, in the examples in this book it's left out to save space.

## IntelliSense and Outlining

Visual Studio .NET provides a number of automatic timesavers through its IntelliSense technology. They are similar to features such as automatic spell checking and formatting in Microsoft Office applications, but much less intrusive. Most of these features are introduced in the following sections, but you'll need several hours of programming before you've become familiar with all of Visual Studio .NET's timesavers. There is not enough space to described advanced tricks, such as special edit commands that comment entire blocks of text, intelligent search and replace, and programmable macros—these features could occupy an entire book of their own.

## Outlining

Outlining allows Visual Studio .NET to "collapse" a subroutine, block structure, or region to a single line. It allows you to see the code that interests you, while hiding unimportant code. To collapse a portion of code, click the minus box next to the first line. Click the box again (which will now have a plus symbol) to expand it (see Figure 8-14).

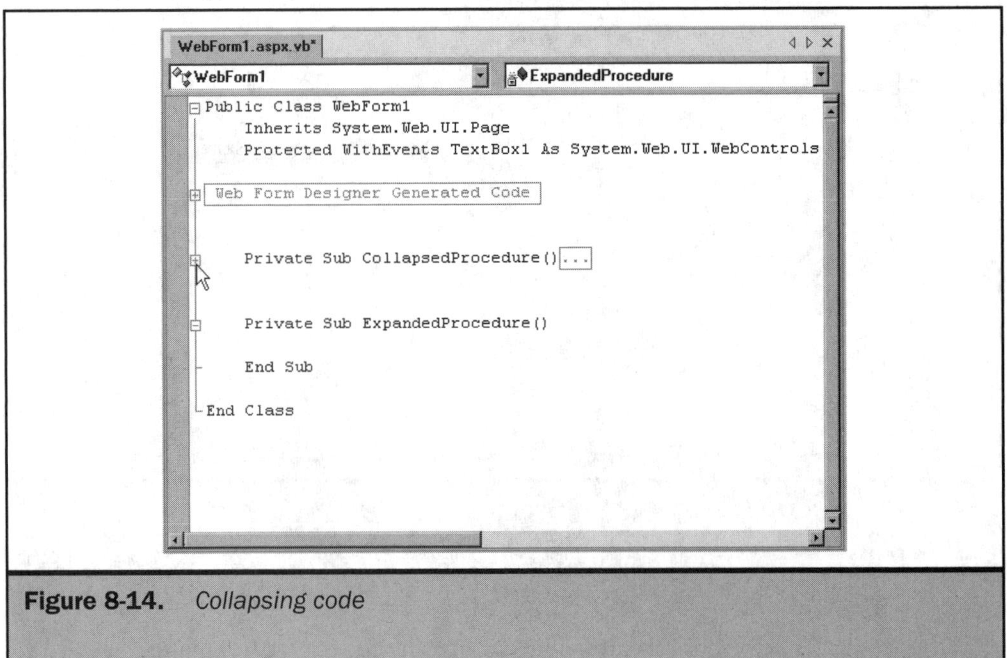


**Figure 8-14.** *Collapsing code*

## Member List

Visual Studio .NET makes it easy for you to interact with controls and classes. When you type a class or object name, it pops up a list of available properties and methods (see Figure 8-15). It uses a similar trick to provide a list of data types when you define a variable, or to provide a list of valid values when you assign an enumeration.

Visual Studio .NET also automatically provides a list of parameters and their data types when you call a method or invoke a constructor. This information is presented in a ToolTip above the code and is shown as you type. Because the .NET class library makes heavy use of function overloading, these methods may have multiple different versions. When they do, Visual Studio .NET indicates the number of versions, and allows you to see the method definitions for each one by clicking the small up and down arrows in the ToolTip. Each time you click the arrow, the ToolTip displays a different version of the overloaded method (see Figure 8-16).

## Block Completion

You'll also save a few keystrokes when typing in common code constructs. For example, Visual Studio .NET will automatically add the End If, End Case, or Next to the end of your code when needed.



## Error Underlining

One of the code editor's most useful features is error underlining. Visual Studio .NET is able to detect a variety of error conditions, such as undefined variables, properties or methods, invalid data type conversions, and missing code elements. Rather than stopping you to alert you that a problem exists (an annoying feature in previous versions of Visual Basic), the Visual Studio .NET editor quietly underlines the offending code. You can hover your mouse over an underlined error to see a brief ToolTip description of the problem (see Figure 8-17).

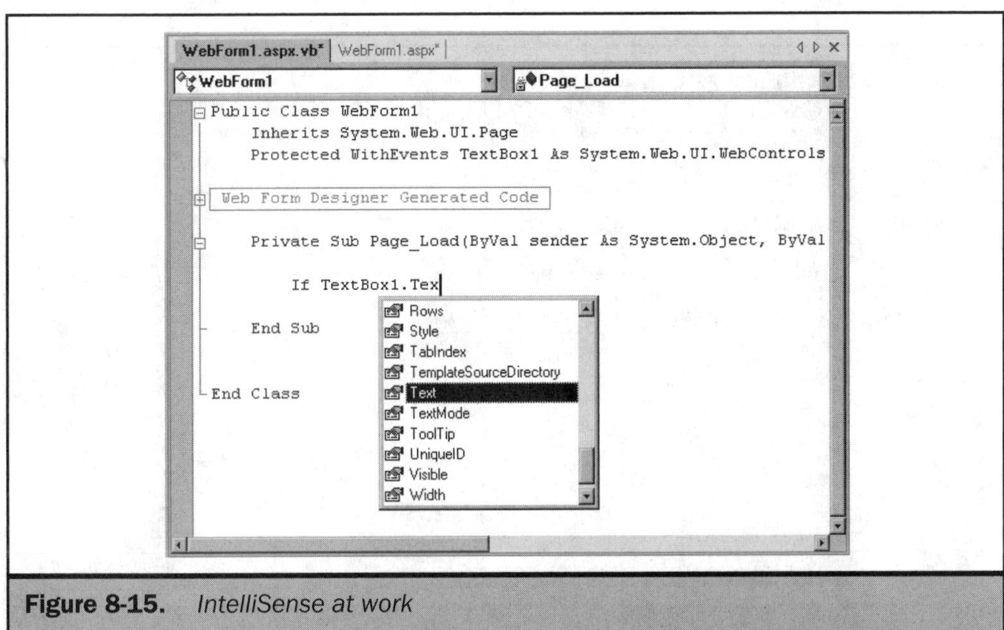


**Figure 8-15.** *IntelliSense at work*

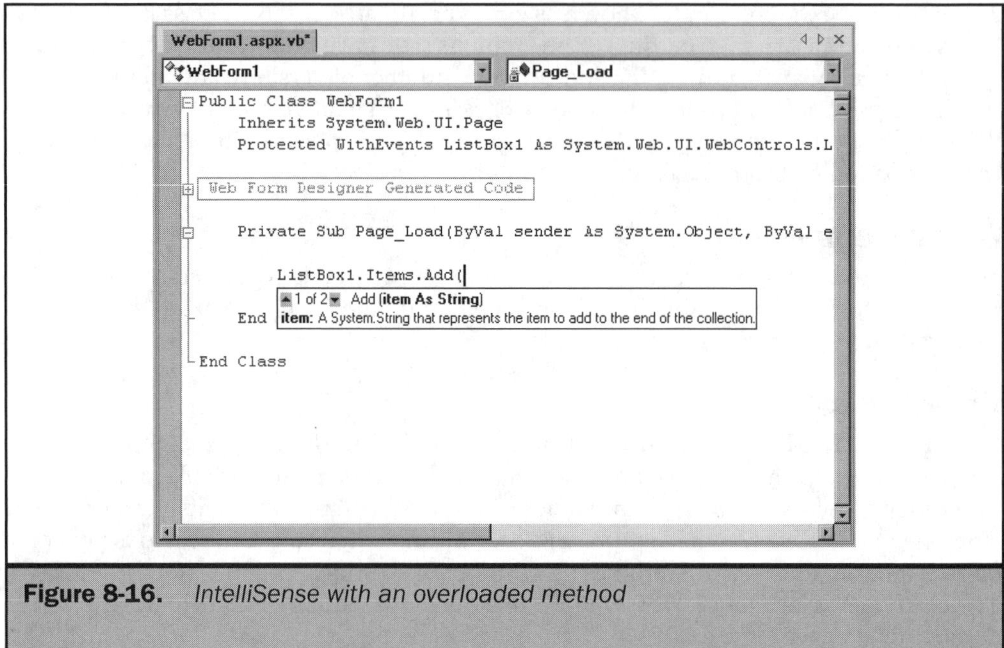


**Figure 8-16.** *IntelliSense with an overloaded method*

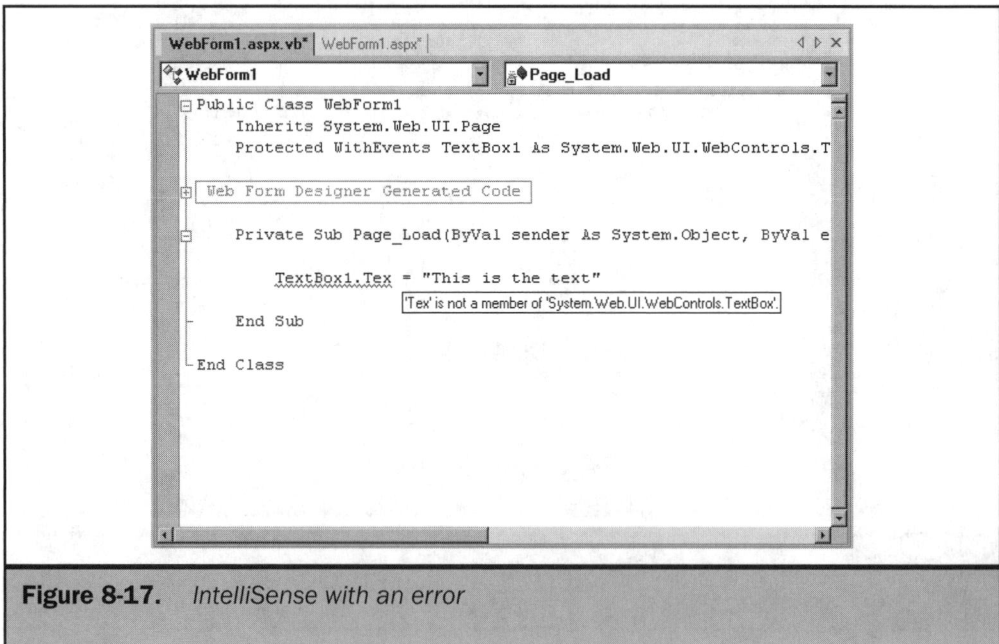


**Figure 8-17.** *IntelliSense with an error*

If you try to compile your program with errors in it, Visual Basic .NET stops you and displays the Task List window with a list of all the errors it detected (see Figure 8-18). You can then jump quickly to a problem by double-clicking it in the list.

Task List - 5 Build Error tasks shown (filtered)

| ! | | ☑ | Description | File | Line |
|---|---|---|---|---|---|
| | | | Click here to add a new task | | |
| ! | | | 'If' must end with a matching 'End If'. | c:\inetpub\...\WebForm1.aspx.vb | 22 |
| ! | | | 'Tex' is not a member of 'System.Web.UI.WebControls.TextBox'. | c:\inetpub\...\WebForm1.aspx.vb | 22 |
| ! | | | Local variable 'x' cannot be referred to before it is declared. | c:\inetpub\...\WebForm1.aspx.vb | 23 |
| ! | | | Name 'y' is not declared. | c:\inetpub\...\WebForm1.aspx.vb | 23 |
| ! | | | Type 'tt' is not defined. | c:\inetpub\...\WebForm1.aspx.vb | 24 |

**Figure 8-18.** *Build errors in the Task List*

### Auto Format and Color

Visual Studio .NET also provides some cosmetic conveniences. It automatically colors your code, making comments green, keywords blue, and normal code black (although you can configure these options). The result is much more readable code.

In addition, Visual Studio .NET is configured by default to automatically format your code. This means you can type your code lines freely without worrying about tabs and positioning. As soon as you move on to the next line, Visual Studio .NET applies the "correct" indenting.

## Project Settings

There are several types of project-wide settings that you can configure. One of the most important is setting your start page. The start page isn't necessarily the page that users will start with (that depends on the URL they use, or it will default to the index.html file if they type in a virtual directory name with no file specified). Instead, the start page is the page that Visual Studio .NET will launch automatically when you are testing and running your application. To set a start page, right-click on the page in the Solution Explorer and select Set As Start Page.

To access the full set of project properties, right-click on your project in the Solution Explorer and select Properties (or select Project | Properties from the menu). The window shown in Figure 8-19 will appear. There are two groups of project settings: Common Properties, which always apply, and Configuration Properties, which are tied to a specific type mode (for example, release mode or debug mode). The Common Properties are explained in Table 8-1.

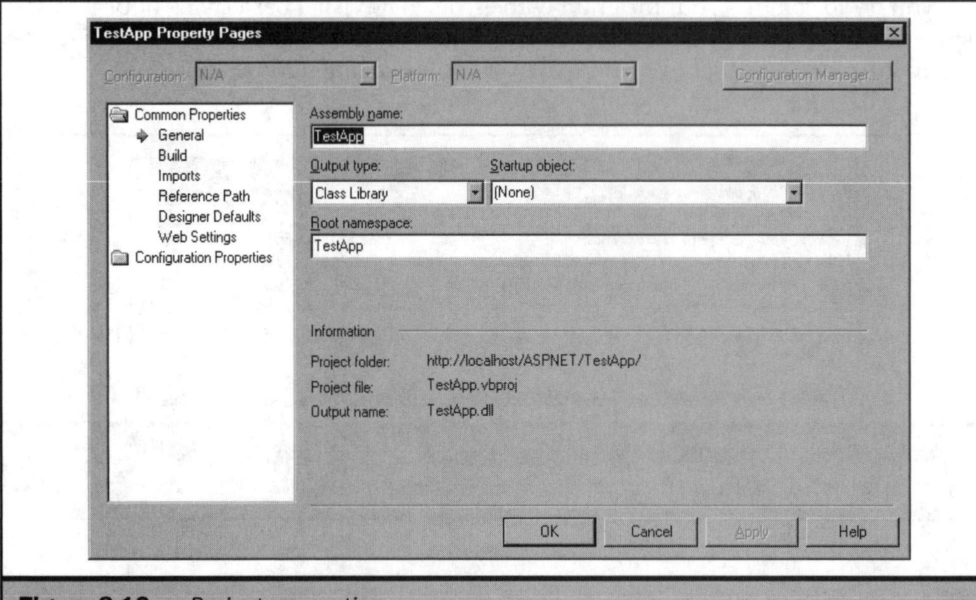


**Figure 8-19.** *Project properties*

| Group | Description |
|---|---|
| General | Configure the Assembly name setting to change the name of the DLL file that Visual Studio .NET generates.<br><br>Change the Root namespace to change the name of the namespace that contains all your web classes (the page directive in the .aspx files will be updated automatically).<br><br>Note that the Output type will always be class library. A web application is not a standalone executable, but a DLL that the ASP.NET engine loads in response to a user request. |
| Build | Allows you to set the project-wide values for Option Explicit, Option Strict, and Option Compare. Option Explicit should always be enabled to prevent variable naming mistakes. Option Strict forces you to use explicit data type conversion (for example, you must use the CType function to convert a string into a number), which can help eliminate accidental errors. |

**Table 8-1.** *Common Project Properties*

| Group | Description |
|---|---|
| Imports | You can use this section to import namespaces and make them locally available to all the code in your project. When you take this approach, you don't need to use the Imports statement at the beginning of each file. |
| Designer Defaults | You can set the default page layout style (grid or layout) that will be used in all new web pages. You can also specify that client event handling and postback code should be created using VBScript. Generally, you won't use this option as it limits your application to Internet Explorer browsers. |

**Table 8-1.** *Common Project Properties (continued)*



# Visual Studio .NET Debugging

Once you have created an application, you can start it by choosing Debug | Start or clicking the Start button in the toolbar. When you compile your project in debug mode, Visual Studio .NET adds special debugging symbols to your code, which allow it to work with the built-in debugging services. When you are ready to deploy your web application, you change the build configuration in the toolbar to Release (see the following illustration), which instructs Visual Studio .NET to compile your program without debug symbols.

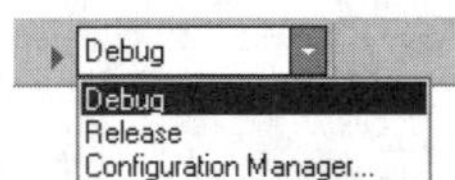


When you compile your application, Visual Studio .NET creates a single DLL file with the name of your project and compiles all the page classes into this file. (This process was described in the explanation of code-behind development in Chapter 5.) Visual Studio .NET then starts one of the pages in your application by launching Internet Explorer and browsing to the .aspx file.

## Single-Step Debugging

Single-step debugging allows you to test your assumptions about how your code works, and see what is really happening under the hood of your application. It's incredibly easy to use:

1. Find a location in your code where you want to pause execution, and start single-stepping (you can use any executable line of code, but not a variable

declaration, comment, or blank line). Click in the margin next to the line code, and a red breakpoint will appear (see Figure 8-20).

2. Now start your program as you would ordinarily. When the program reaches your breakpoint, execution will pause, and you'll be switched back to the Visual Studio .NET code window. The breakpoint statement won't be executed.
3. At this point, you can execute the current line by pressing F8. The following line in your code will be highlighted with a yellow arrow, indicating that this is the next line that will be executed. You can continue like this through your program, running one line at a time by pressing F8, and following the code's path of execution.
4. Whenever the code is in break mode, you can hover over variables to see their current contents (see Figure 8-21). This allows you to verify that variables contain the values you expect.

   You can also use any of the commands listed in Table 8-2 while in break mode. These commands are available from the context menu by right-clicking on the code window, or by using the associated hotkey.

Breakpoints are automatically saved with your application, although they aren't used when you compile the application in release mode. You can also create and then disable a breakpoint. Just click on an active breakpoint, and it will become a transparent gray circle. That allows you to keep a breakpoint to use later, without leaving it active.

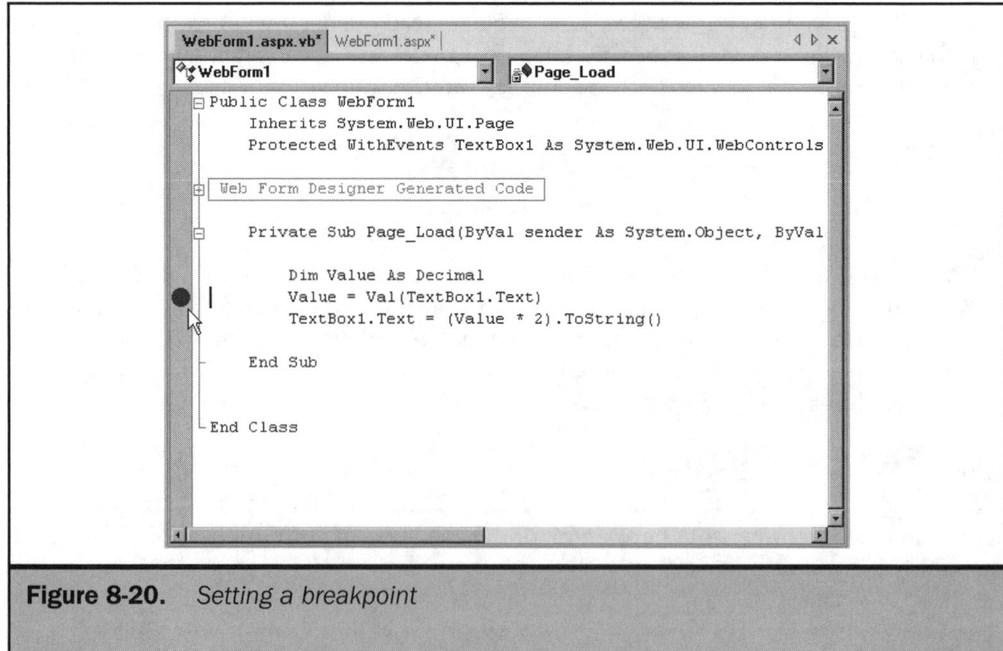


**Figure 8-20.** *Setting a breakpoint*

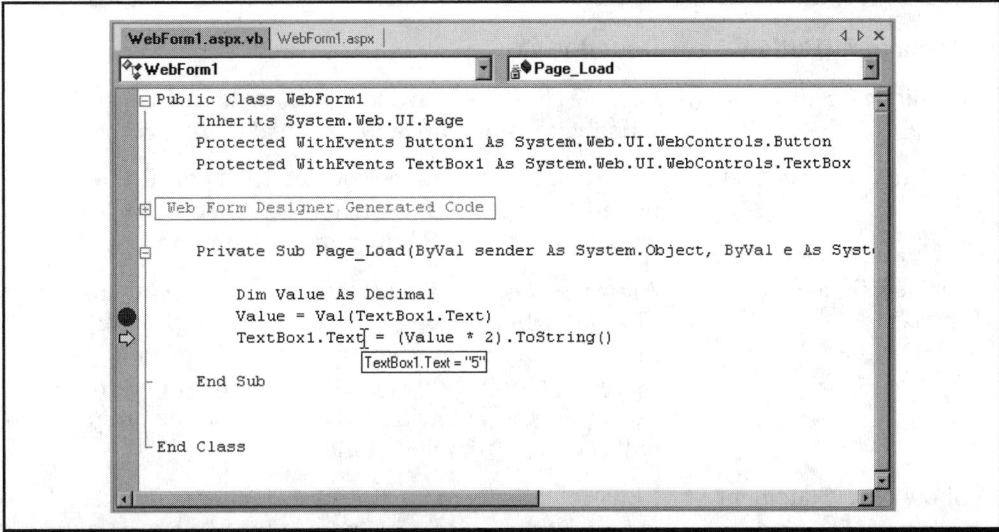


**Figure 8-21.** *Viewing variable contents in break mode*



| Command (Hotkey) | Description |
|---|---|
| Step Into (F8) | Executes the currently highlighted line and then pauses. If the currently highlighted line calls a procedure, execution will pause at the first executable line inside the method or function (which is why this feature is called stepping "into"). |
| Step Over (SHIFT-F8) | The same as Step Into, except it runs procedures as though they are a single line. If you press Step Over while a procedure call is highlighted, the entire procedure will be executed. Execution will pause at the next executable statement in the current procedure. |
| Step Out (CTRL-SHIFT-F8) | Executes all the code in the current procedure, and then pauses at the statement that immediately follows the one that called this method or function. In other words, this allows you to step "out" of the current procedure in one large jump. |

**Table 8-2.** *Commands Available in Break Mode*

| Command (Hotkey) | Description |
|---|---|
| Continue (F5) | Resumes the program and continues to run it normally, without pausing until another breakpoint is reached. |
| Run To Cursor (CTRL-F8) | Allows you to run all the code up to a specific line (where your cursor is currently positioned). You can use this technique to skip a time-consuming loop. |
| Set Next Statement (CTRL-F9) | Allows you to change the path of execution of your program while debugging. It causes your program to mark the current line (where your cursor is positioned) as the current line for execution. When you resume execution, this line will be executed, and the program will continue from that point. |
| Show Next Statement | Moves the focus to the line of code that is marked for execution. This line is marked by a yellow arrow. The Show Next Statement command is useful if you lose your place while editing. |

**Table 8-2.** *Commands Available in Break Mode (continued)*

Choose Debug | Windows | Breakpoints to see a window that lists all the breakpoints in your current project. The Breakpoints window provides a hit count, showing the number of times a breakpoint has been encountered (see Figure 8-22). You can jump to the corresponding location in code by double-clicking on a breakpoint.

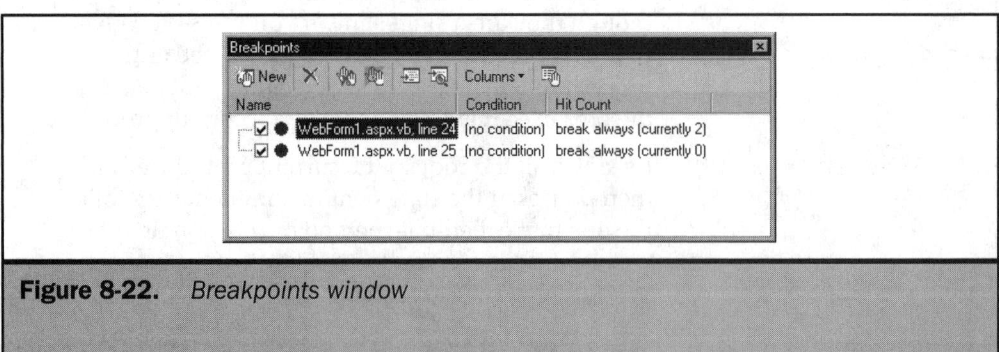


**Figure 8-22.** *Breakpoints window*

### Advanced Breakpoints

Visual Studio .NET allows you to customize breakpoints so they only occur if certain conditions are true. To customize a breakpoint, right-click on it and select Breakpoint Properties. In the window that appears:

- Click the Condition button to set an expression. You can choose to break when this expression is True, or when it has changed since the last time the breakpoint was hit.
- Click the Hit Count button to create a breakpoint that only pauses after a breakpoint has been hit a certain number of times (for example, at least 20), or a specific multiple of times (for example, every fifth time).



## Variable Watches

What if you want to track a variable, but you don't want to stop at a specific point? You can switch your program into break mode at any point by clicking the Pause button in the toolbar or selecting Debug | Break All. You can also track variables across an entire application using the Autos, Locals, and Watch windows, described in Table 8-3.

| Window | Description |
|---|---|
| Locals | Automatically displays all the variables that are in scope in the current procedure. This offers a quick summary of important variables. |
| Autos | Automatically displays variables that Visual Studio .NET determines are important for the current code statement. For example, this might include variables that are accessed or changed in the previous line. |
| Watch | Displays variables you have added. Watches are saved with your project, so you can continue tracking a variable at a later time. To add a watch, right-click on a variable in your code and select Add Watch, or double-click on the last row in the Watch window and type in the variable name. |

**Table 8-3.** *Variable Watch Windows*

Each row in the Locals, Autos, and Watch windows provides information about the type or class of the variable and its current value. If the variable holds an object instance, you can expand the variable and see its private members and properties. For example, in the Locals window you'll see the variable Me, which is a reference to the current page class. If you click on the plus (+) box next to the word Me, a full list will appear that describes many page properties (and some system values), as shown in Figure 8-23.

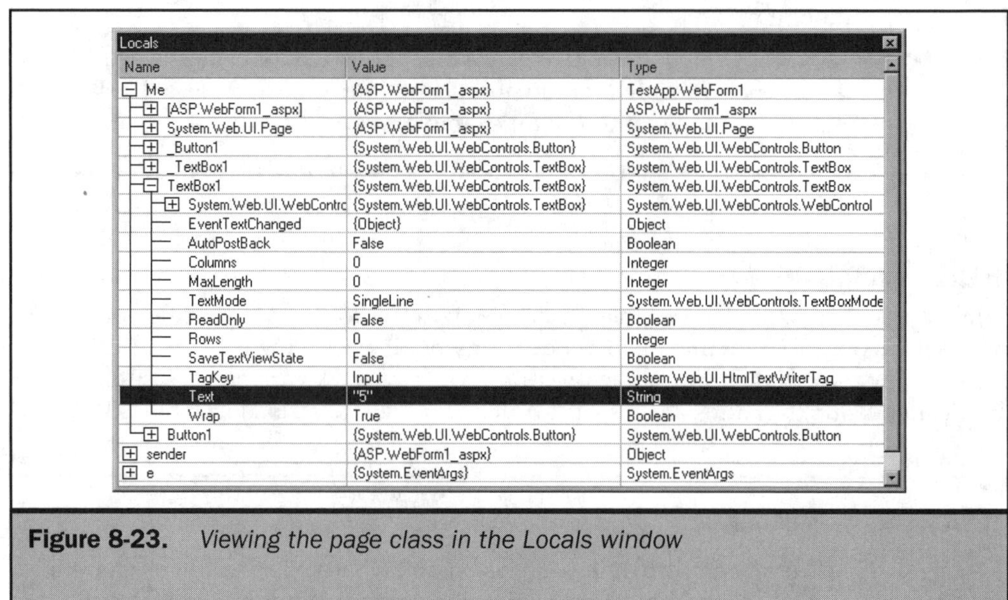

Locals
Name
Value
Type
Me {ASP.WebForm1_aspx} TestApp.WebForm1
[ASP.WebForm1_aspx] {ASP.WebForm1_aspx} ASP.WebForm1_aspx
System.Web.UI.Page {ASP.WebForm1_aspx} System.Web.UI.Page
_Button1 {System.Web.UI.WebControls.Button} System.Web.UI.WebControls.Button
_TextBox1 {System.Web.UI.WebControls.TextBox} System.Web.UI.WebControls.TextBox
TextBox1 {System.Web.UI.WebControls.TextBox} System.Web.UI.WebControls.TextBox
System.Web.UI.WebContrc {System.Web.UI.WebControls.TextBox} System.Web.UI.WebControls.WebControl
EventTextChanged {Object} Object
AutoPostBack False Boolean
Columns 0 Integer
MaxLength 0 Integer
TextMode SingleLine System.Web.UI.WebControls.TextBoxMode
ReadOnly False Boolean
Rows 0 Integer
SaveTextViewState False Boolean
TagKey Input System.Web.UI.HtmlTextWriterTag
Text "5" String
Wrap True Boolean
Button1 {System.Web.UI.WebControls.Button} System.Web.UI.WebControls.Button
sender {ASP.WebForm1_aspx} Object
e {System.EventArgs} System.EventArgs


**Figure 8-23.** *Viewing the page class in the Locals window*

If you are missing one of the Watch windows, you can show it manually by selecting it from the Debug | Windows submenu.

## You Can Modify Variables in Break Mode

The Watch, Locals, and Autos windows allow you to change simple variables while your program is in break mode. Just double-click on the current value in the Value column and type in a new value. This allows you to simulate scenarios that are difficult or time-consuming to recreate manually, or test specific error conditions.

## Working Without Visual Studio .NET

This chapter has extolled the many benefits of Visual Studio .NET. However, if you prefer to work with a simpler, leaner utility (such as Notepad), you can still create equally advanced ASP.NET applications. You might even discover a third-party IDE that you prefer.

The examples with this book are compatible with Visual Studio .NET or with any other type of code-behind development. The online code has standard .aspx and .vb files that you can use independently or use with Visual Studio .NET by using the .vbproj and .sln project and solution files.

# Chapter 9

## Validation and Rich Controls

The ASP.NET web control framework has almost unlimited possibilities. In the coming months, we'll see third-party component developers create increasingly sophisticated control classes that you can plug in to your web applications effortlessly. In this chapter, we start to look at some of the real promise of ASP.NET and the server-control model, and consider controls that have no equivalent in the ordinary HTML world: the Calendar and AdRotator.

The second part of this chapter examines ASP.NET's validation controls. These controls take a previously time-consuming and complicated task—verifying user input and reporting errors—and automate it with an elegant, easy-to-use collection of validators. You'll learn how to add these controls to an existing page, and use regular expression, custom validation functions, and manual validation. And as usual, we'll peer under the hood to take a look at how ASP.NET implements these new features.

Finally, we'll briefly consider the next generation of controls, which promises to bring a new world of rich user interface to the Web. These new controls, prepared by other developers, represent one of the most exciting new directions for ASP.NET.

## The Calendar Control

The Calendar control is one of the most impressive web controls. It's commonly called a rich control because it can be programmed as a single object (and defined in a single, simple tag), but rendered in dozens of lines of HTML output.

```
<asp:Calendar id="Dates" runat="server" />
```

In its default mode, the Calendar control presents a single month view (see Figure 9-1) where the user can navigate from month to month using the navigational areas, at which point the page is posted back, and ASP.NET automatically provides a new page with the correct month values. When the user clicks on a date, it becomes highlighted in a gray box. You can retrieve the day as a DateTime object from the Calendar.SelectedDate property.

This basic set of features may provide everything you need in your application. Alternatively, you can configure different selection modes to allow users to select entire weeks or months, or render the control as a static calendar that doesn't allow selection. The important fact to remember is that if you allow month selection, the user can also select a single week or a day. Similarly, if you allow week selection, the user can also select a single day.

The type of selection is set through the Calendar.SelectionMode property. You may also need to set the Calendar.FirstDayOfWeek property to configure how a week is selected. (For example, set FirstDayOfWeek to the enumerated value Monday, and weeks will be selected from Monday to Sunday.)

When you allow multiple date selection, you need to examine the SelectedDates property, which provides a collection of all the selected dates. You can loop through this collection using the For Each syntax. The following code demonstrates this technique (see Figure 9-2).

```
lblDates.Text = "You selected these dates:<br>"

Dim dt As DateTime
For Each dt In MyCalendar.SelectedDates
    lblDates.Text &= dt.ToLongDateString() & "<br>"
Next
```

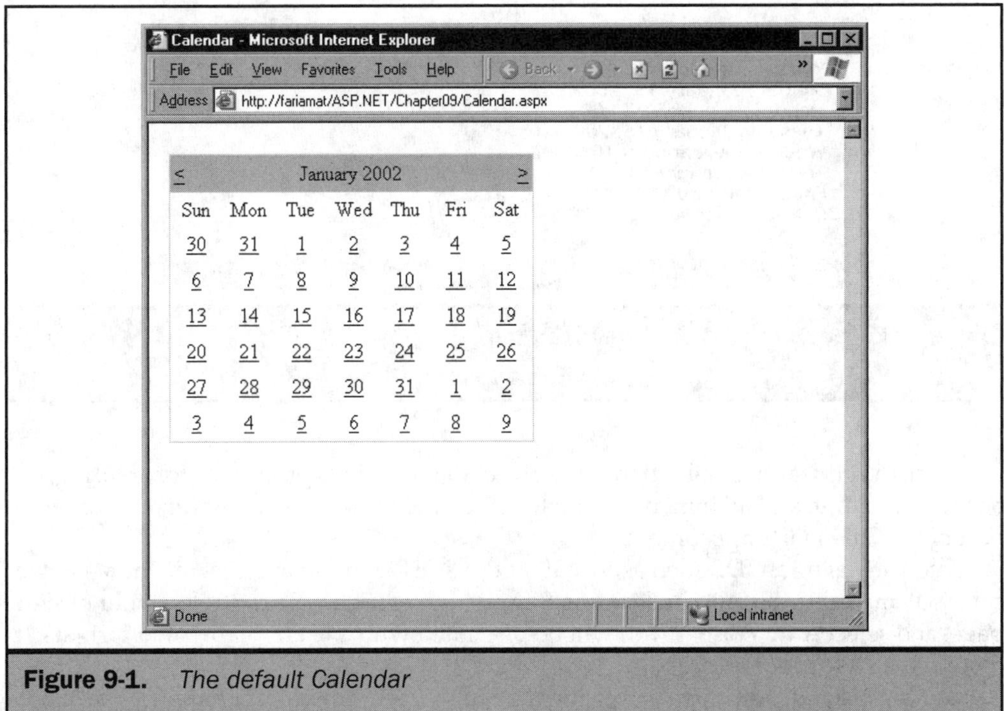


**Figure 9-1.** *The default Calendar*

## Formatting the Calendar

The Calendar control provides a whole host of formatting-related properties. These are described in more detail in Chapter 27. It's enough to note that various parts of the Calendar, like the header, selector, and various day types can be set using one of the style properties (for example, WeekendDayStyle). Each of these style properties

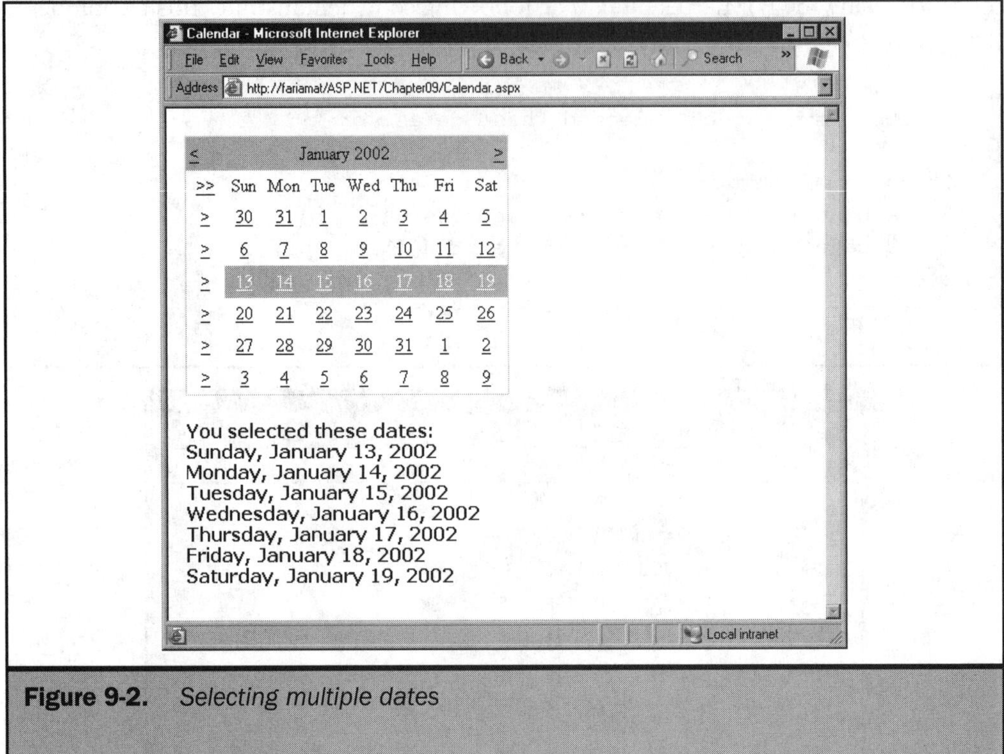


**Figure 9-2.** *Selecting multiple dates*

references a full-featured TableItemStyle object that provides properties for coloring, border style, font, and alignment. Taken together, they allow you to modify almost any part of the Calendar's appearance.

If you are using an IDE such as Visual Studio .NET, you can even set an entire related color scheme using the built-in designer. Simply right-click on the control on your design page, and select Auto Format. You will be presented with a list of predefined formats that set the style properties, as shown in Figure 9-3.

You can also use additional properties to hide some elements or configure the text they display.

## Restricting Dates

In most situations where you need to use a calendar for selection, you don't want to allow the user to select any date in the calendar. For example, the user might be booking an appointment or choosing a delivery date, two services that are generally only provided on set days. The Calendar makes it surprisingly easy to implement this logic. In fact, if you've worked with the date and time controls on the Windows platform, you'll quickly recognize that the ASP.NET versions are far superior.

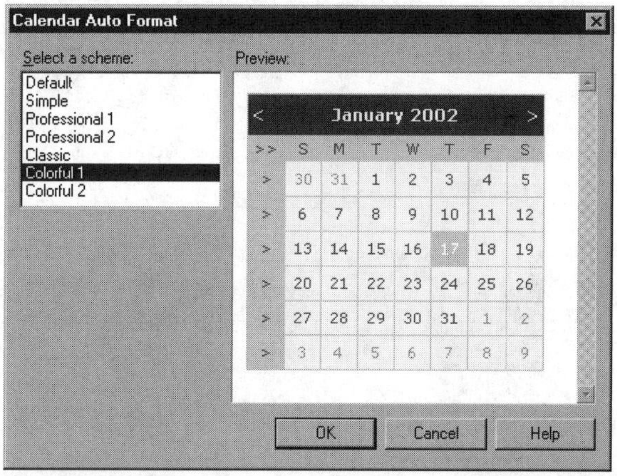

Figure 9-3. *Calendar styles*



The basic approach to restricting dates is to write an event handler for the Calendar.DayRender event. This event occurs when the Calendar is about to create a month to display to the user. This event gives you the chance to examine the date that is being added to the current month (through the e.Day property), and decide whether it should be selectable or restricted.

```
Private Sub DayRender(source As Object, e As DayRenderEventArgs) _
  Handles Calendar.DayRender

    ' Restrict dates after the year 2100, and those on the weekend.
    If e.Day.IsWeekend Or e.Day.Date.Year > 2100 Then
        e.Day.IsSelectable = False
    End If

End Sub
```

The e.Day object is an instance of the CalendarDay class, which provides various useful properties. These are described in Table 9-1.

The DayRender event is extremely powerful. Besides allowing you to tailor what dates are selectable, it also allows you to configure the cell where the date is located through the e.Cell property (the Calendar is really a sophisticated HTML table). For example, you could highlight an important date or even add extra information (see Figure 9-4).

```
Private Sub DayRender(source As Object, e As DayRenderEventArgs) _
  Handles Calendar.DayRender

    ' Check for May 5 in any year, and format it.
    If e.Day.Date.Day = 5 And e.Day.Date.Month = 5 Then
        e.Cell.BackColor = System.Drawing.Color.Yellow

        ' Add some static text to the cell.
        Dim lbl As New Label
        lbl.Text = "<br>My Birthday!"
        e.Cell.Controls.Add(lbl)
    End If

End Sub
```

| Property | Description |
|---|---|
| Date | The DateTime object that represents this date. |
| IsWeekend | True if this date falls on a Saturday or Sunday. |
| IsToday | True if this value matches the Calendar.TodaysDate property, which is set to the current day by default. |
| IsOtherMonth | True if this date does not belong to the current month, but is displayed to fill in the first or last row. For example, this might be the last day of the previous month or the next day of the following month. |
| IsSelectable | Allows you to configure whether the user can select this day. |

**Table 9-1.** *CalendarDay Properties*

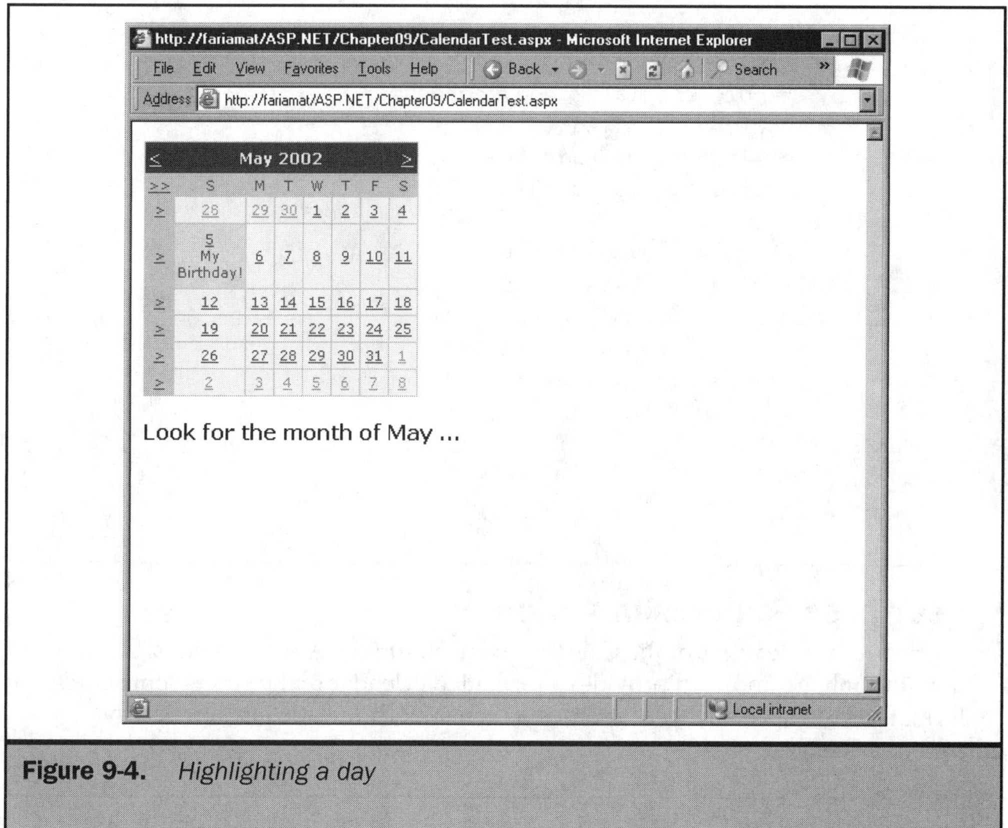


**Figure 9-4.** *Highlighting a day*

The Calendar control provides two other useful events: SelectionChanged and VisibleMonthChanged. These occur immediately after a change, but before the page is returned to the user. You can react to this event and update other portions of the web page to correspond to the current calendar month (for example, setting a list of valid times in a list control).

```
Private Sub SelectionChanged(source As Object, e As EventArgs) _
  Handles Calendar.SelectionChanged

    lstTimes.Items.Clear
```

```
    Select Case Calendar.SelectedDate.DayOfWeek
        Case DayOfWeek.Monday
            ' Apply special Monday schedule.
            lstTimes.Items.Add("10:00")
            lstTimes.Items.Add("10:30")
            lstTimes.Items.Add("11:00")
        Case Else
            lstTimes.Items.Add("10:00")
            lstTimes.Items.Add("10:30")
            lstTimes.Items.Add("11:00")
            lstTimes.Items.Add("11:30")
            lstTimes.Items.Add("12:00")
            lstTimes.Items.Add("12:30")
    End Select
End Sub
```

### See These Features in Action

To try out these features of the Calendar control, run the Appointment.aspx page from the online samples. It provides a formatted calendar that restricts some dates, formats others specially, and updates a corresponding list control when the selection changes.

## The AdRotator

The AdRotator has been available as an ASP component for some time. The new ASP.NET AdRotator adds some new features, such as the ability to filter the full list of banners to the best matches for a given page. The AdRotator also uses a new XML file format.

The basic purpose of the AdRotator is to provide a banner-type graphic on a page (often used as an advertisement link to another site) that is chosen randomly from a group of possible banners. In other words, every time the page is requested, a different banner could be chosen and displayed, which is the "rotation" indicated by the name AdRotator.

In ASP.NET, it wouldn't be too difficult to implement an AdRotator type of design on your own. You could react to the Page.Load event, generate a random number, and then use that number to choose from a list of predetermined image files. You could even store the list in the web.config file so that it can be easily modified separately as part of the application's configuration. Of course, if you wanted to enable several pages with a random banner you would either have to repeat the code or create your own custom control. The AdRotator provides these features for free.

## The Advertisement File

The AdRotator stores its list of image files in a special XML file. This file uses the format shown here.

```
<Advertisements>

  <Ad>
    <ImageUrl>prosetech.jpg</ImageUrl>
    <NavigateUrl>http://www.prosetech.com</NavigateUrl>
    <AlternateText>ProseTech Site</AlternateText>
    <Impressions>1</Impressions>
    <Keyword>Computer</Keyword>
  </Ad>

</Advertisements>
```

This example shows a single possible advertisement. To add more advertisements, you would create multiple <Ad> elements, and place them all inside the root <Advertisements> element.

```
<Advertisements>

  <Ad>
    <!-- First ad here. -->
  </Ad>

  <Ad>
    <!-- Second ad here. -->
  </Ad>
</Advertisements>
```

Each <Ad> element has a number of other important properties that configure the link, the image, and the frequency, as described in Table 9-2.

## The AdRotator Class

The actual AdRotator class only provides a limited set of properties. You specify the appropriate advertisement file in the AdvertisementFile property, and the type of window that the link should follow (the Target window). Note that in Visual Studio .NET, you can't link to an advertisement file unless you have added it to the current project.

| Element | Description |
|---|---|
| ImageUrl | The image that will be displayed. This can be a relative link (a file in the current directory) or a fully qualified Internet URL. |
| NavigateUrl | The link that will be followed if the user clicks on the banner. |
| AlternateText | The text that will be displayed instead of the picture if it cannot be displayed. This text will also be used as a ToolTip in some newer browsers. |
| Impressions | A number that sets how often an advertisement will appear. This number is relative to the numbers specified for other ads. For example, a banner with the value 10 will be shown twice as often as the banner with the value 5. |
| Keyword | A keyword that identifies a group of advertisements. This can be used for filtering. For example, you could create ten advertisements, and give half of them the keyword "Retail" and the other half the keyword "Computer." The web page can then choose to filter the possible advertisements to include only one of these groups. |

**Table 9-2.** *Advertisement File Elements*

The target can name a specific frame, or it can use one of the special values defined in Table 9-3.

| Target | Description |
|---|---|
| _blank | The link opens a new unframed window. |
| _parent | The link opens in the parent of the current frame. |
| _self | The link opens in the current frame. |
| _top | The link opens in the topmost frame of the current window (so the site appears in the full, unframed window). |

**Table 9-3.** *Special Frame Targets*

Optionally, you can set the KeywordFilter property so that the banner will be chosen from a specific keyword group. A fully configured AdRotator tag is shown here.

```
<asp:AdRotator id="Ads" runat="server" AvertisementFile="MainAds.xml"
     Target="_blank" KeywordFilter="Computer" />
```

Additionally, you can react to the AdRotator.AdCreated event. This occurs when the page is being created, and an image is randomly chosen from the file. This event provides you with information about the image that you can use to customize the rest of your page. For example, you might display some related content or a link, as shown in Figure 9-5.

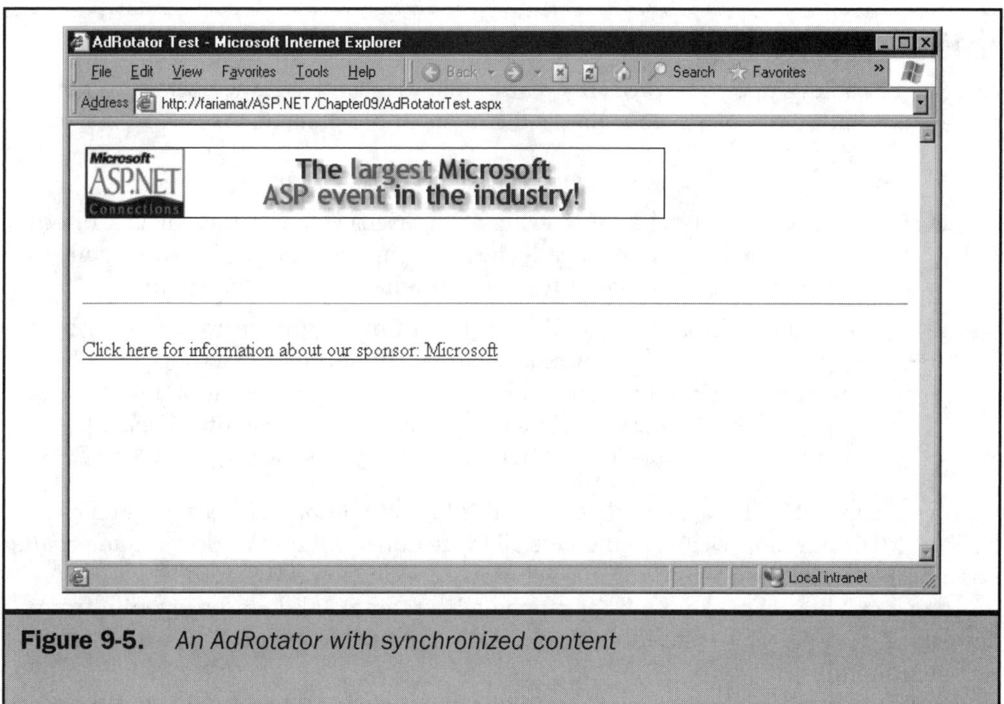


**Figure 9-5.** *An AdRotator with synchronized content*

The event-handling code for this example simply configures a hyperlink control.

```
Private Sub Ads_AdCreated(sender As Object, _
  e As AdCreatedEventArgs) Handles Ads.AdCreated
```

```
        ' Synchronize the Hyperlink control.
        lnkBanner.NavigateUrl = e.NavigateUrl

        ' Syncrhonize the text of the link.
        lnkBanner.Text = "Click here for information about our sponsor: "
        lnkBanner.Text &= e.AlternateText()
    End Sub
```

As you can see, rich controls like the Calendar and AdRotator don't just add a sophisticated HTML output, they also include an event framework that allows you to take charge of the control's behavior and integrate it into your application.

## Validation

As a seasoned developer, you probably realize that you can't assume users won't make mistakes. What's particularly daunting is the range of possible mistakes:

- Users might ignore an important field and leave it blank.
- Users might try to type a short string of "nonsense" to circumvent a required field check, creating endless headaches on your end, such as invalid email addresses that cause problems for your automatic mailing programs.
- Users might make an honest mistake, including a typing error, entering a non-numeric character in a number field, or submitting the wrong type of information. They might even enter several pieces of information that are individually correct, but when taken together are inconsistent (for example, entering a MasterCard number after choosing Visa as the payment type).

A web application is particularly susceptible to these problems, because it relies on basic HTML input controls that don't have all the features of their Windows counterparts. For example, a common technique in a Windows application is to handle the KeyPress event of a text box, check to see if the current character is valid, and prevent it from appearing if it isn't. This technique is commonly used to create text boxes that only accept numeric input.

In web applications, however, you don't have this sort of fine-grained control. In order to handle a KeyPress event the page would have to be posted back to the server every time the user types a letter, slowing an application down hopelessly. Instead, you need to perform all your validation at once when a page (which may contain multiple input controls) is submitted. You then need to create the appropriate user interface to report the mistakes. Some web sites only report the first incorrect field, while others use a special table, list, or window that describes them all. By the time you have perfected your validation routines, a considerable amount of effort has gone into writing validation code.

ASP.NET aims to save you this trouble and provide a reusable framework of validation controls that manages validation details by checking fields and reporting on errors automatically. These controls can even make use of client-side DHTML and JavaScript to provide a more dynamic and responsive interface, while still providing ordinary validation for older, down-level browsers.

## The Validation Controls

ASP.NET provides five different validator controls (see Table 9-4). Four are targeted at specific types of validation, while the fifth allows you to apply custom validation routines.



| Control Class | Description |
|---|---|
| RequiredFieldValidator | Validation succeeds as long as the input control does not contain an empty string. |
| RangeValidator | Validation succeeds if the input control contains a value within a specific numeric, alphabetic, or date range. |
| CompareValidator | Validation succeeds if the input control contains a value that matches the value in another, specified input control. |
| RegularExpressionValidator | Validation succeeds if the value in an input control matches a specified regular expression. |
| CustomValidator | Validation is performed by a user-defined function. |

**Table 9-4.** *Validator Controls*

Each validation control can be bound to a single input control. In addition, you can apply more than one validation control to the same input control to provide multiple types of validation.

Like all other web controls, you add a validator as a tag in the form <asp:ControlClassName />. There is one additional validation control, called ValidationSummary, that doesn't perform any actual control checking. Instead, it can be used to provide a list of all the validation errors for the entire page.

### Validation Always Succeeds for Empty Values

If you use the RangeValidator, CompareValidator, or RegularExpressionValidator, validation will automatically succeed if the input control is empty, because there is no value to validate. If this is not the behavior you want, you should add an additional RequiredFieldValidator to the control. That ensures that two types of validation will be performed, effectively restricting blank values.

## The Validation Process

You can use the validator controls to verify a page automatically when the user submits it, or manually in your code. The first option is the most common:

1. The user receives a normal page, and begins to fill in the input controls.
2. When finished, the user clicks a button to submit the page.
3. Every Button control has a CausesValidation property.

- If this property is False, ASP.NET will ignore the validation controls, the page will be posted back, and your event handling code will run normally.
- If this property is True (the default), ASP.NET will automatically validate the page when the user clicks the button. It does this by performing the validation for each control on the page. If any control fails to validate, ASP.NET will return the page with some error information, depending on your settings. Your click event handling code may or may not be executed—meaning that you will have to specifically check in the event handler whether the page is valid or not.

Based on this description, you'll realize that validation happens automatically when certain buttons are clicked. It does not happen when the page is posted back due to a change event (like choosing a new value in an AutoPostBack list) or if the user clicks a button that has CausesValidation set to False. However, you can still validate one or more controls manually, and then make a decision in your code based on the results. We'll look at this process in more detail a little later.

## The Validator Classes

The validation control classes are found in the System.Web.UI.WebControls namespace and inherit from the BaseValidator class. This class defines the basic functionality for a validation control. Its properties are described in Table 9-5.

## ASP.NET Also Provides Client-Side Validation

In browsers that support it (currently only Internet Explorer 5 and above), ASP.NET will automatically add code for client-side validation. In this case, when the user clicks on a CausesValidation button, the same error messages will appear without the page needing to be submitted and returned from the server. This increases the responsiveness of the application.

However, if the page validates successfully on the client side, ASP.NET will still revalidate it when it is received at the server. This is because it is easy for an experienced user to circumvent client-side validation (for example, by deleting the block of JavaScript validation code). By performing the validation at both ends, your application can be as responsive as possible, but also secure.



| Property | Description |
|---|---|
| ControlToValidate | Identifies the control that this validator will check. Each validator can verify the value in one input control. |
| ErrorMessage, ForeColor, and Display | If validation fails, the validator control can display a text message (set by the ErrorMessage property). The Display property allows you to configure whether this error message will be added dynamically as needed (Dynamic), or whether an appropriate space will be reserved for the message (Static). Static is useful when the validator is in a table, and you don't want the width of the cell to collapse when no message is displayed. |
| IsValid | After validation is performed, this returns True or False depending on whether it succeeded or failed. Generally, you will check the state of the entire page by looking at its IsValid property instead, to find out if all the validation controls succeeded. |

**Table 9-5.** *Properties of the BaseValidator Class*

| Property | Description |
|---|---|
| Enabled | When set to False, automatic validation will not be performed for this control when the page is submitted. |
| EnableClientSideScript | If set to True, ASP.NET will add special JavaScript and DHTML code to allow client-side validation on browsers that support it. |

**Table 9-5.** *Properties of the BaseValidator Class (continued)*

When using a validation control, the only properties you need to use are ControlToValidate and ErrorMessage. In addition, you may need to use the properties that are used for your specific validator. These properties are outlined in Table 9-6.

| Validator Control | Added Members |
|---|---|
| RequiredFieldValidator | None required |
| RangeValidator | MaximumValue, MinimumValue, Type |
| CompareValidator | ControlToCompare, Operator, Type, ValueToCompare |
| RegularExpressionValidator | ValidationExpression |
| CustomValidator | ClientValidationFunction, ServerValidate event |

**Table 9-6.** *Validator-Specific Properties*

A detailed explanation for each validation control is available in Chapter 27. Also, the customer validation form example later in this chapter demonstrates each type of validation.

## A Simple Validation Example

To get an understanding of how validation works, you can create a simple example. This test uses a single Button web control, two TextBox controls, and a RangeValidation control that validates the first text box. If validation fails, an error message will be shown in the RangeValidation control (see Figure 9-6), so this control should be placed immediately next to the TextBox it's validating.

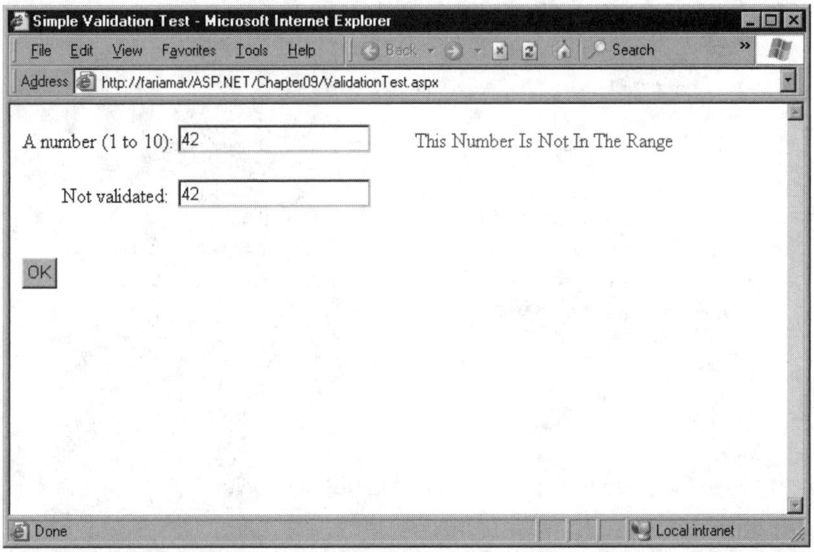

**Figure 9-6.** *Failed validation*

In addition, a Label control is placed at the bottom of the form. This label will report when the page has been successfully posted back and the button click event handling code is executed. Its EnableViewState property is disabled to ensure that it will be cleared every time the page is posted back.

The layout code defines a RangeValidator control, sets the error message, identifies the control that will be validated, and requires an integer from 1 to 10 (shown in bold in the following code example). These properties are set in the .aspx file, but they could also be configured in the event handler for the Page.Load event. The button automatically has its CauseValidation property set to True, as this is the default.

```
<HTML><body>
  <form method="post" runat="server">

    A number (1 to 10):
    <asp:TextBox id=txtValidated runat="server" />
    <asp:RangeValidator id="RangeValidator" runat="server"
         ErrorMessage="This Number Is Not In The Range"
         ControlToValidate="txtValidated"
         MaximumValue="10" MinimumValue="1"
         Type="Integer" />
    <br><br>
    Not validated:
    <asp:TextBox id=txtNotValidated runat="server" /><br><br>
    <asp:Button id=cmdOK runat="server" Text="OK" /><br><br>
    <asp:Label id=lblMessage runat="server"
         EnableViewState="False" />

  </form>
</body></HTML>
```

Finally, here is the code that responds to the button click:

```
Private Sub cmdOK_Click(sender As Object, e As EventArgs) _
  Handles cmdOK.Click
    lblMessage.Text = "cmdOK_Click event handler executed."
End Sub
```

If you are testing this web page in Internet Explorer 5 or later, you'll notice an interesting trick. When you first open the page, the error message is hidden. But if you type an invalid number (remember, validation will succeed for an empty value), and press TAB to the second text box, an error message will appear automatically next to the offending control. This is because ASP.NET adds a special JavaScript function that detects when the focus changes. This code uses the special WebUIValidation.js script library file that is installed on your server with the .NET framework (in the c:\Inetpub\wwwroot\aspnet_client\system_web\[version] directory), and is somewhat complicated. However, ASP.NET handles all the details for you automatically. If you try to click OK with an invalid value in txtValidated, your actions will be ignored, and the page won't be posted back.

## Server-Side Validation

These features are relatively high-level, because they combine DHTML and JavaScript. Clearly, not all browsers will support this client-side validation. To see what will happen on a down-level browser, set the RangeValidator.EnableClientScript property to False and rerun the page. Now error messages won't appear dynamically as you change focus. However, when you click OK, the page will be returned from the server with the appropriate error message displayed next to the invalid control.

The potential problem in this scenario is the fact that the click event-handling code will still execute, even though the page is invalid. To correct this problem, and ensure that your page behaves the same on modern and older browsers, you must specifically abort the event code if validation has not been performed successfully.

```
Private Sub cmdOK_Click(sender As Object, e As EventArgs) _
  Handles cmdOK.Click
    ' Abort the event if the control is not valid.
    If RangeValidator.IsValid = False Then Exit Sub
    lblMessage.Text = "cmdOK_Click event handler executed."
End Sub
```

This code solves our current problem, but would not be of much help if the page contained multiple validation controls. Fortunately, every web form provides a special IsValid property. This property will be False if any validation control has failed. It will be True if all the validation controls completed successfully, or if validation was not performed (for example, if the validation controls are disabled or if the button has CausesValidation set to False).

```
Private Sub cmdOK_Click(sender As Object, e As EventArgs) _
  Handles cmdOK.Click
    ' Abort the event if the page is not valid.
    If Me.IsValid = False Then Exit Sub
    lblMessage.Text = "cmdOK_Click event handler executed."
End Sub
```

Remember, client-side validation is just a nice frosting on top of your application. Server-side validation will *always* be performed, ensuring that crafty users can't "spoof" pages.

## Other Display Options

In some cases, you might have already created a carefully designed form that combines multiple input fields. Perhaps you want to add validation to this page, but you can't reformat the layout to accommodate all the error messages for all the validation controls. In this case, you can save some work by using the ValidationSummary control.

To try this out, set the Display property of the RangeValidator control to None. This ensures that the error message will never be displayed. However, validation will still be performed, and the user will still be prevented from successfully clicking OK if some invalid information exists on the page.

Next, add the ValidationSummary in a suitable location (such as the bottom of the page).

```
<asp:ValidationSummary id="Errors" runat="server" />
```

When you run the page, you won't see any dynamic messages as you enter invalid information and TAB to a new field. However, when you click OK, the Validation-Summary will appear with a list of all error messages, as shown in Figure 9-7. In this case, it retrieves one error message (from the RangeValidator control). However, if you had a dozen validators, it would retrieve all of their error messages and create a list.

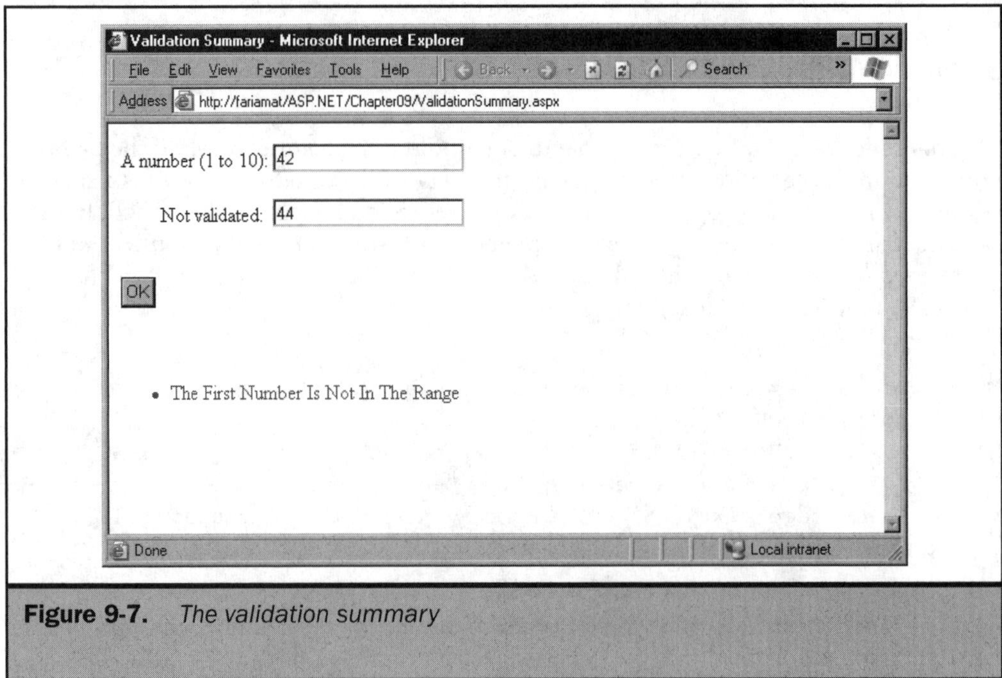


**Figure 9-7.** *The validation summary*

The ValidationSummary control also provides some useful properties you can use to fine-tune the error display. You can set the HeaderText property to display a special title at the top of the list (such as "Your page contains the following errors:"). You can also change the ForeColor and choose a DisplayMode. The possible modes are BulletList (the default), List, and Paragraph.

Finally, you can choose to have the validation summary displayed in a pop-up dialog box instead of on the page (see Figure 9-8). This approach has the advantage of leaving the user interface of the page untouched, but it also forces the user to dismiss the error messages by closing the window before being able to modify the input controls. If users will need to refer to these messages while they fix the page, the inline display is better.

To show the summary in a dialog box, set the ValidationSummary.ShowMessageBox property to True.

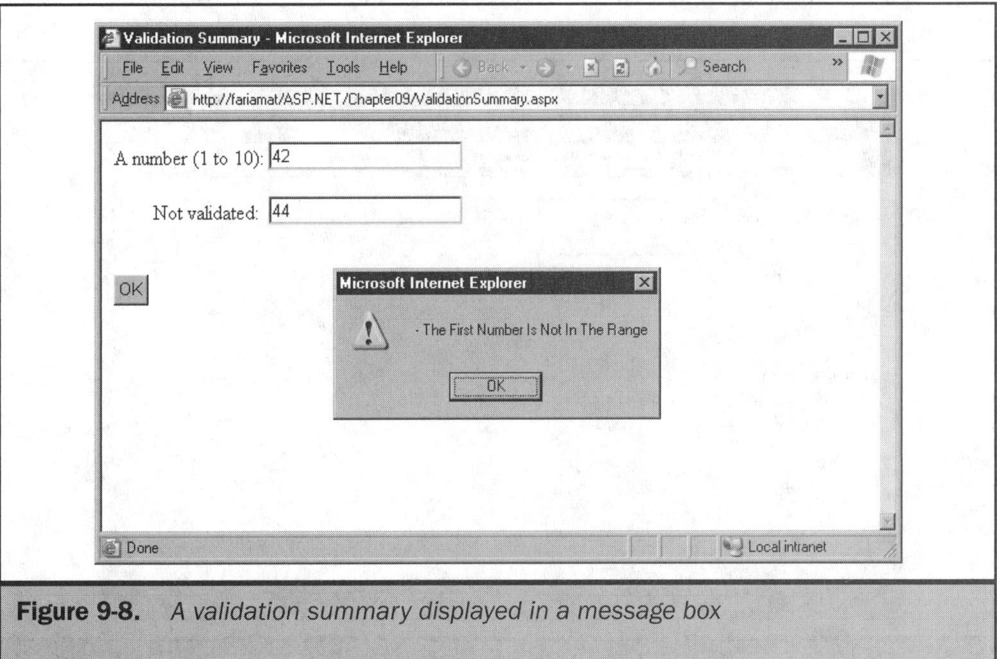


**Figure 9-8.** *A validation summary displayed in a message box*



## Manual Validation

Your final option is to disable validation and perform the work on your own, with the help of the validation controls. This allows you to take other information into consideration, or create a specialized error message that involves other controls (such as images or buttons).

There are three ways that you can create manual validation:

- Use your own code to verify values. In this case, you won't use any of the ASP.NET validation controls.
- Disable the EnableClientScript property for each validation control. This allows an invalid page to be submitted, after which you can decide what to do with it depending on the problems.

- Add a button with CausesValidation set to False. When this button is clicked, manually validate the page by calling the Page.Validate method. Then examine the IsValid property and decide what to do.

The next example follows the second approach. Once the page is submitted, it examines all the validation controls on the page, by looping through the Page.Validators collection. Every time it finds a control that hasn't validated successfully, it retrieves the invalid value from the input control and adds it to a string. At the end of this routine, it displays a message that describes which values were incorrect, as shown in Figure 9-9.

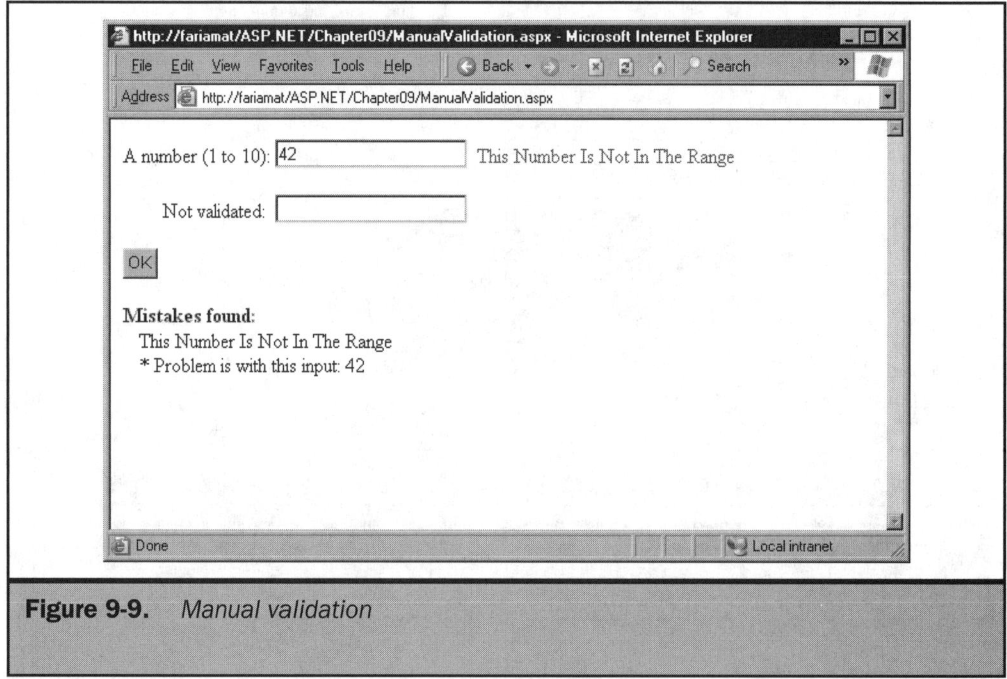


**Figure 9-9.** *Manual validation*

This technique adds a feature that wouldn't be available with automatic validation, which uses the static ErrorMessage property. In that case, it's not possible to include the actual incorrect values in the message.

```
Private Sub cmdOK_Click(sender As Object, e As EventArgs) _
  Handles cmdOK.Click

    Dim ErrorMessage As String = "<b>Mistakes found:</b><br>"
```

```
    ' Create a variable to represent the input control.
    Dim ctrlInput As TextBox

    ' Search through the validation controls.
    Dim ctrl As BaseValidator

    For Each ctrl In Me.Validators
        If ctrl.IsValid = False Then
            ErrorMessage &= ctrl.ErrorMessage & "<br>"

            ' Find the corresponding input control, and change the
            ' generic Control variable into a TextBox variable.
            ' This allows access to the Text property.
            ctrlInput = CType( _
              Me.FindControl(ctrl.ControlToValidate), TextBox)
            ErrorMessage &= " * Problem is with this input: "
            ErrorMessage &= ctrlInput.Text & "<br>"
        End If
    Next

    lblMessage.Text = ErrorMessage
End Sub
```

This example uses an advanced technique: the Page.FindControl method. It's required because the ControlToValidate property is just a string with the name of a control, not a reference to the actual control object. To find the control that matches this name (and retrieve its Text property), you need to use the FindControl method. Once the code has retrieved the matching text box, it can perform other tasks such as clearing the current value, tweaking a property, or even changing the text box color.

## Understanding Regular Expressions

Regular expressions are an advanced tool for matching patterns. They have appeared in countless other languages and gained popularity as an extremely powerful way to work with strings. In fact, Visual Studio .NET even allows programmers to perform a search-and-replace operation through their code using a regular expression (which may represent the new height of computer geekdom).

Regular expressions can almost be considered an entire language of their own. To master all the ways that you can use regular expressions—including pattern matching, back references, and named groups—could occupy an entire small book. Fortunately, you can understand the basics of regular expressions without nearly that much work.

## Literals and Metacharacters

All regular expressions are made up of two kinds of characters: literals and metacharacters. Literals are not unlike the string literals you type in code. They represent a specific, defined character. For example, if you search for the string literal "l" you will find the character "l" and nothing else.

Metacharacters provide the true secret to unlocking the full power of regular expressions. You are probably already familiar with two metacharacters from the DOS world (? and *). Consider the command-line expression shown here:

```
Del *.*
```

The expression *.* contains one literal (the period) and two metacharacters (the asterisks). This translates as "delete every file that starts with any number of characters, contains a dot, and ends with an extension of any number of characters." This has the well-documented effect of deleting everything in the current directory.

Another DOS metacharacter is the question mark, which means "any single character." For example, the following statement deletes any file named "hello" that has an extension of exactly one character.

```
Del hello.?
```

The regular expression language provides many flexible metacharacters—far more than the DOS command line. For example, \s represents any whitespace character (such as a space or tab). \d represents any digit. Thus, the following expression would match any string that starts with the numbers 333, followed by a single whitespace character and *any* three numbers. Valid matches include 333 333, 333 945, but not 334 333 or 3334 945.

```
333\s\d\d\d
```

Part of the reason that regular expressions are confusing to new users is because they use special metacharacters that are more than one character long. In the previous example, \s represents a single character, as does \d, even though they both occupy two characters in the expression.

You can use the plus sign to represent a repeated character. For example 5+7 means "any number of 5 characters, followed by a single 7." The number 57 would match, as would 555557. You can also use brackets to group together a subexpression. For example, (52)+7 would find any string that starts with a sequence of 52. Matches include 527, 52527, 52552527, and so on.

You can also delimit a range of characters using square brackets. [a-f] would match any single character from "a" to "f" (lowercase only). The following expression would match any word that starts with a letter from "a" to "f," contains one or more "word" characters (letters), and ends with "ing"—possible matches include "acting" and "developing."

```
[a-f]\w+ing
```

The following is a more useful regular expression that can match any email address by verifying that it contains the @ symbol. The dot is a metacharacter used to indicate any character except newline. Some invalid email addresses would still be allowed, however, including those that contain spaces, and the regular expression doesn't verify that a dot (.) is present. We'll introduce a better example a little later.

```
.+@.+
```



## Finding a Regular Expression

Clearly, choosing the perfect regular expression may require some testing. In fact, there are numerous reference materials (on the Internet and in paper form) that include useful regular expressions for validating common values such as postal codes. To experiment on your own, you can use the simple RegularExpressionTest page included with the online samples (see Figure 9-10). It allows you to set a regular expression that will be used to validate a control. Then you can try typing in some sample values, and see if the regular expression validator succeeds or fails.

The code is quite simple. The Set This Expression button assigns a new regular expression to the RegularExpressionValidator control (using whatever text you have typed). The Validate button simply triggers a postback, which causes ASP.NET to perform validation automatically. If an error message appears, validation has failed. Otherwise, it is successful.

```
Public Class RegularExpressionTest
  Inherits Page

    Protected txtExpression As TextBox
    Protected txtValidate As TextBox
    Protected lblExpression As Label
```

```
    Protected WithEvents cmdSetExpression As Button
    Protected WithEvents cmdValidate As Button
    Protected TestValidator As RegularExpressionValidator
    Protected ValidationSummary1 As ValidationSummary

    Private Sub cmdSetExpression_Click(sender As Object, _
      e As EventArgs) Handles cmdSetExpression.Click
        TestValidator.ValidationExpression = txtExpression.Text
        lblExpression.Text = "Current Expression: "
        lblExpression.Text &= txtExpression.Text
    End Sub

End Class
```

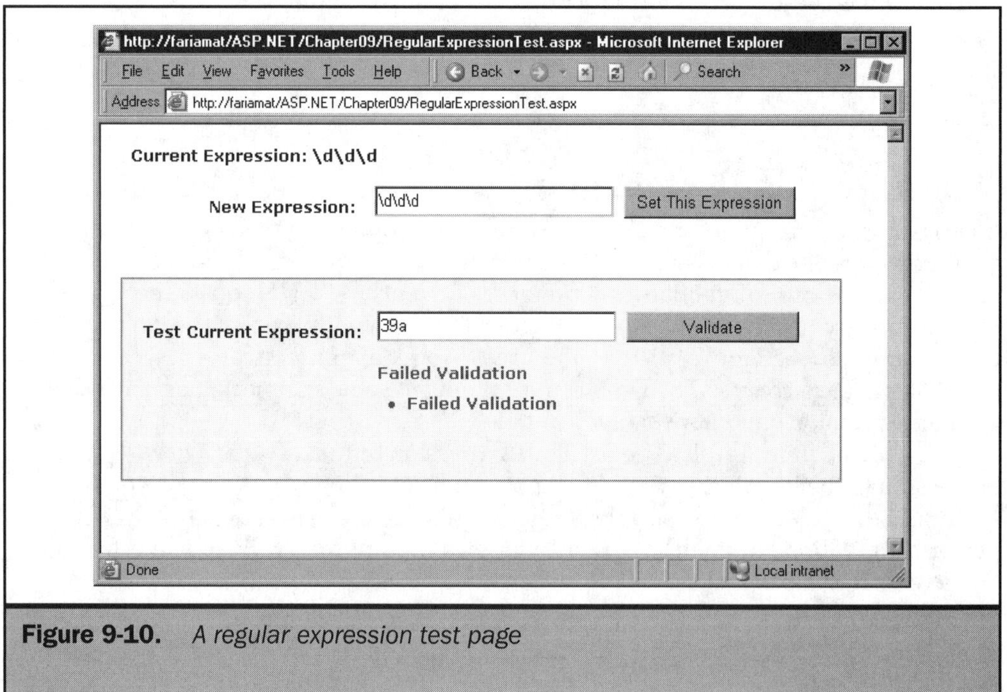


**Figure 9-10.** *A regular expression test page*

Table 9-7 shows some of the fundamental regular expression building blocks. If you need to match a literal character with the same name as a special character, you generally precede it with a \ character. For example *hello* matches the text *hello* in a string, because the special asterisk (*) character is preceded by a slash (\).

Some of the most common (and useful) regular expressions are shown in Table 9-8.

| Character | Description |
|---|---|
| * | Zero or more occurrences of the previous character or subexpression. For example, 7*8 matches 7778 or just 8. |
| + | One or more occurrences of the previous character or subexpression. For example, 7+8 matches 7778 but not 8. |
| ( ) | Groups a subexpression that will be treated as a single element. For example, (78)+ matches 78 and 787878. |
| \| | Either of two matches. For example, 8\|6 matches 8 or 6. |
| [ ] | Matches one character in a range of valid characters. For example, [A-C] matches A, B, or C. |
| [^ ] | Matches a character that is not in the given range. For example, [^A-B] matches any character except A and B. |
| . | Any character except newline. For example, "here" matches "where" and "there." |
| \s | Any whitespace character (such as a tab or space). |
| \S | Any non-whitespace character. |
| \d | Any digit character. |
| \D | Any character that is not a digit. |
| \w | Any "word" character (letter, number, or underscore). |

**Table 9-7.** *Regular Expression Characters*

| Content | Regular Expression | Description |
|---|---|---|
| Email address* | \S+@\S+\.\S+ | Check for an ampersand (@), dot (.), and only allow non-whitespace characters. |
| Password | \w+ | Any sequence of word characters (letter, space, or underscore). |

**Table 9-8.** *Commonly Used Regular Expressions*

| Content | Regular Expression | Description |
|---|---|---|
| Specific-length password | \w{4,10} | A password that must be at least four characters long, but no longer than ten characters. |
| Advanced password | [a-zA-Z]\w{3,9} | As with the specific-length password, this allows four to ten total characters. But the first character must fall in the range of a–z or A–Z (it must start with a letter). |
| Another advanced password | [a-zA-Z]\w*\d+\w* | This password starts with a letter character, followed by zero or more word characters, a digit, and then zero or more word characters. In short, it forces a password to contain a number. You could use a similar pattern to require two numbers or any other special character. |
| Limited-length field | \S{4,10} | Like the password example, this allows four to ten characters, as well as special characters (asterisks, ampersands, and so on). |
| Social Security number | \d{3}-\d{2}-\d{4} | A sequence of three, two, and four digits, with each group separated by a dash. A similar pattern could be used when requiring a phone number. |

* There are many different ways to validate email addresses, with regular expressions of varying complexity. See http://www.4guysfromrolla.com/webtech/validateemail.shtml for a discussion of this subject and numerous examples.

**Table 9-8.** *Commonly Used Regular Expressions (continued)*

Some logic is much more difficult to model in a regular expression. An example is the Luhn algorithm, which verifies credit card numbers by first doubling every second digit, adding these doubled digits together, and then dividing the sum by zero. The number is valid (although not necessarily connected to a real account) if the final result is zero. To use the Luhn algorithm, you need a CustomValidator control that runs this logic on the supplied value.

## A Validated Customer Form

To end our discussion, we'll consider a full-fledged web form (as shown in Figure 9-11) that combines a variety of different pieces of information that might be needed to add a user record (for example, an e-commerce site shopper or a content site subscriber).

There are several types of validation being performed:

- A RequiredFieldValidator is used for the user name and the password.
- A CompareValidator ensures that the two versions of the masked password match.

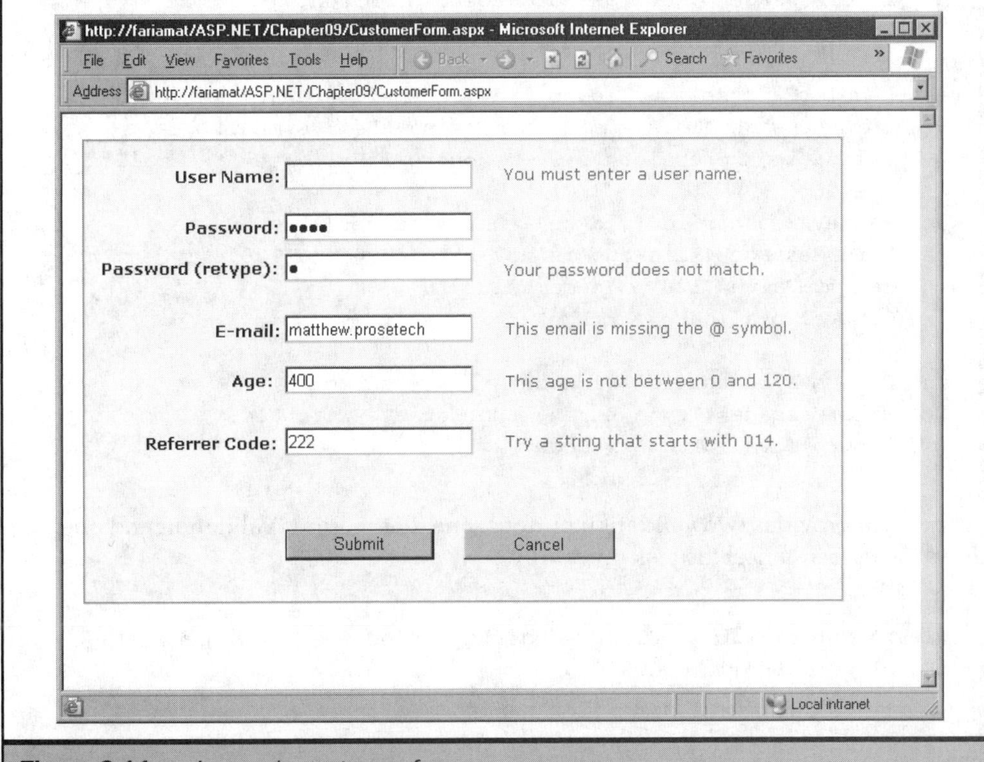


**Figure 9-11.** *A sample customer form*

- A RegularExpressionValidator checks that the email address contains an @ symbol.
- A RangeValidator ensures the age is a number from 0 to 120.
- A CustomValidator performs a special validation on the server of a "referrer code." This code verifies that the first three characters make up a number that is divisible by 7.

The tags for the validator controls are as follows:

```
<asp:RequiredFieldValidator id="vldUserName" runat="server"
     ErrorMessage="You must enter a user name."
     ControlToValidate="txtUserName" />

<asp:RequiredFieldValidator id="vldPassword" runat="server"
     ErrorMessage="You must enter a password."
     ControlToValidate="txtPassword" />

<asp:CompareValidator id="vldRetype" runat="server"
     ErrorMessage="Your password does not match."
     ControlToCompare="txtPassword" ControlToValidate="txtRetype" />

<asp:RegularExpressionValidator id="vldEmail" runat="server"
     ErrorMessage="This email is missing the @ symbol."
     ValidationExpression=".+@.+" ControlToValidate="txtEmail" />

<asp:RangeValidator id="vldAge" runat="server"
     ErrorMessage="This age is not between 0 and 120." Type="Integer"
     MaximumValue="120" MinimumValue="0"
     ControlToValidate="txtAge" />

<asp:CustomValidator id="vldCode" runat="server"
     ErrorMessage="Try a string that starts with 014."
     ControlToValidate="txtCode" />
```

The form provides two validation buttons, one that requires validation and one that allows the user to cancel the task gracefully.

```
Private Sub cmdSubmit_Click(sender As Object, e As EventArgs) _
  Handles cmdSubmit.Click
    If Page.IsValid = False Then Exit Sub
    lblMessage.Text = "This is a valid form."
End Sub
```

```
Private Sub cmdCancel_Click(sender As Object, e As EventArgs) _
  Handles cmdCancel.Click
    lblMessage.Text = "No attempt was made to validate this form."
End Sub
```

The only form-level code that is required for validation is the custom validation code. The validation takes place in the CustomValidator's ServerValidate event handler. This method receives the value it needs to validate (e.Value) and sets the result of the validation to True or False (e.IsValid).



### Custom Validation Is More Secure

In some cases, you might be able to replace custom validation with a particularly ingenious use of a regular expression. However, custom validation can be used to ensure that validation code is only executed at the server. That prevents users from seeing your regular expression template (in the rendered JavaScript code) and using it to determine how they can outwit your validation routine. For example, a user may not have a valid credit card number, but if they know the algorithm you use to test it, they can easily create a false one.

```
Private Sub vldCode_ServerValidate(source As Object, _
  e As ServerValidateEventArgs) Handles vldCode.ServerValidate
    ' Check if the first three digits are divisible by seven.
    If Val(Left(e.Value, 3)) Mod 7 = 0 Then
        e.IsValid = True
    Else
        e.IsValid = False
    End If
End Sub
```

You'll notice that this validation isn't performed until the page is posted back. That means that if you enable the client script code (the default), dynamic messages will appear informing the user when the other values are incorrect, but they will not indicate any problem with the referral code until the page is posted back.

This isn't really a problem, but if it troubles you, use the CustomValidator's ClientValidationFunction property. First, add a client-side JavaScript or VBScript validation function to the .aspx portion of the web page (ideally, it will be JavaScript, for compatibility with browsers other than Internet Explorer). You can't use ASP.NET code, only code that will be recognized by the client browser.

Your JavaScript function will accept two parameters (in true .NET style), which identify the source of the event and the additional validation parameters. In fact, the client-side event is modeled on the .NET ServerValidate event. Just as you did in the ServerValidate event handler, in the client validation function you retrieve the value to validate from the Value property of the event argument object. You then see the IsValid property to indicate whether validation succeeds or fails. The skeleton outline for such a function is shown here, which provides the client-side equivalent of our ServerValidate event handler. You'll notice that the code resembles C# superficially.

```
<script language="JavaScript">
<!--
function MyCustomValidation(objSource, objArgs)
{
    // Get value.
    var number = objArgs.Value;

    // Check value and return result.
    number = number.substr(0, 3);
    if (number % 7 == 0)
    {
        objArgs.IsValid = true;
        return;
    }
    else
    {
        objArgs.IsValid = false;
        return;
    }
}
// -->
</script>
```

Once you've added the function, set the ClientValidationFunction property of the CustomValidator control to the name of the function (shown here in bold).

```
<asp:CustomValidator id="vldCode" runat="server"
    ErrorMessage="Try a string that starts with 014."
    ControlToValidate="txtCode"
    ClientValidationFunction="MyCustomValidation" />
```

ASP.NET will now call this function on your behalf when it is required.

Even when you use client-side validation, you should still include the ServerValidate event handler, both to provide server-side validation for clients that don't support the required JavaScript and DHTML features, and to prevent clients from circumventing your validation by modifying the HTML page they receive.

### You Can Validate List Controls

The examples in this chapter have concentrated exclusively on validating text entry, which is the most common requirement in a web application. While you can't validate RadioButton or CheckBox controls, you can validate most single-select list controls.

When validating a list control, the value that is being validated is the Value property of the selected ListItem object. Remember, the Value property is the special hidden information attribute that can be added to every list item. If you don't use it, you can't validate the control (validating the text of the selection is not a supported option).



## Other Rich Controls

One of the best features of ASP.NET's new control model is that other developers can create their own rich controls, which can then be incorporated into any ASP.NET application. You'll get a taste of this in Chapter 22, when you learn to create your own controls. Even without this knowledge, however, you can already start to use some of these advanced third-party controls. These controls provide features unlike any HTML element—including advanced grids, charting tools, and tree views.

ASP.NET custom controls act like web controls in every sense. Your web page interacts with the appropriate control object, and the final output is rendered automatically every time the page is sent to the client as HTML. That means the controls only need to be installed on your server, and any client can benefit from them. To access a custom control, you generally need to copy the assembly DLL to your application's bin directory (or create a reference to it using Visual Studio .NET). You can then import the namespace, and add the control to the toolbox, as described in Chapter 22. You may even find that some controls support data-binding and templates, and provide specialized designers that let you customize them from the development environment.

The Internet contains many hubs for control sharing. One such location is Microsoft's own http://www.asp.net/, which provides a Control Gallery where developers can submit their ASP.NET web controls (see Figure 9-12). Currently, it's a little underpopulated, but it's sure to heat up soon.

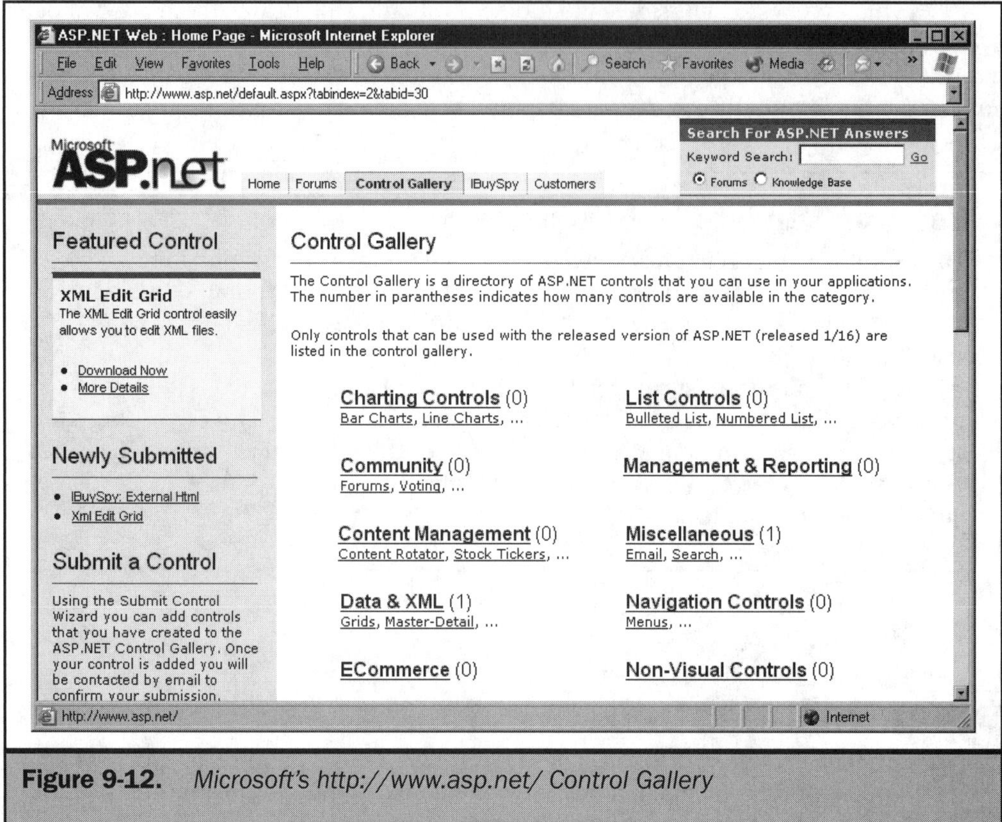


**Figure 9-12.** *Microsoft's http://www.asp.net/ Control Gallery*

# The Microsoft Internet Explorer Controls

Microsoft's Internet Explorer team has developed their own toolkit of controls for the ASP.NET platform. At the time of this book's writing, these controls hadn't yet been updated to support the final release of the .NET platform, but the change is likely imminent, if it hasn't happened already.

The Internet Explorer controls correspond to a few standards seen in the Windows world:

- A toolbar with a collection of graphical buttons.
- A TreeView that displays a hierarchy of items (as used in Windows Explorer to show directories).

- A MultiPage and TabStrip control, which are often used together to provide a set of tabbed "pages." The user can display a different set of controls (contained in one page in a MultiPage) by clicking a different button on the TabStrip.

The Internet Explorer controls can send HTML output for any current browser, but they shine when used with Internet Explorer, where they use special DHTML code automatically to create a more responsive and dynamic user interface. To try out these controls, browse to http://msdn.microsoft.com/workshop/webcontrols/webcontrols_entry.asp. You'll find a download that allows you to install them on your server, and a comprehensive reference that describes the objects used by each control. The latest specific installation instructions are contained at the site, although the process is mostly automatic.

Once you have the controls installed, you can access them through the Microsoft.Web.UI.WebControls namespace. The easiest way to use them is to import the namespace and register a tag prefix so that you can define a control in the .aspx file without having to use the full assembly name. (You'll learn much more about this process in Chapter 22.)

For example, the following code defines a tag prefix "ie" to use for the web controls control.

```
<%@ register TagPrefix="ie"
    Namespace = "Microsoft.Web.UI.WebControls"
    Assembly = "Microsoft.Web.UI.WebControls"
%>
```

You can now declaratively create the TreeView using the ie prefix and the class name.

```
<ie:TreeView runat="server">
  <ie:TreeNode Text="Michigan">
     <ie:TreeNode Text="Detroit" />
     <ie:TreeNode Text="Farmington" />
  </ie:TreeNode>
  <ie:TreeNode Text="Washington" >
     <ie:TreeNode Text="Bellevue" />
     <ie:TreeNode Text="Redmond" />
  </ie:TreeNode>
</ie:TreeView>
```

The result is shown in Figure 9-13.

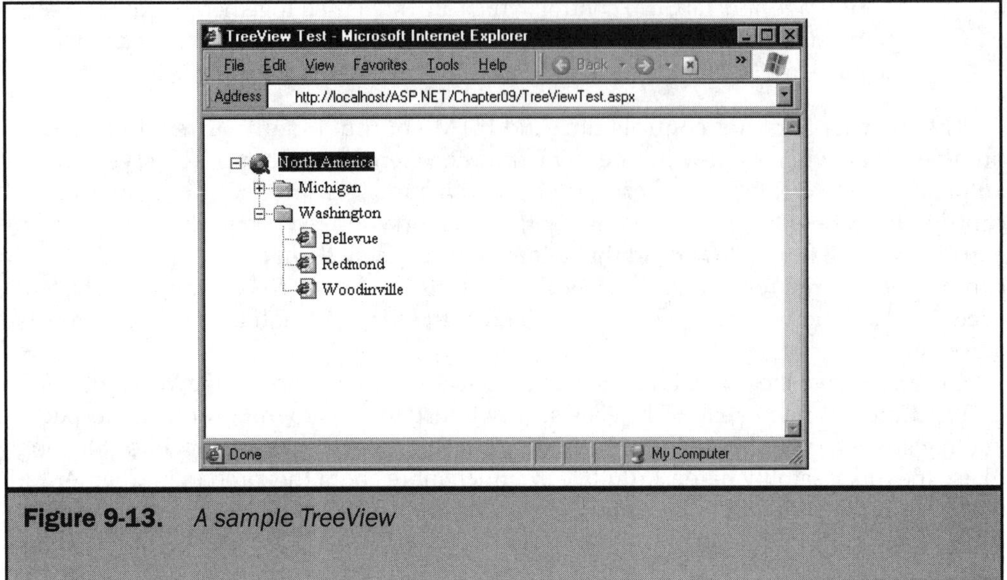


**Figure 9-13.** *A sample TreeView*

You can also use the Internet Explorer controls in much the same way. Figure 9-14 shows a basic sample of a declarative TabStrip and MultiPage control. You'll notice in the code that while the required three tabs are declared, all the PageView objects are empty, except for the one that is currently being displayed.

```
<ie:TabStrip id="tsMail" runat="server">
    <ie:Tab Text="Inbox" />
    <ie:TabSeparator />
    <ie:Tab Text="Compose" />
    <ie:TabSeparator />
    <ie:Tab Text="Addresses" />
    <ie:TabSeparator DefaultStyle="width:100%" />
</ie:TabStrip>

<ie:MultiPage id="mpMail" runat="server"
    <ie:PageView>
    </ie:PageView>

    <ie:PageView>
        <table>
        <tr><td>To:</td><td><asp:TextBox runat="server" /></td></tr>
        <tr><td>From:</td><td><asp:TextBox runat="server" />
        </td></tr>
```

```
            <tr><td>Subject:</td><td><asp:TextBox runat="server" />
            </td></tr>
            </table>
            <asp:TextBox runat="server" rows="5" columns="30"
                 TextMode="Multiline" />
        </ie:PageView>

        <ie:PageView>
        </ie:PageView>
    </ie:MultiPage>
```



As with most web controls, you don't need to define all the user interfaces in the .aspx template—instead, you could configure the properties of the appropriate control object dynamically (typically in the Page.Load event handler). You can also react to a rich set of higher-level events—such as detecting when tabbed pages are changed or a node is expanded or collapsed in a TreeView.

The previous examples show how the Internet Explorer controls look, but only scratch the surface of how you might use this ASP.NET add-on in an application. For more information about the Internet Explorer web controls, and other third-party creations, take your search online to the .NET community. Custom controls are already targeted as one of the fastest growing areas of interest for the .NET platform.

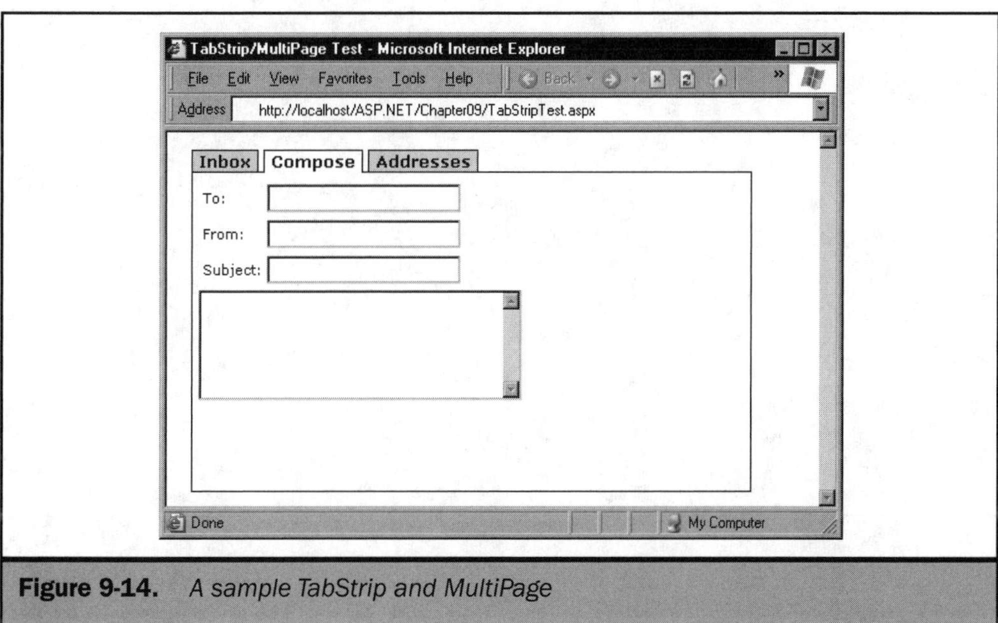


**Figure 9-14.** *A sample TabStrip and MultiPage*

# Chapter 10

## State Management

The most significant difference between programming for the Internet and programming for the desktop is state management. In a traditional Windows application, state is managed automatically and transparently. Memory is plentiful, and always available. In a web application, it's a different story. Thousands of users might simultaneously run the same application on the same computer (the web server), each one communicating over the stateless HTTP protocol of the Internet. These conditions make it impossible to program a web application like a traditional Windows program.

Understanding these state limitations is the key to creating efficient, robust web applications. In this chapter you'll learn why state is no trivial issue in the world of Internet programming, and you'll see how you can use ASP.NET's state management features to store and manage information carefully and consciously. We'll explore different state options, including viewstate, session state, and custom cookies, and consider how to transfer information from page to page using the query string.

### Is ASP.NET State Management Like ASP?

If you're a seasoned ASP programmer, most of the content in this chapter will sound familiar. State management in ASP.NET is refined, not revolutionized. You'll see some changes, such as a new object model (from the .NET class library) and viewstate, which is an entirely new option for storing data. You'll also learn advanced session state configuration options that weren't available in any previous version of ASP. These allow you to persist state to a database or outside process, making it shareable between servers in a web farm and durable between server restarts. On the whole, however, many of the same state considerations that are found in ASP applications apply to ASP.NET.

## The Problem of State

In a traditional Windows program, users interact with a continuously running application. A portion of memory on the desktop computer is allocated to store the current set of working information.

In a web application, the story is quite a bit different. A professional ASP.NET site might look like a continuously running application, but it's really just a clever illusion. Web applications use a highly efficient disconnected access pattern. In a typical web request, the client connects to the web server and requests a page. When the page is delivered, the connection is severed and the web server abandons any information it has about the client. By the time the user receives a page, the "application" has already stopped running.

Because clients only need to be connected for a few seconds, a web server can handle thousands of requests without a performance hit. However, if you need to retain information between user actions (and you almost always do), you need to take special measures.

## Viewstate

In the previous chapters, you've learned how ASP.NET introduces viewstate to allow controls to remember their state. Viewstate information is maintained in a hidden field, and automatically sent back to the server with every postback. Your ASP.NET application can use this information in its programming logic.

Viewstate represents the first option for state management. However, it's worth noting that you don't need to create a control to use viewstate management. Instead, you can add additional bits of information directly to the viewstate collection of the containing page, and retrieve them later on postback. The type of information you add can be just about any .NET object or a custom data object you have created. However, you will need to convert it when you retrieve it, as items are stored as the generic Object type.

The viewstate collection is provided through the Page.ViewState property. This property is an instance of the StateBag collection class. To add and remove items in this class, you use a dictionary system, where every item has a unique string name.

Consider this viewstate example:

```
Me.ViewState("Counter") = 1
```

This places the value 1 (or rather, an Integer object that contains the value 1) into the ViewState collection, and gives it the descriptive name Counter. If there is currently no item with the name Counter, it will be created automatically. If there is already an item indexed under Counter, it will be overwritten.

When retrieving a value, you use the key name and perform the necessary conversion. If you have not enabled Option Strict, you may be able to perform some conversions to strings or simple numeric types automatically. However, it is usually a better idea to always handle the conversion manually. Conversions can be performed to any type using the CType statement, as we saw in Chapters 2 and 3.

```
Counter = CType(Me.ViewState("Counter"), Integer)
```

### ASP.NET Provides Many Dictionary Collections

ASP.NET's dictionary-based collection system is an important concept. ASP.NET provides many collections that use the exact same syntax, including collection for session and application state as well as caching and cookies. We'll look at many of these collections throughout this chapter.

## A Viewstate Example

The following example is a simple counter program that records how many times a button was clicked. Without any kind of state management, the counter will be locked perpetually at 1. With a careful use of viewstate, the task is made much simpler.

```
Public Class SimpleCounter
  Inherits Page

    Protected lblCount As Label
    Protected WithEvents cmdIncrement As Button

    Private Sub cmdIncrement_Click(sender As Object, _
      e As EventArgs) Handles cmdIncrement.Click
        Dim Counter As Integer
        If Me.ViewState("Counter") = Nothing Then
            Counter = 1
        Else
            Counter = CType(Me.ViewState("Counter"), Integer) + 1
        End If

        Me.ViewState("Counter") = Counter
        lblCount.Text = "Counter: " & Counter.ToString()
    End Sub

End Class
```

The code checks first for a null reference before assigning the variable. This is not strictly necessary, as Visual Basic .NET will automatically convert an empty value to the number 0 in an addition statement. The technique is required for more complex objects, however, which may need to be specially created or have various properties set before being placed into state. The output for this page is shown in Figure 10-1.

There are other ways to solve this problem. For example, you could enable state management for a label control and use it to store the counter. Every time the increment button is clicked, you could then retrieve the current value from the label text and convert it to an integer. However, this technique isn't always appropriate. For example, you might create a program that tracks button clicks, but doesn't display them on the screen. In this case, you could still store this information in a web control, but you would have to make it hidden.

That, of course, is exactly what viewstate does: it stores information automatically in a special hidden field in the page. Because ASP.NET handles these lower-level details for you, your code becomes more clear and concise. And as you saw in the previous chapters, viewstate information is automatically compressed and lightly encoded, allowing for basic privacy when needed. This encryption won't deter a dedicated hacker, but it does deter the casual user from peering into some of the low-level details of your page and guessing what is happening behind the scenes.

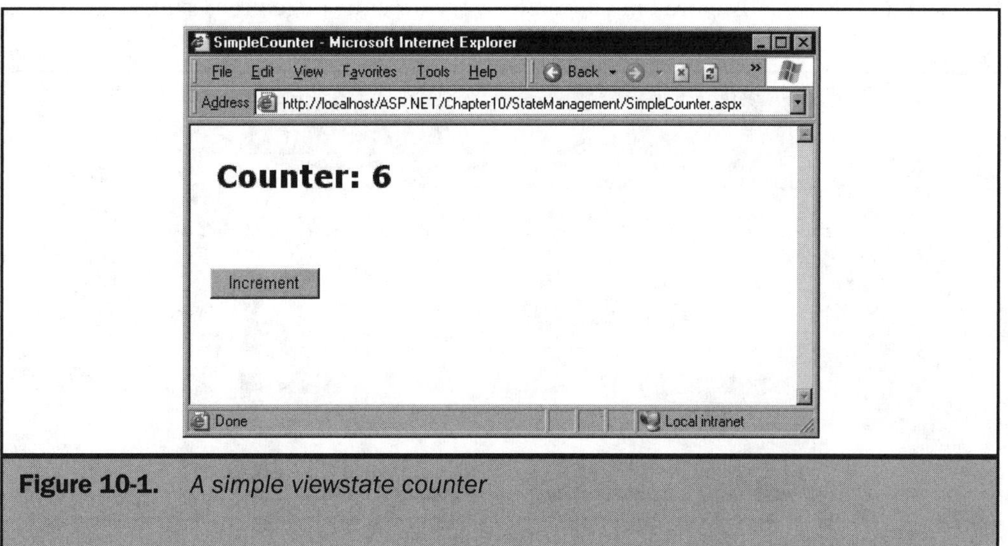


**Figure 10-1.** *A simple viewstate counter*



### Viewstate Is Also Used When Creating Custom Controls

Every control provides a ViewState property. However, in web page code you can only access the ViewState for the current class, which is the custom Page class. If you are deriving a special custom control, you can use that control's ViewState property to store any extra state information you need to maintain the control's appearance and data.

## Retaining Member Variables

You have probably already noticed that any information you set in a member variable for an ASP.NET page is automatically abandoned when the page processing is finished and the page is sent to the client. (The Counter variable in the previous code listing is an example.) Interestingly, you can work around this limitation using viewstate.

The basic principle is to save all member variables to viewstate when the Page.PreRender event occurs, and retrieve them when the Page.Load event occurs. Remember, Page.Load happens every time the page is created. In the case of a postback, the Page.Load event occurs followed by the appropriate event handlers.

The following example uses this technique with a single user variable (named Contents). The page provides a text box and two buttons. The user can choose to save a string of text, and then restore it at a later time (see Figure 10-2). The event handlers save and restore this text from the Contents variable, without having any awareness of the fact that it is actually stored in viewstate every time the page processing is complete.

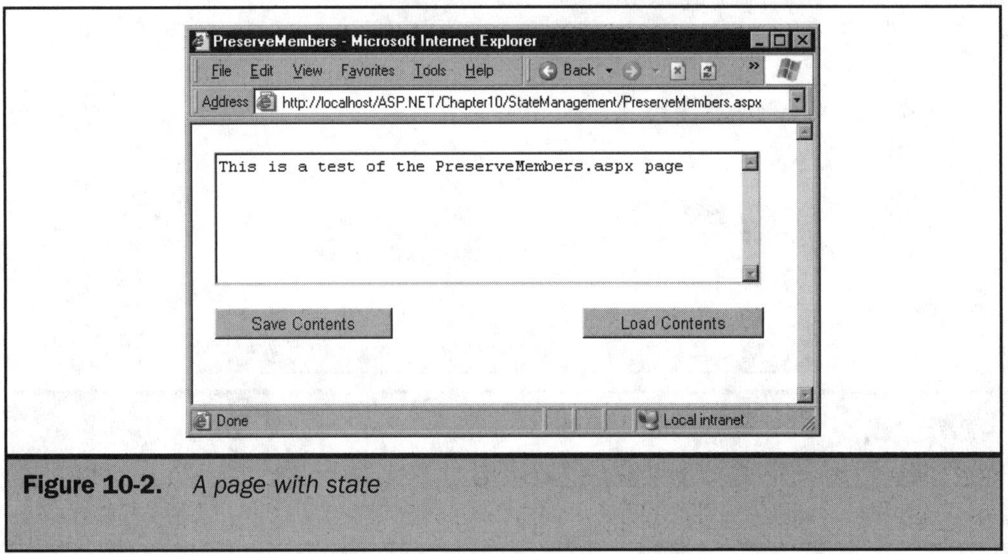


**Figure 10-2.** *A page with state*

```
Public Class PreserveMembers
  Inherits Page

    Protected txtContents As TextBox
    Protected WithEvents cmdSave As Button
    Protected WithEvents cmdLoad As Button

    ' A member variable that will be cleared with every postback.
    Private Contents As String

    Private Sub Page_Load(sender As Object, e As EventArgs) _
      Handles MyBase.Load
        If Me.IsPostBack = True Then
            ' Restore variables.
            Contents = CType(Me.ViewState("Text"), String)
        End If
    End Sub
```

```
    Private Sub Page_PreRender(sender As Object, _
      e As System.EventArgs) Handles MyBase.PreRender
        ' Persist variables.
        Me.ViewState("Text") = Contents
    End Sub

    Private Sub cmdSave_Click(sender As Object, e As EventArgs) _
      Handles cmdSave.Click
        ' Transfer contents of text box to member variable.
        Contents = txtValue.Text
        txtValue.Text = ""
    End Sub

    Private Sub cmdLoad_Click(sender As Object, e As EventArgs) _
      Handles cmdLoad.Click
        ' Restore contents of member variable to text box.
        txtValue.Text = Contents
    End Sub

End Class
```



The addition of the logic in the Load and PreRender events allows your code to work more or less as it would in a desktop scenario. You have to be careful when using this technique not to store needless amounts of information, as it enlarges the size of the final page output, and can slow down page transmission times. The disadvantage with hiding the low-level Internet reality is that you'll forget to respect it and design for it. (You should also refrain from combining methods and saving some viewstate variables at the PreRender stage and others in event handlers, as this is sure to confuse yourself and every other programmer involved.)

### Viewstate Cannot Be Stored in the Page.Unload Event Handler

The previous example reacted to the Page.PreRender event, which occurs just after page processing is complete and just before the page is rendered into HTML. This is an ideal place to store any leftover information that is required. You cannot perform a similar function in an event handler for the Page.Unload event. Though it will not cause an error, the information will not be stored, because the final HTML page output is already rendered.

## Transferring Information

One of the most significant limitations with viewstate is that it is tightly bound to a specific page. If the user navigates to another page, this information is lost. There are several solutions to this problem, and the best approach depends on your requirements. One common approach is to pass information using the query string. This approach is commonly found in search engines. For example, if you perform a search on the popular "Ask Jeeves" web site for organic gardening, you'll be redirected to a new URL that incorporates your search parameters as shown in the following illustration.

The query string is the portion of the URL after the question mark. In this case, it defines a single variable named ask, which contains the string "organic+gardening."

The advantage of the query string is that it is very lightweight and doesn't exert any kind of burden on the server. There are some limitations, however:

- Information is limited to simple strings, which must contain URL-legal characters.
- Information is clearly visible to the user and by anyone else who cares to eavesdrop on the Internet.
- The enterprising user might decide to modify the query string and supply new values, which your program won't expect and can't protect against.
- Many browsers impose a limit on the length of a URL (usually from 1 to 2K). For that reason, you can't place a large amount of information in the query string and still be assured of compatibility with most browsers.

Query string information is still a useful technique. It's particularly well suited to database applications where you present the user with a list of items that correspond to records in a database. The user can then select an item and be forwarded to a detailed information page. This page can receive the unique ID that identifies the record from the sending page, and then look it up in the database for more information. You'll notice this technique in e-commerce sites like Amazon.com.

To store information in the query string, you need to place it there yourself. Unfortunately, there is no collection-based way to do it. Typically, this means using a special HyperLink control, or a special Response.Redirect statement like the one shown here.

```
Response.Redirect("newpage.aspx?recordID=10")
```

Multiple parameters can be sent, as long as they are separated with an ampersand (&).

```
Response.Redirect("newpage.aspx?recordID=10&mode=full")
```

The receiving page has an easier time working with the query string. It can receive the values from the QueryString dictionary collection exposed by the built-in Request object.

```
Dim ID As String = Request.QueryString("recordID")
```

Note that information is always retrieved as a string, which can then be converted to another simple data type. Values in the QueryString collection are indexed by the variable name.



## A Query String Example

The next program presents a table of entries. When the user chooses an item by clicking on the appropriate hyperlink, the user is forwarded to a new page. This page displays the received ID number, which provides a quick and simple query string test. In a sophisticated application, you would want to combine some of the data control features that are described later in this book in the ADO.NET chapters.

The first page provides a list of items, a checkbox, and submission button (see Figure 10-3).

```
Public Class QueryStringSender
  Inherits Page

    Protected lstItems As ListBox
    Protected chkDetails As CheckBox
    Protected WithEvents cmdGo As Button

    Private Sub Page_Load(sender As Object, e As EventArgs) _
      Handles MyBase.Load
        ' Add sample values.
        lstItems.Items.Add("Econo Sofa")
        lstItems.Items.Add("Supreme Leather Drapery")
        lstItems.Items.Add("Threadbare Carpet")
        lstItems.Items.Add("Antique Lamp")
        lstItems.Items.Add("Retro-Finish Jacuzzi")
    End Sub

    Private Sub cmdGo_Click(sender As Object, e As EventArgs) _
```

```
        Handles cmdGo.Click
          If lstItems.SelectedIndex = -1 Then
              lblError.Text = "You must select an item."
          Else
              ' Forward the user to the information page.
              Dim String As String = "QueryStringRecipient.aspx?"
              Url &= "Item=" & lstItems.SelectedItem.Text & "&"
              Url &= "Mode=" & chkDetails.Checked.ToString()
              Response.Redirect(Url)
          End If
      End Sub

End Class
```

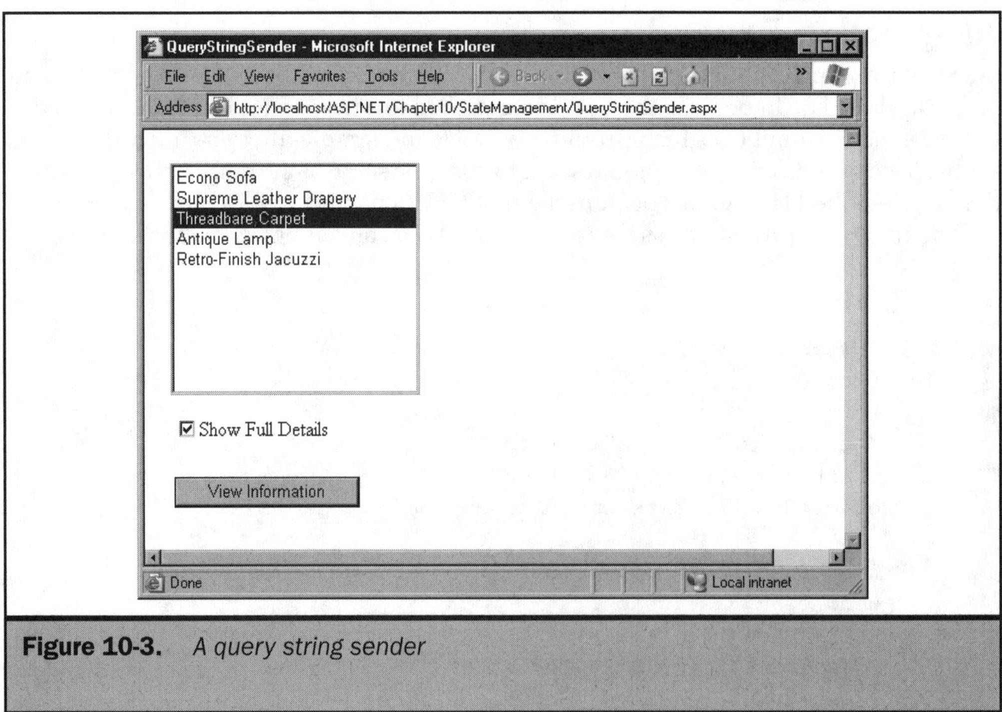


**Figure 10-3.** *A query string sender*

One interesting aspect of this example is that it places information in the query string that really isn't valid, namely the space that appears in the item name. When you run the application, you'll notice that ASP.NET encodes the string for you automatically, converting spaces to the valid %20 equivalent escape sequence. The recipient page reads the original values from the QueryString collection without any trouble. The recipient page is shown in Figure 10-4.

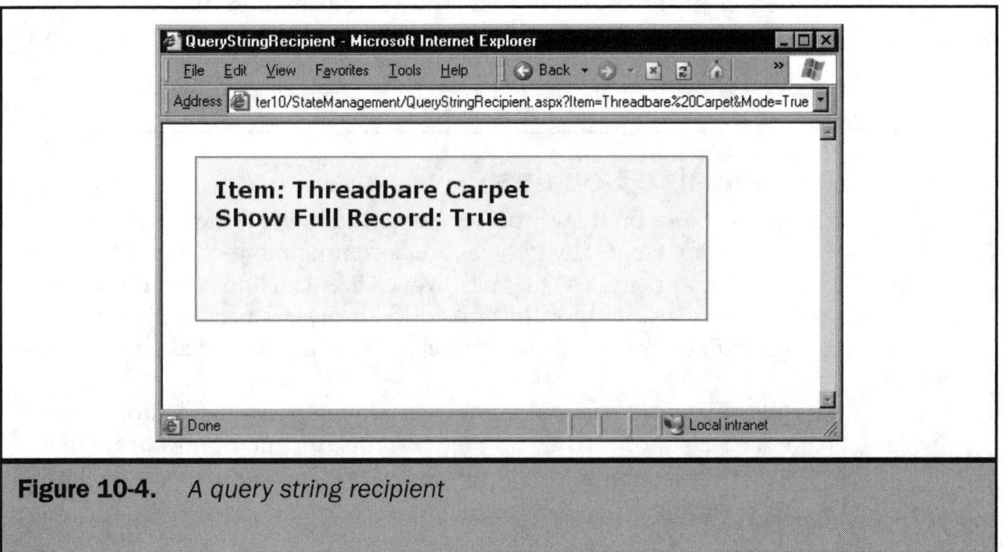


**Figure 10-4.** *A query string recipient*

```
Public Class QueryStringRecipient
  Inherits Page

    Protected lblInfo As Label

    Private Sub Page_Load(sender As Object, e As EventArgs) _
      Handles MyBase.Load
        lblInfo.Text = "Item: " & Request.QueryString("Item")
        lblInfo.Text &= "<br>Show Full Record: "
        lblInfo.Text &= Request.QueryString("Mode")
    End Sub

End Class
```



## Custom Cookies

Custom cookies provide another way that you can store information for later use. Cookies are small files that are created on the client's hard drive (or, if they are temporary, in the Internet browser's memory). One advantage of cookies is that they work transparently without the user being aware that information needs to be stored. They also can be easily used by any page in your application, and even retained in between visits, allowing for truly long-term storage. They suffer from some of the same drawbacks that affect query strings. Namely, they are limited to simple string information, and they are easily accessible and readable if the user finds and opens the corresponding file. They are a poor choice for complex or private information or large amounts of data.

### Some Users Disable Cookies

Some users disable cookies on their browsers, potentially breaking a web application that requires them. Generally, cookies are becoming more widely adopted these days because so many sites use them. However, they can limit your potential audience, and they aren't suited for the embedded browsers used with mobile devices. Also, a user might manually delete a cookie file that is stored on their hard drive.

A good rule of thumb is to use cookies to retain preference-related information, such as a customer's last order. You can then use this information to provide a richer experience, but you shouldn't require the use of cookies or assume that they will always be present.

Before you can use cookies, you should import the System.Net namespace so you can easily work with the appropriate types.

```
Imports System.Net
```

Cookies are fairly easy to use. Both the Request and Response objects (which are provided through Page properties) provide a Cookies collection. The important trick to remember is that you retrieve cookies from the Request object, and you set cookies using the Response object.

To set a cookie, just create a new System.Net.HttpCookie object. You can then fill it with string information (using the familiar dictionary pattern) and attach it to the current web response.

```
' Create the cookie object.
Cookie = New HttpCookie("Preferences")

' Set a value in it.
Cookie("LanguagePref") = "English"
```

```
' Add it to the current web response.
Response.Cookies.Add(Cookie)
```

A cookie added in this way will persist until the user closes the browser and will be sent with every request. To create a longer-lived cookie, you can set an expiration date.

```
' This cookie lives for 1 year.
Cookie.Expires = DateTime.Now.AddYears(1)
```

Cookies are retrieved by cookie name using the Request.Cookies collection.

```
Dim Cookie As HttpCookie = Request.Cookies("Preferences")
Dim Language As String

' Check to see if a cookie was found with this name.
' This is a good precaution to take,
' as the user could disable cookies.
If Not Cookie Is Nothing Then
    Language = Cookie("LanguagePref")
End If
```



## A Cookie Example

The next example shows a typical use of cookies to store a customer name. If the name is found, a welcome message is displayed (see Figure 10-5).

```
Imports System.Net

Public Class CookieExample
  Inherits Page

    Protected lblWelcome As Label
    Protected txtName As TextBox
    Protected WithEvents cmdStore As Button

    Private Sub Page_Load(sender As Object, e As EventArgs) _
      Handles MyBase.Load
        Dim Cookie As HttpCookie = Request.Cookies("Preferences")
        If Cookie Is Nothing Then
            lblWelcome.Text = "<b>Unknown Customer</b>"
```

```
        Else
            lblWelcome.Text = "<b>Cookie Found.</b><br><br>"
            lblWelcome.Text &= "Welcome, " & Cookie("Name")
        End If
    End Sub

    Private Sub cmdStore_Click(sender As Object, e As EventArgs) _
      Handles cmdStore.Click
        Dim Cookie As HttpCookie = Request.Cookies("Preferences")
        If Cookie Is Nothing Then
            Cookie = New HttpCookie("Preferences")
        End If

        Cookie("Name") = txtName.Text
        Cookie.Expires = DateTime.Now.AddYears(1)
        Response.Cookies.Add(Cookie)

        lblWelcome.Text = "<b>Cookie Created.</b><br><br>"
        lblWelcome.Text &= "New Customer: " & Cookie("Name")
    End Sub

End Class
```

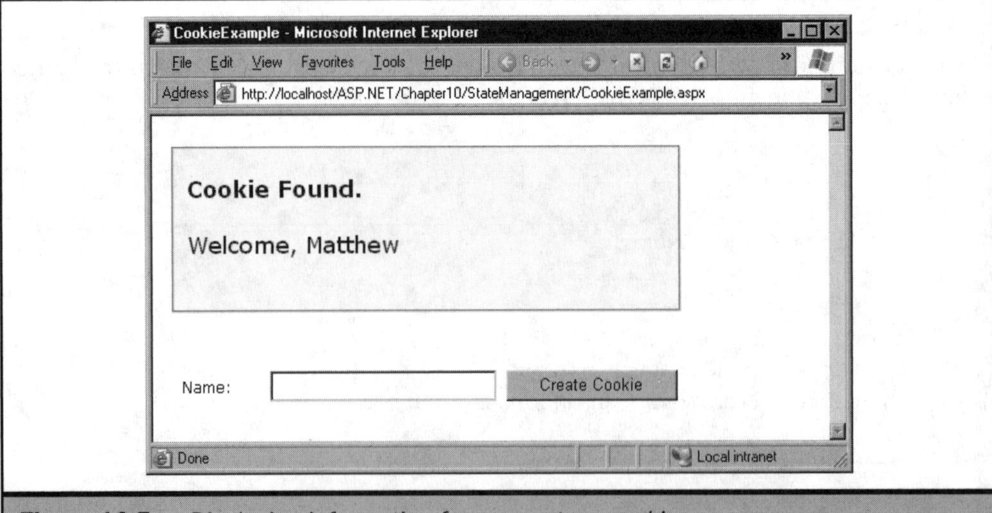


**Figure 10-5.** *Displaying information from a custom cookie*

# Session State

There comes a point in the life of most applications when they begin to have more sophisticated storage requirements. An application might need to store and access complex information such as DataSets or custom data objects, which can't be easily persisted to a cookie or sent through a query string. Or the application might have stringent security requirements that prevent it from storing the client's information in viewstate or a custom cookie. In these situations, you can use ASP.NET's built-in session state facility.

Session state management is one of ASP.NET's premiere features. It allows you to store any type of data in memory on the server. The information is protected, because it is never transmitted to the client, and it is uniquely bound to a specific session. Every client that accesses the application has a different session and a distinct collection of information.



## Session Tracking

ASP.NET tracks each session using a unique 120-bit identifier. ASP.NET uses a special algorithm to generate this value, guaranteeing that it is unique and random, so a malicious user can't reverse engineer or "guess" what session ID a given client will be using. This special ID is the only piece of information that is transmitted between the web server and the client. When the client presents the session ID, ASP.NET looks up the corresponding session, retrieves the serialized data from the state server, converts it to live objects, and places these objects into a special collection so they can be accessed in code. This process takes place automatically.

In order for this system to work, the client must present the appropriate session ID with each request. There are two ways this can be accomplished:

- The session ID can be transmitted in a special cookie (named "ASP.NET_SessionId"), which ASP.NET creates automatically when the session collection is used. This is the default and the system that was used with earlier versions of ASP.
- The session ID can be transmitted in a specially modified (or "munged") URL. This is a new feature in ASP.NET that allows you to create applications that use session state with clients that don't support cookies.

## Using Session State

You can interact with session state using the System.Web.SessionState.HttpSessionState class, which is provided in an ASP.NET web page as the built-in Session object. The syntax for adding items to the collection and retrieving them is basically the same as adding items to a page's viewstate. Table 10-1 shows the HttpSessionState members and their descriptions.

For example, you might store a DataSet in session memory like this:

```
Session("dsInfo") = dsInfo
```

### Session State Doesn't Come for Free

Session state solves many of the problems associated with other forms of state management. However, it requires that the server store additional information. This extra memory requirement, even if it is minute, can quickly grow to performance-destroying levels as hundreds or thousands of clients access the site.

In other words, any use of session state must be carefully thought out. A careless use of session state is the number one cause of applications that are difficult to scale to large numbers of clients (and become victims of their own success). Often, a better approach is to use caching, as described later in this book.

You can then retrieve it with an appropriate conversion operation:

```
dsInfo = CType(Session("dsInfo"), DataSet)
```

Session state is global to your entire application for the current user. Session state can be lost in several ways:

- If the user closes and restarts the browser.
- If the session times out due to inactivity. More information about session timeout can be found in the "Session State Configuration" section.
- If the programmer ends the session in code.
- If the user accesses the same page through a different browser window, although the session will still exist if a web page is accessed through the original browser window. Different browsers differ on how they handle this situation.

| Member | Description |
|---|---|
| Count | The number of items in the current session collection. |
| IsCookieless | Identifies whether this session is tracked with a cookie, or using modified URLs. |
| IsNewSession | Identifies whether this session was just created for the current request. If there is currently no information in session state, ASP.NET won't bother to track the session or create a session cookie. Instead, the session will be recreated with every request. |

**Table 10-1.** *HttpSessionState Members*

| Member | Description |
|---|---|
| Mode | Provides an enumerated value that explains how ASP.NET stores session state information. This storage mode is determined based on the web.config configuration settings discussed later in this chapter. |
| SessionID | Provides a string with the unique session identifier for the current client. |
| StaticObjects | Provides a collection of read-only session items that were declared by <object runat=server> tags in the global.asax. Generally, this technique is not used, and is a holdover from ASP programming that is included for backward compatibility. |
| Timeout | The current number of minutes that must elapse before the current session will be abandoned, provided no more requests are received from the client. This value can be changed programmatically, giving you the chance to make the session collection longer term when required for more important operations. |
| Abandon() | Cancels the current session immediately and releases all the memory it occupied. This is a useful technique in a logoff page to ensure that server memory is reclaimed as quickly as possible. |
| Clear() | Removes all the session items, but does not change the current session identifier. |

**Table 10-1.** *HttpSessionState Members (continued)*



# A Session State Example

The next example uses session state to store several Furniture data objects. The data object combines a few related variables, and uses a special constructor so that it can be created and initialized in one easy line. Rather than use full property procedures, the class takes a shortcut and uses public member variables.

```
Public Class Furniture

    Public Name As String
```

```
    Public Description As String
    Public Cost As Decimal

    Public Sub New(Name As String, Description As String, _
      Cost As Decimal)
        Me.Name = Name
        Me.Description = Description
        Me.Cost = Cost
    End Sub

End Class
```

Three Furniture objects are created the first time the page is loaded, and they are stored in session state. The user can then choose from a list of furniture piece names. When a selection is made, the corresponding object will be retrieved, and its information will be displayed (see Figure 10-6).

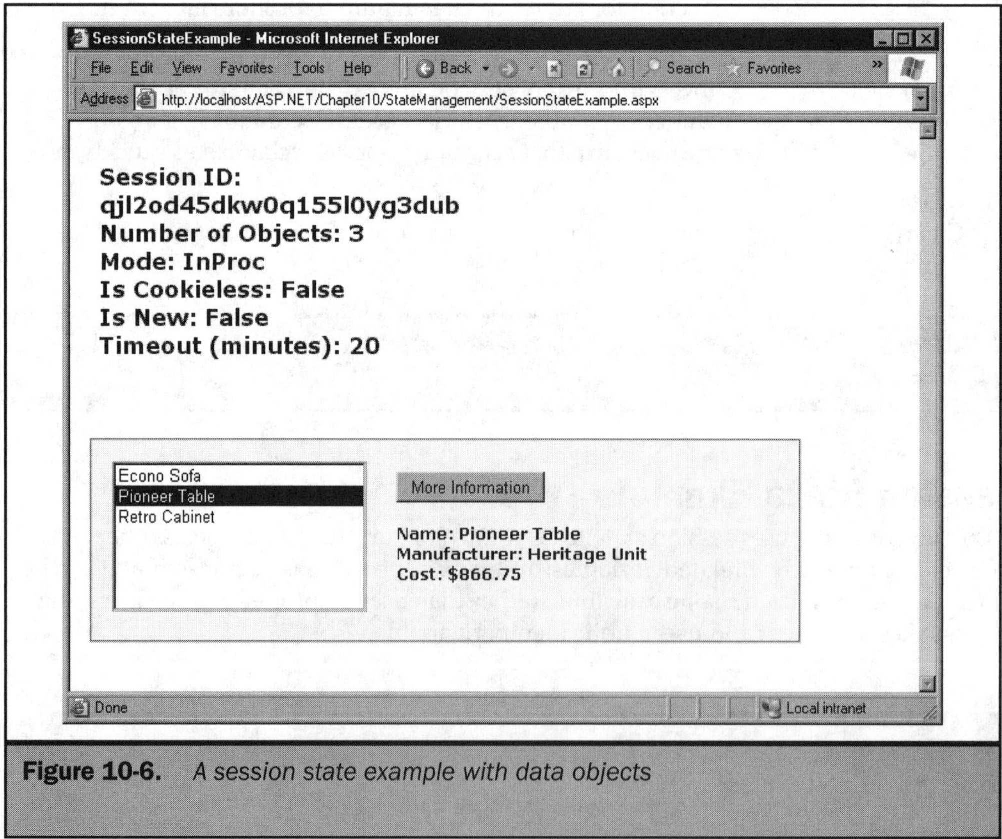


**Figure 10-6.** *A session state example with data objects*

```
Public Class SessionStateExample
  Inherits Page

    Protected cmdMoreInfo As Button
    Protected lblRecord As Label
    Protected lblSession As Label
    Protected lstItems As ListBox

    Private Sub Page_Load(sender As Object, e As EventArgs) _
      Handles MyBase.Load

        If Me.IsPostBack = False Then
            ' Create Furniture objects.
            Dim Piece1 As New Furniture("Econo Sofa", _
                                        "Acme Inc.", 74.99)
            Dim Piece2 As New Furniture("Pioneer Table", _
                                        "Heritage Unit", 866.75)
            Dim Piece3 As New Furniture("Retro Cabinet", _
                                        "Sixties Ltd.", 300.11)

            ' Add objects to session state.
            Session("Furniture1") = Piece1
            Session("Furniture2") = Piece2
            Session("Furniture3") = Piece3

            ' Add rows to list control.
            lstItems.Items.Clear()
            lstItems.Items.Add(Piece1.Name)
            lstItems.Items.Add(Piece2.Name)
            lstItems.Items.Add(Piece3.Name)
        End If

        ' Display some basic information about the session.
        ' This is useful for testing configuration settings.
        lblSession.Text = "Session ID: " & Session.SessionID
        lblSession.Text &= "<br>Number of Objects: "
        lblSession.Text &= Session.Count.ToString()
        lblSession.Text &= "<br>Mode: " & Session.Mode.ToString()
        lblSession.Text &= "<br>Is Cookieless: "
        lblSession.Text &= Session.IsCookieless.ToString()
        lblSession.Text &= "<br>Is New: "
        lblSession.Text &= Session.IsNewSession.ToString()
        lblSession.Text &= "<br>Timeout (minutes): "
        lblSession.Text &= Session.Timeout.ToString()
```

## Making Session State Scalable

Most web developers face a confounding conundrum. They can use session state and ensure excellent performance for a small set of users, but potentially poor scalability for large numbers as the memory cost begins to wear on the server. Alternatively, they can use a database to store temporary session information. This ensures scalability, but slow performance all around as the database must be queried for almost every page request.

There is a compromise, and it involves caching. The basic approach is to create a temporary database record with session information, and store its unique ID in session state. This ensures that the in-memory session information is always minimal, but your web page code can easily find the corresponding session record. To reduce the number of database queries, the session information is also added to the cache (indexed under the session identifier). On subsequent requests, your code can check first in the cache, and use database lookup as a last resort. This process becomes even more transparent if you create a custom component that provides the session information and performs the required cache lookup for you.

For more information, read about custom components in Chapter 21 and caching in Chapter 23.

```
End Sub

Private Sub cmdMoreInfo_Click(sender As Object, _
  e As EventArgs) Handles cmdMoreInfo.Click

    If lstItems.SelectedIndex = -1 Then
        lblRecord.Text = "No item selected."
    Else
        ' Construct the right key name based on the index.
        Dim Key As String
        Key = "Furniture" & _
              (lstItems.SelectedIndex + 1).ToString()

        ' Retrieve the object and display its information.
        Dim Piece As Furniture = CType(Session(Key), Furniture)
        lblRecord.Text = "Name: " & Piece.Name
        lblRecord.Text &= "<br>Manufacturer: "
        lblRecord.Text &= & Piece.Description
```

```
            lblRecord.Text &= "<br>Cost: $" & Piece.Cost.ToString()
        End If

    End Sub

End Class
```

# Session State Configuration

Session state is configured through the web.config file for your current application (which is found in the same virtual directory as the .aspx web page files). The configuration file allows you to set advanced options such as the timeout and the session state mode. If you are creating your web application in Visual Studio .NET, your project will include an automatically generated web.config file.

A typical web.config file is shown below. The settings that don't relate to session state have been omitted.

```
<?xml version="1.0" encoding="utf-8" ?>
<configuration>
    <system.web>
        <!-- Other settings omitted. -->
        <sessionState
            mode="InProc"
            stateConnectionString="tcpip=127.0.0.1:42424"
            sqlConnectionString="data source=127.0.0.1;user id=sa"
            cookieless="false"
            timeout="20"
        />
    </system.web>
</configuration>
```

In total, there are five settings related to session state.

## Cookieless

You can set the cookieless setting to true or false (the default).

```
<sessionState
    cookieless="false"
/>
```

When set to true, the session ID will automatically be inserted into the URL. When ASP.NET receives a request, it will remove the ID, retrieve the session collection, and forward the request to the appropriate directory. A munged URL is shown here:

ASP.NET is even intelligent enough to automatically convert relative links in the web page, adding the special session ID into the URL automatically in the final HTML page that is sent to the client.

For example, consider the following project (included with the samples in the CookielessSessions directory), which contains two pages and uses cookieless mode. The first page (shown in Figure 10-7) contains a hyperlink control and a button. The HyperLink's NavigateUrl property is set to Cookieless2.aspx. When ASP.NET renders this page, it transforms the hyperlink control to an HTML anchor tag (as it always does). However, the anchor has been updated to include the munged URL, and thereby preserve session state.

```
<a id="HyperLink1"
   href="/McGrawHill/State/Cookieless/(ddugkx55qmzqm355bzshxz55)/
   Cookieless2.aspx">HyperLink
</a>
```

Even manual redirects in the code are successfully intercepted and modified to preserve session information. For example, the button uses Response.Redirect code to forward the user to the Cookieless2.aspx page. The following relative redirect statement preserves the munged URL, with no extra steps required.

```
Private Sub cmdLink_Click(sender As Object, As EventArgs) _
  Handles cmdLink.Click
    Response.Redirect("Cookieless2.aspx")
End Sub
```

The only real limitation of the cookieless state is that you cannot use absolute links, because ASP.NET will not insert the session ID into them. For example, if you use the third command button, which uses the code shown below, the current session will be abandoned, and the Cookieless2.aspx page will find an empty session collection (see Figure 10-8).

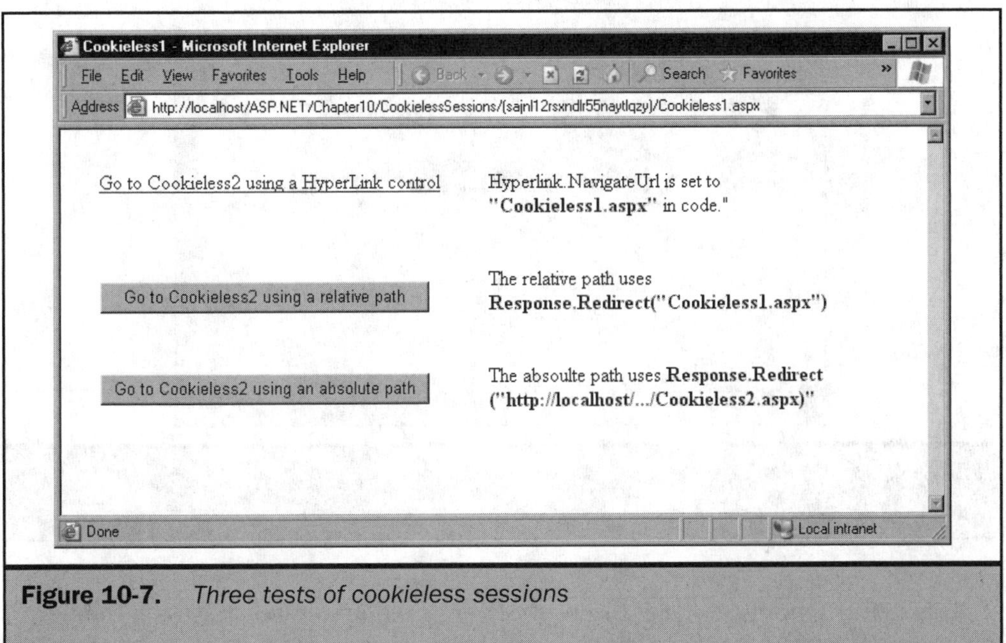


**Figure 10-7.** *Three tests of cookieless sessions*

```
Private Sub cmdLinkAbsolute_Click(sender As Object, e As EventArgs) _
  Handles cmdLinkAbsolute.Click
    Dim Url As String
    Url = "http://localhost/ASP.NET/Chapter10/CookielessSessions/"
    Url &= "Cookieless2.aspx"
    Response.Redirect(Url)
End Sub
```

## Timeout

Another important session state setting in the web.config file is the timeout. This specifies the number of minutes that ASP.NET will wait, without receiving a request, before it abandons the session.

```
<sessionState
    timeout="20"
/>
```

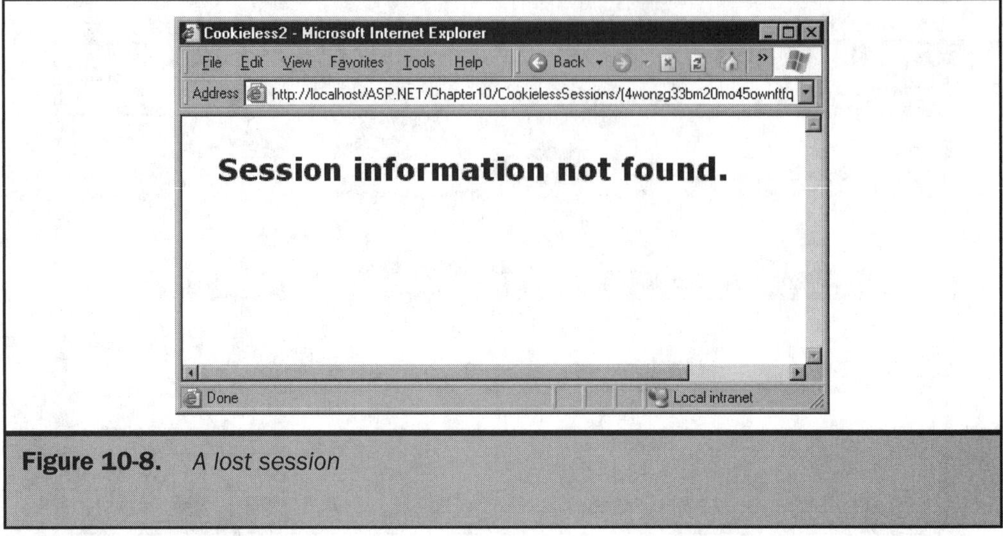


**Figure 10-8.** *A lost session*

This setting represents one of the most important compromises of session state. A difference of minutes can have a dramatic effect on your server's load and your application's performance. Ideally, you will choose a timeframe that is short enough to allow the server to reclaim valuable memory after a client stops using the application, but long enough to allow a client to pause and continue a session without losing it.

## Timeout Can Be Controlled in Code

Remember, you can also programmatically change the session timeout in code. For example, if you know a session contains an unusually large amount of information, you may need to limit the amount of time the session can be stored. You would then warn the user and change the timeout property.

```
Session.Timeout = 10
```

It's also a good practice to provide other session-friendly features in your application. For example, you should always have a logout button that automatically cancels a session using the Session.Abandon method. You might also want to use database storage or caching when large amounts of information are being worked with. You can identify the database record where this temporary information is stored by storing a record ID in session state.

# Mode

The other session state settings allow you to configure special session state services.

```
<sessionState
    mode="InProc"
    stateConnectionString="tcpip=127.0.0.1:42424"
    sqlConnectionString="data source=127.0.0.1;user id=sa;password="
/>
```



## InProc

For the default mode (InProc), the other two settings have no effect, and are just included as place holders to show you the appropriate format. InProc is similar to the way session state was stored in previous versions of ASP. It instructs information to be stored in the same process as the ASP.NET worker threads, providing the best performance, but the least durability. If you restart your server, the state information will be lost.

Generally, InProc is the best option for most web sites. The one most notable exception is in a web farm scenario. In order to allow session state to be shared between servers, you must use the out-of-process or SQL Server-based session state service.

## Off

This setting disables session state management for every page in the application. This can provide a slight performance improvement for web sites that are not using session state.

## StateServer

With this setting, ASP.NET will use a separate Windows Service for state management. This service runs on the same web server, but it is outside the main ASP.NET process, giving it a basic level of protection if the ASP.NET process needs to be restarted. The cost is the increased time delay imposed when state information is transferred between two processes. If you frequently access and change state information, this can make for a fairly unwelcome slowdown.

When using the StateServer setting, you need to specify a value for the state-ConnectionString setting. This string identifies the TCP/IP address of the computer that is running the StateServer service and its port (which is defined by ASP.NET and does not usually need to be changed). This allows you to host the StateServer on another computer. If you don't change this setting, the local server will be used (set as address 127.0.0.1).

Of course, before your application can use the service, you need to start it. The easiest way to do this is to use the Microsoft Management Console. Select Start | Programs | Administrative Tools | Computer Management (you can also access the

Administrative Tools group through the Control Panel). Then select the Services And Applications | Services node. Find the service called ASP.NET State Service in the list (see Figure 10-9).

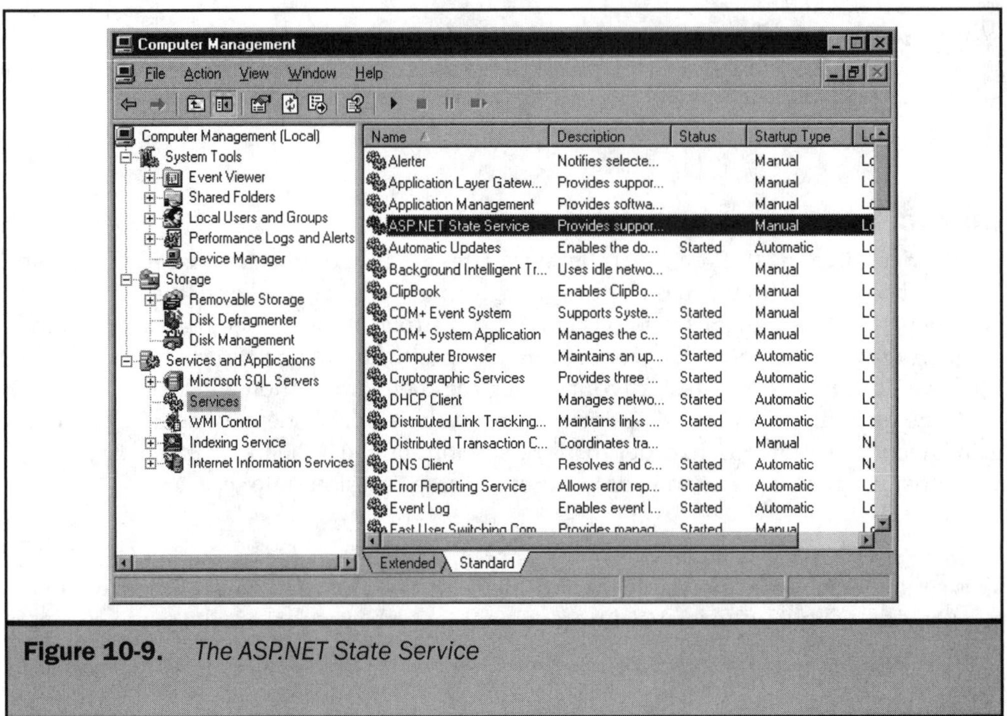


**Figure 10-9.** *The ASP.NET State Service*

Once you find the service in the list, you can manually start and stop it by right-clicking on it.

Generally, you will want to configure Windows to automatically start the service. Right-click on it, select Properties, and modify the Startup type setting to Automatic (see Figure 10-10).

## SqlServer

This setting instructs ASP.NET to use an SQL Server database to store session information, as identified by the sqlConnectionString attribute. This is the most resilient state store, but also the slowest by far. To use this method of state management, you will need to have a server with SQL Server installed.

When setting the sqlConnectionString, you follow the same sort of pattern you use with ADO.NET data access. Generally, you will need to specify a data source (the server address), and a user ID and password, unless you are using SQL integrated security.

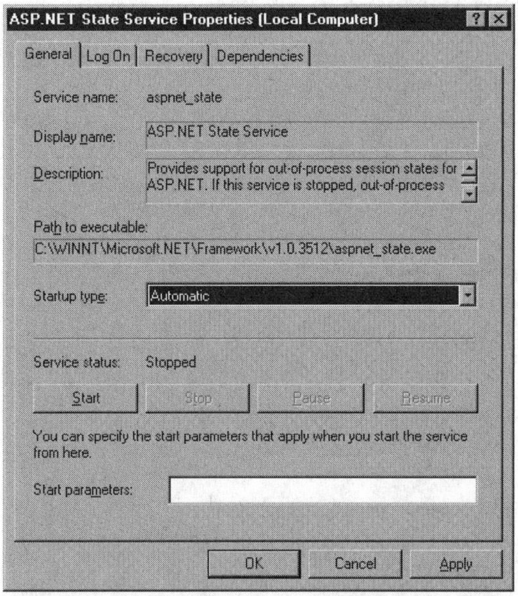

**Figure 10-10.** *Service Properties*



In addition, you need to install the special stored procedures and temporary session databases. These stored procedures take care of storing and retrieving the session information. ASP.NET includes a Transact-SQL script for this purpose called InstallSqlState.sql. It's found in the \WINNT\Microsoft.NET\Framework\[version] directory. You can run this script using an SQL Server utility like OSQL.exe or Query Analyzer. It only needs to be performed once.

## Application State

Application state is the last type of state management that we will consider. It stores global objects that can be accessed by any client. Application state is based on the System.Web.HttpApplicationState class, which is provided in the web page through the Application object.

Application state is very similar to session state. It can store the same type of objects, retain information on the server, and use the same dictionary-based syntax. A common example of the application state is a global counter that tracks how many times an operation has been performed by all of the web application's clients.

For example, you could create a global.asax event handler that tracks how many sessions have been created or how many requests have been received into the application. Or you can use similar logic in the Page.Load event handler to track how many times a given page has been requested by various clients.

```
Private Sub Page_Load(sender As Object, e As EventArgs) _
  Handles MyBase.Load

    Dim Count As Integer = CType(Application("HitCounter", Integer)
    Count += 1
    Application("HitCounter") = Count
    lblCounter.Text = Count.ToString()

End Sub
```

Once again, application state items are stored as objects, so it's always a good idea to convert them manually. Items in application state never time out. They last until the application or server is restarted.

Application state is not often used because it is generally inefficient. In the previous example, the counter would probably not keep an accurate count, particularly in times of heavy traffic. For example, if two clients requested the page at the same time, you could have a sequence of events like this:

1. User A retrieves the current count (432).
2. User B retrieves the current count (432).
3. User A sets the current count to 433.
4. User B sets the current count to 433.

In other words, one request is lost because two clients access the counter at the same time. To prevent this problem, you need to use the Lock() and Unlock() methods, which explicitly allow only one client to access the value at a time.

```
Private Sub Page_Load(sender As Object, e As EventArgs) _
  Handles MyBase.Load

    ' Acquire exclusive access.
    Application.Lock()

    Dim Count As Integer = CType(Application("HitCounter", Integer)
    Count += 1
```

```
    Application("HitCounter") = Count

    ' Release exclusive access.
    Application.Unlock()

    lblCounter.Text = Count.ToString()

End Sub
```



Unfortunately, all other clients requesting the page will now be stalled until the Application collection is released. This can drastically reduce performance. Generally, frequently modified values are poor candidates for application state. In fact, application state is rarely used in the .NET world because its two most common uses have been replaced by easier, more efficient methods:

- In the past, application state was used to store application-wide constants, such as a database connection string. As you saw in Chapter 5, this type of constant can now be stored in the web.config file, which is generally more flexible because you can change it easily without needing to hunt through web page code.
- Application state has also been used to store frequently required information that is time-consuming to create, such as a full product catalog that requires a database lookup. However, using application state to store this kind of information raises all sorts of problems about how to check if the data is valid and replace it when needed. It can also hamper performance if the product catalog is too large. Chapter 23 introduces a similar but much more sensible approach—storing frequently used information in a data cache. In fact, most uses of application state can be replaced more efficiently with caching.

The Complete Reference

# Chapter 11

## Tracing, Logging, and Error Handling

No software can run free from error, and ASP.NET applications are no exception. Sooner or later your code will be interrupted by a programming mistake, invalid data, unexpected circumstances, or even hardware failure. Novice programmers spend sleepless nights worrying about errors. Professional developers recognize that bugs are an inherent part of software applications and code defensively, testing assumptions, logging problems, and writing error-handling code to deal with the unexpected.

In this chapter, you'll learn the error handling and debugging practices that can defend your ASP.NET applications against common errors, track user problems, and help you solve mysterious issues. Some of the error-handling topics we'll discuss include:

- Using VB .NET's new structured exception handling to deal with application errors
- Using logs to keep a record of unrecoverable errors
- Configuring custom web pages for common HTTP errors
- Using page tracing to see diagnostic information about ASP.NET pages

## Common Errors

Errors can occur in a variety of situations. Some of the most common causes of errors include attempts to divide by zero (usually caused by invalid input or missing information) and failed attempts to connect to a limited resource such as a file or a database (which occur when the file doesn't exist, the database connection times out, or the code has insufficient security credentials).

Another infamous type of error is the null reference exception, which usually occurs when a program attempts to use an uninitialized object. As a .NET programmer, you'll quickly learn to recognize and resolve this common, but annoying mistake. The following code example shows the problem in action:

```
Dim conOne As OleDbConnection
' The next line will fail and generate a null reference exception.
' You cannot modify a property (or use a method) of an object that
' doesn't exist!
conOne.ConnectionString = ConnectionString

Dim conTwo As New OleDbConnection()
' This works, because the object has been initialized with the
' New keyword.
conTwo.ConnectionString = ConnectionString
```

When an error occurs in your code, VB .NET checks to see if there are any active error handlers in the current scope. If the error occurs inside a function, VB .NET searches for local error handlers, and then checks for any active error handlers in the calling code. If no error handlers are found, the current procedure is aborted, and an error page is displayed in the browser. Depending on whether the request came from the local computer or a remote client, the error page may show a detailed description (as shown in Figure 11-1) or a generic message. We'll explore this topic a little later in the "Error Pages" section.

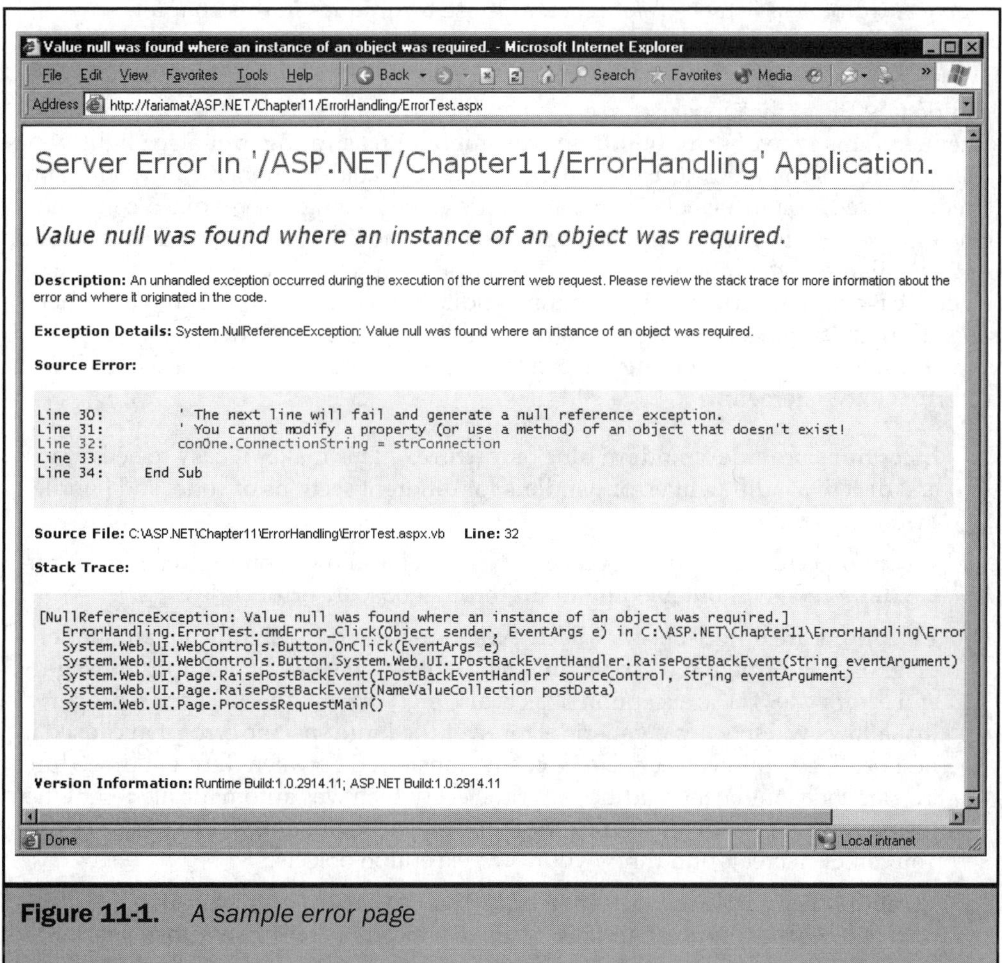


**Figure 11-1.** *A sample error page*

Even if an error is the result of invalid input or the failure of a third-party component, an error page can shatter the professional appearance of any application. The application users end up feeling that the application is unstable, insecure, or of poor quality—and they are at least partially correct.

If an ASP.NET application is carefully designed and constructed, an error page will almost never appear. Errors may still occur due to unforeseen circumstances, but they will be caught in the code and identified. If the error is a critical one that the application cannot solve on its own, it will report a more useful (and user-friendly) page of information that might include a link to a support email or phone number where the customer can receive additional assistance. We'll look at those techniques in this chapter.

## On Error Go Home

Traditional ASP applications use an error-handling system based on the On Error Goto statement. This type of error handling was not only frustrating, but also slightly embarrassing for many ASP.NET developers. It used an old-fashioned Goto command to redirect execution to a labeled portion of code, encouraging disorganized code and unnecessary errors. In order to support backward compatibility, the On Error Goto command is still available in the modern ASP.NET environment. However, you'll probably never use it again, as structured exception handling, a technique found in most other programming languages for years, finally makes its debut in ASP.NET.

Structured exception handling offers a long list of improvements over the traditional On Error Goto statement:

**Exceptions provide a modern block structure.** This makes it easy to activate and deactivate different error handlers for different sections of code, and handle their errors individually.

**Exceptions are caught based on their type.** This allows you to streamline error-handling code without needing to sift through obscure error codes.

**Exceptions are object-based.** Each exception provides a significant amount of diagnostic information wrapped into a neat object, instead of a simple message and error code. These exception objects also support an InnerException property that allows you to wrap a generic error over the more specific error that caused it. Best of all, exception objects can be easily transferred between different procedures in your code, unlike the traditional Err object (which was automatically reset when the point of execution moved to another procedure or another error occurred). You can even create and throw your own exception objects.

**Exception handlers are multi-layered.** You can easily layer exception handlers on top of other exception handlers, some of which may only check for a specialized set of errors.

**Exceptions are a generic part of the .NET framework.** That means they are completely cross-language compatible. Thus, a .NET component written in C# can throw an exception that you can catch in a web page written in Visual Basic.

## The .NET Exception Object

Every exception object derives from the base class System.Exception, which includes some essential functionality. Table 11-1 lists its most important members.

| Member | Description |
|---|---|
| HelpLink | A link to a help document, which can be a relative or fully qualified URL or URN (file:///C:/ACME/MyApp/help.html#Err42). The .NET framework does not use this property intrinsically, but you can set it in your custom exceptions if you want to use it in your web page code. |
| InnerException | A nested exception. For example, a method might catch a simple file IO error, and create a higher-level "operation failed" error. The details about the original error could be retained in the InnerException property of the higher-level error. |
| Message | Contains a text description with a significant amount of information describing the problem. |
| Source | The name of the assembly where the error occurred. |
| StackTrace | A string that contains a list of all the current method calls on the stack, in order of most to least recent. This is useful for determining where the problem occurred. |
| TargetSite | A reflection object (an instance of the System.Reflection.MethodBase class) that provides some information about the method where the error occurred. This information includes generic method details like the procedure name and the data types for its parameter and return value. It does not contain any information about the actual parameter values that were used when the problem occurred. |
| GetBaseException() | This method is useful for nested exceptions that may have more than one layer. It retrieves the original (deepest nested) exception by moving to the base of the InnerException chain. |

**Table 11-1.** *Exception Properties*

Figure 11-2 shows how the InnerException property works. In this case, a FileNotFoundException led to a NullReferenceException, which led to a custom UpdateFailedException. The code returns an UpdateFailedException that references the NullReferenceException, which references the original FileNotFoundException.

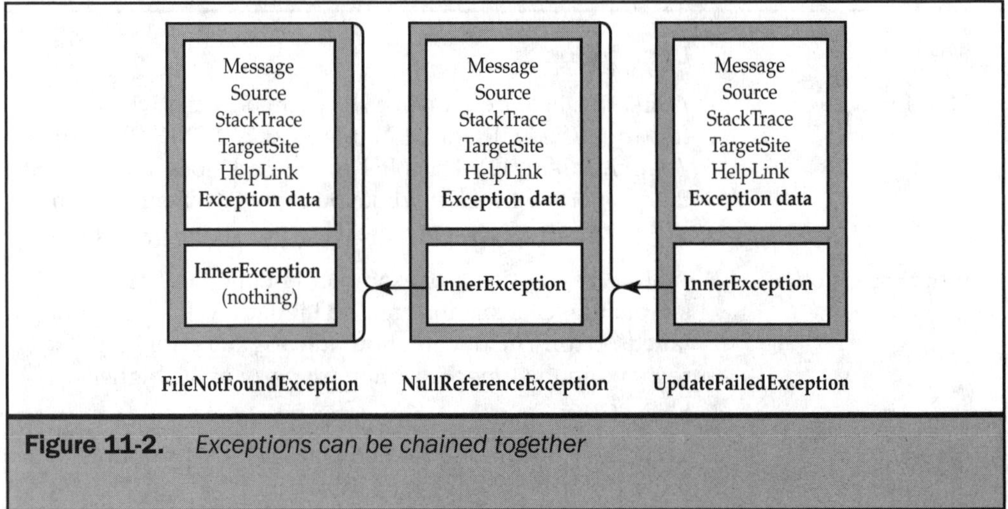


**Figure 11-2.** *Exceptions can be chained together*

## Use the Exception Chain

The InnerException property is an extremely useful tool for component-based programming. Generally, it's not much help if a component reports a low-level problem like a null-reference or a divide-by-zero error. Instead, it needs to communicate a more detailed message about which operation failed, and what input may have been invalid. The calling code can then often correct the problem and retry the operation.

On the other hand, sometimes you are debugging a bug that lurks deep inside the component itself. In this case, you need to know precisely what caused the error—you don't want to replace it with a higher-level exception that could obscure the root problem. Using an exception chain handles both these scenarios: you receive as many linked exception objects as needed, which can specify information from the least to most specific error condition.

# Exception Flavors

When you catch an exception in an ASP.NET, it won't be an instance of the generic System.Exception class. Instead, it will be an object that represents a specific type of error. This object will be based on one of the many classes that inherit from

System.Exception. These include diverse classes like DivideByZeroException, ArithmeticException, System.IO.IOException, System.Security.SecurityException, and many more. Some of these classes provide additional details about the error in additional properties.

Visual Studio .NET provides a useful tool to browse through the exceptions in the .NET class library. Simply select Debug | Exceptions from the menu (you'll need to have a project open in order for this work). The Exceptions window will appear with exceptions organized in a hierarchical tree control, grouped by namespace (see Figure 11-3).

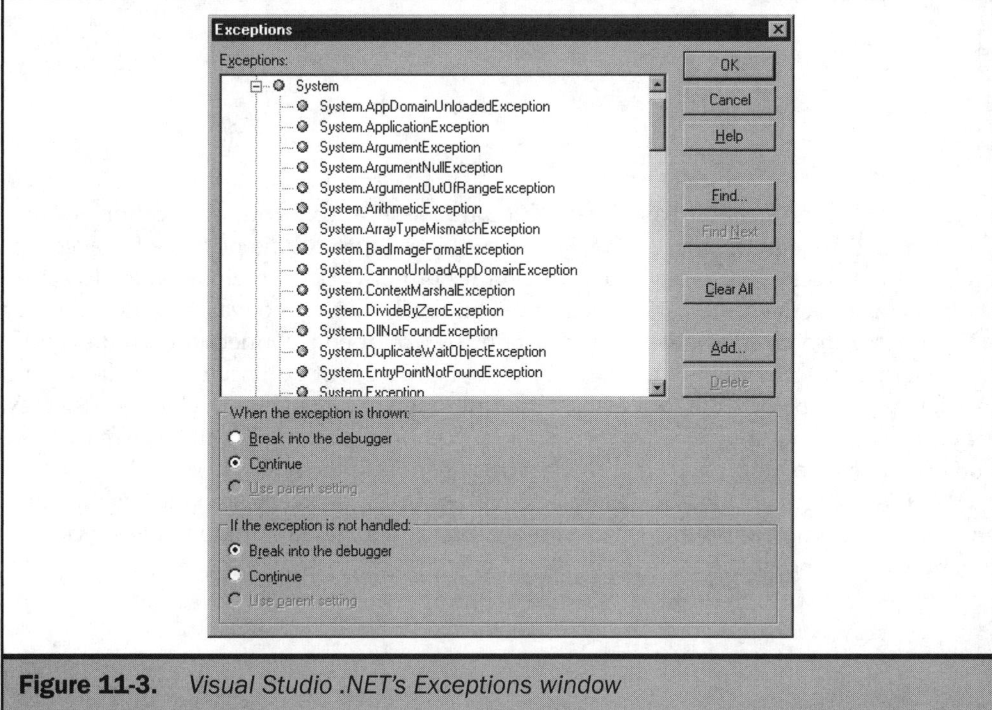


**Figure 11-3.** *Visual Studio .NET's Exceptions window*

## Use the Exceptions Window to Set Debugging Options

The Exceptions window allows you to specify what exceptions should be handled by your code when debugging, and what exceptions will cause Visual Studio .NET to enter break mode immediately. That means you don't need to disable your error-handling code to troubleshoot a problem.

For example, you could choose to allow your program to handle a common FileNotFoundException (which could be caused by an invalid user selection), but instruct Visual Studio .NET to pause execution if an unexpected DivideByZero exception occurs.

## Handling Exceptions

The first line of defense in an application is to check for potential error conditions before performing an operation. For example, a program can explicitly check if the divisor is zero before performing a calculation or if a file exists before attempting to open it.

```
If System.IO.File.Exists("myfile.txt") = True Then
    ' Safe to open the myfile.txt file.
End If

If Divisor <> 0 Then
    ' Safe to divide some number by Divisor.
End If
```

Even if you perform this basic level of "quality assurance," your application is still vulnerable. For example, there is no way to protect against all the possible file access problems that occur, including hardware failures or network problems that could arise spontaneously in the middle of an operation. Similarly, there's no way to validate a user ID and password for a database before attempting to open a connection—and even if there were, that technique would be subject to its own set of potential errors. In some cases, it may not be practical to perform the full range of defensive checks, because they may impose a noticeable performance drag on your application. For all these reasons, you need a way to detect and deal with errors when they occur.

.NET languages provide this technique with structured exception handling. To use structured exception handling, you wrap potentially problematic code in the special block structure shown here:

```
Try
    ' Risky code goes here (i.e. opening a file,
    ' connecting to a database).
Catch
    ' An error has been detected. You can deal with it here.
Finally
    ' Time to clean up, regardless of whether there was an error
    ' or not.
End Try
```

The Try statement enables error handling. Any exceptions that occur in the following lines can be "caught" automatically. The code in the Catch block will be executed when an error is detected. And, whether a bug occurs or not, the optional Finally section of the code will be executed last. This allows you to perform some basic cleanup, like closing a database connection. The Finally code is important because it will execute even if an error has occurred that will prevent the program from continuing. In other words, if an unrecoverable exception halts your application, you will still have the chance to release resources.

### How Do I Stop an Error?

The act of catching an error neutralizes it. If all you want to do is render a specific error harmless, you don't even need to add any code in the Catch block of your error handler. Usually, however, this portion of the code will be used to report the error to the user or log it for future reference. In a separate component (such as a business object), this code might actually create a new exception object with additional information, and throw it to the calling code, which will be in the best position to remedy it or alert the user.



## Catching Specific Exceptions

Structured exception handling is particularly flexible because it allows you to catch specific types of exceptions. To do so, you add multiple Catch statements, each one identifying the type of exception (and providing a new variable to catch it in):

```
Try
    ' Risky database code goes here.
Catch err As System.Data.OleDbException
    ' Catches common problems like connection errors.
Catch err As System.NullReferenceException
    ' Catches problems resulting from an unitialized object.
End Try
```

An exception will be caught as long as it is of the same class, or if it is derived from the indicated class. In other words, the statement Catch err As Exception will catch any exception, because every exception object is derived from the System.Exception base class.

Exception blocks work like an If/End If or Select Case block structure. That means that as soon as a matching exception handler is found, the appropriate catch code is invoked. Therefore, you should organize your Catch statements from most specific to least specific:

```
Try
    ' Risky database code goes here.
Catch err As System.Data.OleDbException
```

```
    ' Catches common problems like connection errors.
Catch err As System.NullReferenceException
    ' Catches problems resulting from an unitialized object.
Catch err As System.Exception
    ' Catches any other errors.
End Try
```

Ending with a Catch statement for the generic Exception class is often a good idea to make sure no errors slip through. However, in component-based programming you should make sure you only intercept an exception you can deal with or recover from. Otherwise, it is better to let the calling code catch the original error.

## Nested Exception Handlers

When an exception is thrown, VB .NET tries to find a matching Catch statement in the current procedure. If the code is not in a local structured exception block, or if none of the Catch statements match the exception, VB .NET will move up the call stack, searching for active exception handlers:

```
Private Sub Page_Load(sender As Object, e As EventArgs) _
  Handles MyBase.Load
    Try
        DivideNumbers(5, 0)
    Catch err As DivideByZeroException
        ' Report error here.
    End Try
End Sub

Private Function DivideNumbers(number As Decimal, _
 divisor As Decimal) As Decimal
    Return (number/divisor)
End Function
```

In this example, the DivideNumbers function lacks any sort of exception handler. However, the DivideNumbers function call is made inside an exception handler, which means that the problem will be caught further upstream in the calling code. This is a good approach because the DivideNumbers routine could be used in a variety of different circumstances (or if it is part of a component, in a variety of different types of applications). It really has no access to any kind of user interface and can't directly report an error. Only the calling code is in a position to determine if the problem is a serious or minor one, and prompt the user for more information or report error details in the web page.

Exception handlers can also be overlapped in such a way that different exception handlers filter out different types of problems:

```
Private Sub Page_Load(sender As Object, e As EventArgs) _
  Handles MyBase.Load
    Try
        Dim Average As Integer = GetAverageCost(DateTime.Now)
    Catch err As DivideByZeroException
        ' Report error here.
    End Try
End Sub

Private Function GetAverageCost(saleDate As Date) As Integer
    Try
        ' Use Database access code here to retrieve all the
        ' sale records for this date, and calculate the average.
    Catch err As OleDbException
        ' Handle a database related problem.
    Finally
        ' Close the database connection.
    End Try
End Function
```



### Interesting Facts About this Code

- If an OleDbException occurs during the database operation, it will be caught in the GetAverageCost function.
- If a DivideByZeroException occurs (for example, the function attempts to calculate an average based on a DataSet that contains no rows), the exception will be caught in the calling Page_Load subroutine.
- If another problem occurs (such as a null reference exception), there is no active exception handler that can catch it. VB .NET will search through the entire call stack without finding a matching Catch statement in an active exception handler. It will then generate a runtime error, end the program, and return a page with exception information.

## Exception Handling in Action

You can use a simple program to test exceptions and see what sort of information is retrieved. This sample program allows a user to enter two values and attempts to divide them. It then reports all the related exception information in the page (see Figure 11-4).

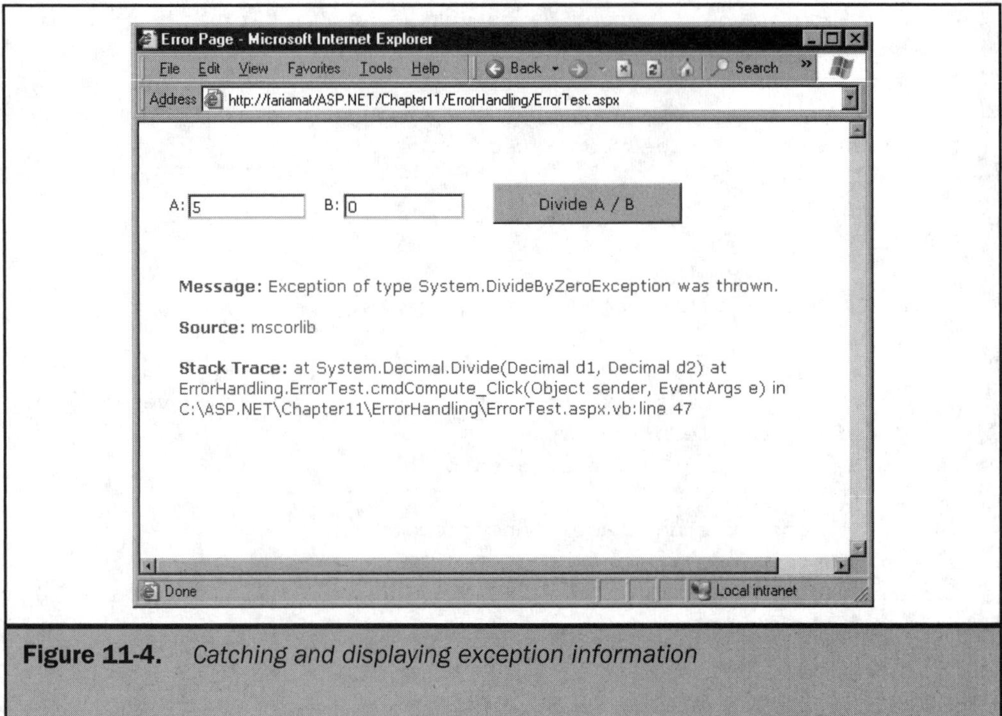


**Figure 11-4.** *Catching and displaying exception information*

Obviously, this problem could be easily avoided with extra code safety checks, or elegantly resolved using the validation controls. However, this code provides a good example of how you can deal with the properties of an exception object. It also gives you a good idea about what sort of information will be returned.

```
Public Class ErrorTest
  Inherits Page
    Protected lblResult As Label
    Protected WithEvents cmdCompute As Button
    Protected txtB As TextBox
    Protected txtA As TextBox

    Private Sub cmdCompute_Click(sender As Object, e As EventArgs) _
      Handles cmdCompute.Click
```

```
        Try
            Dim A, B, Result As Decimal
            A = Val(txtA.Text)
            B = Val(txtB.Text)
            Result = A / B
            lblResult.Text = Result.ToString()
            lblResult.ForeColor = Color.Black
        Catch err As Exception
            lblResult.Text = "<b>Message:</b> " & err.Message
            lblResult.Text &= "<br><br>"
            lblResult.Text &= "<b>Source:</b> " & err.Source
            lblResult.Text &= "<br><br>"
            lblResult.Text &= "<b>Stack Trace:</b> " & err.StackTrace
            lblResult.ForeColor = Color.Red
        End Try

    End Sub

End Class
```



Note that as soon as the error occurs, execution is transferred to an exception handler. The code in the Catch block is not completed. It is for that reason that the contents of the label are set in the Catch block. These lines will only be executed if the division code runs error-free.

You'll see many more examples of exception handling throughout this book. The data access chapters in Part III show the best practices for exception handling when accessing a database.

## Mastering Exceptions

There are a number of useful points to keep in mind when working with ASP.NET's new structured exception handling:

**Break down your code into multiple Try/Catch blocks.** If you put all of your code into one exception handler, you will have trouble determining where the problem occurred. Also, unlike with the On Error Goto system, there is no way to "resume" the code in a Catch block. That means that if an error occurs early on and you have a great deal of code in a single exception handler, many lines will be skipped. The rule of thumb is to use one exception handler for one related task (like opening a file and retrieving information).

**Use ASP.NET's error pages during development.** During development, you may not want to implement portions of your application's error-handling code because it may mask easily correctable mistakes in your application.

**Don't use exception handlers for every statement.** Simple code statements (assigning a constant value to a variable, interacting with a control, and so on) may cause errors during development testing, but will not cause any future problems once perfected. Error handling should be used when you are accessing an outside resource or dealing with supplied data that you have no control over (and thus may be invalid).

## Throwing Your Own Exceptions

You can also define and create your own exception objects to represent special error conditions. All you need to do is create an instance of the appropriate exception class, and then use the Throw statement.

The next example introduces a modified DivideNumbers function. It explicitly checks if the specified divisor is zero, and then manually creates and throws an instance of the DivideByZeroException class to indicate the problem, rather than attempt the operation. Depending on the code, this pattern can save time by eliminating some unnecessary steps, or prevent a task from being initiated if it can't be successfully completed.

```
Private Sub Page_Load(sender As Object, e As EventArgs) _
  Handles MyBase.Load
    Try
        DivideNumbers(5, 0)
    Catch err As DivideByZeroException
        ' Report error here.
    End Try
End Sub

Private Function DivideNumbers(number As Decimal, _
  divisor As Decimal) As Decimal
    If divisor = 0
        Dim err As New DivideByZeroException()
        Throw err
    Else
        Return (number/divisor)
    End If
End Function
```

Alternatively, you can create a .NET exception object, but specify a custom error message by using a different constructor:

```
Private Function DivideNumbers(number As Decimal, _
  divisor As Decimal) As Decimal
    If divisor = 0
```

```
        Dim err As New DivideByZeroException( _
          "You supplied 0 for the divisor parameter." & _
          "You must be stopped.")
        Throw err
    Else
        Return (number/divisor)
    End If
End Function
```

In this case, the DivideByZeroException will still be caught by any ordinary exception handlers. The only difference is that the error object has a modified Message property that contains the custom string. The resulting exception is shown in Figure 11-5.

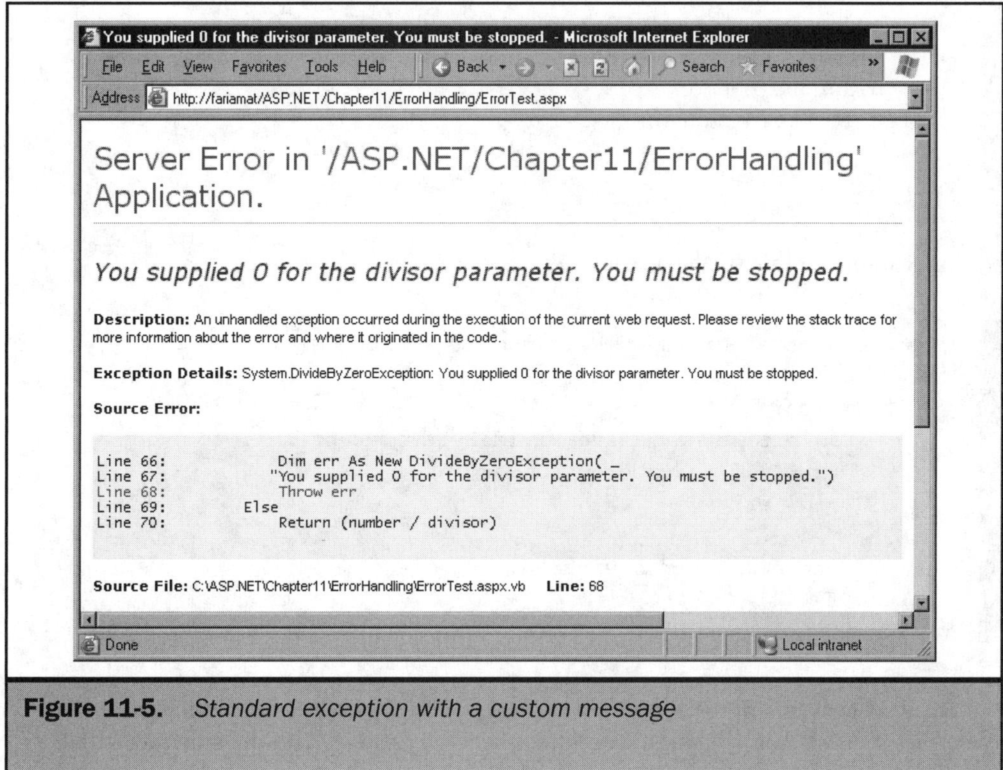


**Figure 11-5.** *Standard exception with a custom message*

Throwing an error is most useful in component-based programming (for example, when your ASP.NET page is creating objects and calling methods from a class defined in a separate compiled assembly). In this case, the component (typically a class in a separate DLL) notifies the calling code of an error. The component should handle recoverable errors quietly, and not throw them back to the calling code. On the other hand, unrecoverable errors should always be indicated with an exception, and never by another method like a return code. For more information about component-based programming, refer to Chapter 21.

If you can find an exception in the class library that accurately reflects the problem that has occurred, you should throw it. If you need to return additional or specialized information, you can create your own custom exception class.

Custom exception classes should always inherit from System.ApplicationException. In addition, you can add properties to record additional information. For example, here is a special class that records information about the failed attempt to divide by zero:

```
Public Class CustomDivideByZeroException
  Inherits ApplicationException

    ' Add a variable to specify the "other" number.
    ' Depending on the circumstance, this might help
    ' diagnose the problem.
    Public DividingNumber As Integer

End Class
```

You can throw this special error like this:

```
Private Function DivideNumbers(number As Integer, _
  divisor As Integer) As Integer
    If divisor = 0
        Dim err As New CustomDivideByZeroException()
        err.DividingNumber = number
        Throw err
    Else
        Return (number/divisor)
    End If
End Function
```

To perfect the custom exception, you need to supply it with the three standard constructors. This allows your exception class to be created with the standards that every exception supports:

- On its own, with no arguments
- With a custom message
- With a custom message and an exception object to use as the inner exception

All these constructors need to do is forward the parameters to the base class (the constructors in the inherited ApplicationException class) using the MyBase keyword:

```
Public Class CustomDivideByZeroException
  Inherits ApplicationException

    ' Add a variable to specify the "other" number.
    ' Depending on the circumstance, this might help
    ' diagnose the problem.
    Public DividingNumber As Integer

    Public Sub New()
        MyBase.New()
    End Sub

    Public Sub New(message As String)
        MyBase.New(message)
    End Sub

    Public Sub New(message as String, inner As Exception)
        MyBase.New(message, inner)
    End Sub

End Class
```

The third constructor is particularly useful for component programming. Using it you could intercept a low-level exception (like DivideByZero) and replace it with a higher-level exception without losing the original exception. The next example shows how you could use this constructor with a component class called ArithmeticUtility:

```
Public Class ArithmeticUtilityException
  Inherits ApplicationException

    Public Sub New()
        MyBase.New()
    End Sub

    Public Sub New(message As String)
        MyBase.New(message)
    End Sub

    Public Sub New(message as String, inner As Exception)
```

```
        MyBase.New(message, inner)
    End Sub

End Class

Public Class ArithmeticUtility

    Private Function Divide(number As Decimal, _
      divisor As Decimal) As Decimal
        Try
            Return (number/divisor)
        Catch err As Exception
            ' Create an instance of the specialized exception class,
            ' and place the original error in the InnerException
            ' property.
            Dim errNew As New ArithmeticUtilityException(err)

            ' Now "rethrow" the new exception.
            Throw errNew
        End Try
    End Function

End Class
```

Remember, custom exception classes are really just a special, standardized way for one class to communicate an error to a different portion of code. If you are not using components or your own utility classes, you probably don't need to create custom exception classes.

## Logging Exceptions

In many cases, it's best not only to detect and catch errors, but to log them as well. For example, some problems may only occur when your web server is dealing with a particularly large load. Other problems might recur intermittently, with no obvious causes. To diagnose these errors and build a larger picture of site problems, you need to log errors automatically so they can be reviewed at a later date.

The .NET framework provides a wide range of logging tools. When certain errors occur, you can send an email, add a database record, or create and write to a file. (Many of these techniques are described in other parts of this book.) However, logging techniques are generally best if they are as simple as possible. For example, you will probably run into trouble if you try to log a database error to another table in the database.

One of the best logging tools is provided in the Windows event logs (see Table 11-2). To view these logs, select Settings | Control Panel | Administrative Tools | Event Viewers from the Start menu. By default, you'll see three logs, as shown in Figure 11-6.

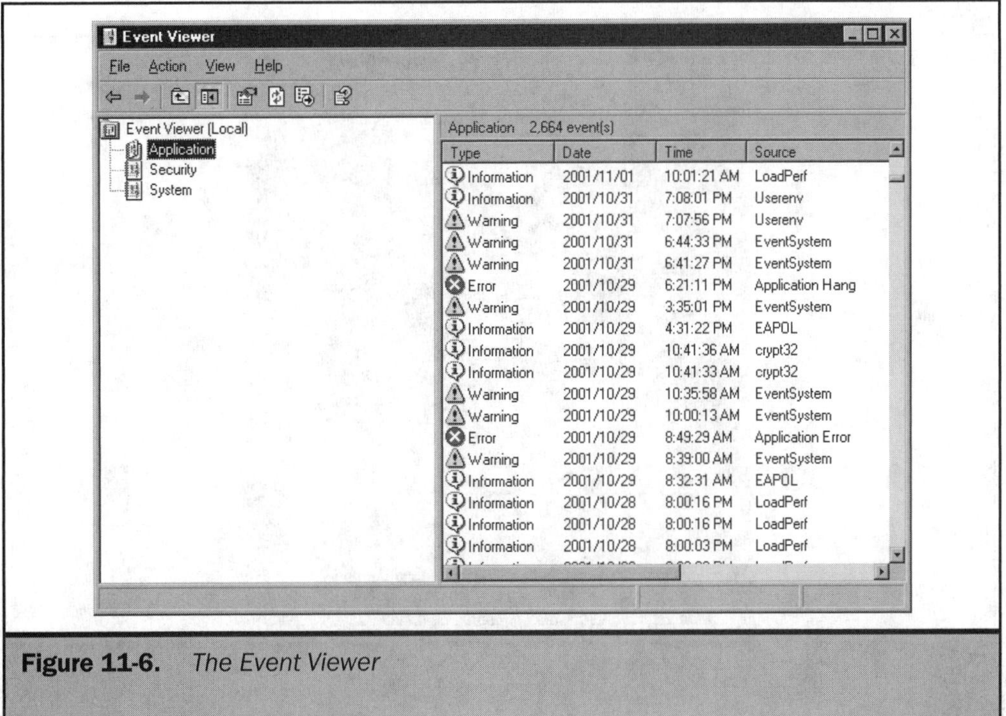


**Figure 11-6.** *The Event Viewer*

| **Log Name** | **Description** |
|---|---|
| Application | Used to track errors or notifications from any application. Generally, you will use this log, or create your own. |
| Security | Used to track security-related problems, but generally used exclusively by the operating system. |
| System | Used to track operating system events. |

**Table 11-2.** *Windows Event Logs*

Each event record identifies the source (generally, the application or service that created the record), the type of notification (error, information, warning), and the time it was left. You can also double-click on a record to view additional information such as a text description (see Figure 11-7).

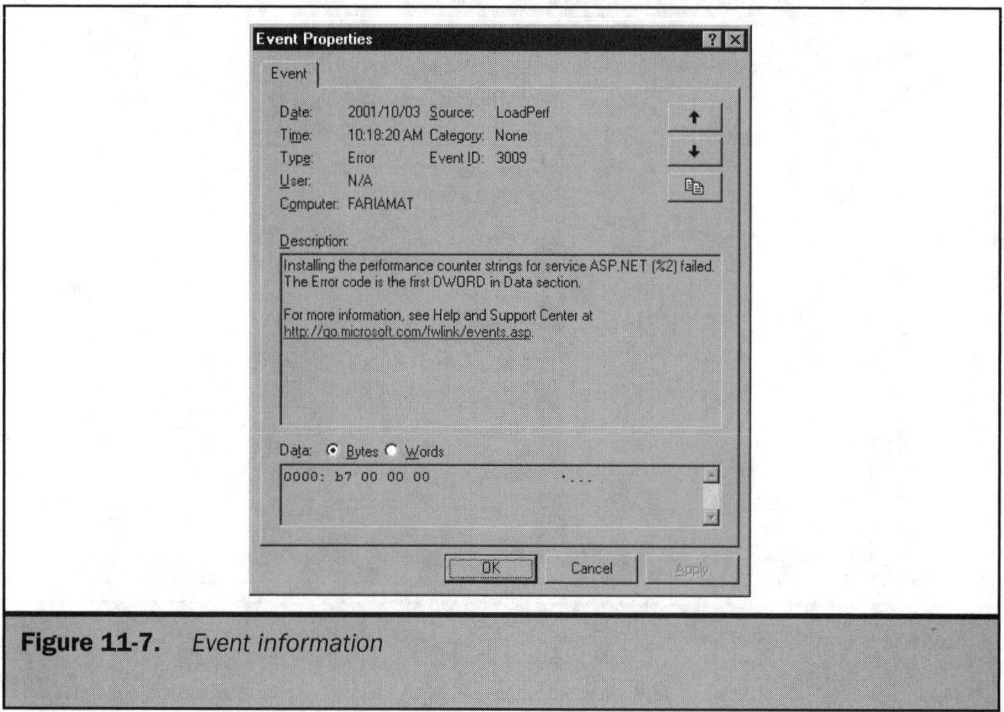


**Figure 11-7.** *Event information*

One of the potential problems with event logs is that they are automatically overwritten when the maximum size is reached (typically half a megabyte) as long as they are of at least a certain age (typically seven days). This means that application logs can't be used to log critical information that you need to retain for a long period of time. Instead, they should be used to track information that is only valuable for a short amount of time. For example, you can use event logs to review errors and diagnose strange behavior immediately after it happens, not a month later.

You do have some ability to configure the amount of time a log will be retained and the maximum size it will be allowed to occupy. To configure these settings, right-click on the application log and select Properties. You'll see the Application Properties window shown in Figure 11-8.

**Figure 11-8.** *Log properties*

Generally, you should not disable automatic log deletion, as it could cause a large amount of wasted space and slowed performance if information is not being regularly removed. Instead, if you want to retain more log information, set a larger disk space limit.

You can use the right-click context menu, shown here, to clear the events in the log, save log entries, and open an external log file.

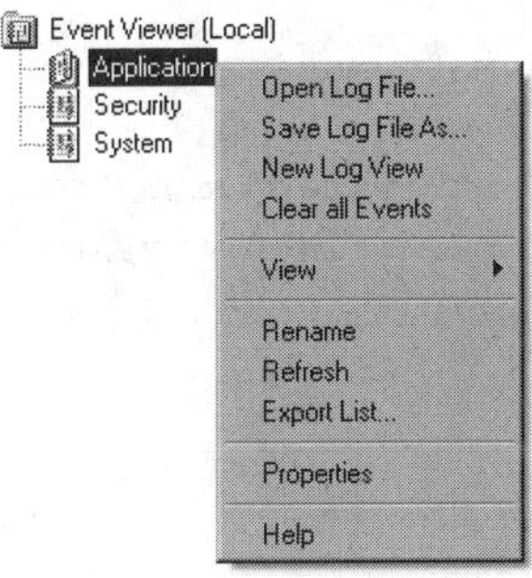

## Using the EventLog Class

You can interact with this log in an ASP.NET page by using the System.Diagnostics class. The following example rewrites the simple ErrorTest page to use event logging:

```
Imports System.Diagnostics

Public Class ErrorTestLog
  Inherits Page
    Protected lblResult As Label
    Protected WithEvents cmdCompute As Button
    Protected txtB As TextBox
    Protected txtA As TextBox

    Private Sub cmdCompute_Click(sender As Object, e As EventArgs) _
      Handles cmdCompute.Click

        Try
            Dim A, B, Result As Decimal
            A = Val(txtA.Text)
            B = Val(txtB.Text)
            Result = A / B
            lblResult.Text = Result.ToString()
            lblResult.ForeColor = Color.Black
        Catch err As Exception
            lblResult.Text = "<b>Message:</b> " & err.Message
            lblResult.Text &= "<br><br>"
            lblResult.Text &= "<b>Source:</b> " & err.Source
            lblResult.Text &= "<br><br>"
            lblResult.Text &= "<b>Stack Trace:</b> " & err.StackTrace
            lblResult.ForeColor = Color.Red

            ' Write the information to the event log.
            Dim log As New EventLog()
            log.Source = "DivisionPage"
            log.WriteEntry(err.Message, EventLogEntryType.Error)
        End Try

    End Sub

End Class
```

The event log record will now appear in the Event Viewer utility, as shown in Figure 11-9. Note that logging is intended for the system administrator or developer. It does not replace the code you use to notify the user that a problem has occurred.

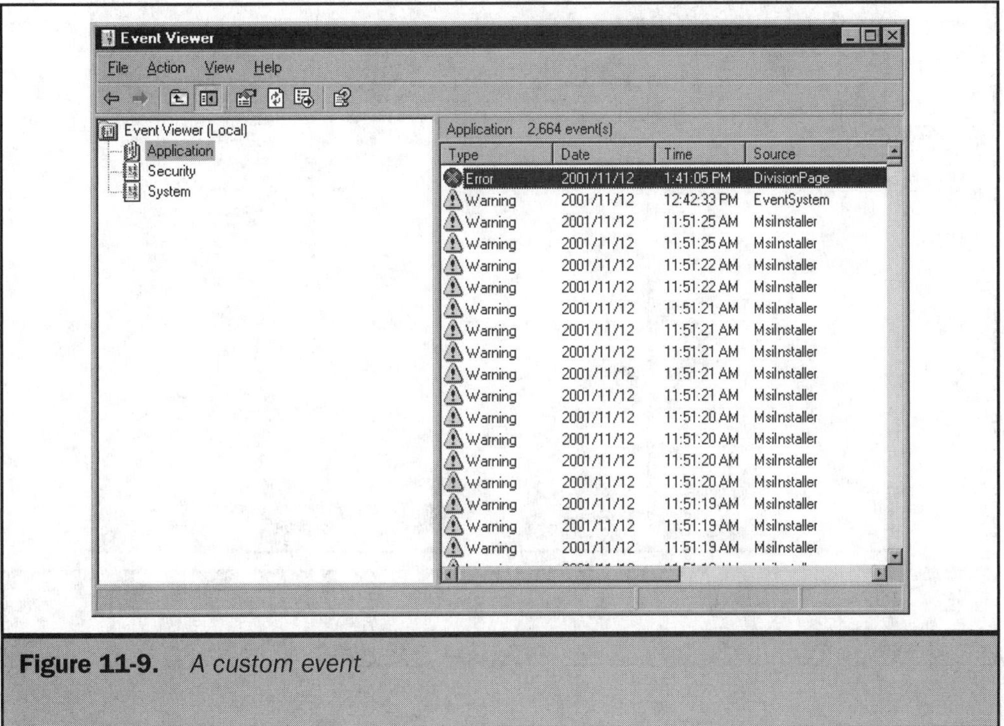

Figure 11-9. *A custom event*

You can also log errors to a custom log. For example, you could create a log with your company name, and add records for all of your ASP.NET applications to it. You might even want to create an individual log for a particularly large application, and use the Source property of each entry to indicate the page (or web service method) that caused the problem.

Creating a custom log is easy—you just need to use a different constructor for the EventLog class:

```
' Create the log if it doesn't exist.
Dim log As New EventLog("MyCompany")
log.Source = "ErrorTestLog_Page"
log.WriteEntry(err.Message, EventLogEntryType.Error)
```

The new log is shown in Figure 11-10.

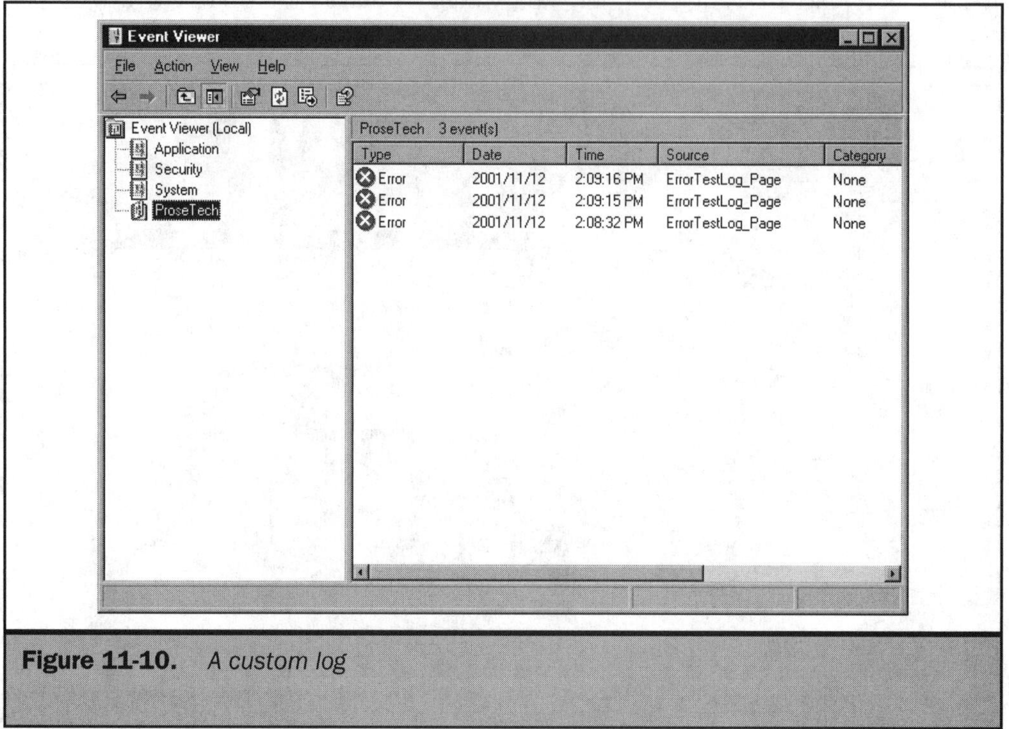


**Figure 11-10.** *A custom log*

### What Should I Log?

Event logging uses disk space and takes processor time away from web applications. Don't store unimportant information, large quantities of data, or information that would be better off in another type of storage (such as a relational database). Generally, an event log should be used to log unexpected conditions or errors, not customer actions or performance tracking information.

## Retrieving Log Information

One of the disadvantages of the event logs is that they are tied to the web server. This can make it difficult to review log entries if you don't have a way to access the server. There are several possible solutions to this problem. One interesting technique involves using a special administration page. This ASP.NET page can use the EventLog class to retrieve and display all the information from the event log.

The following example retrieves all the entries that were left by the ErrorLogTest, and displays them in a simple web page (shown in Figure 11-11). A more sophisticated approach would use similar code, but one of the data controls discussed in Chapter 15.

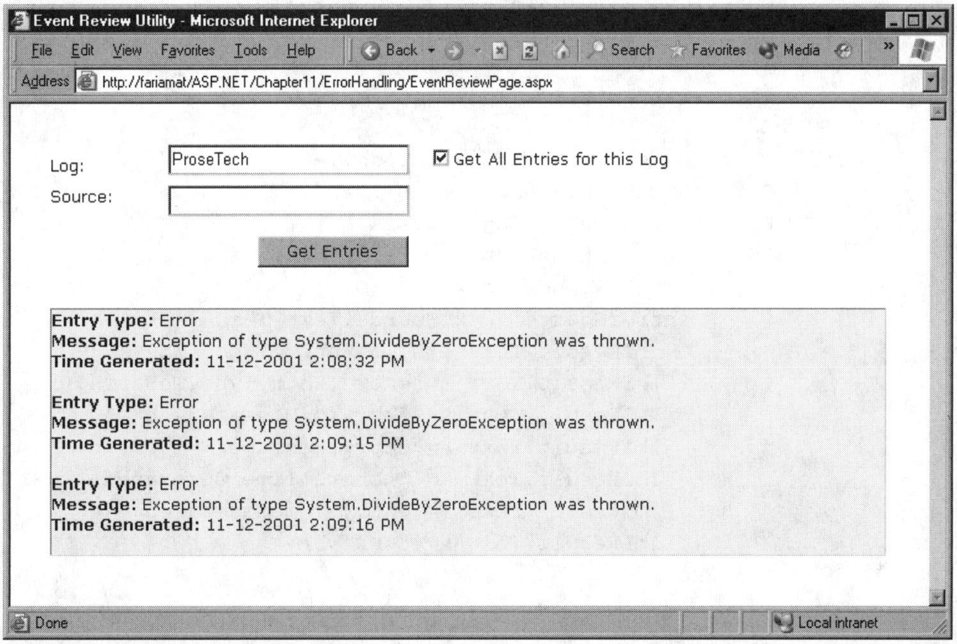

**Figure 11-11.** *A log viewer page*

```
Imports System.Diagnostics

Public Class EventReviewPage
  Inherits Page

    Protected lblResult As Label
    Protected txtSource As TextBox
    Protected WithEvents cmdGet As Button
    Protected WithEvents chkAll As CheckBox
    Protected txtLog As TextBox
```

```
    Private Sub cmdGet_Click(sender As Object, e As EventArgs) _
      Handles cmdGet.Click

        lblResult.Text = ""

        ' Check if the log exists.
        If Not EventLog.Exists(txtLog.Text) Then
            lblResult.Text = "The event log " & txtLog.Text
            lblResult.Text &= " does not exist."
        Else
            Dim log As New EventLog(txtLog.Text)
            Dim entry As EventLogEntry
            For Each entry In log.Entries
                ' Write the event entries to the page.
                If chkAll.Checked = True Or _
                  entry.Source = txtSource.Text Then
                    lblResult.Text &= "<b>Entry Type:</b> "
                    lblResult.Text &= entry.EntryType.ToString()
                    lblResult.Text &= "<br><b>Message:</b> "
                    lblResult.Text &= entry.Message
                    lblResult.Text &= "<br><b>Time Generated:</b> "
                    lblResult.Text &= entry.TimeGenerated
                    lblResult.Text &= "<br><br>"
                End If
            Next
        End If

    End Sub

    Private Sub chkAll_CheckedChanged(sender As Object, _
     e As EventArgs) Handles chkAll.CheckedChanged
        ' The chkAll control has AutoPostback = True.
        If chkAll.Checked = True Then
            txtSource.Text = ""
            txtSource.Enabled = False
        Else
            txtSource.Enabled = True
        End If
    End Sub

End Class
```

### Other Logs

You can get around some of the limitations involved with the event log by using your own custom logging system. All the ingredients you need are built into the common class library. You could store error information in a binary, text, or XML file (as described in Chapters 16 and 17), in a database (as described in Chapter 13), or in an email account (also in Chapter 16).

## Error Pages

As you create and test an ASP.NET application, you'll become familiar with the rich information pages that are shown to describe unhandled errors. These pages are extremely useful for diagnosing problems during development, because they contain a wealth of information. Some of this information includes the source code where the problem occurred (with the offending line highlighted), the type of error, and a detailed error message describing the problem. A sample rich error page is shown in Figure 11-12.

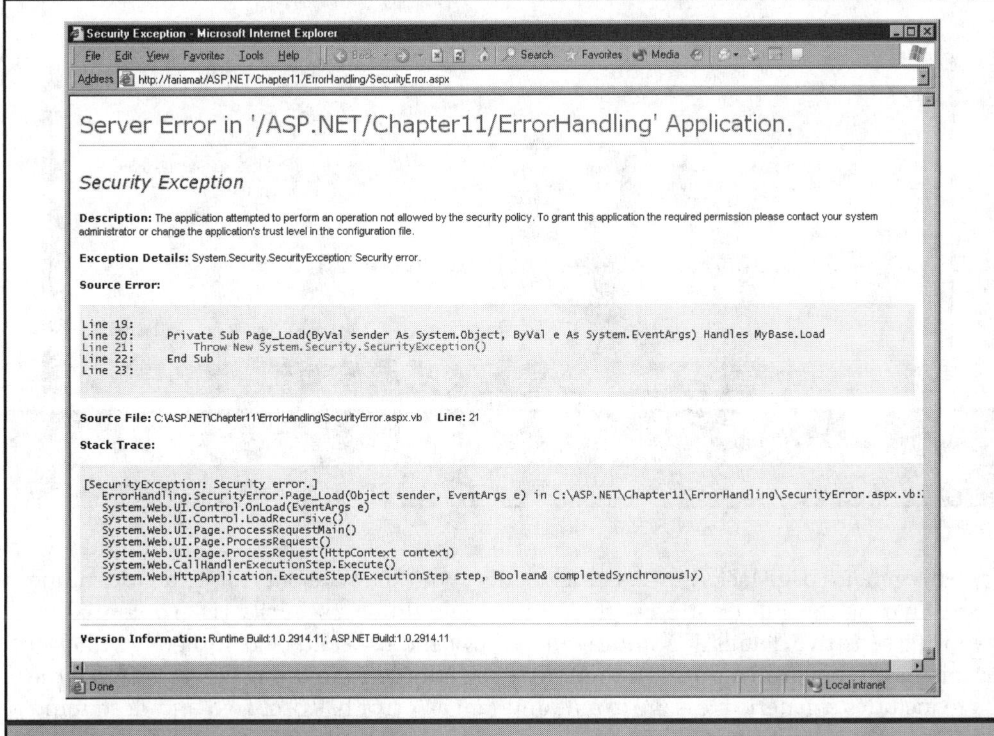


**Figure 11-12.** *A rich ASP.NET error page*

This error page is only shown for local requests that access the ASP.NET application through the http://localhost domain. (This domain always refers to the current computer, regardless of its actual server name or Internet address.) ASP.NET does not create a rich error page for requests from other computers, instead they receive the rather unhelpful generic page shown in Figure 11-13.

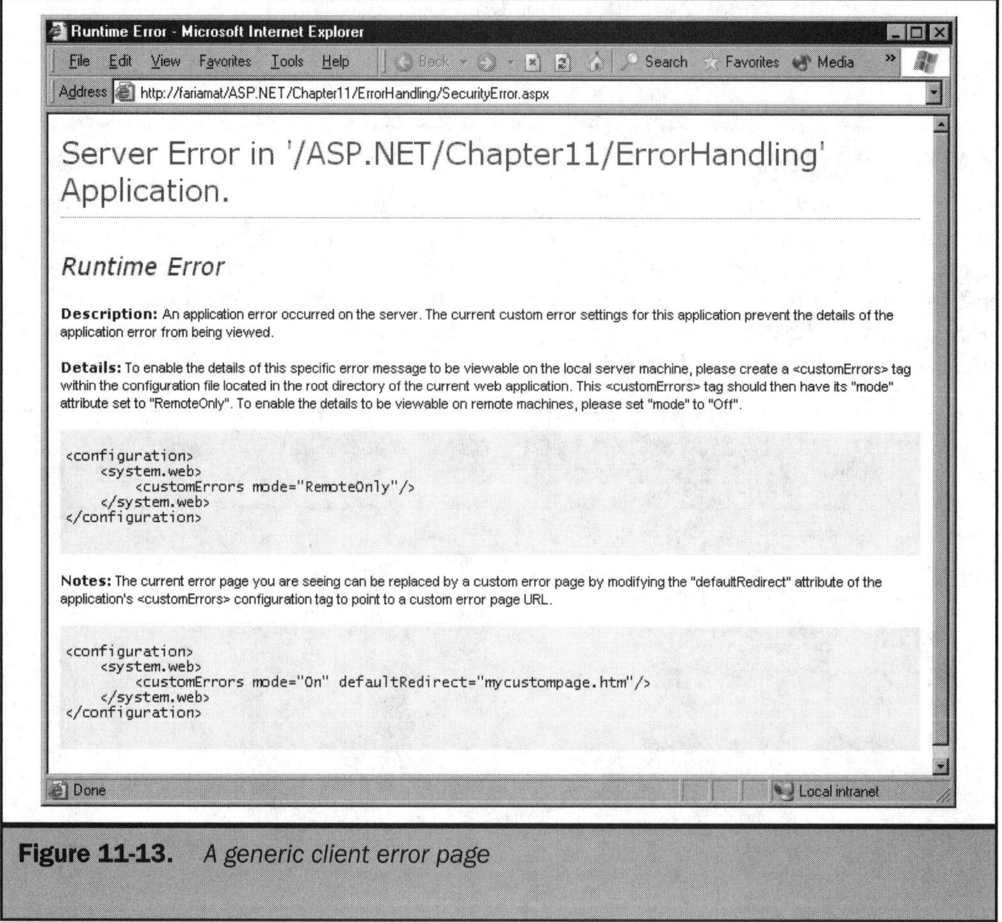


**Figure 11-13.** *A generic client error page*

This generic page lacks any specific details about the type of error or the offending code. Sharing this information with end users would be a security risk (potentially exposing sensitive details about the source code) and it would be completely unhelpful, as clients are never in a position to modify the source code themselves. Instead, the page includes a generic message explaining that an error has occurred and describing how to enable remote error pages.

## Error Modes

Remote error pages remove this restriction, and allow ASP.NET to display detailed information for problems regardless of the source of the request. Remote error pages are intended as a testing tool. For example, in the initial rollout of an application beta, you might use field testers. These field testers would need to report specific information about application errors to aid in the debugging process. Similarly, you could use remote error pages if you are working with a team of developers and testing an ASP.NET application hosted on a live web server. In this case, you might follow the time-honored code, compile, and upload pattern.

To change the error mode, you need to modify the web.config file for the application:

```
<configuration>
  <system.web>
    <customErrors mode="RemoteOnly" />
  </system.web>
</configuration>
```

The different options for the mode attribute are listed in Table 11-3.

| Error Mode | Description |
|---|---|
| RemoteOnly | This is the default setting, which only uses rich ASP.NET error pages when the developer is accessing an ASP.NET application on the current machine. |
| Off | This configures rich error pages (with source code and stack traces) for all unhandled errors, regardless of the source of the request. This setting is helpful in many development scenarios, but should not be used in a deployed application. |
| On | ASP.NET error pages will never be shown. When an unhandled error is encountered, a corresponding custom error page will be shown if one exists. Otherwise, ASP.NET will show the generic message explaining that application settings prevent the error details from being displayed, and describing how to change the configuration. |

**Table 11-3.** *Error Modes*

## A Custom Error Page

In a deployed application, you should use the On or RemoteOnly error mode. Any errors in your application should be dealt with through error-handling code, which can then present a helpful and user-oriented message (rather than the developer-oriented code details in ASP.NET's rich error messages).

However, it is not possible to catch every potential error in an ASP.NET application. For example, a hardware failure could occur spontaneously in the middle of an ordinary code statement that would not normally cause an error. More commonly, the user might encounter an HTTP error by requesting a page that does not exist. ASP.NET allows you to handle these problems with custom error pages.

There are two ways to implement custom error pages. You can create a single generic error page:

```
<configuration>
  <system.web>
    <customErrors defaultRedirect="DefaultError.aspx" />
  </system.web>
</configuration>
```

In this case, if ASP.NET encounters an HTTP error while serving the request, it will forward the user to the DefaultError.aspx web page. If ASP.NET encounters an unhandled application error, and it is not configured to display a rich error page for the current request, it will also forward the user to the DefaultError.aspx page. Remote users will never see the generic ASP.NET error page. If ASP.NET encounters an unhandled application error and it is configured to display a rich developer-targeted error page, it will display the informative error page instead.

### What Happens If an Error Occurs in the Error Page?

If an error occurs in the custom error page (in this case, DefaultError.aspx), ASP.NET will not be able to handle it. It will not try to re-forward the user to the same page. Instead, it will display the normal client error page with the generic message.

## Specific Custom Error Pages

You can also create error pages targeted at specific types of HTTP errors (such as the infamous 404 Not Found error, or Access Denied). This technique is commonly used with web sites to provide friendly equivalents for common problems. Figure 11-14 shows how Excite handles this issue.

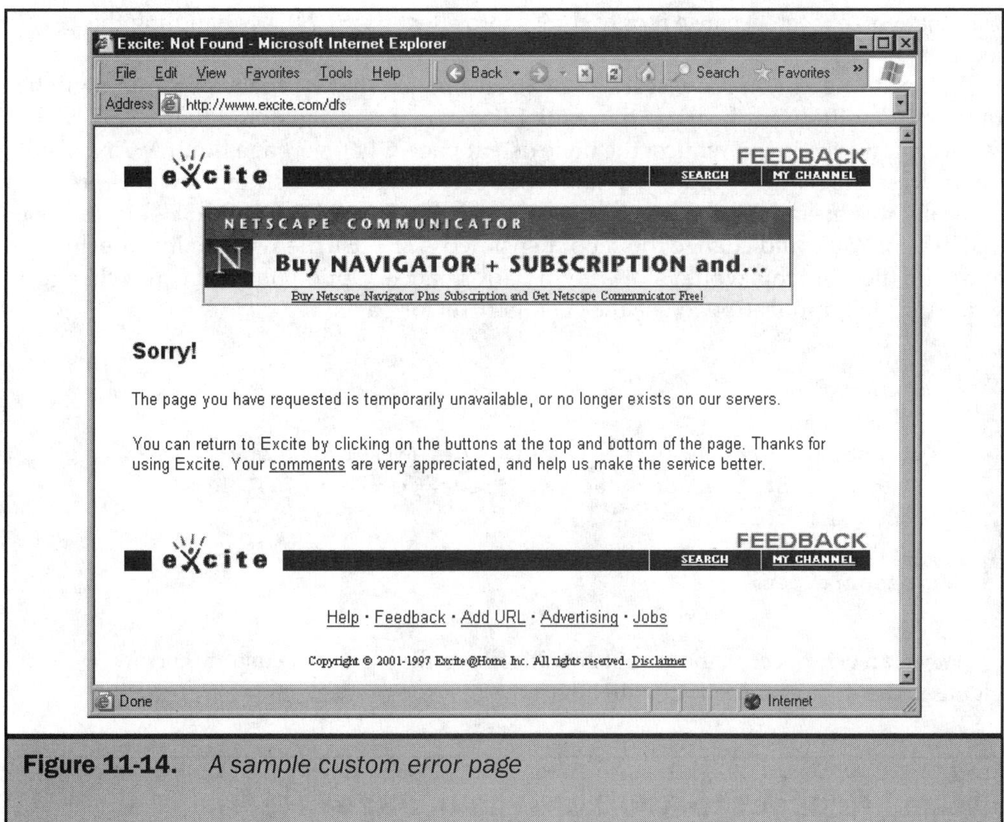


**Figure 11-14.** *A sample custom error page*

To define an error-specific custom page, you add an <error> subelement to the <customErrors> element. The <error> element identifies the HTTP error code and the redirect page.

```
<configuration>
  <system.web>
    <customErrors defaultRedirect="DefaultError.aspx">
      <error statusCode="404" redirect="404.aspx" />
    <customErrors>
  </system.web>
</configuration>
```

In this example, the user will be redirected to the 404.aspx page when requesting an ASP.NET page that does not exist. This custom error page may not work exactly the way that you expect, because it only comes into effect if ASP.NET is handling the request.

For example, if you request the nonexistent page whateverpage.aspx, you will be redirected to 404.aspx, because the .aspx file extension is registered to the ASP.NET service. However, if you request the nonexistent page whateverpage.html, ASP.NET will not process the request, and the default redirect setting specified in IIS will be used. Typically, this means that the user will see the page C:\WINNT\Help\IISHelp\common \404b.htm. You could change the set of registered ASP.NET file types to include .html and .htm files, but this would slow down performance. Optionally, you could change your ASP.NET application to use the custom IIS error page:

```
<configuration>
  <system.web>
    <customErrors defaultRedirect="/defaulterror.aspx">
      <error statusCode="404" redirect="/Errors/404b.htm" />
    <customErrors>
  </system.web>
</configuration>
```

When an error occurs that is not specifically addressed by a custom <error> element, the default error page will be used.

### Can I Redirect to Another Type of Page?

As with the default page, you can redirect to an ASP.NET .aspx page or another valid format such as a simple HTML page.

## Page Tracing

ASP.NET's detailed error pages are extremely helpful when you are testing and perfecting an application. However, sometimes you need more information to verify that your application is performing properly or track down logic errors, which may produce invalid data but no obvious exceptions. In traditional ASP development, programmers often resorted to using Response.Write to display debug information directly on the web page. Unfortunately, this technique is fraught with problems:

**Code entanglement** It is difficult to separate the ordinary code from the debugging code. Before the application can be deployed, you need to painstakingly search through the code and remove or comment out all the Response.Write statements.

**No single point of control** If problems occur later down the road, there's no easy way to "re-enable" the write statements. Response.Write statements are tightly integrated into the code.

**User interface problems** Response.Write outputs information directly into the page. Depending on the current stage of page processing, the information can appear in just about any location, potentially scrambling your layout.

These problems can be overcome with additional effort and some homegrown solutions. However, ASP.NET provides a far more convenient and flexible method built into the framework services. It's called tracing.



## Enabling Tracing

In order to use tracing, you need to explicitly enable it. There are several ways to switch tracing on. One of the easiest ways is with a page directive:

```
<%@ Page Trace="True" %>
```

You can also enable tracing by using the built-in Trace object (which is an instance of the System.Web.TraceContext class):

```
Private Sub Page_Load(sender As Object, e As EventArgs) _
  Handles MyBase.Load
    Trace.IsEnabled = True
End Sub
```

This technique is particularly useful because it allows you to enable or disable tracing for a page programmatically. For example, you could examine the query string collection, and only enable tracing if a special Tracing variable is received. This could allow developers to run tracing diagnostics on deployed pages, without revealing that information for normal requests from end users.

```
Private Sub Page_Load(sender As Object, e As EventArgs) _
  Handles MyBase.Load

    If Request.QueryString("Tracing") = "On"
        Trace.IsEnabled = True
    End If

End Sub
```

Lastly, you can enable application-level tracing with the web.config file. This topic is discussed later in this chapter.

Note that, by default, once you enable tracing it will only apply to local requests. That prevents actual end users from seeing the tracing information. If you need to trace a web page from an offsite location, you should use a technique like the previous one (for query string activation), and you will also need to change some web.config settings to enable remote tracing. Information about modifying these settings is found at the end of this chapter, in the "Application-Level Tracing" section.

### What About Visual Studio .NET?

Visual Studio .NET provides a full complement of debugging tools that allow you to set breakpoints, step through code, and view the contents of variables while your program executes. Though you can use Visual Studio .NET in conjunction with page tracing, you probably won't need to. Instead, page tracing will become more useful for debugging problems *after* you have deployed the application to a web server. Visual Studio .NET error handling is discussed in Chapter 8.

## Tracing Information

ASP.NET tracing automatically provides a lengthy set of standard, formatted information. For example, Figure 11-15 shows a rudimentary ASP.NET page with a single label control and button.

On its own, this page does very little, displaying a single line of text. When you click the button to enable tracing, however, you end up with a lot of extra diagnostic information, as shown in Figure 11-16.

Tracing information is provided in several different categories. Depending on your page, you may not see all the sections. For example, if the page request didn't supply any query string parameters, you won't see the QueryString collection. Similarly, if there's no data currently being held in the application or session state, you won't see those sections either.

### Request Details

The Request Details section, shown in the following illustration, includes some basic information such as the current Session ID, the time the web request was made, and the type of web request and encoding.

| Request Details | | | |
|---|---|---|---|
| **Session Id:** | vqa22245szjcs545kripra45 | **Request Type:** | POST |
| **Time of Request:** | 11-12-2001 6:49:35 PM | **Status Code:** | 200 |
| **Request Encoding:** | Unicode (UTF-8) | **Response Encoding:** | Unicode (UTF-8) |

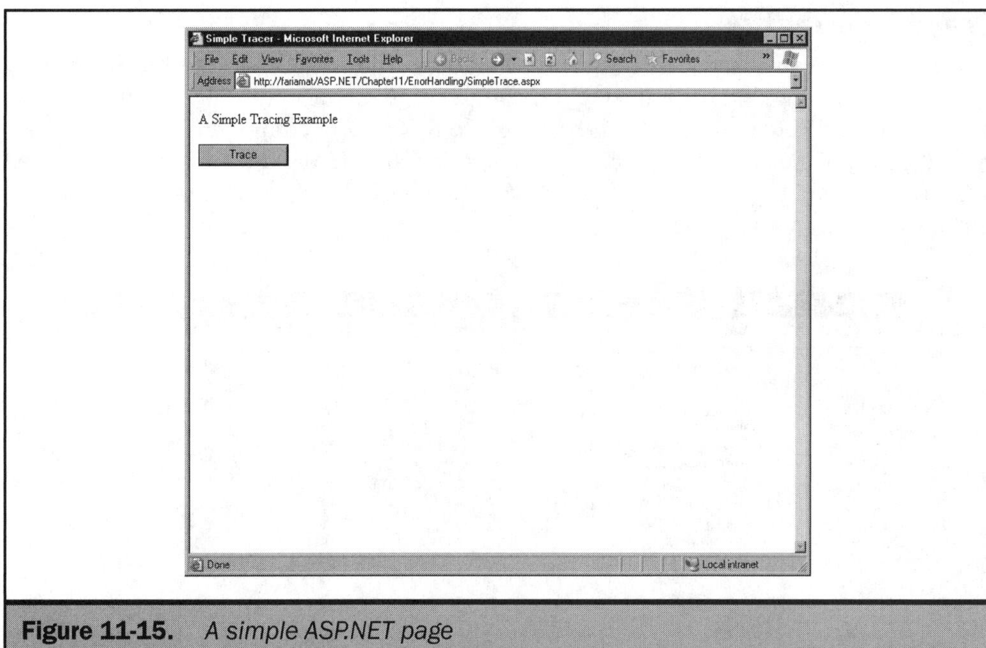


Figure 11-15. *A simple ASP.NET page*

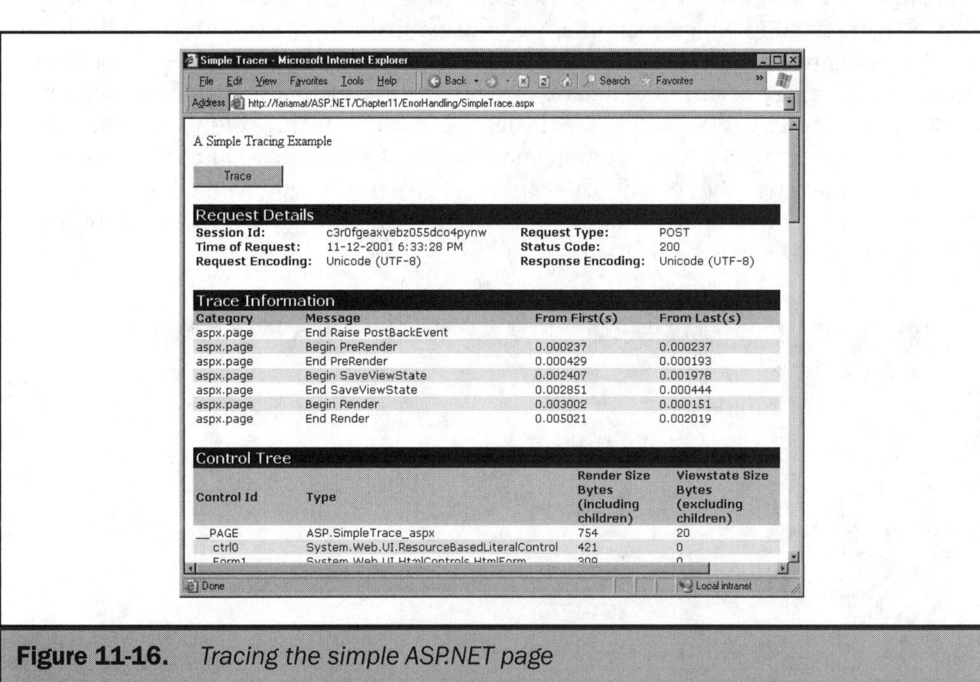


Figure 11-16. *Tracing the simple ASP.NET page*

## Trace Information

The Trace Information section, shown in the following illustration, shows the different stages of processing that the page went through before being sent to the client. Each section has additional information about how long it took to complete, as measured from the start of the first stage (From First) and as measured from the start of the previous stage (From Last). If you add your own trace messages (which you'll see shortly), they will also appear in this section.

| Trace Information | | | |
|---|---|---|---|
| **Category** | **Message** | **From First(s)** | **From Last(s)** |
| aspx.page | Begin ProcessPostData Second Try | | |
| aspx.page | End ProcessPostData Second Try | 0.000164 | 0.000164 |
| aspx.page | Begin Raise ChangedEvents | 0.000320 | 0.000156 |
| aspx.page | End Raise ChangedEvents | 0.000455 | 0.000134 |
| aspx.page | Begin Raise PostBackEvent | 0.000586 | 0.000131 |
| aspx.page | End Raise PostBackEvent | 0.003737 | 0.003152 |
| aspx.page | Begin PreRender | 0.004063 | 0.000326 |
| aspx.page | End PreRender | 0.004235 | 0.000173 |
| aspx.page | Begin SaveViewState | 0.007149 | 0.002914 |
| aspx.page | End SaveViewState | 0.007771 | 0.000621 |
| aspx.page | Begin Render | 0.007975 | 0.000204 |
| aspx.page | End Render | 0.011350 | 0.003375 |

## Control Tree

The control tree, shown in the following illustration, shows you all the controls on the page, indented to show their hierarchy (some controls are contained inside other controls). In our simple page example, the only explicitly created controls are the label (lblMessage) and the web page. However, ASP.NET adds additional literal controls automatically to represent spacing and any other static elements that aren't server controls (such as text or ordinary HTML tags). One useful feature of this section is the Viewstate column, which tells you how many bytes of space are required to persist the current information in the control. This can help you gauge whether enabling the control state is detracting from performance, particularly when working with databound controls like the DataGrid or DataList.

| Control Tree | | | |
|---|---|---|---|
| **Control Id** | **Type** | **Render Size Bytes (including children)** | **Viewstate Size Bytes (excluding children)** |
| __PAGE | ASP.TraceExample_aspx | 1691 | 24 |
| ctrl0 | System.Web.UI.ResourceBasedLiteralControl | 427 | 0 |
| Form1 | System.Web.UI.HtmlControls.HtmlForm | 1236 | 0 |
| ctrl1 | System.Web.UI.LiteralControl | 137 | 0 |
| cmdWrite | System.Web.UI.WebControls.Button | 201 | 0 |
| ctrl2 | System.Web.UI.LiteralControl | 2 | 0 |
| Label1 | System.Web.UI.WebControls.Label | 113 | 0 |
| ctrl3 | System.Web.UI.LiteralControl | 2 | 0 |
| cmdWriteCategory | System.Web.UI.WebControls.Button | 232 | 0 |
| ctrl4 | System.Web.UI.LiteralControl | 2 | 0 |
| cmdError | System.Web.UI.WebControls.Button | 203 | 0 |
| ctrl5 | System.Web.UI.LiteralControl | 2 | 0 |
| cmdSession | System.Web.UI.WebControls.Button | 171 | 0 |
| ctrl6 | System.Web.UI.LiteralControl | 14 | 0 |
| ctrl7 | System.Web.UI.LiteralControl | 28 | 0 |

## Session and Application States

The Session State, shown in the following illustration, and Application State sections display every item that is in the current session or application state. Each item is listed with its name, type, and value. If you are storing simple pieces of string information, the value is straightforward. If you are storing an object, .NET calls the object's ToString method to get an appropriate string representation. For complex objects, the result may just be the class name.

| Session State | | |
|---|---|---|
| Session Key | Type | Value |
| Test | System.String | This is just a string |
| MyDataSet | System.Data.DataSet | System.Data.DataSet |

## Cookies Collection

The Cookies Collection section, shown in the following illustration, displays all the cookies that are sent with the response, and the content and size of each cookie in bytes. Even if you have not explicitly created a cookie, you will see the ASP.NET_SessionId cookie, which contains the current session ID. If you are using forms-based authentication, you will also see the security cookie.

| Cookies Collection | | |
|---|---|---|
| Name | Value | Size |
| ASP.NET_SessionId | vqa22245szjcs545kripra45 | 42 |

## Headers Collection

The Headers Collection section, shown in the following illustration, lists all the HTTP headers. Generally, you don't need to use this information, although it can be useful for troubleshooting unusual network problems.

| Headers Collection | |
|---|---|
| Name | Value |
| Cache-Control | no-cache |
| Connection | Keep-Alive |
| Content-Length | 68 |
| Content-Type | application/x-www-form-urlencoded |
| Accept | image/gif, image/x-xbitmap, image/jpeg, image/pjpeg, application/vnd.ms-excel, application/msword, application/pdf, */* |
| Accept-Encoding | gzip, deflate |
| Accept-Language | en-us |
| Host | fariamat |
| Referer | http://fariamat/ASP.NET/Chapter11/ErrorHandling/TraceExample.aspx |
| User-Agent | Mozilla/4.0 (compatible; MSIE 6.0; Windows NT 5.1; .NET CLR 1.0.2914) |

## Form Collection

The Form Collection section, shown in the following illustration, lists the posted-back form information.

| Form Collection | |
|---|---|
| **Name** | **Value** |
| __VIEWSTATE | dDwtMjA5NDAxOTA1OTs7Pg== |
| cmdSession | Add Session Item |

## Querystring Collection

The Querystring Collection section, shown in the following illustration, lists the variables and values submitted in the query string. Generally, you will be able to see this information directly in the Address box in the browser, so you won't need to refer to the information here.

| Querystring Collection | |
|---|---|
| **Name** | **Value** |
| search | cat |
| style | full |

## Server Variables

This section lists all the server variables and their contents. You do not generally need to examine this information. Note also that if you want to examine a server variable programmatically, you can do so by name with the built-in Request.ServerVariables collection, or by using one of the more useful higher-level properties from the Request object.

# Writing Trace Information

The default trace log provides a set of important information that allows you to monitor some important aspects of your application, such as the current state contents and the time taken to execute portions of code. In addition, you will often want to generate your own tracing messages. For example, you might want to output the value of a variable at various points in execution, so you can compare it with an expected value. Similarly, you might want to output messages when the code reaches certain points in execution, so you can verify that various procedures are being used (and are used in the order you expect).

To write a custom trace message, you use the Write or the Warn method of the built-in Trace object. Both of these methods are equivalent. The only difference is that Warn displays the message in red, which makes it easier to distinguish from other messages in the list.

```
Private Sub cmdWrite_Click(sender As Object, e As EventArgs) _
  Handles cmdWrite.Click
```

```
    Trace.IsEnabled = True
    Trace.Write("About to place an item in session state.")
    Session("Test") = "Contents"
    Trace.Write("Placed item in session state.")

End Sub
```

These messages appear in the Trace Information section of the page, along with the default messages that ASP.NET generates automatically (see Figure 11-17).

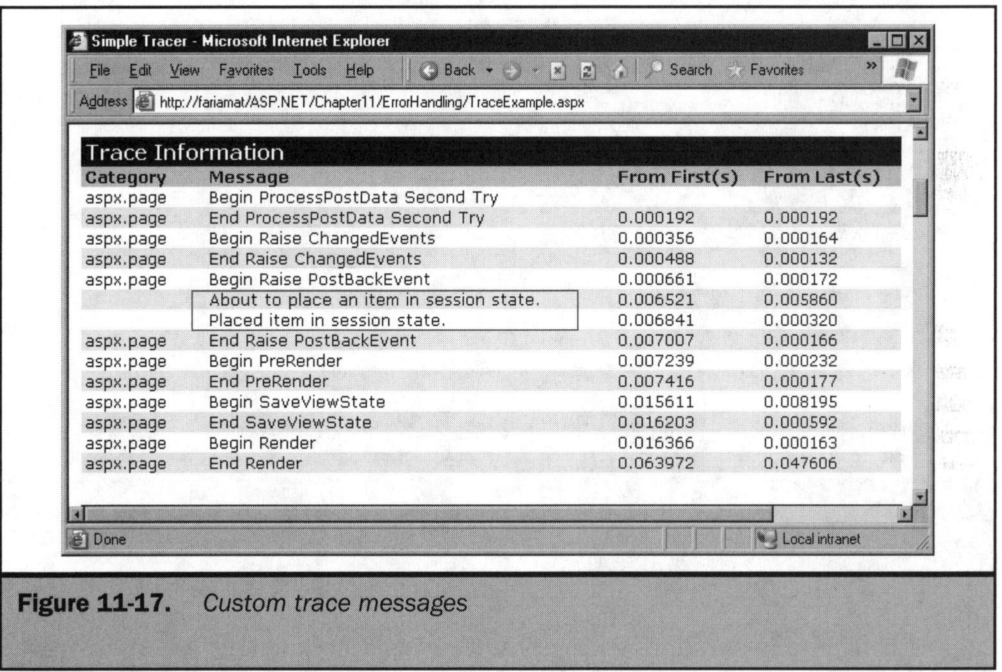


| Category | Message | From First(s) | From Last(s) |
|---|---|---|---|
| aspx.page | Begin ProcessPostData Second Try | | |
| aspx.page | End ProcessPostData Second Try | 0.000192 | 0.000192 |
| aspx.page | Begin Raise ChangedEvents | 0.000356 | 0.000164 |
| aspx.page | End Raise ChangedEvents | 0.000488 | 0.000132 |
| aspx.page | Begin Raise PostBackEvent | 0.000661 | 0.000172 |
| | About to place an item in session state. | 0.006521 | 0.005860 |
| | Placed item in session state. | 0.006841 | 0.000320 |
| aspx.page | End Raise PostBackEvent | 0.007007 | 0.000166 |
| aspx.page | Begin PreRender | 0.007239 | 0.000232 |
| aspx.page | End PreRender | 0.007416 | 0.000177 |
| aspx.page | Begin SaveViewState | 0.015611 | 0.008195 |
| aspx.page | End SaveViewState | 0.016203 | 0.000592 |
| aspx.page | Begin Render | 0.016366 | 0.000163 |
| aspx.page | End Render | 0.063972 | 0.047606 |

**Figure 11-17.** *Custom trace messages*

You can also use an overloaded method of Write or Warn that allows you to specify the category. A common use of this field is to indicate the current procedure, as shown in Figure 11-18.

```
Private Sub cmdWriteCategory_Click(sender As Object, _
  e As System.EventArgs) Handles cmdWriteCategory.Click

    Trace.IsEnabled = True
```

```
    Trace.Write("Page_Load", _
                "About to place an item in session state.")
    Session("Test") = "Contents"
    Trace.Write("Page_Load", "Placed item in session state.")

End Sub
```

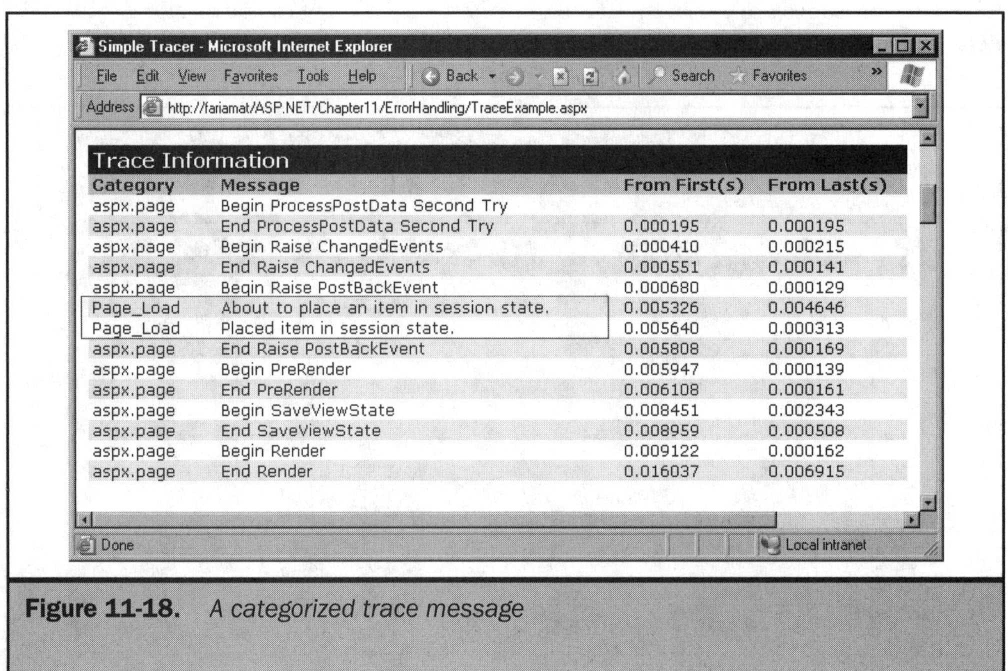


**Figure 11-18.** *A categorized trace message*

Alternatively, you can supply category and message information with an exception object that will automatically be described in the trace log (see Figure 11-19):

```
Private Sub cmdError_Click(sender As Object, e As EventArgs) _
  Handles cmdError.Click

    Try
        DivideNumbers(5, 0)
    Catch err As Exception
        Trace.Warn("cmdError_Click", "Caught Error", err)
    End Try
```

```
End Sub

Private Function DivideNumbers(number As Integer, _
  divisor As Integer) As Integer
    Return (number/divisor)
End Sub
```



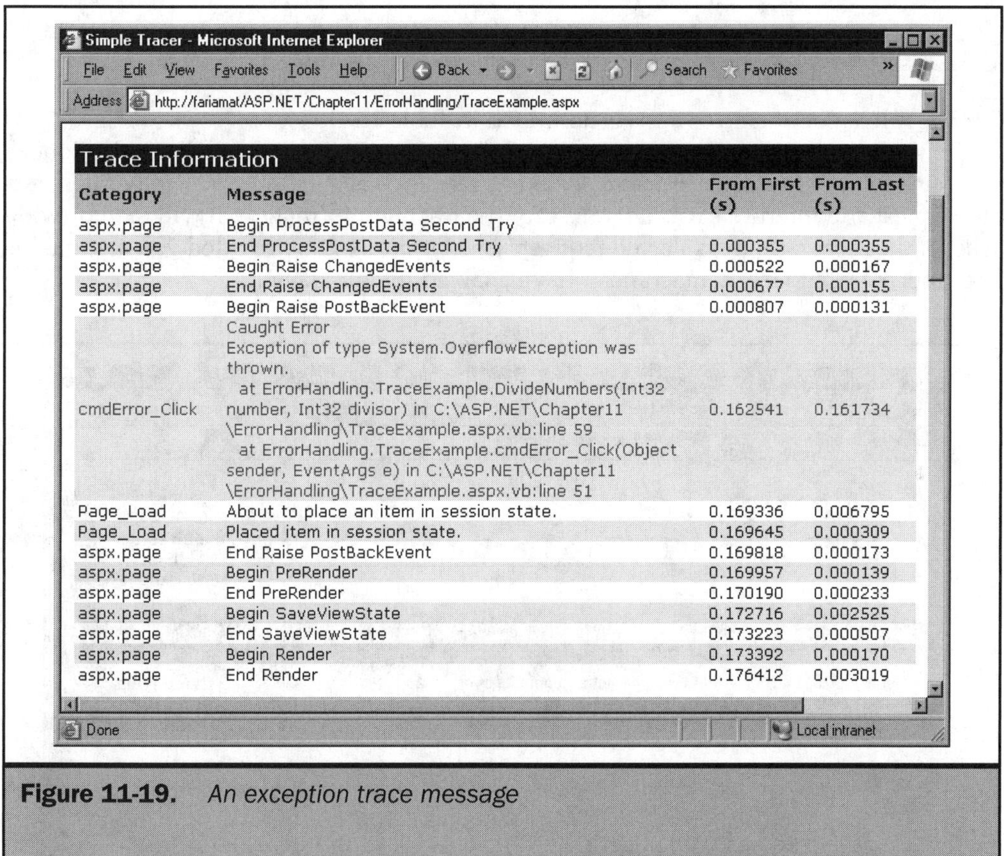


| Category | Message | From First (s) | From Last (s) |
|---|---|---|---|
| aspx.page | Begin ProcessPostData Second Try | | |
| aspx.page | End ProcessPostData Second Try | 0.000355 | 0.000355 |
| aspx.page | Begin Raise ChangedEvents | 0.000522 | 0.000167 |
| aspx.page | End Raise ChangedEvents | 0.000677 | 0.000155 |
| aspx.page | Begin Raise PostBackEvent | 0.000807 | 0.000131 |
| cmdError_Click | Caught Error<br>Exception of type System.OverflowException was thrown.<br>at ErrorHandling.TraceExample.DivideNumbers(Int32 number, Int32 divisor) in C:\ASP.NET\Chapter11\ErrorHandling\TraceExample.aspx.vb:line 59<br>at ErrorHandling.TraceExample.cmdError_Click(Object sender, EventArgs e) in C:\ASP.NET\Chapter11\ErrorHandling\TraceExample.aspx.vb:line 51 | 0.162541 | 0.161734 |
| Page_Load | About to place an item in session state. | 0.169336 | 0.006795 |
| Page_Load | Placed item in session state. | 0.169645 | 0.000309 |
| aspx.page | End Raise PostBackEvent | 0.169818 | 0.000173 |
| aspx.page | Begin PreRender | 0.169957 | 0.000139 |
| aspx.page | End PreRender | 0.170190 | 0.000233 |
| aspx.page | Begin SaveViewState | 0.172716 | 0.002525 |
| aspx.page | End SaveViewState | 0.173223 | 0.000507 |
| aspx.page | Begin Render | 0.173392 | 0.000170 |
| aspx.page | End Render | 0.176412 | 0.003019 |

**Figure 11-19.** *An exception trace message*

By default, trace messages are listed in the order they were outputted by your code. Alternatively, you can specify that messages should be sorted by category, using the TraceMode property of the Trace object:

```
Trace.TraceMode = TraceMode.SortByCategory
```

## Application-Level Tracing

Application-level tracing allows you to enable tracing for an entire application. To do this, you need to modify settings in the web.config file, as shown here:

```
<configuration>
  <system.web>
    <trace enabled="true" requestLimit="10" pageOutput="false"
     traceMode="SortByTime" localOnly="true" />
  </system.web>
</configuration>
```

The full list of tracing options is described in Table 11-4.

To view tracing information, you request the trace.axd file in the web application's root directory. This file doesn't actually exist; instead, ASP.NET automatically intercepts the request and interprets it as a request for the tracing information. It will then provide a list of the most recently collected requests (see Figure 11-20), provided you are making the request from the local machine or have enabled remote tracing.

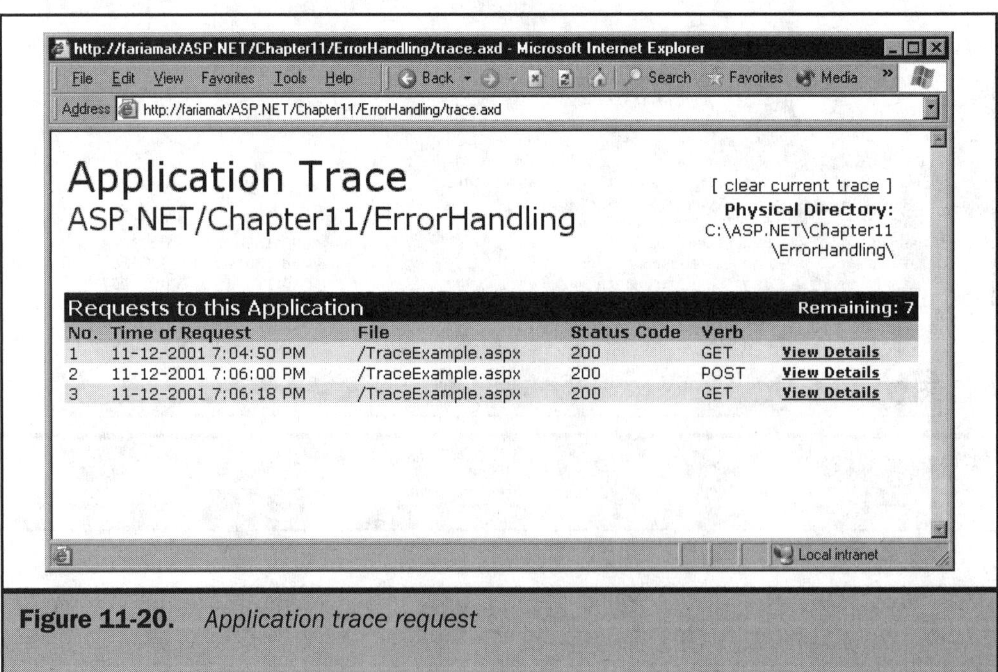


**Figure 11-20.** *Application trace request*

| Attribute | Values | Description |
|---|---|---|
| Enabled | True, False | Turns application-level tracing on or off. |
| requestLimit | Any integer (e.g., 10) | This is the number of HTTP requests for which tracing information will be stored. Unlike page-level tracing, this allows you collect a batch of information from multiple requests. When the maximum is reached, the information for the oldest request is abandoned every time a new request is received. |
| pageOutput | True, False | Determines whether tracing information will be displayed on the page (as it is with page-level tracing). If you choose False, you will still be able to view the collected information by requesting trace.axd from the virtual directory where your application is running. |
| traceMode | SortByTime, SortByCategory | Determines the sort order of trace messages. |
| localOnly | True, False | Determines whether tracing information will be shown only to local clients (clients using the same computer) or to remote clients as well. By default, this is True and remote clients cannot see tracing information. |

**Table 11-4.** *Tracing Options*

You can see the detailed information for any request by clicking the View Details link (see Figure 11-21). This provides a useful way to store tracing information for a short period of time, and review it without needing to see the actual pages. It also works best if you are using Visual Studio .NET's grid layout, which uses absolute positioning that can conflict with the tracing display and lead to overwritten or obscured text.

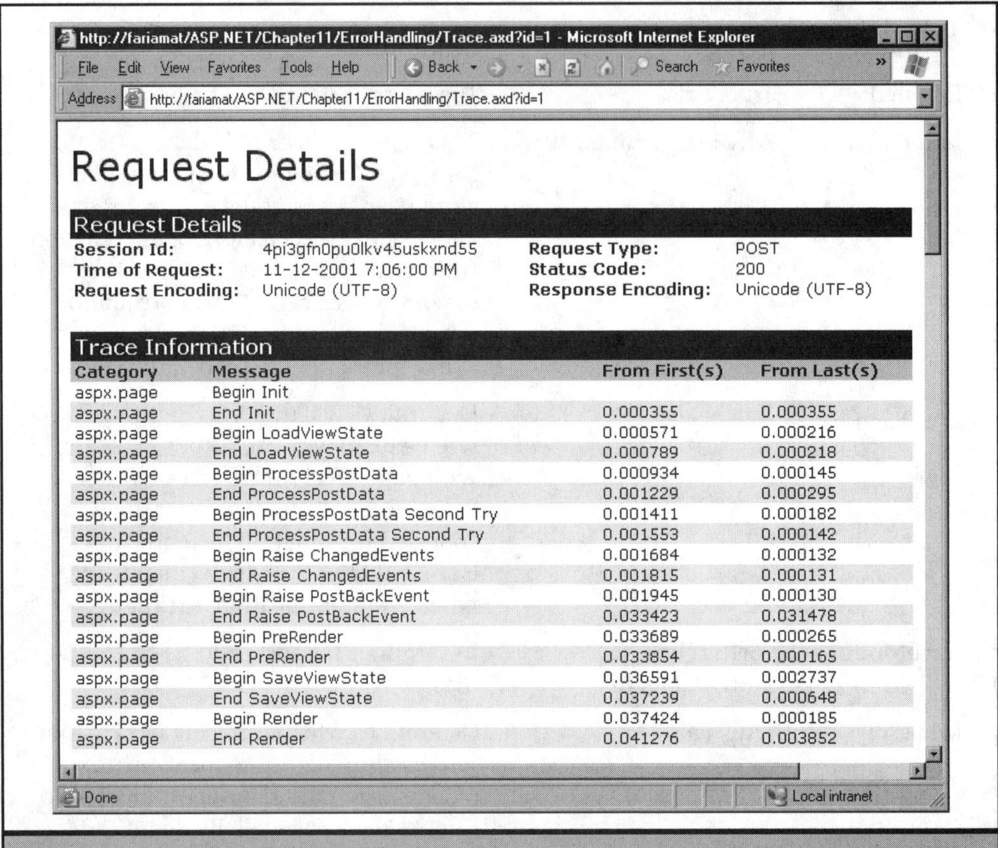


**Figure 11-21.** *Request details of the trace information*

The Complete Reference

# Part III

## Working with Data

# Chapter 12

## Overview of ADO.NET

So far, you've discovered that ASP.NET isn't just a new way to create modern web applications—it's also part of an ambitious multi-layered strategy called .NET. ASP.NET is only one component in Microsoft's .NET platform, which includes a revitalized language (Visual Basic .NET instead of VBScript), a new philosophy for cross-language integration, a new way of looking at components and deployment, and a shared class library with components that allow you to do everything from handling errors to analyzing XML documents. In this chapter, you'll discover that the .NET framework has yet another surprise in store: ADO.NET, the latest version of the Active Data Objects model.

ADO.NET allows you to interact with relational databases and other data sources. Quite simply, ADO.NET is the technology that ASP.NET applications use to communicate with a database, whether they need to add a new customer record, log a purchase, or display a product catalog. If you've worked with ADO before, you'll discover that ADO.NET is much more than a slightly enhanced .NET version of ADO data access technology. As with ASP and Visual Basic, the .NET moniker signals some revolutionary changes. ADO.NET is now optimized for distributed applications (like web applications), based on XML, and outfitted with an entirely new object model.

In this chapter, we'll look at some of the defining features of ADO.NET with a high-level overview. You won't actually get into any real coding—that's all to come in the next few chapters—but you will prepare yourself by learning the basic organization and philosophy of ADO.NET. Along the way, I'll answer some common questions about how ADO and ADO.NET differ, why web developers need a new data access technology, and what ingredients make up a data-driven web application.

## Introducing ADO.NET and Data Management

Almost every piece of software ever written works with data. In fact, a typical Internet application is often just a thin user interface shell on top of a sophisticated database program that reads and writes information from a database on the web server. At its simplest, a database program might allow a user to perform simple searches and display results in a formatted table. A more sophisticated ASP.NET application might use a database "behind the scenes" to retrieve information, which is then processed and displayed in the appropriate format and location in the browser. The user might not even be aware (or care) that the displayed information originates from a database. Using a database is an excellent way to start dividing the user interface logic from the content, which allows you to create a site that can work with dynamic, easily updated data.

In most ASP.NET applications you'll need to use a database for some tasks. Here are some basic examples of data-driven ASP.NET applications:

- **E-commerce sites** involve managing sales, customer, and inventory information. This information might be displayed directly on the screen (as with a product catalog) or used unobtrusively to record transactions or customer information.

- **Online knowledge bases and customized search engines** involve less structured databases that store vast quantities of information, or links to various documents and resources.
- **Information-based sites such as web portals** can't be easily scalable or manageable unless all the information they use is stored in a consistent, strictly defined format. Typically, a site like this is matched with another ASP.NET program that allows an authorized user to add or update the displayed information by modifying the corresponding database records through a browser interface. In Chapter 25, we look at a portal application that is completely configurable and draws all its information from a database.

You probably won't have any trouble thinking about where you need to use database technology in an ASP.NET application. What Internet application couldn't benefit from a guest book that records user comments, or a simple email address submission form that uses a back-end database to store a list of potential customers or contacts?



## A Quick Overview of Databases

The most common way to manage data is by using a database. Database technology is particularly useful for business software, which typically requires hierarchical sets of related information. For example, a typical database for a sales ordering program consists of a list of customers, a list of products, and a list of sales that draws on information from the other two tables. This type of information is best described using a relational model, which is the philosophy that underlies all modern database products, including SQL Server, Oracle, and even Microsoft Access. In a relational model, information is broken down into its smallest and most concise units. A sales record doesn't store all the information about the products that were sold; instead it just stores a product ID that refers to a full record in a product table (see Figure 12-1).

While it's technically possible to create these tables, add all the information you need, and store it as an XML file using ADO.NET, this wouldn't be very flexible. Instead, additional products such as SQL Server are usually required to handle the basic database infrastructure. These products take responsibility for providing the data to multiple users simultaneously and make sure that certain rules are followed (for example, disallowing conflicting changes or invalid data types). These products also provide all the tools that you will usually use to create and modify database information. Figure 12-2 shows SQL Server's Enterprise Manager, which is usually the easiest way to design and create tables in an SQL Server database. As an ASP.NET developer, you may have the responsibility of creating these tables for web applications. Alternatively, they may already exist or may be the responsibility of a dedicated database administrator.

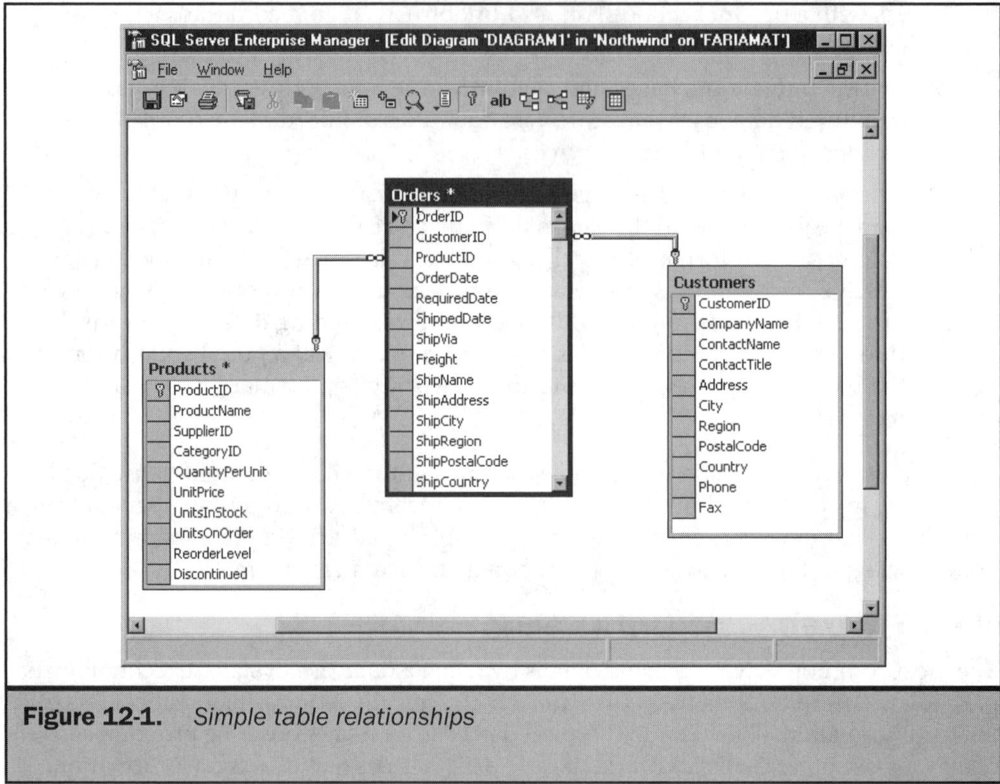


**Figure 12-1.** *Simple table relationships*

That's where ADO.NET comes into the picture. ADO.NET is a technology designed to let an ASP.NET program (or any other .NET program, for that matter) access data. Typically, you'll use ADO.NET to access a relational database, but you could also use it to work with raw XML information, or other data sources such as email messages stored in an Exchange mail server. More and more, ADO.NET is becoming a standard way to access and exchange any type of information.

## Database Access in the Internet World

Accessing a database in an Internet application is a completely different scenario than accessing a database in a typical desktop or client/server program. Most developers hone their database skills in the desktop world, and run into serious problems when they try to apply what they have learned in the world of web applications. Web applications raise a whole new set of considerations and potential problems. These problems have plagued ASP developers for years and are finally dealt with directly by ADO.NET's new design.

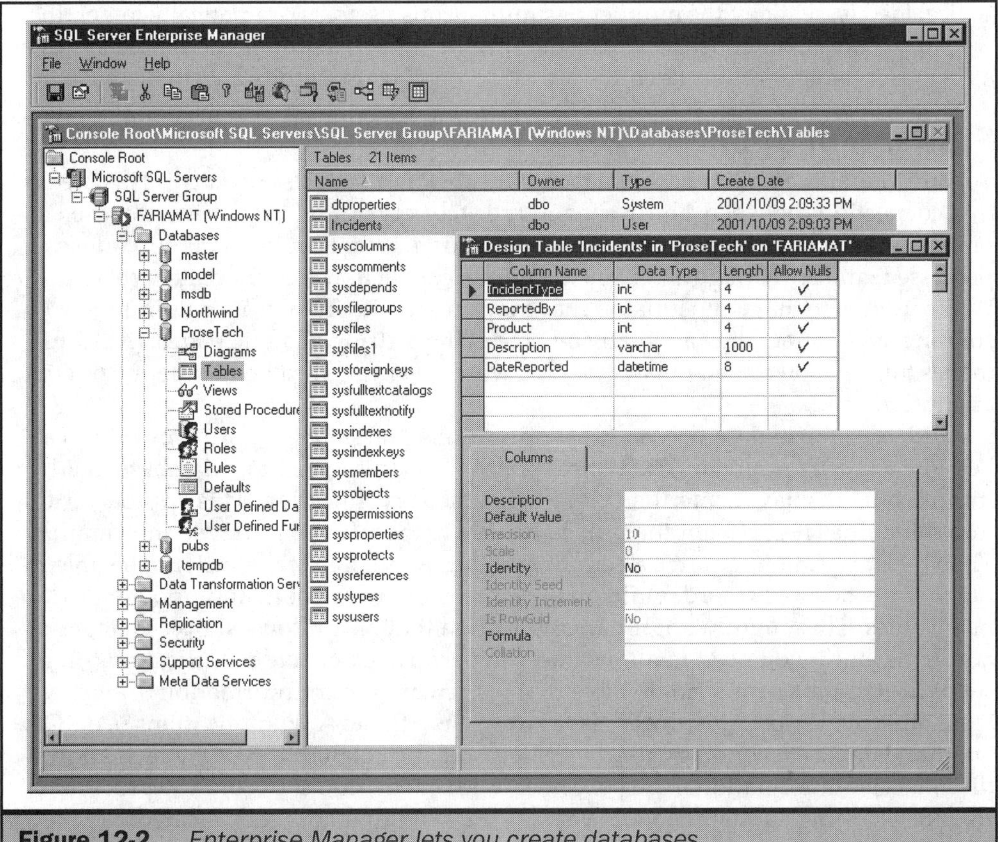


**Figure 12-2.** *Enterprise Manager lets you create databases.*



## Problems of Scale

A web application has the potential to be used by hundreds of simultaneous users. This means that it can't be casual about using server memory or limited resources like database connections. If you design an ASP application that acquires a database connection and holds it for even a few minutes, other users may notice a significant slowdown or even be locked out of the database completely. And if database concurrency issues aren't carefully thought out, problems such as locked records and conflicting updates can make it difficult to provide consistent data to all users.

All of these problems are possible with traditional client/server database development. The difference is that they are far less likely to have any negative effect because the typical load (essentially the number of simultaneous users) is dramatically lower. In a web application, database practices that might slightly hamper the performance of a client/server application can multiply rapidly and cause significant problems.

## Problems of State

You are probably familiar with the fact that HTTP is a stateless protocol. This means that connections between a browser and the web server aren't maintained. When a user browses to a page in an ASP.NET application, a connection is made, code is processed, an HTML page is returned, and the connection is immediately severed. While users may have the illusion that they are interacting with a continuously running application, they are really just receiving a string of static pages. (ASP.NET makes this illusion so convincing that it's worth asking if it can really be considered an illusion at all.)

With traditional data-driven ASP applications, the stateless nature of HTTP can be quite a thorny problem. The typical approach is to connect to a database, read information, display it, and then close the database connection. This approach runs into difficulties if you want the user to be able to modify the retrieved information. Then the application requires a certain amount of intelligence in order to be able to identify the original record, build an SQL statement to select it, and update it to the new values. This might work for an application that only allows simple changes or additions, but if you need to allow a user to perform extensive modifications on a set of related tables (or a single table that was created from information drawn from multiple tables), the process is far from easy. Some ASP applications use RDS, another database technology used by Microsoft and related to ADO, which allows disconnected information to be processed with client-side code, but the process requires learning another new data access technology, and is complicated by questions about browser capability and security.

## Problems of Communication and Compatibility

Sending data over an internal network is easy. Sending information over the Internet is also easy, as long as you stick to standard text and the HTTP protocol. Generally, ADO could be used in a true multi-platform Internet application without any problems because all the actual code is performed on the Windows web server. However, in some occasions the proprietary (and some might say Microsoft-centric) nature of ADO starts to show through. For one thing, using RDS and client-side database scripting imposes some unrealistic requirements on the type of browser. Also, sending data to remote components using ADO requires the use of COM calls or ADO's binary data format, which can run into trouble with a firewall. Don't even ask how you can work with the data in a component on a non-Microsoft platform like Linux or Macintosh—you can't!

# Characteristics of ADO.NET

ADO.NET is interesting because in many ways it inverts Microsoft's previous database access philosophy. Features that were optional add-ons in ADO are now part of the core feature set, and the cursor-driven, COM-based technology that was touted in ADO has been completely eliminated. Following are some of the most dramatic changes that together make up the overall philosophy of ADO.NET data access.

## Disconnected Access

Disconnected access is the most important characteristic of ADO.NET, the greatest change from ADO, and perhaps the single best example of the new .NET philosophy for accessing data. In a typical ADO application, you connect to the database, create a Recordset, use the information to fill a DataGrid or calculate some type of summary information, and then abandon the Recordset and close the connection. While the connection is open, you have a "live" (or cursor-based) connection with the database that allows you to make immediate updates and, in some cases, see the changes made by other users in real time. In a poorly written program, the database connection might be kept open while other tasks are being performed, which means that important resources are being used, potentially limiting the number of other users that can access the database and use the ASP.NET application.

ASP.NET has a different philosophy entirely. In ASP.NET you still create a connection to a database, but you can't use a cursor. Instead, you fill a DataSet with a copy of the information drawn from the database. If you change the information in the DataSet, the information in the corresponding table in the database is not changed. That means you can easily change and manipulate values without worry, because you aren't using a valuable database connection. When needed, the DataSet can be connected back to the original data source, and all the changes can be applied.



### Disconnected Access Raises New Issues

Disconnected access is a key requirement for Internet applications, and it is also an approach that often requires additional consideration and precautions. Disconnected access makes it easy for users to create inconsistent updates, a problem that won't be resolved (or even identified) until the update is applied to the original data source. Disconnected access can also require special considerations because changes are not applied in the order they were entered. This design can cause problems when you add relational data.

Fortunately, ADO.NET provides a rich set of features to deal with all these possibilities and provide performance that is almost always superior to ADO. However, you do need to be aware that the new disconnected model may introduce new considerations and require extra care. We'll examine all these issues in the following ADO.NET chapters.

# Native XML

ADO.NET uses XML natively to store data. This fact is not automatically obvious when you are working with ADO.NET DataSets, because you will usually use the DataSet object's built-in methods and properties to perform all the data manipulation you need. In this case, you will access data in a row-based fashion that resembles ADO. You might also make the reasonable (but incorrect) assumption that XML is just another import and export format supported by ADO.NET for advanced compatibility. In fact, XML plays a far greater role.

In reality, when you retrieve information from a database into an ADO.NET DataSet, the data is stored in memory in an XML format. If you want, you can modify values, remove rows, and add new records using XML Document Object Model (DOM), which is available in .NET through the types in the System.Xml namespaces. Similarly, you could read an appropriately formatted XML document, work with it using the ADO.NET database objects, and conclude by writing it back to an XML file or creating a matching table in a relational database.

Figure 12-3 shows a sample customer table in SQL Server's Enterprise Manager.

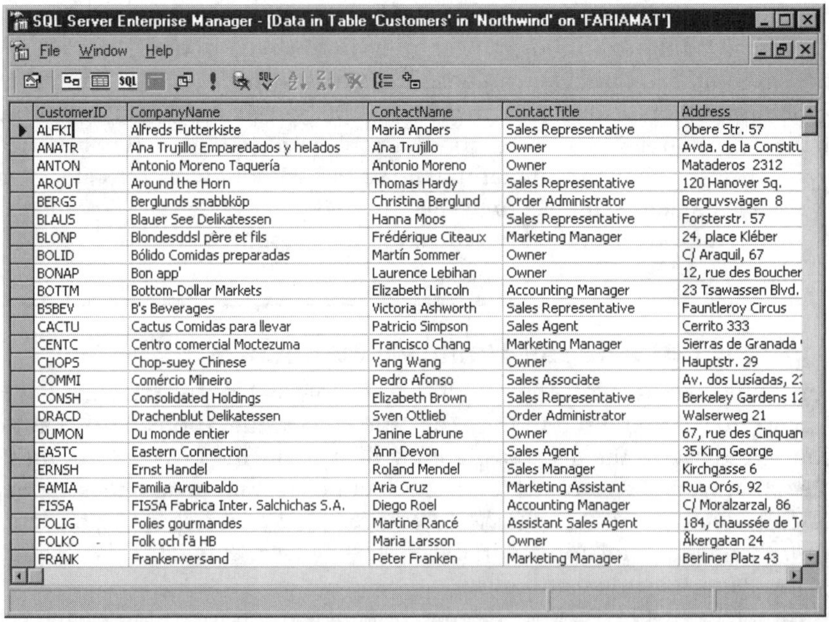

SQL Server Enterprise Manager - [Data in Table 'Customers' in 'Northwind' on 'FARIAMAT']

File Window Help

| CustomerID | CompanyName | ContactName | ContactTitle | Address |
|---|---|---|---|---|
| ALFKI | Alfreds Futterkiste | Maria Anders | Sales Representative | Obere Str. 57 |
| ANATR | Ana Trujillo Emparedados y helados | Ana Trujillo | Owner | Avda. de la Constitu |
| ANTON | Antonio Moreno Taquería | Antonio Moreno | Owner | Mataderos 2312 |
| AROUT | Around the Horn | Thomas Hardy | Sales Representative | 120 Hanover Sq. |
| BERGS | Berglunds snabbköp | Christina Berglund | Order Administrator | Berguvsvägen 8 |
| BLAUS | Blauer See Delikatessen | Hanna Moos | Sales Representative | Forsterstr. 57 |
| BLONP | Blondesddsl père et fils | Frédérique Citeaux | Marketing Manager | 24, place Kléber |
| BOLID | Bólido Comidas preparadas | Martín Sommer | Owner | C/ Araquil, 67 |
| BONAP | Bon app' | Laurence Lebihan | Owner | 12, rue des Boucher |
| BOTTM | Bottom-Dollar Markets | Elizabeth Lincoln | Accounting Manager | 23 Tsawassen Blvd. |
| BSBEV | B's Beverages | Victoria Ashworth | Sales Representative | Fauntleroy Circus |
| CACTU | Cactus Comidas para llevar | Patricio Simpson | Sales Agent | Cerrito 333 |
| CENTC | Centro comercial Moctezuma | Francisco Chang | Marketing Manager | Sierras de Granada |
| CHOPS | Chop-suey Chinese | Yang Wang | Owner | Hauptstr. 29 |
| COMMI | Comércio Mineiro | Pedro Afonso | Sales Associate | Av. dos Lusíadas, 2 |
| CONSH | Consolidated Holdings | Elizabeth Brown | Sales Representative | Berkeley Gardens 1 |
| DRACD | Drachenblut Delikatessen | Sven Ottlieb | Order Administrator | Walserweg 21 |
| DUMON | Du monde entier | Janine Labrune | Owner | 67, rue des Cinquan |
| EASTC | Eastern Connection | Ann Devon | Sales Agent | 35 King George |
| ERNSH | Ernst Handel | Roland Mendel | Sales Manager | Kirchgasse 6 |
| FAMIA | Familia Arquibaldo | Aria Cruz | Marketing Assistant | Rua Orós, 92 |
| FISSA | FISSA Fabrica Inter. Salchichas S.A. | Diego Roel | Accounting Manager | C/ Moralzarzal, 86 |
| FOLIG | Folies gourmandes | Martine Rancé | Assistant Sales Agent | 184, chaussée de T |
| FOLKO | Folk och fä HB | Maria Larsson | Owner | Åkergatan 24 |
| FRANK | Frankenversand | Peter Franken | Marketing Manager | Berliner Platz 43 |

**Figure 12-3.** *Partial listing of a database table*

Figure 12-4 shows the XML document that ADO.NET creates for the customer table automatically. The XML is displayed courtesy of a simple utility included with the online samples for this chapter. I haven't included the code yet because we won't explore the specifics of how to connect to a database until Chapter 13. The important concept to understand now is that this XML shows ADO.NET's internal representation of the selected data. The ASP.NET application does not need to perform any additional steps or conversion.

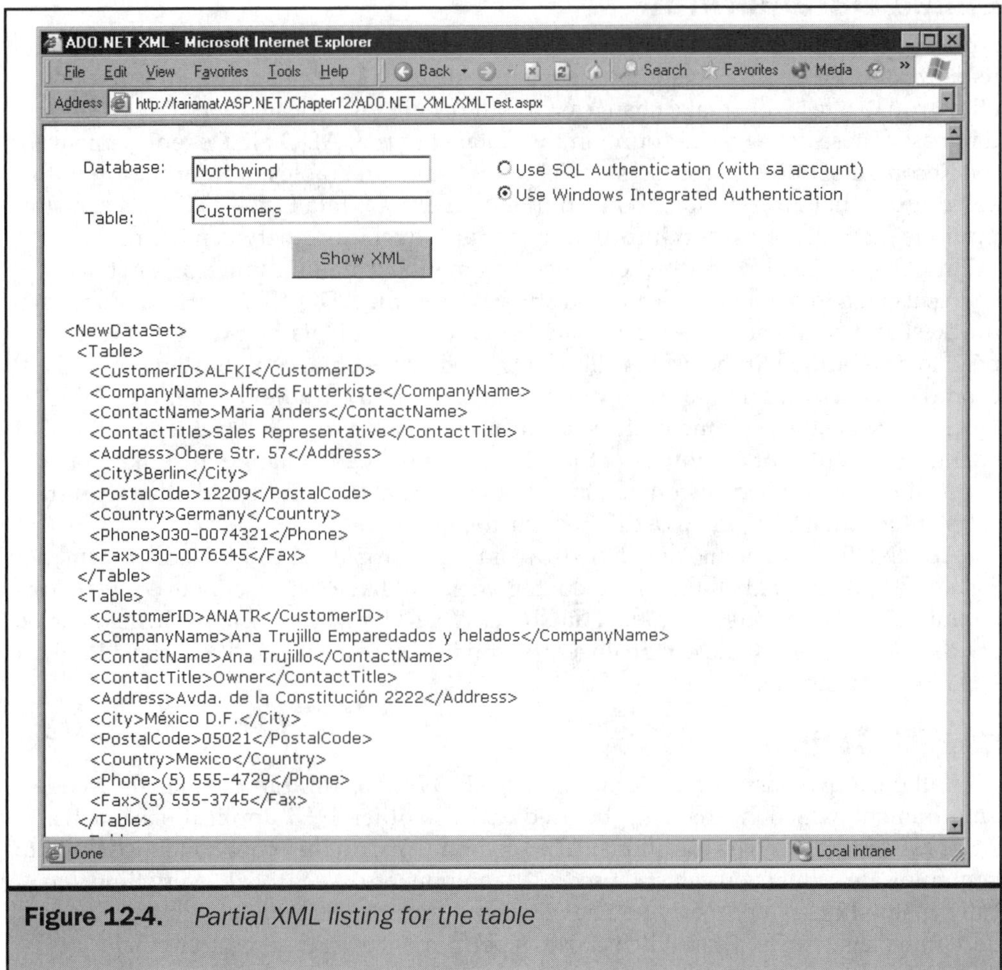


**Figure 12-4.** *Partial XML listing for the table*

In other words, ADO.NET is built on XML technology from the ground up and, as a result, it provides a dual programming model. This book focuses on using the ADO.NET objects rather than the XML document model, because this approach is generally more useful and much more convenient for database access. However, if you are working with a large cross-platform project that uses XML to transfer information from one component to another, this dual functionality can be very useful. Chapter 17 sheds more light on XML programming with ASP.NET.

## Extended Data Format

ADO.NET has a self-sufficiency that ADO never had. Part of this change results from its new role as a disconnected data manager. ADO.NET retains more information to allow you to effectively make changes without needing to repeatedly reconnect to the database. These changes are found in the DataSet object, ADO.NET's replacement for the Recordset. Unlike Recordsets, which were really just tables of information with some additional information about column names and data types, DataSets can store multiple distinct tables, and information about the relations between them.

In ADO, a typical Recordset combines information from multiple tables in the data source using a Join query. This method still works in the ADO.NET world, and it is the quickest and most convenient approach when you are displaying data that doesn't need to be modified. If the user is allowed to modify the data, complications arise. For example, the user might modify a value that corresponds to a field in a linked table (such as the customer name in the sales information report). The problem with this change is that it's not obvious whether the user is trying to change the linked table (correcting a misspelled customer name) or the original table (indicating that a given sales order actually applies to a different customer).

ADO.NET gives you the flexibility to avoid these problems. You can add information for several interrelated tables, link them together, and have the functional equivalent of a miniature, disconnected relational database. When changes need to be flushed back to the data source, each table can be lined up with its original source. (We'll consider these techniques in Chapter 13.)

## Managed Code

Like all the .NET class library components, ADO.NET is built in the managed code environment, which means it can be used easily in other .NET applications (such as ASP.NET programs). The traditional ADO components, on the other hand, use COM to communicate. While you can still use COM components in ASP.NET, every time you call a method or set a property you have to jump over the boundary between managed and unmanaged code. This switch causes a performance lag that reduces efficiency. ADO.NET, however, talks natively to any other .NET component.

### Data Providers

You might wonder where OLE DB fits into all of this. OLE DB was an important standard that supported ADO. In essence, ADO could communicate with any database that had an OLE DB provider. ADO.NET is exactly the same. Of course, communicating with the standard OLE DB providers still means a jump from managed to unmanaged code, but other providers are on the way to provide better performance. In the meantime, you can rest assured that you can connect to almost anything in ADO.NET that was supported in ADO.

One managed provider that is already available for ADO.NET is the SQL Server provider. ADO.NET provides its own set of classes customized for SQL Server access. They work almost exactly the same as the OLE DB equivalents, but they skip the entire OLE DB level and interact directly through SQL's Tabular Data Stream (TDS), guaranteeing excellent performance.

## Comparing ADO and ADO.NET

Earlier versions of ADO were designed for desktop use and added Internet-friendly functionality as an afterthought. ADO.NET is a revolutionary change that inverts this picture. This change allows all .NET programmers to use ADO.NET in exactly the same way—whether they are designing for the desktop, client/server, or web environment. These changes don't come without some growing pains for the ADO programmer, however. Not only has the object model been entirely redesigned, but common tasks like data binding and updating data have changed considerably.

The scenarios that follow illustrate the difference between ADO and ADO.NET in some common situations.



### Scenario 1: Looping Through a Table

Consider the case where you need to display a list of database information by iterating through a table of data. In ADO, you would create a fast-forward, read-only connection with the Connection object, fill a Recordset, and loop through it using the MoveNext method. As soon as the operation was complete, you would close the connection.

In this case, ADO.NET is quite similar. You still use the Connection and Command objects, but instead of going through a Recordset (or DataSet, the ADO.NET replacement), you can use a DataReader, which is a special object designed to move quickly through a read-only set of data.

### Scenario 2: Looping Through Parent-Child Tables

Sometimes you want to display a set of hierarchical information in a way that clearly shows the parent-child relationship. For example, you might need to show a nested table listing sales orders information inside a list of customers.

In ADO, this type of table is easy to create, but requires a significant amount of manual work. One approach is to fill multiple Recordsets (in this case a Customers Recordset and a Sales Recordset). For every record in the Customers table, you would need to search through the Sales table to find any links. Another approach would be to use a Join query to create a single compound Recordset, and sort it by customer. In this case, as you loop through the table you would need to continuously check the current customer. Whenever a new customer appears, you would start a new customer group. These approaches, which are both fairly simple on the surface, often lead to a lot of extra coding and repeated database queries.

In ADO.NET, this type of manual work is greatly simplified through a collection-based approach. You would just retrieve the Customers and Sales tables, add them both separately to a DataSet, and define the relation. You could then loop through all the sales for each customer using a standard For/Each statement like this:

```
For Each CustomerRow In CustomerTable.Rows
    ' Display the customer group.
    For Each SalesRow In CustomerRow.GetChildRows(SalesRelationship)
        ' Display each sale for that customer.
    Next
Next
```

We'll explore this technique in more detail in Chapter 13.

## Scenario 3: Retrieving, Processing, and Updating Data

In ADO, retrieving, processing, and updating data is more or less automatic, because a connection to the database is always present. Typically, you read information using a Connection (and possibly a Command) object, place it in a Recordset, and make changes, which take effect automatically.

In ADO.NET, the DataSet is not directly connected to the database. To get information from the database into the DataSet, and to move changes from the DataSet back to the database, you need to use a special adapter object (either SqlAdapter or OleAdapter). This adapter bridges the gap between the DataSet and the data source, and allows information to shuttle back and forth.

## Scenario 4: Disconnected Use

In ADO, you created a disconnected Recordset by creating a Connection and filling the Recordset as you would normally, and then removing the Connection. To commit changes, you would reconnect and use the Update or UpdateBatch method of the Recordset. As previously discussed, you could have problems updating the original information if your Recordset was composed out of multiple joined tables.

In ADO.NET, no special steps need to be taken. DataSets are automatically disconnected, and information is not transmitted directly, but through the appropriate data adapter object.

### Can I Still Use ADO?

ADO provides some features that ADO.NET cannot. For example, ADO allows you to create a Recordset that automatically refreshes itself when another user changes data on the server, guaranteeing that it is always up to date. ADO also allows you to lock records that you might be about to change, making it easy to guarantee exclusive access without worrying about stored procedures or transactions. However, while these concepts may still play a role in some client/server and desktop programs, they are fundamentally incompatible with Internet applications. No ASP.NET application can effectively maintain a connection for a user over the Internet—and even if you could, it would never make sense for a single user to have exclusive access to information that needs to be shared with a broad community of users. For these reasons, ADO.NET is the only practical database access model for ASP.NET applications.



# The ADO.NET Object Model

This section introduces the ADO.NET components and explains how they interact. These objects are the foundation of ADO.NET programming, and we will return to them consistently over the next three chapters to create, read, update, and process data.

## Data Namespaces

The ADO.NET components live in five main namespaces in the .NET class library. Together, these namespaces hold all the functionality that we call ADO.NET. The following list describes each data namespace:

**System.Data** Contains fundamental classes with the core ADO.NET functionality. These include DataSet and DataRelation, which allow you to manipulate structured relational data. These classes are totally independent of any specific type of database or the way you use to connect to it.

**System.Data.Common** These classes are not used directly in your code. Instead, they are used by other classes in the System.Data.SqlClient and System.Data.OleDb namespaces, which inherit from them and provide specific versions customized for SQL Server and OLE DB providers.

**System.Data.OleDb** Contains the classes you use to connect to the OLE DB provider, including OleDbCommand and OleDbConnection. (These classes support all OLE DB providers except the OLE DB driver for ODBC data sources.)

**System.Data.SqlClient** Contains the classes you use to connect to a Microsoft SQL Server database. These classes, like SqlDbCommand and SqlDbConnection, provide all the same properties and methods as their counterparts in the System. Data.OleDb namespace. The only difference is that they are optimized for SQL Server, and provide better performance by eliminating extra OLE DB/COM layers (and connecting the optimized Tabular Data Stream (TDS) interface directly).

**System.Data.SqlTypes** Contains structures for SQL Server-specific data types such as SqlMoney and SqlDateTime. You can use these types to work with SQL Server data types without needing to convert them into the standard .NET equivalents (such as System.Decimal and System.DateTime). These data types aren't required, but they do allow you to avoid any potential rounding or conversion problems that could adversely affect data. They may also increase speed by eliminating the need for automatic conversions.

## ADO.NET Objects

ADO.NET relies on the functionality in a few core objects. These objects can be divided into two groups: those that are used to contain and manage data (DataSet, DataTable, DataRow, and DataRelation are a few examples) and those that are used to connect to a specific data source (the Connections, Commands, and DataReader classes).

The ADO.NET objects in this second group are provided in two different flavors: the standard version of OLE DB providers, and a special version for SQL Server interaction that increases performance. Both versions work almost exactly the same; the only difference is that the classes designed for SQL Server bypass the OLE DB layer, and provide better performance. Microsoft makes other managed providers available through their web site (including a managed provided for ODBC), and may incorporate them into the .NET framework in the future, allowing you to improve performance without having to significantly alter your code. Remember, both the OLE DB and SQL Server types derive from the same basic classes in System.Data.Common. They also provide the same interface (methods and properties). Only the internal, "behind the scenes" details are different. For example, SqlCommand and OleDbCommand both allow you to execute an SQL statement or stored procedure against a data source.

In the following chapters, you'll become very familiar with all these objects. In the remaining sections of this chapter, I'll briefly introduce them all and give a high-level overview of how they work together.

## The Data Objects

The data objects allow you to store a local, disconnected copy of data. They don't store a connection to a data source—in fact, you can create all the data objects by hand without even using a database. You should also note that no matter what type of data source you use, objects like DataSet and DataRelation are generic.

The object model is shown in Figure 12-5.

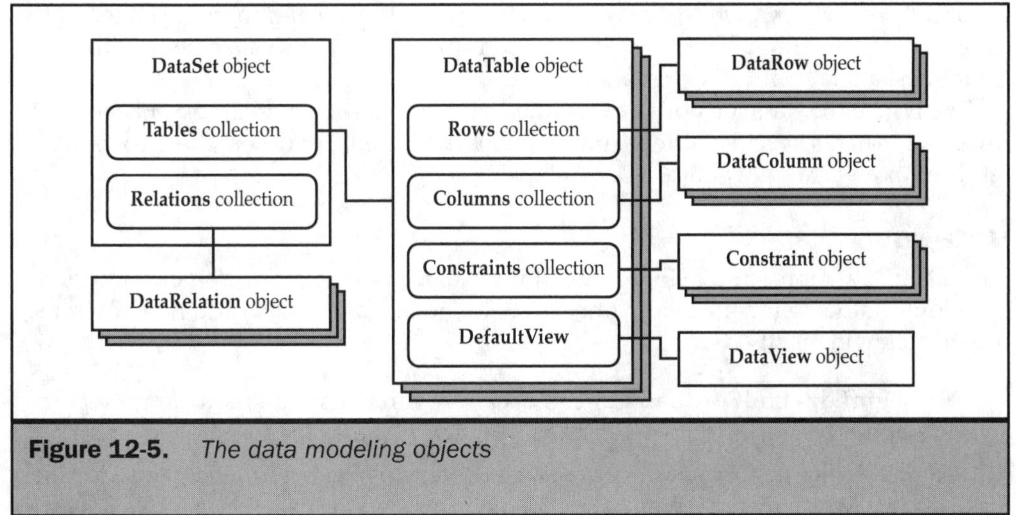


**Figure 12-5.** *The data modeling objects*



## DataSet

This is the core of ADO.NET. The DataSet class stores disconnected information drawn from a database and allows you to manipulate it as a single, neatly packaged object. The DataSet class has no direct connection to a data source. In fact, you can create a DataSet by hand without involving a database at all.

DataSets contains two main types of objects: DataTables (provided in the Tables property) and DataRelations (provided in the Relations property). DataSets support the following methods:

- **WriteXML** and **ReadXML** allow the DataSet to be serialized to an XML file and read back from a file.
- **Merge** adds the contents of one DataSet into another.
- **Clear** removes all the information in the DataSet. You can also just destroy the object (by setting it to Nothing or letting it go out of scope) without using this method.
- **AcceptChanges**, **GetChanges**, and **RejectChanges** allow you to work with the modified data, examining, implementing, or reverting changes. Note that these methods don't update the original data source. Chapter 13 examines the DataSet's ability to store multiple values.

## DataTable

You can add information into a DataSet one table at a time. The DataTable object represents one of these tables. It contains a collection of DataRows (in the Rows property), which contains all the data in the table. It also provides a collection of DataColumns (in the Columns property), which contains information about each column in the table, and a collection of Constraint objects (in the Columns property), which specifies additional column metadata such as the primary key.

The DataTable class includes a Select method that allows you to grab a subset of rows that match a specified filter expression, in a specified sort order. These rows are returned as an array, not another DataTable.

## DataRow

Each DataRow represents a single row of information in the table. You can access individual values using the field name or a field index. You can also add new rows and use the following methods:

- **BeginEdit**, **EndEdit**, and **CancelEdit** allow you to use edit mode to make a series of changes to a row, and apply or cancel them all at once.
- **Delete** marks a row as deleted, and hides it from the default view used for the table, which means it won't appear when you bind the data to a control. However, the row will still be present in the DataTable until you update the data source and refresh the DataSet. (In fact, the row needs to be present so that your program can find and remove the row from the original data source when you update it.) Again, we'll cover this in depth in Chapter 13.
- **GetChildRows** uses the table relations you have defined to get rows from a linked table. For example, when using a Customers table you can use GetChildRows to retrieve all the corresponding order records from the Orders table.

## DataColumn

Unlike the DataRow objects, the DataColumn objects don't contain any actual data. Instead, they store information about the column, such as the column's data type, its default value, and various restrictions (its length, whether null values are allowed, and so on).

## DataRelation

Each DataRelation object specifies a single parent/child relationship between two different tables in a DataSet. For example, a DataRelation could indicate that the CustomerID column in the Orders table corresponds to the CustomerID column in the Customers table. As with any relational database, using a relation implies certain restrictions. For example, you can't create a child row that refers to a nonexistent parent, and you can't delete a parent that has corresponding child rows.

While it is easy to add a table from a data source into a DataSet, there is currently no corresponding way to get information like DataRelations. If you want to create a

DataRelation in a DataSet to mirror the logic in your database, you need to do it manually.

### DataView

The DataView object provides a window onto a DataTable. Each DataTable has at least one DataView (provided through the DefaultView property), which is used for data binding. In many cases, the DataView simply shows all the information in the DataTable, with no changes. In other cases, you can use the DataView to apply special filtering or sorting options. These frills aren't available in a DataTable, because they affect the *presentation* of data. The DataTable object is only concerned with data *content*. DataViews also allow you to format a single DataTable in more than one way by creating separate DataView objects. However, DataViews don't have any capabilities to hide specific columns or change the order of columns. To hide or rearrange columns, you have to work with the actual ASP.NET control.

## The Data Source Interaction Objects

On their own, the data objects can't accomplish much. You might want to add tables, rows, and data by hand, but in most cases the information you need is located in a data source such as a relational database. To access this information, extract it, and insert it into the appropriate data objects, you need the objects described in this section. Remember, each one of these objects has a database-specific implementation. That means you use a different, essentially equivalent object depending on whether you are interacting with SQL Server or an OLE DB provider.

The goal of the data source objects is to create a connection and move information into a DataSet or into a DataReader. The overall interaction of these objects is shown in Figure 12-6. This diagram shows the simplest way of accessing a database—going straight to the source with Command objects and retrieving read-only rows through a DataReader. Figure 12-7 shows your other option: placing data into a disconnected DataSet to work with over a more extended period of time.

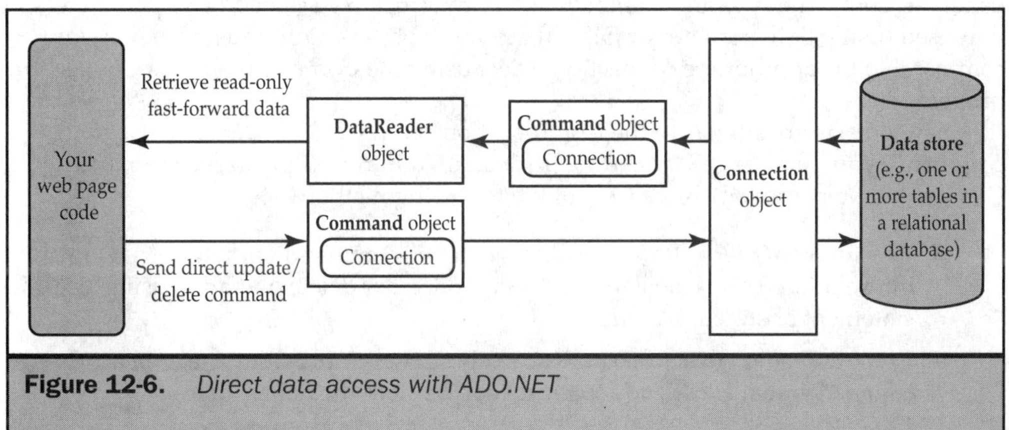


**Figure 12-6.** *Direct data access with ADO.NET*

WORKING WITH DATA

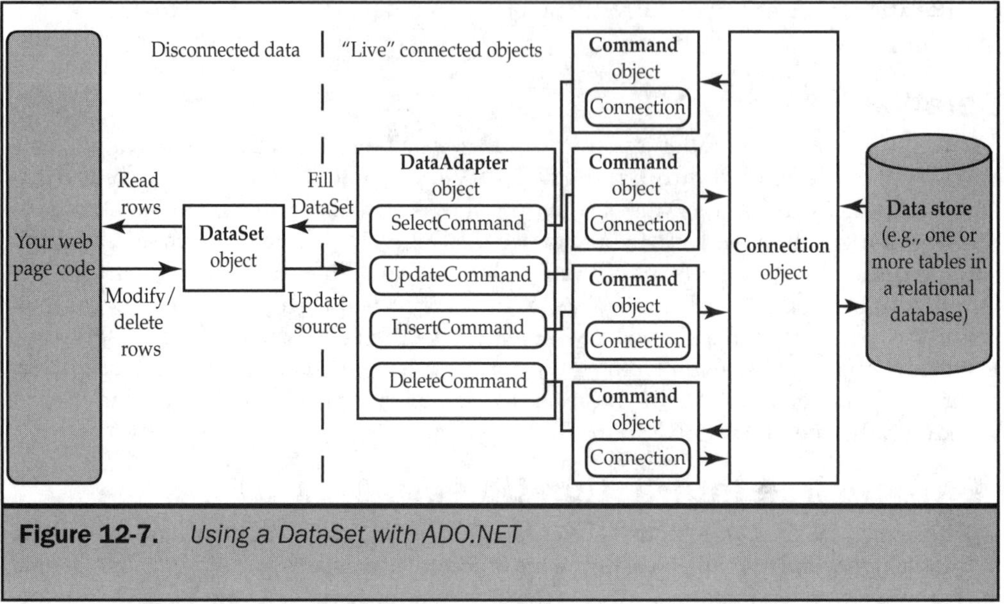


**Figure 12-7.** *Using a DataSet with ADO.NET*

## SqlConnection and OleDbConnection

These objects allow you to establish a connection (using the Open method), which is the first step in any database operation. They also allow you to start a transaction (using the BeginTransaction method). These objects are similar to ADO's Connection object.

## SqlCommand and OleDbCommand

These objects represent an SQL statement or stored procedure that you can use against a data source to retrieve, update, or modify data. You set information into a command using the CommandType and CommandText properties. You can add any parameters you need (using SqlParameter or OleDbParameter objects). You must also link your command to the appropriate connection object using the Command object's Connection property.

These objects are similar to the Command object in ADO. To actually use your command, you must use a DataAdapter (described in the "SqlDataAdapter and OleDataAdapter" section), or use one of the following methods:

- **ExecuteNonQuery** allows you to execute the command without retrieving any information. This is ideal for an insert, update, or delete operation using an SQL statement or stored procedure.
- **ExecuteReader** creates a DataReader object, which provides a fast forward-only connection that allows you to retrieve rows from the data source.

- **ExecuteScalar** also creates a reader, but it only returns a single value: the first column from the first row of the resulting rowset. This method can be used if you are using an SQL statement or stored procedure that returns a value (like a field average or total) instead of a rowset.

## SqlDataReader and OleDbDataReader

The SqlDataReader and OleDbDataReader objects provide a steady stream of data. They are the fastest way to read data when all you want to do is display it in a web page, and you don't need any capability to manipulate or update it later on. These classes are the equivalent of ADO's fast forward-only cursor. They maintain a live connection with a data source, but they don't allow any changes. To get a row of information from an SqlDataReader or OleDbDataReader object, you use the Read method.

## SqlDataAdapter and OleDataAdapter

These objects, which derive from the common DataAdapter class, act as a bridge between a Command and a DataSet. For example, you can create an SQL statement that selects a set of rows, create a Command that represents it, and use the SqlDataAdapter or OleDataAdapter object to automatically retrieve all the matching values and insert them into a supplied DataSet. Similarly, you can use the SqlDataAdapter and OleDataAdapter objects for the reverse procedure, to update a data source based on a modified DataSet.

Every DataAdapter can hold a reference to four different commands, one for each type of operation. You set these commands through the DeleteCommand, InsertCommand, SelectCommand, and UpdateCommand properties. You don't need to create Command objects for all these properties if you don't want to perform the corresponding task. For example, you only need to set the SelectCommand if you're just interested in retrieving rows.

Once you have set the appropriate commands, you can use one of the following methods:

- **Fill** executes the SelectCommand and places the results into the DataSet you supply.
- **FillSchema** uses the SelectCommand to retrieve information about a table, such as column constraints, and add it to a DataSet. No data rows are transferred.
- **Update** scans through the supplied DataSet, and applies all the changes it finds to the data source. In the process, it uses the InsertCommand, UpdateCommand, or DeleteCommand as required. For example, if it finds new rows that didn't exist before, it uses the InsertCommand.

Chapter 13 shows how you use the DataAdapter and the other ADO.NET objects in some practical scenarios.

The Complete Reference

# Chapter 13

## ADO.NET Data Access

Chapter 12 introduced ADO.NET and the family of objects that provides its functionality. This family includes objects for modeling data (representing tables, rows, columns, and relations) and objects designed for communicating with a data source. In this chapter, you'll learn how to put these objects to work by creating pages that use ADO.NET to retrieve information from a database and apply changes. You'll also learn how to retrieve and manage disconnected data, and deal with the potential problems that can occur.

## About the ADO.NET Examples

One of the goals of ADO.NET is to provide data access universally and with a consistent object model. That means you should be able to access data the same way regardless of what type of database you are using (or even if you are using a data source that doesn't correspond to a database). In this chapter, most examples will use the "lowest common denominator" of data access—the OLE DB data types. These types, found in the System.Data.OleDb namespace, allow you to communicate with just about any database that has a matching OLE DB provider, including SQL Server. However, when you develop a production-level application, you'll probably want to use an authentic .NET provider for best performance. These managed providers will work almost exactly the same, but their Connection and Command objects will have different names and will be located in a different namespace. Currently, the only managed provider included with .NET is SQL Server, but many other varieties are planned, and a managed ODBC driver is already available as a download from Microsoft.

In the examples in this chapter, I make note of any differences between the OLE DB and SQL providers. Remember, the underlying technical details differ, but the objects are almost identical. The only real differences are as follows:

- The names of the Connection, Command, and DataReader classes are different, to help you distinguish them.
- The connection string (the information you use to connect to the database) differs depending on the way you connect and several other factors.
- The OLE DB objects support a wider variety of data types, while the SQL Server objects only support valid SQL Server data types.

### Know Your Database

It's best not to worry too much about the differences between OLE DB and SQL providers. They are similar to the differences between different OLE DB data sources, or even between differently configured installations of the same relational database product. When programming with ADO.NET, it always helps to know your database. If you have information on-hand about the data types it uses, the stored procedures it provides, and the user login you require, you'll be able to work more quickly and with less chance of error.

## Obtaining the Sample Database

This chapter uses examples drawn from the pubs database, a sample database included with Microsoft SQL Server and designed to help you test database access code. If you aren't using SQL Server, you won't have this database available. Instead, you can use MSDE, the free data engine included with Visual Studio .NET. MSDE is a scaled-down version of SQL Server that's free to distribute. Its only limitations are that it's restricted to five simultaneous users and that it doesn't provide any graphical tools for creating and managing databases. To install the pubs database in MSDE or SQL Server, you can use the Transact-SQL script included with the samples for this chapter. Alternatively, you can use a different relational database engine, and tweak the examples in this section accordingly.

# SQL Basics

When you interact with a data source through ADO.NET, you use the SQL language to retrieve, modify, and update information. In some cases, ADO.NET will hide some of the details for you and even generate the required SQL statements automatically. However, to design an efficient database application with the minimum amount of frustration, you need to understand the basic concepts of SQL.

SQL (Structured Query Language) is a standard data access language used to interact with relational databases. Different databases differ in their support of SQL or add additional features, but the core commands used to select, add, and modify data are common. In a database product like Microsoft SQL Server, it's possible to use SQL to create fairly sophisticated SQL scripts for stored procedures and triggers (although they have little of the power of a full object-oriented programming language). When working with ADO.NET, however, you will probably only use a few standard types of SQL statements:

- Use a Select statement to retrieve records.
- Use an Update statement to modify records.
- Use an Insert statement to add a new record.
- Use a Delete statement to delete existing records.

If you already have a good understanding of SQL, you can skip the next few sections. Otherwise, read on for a quick tour of SQL fundamentals.

## Experimenting with SQL

If you've never used SQL before, you may want to play around with it and create some sample queries before you start using it in an ASP.NET site. Most database products give you some features for testing queries. If you are using SQL Server, you can try the SQL Query Analyzer, shown in Figure 13-1. This program lets you type in SQL statements, run them, and see the retrieved results, allowing you to test your SQL assumptions and try out new queries.

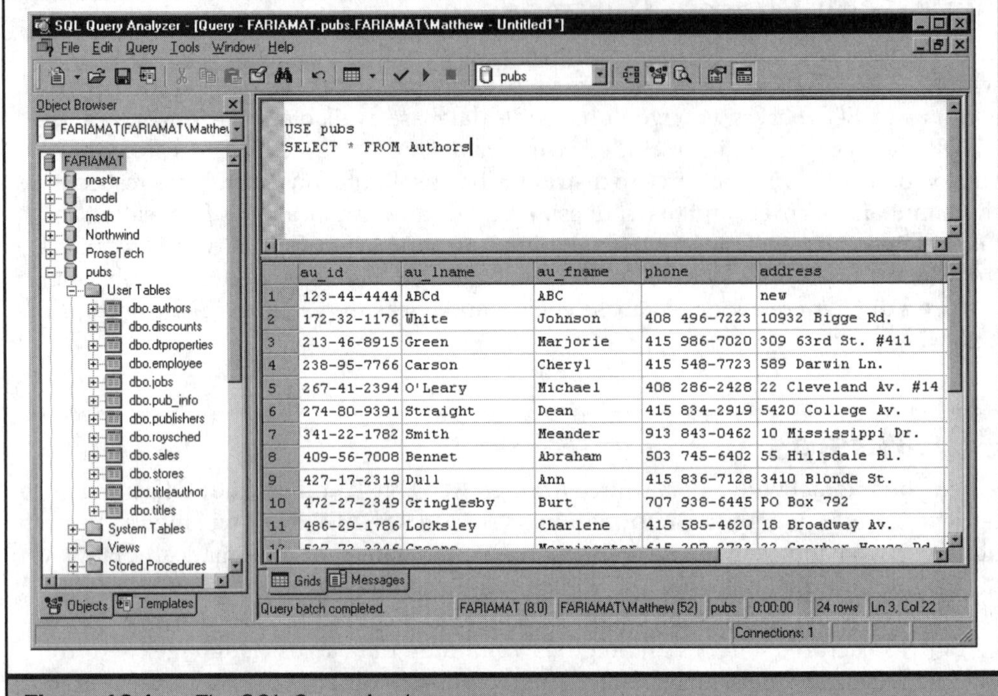

Figure 13-1. *The SQL Query Analyzer*

### More About SQL

You might also want to look at one of the excellent online SQL references available on the Internet. Additionally, if you are working with SQL Server you can use Microsoft's thorough Books Online reference to become a database guru. One topic you might want to investigate is Join queries, which allow you to connect related tables into one set of results.

## The SQL Select Statement

To retrieve one or more rows of data, you use a Select statement:

```
SELECT [columns] FROM [tables] WHERE [search_condition]
      ORDER BY [order_expression ASC | DESC]
```

This format really just scratches the surface of SQL. If you want, you can create advanced statements that use sub-grouping, averaging and totaling, and other options (such as setting a maximum number of returned rows). However, though these tasks can be performed with advanced SQL statements, they are often performed manually by your application code or built into a stored procedure in the database.

## A Sample Select Statement

A typical (and rather inefficient) Select statement for the pubs database is shown here. It works with the Authors table, which contains a list of authors:

```
SELECT * FROM Authors
```

- The asterisk (*) retrieves all the columns in the table. This isn't the best approach for a large table if you don't need all the information. It increases the amount of data that has to be transferred and can slow down your server.
- The From clause identifies that the Authors table is being used for this statement.
- There is no Where clause. That means that all the records will be retrieved from the database, regardless of whether there are ten or ten million. This is a poor design practice, as it often leads to applications that appear to work fine when they are first deployed, but gradually slow down as the database grows. In general, you should *always* include a Where clause to limit the possible number of rows. Often, queries are limited by a date field (for example, all orders that were placed in the last three months).
- There is no Order By clause. This is a perfectly acceptable approach, especially if order doesn't matter or you plan to sort the data on your own using the tools provided in ADO.NET.



### Try These Examples in Query Analyzer

You can try out all the examples in this section without generating an ASP.NET program. Just use the SQL Query Analyzer or a similar query tool. In the Query Analyzer, you can type in the Select statement, and click the green start button. A table of records with the returned information will appear at the bottom of the screen.

Note that you must specify the database you want to use before using any table names. To do this, type the following Use statement first:

```
Use pubs
```

## Improving the Select Statement

Here's another example that retrieves a list of author names:

```
SELECT au_lname, au_fname FROM Authors WHERE State='MI' ORDER BY
au_lname ASC
```

- Only two columns are retrieved (au_lname and au_fname). They correspond to the last and first names of the author.
- A Where clause restricts results to those authors who live in the specified state. Note that the Where clause requires apostrophes around the value you want to match (unless it is a numeric value).
- An Order By clause sorts the information alphabetically by the author's last name.

## An Alternative Select Statement

Here's one last example:

```
SELECT TOP 100 au_lname, au_fname FROM Authors ORDER BY au_lname,
au_fname ASC
```

- This example uses the Top clause instead of a Where statement. The database rows will be sorted, and the first 100 matching results will be retrieved. The Top clause is useful for user-defined search operations where you want to ensure that the database is not tied up in a long operation retrieving unneeded rows.
- This example uses a more sophisticated Order By expression, which sorts authors with identical last names into a subgroup by their first names.

## The Where Clause

In many respects, the Where clause is the most important part of the Select statement. You can combine multiple conditions with the And keyword, and you can specify greater than and less than comparisons by using the greater than (>) and less than (<) operators.

The following is an example with a different table and a more sophisticated Where statement. The international date format is used to compare date values.

```
SELECT * FROM Sales WHERE ord_date < '2000/01/01' AND ord_date >
'1987/01/01'
```

## The SQL Update Statement

The SQL Update statement selects all the records that match a specified search expression and then modifies them all according to an update expression. At its simplest, the Update statement has the following format:

```
UPDATE [table] SET [update_expression] WHERE [search_condition]
```

Typically, you will use an Update statement to modify a single record. The following example adjusts the phone column in a single author record. It uses the unique author ID to find the correct row.

```
UPDATE Authors SET phone='408 496-2222' WHERE au_id='172-32-1176'
```

In the Query Analyzer (see Figure 13-2), this statement will return the number of rows affected, but it will not display the change. To do that, you need to request the row by performing another SQL statement.



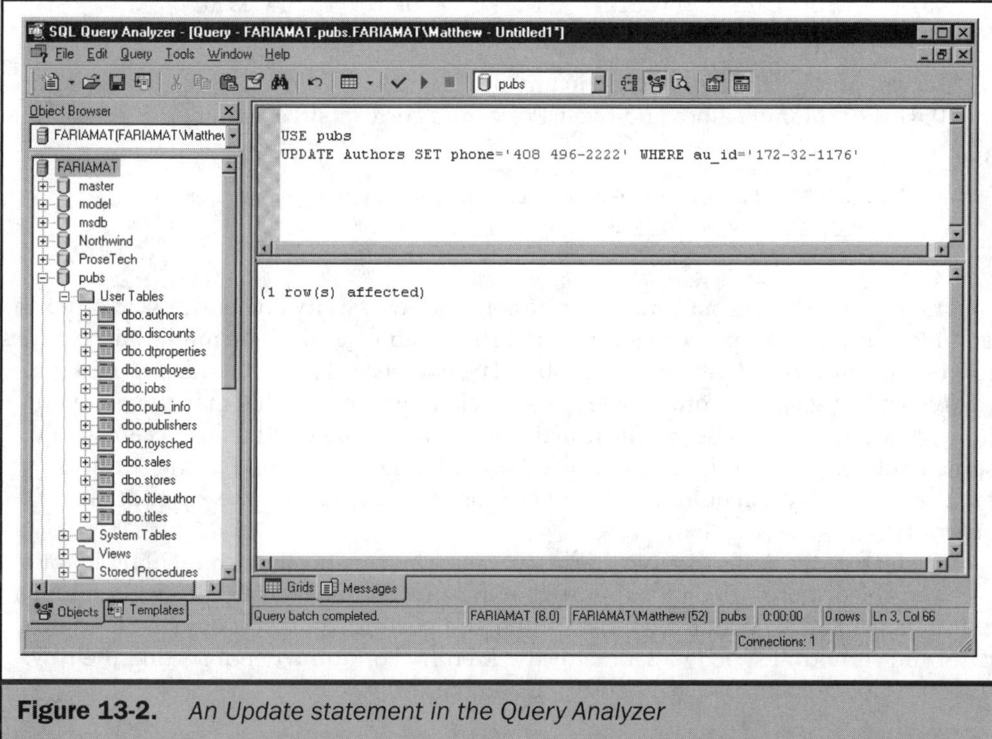


**Figure 13-2.** *An Update statement in the Query Analyzer*

As with a Select statement, you can use an Update statement to make several changes at once or to search for a record based on several different criteria:

```
UPDATE Authors SET au_lname='Whiteson', au_fname='John'
    WHERE au_lname='White' AND au_fname='Johnson'
```

You can even use the Update statement to update an entire range of matching records. The following example modifies the phone number for every author who lives in California:

```
UPDATE Authors SET phone='408 496-2222' WHERE state='CA'
```

## The SQL Insert Statement

The SQL Insert statement adds a new record to a table with the information you specify. It takes the following form:

```
INSERT INTO [table] ([column_list]) VALUES ([value_list])
```

You can provide the information in any order you want, as long as you make sure that the list of column names and the list of values correspond exactly.

```
INSERT INTO Authors (au_id, au_lname, au_fname, zip, contract)
       VALUES ('998-72-3566', 'John', 'Khan', 84152, 0)
```

This example leaves out some information, such as the city and address, in order to provide a simple example. The information shown above is the bare minimum required to create a new record in the Authors table. The new record is featured in Figure 13-3.

Remember, databases often have special field requirements that may prevent you from adding a record unless you fill in all the values with valid information. Alternatively, some fields may be configured to use a default value if left blank. In the Authors table, some fields are required and a special format is defined for the zip code and author ID.

One feature the Authors table doesn't use is an automatically incrementing identity column. This feature, which is supported in most relational database products, assigns a unique value to a specified column when you perform an insert operation. In this case, you shouldn't specify a value for the identity column when inserting the row. Instead, allow the database to choose one automatically.

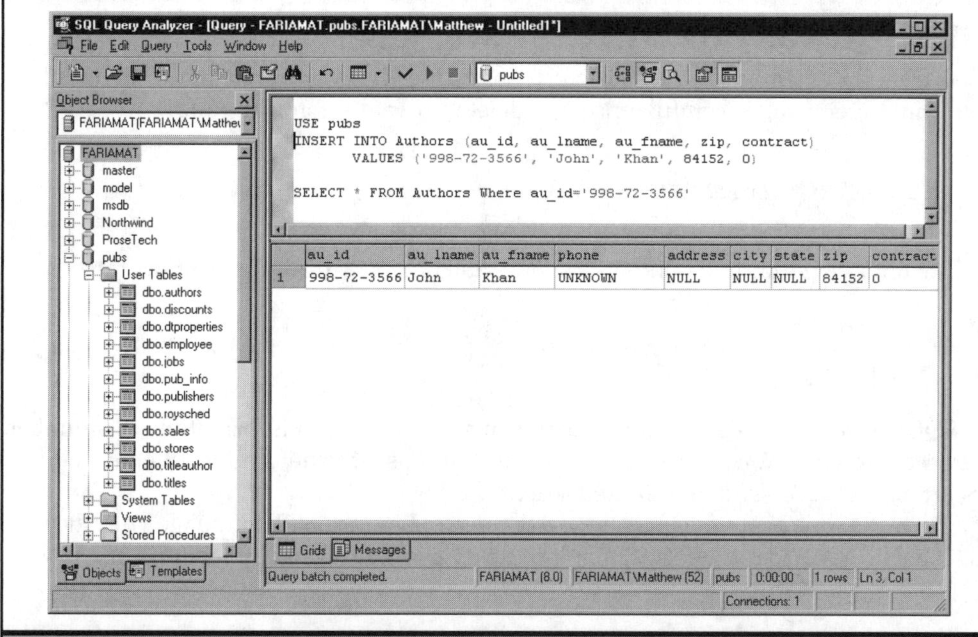


**Figure 13-3.** *Inserting a new record*

## Auto-Increment Fields Are Indispensable

If you are designing a database, make sure that you add an auto-incrementing identity field to every table. It's the fastest, easiest, and least error-prone way to assign a unique "identification number" to every record. Without an automatically generated identity field, you will need to go to considerable effort to create and maintain your own unique field. Often, programmers fall into the trap of using a data field for a unique identifier, such as a Social Security number or name. This almost always leads to trouble at some inconvenient time far in the future, when you need to add a person who doesn't have a SSN number (for example, a foreign national) or account for an SSN number or name change (which will cause problems for other related tables, such as a purchase order table that identifies the purchaser by the name or SSN number field). A much better approach is to use a unique identifier, and have the database engine assign an arbitrary unique number to every row automatically.

If you create a table without a unique identification column, you will have trouble when you need to select that specific row for deletion or updates. Selecting records based on a text field can also lead to problems if the field contains special embedded characters (like apostrophes). You'll also find it extremely awkward to create table relationships.

## The SQL Delete Statement

The Delete statement is even easier to use. It specifies criteria for one or more rows that you want to remove. Be careful: once you delete a row, it's gone for good!

```
DELETE FROM [table] WHERE [search_condition]
```

The following example removes a single matching row from the Authors table:

```
DELETE FROM Authors WHERE au_id='172-32-1176'
```

SQL Delete and Update commands return a single piece of information: the number of affected records. You can examine this value and use it to determine whether the operation was successful or executed as expected.

The rest of this chapter shows how you can combine the SQL language with the ADO.NET objects to retrieve and manipulate data in your web applications.

## Accessing Data the Easy Way

The "easy way" to access data is to perform all your database operations manually and not worry about maintaining disconnected information. This model is closest to traditional ADO programming, and it allows you to side-step potential concurrency problems, which result when multiple users try to update information at once.

Generally, simple data access is ideal if you only need to read information or if you only need to perform simple update operations, such as adding a record to a log or allowing a user to modify values in a single record (for example, customer information for an e-commerce site). Simple data access is not as useful if you want to provide sophisticated data manipulation features, such as the ability to perform multiple edits on several different records (or several tables).

With simple data access, a disconnected copy of the data is not retained. That means that data selection and data modifications are performed separately. Your program must keep track of the changes that need to be committed to the data source. For example, if a user deletes a record, you need to explicitly specify that record using an SQL Delete statement.

### Simple Data Access

To retrieve information with simple data access, follow these steps:

1. Create Connection, Command, and DataReader objects.
2. Use the DataReader to retrieve information from the database and display it in a control on a web form.

3. Close your connection.
4. Send the page to the user. At this point, the information your user sees and the information in the database no longer have any connection, and all the ADO.NET objects have been destroyed.

### Simple Data Updates

To add or update information, follow these steps:

1. Create new Connection and Command objects.
2. Execute the Command (with the appropriate SQL statement).

### Importing the Namespaces

Before continuing any further, make sure you import the ADO.NET namespaces, as shown here. Alternatively, you can add these as project-wide imports by modifying your project's properties in Visual Studio .NET.

```
Imports System.Data
Imports System.Data.OleDb   ' Or System.Data.SqlClient
```



## Creating a Connection

Before you can retrieve or update data, you need to make a connection to the data source. Generally, connections are limited to some fixed number, and if you exceed that number (either because you run out of licenses or because your server can't accommodate the user load), attempts to create new connections will fail. For that reason, you should try to hold a connection open for as short a time as possible. You should also write your database code inside a Try/Catch error-handling structure, so that you can respond if an error does occur.

To create a connection, you need to specify a value for its ConnectionString property. This ConnectionString defines all the information the computer needs to find the data source, log in, and choose an initial database. Out of all the examples in this chapter, the ConnectionString is the one value you might have to tweak before it works for the database you want to use. Luckily, it's quite straightforward.

```
Dim MyConnection As New OleDbConnection()
MyConnection.ConnectionString = "Provider=SQLOLEDB.1;" & _
  "Data Source=localhost;" & _
  "Initial Catalog=Pubs;User ID=sa"
```

The connection string for the SqlConnection object is quite similar, and just leaves out the Provider setting:

```
Dim MyConnection As New SqlConnection()
MyConnection.ConnectionString = "Data Source=localhost;" & _
 "Initial Catalog=Pubs;User ID=sa"
```

## The Connection String

The connection string is actually a series of distinct pieces of information, separated by semicolons (;). In the preceding example, the connection string identifies the following pieces of information:

**Provider** This is the name of the OLE DB provider, which allows communication between ADO.NET and your database. (SQLOLEDB is the OLE DB provider for SQL.) Other providers include MSDAORA (the OLE DB provider for an Oracle database) and Microsoft.Jet.OLEDB.4.0 (the OLE DB provider for Access).

**Data Source** This indicates the name of the server where the data source is located. In this case, the server is on the same computer hosting the ASP.NET site, so localhost is sufficient.

**Initial Catalog** This is the name of the database that this connection will be accessing. It's only the "initial" database because you can change it later, by running an SQL command or by modifying the Database property.

**User ID** This is used to access the database. The user ID "sa" corresponds to the system administrator account provided with databases such as SQL Server.

**Password** By default, the sa account doesn't have a password. Typically, in a production-level site, this account would be modified or replaced. To specify a password for a user, just add the Password settings to the connection string (as in "Password=letmein"). Note that as with all connection string settings, you don't need quotation marks, but you do need to separate the setting with a semicolon.

**ConnectionTimeout** This determines how long your code will wait, in seconds, before generating an error if it cannot establish a database connection. Our example connection string doesn't set the ConnectionTimeout, so the default of 15 seconds is used. Use 0 to specify no limit, which is a bad idea. That means that, theoretically, the user's web page could be held up indefinitely while this code attempts to find the server.

## SQL Server Integrated Authentication

If the example connection string doesn't allow you to connect to an SQL Server database, it could be because the standard SQL Server accounts have been disabled in favor of integrated Windows authentication (in SQL Server 2000, this is the default).

- With **SQL Server authentication**, SQL Server maintains its own user account information.
- With **integrated authentication**, SQL Server automatically uses the Windows account information for the currently logged-in user. In this case, you would use a connection string with the Integrated Security option:

```
MyConnection.ConnectionString = "Provider=SQLOLEDB.1;" & _
 "Data Source=localhost;" & _
 "Initial Catalog=Pubs;Integrated Security=SSPI"
```

For this to work, the currently logged-on Windows user must have the required authorization to access the SQL database. In the case of an ASP.NET application, the "current user" is set based on IIS and web.config options. For more information, refer to Chapter 24, which discusses security.

## Other Connection String Values

There are some other, lesser-used options you can set for a connection string, such as parameters that specify how long you'll wait while trying to make a connection before timing out. For more information, refer to the .NET help files (under SqlConnection or OleDbConnection).

## Connection String Tips

Typically, all the database code in your application will use the same connection string. For that reason, it usually makes the most sense to store a connection string in a globally available variable or class member.

```
Dim ConnectionString As String = "Provider=SQLOLEDB ..."
```

You can also create a Connection object with a preassigned connection string by using a special constructor:

```
Dim MyConnection As New OleDbConnection(ConnectionString)
' MyConnection.ConnectionString is now set to ConnectionString.
```

## Making the Connection

Before you can use a connection, you have to explicitly open it:

```
MyConnection.Open()
```

To verify that you have successfully connected to the database, you can try displaying some basic connection information. The following example uses a label control called lblInfo (see Figure 13-4).

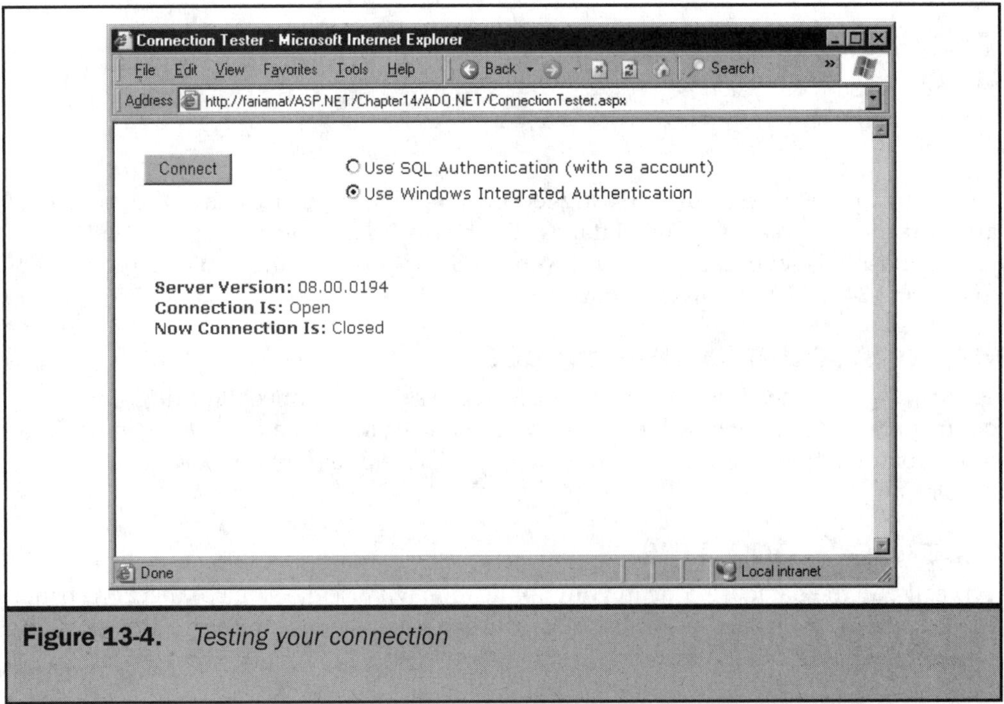


**Figure 13-4.** *Testing your connection*

Here's the code using a Try/Catch error-handling block:

```
' Define the ADO.NET connection object.
Dim MyConnection As New OleDbConnection(ConnectionString)

Try
```

```
    ' Try to open the connection.
    MyConnection.Open()
    lblInfo.Text = "<b>Server Version:</b> "
    lblInfo.Text &= MyConnection.ServerVersion
    lblInfo.Text &= "<br><b>Connection Is:</b> "
    lblInfo.Text &= MyConnection.State.ToString()
Catch err As Exception
    ' Handle an error by displaying the information.
    lblInfo.Text = "Error reading the database. "
    lblInfo.Text &= err.Message
Finally
    ' Either way, make sure the connection is properly closed.
    If (Not Is Nothing MyConnection) Then
        MyConnection.Close()
        lblInfo.Text &= "<br><b>Now Connection Is:</b> "
        lblInfo.Text &=  MyConnection.State.ToString()
    End If
End Try
```

Once you use the Open method, you have a live connection to your database. One of the most fundamental principles of data access code is that you should reduce the amount of time you hold a connection open as much as possible. Imagine that as soon as you open the connection, you have a live, ticking time bomb. You need to get in, retrieve your data, and throw the connection away as quickly as possible to make sure your site runs efficiently.

Closing a connection is just as easy:

```
MyConnection.Close()
```

## Defining a Select Command

The Connection object provides a few basic properties that give information about the connection, but that's about all. To actually retrieve data, you need a few more ingredients:

- An SQL statement that selects the information you want
- A Command object that executes the SQL statement
- A DataReader or DataSet object to catch the retrieved records

Command objects represent SQL statements. To use a Command, you define it, specify the SQL statement you want to use, specify an available connection, and execute the command.

You can use one of the earlier SQL statements as shown here:

```
Dim MyCommand As New OleDbCommand()
MyCommand.Connection = MyConnection
MyCommand.CommandText = "SELECT * FROM Authors"
```

Or you can use the constructor as a shortcut:

```
Dim MyCommand As New OleDbCommand("SELECT * FROM Authors", _
  MyConnection)
```

The process is identical for an SqlCommand:

```
Dim MyCommand As New SqlCommand("SELECT * FROM Authors", MyConnection)
```

## Using a Command with a DataReader

Once you've defined your command, you need to decide how you want to use it. The simplest approach is to use a DataReader, which allows you to quickly retrieve all your results. The DataReader uses a live connection, and should be used quickly and then closed. The DataReader is also extremely simple. It supports fast forward-only, read-only access to your results, which is generally all you need when retrieving information. Because of the DataReader's optimized nature, it provides better performance than the DataSet. It should always be your first choice for simple data access.

Before you can use a DataReader, make sure you have opened the connection:

```
MyConnection.Open()
```

To create a DataReader, you use the ExecuteReader method of the Command object:

```
' You don't need to use the New keyword because
' the Command will create the DataReader.
```

```
Dim MyReader As OleDbDataReader
MyReader = MyCommand.ExecuteReader()
```

The process is identical for the SqlDataReader:

```
Dim MyReader As SqlDataReader
MyReader = MyCommand.ExecuteReader()
```

These two lines of code define a DataReader and create it using your command. (In order for them to work, you'll need all the code we've created so far in the previous sections to define a connection and a command.)

Once you have the reader, you retrieve a row using the Read method:

```
MyReader.Read()   ' The first row in the result set is now available.
```

You can then access values in that row using the corresponding field name. The following example adds an item to a list box with the first name and last name for the current row:

```
lstNames.Items.Add(MyReader("au_lname") & ", " & MyReader("au_fname"))
```

To move to the next row, use the Read method again. If this method returns True, a row of information has been successfully retrieved. If it returns False, you have attempted to read past the end of your result set. There is no way to move backward to a previous row.

As soon as you have finished reading all the results you need, close the DataReader and Connection:

```
MyDataReader.Close()
MyConnection.Close()
```

## Putting It All Together

The next example demonstrates how you can use all the ADO.NET ingredients together to create a simple application that retrieves information from the Authors table.

You can select an author record by last name using a drop-down list box, as shown in Figure 13-5. The full record is then retrieved and displayed in a simple label control, as shown in Figure 13-6.

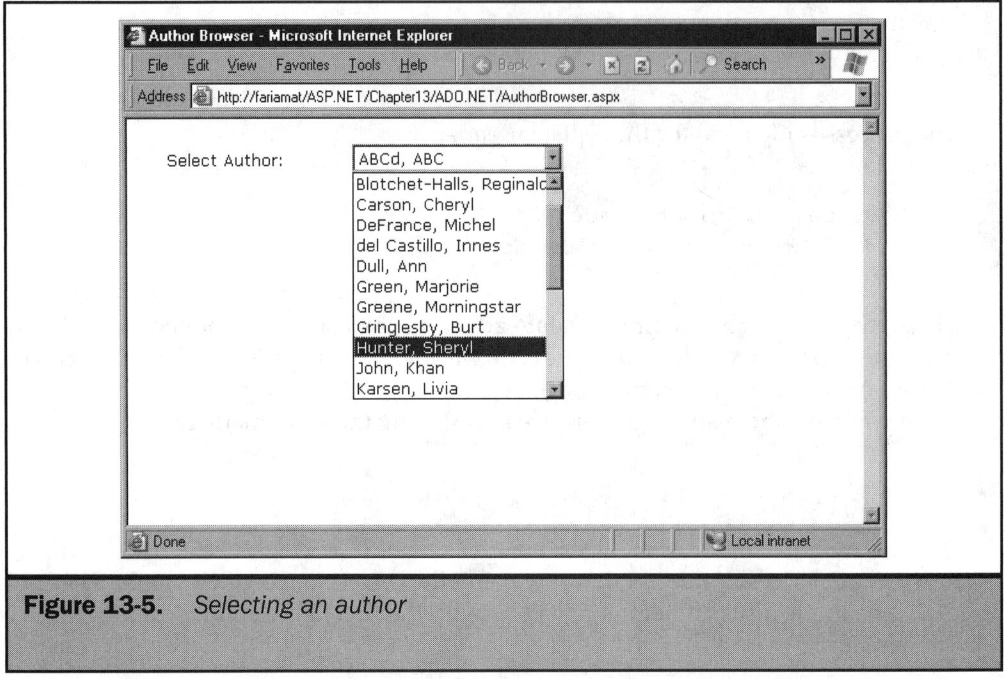


**Figure 13-5.** *Selecting an author*

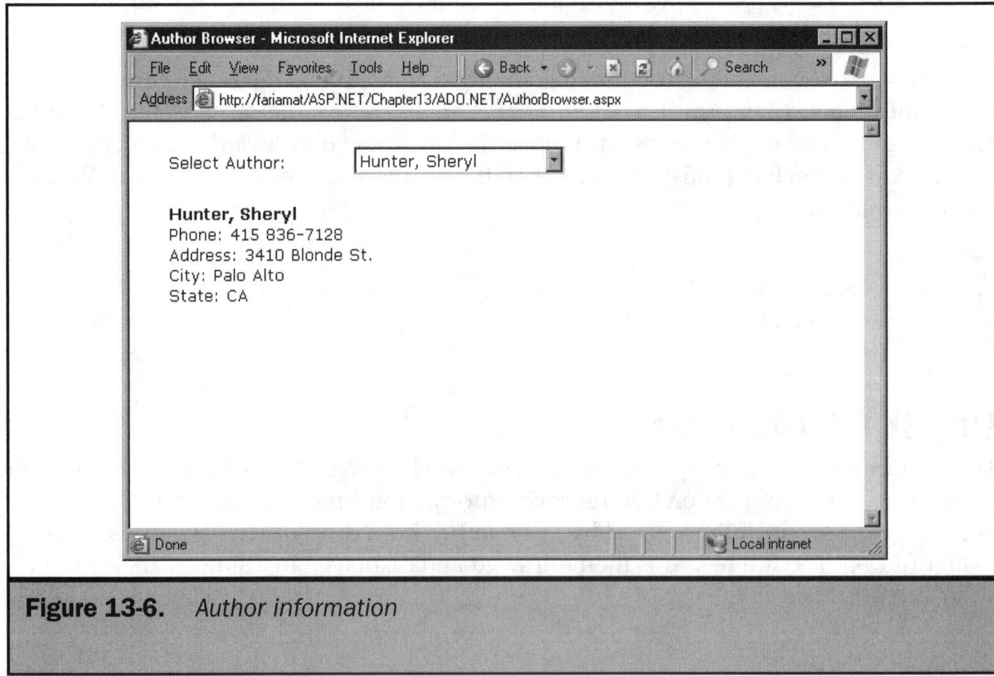


**Figure 13-6.** *Author information*

## Filling the List Box

To start off, the connection string is defined as a private variable for the page class:

```
Private ConnectionString As String = "Provider=SQLOLEDB.1;" & _
 "Data Source=localhost;Initial Catalog=pubs;Integrated Security=SSPI"
```

The list box is filled after the Page.Load event occurs. Because the list box control is set to persist its viewstate information, this information only needs to be retrieved once, the first time the page is displayed. It will be ignored on all postbacks.

```
Private Sub Page_Load(sender As Object, e As EventArgs) _
  Handles MyBase.Load

    If Me.IsPostBack = False Then
        FillAuthorList()
    End If

End Sub

Private Sub FillAuthorList()

    lstAuthor.Items.Clear()

    ' Define the Select statement.
    ' Three pieces of information are needed: the unique id,
    ' and the first and last name.
    Dim SelectSQL As String
    SelectSQL = "SELECT au_lname, au_fname, au_id FROM Authors"

    ' Define the ADO.NET objects.
    Dim con As New OleDbConnection(ConnectionString)
    Dim cmd As New OleDbCommand(SelectSQL, con)
    Dim reader As OleDbDataReader

    ' Try to open database and read information.
    Try
        con.Open()
        reader = cmd.ExecuteReader()

        ' For each item, add the author name to the displayed
        ' list box text, and store the unique ID in the Value property.
```

```
        Do While reader.Read()
            Dim NewItem As New ListItem()
            NewItem.Text = reader("au_lname") & ", " & _
              reader("au_fname")
            NewItem.Value = reader("au_id")
            lstAuthor.Items.Add(NewItem)
        Loop

        reader.Close()

    Catch err As Exception
        lblResults.Text = "Error reading list of names. "
        lblResults.Text &= err.Message
    Finally
        If (Not con Is Nothing) Then
            con.Close()
        End If
    End Try

End Sub
```

## Interesting Facts About this Code

- This example looks more sophisticated than the previous bite-sized snippets in this chapter, but it really doesn't introduce anything new. The standard Connection, Command, and DataAdapter objects are used. The connection is opened inside an error-handling block, so that your page can handle any unexpected errors and provide information. A Finally block makes sure that the connection is properly closed, even if an error occurs.
- The actual code for reading the data uses a loop. With each pass, the Read method is used to get another row of information. When the reader has read all the available information, this method will return False, the While condition will evaluate to False, and the loop will end gracefully.
- The unique ID (the value in the au_id field) is stored in the Value property of the list box for reference later. This is a crucial ingredient that is needed to allow the corresponding record to be queried again. If you tried to build a query using the author's name, you would need to worry about authors with the same name, and invalid characters (such as the apostrophe in O'Leary) that would invalidate your SQL statement.

## Retrieving the Record

The record is retrieved as soon as the user changes the list box selection. To accomplish this effect, the AutoPostBack property of the list box is set to True, so its change events are detected automatically.

```
Private Sub lstAuthor_SelectedIndexChanged(sender As Object, _
  e As EventArgs) Handles lstAuthor.SelectedIndexChanged

    ' Create a Select statement that searches for a record
    ' matching the specific author id from the Value property.
    Dim SelectSQL As String
    SelectSQL = "SELECT * FROM Authors "
    SelectSQL &= "WHERE au_id='" & lstAuthor.SelectedItem.Value & "'"

    ' Define the ADO.NET objects.
    Dim con As New OleDbConnection(ConnectionString)
    Dim cmd As New OleDbCommand(SelectSQL, con)
    Dim reader As OleDbDataReader

    ' Try to open database and read information.
    Try
        con.Open()
        reader = cmd.ExecuteReader()
        reader.Read()
        lblResults.Text = "<b>" & reader("au_lname")
        lblResults.Text &= ", " & reader("au_fname") & "</b><br>"
        lblResults.Text &= "Phone: " & reader("phone") & "<br>"
        lblResults.Text &= "Address: " & reader("address") & "<br>"
        lblResults.Text &= "City: " & reader("city") & "<br>"
        lblResults.Text &= "State: " & reader("state") & "<br>"
        reader.Close()
    Catch err As Exception
        lblResults.Text = "Error getting author. "
        lblResults.Text &= err.Message
    Finally
        If (Not con Is Nothing) Then
            con.Close()
        End If
    End Try

End Sub
```

The process is similar to the procedure used to retrieve the last names. There are only a couple of differences:

- The code dynamically creates an SQL statement based on the selected item in the drop-down list box. It uses the Value property of the selected item, which stores the unique identifier. This is a common (and very useful) technique.
- Only one record is read. The code assumes that only one author has the matching au_id, which is reasonable as this field is unique.

> **What About More Advanced Controls?**
>
> This example shows how ADO.NET works to retrieve a simple result set. Of course, ADO.NET also provides handy controls that go beyond this generic level, and let you provide full-featured grids with sorting and editing. These controls are described in Chapter 15. For now, concentrate on understanding the fundamentals about ADO.NET and how it works with data.

# Updating Data

Now that you understand how to retrieve data, it's not much more complicated to perform simple delete and update operations. Once again, you use the Command object, but this time you don't need a DataReader because no results will be retrieved. You also don't need an SQL Select command. Instead, you can use one of three new SQL commands: Update, Insert, or Delete.

## Using Update, Insert, and Delete Commands

To execute an Update, Insert, or Delete statement, you need to create a Command object. You can then execute the command with the ExecuteNonQuery method. This method returns the number of rows that were affected, which allows you to check your assumptions. For example, if you attempt to update or delete a record and are informed that no records were affected, you probably have an error in your Where clause that is preventing any records from being selected. (If, on the other hand, your SQL command has a syntax error or attempts to retrieve information from a non-existent table, an exception will occur.)

To demonstrate how to Update, Insert, and Delete simple information, the previous example has been enhanced. Instead of being displayed in a label, the information from each field is added to a separate text box. Two additional buttons allow you to update the record (Update), or delete it (Delete). You can also insert a new record by clicking Create New, entering the information in the text boxes, and then clicking Insert New, as shown in Figure 13-7.

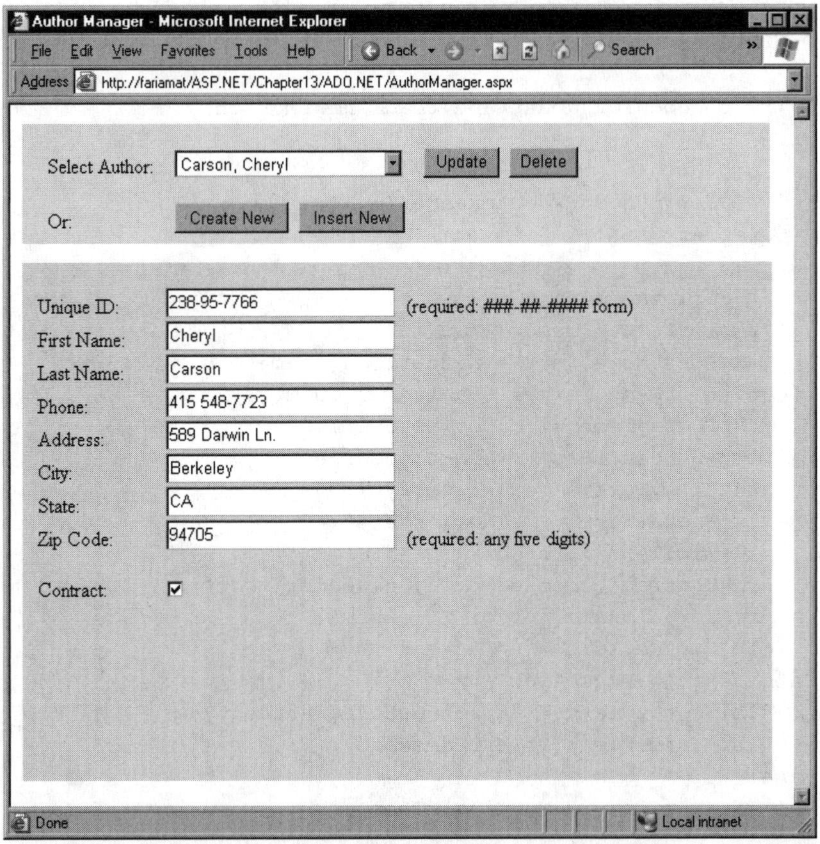

**Figure 13-7.** *A more advanced author manager*



The record selection code is identical from an ADO.NET perspective, but it now uses the individual text box controls.

```
Private Sub lstAuthor_SelectedIndexChanged(sender As Object, _
  e As EventArgs) Handles lstAuthor.SelectedIndexChanged

    ' Define ADO.NET objects.
    Dim SelectSQL As String
    SelectSQL = "SELECT * FROM Authors "
    SelectSQL &= "WHERE au_id='" & lstAuthor.SelectedItem.Value & "'"
    Dim con As New OleDbConnection(ConnectionString)
```

```
    Dim cmd As New OleDbCommand(SelectSQL, con)
    Dim reader As OleDbDataReader

    ' Try to open database and read information.
    Try
        con.Open()
        reader = cmd.ExecuteReader()
        reader.Read()

        ' Fill the controls.
        txtID.Text = reader("au_id")
        txtFirstName.Text = reader("au_fname")
        txtLastName.Text = reader("au_lname")
        txtPhone.Text = reader("phone")
        txtAddress.Text = reader("address")
        txtCity.Text = reader("city")
        txtState.Text = reader("state")
        txtZip.Text = reader("zip")
        chkContract.Checked = CType(reader("contract"), Boolean)
        reader.Close()
        lblStatus.Text = ""
    Catch err As Exception
        lblStatus.Text = "Error getting author. "
        lblStatus.Text &= err.Message
    Finally
        If (Not con Is Nothing) Then
            con.Close()
        End If
    End Try

End Sub
```

To see the full code, refer to the included example files. If you play with the example at length, you'll notice that it lacks a few niceties that would be needed in a professional web site. For example, when creating a new record, the name of the last selected user is still visible, and the Update and Delete buttons are still active, which can lead to confusion or errors. A more sophisticated user interface could prevent these problems by disabling inapplicable controls (perhaps by grouping them in a Panel control) or using separate pages. In this case, however, the page is useful as a quick way to test some basic data access code.

## Updating a Record

When the user clicks the Update button, the information in the text boxes is applied to the database:

```
Private Sub cmdUpdate_Click(sender As Object, _
  e As EventArgs) Handles cmdUpdate.Click

    ' Define ADO.NET objects.
    Dim UpdateSQL As String
    UpdateSQL = "UPDATE Authors SET "
    UpdateSQL &= "au_id='" & txtID.Text & "', "
    UpdateSQL &= "au_fname='" & txtFirstName.Text & "', "
    UpdateSQL &= "au_lname='" & txtLastName.Text & "', "
    UpdateSQL &= "phone='" & txtPhone.Text & "', "
    UpdateSQL &= "address='" & txtAddress.Text & "', "
    UpdateSQL &= "city='" & txtCity.Text & "', "
    UpdateSQL &= "state='" & txtState.Text & "', "
    UpdateSQL &= "zip='" & txtZip.Text & "', "
    UpdateSQL &= "contract='" & Int(chkContract.Checked) & "' "
    UpdateSQL &= "WHERE au_id='" & lstAuthor.SelectedItem.Value & "'"

    Dim con As New OleDbConnection(ConnectionString)
    Dim cmd As New OleDbCommand(UpdateSQL, con)

    ' Try to open database and execute the update.
    Try
        con.Open()
        Dim Updated As Integer
        Updated = cmd.ExecuteNonQuery
        lblStatus.Text = Updated.ToString() & " records updated."
    Catch err As Exception
        lblStatus.Text = "Error updating author. "
        lblStatus.Text &= err.Message
    Finally
        If (Not con Is Nothing) Then
            con.Close()
        End If
    End Try

End Sub
```

The update code is similar to the record selection code. The main differences are:

- No DataReader is used, because no results are returned.
- A dynamically generated Update command is used for the Command object. It selects the corresponding author records, and changes all the fields to correspond to the values entered in the text boxes.
- The ExecuteNonQuery method returns the number of affected records. This information is displayed in a label to confirm to the user that the operation was successful.

## Deleting a Record

When the user clicks the Delete button, the author information is removed from the database. The number of affected records is examined, and if the Delete operation was successful, the FillAuthorList function is called to refresh the page.

```
Private Sub cmdDelete_Click(sender As Object, _
  e As EventArgs) Handles cmdDelete.Click

    ' Define ADO.NET objects.
    Dim DeleteSQL As String
    DeleteSQL = "DELETE FROM Authors "
    DeleteSQL &= "WHERE au_id='" & lstAuthor.SelectedItem.Value & "'"

    Dim con As New OleDbConnection(ConnectionString)
    Dim cmd As New OleDbCommand(DeleteSQL, con)

    ' Try to open database and delete the record.
    Dim Deleted As Integer
    Try
        con.Open()
        Deleted = cmd.ExecuteNonQuery()
    Catch err As Exception
        lblStatus.Text = "Error deleting author. "
        lblStatus.Text &= err.Message
    Finally
        If (Not con Is Nothing) Then
            con.Close()
        End If
    End Try

    ' If the delete succeeded, refresh the author list.
    If Deleted > 0 Then
```

```
            FillAuthorList()
        End If

    End Sub
```

Interestingly, delete operations rarely succeed with the records in the pubs database, because they have corresponding child records linked in another table of the pubs database. Specifically, each author can have one or more related book titles. Unless the author's records are removed from the TitleAuthor table first, the author cannot be deleted. Because of the careful error-handling used in the previous example, this problem is faithfully reported in your application (see Figure 13-8) and does not cause any real problems.

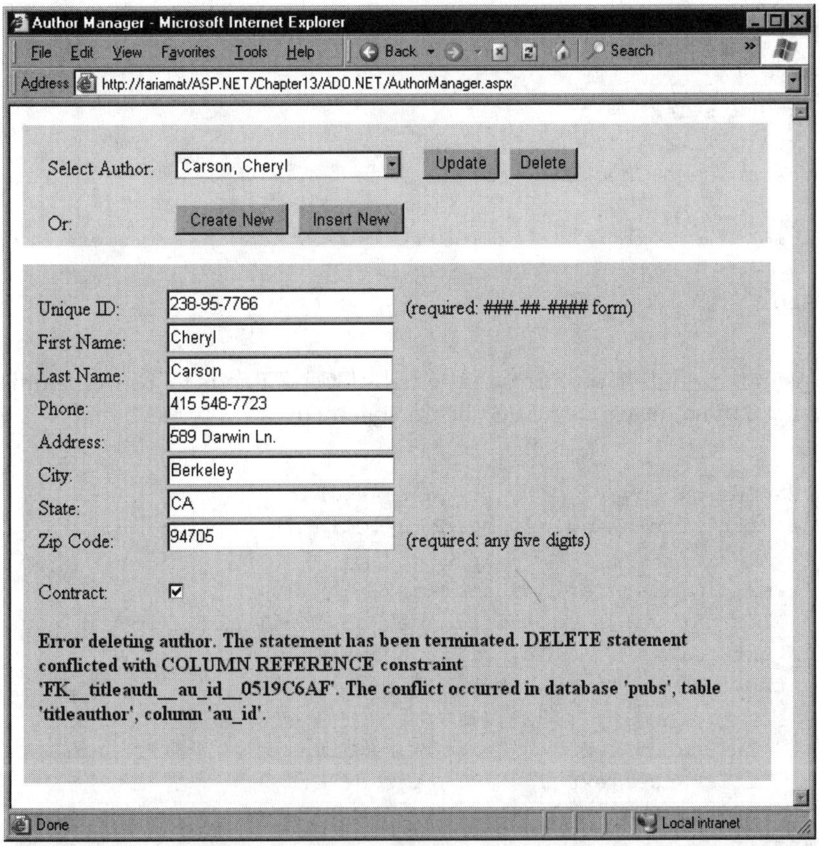

**Figure 13-8.** *A failed delete attempt*

To get around this limitation, you can use the Create New and Insert New buttons to add a new record, and then delete this record. Because it is not linked to any other records, its deletion will be allowed.

## Adding a Record

To start adding a new record, click Create New to clear the fields. Technically speaking, this step isn't required, but it simplifies the user's life.

```
Private Sub cmdNew_Click(sender As Object, _
  e As EventArgs) Handles cmdNew.Click

    txtID.Text = ""
    txtFirstName.Text = ""
    txtLastName.Text = ""
    txtPhone.Text = ""
    txtAddress.Text = ""
    txtCity.Text = ""
    txtState.Text = ""
    txtZip.Text = ""
    chkContract.Checked = False

    lblStatus.Text = "Click Insert New to add the completed record."

End Sub
```

The Insert New button performs the actual ADO.NET code to insert the finished record using a dynamically generated Insert statement:

```
Private Sub cmdInsert_Click(sender As Object, _
  e As EventArgs) Handles cmdInsert.Click

    ' Perform user-defined checks.
    ' Alternatively, you could use RequiredFieldValidator controls.
    If txtID.Text = "" Or txtFirstName.Text = "" Or _
      txtLastName.Text = "" Then

        lblStatus.Text = "Records require an ID, first name,"
        lblStatus.Text &= "and last name."
        Exit Sub
    End If

    ' Define ADO.NET objects.
```

```
    Dim strInsert As String
    strInsert = "INSERT INTO Authors ("
    strInsert &= "au_id, au_fname, au_lname, "
    strInsert &= "phone, address, city, state, zip, contract) "
    strInsert &= "VALUES ('"
    strInsert &= txtID.Text & "', '"
    strInsert &= txtFirstName.Text & "', '"
    strInsert &= txtLastName.Text & "', '"
    strInsert &= txtPhone.Text & "', '"
    strInsert &= txtAddress.Text & "', '"
    strInsert &= txtCity.Text & "', '"
    strInsert &= txtState.Text & "', '"
    strInsert &= txtZip.Text & "', '"
    strInsert &= Int(chkContract.Checked) & "')"

    Dim con As New OleDbConnection(ConnectionString)
    Dim cmd As New OleDbCommand(strInsert, con)

    ' Try to open database and execute the update.
    Dim Added As Integer
    Try
        con.Open()
        Added = cmd.ExecuteNonQuery
        lblStatus.Text = Added.ToString() & " records inserted."
    Catch err As Exception
        lblStatus.Text = "Error inserting record. "
        lblStatus.Text &= err.Message
    Finally
        If (Not con Is Nothing) Then
            con.Close()
        End If
    End Try

    ' If the insert succeeded, refresh the author list.
    If Added > 0 Then
        FillAuthorList()
    End If

End Sub
```

If the insert fails, the problem will be reported to the user in a rather unfriendly way (see Figure 13-9). This is typically a result of not specifying valid values. In a more polished application, you would use validators (as discussed in Chapter 9) and provide more useful error messages.

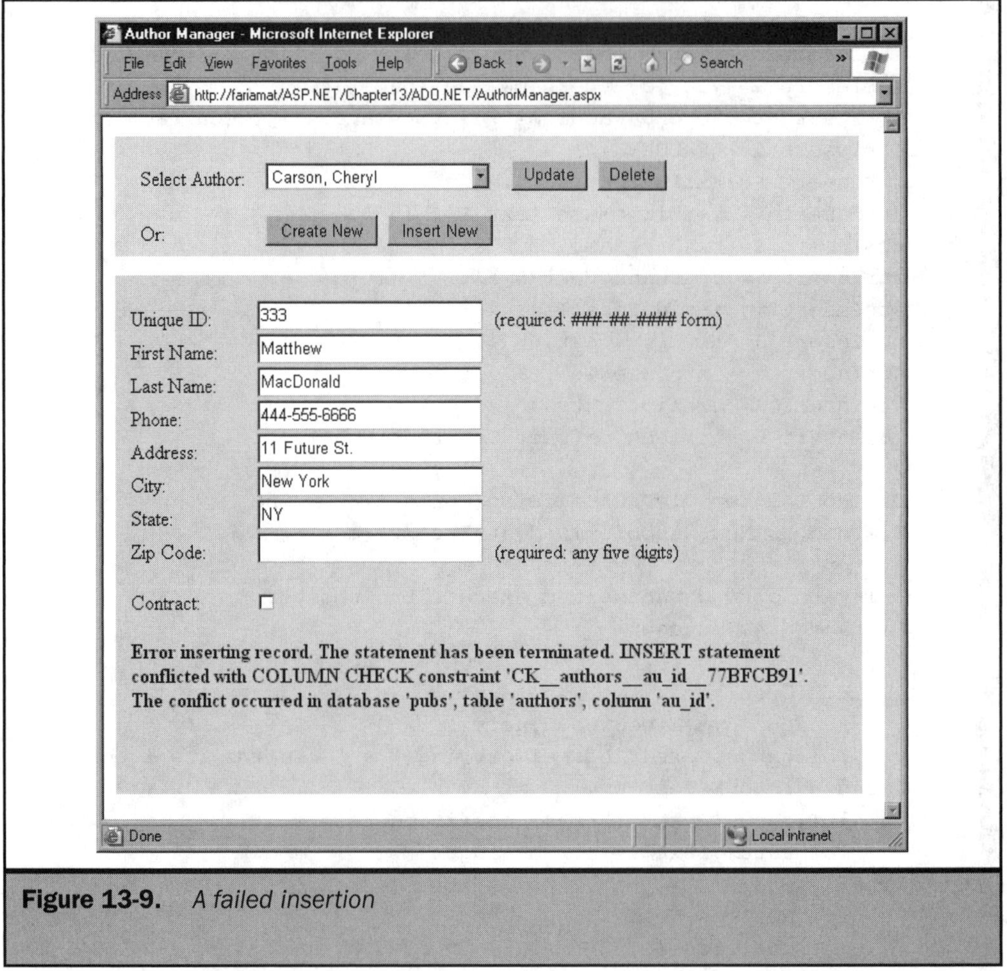


**Figure 13-9.** *A failed insertion*

If the insert operation is successful, the page is updated with the new author list.

## Accessing Disconnected Data

With disconnected data manipulation, your coding is a little different. In many cases, you have less SQL code to write, and you modify records through the DataSet object. However, you need to carefully watch for problems that can occur when you send changes to the data source. In our simple one-page scenario, disconnected data access won't present much of a problem. If, however, you use disconnected data access to make a number of changes and commit them all at once, you are more likely to run into trouble.

With disconnected data access, a copy of the data is retained, briefly, in memory while your code is running. Changes are tracked automatically using the built-in features of the DataSet object. You fill the DataSet in much the same way that you connect a DataReader. However, while the DataReader held a live connection, information in the DataSet is always disconnected.

## Selecting Disconnected Data

The following example shows how you could rewrite the FillAuthorList() subroutine to use a DataSet instead of a DataReader. The changes are highlighted in bold.

```
Private Sub FillAuthorList()

    lstAuthor.Items.Clear()

    ' Define ADO.NET objects.
    Dim SelectSQL As String
    SelectSQL = "SELECT au_lname, au_fname, au_id FROM Authors"
    Dim con As New OleDbConnection(ConnectionString)
    Dim cmd As New OleDbCommand(SelectSQL, con)
    Dim adapter As New OleDbDataAdapter(cmd)
    Dim Pubs As New DataSet()

    ' Try to open database and read information.
    Try
        con.Open()
        ' All the information in transferred with one command.
        adapter.Fill(Pubs, "Authors")
    Catch err As Exception
        lblStatus.Text = "Error reading list of names. "
        lblStatus.Text &= err.Message
    Finally
        If (Not con Is Nothing) Then
            con.Close()
        End If
    End Try

    Dim row As DataRow
    For Each row In Pubs.Tables("Authors").Rows
        Dim NewItem As New ListItem()
```

```
            NewItem.Text = row("au_lname") & ", " & _
              row("au_fname")
            NewItem.Value = row("au_id")
            lstAuthor.Items.Add(NewItem)
        Next

    End Sub
```

Every DataAdapter can hold four different commands: SelectCommand, InsertCommand, UpdateCommand, and DeleteCommand. This allows you to use a single DataAdapter object for multiple tasks. The Command object supplied in the constructor is automatically assigned to the DataAdapter.SelectCommand property.

The DataAdapter.Fill method takes a DataSet and inserts one table of information. In this case, the table is named Authors, but any name could be used. That name is used later to access the appropriate table in the DataSet.

To access the individual DataRows, you can loop through the Rows collection of the appropriate table. Each piece of information is accessed using the field name, as it was with the DataReader.

## Selecting Multiple Tables

Some of the most impressive features of the DataSet appear when you retrieve multiple different tables. A DataSet can contain as many tables as you need, and you can even link these tables together to better emulate the underlying relational data source. Unfortunately, there's no way to connect tables together automatically based on relationships in the underlying data source. However, you can perform this connection manually, as shown in the next example.

In the pubs database, authors are linked to titles using three tables. This arrangement (called a many-to-many relationship, shown in Figure 13-10) allows several authors to be related to one title, and several titles to be related to one author. Without the intermediate TitleAuthor table, the database would be restricted to a one-to-many relationship, which would only allow a single author for each title.

In an application, you rarely need to access these tables individually. Instead, you usually need to combine information from them in some way (for example, to find out what author wrote a given book). On its own, the Titles table indicates only an author ID, but it doesn't provide additional information such as the author's name and address. To link this information together, you can use a special SQL Select statement called a Join query. Alternatively, you can use the features built into ADO.NET.

The next example provides a simple page that lists authors and the titles they have written. The interesting thing about this page is that it is generated using ADO.NET table linking.

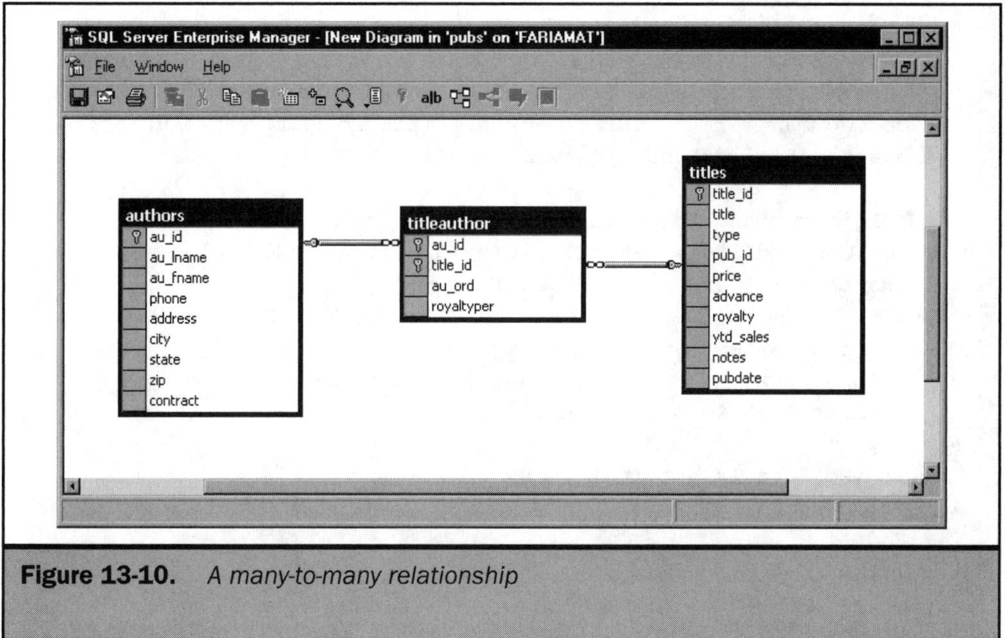


**Figure 13-10.** *A many-to-many relationship*



To start, the standard ADO.NET data access objects are created, including a DataSet. In the online example, all these steps are performed in a custom CreateList subroutine (for clarity), which is called from the Page.Load event handler so that the output is created when the page is first generated.

```
' Define ADO.NET objects.
Dim SelectSQL As String
SelectSQL = "SELECT au_lname, au_fname, au_id FROM Authors"
Dim con As New OleDbConnection(ConnectionString)
Dim cmd As New OleDbCommand(SelectSQL, con)
Dim adapter As New OleDbDataAdapter(cmd)
Dim dsPubs As New DataSet()
```

Next, the information for all three tables is pulled from the database and placed in the DataSet. This task could be accomplished with three separate Command objects, but to make the code a little lighter, this example uses only one, and modifies the CommandText property as needed.

```
Try
    con.Open()
```

```
    adapter.Fill(dsPubs, "Authors")

    ' This command is still linked to the data adapter.
    cmd.CommandText = "SELECT au_id, title_id FROM TitleAuthor"
    adapter.Fill(dsPubs, "TitleAuthor")

    ' This command is still linked to the data adapter.
    cmd.CommandText = "SELECT title_id, title FROM Titles"
    adapter.Fill(dsPubs, "Titles")

Catch err As Exception
    lblList.Text = "Error reading list of names. "
    lblList.Text &= err.Message
Finally
    If (Not con Is Nothing) Then
        con.Close()
    End If
End Try
```

Now that all the information is in the database, two DataRelation objects need to be created to make it easier to navigate through the linked information. In this case, these DataRelation objects match the foreign key restrictions placed at the data source level.

To create a DataRelation, you need to specify the linked fields from two different tables, and you need to give your DataRelation a unique name. (In the following example, a blank string is specified for both names, which instructs ADO.NET to assign a default value automatically.) The order of the linked fields is important. The first field is the parent, and the second field is the child. (The idea here is that one parent can have many children, but each child can only have one parent. In other words, the parent-to-child relationship is another way of saying one-to-many.) In our example, each book title can have more than one entry in the TitleAuthor table. Each author can also have more than one entry in the TitleAuthor table.

```
Dim Titles_TitleAuthor As New DataRelation("", _
  dsPubs.Tables("Titles").Columns("title_id"), _
  dsPubs.Tables("TitleAuthor").Columns("title_id"))
Dim Authors_TitleAuthor As New DataRelation("", _
  dsPubs.Tables("Authors").Columns("au_id"), _
  dsPubs.Tables("TitleAuthor").Columns("au_id"))
```

Once these DataRelation objects have been created, they must be added to the DataSet.

```
dsPubs.Relations.Add(Titles_TitleAuthor)
dsPubs.Relations.Add(Authors_TitleAuthor)
```

The remaining code loops through the DataSet. However, unlike the previous example, which moved through one table, this example uses the DataRelation objects to branch to the other linked tables. It works like this:

1. Select the first record from the Author table.
2. Using the Authors_TitleAuthor relationship, find the child records that correspond to this author. This step uses the GetChildRows method of the DataRow.
3. For each matching record in TitleAuthor, look up the corresponding Title record to get the full text title. This step uses the GetParentRows method of the DataRow.
4. Move to the next Author record, and repeat the process.

The code is dense and economical:

```
Dim rowAuthor, rowTitleAuthor, rowTitle As DataRow

For Each rowAuthor In dsPubs.Tables("Authors").Rows

    lblList.Text &= "<br><b>" & rowAuthor("au_fname")
    lblList.Text &= " " & rowAuthor("au_lname") & "</b><br>"
    For Each rowTitleAuthor In _
      rowAuthor.GetChildRows(Authors_TitleAuthor)

        For Each rowTitle In _
          rowTitleAuthor.GetParentRows(Titles_TitleAuthor)

            lblList.Text &= "  " ' Non-breaking spaces.
            lblList.Text &= rowTitle("title") & "<br>"

        Next

    Next

Next
```

The final result is shown in Figure 13-11.

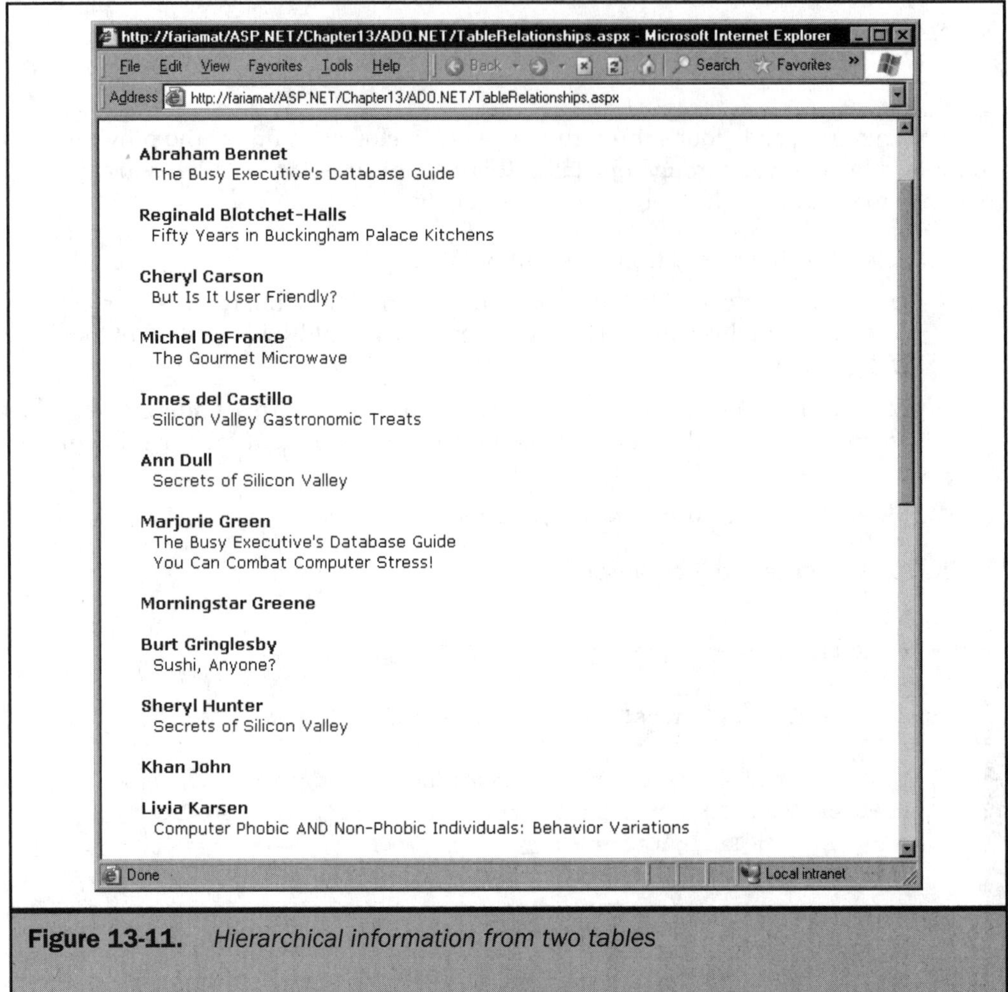


**Figure 13-11.** *Hierarchical information from two tables*

If there were a simple one-to-many relationship between authors and titles, you could leave out the inner For Each statement, and use simpler code:

```
For Each rowAuthor In dsPubs.Tables("Authors").Rows
    ' Display Author
    For Each rowTitleAuthor In rowAuthor.GetChildRows(Authors_Titles)
        ' Display Title
    Next
Next
```

However, having seen the more complicated example, you are ready to create and manage multiple DataRelation objects on your own.

### DataRelations Restrict and Verify Data

Using a DataRelation implies certain restrictions. For example, if you try to create a child row that refers to a nonexistent parent, ADO.NET will generate an error. Similarly, you can't delete a parent that has linked children records. These restrictions are already enforced by the data source, but by adding them to the DataSet, you ensure that they will be enforced by ADO.NET as well. This technique allows you to catch errors as soon as they occur, rather than waiting until you attempt to commit changes to the data source.

# Modifying Disconnected Data

The information in the DataSet can be easily modified. The only complication is that these changes are not committed until you update the data source with a DataAdapter object.

## Modifying and Deleting Rows

Modifying and deleting rows are two of the most common changes you'll make to a DataSet. They are also the easiest. The following example modifies one author's last name. You can place this logic into a function and call it multiple times to swap the last name back and forth.

```
For Each rowAuthor In dsPubs.Tables("Authors").Rows

    If rowAuthor("au_lname") = "Bennet" Then
        rowAuthor("au_lname") = "Samson"
    Else If rowAuthor("au_lname") = "Samson" Then
        rowAuthor("au_lname") = "Bennet"
    End If

Next
```

Deleting a row is just as easy:

```
For Each rowAuthor In dsPubs.Tables("Authors").Rows
```

```
    If rowAuthor("au_fname") = "Cheryl" Then
        rowAuthor.Delete
    End If

Next
```

Alternatively, if you know the exact position of a record, you can modify or delete it using the index number rather than enumerating through the collection:

```
dsPubs.Tables("Authors").Rows(3).Delete
```

The DataSet is always disconnected. Any changes you make will appear in your program, but won't affect the original data source unless you take additional steps. In fact, when you use the Delete method, the row is not actually removed, only marked for deletion. (If the row were removed entirely, ADO.NET would be unable to find it and delete it from the original data source when you reconnect later.)

If you use the Delete method, you need to be aware of this fact and take steps to avoid trying to use deleted rows:

```
For Each row In dsPubs.Tables("Authors").Rows
    If row.RowState <> DataRowState.Deleted Then
        ' It's OK to display the row value, modify it, or use it.
    Else
        ' This record is scheduled for deletion.
        ' You should just ignore it.
    End If
Next
```

If you try to read a field of information from a deleted item, an error will occur. As I warned earlier—life with disconnected data isn't always easy.

### DataSets Also Provide a Remove Method

You can use the Remove method to delete an item completely. However, if you use this method the record won't be deleted from the data source when you reconnect and update it with your changes. Instead, it will just be eliminated from your DataSet.

## Adding Information to a DataSet

You can also add a new row using the Add method of the Rows collection. Before you can add a row, however, you need to use the NewRow method first to get a blank copy. The following example uses this technique with the original web page for viewing and adding authors:

```
Dim rowNew As DataRow
rowNew = dsPubs.Tables("Authors").NewRow
rowNew("au_id") = txtID.Text
rowNew("au_fname") = txtFirstName.Text
rowNew("au_lname") = txtLastName.Text
rowNew("phone") = txtPhone.Text
rowNew("address") = txtAddress.Text
rowNew("city") = txtCity.Text
rowNew("state") = txtState.Text
rowNew("zip") = txtZip.Text
rowNew("contract") = Int(chkContract.Checked)
dsPubs.Tables("Authors").Rows.Add(rowNew)
```

The full code needed to update the data source with these changes is included a little later in this chapter.



# Updating Disconnected Data

Earlier, you saw how the DataAdapter object allows you to retrieve information. Unlike the DataReader, DataAdapter objects can transfer data in both directions.

Updating the data source is a more complicated operation than reading from it. Depending on the changes that have been made, the DataAdapter may need to perform Insert, Update, or Delete operations. Luckily, you don't need to create these Command objects by hand. Instead, you can use ADO.NET's special utility class: the CommandBuilder object (which is provided as SqlCommandBuilder and OleDbCommandBuilder).

## The CommandBuilder

The CommandBuilder examines the DataAdapter object you used to create the DataSet, and it adds the additional Command objects for the InsertCommand, DeleteCommand, and UpdateCommand properties. The process works like this:

```
' Create the CommandBuilder.
Dim cb As New OleDbCommandBuilder(adapter)

' Retrieve an updated DataAdapter.
adapter = cb.DataAdapter
```

## Updating a DataTable

With the correctly configured DataAdapter, you can update the data source using the Update method. You need to use this method once for each table (just like when retrieving the data).

```
Dim RowsAffected As Integer
RowsAffected = adapter.Update(dsPubs, "Authors")
RowsAffected = adapter.Update(dsPubs, "Titles")
```

The DataSet stores information about the current state of all the rows and their original state. This allows ADO.NET to find the changed rows. It adds every new row (rows with the state DataRowState.Added) with the DataAdapter's Insert command. It removes every deleted row (DataRowState.Deleted) using the DataAdapter's Delete command. It also updates every changed row (DataRowState.Modified) with the Update command. There is no guaranteed order in which these operations will take place. Once the update is successfully completed, all rows will be reset to DataRowState.Unchanged.

## Controlling Updates

If you used linked tables, the standard way of updating the data source can cause some problems, particularly if you have deleted or added records. These problems result because changes are usually not committed in the same order that they were made. (To provide this type of tracking, the DataSet object would need to store much more information and waste valuable memory on the server.)

You can control the order in which tables are updated, but that's not always enough to prevent a conflict. For example, if you update the Authors table first, ADO.NET might try to delete an Author record before it deletes the TitleAuthor record that is still using it. It you update the TitleAuthor table first, ADO.NET might try to create a TitleAuthor that references a nonexistent Title. At some point, ADO.NET may be enhanced with the intelligence needed to avoid these problems, provided you use DataRelations. Currently, you need to resort to other techniques for more fine-tuned control.

Using features built into the DataSet, you can pull out the rows that need to be added, modified, or deleted into separate DataSets, and choose an update order that will not place the database into an inconsistent state at any point. Generally, you can safely update a database by performing all the record inserts, followed by all the modifications, and then all the deletions.

By using the DataSet's GetChanges method, you can implement this exact pattern:

```
' Create three DataSets, and fill them from dsPubs.
Dim dsNew As DataSet = dsPubs.GetChanges(DataRowState.Added)
Dim dsModify As DataSet = dsPubs.GetChanges(DataRowState.Deleted)
```

```
Dim dsDelete As DataSet = dsPubs.GetChanges(DataRowState.Modified)

' Update these DataSets separately.
' Remember, each DataSet has three tables!
' Also note that the "add" operation for the Authors and Titles tables
' must be carried out before the add operation for the TitleAuthor
' table.
adapter.Update(dsNew, "Authors")
adapter.Update(dsNew, "Titles")
adapter.Update(dsNew, "TitleAuthor")
adapter.Update(dsModify, "Authors")
adapter.Update(dsModify, "Titles")
adapter.Update(dsModify, "TitleAuthor")
adapter.Update(dsDelete, "Authors")
adapter.Update(dsDelete, "Titles")
adapter.Update(dsDelete, "TitleAuthor")
```

This adds a layer of complexity, and a significant amount of extra code. However, in cases where you make many different types of modifications to several different tables at once, this is the only solution. To avoid these problems, you could commit changes earlier (rather than committing an entire batch of changes at once), or use Command objects directly instead of relying on the disconnected data features of the DataSet.



## An Update Example

The next example rewrites the code for adding a new author in the update page with equivalent DataSet code. You can find this example in the online samples as AuthorManager2.aspx. (AuthorManager.aspx is the original, command-based version.)

```
Private Sub cmdInsert_Click(sender As Object, e As EventArgs) _
  Handles cmdInsert.Click

    ' Define ADO.NET objects.
    Dim SelectSQL As String
    SelectSQL = "SELECT * FROM Authors"
    Dim con As New OleDbConnection(ConnectionString)
    Dim cmd As New OleDbCommand(SelectSQL, con)
    Dim adapter As New OleDbDataAdapter(cmd)
    Dim dsPubs As New DataSet()

    ' Get the schema information.
    Try
        con.Open()
```

```
        adapter.FillSchema(dsPubs, SchemaType.Mapped, "Authors")
    Catch err As Exception
        lblStatus.Text = "Error reading schema. "
        lblStatus.Text &= err.Message
    Finally
        If (Not con Is Nothing) Then
            con.Close()
        End If
    End Try

    Dim rowNew As DataRow
    rowNew = dsPubs.Tables("Authors").NewRow
    rowNew("au_id") = txtID.Text
    rowNew("au_fname") = txtFirstName.Text
    rowNew("au_lname") = txtLastName.Text
    rowNew("phone") = txtPhone.Text
    rowNew("address") = txtAddress.Text
    rowNew("city") = txtCity.Text
    rowNew("state") = txtState.Text
    rowNew("zip") = txtZip.Text
    rowNew("contract") = Int(chkContract.Checked)
    dsPubs.Tables("Authors").Rows.Add(rowNew)

    ' Insert the new record.
    Dim Added As Integer
    Try
        ' Create the CommandBuilder.
        Dim cb As New OleDbCommandBuilder(adapter)
        ' Retrieve an updated DataAdapter.
        adapter = cb.DataAdapter

        ' Update the database using the DataSet.
        con.Open()
        Added = adapter.Update(dsPubs, "Authors")
    Catch err As Exception
        lblStatus.Text = "Error inserting record. "
        lblStatus.Text &= err.Message
    Finally
        con.Close()
    End Try

    ' If the insert succeeded, refresh the author list.
```

```
        If Added > 0 Then
            FillAuthorList()
        End If

    End Sub
```

In this case, the example is quite inefficient. In order to add a new record, a DataSet needs to be created, with the required tables and a valid row. To retrieve information about what this row should look like, the FillSchema method of the data adapter is used. The FillSchema method creates a table with no rows, but with other information about the table, such as the name of each field and the requirements for each column (the data type, the maximum length, any restriction against null values, and so on). If you wanted, you could use the FillSchema method followed by the Fill method.

After this step, the information is entered into a new row in the DataSet, the DataAdapter is updated with the CommandBuilder, and the changes are committed to the database. The whole operation took two database connections and required the use of a DataSet that was then abruptly abandoned. In this scenario, disconnected data is probably an extravagant solution to a problem that would be better solved with ordinary Command objects.



### FillSchema Is Useful with Auto-Increment Columns

Many database tables use identity columns that increment automatically. For example, an alternate design of the Authors table might use au_id as an auto-incrementing column. In this case, the database would automatically assign a unique ID to each inserted author record. To allow this to work with ADO.NET, you need to use the FillSchema method for the appropriate table, so that the column is set to be an auto-increment field. When adding new authors, you wouldn't specify any value for the au_id field; instead, this number would be generated when the changes are committed to the database.

## Concurrency Problems

As you discovered earlier, ADO.NET maintains information in the DataSet about the current and the original value of every piece of information in the DataSet. When updating a row, ADO.NET searches for a row that matches every "original" field exactly, and then updates it with the new values. If another user changes even a single field in that record while your program is working with the disconnected data, an exception is thrown. The update operation is then halted, potentially preventing other valid rows from being updated.

There is an easier way to handle these potential problems: using the DataAdapter's RowUpdated event. This event occurs after every individual insert, update, or delete operation, but before an exception is thrown. It gives you the chance to examine the results, note any errors, and prevent an error from occurring.

The first step is to create an appropriate event handler for the DataAdapter.RowUpdated event:

```
Public Sub OnRowUpdated(sender As Object, e As
OleDbRowUpdatedEventArgs)

    ' Check if any records were affected.
    ' If no records were affected, the statement did not execute
    ' as expected.
    If e.RecordsAffected() < 1 Then
        ' Find out the type of failed error.
        Select Case e.StatementType
            Case StatementType.Delete
                lstErrors.Items.Add("Not deleted: " & e.Row("au_id"))
            Case StatementType.Insert
                lstErrors.Items.Add("Not inserted: " & e.Row("au_id"))
            Case StatementType.Update
                lstErrors.Items.Add("Not updated: " & e.Row("au_id"))
        End Select

        ' Using the OledDbRowUpdatedEventArgs class,
        ' you can tell ADO.NET
        ' to ignore the problem and keep updating the other rows.
        e.Status = UpdateStatus.SkipCurrentRow
    End If

End Sub
```

The OleDbRowUpdatedEventArgs object provides this event handler with information about the row that ADO.NET just attempted to modify (e.Row), the type of modification (e.StatementType), and the result (e.RecordsAffected). In this example, errors are detected, and information about the unsuccessfully updated rows is added to a list control. Now that the problem has been noted, the e.Status property can be used to instruct ADO.NET to continue updating other changed rows in the DataSet.

Remember, this event occurs while the DataAdapter is in mid-update and using a live database connection. For that reason, you should not try to perform anything too complicated or time-consuming in this event handler. Instead, quickly log or display the errors and continue.

Now that the event handler has been created, you need to attach it to the DataSet before you perform the update. To do this, you use the AddHandler statement:

```
' Connect the event handler.
AddHandler adapter.RowUpdated, AddressOf OnRowUpdated

' Perform the update.
Dim RowsAffected As Integer
RowsAffected = adapter.Update(dsPubs, "Authors")
```

## A Concurrency Example

It can be hard to test the code you write to deal with concurrency problems, because it is only executed in specific circumstances. These circumstances may be common for a fully deployed large-scale application, but they are more difficult to recreate when a single developer is doing the testing.

The ConcurrencyHandler.aspx file in the online samples simulates a concurrency problem by making invalid changes to a database using two separate DataSets. When the code attempts to commit these changes, the OnRowUpdated code springs into action and reports the problem (see Figure 13-12).



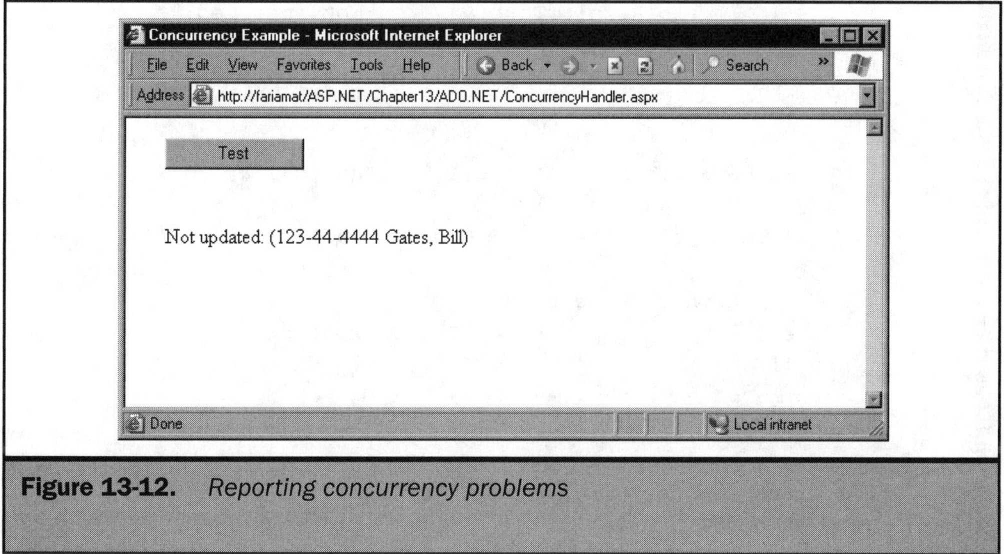


**Figure 13-12.** *Reporting concurrency problems*

The full page code is shown here:

```
Imports System.Data.OleDb
Imports System.Data

Public Class ConcurrencyHandler
  Inherits Page
    Protected WithEvents cmdTest As Button
    Protected lblResult As System.Web.UI.WebControls.Label

    ' Connection string used for all connections.
    Private ConnectionString As String = "Provider=SQLOLEDB.1;" & _
     "DataSource=localhost;Initial Catalog=pubs;" & _
     "Integrated Security=SSPI"

    Public Sub OnRowUpdated(sender As Object, _
      e As OleDbRowUpdatedEventArgs)
        ' Check if any records were affected.
        If e.RecordsAffected() < 1 Then
            ' Find out the type of failed error.
            Select Case e.StatementType
                Case StatementType.Delete
                    lblResult.Text &= "<br>Not deleted: "
                Case StatementType.Insert
                    lblResult.Text &= "<br>Not inserted: "
                Case StatementType.Update
                    lblResult.Text &= "<br>Not updated: "
            End Select

            lblResult.Text &= "(" & e.Row("au_id") & " " & _
              e.Row("au_lname")
            lblResult.Text &= ", " & e.Row("au_fname") & ")"

            ' Continue processing.
            e.Status = UpdateStatus.SkipCurrentRow
        End If

    End Sub

    Private Sub cmdTest_Click(sender As Object, e As EventArgs) _
      Handles cmdTest.Click
```

```
lblResult.Text = ""

' Define ADO.NET objects.
Dim SelectSQL As String
SelectSQL = "SELECT * FROM Authors"
Dim con As New OleDbConnection(ConnectionString)
Dim cmd As New OleDbCommand(SelectSQL, con)
Dim adapter As New OleDbDataAdapter(cmd)

' Create the CommandBuilder.
Dim cb As New OleDbCommandBuilder(adapter)
' Retrieve an updated DataAdapter.
adapter = cb.DataAdapter

' Connect the event handler.
AddHandler adapter.RowUpdated, AddressOf OnRowUpdated

' Create two DataSets... perfect for conflicting data.
Dim dsPubs1 As New DataSet(), dsPubs2 As New DataSet()

Try
    con.Open()

    ' Fill both DataSets with the same table.
    adapter.Fill(dsPubs1, "Authors")
    adapter.Fill(dsPubs2, "Authors")

    ' "Flip" the contract field in the first row of dsPubs1.
    If dsPubs1.Tables(0).Rows(0).Item("contract") = True Then
        dsPubs1.Tables(0).Rows(0).Item("contract") = False
    Else
        dsPubs1.Tables(0).Rows(0).Item("contract") = True
    End If

    ' Update the database
    adapter.Update(dsPubs1, "Authors")

    ' Make a change in the second DataSet.
    dsPubs2.Tables(0).Rows(0).Item("au_fname") = "Bill"
    dsPubs2.Tables(0).Rows(0).Item("au_lname") = "Gates"

    ' Try to update this row. Even though these changes
```

```
            ' don't conflict, the update will fail because the row
            ' has been changed.
            adapter.Update(dsPubs2, "Authors")

        Catch err As Exception
            lblResult.Text &= "Error reading schema. "
            lblResult.Text &= err.Message
        Finally
            If (Not con Is Nothing) Then
                con.Close()
            End If
        End Try

    End Sub

End Class
```

The Complete Reference

# Chapter 14

## Data Binding

In Chapter 13, you learned how to use ADO.NET to retrieve information from a database, work with it in an ASP.NET application, and then apply your changes back to the original data source. These techniques are flexible and powerful, but they aren't always convenient.

For example, you can use the DataSet or the DataReader to retrieve rows of information, format them individually, and add them to an HTML table on a web page. Conceptually, this isn't too difficult. However, it still requires a lot of repetitive code to move through the data, format columns, and display it in the correct order. Repetitive code may be easy, but it's also error-prone, difficult to enhance, and unpleasant to look at. Fortunately, ASP.NET adds a feature that allows you to skip this process and pop data directly into HTML elements and fully formatted controls. It's called data binding.

# Introducing Data Binding

The basic principle of data binding is this: you tell a control where to find your data and how you want it displayed, and the control handles the rest of the details. Data binding in ASP.NET is superficially similar to data binding in the world of desktop or client/server applications, but fundamentally different. In those environments, data binding refers to the creation of a direct connection between a data source and a control in an application window. If the user changes a value in the onscreen control, the data in the linked database is modified automatically. Similarly, if the database changes while the user is working with it (for example, another user commits a change), the display can be refreshed automatically.

This type of data binding isn't practical in the ASP.NET world, because you can't effectively maintain a database connection over the Internet. This "direct" data binding also severely limits scalability and reduces flexibility. It's for these reasons that data binding has acquired a bad reputation.

ASP.NET data binding, on the other hand, has little in common with direct data binding. ASP.NET data binding works in one direction only. Information moves from a data object into a control. Then the objects are thrown away and the page is sent to the client. If the user modifies the data in a databound control, your program can update the database, but nothing happens automatically.

ASP.NET data binding is much more flexible than traditional data binding. Many of the most powerful data binding controls, such as the Repeater, DataList, and DataGrid, allow you to configure formatting options and even add repeating controls and buttons for each record. This is all set up through special templates, which are a new addition to ASP.NET. Templates are examined in detail in Chapter 15.

## Types of ASP.NET Data Binding

There are actually two types of ASP.NET data binding.

### Single-Value or "Simple" Data Binding

This type of data binding is used to add information anywhere on an ASP.NET page. You can even place information into a control property or as plain text inside an HTML tag. Single-value data binding doesn't necessarily have anything to do with ADO.NET. In fact, because ADO.NET usually works with entire lists or tables of information, single-value data binding is rarely of much use. Instead, single-value data binding allows you to take a variable, property, or expression and insert it dynamically into a page.

### Repeated-Value or List Binding

This type of data binding is much more useful for handling complex tasks, such as displaying an entire table or all the values from a single field in a table. Unlike single-value data binding, this type of data binding requires a special control that supports it. Typically, this will be a list control like CheckBoxList or ListBox, but it can also be a much more sophisticated control like the DataGrid. You will know that a control supports repeated-value data binding if it provides a DataSource property. As with single-value binding, repeated-value binding does not necessarily need to use data from a database, and it doesn't have to use the ADO.NET objects. For example, you can use repeated-value binding to bind data from a collection or an array.

## How Data Binding Works

Data binding works a little differently depending on whether you are using single-value or repeated-value binding. In single-value binding, a data binding expression is inserted right into the display portion of the .aspx file (not the code portion or code-behind file). In repeated-value binding, data binding is configured by setting the appropriate control properties (for example, in the Load event for the page). You'll see specific examples of both these techniques later in this chapter.

Once you specify data binding, you need to activate it. You accomplish this task by calling the DataBind method. The DataBind method is a basic piece of functionality supplied in the Control class. It automatically binds a control and any child controls that it contains. With repeated-value binding, you can use the DataBind method for the specific list control you are using. Alternatively, you can bind the whole page at once by calling the DataBind method for the current page. Once you call this method, all the data binding expressions in the page are evaluated and replaced with the specified value.

Typically, you use the DataBind method in the Page.Load event. If you forget to use it, ASP.NET will ignore your data binding expressions, and the client will receive a page that contains empty values.

This is a very general description of the whole process. To really understand what's happening, you need to work with some specific examples.

# Single-Value Data Binding

Single-value data binding is really just a different approach to dynamic text. To use it, you add a special data binding expression into your .aspx files. These expressions have the following format:

```
<%# expression_goes_here %>
```

This may look like a script block, but it isn't. If you try to write any code inside this special tag, you will receive an error. The only thing you can add is valid data binding expressions. For example, if you have a public variable on your page named Country, you could write:

```
<%# Country %>
```

When you call the DataBind method for the page, this text will be replaced with the value for Country (for example, Spain). Similarly, you could use a property or a built-in ASP.NET object:

```
<%# Request.Browser.Browser %>
```

This would substitute a string with the current browser name (for example, IE). In fact, you can even call a built-in function, a public function defined on your page, or execute a simple expression, provided it returns a result that can be converted to text and displayed on the page. The following data binding expressions are all valid:

```
<%# GetUserName(ID) %>
<%# 1 + (2 * 20) %>
<%# "John " & "Smith" %>
```

Remember, these data binding expressions are placed in the HTML code for your .aspx file. That means that if you're relying on Visual Studio .NET to manage your HTML code automatically, you may have to venture into slightly unfamiliar territory. To examine how you can add a data binding expression, and see why you might want to, it helps to review a simple example.

## A Simple Data Binding Example

This section considers a simple example of single-value data binding. The example has been stripped to the bare minimum amount of detail needed to illustrate the concept.

You start with a special variable defined in your Page class, which is called TransactionsCount:

```
Public Class DataBindingPage
  Inherits Page

    Public TransactionCount As Integer

    ' (Additional code omitted.)

End Class
```

Note that this variable must be designated as Public, not Private. Otherwise, ASP.NET will not be able to access it when it is evaluating the data binding expression.

Now, assume that this value is set in the Page.Load event handler using some database lookup code. For testing purposes, our example skips this step and hard-codes a value:

```
Private Sub Page_Load(sender As Object, e As EventArgs) _
  Handles MyBase.Load

    ' You could use database code here to look up a value for
    ' TransactionCount.
    TransactionCount = 10
    ' Now convert all the data binding expressions on the page.
    Me.DataBind()

End Sub
```

Two things actually happen in this event handler: the TransactionCount variable is set to 10, and all the data binding expressions on the page are bound. Currently, there aren't any data binding expressions, so this method has no effect. Notice that this example uses the Me keyword to refer to the current page. You could just write DataBind() without the Me keyword, as the default object is the current Page object. However, using the Me keyword makes it a bit clearer what control is being used.

To actually make this data binding accomplish something, you need to add a data binding expression. Usually, it's easiest to add this value directly to the presentation code in the .aspx file. If you are using Notepad to create your ASP.NET pages, you won't have any trouble with this approach. If, on the other hand, you're using Visual Studio .NET to create your controls, you should probably add a label control, and then configure the data binding expression in the HTML view by clicking the HTML button (see Figure 14-1).

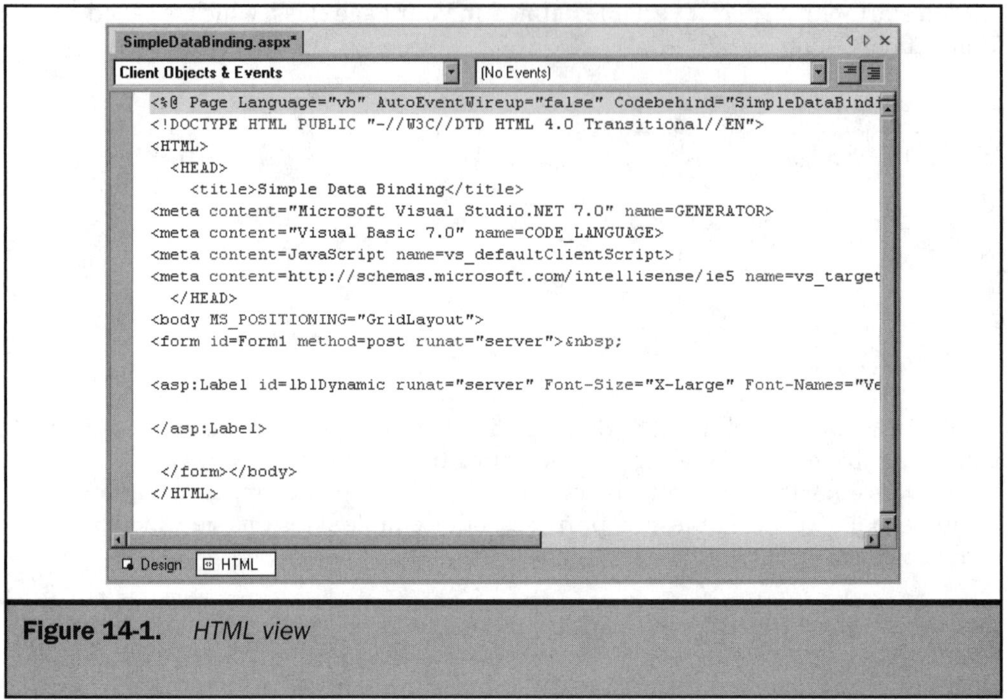


**Figure 14-1.** *HTML view*

You could also type this data binding expression in the Properties window, but Visual Studio .NET does not always refresh this information correctly. In this case, it's better to work on a slightly lower level.

To add your expression, find the tag for the label control. Modify the Text property as shown in the following code. Note that some of the label attributes (such as its size and position) have been left out to help make it clearer. You should not, however, delete this information in your code!

```
<asp:Label id=lblDynamic runat="server" Font-Size="X-Large"
Font-Names="Verdana">
There were <%# TransactionCount %> transactions today. I see that
you are using <%# Request.Browser.Browser %>.
</asp:Label>
```

This example uses two separate data binding expressions, which are inserted along with the normal static text. The first data binding expression references the intTransactionsToday variable, and the second uses the built-in Request object to find out some information about the user's browser. When you run this page, the output looks like Figure 14-2.

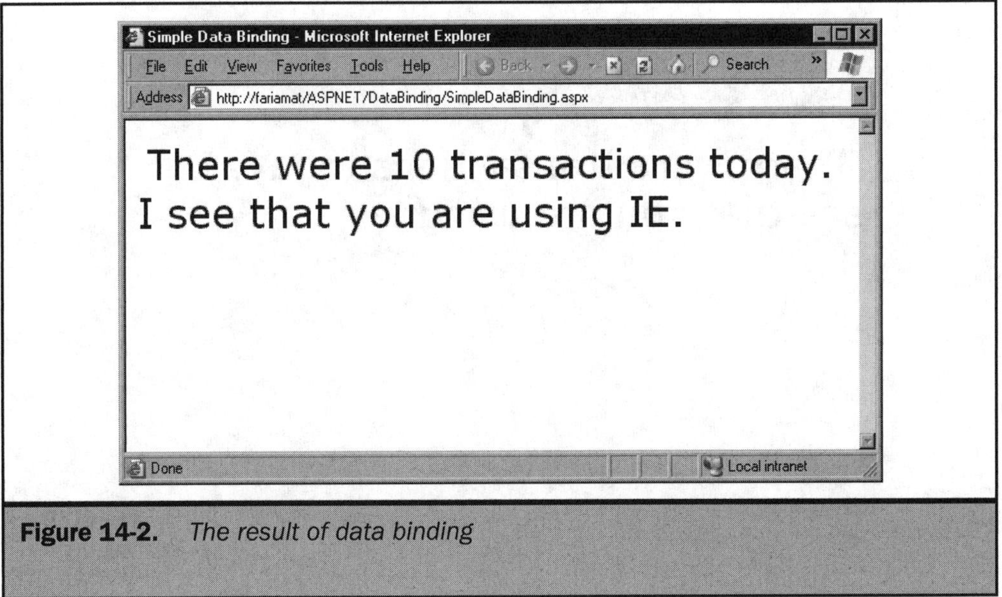


**Figure 14-2.** *The result of data binding*



The data binding expressions have been automatically replaced with the appropriate values. If the page is posted back, you could use additional code to modify TransactionCount, and as long as you called the DataBind method, that information would be popped into the page in the locations you have designated.

If, however, you forgot to call the DataBind method, the expressions would be ignored, and the user would see a somewhat confusing window that looks like Figure 14-3.

You also need to be careful with your databound control in the design environment. If you modify its properties in the Properties window of Visual Studio .NET, the editor can end up thoughtlessly obliterating your data binding expressions.

## Order Is Important

When using single-value data binding, you need to consider when you should call the DataBind method. For example, if you made the mistake of calling it before you set the TransactionCount variable, the corresponding expression would just be converted into 0. Remember, data binding is a one-way street. That means there won't be any visible effect if you change the TransactionCount variable after you've used the DataBind method. Unless you call the DataBind method again, the displayed value won't be updated.

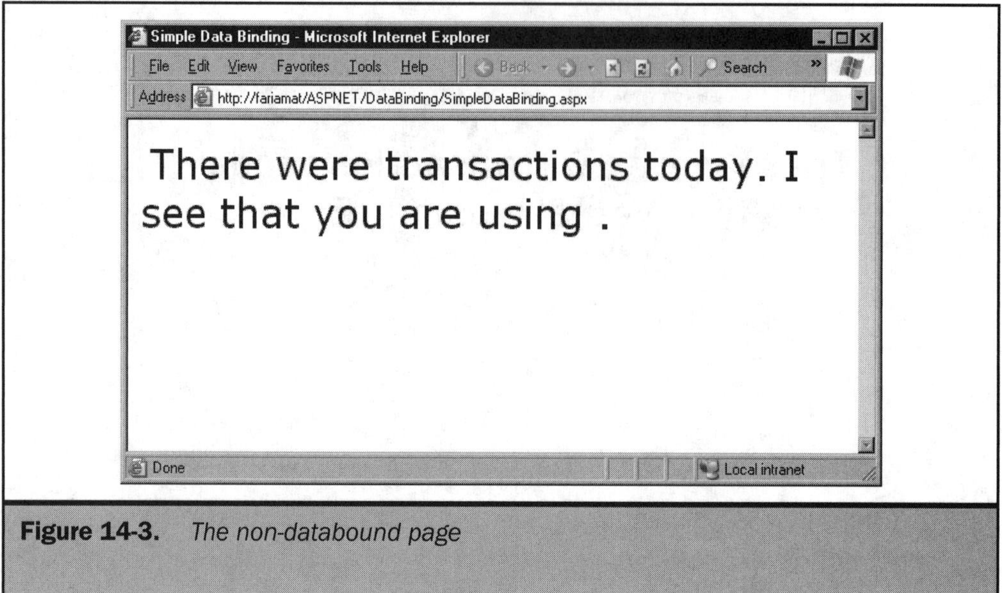


**Figure 14-3.** *The non-databound page*

## Simple Data Binding with Properties

In the example so far, data binding expressions are used to set static text information inside a label tag. However, you can also use single-value data binding to set other types of information on your page, including control properties. To do this, you simply have to know where to put the data binding expression.

For example, consider a page that defines a URL variable and uses it to refer to a picture in the application directory:

```
Public Class DataBindingPage
  Inherits Page

    Public URL As String

    Private Sub Page_Load(sender As Object, e As EventArgs) _
      Handles MyBase.Load
        URL = Server.MapPath("picture.jpg")
        Me.DataBind()
    End Sub

End Class
```

This URL can now be used to create a label as the previous example did:

```
<asp:Label id=lblDynamic runat="server"><%# URL %></asp:Label>
```

You can also use it as a caption for a checkbox:

```
<asp:CheckBox id="chkDynamic" Text="<%# URL %>" runat="server" />
```

Or as a target for a hyperlink control:

```
<asp:Hyperlink id="lnkDynamic" Text="Click here!"
    NavigateUrl="<%# URL %>" runat="server" />
```

Or even as a picture:

```
<asp:Image id="imgDynamic" Src="<%# URL %>" runat="server" />
```



The only trick is that you need to be able to edit these control tags manually. A final combined page that uses all these elements would look something like Figure 14-4.

To examine it in more detail, try out the sample code for this chapter.

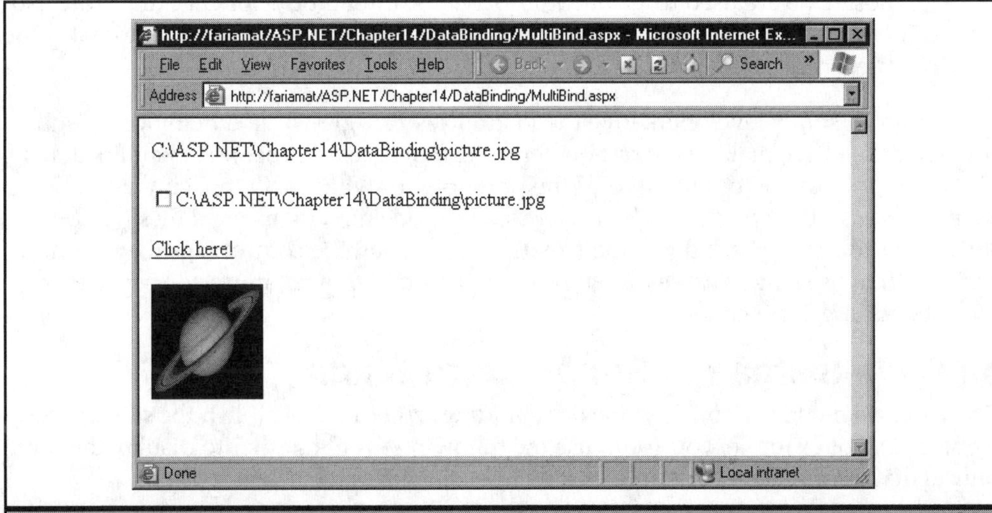


**Figure 14-4.** *Multiple ways to bind the same data*

## Problems with Single-Value Data Binding

Before you start using single-value data binding techniques in every aspect of your ASP.NET programs, you should consider some of the serious drawbacks that this approach can present.

**Putting code into a page's user interface** One of ASP.NET's great advantages is that it finally allows developers to separate the user interface code (the HTML and control tags in the .aspx file) from the actual code used for data access and all other tasks (in the code-behind file). However, over-enthusiastic use of single-value data binding can encourage you to disregard that distinction and start coding function calls and even operations into your page. If not carefully managed, this can lead to complete disorder.

**Code fragmentation** When data binding expressions are used, it may not be obvious to other developers where the functionality resides for different operations. This is particularly a problem if you blend both approaches (modifying the same control using a data binding expression, and then directly in code). Even worse, the data binding code may have certain dependencies that aren't immediately obvious. If the page code changes, or a variable or function is removed or renamed, the corresponding data binding expression could stop providing valid information without any explanation or even an obvious error.

**No design-time error checking** When you type a data binding expression, you need to remember the corresponding variable, property, or method name and enter it exactly. If you don't, you won't realize your mistake until you try to run the page and you receive an error (see Figure 14-5). This is a significant drawback for those who are used to Visual Studio .NET's automatic error checking. You also can't take advantage of Visual Studio .NET's IntelliSense features to automatically complete code statements.

Of course, some developers love the flexibility of single-value data binding, and use it to great effect, making the rest of their code more economical and streamlined. It's up to you to be aware of (and avoid) the potential drawbacks. Often, single-value data binding suits developers who prefer to write code directly in .aspx files without Visual Studio .NET. These developers manually write all the control tags they need, and can thus use single-value data binding to create a shorter, more concise file without adding extra code.

## Using Code Instead of Simple Data Binding

If you decide not to use single-value data binding, you can accomplish the same thing using code. For example, you could use the following event handler to display the same output that our first label example created.

```
Private Sub Page_Load(sender As Object, e As EventArgs) _
  Handles MyBase.Load

    TransactionCount = 10
    lblDynamic.Text = "There were " & TransactionCount.ToString()
    lblDynamic.Text &= "transactions today. "
    lblDynamic.Text &= "I see that you are using " & _
      Request.Browser.Browser

End Sub
```

This code dynamically fills in the label without using data binding. The trade-off is more code. Instead of importing ASP.NET code into the .aspx file, you end up doing the reverse: importing user interface (the specific text) into your code file!

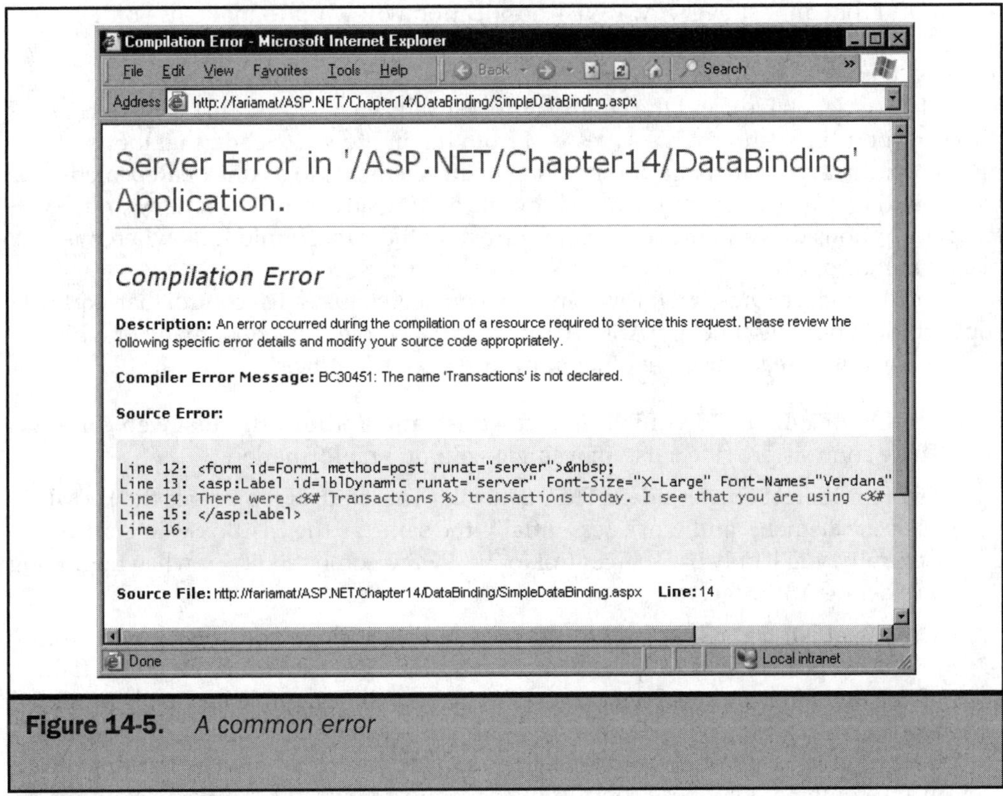


**Figure 14-5.** *A common error*

**Stick to One Approach**

As much as possible, stick to one approach for using dynamic text. If you decide to use data binding, try to reduce the number of times you modify a control's text in code. If you do both, you may end up confusing others, or just canceling your own changes! For example, if you call the DataBind method on a control that uses a data expression after changing its values in code, your data binding expression will not be used.

# Repeated-Value Data Binding

While using simple data binding is an optional choice, repeated-value binding is so useful that almost every ASP.NET application will want to make use of it somewhere. Repeated-value data binding uses one of the special list controls included with ASP.NET. You link one of these controls to a data list source (such as a field in a data table), and the control automatically creates a full list using all the corresponding values. This saves you from having to write code that loops through the array or data table and manually adds elements to a control. Repeated-value binding can also simplify your life by supporting advanced formatting and template options that automatically configure how the data should look when it is placed in the control.

To create a data expression for list binding, you need to use a list control that explicitly supports data binding. Luckily, ASP.NET provides a whole collection, many of which you've probably already used in other applications or examples:

**The ListBox, DropDownList, CheckBoxList, and RadioButtonList web controls** These controls provide a list for a single-column of information.

**The HtmlSelect server-side HTML control** This control represents the HTML <select> element, and works essentially the same as the ListBox web control. Generally, you'll only use this control for backward compatibility or when upgrading an existing ASP page.

**The DataList, DataGrid, and Repeater controls** These controls allow you to provide repeating lists or grids that can display more than one column (or field) of information at a time. For example, if you were binding to a hashtable (a special type of collection), you could display both the key and value of each item. If you were binding to a full-fledged table in a DataSet, you could display multiple fields in any combination. These controls offer the most powerful and flexible options for data binding.

With repeated-value data binding, you can write a data binding expression in your .aspx file, or you can apply the data binding by setting control properties. In the case of the simpler list controls, you will usually just set properties. Of course, you can set properties in many ways, using code in a code-behind file, or by modifying the control tag in the .aspx file, possibly with the help of Visual Studio .NET's Properties window. The approach you take does not matter. The important detail is that you don't use any <%# expression %> data binding expressions.

For more sophisticated and flexible controls, such as the Repeater and DataList, you need to set some properties *and* enter data binding expressions in the .aspx file, generally using a special template format. Understanding the use of templates is the key to mastering data binding, and we'll explore it in detail in Chapter 15.

To continue any further with data binding, it helps to divide the subject into a few basic categories. We'll start by looking at data binding with the list controls.

# Data Binding with Simple List Controls

In some ways, data binding to a list control is the simplest kind of data binding. You only need to follow three steps:

1. **Create and fill some kind of data object.** There are numerous options, including an Array, ArrayList, Collection, Hashtable, DataTable, and DataSet. Essentially, you can use any type of collection that supports the IEnumerable interface, although there are specific advantages and disadvantages that you will discover in each class.
2. **Link the object to the appropriate control.** To do this, you only need to set a couple of properties, including DataSource. If you are binding to a full DataSet, you will also need to set the DataMember property to identify the appropriate table that you want to use.
3. **Activate the binding.** As with single-value binding, you activate data binding by using the DataBind method, either for the specific control or for all contained controls at once by using the DataBind method for the current page.



This process is the same whether you are using the ListBox, DropDownList, CheckBoxList, RadioButtonList, or even HtmlSelect control. All these controls provide the exact same properties and work the same way. The only difference is in the way they appear on the final web page.

# A Simple List Binding Example

To try out this type of data binding, add a ListBox control to a new web page. Use the Page.Load event handler to create a collection to use as a data source:

```
Dim colFruit As New Collection()
colFruit.Add("Kiwi")
```

```
colFruit.Add("Pear")
colFruit.Add("Mango")
colFruit.Add("Blueberry")
colFruit.Add("Apricot")
colFruit.Add("Banana")
colFruit.Add("Peach")
colFruit.Add("Plum")
```

Now, you can link this collection to the list box control.

```
lstItems.DataSource = colFruit
```

Because a collection is a straightforward, unstructured type of object, this is all the information you need to set. If you were using a DataTable (which has more than one field) or a DataSet (which has more than one DataTable), you would have to specify additional information, as you will see in later examples.

To activate the binding, use the DataBind method:

```
Me.DataBind()
' Could also use lstItems.DataBind to bind just the list box.
```

The resulting web page looks like Figure 14-6.

This technique can save quite a few lines of code. In this example, there isn't a lot of savings because the collection is created just before it is displayed. In a more realistic application, however, you might be using a function that returns a ready-made collection to you.

```
Dim colFruit As Collection    ' No New keyword is needed this time.
colFruit = GetFruitsInSeason("Summer")
```

In this case, it is extremely simple to add the extra two lines needed to bind and display the collection in the window.

```
lstItems.DataSource = colFruit
Me.DataBind()
```

Or even change it to this:

```
lstItems.DataSource = GetFruitsInSeason("Summer")
Me.DataBind()
```

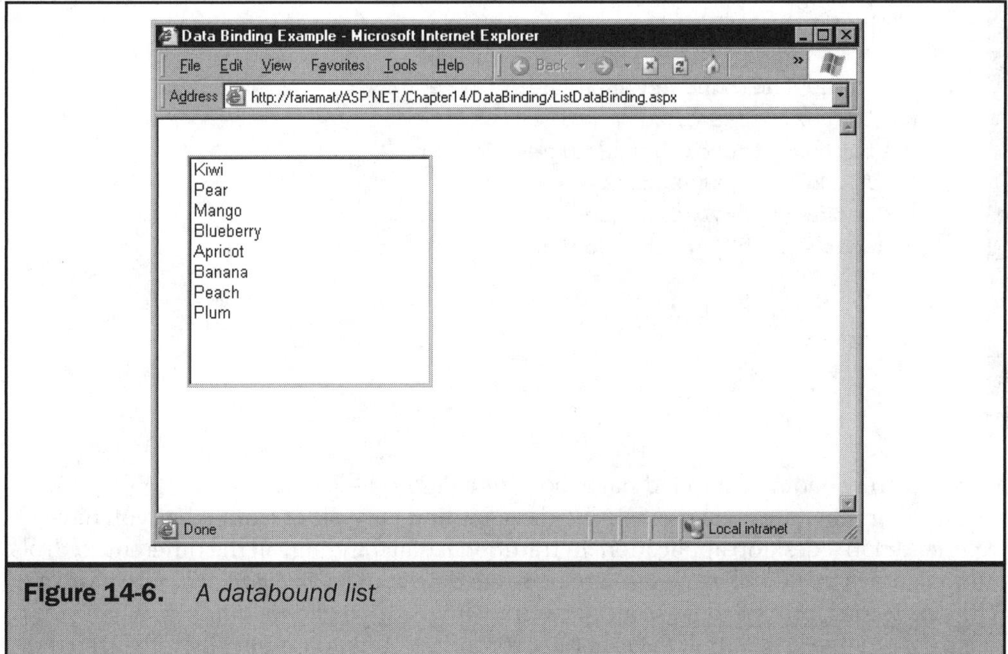


**Figure 14-6.** *A databound list*



On the other hand, consider the extra trouble you would have to go through if you didn't use data binding. This type of savings adds up rapidly, especially when you start to combine data binding with multiple controls, advanced objects like DataSets, or advanced controls that apply formatting through templates.

## Multiple Binding

You can bind the same data list object to multiple different controls. Consider the following example, which compares all the different types of list controls at your disposal by loading them with the same information:

```
Private Sub Page_Load(sender As Object, e As EventArgs) _
  Handles MyBase.Load

    ' Create and fill the collection.
    Dim colFruit As New Collection()
    colFruit.Add("Kiwi")
    colFruit.Add("Pear")
    colFruit.Add("Mango")
    colFruit.Add("Blueberry")
    colFruit.Add("Apricot")
    colFruit.Add("Banana")
    colFruit.Add("Peach")
```

```
    colFruit.Add("Plum")

    ' Define the binding for the list controls.
    MyListBox.DataSource = colFruit
    MyDropDownListBox.DataSource = colFruit
    MyHTMLSelect.DataSource = colFruit
    MyCheckBoxList.DataSource = colFruit
    MyRadioButtonList.DataSource = colFruit

    ' Activate the binding.
    Me.DataBind()

End Sub
```

The corresponding compiled page looks like Figure 14-7.

This is another area where ASP.NET data binding may differ from what you have experienced in a desktop application. In traditional data binding, all the different controls are sometimes treated like "views" on the same data source, and you can only work with one record from the data source at a time. In this type of data binding, when you select Pear in one list control, the other list controls would automatically refresh so that they too have Pear selected (or the corresponding information from the same row). This is not how ASP.NET uses data binding.

## Viewstate

Remember, the original collection is destroyed as soon as the page is completely processed into HTML and sent to the user. However, the information will remain in the controls if you have set their EnableViewstate properties to True. That means that you don't need to recreate and rebind the control every time the Page.Load event occurs, and you should check the IsPostBack property first.

Of course, in many cases, especially when working with databases, you will want to rebind on every pass. For example, if you presented information corresponding to values in a database table, you might want to let the user make changes or specify a record to be deleted. As soon as the page is posted back, you would then want to execute an SQL command and rebind the control to show the new data (thereby confirming to the user that the data source was updated with the change). In this case, you should disable viewstate, because you will be rebinding the data with every postback.

Chapter 15 will examine this situation a little more closely. The important concept to realize now is that you need to be consciously evaluating state options. If you don't need viewstate for a databound list control, you should disable it, as it can slow down response times if a large amount of data is displayed on the screen. This is particularly true for our example with multiple binding, as each control will have its own viewstate and its own separate copy of the identical data.

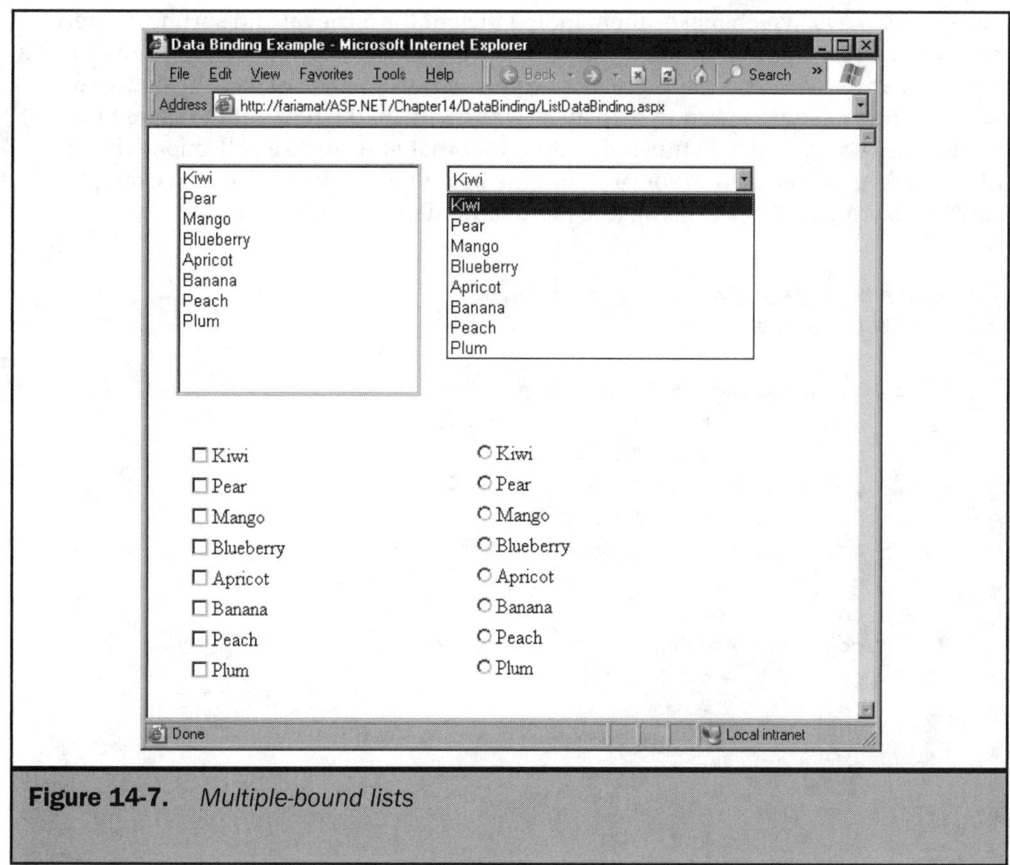


**Figure 14-7.** *Multiple-bound lists*



## Data Binding with a Hashtable

Collections are not the only kind of data source you can use with list data binding. Other popular choices include various types of arrays and specialized collections. The concepts are virtually identical, so this chapter won't spend much time looking at different possibilities. Instead, we'll consider one more example with a hashtable before continuing on to DataSets and DataReaders, which allow information to be displayed from a database.

A hashtable is a special kind of collection where every item has a corresponding key. It's also called a dictionary, because every item (or "definition," to use the dictionary analogy) is indexed with a specific key (or dictionary "word"). This is similar to the way that built-in ASP.NET collections like Session, Application, and Cache work.

You might already know that the standard collection used in the previous example allows you to specify a key for every inserted item. However, it doesn't require one. This is the main difference between a generic collection and the hashtable—hashtables always need keys, which makes them more efficient for retrieval and sorting. Generic collections, on the other hand, are like large black sacks. Generally, you need to go through every item in a generic collection to find what you need, which makes them ideal for cases where you always need to display or work with all the items at the same time.

You create a hashtable in much the same way that you create a collection. The only difference is that you need to supply a unique key for every item. The next example uses the lazy practice of assigning a sequential number for each key:

```
Private Sub Page_Load(sender As Object, e As EventArgs) _
  Handles MyBase.Load

    If Me.IsPostBack = False Then
        Dim colFruit As New Hashtable()
        colFruit.Add(1, "Kiwi")
        colFruit.Add(2, "Pear")
        colFruit.Add(3, "Mango")
        colFruit.Add(4, "Blueberry")
        colFruit.Add(5, "Apricot")
        colFruit.Add(6, "Banana")
        colFruit.Add(7, "Peach")
        colFruit.Add(8, "Plum")

        ' Define the binding for the list controls.
        MyListBox.DataSource = colFruit

        ' Activate the binding.
        Me.DataBind()
    End If

End Sub
```

However, when you try to run this code, you'll receive the unhelpful page shown in Figure 14-8.

What happened? ASP.NET doesn't know how to handle hashtables without additional information. Instead, it defaults to using the ToString method to get the class name for each item in the collection, which is probably not what you had in mind.

To solve this problem, you have to specify the property that you are interested in. Add this line before the Me.DataBind() statement:

```
' Specify that you will use the Value property of each item.
MyListBox.DataTextField = "Value"
```

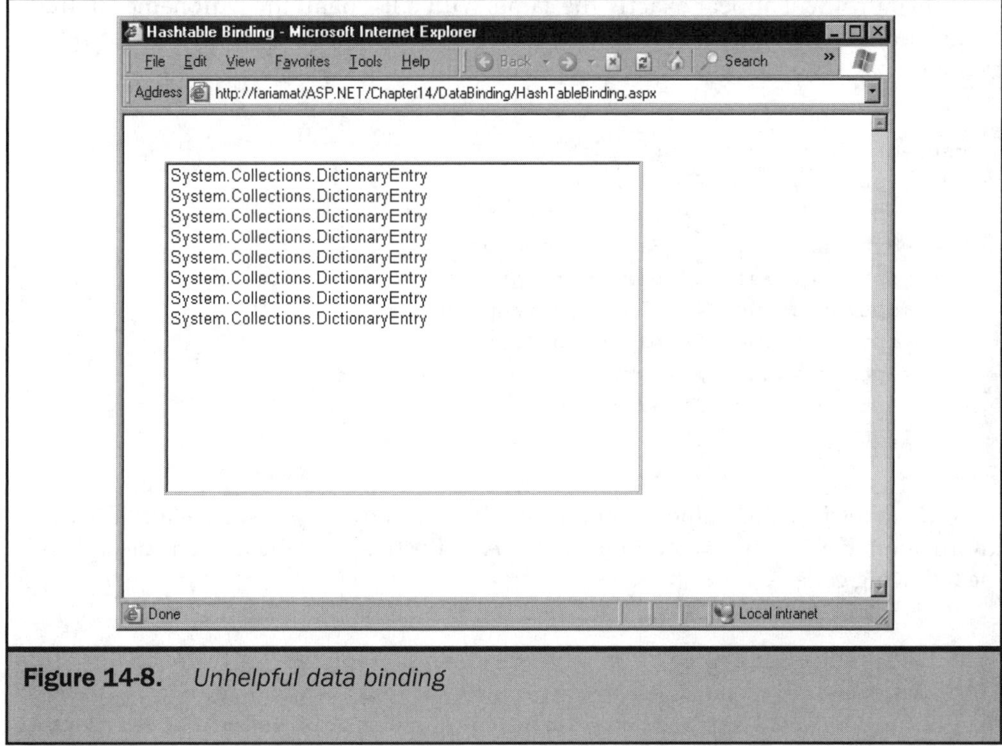


**Figure 14-8.** *Unhelpful data binding*



The page will now appear as expected, with all the fruit names. Notice that you need to enclose the property name in quotation marks. ASP.NET uses reflection to inspect your object and find the property that matches this string at runtime.

You might want to experiment with what other types of collections you can bind to a list control. One interesting option is to use a built-in ASP.NET control such as the Session object. An item in the list will be created for every currently defined Session variable, making this trick a nice little debugging tool to quickly check current information.

## Using the DataValueField Property

Along with the DataTextField property, all list controls that support data binding also provide a DataValueField, which adds the corresponding information to the value attribute in the control element. This allows you to store extra (undisplayed) information that you can access later. For example, you could use these two lines to define your data binding:

```
MyListBox.DataTextField = "Value"
MyListBox.DataValueField = "Key"
```

The control will appear exactly the same, with a list of all the fruit names in the hashtable. If you look at the HTML source of the page, though, you will see that value attributes have been set with the corresponding numeric key for each item:

```
<select name="MyListBox" id="MyListBox" >
    <option value="8">Plum</option>
    <option value="7">Peach</option>
    <option value="6">Banana</option>
    <option value="5">Apricot</option>
    <option value="4">Blueberry</option>
    <option value="3">Mango</option>
    <option value="2">Pear</option>
    <option value="1">Kiwi</option>
</select>
```

You can retrieve this value later on using the SelectedItem class to get additional information. For example, you could enable AutoPostBack for the list control, and add the following code:

```
Private Sub MyListBox_SelectedIndexChanged(sender As Object, _
 e As EventArgs) Handles MyListBox.SelectedIndexChanged
    lblMessage.Text = "You picked: " & MyListBox.SelectedItem.Text
    lblMessage.Text &= " which has the key: " & _
      MyListBox.SelectedItem.Value
End Sub
```

The result is demonstrated in Figure 14-9. This technique is particularly useful with a database. You could embed a unique ID into the value property and be able to quickly look up a corresponding record depending on the user's selection by examining the value of the SelectedItem object.

Note that in order for this to work, you must *not* be regenerating the list with every postback. If you are, the selected item information will be lost, and an error will occur. The preceding example uses the Page.IsPostBack property to determine whether to build the list.

## Data Binding with Databases

So far the examples in this chapter have dealt with data binding that doesn't involve databases or any part of ADO.NET. While this is an easy way to familiarize yourself with the concepts, and a useful approach in its own right, the greatest advantage from data binding is achieved when you use it in conjunction with a database.

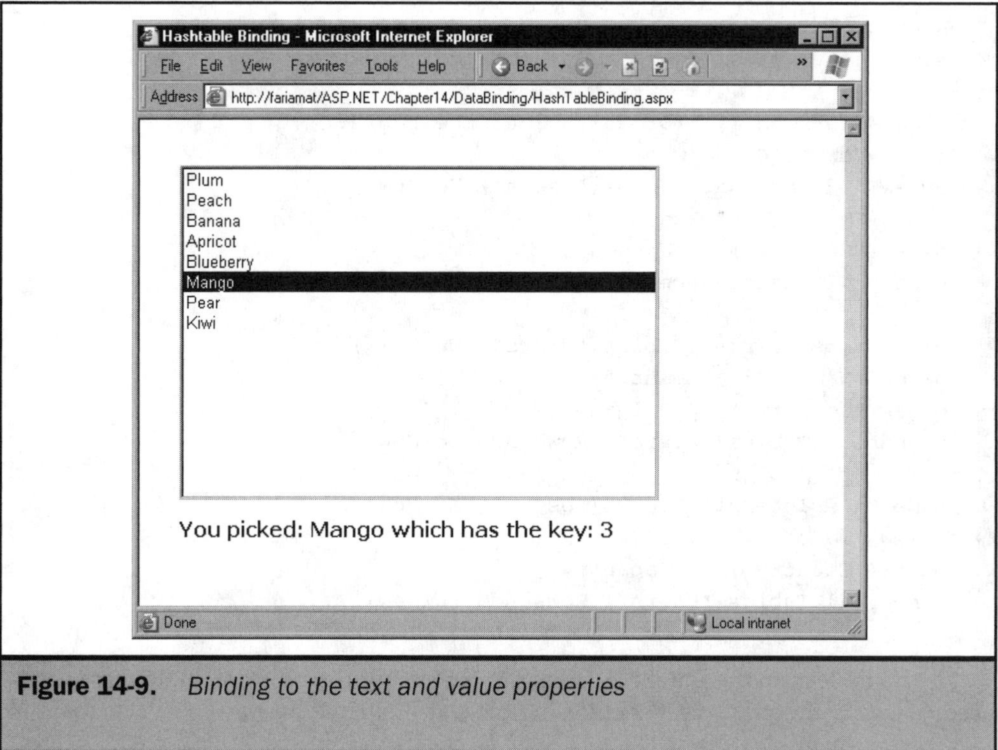


**Figure 14-9.** *Binding to the text and value properties*



Remember, in order to work with databases you should import the related namespaces:

```
Imports System.Data
Imports System.Data.OleDb      ' Or System.Data.SqlDB
```

The data binding process still takes place in the same three steps with a database. First you create your data source, which will be a DataReader or DataSet object. A DataReader generally offers the best performance, but it limits your data binding to a single control, so a DataSet is a more common choice. In the following example, the DataSet is filled by hand, but it could just as easily be filled with a DataAdapter object.

```
' Define a DataSet with a single DataTable.
Dim dsInternal As New DataSet()
dsInternal.Tables.Add("Users")

' Define two columns for this table.
```

```
dsInternal.Tables("Users").Columns.Add("Name")
dsInternal.Tables("Users").Columns.Add("Country")

' Add some actual information into the table.
Dim rowNew As DataRow
rowNew = dsInternal.Tables("Users").NewRow()
rowNew("Name") = "John"
rowNew("Country") = "Uganda"
dsInternal.Tables("Users").Rows.Add(rowNew)

rowNew = dsInternal.Tables("Users").NewRow()
rowNew("Name") = "Samantha"
rowNew("Country") = "Belgium"
dsInternal.Tables("Users").Rows.Add(rowNew)

rowNew = dsInternal.Tables("Users").NewRow()
rowNew("Name") = "Rico"
rowNew("Country") = "Japan"
dsInternal.Tables("Users").Rows.Add(rowNew)
```

Next, a table from the DataSet is bound to the appropriate control. In this case, you need to specify the appropriate field using the DataTextField property:

```
' Define the binding.
lstUser.DataSource = dsInternal.Tables("Users")
lstUser.DataTextField = "Name"
```

Alternatively, you could use the entire DataSet for the data source, instead of just the appropriate table. In this case, you have to select a table by setting the control's DataMember property. This is an equivalent approach, but the code looks slightly different:

```
' Define the binding.
lstUser.DataSource = dsInternal
lstUser.DataMember = "Users"
lstUser.DataTextField = "Name"
```

As always, the last step is to activate the binding:

```
Me.DataBind()
' You could also use lstItems.DataBind to bind just the list box.
```

The final result is a list with the information from the specified database field, as shown in Figure 14-10. The list box will have an entry for every single record in the table, even if it appears more than once, from the first row to the last.

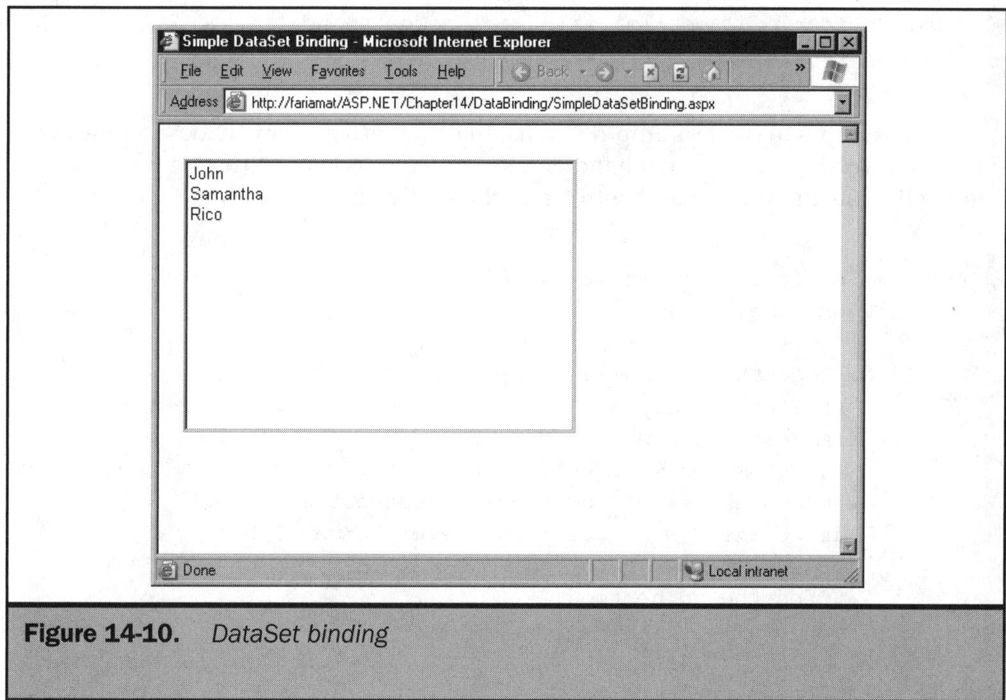


**Figure 14-10.** *DataSet binding*

### Can You Include More than One Field in a List Control?

The simple list controls require you to bind their Text or Value property to a single data field in the data source object. However, much more flexibility is provided by the more advanced data binding controls examined in Chapter 15. They allow fields to be combined in any way using templates.

## Creating a Record Editor

The next example is more practical. It's a good example of how data binding might be used in a full ASP.NET application. This example allows the user to select a record and update one piece of information by using databound list controls. This example uses the

Products table from the Northwind database included with SQL Server. A Private variable in the Page class is used to define a connection string that every part of the code can access:

```
Private ConnectionString As String = "Provider=SQLOLEDB.1;" & _
 "DataSource=localhost;Initial Catalog=Northwind;" & _
 "Integrated Security=SSPI"
```

The first step is to create a drop-down list that allows the user to choose a product for editing. The Page.Load event handler takes care of this task, retrieving the data, binding it to the drop-down list control, and then activating the binding:

```
Private Sub Page_Load(sender As Object, e As EventArgs) _
  Handles MyBase.Load

    If Me.IsPostBack = False Then
        ' Define the ADO.NET objects for selecting Products.
        Dim SelectCommand As String
        SelectCommand = "SELECT ProductName, ProductID FROM Products"
        Dim con As New OleDbConnection(ConnectionString)
        Dim com As New OleDbCommand(SelectCommand, con)

        ' Open the connection.
        con.Open()

        ' Define the binding.
        lstProduct.DataSource = com.ExecuteReader()
        lstProduct.DataTextField = "ProductName"
        lstProduct.DataValueField = "ProductID"

        ' Activate the binding.
        lstProduct.DataBind()

        con.Close()

        ' Make sure nothing is currently selected.
        lstProduct.SelectedIndex = -1

    End If

End Sub
```

The actual database code is very similar to what we covered in Chapter 13. The example uses a Select statement, but carefully limits the returned information to just the ProductName field, which is the only piece of information it will use. The resulting window shows a list of all the products defined in the database, as shown in Figure 14-11.

The drop-down list enables AutoPostBack, so as soon as the user makes a selection, a lstProduct.SelectedItemChanged event fires. At this point, our code performs several tasks:

- It reads the corresponding record from the Products table and displays additional information about it in a label control. In this case, a special Join query is used to link information from the Products and Categories table. The code also determines what the category is for the current product. This is the piece of information it will allow the user to change.
- It reads the full list of CategoryNames from the Categories table and binds this information to a different list control.
- It highlights the row in the category list box that corresponds to the current product. For example, if the current product is a Seafood category, the Seafood entry in the list box will be selected.



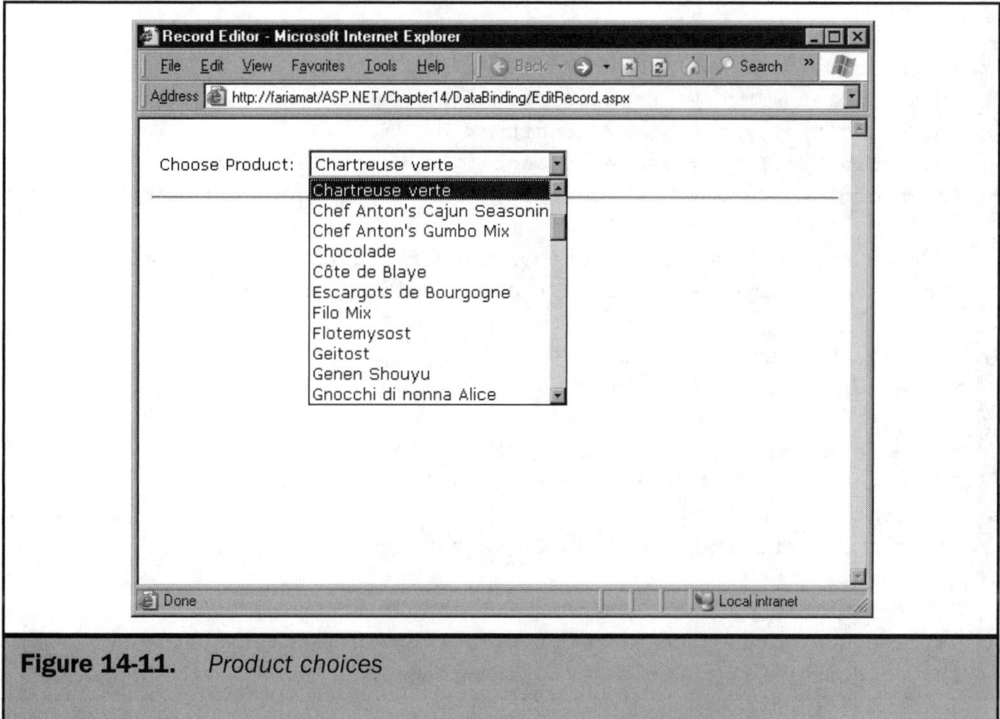


**Figure 14-11.** *Product choices*

This logic appears fairly involved, but it is really just an application of what you have learned over the last two chapters. The full listing is shown here. Remember, all this code is placed inside the event handler for the lstProdcut.SelectedIndexChanged.

```
' Create a command for selecting the matching product record.
Dim ProductCommand As String
ProductCommand = "SELECT ProductName, QuantityPerUnit, " & _
 "CategoryName FROM Products INNER JOIN Categories ON " & _
 "Categories.CategoryID=Products.CategoryID " & _
 "WHERE ProductID='" & lstProduct.SelectedItem.Value & " '"

' Create the Connection and Command objects.
Dim con As New OleDbConnection(ConnectionString)
Dim comProducts As New OleDbCommand(ProductCommand, con)

' Retrieve the information for the selected product.
con.Open()
Dim reader As OleDbDataReader = comProducts.ExecuteReader()
reader.Read()

' Update the display.
lblRecordInfo.Text = "<b>Product:</b> "
lblRecordInfo.Text &= reader("ProductName") & "<br>"
lblRecordInfo.Text &= "<b>Quantity:</b> "
lblRecordInfo.Text = reader("QuantityPerUnit") & "<br>"
lblRecordInfo.Text &= "<b>Category:</b> " & reader("CategoryName")

' Store the corresponding CategoryName for future reference.
Dim MatchCategory As String = reader("CategoryName")

' Close the reader.
reader.Close()

' Create a new Command for selecting categories.
Dim CategoryCommand As String = "SELECT CategoryName, & _
 "CategoryID FROM Categories"
Dim comCategories As New OleDbCommand(CategoryCommand, con)

' Retrieve the category information, and bind it.
lstCategory.DataSource = comCategories.ExecuteReader()
lstCategory.DataTextField = "CategoryName"
lstCategory.DataValueField = "CategoryID"
```

```
lstCategory.DataBind()
con.Close()

' Highlight the matching category in the list.
lstCategory.Items.FindByText(MatchCategory).Selected = True

lstCategory.Visible = True
cmdUpdate.Visible = True
```

This code could be improved in several ways. It probably makes the most sense to remove these data access routines from this event handler, and put them into more generic functions. For example, you could use a function that accepts a ProductName and returns a single DataRow with the associated product information. Another improvement would be to use a stored procedure to retrieve this information, rather than a full-fledged DataReader.

The end result is a window that updates itself dynamically whenever a new product is selected, as shown in Figure 14-12.



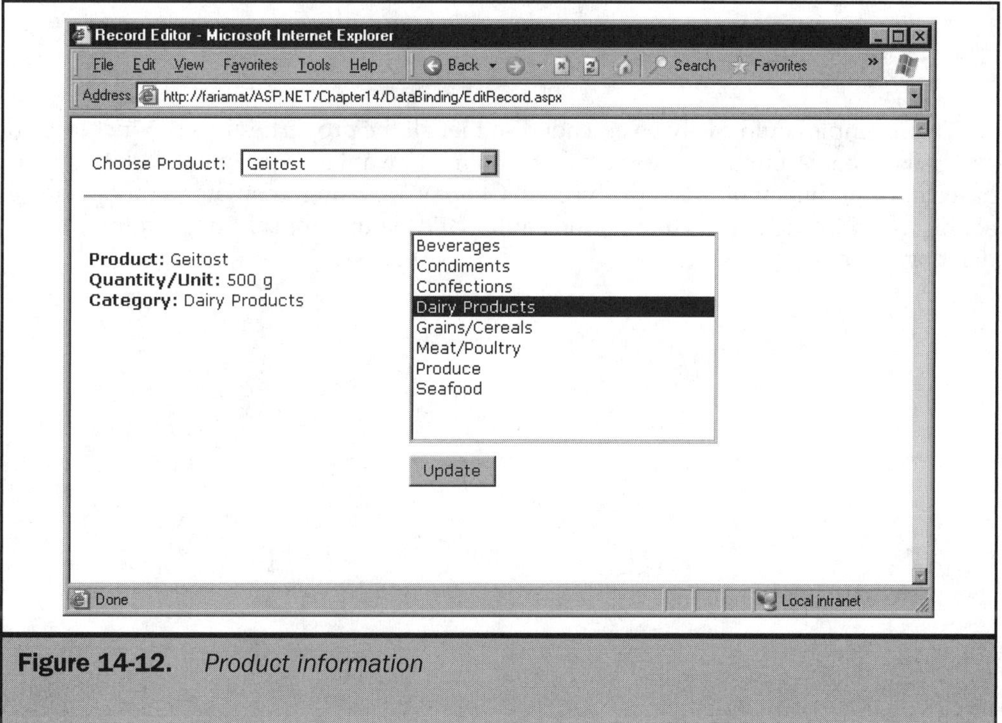


**Figure 14-12.** *Product information*

This example still has one more trick in store. If the user selects a different category and clicks Update, the change is made in the database. Of course, this means creating new Connection and Command objects:

```
Private Sub cmdUpdate_Click(sender As Object, _
 e As EventArgs) Handles cmdUpdate.Click

    ' Define the Command.
    Dim UpdateCommand As String = "UPDATE Products " & _
     "SET CategoryID='" & stCategory.SelectedItem.Value & "' " & _
     "WHERE ProductName='" & lstProduct.SelectedItem.Text & "'"

    Dim con As New OleDbConnection(ConnectionString)
    Dim com As New OleDbCommand(UpdateCommand, con)

    ' Perform the update.
    con.Open()
    com.ExecuteNonQuery()
    con.Close()

End Sub
```

This example could easily be extended so that all the properties in a product record are easily editable, but before you try that, you might want to experiment with template-based data binding, which is introduced in Chapter 15. Using templates, you can create sophisticated lists and grids that provide automatic features for selecting, editing, and deleting records.

The Complete Reference

# Chapter 15

## The DataList, DataGrid, and Repeater

When it comes to data binding, not all ASP.NET controls are created equal. In the last chapter, you saw how data binding could help you automatically insert single values and lists into all kinds of common controls and even ordinary HTML. In this chapter, we'll concentrate on three more advanced controls—the DataList, DataGrid, and Repeater—which allow you to bind entire tables of data. These controls are sometimes known as "templated" controls because they allow you to use significant formatting and customization features by creating templates. Some of these controls even have additional built-in functionality for selecting, editing, and sorting the displayed information.

## Introducing Templates

Templates are special blocks of HTML that allow you to define the content and formatting for part of a control. Controls that support templates allow a great deal of flexibility. Rather than just setting an individual value (such as a Text property) and related formatting properties (such as a Color property), you define an entire block of HTML that can include other controls, styles, and information in any arrangement. The drawback is that you need to enter this information manually in its script form. If you're used to the conveniences of Visual Studio .NET, this may seem like a rather unfriendly approach. However, in many ways templates are just an extension of the data binding syntax you saw in Chapter 14.

### Examples in this Chapter

In this chapter, we return to the pubs database. All the data binding examples use the Authors table, which contains a list of author information. Because the focus of this chapter is on designing and using templates and other features of the ASP.NET data controls, you don't need examples that involve sophisticated data access code. (In fact, you can duplicate these examples by creating and filling a DataSet object manually, and not using a database at all.) Note that unlike single-value data binding, the repeated-value data binding used in the Repeater, DataList, and DataGrid controls almost always uses information drawn from a database and provided in a DataSet object.

## Using Templates with the DataList

To see a simple example of how data binding works with a template control, add a DataList control to your web page. If you are working with Visual Studio .NET, you won't see a default graphical representation. Instead, a special box will appear informing you that this control requires templates (see Figure 15-1).

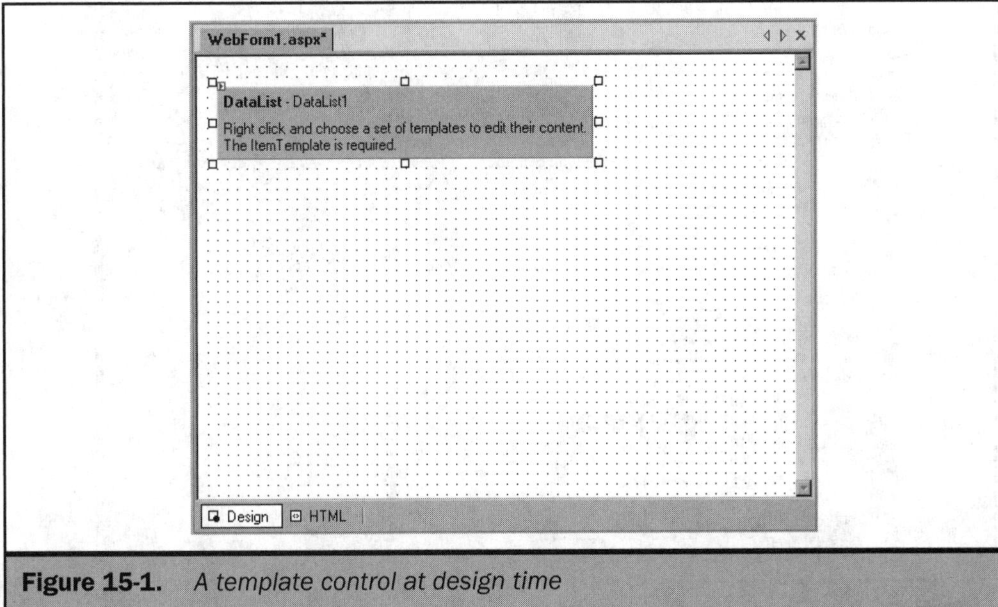


**Figure 15-1.** *A template control at design time*



## Creating a Template

As in Chapter 14, you need to work with the layout code in your .aspx file to implement data binding. All the templates for controls like the DataList are defined in the .aspx file. To view it in Visual Studio .NET, click the HTML button at the bottom of the form designer.

Find the line that represents your DataList control. It's made up of an opening and closing tag. If you are using grid layout for your page, the opening tag will have additional information about the size and position of the list.

```
<asp:DataList id=listAuthor runat="server"></asp:DataList>
```

To make your DataList functional, you need to add at least one template: the item template. All templates are coded in between the opening and ending tags of the DataList control. If you're working with Visual Studio .NET, you'll receive an IntelliSense list that provides you with the names of all the templates as soon as you type the less than (<) character (see Figure 15-2).

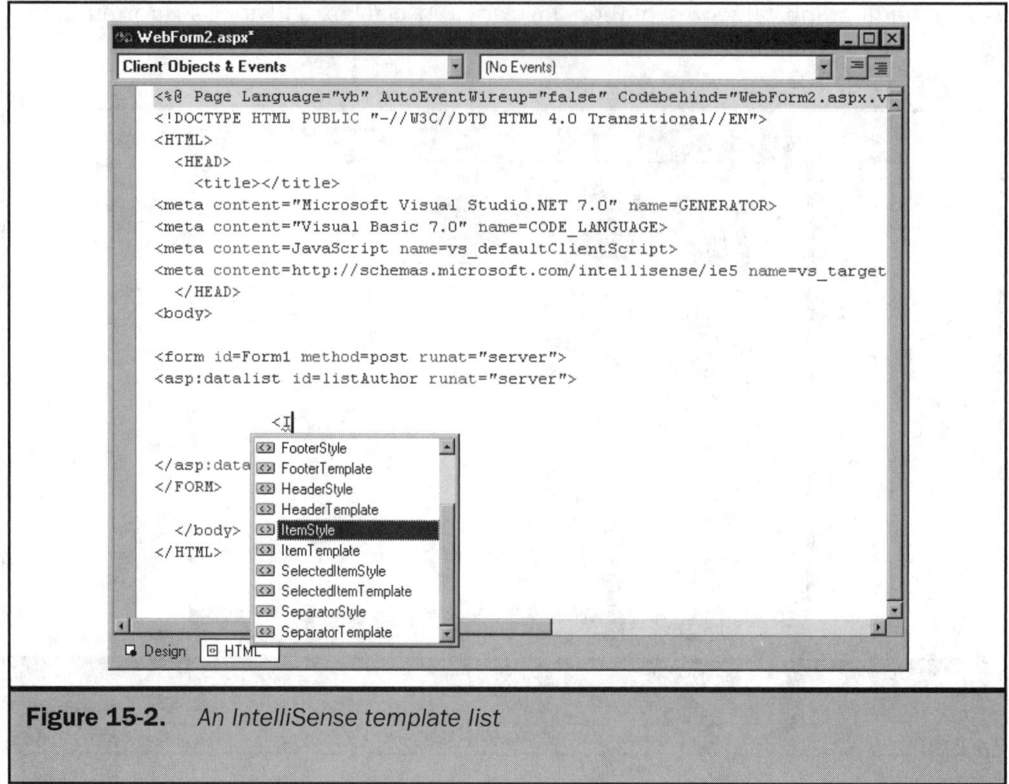

Figure 15-2. *An IntelliSense template list*

The item template is added like this:

```
<asp:DataList id=listAuthor runat="server">
    <ItemTemplate></ItemTemplate>
</asp:DataList>
```

Inside the item template, you can add a data binding expression using the special <%# %> data binding expression syntax. As with the examples in Chapter 14, you can use any combination of expressions and variables inside an expression. You can also use the special Container.DataItem keyword to refer to the object bound to the DataSource property. For example, the DataList that follows binds a table and displays the author's last name (drawn from the au_lname field):

```
<asp:DataList id=listAuthor runat="server">
    <ItemTemplate><%# Container.DataItem("au_lname") %>
    </ItemTemplate>
</asp:DataList>
```

In order for this syntax to work, a DataSet with the au_lname field must be bound to the listAuthor.DataSource property at runtime.

The following example shows a more sophisticated use of data binding that combines two fields to display an author's full name in a standard format. The spacing used is just to make the code more readable. Remember, in an HTML page, whitespace is collapsed (meaning hard returns, tabs, and multiple spaces are ignored).

```
<asp:DataList id=listAuthor runat="server">
    <ItemTemplate><%# Container.DataItem("au_lname") %>,
                  <%# Container.DataItem("au_fname") %>
    </ItemTemplate>
</asp:DataList>
```

## Using a Template

On its own, this template still doesn't accomplish anything. In fact, if you run this page, no information will be displayed in the browser window. To actually create the DataList, you need to bind a data source that has an au_lname and au_fname field. For example, you could create and bind a DataSet in the Page.Load event:



```
Imports System.Data.OleDb
Imports System.Data

Public Class BasicAuthorList
  Inherits Page

    Protected listAuthor As DataList

    Private ConnectionString As String = "Provider=SQLOLEDB.1;" & _
    "DataSource=localhost;Initial Catalog=pubs;" & _
    "Integrated Security=SSPI"

    Private Sub Page_Load(sender As Object, e As EventArgs) _
      Handles MyBase.Load
        ' Create and fill a DataSet.
        Dim Select As String
        Select = "SELECT * FROM Authors"
        Dim con As New OleDbConnection(ConnectionString)
        Dim cmd As New OleDbCommand(Select, con)
        Dim adapter As New OleDbDataAdapter(cmd)
        Dim Pubs As New DataSet()
        adapter.Fill(Pubs, "Authors")
        con.Close()
```

```
        ' Bind the DataSet, and activate the data bindings for the page.
        listAuthor.DataSource = Pubs.Tables("Authors")
        Me.DataBind()
    End Sub

End Class
```

This is standard ADO.NET code. The end result is a list of names in a simple, unformatted HTML table, as shown in Figure 15-3.

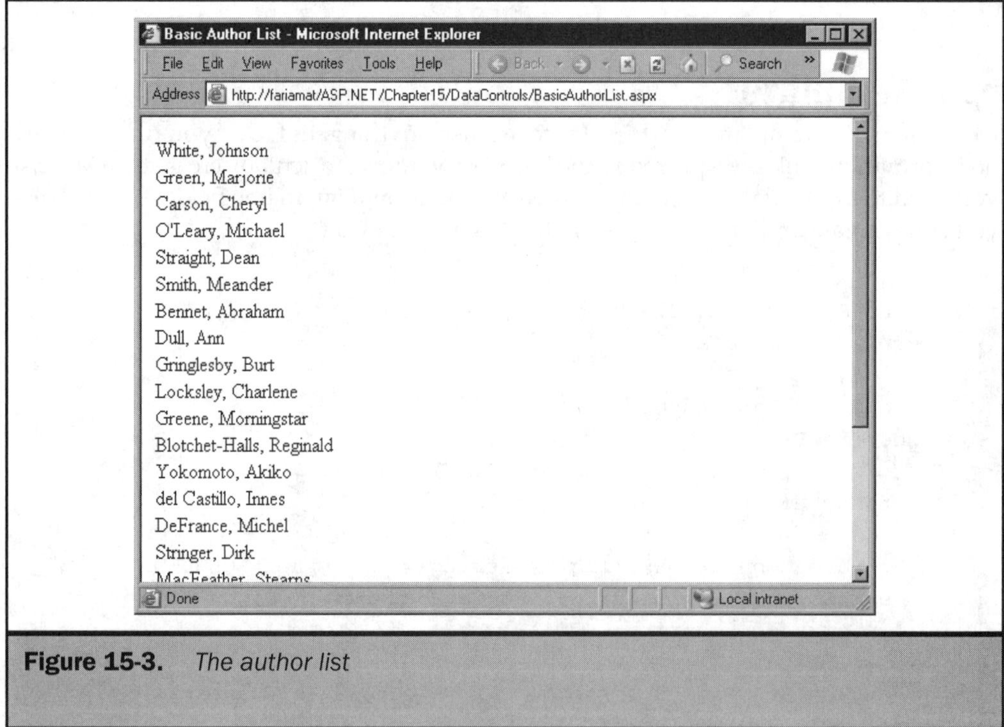


**Figure 15-3.** *The author list*

Unfortunately, at design time you won't see all this information, because the data binding is set up dynamically through code. Instead, in the Visual Studio .NET IDE you'll only see any hard-coded, static elements in the template (in this case, the comma), as shown in Figure 15-4.

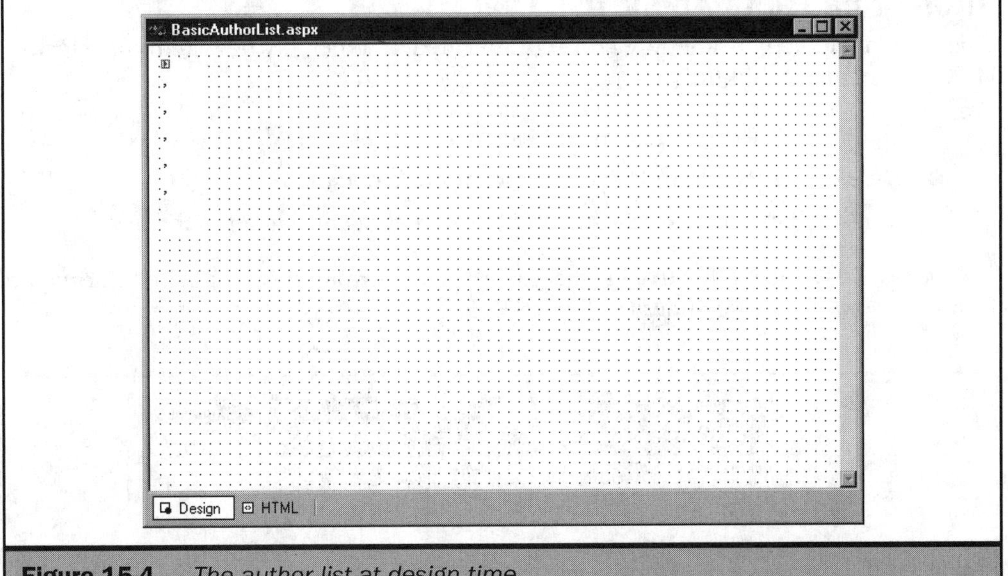


**Figure 15-4.** *The author list at design time*



## Templates with HTML

The item template in the previous example was fairly simple. It combined two data fields, separated by a comma. No special HTML elements were used. For a more advanced template, you can treat the item template as though it is just another portion of your .aspx file, and insert HTML markup tags or even ASP.NET controls. For example, you could make use of special formatting by creating a template like this:

```
<ItemTemplate>
    <font face="Verdana" size="2"><b>
    <%# Container.DataItem("au_fname") %>
    <%# Container.DataItem("au_lname") %></b></font><br>
    <font face="Verdana" size="1">   
    Address: <%#Container.DataItem("address")%>
    <br>   
    City: <%# Container.DataItem("city")%></font><br><br>
</ItemTemplate>
```

## Interesting Facts About this Code

This template looks considerably more complicated, but the only new items are stock HTML elements, including:

- The <font> tag to change the font style and size for the displayed text
- The <b> tag to bold the heading (the author's name)
- Non-breaking spaces ( ) and hard breaks (<br>) to align the text

The result is a more attractive list that incorporates formatting along with information from your data source, as shown in Figure 15-5.

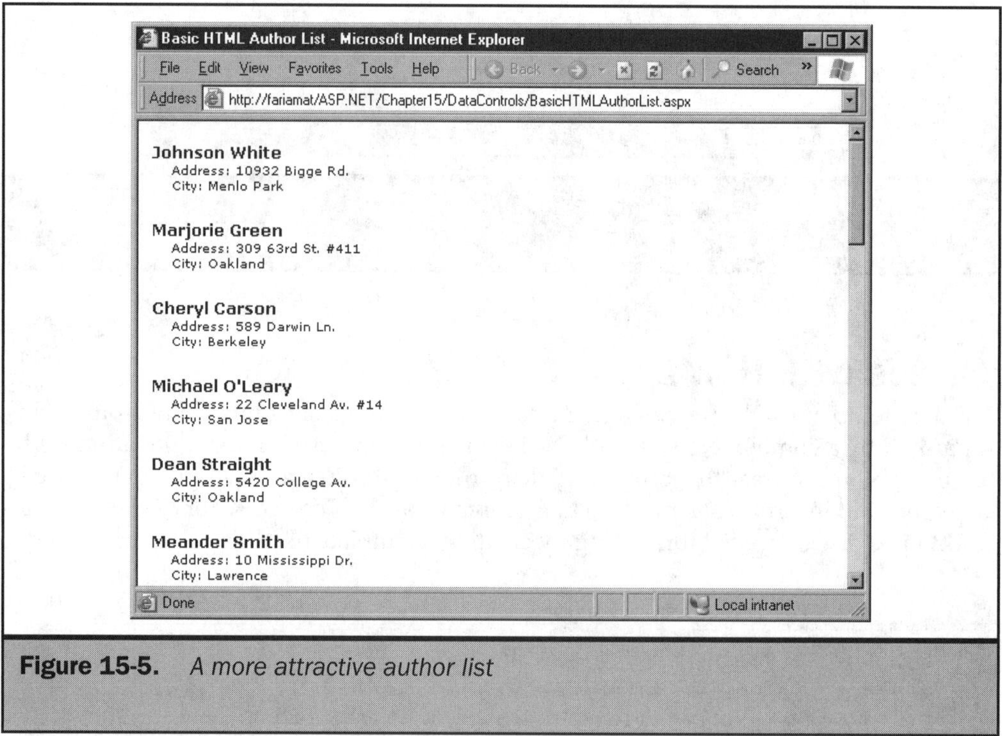


**Figure 15-5.** *A more attractive author list*

At design time, you'll see a list that defaults to five items and only shows the static information (the headings), as shown in Figure 15-6. This gives you an idea why this code is referred to as a template. At runtime, the bound values are inserted into the appropriate slots in the layout you have defined.

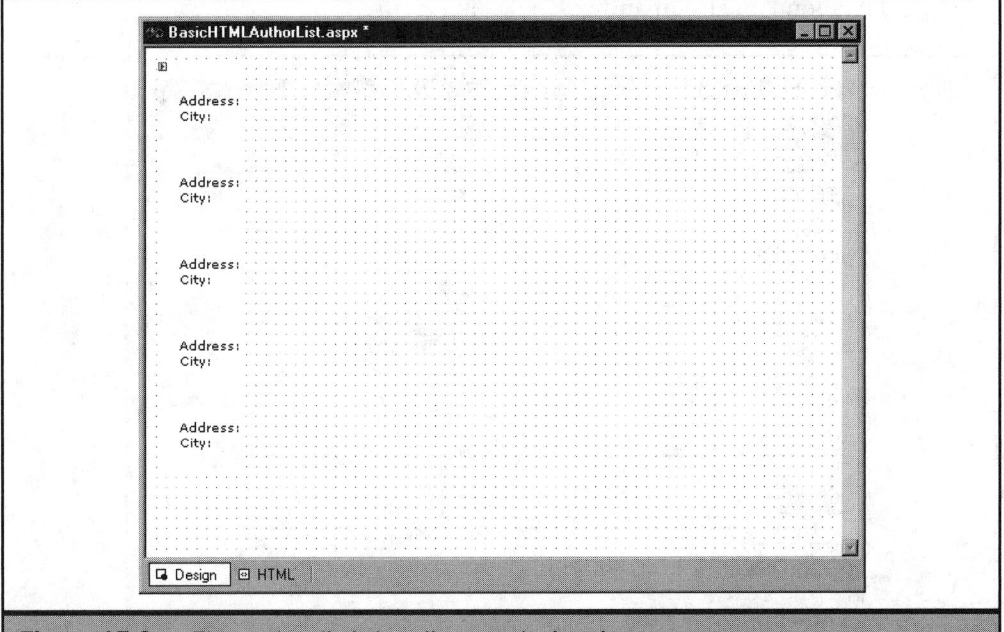


**Figure 15-6.** *The author list's headings at design time*



# Templates with ASP.NET Controls

You can add the tags for ASP.NET controls just as easily as you can add HTML elements. Container.DataItem data binding expressions can then be used to fill in the appropriate control values. In Visual Studio .NET, IntelliSense gives you some assistance with a drop-down list of elements you might want to use when you are typing the .aspx file.

The following template uses text boxes to hold the values returned from the DataSet. It also adds an Update button to each record.

```
<ItemTemplate>
    <b><%# Container.DataItem("au_fname") %>
    <%# Container.DataItem("au_lname") %></b><br>
    <asp:TextBox Text='<%# Container.DataItem("address") %>'
         runat=server /><br>
    <asp:TextBox Text='<%# Container.DataItem("city") %>'
         runat=server /><br>
    <asp:Button id=cmdUpdate Text='Update'
         runat=server /><br><br>
</ItemTemplate>
```

Once databound, the list of authors looks like Figure 15-7.

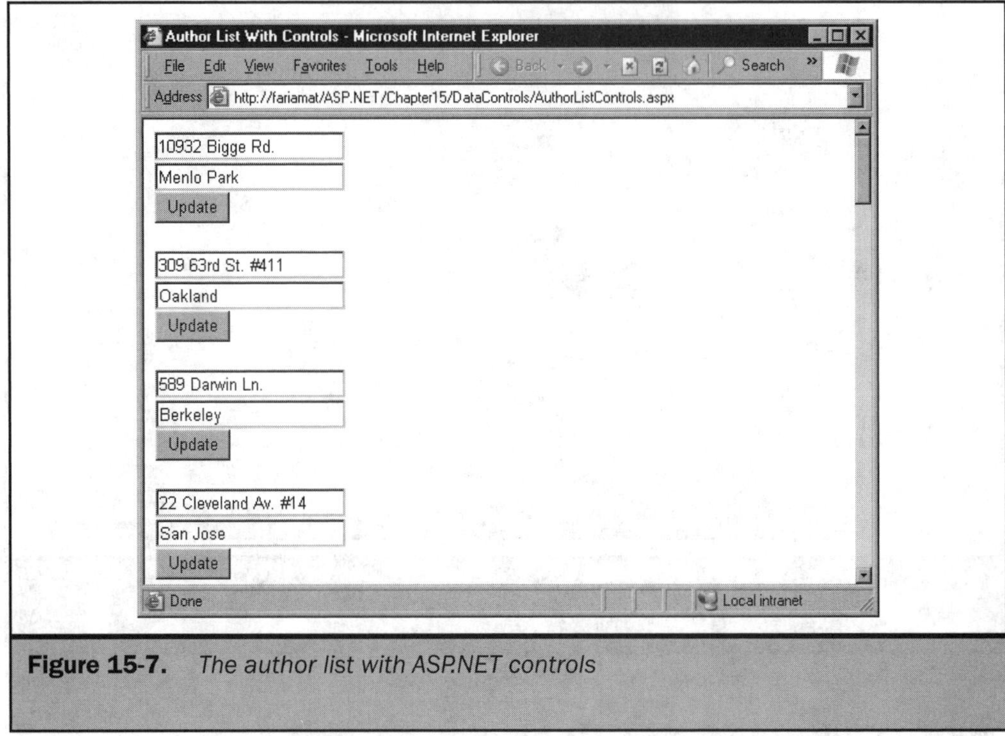


**Figure 15-7.** *The author list with ASP.NET controls*

As it stands, there's one problem: the button isn't connected to any event handler. In fact, even if you do manually connect it by modifying the <asp:Button> tag and specifying a subprocedure for the click event, you won't be able to distinguish one button from another. That means you can't tell which item the button belongs to, and you won't know where to find the corresponding information to update.

The easiest way to resolve this problem is to use an event from the DataList control, not the contained button. The DataList.ItemCommand event serves this purpose. It fires whenever *any* button in the DataList is clicked. It also provides the item where the event occurred (through the e.Item property). Later in this chapter, we'll look at more specific examples that show how you can use this event to update or delete records in a DataList.

## Formatting with DataBinder.Eval

So far, the examples in this chapter have used the Container.DataItem syntax for data binding. There's one other option, which uses the System.Web.UI.DataBinder class. The following example retrieves an author's last name:

```
DataBinder.Eval(Container.DataItem, "au_lname")
```

From a performance standpoint, the DataBinder.Eval data binding expression is slightly slower because it uses runtime type inspection. However, it's useful in some situations where you need to apply additional formatting, because it accepts a format string as an optional third parameter. In the Authors table from the pubs database, this notation isn't very useful because almost all the information is stored in strings. If you need to work with numbers or date values, however, this formatting can become extremely useful.

## Format Strings

Format strings are generally made up of a placeholder and format indicator, which are wrapped inside curly brackets. It looks something like this:

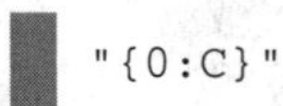

```
"{0:C}"
```

In this case, the 0 represents the value that will be formatted, and the letter indicates a predetermined format style. Here, C means currency format, which formats a number as a dollar figure (so 3400.34 becomes $3,400.34). To use this format string when data binding, you could use code like this:

```
DataBinder.Eval(Container.DataItem, "Price", "{0:C}")
```

Some of the other formatting options for numeric values are shown in Table 15-1.

| Type | Format String | Example |
|---|---|---|
| Currency | {0:C} | $1,234.50<br>Brackets indicate negative values: ($1,234.50). Currency sign is locale-specific: (£1,234.50). |
| Scientific (Exponential) | {0:E} | 1.234.50E+004 |
| Percentage | {0:P} | 45.6% |
| Fixed Decimal | {0:F?} | Depends on the number of decimal places you set. {0:F3} would be 123.400. {0:F0} would be 123. |

**Table 15-1.** *Numeric Format Strings*

Other examples can be found in the MSDN help. For date or time values, there is also an extensive list. Some examples are shown in Table 15-2.

| Type | Format String | Example |
|---|---|---|
| Short Date | {0:d} | M/d/yyyy (for example: 10/30/2002) |
| Long Date | {0:D} | dddd, MMMM dd, yyyy (for example: Monday, January 30, 2002) |
| Long Date and Short Time | {0:f} | dddd, MMMM dd, yyyy HH:mm aa (for example: Monday, January 30, 2002 10:00 AM) |
| Long Date and Long Time | {0:F} | dddd, MMMM dd, yyyy HH:mm:ss aa (for example: Monday, January 30, 2002 10:00:23 AM) |
| ISO Sortable Standard | {0:s} | yyyy-MM-dd HH:mm:ss (for example: 2002-01-30 10:00:23) |
| Month and Day | {0:M} | MMMM dd (for example: January 30) |
| General | {0:G} | M/d/yyyy HH:mm:ss aa (depends on locale-specific settings) (for example: 10/30/2002 10:00:23 AM) |

**Table 15-2.** *Time and Date Format Strings*

## You Can Also Format Values Manually

Another approach to formatting values is to change them before you bind the data. For example, you could fill a DataSet, and then loop through it, either modifying each row or creating another DataTable or DataSet to hold the "processed" values.

## Data Binding with Multiple Templates

The examples so far have worked exclusively with the item template. Part of the power of template controls is that they define several different styles that allow you to configure different types of rows. For example, you can also create a template for the header row (HeaderTemplate) and the divider in between rows (SeparatorTemplate). You can also set items to alternate row by row (by adding an AlternateItemTemplate).

The following example shows a number of different templates in a DataList control.

```
<asp:datalist id=listAuthor runat="server">
    <HeaderTemplate>
        <h2>Author List</h2><br><hr>
    </HeaderTemplate>
    <ItemTemplate>
        <b><%# Container.DataItem("au_fname") %>
        <%# Container.DataItem("au_lname") %></b><br>
        Address: <%# Container.DataItem("address") %><br>
        City: <%# Container.DataItem("city") %>
    </ItemTemplate>
    <AlternatingItemTemplate>
            <b><%# Container.DataItem("au_fname") %>
        <%# Container.DataItem("au_lname") %></b><br>    
        Address: <%# Container.DataItem("address") %><br>
            City: <%# Container.DataItem("city") %>
    </AlternatingItemTemplate>
    <SeparatorTemplate>
        <br><hr><br>
    </SeparatorTemplate>
    <FooterTemplate>
        <br>This list provided on <%# System.DateTime.Now %>
    </FooterTemplate>
</asp:datalist>
```

Note that these templates can be listed in the .aspx file in any order. The resulting DataList looks quite a bit different, as shown in Figure 15-8.

Special templates are also the key to unlocking the selecting and editing features we'll consider shortly.

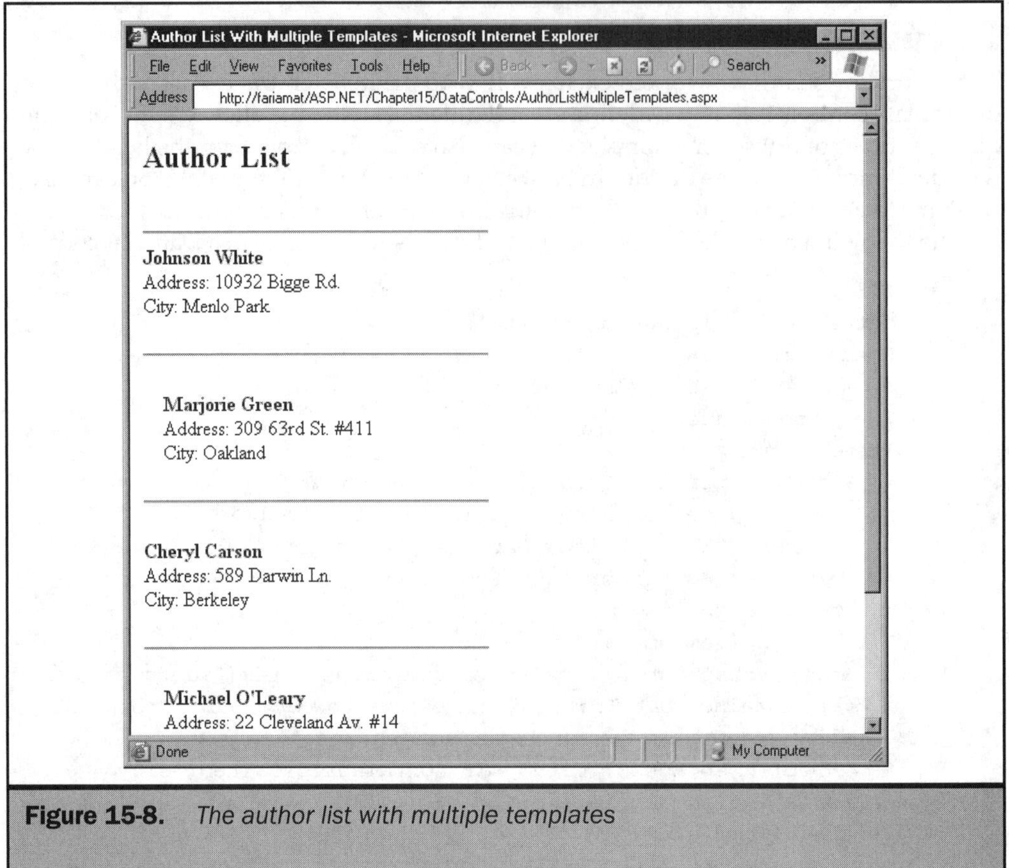


**Figure 15-8.** *The author list with multiple templates*

## Formatting with Template Styles

Every template has a corresponding style. For example, you can configure the appearance of a header template inside a <HeaderStyle> tag. You can manually code these tags in the .aspx file, or you can set them using the Properties window in Visual Studio .NET, which will add the corresponding information to your code automatically (see Figure 15-9).

Each style has a significant amount of associated information, allowing you to set background and foreground colors, borders, fonts, and alignment as attributes of the style tag. Here's an example of a control that makes full use of the different styles:

```
<asp:datalist id=listAuthor runat="server" BorderColor="#DEBA84"
BorderStyle="None" CellSpacing="2" BackColor="#DEBA84"
```

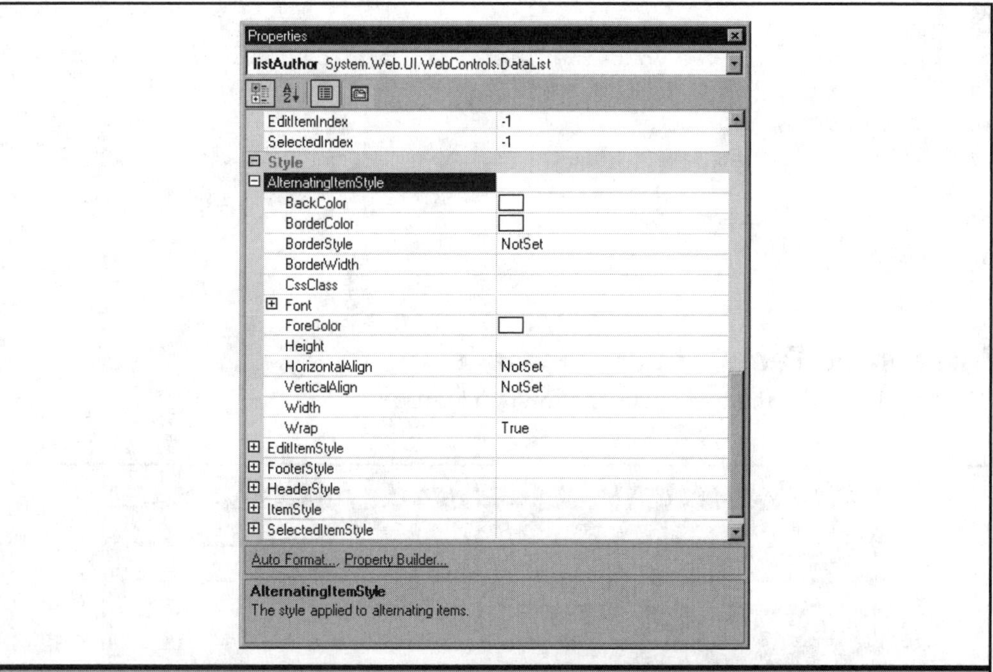


**Figure 15-9.** *Configuring styles in Visual Studio .NET*



```
CellPadding="3" GridLines="Both" BorderWidth="1px">
    <HeaderStyle Font-Bold="True" ForeColor="White"
     BackColor="#A55129"></HeaderStyle>
        <ItemStyle Font-Size="Smaller" Font-Names="Verdana"
      ForeColor="#8C4510" BackColor="#FFF7E7"></ItemStyle>
    <AlternatingItemStyle BackColor="#FFE0C0"></AlternatingItemStyle>
    <FooterStyle ForeColor="#8C4510" BackColor="#F7DFB5">
      </FooterStyle>

    <HeaderTemplate>
        <h2>Author List</h2>
    </HeaderTemplate>
    <FooterTemplate>
        <br>This list provided on <%# System.DateTime.Now %>
    </FooterTemplate>
    <ItemTemplate>
        <b><%# Container.DataItem("au_fname") %>
```

```
            <%# Container.DataItem("au_lname") %></b><br>
            Address: <%# Container.DataItem("address") %><br>
            City: <%# Container.DataItem("city") %>
        </ItemTemplate>
        <SeparatorTemplate>
            <hr>
        </SeparatorTemplate>
</asp:datalist>
```

## Interesting Facts About this Code

The template, with the basic data, is shown in Figure 15-10.

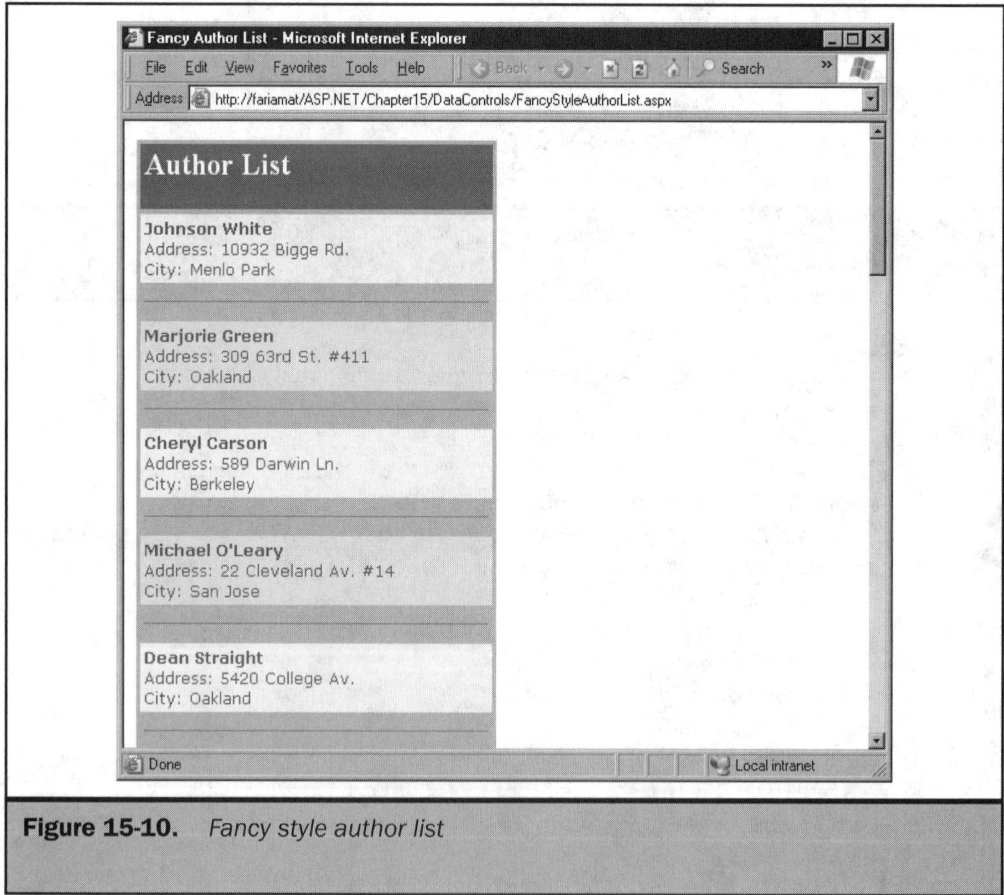


**Figure 15-10.** *Fancy style author list*

- The actual templates make much less use of spacing and line breaks (<br> elements) because some basic information is set for the DataList border style and cell padding for the table that will contain all the rows.
- Initially, all the styles inherit the basic color properties from the containing control (in this case, the DataList). In addition, the AlternatingItemStyle tag inherits all the formatting you apply to the ItemStyle element.

The templates, combined with the corresponding style tags, allow you to have very tight control over every aspect of your data control's appearance. This control is quite different than the features historically offered by data binding. In fact, data binding has acquired a bad reputation because it is typically very *inflexible*, often allowing no way to modify or combine values, and forcing you to use every field retrieved from a database with no control over order or layout. With ASP.NET templates, the situation is reversed. Every field is explicitly placed using a Container.DataItem statement, and additional formatting can be applied at every level using the DataBinder.Eval method and the powerful set of built-in styles.

## Auto Format

One other interesting feature is Visual Studio .NET's "auto format" ability for data controls. (You may have already used a similar feature when formatting tables in Microsoft Word.) To automatically format a DataList, click the Auto Format link at the bottom of the Properties window. A window will appear that allows you to choose a grouped set of themed styles, as shown in Figure 15-11.

When you choose a style set from this window, all the code is added to configure the DataList control and the corresponding styles. You can then fine-tune it with the Properties window or manually in the .aspx code view.



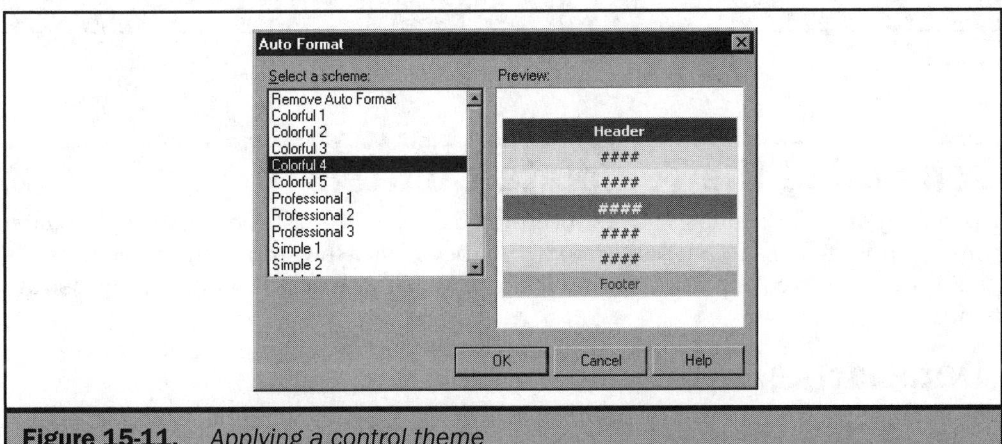


**Figure 15-11.** *Applying a control theme*

Similarly, you can set styles and formatting options in an integrated window by clicking the Property Builder link at the bottom of the Properties window. This gives you yet another way to adjust the same style settings (see Figure 15-12). While you are essentially on your own for creating the templates and inserting the data binding syntax, there is no shortage of tools for configuring the look of your data control.

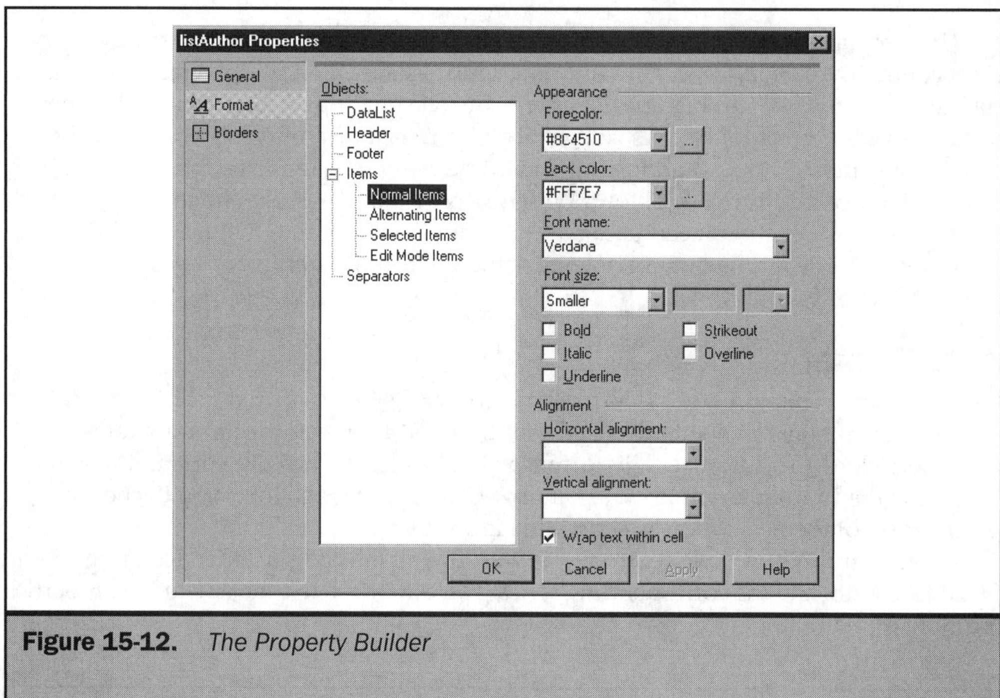


**Figure 15-12.** *The Property Builder*

## Comparing the Template Controls

Up to this point, the examples have concentrated on the DataList control. The other data controls provided in ASP.NET are similar, but they have a few important differences. As you design your web applications, you will need to choose the ideal tool for the task at hand.

### The DataList

The DataList is a versatile control that displays a list of items in an HTML table. Generally, each item is contained in a single column on a single row. That makes the DataList ideal for customized displays where multiple fields are grouped and formatted in one block of HTML. If you look at the HTML code that is generated for the page when it is sent to the client, you'll see that a DataList encloses every item in a separate table row. (Alternatively, you can use the DataGrid control for a multi-columned grid display.)

The DataList supports automatic selection and editing. Compared to the DataGrid, it lacks automatic paging (breaking a table into multiple pages for separate display) and sorting.

## DataList Layout

The DataList provides some additional layout features that let you change how the cells in the table are ordered. For example, you can set the RepeatDirection property to Horizontal to make a row of cells from left to right. Every item will occupy a separate column on the same row. In Figure 15-13, you can see the result when the RepeatDirection is changed for the previous example with a list of authors.

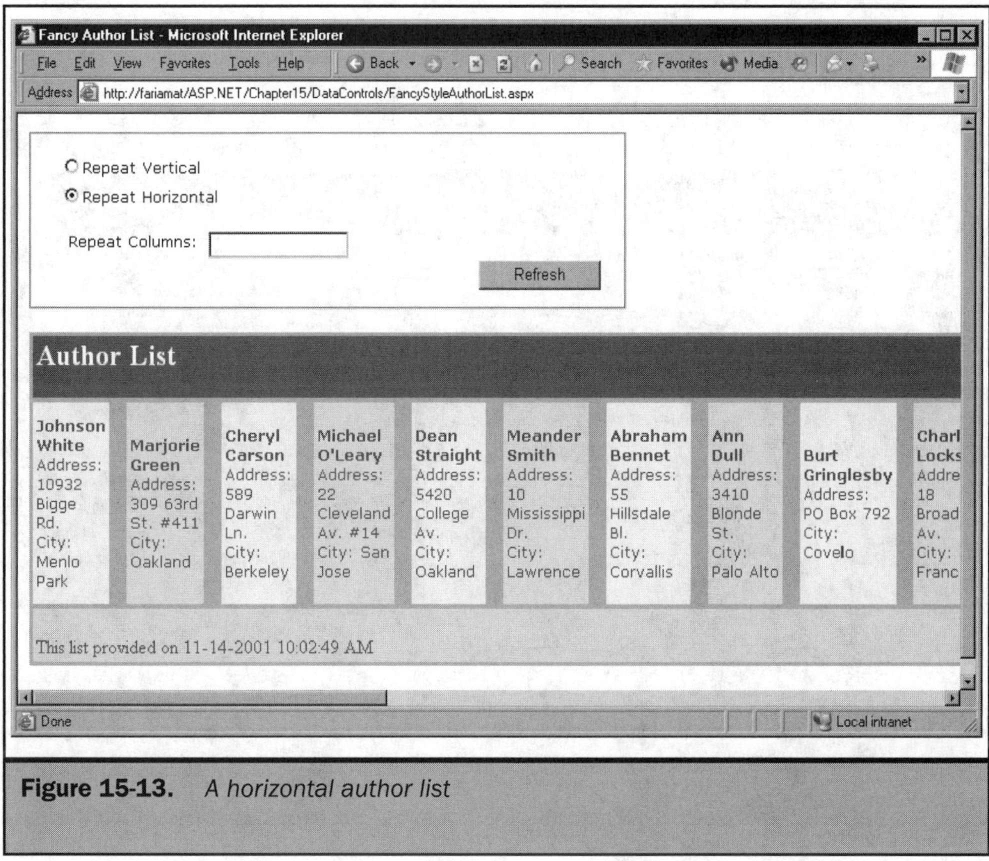


**Figure 15-13.** *A horizontal author list*

You can also create a DataList that lays out items in a grid with a maximum number of columns using the RepeatColumns property. By default, RepeatColumns is set to 0 and no specific maximum number of columns is used. In Horizontal alignment, the table will have one column for each item, and in Vertical alignment, the table will have only one column, with all the items in separate rows.

Once you set the RepeatColumns property, ASP.NET will create a table with that many columns (provided enough items exist) and will fill it from left to right (if RepeatDirection is Horizontal) or top to bottom (if RepeatDirection is Vertical). Figure 15-14 shows the results of setting RepeatColumns to 5 and RepeatDirection to Horizontal.

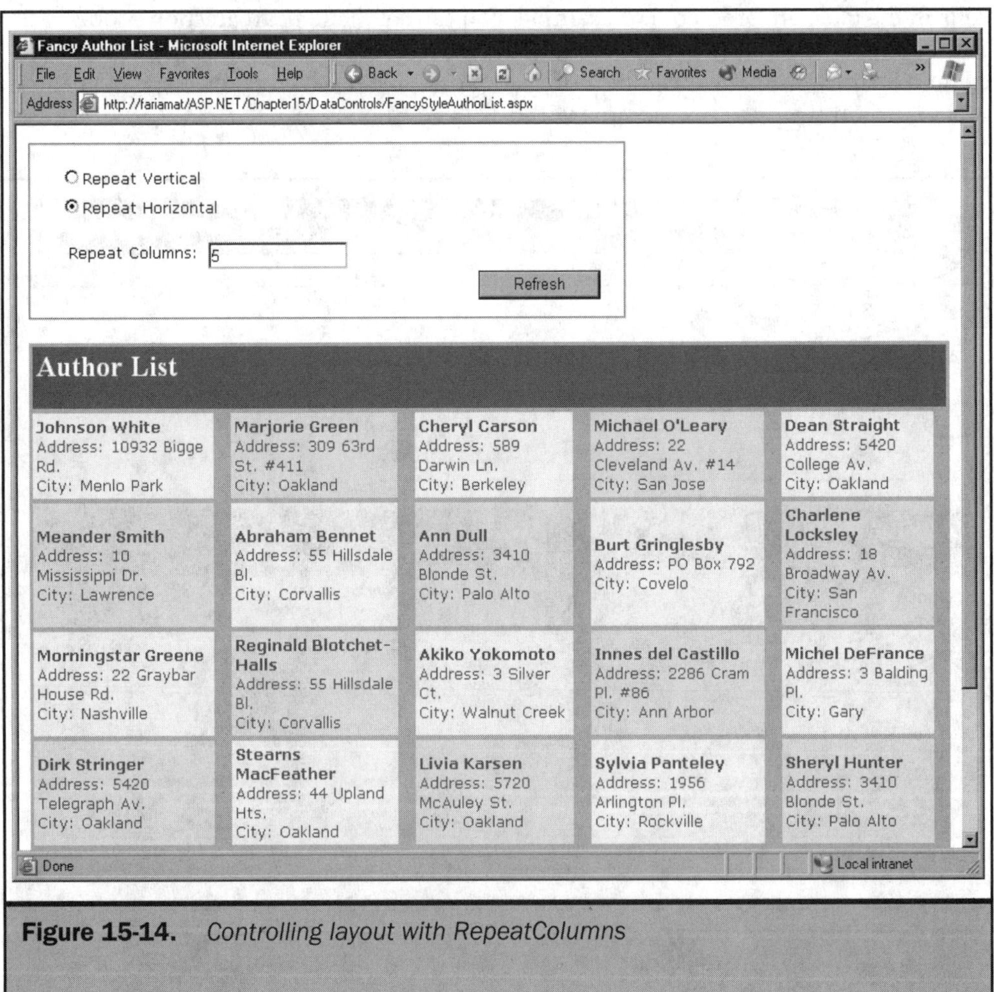


**Figure 15-14.** *Controlling layout with RepeatColumns*

To play around with these different layout options, try the sample code for this chapter, which includes an example that lets the user choose the RepeatDirection and number of RepeatColumns for a table (the file FancyStyleAuthorList.aspx). The important point for DataLists is that each item is fully contained in a single cell.

# The DataGrid

DataGrids are designed for displaying multi-column tables, where every item in a list has a single row with multiple columns. Typically, each column corresponds to information in an individual database field, although templates allow you to precisely configure the content.

The DataGrid is probably the most powerful data control, as it comes equipped with the most ready-made functionality. This includes features for automatic paging, sorting, selecting, and editing.

## Automatically Generating Columns

Interestingly, the DataGrid is the only data control described in this chapter that can work without templates. As long as you have the AutoGenerateColumns property set to True (the default), columns will be created for every field in a DataSet as soon as you bind it.



```
' (Data access code omitted.)
gridAuthor.AutoGenerateColumns = True
gridAuthor.DataSource = Pubs.Tables("Authors")
' Columns are generated automatically when the DataGrid is bound.
' No templates are required.
Me.DataBind()
```

The output is automatic, and appears in the exact same way that it is stored in the DataSet (see Figure 15-15).

This approach loses many of the advantages of data binding, however, because you cannot precisely define the order, appearance, and formatting of the columns. In other words, you should be aware of this functionality, but you will probably want to avoid it, and explicitly set AutoGenerateColumns to False and define specific column tags.

## Defining Columns

With DataGrids, the content and formatting of each column is defined in a special nested <Columns> tag. Inside this tag, you add one column control tag for each column you want in your DataGrid. Columns are displayed from right to left in the grid, based on the order in which the column tags are listed in the .aspx file.

| au_id | au_lname | au_fname | phone | address | city | state | zip | contract |
|---|---|---|---|---|---|---|---|---|
| 172-32-1176 | White | Johnson | 408 496-2222 | 10932 Bigge Rd. | Menlo Park | CA | 94025 | True |
| 213-46-8915 | Green | Marjorie | 415 986-7020 | 309 63rd St. #411 | Oakland | CA | 94618 | True |
| 238-95-7766 | Carson | Cheryl | 415 548-7723 | 589 Darwin Ln. | Berkeley | CA | 94705 | True |
| 267-41-2394 | O'Leary | Michael | 408 286-2428 | 22 Cleveland Av. #14 | San Jose | CA | 95128 | True |
| 274-80-9391 | Straight | Dean | 415 834-2919 | 5420 College Av. | Oakland | CA | 94609 | True |
| 341-22-1782 | Smith | Meander | 913 843-0462 | 10 Mississippi Dr. | Lawrence | KS | 66044 | False |
| 409-56-7008 | Bennet | Abraham | 503 745-6402 | 55 Hillsdale Bl. | Corvallis | OR | 94705 | False |
| 427- | | | | | | | | |

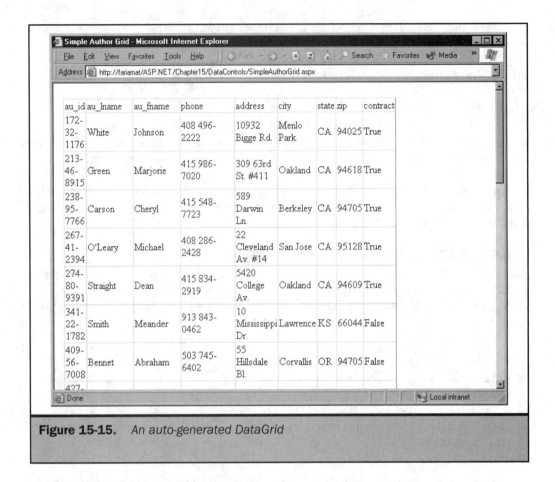

**Figure 15-15.** *An auto-generated DataGrid*

When you create a column, you have several possible choices. Each of these column types corresponds to a control class in the System.Web.UI.WebControls namespace.

- A BoundColumn, which displays text from a field in the DataSource
- A ButtonColumn, which displays a command button for each item in the list
- An EditCommandColumn, which displays editing buttons for each item in the list
- A HyperlinkColumn, which displays the contents (a field from the data source or static text) as a hyperlink
- A TemplateColumn, which allows you to specify multiple fields, custom controls, and anything you would normally put in an item template for a DataList control

To create a DataGrid with these column types, set the AutoGenerateColumns property of your DataGrid to False. You can then add the columns using the Property Builder available in Visual Studio .NET or by writing the appropriate tags in the .aspx file. The latter approach is the best way to understand what is actually taking place, and it's similar to creating templates for a DataList.

The layout code for a sample grid is shown here:

```
<asp:DataGrid id=gridAuthor runat="server" AutoGenerateColumns=
"False">
  <Columns>
     <asp:TemplateColumn HeaderText="Author Name">
        <ItemTemplate><%# Container.DataItem("au_fname") %>
        <%# Container.DataItem("au_lname") %></ItemTemplate>
     </asp:TemplateColumn>

     <asp:BoundColumn DataField="city" HeaderText="City" />
     <asp:BoundColumn DataField="address" HeaderText="Address" />
  </Columns>
</asp:DataGrid>
```

Once the DataGrid is bound to the author information in the DataSet, a grid is generated, as shown in Figure 15-16.

## Interesting Facts About this Code

- Columns are the first level of nested items in the DataGrid tag, not templates.
- Predefined columns are added by using the appropriate ASP.NET column control with the properties configured through tag attributes.
- For greater control, you can insert a TemplateColumn, which can contain a series of templates specifying the header, footer, and item appearance. The preceding example uses the item template to create a column that displays an author's first and last name together. Note that this is the only case where data binding expressions are required. The bound columns take care of data binding automatically when you specify the DataField attribute.

## Styles

Styles can be configured in the same way they were for the DataList, through the Property Builder window or by using the Auto Format window to apply a themed set of matching styles. The following example adds three styles.

```
<asp:DataGrid id=gridAuthor runat="server" AutoGenerateColumns=
"False" BorderColor="#DEBA84" BorderStyle="None" CellSpacing="2"
BackColor="#DEBA84" CellPadding="3" BorderWidth="1px">
```

```
    <FooterStyle ForeColor="#8C4510" BackColor="#F7DFB5">
    </FooterStyle>
    <HeaderStyle ForeColor="White" BackColor="#A55129"></HeaderStyle>
    <ItemStyle ForeColor="#8C4510" BackColor="#FFF7E7"></ItemStyle>

    <Columns>
      <!-- Column information omitted. -->
    </Columns>

</asp:DataGrid>
```

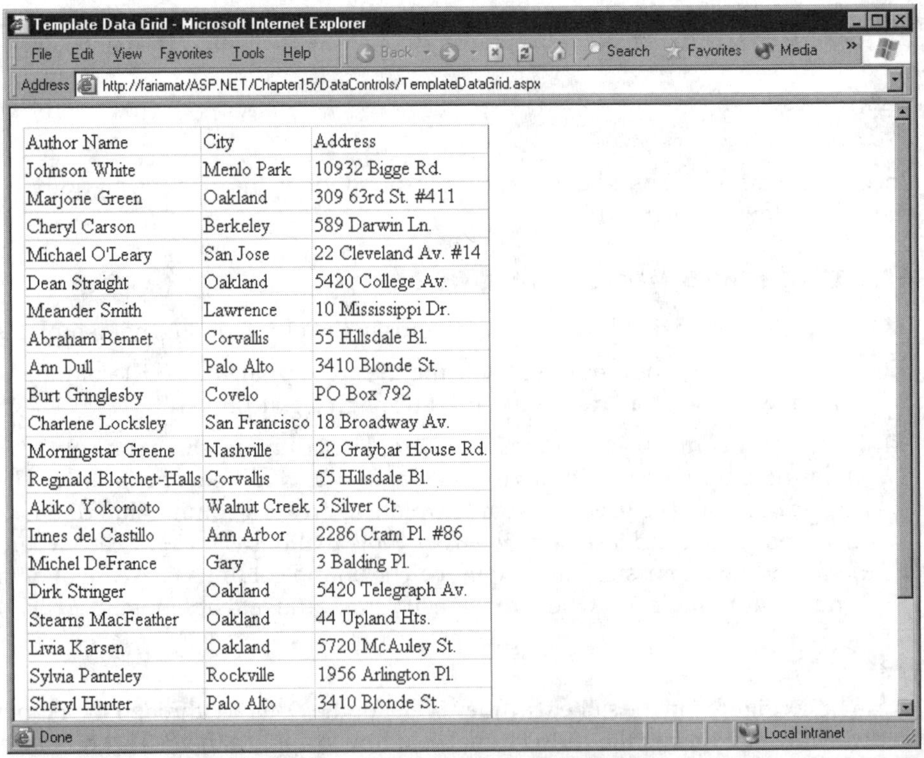

| Author Name | City | Address |
|---|---|---|
| Johnson White | Menlo Park | 10932 Bigge Rd. |
| Marjorie Green | Oakland | 309 63rd St. #411 |
| Cheryl Carson | Berkeley | 589 Darwin Ln. |
| Michael O'Leary | San Jose | 22 Cleveland Av. #14 |
| Dean Straight | Oakland | 5420 College Av. |
| Meander Smith | Lawrence | 10 Mississippi Dr. |
| Abraham Bennet | Corvallis | 55 Hillsdale Bl. |
| Ann Dull | Palo Alto | 3410 Blonde St. |
| Burt Gringlesby | Covelo | PO Box 792 |
| Charlene Locksley | San Francisco | 18 Broadway Av. |
| Morningstar Greene | Nashville | 22 Graybar House Rd. |
| Reginald Blotchet-Halls | Corvallis | 55 Hillsdale Bl. |
| Akiko Yokomoto | Walnut Creek | 3 Silver Ct. |
| Innes del Castillo | Ann Arbor | 2286 Cram Pl. #86 |
| Michel DeFrance | Gary | 3 Balding Pl. |
| Dirk Stringer | Oakland | 5420 Telegraph Av. |
| Stearns MacFeather | Oakland | 44 Upland Hts. |
| Livia Karsen | Oakland | 5720 McAuley St. |
| Sylvia Panteley | Rockville | 1956 Arlington Pl. |
| Sheryl Hunter | Palo Alto | 3410 Blonde St. |

**Figure 15-16.** *A DataGrid using templates*

### You Can Hide or Show Columns

One useful feature of the DataGrid is the ability to hide individual columns. For example, you could allow the user to set certain preferences that configure the display to be either verbose or streamlined with only a few important columns. This differs from the DataList, which contains all its information in a single cell and cannot be dynamically configured. To hide a column, use the Columns collection for the DataGrid. For example, gridAuthors.Columns(2).Visible = False would hide the third column (columns are numbered starting at zero).

## The Repeater

The Repeater is the most primitive of the template controls, and it doesn't provide any extra support for selection, editing, or sorting. For that reason, the Repeater is mostly left out of our discussion in this chapter.

One interesting feature about the Repeater is that it doesn't apply any of its own formatting. In other words, the item template you define for a Repeater is simply repeated the required number of times on a page with no additional HTML tags. The DataList and DataGrid, on the other hand, supply a basic HTML table to delimit items. Consider the Repeater shown here:

```
<asp:Repeater id=repeatAuthor runat="server">
    <ItemTemplate><%# Container.DataItem("au_fname") %>
</ItemTemplate>
</asp:Repeater>
```

This Repeater creates the list of first names shown in Figure 15-17, which run together into a single long string of text.

To create a table in a Repeater, you must include the begin table tag (<table>) in the HeaderTemplate, a single table row tag (<tr>) in the ItemTemplate, and the end table tag (</table>) in the FooterTemplate.

```
<asp:Repeater id=repeatAuthor runat="server">
    <HeaderTemplate><table></HeaderTemplate>
    <ItemTemplate><tr><%# Container.DataItem("au_fname") %>
    </tr></ItemTemplate>
    <FooterTemplate></table></FooterTemplate>
</asp:Repeater>
```

WORKING WITH DATA

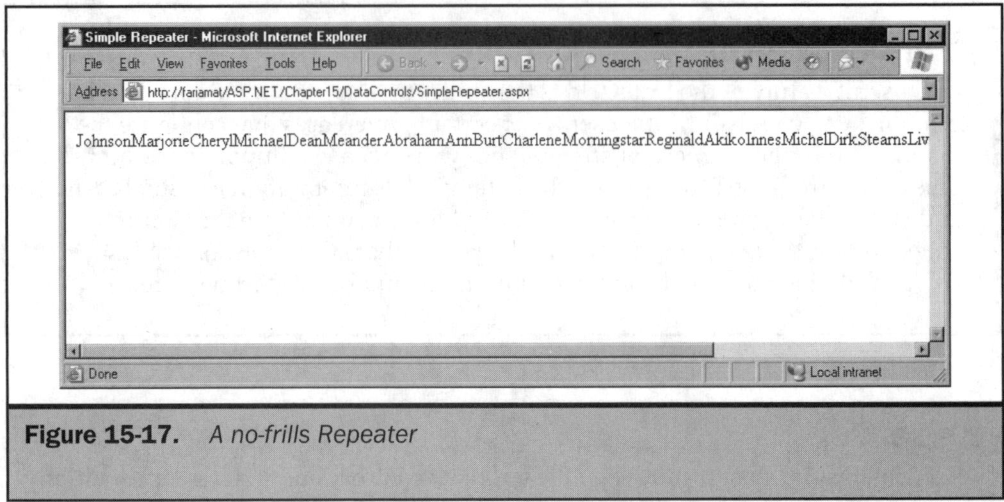


**Figure 15-17.** *A no-frills Repeater*

This construct is underlined in red in the Visual Studio .NET editor because the <table> tag overlaps the template tags. However, it is perfectly valid for a Repeater, and it creates the desired output (see Figure 15-18).

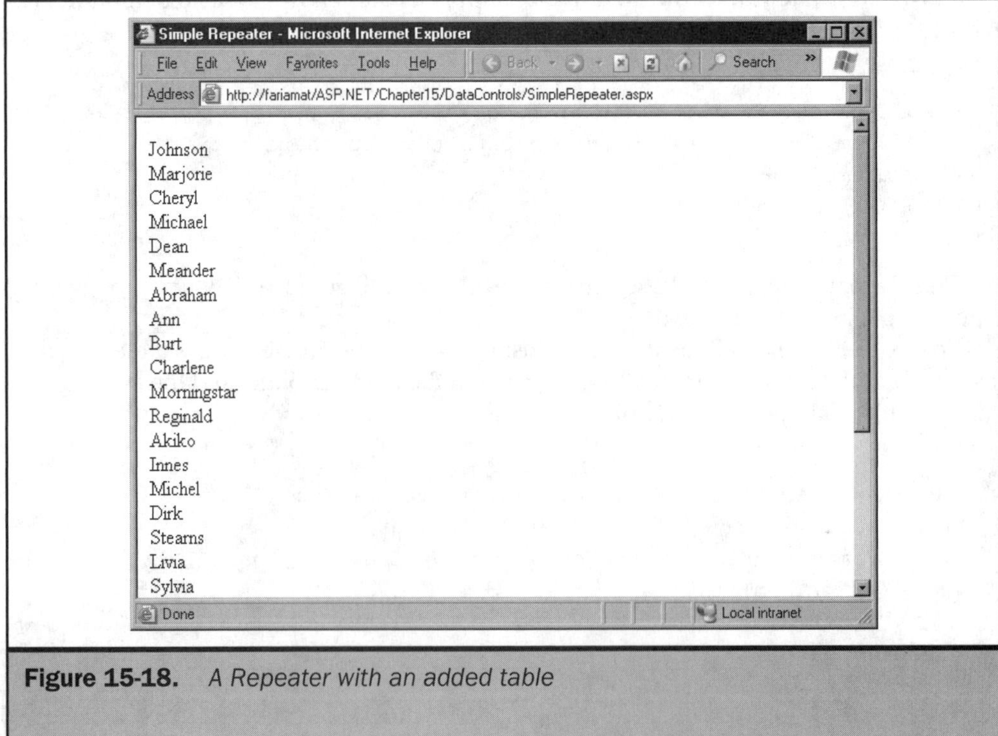


**Figure 15-18.** *A Repeater with an added table*

Incidentally, this ability to overlap tags and the complete lack of any preset formatting gives the Repeater control its flexibility. You can create a Repeater control with tags that span templates, which just isn't possible for the DataList or DataGrid. Usually, however, you'll prefer one of these more fully featured controls.

## Styles and Templates

The DataList, DataGrid, and Repeater are described in detail in the MSDN reference. Tables 15-3 and 15-4 present an overview that compares what styles and templates each control offers. You should also examine the additional properties of the DataGrid and DataList controls. For example, both allow you to configure a default background color and cell padding, and hide or display the header and footer.

| DataList | DataGrid | Repeater |
|---|---|---|
| AlternatingItemStyle | AlternatingItemStyle | No predefined styles |
| EditItemStyle | EditItemStyle | |
| FooterStyle | FooterStyle | |
| HeaderStyle | HeaderStyle | |
| ItemStyle | ItemStyle | |
| SelectedItemStyle | SelectedItemStyle | |
| SeparatorStyle | PagerStyle | |

**Table 15-3.** *Data Control Styles*

| DataList | DataGrid (only supported by the TemplateColumn) | Repeater |
|---|---|---|
| AlternatingItemTemplate | HeaderTemplate | ItemTemplate |
| EditItemTemplate | ItemTemplate | AlternatingItemTemplate |
| HeaderTemplate | EditItemTemplate | SeparatorTemplate |

**Table 15-4.** *Data Control Templates*

| DataList | DataGrid (only supported by the TemplateColumn) | Repeater |
|---|---|---|
| ItemTemplate | FooterTemplate | FooterTemplate |
| SelectedItemTemplate | | |
| SeparatorTemplate | | |
| FooterTemplate | | |

**Table 15-4.** *Data Control Templates (continued)*

## Preparing Your List for Selection and Editing

Before you can use more advanced features with your template control, you need to straighten out a couple of details. First of all, you should move the code for querying the database and binding the grid to a separate subprocedure. You will need to call this procedure frequently, so that you can update the grid when it is changed or sorted. However, you will also need to make sure that the grid is not indiscriminately rebound. For example, if you bind the grid in the Page.Load event with every postback, you will end up losing information about what button was clicked or what item was selected.

Your code should follow a pattern as shown here:

```
Private Sub Page_Load(sender As Object, e As EventArgs) _
  Handles MyBase.Load
    If Me.IsPostBack = False Then
        Dim ds As DataSet = GetDataSet()
        BindGrid(ds)
    End If
End Sub

Public Function GetDataSet() As DataSet
    Dim Select As String
    Select = "SELECT * FROM Authors"
    Dim con As New OleDbConnection(ConnectionString)
```

```
    Dim cmd As New OleDbCommand(Select, con)
    Dim adapter As New OleDbDataAdapter(cmd)
    Dim dsPubs As New DataSet()
    adapter.Fill(dsPubs, "Authors")
    con.Close()
    Return dsPubs
End Sub

Public Sub BindGrid(ds As DataSet)
    gridAuthor.DataSource = ds.Tables("Authors")
    Me.DataBind()
End Sub
```

# Selecting Items

"Selecting" an item generally refers to the ability to click on a row and have it change color (or become highlighted) to indicate that the user is currently working with this record. At the same time, you might want to display additional information about the record in another control. With the DataGrid and DataList, selection happens almost automatically.

Before you can use item selection, you must define a different style for selected items. The SelectedItemStyle determines how the selected row or cell will appear. If you don't set this style, it will default to the same value as ItemStyle, which means the user won't be able to determine which row is currently selected. If you are using a DataList, you will also need to define a SelectedItemTemplate.

To find out what item is currently selected (or to change the selection) you can use the SelectedItem property. It will be set to -1 if no item is currently selected. Also, you can react to the SelectedIndexChanged event to handle any additional related tasks, like updating another control with the information from the selected record.



## Selection with the DataGrid

To start, define formatting for the selected item, as shown here. Remember, you can also set this style using the Properties window at design time.

```
<SelectedItemStyle Font-Bold="True" ForeColor="White"
 BackColor="#738A9C">
</SelectedItemStyle>
```

Next, you need to create a button the user can click to select the row. For a DataGrid, this means adding a bound button column with the CommandName property set to

Select. You also need to specify the text that will appear in the button. Depending on the ButtonType you set, this button can appear as a hyperlink or a graphical push button.

```
<asp:ButtonColumn Text="Select" ButtonType="PushButton"
     CommandName="Select">
</asp:ButtonColumn>
```

When you compile and run the page, the button will automatically select the column and change the appearance when clicked (see Figure 15-19).

**Figure 15-19.** *DataGrid selection*

## Selection with the DataList

To start, define the SelectedItemStyle and SelectedItemTemplate. You will also need to add a Select button of some sort to the ItemTemplate (shown in bold in the following example). A complete example is shown here:

```
<asp:DataList id=listAuthor runat="server" BorderColor="#DEBA84"
BorderStyle="None" CellSpacing="2" BackColor="#DEBA84"
CellPadding="3" GridLines="Both" BorderWidth="1px">
```

```
    <HeaderStyle Font-Bold="True" ForeColor="White"
     BackColor="#A55129">
    </HeaderStyle>
    <ItemStyle Font-Names="Verdana" ForeColor="#8C4510"
     BackColor="#FFF7E7">
    </ItemStyle>
    <AlternatingItemStyle BackColor="#FFE0C0"></AlternatingItemStyle>
    <SelectedItemStyle Font-Italic="True" BorderColor="Aqua"
     BackColor="#FFC0FF">
    </SelectedItemStyle>

    <HeaderTemplate>
       <h2>Author List</h2>
    </HeaderTemplate>

    <ItemTemplate>
       <b><%# Container.DataItem("au_fname") %>
       <%# Container.DataItem("au_lname") %></b><br>
       Address: <%# Container.DataItem("address") %><br>
       City: <%# Container.DataItem("city") %><br>
       <asp:Button CommandName="Select" Text="Select"
            Runat=server ID="Button1"/>
    </ItemTemplate>

    <SelectedItemTemplate>
       <b><%# Container.DataItem("au_fname") %>
       <%# Container.DataItem("au_lname") %></b><br>
       Address: <%# Container.DataItem("address") %><br>
       City: <%# Container.DataItem("city") %><br>
    </SelectedItemTemplate>
</asp:DataList>
```

There are two differences between selected and unselected items in this example. Selected items have a different style (and appear with a rather garish aqua background) and selected items also use a different template (appearing without a Select button).

Unlike the DataGrid, the DataList does not natively recognize a special type of select button column. That means you need to handle the DataList.ItemCommand event and make sure the corresponding row is selected. The ItemCommand event is fired whenever any button is clicked in a DataList. You need to examine either the source parameter or the e.CommandName property to determine what button was clicked.

```
Private Sub listAuthor_ItemCommand(source As Object, _
  e As DataListCommandEventArgs) Handles listAuthor.ItemCommand
```

WORKING WITH DATA

```
        ' Was the select button clicked?
        If e.CommandName = "Select" Then
            ' Select the appropriate row.
            listAuthor.SelectedIndex = e.Item.ItemIndex

            ' Rebind the grid to update its appearance.
            Dim ds As DataSet = GetDataSet()
            BindGrid(ds)
        End If

    End Sub
```

To select a row, all you need to do is set the SelectedIndex property of the DataList. The ItemCommand event makes it easy, by supplying the row that was clicked in the e.Item property. A DataList with a selected item is shown in Figure 15-20.

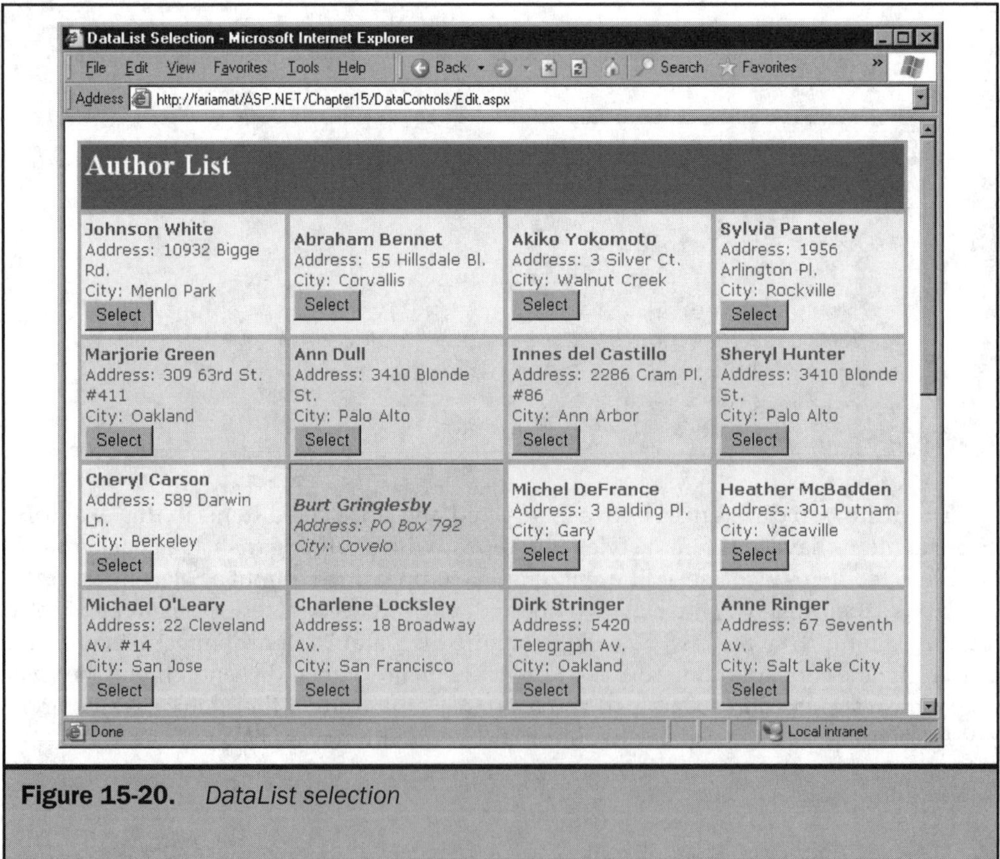


**Figure 15-20.** *DataList selection*

# Editing Items

Editing an item in ASP.NET is similar to selecting it. The only difference is that you use the EditItemIndex property instead of SelectedIndex. You also need to add additional database code to change the information in the data source.

## Editing with the DataGrid

The DataGrid uses a special type of column that automatically displays the Edit buttons, called EditCommandColumn. Initially, this column displays an Edit button for every row. Once this button is clicked, the corresponding row switches into edit mode, and the EditCommandColumn displays two buttons: Cancel and Update. Cancel returns the row to normal, while Update applies the changes and updates the database (with the help of your code).

The following is a sample DataGrid with an edit column. The bold code specifies the text for the Edit, Cancel, and Update buttons. Otherwise, these buttons will not be displayed. There is no default text.

```
<asp:DataGrid id=gridAuthor runat="server"
 AutoGenerateColumns="False" >
  <Columns>
     <asp:BoundColumn DataField="au_id" HeaderText="ID" />
     <asp:TemplateColumn HeaderText="Author Name">
        <ItemTemplate>
           <%# Container.DataItem("au_fname") %>
           <%# Container.DataItem("au_lname") %>
        </ItemTemplate>
     </asp:TemplateColumn>
     <asp:BoundColumn DataField="city" HeaderText="City" />
     <asp:BoundColumn DataField="address" HeaderText="Address" />
     <asp:EditCommandColumn EditText="Edit" CancelText="Cancel"
      UpdateText="Update" ButtonType="PushButton" />
  </Columns>
</asp:DataGrid>
```

The DataGrid automatically converts the bound columns in the current row to text boxes when the user switches into edit mode. You can prevent a user from editing a bound column by setting its ReadOnly property to True. In this case, a text box will not appear, and editing will not be allowed. This is a good idea for the ID column, which cannot be changed because it is the index of the table.

```
<asp:BoundColumn DataField="au_id" HeaderText="ID" ReadOnly=True />
```

In our example, no edit box is provided for the first column (the author name), because it is a special template column. In order for it to be placed into edit mode, it must have an EditItemTemplate as well as an ItemTemplate.

```
<asp:TemplateColumn HeaderText="Author Name">
    <ItemTemplate>
        <%# Container.DataItem("au_fname") %>
        <%# Container.DataItem("au_lname") %>
    </ItemTemplate>
    <EditItemTemplate>
        <asp:TextBox Text='<%# Container.DataItem("au_fname") %>'
                     id="txtfname" runat=server /><br>
        <asp:TextBox Text='<%# Container.DataItem("au_lname") %>'
                     id="txtlname" runat=server /><br>
    </EditItemTemplate>
</asp:TemplateColumn>
```

You might also want to use TemplateColumns with special edit templates to allow the user to use controls other than text boxes to edit the data. For example, you could create a drop-down list box and fill it in the Page.Load event.

## The EditCommand Event

To actually add some functionality to the Edit buttons, you need to react to a few basic DataGrid events. To start, you must use the EditCommand event to put the appropriate row in your list into edit mode.

```
Private Sub gridAuthor_EditCommand(source As Object, _
  e As DataGridCommandEventArgs) Handles gridAuthor.EditCommand
    gridAuthor.EditItemIndex = e.Item.ItemIndex
    Dim ds As DataSet = GetDataSet()
    BindGrid(ds)
End Sub
```

When you place a DataGrid into edit mode, it automatically provides a text box that allows the user to edit every field, as shown in Figure 15-21.

## The CancelCommand Event

The next possible event is CancelCommand, which occurs when the user clicks Cancel to end editing. In this event handler, you need to switch off editing for the DataGrid and rebind the row.

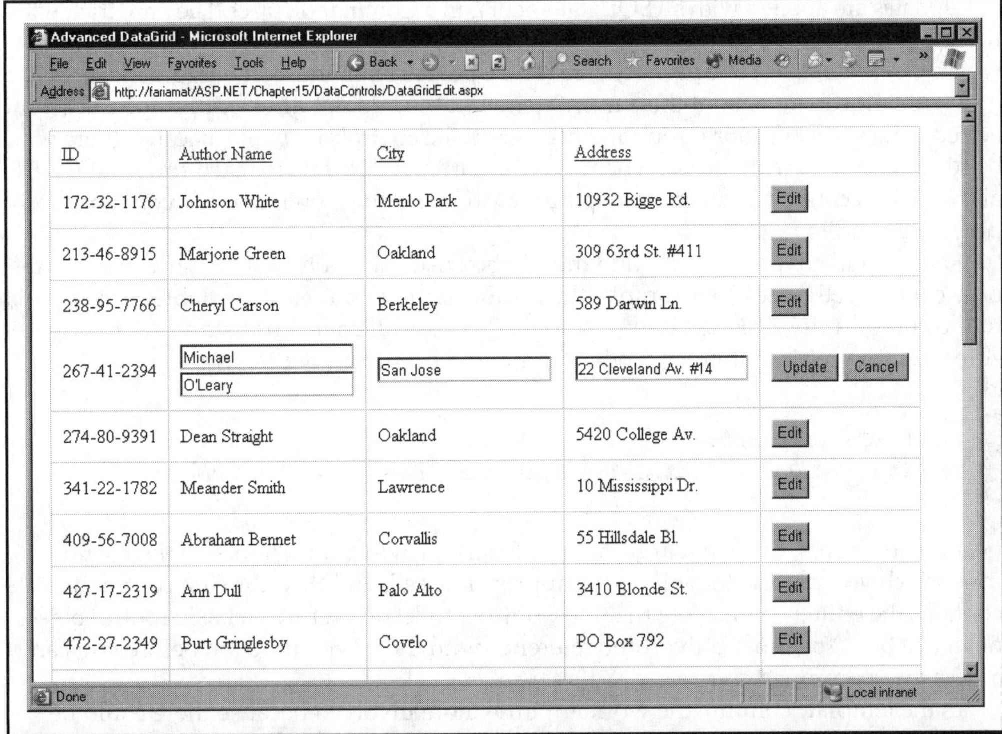


**Figure 15-21.** *DataGrid editing*

```
Private Sub gridAuthor_CancelCommand(source As Object, _
  e As DataGridCommandEventArgs) Handles gridAuthor.CancelCommand
    gridAuthor.EditItemIndex = -1
    Dim ds As DataSet = GetDataSet()
    BindGrid(ds)
End Sub
```

## The UpdateCommand Event

The UpdateCommand event is probably the most important event. It has two tasks: to apply the change to the database, and to switch the row out of edit mode, as the CancelCommand event handler does. You don't need to actually modify the DataGrid itself, because the new values will appear automatically when the data is retrieved from the data source and rebound.

Updates are applied with an SQL statement and a Command object. The only trick with updating the data is that you need to find the appropriate text boxes (or other controls) where the new values have been entered. The UpdateCommand event arguments provide you with information about the current item, but they do not directly provide the actual edited values. What's more, you can't just access the controls by name, because there will be several controls with the same name on the current page (one for each row). (ASP.NET allows this because it automatically places each row into its own naming container to prevent a conflict.)

For a bound control, you can find the text box using an index number, because it is the only control in the cell. For example, the third column in our example table corresponds to the author's city. This cell is at position 2 (because all collections start numbering at zero). You can retrieve it in the UpdateCommand event handler like so:

```
Dim NewCity As String
NewCity = CType(e.Item.Cells(2).Controls(0), TextBox).Text
```

In other words, the event argument's object e provides a reference to the current row, which you can use to look up the appropriate cell, and then the first control, which contains the edited value. Note that the Controls collection returns a basic control object, not a text box. You must convert the reference with the CType function before you can access the text property.

In the template column, the work is a little more involved because there could be several controls. The easiest approach is to use the FindControl method. You can retrieve the author's first name from the first column in our example as follows:

```
Dim NewFirstName As String
NewFirstName = CType(e.Item.FindControl("txtfname"), TextBox).Text
```

Now that you know the fundamentals, you can combine them with some standard ADO.NET code to create a fully functional update routine like the one shown here:

```
Private Sub gridAuthor_UpdateCommand(source As Object, _
 e As DataGridCommandEventArgs) Handles gridAuthor.UpdateCommand

     ' Create variables to hold new values.
     Dim NewFirstName, NewLastName As String
     Dim NewCity, NewAddress As String

     ' Retrieve the new values.
     NewFirstName = CType(e.Item.FindControl("txtfname"), _
       TextBox).Text
     NewLastName = CType(e.Item.FindControl("txtlname"), TextBox).Text
```

```
    NewCity = CType(e.Item.Cells(2).Controls(0), TextBox).Text
    NewAddress = CType(e.Item.Cells(3).Controls(0), TextBox).Text

    ' Retrieve the author ID to look up the record.
    Dim ID As String
    ID = e.Item.Cells(0).Text

    ' Define the SQL Update statement.
    Dim Update As String
    Update = "UPDATE Authors SET "
    Update &= "au_fname='" & NewFirstName & "', "
    Update &= "au_lname='" & NewLastName & "', "
    Update &= "city='" & NewCity & "', "
    Update &= "address='" & NewAddress & "' "
    Update &= "WHERE au_id='" & ID & "'"

    ' Create the ADO.NET objects.
    Dim con As New OleDbConnection(ConnectionString)
    Dim cmd As New OleDbCommand(Update, con)

    ' Try to open database and execute the update.
    Try
        con.Open()
        Dim NumberUpdated As Integer
        NumberUpdated = cmd.ExecuteNonQuery()
        lblStatus.Text = NumberUpdated.ToString()
        lblStatus.Text &= " records updated."
    Catch err As Exception
        lblStatus.Text = "Error updating author. "
        lblStatus.Text &= err.Message
    Finally
        If Not (con Is Nothing) Then
            con.Close()
        End If
    End Try

    ' Cancel edit mode.
    gridAuthor.EditItemIndex = -1

    ' Rebind the grid.
    Dim ds As DataSet = GetDataSet()
    BindGrid(ds)

End Sub
```

## Editing with the DataList

DataList editing is very similar to DataGrid editing:

- The DataList uses templates. Editing for a DataList item works the same as it does for a TemplateColumn in a DataGrid. That means you need to explicitly create an EditItemTemplate and use Container.DataItem statements to place information into text boxes or other controls.
- The DataList goes into and out of edit mode by setting the EditItemIndex, exactly like the DataGrid.
- The DataList raises EditCommand, UpdateCommand, and CancelCommand events, just like the DataGrid. The code you use in your event handlers is essentially the same.
- The DataList does not have predefined editing controls. That means you need to add your own buttons for editing. Usually, you accomplish this by adding the required Edit button to the SeletecedItemTemplate or ItemTemplate, and the Cancel and Update buttons to the EditItemTemplate.
- The DataList does provide some built-in smarts. If you set the command name of your button to Edit, Update, or Cancel, the corresponding EditCommand, UpdateCommand, or CancelCommand event will be fired automatically, along with the more generic ItemCommand. This is different than record selection, where you needed to use the generic ItemCommand event and check the command name to find out what type of button was clicked.

### The Templates

When you examine the DataList editing code, you'll recognize that it's very similar to the DataGrid and DataList selection examples. First you define the appropriate templates. The following example creates an Edit button and allows editing for two fields (in the txtCity and txtAddress text boxes) as shown in Figure 15-22.

```
<asp:DataList id=listAuthor style="Z-INDEX: 101; LEFT: 31px;
POSITION: absolute; TOP: 39px" runat="server" Width="189px"
Height="556px" BorderStyle="Ridge" BorderWidth="3px" CellPadding="5">
    <ItemTemplate>
        <b><%# Container.DataItem("au_fname") %>
        <%# Container.DataItem("au_lname") %></b>
        (<%# Container.DataItem("au_id") %>)<br>
        Address: <%# Container.DataItem("address") %><br>
        City: <%# Container.DataItem("city") %><br>
        <asp:Button CommandName="Edit" Text="Edit" Runat=server />
    </ItemTemplate>

    <EditItemTemplate>
        <b><%# Container.DataItem("au_fname") %>
```

```
        <%# Container.DataItem("au_lname") %></b>
        (<asp:Label Text='<%# Container.DataItem("au_id") %>'
                    id=lblID runat=server />)<br>
        Address:
        <asp:TextBox Text='<%# Container.DataItem("address") %>'
                     id="txtAddress" runat=server /><br>
        City:
        <asp:TextBox Text='<%# Container.DataItem("city") %>'
                     id="txtCity" runat=server /><br>
        <asp:Button CommandName="Update" Text="Update" Runat=server />
        <asp:Button CommandName="Cancel" Text="Cancel" Runat=server />
    </EditItemTemplate>

    <SeparatorTemplate><hr></SeparatorTemplate>

</asp:DataList>
```



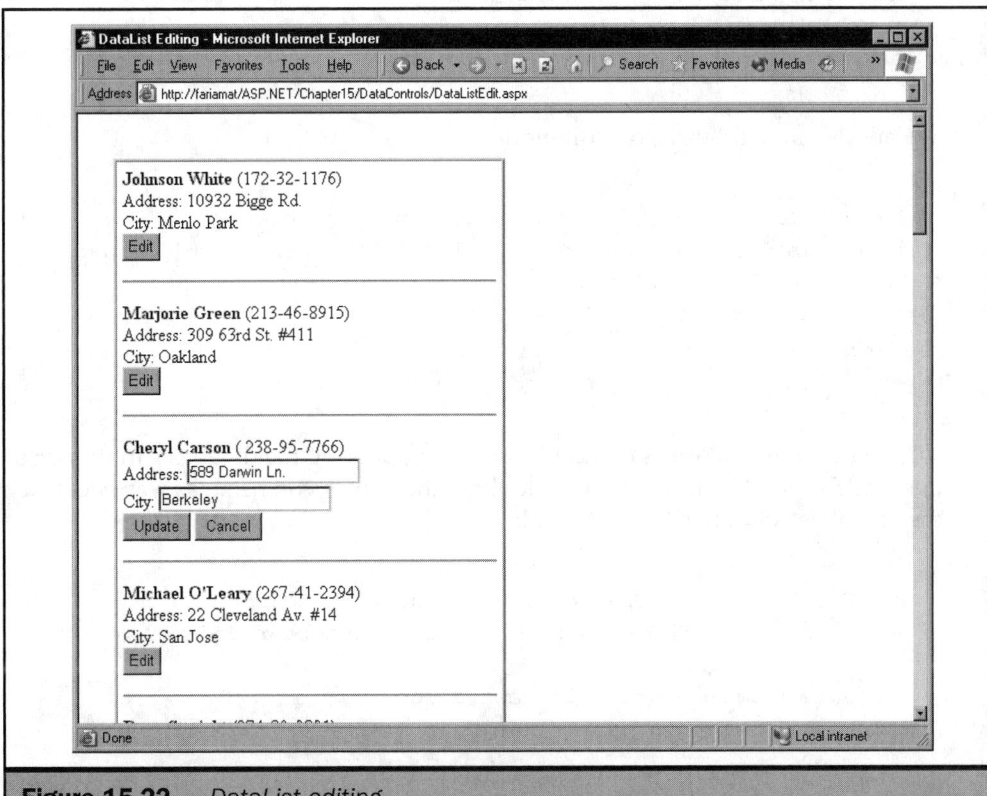


**Figure 15-22.** *DataList editing*

One interesting trick in this code is that the edit template stores the author ID in a label control so that it can be retrieved easily with the FindControl method and used to look up the corresponding database record for the update. There are other possible approaches to retrieving the author ID of the record in edit mode. For example, you can set the DataList.DataKeyField property to the name of the key field (like "au_id"). You can then find the key for a given row using the DataList.DataKeys collection. This approach allows you to store a key that you don't want to display in the control. It's also quite a convenience—as long as you've set the DataKeyField property before filling the control, the DataKeys collection will be populated automatically from the data source.

## The Event Handler Code

The basic event handler code is almost identical to the DataGrid example. The EditCommand event turns on edit mode:

```
Private Sub listAuthor_EditCommand(source As Object, _
 e As DataListCommandEventArgs) Handles listAuthor.EditCommand
    listAuthor.EditItemIndex = e.Item.ItemIndex
    Dim ds As DataSet = GetDataSet()
    BindGrid(ds)
End Sub
```

The CancelCommand turns off edit mode:

```
Private Sub listAuthor_CancelCommand(source As Object, _
 e As DataListCommandEventArgs) Handles listAuthor.CancelCommand
    listAuthor.EditItemIndex = -1
    Dim ds As DataSet = GetDataSet()
    BindGrid(ds)
End Sub
```

The UpdateCommand turns off edit mode after updating the database. In this case, you must use the FindControl method to look up the values you need, as was necessary with the TemplateColumn in the DataGrid:

```
Private Sub listAuthor_UpdateCommand(source As Object, _
  e As DataListCommandEventArgs) Handles listAuthor.UpdateCommand

    ' Create variables to hold new values.
    Dim NewCity, NewAddress As String
```

```
    ' Retrieve the new values.
    NewCity = CType(e.Item.FindControl("txtCity"), TextBox).Text
    NewAddress = CType(e.Item.FindControl("txtAddress"), TextBox).Text

    ' Retrieve the author ID to look up the record.
    Dim ID As String
    ID = CType(e.Item.FindControl("lblID"), Label).Text

    ' Define the SQL Update statement.
    Dim Update As String
    Update = "UPDATE Authors SET "
    Update &= "city='" & NewCity & "', "
    Update &= "address='" & NewAddress & "' "
    Update &= "WHERE au_id='" & ID & "'"

    ' Create the ADO.NET objects.
    Dim con As New OleDbConnection(ConnectionString)
    Dim cmd As New OleDbCommand(Update, con)

    ' Try to open database and execute the update.
    Try
        con.Open()
        Dim NumberUpdated As Integer
        NumberUpdated = cmd.ExecuteNonQuery
        lblStatus.Text = NumberUpdated.ToString() & " records updated."
    Catch err As Exception
        lblStatus.Text = "Error updating author. "
        lblStatus.Text &= err.Message
    Finally
        If Not (con Is Nothing) Then
            con.Close()
        End If
    End Try

    ' Cancel edit mode.
    listAuthor.EditItemIndex = -1

    ' Rebind the grid.
    Dim ds As DataSet = GetDataSet()
    BindGrid(ds)

End Sub
```

## Paging with the DataGrid

Often, a database search will return too many rows to be realistically displayed in a single page. If the client is using a slow connection, sending an extremely large DataGrid can take a frustrating amount of time. Once the data is retrieved, the user may find out that it doesn't contain the right content anyway, or that the search was too broad and there is no easy way to wade through all the results to find the important information.

The DataGrid handles this scenario by providing automatic paging logic. When you use automatic paging, the full results are retrieved from the data source and placed into a DataSet. Once you bind that DataSet to the DataGrid, however, it is subdivided into smaller groupings (typically of 10 or 20 rows) and only the first batch is sent to the user (the other groups are abandoned when the page finishes processing). The DataGrid automatically displays a special group of pager controls that allow the user to skip from page to page. These look like less than (<) and greater than (>) signs.

Implementing automatic paging is quite easy:

1. Set the AllowPaging property of the DataGrid to True, and specify a number of rows for the PageSize property. This ensures that the paging controls will be displayed at the bottom of the grid.
2. Configure the PagerStyle as desired. These settings determine the color and appearance of the pager row, and they also determine the type of pager controls. For example, you can set DataGrid.PagerStyle.Mode to NextPrev to show next and previous buttons for stepping through the pages (< and >). Or you can set it to NumericPages to show a group of number buttons that allow the user to jump immediately to the specified page (1 2 3 4 5 ...).
3. Handle the PageIndexChanged event, and use it to set the CurrentPageIndex and rebind the DataGrid. The value you should use for the CurrentPageIndex is provided in the event arguments.

```
Private Sub gridAuthor_PageIndexChanged(source As Object, _
 e As DataGridPageChangedEventArgs) _
 Handles gridAuthor.PageIndexChanged

    ' Set the new page.
    gridAuthor.CurrentPageIndex = e.NewPageIndex
    ' Rebind the grid.
    Dim ds As DataSet = GetDataSet()
    BindGrid(ds)

End Sub
```

Every time a new page is requested, the full DataSet is queried from the database, meaning that there is no performance increase on the database side. However, only the requested subset of rows is sent to the client, thus improving transmission time and reducing the client's wait. The end result is a more responsive and manageable page (see Figure 15-23).

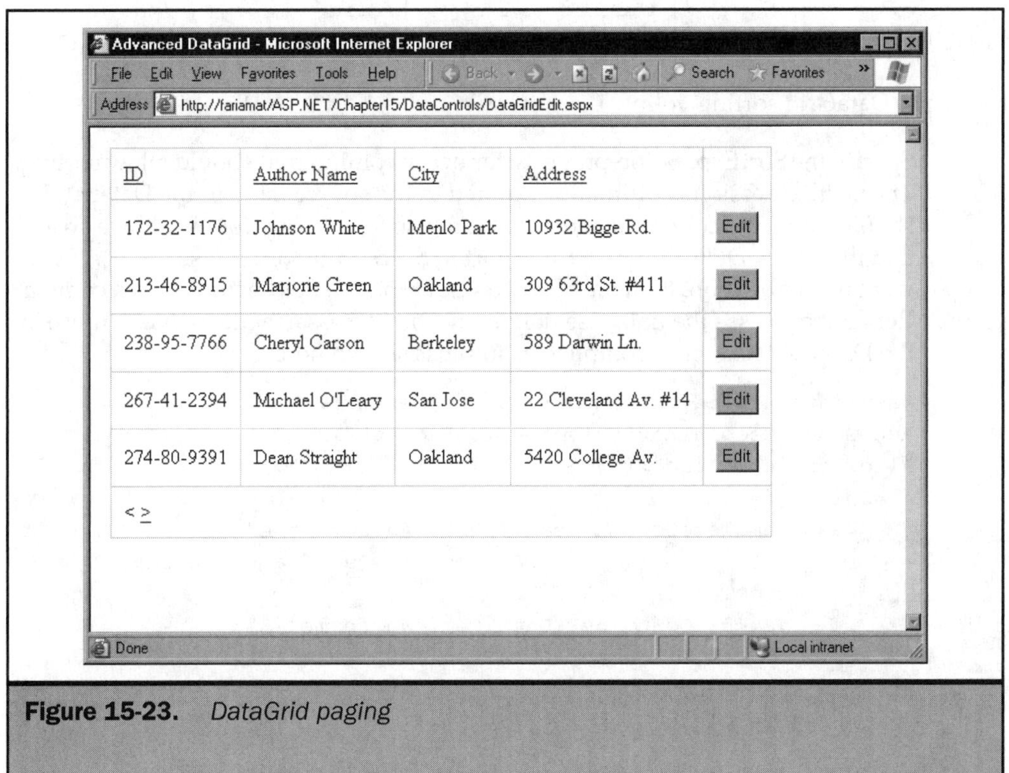


**Figure 15-23.** *DataGrid paging*



## Sorting with the DataGrid

Sorting is a standard feature in most rich grid controls, such as those seen in Windows applications. In a web application, the process is not quite as easy, because the DataSet object is not maintained in memory. That means that the data needs to be requeried and rebound when the page is posted back.

DataGrid sorting is accomplished by sorting the data in the DataSet before binding it to the DataGrid control. However, the DataGrid includes a couple of built-in features that make the process much simpler. Namely, it allows you to use column hyperlinks to implement automatic sorting as shown in the following illustration.

| ID | Author Name | City | Address |
|---|---|---|---|

To use DataGrid sorting, follow these steps:

1. Specify the SortExpression property for every column that should allow sorting. The SortExpression is ultimately applied to the source table in the DataSet. It should name the column that you want to use for sorting (followed by a space and the letters DESC if you want to sort in descending or reverse order). If you want to sort by more than one row, you can separate field names with a comma. Remember, this is the database field name, not necessarily the name you use in the DataGrid header. A complete example is shown here:

```
<asp:datagrid id=gridAuthor runat="server"
AutoGenerateColumns="False" AllowPaging="True"
AllowSorting="True">
  <Columns>
    <asp:TemplateColumn HeaderText="Author Name"
                        SortExpression="au_fname, au_lname">
        <ItemTemplate>
            <%# Container.DataItem("au_fname") %>
            <%# Container.DataItem("au_lname") %>
        </ItemTemplate>
    </asp:TemplateColumn>

    <asp:BoundColumn DataField="city" HeaderText="City"
                     SortExpression="city"></asp:BoundColumn>
    <asp:BoundColumn DataField="address" HeaderText="Address"
                     SortExpression="address"></asp:BoundColumn>
  </Columns>
</asp:datagrid>
```

2. Set the AllowSorting property of the DataGrid to True. This ensures that the column headings appear as hyperlinks.
3. Handle the SortCommand event. This event provides you with the name of the column that was clicked. You can use this information to build a sort expression and apply it before rebinding the data.

```
Private Sub gridAuthor_SortCommand(source As Object, _
 e As DataGridSortCommandEventArgs) Handles
gridAuthor.SortCommand

    Dim ds As DataSet = GetDataSet()
    ' Apply the sort expression to the table's default view.
    ds.Tables("Authors").DefaultView.Sort = e.SortExpression
    BindGrid(ds)

End Sub
```

## You Can Also Implement Sorting for a DataList

You now know enough about sorting to implement it for a DataList control. In fact, the process is very similar, but requires a few extra steps. First of all, you need to add your own sort buttons, either in the control or, more likely, as separate controls above or below the DataList. When one of these sort buttons is clicked, you would then programmatically set a sort expression for your DataSet and rebind the data. The only difference between a DataGrid and a DataList control is that the DataGrid provides a convenient set of sort buttons (the column headers) and allows you to specify the corresponding sort expression directly in the column tag.

# Chapter 16

## Files, Streams, and Email

There's a good reason why we examined ADO.NET before considering simpler data access techniques such as writing and reading to ordinary files. Traditional file access is generally much less useful in a web application than it is in a desktop program. Databases, on the other hand, are designed from the ground up to support a large load of simultaneous users with speed, safety, and efficiency. Most web applications will rely on a database for some feature, but many won't have any use for straight file access.

Of course, enterprising ASP.NET developers can find a use for almost any technology. There's no doubt in my mind that if file access was left out of this book, many developers would be frustrated when they designed web applications with legitimate (and innovative) uses for ordinary files. In fact, file access is so easy and straightforward in .NET that it may be the perfect ticket for simple, small-scale solutions that don't need a full external database.

This chapter explains how you can use the input/output classes in .NET to read and change file system information, create simple text and binary files, and allow users to upload their own files. The chapter winds up with another important ASP.NET feature: emailing. You'll learn how you can send an email message from your web server just by creating and configuring the right .NET object.

## Files and Web Applications

Why is it that most web applications don't make direct use of files? There are actually several limitations:

**File naming** Every file you create needs to have a unique name (or it will overwrite another file). Unfortunately, there is no easy way to ensure that a file's name is unique. While relational databases provide auto-incrementing fields that automatically fill with a unique number when you create the record, files have no such niceties. Usually, you need to fall back on some random number system that incorporates the current date (and is thus statistically unique), or let the user specify the filename.

**Security risks** Your ASP.NET code usually runs at a highly trusted level, and won't be prevented from potential dangerous or damaging file operations. However, if a file or path name is specified by the user, there's a chance the user could devise some way to submit the name of an existing or protected file and "trick" your program into overwriting or deleting it. Even without this ability, a malicious or careless user might use an ASP.NET page that creates or uploads a file to fill up your web server hard drive and cause it to stop working.

**Multi-user limitations** As you've seen in the ADO.NET chapters, relational databases provide features to manage locking, inconsistent updates, and transactions. Comparatively, the web server's file system is woefully backward. Opening a file generally locks other users out of it, and there is no possibility for more than one user to update a file at once without catastrophe.

**Scalability problems** File operations suffer from some overhead. In a simple scenario, file access may be faster than connecting to a database and performing a query. When multiple users are working with files at the same time, however, these advantages disappear, and your web server may slow down dramatically.

Generally, file access is best for smaller internal applications (such as those hosted on an intranet). In these situations, you can assume a smaller number of simultaneous users, as well as a set of trusted users who are less likely to try to battle your web server. (Alternatively, you can force internal users to be explicitly authenticated using their network accounts before being allowed access to your site. This topic is discussed in more detail in Chapter 24.)

## File System Information

Many of the considerations listed previously apply to web applications that create their own files. However, the simplest level of file access just involves retrieving information about existing files and directories, and performing typical file system operations such as copying files and creating directories.

ASP.NET provides four basic classes for retrieving this sort of information. They are all located in the System.IO directory (and, incidentally, can be used in desktop applications in the exact same way that they are used in web applications).

- The Directory and File classes provide shared methods that allow you to retrieve information about any files and directories that are visible from your server. They are best suited for quick "one off" operations.
- The DirectoryInfo and FileInfo classes use similar instance methods and properties to retrieve the same sort of information. They are ideal for situations when you need to perform a series of operations or retrieve several pieces of information from the same file or directory.

### Shared versus Instance Members

In Chapter 3, we saw how a class can provide two different types of members. Shared members are always available—you just use the name of the class. To access an instance member, you need to create an object first, and then access the property or method through the object's variable name.

With the file access classes, shared methods are more convenient to use because they don't require you to instantiate the class. On the other hand, if you need to retrieve several pieces of information, it's easier to use an instance class. That way you don't need to keep specifying the name of the directory or file each time you call a method. It's also faster. That's because the FileInfo and DirectoryInfo classes perform their security checks once—when you create the actual object instance. The Directory and File classes perform a security check every time you invoke a method.

## The Directory and File Classes

The Directory and File classes provide a number of useful methods. Tables 16-1 and 16-2 tell the whole story. Note that every method takes the same parameter: a fully qualified path name identifying the directory or file you want the operation to act on. A few methods, like Delete, have optional additional parameters.

| Method | Description |
|---|---|
| CreateDirectory() | Creates a new directory. If you specify a directory inside another nonexistent directory, ASP.NET will thoughtfully create *all* the required directories. |
| Delete() | Deletes the corresponding empty directory. To delete a directory along with its contents (subdirectories and files), add the optional second parameter of True. |
| Exists() | Returns True or False to indicate if the specified directory exists. |
| GetCreationTime(), GetLastAccessTime(), and GetLastWriteTime() | Returns a DateTime object that represents the the time the directory was created, accessed, or written to. Each "Get" method has a corresponding "Set" method, which isn't shown in this table. |
| GetDirectories(), GetFiles(), and GetLogicalDrives() | Returns an array of strings, one for each sub-directory, file, or drive in the specified directory (depending on which method you are using). This method can accept a second parameter that specifies a search expression (like "ASP*.*"). Drive letters are in the format "C:\". |
| GetParent() | Parses the supplied directory string and tells you what the parent directory is. You could do this on your own by searching for the \ character, but this function makes life a little easier. |

**Table 16-1.** *Directory Class Methods*

| Method | Description |
|---|---|
| GetCurrentDirectory() and SetCurrentDirectory() | Allows you to set and retrieve the current directory, which is useful if you need to use relative paths instead of full paths. Generally, these functions shouldn't be relied on and aren't necessary. |
| Move() | Accepts two parameters: the source path and the destination path. The directory and all its contents can be moved to any path, as long as it is located on the same drive. |

**Table 16-1.** *Directory Class Methods (continued)*

| Method | Description |
|---|---|
| Copy() | Accepts two parameters: the fully qualified source filename and the fully qualified destination filename. To allow overwriting, add the optional third parameter set to True. |
| Delete() | Deletes the specified file, but does not throw an exception if the file can't be found. |
| Exists() | Indicates True or False whether a specified file exists. |
| GetAttributes() and SetAttributes() | Retrieves or sets an enumerated value that can include any combination of the values from the FileMode enumeration. |
| GetCreationTime(), GetLastAccessTime(), and GetLastWriteTime() | Returns a DateTime object that represents the time the file was created, accessed, or last written to. Each "Get" method has a corresponding "Set" method, which isn't shown in this table. |

**Table 16-2.** *File Class Methods*

The File class also includes some methods that allow you to create and open files as streams. We'll explore these features a little later in the chapter. The only feature that the File class lacks (and the FileInfo class provides) is the ability to retrieve the size of a specified file.

The File and Directory methods are completely intuitive. For example, consider the code for a simple page that displays some information about the files in a specific directory. You might use this code to create a simple admin page that allows you to review the contents of an FTP directory clients use to upload their documents and delete suspicious files (see Figure 16-1).

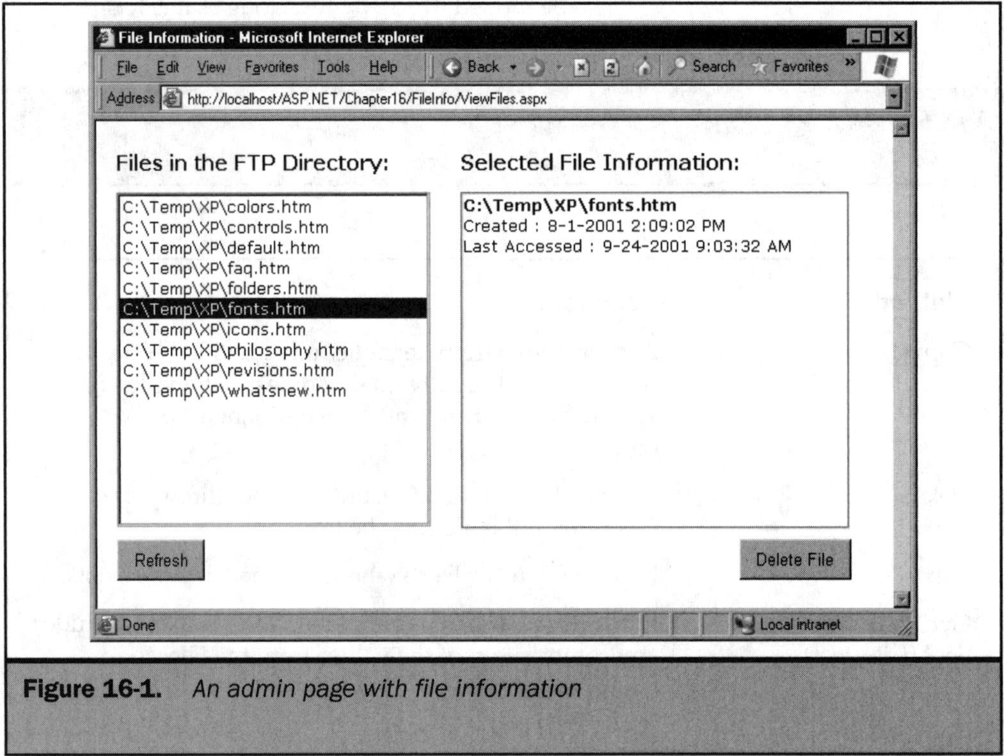


**Figure 16-1.** *An admin page with file information*

The code for this page is as follows:

```
' Import the namespace that includes the I/O classes.
Imports System.IO

Public Class ViewFiles
```

```
Inherits Page

  Protected WithEvents lstFiles As ListBox
  Protected WithEvents cmdRefresh As Button
  Protected lblFileInfo As Label
  Protected WithEvents cmdDelete As Button

  Public FTPDirectory As String = "C:\FTPSite\Current"

  Private Sub Page_Load(sender As Object, e As EventArgs) _
    Handles MyBase.Load
      If Me.IsPostBack = False Then
          CreateFileList()
      End If
  End Sub

  Private Sub CreateFileList()
      ' Retrieve the list of files, and display it in the page.
      ' This code also disables the delete button, ensuring the
      ' user must view the file information before deleting it.
      Dim FileList As Array = Directory.GetFiles(FTPDirectory)
      lstFiles.DataSource = FileList
      lstFiles.DataBind()
      lblFileInfo.Text = ""
      cmdDelete.Enabled = False
  End Sub

  Private Sub cmdRefresh_Click(sender As Object, e As EventArgs) _
    Handles cmdRefresh.Click
      CreateFileList()
  End Sub

  Private Sub lstFiles_SelectedIndexChanged(sender As Object, _
    e As EventArgs) Handles lstFiles.SelectedIndexChanged

      ' Display the selected file information.
      ' This control has AutoPostback = True.
      Dim FileName As String = lstFiles.SelectedItem.Text
      lblFileInfo.Text = "<b>" & FileName & "</b><br>"
      lblFileInfo.Text &= "Created : "
      lblFileInfo.Text &= File.GetCreationTime(FileName).ToString()
      lblFileInfo.Text &= "<br>Last Accessed : "
```

```
        lblFileInfo.Text &= File.GetLastAccessTime(FileName).ToString()
        lblFileInfo.Text &= "<br>"

        ' Show attribute information. GetAttributes can return a
        ' combination of enumerated values, so you need to
        ' evaluate it with the And keyword.
        Dim Attr As FileAttributes = File.GetAttributes(FileName)
        If (Attr And FileAttributes.Hidden) = _
          FileAttributes.Hidden Then
            lblFileInfo.Text &= "This is a hidden file." & "<br>"
        End If
        If (Attr And FileAttributes.ReadOnly) = _
          FileAttributes.ReadOnly Then
            lblFileInfo.Text &= "This is a read-only file." & "<br>"
        End If

        ' Allow the file to be deleted.
        If (Attr And FileAttributes.ReadOnly) <> _
         FileAttributes.ReadOnly Then
            cmdDelete.Enabled = True
        End If

    End Sub

    Private Sub cmdDelete_Click(sender As Object, e As EventArgs) _
      Handles cmdDelete.Click
        File.Delete(lstFiles.SelectedItem.Text)
        CreateFileList()
    End Sub

End Class
```

## Interesting Facts About this Code

- The CreateFileList procedure is easy to code, because it uses the data-binding feature of the ListBox. The array returned from the GetFiles methods can be attached to the list with no extra code.
- When the user chooses an item in the list, the control posts back immediately and allows your code to refresh the file information.
- When evaluating the FileAttributes enumeration, you need to use the And keyword (this is called bitwise comparison). The reason is that the value returned from GetAttributes can actually contain a combination of more than one attribute.

- The code that displays file information could benefit from a switch to the FileInfo class. As it is, every method needs to respecify the file, which requires a separate security check.

## The DirectoryInfo and FileInfo Classes

The DirectoryInfo and FileInfo classes mirror the functionality in the Directory and File classes. In addition, they make it easy to walk through directory/file relationships. For example, you can easily retrieve the FileInfo objects of files in a directory represented by a DirectoryInfo object.

Note that while the Directory and File classes only expose methods, DirectoryInfo and FileInfo provide a combination of properties and methods. For example, while the File class had separate GetAttributes and SetAttributes methods, the FileInfo class exposes a read-write Attributes property.

Another nice thing about the DirectoryInfo and FileInfo classes is that they share a common set of properties and methods. Table 16-3 describes the members they have in common.

| Member | Description |
|---|---|
| Attributes | Allows you to retrieve or set attributes using a combination of values from the FileAttributes. |
| CreationTime, LastAccessTime, and LastWriteTime | Allow you to set or retrieve the creation time, last access time, and last write time, using a DateTime object. |
| Exists | Returns True or False depending on whether the file or directory exists. In other words, you can create FileInfo and DirectoryInfo objects that don't actually correspond to current physical directories (although you obviously won't be able to use properties like CreationTime and methods like MoveTo). |
| FullName, Name and Extension | Returns a string that represents the fully qualified name, the directory or filename (with extension), or the extension on its own, depending on which property you use. |
| Delete() | Removes the file or directory, if it exists. When deleting a directory, it must be empty or you must specify an optional parameter set to True. |

**Table 16-3.** *DirectoryInfo and File Members*

| Member | Description |
|---|---|
| Refresh() | Updates the object so it is synchronized with any file system changes that have happened in the meantime (for example, if an attribute was changed manually using Windows Explorer). |
| Create() | Creates the specified directory or file. |
| MoveTo() | Copies the directory and its contents or the file. For a DirectoryInfo object, you need to specify the new path; for a FileInfo object you specify a path and filename. |

**Table 16-3.** *DirectoryInfo and File Members (continued)*

In addition, the FileInfo and DirectoryInfo classes have a couple of unique members, as indicated in Tables 16-4 and 16-5.

| Member | Description |
|---|---|
| Parent, and Root | Returns a DirectoryInfo object that represents the parent or root directory. |
| CreateSubdirectory() | Creates a directory with the specified name in the directory represented by the DirectoryInfo object. It also returns a new DirectoryInfo object that represents the subdirectory. |
| GetDirectories() | Returns an array of DirectoryInfo objects that represent all the subdirectories contained in this directory. |
| GetFiles() | Returns an array of FileInfo objects that represent all the files contained in this directory. |

**Table 16-4.** *Unique DirectoryInfo Members*

| Member | Description |
|---|---|
| Directory | Returns a DirectoryInfo object that represents the parent directory. |
| DirectoryName | Returns a string that identifies the name of the parent directory. |
| Length | Returns a Long with the file size in bytes. |
| CopyTo() | Copies a file to the new path and filename specified as a parameter. It also returns a new FileInfo object that represents the new (copied) file. You can supply an optional additional parameter of True to allow overwriting. |

**Table 16-5.** *Unique FileInfo Members*



When you create a DirectoryInfo or FileInfo object, you specify the full path in the constructor.

```
Dim MyDirectory As New DirectoryInfo("C:\Temp")
Dim MyFile As New FileInfo("C:\Temp\readme.txt")
```

This path may or may not correspond to a real physical file or directory. If it doesn't, you can always use the Create method to create the corresponding file or directory.

```
' Define the new directory and file.
Dim MyDirectory As New DirectoryInfo("C:\Temp\Test")
Dim MyFile As New FileInfo("C:\Temp\Test\readme.txt")

' Now create them. Order here is important.
' You can't create a file in a directory that doesn't exist yet.
MyDirectory.Create()
MyFile.Create()
```

## A Sample File Browser

You can use methods such as DirectoryInfo.GetFiles() and DirectoryInfo.GetDirectories() to create a simple file browser. Be warned that while this code is a good example of how to use the DirectoryInfo and FileInfo classes, it is *not* a good example of security.

Generally, you wouldn't want a user to find out so much information about the files on your web server.

## ASP.NET Works in a Trusted Environment

In a typical web site, you will disable file browsing for the virtual directory where a web application is hosted. This restricts clients from accessing the information in a browser or through Windows Explorer, but it does not affect what your ASP.NET application can do. Remember, ASP.NET code executes under a special trusted account and can expose security gaps that IIS would not normally allow. You can change this behavior using impersonation, as described at the end of Chapter 24.

The sample file browser program allows the user to see information about any file in any directory in the current drive, as shown in Figure 16-2.

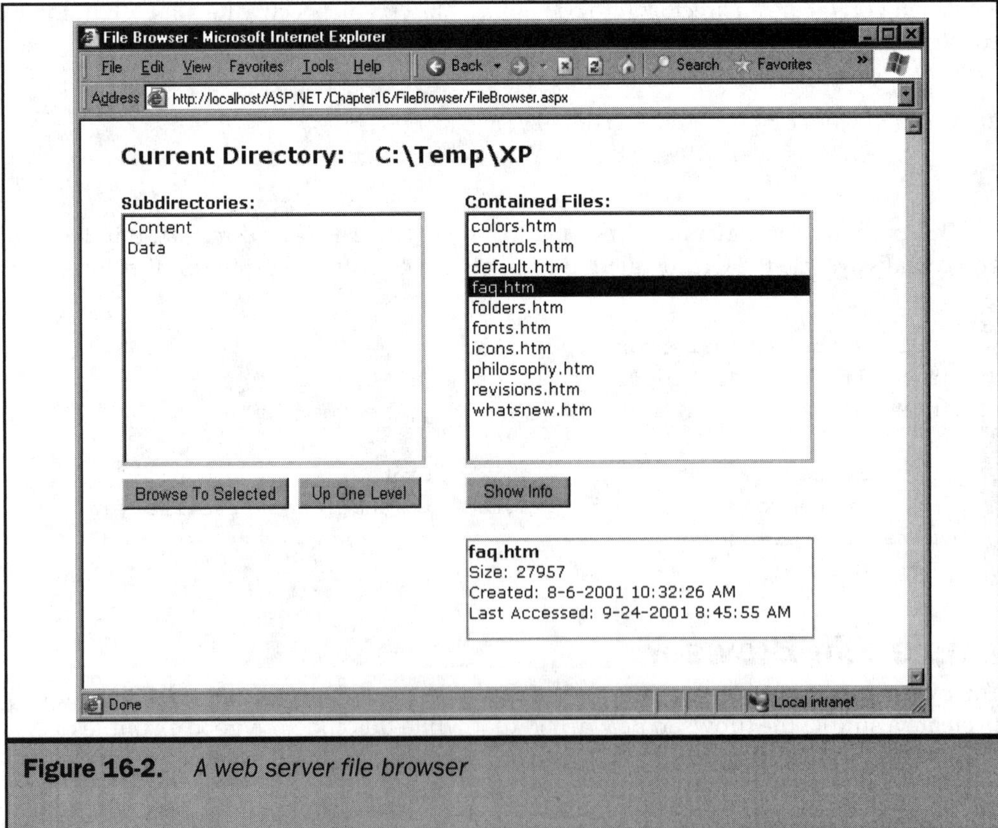


**Figure 16-2.** *A web server file browser*

```
Imports System.IO

Public Class FileBrowser
  Inherits Page

    Protected WithEvents cmdBrowse As Button
    Protected lblFileInfo As Label
    Protected lstDirs As ListBox
    Protected lstFiles As ListBox
    Protected lblCurrentDir As Label
    Protected WithEvents cmdParent As Button
    Protected WithEvents cmdShowInfo As Button

    Private Sub Page_Load(sender As Object, e As EventArgs) _
      Handles MyBase.Load
        If Me.IsPostBack = False Then
            Dim StartingDir As String = "C:\Temp"
            lblCurrentDir.Text = StartingDir
            ShowFilesIn(StartingDir)
            ShowDirectoriesIn(StartingDir)
        End If
    End Sub

    Private Sub ShowFilesIn(Dir As String)
        Dim DirInfo As New DirectoryInfo(Dir)
        Dim FileItem As FileInfo

        lstFiles.Items.Clear()
        For Each FileItem In DirInfo.GetFiles()
            lstFiles.Items.Add(FileItem.Name)
        Next
    End Sub

    Private Sub ShowDirectoriesIn(Dir As String)
        Dim DirInfo As New DirectoryInfo(Dir)
        Dim DirItem As DirectoryInfo

        lstDirs.Items.Clear()
        For Each DirItem In DirInfo.GetDirectories()
            lstDirs.Items.Add(DirItem.Name)
        Next
    End Sub

    Private Sub cmdBrowse_Click(sender As Object, e As EventArgs) _
```

```
     Handles cmdBrowse.Click
        ' Browse to the currently selected subdirectory.
        If lstDirs.SelectedIndex <> -1 Then
            Dim NewDir As String = lblCurrentDir.Text.TrimEnd("\")
            NewDir &= "\" & lstDirs.SelectedItem.Text
            lblCurrentDir.Text = NewDir
            ShowFilesIn(NewDir)
            ShowDirectoriesIn(NewDir)
        End If
    End Sub

    Private Sub cmdParent_Click(sender As Object, e As EventArgs) _
      Handles cmdParent.Click
        ' Browse up to the current directory's parent.
        ' The Directory.GetParent method helps us out.
        Dim NewDir As String
        If Directory.GetParent(lblCurrentDir.Text) Is Nothing Then
            ' This is the root directory; there are no more levels.
            Exit Sub
        Else
            NewDir = Directory.GetParent(lblCurrentDir.Text).FullName
        End If

        lblCurrentDir.Text = NewDir
        ShowFilesIn(NewDir)
        ShowDirectoriesIn(NewDir)
    End Sub

    Private Sub cmdShowInfo_Click(sender As Object, e As EventArgs) _
      Handles cmdShowInfo.Click
        ' Show information for the currently selected file.
        If lstFiles.SelectedIndex <> -1 Then
            Dim FileName As String = lblCurrentDir.Text.TrimEnd("\")
            FileName &= "\" & lstFiles.SelectedItem.Text
            Dim SelFile As New FileInfo(FileName)
            lblFileInfo.Text = "<b>" & SelFile.Name & "</b><br>"
            lblFileInfo.Text &= "Size: " & SelFile.Length & "<br>"
            lblFileInfo.Text &= "Created: "
            lblFileInfo.Text &= SelFile.CreationTime.ToString()
            lblFileInfo.Text &= "<br>Last Accessed: "
            lblFileInfo.Text &= SelFile.LastAccessTime.ToString()
        End If
    End Sub

End Class
```

### Interesting Facts About this Code

- The list controls in this example don't post back immediately. Instead, the web page relies on Browse To Selected and Show Info buttons.
- By default, directory names don't end with a trailing backslash (\) character. (For example, C:\Temp is used instead of C:\Temp\.) However, when referring to the root drive, a slash is required. This is because only C:\ refers to the root drive; C: refers to the current directory, whatever it may be. This can cause problems when handling filenames because you don't want to add an extra trailing slash to a path (as in the invalid path C:\\myfile.txt). To solve this problem, the preceding code uses the String.TrimEnd method, which removes the slash if it is present.
- The ShowFilesIn and ShowDirectoriesIn subroutines loop through the file and directory collections to build the lists. Another approach is to use data binding instead. Just remember that when you bind a collection of objects, you need to specify which property will be used for the list. In this case, it is the DirectoryInfo.Name or FileInfo.Name property.

```
' Another way to fill lstFiles.
lstFiles.DataSource = DirInfo.GetFiles()
lstFiles.DataMember = "Name"
lstFiles.DataBind()
```



## Reading and Writing with Streams

The .NET framework makes it easy to create simple "flat" files in text or binary format. Unlike a database, these files don't have any internal structure (that's why they are called "flat"). Instead, these files are really just a list of whatever information you want—the programmer's equivalent to a large black sack.

### Text Files

You write to and read from a file using a stream writer and stream reader—special classes that abstract away the process of interacting with a file. There's really not much to it. You can create the classes on your own, or you can use one of the helpful shared methods included in the File class.

```
' Define a StreamWriter (which is designed for writing text files).
Dim w As StreamWriter

' Create the file, and get a StreamWriter for it.
w = File.CreateText("c:\myfile.txt")
```

Once you have the StreamWriter, you can use the WriteLine method to add information into the file. The WriteLine method is overloaded so that it can write many simple data types, including strings, integers, and other numbers. These values are essentially all converted into strings when they are written to a file, and must be converted back into the appropriate types manually when you read the file.

```
w.WriteLine("This file generated by ASP.NET")   ' Write a string.
w.WriteLine(42)                                  ' Write a number.
```

When you finish with the file, you must make sure to close it. Otherwise, the changes may not be properly written to disk, and the file could be locked open.

```
' Tidy up.
w.Close()
```

It's always a good idea to take a look at what you wrote in Notepad, while debugging an application that writes to files (see Figure 16-3).

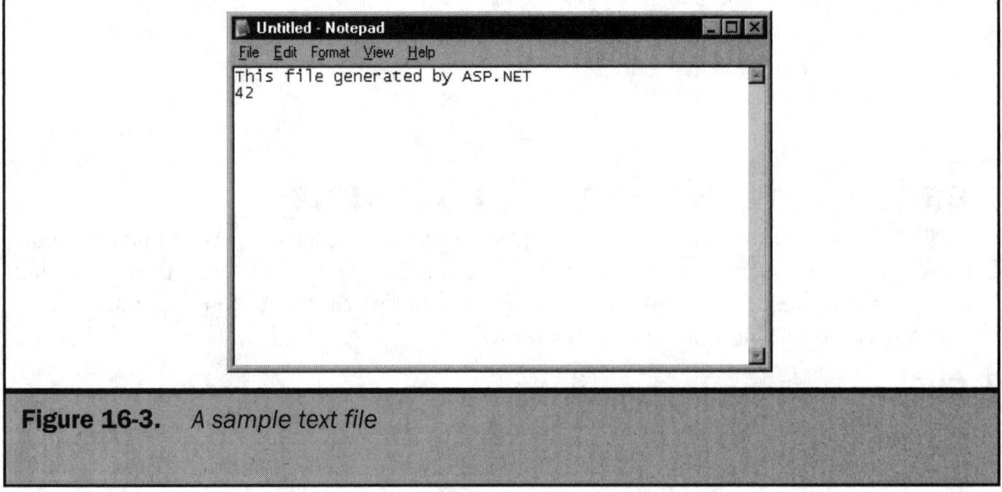


**Figure 16-3.** *A sample text file*

To read the information, you use the corresponding StreamReader class. It provides a ReadLine method that returns a string.

```
Dim r As StreamReader = File.OpenText("c:\myfile.txt")
Dim InputString As String
InputString = r.ReadLine()     ' = "This file generated by ASP.NET"
InputString = r.ReadLine()     ' = "42"
```

### You Can Also Create Text Cookies

In Chapter 10, you saw how you could create a cookie for the current user, which could be persisted to disk as a simple text file. This is probably a more common technique for a web application, but it is quite a bit different than the file access code we've looked at in this chapter. Cookies are created on the client side rather than on the server. That means your ASP.NET code may be able to use them on subsequent requests, but they aren't any use for tracking other information that you need to retain.

## Binary Files

You can also write to a binary file. Binary data uses space more efficiently, but also creates files that aren't as easy to read on your own. If you open a file in Notepad, you'll see a lot of extended ASCII characters (politely known as gibberish).

To open a file for binary writing, you need to create a new BinaryWriter class. The class constructor accepts a stream, which you can retrieve using the File.OpenWrite method.

```
Dim w As New BinaryWriter(File.OpenWrite("c:\binaryfile"))
```

.NET concentrates on streams, rather than the source or destination for the data. In other words, you can write to a binary file in almost the same way as you write to a text file, because you are still using streams. The only difference is the *backing store*—in this case, the format of the file.

```
Dim str As String = "ASP.NET Binary File Test"
Dim int As Integer = 42
w.Write(str)
w.Write(int)
```

Unfortunately, binary files require that you know the data type you want to retrieve. To retrieve a string, you use the ReadString method. To retrieve an integer, you must use ReadInt32. That's why the preceding code example writes variables instead of literal values. If the value 42 were hard-coded as the parameter for the Write method, it wouldn't be clear if the value would be written as a 16-bit integer, 32-bit integer, decimal, or something else. Unfortunately, you may need to micromanage binary files in this way to prevent errors.

```
Dim r As New BinaryReader(File.OpenRead("c:\binaryfile"))
Dim str As String
```

```
Dim int As Integer
w.ReadString(str)
w.ReatInt32(int)
```

### Non-Sequential Access

There's no easy way to jump to a location in a text or binary file without reading through all the information in order. While you can use methods like Seek on the underlying stream, you need to specify an offset in bytes, which involves some fairly involved calculations to determine variable sizes. If you need to store a large amount of information and move through it quickly, you need a dedicated database, not a binary file.

## A Simple Guest Book

The next example demonstrates the file access techniques described in the previous sections to create a simple guest book. The page actually has two parts. If there are no current guest entries, the client will only see the controls for adding a new entry (see Figure 16-4).

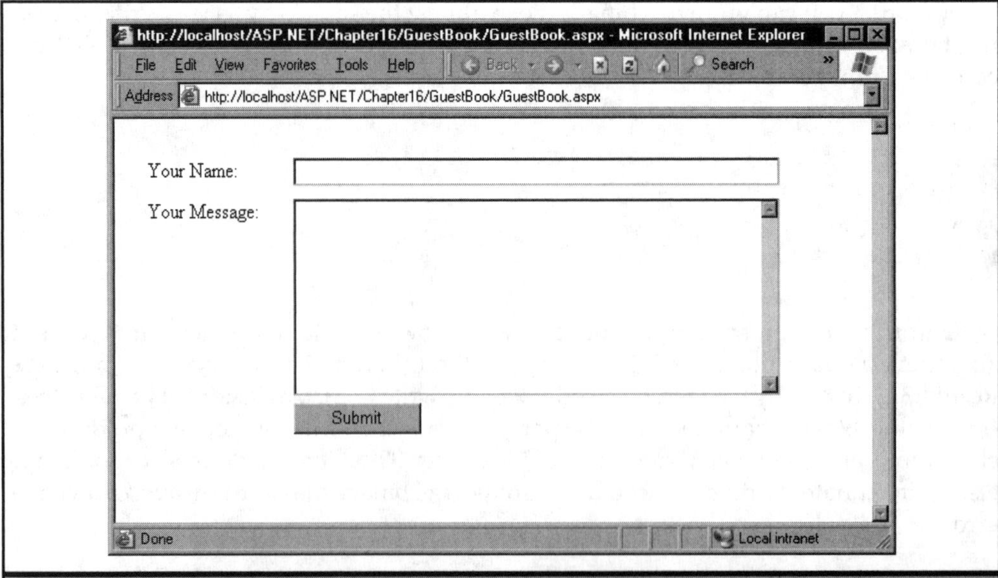


**Figure 16-4.** *The initial guest book page*

When the user clicks Submit, a file will be created for the new guest book entry. As long as there is at least one guest book entry, a DataList control will appear at the top of the page (see Figure 16-5).

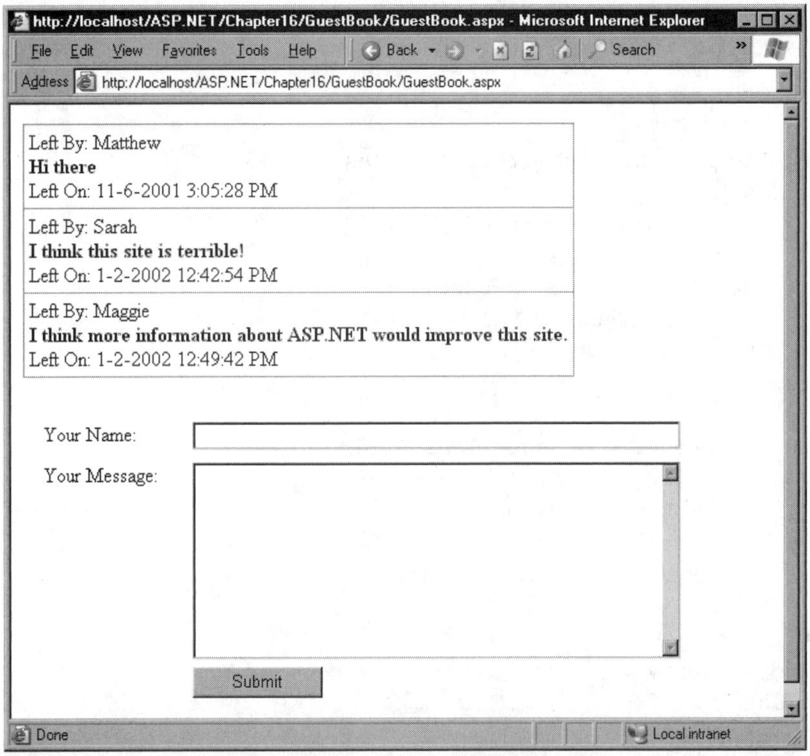

**Figure 16-5.** *The full guest book page*

The DataList that represents the guest book is constructed using data binding, which we explored in Chapters 14 and 15. Technically speaking, the DataList is bound to an ArrayList collection that contains instances of the BookEntry class. The class definition is included in our code-behind file, and looks like this:

```
Public Class BookEntry
    Public _Author As String
    Public _Submitted As Date
    Public _Message As String
```

```
    Public Property Author() As String
        Get
            Return _Author
        End Get
        Set(ByVal Value As String)
            _Author = Value
        End Set
    End Property

    Public Property Submitted() As Date
        Get
            Return _Submitted
        End Get
        Set(ByVal Value As Date)
            _Submitted = Value
        End Set
    End Property

    Public Property Message() As String
        Get
            Return _Message
        End Get
        Set(ByVal Value As String)
            _Message = Value
        End Set
    End Property
End Class
```

The DataList uses this item template to fish out the values it needs to display:

```
<ItemTemplate>
  Left By: <%# Databinder.Eval(Container.DataItem, "Author") %><br>
  <b><%# Databinder.Eval(Container.DataItem, "Message") %></b><br>
  Left On: <%# Databinder.Eval(Container.DataItem, "Submitted") %>
</ItemTemplate>
```

It also adds some style information that isn't included here, as it's not necessary to understand the logic of the program. In fact, these styles were applied using the DataList's Auto Format feature in Visual Studio .NET.

As for the entries, the guest book page uses a special directory (GuestBook) to store a collection of files. Each file represents a separate entry in the guest book. A better approach would usually be to create a GuestBook table in a database, and make each entry a separate record.

The code for the web page is shown here.

```
Imports System.IO

Public Class GuestBook
  Inherits Page

    Protected GuestBookList As DataList
    Protected WithEvents cmdSubmit As Button
    Protected txtMessage As TextBox
    Protected txtName As TextBox

    Private GuestBookName As String
    GuestBookName = "C:\ASP.NET\Chapter16\GuestBook\GuestBook"

    Private Sub Page_Load(sender As Object, e As EventArgs) _
      Handles MyBase.Load
        If Me.IsPostBack = False Then
            GuestBookList.DataSource = GetAllEntries()
            GuestBookList.DataBind()
        End If
    End Sub

    Private Sub cmdSubmit_Click(sender As Object, e As EventArgs) _
      Handles cmdSubmit.Click
        ' Create a new BookEntry object.
        Dim NewEntry As New BookEntry()
        NewEntry.Author = txtName.Text
        NewEntry.Submitted = DateTime.Now
        NewEntry.Message = txtMessage.Text

        ' Let the SaveEntry procedure create the corresponding file.
        SaveEntry(NewEntry)

        ' Refresh the display.
        GuestBookList.DataSource = GetAllEntries()
        GuestBookList.DataBind()

        txtName.Text = ""
        txtMessage.Text = ""
    End Sub

    Private Function GetAllEntries() As ArrayList
        ' Return an ArrayList that contains BookEntry objects
```

```
        ' for each file in the GuestBook directory.
        ' This function relies on the GetEntryFromFile function.
        Dim Entries As New ArrayList()
        Dim GuestBookDir As New DirectoryInfo(GuestBookName)

        Dim FileItem As FileInfo
        For Each FileItem In GuestBookDir.GetFiles()
            Entries.Add(GetEntryFromFile(FileItem))
        Next

        Return Entries
    End Function

    Private Function GetEntryFromFile(ByVal EntryFile As FileInfo) _
      As BookEntry
        ' Turn the file information into a Book Entry object.
        Dim NewEntry As New BookEntry()
        Dim r As StreamReader = EntryFile.OpenText()
        NewEntry.Author = r.ReadLine()
        NewEntry.Submitted = DateTime.Parse(r.ReadLine())
        NewEntry.Message = r.ReadLine()
        r.Close()

        Return NewEntry
    End Function

    Private Sub SaveEntry(ByVal Entry As BookEntry)
        ' Create a new file for this entry, with a filename that
        ' should be unique.
        Dim Rand As New Random()
        Dim FileName As String = GuestBookName & "\"
        FileName &= DateTime.Now.Ticks.ToString() & Rand.Next(100)
        Dim NewFile As New FileInfo(FileName)
        Dim w As StreamWriter = NewFile.CreateText()

        ' Write the information to the file.
        w.WriteLine(Entry.Author)
        w.WriteLine(Entry.Submitted.ToString())
        w.WriteLine(Entry.Message)
        w.Close()
    End Sub
End Class
```

### Interesting Facts About this Code

- The code uses text files so you can easily review the information on your own with Notepad. Binary files could be used just as easily and would save a small amount of space.
- The filename for each entry is generated using a combination of the current date and time (in ticks) and a random number. Practically speaking, this makes it impossible for a file to be generated with a duplicate filename.
- This program does not use any error handling, which is an obvious limitation. Whenever you try to access a file, you should use a Try/Catch block, as all kinds of unexpected events can occur and cause problems.
- Careful design makes sure that this program isolates file writing and reading code in separate functions, such as SaveEntry, GetAllEntries, and GetEntryFromFile. For even better organization, you could move these routines into a separate class or even a separate component. For more information, read Chapter 21.



## Allowing File Uploads

Although you've seen detailed examples about how to work with files and directories on the web server, we haven't considered the question of how to allow file uploads. The problem with file uploading is that you need some way to retrieve information from the client—and as you already know, all ASP.NET code executes on the server.

Fortunately, ASP.NET includes a special HTML server control that can help you with this task. It's called HtmlInputFile, and it represents the <input type="file"> HTML tag. While it doesn't give you much choice as far as user interface is concerned (it's limited to a text box that contains a filename and a Browse button), it does accomplish what you need.

To create a working file upload page, you need three ingredients:

- You must set the encoding type of the form to "multipart/form-data." You can do this by setting a property of the HtmlForm control class, or you can just find the tag in your .aspx file and modify it as shown next. If you don't make this change, your uploading code will not work.

```
<form id="Form1" enctype="multipart/form-date" runat="server">
  <!— Server controls go here, including the HtmlInput
      control. —>
</form>
```

- You need to add the HtmlInputFile control, either by hand as an <input type= "file" runat="server"> tag, or using Visual Studio .NET, in which case you must right-click on the HTML control and select Run As Server Control.

- You need to add a button that triggers the upload and saves the file to the server's hard drive. (The Browse button functionality is hard-wired into the browser.) You can use the HtmlInputFile.PostedFile.SaveAs method.

```
FileInput.PostedFile.SaveAs("c:\newfile")
```

Figure 16-6 shows a complete web page that demonstrates how to upload a user-specified file.

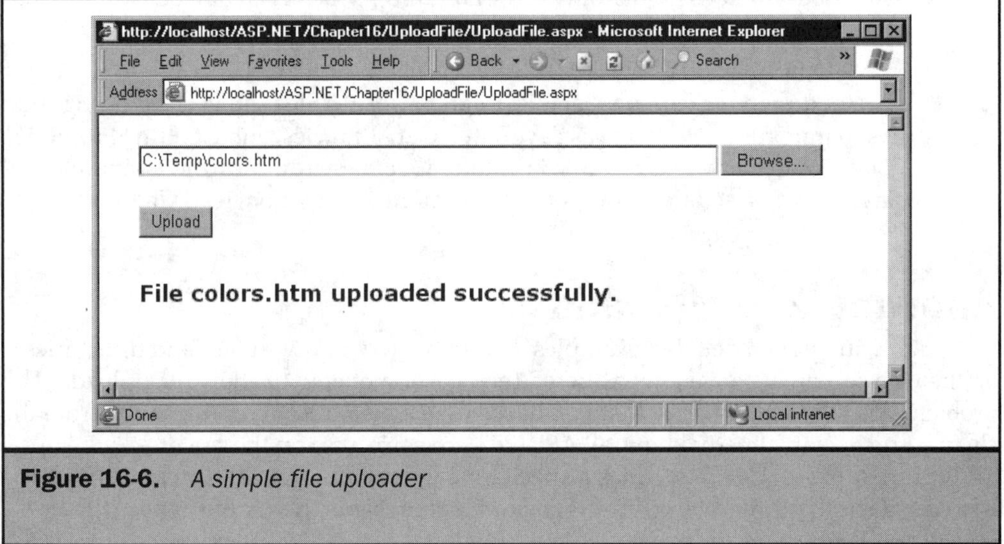


**Figure 16-6.** *A simple file uploader*

```
Imports System.IO

Public Class UploadFile
  Inherits Page
    Protected WithEvents cmdUpload As Button
    Protected lblInfo As Label
    Protected FileInput As HtmlInputFile

    Private Sub Page_Load(sender As Object, e As EventArgs) _
      Handles MyBase.Load
        ' Only accept image types.
        FileInput.Accept = "image/*"
    End Sub

    Private Sub cmdUpload_Click(sender As Object, e As EventArgs) _
```

```
        Handles cmdUpload.Click

        ' Check that a file is actually being submitted.
        If FileInput.PostedFile Is Nothing Then
            lblInfo.Text = "No file specified."
        Else
            Try
                ' The saved file will retain its original filename,
                ' but be stored in the current server application
                ' directory.
                Dim ServerFileName As String
                ServerFileName = Path.GetFileName _
                  (FileInput.PostedFile.FileName)
                FileInput.PostedFile.SaveAs("C:\Uploads\" & _
                                            ServerFileName)
                lblInfo.Text = "File " & ServerFileName
                lblInfo.Text &= " uploaded successfully."
            Catch err As Exception
                lblInfo.Text = err.Message
            End Try
        End If

    End Sub

End Class
```



## Interesting Facts About this Code

- The saved file keeps its original (client-side) name. The code uses the Path.GetFileName shared method, to transform the fully qualified name provided by FileInput.PostedFile.FileName and retrieve just the file, without the path.
- When using file uploading, you may need to make some configuration changes. Specifically, you should specify the maxRequestLength setting in the web.config to set the largest file size that can be transmitted. The following sample setting configures the server to accept the default of 4096 bytes and reject anything larger.

```
<?xml version="1.0" encoding="utf-8" ?>
<configuration>
  <system.web>
```

```
    <!-- Other settings omitted for clarity. -->
    <httpRuntime maxRequestLength="4096"
    />
  </system.web>
</configuration>
```

- The FileInput.PostedFile object only contains a few properties. One interesting property is ContentLength, which returns the size of the file in bytes. You could examine this setting and use it to prevent a user from uploading excessively large files.

## Sending Mail

I've saved the easiest for last. Sending mail in an ASP.NET application involves little more than creating a single object. Behind the scenes, these mailing features use the built-in SMTP service included with IIS. The technology is similar to the CDO component often used in traditional ASP development.

The first step when working with mail messages is to import the appropriate namespace.

```
Import System.Web.Mail
```

Next, you create a new MailMessage object, and set properties to identify the recipient, the priority, the subject, and the message itself. When entering the message, you can use standard HTML tags, provided you've set the BodyFormat property to MailFormat.Html.

```
Dim MyMessage As New MailMessage()
MyMessage.To = "someone@mycompany.com"
MyMessage.From = "ASP.NET Test Application"
MyMessage.Subject = "This is a test"
MyMessage.Priority = MailPriority.High
MyMessage.Body = "<b>Hello world (of e-mail).</b>"
```

To send the mail, you use the shared Send method of the SmtpMail class.

```
SmtpMail.Send(MyMessage)
```

Imagine the warm feeling you'll get when your application sends you its first email, as shown in Figure 16-7.

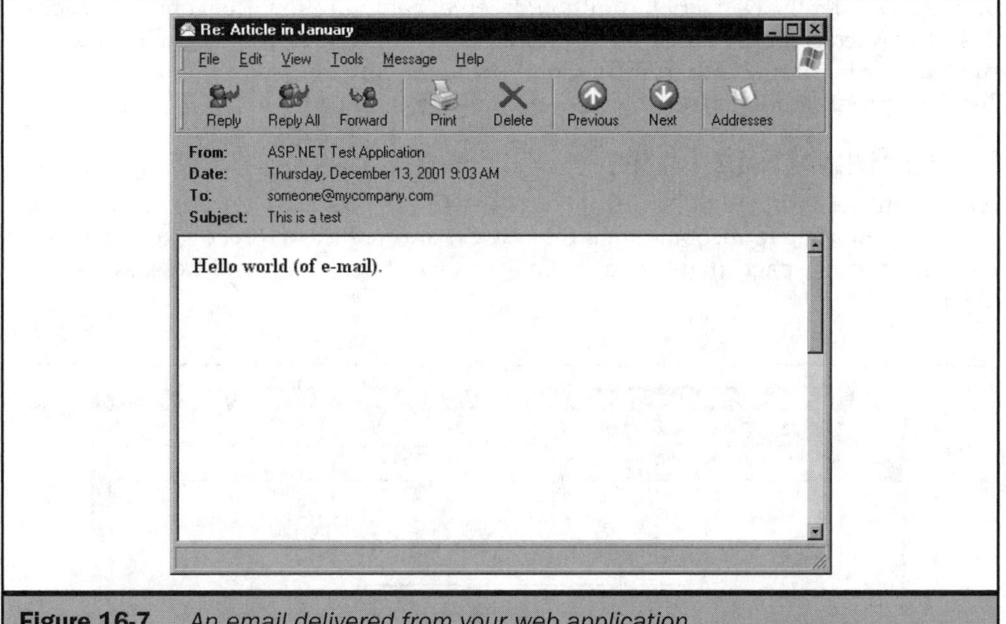


**Figure 16-7.** *An email delivered from your web application*



## Adding Attachments

You can add an attachment to an email message by creating a MailAttachment object. This class has two important properties: Encoding (which is set to MailEncoding.UUEncode by default), and Filename, which identifies a file on the server. You can set the Filename property in the MailAttachment constructor.

```
Dim MyAttachment As New MailAttachment("C:\Temp\SampleFile.rtf")
```

You then link the MailAttachment to a MailMessage using the Attachments collection.

```
MyMessage.Attachments.Add(MyAttachment)
```

The only catch is that in order to use this mail ability, you will need to have your SMTP server properly configured. To accomplish this, fire up IIS Manager again, and select Default SMTP Server under your computer name (or the name of the computer that is the SMTP server). Right-click, and select properties. The important configuration details are under the Delivery tab, although server configuration is beyond the scope of this book. Microsoft provides an excellent introduction to Internet email and mail servers (with a little bit of traditional ASP code thrown in) at http://www.microsoft.com/TechNet/prodtechnol/iis/deploy/config/mail.asp.

## An Issue Reporting Form

A common place where ASP.NET's mail features can be put to use is the common issue/comment reporting form. Sometimes these pages are connected directly to a database. In other cases, the page might send an email to a technical support address, as shown in Figure 16-8.

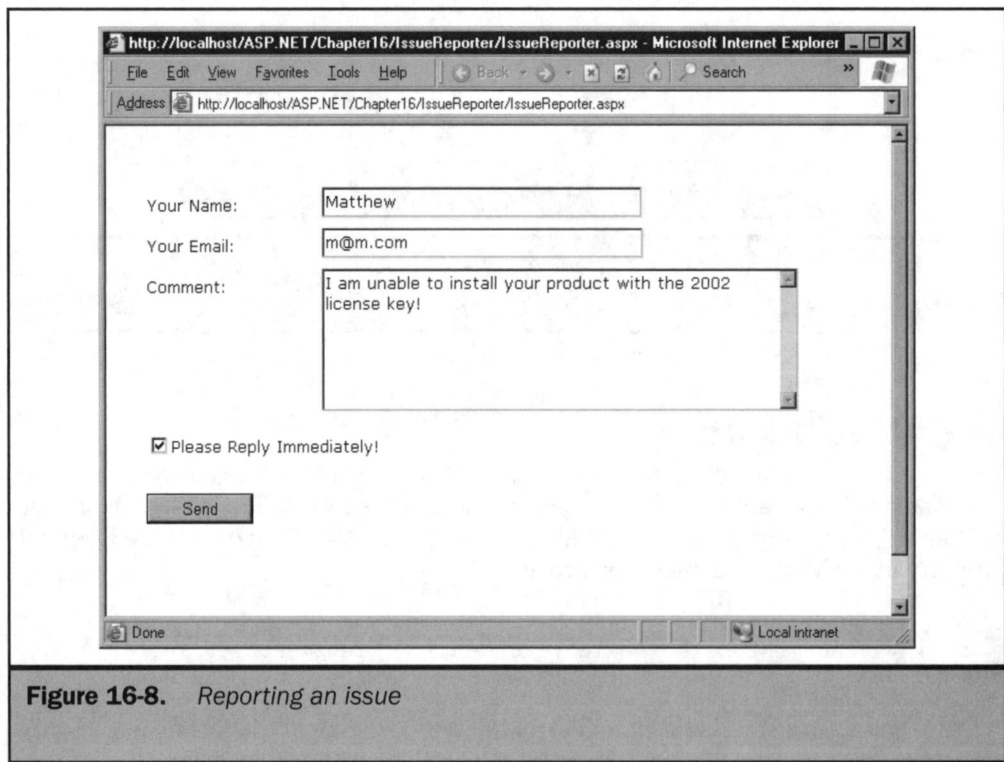


**Figure 16-8.** *Reporting an issue*

```
Imports System.Web.Mail
Public Class IssueReporter
  Inherits Page

    Protected chkPriority As CheckBox
    Protected txtName As TextBox
```

```
    Protected txtSender As TextBox
    Protected txtComment As TextBox
    Protected WithEvents cmdSend As Button
    Protected lblResult As Label

    Private Sub cmdSend_Click(sender As Object, e As EventArgs) _
      Handles cmdSend.Click
        ' Create the message.
        Dim Msg As New MailMessage()
        Msg.Subject = "Issue Report"
        Msg.Body = "Submitted By: " & txtName.Text & Chr(10)
        Msg.Body &= txtComment.Text
        Msg.From = txtSender.Text
        If chkPriority.Checked Then Msg.Priority = MailPriority.High

        ' Send the message.
        SmtpMail.Send(Msg)
    End Sub

End Class
```



## Email Can Be Used for Automatic Logging

In the previous example, you saw how a customer can fill out a form that triggers the sending of an email. Many sites take this idea a step further, and automatically report on problems with the web application by sending an email to an administrator's account. This is an extremely interesting technique, but requires a few considerations:

- Don't attach an automatic email feature to a non-critical error or a known issue that occurs occasionally. In these cases, it's better to log some sort of aggregate information to a database table that can be examined later, rather than clogging up an important email account.
- Will someone actually read the mail? If the messages aren't being checked, they do little good.
- In some cases, an error could occur with the email service, preventing this technique from working. In this case, an even simpler error logging method is better.

The Complete Reference

# Chapter 17

## Using XML

XML features are no longer an optional add-on for ASP applications. XML is woven right into the fabric of .NET, and it powers key parts of ASP.NET technology. In this chapter, you'll learn why XML plays in every ASP.NET web application—whether you realize it or not.

You'll also learn how you can create and read XML documents on your own, by using the classes of the .NET library. Along the way, we'll sort through some of the near-hysteric XML hype and consider what a web application can use XML for in *practical* terms. You may find that ASP.NET's low-level XML support is all you need, and decide that you don't want to manually create and manipulate XML data. On the other hand, you might want to use the XML classes to communicate with other applications or components, manage relational data, or just as a convenient replacement for simple text files. We'll assess all these issues realistically—which is a major departure from most of today's ASP.NET articles, seminars, and books. We'll also start with a whirlwind introduction to XML and why it exists, in case you aren't already familiar with its syntax.

## XML's Hidden Role in .NET

The most useful place for XML isn't in your web applications, but in the infrastructure that supports them. Microsoft has taken this philosophy to heart with ASP.NET. Instead of providing separate components that allow you to add in a basic XML parser or similar functionality, ASP.NET uses XML quietly behind the scenes to accomplish a wide range of different tasks. If you don't know much about XML yet, the most important thing you should realize is that you are already using it.

### ADO.NET Data Access

Although you interact with data using a combination of .NET objects and properties, the internal format these components use to store the data is actually XML. This has a number of interesting consequences. One change (which you won't see in this book) occurs with distributed programming, which uses multiple components on different computers that communicate over a network. With ADO, these components would exchange data in a proprietary binary format, which would have difficulty crossing firewall boundaries. With ADO.NET, these components exchange pure XML, which can flow over normal channels because it is text-based. This XML data exchange could even be extended to components on another operating system or in a non-Microsoft development language. All they need to do is be able to read XML.

As an ASP.NET developer, you are more likely to see some interesting but less useful features. For example, you can store the results of a database query in an XML file, and retrieve it later in the same page or in another application. You can also manipulate the information in a DataSet by changing an XML string. This technique, which is introduced at the end of the chapter, is not that useful in most scenarios because it effectively bypasses the basic DataSet features for error checking. However, the reverse—manipulating XML documents through ADO.NET objects—can be quite handy.

### Configuration Files

ASP.NET stores settings in a human-readable XML format using configuration files such as machine.config and web.config, which were first introduced in Chapter 5. Arguably, a plain text file could be just as efficient, but then the designers of the ASP.NET platform would have to create their own proprietary format, which developers would then need to learn. XML provides an all-purpose language that is designed to let programmers store data in a customized, yet very consistent and standardized way using tags. Anyone who understands XML will immediately understand how the ASP.NET configuration files work.

### Web Services

We haven't explored Web Services yet, but it's worth pointing out that they are one of ASP.NET's most important examples of integrated XML use. In order to create or use a Web Service in a .NET program, you don't actually have to understand anything about XML, because the framework handles all the details for you. However, because Web Services are built on these familiar standards, other programmers can develop clients for your Web Services in completely different programming languages, operating systems, and computer hardware platforms, with just a little more work. In fact, they can even use a competing toolkit to create a Web Service that you can consume in .NET! Cross-platform programming is clearly one of XML's key selling points.

### Anywhere Miscellaneous Data Is Stored

Just when you think you've identified everywhere that XML markup is used, you'll find it appearing in another new place. You'll find XML when you write an advertisement file defining the content for the AdRotator control, or if you use .NET serialization to write an object to a file. The developers of the .NET platform have embraced XML in unprecedented ways, partially abandoning Microsoft's traditional philosophy of closed standards and proprietary technologies.

## XML Explained

The basic premise of XML is fairly simple, although the possible implementations of it (and the numerous extensions to it) can get quite complex. XML is designed as an all-purpose format for encoding data. In almost every case, when you decide to use XML, you are deciding to store data in a standardized way, rather than creating your own new (and to other developers, unfamiliar) format. The actual location of this data—in memory, in a file, in a network stream—is irrelevant.

For example, consider a simple program that stores product items as a list in a file. When you first create this program, you decide that it will store three pieces of product information (ID, name, and price), and that you will use a simple text file format for easy debugging and testing. The file format you use looks like this:

```
1
Chair
49.33
2
Car
43399.55
3
Fresh Fruit Basket
49.99
```

This is the sort of format that you might create by using .NET classes like the StreamWriter. It's easy to work with—you just write all the information, in order, from top to bottom. Of course, it's a fairly fragile format. If you decide to store an extra piece of information in the file (such as a flag that indicates if an item is available), your old code won't work. Instead you might need to resort to adding a header that indicates the version of the file.

```
SuperProProductList
Version 2.0
1
Chair
49.33
True
2
Car
43399.55
True
3
Fresh Fruit Basket
49.99
False
```

Now, you could check the file version when you open it and use different file reading code appropriately. Unfortunately, as you add more and more possible versions, this code will become incredibly tangled, and you may accidentally break one of the earlier file formats without realizing it. A better approach would be to create a file format that indicates where every product record starts and stops. Your code would then just set some appropriate defaults if it encounters missing information in an older file format.

```
SuperProProductList
Version 3.0
##Start##
1
Chair
49.33
True
3
##Start##
2
Car
43399.55
True
3
##Start##
3
Fresh Fruit Basket
49.99
False
4
```



All in all, this isn't a bad effort. Unfortunately, you may as well use the binary file format at this point—the text file is becoming hard to read, and it's even harder to guess what piece of information each value represents. On the code side, you'll also need some basic error-checking abilities of your own. For example, you should make your code able to skip over accidentally entered blank lines, detect a missing ##Start## tag, and so on, just to provide a basic level of protection.

The central problem with this homegrown solution is that you're reinventing the wheel. While you are trying to write basic file access code and create a reasonably flexible file format for a simple task, other programmers around the world are creating their own private, ad hoc solutions. Even if your program works fine and you can understand it, other programmers will definitely not find it as easy.

## Improving the List with XML

This is where XML comes into the picture. XML is an all-purpose way to identify data using tags. These tags use the same sort of format found in an HTML file, but while

HTML tags indicate formatting, XML tags indicate content. (Because an XML file is just about data, there is no standardized way to display it in a browser.)

The SuperProProductList could use the following, clearer XML syntax:

```
<?xml version="1.0"?>
<SuperProProducList>
    <Product>
        <ID>1</ID>
        <Name>Chair</Name>
        <Price>49.33</Price>
        <Available>True</Available>
        <Status>3</Status>
    </Product>
    <Product>
        <ID>2</ID>
        <Name>Car</Name>
        <Price>43399.55</Price>
        <Available>True</Available>
        <Status>3</Status>
    </Product>
    <Product>
        <ID>3</ID>
        <Name>Fresh Fruit Basket</Name>
        <Price>49.99</Price>
        <Available>False</Available>
        <Status>4</Status>
    </Product>
</SuperProProductList>
```

This format is clearly readable. Every product item is enclosed in a <Product> tag, and every piece of information has its own tag with an appropriate name. Tags are nested several layers deep to show relationships. Essentially, XML provides the basic tag syntax, and you (the programmer) define the tags that you want to use.

Best of all, when you read this XML document in most programming languages (including those in the .NET framework), you can use XML parsers to make your life easier. In other words, you don't need to worry about detecting where a tag starts and stops, collapsing whitespace, and identifying attributes (although you do need to worry about case, as XML is case-sensitive). Instead, you can just read the file into some helpful XML data objects that make navigating through the entire document much easier.

### XML versus Databases

XML can do an incredible number of things—perhaps including some that it was never designed for. This book is not intended to teach you XML programming, but good ASP.NET application design. For most ASP.NET programmers, XML is an ideal replacement for custom file access routines, and works best in situations where you need to store a small amount of data for relatively simple tasks.

XML files are not a good substitution for a database, because they have the same limitations as any other type of file access. Database products provide a far richer set of features for managing multi-user concurrency and providing optimized performance. XML documents also can't enforce table relations or provide the same level of error checking.

## XML Basics

Part of XML's popularity is the result of its simplicity. When creating your own XML document, there are only a few rules you need to remember. The following two considerations apply to XML and HTML markup:

- Whitespace is automatically collapsed, so you can freely use tabs and hard returns to properly align your information. To add a real space, you need to use the   entity equivalent, as in HTML.
- You can only use valid characters. Special characters, such as the angle brackets (< >) and the ampersand (&), can't be entered as content. Instead, you'll have to use the entity equivalents (such as < and > for angle brackets, and & for the ampersand). These equivalents are the same as in HTML coding, and will be automatically converted back to the original characters when you read them into your program with the appropriate .NET classes.

In addition, XML imposes rules that are not found in ordinary HTML:

- XML tags are case-sensitive, so <ID> and <id> are completely different tags.
- Every start tag must have an end tag, or you must use the special "empty tag" format, which includes a forward slash at the end. For example, you can use <Name>Content</Name> or <Name />, but you cannot use <Name> on its own. This is similar to the syntax for ASP.NET controls.
- All tags must be nested in a root tag. In the SuperProProductList example, the root tag is <SuperProProductList>. As soon as the root tag is closed, the document is finished, and you cannot add any more content. In other words, if you omit the <SuperProProductList> tag and start with a <Product> tag, you will only be able to enter information for one product, because as soon as you add the closing </Product> the document is complete.

- Every tag must be fully enclosed. In other words, when you open a subtag, you need to close it before you can close the parent. <Product><ID></ID> </Product> is valid, but <Product><ID></Product></ID> is not. As a general rule, indent when you open a new tag, as this will allow you to see the document's structure and notice if you accidentally close the wrong tag first.

If you meet these requirements, your XML document can be parsed and displayed as a basic tree. This means that your document is *well formed*, but it does not mean that it is valid. For example, you may still have your elements in the wrong order (for example, <ID><Product></Product></ID>), or you may have the wrong type of data in a given field (for example, <ID>Chair</ID><Name>2</Name). There are ways to impose these additional rules on your XML documents, as you'll see shortly.

XML tags are also known as elements. These elements are the primary units for organizing information, but they aren't the only option. You can also use attributes.

## Attributes

Attributes are used to add extra information to an element. Instead of putting information into a subtag, you can use an attribute. In the XML community, deciding whether to use subtags or attributes—and what information should go into an attribute—is a matter of great debate, with no clear consensus.

Here's the SuperProProductList example with an ID and Name attribute instead of an ID and Name subtag:

```
<?xml version="1.0"?>
<SuperProProducList>
    <Product ID="1" Name="Chair">
        <Price>49.33</Price>
        <Available>True</Available>
        <Status>3</Status>
    </Product>
    <Product ID="2" Name="Car">
        <Price>43399.55</Price>
        <Available>True</Available>
        <Status>3</Status>
    </Product>
    <Product ID="3" Name="Fresh Fruit Basket">
        <Price>49.99</Price>
        <Available>False</Available>
        <Status>4</Status>
    </Product>
</SuperProProductList>
```

Of course, you've already seen this sort of syntax with HTML tags and ASP.NET server controls.

```
<asp:DropDownList id="lstBackColor" AutoPostBack="True"
                  runat="server"
                  Width="194px"
                  Height="22px"/>
```

Attributes are also common in the configuration file.

```
<sessionState mode="Inproc "
              cookieless="false"
              timeout="20" />
```

Note that the use of attributes in XML is more stringent than in HTML. In XML, Attributes must always have values, and these values must use quotation marks. For example, <Product Name="Chair" /> is acceptable, but <Product Name=Chair /> or <Product Name /> is not. (ASP.NET control tags do not always follow these rules.)

## Comments

You can also add comments to an XML document. Comments go anywhere and are ignored for data processing purposes. Comments are bracketed by the <!— and —> codes.

```
<?xml version="1.0"?>
<SuperProProducList>
<!-- This is a test file. -->
    <Product ID="1" Name="Chair">
        <Price>49.33<!-- Why so expensive? --></Price>
        <Available>True</Available>
        <Status>3</Status>
    </Product>
    <!-- Other products omitted for clarity. -->
</SuperProProductList>
```

# The XML Classes

.NET provides a rich set of classes for XML manipulation in several namespaces. One of the most confusing aspects of using XML with .NET is deciding which combination of classes you should use. Many of them provide similar functionality in a slightly different way, optimized for specific scenarios or for compatibility with specific standards.

The majority of the examples we'll explore use the types in this namespace, which allow you to read and write XML files, manipulate XML data in special objects, and even validate XML documents. We'll consider several options for dealing with XML data:

- Dealing with XML as a special type of text file, using XmlTextWriter and XmlTextReader.
- Dealing with XML as a collection of in-memory objects, such as XmlDocument and XmlNode.
- Dealing with XML as a special interface to relational data, using the XmlDataDocument class.

## The XML TextWriter

One of the simplest ways to create or read any XML document is to use the basic XmlTextWriter and XmlTextReader classes. These classes work like their StreamWriter and StreamReader relatives, except for the fact that they write and read XML documents instead of ordinary text files. That means that you follow the same process that you saw in Chapter 16 for creating a file. First, you create or open the file. Then you write to it or read from it, moving from top to bottom. Finally, you close it, and get to work using the retrieved data in whatever way you'd like.

Before beginning this example, you'll need to import the namespaces for file handling and XML.

```
Imports System.IO
Imports System.Xml
```

Here's an example that creates a simple version of the SuperProProductList document.

```
Dim fs As New FileStream("c:\SuperProProductList.xml", _
                         FileMode.Create)
Dim w As New XmlTextWriter(fs, Nothing)

w.WriteStartDocument()
w.WriteStartElement("SuperProProducList")
w.WriteComment("This file generated by the XmlTextWriter class.")

' Write the first product.
w.WriteStartElement("Product")
w.WriteAttributeString("ID", "", "1")
w.WriteAttributeString("Name", "", "Chair")

w.WriteStartElement("Price")
w.WriteString("49.33")
```

```
w.WriteEndElement()

w.WriteEndElement()

' Write the second product.
w.WriteStartElement("Product")
w.WriteAttributeString("ID", "", "2")
w.WriteAttributeString("Name", "", "Car")

w.WriteStartElement("Price")
w.WriteString("43399.55")
w.WriteEndElement()

w.WriteEndElement()

' Write the third product.
w.WriteStartElement("Product")
w.WriteAttributeString("ID", "", "3")
w.WriteAttributeString("Name", "", "Fresh Fruit Basket")

w.WriteStartElement("Price")
w.WriteString("49.99")
w.WriteEndElement()

w.WriteEndElement()

' Close the root element.
w.WriteEndElement()
w.WriteEndDocument()
w.Close()
```



## Formatting Your XML

By default, the XmlTextWriter will create an XML file that has all its tags lumped together in a single line without any helpful carriage returns or indentation. Although additional formatting isn't required, it can make a significant difference if you want to read your XML files in Notepad or another text editor. Fortunately, the XmlTextWriter supports formatting; you just need to enable it, as follows:

```
' Set it to indent output.
w.Formatting = Formatting.Indented

' Set the number of indent spaces.
w.Indentation = 5
```

The code on the previous page is similar to the code used for writing a basic text file. It does have a few advantages, however. You can close elements quickly and accurately, the angle brackets (< >) are included for you automatically, and some errors (such as closing the root element too soon) are caught automatically, ensuring a well-formed XML document as the final result.

To check that your code worked, open the file in Internet Explorer, which automatically provides a collapsible view for XML documents (see Figure 17-1).

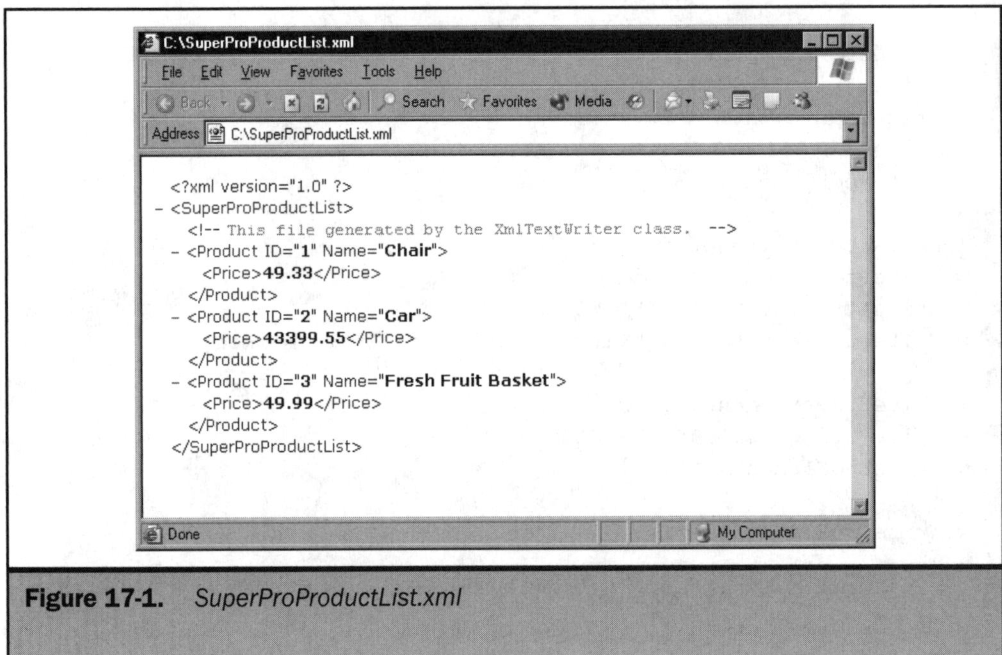


**Figure 17-1.** *SuperProProductList.xml*

# The XML Text Reader

Reading the XML document in your code is just as easy with the corresponding XmlTextReader class. The XmlTextReader moves through your document from top to bottom, one node at a time. You call the XmlTextReader.Read method to move to the next node. This method returns True if there are more nodes to read, or False once it has read the final node. The current node is provided through the properties of the XmlTextReader class, like NodeType and Name.

A *node* is a designation that includes comments, whitespace, opening tags, closing tags, content, and even the XML declaration at the top of your file. To get a quick understanding of nodes, you can use the XmlTextReader to run through your entire document from start to finish, and display every node it encounters. The code for this task is shown next.

```
Dim fs As New FileStream("c:\SuperProProductList.xml", FileMode.Open)
Dim r As New XmlTextReader(fs)

' Parse the file and read each node.
Do While r.Read()
    lblStatus.Text &= "<b>Type:</b> " & r.NodeType.ToString & "<br>"

    If r.Name <> "" Then
        lblStatus.Text &= "<b>Name:</b> " & r.Name & "<br>"
    End If

    If r.Value <> "" Then
        lblStatus.Text &= "<b>Value:</b> " & r.Value & "<br>"
    End If

    If r.AttributeCount > 0 Then
        lblStatus.Text &= "<b>Attributes:</b> "
        Dim i As Integer
        For i = 0 To r.AttributeCount() - 1
            lblStatus.Text &= "  " & r.GetAttribute(i) & " "
        Next
        lblStatus.Text &= "<br>"
    End If

    lblStatus.Text &= "<br>"
Loop
```



To test this out, try the XmlText.aspx page included with the online samples (as shown in Figure 17-2). The following is a list of all the nodes that are found, shortened to include only one product:

```
Type: XmlDeclaration
Name: xml
Value: version="1.0"
Attributes: 1.0

Type: Element
Name: SuperProProductList

Type: Comment
Value: This file generated by the XmlTextWriter class.

Type: Element
```

```
Name: Product
Attributes: 1, Chair

Type: Element
Name: Price

Type: Text
Value: 49.33

Type: EndElement
Name: Price

Type: EndElement
Name: Product

Type: EndElement
Name: SuperProProductList
```

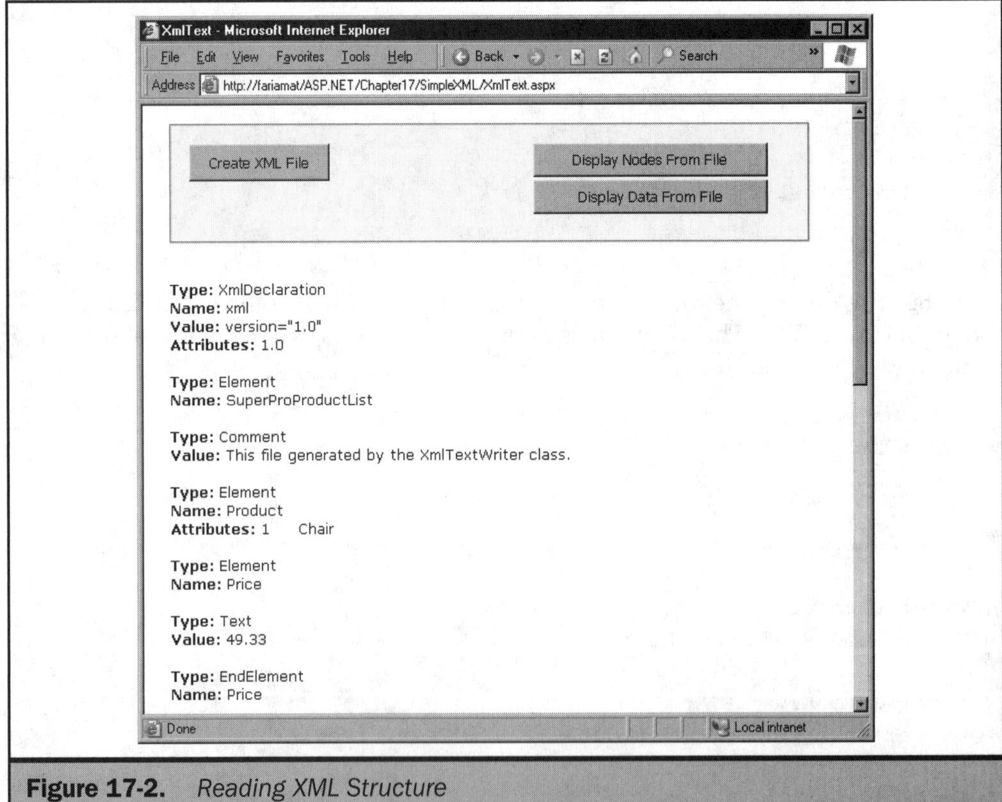


**Figure 17-2.** *Reading XML Structure*

In a typical application, you would need to go "fishing" for the elements that interest you. For example, you might read information from an XML file such as SuperProPriceList.xml and use it to create Product objects, based on the Product class shown here:

```
Public Class Product
    Private _ID As Integer
    Private _Name As String
    Private _Price As Decimal

    Public Property ID() As Integer
        Get
            Return _ID
        End Get
        Set(ByVal Value As Integer)
            _ID = Value
        End Set
    End Property

    Public Property Name() As String
        Get
            Return _Name
        End Get
        Set(ByVal Value As String)
            _Name = Value
        End Set
    End Property

    Public Property Price() As Decimal
        Get
            Return _Price
        End Get
        Set(ByVal Value As Decimal)
            _Price = Value
        End Set
    End Property

End Class
```

There's nothing particularly special about this class—all it does is allow you to store three related pieces of information (a price, name, and ID). Note that this class uses property procedures and so is eligible for data binding.

A typical application might read data out of an XML file and place it directly into the corresponding objects. The next example (also a part of the XmlText.aspx page) shows how you can easily create a group of Product objects based on the SuperProProductList.xml file.

```
' Open a stream to the file.
Dim fs As New FileStream("c:\SuperProProductList.xml", FileMode.Open)
Dim r As New XmlTextReader(fs)

Dim Products As New ArrayList()

' Loop through the products.
Do While r.Read()

    If r.NodeType = XmlNodeType.Element And r.Name = "Product" Then
        Dim NewProduct As New Product()
        NewProduct.ID = Val(r.GetAttribute(0))
        NewProduct.Name = r.GetAttribute(1)

        ' Get the rest of the subtags for this product.
        Do Until r.NodeType = XmlNodeType.EndElement
            r.Read()

            ' Look for Price subtags.
            If r.Name = "Price" Then
                Do Until (r.NodeType = XmlNodeType.EndElement)
                    r.Read()
                    If r.NodeType = XmlNodeType.Text Then
                        NewProduct.Price = Val(r.Value)
                    End If
                Loop
            End If

            ' We could check for other Product nodes
            ' (like Available, Status, etc.) here.
        Loop

        ' Add the product to the list.
        Products.Add(NewProduct)
    End If
Loop

r.Close()

' Display the retrieved document.
```

```
dgResults.DataSource = Products
dgResults.DataBind()
```

## Interesting Facts About this Code

- This code uses a nested looping structure. The outside loop iterates over all the products, and the inner loop searches through all the product tags (in this case, there is only a possible Price tag). This keeps the code well organized. The EndElement node alerts us when a node is complete and the loop can end. Once all the information is read for a product, the corresponding object is added into the ArrayList collection.
- All the information is retrieved from the XML file as a string. Thus, the Val function is used to extract numbers, although there are other possibilities.
- Data binding is used to display the contents of the collection. A DataGrid set to generate columns automatically creates the table shown in Figure 17-3.



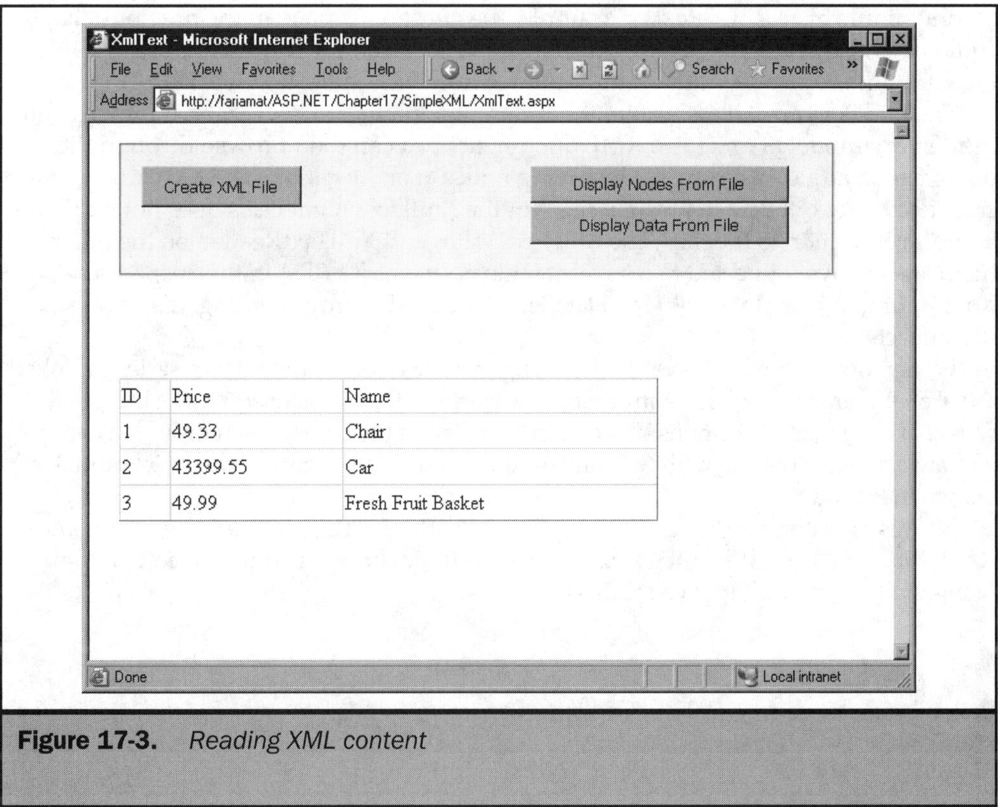


**Figure 17-3.** *Reading XML content*

### Other XmlTextReader Properties

The XmlTextReader provides many more properties and methods. These additional members don't add new functionality, they allow for increased flexibility. For example, you can read a portion of an XML document into a string using methods such as ReadString, ReadInnerXml, and ReadOuterXml. These members are all documented in the MSDN class library reference. Generally, the most straightforward approach is just to work your way through the nodes as shown in the SuperProProductList example.

## Working with XML Documents

The XmlTextReader and XmlTextWriter use XML as a backing store. They are streamlined for getting data into and out of a file quickly. You won't actually work with the XML data in your program. Instead, you open the file, use the data to create the appropriate objects or fill the appropriate controls, and close it soon after. This approach is ideal for storing simple blocks of data. For example, the guest book page in the previous chapter could be slightly modified to store data in an XML format, which would provide greater standardization, but wouldn't change how the application works.

The XmlDocument class provides a different approach to XML data. It provides an in-memory model of an entire XML document. You can then browse through the document, reading, inserting, or removing nodes at any location. The XML document can be saved to or retrieved from a file, but the XmlDocument class does not maintain a direct connection to the file. (The XmlTextWriter and XmlTextReader, on the other hand, are always connected to a stream, which is usually a file.) In this respect, the XmlDocument is analogous to the DataSet in ADO.NET programming: it's always disconnected.

When you use the XmlDocument class, your XML file is created as a series of linked .NET objects in memory. It's similar to the object relationships used with ADO.NET, where every DataSet contains more than one DataTable object, each of which can contain DataRow objects with the information for a single record. The object model is shown in Figure 17-4.

Next is an example that creates the SuperProProductList in memory, using an XmlDocument class. When it's finished, the XML document is transferred to a file using the XmlDocument.Save method.

```
' Start with a blank in memory document.
Dim doc As New XmlDocument()
```

```
' Create some variables that will be useful for
' manipulating XML data.
Dim RootElement, ProductElement, PriceElement As XmlElement
Dim ProductAttribute As XmlAttribute
Dim Comment As XmlComment

' Create the declaration.
Dim Declaration As XmlDeclaration
Declaration = doc.CreateXmlDeclaration("1.0", Nothing, "yes")

' Insert the declaration as the first node.
doc.InsertBefore(Declaration, doc.DocumentElement)

' Add a comment.
Comment = doc.CreateComment("Created with the XmlDocument class.")
doc.InsertAfter(Comment, Declaration)

' Add the root node.
RootElement = doc.CreateElement("SuperProProductList")
doc.InsertAfter(RootElement, Comment)

' Add the first product.
ProductElement = doc.CreateElement("Product")
RootElement.AppendChild(ProductElement)

' Set and add the product attributes.
ProductAttribute = doc.CreateAttribute("ID")
ProductAttribute.Value = "1"
ProductElement.SetAttributeNode(ProductAttribute)
ProductAttribute = doc.CreateAttribute("Name")
ProductAttribute.Value = "Chair"
ProductElement.SetAttributeNode(ProductAttribute)

' Add the price node.
PriceElement = doc.CreateElement("Price")
PriceElement.InnerText = "49.33"
ProductElement.AppendChild(PriceElement)

' (Code to add two more products omitted.)

' Save the document.
doc.Save("c:\SuperProProductList.xml")
```

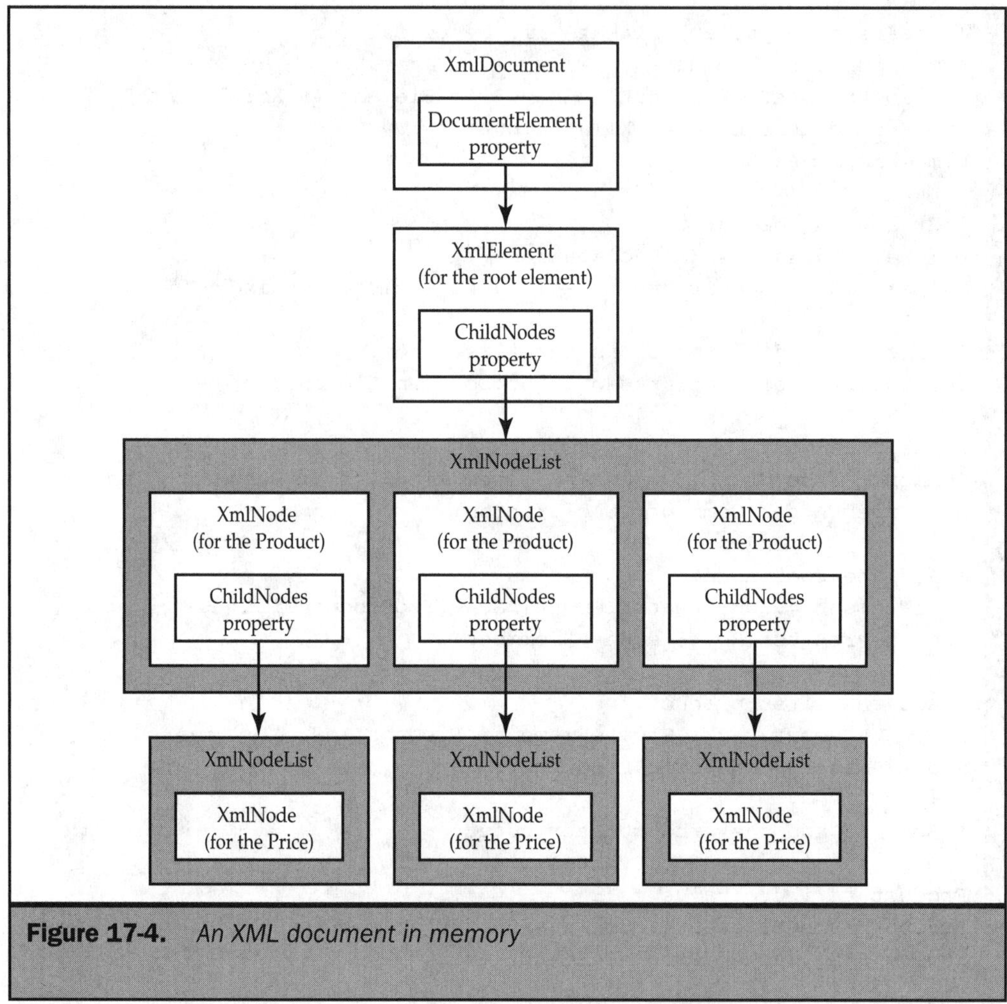


**Figure 17-4.** *An XML document in memory*

One of the best features of the XmlDocument class is that it does not rely on any underlying file. When you use the Save method, the file is created, a stream is opened, the information is written, and the file is closed, all in one line of code. That means that this is probably the only line that you need to put inside a Try/Catch error-handling block.

While you are manipulating data with the XML objects, your text file is not being changed. Once again, this is conceptually similar to the ADO.NET DataSet.

## Interesting Facts About this Code

- Every separate part of the XML document is created as an object. Elements (tags) are created as XmlElement objects, comments are created as XmlComment objects, and attributes are represented as XmlAttribute objects.
- To create a new element, comment, or attribute for your XML document, you need to use one of the XmlDocument class methods, such as CreateComment, CreateAttribute, or CreateElement. This ensures that the XML is generated correctly for your document, but it does not actually place any information into the XmlDocument.
- Once you have created the object and entered any additional inner information, you need to add it to your document. You can do so using methods such as InsertBefore or InsertAfter (from the XmlDocument object) to place your root node. To add a child element (such as the Product element inside the SuperProProductList element), you need to find the appropriate parent object and use its AppendChild method. In other words, you need to keep track of some object references; you can't write a child element directly to the document in the same way that you could with the XmlTextWriter.
- You can insert nodes anywhere. While the XmlTextWriter and XmlTextReader forced you to read every node, from start to finish, the XmlDocument is a much more flexible collection of objects.
- The file written by this code is shown in Figure 17-5 (as displayed by Internet Explorer).



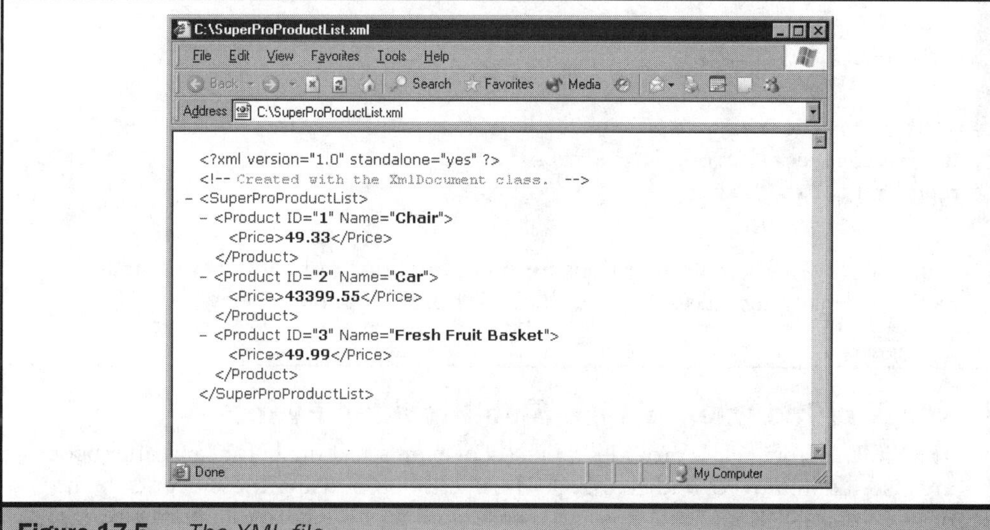


**Figure 17-5.** *The XML file*

## Reading an XML Document

To read information from your XML file, all you need to do is create an XmlDocument object and use its Load method. Depending on your needs, you may want to keep the data in its XML form, or you can extract by looping through the collection of linked XmlNode objects. This process is similar to the XmlTextReader example, but the code is noticeably cleaner.

```
' Create the document.
Dim doc As New XmlDataDocument()
doc.Load("c:\SuperProProductList.xml")

' Loop through all the nodes, and create the ArrayList..
Dim Element As XmlElement
Dim Products As New ArrayList()

For Each Element In doc.DocumentElement.ChildNodes
    Dim NewProduct As New Product()
    NewProduct.ID = Element.GetAttribute("ID")
    NewProduct.Name = Element.GetAttribute("Name")

    ' If there were more than one child node, you would probably use
    ' another For Each loop here, and move through the
    ' Element.ChildNodes collection.
    NewProduct.Price() = Element.ChildNodes(0).InnerText()

    Products.Add(NewProduct)
Next

' Display the results.
dgResults.DataSource = Products
dgResults.DataBind()
```

You have a variety of other options for manipulating your XmlDocument and extracting or changing pieces of data. Table 17-1 provides an overview.

### The XmlDocument Class Also Provides Events

The XmlDocument class provides a rich set of events that fire before and after nodes are inserted, removed, and changed. The likelihood of using these events in an ordinary ASP.NET application is fairly slim, but it represents an interesting example of the features .NET puts at your fingertips.

## The Difference Between XmlNode and XmlElement

You may have noticed that the XmlDocument is created with specific objects like XmlComment and XmlElement, but read back as a collection of XmlNode objects. The reason is that XmlComment and XmlElement are customized classes that inherit their basic functionality from XmlNode.

The ChildNodes collection allows you to retrieve all the content contained inside any portion of an XML document. Because this content could include comments, elements, and any other types of node, the ChildNodes collection uses the lowest common denominator. Thus, it provides child nodes as a collection of standard XmlNode objects. Each XmlNode has basic properties similar to what you saw with the XmlTextReader, including NodeType, Name, Value, and Attributes. You'll find that you can do all of your XML processing with XmlNode objects.

| Technique | Description |
| --- | --- |
| Finding a node's relative | Every XmlNode leads to other XmlNode objects. You can use properties such as FirstChild, LastChild, PreviousSibling, NextSibling, and ParentNode to return a reference to a related node.<br><br>An example is ParentNode = MyNode.ParentNode. |
| Cloning a portion of an XmlDocument | You can use the CloneNode method with any XmlNode to create a duplicate copy. You need to specify True or False to indicate whether you want to clone all children (True) or just the single node (False).<br><br>An example is NewNode = MyNode.Clone(True). |
| Removing or adding nodes | Find the parent node, and then use one of its node adding methods. You can use AppendChild (adds the child to the end of the child list) and PrependChild (to add the node to the start of the child list). You can also remove nodes with RemoveChild, ReplaceChild, and RemoveAll (deletes all children and all attributes for the current node).<br><br>An example is MyNode.RemoveChild(NodeToDelete). |

**Table 17-1.** *XmlNode Manipulation*

| Technique | Description |
|---|---|
| Adding inner content | Find the node, and add a NodeType.Text child node. One possible shortcut is just to set the InnerText property of your node, but that will erase any existing child nodes. |
| Manipulating attributes | Every node provides an XmlAttributeCollection of all its attributes through the XmlNode.Attributes property. To add an attribute, you must create an XmlAttribute object, and use methods such as Append, Prepend, InsertBefore, or InsertAfter. To remove an attribute, you can use Remove and RemoveAll.<br>An example is MyNode.Attributes.Remove (AttributeToDelete). |
| Working with content as string data | You can retrieve or set the content inside a node using properties such as InnerText, InnerXml, and OuterXml. Be warned that the inner content of a node includes all child nodes. Thus, setting this property carelessly could wipe out other information, like subtags. |

**Table 17-1.** *XmlNode Manipulation (continued)*

## Searching an XML Document

One of the pleasures of the XmlDocument is its support of searching, which allows you to find nodes when you know they are there—somewhere—but you aren't sure how many matches there are or where the element is.

To search an XmlDocument, all you need to do is use the GetElementById or GetElementsByTagName method. The following code example puts the GetElementsByTagName method to work, and creates the output shown in Figure 17-6.

```
Dim doc As New XmlDataDocument()
doc.Load("c:\SuperProProductList.xml")
Dim Results As XmlNodeList
Dim Result As XmlNode
```

```
' Find the matches.
 Results = doc.GetElementsByTagName("Price")

' Display the results.
lblStatus.Text = "<b>Found " & Results.Count.ToString() & " Matches "
lblStatus.Text &= " for the Price tag: </b><br><br>"
For Each Result In Results
    lblStatus.Text &= Result.FirstChild.Value & "<br>"
Next
```

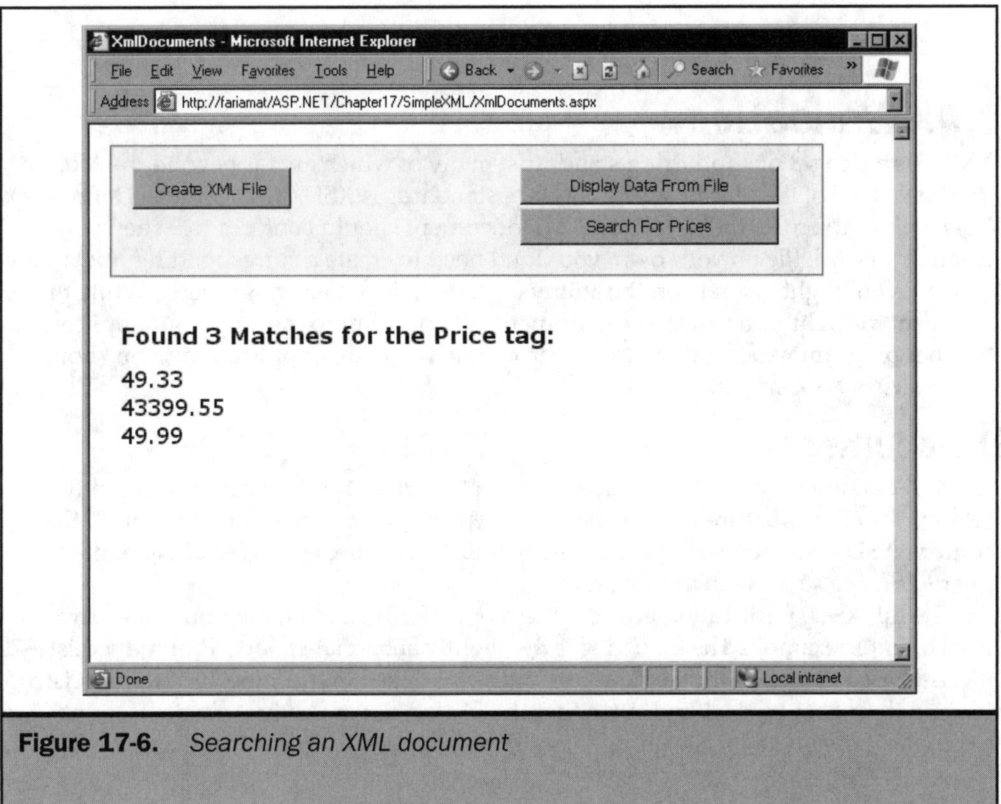


**Figure 17-6.** *Searching an XML document*

This technique works well if you want to find an element based on its name. If you want to use more sophisticated searching, match only part of a name, or examine only part of a document, you'll have to fall back on the traditional standard: looping through all the nodes in the XmlDocument.

### You Can Also Use XPath Classes

The search method provided by the XmlDocument class is relatively primitive. For a more advanced tool, you might want to learn the XPath language, which is a W3C recommendation (defined at http://www.w3.org/TR/xpath/) designed for performing queries on XML data. .NET provides XPath support through the classes in the System.Xml.XPath namespace, which include an XPath parser and evaluation engine. Of course, these aren't much use unless you learn the syntax of the XPath language itself.

# XML Validation

XML has a rich set of supporting standards, many of which are far beyond the scope of this book. One of the most useful secondary standards is XSD (XML Schema Definition). XSD defines the rules that a specific XML document should conform to. When you are creating an XML file on your own, you don't need to create a corresponding XSD file—instead, you might just rely on the ability of your code to behave properly. While this is sufficient for tightly controlled environments, if you want to open up your application to other programmers, or allow it to interoperate with other applications, you should create an XSD document.

## XSD Documents

An XSD document can define what elements a document should contain and in what relationship (its structure). It can also identify the appropriate data types for all the content. XSD documents are written using an XML syntax with special tag names. Every XSD tag starts with the xs: prefix.

The full XSD specification is out of the scope of this chapter, but you can learn a lot from a simple example. The following is the slightly abbreviated SuperProProductList.xsd file. All it does is define the elements and attributes used in the SuperProProductList.xml file and their data types. It indicates that the file is a list of Product elements, which are a complex type made up of a string (Name), a decimal value (Price), and an integer (ID).

```
<?xml version="1.0"?>
<xs:schema id="SuperProProductList"
    targetNamespace="SuperProProductList" >
  <xs:element name="SuperProProductList">
```

```
    <xs:complexType>
      <xs:choice maxOccurs="unbounded">
        <xs:element name="Product">
          <xs:complexType>
            <xs:sequence>
              <xs:element name="Price" type="xs:decimal"
                  minOccurs="0" />
            </xs:sequence>
            <xs:attribute name="ID" form="unqualified"
                type="xs:string" />
            <xs:attribute name="Name" form="unqualified"
                type="xs:int" />
          </xs:complexType>
        </xs:element>
      </xs:choice>
    </xs:complexType>
  </xs:element>
</xs:schema>
```

To associate this file with SuperProProductList.xml, you should make sure that they both use the same XML namespace. SuperProProductList.xsd defines a targetNamespace attribute, which is set to SuperProProductList. To specify the namespace for SuperProProductList.xml, modify the SuperProProductList element by adding the xmlns attribute.

```
<SuperProProductList xmlns="SuperProProductList" >
```

ASP.NET allows you to validate your document to make sure that it follows the rules specified in the XSD schema file, using an XmlValidatingReader class. This class enhances an existing XmlTextReader, and throws an exception (or raises an event) to indicate errors as you move through the XML file.

## Validating an XML File

Before using XSD schemas, you need to import the namespace System.Xml.Schema namespace, which contains types like XmlSchema and XmlSchemaCollection.

```
Imports System.Xml.Schema
```

The code snippet that follows shows how you can create an XmlValidatingReader that uses the SuperProProductList.xsd file, and use it to verify that the XML in SuperProProductList.xml is valid.

```
' Open the XML file.
Dim fs As New FileStream(Request.ApplicationPath & _
  "\SuperProProductList.xml", FileMode.Open)
Dim r As New XmlTextReader(fs)

' Create the validating reader.
Dim vr As New XmlValidatingReader(r)
vr.ValidationType = ValidationType.Schema

' Add the XSD file to the validator.
Dim Schemas As New XmlSchemaCollection()
Schemas.Add("SuperProProductList", _
  Request.ApplicationPath & "\SuperProProductList.xsd")
vr.Schemas.Add(Schemas)

' Read through the document.
Do While vr.Read()
    ' Process document here.
    ' If an error is found, an exception will be thrown.
Loop

vr.Close()
```

Using the current file, this code will succeed, and you will be able to access the current node through the XmlValidatingReader object in the same way that you could with the XmlTextReader. However, consider what happens if you make the minor modification shown here.

```
<Product ID="A" Name="Chair">
```

Now when you try to validate the document, an XmlSchemException (from the System.Xml.Schema namespace) will be thrown, alerting you of the invalid data type, as shown in Figure 17-7.

Instead of catching errors, you can react to the ValidationEventHandler event. If you react to this event, you will be provided with information about the error, but no exception will be thrown. Typically, you would use the AddHandler statement to connect your event handling procedure to the XmlValidatingReader.ValidationEventHandler event just before you started to read the XML file.

```
AddHandler vr.ValidationEventHandler, AddressOf MyValidateHandler
```

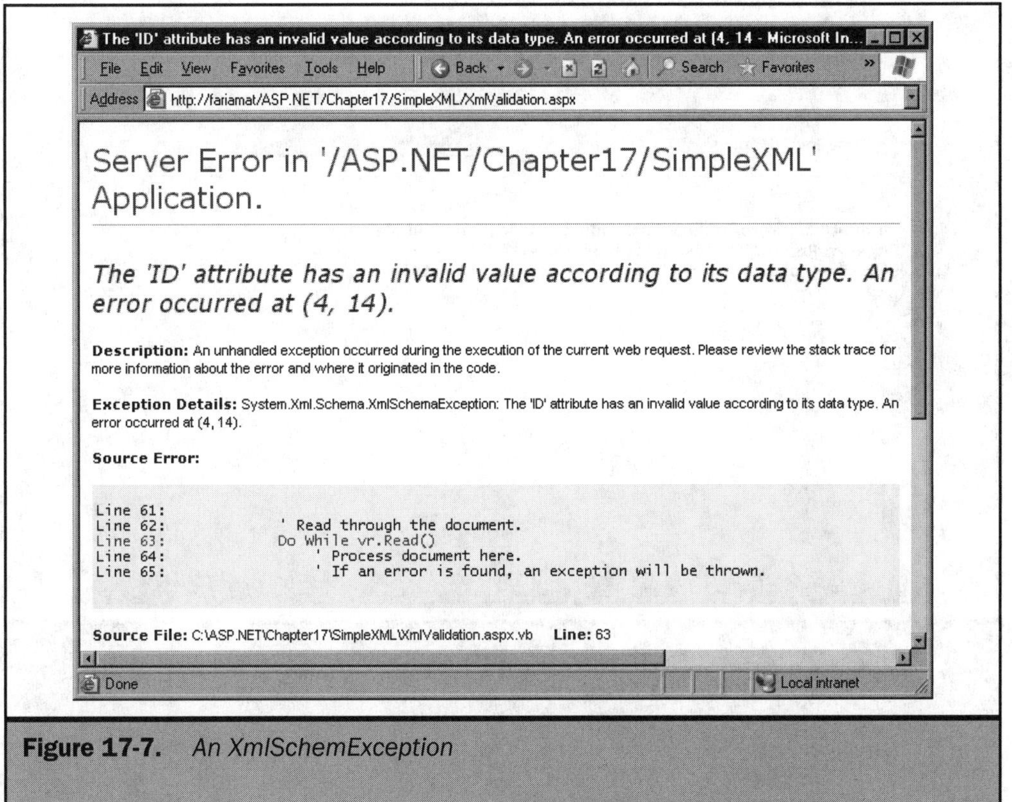


**Figure 17-7.** *An XmlSchemException*

The event handler receives a ValidationEventArgs class, which contains the exception, a message, and a number representing the severity:

```
Public Sub MyValidateHandler(sender As Object, _
  e As ValidationEventArgs)
    lblStatus.Text &= "Error: " & e.Message & "<br>"
End Sub
```

To try out validation, you can use the XmlValidation.aspx page in the online samples. It allows you to validate a valid SuperProProductList, as well as two other versions, one with incorrect data and one with an incorrect tag (see Figure 17-8).

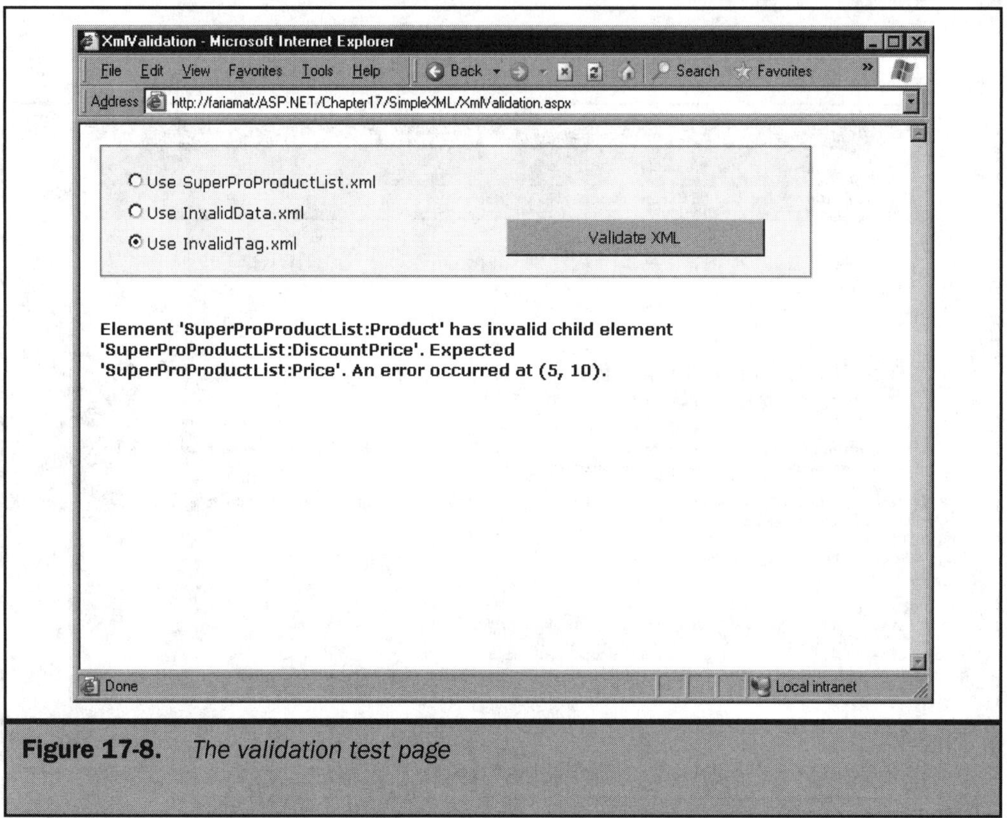


**Figure 17-8.** *The validation test page*

## Creating XSD Files in Visual Studio .NET

To create a schema for your XML files, you don't have to master the subtleties of XSD syntax. Visual Studio .NET provides an impressive graphical designer that lets you point-and-click your way to success.

Start by adding the appropriate XML file to your project. You can then edit your XML data in one of two ways: in direct text view, which provides a color-coded display of the XML tags, or through a graphical editor that makes your XML content look like one or more database tables (see Figure 17-9). You can add new rows or change existing data with ease.

To create the schema, just right-click anywhere on either of the XML views, and choose Create Schema from the context menu. An XSD file with the same name as your XML file will be generated automatically and added to your project.

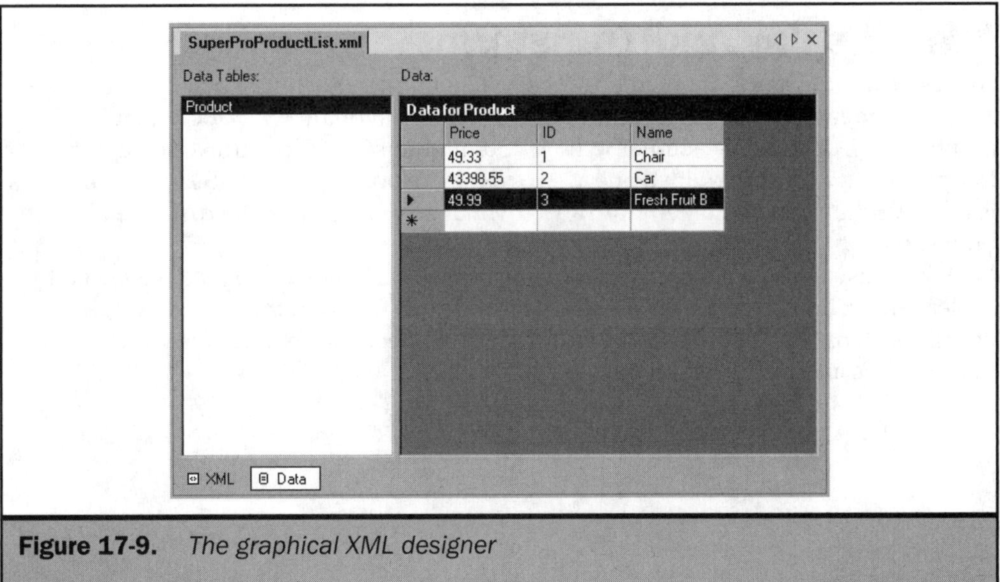


**Figure 17-9.** *The graphical XML designer*



There are also two views for editing your XSD file: text view and another graphical designer. By default, Visual Studio .NET will assume that all the data in an XML file is made up of strings. You can use the graphical tool to choose better options for each field (see Figure 17-10), and the XSD code will be updated automatically.

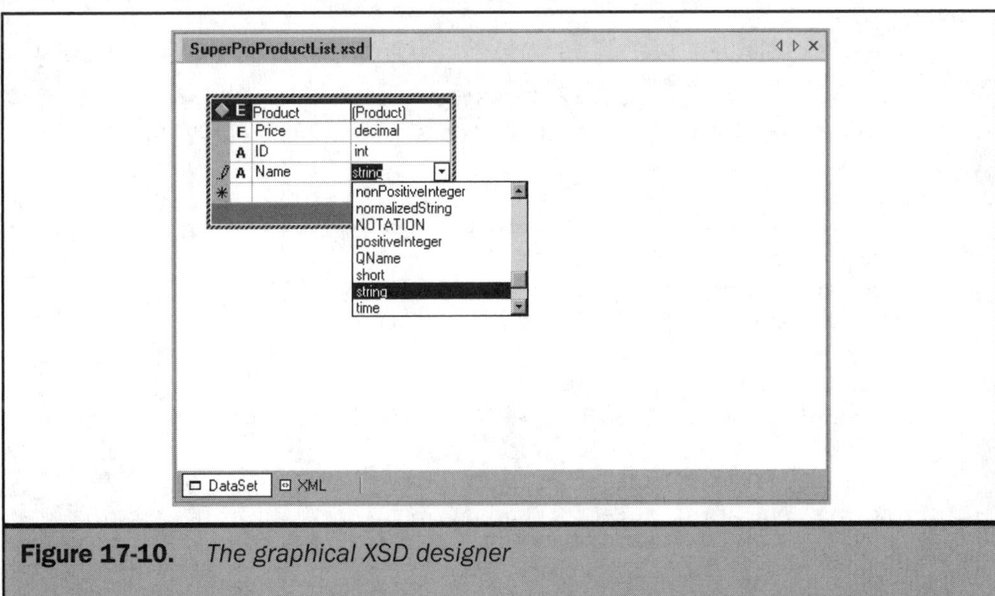


**Figure 17-10.** *The graphical XSD designer*

## XML Display and Transforms

Another standard associated with XML is XSL, which uses a stylesheet to transform an XML document. XSL can be used to retrieve a portion of an XML document into another XML document—similar to how you might use SQL to retrieve some of the information in a database with a query. An even more popular use of XSL transformations is to convert an XML document into an HTML document that can be displayed in a browser.

XSL is easy to use from the point of view of the .NET class library. All you need to understand is how to create an XmlTransform object (found in the System.Xml.Xsl namespace), use its Load method to specify a stylesheet and its Transform method to output the result to a file or stream.

```
Dim Transformer As New XmlTransform

' Load the XSL stylesheet.
Transformer.Load("SuperProProductList.xslt")

' Create a transformed XML file.
' SuperProProductList.xml is the starting point.
Transformer.Transform("SuperProProductList.xml", "New.xml")
```

However, that doesn't spare you from needing to learn the XSL syntax. Once again, the intricacies of XSL are a bit of a tangent from core ASP.NET programming, and outside the scope of this book. To get started with XSL, however, it helps to review a simple example.

```
<?xml version="1.0" encoding="UTF-8" ?>
<xsl:stylesheet xmlns:xsl="http://www.w3.org/1999/XSL/Transform"
    version="1.0" >

  <xsl:template match="SuperProProductList">
    <html><body><table border="1">
    <xsl:apply-templates select="Product"/>
    </table></body></html>
  </xsl:template>

  <xsl:template match="Product">
    <tr>
    <td><xsl:value-of select="@ID"/></td>
    <td><xsl:value-of select="@Name"/></td>
    <td><xsl:value-of select="Price"/></td>
```

```
    </tr>
  </xsl:template>

</xsl:stylesheet>
```

Every XSL file has a root xsl:stylesheet element. The stylesheet can contain one or more templates (the sample file SuperProProductList.xslt has two). In this example, the first template searches for the root SuperProProductList element. When it finds it, it outputs the tags necessary to start an HTML table, and then uses the xsl:apply-templates command to branch off and perform processing for any contained Product elements.

```
<xsl:template match="SuperProProductList">
  <html><body><table border="1">
  <xsl:apply-templates select="Product"/>
```

When that process is complete, the HTML tags for the end of the table will be written.

```
</table></body></html>
```

When processing each Product element, information about the ID, Name, and Price is extracted and written to the output using the xsl:value-of command. The @ sign indicates that the value is being extracted from an attribute, not a subtag. Every piece of information is written inside a table row. For more advanced formatting, you could use additional HTML tags to format some text in bold or italics, for example.

```
<xsl:template match="Product">
  <tr>
  <td><xsl:value-of select="@ID"/></td>
  <td><xsl:value-of select="@Name"/></td>
  <td><xsl:value-of select="Price"/></td>
  </tr>
</xsl:template>
```

The final result of this process is the HTML file shown here.

```
<html>
  <body>
    <table border="1">
```

```
      <tr>
        <td>1</td>
        <td>Chair</td>
        <td>49.33</td>
      </tr>
      <tr>
        <td>2</td>
        <td>Car</td>
        <td>43398.55</td>
      </tr>
      <tr>
        <td>3</td>
        <td>Fresh Fruit Basket</td>
        <td>49.99</td>
      </tr>
    </table>
  </body>
</html>
```

We'll take a look at how this output appears in an Internet browser in the next section.

Generally speaking, if you aren't sure that you need XSL, you probably don't. The .NET framework provides a rich set of tools for searching and manipulating XML files the easy way, which is the best approach for small-scale XML use.

## The Xml Web Control

Instead of manually writing an HTML file, you might want to display the information in a page. The XmlTransform file just converts XML files—it doesn't provide any way to insert the output into your web page. However, ASP.NET includes a web control called Xml (found in the System.Web.UI.WebControls namespace) that displays XML content. You can specify the XML content for this control in several ways: by assigning an XmlDocument object to the Document property, by assigning a string containing the XML content to the DocumentContent property, or by specifying a string that refers to an XML file using the DocumentSource property.

```
' Display the information from an XML file in the Xml control.
MyXml.DocumentSource = Request.ApplicationPath & _
  "\SuperProProductList.xml"
```

If you assign the SuperProProductList.xml file to the Xml control, you're likely to be disappointed. The result is just a string of the inner text (the price for each product), bunched together without a space (see Figure 17-11).

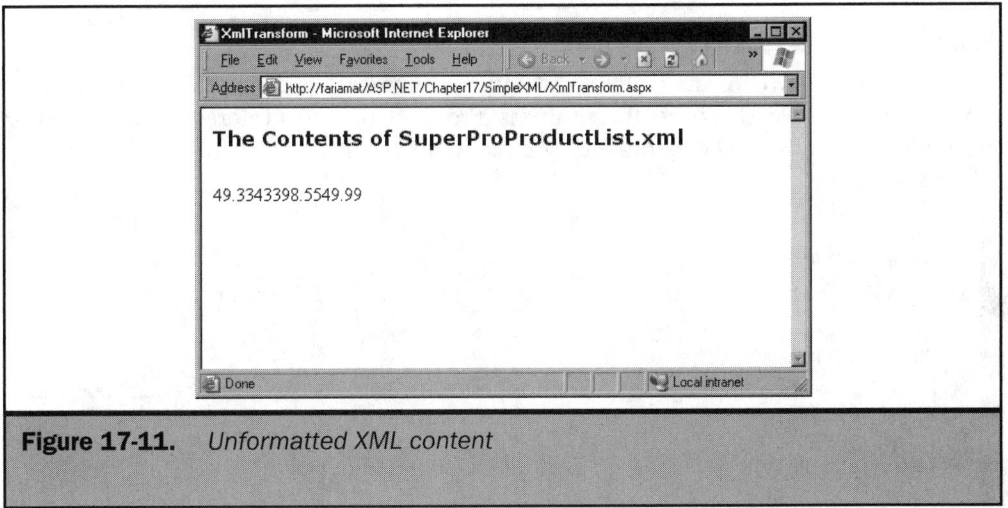


**Figure 17-11.** *Unformatted XML content*

However, you can also apply an XSL transformation, either by assigning an XslTransform object to the Transform property or by using a string that refers to the XSLT file with the TransformSource property.

```
' Specify a XSLT file.
MyXml.TranformSource = Request.ApplicationPath & _
  "\SuperProProductList.xslt"
```

Now the output is automatically formatted according to your stylesheet (see Figure 17-12).

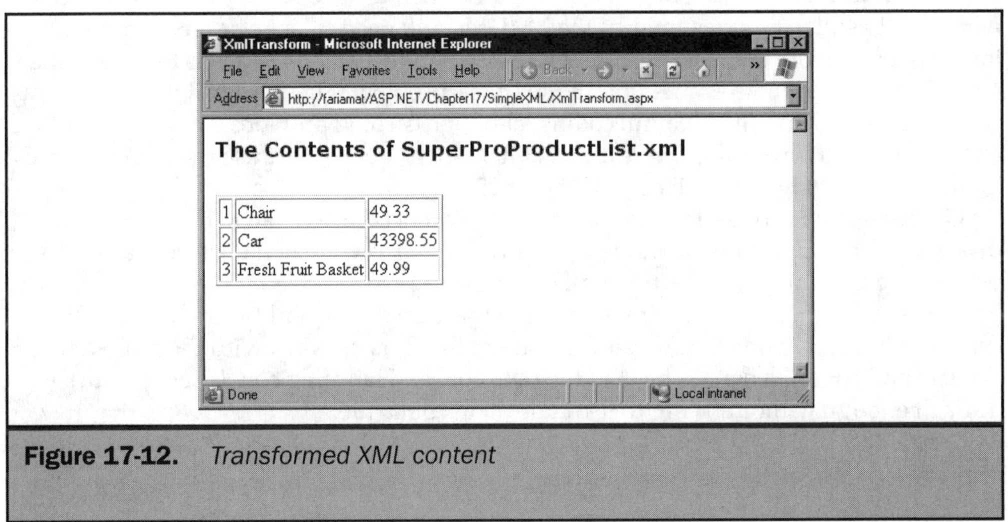


**Figure 17-12.** *Transformed XML content*

## XML in ADO.NET

The integration between ADO.NET and XML is straightforward and effortless, but it's not likely to have a wide range of usefulness. Probably the most interesting feature is the ability to serialize a DataSet to an XML file (with or without a corresponding XSD schema file).

```
' Save a DataSet.
MyDataSet.WriteXml(Request.ApplicationPath & "datasetfile.xml")

' Save a DataSet schema.
MyDataSet.WriteSchema(Request.ApplicationPath & "datasetfile.xsd")
```

It's then very easy to retrieve the complete DataSet later on.

```
' Retrieve the DataSet with its schema (just to be safe, and make
' sure no data types are corrupted or tags have been changed).
Dim MyDataSet As NewDataSet()
MyDataSet.ReadXmlSchema(Request.ApplicationPath & "datasetfile.xsd")
MyDataSet.ReadXml(Request.ApplicationPath & "datasetfile.xml")
```

This technique could be useful for permanently storing the results of a slow-running query. A web page that needs this information could first check for the presence of the file before trying to connect to the database. This type of system is similar to many homegrown solutions used in traditional ASP programming. It's useful, but it raises additional issues.

For example, every web page that needs the data must check the file age to determine whether it is still valid. Presumably, the XML file will need to be refreshed at periodic intervals, but if more than one executing web page finds that the file needs to be refreshed and tries to create it at the same time, a file access problem will occur. All these problems can be resolved with a little painful coding, although caching provides a more streamlined and elegant solution. It also offers much better performance, because the data is stored in memory. Caching is described in Chapter 23.

Of course, there could be some cases where you need to exchange the results of a query with an application on another platform, or when you need to store the results permanently (caching information will be automatically removed if it is not being used or the server memory is becoming scarce). In these cases, the ability to save a DataSet can come in quite handy. But whatever you do, don't try to work with the retrieved DataSet and commit changes back to the data source. Handling concurrency issues is difficult enough without trying to use stale data from a file!

## The XmlDataDocument

Another option provided by the DataSet is the ability to access it through an XML interface. If you wanted to do this with a database, you would need to perform the slightly awkward work of saving the DataSet to a file and then retrieving it into an XmlDataDocument. You would also lose your ability to enforce many relationships, unique constraints, and have a much more difficult time managing data updates.

A more useful way to use the XmlDataDocument is to access an ordinary XML file as though it is a database. This means you don't need to work with the XML syntax we have explored, and you don't need to go to the work of extracting all the information and creating the appropriate objects and collections. Instead, you can use the familiar ADO.NET objects to manipulate the underlying XML document.

Consider these remarkable few lines of code:

```
Dim DataDoc As New XmlDataDocument()

' Set the schema and retrieve the data.
DataDoc.DataSet.ReadXmlSchema(Request.ApplicationPath & _
  "\SuperProProductList.xsd")
DataDoc.Load(Request.ApplicationPath & "\SuperProProductList.xml")

' Display the retrieved data.
dgResults.DataSource = DataDoc.DataSet
dgResults.DataBind()
```

In this example, a new XmlDataDocument is created, an XML file is loaded into it, and the information is automatically provided through a special DataSet that is "attached" to the XmlDataDocument. This allows you to use the ADO.NET objects to work with data (like the DataTable and DataRow objects), as well as the standard XmlDocument members (like the GetTagsByElementName method and the ChildNodes property). You could even use both approaches at the same time, because both the XML and the ADO.NET interface access the same underlying data. The retrieved data is shown in Figure 17-13.

The only catch is that your XML file must have a schema in order for ASP.NET to be able to determine the proper structure of your data. Before you retrieve the XML file, you must use the XmlDataDocument.DataSet.ReadXmlSchema method. Otherwise, you won't be able to access the data through the DataSet.

Clearly, if you need to store hierarchical data in an XML file and are willing to create an XSD schema, the XmlDataDocument is a great convenience. It also allows you to bridge the gap between ADO.NET and XML—some clients can look at the data as XML, while others can access it through the database objects without losing any information or requiring an error-prone conversion process.

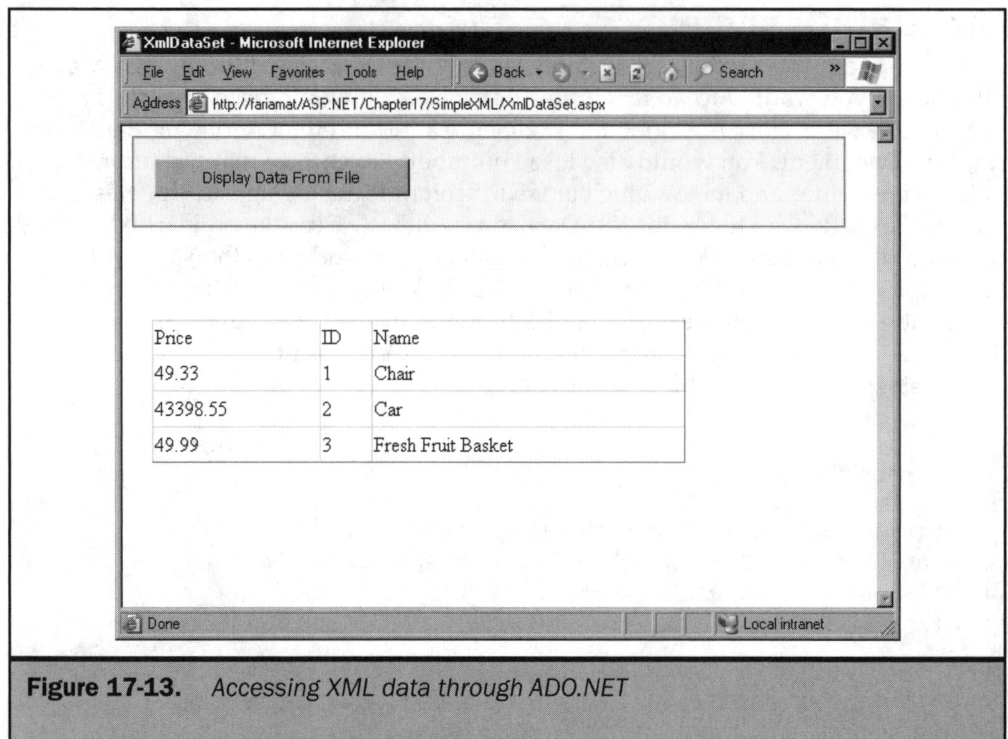


**Figure 17-13.** *Accessing XML data through ADO.NET*

The Complete Reference

# Part IV

## Web Services

The Complete Reference

# Chapter 18

## Web Services Architecture

Microsoft has promoted ASP.NET's new Web Services more than almost any other part of the .NET framework. But despite its efforts, confusion is still widespread about what a Web Service is and, more importantly, what it's meant to accomplish. This chapter introduces Web Services and explains their role in Microsoft's vision of the programmable Web. Along the way, you'll learn about the open standards plumbing that allows Web Services to work, and clear up the confusion around technical terms like WSDL, SOAP, and UDDI.

# Internet Programming Then and Now

In order to understand the place of Web Services, you have to understand the shortcomings of the current architecture in Internet applications. In many respects, Internet applications are at the same point in their development that client/server desktop applications were five years ago. This is the "monolithic" era, dominated by full-featured sites that provide a collection of distinct, but related, services.

## The Era of Monolithic Applications

Most of the applications you use over the Internet today can be considered "monolithic" because they combine a variety of different services behind a single proprietary user interface. For example, you may already use your bank's web site to do everything from checking exchange rates and reviewing stock quotes to paying bills and transferring funds. This is a successful model of development, but in several ways it's limited by its own success:

- Monolithic applications take a great deal of time and resources to create. They are often tied to a specific platform or to specific technologies, and they can't be easily extended and enhanced.
- Getting more than one application to work together is a full project of its own. Usually, an integration project involves a lot of custom work that's highly specific to a given scenario. Furthermore, every time you need to interact with another business, you need to start the integration process all over again. Currently, most web sites limit themselves to extremely simple methods of integration. For example, you might be provided with a link that opens up another web site in an existing frame on the current web page.
- Most importantly, units of application logic can't easily be reused between one application and another. With ASP.NET, source code can be shared using .NET classes, but deployed applications often don't provide the same opportunities. And if you want to perform more sophisticated or subtle integration, such as between a web site and a Windows application, or between applications hosted on different platforms, there are no easy solutions available.

- Sometimes, you might want to get extremely simple information from a web application, such as an individual stock quote. In order to get this information, you usually need to access and navigate through the entire web application, locate the correct page, and then perform the required task. There's no way to access information or perform a task without working through the graphical user interface, which can be cumbersome over a slow connection or unworkable on a portable device like a cell phone.

## Components and the COM Revolution

This state of affairs may sound familiar to you if you've followed the history of the Windows platform. A similar situation existed in the world of desktop applications, and developers found that they were spending the majority of their programming time solving problems they had already solved before. Programmers needed to structure in-house applications very carefully with DLLs or source code components in order to have any chance of reusing their work. Third-party applications usually could only be integrated through specific "pipelines." For example, one program might need to export to a set file format, which would then be manually imported into a different application.

The story improved dramatically when Microsoft introduced their COM technology (parts of which also go by the more market-friendly name ActiveX). With COM, developers found that they could develop components in their language of choice, and reuse them in a variety of different programming environments, without needing to share source code. Similarly, there was less of a need to export and import information using proprietary file formats. Instead, COM components allowed developers to package functionality into succinct and reusable chunks with well-defined interfaces.

COM helped end the era of monolithic applications. Even though you still use database and office productivity applications like Microsoft Word that seem to be single, integrated applications, much of the application's functionality is delegated to separate components behind the scenes. As with all object-oriented programming, this makes code easier to debug, alter, and extend.

## Web Services and the Programmable Web

Web Services enable the same evolution that COM did, with a twist. Web Services are individual units of programming logic that exist on a web server. They can be easily integrated into all sorts of applications, including everything from other ASP.NET applications to simple console (command-line) applications. The twist is that, unlike COM, which is a platform-specific binary standard, Web Services are built on a foundation of open standards. These standards allow Web Services to be created with .NET, but consumed on other platforms—or vice versa. In fact, the idea of Web Services didn't originate at Microsoft. Other major computer forces like IBM and Ariba are pursuing Web Services and supporting some of the standards, such as WSDL, that Microsoft uses natively in ASP.NET.

The root standard for all the individual Web Service standards is XML. Because XML is text-based, Web Service invocations can pass over normal HTTP channels, unlike remote DCOM calls, which are often blocked by corporate firewalls. So not only are Web Services governed by cross-platform standards, they're also easy to access.

The starting point for understanding a Web Service is seeing it as an individual function that is called over the Internet. Of course, this "function" has all the powerful capabilities that ASP.NET programmers are used to, such as the automatic security (see Chapter 24) and session state facilities (see Chapter 10).

## The Open Standards Plumbing

Before using Web Services, it helps to understand a little about the architecture that makes it all possible. Strictly speaking, this knowledge isn't required to work with Web Services. In fact, you could skip to the next chapter and start creating your first Web Service right now. However, understanding a little bit about the way Web Services work can help you determine how best to use them.

Remember, Web Services are designed from the ground up with open standard compatibility in mind. To ensure the greatest possible compatibility and extensibility, the Web Service architecture has been made as generic as possible. That means that very few assumptions are made about the format and encoding used to send information to and from a Web Service. Instead, all of these details are explicitly defined, in a very flexible way, using standards like SOAP and WSDL. And as you'll see, in order for a client to be able to connect to a Web Service, a lot of mundane work has to go on behind the scenes processing and interpreting this SOAP and WSDL information. This mundane work does exert a bit of a performance overhead, but it won't hamper most well-designed Web Services.

Table 18-1 summarizes the standards this chapter examines. It's worth noting that WSDL is really the only standard "baked in" to Web Services.

| Standard | Description |
|---|---|
| WSDL | The Web Service Description Language tells a client what methods are present in a Web Service, what parameters and return values each method uses, and how to communicate with them. |
| SOAP | The preferred way to encode information (such as data values) before sending it to or from a Web Service. HTTP GET and HTTP POST can also be used. |

**Table 18-1.** *Web Service Standards*

| Standard | Description |
|---|---|
| HTTP | The protocol over which communication takes place. For example, SOAP message are sent over HTTP channels. |
| DISCO | The discovery standard contains links to Web Services, or it can be used to provide a dynamic list of Web Services in a specified path. |
| UDDI | The business registry that lists information about companies, the Web Services they provide, and the corresponding URLs for DISCO file or WSDL contracts. Unfortunately, it's still too new to be widely accepted and useful. |

**Table 18-1.** *Web Service Standards (continued)*

## WSDL

WSDL is the Web Service Description Language. It's an XML-based standard that specifies how a client can interact with a Web Service, including details like how parameters and return values should be encoded in a message, and what protocol should be used for transmission over the Internet. Currently, three standards are supported for the actual transmission of Web Service information: HTTP GET, HTTP POST, and SOAP (over HTTP).

The full WSDL standard can be found at http://www.w3.org/TR/2001/NOTE-wsdl-20010315. The standard is fairly complex, but its underlying logic is abstracted away from the developer in ASP.NET programming, just as ASP.NET web controls abstract away the messy details of HTML tags and attributes. As you'll see in Chapter 19, ASP.NET creates WSDL documents for your Web Services *automatically*. ASP.NET can also create a proxy class based on the WSDL document automatically. Even on other platforms, tools will likely be available to make these chores relatively painless.

In the next few sections, we'll analyze a sample WSDL document for a very simple Web Service, made up of a single method called GetStockQuote. This method accepts a string specifying a stock ticker and returns a numeric value that represents a current price quote. The Web Service itself is called MyWebService, and we'll peer into its actual ASP.NET code in Chapter 19.

### What Doesn't the WSDL Document Contain?

The WSDL document contains information for communication between a Web Service and client. It doesn't contain any information that has anything to do with the code or implementation of your Web Service methods (that is unnecessary and could compromise security). Incidentally, .NET includes types that represent all the language elements of a WSDL document in the System.Web.Services.Description namespace.

## The <definitions> Element

The WSDL document is quite long, so we'll look at it section by section, in order. Don't worry about understanding it in detail—the ASP.NET framework will handle that—but do use it to get an idea about how Web Services communicate.

The header and root namespace looks like this:

```
<?xml version="1.0" encoding="utf-8" ?>
<definitions xmlns:s="http://www.w3.org/2001/XMLSchema"
  xmlns:http="http://schemas.xmlsoap.org/wsdl/http/"
  xmlns:mime="http://schemas.xmlsoap.org/wsdl/mime/"
  xmlns:tm="http://microsoft.com/wsdl/mime/textMatching/"
  xmlns:soap="http://schemas.xmlsoap.org/wsdl/soap/"
  xmlns:soapenc="http://schemas.xmlsoap.org/soap/encoding/"
  xmlns:s0="http://tempuri.org/" targetNamespace="http://tempuri.org/"
  xmlns="http://schemas.xmlsoap.org/wsdl/">

  <!-- This is where all the rest of the WSDL document goes.
  I've snipped it into the individual pieces shown in the
  rest of the chapter. -->

</definitions>
```

Looking at the WSDL document, you'll notice that an XML tag structure is used. All the information is contained in a root <definitions> element.

## The <types> Element

The first element contained inside the <description> element is a <types> element that defines information about the data types of the return value and parameters your Web Service method uses. If your Web Service returns an instance of a custom class, ASP.NET will add an extra entry to define your class (although only data members will be preserved, not methods, which can't be converted into an XML representation).

The <types> element for our sample MyWebService is shown below. By looking at it, we can tell that our function, GetStockQuote, uses a string parameter, called Ticker, and a decimal return value. The corresponding lines are highlighted in bold.

```
<types>
   <s:schema attributeFormDefault="qualified"
    elementFormDefault="qualified"
   targetNamespace="http://tempuri.org/">
     <s:element name="GetStockQuote">
       <s:complexType>
         <s:sequence>
           <s:element minOccurs="1" maxOccurs="1" name="Ticker"
              nillable="true" type="s:string"/>
         </s:sequence>
       </s:complexType>
     </s:element>
     <s:element name="GetStockQuoteResponse">
       <s:complexType>
         <s:sequence>
           <s:element minOccurs="1" maxOccurs="1"
              name="GetStockQuoteResult" type="s:decimal"/>
         </s:sequence>
       </s:complexType>
     </s:element>
     <s:element name="decimal" type="s:decimal"/>
   </s:schema>
 </types>
```

## The <message> Elements

Messages represent the information exchanged between a Web Service method and a client. When you request a stock quote from our simple Web Service, ASP.NET sends a message, and the Web Service sends a different message back. The data type can be defined in the message element, as it is for the GetStockQuoteHttpPostIn message in the following example, or it can be defined using one of the data types in the <types> element, as it is for the GetStockQuoteSoapIn message (both shown in bold).

```
<message name="GetStockQuoteSoapIn">
   <part name="parameters" element="s0:GetStockQuote"/>
 </message>
 <message name="GetStockQuoteSoapOut">
   <part name="parameters" element="s0:GetStockQuoteResponse"/>
 </message>
```

```
<message name="GetStockQuoteHttpGetIn">
  <part name="Ticker" type="s:string"/>
</message>
<message name="GetStockQuoteHttpGetOut">
  <part name="Body" element="s0:decimal"/>
</message>
<message name="GetStockQuoteHttpPostIn">
  <part name="Ticker" type="s:string"/>
</message>
<message name="GetStockQuoteHttpPostOut">
  <part name="Body" element="s0:decimal"/>
</message>
```

In this example, you'll notice that ASP.NET creates both a GetStockQuoteSoapIn and a GetStockQuoteSoapOut message. The naming is optional, but it underscores the fact that a separate message is required for input (sending parameters and invoking a Web Service method) and output (retrieving a return value from a Web Service method). You'll also notice that there is a corresponding "in" and "out" message defined for each of the three protocols supported by ASP.NET Web Services: HTTP POST, HTTP GET, and SOAP. Remember, MyWebService only contains one method. The three versions of it that you see in WSDL are provided and supported by ASP.NET automatically to allow the client the chance to choose a preferred method of communication.

## The <portType> Elements

The <portType> elements match <message> elements to corresponding <operation> elements. In other words, the <message> elements define the structure of a message, but the <operation> elements specify what messages are required for a specific operation. For example, you'll see that for the SOAP port type (MyWebServiceSoap), the GetStockQuote method requires an input message called GetStockQuoteIn and a matching output message called GetStockQuoteOut.

```
<portType name="MyWebServiceSoap">
  <operation name="GetStockQuote">
    <input message="s0:GetStockQuoteSoapIn"/>
    <output message="s0:GetStockQuoteSoapOut"/>
  </operation>
</portType>
<portType name="MyWebServiceHttpGet">
  <operation name="GetStockQuote">
    <input message="s0:GetStockQuoteHttpGetIn"/>
    <output message="s0:GetStockQuoteHttpGetOut"/>
```

```
  </operation>
</portType>
<portType name="MyWebServiceHttpPost">
  <operation name="GetStockQuote">
    <input message="s0:GetStockQuoteHttpPostIn"/>
    <output message="s0:GetStockQuoteHttpPostOut"/>
  </operation>
</portType>
```

## The <binding> Elements

The <binding> elements link the abstract data format to the concrete protocol used for transmission over an Internet connection. So far, the WSDL document has specified the data type used for various pieces of information, the required messages used for an operation, and the structure of each message. With the <binding> element, the WSDL document specifies the low-level communication protocol that you can use to talk to a Web Service.

For example, the MyWebService WSDL document specifies that the SOAP-specific GetStockQuote operation communicates using SOAP messages. The HTTP POST and HTTP GET operations receive information as an XML document (type “mimeXML”), and send it encoded as either a query string argument (“http:urlEncded”) or in the body of a posted form (type “application/x-www-form-urlencoded”).

```
<binding name="MyWebServiceSoap" type="s0:MyWebServiceSoap">
  <soap:binding transport="http://schemas.xmlsoap.org/soap/http"
   style="document"/>
  <operation name="GetStockQuote">
    <soap:operation soapAction="http://tempuri.org/GetStockQuote"
     style="document"/>
    <input>
      <soap:body use="literal"/>
    </input>
    <output>
      <soap:body use="literal"/>
    </output>
  </operation>
</binding>
<binding name="MyWebServiceHttpGet" type="s0:MyWebServiceHttpGet">
  <http:binding verb="GET"/>
  <operation name="GetStockQuote">
    <http:operation location="/GetStockQuote"/>
```

```
      <input>
        <http:urlEncoded/>
      </input>
      <output>
        <mime:mimeXml part="Body"/>
      </output>
    </operation>
  </binding>
  <binding name="MyWebServiceHttpPost" type="s0:MyWebServiceHttpPost">
    <http:binding verb="POST"/>
    <operation name="GetStockQuote">
      <http:operation location="/GetStockQuote"/>
      <input>
        <mime:content type="application/x-www-form-urlencoded"/>
      </input>
      <output>
        <mime:mimeXml part="Body"/>
      </output>
    </operation>
  </binding>
```

## The <service> Element

The <service> element represents "entry points" into your Web Service. This is how a client accesses the Web Service.

An ASP.NET Web Service defines three different <port> elements in the <service> element, one for each protocol. Inside each <port> element is another element that identifies the Internet address (URL) needed to access the Web Service. Most Web Services will use the same URL address for all types of communication.

```
<service name="MyWebService">

<port name="MyWebServiceSoap"
 binding="s0:MyWebServiceSoap">
  <soap:address
   location="http://localhost/MyWebService/MyWebService.asmx"/>
</port>
<port name="MyWebServiceHttpGet"
 binding="s0:MyWebServiceHttpGet">
  <http:address
   location="http://localhost/MyWebService/MyWebService.asmx"/>
```

```
</port>
<port name="MyWebServiceHttpPost"
 binding="s0:MyWebServiceHttpPost">
  <http:address
   location="http://localhost/MyWebService/MyWebService.asmx"/>
</port>

</service>
```

### Can I See a WSDL for an Existing Web Service?

Here's a neat trick: any existing ASP.NET service will display its corresponding WSDL document if you add **?WSDL** to the query string. For example, you could look at the WSDL document for the preceding Web Service example by navigating to http://localhost/MyWebService/MyWebService.asmx?WSDL. This can be secured with normal web security measures such as passwords or client certificates, but you generally won't need to take these steps. Remember, the WSDL document is equivalent to a list of methods; it doesn't provide code or implementation details. The greatest benefits of Web Services are their auto-discovery and self-description features.

## SOAP

As the WSDL document shows, there are three different protocols a client can use to communicate with a Web Service:

- HTTP GET, which communicates with a Web Service by encoding information in the query string, and retrieves information as a standard XML document page.
- HTTP POST, which places parameters in the request body (as form values), and retrieves information as a standard XML document page.
- SOAP (Simple Object Access Protocol), which is the default for ASP.NET's automatically generated proxy classes. SOAP works over HTTP, but uses a special XML-like format for bundling up information. This format revolves around the idea of SOAP messages.

## A Sample SOAP Message

Essentially, when you use the SOAP protocol, you are simply using the SOAP standard to encode the information in your messages. SOAP messages follow an XML-based standard, and look something like this:

```
<?xml version="1.0" encoding="UTF-8" standalone="no"?>
<soap:Envelope xmlns="http://schemas.xmlsoap.org/soap/envelope/">
  <soap:Body>
    <GetStockQuote xmlns ="http://tempuri.org/message/">
    <Ticker>MSFT</Ticker>
    </GetStockQuote>
  </soap:Body>
</soap:Envelope>
```

You may have already noticed why the SOAP message format is superior to HTTP GET and HTTP POST. HTTP requests send information as simple name/value pairs. SOAP messages, on the other hand, use a well-formatted XML document, which can accommodate more complex information like an instance of a special class.

Looking at the preceding SOAP message, you can see that the root element is a <soap:envelope>, which contains the <soap:body> of the request. Inside the body is information indicating that the GetStockQuote method is being called, with a Ticker parameter of MSFT. While this is a fairly straightforward method call, SOAP messages can easily contain entire structures representing custom objects or DataSets.

In response to this request, a SOAP output message will be returned. For information about the SOAP standard, you can read the full specification at http://www.w3.org/TR/SOAP. (Once again, these technical details explain a lot about how SOAP works, but are rarely used in day-to-day programming.)

# Communicating with a Web Service

The WSDL and SOAP standards enable the communication between Web Service and client, but they don't show how it happens. The following three components play a role:

- A custom Web Service class that provides some piece of functionality.
- A client application that wants to use this functionality.
- A proxy class that acts as the interface between the two. The proxy class contains a representation of all the Web Service methods, and takes care of the details involved in communicating with the Web Service by the chosen protocol.

The actual process works like this (see Figure 18-1):

1. The client creates an instance of a proxy class.

2. The client invokes the method on the proxy class, exactly as though it were using a normal, local class.
3. Behind the scenes, the proxy class sends the information to the Web Service in the appropriate format (usually SOAP) and receives the corresponding response, which is deserialized into the corresponding data or object.
4. The proxy class returns the result to the calling code.

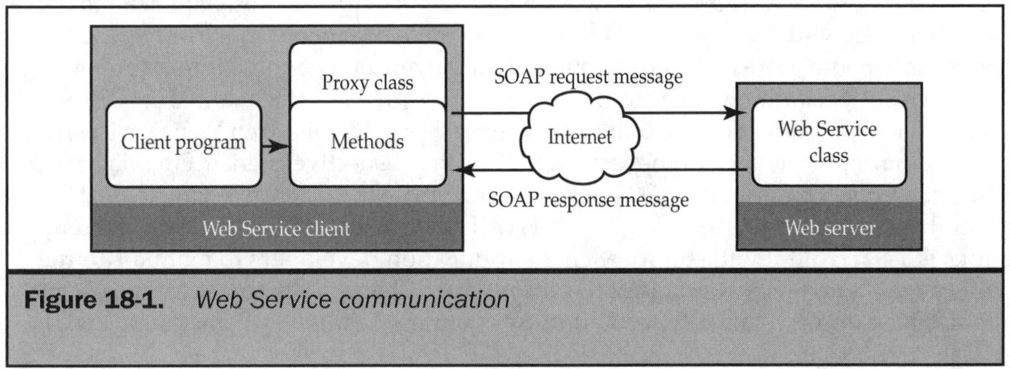


**Figure 18-1.** *Web Service communication*

Perhaps the most significant detail lies in the fact that the client does not need to be aware that a remote function call to a Web Service is being made. The process is completely transparent and works as though you were calling a function in your own local code!

Of course, some additional limitations and considerations apply:

- Not all data types are supported for method parameters and return values. For example, you can't pass many .NET class library objects (the DataSet is one important exception).
- The network call takes a short, but measurable, amount of time. If you need to use several Web Service methods in a row, this delay can start to add up.
- Unless the Web Service takes specific steps to remember its state information, this data will be lost. Basically, that means that you should treat a Web Service like a utility class, composed of as many independent methods as you need. You shouldn't think of a Web Service as an ordinary object with properties and member variables.
- There are a variety of new errors that can occur and interrupt your web method (for example, network problems). You may need to take this into account when building a robust application.

We'll examine all of these issues in detail throughout Chapters 19 and 20.

## Web Service Discovery and UDDI

Imagine you've created a Web Service that uses WSDL to describe how it works and transmits information in SOAP packets. Inevitably, you start to ask how clients can find your Web Services. At first, it seems to be a trivial question. Clearly, a Web Service is available at a specific URL address. Once the client has this address, the WSDL document can be retrieved by adding ?WSDL to the URL, and all the necessary information is available. So why is a discovery standard required at all?

The straightforward process described above works great if you only need to share a Web Service with specific clients or inside a single organization. However, as Web Services become more and more numerous and eventually evolve into a common language for performing business transactions over the Web, this manual process seems less and less practical. For one thing, if a company provides a dozen Web Services, how does it communicate each of these twelve URLs to prospective clients? Emailing them on a per-request basis is sure to take up time and create inefficiency. Trying to recite them over the telephone is worse. Providing an HTML page that consolidates all the appropriate links is a start, but it will still force client application developers to manually enter information into their programs. If this information changes later on, it will result in painstaking minor changes that could cause countless headaches. Sometimes, trivial details aren't so trivial.

### The DISCO Standard

The DISCO standard picks up where the "HTML page with links" concept ends. When following the DISCO standard you provide a .disco file that specifies where a Web Service is located. ASP.NET tools such as Visual Studio .NET can read the discover file and automatically provide you with the list of corresponding Web Services.

Here is a sample .disco file:

```
<disco:discovery  xmlns:disco="http://schemas.xmlsoap.org/disco"
  xmlns:wsdl="http://schemas.xmlsoap.org/disco/wsdl">
    <wsdl:contractRef
     ref="http://localhoust/MyWebService/MyWebService.asmx?WSDL"/>
</disco:discovery>
```

The benefit of a .disco file is that it is clearly used for Web Services (while .html and .aspx files can contain any kind of content). The other advantage is that you can insert <disco> elements for as many Web Services as you want, including ones that reside on other web servers. In other words, a .disco file provides a straightforward way to create a repository of Web Service links that can be used automatically by .NET.

## Dynamic Discovery

ASP.NET can also use dynamic discovery. An example is shown here:

```
<?xml version="1.0" encoding="utf-8" ?>
<dynamicDiscovery
  xmlns="urn:schemas-dynamicdiscovery:disco.2000-03-17">
<exclude path="_vti_cnf" />
<exclude path="_vti_pvt" />
<exclude path="_vti_log" />
<exclude path="_vti_script" />
<exclude path="_vti_txt" />
<exclude path="Web References" />
</dynamicDiscovery>
```

A <dynamicDiscovery> element does not specifically reference individual Web Services. Instead, it instructs ASP.NET to search all the subdirectories under the current directory for Web Services. By creating a dynamic discovery file, you can be certain that your discovery will always provide an up-to-date list of all the Web Services you have.

The <exclude> elements tell the discovery process not to look in those folders. This can be used to save time (for example, by restricting directories that just contain images). It can also restrict a Web Service from appearing publicly in a discovery process, although it will still be accessible unless you have specifically written authentication or security code.

### Do I Need DISCO?

ASP.NET Web Services don't require any kind of discovery file. You may not need to make a Web Service easily available. But in many scenarios this standard makes the business aspect of using Web Services a lot easier. Visual Studio .NET automatically creates a discovery document for your computer that references all the Web Services you create. When Visual Studio .NET creates a discovery file, it uses the extension .vsdisco.



## UDDI

UDDI is possibly the youngest and most rapidly developing standard in the whole collection. UDDI (Universal Description, Discovery, and Integration) is a Microsoft-led initiative designed to make it easier for you to locate Web Services on any server.

With discovery files, the client still needs to know the specific URL location of the discovery file. It may make life easier by consolidating multiple Web Services into one directory, but it still doesn't provide any obvious way to examine the Web Services offered by a company without navigating to their web site and looking for a .disco hyperlink. The goal of UDDI, on the other hand, is to provide a repository where businesses can advertise all the Web Services they have. For example, a company might list the services it has for business document exchange, which describe how purchase orders can be submitted and tracking information can be retrieved. In order to submit this information, a business must be registered with the service. In some ways, UDDI is the equivalent of a Yahoo! for Web Services.

There are three main sections to the UDDI:

- White pages, which provide business contact information
- Yellow pages, which organize XML Web Services into categories (for example, Document Exchange Services)
- Green pages, which provide detailed technical information about individual services (this information may be provided by referencing discovery documents or WSDL contracts)

Interestingly enough, the UDDI registry defines a complete programming interface that specifies how SOAP messages can be used to retrieve information about a business or register the Web Services for a business. In other words, the UDDI registry is itself a Web Service! This standard is still too new to really be of use, but you can find detailed specifications at http://uddi.microsoft.com.

The Complete Reference

# Chapter 19

## Creating Web Services

Web Services have the potential to simplify web development dramatically. They might even lead to a new generation of applications that seamlessly integrate multiple remote services into a single web page or desktop interface. However, the greatest programming concept in the world is doomed to fail if it isn't supported by powerful, flexible tools that make its use not only possible, but convenient. Fortunately, ASP.NET does not disappoint, providing classes that allow you to create a Web Service quickly and easily.

In Chapter 18 we looked at the philosophy that led to the creation of Web Services, and the XML infrastructure that makes it all possible. This chapter delves into the practical side of Web Services, leading you through the process of designing and coding web method files. We'll also consider how a Web Service can use transactions, caching, and security.

# Web Service Basics

As you've already seen in this book, ASP.NET is based on object-oriented principles. The traditional (and primitive) script-based programming used in ASP has been replaced with classes that wrap code into neat reusable objects. Web Services follow that pattern—in fact, every Web Service is really an ordinary class. A client can create an instance of your Web Service and use its methods just as though it were any other locally defined class. The underlying HTTP transmission and data type conversion that must happen are handled behind the scenes.

How does this magic work? It's made possible by a class in the .NET class library called WebService, which provides the prefabricated functionality you need. When designing a Web Service, you create a custom class that inherits from the ready-made WebService class, and you add the business functions that are required for your application. Because your custom class derives from WebService, it has the built-in knowledge that allows it to automatically generate its own WSDL (Web Service Description Language) document and work with ASP.NET to provide services to clients over the Internet. The only layer you need to worry about is the code specific to your business. This code can be written like an ordinary Visual Basic .NET function.

## Web Service Ingredients

A Web Service consists of a few special ingredients:

- An .asmx text file that contains the Web Service code. Alternatively, if you're using Visual Studio .NET you will use a code-behind module with the Web Service code. I'll demonstrate both of these techniques in this chapter.
- A Web Service class that inherits from System.Web.Services.WebService.
- A Web Service method marked with a System.Web.Services.WebMethodAttribute. This attribute indicates the individual functions and subroutines that you want to make available over the Internet.

# The StockQuote Web Service

Chapter 18 examined the WSDL document generated for a simple Web Service that contained only one method. The following example shows the corresponding code in an .asmx text file.

```
<%@ WebService Language="VB" Class="StockQuote" %>

Imports System.Web.Services

Public Class StockQuote
    Inherits WebService

    <WebMethod> Public Function GetStockQuote(Ticker As String) _
      As Decimal
        ' Insert some database code here to look up
        ' and return the quote.
    End Function

End Class
```

An .asmx file is similar to the standard .aspx file used for graphical ASP.NET pages. Like .aspx files, .asmx files start with a directive specifying the language, are compiled the first time they are requested in order to increase performance, and can be created with Notepad or any other text editor. The letter "m" indicates "method"—as all Web Services are built out of one or more web methods that provide the actual functionality.

## Understanding the StockQuote Service

The code for the StockQuote Web Service is quite straightforward. The first line specifies that the file is used for a Web Service and is written in Visual Basic .NET code. The next line imports the Web Service namespace so that all the classes you need are at your fingertips. As with other core pieces of ASP.NET technology, Web Service functionality is provided through prebuilt types in the .NET class library.

The remainder of the code is the actual Web Service, which is built out of a single class that derives from WebService. In the example above, the Web Service class contains a custom function called GetStockQuote. This is a normal Visual Basic .NET function, with a special <WebMethod> attribute before its definition.

.NET attributes are used to describe code. The WebMethod attribute doesn't change how your function works, but it does tell ASP.NET that this is one of the procedures it must make available over the Internet. Functions or subroutines that don't have this attribute won't be accessible (or even visible) to remote clients, regardless of whether they are defined with the Private or Public keyword.

### You Don't Need to Inherit from WebService

The .NET framework contains the functionality for communicating over the Internet and generating WSDL documents for your code. This functionality is automatically provided to any method marked with the WebMethod attribute, even if you don't inherit from the WebService class. So why bother?

Inheriting from WebService is a convenience that makes sure you can access the built-in ASP.NET objects (such as Application Session, and User) just as easily as you can in a web form. These objects are provided as properties of the WebService class, which your Web Service acquires through inheritance. If you don't need to use any of these objects (or if you're willing to go through the static HttpContext. Current property to access them), you don't need to inherit.

The best way to understand a Web Service is to think of it as a business object. Business objects support your programs, but don't take part in creating any user interface. For example, business objects might have helper functions that retrieve information from a database, perform calculations, or process custom data and return the results. Your code creates business objects whenever it needs to retrieve or store specific information, such as report information from a database.

Probably the most amazing part of this example is that the StockQuote Web Service is now complete. All you need to do is copy the .asmx file to your web server in a virtual directory that other clients can access over the Internet, as you would with an .aspx page. Other clients can then start creating instances of your class and can call the GetStockQuote function as though it were a locally defined procedure. All they need to do is use .NET to create a proxy class. The process of creating a client is demonstrated in Chapter 20.

## Web Services in Visual Studio .NET

Visual Studio .NET uses code-behind classes that allow you to separate design and code. In the case of .asmx files, this feature is not really necessary. Web Service files consist entirely of code and do not contain any user interface elements. However, to maintain consistency, Visual Studio .NET uses the same system as it does with Web Forms pages, which means every Web Service you create will have both an .asmx and a .vb file. You won't notice this while you are using the Visual Studio .NET IDE, because the .asmx file is hidden from you. However, when you deploy your Web Service to the server, you will have to be sure to copy both the .asmx file and the compiled code behind DLL.

The code-behind version of the StockQuote Web Service would look like this:

**StockQuote.asmx**

```
<%@ WebService Language="vb"
    Codebehind="StockQuote.asmx.vb"
    class="StockApp.StockQuote" %>
```

**StockQuote.asmx.vb**

```
Imports System.Web.Services

Public Class StockQuote
    Inherits WebService

    #Region " Web Services Designer Generated Code "
        ' < code left out of listing >
        ' The infrastructure code in this region is added
        ' automatically. It contains information for any
        ' components you add from the toolbox.
        ' Generally, this region won't have any important code for
        ' Web Services.
    #End Region

    <WebMethod()> Public Function GetStockQuote(Ticker As String) _
      As Decimal
        ' Lookup code goes here.
    End Function

End Class
```

Note that the client *always* connects through the .asmx file.

Interestingly, you can also create an .asmx file that refers to a compiled WebService class. Just place the compiled assembly DLL containing the WebService class in your application's \bin directory, and specify the appropriate class name in your .asmx file. You should also leave out the Codebehind attribute.

# Documenting Your Web Service

Web Services are self-describing, which means that ASP.NET automatically provides all the information the client needs about what methods are available and what parameters they require. This is all accomplished through the WSDL document. However, while the WSDL document describes the mechanics of the Web Service, it doesn't describe its purpose, or the meaning of the information supplied to and returned from each method. Most Web Services will provide this information in separate developer documents. However, you can (and should) include a bare minimum of information with your Web Service using attributes.

### What Are Attributes?

Attributes are a special language construct built into the .NET framework. Essentially, attributes describe your code to the .NET runtime by adding extra metadata. The attributes you use for Web Service description are recognized by the .NET framework, and provided to clients in automatically generated description documents and the Internet Explorer test page. Attributes are used in many other situations, and even if you haven't encountered them before, you are sure to encounter them again in .NET programming.

## Descriptions

You can add descriptions to each function through the WebMethod attribute, and to the entire Web Service as a whole using a WebService attribute. For example, the StockQuote service could be described like this:

```
<WebService(Description:="Provides stock price lookup.")> _
Public Class StockQuote
    Inherits WebService

    <WebMethod(Description:="Gets a quote for a stock.")> _
    Public Function GetStockQuote(Ticker As String) As Decimal
        ' Lookup code goes here.
    End Function

End Class
```

In this example, the line continuation character (_) is used to put the attributes on a separate line. You might also notice that the Description is added as a named argument using the := operator.

These custom descriptions will appear in two important places:

- In the automatically generated WSDL document as <documentation> tags.

```
<service name="StockQuote">
  <documentation>Provides stock price lookup.
  </documentation>
  <!-- Port elements are defined here. -->
</service>
```

- In the automatically generated Internet Explorer test page (which is more likely to be viewed by the client). The test page is described in the next section, "Testing Your Web Service."

## Specifying an XML Namespace

You should also specify a unique namespace for your Web Service that can't be confused with the namespaces used for other Web Services on the Internet. Note that this is an XML namespace, not a .NET namespace, and it doesn't affect the client's code. Instead, this namespace is used to identify your Web Service in the WSDL document. XML namespaces look like URLs, but they don't need to correspond to a valid Internet location.

Ideally, the namespace you use will refer to a URL address that you control. For example, you could use your company's Internet domain name as part of the namespace. If you do not specify a namespace, the default (http://tempuri.org/) will be used. This is fine for development, but you will receive a warning message in the test page advising you to select something more distinctive.

The namespace is specified through the WebService attribute, as shown below. As with any Visual Basic code statement, you need to use the line continuation character (an underscore) to split it over more than one line.

```
<WebService(Description:="Methods to ...", _
Namespace:="http://www.prosetech.com/Stocks")>
```

### Specify a Namespace to Avoid Warnings

Before you continue, you should specify a custom namespace using the Description property of the WebService attribute. Without it, you will receive a warning message and the Internet Explorer test page will contain a lengthy (and somewhat annoying) description about how to change namespaces.

## Testing Your Web Service

Even without creating a client for your Web Service, you can use the ASP.NET framework to view information about it and test it. The most useful testing feature is the Internet Explorer test page: an automatically generated HTML page that lets you execute a Web Service's methods and review its WSDL document.

Before continuing any further, you should modify the GetStockQuote method so that it returns a hard-coded number. This will allow you to test that it is working from the IE test page. For example, you could use the statement Return Ticker.Length. That way, the return value will be the number of characters you supplied in the Ticker parameter.

To view the IE test page, you can do one of two things:

- If you are creating an .asmx file in a text editor, place this text file in an appropriate virtual directory with script running permissions. You can then double-click on it.
- If you are creating your Web Service in Visual Studio .NET, just click the Run button.

### The Internet Explorer Test Page

This window (shown in Figure 19-1) lists all the available Web Service methods (in this case, only one, GetStockQuote, is available). It also lists whatever description information you may have added through attributes.

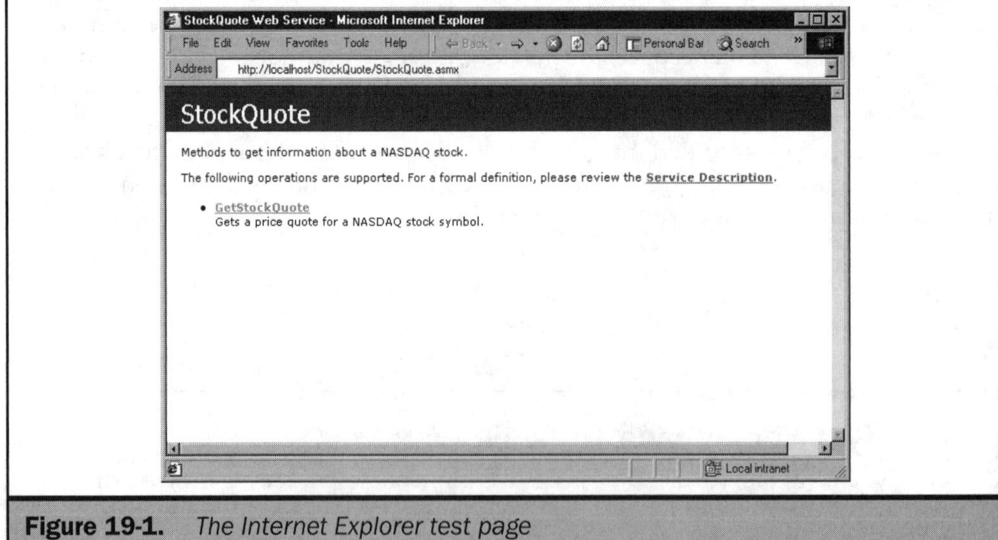


**Figure 19-1.** *The Internet Explorer test page*

Remember, you don't need to write any special code to make this page appear. It's generated for you by ASP.NET and Internet Explorer, and is intended purely as a testing convenience. Clients using your Web Service won't browse to this page to interact with your Web Service, but they might use it to find out some basic information about how to use your Web Service.

## Service Description

You can also click the Service Description link to display the WSDL description of your Web Service (see Figure 19-2), which we examined in detail in Chapter 18.

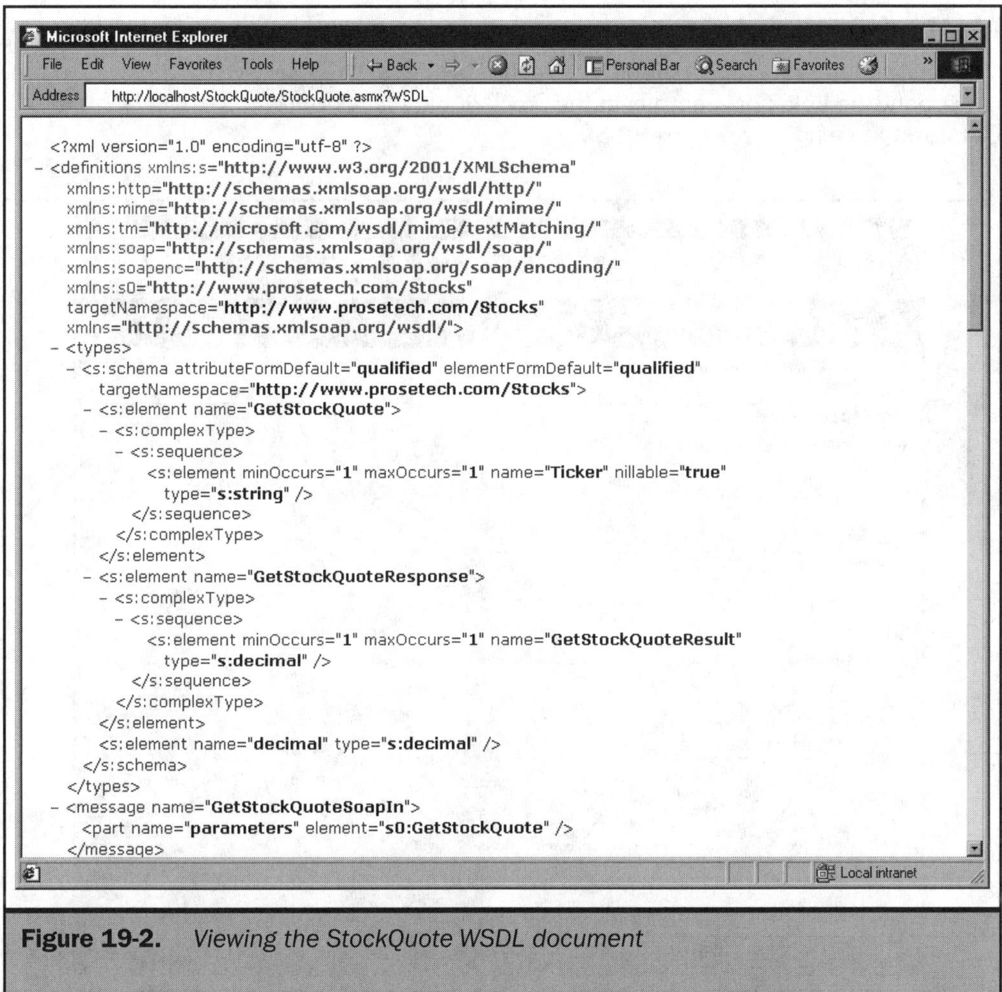


**Figure 19-2.** *Viewing the StockQuote WSDL document*

To display this document, Internet Explorer accesses your .asmx file with a WSDL parameter in the query string.

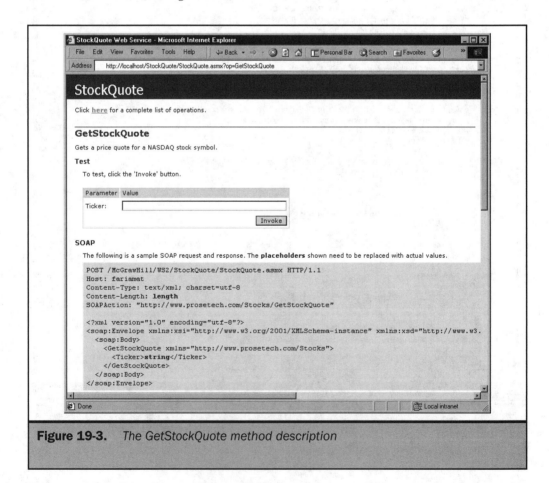

```
http://localhost/StockQuote/StockQuote.asmx?WSDL
```

If you know the location of an ASP.NET Web Service file, you can always retrieve its WSDL document by adding ?WSDL to the URL. This provides a standard way for a client to find all the information it needs to make a successful connection. ASP.NET generates this document automatically.

## Method Description

You can find out information about the methods in your Web Service by clicking on the corresponding link. For example, in the StockQuote Web Service you can click on the GetStockQuote link (see Figure 19-3).

**Figure 19-3.** *The GetStockQuote method description*

This window provides two sections. The first part is made up of a text box and Invoke button that allow you to run the function without needing to create a client. The second part is a list of the different protocols you can use to connect with the Web Service (HTTP POST, HTTP GET, and SOAP), and a technical description of the message format for each.

## Testing a Method

To test your method, enter a ticker and click the Invoke button. The result will be returned to you as an HTML page (see Figure 19-4).

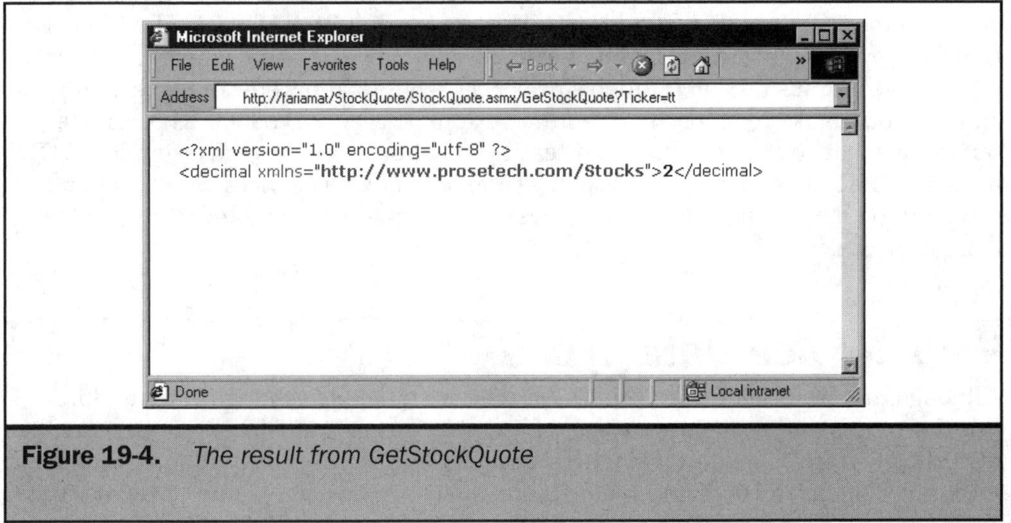


**Figure 19-4.** *The result from GetStockQuote*

This may not be the result you expected, but the information is there—wrapped inside the tags of an XML document. This format allows a Web Service to return complex information, such as a class with several members or even an entire DataSet. If you followed the suggestions for modifying the StockQuote service, you should see a number representing the length of the stock ticker you supplied.

The IE test page is a relatively crude way of accessing a Web Service. It's never used for any purpose other than testing. In addition, it supports a smaller range of data types. For example, there is no way to run a function that requires a custom structure or DataSet as a parameter, and you won't be able to test such a function through this page.

One question that many users have after seeing this page is "Where does this functionality come from?" For example, you might wonder if the Internet Explorer test page has additional script code for running your method, or if it relies on features built into the latest version of Internet Explorer. In fact, all that happens when you click the Invoke button is a normal HTTP GET request. You can see it in the browser string.

```
http://localhost/StockQuote/StockQuote.asmx/GetStockQuote?Ticker=MSFT
```

You could receive the same XML document with the same information by typing this information into your address bar manually.

The URL follows a format like this:

```
http://localhost/[AppName]/[AsmxFile]/[Method]?[Parameters]
```

The parameters are supplied as a list of query string variables after the question mark.

What you see in this example is a case of invoking a Web Service using HTTP GET (HTTP POST would be similar, except the parameters would be encoded in the message body, not the URL, and thus would not be visible to you). Both HTTP GET and HTTP POST retrieve results in an XML document. Generally, clients using your Web Service will use SOAP transmission through a proxy class. SOAP allows for more flexibility, and lets you invoke functions that require custom objects or DataSets as parameters. But the fact that you can run your code easily and effortlessly through a simple HTTP request in the browser string attests to the simplicity of Web Services. Surely, if you can run your code this easily in a simple browser, true cross-platform integration can't be that much harder.

## Web Service Data Types

Although the client can interact with a Web Service method as though it were a local function or subroutine, there are some differences. The most significant of these are the restrictions on the data types that you can use. As Web Services are built on top of the XML serialization architecture, web methods can use quite a few predefined data types. Table 19-1 provides a list of data types that are supported for Web Service parameters and return values.

| Data Type | Description |
|---|---|
| The Basics | Standard types such as integers and floating point numbers, Boolean variables, dates and times, and strings are fully supported. |
| Enumerations | Enumerations types (defined in Visual Basic .NET with the Enum keyword) are fully supported. |
| DataSets | ADO.NET DataSets allow you to use information from a relational database in your methods. DataTables and DataRows, however, are not supported. |

**Table 19-1.** *Web Service Data Types*

| Data Type | Description |
|---|---|
| XmlNode | Objects based on System.Xml.XmlNode are representations of a portion of an XML document. Under the hood, all Web Service data is passed as XML. This class allows you to directly support a portion of XML information whose structure may change. |
| Custom Objects | You can pass any object you create based on a custom class or structure. The only limitation is that only data members can be transmitted. If you use a class with defined methods, the copy of the object that is transmitted will only have its properties and variables. You won't be able to successfully use most other .NET classes (except DataSets and XmlNodes). |
| Arrays | You can use arrays of any supported type, including DataSets, XmlNodes, and custom objects. |

**Table 19-1.** *Web Service Data Types (continued)*

### Some Types Need SOAP

The full set of objects is supported for return values, and for parameters when you are communicating through SOAP. If you are communicating through HTTP GET or HTTP POST, you will only be able to use basic types, enumerations, and arrays of basic types or enumerations. This is because complex classes and other types cannot be represented in the query string (for HTTP GET) or form body (for an HTTP POST operation).



## The StockQuote Service with a Data Object

If you've ever used stock quoting services over the Internet, you have probably noticed that our example so far is somewhat simplified. The GetStockQuote function returns one piece of information—a price quote—whereas popular financial sites usually produce a full quote with a 52-week high and 52-week low, and other information about the volume of shares traded on a particular day. You could add more methods to the Web

Service to supply this information, but that would require multiple similar function calls, which would slow down performance because more time would be spent sending messages back and forth over the Internet. The client code would also become more tedious.

A better solution is to use a data object that encapsulates all the information you need. You can define the class for this object in the same file, and then use it as a parameter or return value for any of your functions. The data object is a completely ordinary Visual Basic .NET class, and shouldn't derive from System.Web.Services.WebService. It can contain public member variables that use any of the data types supported for Web Services. It can't contain methods (if it does, they will simply be ignored). Similarly, you shouldn't use full property procedures, as they would just be converted into ordinary public variables on the client side.

The client will receive the data object and be able to work with it exactly as though it were defined locally. In fact, it will be—the automatically generated proxy class will contain a copy of the class definition, as you'll see in Chapter 20.

Here's how the StockQuote service would look with the addition of a convenient data object:

```
Imports System.Web.Services

<WebService(Description:="Provides stock price lookup.", _
Namespace:="http://www.prosetech.com/Stocks")> _
Public Class StockQuote_BusinessObject
  Inherits System.Web.Services.WebService

    <WebMethod(Description:="Gets a quote for a stock.")> _
    Public Function GetStockQuote(Ticker As String) As StockInfo
        Dim Quote As New StockInfo()
        Quote.Symbol = Ticker
        Quote = FillQuoteFromDB(Quote)
        Return Quote
    End Function

    Private Function FillQuoteFromDB(Lookup As StockInfo) _
      As StockInfo
        ' You can add the appropriate database code here.
        ' For test purposes this function hard-codes
        ' some sample information.
        Lookup.CompanyName = "Trapezoid"
        Lookup.Price = 400
        Lookup.High_52Week = 410
```

```
        Lookup.Low_52Week = 20
        Return Lookup
    End Function

End Class

Public Class StockInfo
    Public Price As Decimal
    Public Symbol As String
    Public High_52Week As Decimal
    Public Low_52Week As Decimal
    Public CompanyName As String
End Class
```

Here's what happens in the GetStockQuote function:

1. A new StockInfo object is created.
2. The corresponding Symbol is specified for the StockInfo object.
3. The StockInfo object is passed to another function that fills it with information. This function is called FillQuoteFromDB.

The FillQuoteFromDB function is not visible to remote clients because it lacks the WebMethod attribute. It isn't even visible to other classes or code modules, because it is defined with the Private keyword. Typically, this function will perform some type of database lookup. It might return information that is confidential and should not be made available to all clients. By putting this logic into a separate function, you can separate the code that determines what information the client should receive, and still have the ability to retrieve the full record if your Web Service code needs to examine or modify other information. Generally, most of the work that goes into creating a Web Service—once you understand the basics—is trying to decide the best way to divide its functionality into separate procedures.

You might wonder how the client will understand the StockInfo object. In fact, the object is really just returned as a blob of XML or SOAP data. If you invoke this method through the IE test page, you'll see the result shown in Figure 19-5.

But ASP.NET is extremely clever about custom objects. When you use a class like StockInfo in your Web Service, it adds the definition directly into the WSDL document:

```
<types>
  <-- Other types omitted. -->
  <s:complexType name="StockInfo">
```

```
      <s:sequence>
        <s:element minOccurs="1" maxOccurs="1" name="Price"
           type="s:decimal" />
        <s:element minOccurs="1" maxOccurs="1" name="Symbol"
           nillable="true"
           type="s:string" />
        <s:element minOccurs="1" maxOccurs="1" name="High_52Week"
           type="s:decimal" />
        <s:element minOccurs="1" maxOccurs="1" name="Low_52Week"
           type="s:decimal" />
        <s:element minOccurs="1" maxOccurs="1" name="CompanyName"
           nillable="true" type="s:string" />
      </s:sequence>
    </s:complexType>
  </types>
```

When you generate a client for this Web Service, a proxy class will be created automatically. It will define the StockInfo class and convert the XML data back into a StockInfo object. The end result is that all the information will return to your application in the form you expect, just as if you had used a local function.

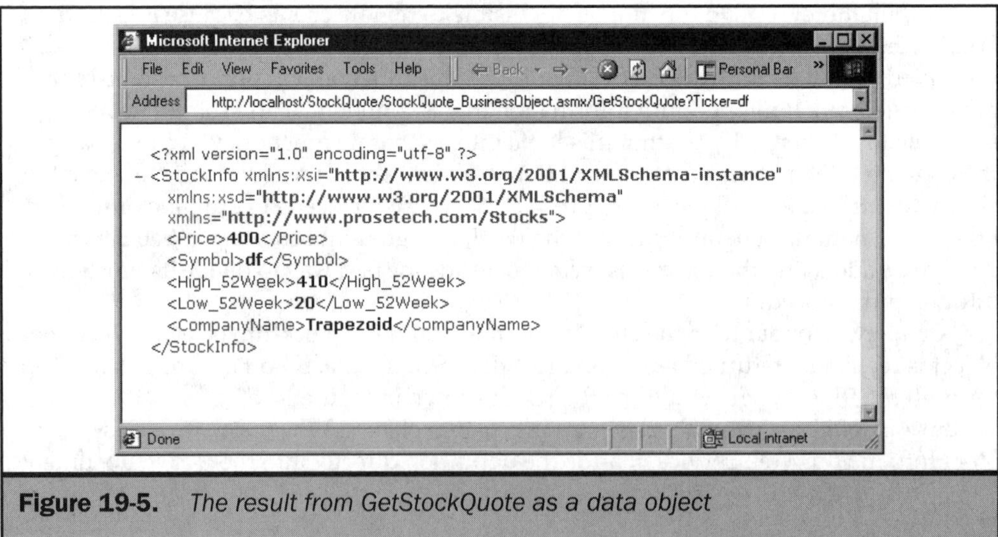


**Figure 19-5.** *The result from GetStockQuote as a data object*

### Returning Historical Data from StockQuote

It may interest you to model a class for a Web Service that returns historical information that can be used to create a price graph. You could implement this in a few different ways. For example, you might use a function that requires the starting and ending dates, and returns an array that contains a number of chronological price quotes. Your client code would then determine how much information was returned by checking the upper bound of the array. The web method definition would look something like this:

```
<WebMethod()> Public Function GetHistory _
  (Ticker As String, Start As DateTime, End As DateTime) _
  As Decimal()
```

Alternatively, you might use a function that accepts a parameter specifying the number of required entries and the time span.

```
<WebMethod()> Public Function GetHistory ( _
  Ticker As String, Period As TimeSpan, _
  NumberOfEntries As Integer) _
  As Decimal()
```

In either case, it's up to you to find the best way to organize a Web Service. The process is a long and incremental one that often involves performance tuning and usability concerns. Of course, it also gives you a chance to put everything you've learned into practice, and get right into the technical details of ASP.NET programming.



## The ASP.NET Intrinsic Objects

When you inherit from System.Web.Services.WebService, you gain access to several of the standard built-in ASP.NET objects that you can use in an ordinary Web Forms page. These include:

**Application** Used for global variables available to all clients

**Server** Used for utility functions such as URL encoding and the creation of COM objects

**Session** Used for per-client variables

**User** Used to retrieve information about the current client

**Context** Provides access to Request and Response and, more usefully, the Cache object

These objects are described in more detail throughout this book.

On the whole, these built-in objects won't often be used in Web Service programming, with the possible exception of the Cache object. Generally, a Web Service should look and work like a business object, and not rely on retrieving or setting additional information through a built-in ASP.NET object. However, if you need to use per-user security or state management, these objects will be very useful. For example, you could create a Web Service that requires the client to log on, and subsequently stores important information in the Session collection. Or you could create a Web Service that creates a custom object on the server (such as a DataSet), stores it in the Session collection, and returns whatever information you need through various separate functions that can be invoked as required. When approaching a design like this, you need to be very conscious of the possible performance toll.

## State Management

There are several different kinds of state management available in ASP.NET, including using the Application and Session collections or custom cookies in the Response and Request objects. All of these methods are possible with Web Services. However, Session management requires an initial performance hit with every method call, because the server has to look up the matching Session collection for the client, even if it is empty. It is disabled by default. You can enable Session state management for a specific method by using the EnableSession property of the WebMethod attribute.

```
<WebMethod(EnableSession:=True)>
```

Before you implement state management, make sure you review whether there is another way to accomplish your goal. Some ASP.NET gurus believe that maintaining state is at best a performance drag, and at worst a contradiction to the philosophy of lightweight stateless Web Services. For example, instead of using a dedicated function to submit client preferences, you could add extra parameters to all your functions to accommodate the required information. Similarly, instead of allowing a user to manipulate a large DataSet stored in the Session collection on the server, you could return the entire object to the client and then clear it from memory. In cases like these, you have to consider many application-specific details. For example, transmitting a large DataSet could greatly increase network traffic, which could also reduce performance. But in general, it is always a good idea to reduce the amount of information stored in memory on the server if you want to create a Web Service that can scale to hundreds or thousands of simultaneous connections.

### Disabling Session State Does Not Destroy the Session Collection

What happens when you have a Web Service that enables Session state management for some methods but disables it for others? Essentially, disabling Session management just tells ASP.NET to ignore any in-memory Session information, and withhold the Session collection from the current procedure. It does not cause existing information to be cleared out of the collection (that will only happen when the Session times out). However, the server still has to allocate memory to store any Session data you have added—the only performance benefit you're receiving is not having to look up Session information when it isn't required.

## The StockQuote Service with State Management

The following example introduces state management into the StockQuote Web Service.

```
Public Class StockQuote_SessionState
  Inherits WebService

    <WebMethod(EnableSession:=True)> _
    Public Function GetStockQuote(Ticker As String) As Decimal
        ' Increment counters. This function locks the application
        ' collection to prevent synchronization errors.
        Application.Lock()
        Application(Ticker) = Application(Ticker) + 1
        Application.UnLock()
        Session(Ticker) = Session(Ticker) + 1

        ' Return a sample value representing the length of the ticker.
        Return Ticker.Length
    End Function

    <WebMethod(EnableSession:=True)> _
    Public Function GetStockUsage(Ticker As String) As CounterInfo
        Dim Result As New CounterInfo()
        Result.GlobalRequests = Application(Ticker)
        Result.SessionRequests = Session(Ticker)
```

```
        Return Result
    End Function

End Class

Public Class CounterInfo
    Public GlobalRequests As Integer
    Public SessionRequests As Integer
End Class
```

This example allows our StockQuote service to record how much it has been used. Every time the GetStockQuote function is used, two counters are incremented. One is a global counter that tracks the total number of requests for that stock quote from all clients. The other one is a session-specific counter that represents how many times the current client has requested a quote for the specified stock. The Ticker string is used to name the stored item. That means that if a client requests quotes for 50 different stocks, 50 different counter variables will be created. Clearly, this system wouldn't be practical for large-scale use. One practice that this example does follow correctly is that of locking the Application collection before updating it. This can cause a significant performance slowdown, but it guarantees that the value will be accurate even if multiple clients are accessing the Web Service simultaneously.

To view the counter information, you can call the GetStockUsage function with the ticker for the stock you are interested in. A custom object, CounterInfo, is returned to you with both pieces of information. Note that if this Web Service used strict type checking, it would need to convert the counter from a string to an integer, and vice versa, as shown here:

```
' Incrementing the Application counter.
Application(Ticker) = CType(Application(Ticker), Integer) + 1

' Retrieving the Application counter.
Result.GlobalRequests = CType(Application(Ticker), Integer)
```

It's unlikely that you'd ever see an application designed to store this much usage information in memory, but it gives you a good indication of how you can use Session and Application state management in a Web Service just as easily as you can an ASP.NET page. Note that Session state automatically expires after a preset amount of time, and both the Session and Application collections will be emptied when the application is stopped. For more information about ASP.NET state management, refer to Chapter 10.

### Clients Need Additional Changes to Support Session State

As you've seen, a Web Service needs to specifically enable Session state with the WebMethod attribute. This allows Session state to work for one method. However, in most cases you want Session state to persist between method calls. For example, you might want to set Session state data in one web method and retrieve it in another. To allow this, the client must support ASP.NET's Session state cookie. This technique is described in detail in Chapter 20.

# Other Web Service Options

The final section of this chapter explores how you can extend your Web Services with support for transactions, caching, and ASP.NET security. None of these features are customized for Web Service use. Instead, they are built into the ASP.NET framework or Windows architecture. This section shows you how to access them.

## Transactions

Transactions are an important feature in many business applications. They ensure that a series of operations either succeeds or fails as a unit. Transactions also prevent the possibility of inconsistent or corrupted data that can occur if an operation fails midway through after committing only some of its changes. Web Services can participate in standard COM+ transactions, but in a somewhat limited way. Because of the stateless nature of the HTTP protocol, Web Service methods can only act as the root object in a transaction. That means that a Web Service method can start a transaction and use it to perform a series of related tasks, but multiple Web Services cannot be grouped into one transaction. This means you may have to put in some extra thought when you are creating a transactional Web Service. For example, it might not make sense to create a financial Web Service with a DebitAccount and a CreditAccount function. Instead, you might want to make sure both functions happen as a single unit using a transaction TransferFunds method.

To use a transaction, you first have to make a reference to the System.EnterpriseServices assembly. In order to do this in Visual Studio .NET, right-click on References in the Solution Explorer, select Add Reference, and choose System.EnterpriseServices (see Figure 19-6).

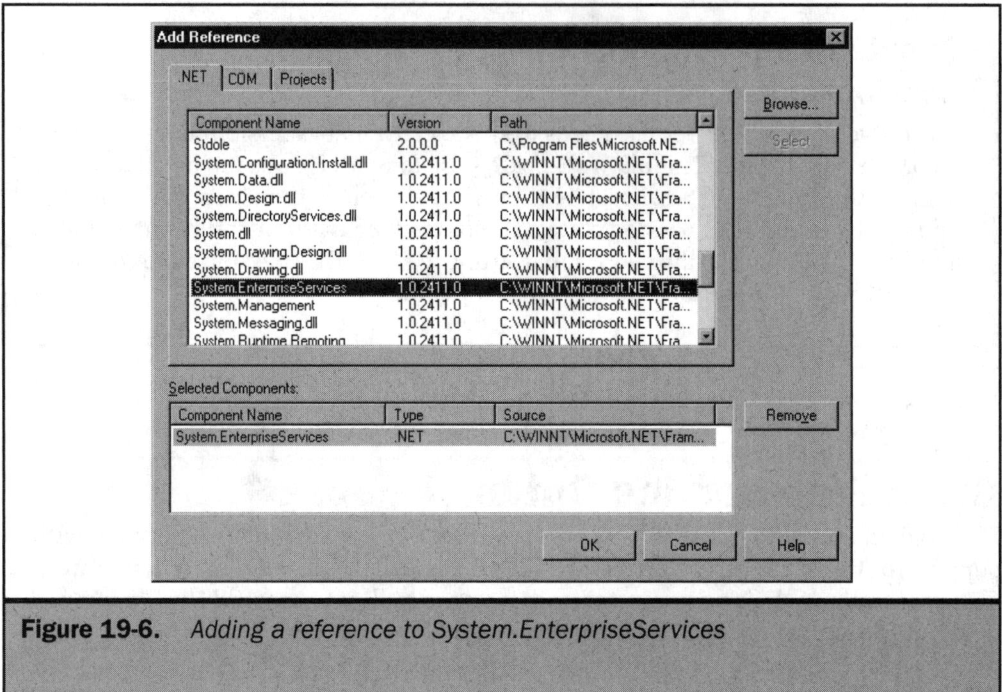


**Figure 19-6.** *Adding a reference to System.EnterpriseServices*

You can now import the corresponding namespace so the types you need (TransactionOption and ContextUtil) are at your fingertips.

```
Imports System.EnterpriseServices
```

To start a transaction in a Web Service method, set the TransactionOption property of the WebMethod attribute. TransactionOption is an enumeration that provides several values that allow you to specify whether a code component uses or requires transactions. Because Web Services must be the root of a transaction, most of these options do not apply. To create a Web Service method that starts a transaction automatically, use the following attribute:

```
<WebMethod(TransactionOption:=TransactionOption.RequiresNew)>
```

This method can then create and use other COM objects that support or require transactions. A transaction started in this way will be automatically committed once the method ends, unless one of the Web Services or components specifies that the transaction has failed. To cause a transaction to fail in the web method code, you can call the shared

SetAbort method of the ContextUtil object. The transaction will also be aborted if an unhandled error occurs.

Now consider the following example, which shows a method that allows a user to buy a stock. A transaction is required for this operation to make sure the account withdrawal and stock credit both succeed or fail as a unit.

```
<WebMethod(TransactionOption := TransactionOption.RequiresNew)> _
Public Sub BuyStock (Ticker As String, Shares As Integer, _
  AcctNumber As String)

    Dim TotalPrice As Decimal = Shares * GetPricePerShare(Ticker)
    Dim objBank As New MyCOMObject()

    If objBank.GetBalance(AcctNumber) < TotalPrice Then
        ' Explicitly abort the transaction.
        ContextUtil.SetAbort()
    Else
        objBank.AddToStockPortfolio(AcctNumberTo, Ticker, Shares)
        objBank.Debit(AcctNumber, TotalPrice)
    End If

End Sub
```

This code sample is purely conceptual and uses a few ingredients that aren't shown, such as the GetPricePerShare function and the objBank COM object. The important aspect to understand is that when you invoke the AddToStockPortfolio and Debit methods, that code has a chance to abort the whole transaction by using the SetAbort method. If any one of the methods you call votes to abort the transaction, the whole process will be automatically rolled back.

Does a Web Service need to use COM+ transactions? It all depends on the situation. If multiple updates are required in separate data stores, you may need to use transactions to ensure your data's integrity. If, on the other hand, you are only modifying values in a single database (such as SQL 2000) you can probably make use of the data provider's built-in transaction features instead, as explained in Chapter 13. Remember, transactions can be used in any ASP.NET application. The only part that is specific to Web Services is the TransactionOption property of the <WebMethod> attribute, which automatically starts your transaction.



## Caching

As with all ASP.NET code, you can use data caching through the Cache object (which is available through the Context.Cache property in your Web Service code). This object can temporarily store information that is expensive to create so that it can be reused by other clients calling the same method, or even other methods or ASP.NET Web Forms pages. For more information on data caching, refer to Chapter 23.

In addition, you can use output caching. Output caching works on the same principle as Web Forms pages: identical requests (in this case, requests for the same method and with the same parameters) will receive identical responses from the cache, until it expires. This can greatly increase performance in heavily trafficked sites, even if you only store a response for a few seconds.

Output caching should only be used in information retrieval or data processing functions. It should not be used in a method that needs to perform other work, such as changing Session or Application items or modifying a database. This is because subsequent calls to a cached method will receive the cached result, but the actual code will not be executed.

To enable caching for a function, you use the CacheDuration property of the WebMethod attribute.

```
<WebMethod(CacheDuration:=30)>
```

The previous example states that the result for this method will be stored in ASP.NET's output cache for 30 seconds, and will be reused for any identical requests that are received in that time. Generally, you should determine the amount of time based on how long the underlying data will remain valid. For example, if a stock quote were being retrieved, you would use a much smaller number of seconds than you might for a weather forecast. If you were storing a piece of information that seldom changes, like the results of a yearly census poll, your considerations would be entirely different. In this case, the information is almost permanent, but the amount of returned information will be larger than the capacity of ASP.NET's output cache. Your goal in this situation would be to limit the cache duration enough to ensure that only the most popular requests are stored.

Of course, caching decisions should also be based on how long it will take to recreate the information and how many clients will be using the Web Service. You may need to perform substantial real-world testing and tuning to achieve perfection.

## Security

You have two options for Web Service security. You can create and use your own login and authentication features, or you can use the standard ASP.NET security methods. The standard ASP.NET security features are described in detail in Chapter 24. Note that because Web Service does not present any user interface, it cannot request user credentials on its own. It has to rely on the calling code, or rely on having the user logged on under an authorized account.

If you are using your own login procedure, you will probably add a dedicated login method that creates a license key, stores it in a database, and returns it to the user. Every other method will then require the same license key as an additional parameter.

The following example shows how the StockQuote service uses this system. Once again, only the conceptual design is shown. To actually finish this into a full-featured application, you'd need to add some rudimentary database code, as described in Chapter 13.

```
Public Class StockQuote_Security
  Inherits System.Web.Services.WebService

    <WebMethod> _
    Public Function Login(ID As String, Password As String) _
     As LicenseKey
        If VerifyUser(ID, Password) = True Then
            ' Generate a license key made up of
            ' some random sequence of characters.
            Dim Key As LicenseKey

            ' A value is hard-coded here. Typically, it would be
            ' generated using some algorithm (maybe incorporating the
            ' current time of day and user ID).
            Key.Key = "s0d343520lgfgfg"

            ' The key would then be added to some temporary
            ' license database.
        Else
            ' Cause an error that will be returned to the client.
            ' The function uses a special SecurityEexception
            ' from the .NET class library.
            Throw New System.Security.SecurityException()
        End If
    End Function

    <WebMethod> _
    Public Function GetStockQuote(Ticker As String, _
     Key As LicenseKey) As Integer
        If VerifyKey(Key) = False Then
            Throw New System.Security.SecurityException()
```

```
        Else
            ' Normal GetStockQuote code goes here.
            Return (Ticker.Length)
        End If
    End Function

    Private Function VerifyUser(ID As String, Password As String) _
     As Boolean
        ' Add database lookup code here to verify the user.
        Return True
    End Function

    Private Function VerifyKey(Key As LicenseKey) As Boolean
        ' Look up key in key database. If it's not there
        ' (or it's expired, return False).
        Return True
    End Function
End Class

Public Class LicenseKey
    Public Key As String
End Class
```

## Interesting Facts About this Code

- Before using any method in this class, the client must call the Login method and store the received license key. Every other web method will require that license key.
- The same private function—VerifyKey—is used regardless of what web method is invoked. This ensures that the license verification code is only written in one place, and is used consistently.
- Currently, this design requires a trip to the database to verify that a license key exists for each web method invocation. Data caching could be added to this design to solve this problem. In this case, every key would be stored in two places—in the database, which would be used as a last resort, and duplicated in the in-memory cache. The VerifyKey function would only perform the database lookup if the cached item was not found. For more information about caching, refer to Chapter 23.

## Security with SOAP Headers

The potential problem with this example is that it requires a license key (or a user ID and password, depending on your design) to be submitted with each method call as a parameter. This can be a bit tedious. To streamline this process, you can use a custom SOAP header.

SOAP headers are special pieces of information that are sent with every SOAP message. They can contain any type of data that you could use as a method parameter or return value for a Web Service method. The advantage of SOAP headers is just the convenience. The client specifies a SOAP header once, and the header is automatically sent to every method that needs it, making the coding clearer and more concise.

To create a custom SOAP header, you first need to define it.

```
Public Class SecurityHeader
  Inherits System.Web.Services.Protocols.SoapHeader

    Public UserID As String
    Public Password As String
    Public Key As String
End Class
```

The SOAP header class must inherit from System.Web.Services.Protocols.SoapHeader. You can then add all the additional pieces of information you want it to contain as member variables. In the following example, three pieces of information are added.

Next, your Web Service needs a public member variable to receive the SOAP header.

```
Public Class StockQuote_SoapSecurity
  Inherits System.Web.Services.WebService

    Public KeyHeader As SecurityHeader

    ' (Other Web Service code goes here.)
End Class
```

The client can create an instance of the SecurityHeader, set the UserID and Password, and attach the SecurityHeader to the Web Service by assigning it to the KeyHeader variable of the proxy class. This process is demonstrated in Chapter 20, in the section "Using Custom SOAP Headers."

The Web Service requires one last ingredient. Each Web Service method that wants to access the SecurityHeader must explicitly indicate this requirement with a

SoapHeader attribute. The attribute indicates the Web Service member variable where the header should be placed.

```
Public Class StockQuote_SoapSecurity
  Inherits System.Web.Services.WebService

    Public KeyHeader As SecurityHeader

    <WebMethod, SoapHeader("KeyHeader", _
    Direction := SoapHeaderDirection.InOut)> _
    Public Function GetStockQuote(Ticker As String) As Integer
        ' (Code omitted.)
    End Function

End Class
```

In this example, the header is sent bidirectionally. It goes to the web method and back to the client. The result is a useful trick: the user can set the user ID and password, and the Web Service can remove these pieces of information from the header (for security) and replace them with a key once the verification has been performed. The advantage of this method is that the client doesn't need to explicitly call the Login method. It's all handled transparently.

The complete Web Service would look like this (the SecurityHeader definition is left out):

```
Public Class StockQuote_Security
  Inherits System.Web.Services.WebService

    Public KeyHeader As SecurityHeader

    <WebMethod, SoapHeader("KeyHeader", _
      SoapHeaderDirection.InOut)> _
    Public Function GetStockQuote(Ticker As String) As Integer
        If VerifyKey(KeyHeader) = False Then
            Throw New System.Security.SecurityException()
        Else
            ' Normal GetStockQuote code goes here.
            Return (Ticker.Length)
        End If
    End Function
```

```
    Private Function VerifyKey(Key As SecurityHeader) As Boolean
        If Key.Key = "" Then
            ' Look up the user in the database and assign the key.
            ' Add the key to temporary database and return True.
        Else
            ' Look up key in key database. If it's not there
            ' (or it's expired, return False).
        End If

        ' This test function always returns true.
        Return True
    End Function

End Class
```

# Chapter 20

## Using Web Services

The past couple of chapters examined how to design and code Web Services. By now you realize that Web Services are really standard business objects that provide a powerful built-in communication framework, which allows you to interact with them over the Internet. However, you still don't know how this interaction takes place. In this chapter, we'll examine how to create a simple ASP.NET client for our StockQuote Web Service. Then, for a little more fun, I'll show you how to access a real, mature Web Service on the Internet: Microsoft's TerraService, which exposes a vast library of millions of satellite pictures from a database that is 1.5 terabytes in size.

## Consuming a Web Service

Microsoft has repeatedly declared that its ambition for programming tools such as Visual Studio .NET, the Common Language Runtime, and the .NET class library is to provide the common infrastructure for application developers, who will then only need to create the upper layer of business-specific logic. Web Services hold true to that promise, with ASP.NET automating communication between Web Services and clients. Before this chapter is finished, you'll see how you can call a Web Service method as easily as a method in a local class.

Web Services communicate with other .NET applications through a special proxy class. You can create this proxy class automatically through Visual Studio .NET or by using a command-line tool. When you wish to call a web method, you call the corresponding method of the proxy object, which then fetches the results for you using SOAP calls. Strictly speaking, you don't need to use a proxy class—you could create and receive the SOAP messages on your own. However, this process is quite difficult and involves a degree of understanding and complexity that would make Web Services much less useful.

### Configuring a Web Service Client in Visual Studio .NET

When developing and testing a Web Service in Visual Studio .NET, it's often easiest to add both the Web Service and the client application to the same solution. This allows you to test and change both pieces at the same time. You can even use the integrated debugger to set breakpoints and step through the code in both the client and the server, as though they were really a single application!

To work with both projects at once in Visual Studio .NET, follow these steps:

1. Open the Web Service project (in this case, the StockQuote service).
2. Select File | Add Project | New Project.
3. Choose ASP.NET Web Application, title it (for example, StockQuoteClient), and click OK.
4. You should set the new project as the startup project (otherwise, you will just see the Web Service test page when you click the Start button). To make this

adjustment, right-click on the new project in the Solution Explorer, and choose Set As StartUp Project.

5. If you create the projects in this order, the build order will be automatically set correctly, and the Web Service will be compiled before the ASP.NET application is compiled and launched. To verify the build order, right-click one of the projects in the Solution Explorer, and click Project Build Order. The StockQuote service should be first in the list.

Your Solution Explorer should now look like Figure 20-1.

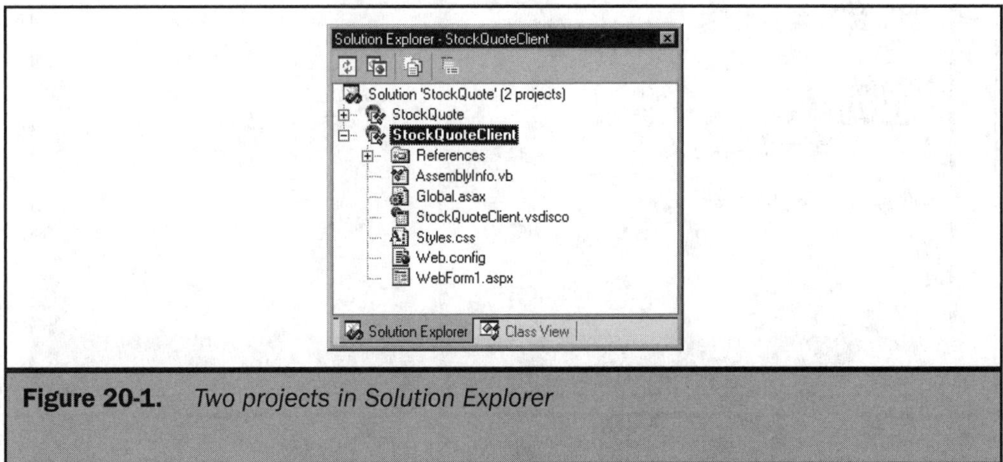


**Figure 20-1.** *Two projects in Solution Explorer*

## Creating a Web Reference in Visual Studio .NET

Even after you add two projects to the same solution, they still have no way to communicate with each other. To set up this layer of interaction, you need to create a special proxy class. In Visual Studio .NET, you create this proxy class by adding a web reference. Web references are similar to ordinary references, but instead of pointing to assemblies with ordinary .NET types, they point to a URL with a WSDL contract for a Web Service.

To create a web reference, follow these steps:

1. Right-click on the client project in the Solution Explorer, and select Add Web Reference.
2. The Add Web Reference window opens, as shown in Figure 20-2. This window provides options for searching web registries or entering a URL directly. You can browse directly to your Web Service by entering the appropriate web address for the discovery document, using the virtual directory (such as http://localhost/StockQuote/StockQuote.asmx?WSDL). Remember, the discovery document is the Web Service address, followed by ?WSDL.

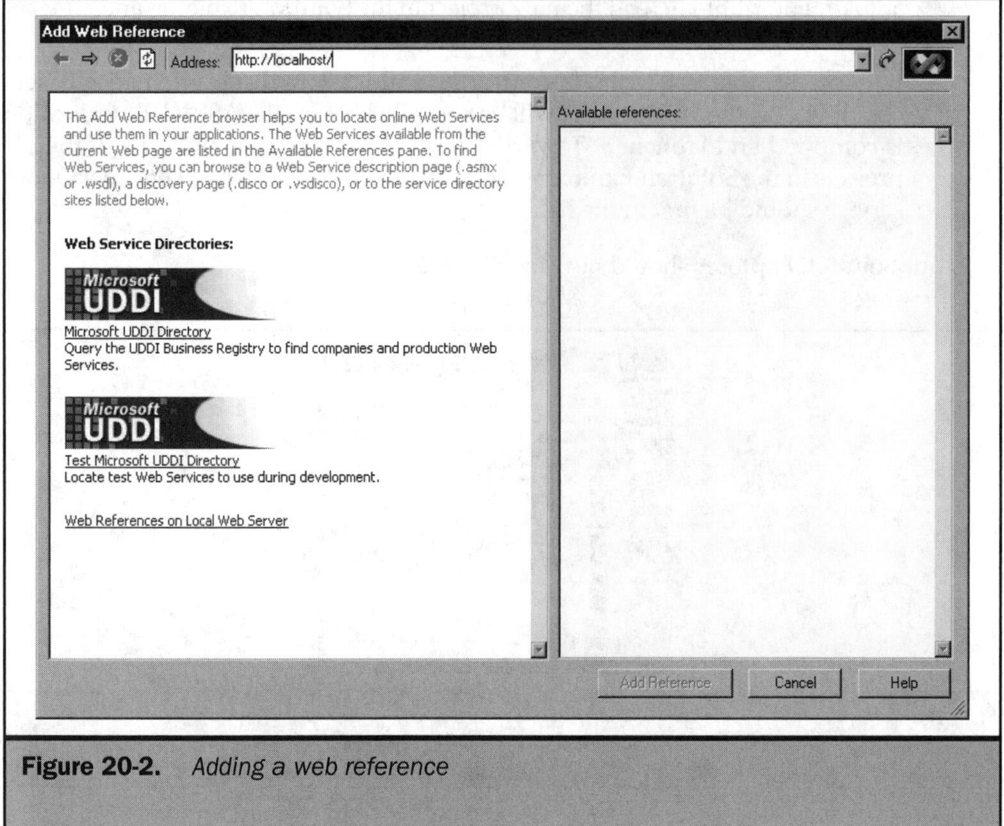


**Figure 20-2.** *Adding a web reference*

3. Alternatively, you can use a discovery file to find your Web Service. The discovery file will be shown on the left, and the linked Web Services will be shown on the right. Figure 20-3 shows the StockQuote.vsdisco file, which provides links to all the different StockQuote variations we saw in the last chapter.
4. You can click View Contract to see the WSDL document, or View Documentation to see the test page. To add the reference to this Web Service, click Add Reference at the bottom of the window.
5. Now your computer (the web server for this service) will appear in the Web References group for your project in the Solution Explorer window. A copy of the corresponding discovery document and WSDL contract will also be added to the client project, and you can browse them as well (see Figure 20-4).

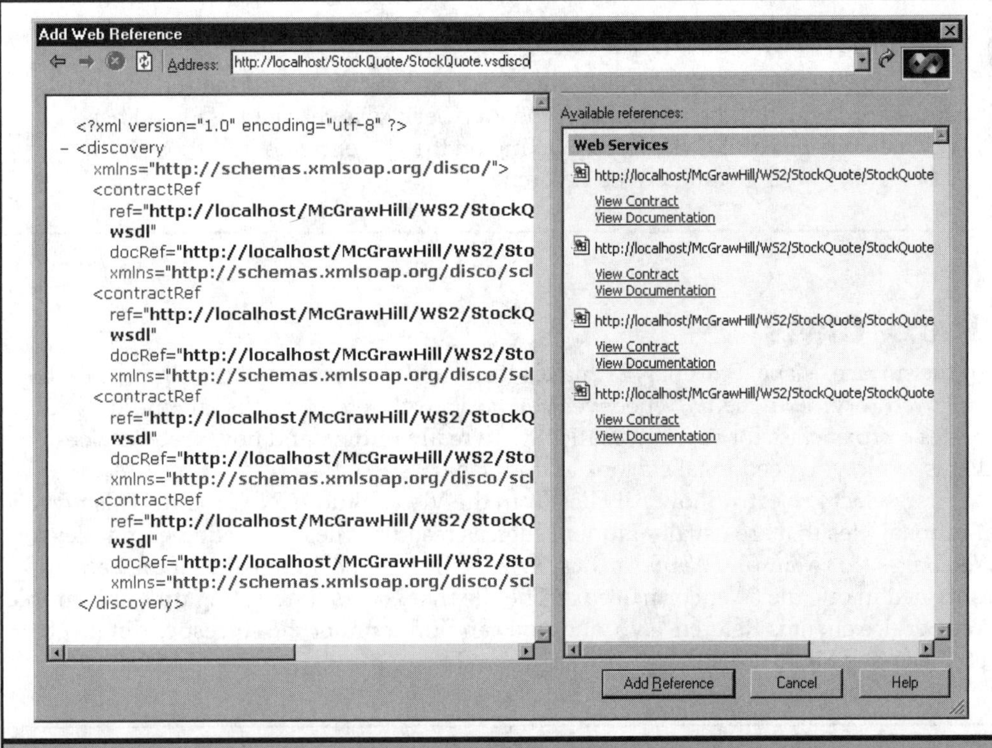


**Figure 20-3.** *Finding a Web Service through a discovery file*

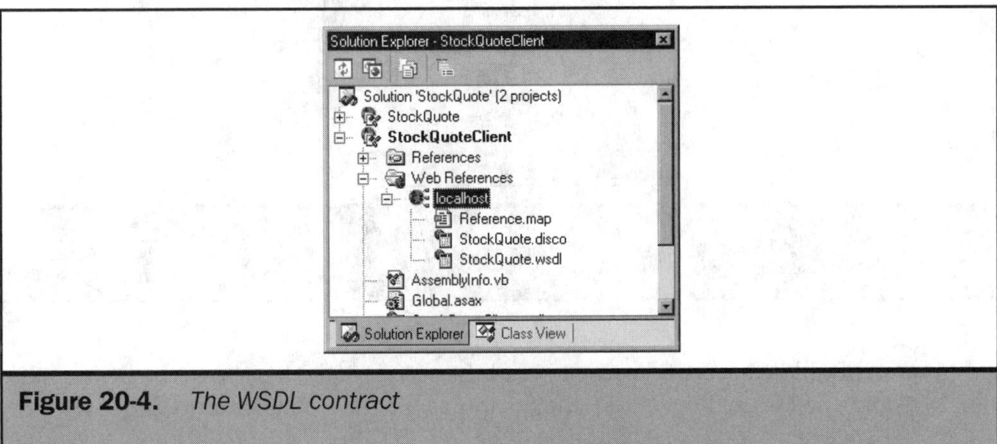


**Figure 20-4.** *The WSDL contract*

### Web References Are Static

The web reference you create uses the WSDL contract and information that exists at the time you add the reference. If the Web Service is changed, you will need to update your proxy class by right-clicking on the server name (localhost, in this case) and choosing Update Web Reference.

## The Proxy Class

On the surface, Visual Studio .NET makes it seem like all you need is a simple link to your Web Service. In reality, whenever you add a web reference, Visual Studio .NET creates a proxy class for you automatically. To really understand how Web Service clients work, you need to take a look at this class.

First, select Project | Show All Files from the Visual Studio .NET menu. This reveals additional files that are usually hidden, such as resource files and code-behind files for Web Pages (for example, WebForm1.aspx.vb), which usually appear as if they are all contained in one file (WebForm1.aspx). The file that is most interesting for our example Web Service client is Reference.vb, and you can find it under the corresponding web reference (see Figure 20-5).

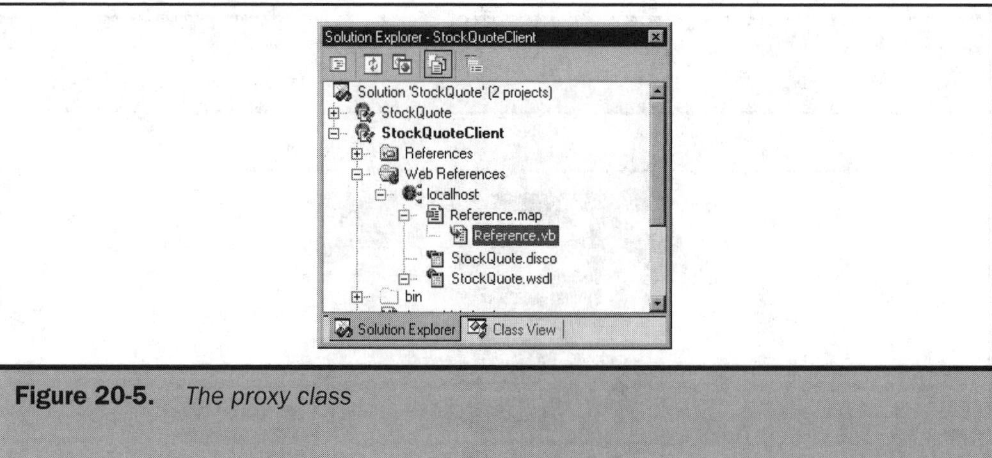


**Figure 20-5.** *The proxy class*

You can double-click the filename to read the source code. It's shown below, in a slightly simplified form. I've left out the attributes that tell Visual Studio .NET how to treat this code when debugging, and replaced some of the attributes that configure the SOAP transmission with comments.

```
'------------------------------------------------------------------------
'     This code was generated by a tool.
'     Runtime Version: 1.0.2914.11
'------------------------------------------------------------------------
Imports System
Imports System.Diagnostics
Imports System.Web.Services
Imports System.Web.Services.Protocols
Imports System.Xml.Serialization

Namespace localhost

    ' (A WebServiceBindingAttribute is declared here.)
    Public Class StockQuote
        Inherits System.Web.Services.Protocols.SoapHttpClientProtocol

        Public Sub New()
            MyBase.New
            Me.Url = "http://localhost/Chapter17/StockQuote.asmx"
        End Sub

        ' (A SoapDocumentMethodAttribute is declared here.)
        Public Function GetStockQuote(ByVal Ticker As String) _
          As StockInfo
            Dim results() As Object = Me.Invoke ( _
             "GetStockQuote", New Object() {Ticker})
            Return CType(results(0),StockInfo)
        End Function

        Public Function BeginGetStockQuote(Ticker As String, _
          callback As AsyncCallback, asyncState As Object) _
          As IAsyncResult

           Return Me.BeginInvoke("GetStockQuote", New Object(), _
             {Ticker}, callback, asyncState)

End Function
```

```
        Public Function EndGetStockQuote( _
          asyncResult As IAsyncResult) As StockInfo
            Dim results() As Object = Me.EndInvoke(asyncResult)
            Return CType(results(0),StockInfo)
        End Function

    End Class

    Public Class StockInfo
        Public Price As Decimal
        Public Symbol As String
        Public High_52Week As Decimal
        Public Low_52Week As Decimal
        Public CompanyName As String
    End Class

End Namespace
```

## Interesting Facts About this Code

- The entire class is contained inside a namespace that is named after the server. For example, to use the StockQuote proxy code (and the StockQuote Web Service), you have to access the .NET namespace called localhost.
- At the end of this file, a copy of the StockInfo class definition is provided. This class is used to return some information from the StockQuote service. Now that Visual Studio .NET has placed its definition in the proxy class, you can create your own StockInfo objects, without needing to add any new code. (The StockInfo class is available as localhost.StockInfo.) Unlike the StockQuote proxy class, the StockInfo class does not participate in any SOAP messages or Internet communication; it is just a simple data class.
- A StockQuote class contains the functionality for the StockQuote Web Service. This class acts as a "stand-in" for the remote StockQuote Web Service. When you call a StockQuote method, you are really calling a method of this local class. This class then performs the SOAP communication as required to contact the "real" remote Web Service. The proxy class acquires its ability to communicate in SOAP through the .NET class library. It inherits from the SoapHttpClientProtocol class, and binds its local methods to Web Service methods with prebuilt .NET attributes. In other words, the low-level SOAP details are hidden not only from you, but also from the proxy class, which relies on ready-made .NET components from the System.Web.Services.Protocols namespace.

- If you peer into the GetStockQuote method, you'll notice that it doesn't actually retrieve a StockInfo object from the remote Web Service. Instead, it receives a generic Object type (which corresponds to a blob of XML data). It then handles the conversion into a StockInfo object before it returns the information to your code. In other words, the proxy layer not only handles the SOAP communication layer, it also handles the conversion from XML to .NET objects and data types, as needed. If .NET types were used directly with Web Services, it would be extremely difficult to use them from other non-Microsoft platforms.
- The proxy class has three methods for every method in the remote Web Service. The first method, which is named after the corresponding Web Service method (such as GetStockQuote), is used like an ordinary Visual Basic function. The other two methods are used to retrieve the same information from the same method asynchronously. In other words, you submit a request with the BeginGetStockQuote method, and pick up your results later with the EndGetStockQuote method. This is a useful technique in desktop applications where you don't want to become bogged down waiting for a slow Internet connection. However, the examples in this chapter use only ASP.NET clients, which do not really benefit from asynchronous consumption because the web page is not returned to the client until all the code has finished processing.
- The proxy class uses a constructor that sets the URL property to point to the Web Service .asmx file. You can query this property in your code to find out what Web Service the proxy is using, or you could change it to connect to an identical Web Service at another location.

## Creating a Proxy with WSDL.exe

Even if you aren't using Visual Studio to design your client application, you still interact with a Web Service through a proxy class. However, this proxy class needs to be generated with another tool. In this case, you must use the WSDL.exe utility that is included with the .NET framework. (You can find this file in the .NET framework directory, such as C:\Program Files\Microsoft.NET\FrameworkSDK\Bin. Visual Studio .NET users have the WSDL.exe utility in the C:\Program Files\Microsoft Visual Studio .NET\FrameworkSDK\Bin directory.) This file is a command-line utility, so it's easiest to use by opening a DOS-style command prompt window.

The syntax for WSDL.exe is as follows:

```
Wsdl /language:language /protocol:protocol
     /namespace:myNameSpace /out:filename
     /username:username /password:password
     /domain:domain <url or path>
```

Each field is described in the Table 20-1.

| Parameter | Meaning |
|---|---|
| Language | This is the language the class is written in. The language is not really important because you shouldn't modify the proxy class anyway; your changes will be lost every time you need to regenerate it. However, if you want to examine it and understand the proxy class, you should probably specify VB. If you don't make a choice, the default is C#. |
| Protocol | Usually, you will omit this option and use the default (SOAP). However, you could also specify HttpGet and HttpPost, for slightly more limiting protocols. |
| Namespace | This is the .NET namespace that your proxy class will use. If you omit this parameter, no namespace is used, and the classes in this file are available globally. For better organization, you should probably choose a logical namespace. |
| Out | This allows you to specify the name for the generated file. By default this is the name of the service, followed by an extension indicating the language (such as StockQuote.vb). You can always rename this file after it is generated. |
| Username, Password, and Domain | You should specify these values if the web server requires authentication to access the discovery and WSDL documents. |
| URL or Path | This is the last portion of the Wsdl command line, and it specifies the location of the WSDL file for the Web Service. |

**Table 20-1.** *WSDL.exe Command-Line Parameters*

A typical WSDL.exe command might look something like this (split over two lines):

```
wsdl /language:VB /namespace:localhost
http://localhost/StockQuote.asmx?WSDL
```

In this case, a StockQuote.vb file would be created, and it would look almost identical to the example shown in the previous section. Before you can use this class in an ASP.NET application, you will need to compile the file. Assuming that it's a VB .NET file, you must use the vbc.exe compiler included with the .NET framework (C# developers use csc.exe instead). To turn your StockQuote class into a DLL, use the following code:

```
vbc /t:library /out:StockQuote.dll StockQuote.vb
```

Now you can copy the .dll file to the bin directory of your ASP.NET client application. Web pages in that application can access the classes in this DLL as long as they use the correct namespace. (As you'll see in Chapter 21, ASP.NET searches the bin directory to find available classes automatically.)

### You Don't Need a Proxy Class

You can use a Web Service without WSDL.exe or Visual Studio .NET. In fact, you don't even need a proxy class. All you need is a program that can send and receive SOAP messages. After all, Web Services are designed to be cross-platform. However, unless you have significant experience with another tool (such as the Microsoft SOAP toolkit), the details are generally frustrating and unpleasant. The .NET types provide the prebuilt infrastructure you need to guarantee easy, error-free operation.

## Using the Proxy Class

Using the proxy class is incredibly easy. In most respects, it's not any different than using a local class. The following sample page uses the StockQuote service and displays the information it retrieves in a label control. You could place this snippet of code into the Page.Load event.

```
' Create a StockInfo object for our results.
Dim WSInfo As New localhost.StockInfo()

' Create the actual Web Service proxy class.
Dim WS As New localhost.StockQuote()

' Call the Web Service method.
WSInfo = WS.GetStockQuote("")

lblResult.Text = WSInfo.CompanyName & " is at: " & WSInfo.Price
```

The whole process is quite straightforward. First, the code creates a StockInfo object to hold the results. Then the code creates an instance of the proxy class, which allows access to all the Web Service functionality. Finally, the code calls the Web Service method using the proxy class and catches the returned data in the StockInfo object. On the surface, it looks the same as the code for any other local class. As you experiment with your project, remember that it does not have a direct connection to your Web Service. Whenever you change the Web Service, you will have to rebuild the Web Service (right-click on the Web Service project and select Build), and then update the web reference (right-click on the client project's localhost reference and select Update Web Reference). Until you perform these two steps, your client will not be able to access the changed Web Service.

## Waiting and Timeouts

You might have noticed that the proxy class (StockQuote) really contains many more members than just the three methods shown in the source code. In fact, it acquires a substantial amount of extra functionality because it inherits from the SoapHttp-ClientProtocol class. In many scenarios, you won't need to use any of these additional features. In some cases, however, they will become very useful. One example is when you use the Timeout property.

The Timeout property allows you to specify the maximum amount of time you are willing to wait, in milliseconds. The default (-1) indicates that you will wait as long as it takes, which could make your web application unacceptably slow if you perform a number of operations to an unresponsive Web Service.

When using the Timeout property, you need to include error handling. If the timeout period expires without a response, an exception will be thrown, giving you the chance to notify the user about the problem.

In the following example, the simple StockQuote client is rewritten to use a timeout.

```
Dim WSInfo As New localhost.StockInfo()
Dim WS As New localhost.StockQuote()

' This timeout will apply to all WS method calls, until it is changed.
WS.Timeout = 3000  ' 3000 milliseconds is 3 seconds.

Try
    ' Call the Web Service method.
    WSInfo = WS.GetStockQuote("")
    lblResult.Text = WSInfo.CompanyName & " is at: " & WSInfo.Price
Catch e As Exception
    lblResult.Text = "Web Service timed out after 3 seconds."
End Try
```

## Connecting Through a Proxy

The proxy class also has some built-in intelligence that allows you to reroute its HTTP communication with special Internet settings. By default, the proxy class uses the default Internet settings for the current computer. In some networks, this may not be the best approach. You can override these settings by using the Proxy property of the Web Service proxy class. (In this case "proxy" is being used in two different ways: as a proxy that manages communication between a client and a Web Service, and as a proxy server in your organization that manages communication between a computer and the Internet.)

For example, if you need to connect through a computer called ProxyServer using port 80, you could use the following code before you called any Web Service methods:

```
Dim ConnectionProxy As New WebProxy("ProxyServer", 80)

Dim WS As New localhost.StockQuote()
WS.Proxy = WebProxy
```

There are many other options for the WebProxy class that allow you to configure connections in a more complicated scenario.

## State Management

Generally, a Web Service is not well suited for operations that require maintaining state. The ultimate performance penalty, when you factor in the need for repeated network calls and server memory, is generally prohibitive. However, it is possible using the EnableTransaction attribute on the appropriate WebMethod if you decide to use state management and the built-in Session object.

If you try to use state with a proxy class, you're likely to be disappointed. Every time you recreate the proxy class, a new Session ID is automatically assigned, which means you won't be able to access the Session state collection from the previous request. To counter this problem, you need to take extra steps to retrieve the cookie with the Session ID information for your Web Service, store it somewhere between web requests, and then reapply it to the proxy class later. Just about any type of storage can be used: a database, a local cookie, view state, or even the Session collection for the current web page. In other words, you could store information for your Web Service session in your current (local) page session.

If this discussion seems a little confusing, it's because you need to remind yourself that there are really two active sessions in this example. The Web Service client has one session, which is maintained as long as the user reading your site doesn't close his browser. The Web Service itself also has its own session (in fact, it could even be hosted on a different server). The Web Service session can't be maintained automatically because you don't communicate with it directly. Instead, the proxy class bears the burden of holding the Web Service session information. Figure 20-6 illustrates the difference.

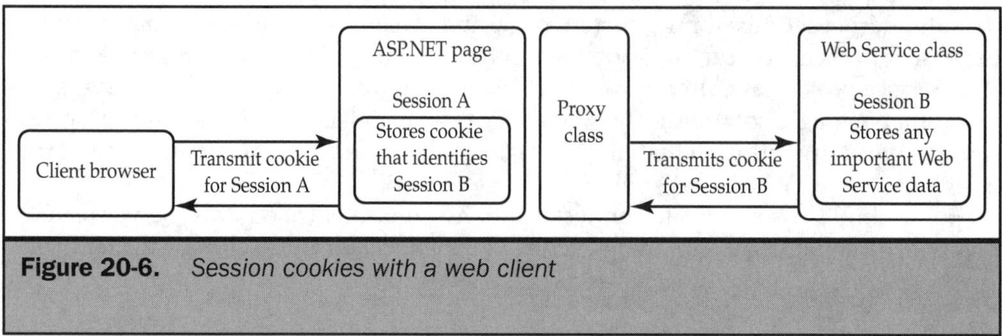


**Figure 20-6.** *Session cookies with a web client*

The next example sheds some light on this situation. This example uses a variant of our original Web Service, called StockQuote_SessionState, which you saw in Chapter 19. It provides two methods: the standard GetStockQuote method and a GetStockUsage method that returns a CounterInfo object with information about how many times the web method was used.

Our client is a simple web page with two buttons and a label control. Every time the Call Service button is clicked, the GetStockQuote method is invoked with a default parameter. When the Get Usage Info button is clicked, the GetStockUsage method is called, which returns the current usage statistics. Information is added to the label, creating a log that records every consecutive action.

```
Public Class FailedSessionServiceTest
  Inherits Page
    Protected WithEvents cmdCallService As Button
    Protected lblResult As Label
    Protected WithEvents cmdGetCounter As Button

    Private WS As New localhost.StockQuote_SessionState()

    Private Sub cmdGetCounter_Click(sender As Object, e As EventArgs) _
      Handles cmdGetCounter.Click
        Dim WSInfo As New localhost.CounterInfo()
        WSInfo = WS.GetStockUsage("MSFT")

        ' Add usage information to the label.
        lblResult.Text &= "<b>Global: "
        lblResult.Text &= WSInfo.GlobalRequests.ToString()
        lblResult.Text &= "<br>Session: "
```

```
        lblResult.Text &= WSInfo.SessionRequests.ToString()
        lblResult.Text &= "<br></b>"
    End Sub

    Private Sub cmdCallService_Click(sender As Object, _
      e As EventArgs) Handles cmdCallService.Click
        Dim Result As Decimal = WS.GetStockQuote("MSFT")

        ' Add confirmation message to the label.
        lblResult.Text &= "GetStockQuote With MSFT Returned "
        lblResult.Text &= Result.ToString() & "<br>"
    End Sub

End Class
```

Unfortunately, every time this button is clicked, the proxy class is recreated, and a new session is used. The output on the page tells an interesting story: after clicking cmdCallService four times and cmdGetCounter once, the Web Service reports the right number of global application requests, but the wrong number of session requests, as shown in Figure 20-7.

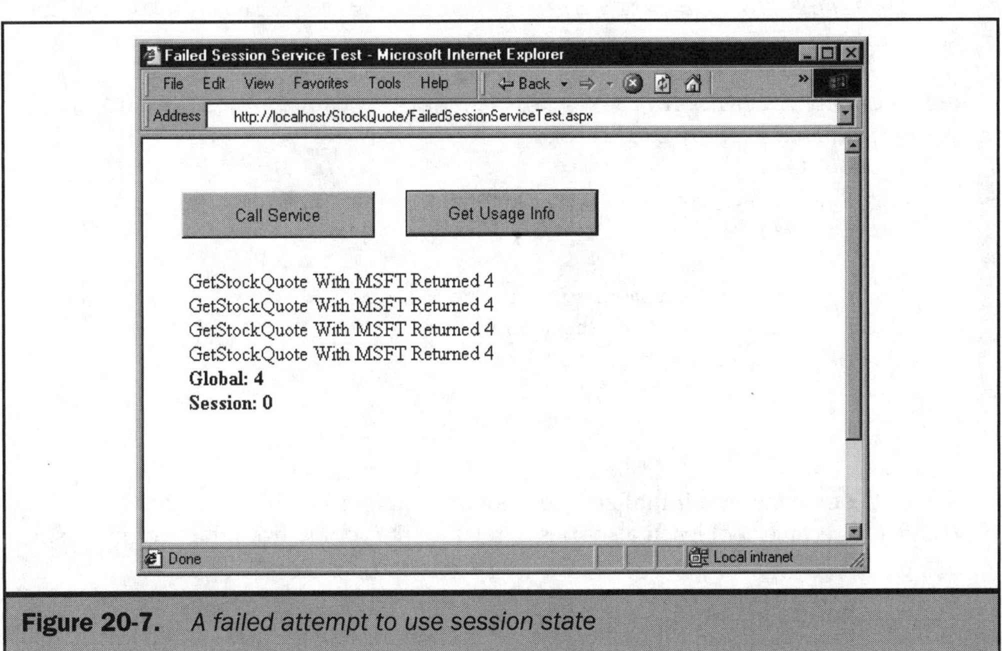


**Figure 20-7.** *A failed attempt to use session state*

To fix this problem, you need to set the CookieContainer property of the proxy class. First, be sure to import the System.Net class, which has the cookie classes this example needs:

```
Imports System.Net
```

The event handlers are modified to add calls to two special functions: GetCookie and SetCookie. These events take place immediately before and after the web method call.

```
Private Sub cmdGetCounter_Click(sender As Object, e As EventArgs) _
  Handles cmdGetCounter.Click
    Dim WSInfo As New localhost.CounterInfo()
    GetCookie()
    WSInfo = WS.GetStockUsage("MSFT")
    SetCookie()

    ' Add usage information to the label.
    lblResult.Text &= "<b>Global: "
    lblResult.Text &= WSInfo.GlobalRequests.ToString()
    lblResult.Text &= "<br>Session: "
    lblResult.Text &= WSInfo.SessionRequests.ToString() & "<br></b>"
End Sub

Private Sub cmdCallService_Click(sender As Object, e As EventArgs) _
  Handles cmdCallService.Click
    GetCookie()
    Dim Result As Decimal = WS.GetStockQuote("MSFT")
    SetCookie()

    ' Add confirmation message to the label.
    lblResult.Text &= "GetStockQuote With MSFT Returned "
    lblResult.Text &= Result.ToString() & "<br>"

End Sub
```

The GetCookie method initializes the CookieContainer for the proxy class, enabling it to send and receive cookies. It also tries to retrieve the cookie from the current session.

```
Private Sub GetCookie()
```

```
    ' Initialize the proxy class CookieContainer so it can
    ' receive cookies.
    WS.CookieContainer = New CookieContainer()

    ' Create a cookie object, and try to retrieve it from
    ' session state.
    Dim SessionCookie As New Cookie()
    SessionCookie = CType(Session("WebServiceCookie"), Cookie)

    ' If a cookie was found, place it in the proxy class.
    ' The only reason it won't be found is if this is the first time
    ' the button has been clicked.
    If IsNothing(SessionCookie) = False Then
        WS.CookieContainer.Add(SessionCookie)
    End If

End Sub
```

The SetCookie method explicitly stores the Web Service Session cookie in session state.

```
Private Sub SetCookie()

    ' Retrieve and store the current cookie for next time.
    ' We know that the session is always stored in a special cookie
    ' called ASP.NET_SessionId.

    Dim WSUri As New Uri("http://localhost")

    Dim Cookies As CookieCollection
    Cookies = WS.CookieContainer.GetCookies(WSUri)
    Session("WebServiceCookie") = Cookies("ASP.NET_SessionId")

End Sub
```



The code could have been simplified somewhat if it stored the whole cookie collection instead of just the Session cookie, but this approach is more controlled.

Now the page works correctly, as shown in Figure 20-8.

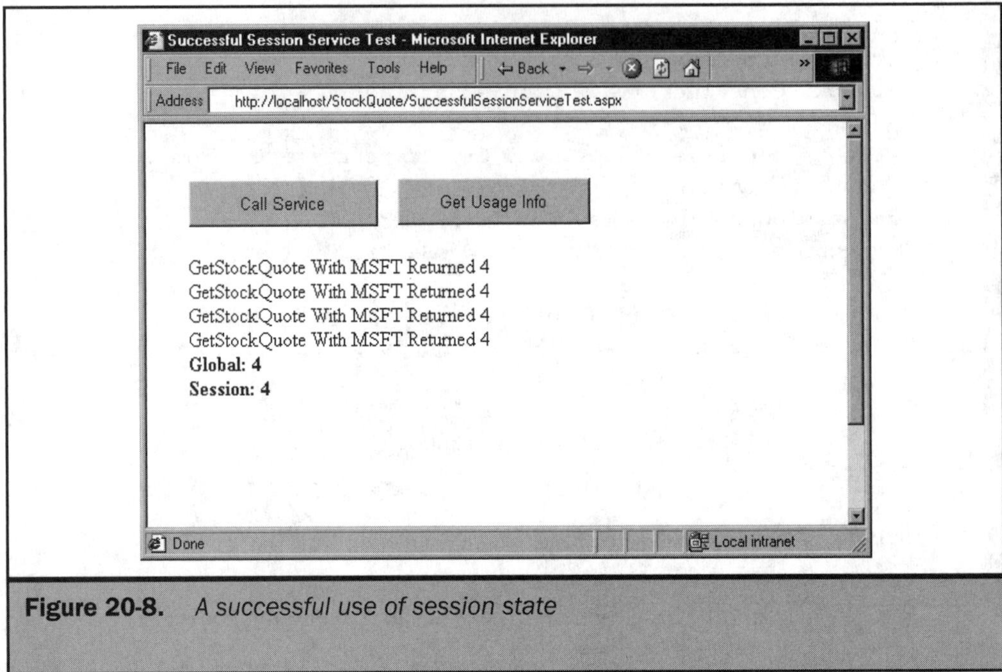


**Figure 20-8.** *A successful use of session state*

## Using SOAP Headers

Some Web Services allow information to be specified once and used for multiple methods automatically. This technique works through SOAP headers. In Chapter 19, you saw a Web Service that used a SOAP header to receive and maintain security credentials. When you create a client for this service, the custom SoapHeader class is copied into the proxy file.

```
Public Class SecurityHeader
  Inherits System.Web.Services.Protocols.SoapHeader

    Public UserID As String
    Public Password As String
    Public Key As String
End Class
```

To use the Web Service, you create an instance of this header, supply the appropriate information, and then attach it to the appropriate variable in the proxy class.

```
' Create an instance of the header.
Dim Header As New SecurityHeader()
Header.UserID = "Matthew"
Header.Password = "OpenSesame"

' Create the proxy class.
Dim WS As New localhost.StockQuote_SoapSecurity()

' Assign the header.
WS.SecurityHeaderValue = Header
```

When you assign the custom header to the proxy class, no information is transmitted. However, from this point on, whenever you call a web method that needs the SecurityHeader, it will be transmitted automatically. In other words, you set the header once and don't need to worry about supplying any additional security information, as long as you use the same instance of the proxy class. The online examples include a simple example of a Web Service client that uses a SOAP header for authentication.

## An Example with TerraService

Now that you know how to use a Web Service, you are not limited to using just the Web Services that you create. In fact, the Internet is brimming with sample services that you can use to test your applications or try out new techniques. In the future, you will even be able to buy prebuilt functionality that you can integrate into your ASP.NET applications by calling a Web Service. Typically, you will pay for these services using some kind of subscription model. Because they are implemented through .NET Web Services and WSDL contracts, you won't need to install anything extra on your web server.

The next section considers how to use one of the more interesting Web Services: Microsoft's TerraService. TerraService is based on the hugely popular TerraServer site where web surfers can view topographic maps and satellite photographs of most of the globe. The site was developed by Microsoft's research division to test SQL Server and increase Microsoft's boasting ability. Under the hood, a 1.5 terabyte SQL Server 2000 database stores all the pictures that are used, as a collection of millions of different tiles. You can find out more about TerraServer at http://terraserver.homeadvisor.msn.com.

To promote .NET, Microsoft has equipped TerraServer with a Web Service interface that allows you to access the TerraServer information. Using this interface (called TerraService) isn't difficult, but creating a polished application with it would be. Before you can really understand how to stitch together different satellite tiles to create a large picture, you need to have some basic understanding of geography and projection systems. There's plenty of additional information about it at the TerraServer site (and the companion TerraService site, http://terraservice.net/). However, because this book is about .NET and not geography, our use of the TerraService will be fairly straightforward. Once you understand the basics, you can continue experimenting with additional web methods and create a more extensive application based on TerraService.

## Adding the Reference

The first step is to create a new ASP.NET application and add a web reference. In Visual Studio .NET, you start by returning to the Add Web Reference window. If you don't know where the specific Web Service file is located (a logical assumption), you can start with the location http://terraservice.net/. Type it into the Address text box, and press ENTER. The home page for TerraService will appear, as shown in Figure 20-9. Scroll through it, and click on the TerraService ASMX link.

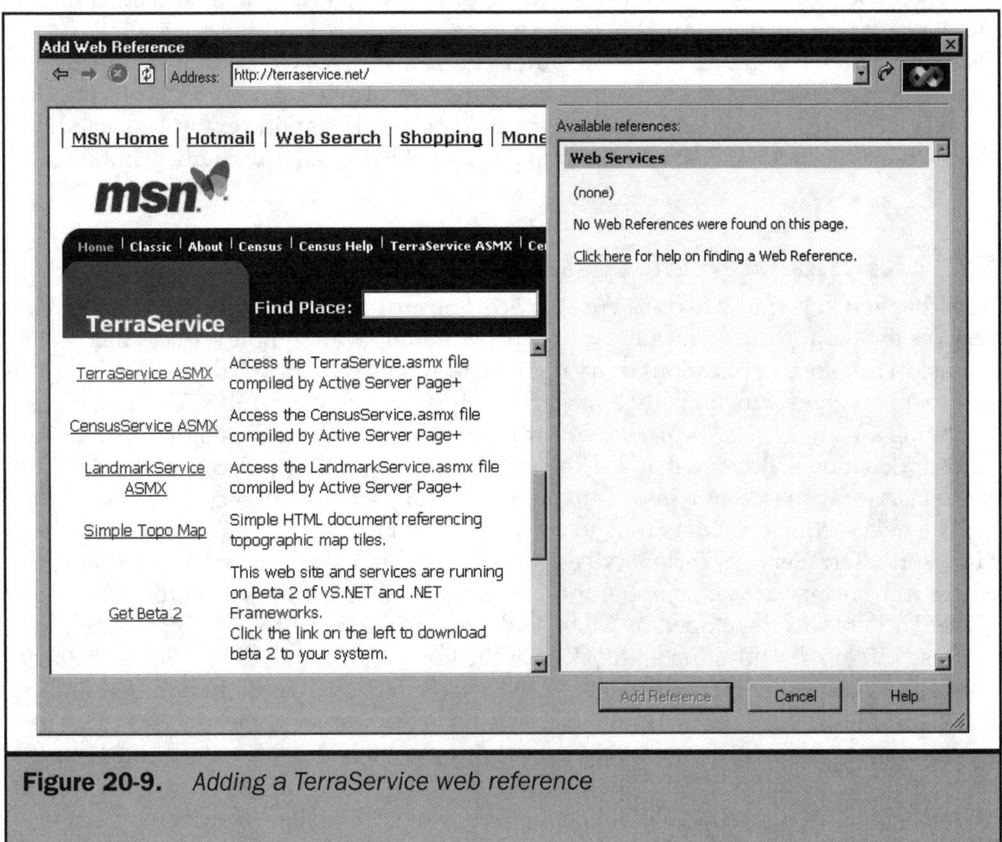


**Figure 20-9.** *Adding a TerraService web reference*

This location (http://terraservice.net/TerraService.asmx?wsdl) is the URL you can bind to with the WSDL.exe utility. You can see from the displayed test page that there are approximately 15 functions. At the time of this writing, no additional information is provided on the test page (indicating that Microsoft doesn't always follow its own recommendations). To read about these methods, you'll have to browse the site on your own.

Click Add Reference to create the web reference. The WSDL document, discovery file, and proxy class will be created under the namespace net.terraservice, as shown in Figure 20-10.

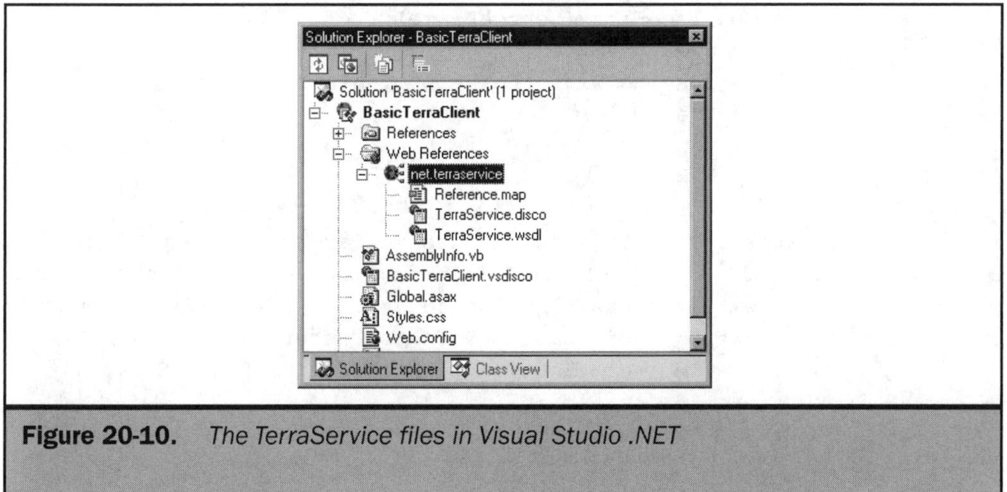


**Figure 20-10.** *The TerraService files in Visual Studio .NET*



## Trying It Out

Before continuing too much further, it makes sense to try out a simple method to see if the Web Service works as expected. A good choice to start is the simple GetPlaceFacts method, which retrieves some simple information about a geographic location that you supply. In this case, the TerraService documentation (and Visual Studio .NET IntelliSense) informs us that this method requires the use of two special classes: a Place class (which specifies what you are searching for), and a PlaceFacts class (which provides you with the information about your place). These classes are available in the net.terraservice namespace.

The following example retrieves information about a place named "Seattle" when a button is clicked, and displays it in a label control. The process is split into two separate subroutines for better organization, although this is not strictly required.

```
Private Sub cmdShow_Click(sender As Object, e As EventArgs) _
  Handles cmdShow.Click

    ' Create the Place object for Seattle.
```

```
    Dim SearchPlace As New net.terraservice.Place()
    SearchPlace.City = "Seattle"

    ' Create the PlaceFacts objects to retrieve our information.
    Dim Facts As New net.terraservice.PlaceFacts()

    ' Call the Web Service method.
    Facts = ts.GetPlaceFacts(SearchPlace)

    ' Display the results with the help of a subroutine.
    ShowPlaceFacts(Facts)

End Sub

Private Sub ShowPlaceFacts(Facts As net.terraservice.PlaceFacts)
    lblResult.Text &= "<b>Place: " & Facts.Place.City & "</b><br><br>"
    lblResult.Text &= Facts.Place.State & ", " & Facts.Place.Country
    lblResult.Text &= "<br> Lat: " & Facts.Center.Lat.ToString()
    lblResult.Text &= "<br> Long: " & Facts.Center.Lon.ToString()
    lblResult.Text &= "<br><br>"
End Sub
```

The result is a successful retrieval of information about the city of Seattle, including its longitude, latitude, and country, as shown in Figure 20-11.

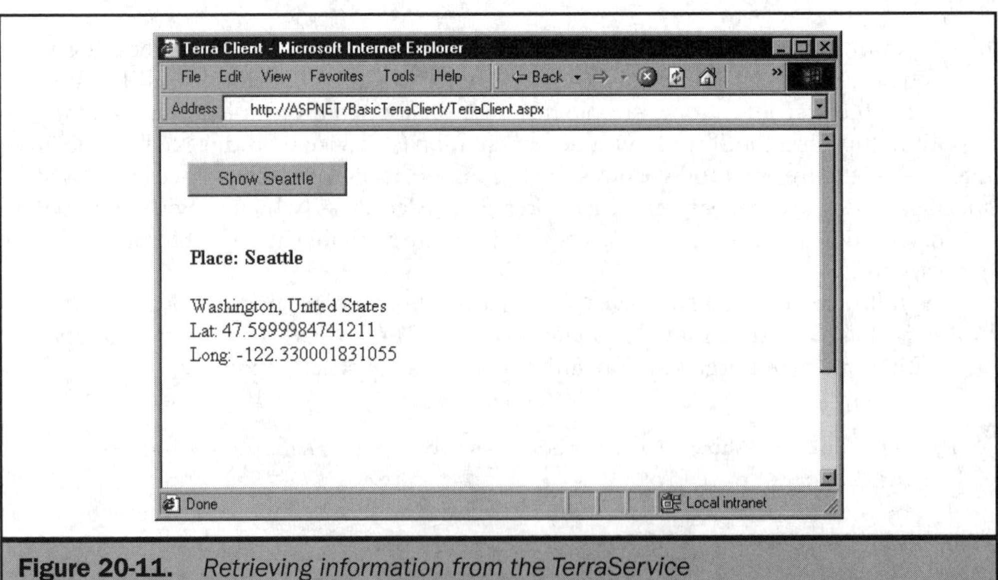


**Figure 20-11.** *Retrieving information from the TerraService*

## Searching for More Information

The TerraService documentation does not recommend using the GetPlaceFacts method, because it is only able to retrieve information about the first place with the matching name. Typically, there are many locations that share the same name. Even in the case of Seattle, there are several landmark locations stored in the TerraServer database along with the city itself. All of these places start with the word "Seattle."

The GetPlaceList method provides a more useful approach, because it returns an array with all the matches. When using GetPlaceList you have to specify a maximum number of allowed matches, to prevent your application from becoming tied up with an extremely long query. You also have a third parameter, which you can set to True to retrieve only results that have corresponding picture tiles in the database, or False to return any matching result. Typically, you would use True if you were creating an application that displays the satellite images for searched locations. You'll also notice that the GetPlaceList function accepts a place name directly and does not use a Place object.

To demonstrate this method, add a second button to the test page and use the following code:

```
Private Sub txtShowAll_Click(sender As Object, e As EventArgs) _
  Handles txtShowAll.Click

    ' Create the TerraService objects.
    Dim FactsArray() As net.terraservice.PlaceFacts
    Dim Facts As net.terraservice.PlaceFacts

    ' Retrieve the matching list (for the city "Kingston").
    FactsArray = ts.GetPlaceList("Kingston", 100, False)

    ' Loop through all the results, and display them.
    For Each Facts In FactsArray
        ShowPlaceFacts(Facts)
    Next

End Sub
```

The result is a list of about 50 matches for places with the name "Kingston," as shown in Figure 20-12.

## Displaying a Tile

By this point, you've realized that using the TerraService is not really different than using any other DLL or code library. The only difference is that you are accessing it over the Internet. In this case, it's no small feat; the TerraServer database contains so much information that it would never be practical to create a network-based or local application.

Also, this information, if not carefully managed, would be extremely difficult to download over the Internet. Providing it through a Web Service interface solves all these problems.

The next example shows our last trick for a Web Service. It retrieves the closest matching tile for the city of Seattle and displays it. To display the tile, the example takes the low-level approach of using Response.WriteBinary. In a more advanced application, a significant amount of in-memory graphical manipulation might be required to get the result you want. The retrieved tile is shown in Figure 20-13.

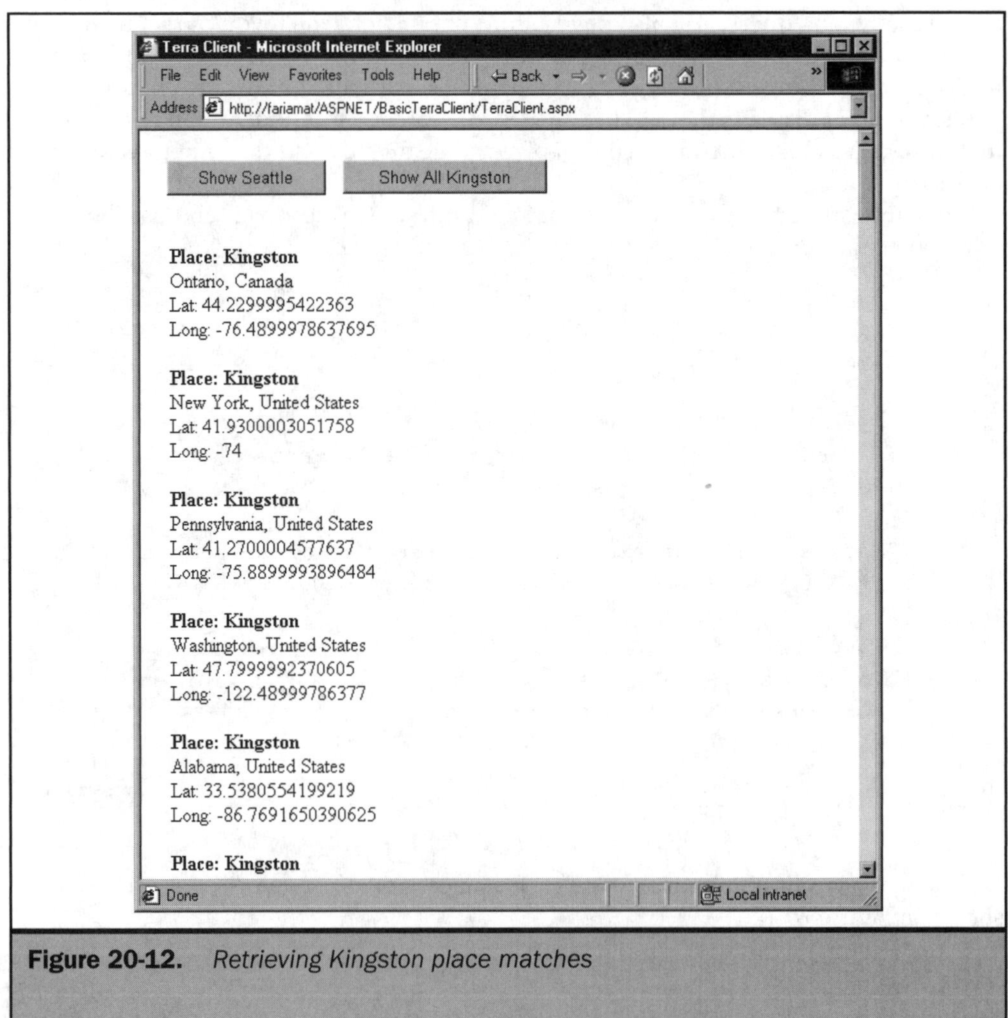


**Figure 20-12.** *Retrieving Kingston place matches*

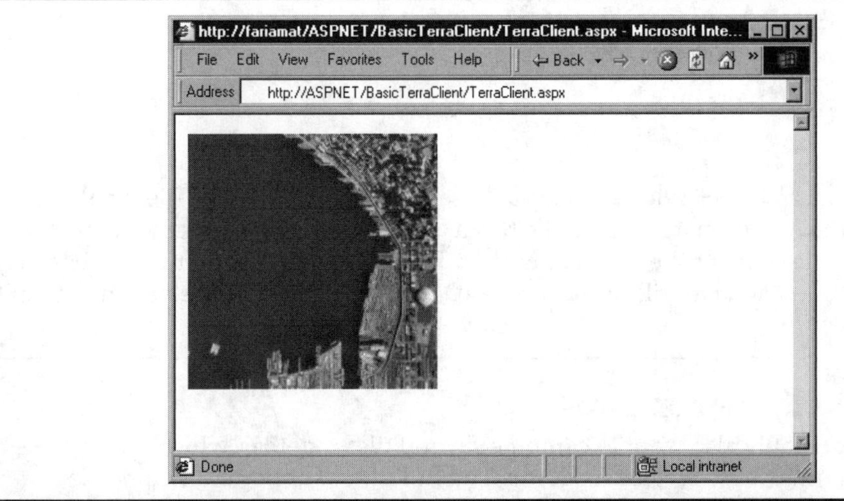


**Figure 20-13.** *A tile From TerraService*

```
Private Sub cmdShowPic_Click(sender As Object, e As EventArgs) _
  Handles cmdShowPic.Click
    ' Define the search.
    Dim SearchPlace As New net.terraservice.Place()
    SearchPlace.City = "Seattle"

    ' Get the PlaceFacts for Seattle.
    Dim Facts As New net.terraservice.PlaceFacts()
    Facts = ts.GetPlaceFacts(SearchPlace)

    ' Retrieve information about the tile at the center of Seattle,
    ' using the Scale and Theme enumerations from the
    ' terraservice namespace.
    Dim TileData As net.terraservice.TileMeta
    TileData = ts.GetTileMetaFromLonLatPt(Facts.Center, _
     net.Terraservice.Theme.Photo, net.terraservice.Scale.Scale16m)

    ' Retrieve the image.
    Dim Image() As Byte
    Image = ts.GetTile(TileData.Id)
```

```
    ' Display the image.
    Response.BinaryWrite(Image)

End Sub
```

Two additional TerraService methods are used in this example. GetTileMetaFromLonLatPt retrieves information about the tile at a given point. This function is used to find out what tile contains the center of Seattle. The GetTile method retrieves the binary information representing the tile, using the TileID provided by GetTileMetaFromLonLatPt.

### Possible Enhancements

You will probably also want to combine several tiles together, which requires the use of other TerraService methods. The full set of supported methods is documented at http://terraservice.net/. Once again, using these methods requires an understanding of graphics and geography, but it does not require any unusual use of Web Services. The core concept—remote method calls through SOAP communication—remains the same.

## Windows Clients

Because this book is focused squarely on ASP.NET, you haven't had the chance to see one of the main advantages of Web Services. Quite simply, they allow desktop applications to use pieces of functionality from the Internet. This allows you to provide a rich, responsive desktop interface that periodically retrieves any real-time information it needs from the Internet. The process is almost entirely transparent. As high-speed access becomes more common, you may not even be aware which portions of functionality depend on the Internet and which ones don't.

You can use Web Service functionality in a Windows application in exactly the same way that you would use it in an ASP.NET application. First, you would create the proxy class using Visual Studio .NET or the WSDL.exe utility. Then you would add code to create an instance of your Web Service and call a web method. The only difference is the upper layer (the user interface the application uses).

If you haven't explored desktop programming with .NET yet, you'll be happy to know that you can reuse much of what you've learned in ASP.NET development. Many web controls (such as labels, buttons, text boxes, and lists) closely parallel their .NET desktop equivalents, and the code you write to interact with them can often be transferred from one environment to the other with very few changes. In fact, the main difference between desktop programming and web programming in .NET is the extra steps you need to take in web applications to preserve information between postbacks, and when transferring the user from one page to another.

The following example shows the form code for a simple Windows TerraService client that uses the GetPlaceList web method. It's been modified to search for a place that the user enters in a text box, and display the results in a list box control. The basic designer code, which creates the controls and sets their initial properties, has been omitted. (This is similar to the control tags in the .aspx template file.)

```
Public Class WindowsTerraClient
  Inherits System.Windows.Forms.Form

    ' (Windows designer code omitted.)

    Private ts As New net.terraservice.TerraService()

    Private Sub cmdShow_Click(sender As Object, e As EventArgs) _
      Handles cmdShow.Click

        ' Create the TerraService objects.
        Dim FactsArray() As net.terraservice.PlaceFacts
        Dim Facts As net.terraservice.PlaceFacts

        ' Retrieve the matching list.
        FactsArray = ts.GetPlaceList(txtPlace.text, 100, False)

        ' Loop through all the results, and display them.
        For Each Facts In FactsArray
            ShowPlaceFacts(Facts)
        Next

    End Sub

    Private Sub ShowPlaceFacts(Facts As net.terraservice.PlaceFacts)

        Dim NewItem As String
        NewItem = "Place: " & Facts.Place.City & ", "
        NewItem &= Facts.Place.State & ", " & Facts.Place.Country
        lstPlaces.Items.Add(NewItem)

    End Sub

End Class
```

The interface for this application is shown in Figure 20-14.

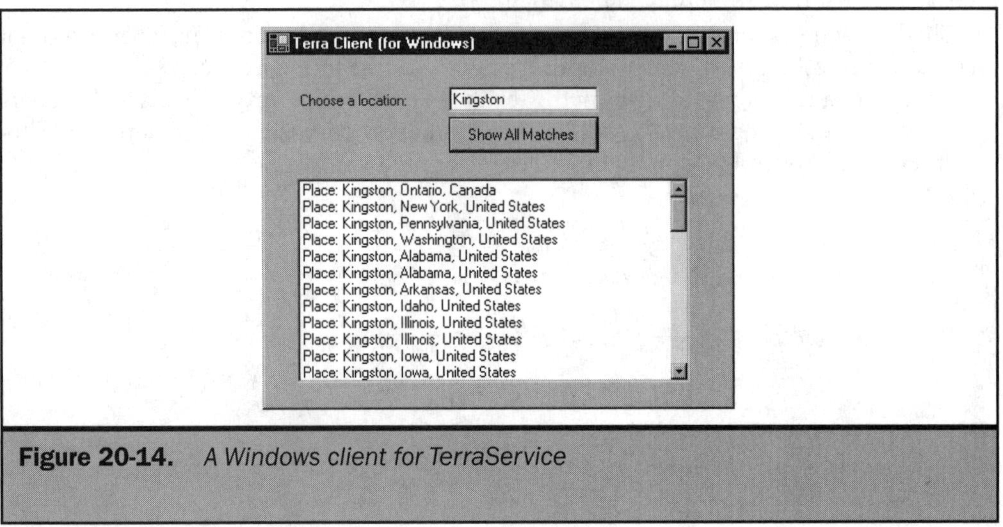


**Figure 20-14.** *A Windows client for TerraService*

Of course, there are many other possibilities available in Windows development, which are covered in many other excellent books. The interesting part from our vantage point is the way that a Windows client can interact with a Web Service just like an ASP.NET application does. This raises a world of new possibilities for integrated Windows/web applications.

The Complete Reference

# Part V

## Advanced ASP.NET

The Complete Reference

# Chapter 21

## Component-Based Programming

Component-based programming is a simple, elegant idea. When used properly, it allows your code to be more organized, consistent, and reusable. It's also incredibly easy to implement in a .NET application, because you never need to touch the registry or perform any special configuration.

To create a component, you separate a portion of your program's functionality and compile it to a separate assembly (DLL file). Your web pages (or any other .NET application) can then use this component in the same way that they use ordinary .NET classes. Best of all, your component provides *exactly* the features your code requires, and hides all the other messy details.

When combined with careful organization, component-based programming is the basis of good ASP.NET application design. In this chapter, we'll examine how you can create components (and why you should), and consider examples that show you how to encapsulate database functionality with a well-written business object. We'll also take a detour into the world of COM, and show how you can access legacy components by adding .NET wrappers around them.

## Why Use Components?

To master ASP.NET development, you need to become a skilled user of the .NET class library. So far, you've learned how to use .NET components designed for sending mail, reading files, and interacting with databases. Though these class library ingredients are powerful, they aren't customizable, which is both an advantage and a weakness.

For example, it's convenient to be able to access any database in almost exactly the same way, irrespective of what type of information it contains. However, it's much less helpful to have to weave database details (such as SQL queries and connection strings) directly into your web page code. Though you can improve on this situation by storing database constants in a web.config application file (as described in Chapter 5), you still need to retrieve data using specific field names. If the structure of a commonly used database changes even slightly, you could be left with dozens of pages to update and retest. To solve these problems, you need to create an extra layer between your web page code and the database. This "extra layer" takes the form of custom component.

This database scenario is only one of the reasons you might want to create your own components. Component-based programming is really just a logical extension of good code organizing principles, and it offers a long list of advantages:

**Increased security** For example, you could configure your component to only allow access to certain tables, fields, or rows in a database. This is often easier than setting up complex permissions in the database itself. Because the application has to go through the component, it needs to play by its rules.

**Better organization** Components move the clutter out of your web page code. It also becomes easier for other programmers to understand your application's logic when it is broken down into separate components.

**Easier troubleshooting** It's impossible to oversell the advantage of components when testing and debugging an application. Component-based programs are broken down into smaller, tighter blocks of code, making it easier to isolate exactly where a problem is occurring.

**More manageable** Component-based programs are much easier to enhance and modify because common tasks are coded once (in the component), and used in as many places as required. Without components, commonly used code has to be copied and pasted throughout an application, making it extremely difficult to change and synchronize.

**Code reuse** Components can be shared with any ASP.NET application that needs the component's functionality. Even better, a component can be used by *any* .NET application, meaning you could create a common "backbone" of logic that's used by a web application and an ordinary Windows application.

**Simplicity** Components can provide multiple related tasks for a single client request (writing several records to a database, opening and reading a file in one step, or even starting and managing a database transaction). Similarly, components hide details—an application programmer can use a database component without worrying about the database name, location of the server, or the user account needed to connect. Even better, you can perform a search using certain criteria, and the component itself can decide whether to use a dynamically generated SQL statement or stored procedure.

**Performance** If you need to perform a long, time-consuming operation, you can create an asynchronous component to handle the work for you. That allows you to perform other tasks with the web page code, and return to pick up the result at a later time.

## Components in ASP

In ASP programming, components were also a requirement to overcome the limitations of VBScript. Unlike ASP pages, components could be written in Visual Basic 6, which provided a richer syntax, a speedier compiled language, and the ability to perform tasks that just weren't allowed in ordinary script code. ASP.NET, as you've learned, doesn't suffer from any of these limitations, and hence components aren't required to compensate for ASP deficiencies. However, components still make good sense and are required to design a large-scale, well-organized ASP.NET application.

## Component Jargon

Component-based programming is sometimes shrouded in a fog of specialized jargon. Understanding these terms helps sort out exactly what a component is supposed to do, and it also allows you to understand MSDN articles about application design. If you are already familiar with the fundamentals of components, feel free to skip ahead.

### Three-Tier Design

The idea of three-tier design is that the functionality of most complete applications can be divided into three main levels (see Figure 21-1). The first level is the user interface (or presentation tier), which displays controls, and receives and validates user input. All the event handlers in your web page are in this first level. The second level is the "business" layer, where the application-specific logic takes place. For an e-commerce site, application-specific logic includes rules such as how shipping charges are applied to an order, when certain promotions are valid, and what customer actions should be logged. It doesn't involve generic .NET details such as how to open a file or connect to a database. The third layer is the data layer, where the application's information is stored in files or a database. The third layer contains logic about how to retrieve and update data, such as SQL queries or stored procedures.

The important detail about three-tier design is that information only travels from one level to an adjacent level. In other words, your user interface code should not try to directly access the database and retrieve information. Instead, it should go through the second layer and then arrive at the database.

This basic organization principle can't always be adhered to, but it's a good ideal. When you create a component, it's almost always used in the second layer to bridge the gap between the data and the user interface. In other words, if you want to fill a list of product categories in a list box, your user interface code would call a component, which would get the list from the database, and then return it to your code. Your web page code is isolated from the database—and if the database structure changes you need to change one concise component, instead of every page on your site.

### Encapsulation

If three-tier design is the overall goal of component-based programming, encapsulation is the best rule of thumb. Encapsulation is the principle that you should create your application out of "black boxes" that hide information. For example, if you have a component that logs a purchase on an e-commerce site, that component handles all the details and allows only the essentially variables to be specified.

For example, this component might accept a user ID and an order item ID, and then handle all the other details. The calling code would not need to worry about how the component works or where the data is coming from—it just needs to understand how to use the component. (This principle is described in a lot of picturesque ways. For example, you know how to drive a car because you understand its component interface—the steering wheel and pedals—not because you understand the low-level details about combustion and the engine.)

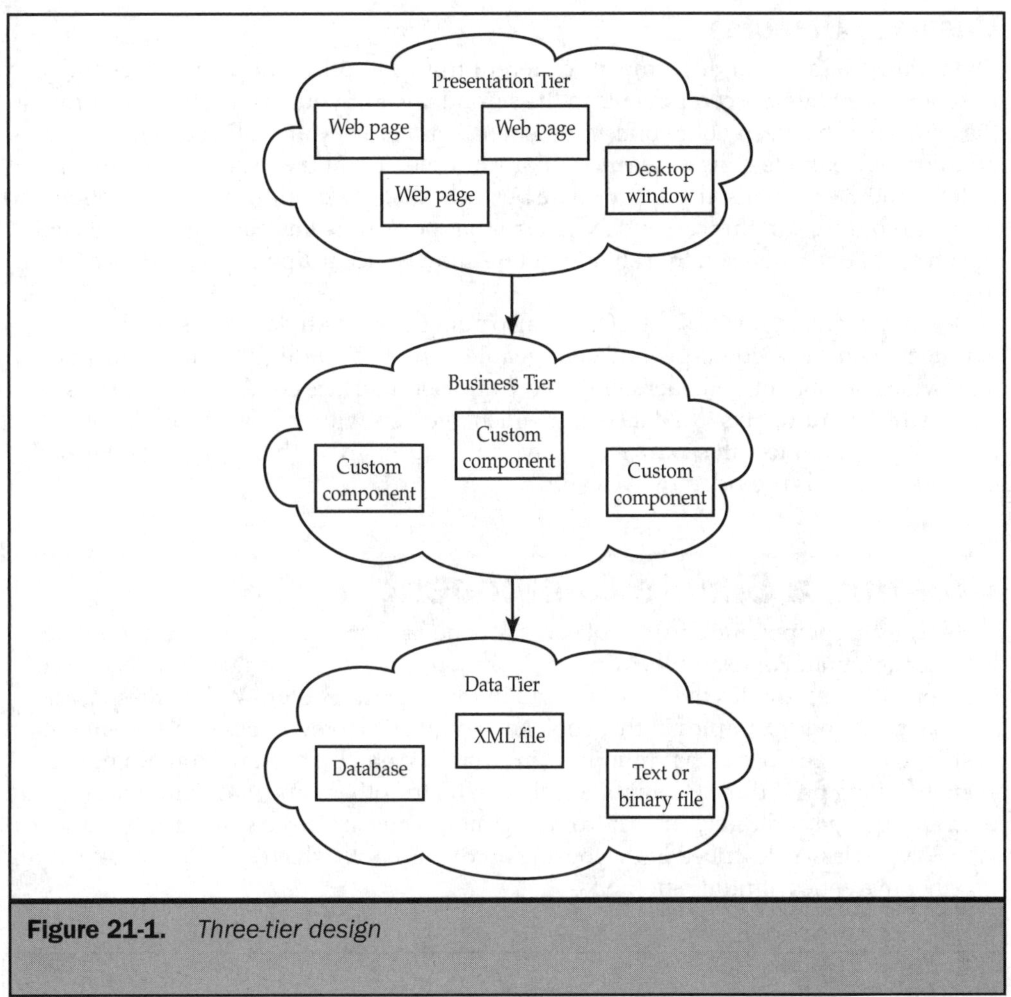


**Figure 21-1.** *Three-tier design*

## Data Objects

Data objects are used in a variety of ways. In this book, we'll use the term to mean a custom object you make that represents a certain grouping of data. For example, you could create a Person class that has properties like Height, Age, and EyeColor. Your code can then create data objects based on this class. You might want to use a data object to pass information from one portion of code to another. (Note that data objects are sometimes used to describe objects that handle data management. This is *not* the use we will follow in this book.)

### Business Objects

The term *business object* often means different things to different people. Generally, business objects are the components in the second layer of your application that provide the extra layer between your code and the data source. They are called business objects because they enforce "business rules." For example, if you try to submit a purchase order without any items, the appropriate business object would throw an exception and refuse to continue. In this case, no .NET error has occurred—instead, you've detected the presence of a condition that should not be allowed according to your application's logic.

In our examples, business objects are also going to contain data access code. In an extremely complicated, large, and changeable system, you might want to further subdivide components, and actually have your user interface code talking to a business object which in turn talks to a data object which interacts with the data source. However, for most programmers this extra step is overkill, especially with the increased level of consistency that is provided by ADO.NET.

## Creating a Simple Component

Technically, a component is just a collection of one or more classes that are compiled together as a unit. For example, Microsoft's System.Web.dll is a single (but very large) component that provides the objects found in many of the System.Web namespaces.

So far, the code examples in this book have only used a few types of class—mainly custom web page classes that inherit from System.Web.UI.Page and contain mostly event handling procedures. Component classes, on the other hand, won't interact directly with a web page and rarely inherit from anything. They are more similar to the custom Web Service classes described in the fourth part of this book, which collect related features together in a series of utility methods.

### Web Services versus Components

Web Services provide some of the same opportunities for code reuse as custom components. However, Web Services are primarily designed as an easy way to share functionality across different computers and platforms. A component, on the other hand, is not nearly as easy to share with the wide world of the Internet, but is far more efficient for sharing *internally* (for example, between different applications in the same company or different web sites on the same server). For that reason, Web Services and components don't directly compete—in fact, a Web Service could even make use of a component (or vice versa). In some cases you might find yourself programming a site with a mixture of the two, putting the code that needs to be reused in-house into components, and the functionality that needs to be made publicly available into Web Services.

## The Component Class

You have two options when writing a component.

- You can code it by hand in a .vb text file, and then compile it with the vbc.exe command-line compiler described in earlier chapters.
- You can use Visual Studio .NET, and start a new Class Library project. When choosing the project directory, you need to specify a real (physical) directory, not the virtual directory name. Figure 21-2 shows Visual Studio .NET's New Project window with a Class Library project.

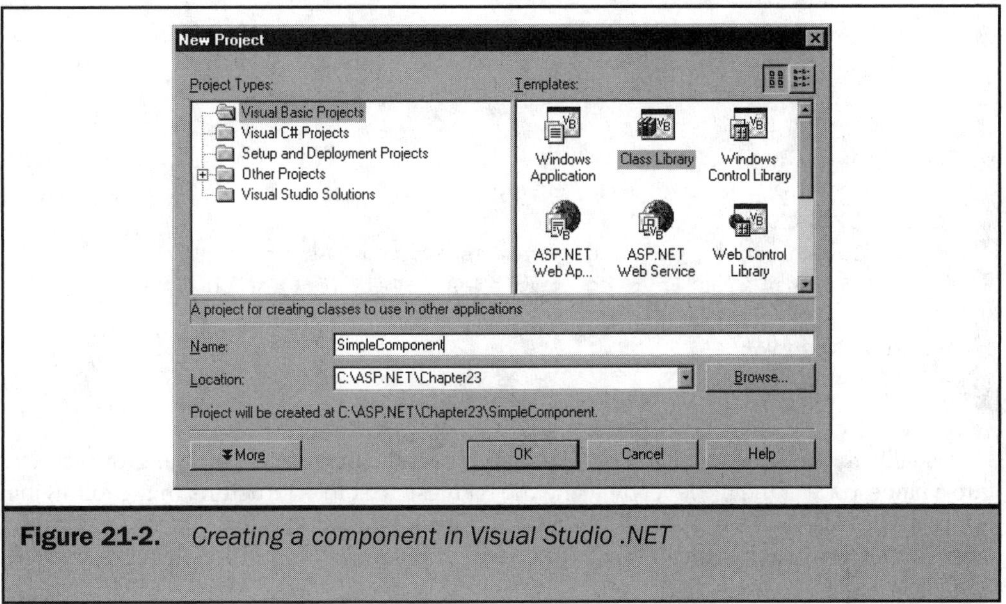


**Figure 21-2.** *Creating a component in Visual Studio .NET*

These options are equivalent. In your .vb file, you define the component as a class.

```
Public Class SimpleTest
End Class
```

Remember, a component can contain more than one class. You can create this other classes in the same file, or in separate files, which will be compiled together into one assembly.

```
Public Class SimpleTest
End Class
```

```
Public Class SimpleTest2
End Class
```

To add functionality to your class, you add public methods (functions or subroutines). The web page code calls these methods to retrieve information or perform a task. The following example shows one of the simplest possible components, which does nothing more than return a string to the calling code.

```
Public Class SimpleTest
    Public Function GetInfo(param As String) As String
        Return "You invoked SimpleTest.GetInfo() with '" & _
                 param & "'"
    End Function
End Class

Public Class SimpleTest2
    Public Function GetInfo(param As String) As String
        Return "You invoked SimpleTest2.GetInfo() with '" & _
                 param & "'"
    End Function
End Class
```

Usually, these classes will be organized in a special namespace. You can group classes into a namespace at the file level by using the Namespace block structure. In the following example, the classes will be accessed in other applications as SimpleComponent.SimpleTest and SimpleComponent.SimpleTest2. If needed, you can create multiple levels of nested namespaces.

```
Namespace SimpleComponent

    Public Class SimpleTest
        ' (Class code omitted.)
    End Class

    Public Class SimpleTest2
        ' (Class code omitted.)
    End Class

End Namespace
```

In Visual Studio .NET, your component is automatically placed in a root namespace that has the project name. This code doesn't appear in the .vb file (although you can add additional namespaces there). To change the name of your root namespace, right-click on the project in the Solution Explorer and select Properties. Look under the Common Properties | General group for the root namespace setting (see Figure 21-3). You can also use this window to configure the name that will be given to the compiled assembly file.

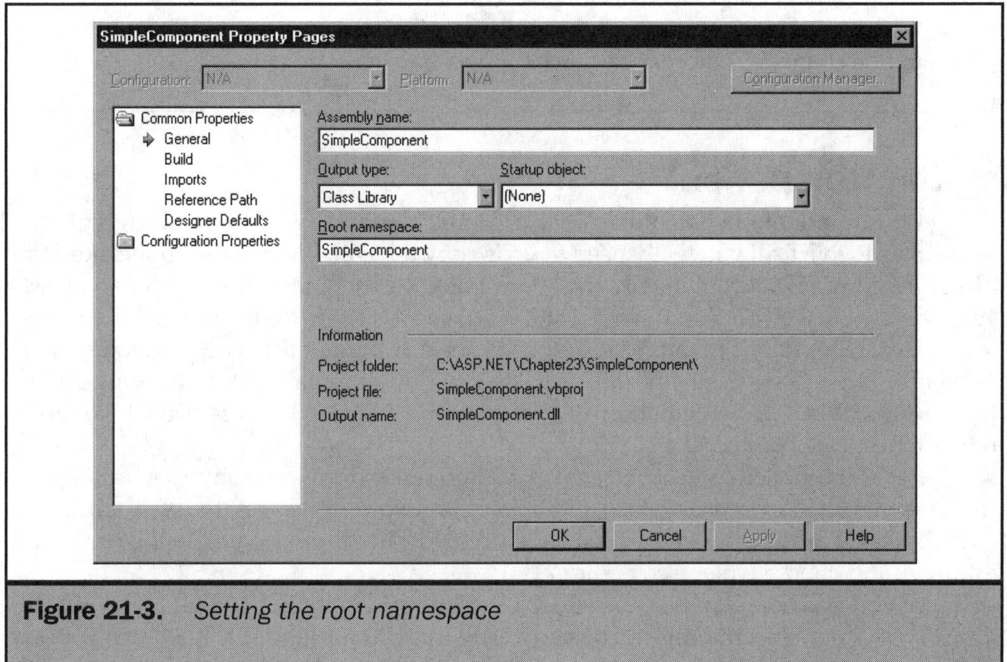


**Figure 21-3.** *Setting the root namespace*

## Compiling the Component Class

In Visual Studio .NET, you can compile this class just by right-clicking on the project in the Solution Explorer and choosing Build. You can't actually run the project, because it isn't an application, and it doesn't provide any user interface.

If you are writing the class by hand in a text file, you can compile it in more or less the same way as you compile a .aspx code-behind file or .asmx web service.

```
vbc /t:library /r:System.dll /r:System.Web.dll SimpleComponent.vb
```

The /t:library parameter indicates that you want to create a DLL assembly instead of an EXE assembly. The compiled assembly will have the name SimpleComponent.dll. The /r parameter specifies any dependent assemblies you use. The compilation process is the same as that described with web pages in Chapter 5.

### All Components Must Be Compiled

Unlike web pages and Web Services, you *must* compile a component before you can use it. Components are not hosted by the ASP.NET service and IIS, and thus cannot be compiled automatically when they are needed.

## Using the Component

Using the component in an actual ASP.NET page is easy. If you are working without Visual Studio .NET, all you really need to do is copy the DLL file into the application's bin directory. ASP.NET automatically monitors this directory, and makes all of its classes available to any web page in the application, just as it does with the native .NET types.

In Visual Studio .NET, you need to specify the component that you plan to use as a reference. This allows Visual Studio .NET to provide its usual syntax checking and IntelliSense. Otherwise, it will interpret your attempts to use the class as mistakes and refuse to compile your code.

To link a component, select Project | Add Reference from the menu (you can also right-click on the References group in the Solution Explorer). Select the .NET tab, and click Browse. Find and select the SimpleComponent.dll file we created in the previous example, and choose Open (see Figure 21-4).

Once you add the reference, the DLL file will be automatically copied to the bin directory of your current project. You can verify this by checking the Full Path property of the SimpleComponent reference, or just browsing to the directory in Windows Explorer. The nice thing is that this file will automatically be overwritten with the most recent compiled version of the assembly every time you run the project.

### Project References

You can also create a Visual Studio .NET solution that combines a class library project with an ASP.NET application project. This technique, which we examined with Web Services in Chapter 20, allows you to debug a component while it is in use alongside the application. In this case, you don't add a reference to the DLL file. Instead, you add a special project reference to the class library project in the same solution, using the Projects tab of the Add Reference window. With project references, Visual Studio .NET automatically compiles the component for you when needed.

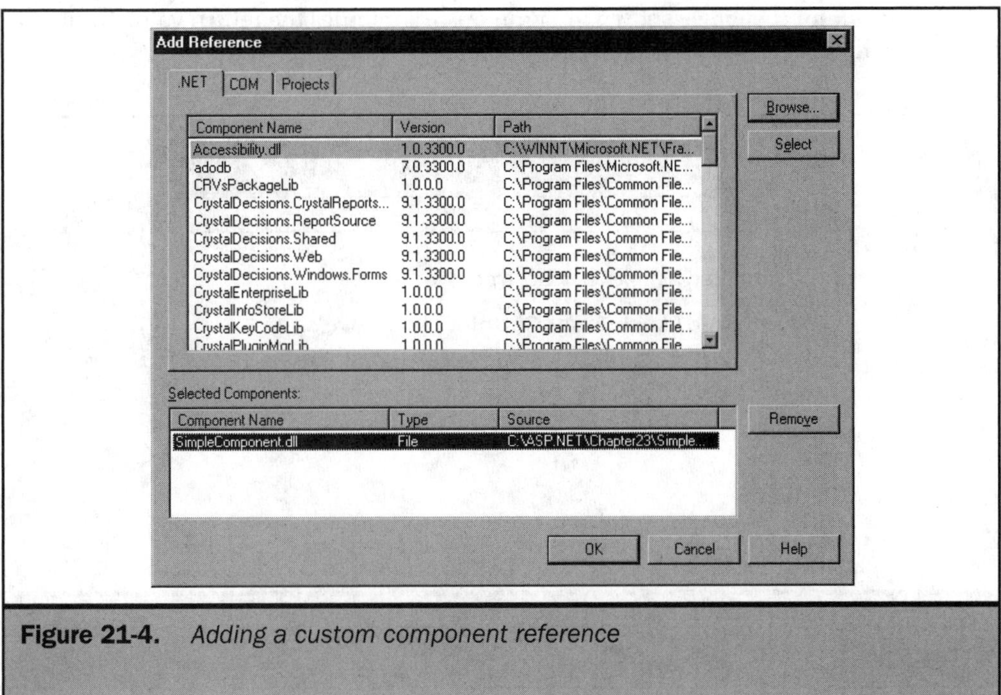


**Figure 21-4.** *Adding a custom component reference*

You can now use the component by creating instances of the SimpleTest or SimpleTest2 class.

```
Public Class TestPage
  Inherits Page

    Protected lblResult As Label

    Private Sub Page_Load(sender As Object, e As EventArgs) _
      Handles MyBase.Load
        Dim TestComponent As New SimpleComponent.SimpleTest()
        Dim TestComponent2 As New SimpleComponent.SimpleTest2()
        lblResult.Text = TestComponent.GetInfo("Hello") & "<br><br>"
        lblResult.Text &= TestComponent2.GetInfo("Bye")
    End Sub

End Class
```

The output for this page, shown in Figure 21-5, combines the return value from both GetInfo methods.

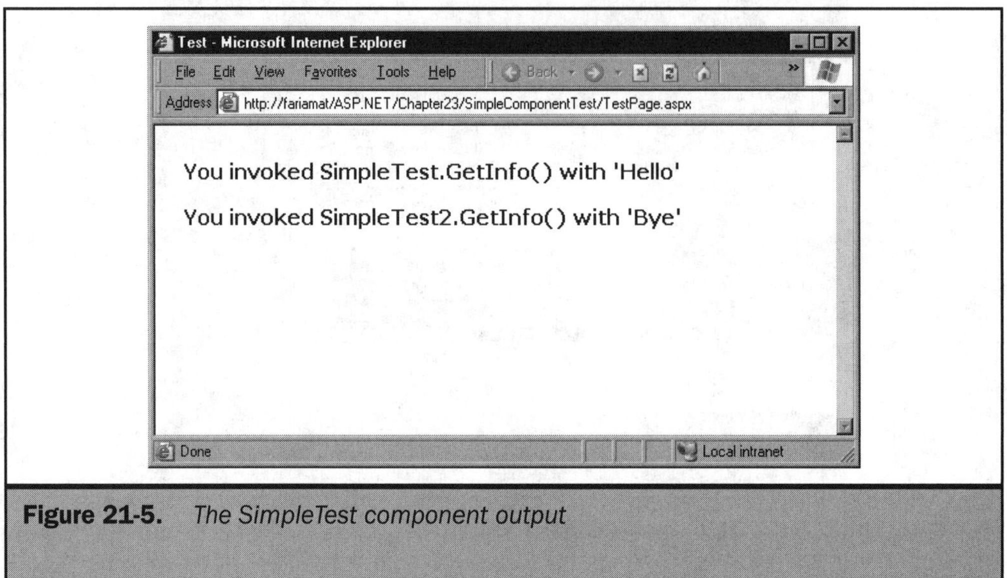


**Figure 21-5.** *The SimpleTest component output*

To make this code slightly simpler, you could have chosen to use shared methods, which don't need a valid instance. A shared GetInfo method would look like this:

```
Public Class SimpleTest
    Public Shared Function GetInfo(param As String) As String
        Return "You invoked SimpleTest.GetInfo() with '" & _
               param & "'"
    End Function
End Class
```

The web page would access the shared GetInfo method through the class name, and would not need to create an object.

```
Private Sub Page_Load(sender As Object, e As EventArgs) _
  Handles MyBase.Load
    lblResult.Text = SimpleComponent.SimpleTest.GetInfo("Hello")
End Sub
```

## Properties and State

The SimpleTest classes provide functionality through public methods. If you're familiar with class-based programming (or if you've read Chapter 3), you'll remember that classes can also store information in private member variables, and provide property procedures that allow the calling code to modify this information. For example, a Person class might have a FirstName property.

When you create classes that use property procedures, you are using *stateful* design. In stateful design, the class has the responsibility of maintaining certain pieces of information. In *stateless* design, like that found in our SimpleTest component, no information is retained between method calls. Compare that to a stateful SimpleTest class.

```
Public Class SimpleTest

    Private _Data As String
    Public Property Data() As String
        Get
            Return _Data
        End Get
        Set(Value As String)
            _Data = Value
        End Set
    End Property

    Public Function GetInfo() As String
        Return "You invoked SimpleTest.GetInfo()," & _
              "and _Data is '" & _Data & "'"
    End Function

End Class
```

In the programming world, there have been a number of great debates arguing whether stateful or stateless programming is best. Stateful programming is the most natural, object-oriented approach, but it also has a few disadvantages. In order to accomplish a common task, you might need to set several properties before calling a method. Each of these individual steps adds a little bit of unneeded overhead. A stateless design, on the other hand, often performs all its work in a single method call. However, because no information is retained in state, you may need to specify several parameters, which can make for tedious programming. A good example of stateful versus stateless objects is shown by the FileInfo and File classes, which are described in Chapter 16.

There is no short answer about whether stateful or stateless design is best, and it often depends on the task at hand. However, stateful designs have some important shortcomings that are difficult to circumvent. The most important of these is the fact that properties need to be changed individually, and that can allow classes to be placed in inconsistent or invalid states. Even if this state is temporary, it can lead to a problem if a software or hardware failure occurs. This type of problem is most commonly seen with transactions.

The next example illustrates the difference with two ways to design an Account class.

## A Stateful Account Class

Consider a stateful account class that represents a single customers account. Information is read from the database when it is first created in the constructor method, and can be updated using the Update method.

```
Public Class Account

    Private _AccountNumber As Integer
    Private _Balance As Decimal

    Public Property Balance() As Decimal
        Get
            Return _Balance
        End Get
        Set(Value As Decimal)
            _Balance = Value
        End Set
    End Property

    Public Sub New(AccountNumber As Integer)
        ' (Code to read account record from database goes here.)
    End Sub

    Public Sub Update()
        ' (Code to update database record goes here.)
    End Sub

End Class
```

If you have two Account objects that expose a Balance property, you need to perform two separate steps to transfer money from one account to another. Conceptually, the process works like this:

```
' Create an account object for each account,
' using the account number.
Dim AccountOne As New Bank.CustomerAccount(122415)
Dim AccountTwo As New Bank.CustomerAccount(123447)
Dim Amount As Decimal = 1000

' Withdraw money from one account.
AccountOne.Balance -= Amount

' Deposit money in the other account.
AccountTwo.Balance += Amount

' Update the underlying database records using an Update method.
AccountOne.Update()
AccountTwo.Update()
```

The problem here is that if this task is interrupted halfway through by an error, you'll end up with at least one unhappy customer.

## A Stateless AccountUtility Class

A stateless object, on the other hand, might only expose a shared method called FundTransfer, which performs all its work in one method.

```
Public Class AccountUtility

    Public Shared Sub FundTransfer(AccountOne As Integer, _
      AccountTwo As Integer, Amount As Decimal)
        ' (The code here retrieves the two database records,
        '  changes them, and updates them.)
    End Sub

End Class
```

The calling code can't use the same elegant Account objects, but it can be assured that account transfers are protected from error. Because all the database operations are performed at once, they can use a database stored procedure for greater performance, and a transaction to ensure that the withdrawal and deposit either succeed or fail as a whole.

```
' Store the account and transfer details.
Dim Amount As Decimal = 1000
Dim AccountIDOne As Integer = 122415
Dim AccountIDTwo As Integer = 123447

Bank.AccountUtility.FundTransfer(AccountIDOne, AccountIDTwo, _
                                 Amount)
```

In a mission-critical system, transactions are often a requirement. For that reason, classes that retain very little state information are often the best design approach, even though they are not quite as elegant or as well organized.

## Database Components

Clearly, components are extremely useful. But if you're starting a large programming project, you may not be sure what features are the best candidates for being made into separate components. Learning how to break an application into components and classes is one of the great arts of programming, and it takes a good deal of practice and fine-tuning.

One of the most common types of components is a database component. Database components are an ideal application of component-based programming for several reasons:

- Databases require extraneous details (connection strings, field names, and so on) that can distract from the application logic, and could easily be encapsulated by a well-written component.
- Databases frequently change. Even if the underlying table structure remains constant and additional information is never required (which is far from certain), queries may be replaced by stored procedures, and stored procedures may be redesigned.
- Databases have special connection requirements. You may even need to change the database access code for reasons unrelated to the application. For example, after profiling and testing a database, you might discover that you can replace a single query with two queries or a more efficient stored procedure. In either case, the returned data remains constant, but the data access code is dramatically different.

- Databases are used repetitively in a finite set of ways. In other words, a common database routine should be written once and is certain to be used many times over.

## A Simple Database Component

To examine the best way to create a database component, we'll consider a simple application that provides a classifieds page listing items that various individuals have for sale. The database uses two tables: an Item table that lists the description and price of a specific sale item, and a Categories table with possible groupings under which items can be grouped. The relationship is shown in Figure 21-6.

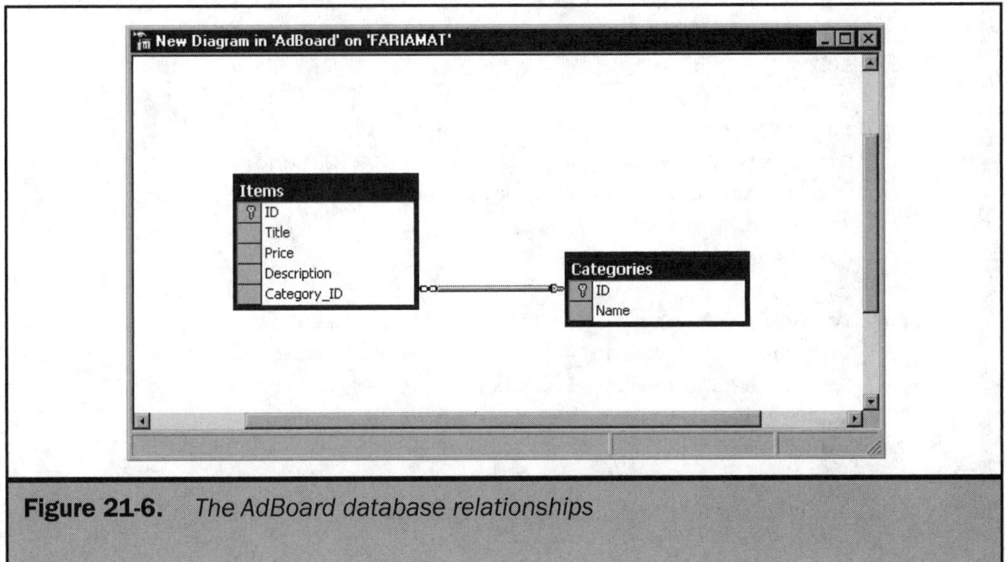


**Figure 21-6.** *The AdBoard database relationships*

In our example, we are connecting with an SQL server database using the OLE DB part of the class library. You can create this database yourself, or you can refer to the online samples, which include the SQL code that will generate it automatically. To start, the Categories table is preloaded with a standard set of allowed categories.

The database component is simple. It's an instance class that retains some basic information (such as the connection string to use), but it does not allow the client to change this information, and therefore does not need any property procedures. Instead, it performs most of its work in methods such as GetCategories and GetItems. These methods return DataSets with the appropriate database records. This type of design creates a fairly thin layer over the database—it handles some details, but the client is still responsible for working with familiar ADO.NET classes such as the DataSet.

```
Imports System.Data
Imports System.Data.OleDb
Imports System.Configuration

Public Class DBUtil
    Private ConnectionString As String

    Public Sub New()
        ConnectionString = ConfigurationSettings.AppSettings( _
                               "ConnectionString")
    End Sub

    Public Function GetCategories() As DataSet
        Dim Query As String = "SELECT * FROM Categories"
        Dim ds As DataSet = FillDataSet(Query, "Categories")
        Return ds
    End Function

    Public Overloads Function GetItems() As DataSet
        Dim Query As String = "SELECT * FROM Categories"
        Dim ds As DataSet = FillDataSet(Query, "Items")
        Return ds
    End Function

    Public Overloads Function GetItems(categoryID As Double) _
      As DataSet
        Dim Query As String = "SELECT * FROM Items "
        Query &= "WHERE Category_ID='" & categoryID & "'"
        Dim ds As DataSet = FillDataSet(Query, "Items")
        Return ds
    End Function

    Public Sub AddCategory(name As String)
        Dim Insert As String = "INSERT INTO Categories "
        Insert &= "(Name) VALUES ('" & name & "')"

        Dim con As New OleDbConnection(ConnectionString)
```

```
        Dim cmd As New OleDbCommand(Insert, con)

        con.Open()
        cmd.ExecuteNonQuery()
        con.Close()
    End Sub

    Public Sub AddItem(title As String, description As String, _
                       price As Decimal, categoryID As Integer)
        Dim Insert As String = "INSERT INTO Items "
        Insert &= "(Title, Description, Price, Category_ID)"
        Insert &= "VALUES ('" & title & "', '" & description & "', "
        Insert &= price & ", '" & categoryID & "')"

        Dim con As New OleDbConnection(ConnectionString)
        Dim cmd As New OleDbCommand(Insert, con)
        con.Open()
        cmd.ExecuteNonQuery()
        con.Close()
    End Sub

    Private Function FillDataSet(query As String, _
                                 tableName As String) As DataSet
        Dim con As New OleDbConnection(ConnectionString)
        Dim cmd As New OleDbCommand(query, con)
        Dim adapter As New OleDbDataAdapter(cmd)

        Dim ds As New DataSet()
        adapter.Fill(ds, tableName)
        con.Close()

        Return ds
    End Function

End Class
```

## Interesting Facts About this Code

- This code automatically retrieves the connection string from the web.config file when the class is created, as described in Chapter 5. This trick enhances encapsulation, but if the client web application does not have the appropriate setting, the component will not work. If you are creating a component that needs to handle ASP.NET and Windows applications, this design wouldn't be suitable.

- This class uses an overloaded GetItems method. This means the client can call GetItems with no parameters to return the full list, or with a parameter indicating the appropriate category. (Chapter 2 provides an introduction to overloaded functions.)
- Each method that accesses the database opens and closes the connection. This is a far better approach than trying to hold a connection open over the lifetime of the class, which is sure to result in performance degradation in multi-user scenarios.
- The code uses its own private FillDataSet function to make the code more concise. This is not made available to clients. Instead, the FillDataSet function is then used by the GetItems and GetCategories methods.

## Consuming the Database Component

To use this component in a web application, we first have to make sure that the appropriate connection string is configured in the web.config file, as shown here.

```
<?xml version="1.0" encoding="utf-8" ?>
<configuration>

  <appSettings>
    <add key="ConnectionString"
         value="Provider=SQLOLEDB.1;Data Source=localhost;Initial
                Catalog=AdBoard;Integrated Security=SSPI" />
  </appSettings>

  <system.web>
    <!-- Configuration sections go here. -->
  </system.web>

</configuration>
```

Next, compile and copy the component DLL file, or add a reference to it if you are using Visual Studio .NET. The only remaining task is to add the user interface.

To test out this component, you can create a simple test page. In our example, shown in Figure 21-7, this page allows users to browse the current listing by category and add new items. When the user first visits the page, it prompts the user to select a category.

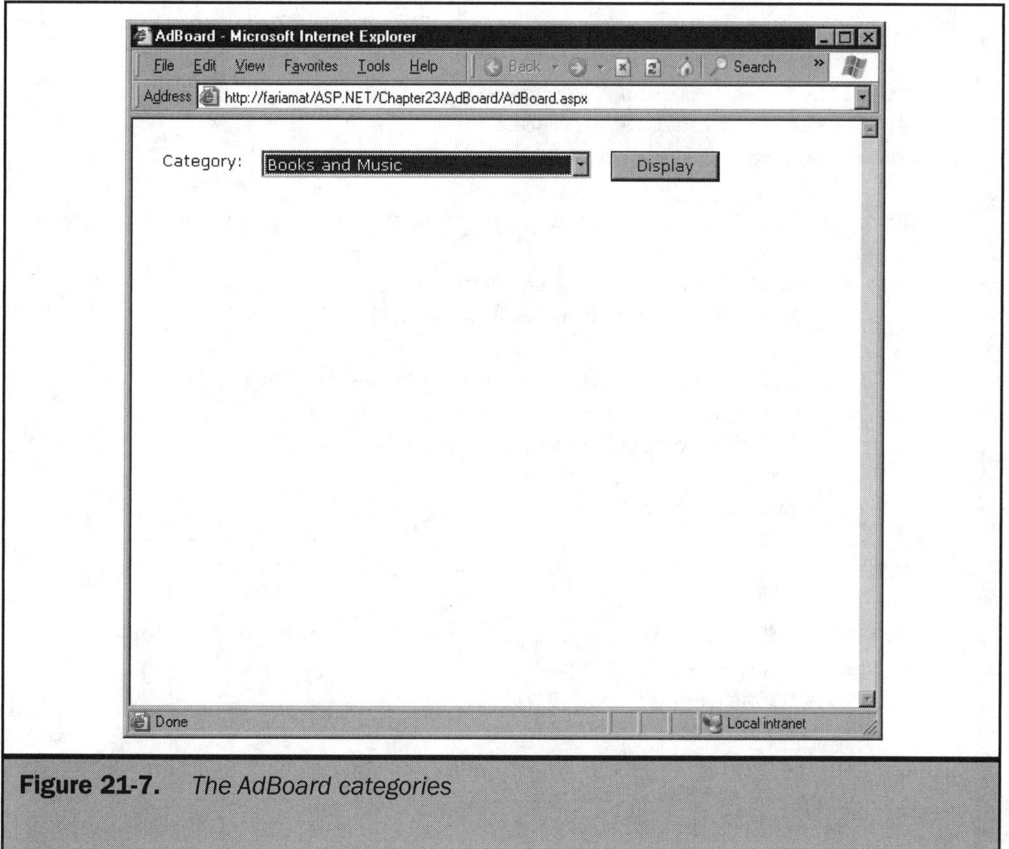


**Figure 21-7.** *The AdBoard categories*

Once a category is chosen, the matching items are displayed, and a panel of controls appears, which allows the user to add a new entry to the ad board under the current category (see Figure 21-8).

The page code creates the component when needed, and displays the appropriate database information by binding the DataSet to the drop-down list or DataGrid control.

```
Public Class AdBoard
  Inherits Page

    Protected lstCategories As DropDownList
    Protected WithEvents cmdDisplay As Button
    Protected pnlNew As Panel
```

```
    Protected txtDescription As TextBox
    Protected txtPrice As TextBox
    Protected txtTitle As TextBox
    Protected gridItems As DataGrid
    Protected WithEvents cmdAdd As Button

    Private Sub Page_Load(sender As Object, e As EventArgs) _
      Handles MyBase.Load
        If Me.IsPostBack = False Then
            Dim DB As New SimpleDB.DBUtil()

            lstCategories.DataSource = DB.GetCategories()
            lstCategories.DataTextField = "Name"
            lstCategories.DataValueField = "ID"
            lstCategories.DataBind()
            pnlNew.Visible = False
        End If
    End Sub

    Private Sub cmdDisplay_Click(sender As Object, e As EventArgs) _
      Handles cmdDisplay.Click
        Dim DB As New SimpleDB.DBUtil()

        gridItems.DataSource = DB.GetItems( _
          lstCategories.SelectedItem.Value)
        gridItems.DataBind()
        pnlNew.Visible = True
    End Sub

    Private Sub cmdAdd_Click(sender As Object, e As EventArgs) _
      Handles cmdAdd.Click
        Dim DB As New SimpleDB.DBUtil()

        DB.AddItem(txtTitle.Text, txtDescription.Text, _
                   txtPrice.Text, lstCategories.SelectedItem.Value)

        gridItems.DataSource = DB.GetItems(_
          Val(lstCategories.SelectedItem.Value))
        gridItems.DataBind()
    End Sub

End Class
```

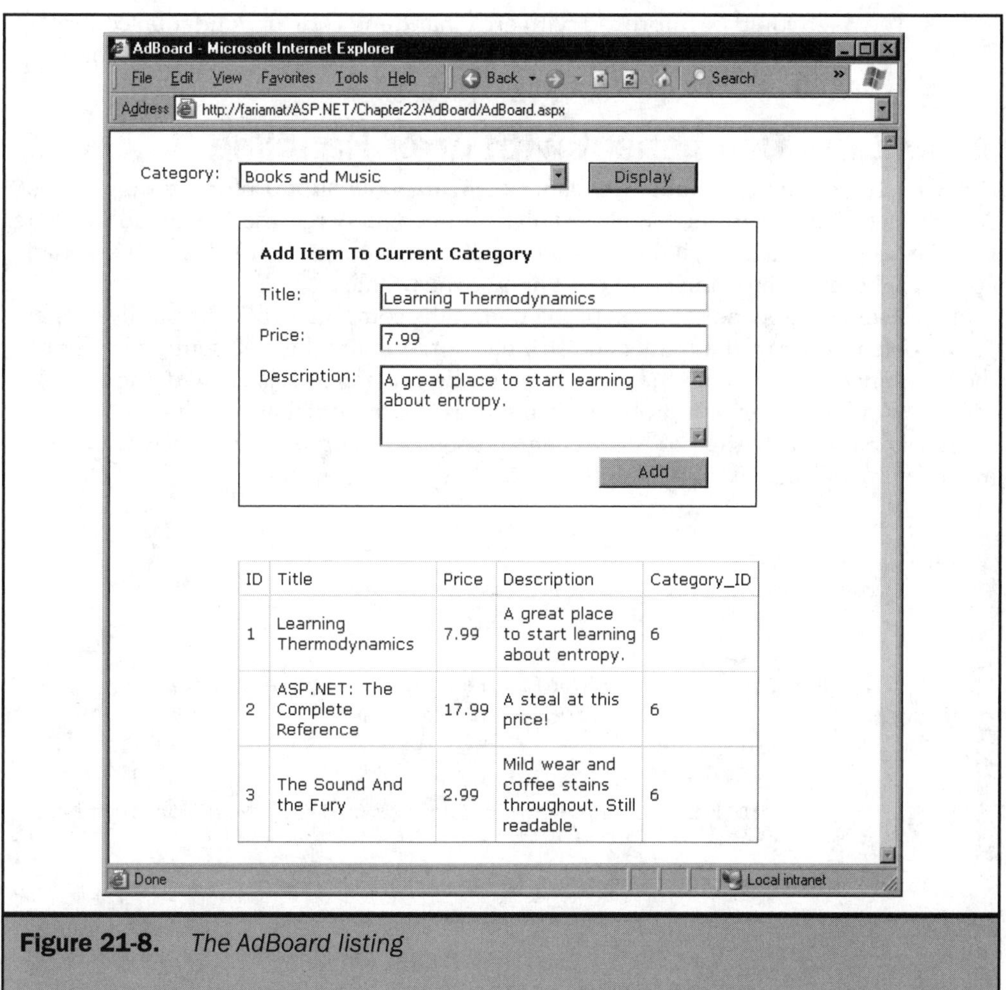


**Figure 21-8.** *The AdBoard listing*

## Interesting Facts About this Code

- Not all the functionality of the component is used in this page. For example, the page does not use the AddCategory method or the version of GetItems that does not require a category number. This is completely normal. Other pages may use different features from the component.
- The page is free of data access code. It does, however, need to understand how to use a DataSet, and it would need to know specific field names in order to create a more attractive DataGrid with custom templates for layout (instead of automatically generated columns).

- The page could be improved with error handling code or validation controls. As it is, no validation is performed to ensure that the price is numeric, or to even ensure that the required values are supplied.

## Enhancing the Component with Error Handling

One way the component could be enhanced is with better support for error reporting. As it is, any database errors that occur will be immediately returned to the calling code. In some cases (for example, if there is a legitimate database problem), this is a reasonable approach, because the component can't handle the problem.

However, there is one common problem that the component fails to handle properly. This problem occurs if the connection string is not found in the web.config file. Though the component tries to read the connection string as soon as it is created, the calling code won't realize there is a problem until it tries to use a database method.

A better approach is to notify the client as soon as the problem is detected, as shown in the following code example.

```
Public Class DBUtil
    Private ConnectionString As String

    Public Sub New()
        ConnectionString = ConfigurationSettings.AppSettings(_
                           "ConnectionString")
        If ConnectionString = "" Then
            Throw New ApplicationException(_
              "Missing ConnectionString variable in web.config file.")
        End If
    End Sub

    ' (Other class code omitted.)

End Class
```

### You Can Debug Component Code

If you are debugging your code in Visual Studio .NET, you'll find that you can single step from your web page code right into the code for the component, even if it isn't a part of the same solution. The appropriate source code file will be loaded into your editor automatically, as long as it is available.

This code throws an ApplicationException with a custom error message that indicates the problem. To provide even better reporting, you could create your own exception class that inherits from ApplicationException, as described in Chapter 11.

## Enhancing the Component with Aggregate Information

The component doesn't have to limit the type of information it provides to DataSets. Other information can also be useful. For example, you might provide a read-only property called ItemFields that returns an array of strings representing the names for fields in the Items table. Or you might add another method that retrieves aggregate information about the entire table, such as the average cost of an item or the total number of currently listed items.

```
Public Class DBUtil
    ' (Other class code omitted.)

    Public Function GetAveragePrice() As Decimal
        Dim Query As String = "SELECT AVG(Price) FROM Items"

        Dim con As New OleDbConnection(ConnectionString)
        Dim cmd As New OleDbCommand(Query, con)

        con.Open()
        Dim Average As Decimal = cmd.ExecuteScalar()
        con.Close()

        Return Average
    End Function

    Public Function GetTotalItems() As Integer
        Dim Query As String = "SELECT Count(*) FROM Items"

        Dim con As New OleDbConnection(ConnectionString)
        Dim cmd As New OleDbCommand(Query, con)

        con.Open()
        Dim Count As Integer = cmd.ExecuteScalar()
        con.Close()

        Return Count
    End Function

End Class
```

These commands use some customized SQL that may be new to you (namely, the Count and AVG functions). However, these methods are just as easy to use from the client's perspective as GetItems and GetCategories.

```
Dim DB As New SimpleDB.DBUtil()
Dim AveragePrice As Decimal = DB.GetAveragePrice()
Dim TotalItems As Integer = DB.GetTotalItems()
```

### Read-Only Properties versus Methods

It may have occurred to you that you could return information such as the total number of items through a read-only property procedure (like TotalItems) instead of a method (in this case, GetTotalItems). Though this would work, property procedures are better left to information that is maintained with the class (in a private variable) or is easy to reconstruct. In this case, it takes a database operation to count the number of rows, and this database operation could cause an unusual problem or slow down performance if used frequently. To help reinforce that fact, a method is used instead of a property.

## Enhancing the Component with a Data Object

Sometimes a DataSet is not the best way to return information to the client. One possible reason could be that the field names are unusual, unintuitive, or subject to change. Another reason might be that the client isn't using data binding, and doesn't want to worry about using the ADO.NET objects to extract the appropriate information.

In these cases, you can create a more advanced component that returns information using a custom data class. This approach takes encapsulating one step further, and isolates the calling code from most of the underlying database details. For example, you could create the following classes to represent the important details for items and categories.

```
Public Class Item
    Public ID As Integer
    Public Title As String
    Public Price As Decimal
    Public Description As String
    Public Category As String
End Class

Public Class Category
    Public ID As Integer
    Public Name As String
End Class
```

For the most part, the member variable names match the actual field names, although they don't need to do so. You can add these classes directly to the .vb file that contains the DBUtil component class.

The DBUtil class requires a slight bit of rewriting to use the new classes. To simplify matters, this version only uses the category-specific version of the GetItems method. You'll notice, however, that this method has been enhanced to perform a join query, and return the matching category name (instead of just the ID) for each item row.

```
Public Class DBUtil
    ' (Other class code omitted.)

    Public Function GetCategories() As Collection
        Dim Query As String = "SELECT * FROM Categories"
        Dim ds As DataSet = FillDataSet(Query, "Categories")
        Dim dr As DataRow
        Dim Categories As New Collection()

        For Each dr In ds.Tables("Categories").Rows
            Dim Entry As New Category()
            Entry.ID = dr("ID")
            Entry.Name = dr("Name")
            Categories.Add(Entry)
        Next

        Return Categories
    End Function

    Public Function GetItems(categoryID As Double) As Collection
        Dim Query As String = "SELECT * FROM Items "
        Query &= "INNER JOIN Categories ON "
        Query &= Category_ID=Categories.ID "
        Query &= "WHERE Category_ID='" & categoryID & "'"
        Dim ds As DataSet = FillDataSet(Query, "Items")
        Dim dr As DataRow
        Dim Items As New Collection()

        For Each dr In ds.Tables("Items").Rows
            Dim Entry As New Item()
            Entry.ID = dr("ID")
            Entry.Title = dr("Title")
            Entry.Price = dr("Price")
            Entry.Description = dr("Description")
            Entry.Category = dr("Name")
            Items.Add(Entry)
```

```
        Next

        Return Items
    End Function

End Class
```

Now the GetCategories and GetItems methods return a collection of Category or Item objects. Whether this information is drawn from a file, database, or created manually is completely transparent to the calling code.

Unfortunately, this change has broken the original code. The problem is that you can't use data binding with the member variables of an object. Instead, your class needs to provide property procedures. For example, you can rewrite the classes for a quick test, using the following code.

```
Public Class Item
    Public ID As Integer
    Public Price As Decimal
    Public Description As String

    Private _Title As String
    Public Property Title() As String
        Get
            Return _Title
        End Get
        Set(Value As String)
            _Title = Value
        End Set
    End Property

    Private _Category As String
    Public Property Category() As String
        Get
            Return _Category
        End Get
        Set(Value As String)
            _Category = Value
        End Set
    End Property
End Class
```

```
Public Class Category

    Private _ID As Integer
    Public Property ID() As Integer
        Get
            Return _ID
        End Get
        Set(Value As Integer)
            _ID = Value
        End Set
    End Property

    Private _Name As String
    Public Property Name() As String
        Get
            Return _Name
        End Get
        Set(Value As String)
            _Name = Value
        End Set
    End Property

End Class
```

Now data binding will be supported for the ID and Name properties of any Category objects, and the Title and Category properties of all Item objects. The original AdBoard code won't require any changes (unless you have changed the component's namespace or class names), but it will work with one slight difference. Because the DataGrid can only bind to two pieces of information, it will only display two columns (see Figure 21-9).

Of course, the calling code doesn't need to use data binding. Instead, it can work with the Item and Category objects directly, just as you can work with .NET structures such as DateTime and Font. Here's an example of how you could fill the list box manually.

```
Dim DB As New DataObjectDB.DBUtil()
Dim Item As New DataObjectDB.Category()
Dim Categories As Collection = Components.GetCategories()

For Each Item In Categories
    lstCategories.Items.Add(New ListItem(Item.Name, Item.ID))
Next
```

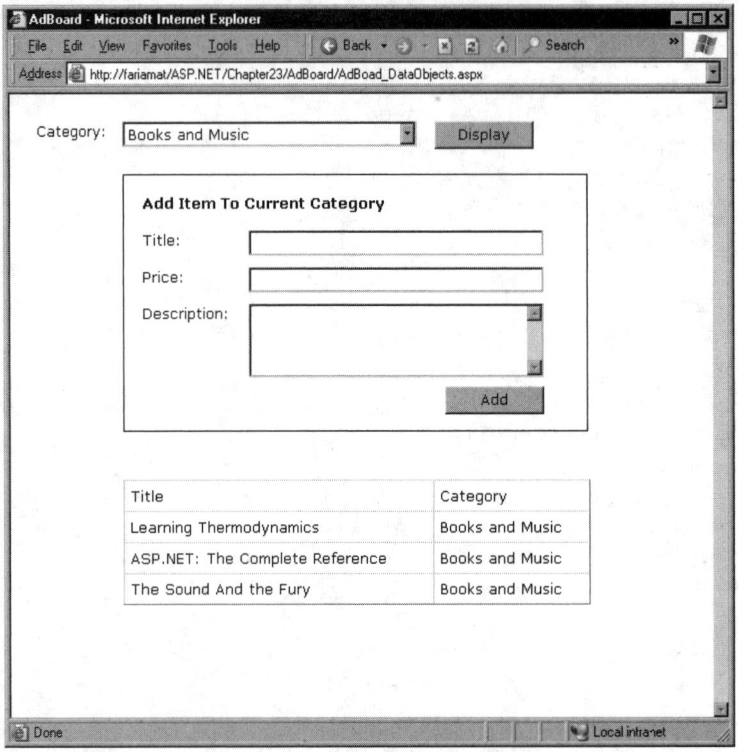

Figure 21-9. *The AdBoard with the new component*

## Data Objects Can Also Add Functionality

The Category and Item objects are really just special structures that group together related data. You can also add methods and other functionality into this class. For example, you could rewrite the AddItem method in the DBUtil component so that it required an Item object parameter. The Item object could provide some basic error checking when you create and set its properties that would notify you of invalid data before you attempt to add it to the database.

This approach can streamline a multi-layered application, but it can also add unneeded complexity, and risk mingling database details deep into your classes and code. For more information, you might want to read a book on three-tier design, or refer to the architectural white papers provided by Microsoft in the MSDN Knowledge Base.

# Using COM Components

If you're a longtime ASP developer, you probably have developed your own components at one time or another. You may even have legacy COM components that you need to use in an ASP.NET application. While the ideal approach is to redesign and recode these components as .NET assemblies, time constraints don't always allow for these changes, particularly if you are already involved in a large migration effort to convert existing web pages. There is no way to directly mingle the unmanaged code in a COM component with .NET code, as this would violate the security and verification services built into the Common Language Runtime.

Fortunately, .NET does provide a method to interact with COM components. It's called a Runtime Callable Wrapper (RCW)—a special .NET proxy class that sits between your code and the COM component (see Figure 21-10). The RCW handles the transition from managed Visual Basic .NET code to the unmanaged COM component. Though this may seem simple, it actually involves marshalling calls across application domains, converting data types, and using traditional COM interfaces. It also involves converting COM events to the completely different .NET event framework.

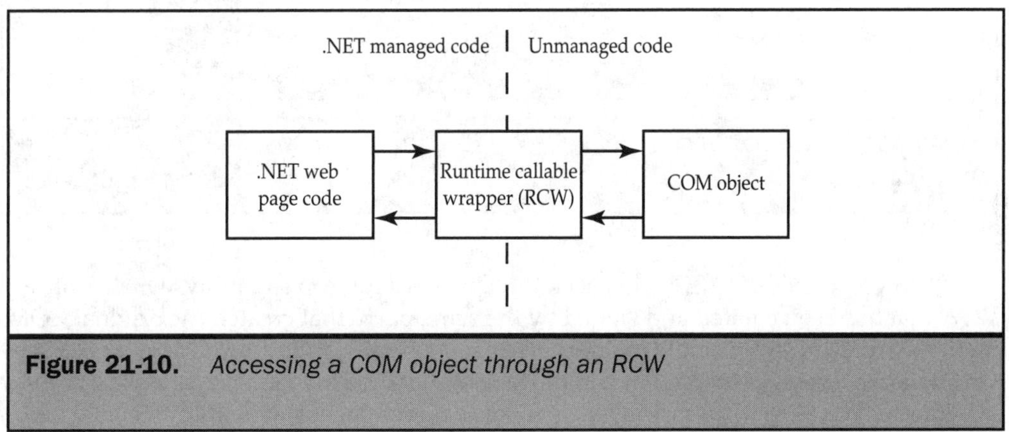


**Figure 21-10.** *Accessing a COM object through an RCW*

The RCW presents your code with an interface that mimics the underlying COM object—it's the same idea as the Web Service proxy class, which "pretends" to be the Web Service in order to simplify your coding. Once you have created an RCW, you can use it in the same way that you would use the actual COM component, invoking its methods, using its properties, and receiving its events.

## Creating an RCW in Visual Studio .NET

There are two basic ways to generate an RCW. The first method is to use Visual Studio .NET. In this case, select Project | Add Reference from the menu, and then select the COM tab to display a list of currently installed COM objects. Find the COM object you want to use and double-click on it, or browse to it using the Browse button (see Figure 21-11).

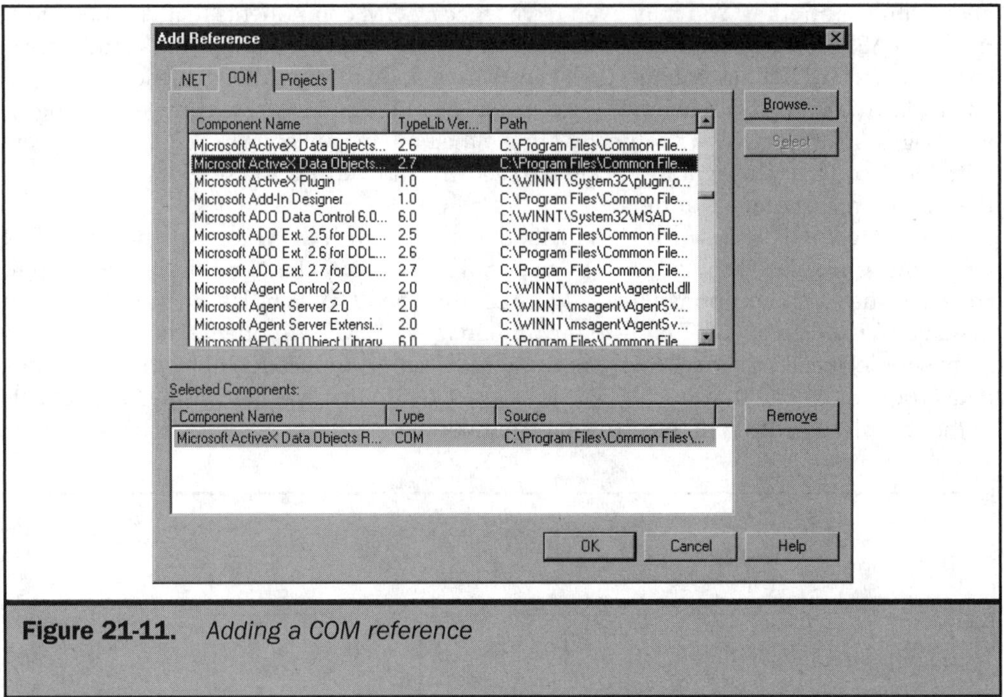


**Figure 21-11.** *Adding a COM reference*

When you click OK, .NET will check for a primary Interop assembly, which is an RCW that has been created and signed by the same party that created the original COM component. If it cannot find a primary Interop assembly, it will prompt you with a warning and generate the RCW DLL file automatically. This file will be placed in the bin directory of your application (as are all components), and will automatically be given the name of the COM component's type library.

For example, in Figure 21-11, a reference is being added to the COM-based ADO data access library (the precursor to ADO.NET). The RCW has the name ADODDB.dll and is made available through the namespace ADODB. This primary Interop assembly is provided with the .NET framework, but you can create your own RCW assemblies for other COM components just as easily.

You can find the component's namespace by examining the current references for your project in the Solution Explorer (see Figure 21-12).

You can now create classes from the COM component, and use them as though they are native .NET classes (which, of course, they now are). That means you use the .NET syntax to create an object or receive an event using the classes in the RCW (see Figure 21-13).

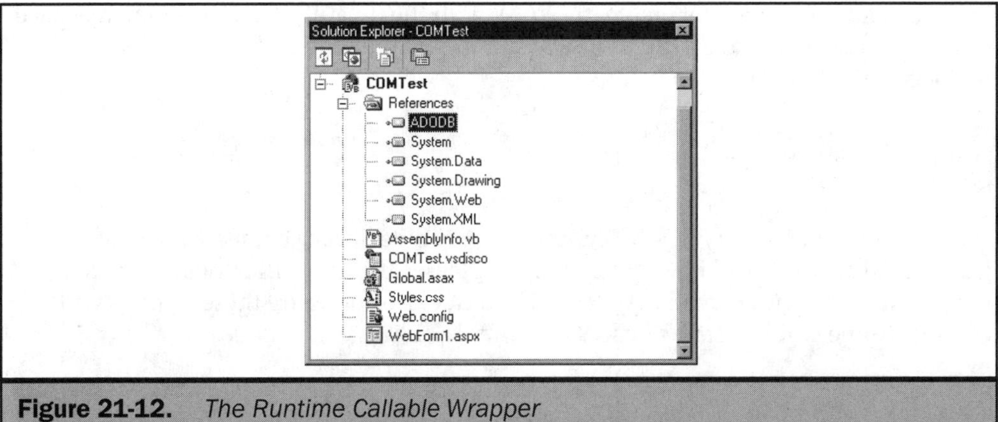


**Figure 21-12.** *The Runtime Callable Wrapper*

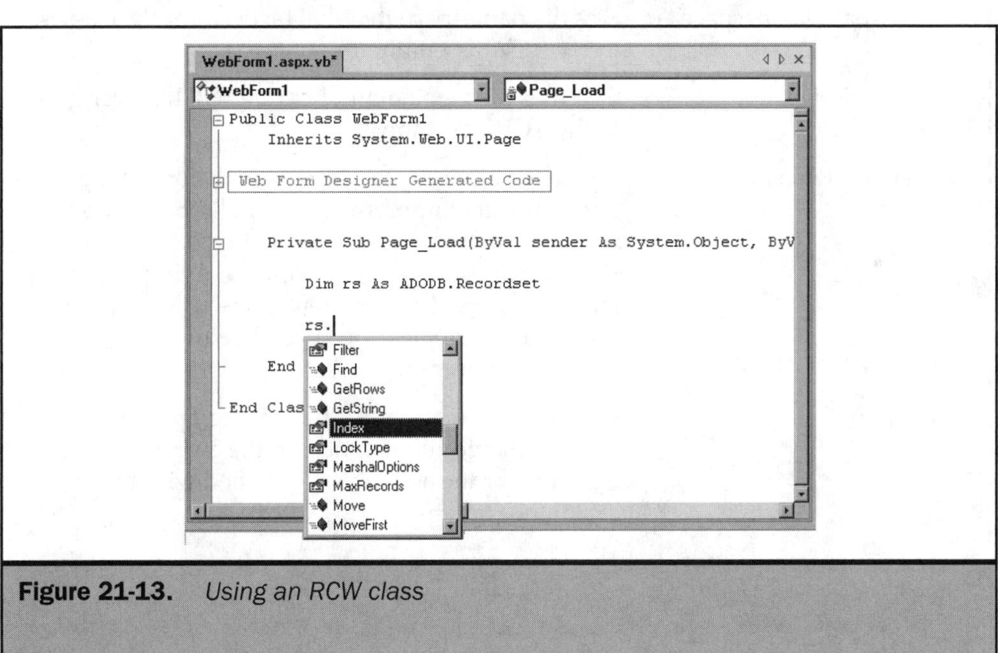


**Figure 21-13.** *Using an RCW class*

## Creating an RCW with Type Library Import

If you aren't using Visual Studio .NET, you can create a wrapper assembly using a command-line utility that is included with the .NET framework. This utility, which is known as the type library import tool, is quite straightforward. The only piece of information you need is the filename that contains the COM component.

The following statement creates an RCW with the default filename and namespace (as it would be in Visual Studio .NET), assuming that the MyCOMComponent.dll file is in the current directory.

```
tlbimp MyCOMComponent.dll
```

Assuming that the MyCOMComponent has a type library named MyClasses, the generated RCW file will have the name MyClasses.dll and will expose its classes through a namespace named MyClasses. You can also configure these options with command-line parameters, as described in Table 21-1.

| Parameter | Description |
|---|---|
| /out:Filename | Sets the name of the RCW file that will be generated. |
| /namespace:Namespace | Sets the namespace that will be used for the classes in the RCW assembly. |
| /asmversion: VersionNumber | Specifies the version number that will be given to the RCW assembly. |
| /reference:Filename | If you do not specify the /reference option, tlbimp.exe automatically imports any external type libraries that are referenced by the current type library. If you specify the /reference option, tlbimp.exe attempts to resolve these references using types in the .NET assemblies you specify before it imports other type libraries. |
| /strictref | Does not import a type library if the Tblimp.exe cannot resolve all references in the current assembly or the assemblies specified with the /reference option. |

**Table 21-1.** *Type Library Import Parameters*

There are also additional options for creating signed assemblies, which is useful if you are a component vendor who needs to distribute a .NET assembly to other clients. These features are described in the MSDN reference. Additionally, you can use .NET classes to manually write your own wrapper class. This process is incredibly painstaking, however, and in the words of Microsoft's own documentation, "seldom performed."

# Chapter 22

## Custom Controls

Component-based development encourages you to divide the logic in your application into discrete, independent blocks. Once you've made the jump to custom classes and objects, you can start creating modular web applications (and even desktop applications) that are built out of reusable units of code. But while these objects help work out thorny data access procedures or custom business logic, they don't offer much when it comes to simplifying your user interface code. If you want to create web applications that reuse a customized portion of user interface, you're still stuck rewriting control tags and reconfiguring page initialization code in several different places.

It doesn't have to be this way. ASP.NET includes tools for modularizing and reusing portions of user interface code that are just as powerful as those that allow you to design custom business objects. There are two main tools at your fingertips, both of which we'll explore in this chapter:

- **User controls** allow you to reuse a portion of a page, by placing it in a special .ascx file. ASP.NET also allows you to make smart user controls that provide methods and properties, and configure their contained controls automatically.
- Custom or **derived controls** allow you to build a new control by inheriting from an ASP.NET control class. With custom controls there is no limit to what you can do, whether it's adding a new property or tweaking the rendered HTML output.

## User Controls

User controls look pretty much the same as ASP.NET web forms. Like web forms, they are composed of an HTML-like portion with control tags (the .ascx file) and can optionally use a .vb code-behind file with event-handling logic. They can also include the same range of HTML content and ASP.NET controls, and they experience the same events as the Page object (such as Load and PreRender). The only differences between user controls and web pages are:

- User controls begin with a <%@ Control %> directive instead of a <%@ Page %> directive.
- User controls use the file extension .ascx instead of .aspx, and their code-behind files inherit from the System.Web.UI.UserControl class. In fact, the UserControl class and the Page class both inherit from the same base classes, which is why they share so many of the same methods and events, as shown in the inheritance diagram in Figure 22-1.
- User controls can't be requested directly by a client. Instead, user controls are embedded inside other web pages.

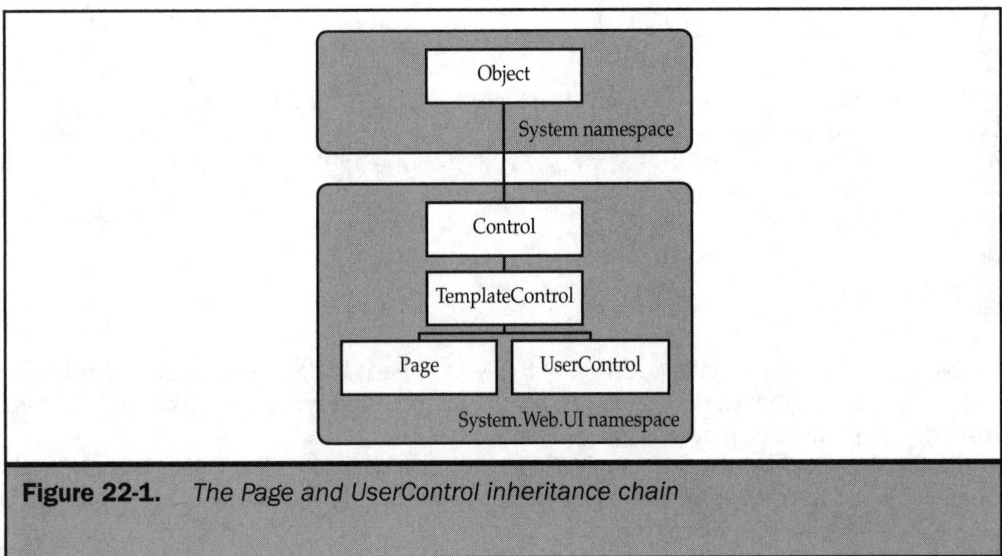


**Figure 22-1.** *The Page and UserControl inheritance chain*

## Creating a Simple User Control

You can create a user control in Visual Studio .NET in much the same way as you add a web page. Just right-click on the project in the Solution Explorer, and select Add | Add User Control. If you aren't using Visual Studio .NET, you simply begin by creating an .ascx text file.

The following user control contains a single label control.

```
<%@ Control Language="VB" AutoEventWireup="false"
    Inherits="Footer" %>

<asp:Label id="lblFooter" runat="server" />
```

Note that the Control directive uses the same attributes that are used in the Page directive for a web page, including Language, AutoEventWireup, and Inherits. Optionally, you could add a Src attribute if you aren't precompiling your code-behind class (and Visual Studio .NET will add a Codebehind attribute to track the file while editing). To refresh your memory about page attributes, refer to Chapter 5.

The code-behind class for this sample user control is similarly straightforward. It uses the UserControl.Load event to add some text to the label.

```
Public MustInherit Class Footer
  Inherits UserControl
```

```
    Protected lblFooter As Label

    Private Sub Load(sender As Object, e As EventArgs) _
      Handles MyBase.Load
        lblFooter.Text = "This page was served at "
        lblFooter.Text &= DateTime.Now.ToString()
    End Sub

End Class
```

Note that the class has the addition of the MustInherit keyword in its class definition. This indicates that the user control cannot be accessed directly; instead, a control derived from this class must be placed on a web page.

To test this user control, you need to insert it into a web page. Two steps are required. First, you need to add a <%@ Register %> directive that identifies the control you want to use and associates it with a unique control prefix.

```
<%@ Register TagPrefix="cr" TagName="Footer" Src="Footer.ascx" %>
```

The Register directive specifies a tag prefix and name. Tag prefixes group sets of related controls (for example, all ASP.NET web controls use the tag prefix "asp"). Tag prefixes are usually lowercase—technically, they are case-insensitive—and should be unique for your company or organization. The Src directive identifies the location of the user control template file, not the code-behind file.

You can then add the user control whenever you want (and as many times as you want), by inserting its control tag. Consider this page example (shown in Figure 22-2).

```
<%@ Page Language="VB" AutoEventWireup="false"
    Inherits="FooterHost"%>
<%@ Register TagPrefix="cr" TagName="Footer" Src="Footer.ascx" %>

<HTML>
<body>

<form id=Form1 method=post runat="server">
    <h2>A Page With a Footer</h2><hr>
    Static Page Text<br><br>
    <cr:Footer id=Footer1 runat="server" />
</form>

</body>
</HTML>
```

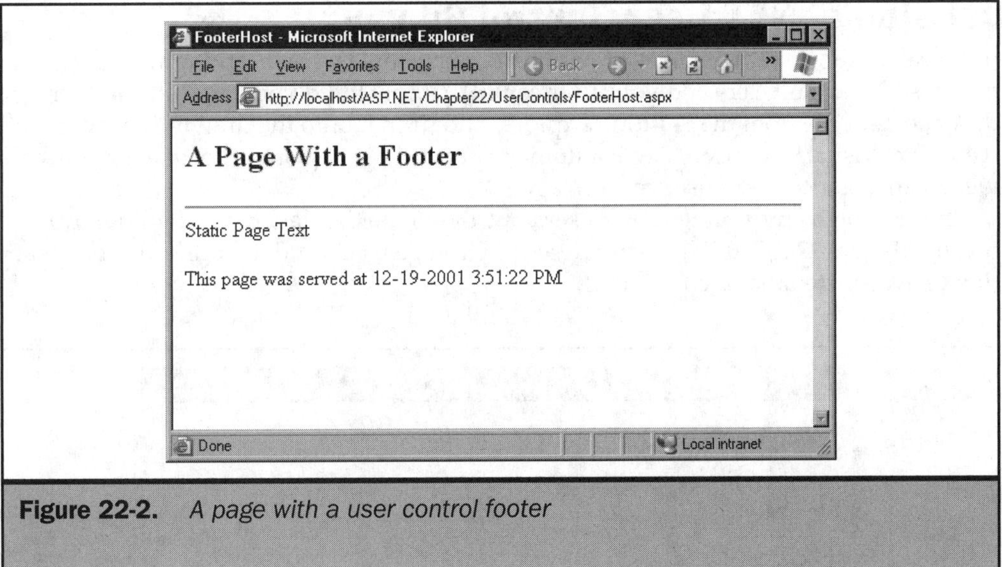


**Figure 22-2.** *A page with a user control footer*

This example shows a simple way that you could create a header or footer and reuse it in all the pages in your web site, simply by adding the user control declaration. In the case of our simple footer, the actual code savings is limited, but it could become much more useful for a complex control with extensive formatting or several contained controls.

Of course, this only scratches the surface of what you can do with a user control. In the following sections, you'll learn how to enhance a control with properties, methods, and events—transforming it from a simple "include file" into a full-fledged object.

## Dynamically Loaded User Controls

The Page class provides a special LoadControl method that allows you to create a user control dynamically at runtime from an .ascx file. The user control is returned to you as a control object, which you can then add to the Controls collection of a container control on the web page (like PlaceHolder or Panel) to display it on the page. This technique is not recommended as a substitute for declaratively using a user control, but it does have some interesting applications if you need to generate user interface dynamically. Chapter 25 shows how the LoadControl method is used with the IBuySpy portal application.

## Visual Studio .NET User Control Support

In Visual Studio .NET, you have a few shortcuts available when working with user controls. Once you've created your user control, simply build your project, and then drag the .ascx file from the Solution Explorer and drop it onto the drawing area of a web form. Visual Studio .NET will automatically add the Register directive for you, as well as an instance of the user control tag.

In the design environment, the user control will be displayed as a familiar gray box (see Figure 22-3)—the same nondescript package used for databound controls that don't have any templates configured.

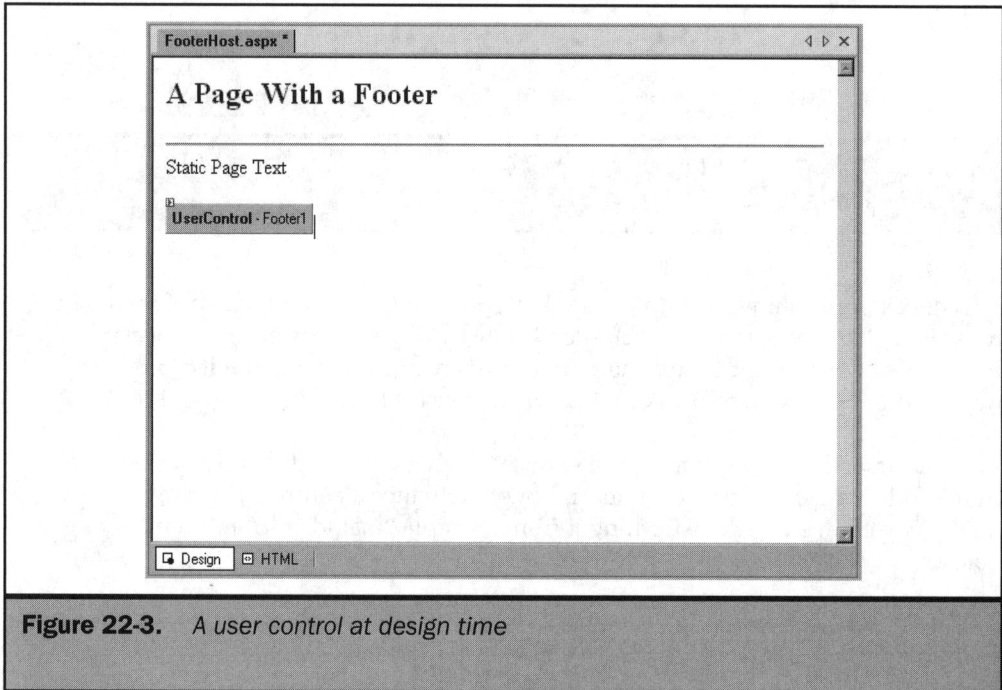


**Figure 22-3.** *A user control at design time*

## Independent User Controls

Conceptually, there are really two types of user controls: independent and integrated. Independent user controls don't interact with the rest of the code on your form. The Footer user control is one such example. Another example might be a list of buttons that offer links to other pages. A Menu user control like this could handle the events for all the buttons, and then run the appropriate Response.Redirect code to move to another web page. Or it could just include ordinary HyperLink controls that don't have any associated server-side code. Every page in the web site could then include the same Menu user control—enabling painless web site navigation with no need to worry about frames. In fact, this is exactly the approach you'll see in practice in Chapter 25 with the IBuySpy e-commerce application.

The following sample defines a simple Menu footer control that just requests a given page with a different query string argument. Note that the style attribute of the <div> tag (which defines fonts and formatting) is omitted for clarity. I've also left out the Inherits attribute in the Control tag, because the user control does not require any code-behind logic.

```
<%@ Control Language="VB" AutoEventWireup="false" %>

<div>
  Products:
  <asp:HyperLink id="lnkBooks" runat="server"
    NavigateUrl="MenuHost.aspx?product=Books">Books
  </asp:HyperLink><br>
  <asp:HyperLink id=lnkToys runat="server"
    NavigateUrl="MenuHost.aspx?product=Toys">Toys
  </asp:HyperLink><br>
  <asp:HyperLink id=lnkSports runat="server"
    NavigateUrl="MenuHost.aspx?product=Sports">Sports
  </asp:HyperLink><br>
  <asp:HyperLink id=lnkFurniture runat="server"
    NavigateUrl="MenuHost.aspx?product=Furniture">Furniture
  </asp:HyperLink>
</div>
```

The MenuHost.aspx file includes two controls, the Menu control and a label that displays the product query string parameter.

```
<%@ Page Language="VB" AutoEventWireup="false" Inherits="MenuHost"%>
<%@ Register TagPrefix="cr" TagName="Menu" Src="Menu.ascx" %>

<HTML>
<body>

<form id=Form1 method=post runat="server">
    <cr:Menu id="Menu1" runat="server" />
    <asp:Label id="lblSelection" / >
</form>

</body>
</HTML>
```

When the MenuHost.aspx page loads, it adds the appropriate information to the lblSelection control.

```
Private Sub Page_Load(sender As Object, e As EventArgs) _
  Handles MyBase.Load
    If Request.Params("product") <> "" Then
        lblSelection.Text = "You chose: "
        lblSelection.Text &= Request.Params("product")
    End If
End Sub
```

The end result is shown in Figure 22-4. Whenever you click a link, the page is posted back, and the text updated.

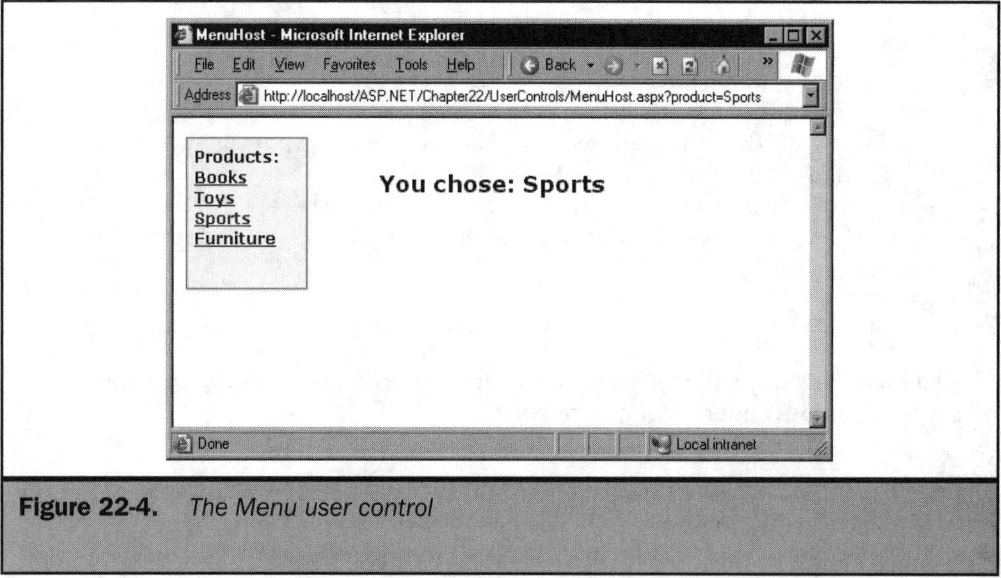


**Figure 22-4.** *The Menu user control*

# Integrated User Controls

Integrated user controls interact with the web page that hosts them, in one way or another. When designing these controls, the class-based design tips you learned in Chapter 3 really become useful.

A typical example is a user control that allows some level of configuration through properties. For example, you could create a footer that supports two different display formats: long date and short time. To add a further level of refinement, the Footer user control allows the web page to specify the appropriate display format using an enumeration.

The first step is to create an enumeration in the custom Footer class. Remember, an enumeration is simply a type of constant that is internally stored as an integer, but is set in code by using one of the allowed names that you specify. Variables that use the FooterFormat enumeration can take the value FooterFormat.LongDate or FooterFormat.ShortTime.

```
Public Enum FooterFormat
    LongDate
    ShortTime
End Enum
```

The next step is to add a property to the Footer class that allows the web page to retrieve or set the current format applied to the footer. The actual format is stored in a private variable called _Format, which is set to the long data format by default when the class is first created. (The same effect could be accomplished, in a slightly sloppier way, by using a public member variable named Format instead of a full property procedure.) If you're hazy on how property procedures work, feel free to review the explanation in Chapter 3.

```
Private _Format As FooterFormat

Public Property Format() As FooterFormat = FooterFormat.LongDate
    Get
        Return _Format
    End Get
    Set(ByVal Value As FooterFormat)
        _Format = Value
    End Set
End Property
```

Finally, the UserControl.Load event needs to take account of the current footer state and format the output accordingly. The full Footer class code is shown here:

```
Public MustInherit Class Footer
  Inherits UserControl

    Protected lblFooter As Label
```

```
    Public Enum FooterFormat
        LongDate
        ShortTime
    End Enum

    Private _Format As FooterFormat = FooterFormat.LongDate
    Public Property Format() As FooterFormat
        Get
            Return _Format
        End Get
        Set(ByVal Value As FooterFormat)
            _Format = Value
       End Set
    End Property

    Private Sub Page_Load(sender As Object, e As EventArgs) _
      Handles MyBase.Load
        lblFooter.Text = "This page was served at "

        If _Format = FooterFormat.LongDate Then
            lblFooter.Text &= DateTime.Now.ToLongDateString()
        ElseIf _Format = FooterFormat.ShortTime Then
            lblFooter.Text &= DateTime.Now.ToShortTimeString()
        End If
    End Sub

End Class
```

To test out this footer, you need to create a page that includes the user control and defines a variable in the custom Page class that represents the user control. (Note that Visual Studio .NET does not add this variable automatically when you create the control, as it does for ordinary web controls.) You can then modify the Format property through the user control variable. An example is shown in Figure 22-5, which automatically sets the Format property for the user control to match a radio button selection whenever the page is posted back.

Note that the user control property is modified in the Page.Load event handler, not the cmdRefresh.Click event handler. The reason is that the Load event occurs before the user control has been rendered each time the page is created. The Click event occurs after the user control has been rendered, and though the property change will be visible in your code, it won't affect the user control's HTML output, which has already been added to the page.

```
Public Class FooterHost
  Inherits Page

    Protected optShort As RadioButton
    Protected optLong As RadioButton
    Protected cmdRefresh As Button
    Protected Footer1 As Footer

    Private Sub Page_Load(sender As Object, e As EventArgs) _
      Handles MyBase.Load

        If optLong.Checked = True Then
            Footer1.Format = Footer.FooterFormat.LongDate
        ElseIf optShort.Checked = True Then
            Footer1.Format = Footer.FooterFormat.ShortTime
        Else
            ' The default value in the Footer class will apply.
        End If

    End Sub

End Class
```

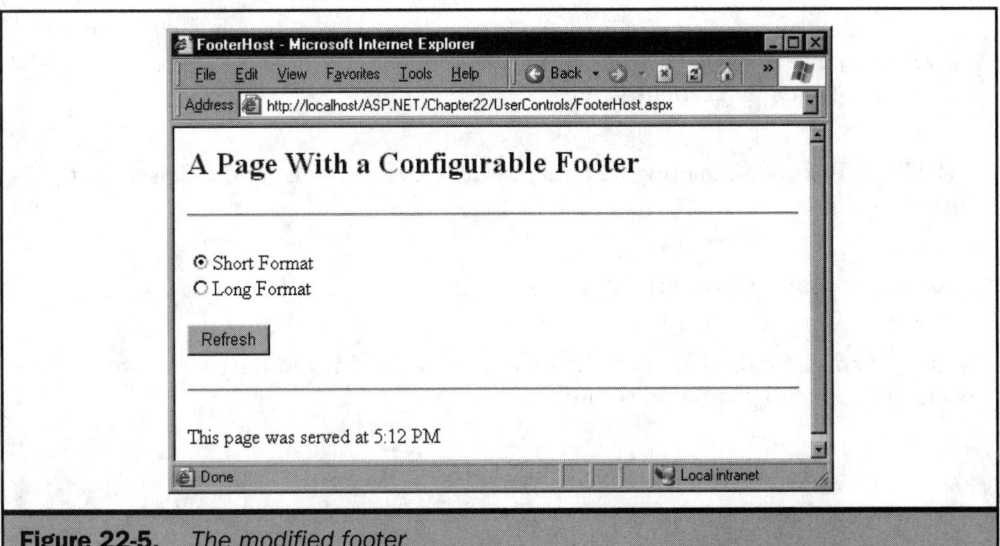


**Figure 22-5.** *The modified footer*

You could also set the initial appearance of the footer in the control tag.

```
<cr:Footer Format="ShortTime" id="Footer1" runat="server" />
```

## User Control Events

Another way that communication can occur between a user control and a web page is through events. Events are really the inverse of properties or methods, where the user control reacts to a change made by the web page code. With events, the user control notifies the web page about an action, and the web page code responds.

Creating a web control that uses events is fairly easy. Consider the next example, which uses a special login box that verifies a user's credentials. This type of control could be used in a variety of sources to restrict access to a variety of different pages. For that reason, you can't hardcode any logic in the user control that redirects the user to a specific page. Instead, the LoginBox user control needs to raise an event to alert the web page code if the login process was successful. At that point, the web page can display the appropriate resource or message.

The first step in creating the LoginBox user control is to define the events using the Event keyword. Remember, events are always declared at the public level, so they don't need an access qualifier keyword. (You can refer to Chapter 3 for a quick overview of how to use events in .NET.)

The LoginBox control defines two events, one that indicates a failed login attempt and one that indicates success.

```
Event LoginFailed()
Event LoginAuthenticated()
```

The LoginBox code can now fire either of these events by using the RaiseEvent command.

```
RaiseEvent LoginFailed()
```

These events are raised after the Login button is clicked, and the user's information is examined. The full page code is shown here:

```
Public MustInherit Class LoginBox
  Inherits UserControl
```

```
    Protected txtUser As TextBox
    Protected txtPassword As TextBox
    Protected WithEvents cmdLogin As Button

    Event LoginFailed()
    Event LoginAuthenticated()

    Private Sub cmdLogin_Click(sender As Object, e As EventArgs) _
      Handles cmdLogin.Click

        ' Typically, this code would use the FormsAuthentication
        ' class described in Chapter 24, or some custom
        ' database-lookup code to authenticate the user.
        ' Our example simply checks for a "secret" code.
        If txtPassword.Text = "opensesame" Then
            RaiseEvent LoginAuthenticated()
        Else
            RaiseEvent LoginFailed()
        End If

    End Sub

End Class
```

The page hosting this code can then add an event handler for either one of these events, in the same way that event handlers are created for any control—by declaring the control variable with the WithEvents keyword, and adding a Handles statement to a procedure with the appropriate signature.

Figure 22-6 shows a simple example of a page that uses the LoginBox control. If the login fails three times, the user is forwarded to another page. If the login succeeds, the LoginBox control is disabled and a message is displayed.

The code for this example is refreshingly straightforward.

```
Public Class ProtectedPage
  Inherits Page

    Protected lblSecretMessage As Label
    Protected pnlControls As Panel
    Protected WithEvents Login As UserControls.LoginBox

    Private Sub Failed() Handles Login.LoginFailed
```

```
        ' Retrieve the number of failed attempts from viewstate.
        Dim Attempts As Integer
        Attempts = CType(Viewstate("Attempts"), Integer)

        Attempts += 1
        If Attempts >= 3 Then Response.Redirect("default.aspx")

        ' Store the new number of failed attempts in viewstate.
        Viewstate("Attempts") = Attempts
    End Sub

    Private Sub Succeeded() Handles Login.LoginAuthenticated
        pnlControls.Enabled = False
        lblSecretMessage.Text = "You are now authenticated" & _
                                "to see this page."
    End Sub

End Class
```

Note that the user control is declared using the full namespace name (UserControls. LoginBox). This is always a good idea, and it's required if the namespace used for the user control is different than that used for the web page.

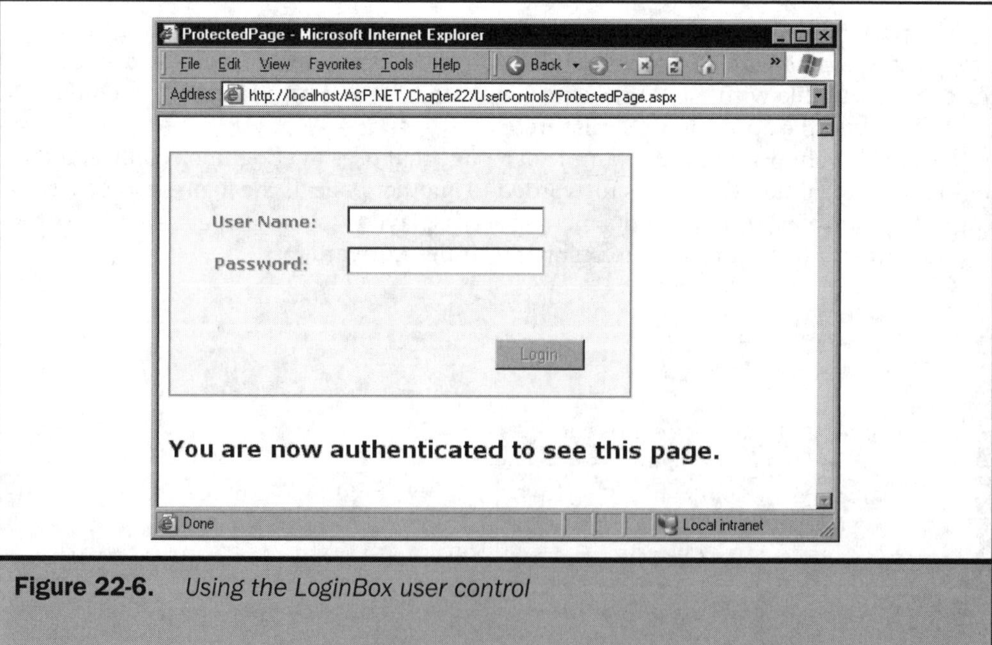


**Figure 22-6.** *Using the LoginBox user control*

## Using Events with Parameters

In the LoginBox example, there is no information passed along with the event. In many cases, however, you want to convey additional information that relates to the event. For example, you could create a LoginRequest event that passes information about the user ID and password that were entered. This would allow your code to decide whether the user has sufficient security permissions for the requested page, while retaining a common look for login boxes throughout your web application.

The .NET standard for events specifies that every event should use two parameters. The first one provides a reference to the control that sent the event, while the second one incorporates any additional information. This additional information is wrapped into a custom EventArgs object, which inherits from the System.EventArgs class. (If your event doesn't require any additional information, you can just use the generic System.EventArgs object, which doesn't contain any additional data. Many framework events, such as Page.Load or Button.Click, follow this pattern.)

The EventArgs class that follows allows the LoginBox user control to pass the name of the authenticated user to the event handler.

```
Public Class LoginAuthenticatedEventArgs
  Inherits EventArgs

    Public UserName As String

End Class
```

To use this class, you need to modify the LoginAuthenticated event definition to the .NET standard shown below. At the same, you should also modify the LoginFailed event definition, which can use the default (empty) System.EventArgs class.

```
Event LoginAuthenticated(sender As Object, _
  e As LoginAuthenticatedEventArgs)
Event LoginFailed(sender As Object, e As EventArgs)
```

Next, your code for raising the event needs to submit the required two pieces of information as event parameters.

```
Private Sub cmdLogin_Click(sender As Object, e As EventArgs) _
  Handles cmdLogin.Click

    If txtPassword.Text = "opensesame" Then
        Dim EventInfo As New LoginAuthenticatedEventArgs()
```

```
        EventInfo.UserName = txtUser.Text
        RaiseEvent LoginAuthenticated(Me, EventInfo)
    Else
        ' You can define the EventArgs object on the same line
        ' that you use it to make more economical code.
        RaiseEvent LoginFailed(Me, New EventArgs())
    End If

End Sub
```

Lastly, your receiving code needs to update its event handler to use the new signature.

```
Private Sub Succeeded(sender As Object, _
  e As LoginAuthenticatedEventArgs) _
  Handles Login.LoginAuthenticated

    pnlControls.Enabled = False
    lblSecretMessage.Text = "You are now authenticated"
    lblSecretMessage.Text &= "to see this page, " & e.UserName

End Sub

Private Sub Failed(sender As Object, e As EventArgs) _
  Handles Login.LoginFailed

        ' Retrieve the number of failed attempts from viewstate.
        Dim Attempts As Integer
        Attempts = CType(Viewstate("Attempts"), Integer)

        Attempts += 1
        If Attempts >= 3 Then Response.Redirect("default.aspx")

        ' Store the new number of failed attempts in viewstate.
        Viewstate("Attempts") = Attempts

End Sub
```

Now the user will see a page like the one shown in Figure 22-7 after a successful login.

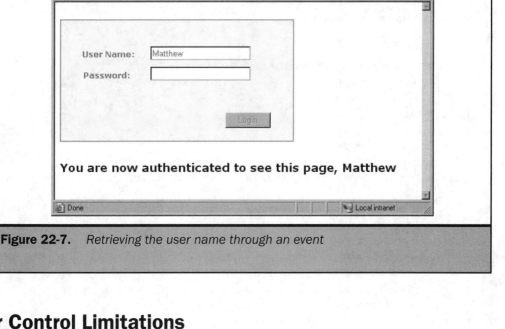

Figure 22-7. *Retrieving the user name through an event*

## User Control Limitations

User controls provide a great deal of flexibility when you want to combine several web controls (and additional HTML content) in a single unit, and possibly add some higher-level business logic. However, they are less useful when you want to modify or extend individual web controls.

For example, imagine you want to create a text box–like control for name entry. This text box might provide GetFirstName and GetLastName methods, which examine the entered text and parse it into a first and last name using one of two recognized formats: space-separated ("FirstName LastName") or comma-separated ("LastName, FirstName"). This way the user can enter a name in either format, and your code doesn't have to go through the work of parsing the text. Instead, the user control handles it automatically.

The full code for this user control would look something like this:

```
Public MustInherit Class NameTextBox
  Inherits System.Web.UI.UserControl

    Protected txtName As TextBox

    Private _FirstName As String
```

```
    Private _LastName As String

    Public Function GetFirstName() As String
        UpdateNames()
        Return _FirstName
    End Function

    Public Function GetLastName() As String
        UpdateNames()
        Return _LastName
    End Function

    Private Sub UpdateNames()
        Dim CommaPos As Integer = txtName.Text.IndexOf(",")
        Dim SpacePos As Integer = txtName.Text.IndexOf(" ")

        Dim NameArray() As String
        If CommaPos <> -1 Then
            NameArray = txtName.Text.Split(",")
            _FirstName = NameArray(1)
            _LastName = NameArray(0)
        ElseIf SpacePos <> -1 Then
            NameArray = txtName.Text.Split(" ")
            _FirstName = NameArray(0)
            _LastName = NameArray(1)
        Else
            ' The text has no comma or space.
            ' It cannot be converted to a name.
            Throw New InvalidOperationException()
        End If
    End Sub

End Class
```

The online samples include a simple page that allows you to test this control (shown in Figure 22-8). It retrieves the first and last names that are entered in the text box when the user clicks a button.

```
Private Sub cmdGetNames_Click(sender As Object, e As EventArgs) _
  Handles cmdGetNames.Click
    lblNames.Text = "<b>First name:</b> "
    lblNames.Text &= NameTextBox1.GetFirstName()
```

```
        lblNames.Text &= "<br><b>Last name:</b> " &
        lblNames.Text &= NameTextBox1.GetLastName()
    End Sub
```

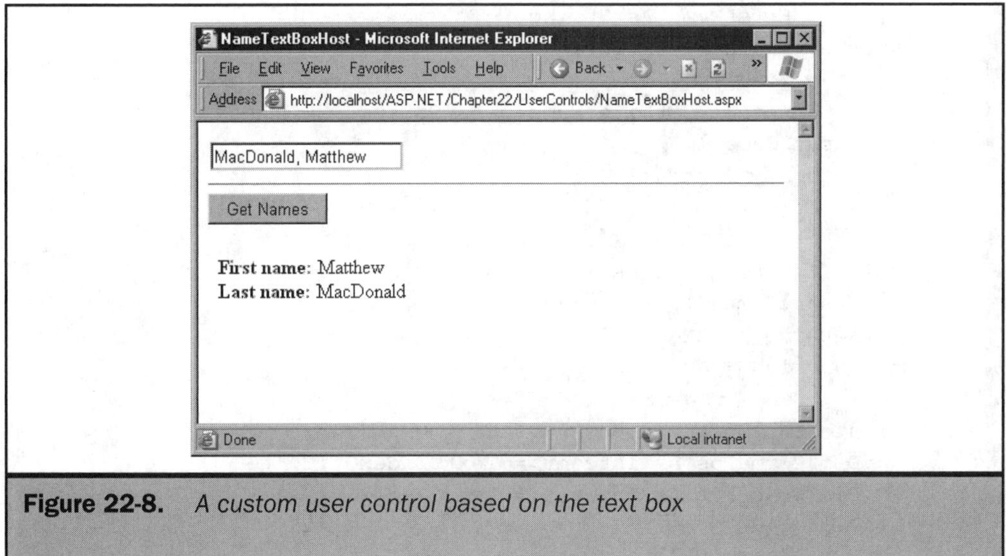


**Figure 22-8.** *A custom user control based on the text box*

Using a full user control is overkill in this case, and it also makes it difficult for the web page programmer to further configure the text box. For example, if a programmer wants to set the text box font or change its size, you either need to add the corresponding properties to the user control class or provide access to the text box through a public member variable. (Technically, the web page programmer could access the text box by using the Controls collection of the user control, but this is a less structured approach that can run into problems if other controls are added to the user control or the ID of the text box changes.) There's also no way to set these values in the user control tag.

The next section describes a better approach for extending or fine-tuning individual controls.



## Deriving Custom Controls

Thanks to the class-based framework of .NET, an easier solution for extending a specialized control is possible using inheritance. All you need to do is find the control you want to extend in the .NET class library, and derive a new class from it that adds the additional functionality you need.

Here's an example of the name text box implemented through a custom control.

```
Public Class NameTextBox
  Inherits System.Web.UI.WebControls.TextBox

    Private _FirstName As String
    Private _LastName As String

    Public Function GetFirstName() As String
        UpdateNames()
        Return _FirstName
    End Function

    Public Function GetLastName() As String
        UpdateNames()
        Return _LastName
    End Function

    Private Sub UpdateNames()
        Dim CommaPos As Integer = Text.IndexOf(",")
        Dim SpacePos As Integer = Text.IndexOf(" ")

        Dim NameArray() As String
        If CommaPos <> -1 Then
            NameArray = Text.Split(",")
            _FirstName = NameArray(1)
            _LastName = NameArray(0)
        ElseIf SpacePos <> -1 Then
            NameArray = Text.Split(" ")
            _FirstName = NameArray(0)
            _LastName = NameArray(1)
        Else
            ' The text has no comma or space.
            ' It cannot be converted to a name.
            Throw New InvalidOperationException()
        End If
    End Sub

End Class
```

In this example, the custom NameTextBox class inherits from the .NET TextBox class (which is found in the System.Web.UI.WebControls namespace). Because the

NameTextBox class extends the TextBox class, all the original TextBox members (such as Font and ForeColor) are still available to the web page programmer, and can be set in code or through the control tag. The only differences in the code between the user control version and the custom control version is that the custom version adds an Inherits statement and works natively with the Text property of the NameTextBox class (not a TextBox member variable).

## Consuming a Custom Control

To test the control, you should compile it into an assembly using the vbc.exe compiler, and place it in the bin directory for the application. This is the exact same process you used in Chapter 21 for custom components. You can then register the custom control using a Register directive with a slightly different set of attributes than the one you used for user controls.

```
<%@ Register TagPrefix="CR" Namespace="CustomControls"
    Assembly="CustomCtrls" %>
```

This Register directive identifies the compiled assembly file and the namespace that holds the custom control. When you register a custom control assembly in this fashion, you gain access to all the control classes in it. You can insert a control by using the tag prefix, followed by a colon (:) and the class name.

```
<CR:NameTextBox id="NameTextBox1" runat="server" />
```

You can set properties of the NameTextBox in code or through the tag. These can include any additional properties you have defined or the properties from the base class:

```
<CR:NameTextBox id="NameTextBox1" BackColor="LightYellow"
  Font="Verdana "Text="Enter Name Here" runat="server" />
```

The technique of deriving custom control classes is known as subclassing, and it allows you to easily add the functionality you need without losing the basic set of features inherent in a control. Subclassed controls can add new properties, events, and methods, or override the existing ones. For example, you could add a ReverseText or EncryptText method to the NameTextBox class that loops through the text contents and modifies them. The process of defining and using custom control events, methods, and properties is the same as with user controls.

One common reason for subclassing a control is to add default values. For example, you might create a custom Calendar control that automatically modifies some properties in its constructor. When the control is first created, these default properties will automatically be applied.

```
Public Class FormattedCalendar
  Inherits Calendar

    Public Sub New()
        ' Configure the appearance of the calendar table.
        Me.CellPadding = 8
        Me.CellSpacing = 8
        Me.BackColor = Color.LightYellow
        Me.BorderStyle = BorderStyle.Groove
        Me.BorderWidth = Unit.Pixel(2)
        Me.ShowGridLines = True

        ' Configure the font.
        Me.Font.Name = "Verdana"
        Me.Font.Size = FontUnit.XXSmall

        ' Set some special calendar settings.
        Me.FirstDayOfWeek = FirstDayOfWeek.Monday
        Me.PrevMonthText = "<--"
        Me.NextMonthText = "-->"

        ' Select the current date by default.
        Me.SelectedDate = Date.Today
    End Sub

End Class
```

You could even add additional event-handling logic to this class that will use the Calendar's DayRender event to configure custom date display. This way, the Calendar class itself handles all the required formatting and configuration; your page code does not need to work at all! Note that the Handles clause specifies the MyBase keyword, indicating an event of the current (inherited) class.

```
Private Sub FormattedCalendar_DayRender(sender As Object, _
  e As DayRenderEventArgs) Handles MyBase.DayRender
```

```
    If e.Day.IsOtherMonth Then
        e.Day.IsSelectable = False
        e.Cell.Text = ""
    Else
        e.Cell.Font.Bold = True
    End If

End Sub
```

The preferred way to handle this is actually to override the OnDayRender method, and make sure to call the base method to ensure that the basic tasks (such as notifying event recipients) are met. The effect of the following code is equivalent.

```
Protected Overrides Sub OnDayRender(cell As TableCell, _
  day As CalendarDay)

    ' Call the base Calendar.OnDayRender method.
    MyBase.OnDayRender(cell, day)

    If day.IsOtherMonth Then
        day.IsSelectable = False
        cell.Text = ""
    Else
        cell.Font.Bold = True
    End If

End Sub
```

Figure 22-9 contrasts two Calendar controls: the normal one, and the custom FormattedCalendar control class.

## Control Tag Settings Override Constructor Defaults

Even though you set these defaults in the custom class code, that doesn't prevent you from modifying them in your web page code. The constructor code runs when the Calendar control is created, after which the control tag settings are applied, and then any event-handling code in your web page also has the chance to modify the FormattedCalendar properties.

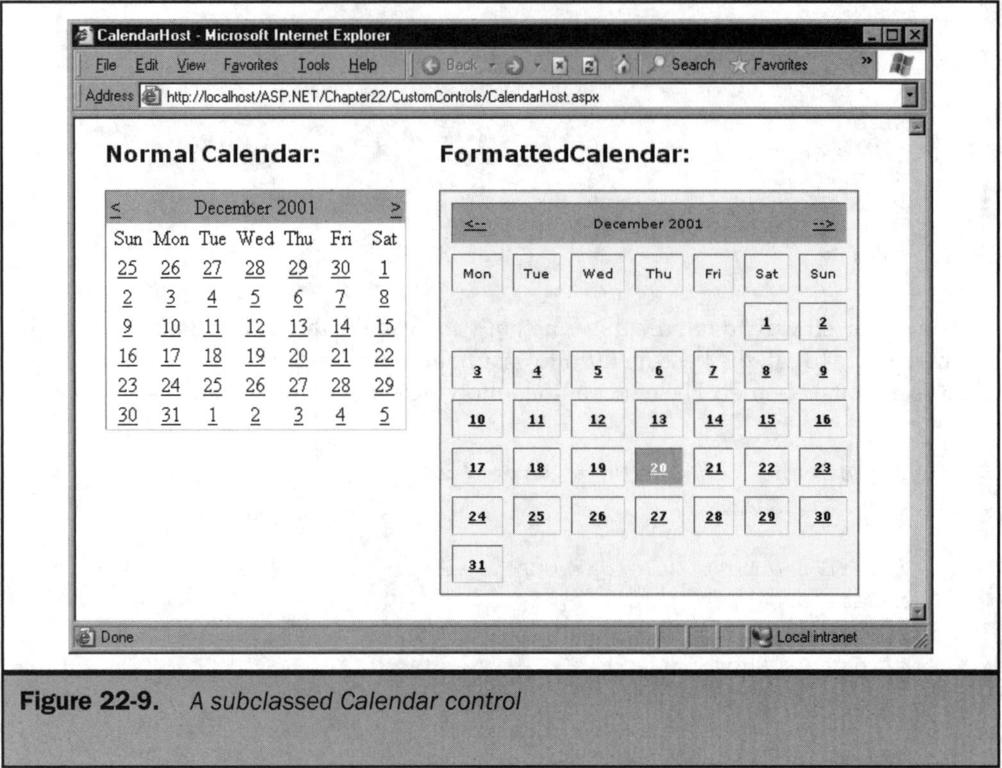


**Figure 22-9.** *A subclassed Calendar control*

## Visual Studio .NET Custom Control Support

In Visual Studio .NET, it's often easiest to develop custom controls in a separate project, compile the assembly, and add a reference to the assembly in the new project. This allows you to easily place the custom controls and the web page classes in separate namespaces, and update them separately.

The process of adding a reference to a custom control assembly is very similar to the process you used to add a reference to a normal compiled component. Start by right-clicking on the Control Box, and choosing Customize Toolbox. Click on the .NET Framework Components tab (see Figure 22-10), and then click the Browse button. Then choose the custom control assembly from the file browser. The controls will be added to the list of available .NET controls.

All checkmarked controls will appear in the Toolbox (see Figure 22-11). You can then draw them on your web forms just like you would with an ordinary control. Note that controls are not added on a per-project basis. Instead, they will remain in the Toolbox until you delete them. To remove a control, right click it and select Delete. This removes the icon only, not the referenced assembly.

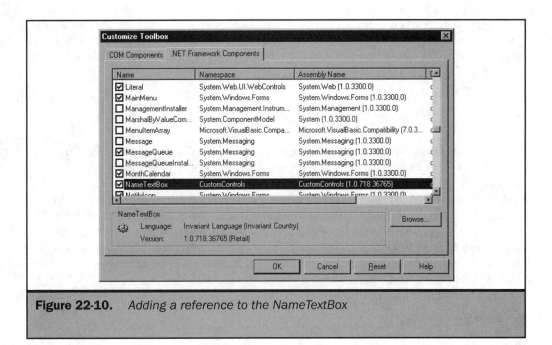

**Figure 22-10.** *Adding a reference to the NameTextBox*

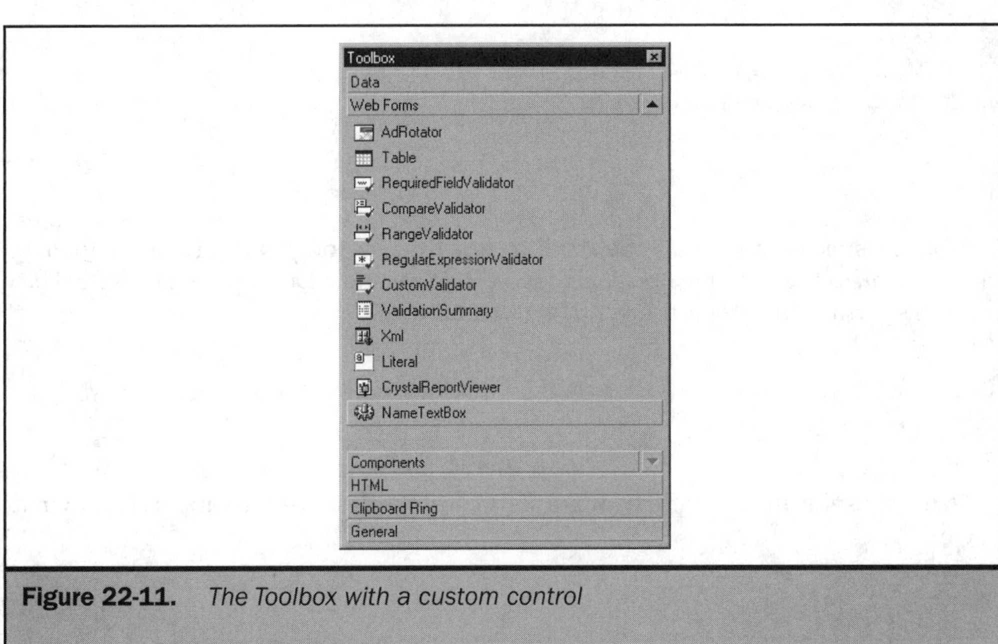


**Figure 22-11.** *The Toolbox with a custom control*

Any properties you add for the custom control automatically appear in the Properties window under the Misc heading. You can further customize the design-time behavior of your control by using various attributes from the System.ComponentModel namespace.

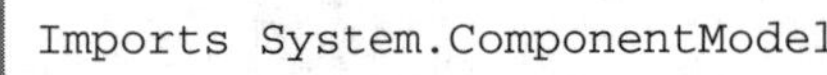

```
Imports System.ComponentModel
```

For example, the property defined below (part of the ConfigurableRepeater control we will consider later in this chapter) will always appear in a "Layout" category in the Properties window. It indicates this to Visual Studio .NET through a System.ComponentModel.Category attribute. Note that attributes are always enclosed in angled brackets and must appear on the same line as the code element they refer to (in this case, the property procedure declaration) or be separated from it using the underscore line continuation character. (You may remember that .NET attributes were also used when programming Web Services. In that case, the attributes were named WebMethod and WebService.)

```
<Category("Layout")> _
Public Property RepeatTimes() As Integer
    Get
        Return _RepeatTimes
    End Get
    Set(ByVal Value As Integer)
        _RepeatTimes = Value
    End Set
End Property
```

You can specify more than one attribute at a time, as long as you separate them using commas. The example here includes a Category and a Description attribute. The result is shown in the Properties window in Figure 22-12.

```
<Description("Sets the number of times Text will be repeated"), _
 Category("Layout"), > _
```

A list of useful attributes for configuring a control's design-time support is shown in Table 22-1.

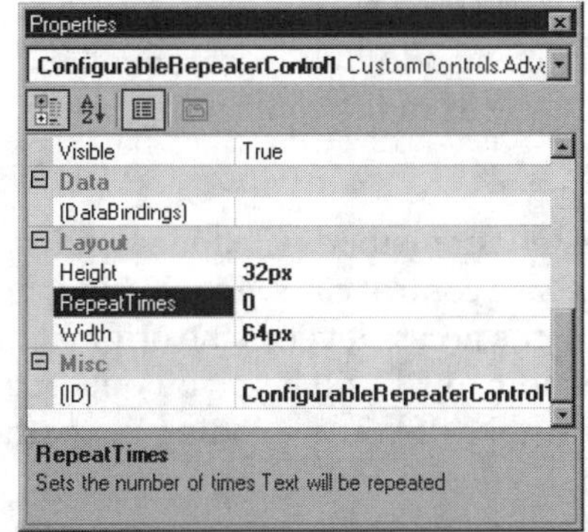


**Figure 22-12.** *Configuring custom control design-time support*

<table>
<tr><th>Attribute</th><th>Description</th></tr>
<tr><td><Browsable(True | False)></td><td>If False, this property will not appear in the Properties window (although the programmer can still modify it in code or by manually adding the control tag attribute, as long as you include a Set property procedure).</td></tr>
<tr><td><Bindable(True | False)></td><td>If True, Visual Studio .NET will display this property in the DataBindings dialog and allow it to be bound to a field in a data source.</td></tr>
<tr><td><Category("")></td><td>A string that indicates the category the property will appear under in the Properties window.</td></tr>
<tr><td><Description("")></td><td>A string that indicates the description the property will have when selected in the Properties window.</td></tr>
<tr><td><DefaultValue()></td><td>Sets the default value that will be displayed for the property in the Properties window.</td></tr>
<tr><td><ParenthesizeProperty-Name(True | False)></td><td>If True, Visual Studio .NET will display parentheses around this property in the Properties window (as it does with the ID property).</td></tr>
</table>

**Table 22-1.** *Attributes for Design-Time Support*

## Other Custom Control Tricks

You can also subclass a control and add low-level refinements by manually configuring the HTML that will be generated from the control. To do this, you only need to follow a few basic guidelines:

- Override one of the Render methods (Render, RenderContents, RenderBeginTag, and so on) from the base control class. To override the method successfully, you need to specify the same access level as the original method (such as Public or Protected). Visual Studio .NET will help you out on this account by warning you if you make a mistake. If you are coding in another editor, just check the MSDN reference first.
- Use the MyBase keyword to call the base method. In other words, you want to make sure you are adding functionality to the method, not replacing it with your code. Also, the original method may perform some required cleanup task that you aren't aware of, or it may raise an event that the web page could be listening for.
- Add the code to write out any additional HTML. Usually, this code will use the HtmlWriter class, which supplies a helpful Write method for direct HTML output.

The following is an example of a text box control that overrides the Render method to add a static title. (Optionally, the content for this title could be taken from a property procedure that the user can configure.)

```
Public Class TitledTextBox
  Inherits TextBox

    Protected Overrides Sub Render(writer As HtmlTextWriter)
        ' Add new HTML.
        writer.Write("<h1>Here is a title</hi><br>")

        ' Call the base method (so the text box portion is rendered).
        MyBase.Render(writer)
    End Sub

End Class
```

Figure 22-13 shows what the TitledTextBox control looks like in the design environment.

Remember, ASP.NET creates a page by moving through the list of controls and instructing each one to render itself (by calling the Render method). It collects the total HTML output and sends it as a complete page (nested in root <HTML><body> tags).

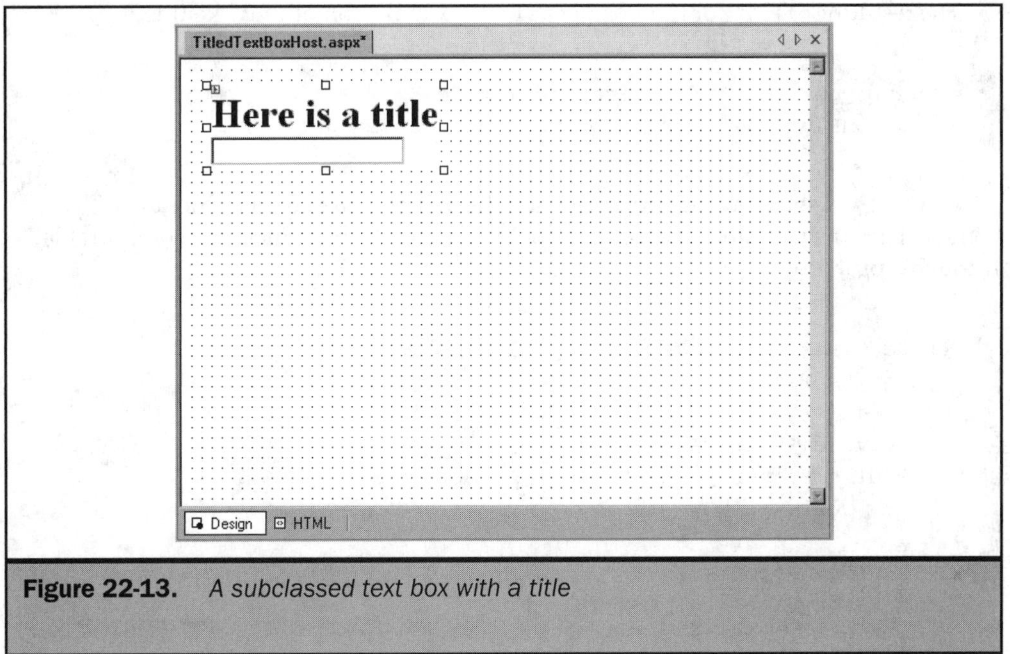


**Figure 22-13.** *A subclassed text box with a title*

You can use a similar technique to add attributes to the HTML text box tag. For example, you might want to add a piece of JavaScript code to the OnBlur attribute to make a message box appear when the control loses focus. There is no TextBox property that exposes this attribute, but you can add it manually in the AddAttributesToRender method.

```
Public Class LostFocusTextBox
  Inherits TextBox

    Protected Overrides Sub AddAttributesToRender( _
      writer As HtmlTextWriter)

        MyBase.AddAttributesToRender(writer)
        writer.AddAttribute("OnBlur", _
          "javascript:alert('You Lost Focus')")

    End Sub

End Class
```

The resulting HTML for the LostFocusTextBox looks something like this:

```
<input type="text" id="LostFocusTextBox2"
      OnBlur="javascript:alert('You Lost Focus')" />
```

Figure 22-14 shows what happens when the text box loses focus. Once again, you could extend the usefulness of this control by making the alert message configurable through a property.

```
Public Class LostFocusTextBox
  Inherits TextBox

    Private _Alert As String
    Public Property AlertCode() As String
        Get
            Return _Alert
        End Get
        Set(Value As String)
            _Alert = Value
        End Set
    End Property

    Protected Overrides Sub AddAttributesToRender( _
      writer As HtmlTextWriter)

        MyBase.AddAttributesToRender(writer)
        writer.AddAttribute("OnBlur", _
          "javascript:alert('" & _Alert & "')")

    End Sub

End Class
```

## Creating a Web Control from Scratch

Once you start experimenting with altering the TextBox control's HTML, it might occur to you to design a control entirely from scratch. This is an easy task in ASP.NET—all you need to do is inherit from the System.Web.UI.WebControls.WebControl class, which is the base of all ASP.NET web controls. Figure 22-15 shows the inheritance hierarchy for web controls.

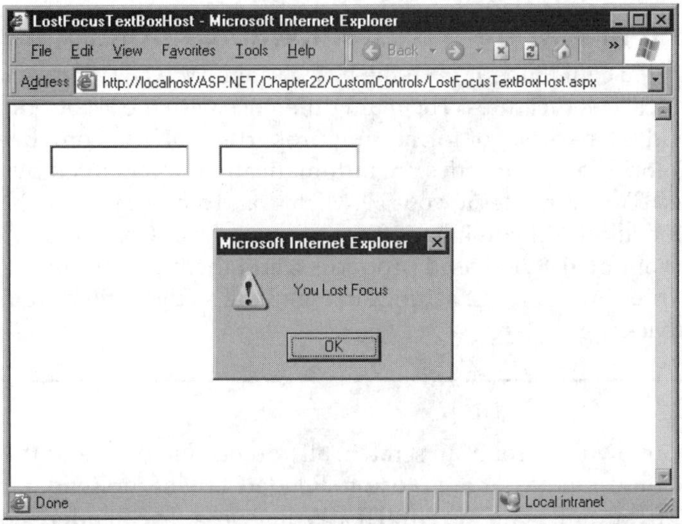

Figure 22-14. *The LostFocusTextBox control*

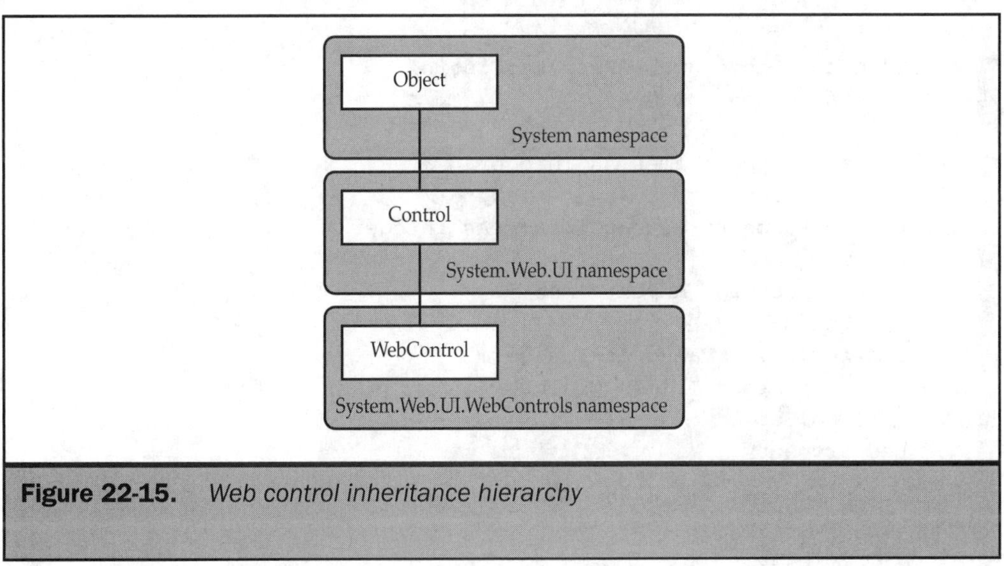


Figure 22-15. *Web control inheritance hierarchy*

### You Could Inherit from System.Web.UI.Control Instead

Technically, you could inherit from the base System.Web.UI.Control class instead, but it provides fewer features. The main difference with the WebControl class is that it provides a basic set of formatting properties such as Font, BackColor, and ForeColor. These properties are automatically implemented by adding the appropriate HTML attributes to your HTML tag, and are also persisted in viewstate for you automatically. If you inherit from the more basic Control class, you need to provide your own style-based properties, add them as attributes using the HtmlTextWriter, and store the settings in viewstate so they will be remembered across postbacks.

To create your own control from scratch, all you need to do is add the appropriate properties, and implement your own custom RenderContents or Render method, which writes the HTML output using the HtmlTextWriter class. The RenderContents method takes place after the Render method, which means that the formatting attributes have already been applied.

The code is quite similar to the earlier TextBox examples. It creates a repeater type of control that lists a given line of text multiple times. The number of repeats is set by the RepeatTimes property.

```
Public Class ConfigurableRepeaterControl
  Inherits WebControl

    Private _RepeatTimes As Integer = 3
    Private _Text As String = "Text"
    Public Property RepeatTimes() As Integer
        Get
            Return _RepeatTimes
        End Get
        Set(ByVal Value As Integer)
            _RepeatTimes = Value
        End Set
    End Property

    Public Property Text() As String
        Get
            Return _Text
        End Get
        Set(ByVal Value As String)
```

```
            _Text = Value
        End Set
    End Property

    Protected Overrides Sub RenderContents(writer As HtmlTextWriter)
        MyBase.RenderContents(writer)
        Dim i As Integer
        For i = 1 To _RepeatTimes
            writer.Write(_Text & "<br>")
        Next
    End Sub

End Class
```

Because we've used a WebControl-derived class instead of an ordinary Control-derived class, and because the code writes the output inside the RenderContents method, the web page programmer can set various style attributes. A sample formatted ConfigurableRepeaterControl is shown in Figure 22-16. If you want to include a title or another portion that you don't want rendered with formatting, add it to the Render method.

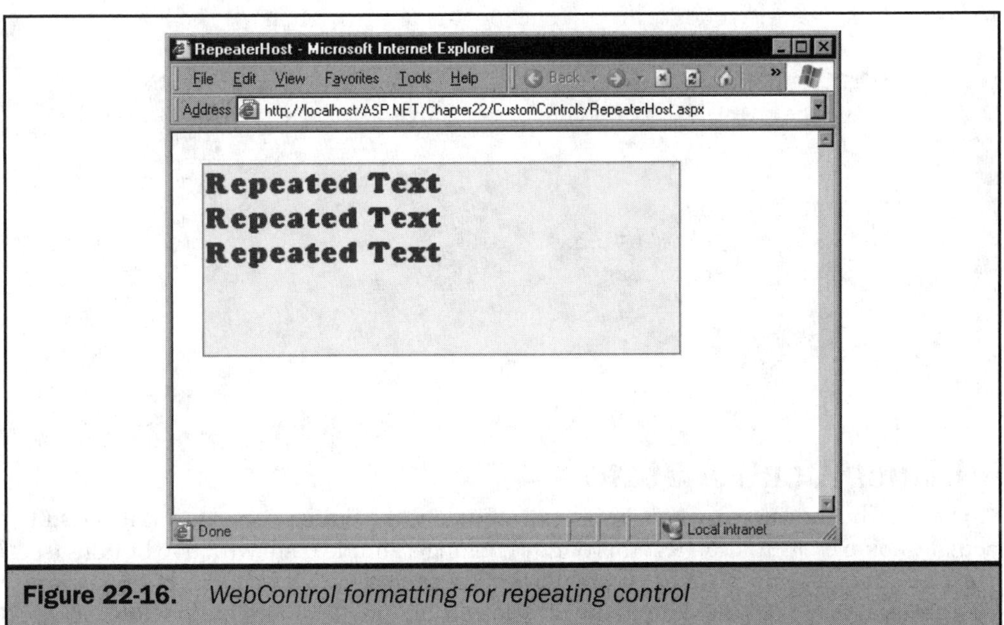


**Figure 22-16.** *WebControl formatting for repeating control*

## Creating Adaptive Controls

One interesting approach you can take with custom controls is to vary their output based on the browser. This is actually a process that ASP.NET carries out automatically for some of its more complex controls (such as the validators), ensuring that they are always rendered in the form best suited to the client's browser.

Depending on the sophistication of your control, a lot of thought may need to go into making it support multiple browsers. (Cross-browser support is one of the main criteria that will distinguish the best-of-breed custom ASP.NET controls from third-party vendors.) However, the actual implementation details are trivial—all you need to do is retrieve the browser type and respond accordingly in the Render or RenderContents method.

A sample control is shown next that simply evaluates the capabilities of its container. It generates the output shown in Figure 22-17.

```
Protected Overrides Sub RenderContents(writer As HtmlTextWriter)
    MyBase.RenderContents(writer)

    If Me.Page.Request.Browser.JavaScript = True Then
        writer.Write("<i>You support JavaScript.</i><br>")
    End If

    If Me.Page.Request.Browser.Browser = "IE" Then
        writer.Write("<i>Output configured for IE.</i><br>")
    ElseIf Me.Page.Request.Browser.Browser = "Netscape" Then
        writer.Write("<i>Output configured for Netscape.</i><br>")
    End If

    Dim i As Integer
    For i = 1 To _RepeatTimes
        writer.Write(_Text & "<br>")
    Next

End Sub
```

## Maintaining Control State

Currently, the repeater control provides an EnableViewState property, but it doesn't actually abide by it. You can test this out by creating a simple page with two buttons (see Figure 22-18). One button changes the RepeatTimes to 5, while the other button simply triggers a postback. You'll find that every time you click the Postback button, RepeatTimes is reset to the default of 3. If you change the Text property in your code, you'll also find that it reverts to the value specified in the control tag.

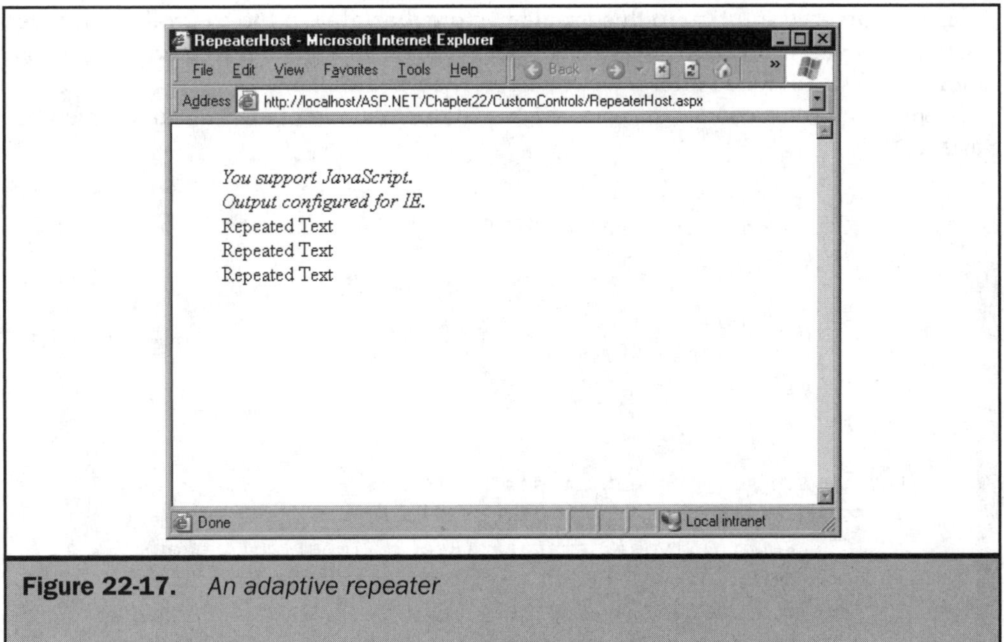


**Figure 22-17.** *An adaptive repeater*

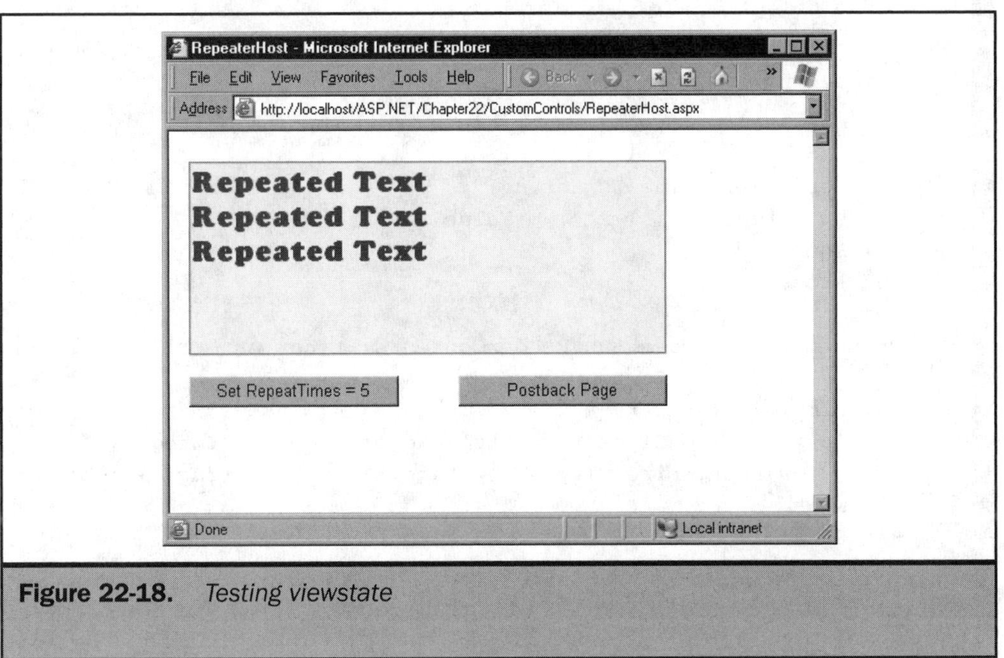


**Figure 22-18.** *Testing viewstate*

There's an easy solution to this problem: store the value in the control's viewstate. As with web pages, the value in any member variables in a custom web control class is automatically abandoned after the page is returned to the client.

Here's a rewritten control that uses a variable stored in viewstate instead of a member variable.

```
Public Class ConfigurableRepeaterControl
  Inherits WebControl

    Public Sub New()
        Viewstate("RepeatTimes") = 3
        Viewstate("Text") = "Text"
    End Sub

    Public Property RepeatTimes() As Integer
        Get
            Return CType(Viewstate("RepeatTimes"), Integer)
        End Get
        Set(ByVal Value As Integer)
            Viewstate("RepeatTimes") = Value
        End Set
    End Property

    Public Property Text() As String
        Get
            Return CType(Viewstate("Text"), String)
        End Get
        Set(ByVal Value As String)
            Viewstate("Text") = Value
        End Set
    End Property

    Protected Overrides Sub RenderContents(writer As HtmlTextWriter)
        MyBase.RenderContents(writer)
        Dim i As Integer
        For i = 1 To CType(Viewstate("RepeatTimes"), Integer)
            writer.Write(CType(Viewstate("Text"), String) & "<br>")
        Next
    End Sub

End Class
```

The code is essentially the same, although it now uses a constructor to initialize the RepeatTimes and Text values. Extra care must also be taken to make sure that the Viewstate object is converted to the correct data type. Performing this conversion manually ensures that you won't end up with bugs or quirks that are difficult to find. Note that though the code looks the same as the code used to store a variable in a Page object's viewstate, the collections are different. That means that the web page programmer won't be able to access the control's viewstate directly.

You'll find that if you set the EnableViewState property to False, changes will not be remembered, but no error will occur. When viewstate is disabled, ASP.NET still allows you to write items to viewstate, but they won't persist across postbacks.

## Creating a Composite Control

So far, we've seen how user controls are generally used for aggregate groups of controls with some added higher-level business logic, while custom controls provide you with more control that allows you to modify or create the final HTML output from scratch. This distinction is usually true. You'll also find that user controls are generally quicker to create, easier to work with in a single project, and simpler to program. Custom controls, on the other hand, provide extensive low-level control features we haven't even considered in this chapter, such as templates and data binding.

One technique we haven't considered is composite controls—custom controls that are built out of other controls. Composite controls are a little bit closer to user controls, because they render their user interface at least partly out of other controls. For example, you might find that you need to generate a complex user interface using an HTML table. Rather than write the entire block of HTML manually in the Render method (and try to configure it based on various higher-level properties), you could dynamically create and insert a Table web control. This pattern is quite common with ASP.NET server controls—for example, it's logical to expect that advanced controls such as the Calendar and DataGrid rely on simpler table-based controls like Table to generate their user interface.

Generating composite controls is quite easy. All you need to do is create the control objects you want to use and add them to the Controls collection of your custom control. (Optionally, you could use one or more container controls, such as the PlaceHolder or Panel, and add the controls to the Controls collection of a container control.) By convention, this task is carried out by overriding the CreateChildControls method.

The following example creates a grid of buttons, based on the Rows and Cols properties. A simple test page for this control is pictured in Figure 22-19.

```
Public Class ButtonGrid
  Inherits WebControl

    Public Sub New()
```

```
        Viewstate("Rows") = 2
        Viewstate("Cols") = 2
    End Sub

    Public Property Cols() As Integer
        Get
            Return CType(Viewstate("Cols"), Integer)
        End Get
        Set(ByVal Value As Integer)
            Viewstate("Cols") = Value
        End Set
    End Property

    Public Property Rows() As Integer
        Get
            Return CType(Viewstate("Rows"), Integer)
        End Get
        Set(ByVal Value As Integer)
            Viewstate("Rows") = Value
        End Set
    End Property

    Protected Overrides Sub CreateChildControls()
        Dim i, j, k As Integer

        For i = 1 To CType(Viewstate("Rows"), Integer)

            For j = 1 To CType(Viewstate("Cols"), Integer)
                k += 1

                ' Create and configure a button.
                Dim ctrlB As New Button()
                ctrlB.Width = Unit.Pixel(60)
                ctrlB.Text = k.ToString()

                ' Add the button.
                Me.Controls.Add(ctrlB)
            Next

            ' Add a line break.
            Dim ctrlL As New LiteralControl("<br>")
```

```
            Me.Controls.Add(ctrlL)
        Next
    End Sub

End Class
```

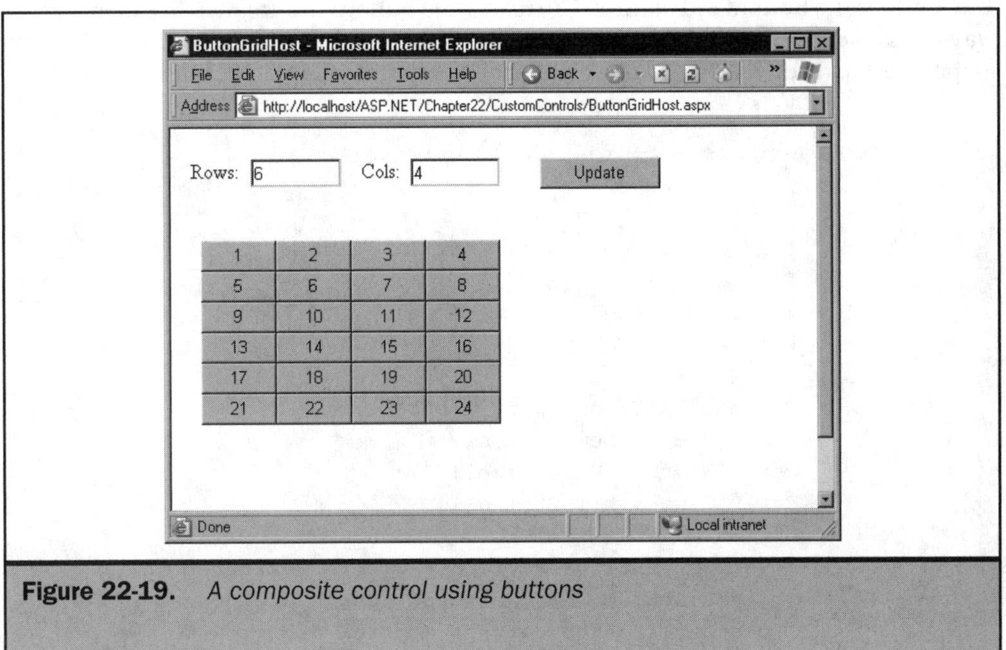


**Figure 22-19.** *A composite control using buttons*

# Custom Control Events

Raising an event from a control is just as easy as it was with a user control. All you need to do is define the event (and any special EventArgs class) and then fire it with the RaiseEvent statement.

However, to raise an event, your code needs to be executing—and for your code to be triggered, the web page needs to be posted back from the server. If you need to create a control that reacts to user actions instantaneously, and then refreshes itself or fires an event to the web page, you need a way to trigger and receive a postback.

In an ASP.NET web page, web controls fire postbacks by calling a special JavaScript function called __doPostBack. The __doPostBack function accepts two parameters: the name of the control that triggered the postback, and a string representing additional postback data. You can retrieve a reference to this function using the special Page.GetPostBackEventReference property from your control. (Every control provides the Page property, which gives a reference to the web page where the control is situated.)

The GetPostBackEventReference reference allows you perform an interesting trick—namely, creating a control or HTML link that invokes the __doPostBack function. The easiest way to perform this magic is usually to add an OnClick attribute to an HTML element (anchors, images, and buttons all support this attribute).

Consider the ButtonGrid control. Currently, the buttons are created, but there is no way to receive their events. This can be changed by setting each button's OnClick event to the __doPostBack function. The single added line is highlighted in bold:

```
Protected Overrides Sub CreateChildControls()
    Dim i, j, k As Integer

    For i = 1 To CType(Viewstate("Rows"), Integer)

        For j = 1 To CType(Viewstate("Cols"), Integer)
            k += 1

            ' Create and configure a button.
            Dim ctrlB As New Button()
            ctrlB.Width = Unit.Pixel(60)
            ctrlB.Text = k.ToString()

            ' Set the OnClick attribute with a reference to
            ' __doPostBack. When clicked, ctrlB will cause a
            ' postback to the current control and return
            ' the assigned text of ctrlB.
            ctrlB.Attributes("OnClick") = _
              Page.GetPostBackEventReference(Me, ctrlB.Text)

            ' Add the button.
            Me.Controls.Add(ctrlB)
        Next

        ' Add a line break.
        Dim ctrlL As New LiteralControl("<br>")
        Me.Controls.Add(ctrlL)
    Next
End Sub
```

To handle the postback, your custom control needs to implement the IPostBackEventHandler interface.

```
Public Class ButtonGrid
  Inherits WebControl
  Implements IPostBackEventHandler
```

You then need to create a method that implements IPostBackEventHandler.RaisePostBackEvent. This method will be triggered when your control fires the postback, and it will receive the additional information submitted with the GetPostBackEventReference method (in this case, the text of the button).

```
Public Overridable Overloads Sub RaisePostBackEvent(eventArgument _
  As String) Implements IPostBackEventHandler.RaisePostBackEvent

    ' Respond to postback here.

End Sub
```

Once you receive the postback, you can modify the control, or even raise another event to the web page. To enhance the ButtonGrid example to use this method, we'll define an additional event in the control:

```
Event GridClick(ByVal ButtonName As String)
```

This event handler raises an event to the web page, with information about the button that was clicked. You'll notice that the event definition doesn't follow the .NET standard for simplicity's sake.

The RaisePostBackEvent method can then trigger the event.

```
Public Overridable Overloads Sub RaisePostBackEvent(eventArgument _
  As String) Implements IPostBackEventHandler.RaisePostBackEvent

    RaiseEvent GridClick(eventArgument)

End Sub
```

A web page client that wants to handle the event might use event-handling code that looks something like this:

```
Private Sub ButtonGrid1_GridClick(ButtonName As String) _
  Handles ButtonGrid1.GridClick

    lblInfo.Text = "You clicked: " & ButtonName

End Sub
```

Figure 22-20 shows the ButtonGrid events in action.

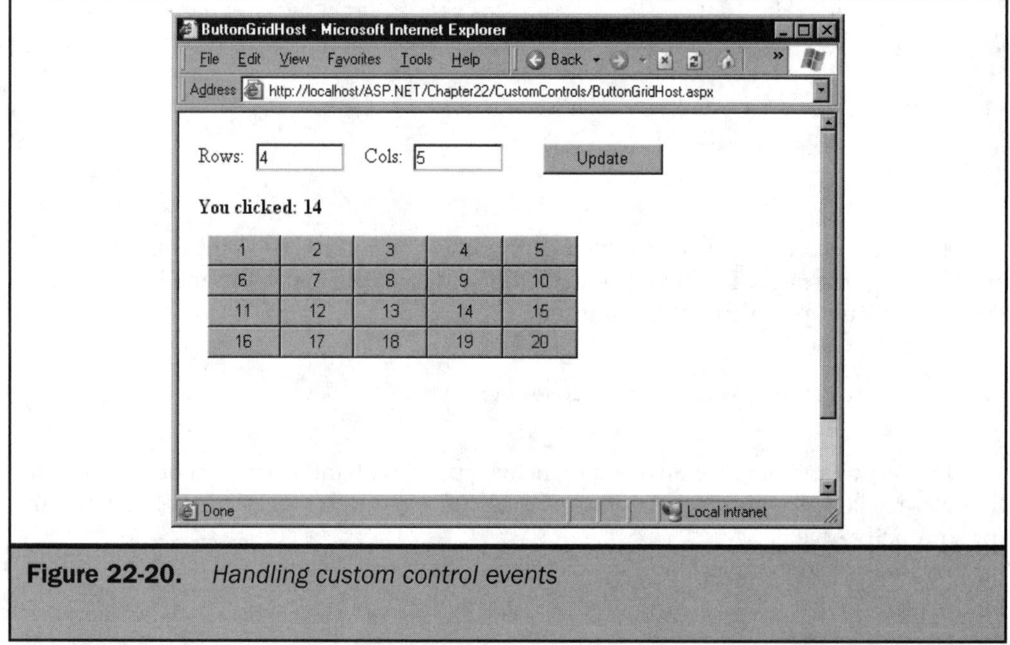


**Figure 22-20.** *Handling custom control events*

ASP.NET custom control creation could be a book in itself. To master it, you'll want to experiment with the online samples for this chapter (provided in a CustomControls project for Visual Studio .NET users). Once you've perfected your controls, pay special attention to the attributes described in Table 22-1. These are key to making your control behave properly and work conveniently in design environments like Visual Studio .NET.

The Complete Reference

# Chapter 23

## Caching and Performance Tuning

ASP.NET applications are a bit of a contradiction. On one hand, because they are hosted over the Internet they have unique requirements—namely, they need to be able to serve hundreds of clients as easily and quickly as they deal with a single user. On the other hand, ASP.NET includes some remarkable "tricks" that let you design and code a web application in a similar way as you might program a desktop application. This uniqueness can lead developers into trouble. ASP.NET makes it easy to forget you are creating a web application—so easy that you might introduce programming practices that will slow or cripple your application when it's heavily used in the real world.

Fortunately, there is a middle ground. You can use the incredible time-saving features like viewstate, server postbacks, and session state that you have spent the last twenty-some chapters learning about, and still create a robust web application. But you need to finish the job, and spend the extra 10 percent of time necessary at every stage of your programming to ensure that your application will perform. This chapter discusses these strategies, which fall into three main categories:

**Design for scalability** There are a few key guidelines that, if kept in mind, can steer you toward efficient, scalable designs.

**Profile your application** One problem with web applications is that it's sometimes hard to test them under the appropriate conditions and really get an idea of what their problems may be. However, Microsoft provides several useful tools that allow you to benchmark your application and put it through a rigorous checkup.

**Implement caching** A little bit of caching may seem like a novelty in a single-user test, but it can make a dramatic improvement in a real-world scenario. You can easily incorporate output and fragment caching into most pages, and use data caching to replace memory-unfriendly state management.

## Designing for Scalability

Throughout this book, the chapters have combined practical how-to information with some tips and insight about the best designs (and possible problems). However, now that you are a more accomplished ASP.NET programmer, it's a good idea to review a number of considerations—and a few minor ways that you can tune up all aspects of your application.

### ASP versus ASP.NET

ASP.NET provides dramatically better performance than ASP, although it's hard to quote a hard statistic because the performance increases differ widely depending on the ways you structure your pages and the type of operations you perform. By far, the greatest performance increase results from the new automatic code compilation. With ASP, your web pages and their script code were processed for every client request. With ASP.NET, each page class is compiled to native code the first time it is requested, and then cached for future requests.

This system does have one noticeable side effect, however. The very first time that a user accesses a particular web page (or the first time the user accesses it after it has been modified), there will be a longer delay while the page is compiled. In some cases, this time for the first request may actually be slightly slower than the equivalent ASP page request. However, this phenomenon will be much more common during development than in an actual deployed web site. With a live web site, a page will be quickly compiled for the first request and then reused for the rest of the application's lifetime. With ASP.NET's ability to automatically recycle memory and recover from most problems without requiring a restart, and with the increased stability of the Windows 2000 and Windows XP platform, an ASP.NET application could be running around the clock for weeks and months with little user intervention and very few page recompiles.

### The Ideal Web Server

Microsoft recommends a two-processor web server for the best price/performance ratio. A single-CPU computer is only marginally cheaper and will provide reduced performance, particularly for applications that use ADO.NET extensively, or in cases where an administrator is using a logging or administrative tool on the web server computer itself (which is almost never a good idea). More sophisticated servers, such as those with four CPUs, are significantly more expensive. A better way to achieve a similar performance increase for a heavily trafficked web site is by using multiple servers to host it (this is known as a web farm or web garden).

These techniques won't be required for typical web sites, unless you are building the next Amazon.com. If you plan to host an ASP.NET application with a web farm or web garden, you'll probably also need some outside technical help. At least one book is in print that is completely dedicated to describing the hardware and software configuration for these large-scale setups.

## Server Controls

In most of the examples in this book, we've used server controls extensively. Server controls are the basic ingredient in an ASP.NET page, and they don't carry a significant performance overhead—in fact, they probably provide better performance than trying to dynamically write a page with tricks such as Response.Write and other involved logic.

However, ASP.NET server controls can be unnecessary in some situations. For example, if you have static text that never needs to be accessed or modified in your code, you don't need to use a Label web control. Instead, you can enter the text as static HTML in your .aspx layout file. In Visual Studio .NET, you can use the HTML label control, which is actually created as an ordinary <div> tag. Unless you specifically check the Run As Server Control option, it will be created as a static element rather than a full server control.

Another potential refinement involves viewstate. If you don't need viewstate for a control, you should disable it by setting the control's EnableViewState to False. Two cases where you don't need viewstate are if the control is set at design time and never changes, or if the control is refreshed with every postback, and doesn't need to keep track of its previous set of information. The latter scenario is the case with data binding, but there is one catch—if you need to access the user's current selection, you still need to have viewstate enabled.

Generally, viewstate becomes most significant when dealing with large controls that can contain significant amounts of data. The problem is that this data exerts a multiple toll on your application—it's encoded twice: once in the hidden label control used for viewstate and directly in the visible control. It's also sent both to the client and then back to the server with each postback. To get a handle on whether viewstate could be an issue, use page tracing (as described in Chapter 11) to see how many bytes the current page's viewstate is consuming.

### Server Control Issues Are Minor

Both of these issues (static text and viewstate) are fairly minor refinements. They can speed up download times, particularly if your application is being used by clients with slow Internet connections. However, they will almost never cause a serious problem in your application the way poor database or session state code can. Don't spend too much time tweaking your controls, but do keep these issues in mind while programming so that you can optimize your pages where the opportunity presents itself.

## ADO.NET Database Access

The rules for accessing a database are relatively straightforward, but they can't be overemphasized. Open a connection to the database only at the point where you need it, and close it properly as soon as possible. Database connections are a limited resource, and represent a potential bottleneck if you don't design carefully.

In addition to making sure you treat your database with this basic degree of respect, there are a number of additional steps you can take to improve performance:

**Improve your database with stored procedures.** RDBMS (Relation Database Management Software) applications such as SQL Server are remarkably complex and provide a great number of performance options that have nothing to do with ASP.NET, but can make a substantial difference in performance. For example, a database that uses intelligently designed stored procedures instead of dynamically generated queries will probably perform much better, because stored procedures are compiled and optimized in advance. This is particularly true if a stored procedure needs to perform several related operations at once.

**Improve your database with profiling and indexes.** Defining indexes that match the types of searches you need to perform can result in much quicker row lookup. To perfect your database, you will need to examine it with a profiling tool (such as Profiler for SQL Server). These tools record database activity into a special log that can be reviewed, analyzed, and replayed. The profiling utility can usually identify problem areas (such as slow executing queries) and even recommend a new set of indexes that will provide better performance. However, to properly profile the database you will need to simulate a typical load by running your application.

**Get only the information you need.** One of the simplest ways to improve any database code is to reduce the amount of information it retrieves, which will reduce the network load, the amount of time the connection needs to be open, and the size of the final page. For example, all searches should be limited to present a small set of rows at a time (often by filtering by date) and should only include the fields that are truly important. Note, however, that while this is an excellent rule of thumb, it is not always the right solution. For example, if you are providing a page that allows a user to edit a database record, it is often easier to retrieve all the information for all the rows at once, rather than requery the database later to get specific information about the selected record.

**Use connection pooling.** In a typical web application, your RDBMS receives requests on behalf of countless different clients, from several different web pages. Generally, these connections are open and active for only a short amount of time, and creating them is the most time-consuming step. However, if every web page uses the exact same connection string, database products such as SQL Server will be able to use their built-in connection pooling to reuse a connection for more than one consecutive client, speeding up the process dramatically. This happens transparently and automatically, provided you always use the exact same connection string (even a minor difference like the order of settings will prevent a connection from being reused). To ensure that the connection string is the same, centralize it in the web.config file, as described in Chapter 5.

**Use data binding.** The fastest way to get information out of a database and into a page is to use a DataReader and bind it directly to a data control. This approach may involve a little more work with custom templates, but it is better than moving through the rows manually and writing to the page yourself.

**Use caching.** If a certain set of data is frequently requested and changes slowly, it's an ideal candidate for caching. With caching, the information will be read from the database and loaded into temporary memory the first time a client requests it, and made directly available to future requests without any database access required. Output and data caching are discussed later in this chapter.

## Session State

Session state was the single greatest restriction on performance in traditional ASP development. Although ASP.NET introduces some features that make session state more scalable, it still needs to be used carefully.

Generally, you won't run into problems if you are just storing a customer's ID in session state. You can probably even accommodate a list of currently selected items (as in a shopping basket). However, if you plan to store large amounts of information such as a DataSet, you need to tread carefully and consider the multiplying effect of a successful application. If each session reserves about 100 kilobytes, 100 simultaneous sessions (not necessarily all corresponding to users who are still at your site) can easily chew up more than 100 megabytes of memory. To solve this sort of problem, you have two design choices:

- Store everything in a database record, and store the ID for that database in session state. When the client returns, look up the information. Nothing is retained in memory, and the information is durable—it won't expire until you remove the record. Of course, this option can reclaim server memory, but slow down the application with database access, the other vulnerable part of your application.
- A better solution is often to store information in a database record, and then cache some of the information in memory. Then the information can still be retrieved quickly when needed, but the memory can be reclaimed by ASP.NET if the server's performance is suffering. More information about data caching can be found later in this chapter.

Also keep in mind that with session state, the best state facility is almost always the default in-process session state store. The other options (such as storing session state in an SQL database) impose additional performance overhead, and are only necessary in web farm scenarios.

# Profiling

To judge the success of an attempted performance improvement, you need to be able to measure the performance of your application. In cases where performance is lagging, you also need enough information to diagnose the possible bottleneck, so you can make a meaningful change.

## The Process Model

The simplest option you have to see how ASP.NET is functioning is to retrieve its vital statistics through the ProcessModelInfo class. This class (in the System.Web namespace) provides two useful shared methods. The first, GetProcessInfo, retrieves a ProcessInfo object that contains information about the current ASP.NET worker process running on the server. The second method, GetProcessHistory, returns an array with up to 100 ProcessInfo objects that contain information about recent worker processes. For example, if ASP.NET has been restarted three times since the server was powered on, you will be able to retrieve up to three ProcessInfo objects. (ASP.NET restarts aren't necessarily due to errors or instability. You might be using advanced configuration settings to automatically restart the ASP.NET worker process after a certain period of idle time or when a certain amount of memory is used, as described in Chapter 28.) The ProcessInfo object provides several useful pieces of information, as shown in Table 23-1.

| Property | Description |
|---|---|
| Age | A TimeSpan object that indicates the length of time that the process was in use (or the length of time since inception for a currently running process). |
| PeakMemoryUsed | The maximum amount of memory, in megabytes (MB), that this process has used at any one time. |
| ProcessID | The ASP.NET-assigned ID number. |
| RequestCount | The number of requests that have been served by this process. |
| ShutdownReason | If the process has shut down, this indicates a value from the ProcessShutdownReason enumeration. This can be an automatic process recycling (such as MemoryLimitExceeded, RequestsLimit, or Timeout), or it could be a serious failure (such as PingFailed or Unexpected). |
| StartTime | A DateTime object indicating when the process started. |
| Status | A value from the ProcessStatus enumeration that indicates the current state of the process (such as Alive, ShutDown, ShuttingDown, or Terminated). |

**Table 23-1.** *ProcessInfo Properties*

To keep an eye on the ASP.NET worker process from another computer, you can create a simple test page that displays the current process information. The following

ProcessModelReport.aspx page does exactly that, displaying all the statistics for the current process when the user clicks a button. The results are shown in Figure 23-1.

```
Dim Current As ProcessInfo = ProcessModelInfo.GetCurrentProcessInfo
lblInfo.Text = "<b>Process: </b>" & Current.ProcessID.ToString()
lblInfo.Text &= "<br><b>Start: </b>" & Current.StartTime.ToString()
lblInfo.Text &= "<br><b>Age: </b>" & Current.Age.ToString()
lblInfo.Text &= "<br><b>Peak Memory: </b>"
lblInfo.Text &= Current.PeakMemoryUsed.ToString()
lblInfo.Text &= "<br><b>Status: </b>" & Current.Status.ToString()
```

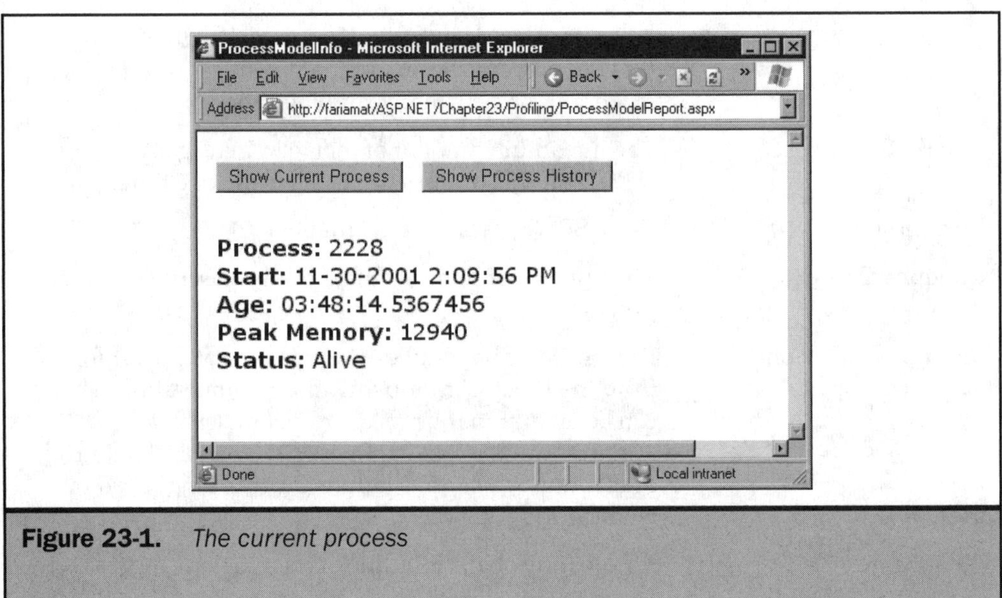


**Figure 23-1.** *The current process*

The same page also provides summary information about the recent worker processes. Thanks to ASP.NET's data binding, the most important information in the ProcessInfo array can be sent straight into the DataGrid control in two easy lines, as shown in Figure 23-2.

```
dgProcess.DataSource = ProcessModelInfo.GetHistory(100)
dgProcess.DataBind()
```

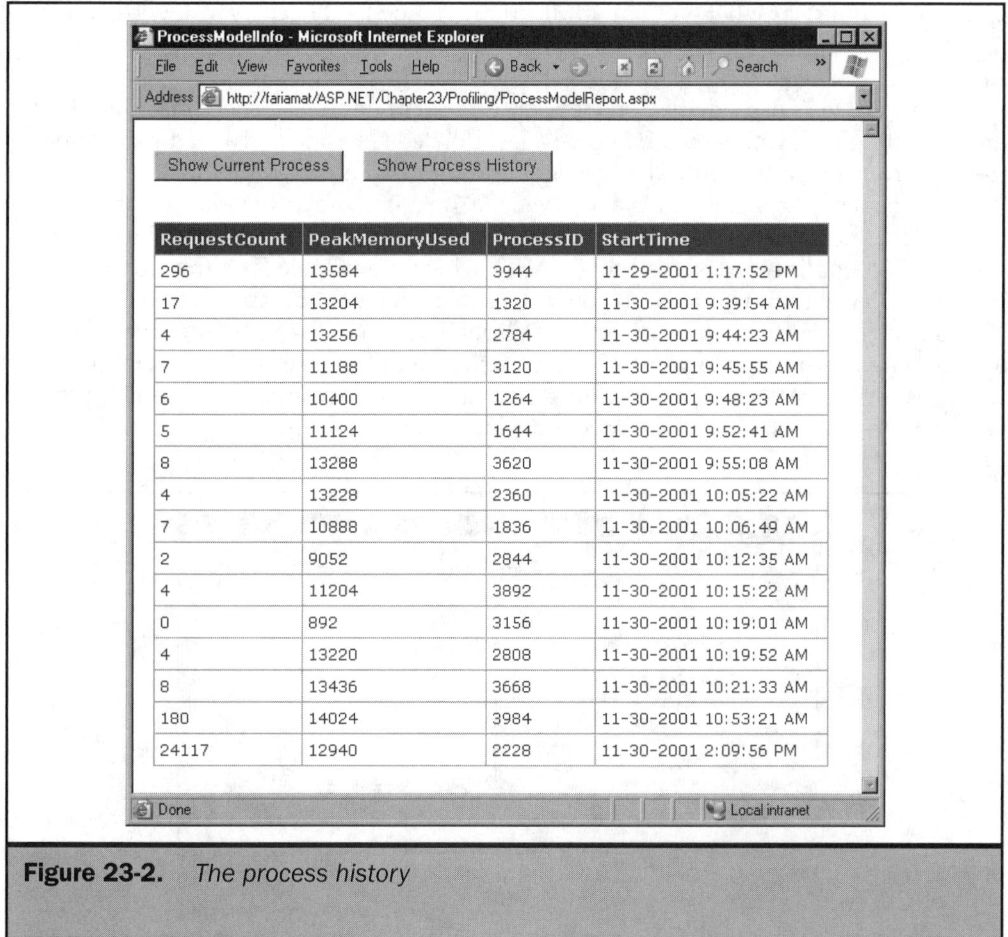


| RequestCount | PeakMemoryUsed | ProcessID | StartTime |
|---|---|---|---|
| 296 | 13584 | 3944 | 11-29-2001 1:17:52 PM |
| 17 | 13204 | 1320 | 11-30-2001 9:39:54 AM |
| 4 | 13256 | 2784 | 11-30-2001 9:44:23 AM |
| 7 | 11188 | 3120 | 11-30-2001 9:45:55 AM |
| 6 | 10400 | 1264 | 11-30-2001 9:48:23 AM |
| 5 | 11124 | 1644 | 11-30-2001 9:52:41 AM |
| 8 | 13288 | 3620 | 11-30-2001 9:55:08 AM |
| 4 | 13228 | 2360 | 11-30-2001 10:05:22 AM |
| 7 | 10888 | 1836 | 11-30-2001 10:06:49 AM |
| 2 | 9052 | 2844 | 11-30-2001 10:12:35 AM |
| 4 | 11204 | 3892 | 11-30-2001 10:15:22 AM |
| 0 | 892 | 3156 | 11-30-2001 10:19:01 AM |
| 4 | 13220 | 2808 | 11-30-2001 10:19:52 AM |
| 8 | 13436 | 3668 | 11-30-2001 10:21:33 AM |
| 180 | 14024 | 3984 | 11-30-2001 10:53:21 AM |
| 24117 | 12940 | 2228 | 11-30-2001 2:09:56 PM |

**Figure 23-2.** *The process history*

The process model information is a basic starting point when checking up on the health of your application. However, it won't give you any idea about the strengths and shortcomings of your code. For that, you need to perform stress testing.

## Stress Testing

There is no shortage of testing tools and framework features you can use to profile your ASP.NET applications. Being able to bridge the gap from test results to application insight is often not as easy. You may be able to record important information such as TTFB and TTLB (the time taken to serve the first byte, and the time taken to deliver the last byte and complete the delivery). But without a way to gauge the meaning of these settings, it's not clear whether your application is being held back by a slow hard drive, a poor choice of ASP.NET settings, an overtasked database, or bad application design. In fact, performance testing is an entire science of its own.

Most basic tests use a dedicated web server, a set of dedicated client machines that are interacting with your web server over a fast isolated network, and a load-generating tool that runs on each client. The load-generating tool automatically requests a steady stream of pages, simulating a heavy load. You might use a utility like Application Center Test (included with some versions of Visual Studio .NET) or the ASP favorite Web Service Applications Stress Tool (WAST), which is available for a free download from http://webtool.rte.microsoft.com/. (The nice thing about Application Center Test is that you can create tests directly in Visual Studio .NET simply by adding the appropriate project type to your solution, as shown in Figure 23-3.) Note that if you try to test the server using a load-testing tool running from the same computer, you will retrieve data that is much less accurate and much less useful.

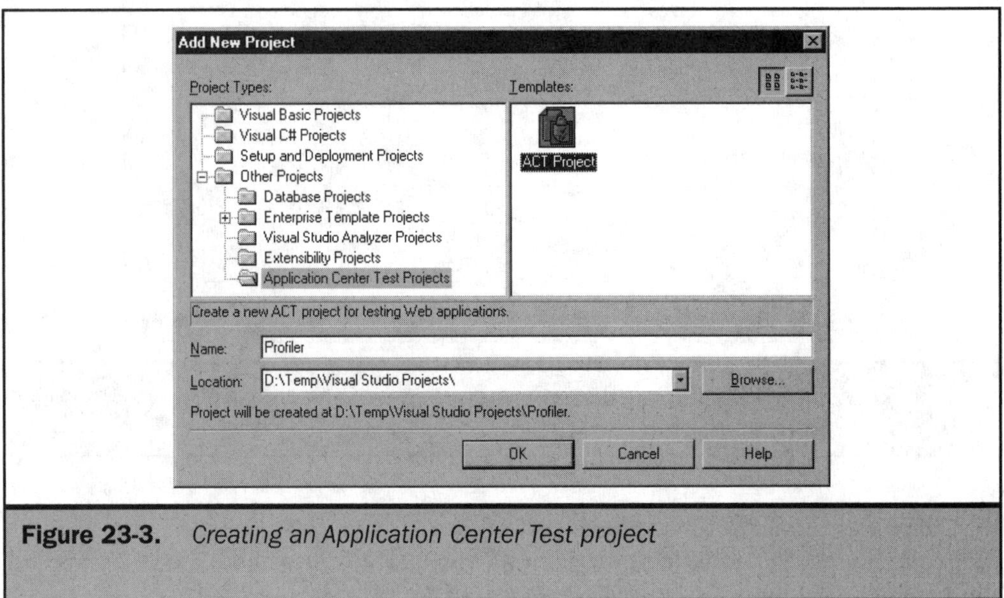


**Figure 23-3.** *Creating an Application Center Test project*

Both Application Center Test and Web Service Applications Stress Tool simulate real-world conditions by continuously requesting pages through several different connections simultaneously. You can configure how many requests are made at once and what files are requested. You can even use a wizard that records typical browser activity while you use the site, and then replays it. Figure 23-4 shows an Application Center Test in progress.

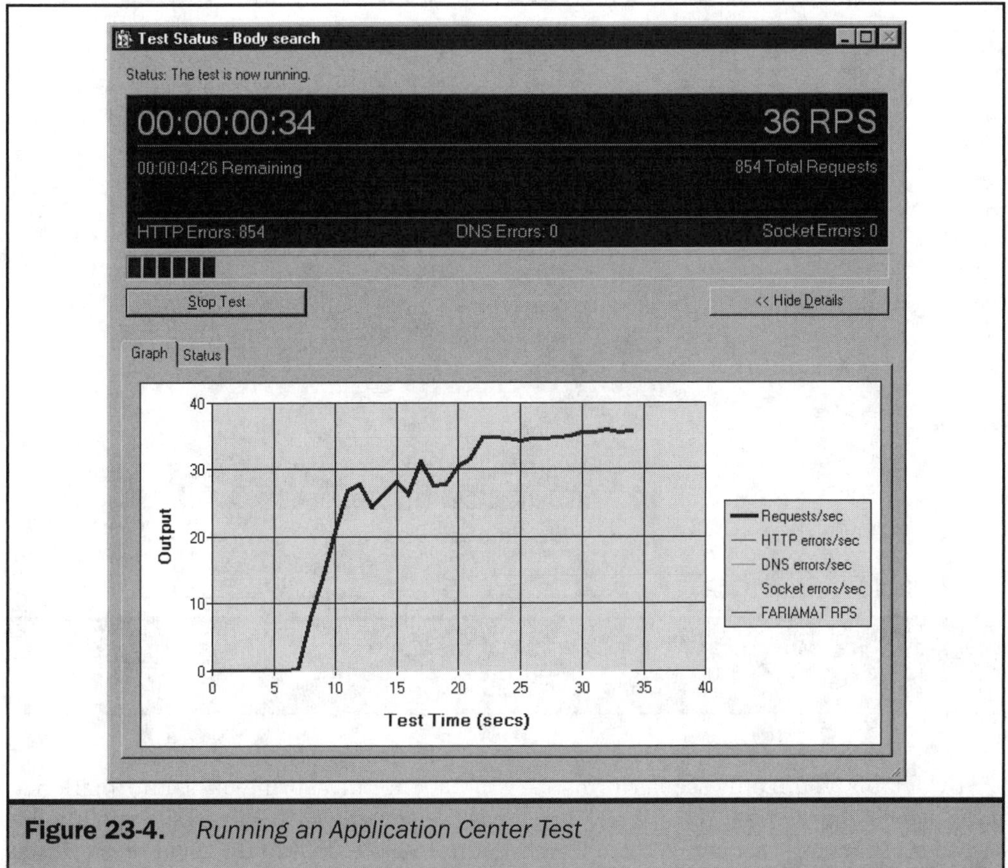


**Figure 23-4.** *Running an Application Center Test*

Most load-generating tools record some kind of report as they work. Both Application Center Test and Web Service Application Stress Tool create text summaries. Additionally, you can record results using Windows Performance Counters, which we'll examine in the next section.

## Performance Counters

Windows Performance Counters are the basic unit of measurement for gauging the performance of your application. You can add or configure counters from a testing utility like Web Service Application Stress Tool, or you can monitor performance directly from the system Performance window. To do so, choose Settings | Control Panel from the Start menu, and choose Administrative Tools | Performance, as shown in Figure 23-5.

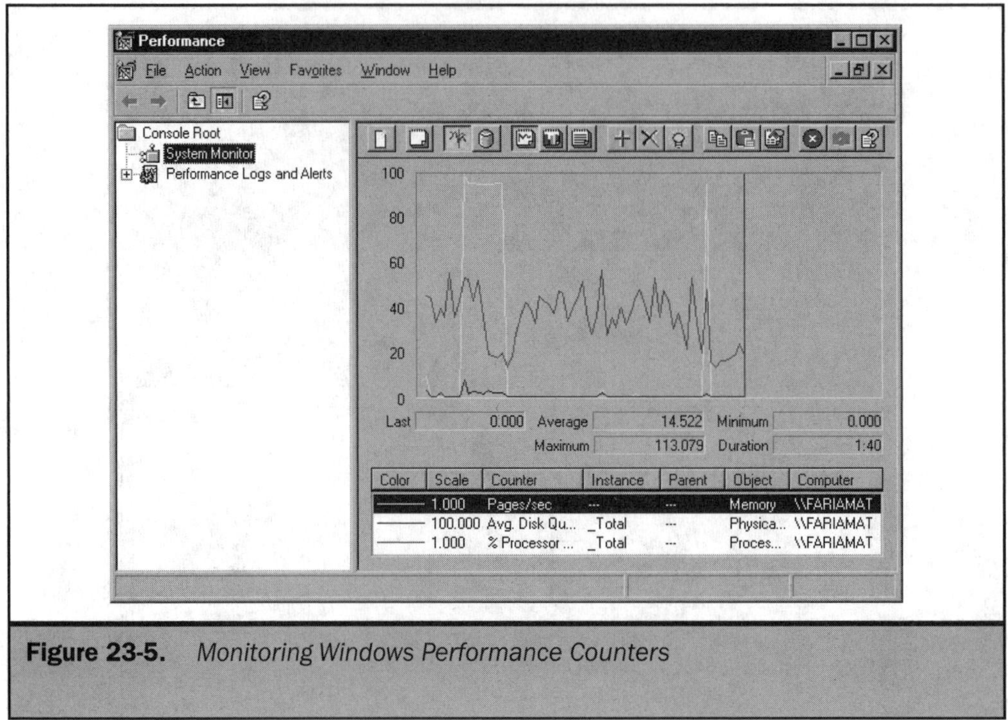


**Figure 23-5.** *Monitoring Windows Performance Counters*

By default, you'll only see Performance Counters for measuring basic information such as the computer's CPU and disk drive use. However, ASP.NET installs much more useful counters for tracking web application performance. To add these counters, right-click on the counter list and choose Properties. You can configure numerous options (such as changing the appearance of the graph and logging information to a report), but the most important tab is Data, which allows you to add and remove counters from the current list. To start, remove the default counters, and click Add to choose more useful ones (see Figure 23-6).

You'll notice several important features about the Add Counters window. First of all, you can specify a computer name—in other words, you can monitor the performance of a remote computer. Monitoring the web server's performance on a client computer is ideal, because it ensures that the act of monitoring doesn't have as much of an effect on the server. The next important feature of this window is the "performance object." These are dozens of different categories of performance counters.

For ASP.NET, you'll find four main categories. The ASP.NET category provides information about the overall performance of ASP.NET, while the ASP.NET Applications category provides information about a single specified web application. There are also two similar categories that include the version number (such as ASP.NET [version] and ASP.NET Apps [version]). These categories provide the same list of counters as the corresponding categories that don't indicate the version. This design supports the side-by-side execution features of .NET, which allow you to install two (or more) versions of the ASP.NET framework at the same time for backward compatibility purposes. In this case, you would find one ASP.NET [version] and ASP.NET Apps [version] category for each version of ASP.NET that is installed on your server. The ASP.NET and ASP.NET Application categories would automatically map to the latest version.

Table 23-2 lists some of the most useful counter types by category and name. The asterisked rows indicate counters that can help you diagnose a problem, while the other rows represent counters that are always useful.

## .NET Includes Performance Counter Classes

.NET provides some interesting features that let you interact with the system Performance Counters programmatically. For example, you can add new performance counters, or retrieve the current value of a performance counter in your code, and display relevant information in a web page or desktop application. To use these features, you simply need to explore the types in the System.Diagnostics namespace.

| Class | Description |
|---|---|
| PerformanceCounter | Represents an individual counter, which includes information like the counter name and the type of data it records. You can create your own counter to represent application-specific performance measures (such as number of purchases/second). |
| PerformanceCounterCategory | Represents a counter category, which will contain one or more counters. |
| CounterCreationData | Represents the data required to create a new counter. It can be used for more control or as a shortcut when creating PerformanceCounter objects. |
| CounterSample | Represents a single piece of information recorded by the counter. It provides a RawValue (the recorded number), a TimeStamp (when the value was recorded), and additional information about the type of counter and how frequently the counter is read. A typical performance counter might create samples several times per second. |

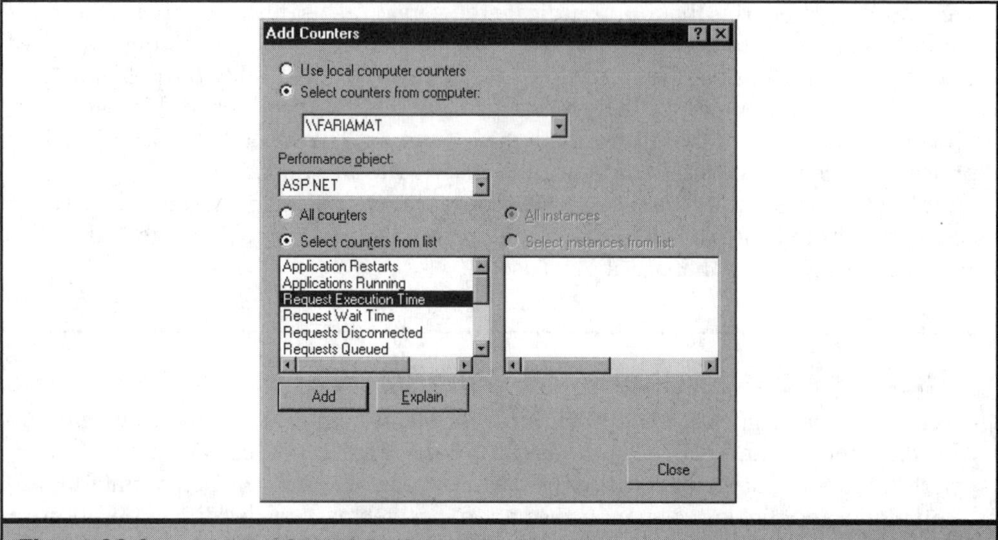


**Figure 23-6.** *Adding ASP.NET Performance Counters*

| Category | Counter | Description |
|---|---|---|
| Processor | % CPU Utilization | The percentage of the CPU's processing time that is being used. If your CPU use remains consistently low regardless of the client load, your application may be trapped waiting for a limited resource. |
| ASP.NET | Requests Queued | The number of requests waiting to be processed. Use this counter to gain an idea about the maximum load that your web server can support. The default machine.config setting specifies a limit of 5,000 queued requests. |

**Table 23-2.** *Useful Performance Counters*

| Category | Counter | Description |
|---|---|---|
| ASP.NET Applications | Requests/Sec | The throughput of the web application. |
| ASP.NET Applications | * Errors Total | This counter should remain at or close to zero. If a web application generates errors, it can exert a noticeable performance slow-down (required for handling the error) which will skew performance results. |
| ASP.NET | * Application Restarts, ASP.NET, Worker Process Restarts | The ASP.NET process may restart based on a fatal crash, or automatically in response to recycling options set in the machine.config file (see the <processModel> settings in Chapter 28 for more information). These counters can give you an idea about how often the ASP.NET process is being reset, and can indicate unnoticed problems. |
| System | * Context Switches/sec | Indicates the rate that thread contexts are switched. A high number may indicate that various threads are competing for a limited resource. |
| ASP.NET Applications | Pipeline Instance Count | The number of request pipelines that exist for an application. This gives an idea of the maximum number of concurrent requests that are being served. If this number is low under a load, it often signifies that the CPU is being well used. |

*Useful when diagnosing problems.

**Table 23-2.** *Useful Performance Counters (continued)*

| Category | Counter | Description |
|---|---|---|
| .NET | * CLR Exceptions, # of Exceps Thrown | The number of exceptions thrown in a .NET application. This can indicate that unexpected errors are occurring (as with the ErrorsTotal counter), but it can also indicate the normal operation of error handling code in response to a missing file or invalid user action. |

*Useful when diagnosing problems.

**Table 23-2.** *Useful Performance Counters (continued)*

## Caching

ASP.NET has taken some dramatic steps forward with caching. Many developers who first learn about caching see it as a bit of a frill—but nothing could be further from the truth. Used intelligently, caching could provide a two-fold, three-fold, or even ten-fold performance improvement by retaining important data for just a short period of time.

In ASP.NET, there are really two types of caching. Your applications can and should use both types, as they complement each other.

- **Output caching** is the simplest type of caching. It stores a copy of the final rendered HTML page that is sent to the client. The next client that submits a request for this page doesn't actually run the page. Instead, the final HTML output is sent automatically. The time that would have been required to run the page and its code is completely reclaimed.
- **Data caching** is carried out manually in your code. To use data caching, you store important pieces of information that are time-consuming to reconstruct (such as a DataSet retrieved from a database) in the cache. Other pages can check for the existence of this information, and use it, bypassing the steps ordinarily required to retrieve it. Data caching is conceptually the same as using Application state (described in Chapter 10), but it's much more server-friendly because items will be removed from the cache automatically when it grows too large and performance could be affected. Items can also be set to expire automatically.

- **Fragment caching** is really a specialized type of output caching. It stores and reuses the compiled HTML output of a portion of a user control on a page. Thus, when the page is requested some code may be executed, but the code for the appropriate user control is not.

## Output Caching

To see output caching in action, you can create a simple page that displays the current time of day, as shown in Figure 23-7.

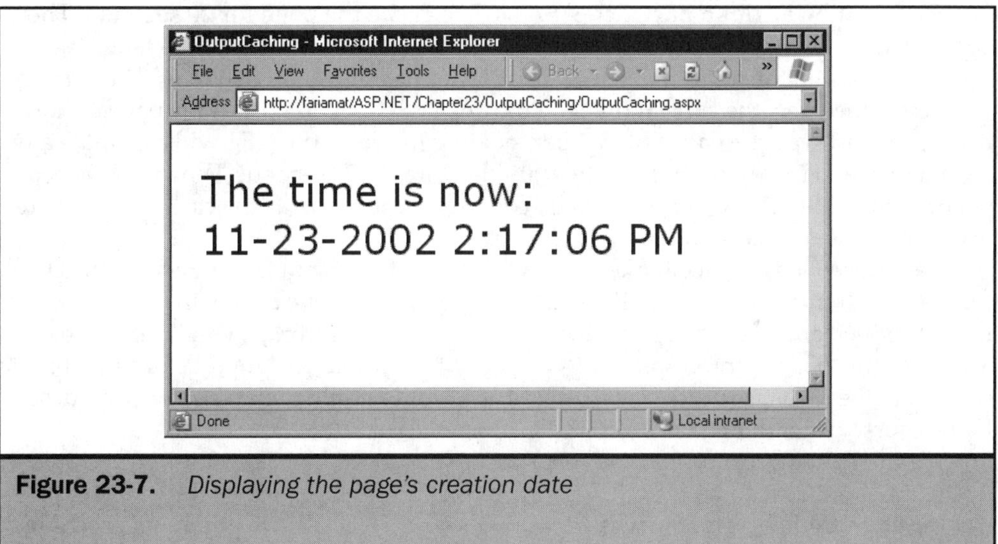


**Figure 23-7.** *Displaying the page's creation date*

The code for this task is elementary:

```
Public Class OutputCaching
  Inherits Page
    Protected lblDate As Label

    Private Sub Page_Load(sender As Object, e As EventArgs) _
      Handles MyBase.Load

        lblDate.Text = "The time is now:<br>"
        lblDate.Text &= DateTime.Now.ToString()
```

```
    End Sub

End Class
```

There are two ways to cache an ASP.NET page. The most common approach is to insert the OutputCache directive at the top of your .aspx file.

```
<%@ OutputCache Duration="20" VaryByParam="None" %>
```

The Duration attribute instructs ASP.NET to cache the page for 20 seconds. The VaryByParam attribute is also required—but we'll discuss its effect a little later.

When you run the test page, you'll discover some interesting behavior. The first time you access the page, the current date will be displayed. If you refresh the page a short time later, however, the page will not be updated. Instead, ASP.NET will automatically send the cached HTML output to you, until it expires in 20 seconds. When the cached page expires, ASP.NET will run the page code again, generate a new cached copy, and use that for the next 20 seconds.

Twenty seconds may seem like a trivial amount of time, but in a high-volume site, it can make a dramatic difference. For example, you might cache a page that provides a list of products from a catalog. By caching the page for 20 seconds, you limit database access for this page to three operations per minute. Without caching, the page will try to connect to the database once for each client, and could easily make dozens of requests in the course of a minute.

Of course, just because you request that a page should be stored for 20 seconds doesn't mean that it actually will. The page could be evicted out of the cache early if the system finds that memory is becoming scarce. This allows you to use caching freely, without worrying too much about hampering your application by using up vital memory.

### Testing with Cached Pages

You may want to add caching to your application in its final development. Otherwise, caching can cause serious programming confusion. For example, you might update information in a database, but forget that your page will still use the cached information. Then, when you test your page, you might assume that the invalid data it returns is the result of an error in your code.

To test if your code is actually running at any time, try setting breakpoints. If you are just receiving a cached HTML page, these breakpoints will not be triggered. Any time you modify and recompile the page, any cached versions will be automatically invalidated. However, Visual Studio .NET may not compile your page if you have not made any changes!

## Caching on the Client Side

Another option is to cache the page exclusively on the client side. In this case, the browser stores a copy, and will automatically use this page if the client browses back to the page or retypes the page's URL. However, if the user clicks the Refresh button, the cached copy will be abandoned and the page will be re-requested from the server, which will run the appropriate page code once again. You can cache a page on the client side using the Location attribute, which specifies a value from the System.Web.UI.OutputCacheLocation enumeration. Possible values include Server (the default), Client, None, and All.

```
<%@ OutputCache Duration="20" VaryByParam="None" Location="Client" %>
```

### When to Use Client-Side Caching

Client-side caching is less common, and less useful when it comes to improving performance because the page is still recreated for every separate user, which doesn't cut down on code execution or database access nearly as dramatically as server-side caching (which shares a single cached copy among all users). However, client-side caching can be a useful technique if your cached page uses some sort of session data. For example, there is no point in caching a page on the server that displays a "hello" message with the user's name. Even though each user is in a separate session, the page will only be created once and reused for all clients, ensuring that most will receive the wrong greeting. Instead, you can either use fragment caching to cache the generic portion of the page, or client-side caching to store a user-specific version on each client's computer.

## Caching and the Query String

One of the main considerations in caching is deciding when a page can be reused and when information must be accurate up to the latest second. Developers, with their love of instant gratification (and arguable lack of patience), generally tend to overemphasize the importance of real-time information. You can usually use caching to efficiently reuse slightly stale data without a problem, and with a considerable performance improvement.

Of course, sometimes information needs to be dynamic. One example is if the page uses information from the current user's session to tailor the user interface. In this case, full page caching just isn't appropriate (although fragment caching may help). Another example is if the page is receiving information from another page through the query string. In this case, the page is too dynamic to cache—or is it?

Our current example sets the VaryByParam attribute to None, which effectively tells ASP.NET that you only need to store one copy of the cached page, which is suitable for all scenarios. If the request for this page adds some query string arguments to the URL, it makes no difference. ASP.NET will always reuse the same output until it expires. You can test this by adding a query string parameter manually in the browser window (such as ?a=b), as shown in Figure 23-8.

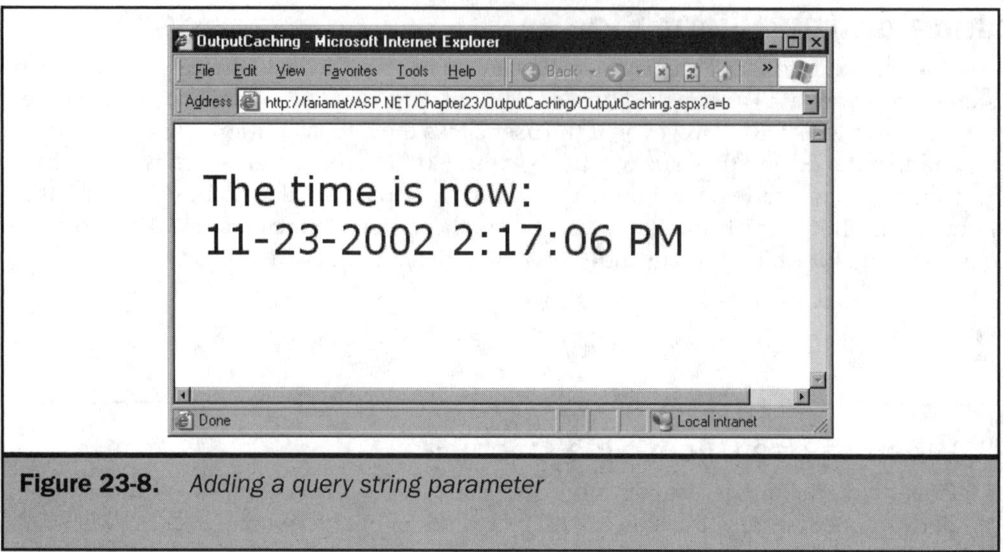


**Figure 23-8.** *Adding a query string parameter*

## Caching Multiple Page Versions

Based on this experiment, you might assume that output caching is not suitable for pages that use query string arguments. But ASP.NET actually provides another option. You can set the VaryByParam attribute to "*" to indicate that the page uses the query string, and to instruct ASP.NET to cache separate copies of the page for different query string arguments.

```
<%@ OutputCache Duration="20" VaryByParam="*" %>
```

Now, when you request the page with additional query string information, ASP.NET will examine the query string. If the string matches a previous request, and a cached copy of that page exists, it will be reused. Otherwise, a new copy of the page will be created and cached separately.

To get a better idea how this process works, consider a series of requests:

1. You request a page without any query string parameter, and receive page copy A.
2. You request the page with the parameter ProductID=1. You receive page copy B.
3. Another user requests the page with the parameter ProductID=2. That user receives copy C.

4. Another user requests the page with ProductID=1. If the cached output B has not expired, it's sent to the user.
5. The user than requests the page with no query string parameters. If copy A has not expired, it's sent from the cache.

You can try this out on your own, although you might want to lengthen the amount of time that the cached page is retained to make it easier to test.

## Caching with Specific Parameters

Setting VaryByParam to the wildcard asterisk (*) is unnecessarily vague. It's usually better to specifically identify an important query string variable by name.

```
<%@ OutputCache Duration="20" VaryByParam="ProductID" %>
```

In this case, ASP.NET will examine the query string looking for the ProductID parameter. Requests with different ProductID parameters will be cached separately, but all other parameters will be ignored. This is particularly useful if the page may be passed additional query string information that it doesn't use. ASP.NET has no way to distinguish the "important" query string parameters without your help.

You can specify several parameters, as long as you separate them with semicolons.

```
<%@ OutputCache Duration="20" VaryByParam="ProductID;CurrencyType" %>
```

In this case, query string will cache separate versions provided the query string differs by ProductID or CurrencyType.

### Problems with VaryByParam="*"

Setting VaryByParam="*" allows you to use caching with dynamic pages that vary their output based on the query string. This approach could be extremely useful for a product detail page, which receives a product ID in its query string. With vary-by-parameter caching, a separate page could be stored for each product, saving a trip to the database. However, to gain performance benefits you might have to increase the cached output lifetime to several minutes or longer.

Of course, there are some potential problems with this technique. Pages that accept a wide range of different query string parameters (such as a page that receives numbers for a calculation, client information, or search keywords) just aren't suited to output caching. The possible number of variations is enormous, and the potential reuse is very low. Though these pages will be evicted from the cache when the memory is needed, they could inadvertently force other more important information out of the cache first.

## A Multiple Caching Example

The following example uses two web pages to demonstrate how multiple versions of a web page can be cached separately. The first page, QueryStringSender.aspx, is not cached. It provides three buttons (see Figure 23-9).

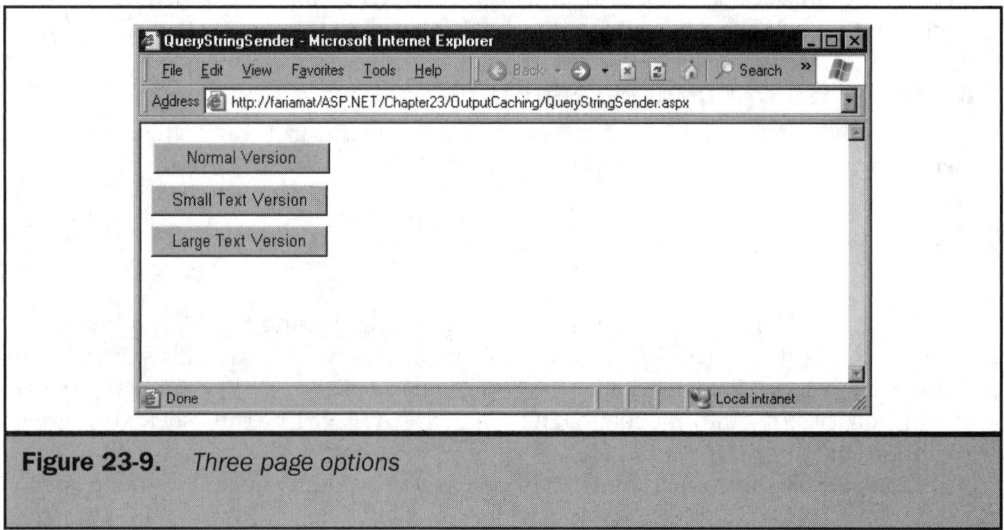


**Figure 23-9.** *Three page options*

A single event handler handles the Click event for all three buttons. The event handler navigates to the QueryStringRecipient.aspx page, and adds a Version parameter to the query string to indicate which button was clicked—cmdNormal, cmdLarge, or cmdSmall.

```
Private Sub cmdVersion_Click(sender As Object, e As EventArgs) _
  Handles cmdLarge.Click, cmdNormal.Click, cmdSmall.Click

        Response.Redirect(Request.Path & "?Version=" & _
          CType(sender, Control).ID)

End Sub
```

The QueryStringRecipient.aspx destination page displays the familiar date message. The page uses an OutputCache directive that looks for a single query string parameter (named Version).

```
<%@ OutputCache Duration="60" VaryByParam="Version" %>
```

In other words, there are three separately maintained HTML outputs for this page, one where Version equals cmdSmall, one where Version equals cmdLarge, and one where Version equals cmdNormal.

Although it's not necessary for our example, the Page.Load event handler tailors the page by changing the font size of the label accordingly. This makes it easy to distinguish the three different versions of the page, and verify that the caching is working as expected.

```
Private Sub Page_Load(sender As Object, e As EventArgs) _
  Handles MyBase.Load

    lblDate.Text = "The time is now:<br>" & DateTime.Now.ToString()
    Select Case Request.QueryString("Version")
        Case "cmdLarge"
            lblDate.Font.Size = FontUnit.XLarge
        Case "cmdNormal"
            lblDate.Font.Size = FontUnit.Large
        Case "cmdSmall"
            lblDate.Font.Size = FontUnit.Small
    End Select

End Sub
```

Figure 23-10 shows one of the cached outputs for this page.

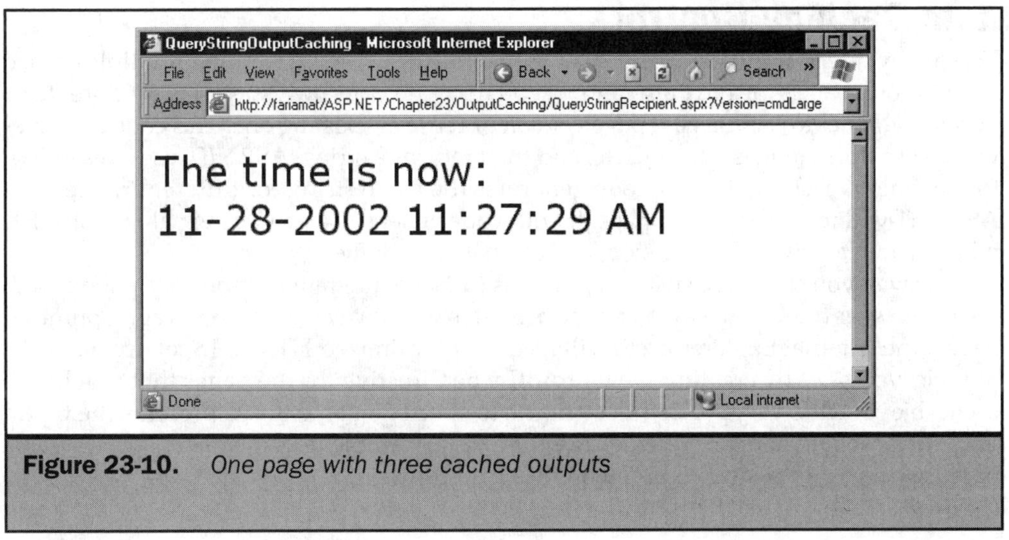


**Figure 23-10.** *One page with three cached outputs*

## Caching and Events

The same problems you witnessed with cached pages and query string values can occur with a cached page that runs events. With VaryByParam="None" ASP.NET will cache one version of the page for all POST requests, and reuse that when any postback is triggered. That means that if you click a button multiple times, it will really only be executed once. Even worse, if you have a page with multiple buttons, their Click events may be ignored altogether. A static page will be resent no matter what button the user clicks, effectively disabling the page.

To compensate for these problems, you can specify the specific postback values that will require separately cached versions of the page using the VaryByParam attribute. For example, set VaryByParam="txtName" to vary the result based on the txtName contents that are posted back with the page. However, this is generally *not* a recommended approach. Because you can't directly see the values that are being posted back (as you can with query string information), it's very easy to create a problem for yourself.

One such problem occurs with viewstate, which is contained in a special hidden control. This hidden input control is sent back to the page with each postback. That means that if you include a VaryByParam="*" attribute with a page that maintains viewstate, you could quickly end up with dozens of versions of the cached page. Every time ASP.NET receives the page, it will examine the posted-back information, determine that it is not the same because the hidden field has changed, and cache another unnecessary version of the page. This could potentially force other important information out of the cache. If, on the other hand, you try to solve this problem by using VaraByParams="None", the caching won't be conditional, and some values may not be correctly restored.

The bottom line is this: for effective, straightforward caching, do not try to implement caching strategies with an event-driven page.

## Custom Caching Control

Varying by query string parameters is not the only option when storing multiple cached versions of a page. ASP.NET also allows you to create your own special procedure that decides whether to cache a new page version or reuse an existing one. This code examines whatever information is appropriate, and then returns a string. ASP.NET uses this string to implement caching. If your code generates the same string for different requests, ASP.NET will reuse the cached page. If your code generates a new string value, ASP.NET will generate a new cached version, and store it separately.

One way you could use custom caching is to cache different versions of a page based on the browser type. That way, Netscape browsers will always receive Netscape-optimized pages, and Internet Explorer users will receive IE-optimized HTML. To set up this sort of logic, you start by creating the OutputCache directive for the pages that will be cacheable. Use the VaryByCustom attribute to specify a name that represents the type of custom caching you are creating. The following example uses the name "Browser" because pages will be cached based on the client browser.

```
<%@ OutputCache Duration="10" VaryByParam="None"
VaryByCustom="Browser" %>
```

Next, you need to create the procedure that will generate the custom caching string. This procedure must be coded in the global.asax application file (or its code-behind file), and must use the syntax shown here.

```
Public Overrides Function GetVaryByCustomString( _
  context As HttpContext, arg As String) As String

    ' Check for the requested type of caching.
    If arg = "Browser"
        ' Determine the current browser.
        Dim BrowserName As String
        BrowserName = Context.Request.Browser.Browser

        ' Indicate that this string should be used to vary caching.
        Return BrowserName
    End If

End Function
```

The GetVaryByCustomString function passes the VaryByCustom name in the arg parameter. This allows you to create an application that implements several different types of custom caching in the same function. Each different type would use a different VaryByCustom name (such as “Browser”, “BrowserVersion”, or “DayOfWeek”). Your GetVaryByCustomString function would examine the VaryByCustom name, and then return the appropriate caching string. If the caching strings for different requests match, ASP.NET will reuse the cached copy of the page. Or to look at it another way, ASP.NET will create and store a separate cached version of the page for each caching string it encounters.

### You Can Also Use VaryByHeader

The OutputCache directive has a third attribute that you can use to define caching. This attribute, VaryByHeader, allows you to store separate versions of a page based on the value of an HTTP header received with the request. You can specify a single header or a list of headers separated by semicolons. This technique could be used with multi-lingual sites, to cache different versions of a page based on the client browser language.

```
<%@ OutputCache Duration="20" VaryByParam="None"
    VaryByHeader="Accept-Language" %>
```

## Caching with the HttpCachePolicy Class

Using the OutputCache directive is generally the preferred way to cache a page, because it separates the caching instruction from the rest of your code. The OutputCache directive also makes it easy to configure several advanced properties in one line.

However, there is one other choice: you can create code that interacts with the special Response.Cache object (an instance of the System.Web.HttpCachePolicy class). This object provides properties that allow you to turn on caching for the current page.

In the following example, the date page has been rewritten so that it automatically enables caching when the page is first loaded. This code enables caching with the SetCacheability method, which specifies that the page will be cached on the server, and that any other client can use the cached copy of the page. The SetExpires method defines the expiration date for the page, which is set to be the current time plus 60 seconds.

```
Private Sub Page_Load(sender As Object, e As EventArgs) _
  Handles MyBase.Load

    ' Cache this page on the server.
    Response.Cache.SetCacheability(HttpCacheability.Public)

    ' Use the cached copy of this page for the next 60 seconds.
    Response.Cache.SetExpires(DateTime.Now.AddSeconds(60))

    ' This additional line ensures that the browser can't
    ' invalidate the page when the user clicks the Refresh button
    ' (which some rogue browsers attempt to do).
    Response.Cache.SetValidUntilExpires(True)

    lblDate.Text = "The time is now:<br>" & DateTime.Now.ToString()

End Sub
```

### The HttpCachePolicy Object Exhibits Slight Differences!

Always test your caching strategies after implementing them. For some completely mysterious reason, caching with the HttpCachePolicy class works slightly different than with the OutputCache directive. Namely, event procedures bypass the cached page unless you set the HttpCachePolicy.VaryByParam property. That means that you can enable caching for an event-driven page, and this caching will only be used for ordinary GET requests, not postbacks. Strange, but true.

## Fragment Caching

In some cases, you may find that you can't cache an entire page, but you would still like to cache a portion that is expensive to create and doesn't vary. One way to implement this sort of scenario is to use data caching to store just the underlying information used for the page. We will examine this technique in the next section. Another option is to use fragment caching.

To implement fragment caching, you need to create a user control for the portion of the page you want to cache. You can then add the OutputCache directive to the user control. The result is that the page will not be cached, but the user control will.

Fragment caching is conceptually the same as page caching. There is only one catch—if your page retrieves a cached version of a user control, it cannot interact with it in code. For example, if your user control provides properties, your web page code cannot modify or access these properties. When the cached version of the user control is used, a block of HTML is simply inserted into the page. The corresponding user control object is not available.

# Data Caching

Data caching is the most flexible type of caching, but it also forces you to take specific additional steps in your code to implement it. The basic principle of data caching is that you add items that are expensive to create to a special built-in collection object (called Cache). This object works much like the Application object you saw in Chapter 10: it's globally available to all requests from all clients in the application. There are really only two differences:

- The Cache object is thread-safe, which means that you don't need to explicitly lock or unlock the Cache collection before adding or removing an item. However, the objects in the Cache collection will still need to be thread-safe themselves. For example, if you create a custom business object, more than one client could try to use that object at once, which could lead to invalid data. There are various ways to code around this limitation—one easy approach that you'll see in this chapter is just to make a duplicate copy of the object if you need to work with it in a web page.
- Items in the Cache collection are automatically removed if they expire, server memory becomes limited, or one of their dependent objects or files changes. This means you can freely use the cache without worrying about wasting valuable server memory, as ASP.NET will remove items as needed. But because items in the cache can be removed, you *always* need to check if a cache object exists before you attempt to use it. Otherwise, you could generate a null-reference exception.

There are several ways to insert an object into the cache. You can simply assign it to a new key name (as you would with the Session or Application collections), but this approach is generally discouraged because it does not allow you to have any control over the amount of time the object will be retained in the cache. A better approach is to use the Insert method.

The Insert method has four overloaded versions. The most useful and commonly used one requires four parameters and is shown here.

```
Cache.Insert(key, item, dependencies, absoluteExpiration, _
          slidingExpiration)
```

The parameters are described in Table 23-3.

| Parameter | Description |
| --- | --- |
| key | A string that assigns a name to this cached item in the collection and allows you to look it up later. |
| item | The actual object that you want to cache. |
| dependencies | A CacheDependency object that allows you to create a dependency for this item in the cache. If you don't want to create a dependent item, just specify Nothing for this parameter. |
| absoluteExpiration | A DateTime object representing the time at which the item will be removed from the cache. |
| slidingExpiration | A TimeSpan object represents how long ASP.NET will wait between requests before removing a cached item. For example, if this value is 20 minutes, ASP.NET will evict the item if it is not used by any code for a 20-minute period. |

**Table 23-3.** *Cache.Insert Parameters*

Typically, you won't use all of these parameters at once. (Cache dependencies, for example, are a special tool we'll consider a little later in this chapter.) Also, you cannot set both a sliding expiration and an absolute expiration policy at the same time. If you want to use an absolute expiration, set the slidingExpiration parameter to TimeSpan.Zero.

```
Cache.Insert("MyItem", obj, Nothing, _
             DateTime.Now.AddMinutes(60), TimeSpan.Zero)
```

Absolute expirations are best when you know the information in a given item can only be considered valid for a specific amount of time (such as a stock chart or weather report). Sliding expiration, on the other, is more useful when you know that a cached item will always remain valid (such as historical data or a product catalog), but should still be allowed to expire if it isn't being used. To set a sliding expiration policy, set the absoluteExpiration parameter to DateTime.Max, as shown here.

```
Cache.Insert("MyItem", obj, Nothing, _
             DateTime.MaxValue, TimeSpan.FromMinutes(10))
```

## A Simple Cache Test

The following presents a simple caching test. An item is cached for 30 seconds and reused for requests in that time. The page code always runs (because the page itself is not cached), checks the cache, and retrieves or constructs the item as needed. It also reports whether the item was found in the cache.

```
Public Class SimpleCacheTest
  Inherits Page

    Protected lblInfo As Label

    Private Sub Page_Load(sender As Object, e As EventArgs) _
      Handles MyBase.Load

        If Me.IsPostBack = True Then
            lblInfo.Text &= "Page posted back.<br>"
        Else
            lblInfo.Text &= "Page created.<br>"
        End If

        If Cache("TestItem") Is Nothing Then
            lblInfo.Text &= "Creating TestItem...<br>"
            Dim TestItem As Date = DateTime.Now()
```

```
                lblInfo.Text &= "Storing TestItem in cache"
                lblInfo.Text &= for 30 seconds.<br>"
                Cache.Insert("TestItem", TestItem, Nothing, _
                             DateTime.Now.AddSeconds(30), TimeSpan.Zero)
            Else
                lblInfo.Text &= "Retrieving TestItem...<br>"
                Dim testitem As Date = CType(Cache("TestItem"), Date)
                lblInfo.Text &= "TestItem is '" & TestItem.ToString()
                lblInfo.Text &= "'<br>"
            End If

            lblInfo.Text &= "<br>"

        End Sub

    End Class
```

Figure 23-11 shows the result after the page has been loaded and posted back several times in the 30-second period.

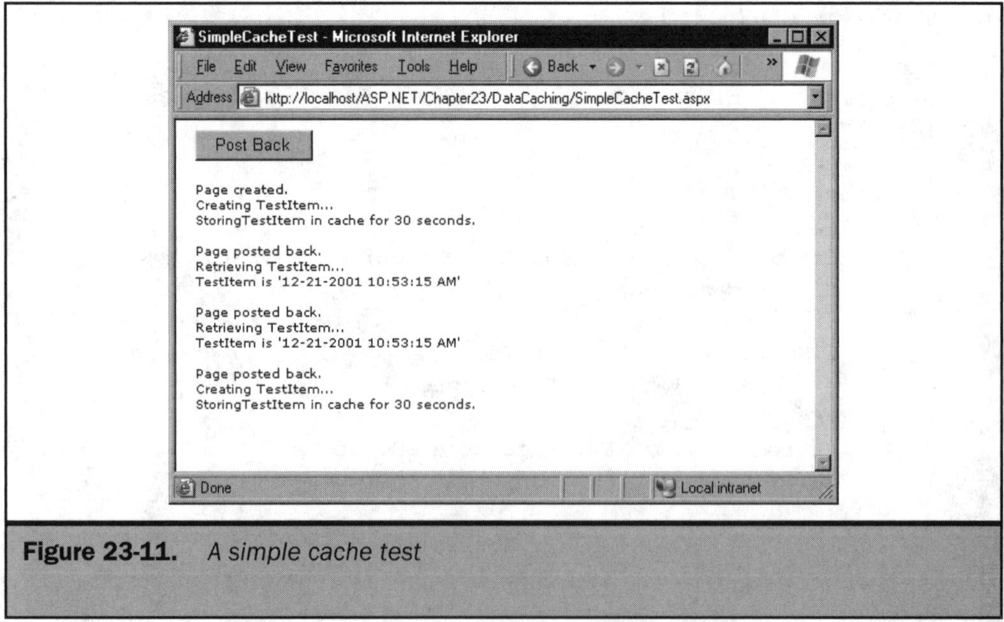


**Figure 23-11.** *A simple cache test*

## Caching to Provide Multiple Views

A more interesting demonstration of caching is shown in the next example, which retrieves information from a database and stores it in a DataSet. This information is then displayed in a web page. However, the output for the web page can't be efficiently cached because the user is given the chance to customize the display by hiding any combination of columns. Note that even with just ten columns, there are more than 1,000 different possible views that can be constructed by hiding and showing various columns, which is far too many versions for successful output caching! Figure 23-12 shows the page.

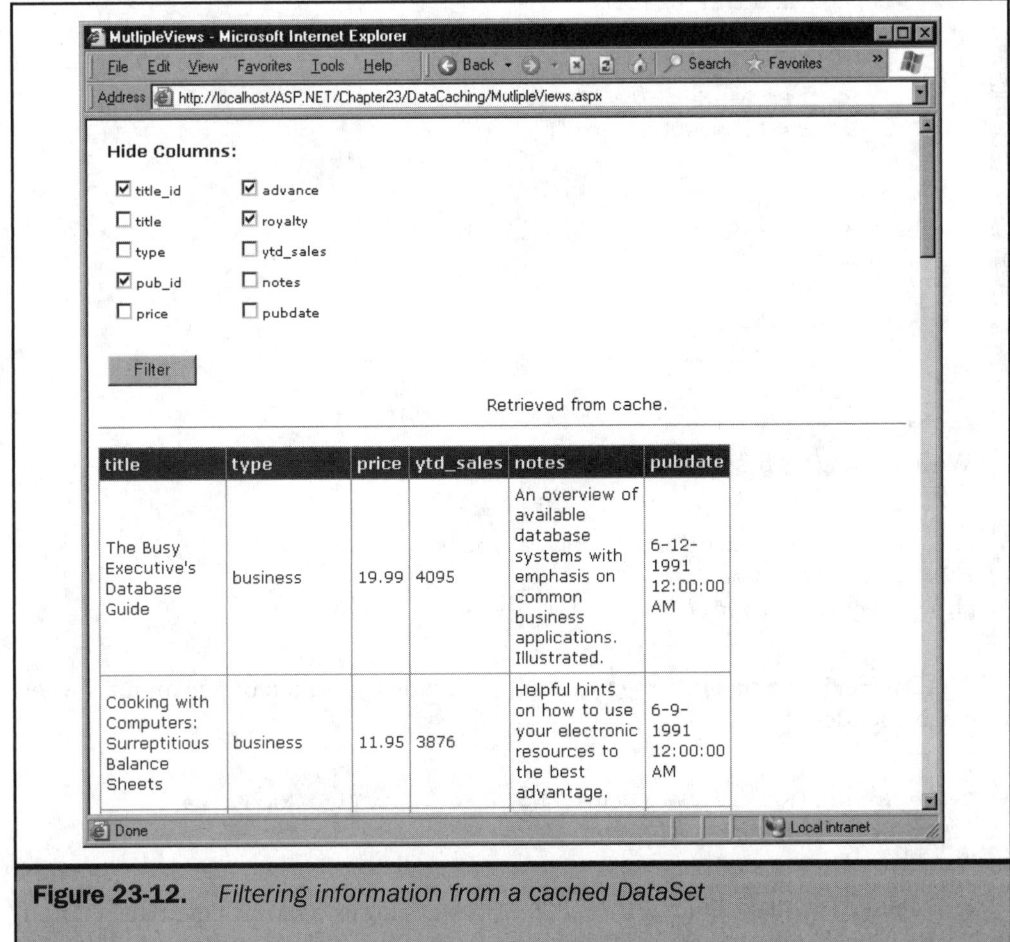


**Figure 23-12.** *Filtering information from a cached DataSet*

The DataSet is constructed in the dedicated RetrieveData function shown here:

```
Private Function RetrieveData() As DataSet
    Dim ConnectionString As String
    ConnectionString = "Provider=SQLOLEDB.1; " & _
      "Data Source=localhost;Initial Catalog=Pubs;User ID=sa"

    Dim SQLSelect As String
    SQLSelect = "SELECT * FROM Titles"

    ' Define ADO.NET objects.
    Dim con As New OleDbConnection(ConnectionString)
    Dim cmd As New OleDbCommand(SQLSelect, con)
    Dim adapter As New OleDbDataAdapter(cmd)
    Dim dsPubs As New DataSet()

    con.Open()
    adapter.Fill(dsPubs, "Titles")
    con.Close()

    Return dsPubs

End Function
```

When the page is first loaded, the checkbox list of columns is filled.

```
chkColumns.DataSource = dsPubs.Tables(0).Columns
chkColumns.DataMember = "Item"
chkColumns.DataBind()
```

The DataSet is inserted into the cache with a sliding expiration of two minutes when the page is loaded.

```
Cache.Insert("Titles", dsPubs, Nothing, DateTime.MaxValue, _
  TimeSpan.FromMinutes(2))
```

Every time the Filter button is clicked, the page attempts to retrieve the DataSet from the cache. If it cannot retrieve the DataSet, it calls the RetrieveData function and then adds the DataSet to the cache. It then reports on the page whether the DataSet was retrieved from the cache or generated manually.

To provide the configurable grid, the code actually loops through the DataTable, removing all the columns that the user has selected to hide before binding the data. Many other alternatives are possible (another approach is just to hide columns), but this strategy demonstrates an important fact about the cache. When you retrieve an item, you actually retrieve a reference to the cached object. If you modify that object, you are actually modifying the cached item as well. For our page to be able to delete columns without affecting the cached copy of the DataSet, the code needs to create a duplicate copy before performing the operations, using the DataSet's Copy method.

The full code for the Filter button is shown here.

```
Private Sub cmdFilter_Click(sender As Object, e As EventArgs) _
  Handles cmdFilter.Click

    Dim dsPubs As DataSet
    If Cache("Titles") Is Nothing Then
        dsPubs = RetrieveData()
        Cache.Insert("Titles", dsPubs, Nothing, DateTime.MaxValue, _
                     TimeSpan.FromMinutes(2))
        lblCacheStatus.Text = "Created and added to cache."
    Else
        dsPubs = CType(Cache("Titles"), DataSet)
        dsPubs = dsPubs.Copy()
        lblCacheStatus.Text = "Retrieved from cache."
    End If

    Dim Item As ListItem
    For Each Item In chkColumns.Items
        If Item.Selected = True Then
            dsPubs.Tables(0).Columns.Remove(Item.Text)
        End If
    Next

    gridPubs.DataSource = dsPubs.Tables(0)
    gridPubs.DataBind()

End Sub
```

## Caching with Dependencies

You can also specify that a cache item will expire automatically when another cache item expires or when a file is modified. This logic is referred to as a cache dependency, because your cached item is dependent on another resource, and is only valid while that resource remains unchanged.

To create a cache dependency, you need to create a CacheDependency object, and then use it when adding the dependent cached item. For example, the following code creates a cached item that will automatically be evicted from the cache when an XML file is changed.

```
' Create a dependency for the ProductList.xml file.
Dim ProdDependency As New CacheDependency( _
  Server.MapPath("ProductList.xml"))

' Add a cache item that will be dependent on this file.
Cache.Insert("ProductInfo", ProdInfo, ProdDependency)
```

CacheDependency monitoring begins as soon as the object is created. If the XML file changes before you have added the dependent item to the cache, the item will expire immediately once it is added.

The CacheDependency object provides several different constructors. You've already seen how it can make a dependency based on a file by using the filename constructor. You can also specify a directory that needs to be monitored for changes, or you can use a constructor that accepts an array of strings that represent multiple files and directories.

Yet another constructor accepts an array of filenames and an array of cache keys. The following example uses this constructor to create an item that is dependent on another item in the cache.

```
Cache("Key 1") = "Cache Item 1"

' Make Cache("Key 2") dependent on Cache("Key 1").
Dim DependencyKey(0) As String
DependencyKey(0) = "Key 1"
Dim Dependency As New CacheDependency(Nothing, dependencyKey)

Cache.Insert("Key 2", "Cache Item 2", dependency)
```

Now, when Cache("Key 1") changes or is removed from the cache, Cache("Key 2") will automatically be dropped.

Figure 23-13 shows a simple test page that is included with the online samples for this chapter. It sets up a dependency, modifies the file, and allows you to verify that the cache item has been dropped from the cache.

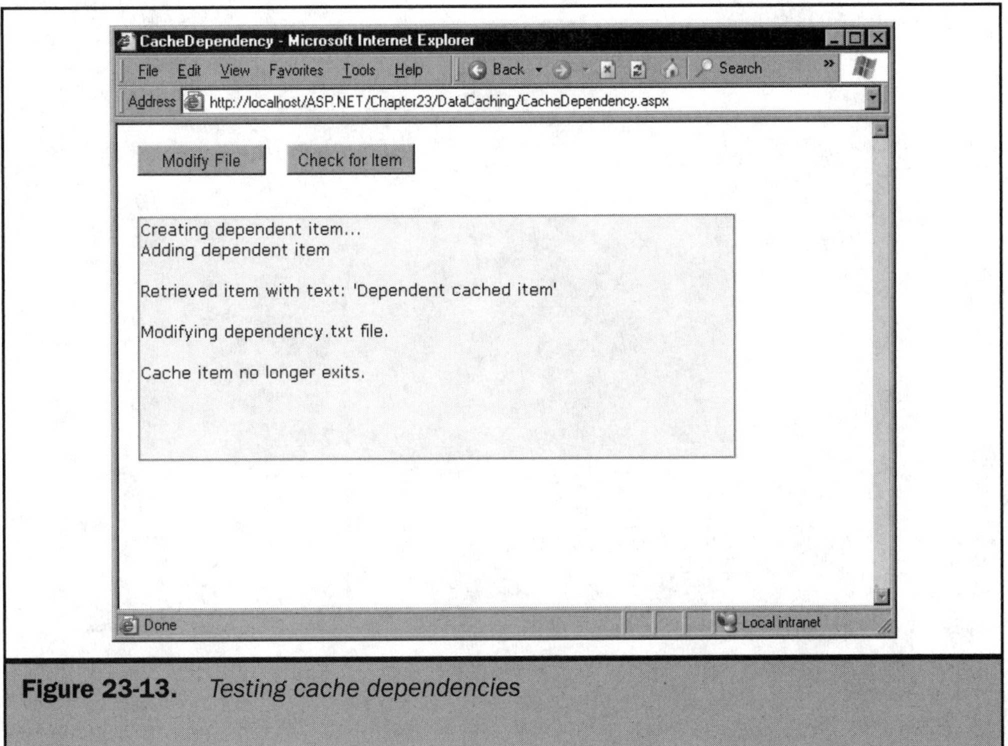


**Figure 23-13.** *Testing cache dependencies*

## Web Service Caching

You can also use caching in a Web Service. You can use data caching in the same way you would use it in a web page, and you can enable output caching on a method-by-method basis to cache the returned value. When a Web Service uses this type of output caching, you do not need to enable any type of cache varying. Responses are only reused for requests with identical parameters.

To enable Web Service output caching, you need to add the CacheDuration value to the WebMethod before the appropriate method declaration. The following example caches a web method's result for 30 seconds.

```
<WebMethod(CacheDuration:=30)> _
```

The Complete Reference

# Chapter 24

## Implementing Security

By default, your ASP.NET applications are available to any user who can access the Internet. While this is ideal for many web applications (and it suits the original spirit of the Internet), it's not always appropriate. For example, an e-commerce site needs to provide a secure shopping experience in order to win customers. A subscription-based site needs to limit content or site access in order to extract a fee. Even a wide-open public site may provide some resources or features (such as an administrative report or configuration page) that shouldn't be available to all users.

ASP.NET provides a multi-layered security model that makes it easy to protect your web applications. While this security is powerful and profoundly flexible, it can appear somewhat confusing, due in large part to the number of different layers where security can be applied. Most of the work in applying security to your application doesn't come from writing code, but from determining the appropriate places to implement your strategy.

In this chapter, we'll sort out the different security subsystems, and consider how you can use Windows, IIS, and ASP.NET services to protect your application. We'll also look at some custom examples that use ASP.NET's new form-based security, which provides a quick and convenient framework for adding user account capabilities.

# Determining Security Requirements

Over the past few years, security has become one of the hottest buzzwords of application design. Media reports constantly emerge about nefarious hackers lifting mailing lists or credit card numbers from e-commerce sites. In most cases, these break-ins are not due to computer wizardry, but to simple carelessness or the lack of a security policy.

The first step in securing your applications is deciding what you need security for. For example, you may need to block access in order to protect private information or just to enforce a subscription policy. Perhaps you don't need any sort of security at all, but you want a login/user account system to provide personalization for frequent visitors. These requirements will determine the approach you use.

Security doesn't need to be complex, but it does often need to be wide-ranging. For example, even if you force users to log in to a part of your site, you still need to make sure that the information is stored in the database under a secure account with a password that couldn't easily be guessed by a user on your local network. You also need to guarantee that your application can't be tricked into sending private information (a possibility if the user modifies a page or a query string to post back different information than you expect).

## Restricted File Types

ASP.NET automatically provides a basic level of security by blocking requests for certain file types (such as configuration and source code files). These file types are identified in the web server's machine.config file in the framework configuration directory (typically C:\WINNT\Microsoft.NET\Framework\[version]\Config), and are assigned to the special HttpForbiddenHandler.

```
<add verb="*" path="*.asax"
     type="System.Web.HttpForbiddenHandler" />
<add verb="*" path="*.ascx"
     type="System.Web.HttpForbiddenHandler" />
<add verb="*" path="*.config"
     type="System.Web.HttpForbiddenHandler" />
<add verb="*" path="*.cs"
     type="System.Web.HttpForbiddenHandler" />
<add verb="*" path="*.csproj"
     type="System.Web.HttpForbiddenHandler" />
<add verb="*" path="*.vb"
     type="System.Web.HttpForbiddenHandler" />
<add verb="*" path="*.vbproj"
     type="System.Web.HttpForbiddenHandler" />
<add verb="*" path="*.webinfo"
     type="System.Web.HttpForbiddenHandler" />
<add verb="*" path="*.asp"
     type="System.Web.HttpForbiddenHandler" />
<add verb="*" path="*.licx"
     type="System.Web.HttpForbiddenHandler" />
<add verb="*" path="*.resx"
     type="System.Web.HttpForbiddenHandler" />
<add verb="*" path="*.resources"
     type="System.Web.HttpForbiddenHandler" />
```

## Security Concepts

There are three concepts that form the basis of any discussion about security:

**Authentication** This the process of determining a user's identity and forcing users to prove they are who they claim.

**Authorization** Once a user is authenticated, authorization is the process of determining if that user has sufficient permissions to perform a given action (such as viewing a page or retrieving information from a database).

**Impersonation** This is the process where certain operations are performed under a different identity. It's sometimes used to refer to the process where anonymous web site users are authenticated under a default IIS_[ServerName] account. In ASP.NET, impersonation also refers to changing the identity the code assumes when executing system operations.

## The ASP.NET Security Model

As you've seen in previous chapters, web requests are fielded first by IIS, which then passes the request on to ASP.NET, if the file type is registered with the ASP.NET service. Figure 24-1 shows this process.

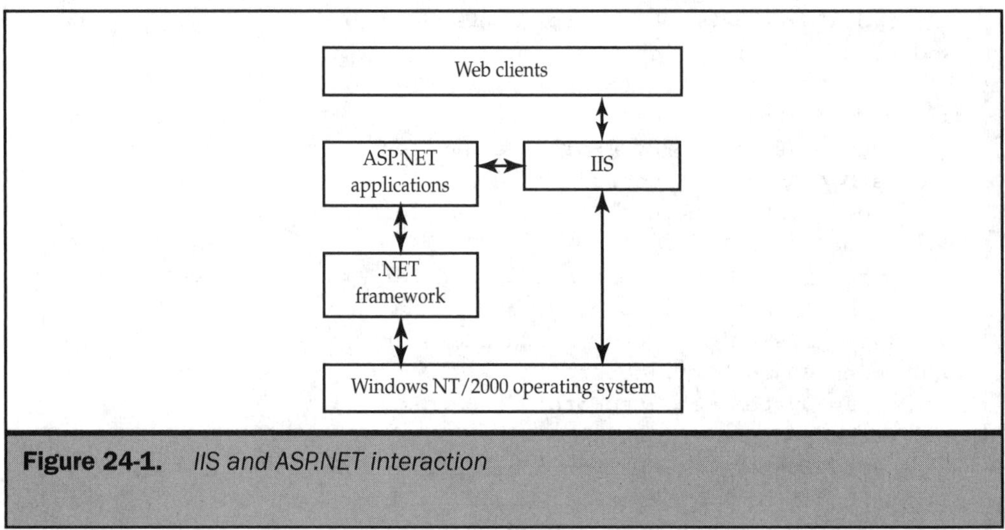


**Figure 24-1.** *IIS and ASP.NET interaction*

Security can be applied at several different places in this chain. First, consider the process for an ordinary (non-ASP.NET) web page request:

1. IIS attempts to authenticate the user. Generally, IIS allows requests from all anonymous users and automatically logs them in under the IUSR_[ServerName] account. IIS security settings are configured on a per-directory basis.
2. If IIS authenticates the user successfully, it attempts to send the user the appropriate HTML file. The operating system performs its own security checks to verify that the authenticated user (typically IUSR_[ServerName] in a public web site) is allowed access to the specified file and directory.

The first and last steps are similar for an ASP.NET request, but there are several additional intermediary layers:

1. IIS attempts to authenticate the user. Generally, IIS allows requests from all anonymous users and automatically logs them in under the IUSR_[ServerName] account.
2. If IIS authenticates the user successfully, it passes the request to ASP.NET with additional information about the authenticated user. ASP.NET can then use its

own security services, depending on the settings in the web.config file and the page that was requested.

3. If ASP.NET authenticates the user, it allows a request to the .aspx page or .asmx Web Service. Then the code itself may run additional custom security checks (for example, manually asking for another password before allowing a specific operation).
4. When the ASP.NET code requests resources (for example, tries to open a file or connect to a database) the operating system performs its own security checks. Usually, the ASP.NET application code runs under a special system account, which allows wide-ranging privileges. However, if you enable impersonation, these system operations will be performed under the account of the authenticated user (or a different account you specify).

The entire process is shown in detail in Figure 24-2.

### ASP.NET Code Runs Under the System Process

One very important and easily missed concept is the fact that the ASP.NET code does *not* run under the IUSR_[ServerName] account, even if you are using anonymous user access. The reason is that the IUSR_[ServerName] account does not have sufficient privileges for ASP.NET code, which needs to be able to create and delete temporary files in order to manage the compilation process. A side effect of this change is that ASP.NET code is no longer "sandboxed" from the web server and operating system. When designing ASP.NET pages, you must keep this fact in mind, and make sure that there is no way your program could be used to make dangerous modifications or delete important files.

Later in this chapter, we'll consider how you can use impersonation to change this behavior. However, the account used for ASP.NET code will always require more access rights than those required for ASP applications.

## Security Strategies

There are a number of different ways that the IIS and ASP.NET security settings can interact, and these combinations often give new ASP.NET developers endless headaches. In reality, there are two central strategies that can be used to add ASP.NET security or personalization to a site:

- Allow anonymous users, but use ASP.NET's Forms authentication model to secure parts of your site. This allows you to create a subscription site or e-commerce store, allows you to manage the login process easily, and lets you write your own login code for authenticating users against a database or simple user account list.

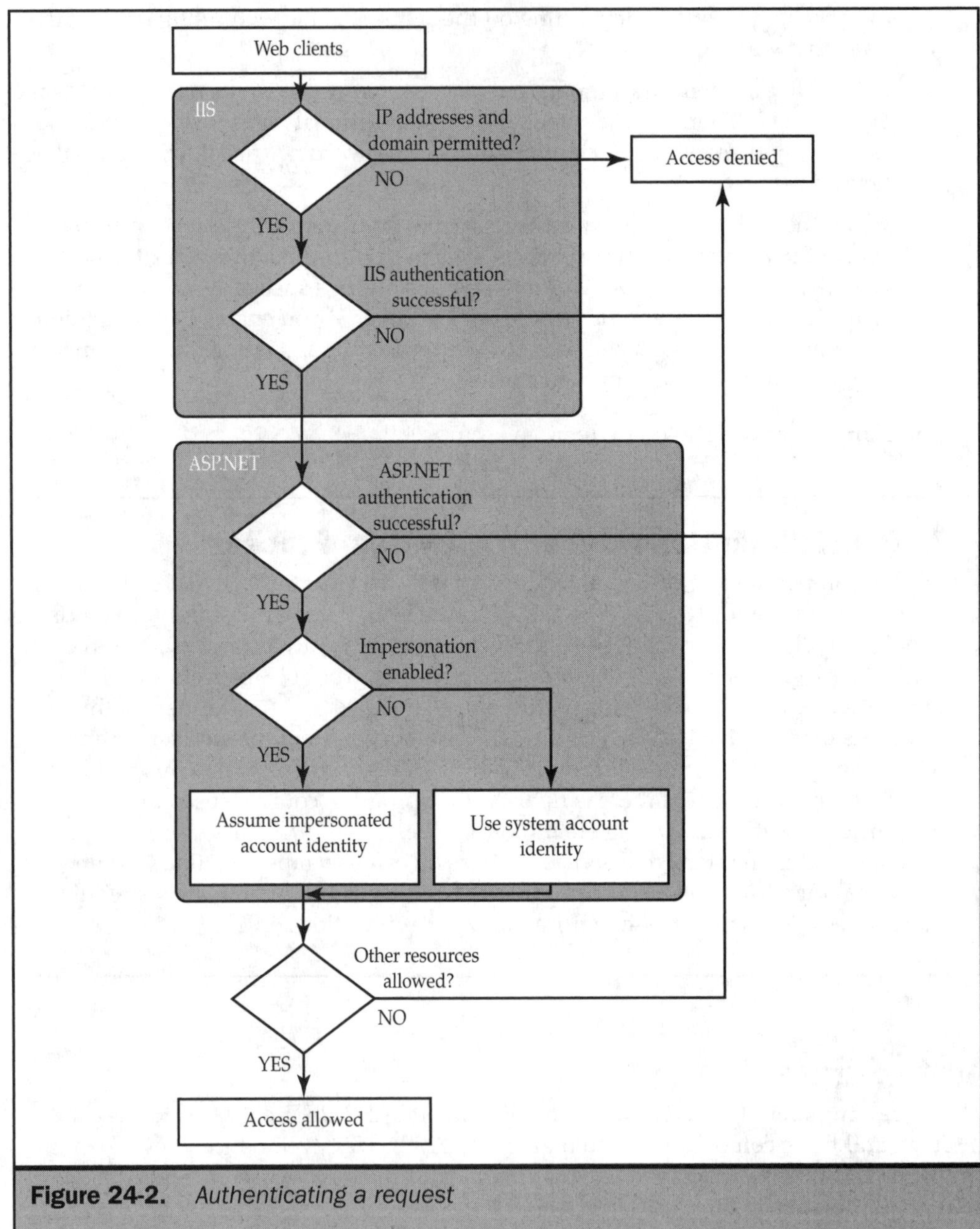


**Figure 24-2.** *Authenticating a request*

- Forbid anonymous users, and use IIS authentication to force every user to log in using Basic, Digest, or Integrated Windows authentication. This system requires that every user has a Windows user account on the server (although users could share accounts). This scenario is poorly suited for a public web application, but often ideal with an Intranet or company-specific site designed to provide resources for a limited set of users.

We'll concentrate on these two approaches in this chapter.

## Certificates

One topic this chapter doesn't treat in detail is user server certificates and SSL connections. These technologies are supported by IIS and are really independent from ASP.NET programming.

Essentially, certificates allow you to demonstrate that your site and your organization information are registered and verified with a certificate authority. This generally encourages customer confidence, although it doesn't guarantee that the company or organization acts responsibly or fairly. To add a certificate to your site, you first need to purchase one from a certificate authority.

IIS Manager allows you to create a certificate request automatically. First, start IIS Manager (select Settings | Control Panel | Administrative Tools | Internet Services Manager from the taskbar). Expand the Web Sites group, and right-click on your web site item (often titled Default Web Site) and choose Properties. Under the Directory Security tab, you'll find a Server Certificate button (see Figure 24-3). Click this button to start a Web Server Certificate Wizard that requests some basic organization information and generates a request file. You'll also need to supply a bit length for the key—the higher the bit length, the stronger the key.

The generated file can be saved as a text file, but it must ultimately be emailed to a certificate authority (along with the required fee). A sample (slightly abbreviated) request file is shown next.

```
Webmaster: administrator@certificatecompany.com
Phone: (555) 555-5555
Server: Microsoft Key Manager for IIS Version 4.0

Common-name: www.yourcompany.com
Organization: YourOrganization

-----BEGIN NEW CERTIFICATE REQUEST-----
MIIB1DCCAT0CAQAwgZMxCzAJBgNVBAYTAlVTMREwDwYDVQQIEwhOZXcgWW9yazEQ
MA4GA1UEBxMHQnVmZmFsbzEeMBwGA1UEChMVVW5pdmVyc2l0eSBhdCBCdWZmYWxv
MRwwGgYDVQQLExNSZXNlYXJjaCBGb3VuZGF0aW9uMSEwHwYDVQQDExh3d3cucmVz
ZWFyY2guYnVmZmFsby5lZHUwgZ8wDQYJKoZIhvcNAQEBBQADgY0AMIGJAoGBALJO
```

ADVANCED ASP.NET

```
hbsCagHN4KMbl7uz0GwvcjJeWH8JqIUFVFi352tnoA15PZfCxW18KNtFeBtrb0pf
-----END NEW CERTIFICATE REQUEST-----
```

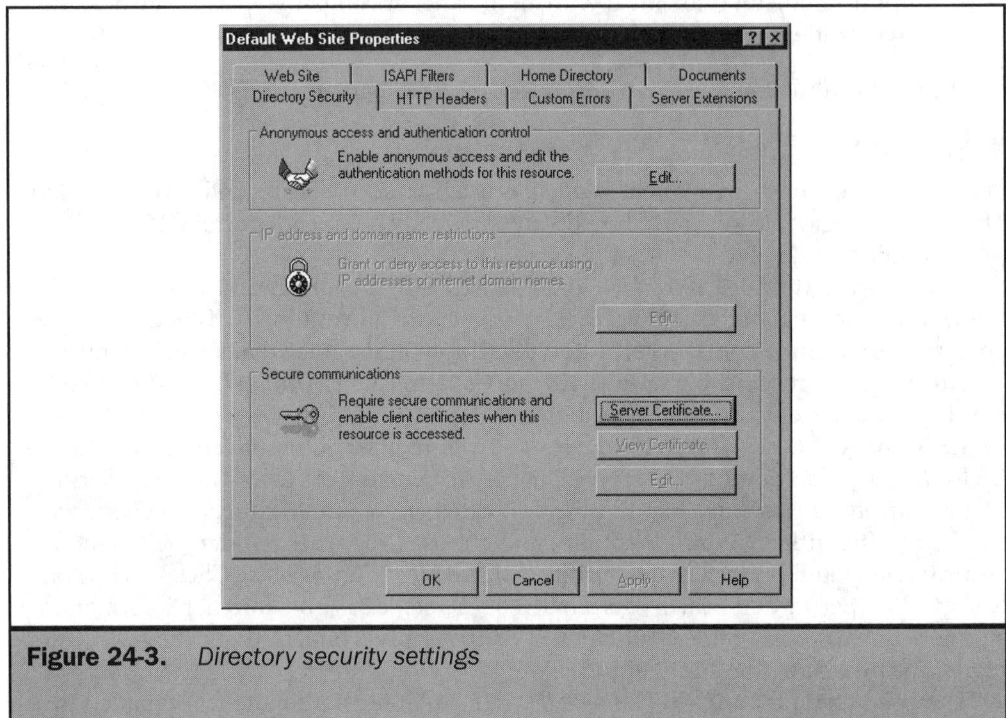


**Figure 24-3.** *Directory security settings*

The certificate authority will return a certificate that you can install according to their instructions.

# SSL

SSL (Secure Sockets Layer) technology is used to encrypt communication between a client and a web site. Although it slows performance, it's often used in a scenario where private or sensitive information needs to be transmitted between an authenticated user and a web application.

To use SSL, you need to have an installed certificate. You can then set IIS directory settings specifying that individual folders require an SSL connection. To access this page over SSL, the client simply types the URL with a preceding https instead of http at the beginning of the request.

In your ASP.NET code, you can check if a user is connecting over a secure connection (see Figure 24-4).

```
Private Sub Page_Load(sender As Object, e As EventArgs) _
  Handles MyBase.Load

    If Request.IsSecureConnection = True Then
        lblStatus.Text = "This page is running under SSL."
    Else
        lblStatus.Text = "This page is not secure."
        lblStatus.Text &= "<br>Please request it with the "
        lblStatus.Text &= "prefix https:// instead of http://"
    End If

End Sub
```

Some browsers still do not support SSL, and some clients may not have the required key installed if you require 128-bit encryption. For those reasons, you should provide an unsecured version of a page for clients that can't connect over SSL.

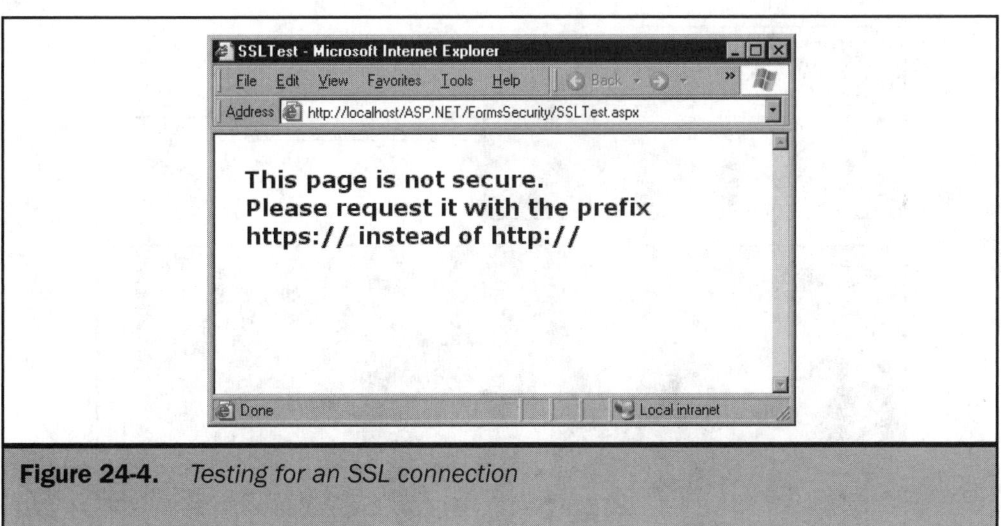


**Figure 24-4.** *Testing for an SSL connection*

## Forms Authentication

In traditional ASP programming, developers usually created their own security systems. A common approach was to add a little snippet of code to the beginning of every secured page, which would then check for the existence of a custom cookie. If the cookie didn't exist, the user would be redirected to a login page, where the cookie would be created after a successful login.

ASP.NET uses the same approach in its Forms authentication model. You are still responsible for writing the code for your login page. However, you no longer have to create or check for the cookie manually, and you don't need to add any code to secured pages. You also benefit from ASP.NET's support for sophisticated hashing and encryption algorithms, which make it all but impossible for users to spoof their own cookies or try other hacking tricks to fool your application into giving them access. Figure 24-5 shows a simplified security diagram that focuses on Forms authentication.

To implement Forms-based security, you need to follow three steps:

- Set the authentication mode in the web.config file.
- Restrict anonymous users from a specific page or directory in your application.
- Create the login page.

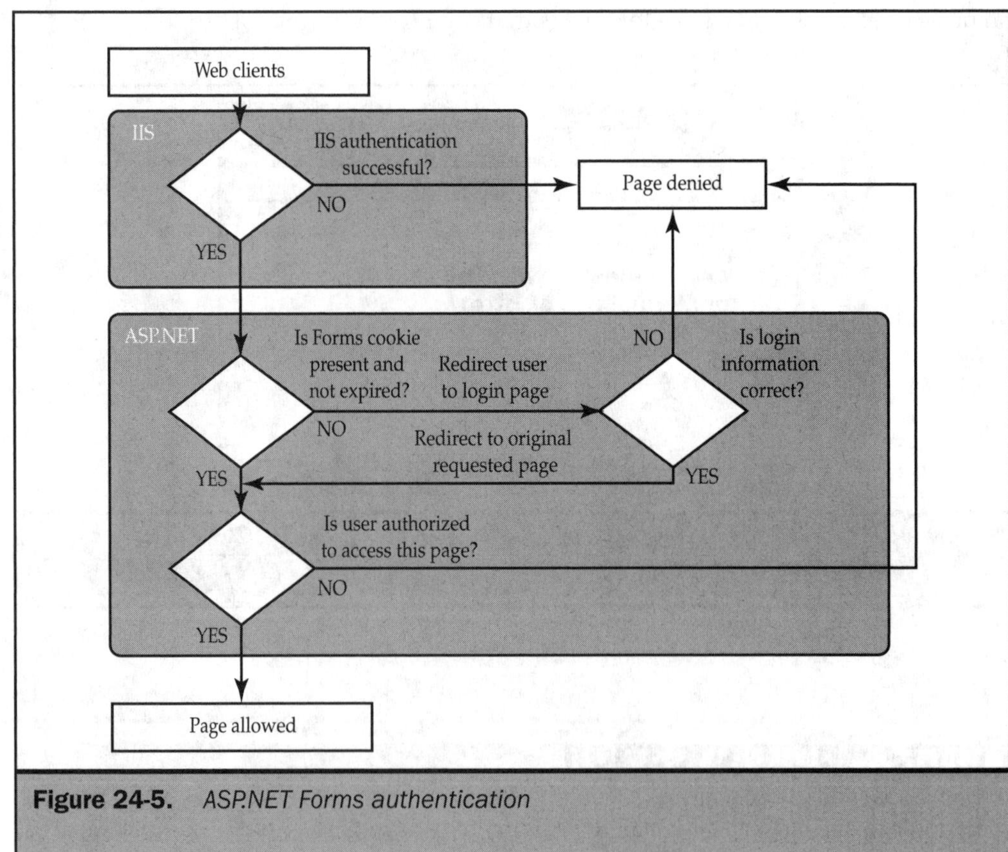


**Figure 24-5.** *ASP.NET Forms authentication*

## Web.config Settings

The type of security used by ASP.NET is defined in the web.config file, through three central configuration sections: <authentication>, <authorization>, and <identity>. For an overview of all of these sections and their settings, you can refer to Chapter 28.

The <authentication> tag defines the ASP.NET authentication mode that will be used to validate the user. In the following listing, the application is configured to use ASP.NET's Forms authentication model. In addition, a <forms> subtag defines some additional settings required for this mode. Namely, it sets the name of the security cookie, the length of time it will be considered valid, and the page that will be used for user login.

```
<configuration>
    <system.web>
        <!-- Other settings omitted. -->
        <authentication mode="Forms">
            <forms name="MyAppCookie"
                   loginUrl="Login.aspx"
                   protection="All"
                   timeout="30" path="/" />
        </authentication>
    </system.web>
</configuration>
```

The settings are described briefly in Table 24-1. They all supply default values and do not need to be set explicitly.

| Attribute Setting | Description |
|---|---|
| Name | The name of the HTTP cookie to use for authentication (defaults to .ASPXAUTH). If multiple applications are running on the same web server, you should give each application's security cookie a unique name. |
| loginUrl | Your custom login page, where the user is redirected if no valid authentication cookie is found. The default value is default.aspx. |

**Table 24-1.** *Form Authentication Settings*

| Attribute Setting | Description |
| --- | --- |
| protection | The type of encryption and validation used for the security cookie (can be All, None, Encryption, or Validation). Validation ensures that the cookie is not changed during transit, and encryption (typically Triple-DES) is used to encode its contents. The default value is All. |
| Timeout | The number of minutes before the cookie expires. ASP.NET will refresh the cookie when it receives a request, as long as half of the cookie's lifetime has expired. The default value is 30. |
| Path | The path for cookies issued by the application. The default value (\) is recommended, because most browsers are case-sensitive and a path case-mismatch could prevent the cookie from being sent with the request. |

**Table 24-1.** *Form Authentication Settings (continued)*

## Authorization Rules

If you make these changes to an application's web.config file and request a page, you'll notice that nothing unusual happens, and the web page is served in the normal way. This is because even though you have enabled Forms authentication for your application, you have not restricted anonymous users.

If you created your project in Visual Studio .NET, you'll find the following access control rule in your web.config file.

```
<configuration>
    <system.web>
        <!-- Other settings omitted. -->
        <authorization>
            <allow users="*" />
        </authorization>
    </system.web>
</configuration>
```

The asterisk (*) is a wildcard character that explicitly permits all users to use the application, even those that have not been authenticated. Even if you delete this line from your application's web.config file, you won't see any change, because the default settings inherited from the machine.config file allow all users. In order to change this behavior, you need to explicitly override the web.config permissions, as shown here.

```
<configuration>
    <system.web>
        <!-- Other settings omitted. -->
        <authorization>
            <deny users="?" />
        </authorization>
    </system.web>
</configuration>
```

The question mark (?) is a wildcard character that includes all anonymous users. By including this rule in your web.config file, you specify that anonymous users are not allowed. Every user must be authenticated, and every user request will require the security cookie. If you request a page in the application directory now, ASP.NET will detect that the request is not authenticated, and attempt to redirect the request to the login page (which will probably cause an error, unless you have already created this file).

Note that you cannot include both rules in the authorization section. For example, the following settings will allow all users.

```
<authorization>
    <allow users="*" />
    <deny users="?" />
</authorization>
```

When evaluating rules, ASP.NET scans through the list from top to bottom, and then continues with the settings in any .config file inherited from a parent directory, ending with the settings in the base machine.config file. As soon as it finds an applicable rule, it stops its search. Thus, in the case above, it will determine that the user <allow users="*"> applies to the current request, and will not evaluate the second line. Reversing the order of these two lines, however, will deny anonymous users (by matching the first rule) and allow all other users (by matching the second rule).

```
<authorization>
    <deny users="?" />
    <allow users="*" />
</authorization>
```

Remember, if the second line is omitted, ASP.NET will search the parent directory, and ultimately match the <allow users="*"> rule in the machine.config file for all non-anonymous users.

## Controlling Access to Specific Directories

A common application design is to place files that require authentication into a separate directory. With ASP.NET configuration files, this approach is easy. Just leave the default <authorization> settings in the normal parent directory, and add a web.config file that specifies stricter settings in the secured directory. This web.config simply needs to deny anonymous users (all other settings and configuration sections can be left out).

```
<configuration>
    <system.web>
        <authorization>
            <deny users="?" />
        </authorization>
    </system.web>
</configuration>
```

### An Application Can Only Use One Authentication Method

You cannot change the <authentication> tag settings in the web.config file of a subdirectory in your application. Instead, all the directories in the application must use the same authentication system. However, each directory can have its own authorization rules.

## Controlling Access to Specific Files

Generally, setting file access permissions by directory is the cleanest and easiest approach. However, you also have the option of restricting specific files by adding <location> tags to your web.config file. This is the technique used in Microsoft's IBuySpy store case study.

The location tags sit outside of the main <system.web> tag and are nested directly in the base <configuration> tag, as shown here.

```
<configuration>
    <system.web>
        <!-- Other settings omitted. -->
        <authorization>
```

```
            <allow users="*" />
        </authorization>
    </system.web>

    <location path="SecuredPage.aspx">
        <system.web>
            <authorization>
                <deny users="?" />
            </authorization>
        </system.web>
    </location>

    <location path="AnotherSecuredPage.aspx">
        <system.web>
            <authorization>
                <deny users="?" />
            </authorization>
        </system.web>
    </location>

</configuration>
```

In this example, all files in the application are allowed, except SecuredPage.aspx and AnotherSecuredPage.aspx, which have an additional access rule denying anonymous users.

## Web Farm Settings

If you are using Forms-based authentication in a web farm, you also need to make sure that each server is using the same machine key. These keys are used to encrypt and decrypt the contents of the security cookie. If they differ from server to server, only the server that creates the cookie will be able to successfully authenticate the user.

The <machineKey> setting is found in the machine.config file. By default, it is generated automatically. Modify this setting by specifying a string of 40–128 hexadecimal characters (the longer the better).

```
<machineKey
validationKey="1234567890123456789012345678901234567890"
 decryptionKey="1234567890123456789012345678901234567890" />
```

## Controlling Access for Specific Users

The <allow> and <deny> rules don't need to use the asterisk or question mark wildcards. Instead, they can specifically identify a user name or a list of comma-separated user names. For example, the following list specifically restricts access from three users. These users will not be able to access the pages in this directory. All other authenticated users will be allowed.

```
<authorization>
    <deny users="matthew,sarah" />
    <deny users="john" />
    <deny users="?" />
</authorization>
```

The following rules explicitly allow two users. All other user requests will be denied access, even if they are authenticated.

```
<authorization>
    <allow users="matthew,sarah" />
    <deny users="*" />
</authorization>
```

# The Login Page

Once you've specified the authentication mode and the authorization rules, you need to build the actual login page, which is an ordinary .aspx page that requests information from the user and decides whether the user should be authenticated.

ASP.NET provides a special FormsAuthentication class in the System.Web.Security namespace, which provides shared methods that help manage the process. The most important methods of this class are described in Table 24-2.

| Method | Description |
|---|---|
| FormsCookieName | A read-only property that provides the name of the Forms authentication cookie. |
| FormsCookiePath | A read-only property that provides the path set for the Forms authentication cookie. |

**Table 24-2.** *Members of the FormsAuthentication Class*

| Method | Description |
|---|---|
| Authenticate() | Checks a user name and password against a list of accounts that can be entered in the web.config file. |
| RedirectFromLoginPage() | Logs the user in to an ASP.NET application by creating the cookie, attaching it to the current response, and redirecting the user to the page that was originally requested. |
| SignOut() | Logs the user out of the ASP.NET application by removing the current encrypted cookie. |
| SetAuthCookie() | Logs the user in to an ASP.NET application by creating and attaching the Forms authentication cookie. Unlike the RedirectFromLoginPage method, it does not forward the user back to the initially requested page. |
| GetRedirectUrl() | Provides the URL of the originally requested page. You could use this with SetAuthCookie() to log a user into an application and make a decision in your code whether to redirect to the requested page or use a more suitable default page. |
| GetAuthCookie() | Creates the authentication cookie but does not attach it to the current response. You can perform additional cookie customization, and then add it manually to the response, as described in Chapter 10. |
| HashPasswordFor-StoringInConfigFile() | Encrypts a string of text using the specified algorithm (SHA1 or MD5). This hashed value provides a secure way to store an encrypted password in a file or database. |

**Table 24-2.** *Members of the FormsAuthentication Class (continued)*

A simple login page can put these methods to work with very little code. Consider the simple Login.aspx page in Figure 24-6.

This page checks if the user has typed in the password "Secret" and then uses the RedirectFromLoginPage method to log the user in.

```
Imports System.Web.Security
```

```
Public Class Login
  Inherits Page

    Protected txtName As TextBox
    Protected txtPassword As TextBox
    Protected lblStatus As Label
    Protected WithEvents cmdLogin As Button

    Private Sub cmdLogin_Click(sender As Object, e As EventArgs) _
      Handles cmdLogin.Click
        If txtPassword.Text.ToLower() = "secret" Then
            FormsAuthentication.RedirectFromLoginPage( _
              txtName.Text, False)
        Else
            lblStatus.Text = "Try again."
        End If
    End Sub

End Class
```

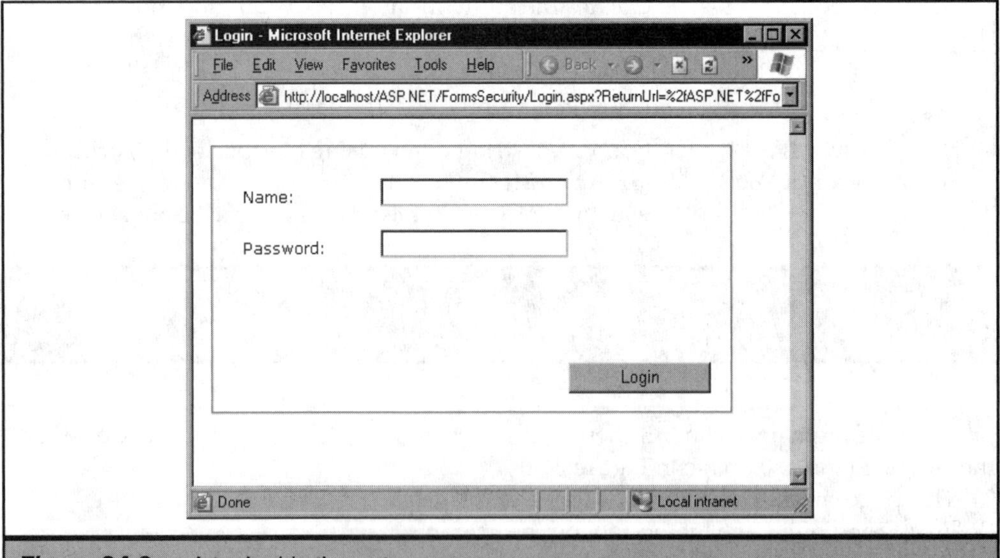


**Figure 24-6.** *A typical login page*

The RedirectFromLoginPage method requires two parameters. The first sets the name of the user. The second is a Boolean variable that creates a persistent Forms authentication cookie when set to True, or an ordinary Forms cookie when set to False. A persistent cookie will be stored on the user's hard drive with an expiration data set to 50 years in the future. This is a convenience that's sometimes useful when you are using the Forms authentication login for personalization instead of security. It's also a security risk because another user could conceivably log in from the same computer, acquiring the cookie and the access to the secured pages. If you want to allow the user to create a persistent cookie, you should make it optional, as the user may want to access your site from a public or shared computer. Generally, sites that use this technique include a checkbox with text such as "Persist Cookie" or "Keep Me Logged In."

```
FormsAuthentication.RedirectFromLoginPage(txtName.Text, _
  chkPersist.Checked)
```

You can test this example with the FormsSecurity sample included with the online code. If you request the SecuredPage.aspx file, you will be redirected to Login.aspx. After entering the correct password, you will return to SecuredPage.aspx, as shown in Figure 24-7. As the user is logged in, the identity can be retrieved through the built-in User object.

```
Private Sub Page_Load(sender As Object, e As EventArgs) _
  Handles MyBase.Load

    lblMessage.Text = "You have reached the secured page, "
    lblMessage.Text &= User.Identity.Name & "."

End Sub
```

Your application should also feature a prominent logout button that destroys the Forms authentication cookie.

```
Private Sub cmdSignOut_Click(sender As Object, e As EventArgs) _
  Handles cmdSignOut.Click

    FormsAuthentication.SignOut()
    Response.Redirect("..\login.aspx")

End Sub
```

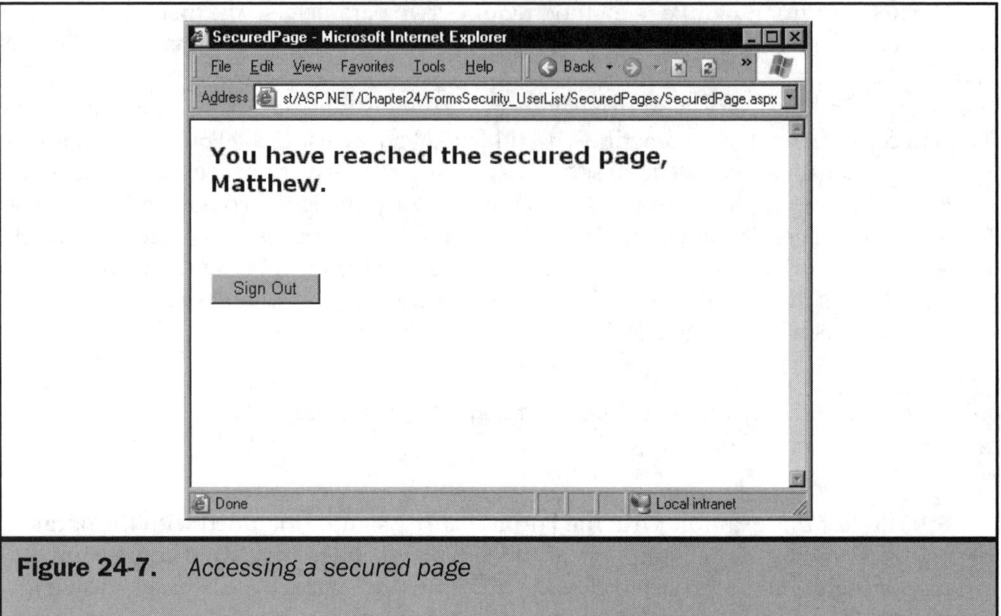


**Figure 24-7.** *Accessing a secured page*

# User Lists

The sample login page uses a password that's hard-coded in the page code. This is an awkward approach that's not suitable for most applications. Typically, the code that responds to the Click event of the Login button would look for a user name and password match in a database table (using trivial ADO.NET data access code).

```
Dim ConnectionString As String = "Provider=SQLOLEDB.1;" & _
  "Data Source=localhost;Initial Catalog=pubs;" & _
  "Integrated Security=SSPI"

Dim SQLSelect As String
SQLSelect = "SELECT Name, Password FROM Users Where Name='"
SQLSelect &= txtUser.Name & "' AND Password='"
SQLSelect &= txtPassword.Text & "'"

' Define the ADO.NET objects.
Dim con As New OleDbConnection(ConnectionString)
Dim cmd As New OleDbCommand(SQLSelect, con)
Dim reader As OleDbDataReader

' Try to open database and read information.
```

```
Try
    con.Open()
    reader = cmd.ExecuteReader()
    reader.Read()

    ' Verify the returned row for a case-sensitive match.
    If txtPassword.Text = reader("Password") Then
        FormsAuthentication.RedirectFromLoginPage( _
          txtName.Text, False)
    Else
        lblStatus.Text = "No match."
    End If
    reader.Close()

Catch err As Exception
    lblStatus.Text = "No match."
Finally
    If (Not con Is Nothing) Then
        con.Close()
    End If
End Try
```

Other approaches are possible. For example, you could use the file or XML access techniques described in Chapters 16 and 17. You could even cache user login information in memory.

ASP.NET also provides a quick and convenient method for storing user account information directly in the web.config file. The disadvantage of this system is that you can't store additional user information (such as a credit card number or shipping address). An advantage is the fact that you can use the Authenticate method of the FormsAuthentication password to check the supplied user information against the list, without needing to write your own file or database access code. To add a user account, insert a <credentials> subtag to the <forms> tag, and add as many <user> subtags as you need inside the <credentials> tag.

The following example defines two valid users.

```
<configuration>
    <system.web>
        <!-- Other settings omitted. -->
        <authentication mode="Forms">
            <forms name="MyAppCookie"
                   loginUrl="Login.aspx"
                   protection="All"
                   timeout="30" path="/" >
```

```
                <credentials passwordFormat="Clear" >
                    <user name="matthew" password="secret" />
                    <user name="sarah" password="opensesame" />
                </credentials>
            </forms>
        </authentication>
    </system.web>
</configuration>
```

Now the login page can use the FormsAuthentication.Authenticate method, which accepts a user name and password, and returns true if a match can be found in the web.config user list. Note that the password is case-sensitive, but the user name is not.

```
If FormsAuthentication.Authenticate(txtName.Text, _
  txtPassword.Text) Then
    FormsAuthentication.RedirectFromLoginPage(txtName.Text, False)
Else
    lblStatus.Text = "Try again."
End If
```

## Protecting User Passwords with Encryption

In the previous user list example, passwords were stored in a clear format that's visible to anyone who reads the web.config file. This isn't necessarily a serious security risk—remember, web requests for .config files are automatically rejected—but it does expose a potential vulnerability, especially if the server is accessible over a local network. To remedy this problem, you can replace the password in the web.config file with a special hash value. The hashed value is not human-readable, and cannot be converted back into the original password by ordinary means. When the user submits login information and you call the Authenticate method, ASP.NET will hash the password and compare it to the hashed value stored in the web.config file.

To add the hashed password to the web.config file, you need to create a simple utility page that can encrypt a text string for you. This is trivially easy, thanks to the Hash-PaswordForStoringInConfigFile method, which is provided by the FormsAuthentication class we have been examining. The page in Figure 24-8 shows an example that encodes the supplied text and places it in another text box so it can be easily copied to the clipboard. Both SHA1 and MD5 algorithm are supported.

```
Private Sub cmdHash_Click(sender As Object, e As EventArgs) _
  Handles cmdHash.Click

    Dim Algorithm As String
```

```
    If optSHA1.Checked = True Then
        Algorithm = "SHA1"
    Else
        Algorithm = "MD5"
    End If

    txtHash.Text = _
      FormsAuthentication.HashPasswordForStoringInConfigFile(_
      txtPassword.Text, Algorithm)

End Sub
```

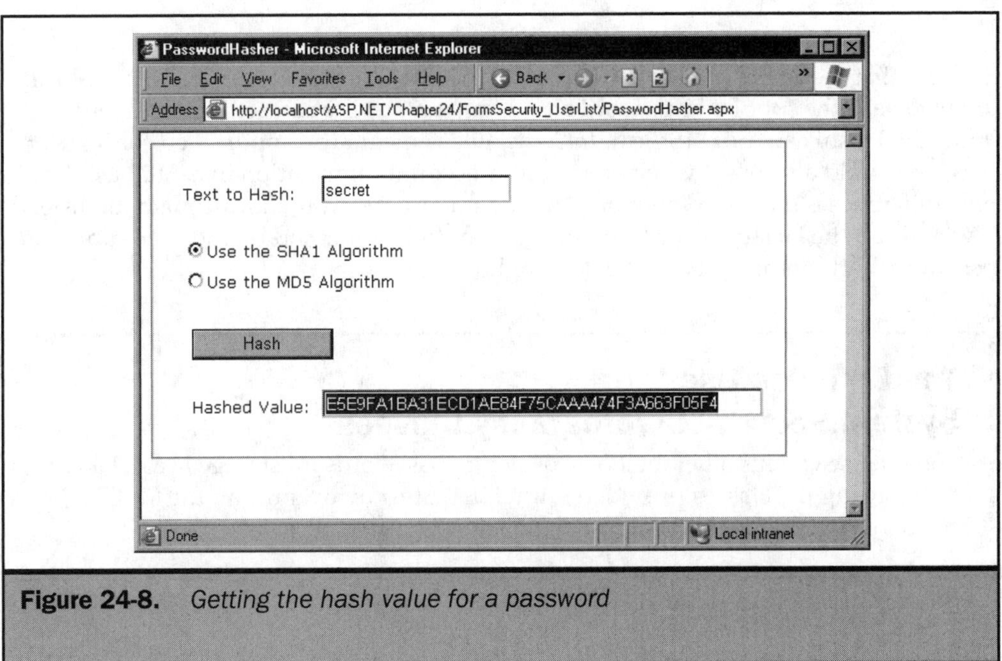


**Figure 24-8.** *Getting the hash value for a password*



You can now update the web.config file with the hashed values by modifying the passwordFormat attribute of the <credentials> tag.

```
<configuration>
    <system.web>
        <!-- Other settings omitted. -->
```

```
        <authentication mode="Forms">
        <forms name="MyAppCookie"
          loginUrl="Login.aspx"
          protection="All"
          timeout="30" path="/" >
            <credentials passwordFormat="SHA1" >
            <user name="matthew"
             password="E5E9FA1BA31ECD1AE84F75CAAA474F3A663F05F4" />
            <user name="sarah"
             password="17618F01A3A21B911C925BCB525A1D21ABD30673" />
            </credentials>
        </forms>
        </authentication>
    </system.web>
</configuration>
```

Note that the actual code in the Login page does not need to change. ASP.NET will know to hash the supplied password based on your application settings. Incidentally, while the HashPaswordForStoringInConfigFile is meant to support web.config user lists, you could also use it when storing user account information in a database. The only difference is that your login page would not use the Authenticate method. Instead, it would call the HashPaswordForStoringInConfigFile method on the user-supplied password, and compare that to the field in the database.

### You Can Also Use the System.Security.Cryptography Classes

You can use various other methods to encrypt passwords for storage in a database or file using the classes provided with .NET. Start by examining the MSDN reference for the System.Security.Cryptography namespace.

## Custom Roles

The authentication strategy we have examined so far provides an all-or-nothing approach that either forbids or allows a user. In many cases, however, an application needs to recognize different levels of users. Some users will be provided with a limited set of capabilities, while other users might be allowed to perform potentially dangerous changes or use the administrative portions of a web site.

To allow this type of multi-tiered access, your code needs to examine the current user identity, and use that information to forbid or allow specific actions. By default, the generic User.Identity object doesn't provide much that can help. Its properties are listed in Table 24-3.

| Property | Description |
|---|---|
| Name | The name of the signed-on user (technically, the user name of the account). |
| IsAuthenticated | True if the user has been authenticated. You could check this property and decide programmatically whether you need to redirect the user to the login page. Note that if the user is not logged in, the other properties (such as Name) will be empty. |
| AuthenticationType | A string that represents the type of authentication that was used (such as Forms or Basic). |

**Table 24-3.** *Identity Properties*

The User object also provides a method called IsInRole which is designed to let you evaluate whether a user is a member of a group. For example, a user who is a member of an Administrators group can be given more access rights.

```
Private Sub Page_Load(sender As Object, e As EventArgs) _
  Handles MyBase.Load

    If User.IsInRole("Administrators")
        ' Do nothing, the page should be accessed as normal because
        ' the user has administrator privileges.
    Else
        ' Don't allow this page. Instead, redirect to the home page.
        Response.Redirect("default.aspx")
    End If

End Sub
```

Unfortunately, with Forms authentication there is no way to associate a user account with a role declaratively in the web.config file. However, you can react to the Application_Authenticate event in the global.asax file (which fires when the user logs in) and assign roles to the current user. The process works like this:

- Check if the user is authenticated. The Application_Authenticate event happens several times during request processing. If the user is not yet authenticated, you can't take any action.
- If the user is authenticated, decide programmatically what role the user should have. For example, you might look up the user's name in a database or XML file, and retrieve a list of roles. In our simple example, the logic is hard-coded in the routine.
- Create a new identity using the GenericPrincipal class. You do this by supplying the current (authenticated) identity and adding the appropriate roles as an array of strings.
- Assign the new identity to the user.

The following global.asax code shows this process in action. In order to use it as written, you must have imported the System.Security.Principal namespace.

```
Sub Application_AuthenticateRequest(sender As Object, _
  e As EventArgs)
    If Request.IsAuthenticated Then

        ' Check who the user is.
        If User.Identity.Name.ToLower() = "matthew" Then

            ' Create an array with the names of the appropriate
            ' roles. In our simple example, matthew is an
            ' Administrator and User.
            ' Typically, this information would be retrieved from
            ' another source (like a database).
            Dim Roles() As String = {"Administrator", "User"}

            ' Assign the new identity.
            ' It's the old identity, with the roles added.
            Context.User = New _
              GenericPrincipal(User.Identity, Roles)
        End If

    End If
End Sub
```

One detail is extremely important in this example. To retrieve the identity, you can use the User property of the Application class (as this example does), or you can use the Context.User property, which is equivalent. However, when assigning the new identity, you need to use the Context.User property. That's because the User property of the Application class is always read-only.

Once you've assigned a role, you can test for it in another page with the User.IsInRole method (see Figure 24-9).

```
Private Sub Page_Load(sender As Object, e As EventArgs) _
  Handles MyBase.Load

    lblMessage.Text = "You have reached the secured page, "
    lblMessage.Text &= User.Identity.Name & "."
    If User.IsInRole("Administrator") Then
        lblMessage.Text &= "<br><br>Congratulations:"
        lblMessage.Text &= "you are an administrator."
    End If

End Sub
```

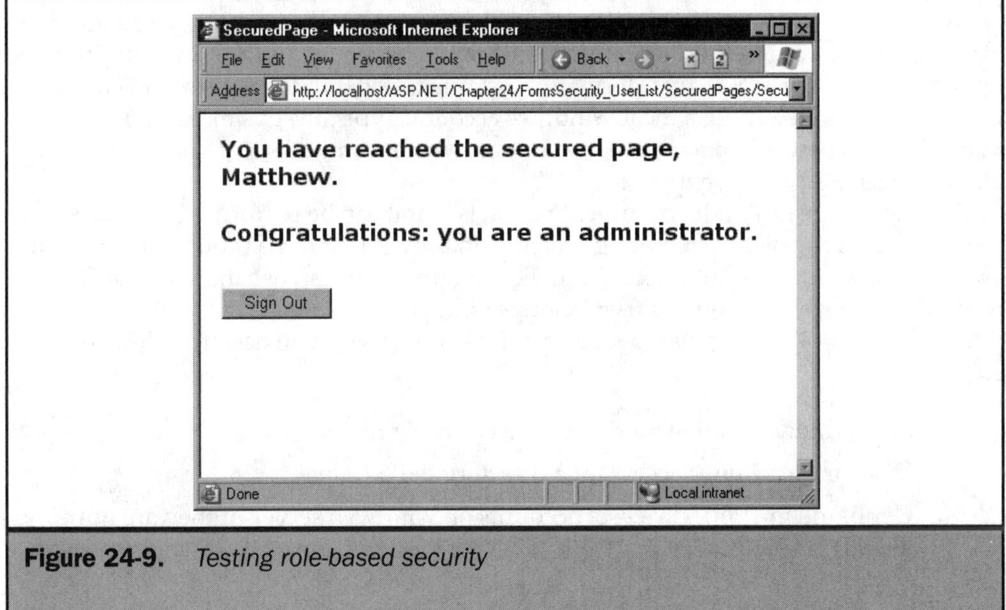


**Figure 24-9.** *Testing role-based security*

### Passport Authentication Is Another Option

This chapter doesn't cover ASP.NET's Passport authentication, which allows you to authenticate a user using Microsoft's Passport service, which is a part of the My Services initiative. Passport is currently in late beta and scheduled for a yearly user fee based on unique web site visitors. Some reference information about enabling the Passport settings is provided in Chapter 28.

Most sites will not need to use Passport authentication. Its main benefit is that it provides a far richer set of user information, which can be drawn from Microsoft's Passport database (the same technology that powers the free Hotmail email site).

## Windows Authentication

With Windows authentication, you rely on ASP.NET to perform the required authentication for you. ASP.NET simply uses the authenticated IIS user. If your web site uses the default settings, this means the user will be authenticated under the anonymous IUSER_[ServerName] account.

When people refer to Windows authentication for a web site, what they usually mean is using IIS to force users to log in before allowing access. There are several different options for how the user login information is transmitted, but the end result is that the user is authenticated using a local Windows account. Typically, this makes Windows authentication best suited to intranet scenarios, where a limited set of known users are already registered on a network server.

The advantage of Windows authentication is that it can be performed transparently (depending on the client's operating system and browser) and that your ASP.NET code can examine all the account information. For example, you can use the User.IsInRole method to check what groups a user belongs to.

To implement Windows-based security with known users, you need to follow three steps:

1. Set the authentication mode in the web.config file.
2. Disable anonymous access for a directory in IIS Manager.
3. Configure the Windows user accounts on your web server (if they are not already present).

### IIS Settings

To disable anonymous access, start IIS Manager (select Settings | Control Panel | Administrative Tools | Internet Services Manager). Then right-click on a virtual directory or a subdirectory inside a virtual directory, and choose Properties. Select the Directory Security tab (see Figure 24-10).

Click the Edit button to modify the directory security settings (see Figure 24-11). In the bottom half of the window, you can enable one of the Windows authentication methods. However, none of these methods will be used unless you explicitly clear the Anonymous access checkbox. The different authentication methods are described in Table 24-4. When users request a page from a Windows authenticated virtual directory, the browser may send a hash of their user information automatically or display a generic login box. It depends on the client's browser and operating system, and the chosen authentication method.

You can enable more than one authentication method, in which case the client will use the method it supports. If anonymous access is enabled, it's always used.

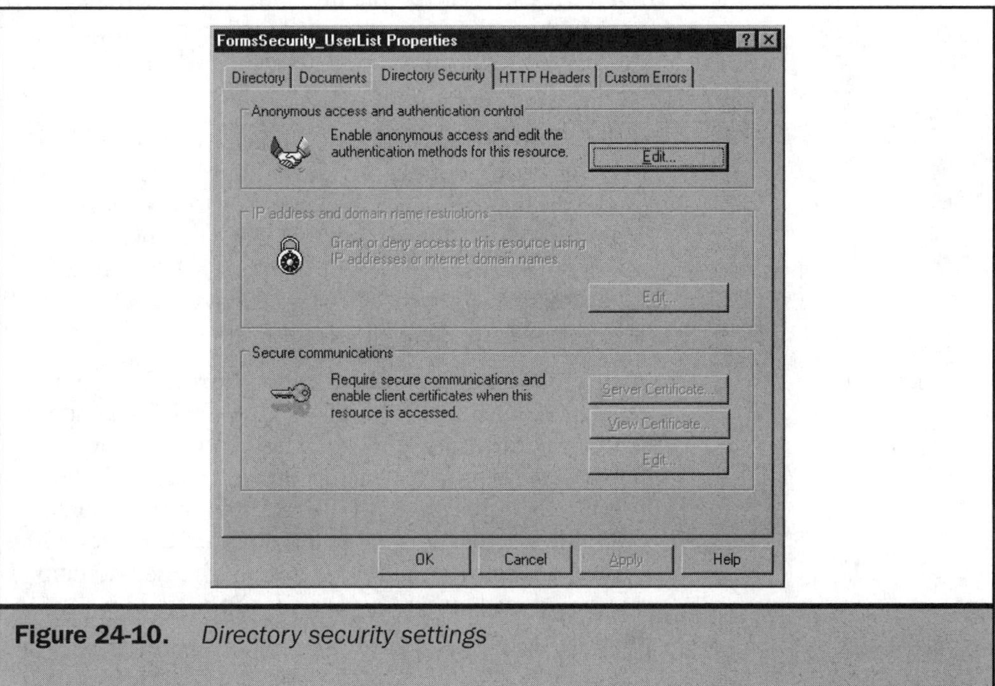


**Figure 24-10.** *Directory security settings*

| Mode | Description |
|---|---|
| Anonymous | Anonymous authentication is technically not a true authentication method, because the client is not required to submit any information. Instead, users are given free access to the web site under a special user account, IUSR_[ServerName]. Anonymous authentication is the default. |

**Table 24-4.** *Windows Authentication Methods*

| Mode | Description |
| --- | --- |
| Basic | Basic authentication is a part of the HTTP 1.0 standard, and it is supported by almost all browsers and web servers. When using basic authentication, the browser presents the user with a login box with a user name and password field. This information is then transmitted to IIS, where it is matched with a local Windows user account. The disadvantage of Basic authentication is that it uses an insecure method of transmission that essentially makes the password visible over the Internet (unless you combine it with SSL technology). |
| Digest | Digest authentication remedies the primary weakness of Basic authentication: sending passwords in plain text. Digest authentication sends a digest (also known as a hash) instead of a password over the network. The primary disadvantage is that Digest authentication is only supported by Internet Explorer 5.0 and later. Your web server also needs to use Active Directory or have access to an Active Directory server. |
| Integrated | Integrated Windows authentication (formerly known as NTLM authentication and Windows NT Challenge/Response authentication) is the best choice for most intranet scenarios. When using Integrated authentication, Internet Explorer can send the required information automatically, using the currently logged-in Windows account on the client, provided it is on a trusted domain. Integrated authentication is only supported on Internet Explorer 2.0 and later. |

**Table 24-4.** *Windows Authentication Methods (continued)*

## Web.config Settings

Once you've enabled the appropriate virtual directory security settings, you should make sure that your application is configured to use Windows authentication. In a Visual Studio .NET project, this is the default.

```
<configuration>
    <system.web>
        <!-- Other settings omitted. -->
        <authentication mode="Windows" />
    </system.web>
</configuration>
```

Next, you can add <allow> and <deny> elements to specifically allow or restrict users from specific files or directories. You can also restrict certain types of users, provided their accounts are members of the same Windows group, by using the roles attribute.

```
<authorization>
    <deny users="matthew" />
    <allow roles="Administrator,SuperUser" />
</authorization>
```

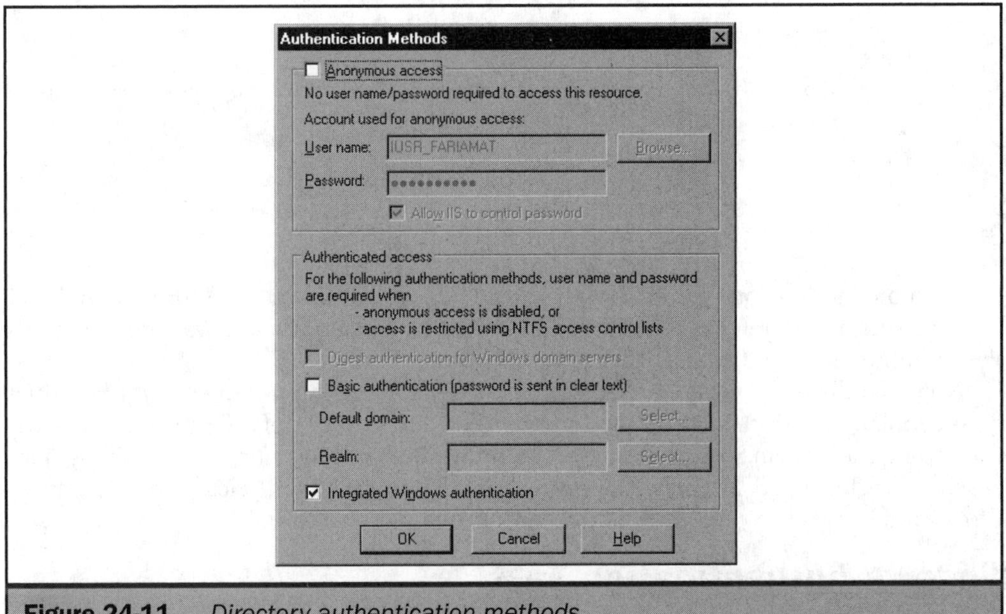


**Figure 24-11.** *Directory authentication methods*

In this example, all users who are members of the Administrator or SuperUser group will be automatically authorized to access ASP.NET pages in this directory. Requests from the user named "matthew" will be denied, even if he is a member of the Administrator or SuperUser group. Remember, ASP.NET examines rules in the order they appear, and stops when it finds a match. Reversing the two lines above would ensure that the user "matthew" is denied only if he is *not* a member of the Administrator or SuperUser group.

If the user accounts are located in a different domain, you should follow the more explicit syntax shown here, which precedes the user name with the name of the domain or server.

```
<allow users="MyDomainName\matthew" />
```

You can also examine a user's group membership programmatically in your code.

```
Private Sub Page_Load(sender As Object, e As EventArgs) _
  Handles MyBase.Load

    If User.IsInRole("MyDomainName\Administrators")
        ' Do nothing, the page should be accessed as normal because
        ' the user has administrator privileges.
    Else
        ' Don't allow this page. Instead, redirect to the home page.
        Response.Redirect("default.aspx")
    End If

End Sub
```

For more information about the <allow> and <deny> rules, and configuring individual files and directories, refer to the discussion under the *Authorization Rules* section in the Forms authentication section earlier in this chapter.

Note that there is no way to retrieve a list of available groups on the web server (that would violate security), but you can find out the names of the default built-in Windows roles using the System.Security.Principal.WindowsBuiltInRole enumeration. These roles are shown in Table 24-5. Not all will apply to ASP.NET use, although at least Administrator, Guest, and User will.

## A Windows Authentication Test

One of the nice things about Windows authentication is that no login page is required. Once you enable it in IIS, your web application can retrieve information directly from the User object. You can access some additional information by converting the generic Identity object to a WindowsIdentity object (which is contained in the System.Security.-Principal namespace). The following is a sample test page, shown in Figure 24-12.

```
Imports System.Security.Principal
Imports System.Web.Security

Public Class SecuredPage
  Inherits Page

    Protected lblMessage As Label
```

| Role | Description |
|---|---|
| AccountOperator | Users with the special responsibility of managing the user accounts on a computer or domain. |
| Administrator | Users with complete and unrestricted access to the computer or domain. |
| BackupOperator | Users who can override certain security restrictions only as part of backing up or restore operations. |
| Guest | Like the User role, but even more restrictive. |
| PowerUser | Similar to Administrator, but with some restrictions. |
| PrintOperator | Like a User, but with additional privileges for taking control of a printer. |
| Replicator | Like a User, but with additional privileges to support file replication in a domain. |
| SystemOperator | Similar to Administrator, with some restrictions. Generally, system operators manage a computer. |
| User | Users are prevented from making system-wide changes, and can only run "certified" applications. |

**Table 24-5.** *Default Windows Roles*

```
    Private Sub Page_Load(sender As Object, e As EventArgs) _
      Handles MyBase.Load
        lblMessage.Text = "You have reached the secured page, "
        lblMessage.Text &= User.Identity.Name & "."

        Dim WinIdentity As WindowsIdentity
        WinIdentity = CType(User.Identity, WindowsIdentity)
        lblMessage.Text &= "<br><br>Authentication Type: "
        lblMessage.Text &= WinIdentity.AuthenticationType
        lblMessage.Text &= "<br>Anonymous: "
        lblMessage.Text &= WinIdentity.IsAnonymous
        lblMessage.Text &= "<br>Authenticated: "
        lblMessage.Text &= WinIdentity.IsAuthenticated
        lblMessage.Text &= "<br>Guest: " & WinIdentity.IsGuest
        lblMessage.Text &= "<br>System: " & WinIdentity.IsSystem
    End Sub

End Class
```

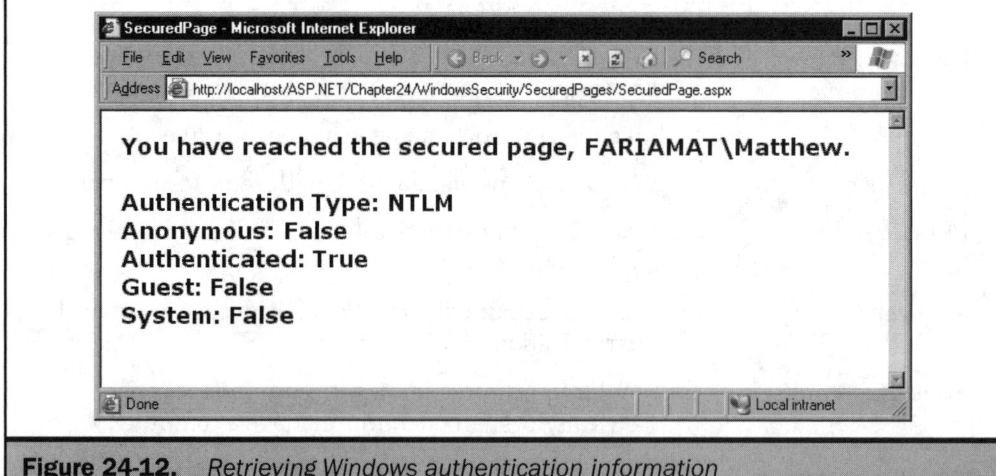


**Figure 24-12.** *Retrieving Windows authentication information*

## Impersonation

Impersonation is an additional option that's available in Windows or Forms authentication, although it's most common with Windows users in an intranet scenario. In order for impersonation to work, the authenticated user account must correspond to a Windows account, which is not guaranteed (or even likely) with Forms authentication.

With impersonation, your ASP.NET code interacts with the system under the identity of the authenticated user—not the normal system account. This technique is usually chosen when you don't want to worry about authorization details in your code.

For example, if you have a simple application that displays XML files, you can set specific permissions for each XML file, restricting them from some users and allowing them to others. Unfortunately, your ASP.NET XML viewer utility always executes under the local system account, which has authority to view all these files. Thus, any authenticated user can view any file. To remedy this situation, you can specifically add additional user verification checks in your code, and refuse to open files that aren't allowed. However, this will typically result in a lot of extra code. If impersonation is enabled, your ASP.NET code will be prevented from accessing an XML file the current user is not allowed to view. This will likely lead to an error—so the ASP.NET application will have to use exception handling to deal with the situation gracefully.

The web.config file uses an <identity> tag to enable impersonation.

```
<configuration>
    <system.web>
        <!-- Other settings omitted. -->
        <identity impersonate="true" >
    </system.web>
</configuration>
```

Keep in mind that the user account will require read/write access to the Temporary ASP.NET Files directory where the compiled ASP.NET files are stored, or the user will not be able to access any pages. This directory is located under the path C:\WINNT\Microsoft.NET\Framework\[version]\Temporay ASP.NET Files.

ASP.NET also provides the option to specifically set an account that will be used for running code. This technique is less common, although it can be useful if you want different ASP.NET applications to execute with different, but fixed, permissions. In this case, the user's authenticated identity is not used by the ASP.NET code.

```
<configuration>
    <system.web>
        <!-- Other settings omitted. -->
        <identity impersonate="true" userName="matthew"
                  password="secret" >
    </system.web>
</configuration>
```

Unfortunately, the password for the impersonated account cannot be encrypted in the web.config file, which can constitute a security risk if local users have access to the computer.

## Programmatic Impersonation

Sometimes it's more useful to use impersonation programmatically through the WindowsIdentity.Impersonate method. This allows you to execute some code in the identity of a specific user (like your file access routine), but allows the rest of your code to run under the local system account, guaranteeing that it won't encounter any problems.

In order to accomplish this, you need to use Windows authentication, but disable impersonation in the ASP.NET file. That means the Windows identity object will be available for you to use when you need it. The following code shows how your code can use the Impersonate method to switch identities:

```
If User.GetType() Is WindowsPrincipal
    Dim ID As WindowsIdentity
    ID = CType(User.Identity, WindowsIdentity)
    Dim ImpersonateContext As WindowsImpersonationContext

    ImpersonateContext = ID.Impersonate()
    ' (Now perform tasks under the impersonated ID.)

    ' Revert to the original.
    ImpersonateContext.Undo()
Else
    ' User is not Windows authenticated.
    ' Throw an error to or take other steps.
End If
```

# Chapter 25

## The IBuySpy Case Studies

Over the last 24 chapters, you've learned about the individual features, technologies, and design patterns that you can use in a professional ASP.NET application. The next step is to start combining these ingredients in your own creations.

Making the transition from simple sites to multi-tier web applications is not always easy. Building a successful ASP.NET application requires knowledge, planning, and the occasional painful experience. Fortunately, Microsoft provides some invaluable help with the IBuySpy case studies, a pair of full-featured web applications that demonstrate best practices for an e-commerce storefront and a web portal. The IBuySpy case studies generated a great deal of excitement when they first appeared in the early beta days of ASP.NET, but have since been overshadowed by the foggy cloud of .NET hype. They don't ship with Visual Studio .NET or the .NET framework, aren't mentioned in the online help, and aren't heavily promoted on Microsoft's MSDN site. In fact, the IBuySpy case studies are poised to become one of ASP.NET's best-kept secrets.

In this chapter, you'll learn everything you need to know to install, configure, and find your way around the IBuySpy case studies. You'll learn how the applications are structured, what tricks they use, and where the techniques you've learned—such as data binding, component-based development, forms security, and user controls—are put to use. Even experienced developers are sure to find a few new insights in the IBuySpy code. Best of all, Microsoft encourages developers to reuse the logic and code from the IBuySpy applications in their own solutions.

### IBuySpy Uses Components and Tiers

Before reading this chapter, make sure you've read Chapter 21, which explains how a large-scale application can be divided into layers with separate functions. The IBuySpy case studies make good use of components and layered design. It's also a good idea to be familiar with Chapter 22, as custom user controls are used extensively.

## Installing the IBuySpy Applications

The IBuySpy samples aren't included on the Visual Studio .NET setup CDs. You need to visit the http://www.ibuyspy.com/ web site (shown in Figure 25-1). On the left are links that allow you to run one of the IBuySpy applications from the Internet, or download a setup program that lets you install it on your local computer.

The best way to work with the case studies is to install them locally, where you can tweak the code and use debugging tools to study how it works. To install the IBuySpy case studies, click the Download Now link, which brings you to a download page with additional options (see Figure 25-2).

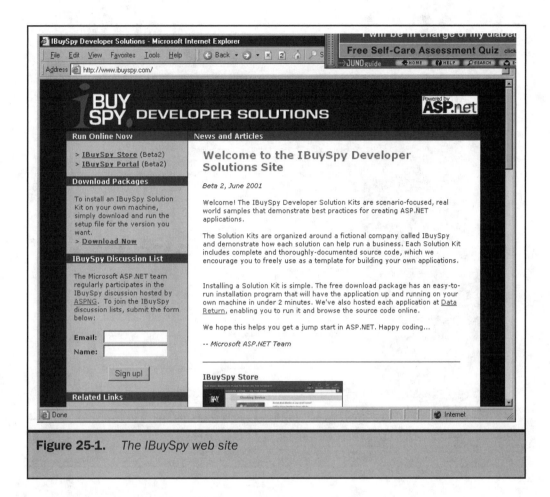

**Figure 25-1.** *The IBuySpy web site*

There are currently two IBuySpy case studies, although a third is planned for the near future. Both IBuySpy case studies use common ASP.NET features such as ADO.NET data access, server controls, caching, and user controls.

- **The IBuySpy store** provides a full-featured three-tier e-commerce site. It incorporates a shopping basket, customer account information and login, high-performance data caching, and transactions. There are even Web Services for order entry and status retrieval.
- **The IBuySpy portal** provides a configurable web portal for an intranet or the Internet that's built out of custom user controls. By default, it's designed as an employee portal for the fictitious IBuySpy company, but you can easily replace the content to create your own custom portal. Best of all, it includes ASP.NET administration pages that allow you to customize its content and behavior without altering a line of code.

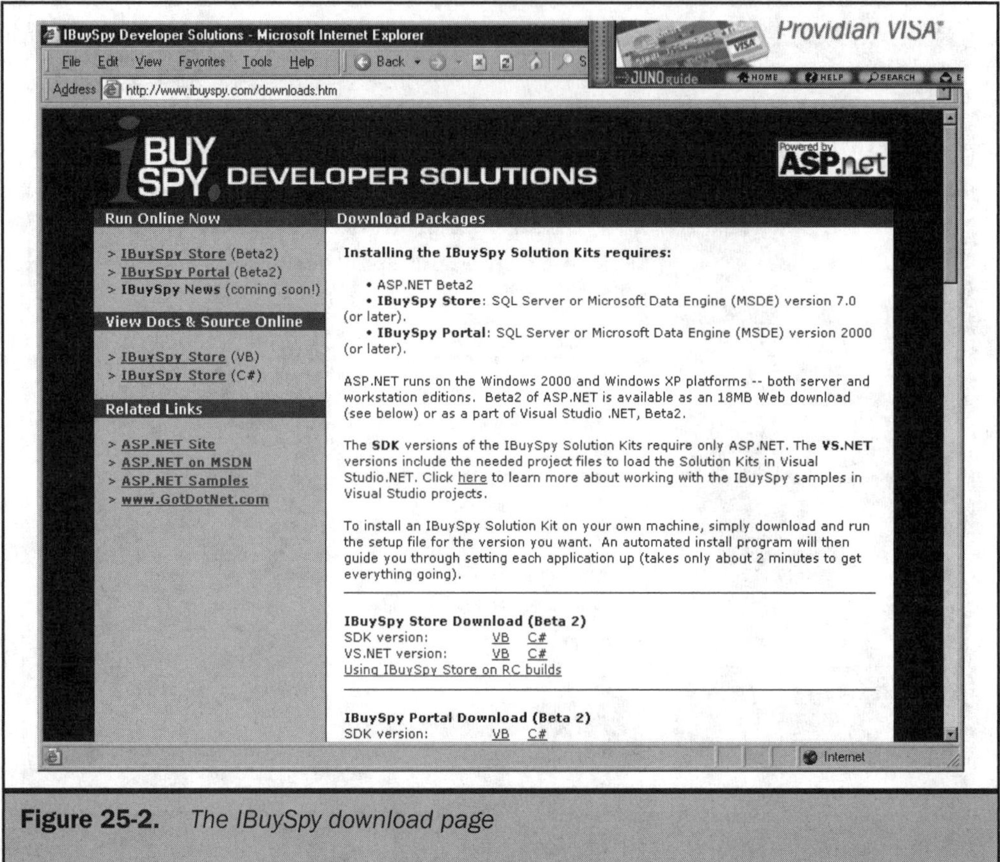


**Figure 25-2.** *The IBuySpy download page*

From the download page you can choose to install the VB or C# versions of an IBuySpy application. Once you've determined your language choice, you have two additional options. You can install what's referred to as the SDK version or the Visual Studio .NET version. The SDK version uses .aspx files with script blocks. The Visual Studio .NET version uses code-behind, and includes all the necessary project files for opening the file in the Visual Studio .NET editor. I recommend that you use the Visual Studio .NET version, even if you develop with another editor (or with Notepad). The code-behind development shown there is most similar to the examples in this book.

When you make your decision and click the appropriate download link, you'll be prompted to save or run a single executable file. This setup program (shown in Figure 25-3) copies the code files, and configures your computer to run the IBuySpy sample site.

Once the IBuySpy files are copied to your computer, the setup application installs the required database (and some sample data) using the SQL Server or MSDE database engine. Before you can perform this step, you need to enter the appropriate user information for your database (see Figure 25-4).

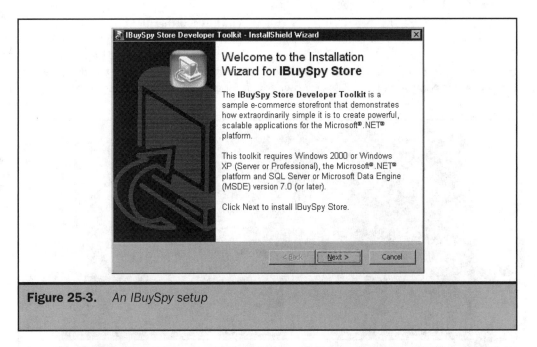

**Figure 25-3.** *An IBuySpy setup*

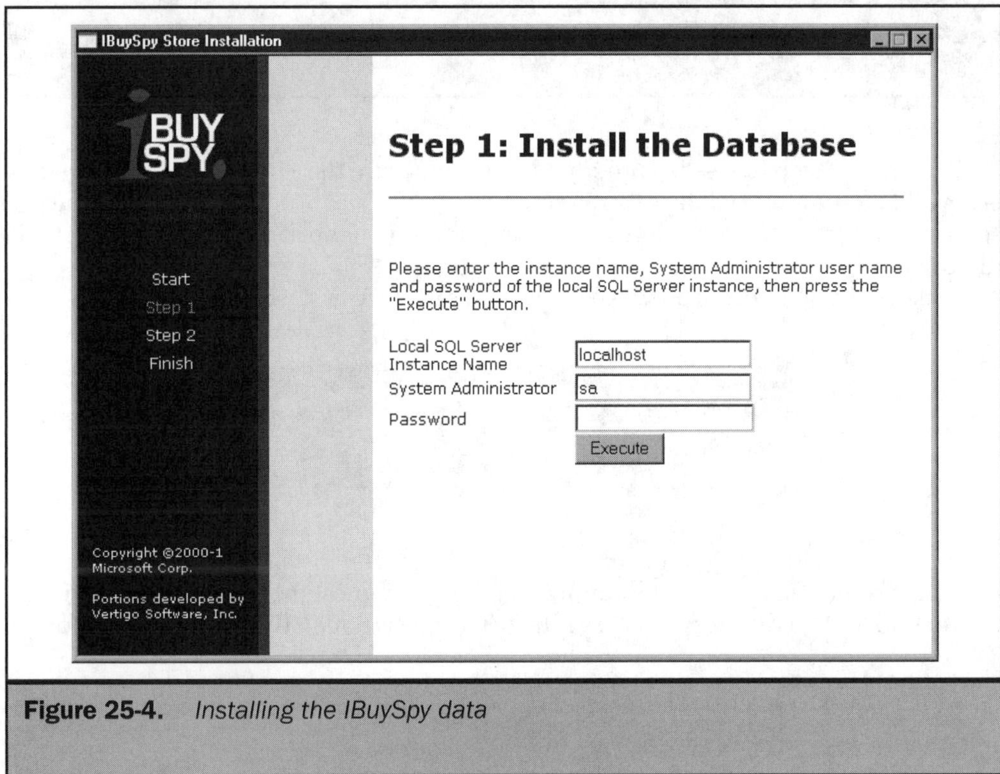


**Figure 25-4.** *Installing the IBuySpy data*

If you are using SQL Server with integrated Windows authentication, this process won't work—instead, you'll need to explicitly modify your security settings (using Enterprise Manager) to allow both Windows Integrated and SQL Server logins. Then click Execute to run the database script. You can reconfigure your security settings when the process is complete. Figure 25-5 shows the database creation script in progress.

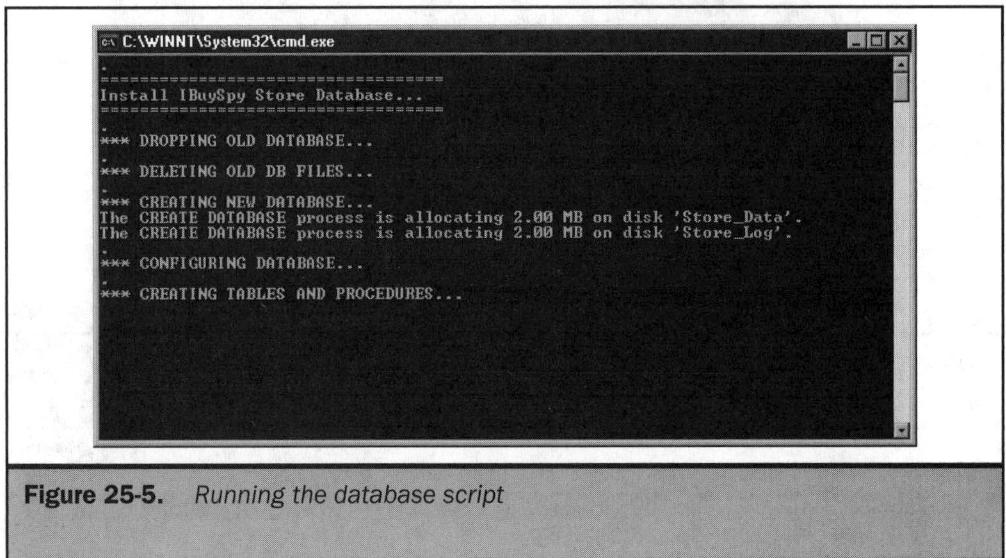


**Figure 25-5.** *Running the database script*

For the next step, the setup program has to configure the directory where the site is installed to be a virtual directory. Remember, the Visual Studio .NET project files specify both the physical location of a web application on the hard drive and its virtual directory.

A message will inform you when the virtual directory has been set:

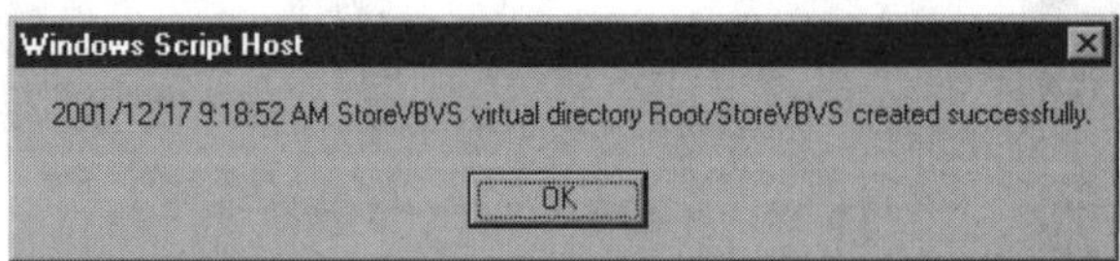


At this point, you can run the IBuySpy application you installed, or you can load it in Visual Studio .NET. To run the application, simply request the start page from the appropriate virtual directory (such as http://localhost/StoreVBVS/Default.aspx for the IBuySpy store). To load the application in Visual Studio .NET, use the desktop shortcut, or look for the .vbproj file in the appropriate directory (such as C:\StoreVBVS\StoreVBVS.proj for the IBuySpy store).

Before you can run the IBuySpy application in Visual Studio .NET, you need to perform two minor modifications. First, you need to enable debugging in the web.config file by adding the line shown below to the <system.web> section. When you create your own .NET projects in Visual Studio .NET, this line is added automatically.

```
<compilation debug="true" />
```

The second step is to right-click on the default.aspx page, and choose Set As Startup. By default, the project has no designated startup page. Default.aspx makes a good choice for a startup page, because it is the home page that will be processed automatically if users make a request to the http://localhost/StoreVBVS/ virtual directory without specifying a page file.

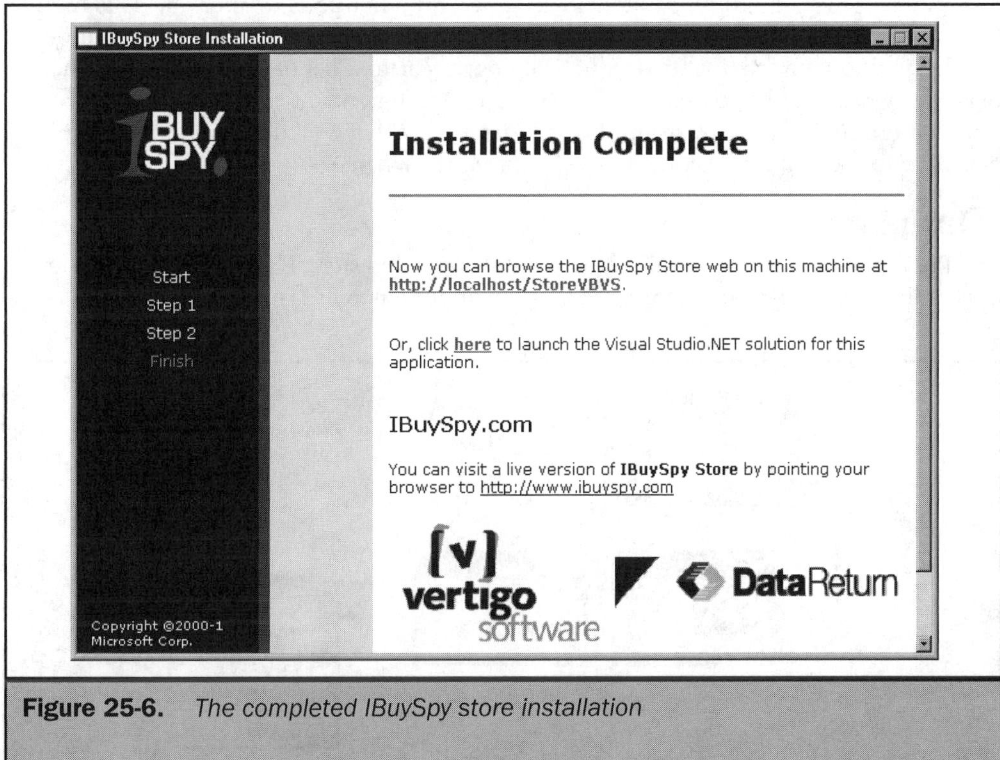


**Figure 25-6.** *The completed IBuySpy store installation*

### Requirements for the IBuySpy Portal

The IBuySpy portal has an additional web server requirement. It provides support for mobile browsers (browsers that might be used in an embedded device like a PDA). Unless you've installed the Mobile Toolkit on your web server, you'll need to remove the code files that attempt to use these features before you can compile the application in Visual Studio .NET. This process is quite simple—just delete any files that have the word "mobile" in their name using Visual Studio .NET's Solution Explorer.

# The IBuySpy Store

The IBuySpy store is an example of one of the most common types of web applications: e-commerce sites. The IBuySpy store is designed for a fictitious retailer that sells high-tech spy gadgets. It includes all the staples you would expect to find from an online retailer, including a searchable product catalog, a featured list of best-selling products, user reviews, and a shopping cart. If you need to implement your own online storefront, you'll find that the IBuySpy example provides you with a well designed and carefully tested template that can become the basis for your own site.

## The Data Layer

The IBuySpy store uses seven tables in a database called *store*. Figure 25-7 shows the part of the database used to store information about customers and their orders.

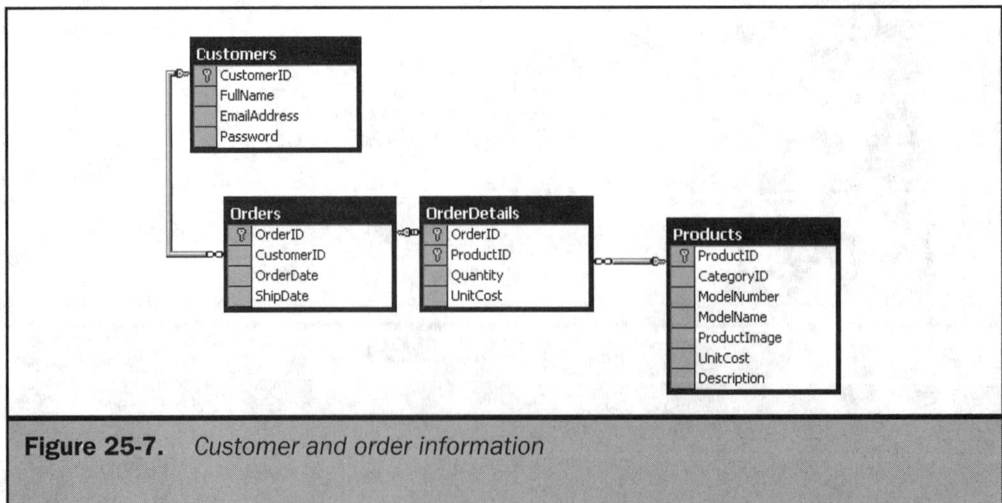


**Figure 25-7.** *Customer and order information*

Each customer record can be linked to any number of child order records. The order information is split into two tables, Order and OrderDetails, which can improve performance for queries that only need to retrieve information from one table. Note that, as a bare minimum, an order record needs to track the date the product was ordered and shipped, the corresponding product, and the cost. The cost in the linked product record is subject to change, and thus cannot be relied upon when calculating the total cost of the order.

Figure 25-8 shows the remainder of the database. (You'll notice that the Products table from Figure 25-7 is repeated with some additional information.)

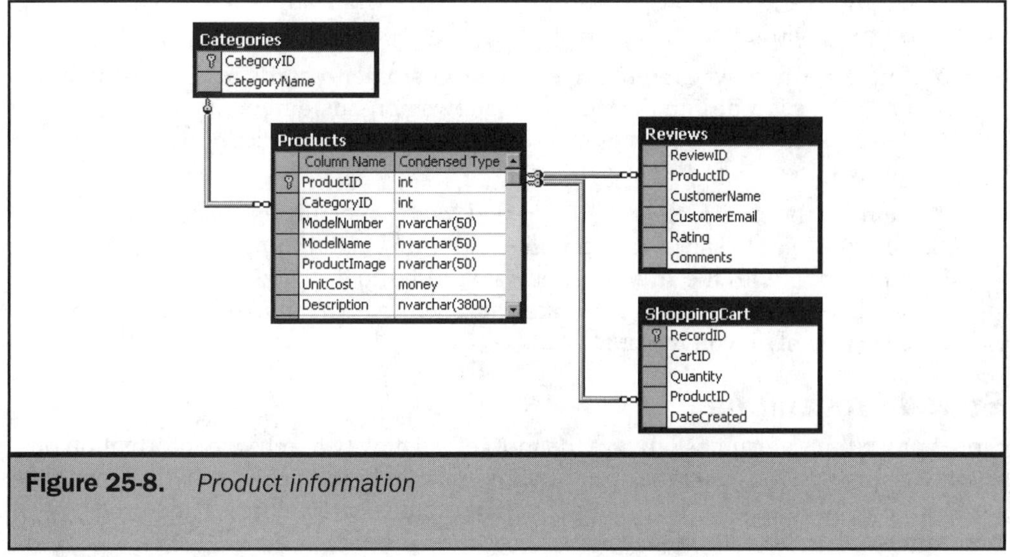


**Figure 25-8.** *Product information*

Every product must be assigned inside an existing category (such as General, Tools, or Travel, to name a few). In addition, every product can have an unlimited number of customer reviews. Finally, a ShoppingCart table stores user selections that haven't been ordered. This information could be stored in session state, but using a database table can provide better scalability, and it allows the information to remain for future visits, rather than timing out after a predetermined amount of time. To find all the items in a given user's cart, you would look for all the records with the same CartID.

Some points of interest:

- User passwords are not encrypted in the database. Thus, you should assume that this application would store its information in a carefully guarded SQL Server database that is not accessible to most users.

- Product images are stored as filenames (such as "image.gif"). Your ASP.NET application can use this name as a relative URL with an image control. However, the file must be present in the application directory on the web server. No error checking will be performed to enforce this restriction or alert you about a missing file. Another option would be to store the binary picture information in the database itself. This approach would solve the problem of missing pictures, but it could hamper performance and would make the pictures inaccessible to static HTML pages that might need to use them. You'll notice when running the IBuySpy store locally that a blank sample image is used for every product. If you run IBuySpy online (or configure the Products table on your own), each product will have its own individual image.
- Customer reviews are not linked to the customer records in the Customers table. This is a design decision that allows non-customers to add their comments. Other web sites (such as Amazon.com) restrict reviews to known users.
- Items in the shopping cart are not tied to any specific user record. This allows a user to start picking items and filling a shopping cart before registering with the site. Most users would find any other arrangement (such as one that forced you to register before being allowed to shop) to be extremely inconvenient.

## Stored Procedures

Stored procedures are almost always the most efficient way to retrieve information or commit changes to the database. The IBuySpy store takes this philosophy to heart, and performs all of its data access through 23 separate stored procedures. The stored procedures are outlined in Table 25-1.

| Stored Procedure | Description |
|---|---|
| CustomerAdd | Inserts a new customer into the Customers table. |
| CustomerDetail | Retrieves information about a specified customer. |
| CustomerLogin | Looks for a customer record with the corresponding name and password. If no record is found, the login has failed. |

**Table 25-1.** *Stored Procedures in the IBuySpy Store*

| Stored Procedure | Description |
|---|---|
| CustomerAlsoBought | Uses a complicated stored procedure that accepts a product ID, and selects the five most popular products that were also purchased by users who bought the identified product. This type of query allows the web site to provide a hook like "if you like product X, you may also like products Y and Z." |
| OrdersAdd | Adds a new order at the end of the checkout process by retrieving all the records from the appropriate shopping cart. Uses a transaction to ensure that there is never a partial (inconsistent) update. |
| OrdersDetail | Retrieves information about a specified order. This information is retrieved in several separate pieces. |
| OrdersList | Retrieves a list of products that have been ordered by a specified customer. |
| ProductCategoryList | Retrieves a list of product categories. |
| ProductDetail | Retrieves detailed information about a specified product. |
| ProductsByCategory | Retrieves a list of products in a specified category. |
| ProductSearch | Retrieves product records using a text-based search with the SQL Like keyword. The search examines the information in the ModelNumber, ModelName, and Description fields, looking for the user-supplied keywords. |
| ProductsMostPopular | Retrieves the top five most popular products. |
| ReviewsAdd | Adds a user review. |
| ReviewsList | Retrieves a list of all the reviews for a given product. |
| ShoppingCartAddItem | Adds the specified product to the specified shopping cart by inserting a new ShoppingCart record. If the product already exists in the shopping cart, the quantity field of the current record is updated instead. |

**Table 25-1.** *Stored Procedures in the IBuySpy Store (continued)*

| Stored Procedure | Description |
|---|---|
| ShoppingCartEmpty | Removes all the records with the specified shopping cart ID. |
| ShoppingCartItemCount | Returns the number of items in the specified shopping cart. |
| ShoppingCartList | Returns the list of items in the specified shopping cart. |
| ShoppingCartMigrate | Moves a temporary shopping cart (created for a user who does not have an account or is not logged in) to the final account for the logged-on user. This occurs just before the item is purchased. |
| ShoppingCartRemove-Abandoned | Deletes shopping carts that have been on the system for more than a day. |
| ShoppingCartRemoveItem | Removes the specified product from the specified shopping cart. |
| ShoppingCartTotal | Calculates the total cost of all the items that are in the specified shopping cart. |
| ShoppingCartUpdate | Modifies the quantity field for the specified product and shopping cart. |

**Table 25-1.** *Stored Procedures in the IBuySpy Store (continued)*

## The Business Components

The IBuySpy store web pages never access the database directly. Instead, they work through a layer of five components that encapsulate all the database code for the site. This allows the database code to be changed without affecting the page code, and it also provides a more logical interface for programming. For example, the page code for working with the shopping cart is extremely intuitive because the underlying database details are handled transparently. The multi-tiered organization in the IBuyStore is shown in Figure 25-9. To see the methods that are provided by any one of the IBuySpy component classes, you can use the Solution Explorer, as shown in Figure 25-10.

The code in the IBuySpy store components is straightforward and well commented. You will also find that it is somewhat lengthy, as every stored procedure call requires several parameter objects, which must each be constructed separately.

The IBuySpy store web pages

**Business Components**

CustomersDB
OrdersDB
ProductsDB
ReviewsDB
ShoppingCartDB

**Stored Procedures**

CustomerDetail
CustomerAdd
CustomerLogin

OrdersList
OrdersAdd

ProductCategoryList
ProductsByCategory
ProductDetail
CustomerAlsoBought
ProductsMostPopular
ProductSearch

ReviewsList
ReviewsAdd

ShoppingCartList
ShoppingCartAddItem
ShoppingCartUpdate
ShoppingCartRemoveItem
ShoppingCartItemCount
ShoppingCartTotal
ShoppingCartMigrate
ShoppingCartEmpty

Store
database

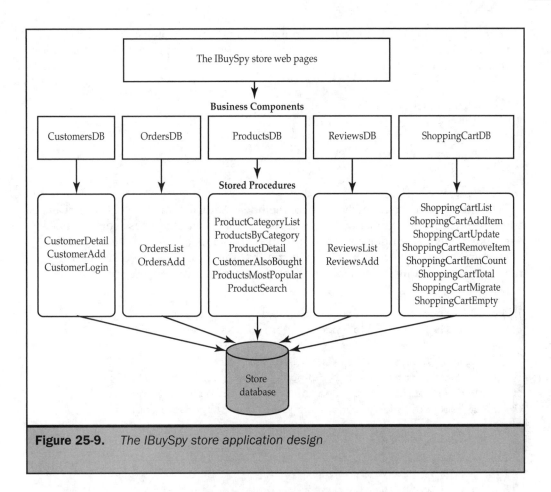

**Figure 25-9.** *The IBuySpy store application design*

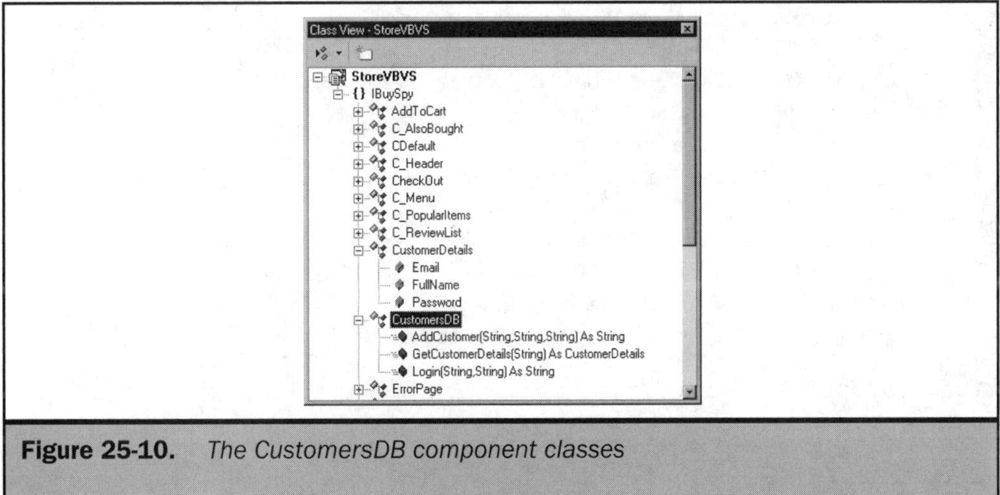


**Figure 25-10.** *The CustomersDB component classes*

For example, the CustomersDB component provides two classes: the utility class CustomersDB and the CustomerDetails data class, which encapsulates the information for a single customer record.

```
Public Class CustomerDetails
    Public FullName As String
    Public Email As String
    Public Password As String
End Class
```

The CustomersDB class includes three methods: AddCustomer, GetCustomerDetails, and Login. The AddCustomer method accepts the name, email, and password for a new user, and creates the underlying record in the Customers table with the help of the CustomerAdd stored procedure. To confirm that the process worked successfully, the customer's unique ID (generated by the database) is returned as a string.

```
Public Function AddCustomer(fullName As String, _
  email As String, password As String) As String

    Dim myConnection As New SqlConnection( _
      ConfigurationSettings.AppSettings("ConnectionString"))
    Dim myCommand As SqlCommand("CustomerAdd", myConnection)
    myCommand.CommandType = CommandType.StoredProcedure

    ' Add Parameters
    Dim parameterFullName As New SqlParameter("@FullName", _
      SqlDbType.NVarChar, 50)
    parameterFullName.Value = fullName
    myCommand.Parameters.Add(parameterFullName)

    Dim parameterEmail As New SqlParameter("@Email", _
      SqlDbType.NVarChar, 50)
    parameterEmail.Value = email
    myCommand.Parameters.Add(parameterEmail)

    Dim parameterPassword As New SqlParameter("@Password", _
      SqlDbType.NVarChar, 50)
    parameterPassword.Value = password
    myCommand.Parameters.Add(parameterPassword)
```

```
    Dim parameterCustomerID As New SqlParameter("@CustomerID", _
      SqlDbType.Int, 4)
    parameterCustomerID.Direction = ParameterDirection.Output
    myCommand.Parameters.Add(parameterCustomerID)

    myConnection.Open()
    myCommand.ExecuteNonQuery()
    myConnection.Close()

    ' Calculate the CustomerID using output parameter
    ' from the stored procedure.
    Dim customerId As Integer = CInt(parameterCustomerID.Value)
    Return customerId.ToString()

End Function
```

## Lowercase Indicates a Private Variable

The IBuySpy examples follow the C# naming convention of starting variables with a lowercase first letter, unless they are publicly visible (like a class property). The IBuySpy examples also don't use variable control prefixes (such as txtName to indicate a text box that contains a user's name).

There's nothing unusual about this example—it's exactly like the database components we considered in Chapter 21. You'll also notice that the connection string is retrieved from the web.config configuration file.

To use this component, the client needs to create an instance of the CustomerDB class and submit the appropriate information. Here's the logic used in the Register.aspx page:

```
' Add New Customer to CustomerDB database
Dim accountSystem As New IBuySpy.CustomersDB()
Dim customerId As String
customerID = accountSystem.AddCustomer(Name.Text, Email.Text, _
                                       Password.Text)

If customerId <> "" Then
    ' The user was created. You can continue with the task at hand.
End If
```

Now consider the GetCustomerDetails method, which returns information as a CustomerDetails object.

```
Public Function GetCustomerDetails(customerID As String) _
  As CustomerDetails

    Dim myConnection As New SqlConnection( _
      ConfigurationSettings.AppSettings("ConnectionString"))
    Dim myCommand As New SqlCommand("CustomerDetail", myConnection)
    myCommand.CommandType = CommandType.StoredProcedure

    ' Add Parameters to stored procedure.
    Dim parameterCustomerID As New SqlParameter("@CustomerID", _
      SqlDbType.Int, 4)
    parameterCustomerID.Value = CInt(customerID)
    myCommand.Parameters.Add(parameterCustomerID)

    Dim parameterFullName As New SqlParameter("@FullName", _
      SqlDbType.NVarChar, 50)
    parameterFullName.Direction = ParameterDirection.Output
    myCommand.Parameters.Add(parameterFullName)

    Dim parameterEmail As New SqlParameter("@Email", _
      SqlDbType.NVarChar, 50)
    parameterEmail.Direction = ParameterDirection.Output
    myCommand.Parameters.Add(parameterEmail)

    Dim parameterPassword As New SqlParameter("@Password", _
      SqlDbType.NVarChar, 50)
    parameterPassword.Direction = ParameterDirection.Output
    myCommand.Parameters.Add(parameterPassword)

    myConnection.Open()
    myCommand.ExecuteNonQuery()
    myConnection.Close()

    ' Create CustomerDetails object.
    Dim myCustomerDetails As New CustomerDetails()

   ' Populate CustomerDetails object using output parameters.
    myCustomerDetails.FullName = CStr(parameterFullName.Value)
    myCustomerDetails.Password = CStr(parameterPassword.Value)
    myCustomerDetails.Email = CStr(parameterEmail.Value)
    Return myCustomerDetails
```

```
End Function
```

The Login method follows similar logic, but throws an exception if a matching user record cannot be found. All of the other components follow the same series of methodical steps—first creating the appropriate parameter objects, then calling the procedure, and finally retrieving the important information from the output parameters to use as a return value if needed.

### The Web Services

The IBuySpy store Web Services are not integrated into the core application. Instead, they provide another approach you can use for ordering a product and checking on its status. However, to make the best use of these Web Services, you would need to create another client application (such as a desktop Windows program) that uses them.

If you'd like to view the Web Services using the Internet Explorer test page, request the InstantOrder.asmx page. Two web methods are provided: OrderItem and CheckStatus. They use the same components used by the web pages in the IBuySpy store application.

## The Application Configuration

The web.config file for the IBuySpy store is short and simple. It serves five main purposes:

- It defines the connection string used for the database. The setup program configures this information when you install the IBuySpy store site.

```
<appSettings>
    <add key="ConnectionString"
         value="server=localhost;uid=sa;database=store" />
</appSettings>
```

- It disables session state management for the entire application, ensuring optimum performance.

```
<sessionState mode="Off" />
```

- It identifies a custom error page to be used in case of an application error.

```
<customErrors mode="RemoteOnly"
              defaultRedirect="ErrorPage.aspx" />
```

- It enables forms-based security.

```
<authentication mode="Forms">
    <forms name="IBuySpyStoreAuth" loginUrl="login.aspx"
           protection="All" path="/" />
</authentication>
```

- It specifies that certain pages (those used for ordering or checking order item status) require an authenticated user.

```
<location path="Checkout.aspx">
    <system.web>
        <authorization>
            <deny users="?" />
        </authorization>
    </system.web>
</location>
<location path="OrderList.aspx">
    <system.web>
        <authorization>
            <deny users="?" />
        </authorization>
    </system.web>
</location>
<location path="OrderDetails.aspx">
    <system.web>
        <authorization>
            <deny users="?" />
        </authorization>
    </system.web>
</location>
```

## The Web Pages

The IBuySpy store includes thirteen .aspx pages, five .ascx user controls, and one .asmx Web Service. Because so much of the IBuySpy store logic is handled by the business components and stored procedures in the database, the web page code is brief, simple, and easily readable.

### The Default.aspx Page

The initial Default.aspx (shown in the browser in Figure 25-11) has a code-behind class with barely five lines of code. It looks for a cookie called IBuySpy_FullName, and uses it to configure a welcome message.

```
Private Sub Page_Load(sender As Object, e As EventArgs) _
  Handles MyBase.Load

    ' Customize welcome message if personalization cookie is present
    If Not Request.Cookies("IBuySpy_FullName") Is Nothing Then
        WelcomeMsg.Text = "Welcome "
        WelcomeMsg.Text &= Request.Cookies("IBuySpy_FullName").Value
    End If

End Sub
```

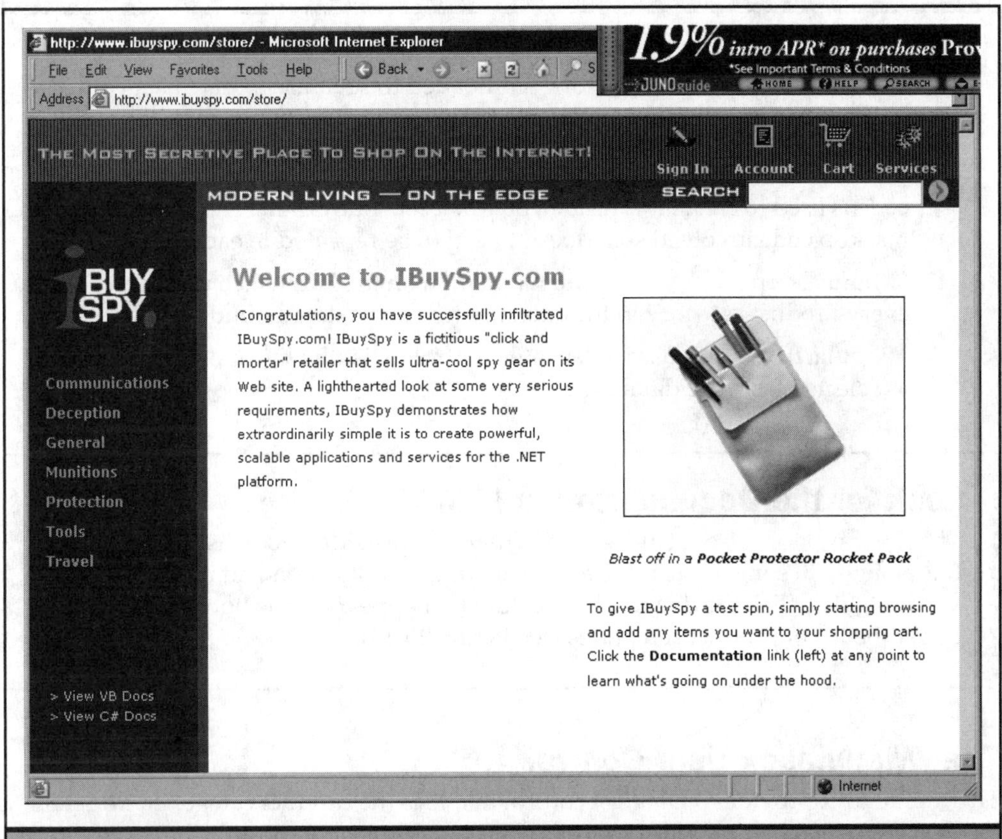


**Figure 25-11.** *The IBuySpy store homepage*

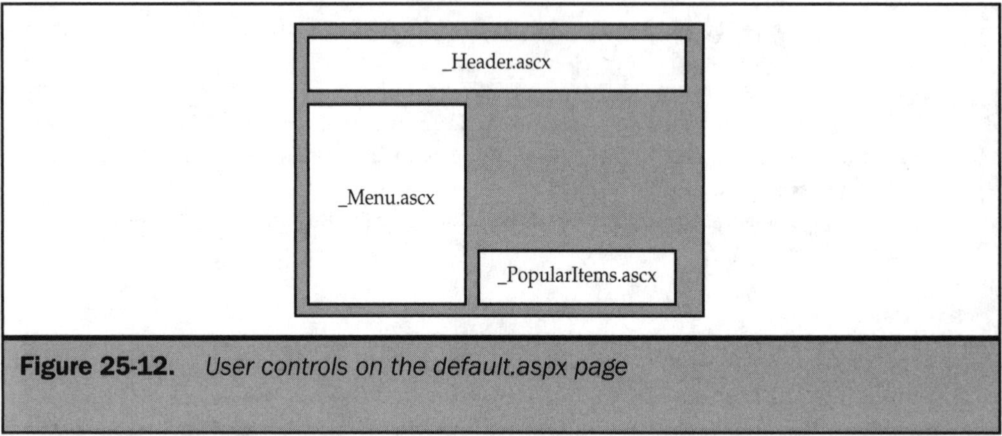


**Figure 25-12.** *User controls on the default.aspx page*

The rest of the page processing work is offloaded to several separate user controls (as diagrammed in Figure 25-12):

- **_Header.ascx** provides the graphical header at the top of the page. No ASP.NET code is used to create this header, but the user control still centralizes the HTML markup code involved so it doesn't need to be repeated in each page.
- **_Menu.ascx** provides the menu navigation on the left, which provides a link for every product category in the database through a data-bound DataList control.
- **_PopularItems.ascx** uses a Repeater control to list the five most popular items, as selected from the database.

### Look for the Documentation Link

The IBuySpy store also includes HTML files that provide a code listing for each file, along with some basic information about the application and its design. To see these files, click the documentation link that appears at the bottom right, under the list of product categories (see Figure 25-13).

## The _Menu.ascx User Control

The _Menu.ascx provides a DataList control that lists the product categories from the database. The DataList provides two templates, which format the appearance of the category differently depending on whether it is currently selected. Each template creates the category as a hyperlink, with the text drawn from the CategoryName database field. The hyperlink jumps to the productslist.aspx page, and passes the selected category ID through the query string.

```
<asp:DataList id="MyList" cellpadding="3" cellspacing="0"
     width="145" SelectedItemStyle-BackColor="dimgray"
     EnableViewState="false" runat="server" >

    <ItemTemplate>
        <asp:HyperLink cssclass="MenuUnselected" id="HyperLink1"
         Text='<%# DataBinder.Eval(Container.DataItem,
              "CategoryName") %>'
         NavigateUrl='<%# "productslist.aspx?CategoryID=" &
         DataBinder.Eval(Container.DataItem, "CategoryID") &
         "&selection=" & Container.ItemIndex %>' runat="server" />
    </ItemTemplate>
    <SelectedItemTemplate>
        <asp:HyperLink cssclass="MenuSelected" id="HyperLink2"
         Text='<%# DataBinder.Eval(Container.DataItem,
              "CategoryName") %>'
         NavigateUrl='<%# "productslist.aspx?CategoryID=" &
         DataBinder.Eval(Container.DataItem, "CategoryID") &
         "&selection=" & Container.ItemIndex %>' runat="server" />
    </SelectedItemTemplate>

</asp:DataList>
```

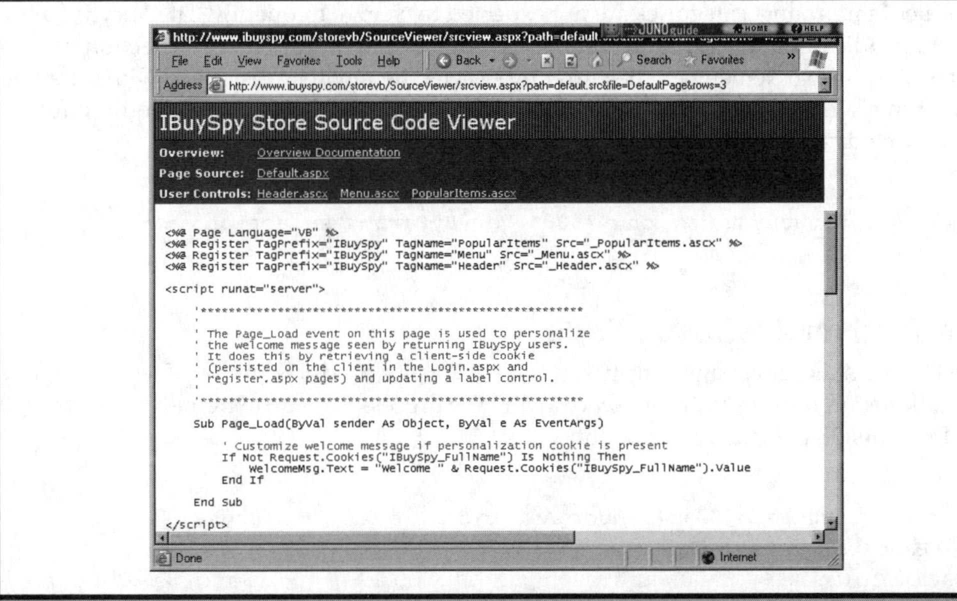


**Figure 25-13.** *The IBuySpy online documentation*

The user control code binds the DataList, with the help of the ProductsDB class. First, however, the code checks if a selection has already been made and sent back in the current query string, in which case it sets the DataList's SelectedIndex property accordingly.

```
Private Sub Page_Load(sender As Object, e As EventArgs) _
  Handles MyBase.Load

    ' Set the current selection of list.
    Dim selectionId As String = Request.Params("selection")

    If Not selectionId Is Nothing Then
        MyList.SelectedIndex = CInt(selectionId)
    End If

    ' Obtain list of menu categories and bind to the list control.
    Dim products As New IBuySpy.ProductsDB()

    MyList.DataSource = products.GetProductCategories()
    MyList.DataBind()

End Sub
```

Finally, to improve performance the menu user control is cached for one hour, which indicates that product categories are not expected to change frequently. The VaryByParam attribute indicates that a separate version is required depending on the selection value in the query string. Remember, the currently selected item will be displayed with different formatting, which means that a separate cached version of the control is required for each selected category.

```
<%@ OutputCache Duration="3600" VaryByParam="selection" %>
```

## The ProductsList.aspx Page

The ProductsList.aspx page simply retrieves the list of products in the selected category (as indicated in the query string). Once again, the process is made extremely easy through the ProdcutsDB database component.

```
Private Sub Page_Load(sender As Object, e As EventArgs)_
  Handles MyBase.Load

    ' Obtain categoryId from QueryString
```

```
    Dim categoryId As Integer = CInt(Request.Params("CategoryID"))

    ' Obtain products and databind to an asp:datalist control
    Dim productCatalogue As New IBuySpy.ProductsDB()

    MyList.DataSource = productCatalogue.GetProducts(categoryId)
    MyList.DataBind()

End Sub
```

The DataList uses an attractive layout that displays a picture and an Add To Cart link (see Figure 25-14). It uses a single template (ItemTemplate), and a sophisticated HTML layout that places it as a table nested inside another table. This ensures that the DataList and the required user controls can be organized precisely on the page. Another approach would be to use HTML frames.

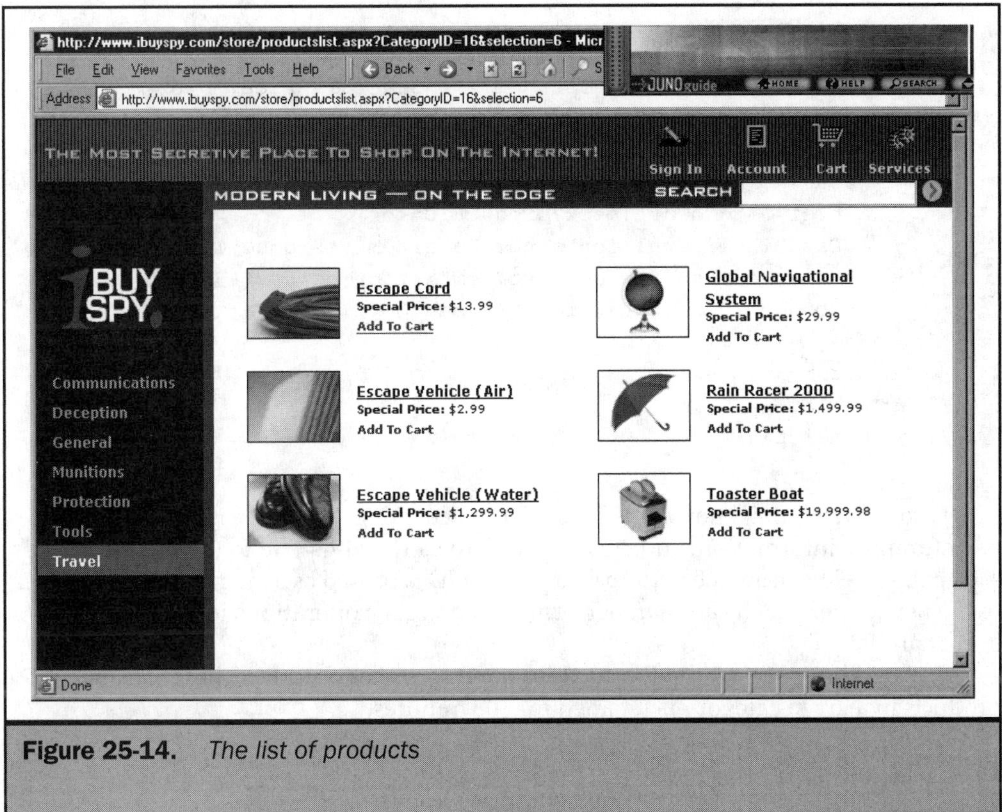


**Figure 25-14.** *The list of products*

```
<asp:DataList id="MyList" RepeatColumns="2" runat="server">
<ItemTemplate>
    <table border="0" width="300"><tr><td width="25"> </td>
    <td width="100" valign="middle" align="right">
      <a href='ProductDetails.aspx?productID=<%#
         DataBinder.Eval(Container.DataItem, "ProductID") %>'>
         <img src='ProductImages/thumbs/
            <%# DataBinder.Eval(Container.DataItem,
                "ProductImage") %>'
            width="100" height="75" border="0">
      </a>
    </td>
    <td width="200" valign="middle">
      <a href='ProductDetails.aspx?productID=<%#
         DataBinder.Eval(Container.DataItem, "ProductID") %>'>
         <span class="ProductListHead">
           <%# DataBinder.Eval(Container.DataItem, "ModelName") %>
         </span><br>
      </a>
      <span class="ProductListItem"><b>Special Price: </b>
        <%# DataBinder.Eval(Container.DataItem,
            "UnitCost", "{0:c}") %>
      </span><br>
      <a href='AddToCart.aspx?productID=<%#
         DataBinder.Eval(Container.DataItem, "ProductID") %>'>
         <span class="ProductListItem"><font color="#9D0000">
         <b>Add To Cart<b></font></span>
      </a>
  </td></tr></table>
</ItemTemplate>
</asp:DataList>
```

The logic is still straightforward: clicking on an item brings you to the ProductDetails.aspx page for more information, and clicking Add To Cart brings you to the AddoToCart.aspx page. In either case, the appropriate product ID is passed as a query string parameter to the new page, which can then perform the necessary operations in its Page_Load event handler.

As would be expected, the ProductList.aspx page uses output caching. The list of products in a given category is retained for 100 minutes.

```
<%@ OutputCache Duration="6000" VaryByParam="CategoryID" %>
```

## The AddToCart.aspx Page

The AddToCart.aspx page actually has no server controls or HTML output. Instead, it performs the processing required for adding the item to the shopping cart, and then it forwards the user to the ShoppingCart.aspx page. This extra step ensures that if the user hits the Refresh button, the item will not be added again (as the AddToCart.aspx page code will not run).

```
Private Sub Page_Load(sender As Object, e As EventArgs) _
  Handles MyBase.Load

    If Not Request.Params("ProductID") Is Nothing Then
        Dim cart As New IBuySpy.ShoppingCartDB()

        ' Obtain current user's shopping cart ID.
        Dim cartId As String = cart.GetShoppingCartId()

        ' Add Product Item to Cart.
        cart.AddItem(cartId, CInt(Request.Params("ProductID")), 1)
    End If

    Response.Redirect("ShoppingCart.aspx")
End Sub
```

The first step when using the ShoppingCartDB component is to call the GetShoppingCartID method. It returns a unique ID for the shopping cart, which will be one of two things. If the user has already logged in, the shopping cart ID will be their unique ID. If the user is a guest or a customer who has not logged in, a randomly generated GUID will be calculated, ensuring that the shopping cart ID is unique. The shopping cart ID is then stored in a special cookie called IBuySpy_CartID. Calling GetShoppingCartID at a later point simply retrieves the value from the cookie, ensuring that the same value is used for a user's entire session. This ID is required to use all of the other ShoppingCartDB methods—without it there is no way to find the user's items in the ShoppingCart table.

The code for the ShoppingCartDB function is shown next.

```
Public Function GetShoppingCartId() As String

    Dim context As HttpContext = HttpContext.Current

    ' If the user is authenticated,
    ' use their customer ID as a shopping cart ID.
    If context.User.Identity.Name <> "" Then
```

```
            Return context.User.Identity.Name
        End If

        ' If user is not authenticated,
        ' either fetch (or issue) a new temporary ID.
        If Not context.Request.Cookies("IBuySpy_CartID") Is Nothing Then
            Return context.Request.Cookies("IBuySpy_CartID").Value
        Else
            ' Generate a new random GUID using System.Guid class.
            Dim tempCartId As Guid = Guid.NewGuid()

            ' Send tempCartId back to client as a cookie
            context.Response.Cookies("IBuySpy_CartID").Value = _
              tempCartId.ToString()
            Return tempCartId.ToString()
        End If

    End Function
```

Remember, there is no item in the database that represents a shopping cart. Instead, each record in the ShoppingCart table represents an individual shopping cart *item*. If there are no items for a given shopping cart ID, there is effectively no shopping cart. At any given time, you would expect to find that the ShoppingCart table has a range of records representing various items from a host of different users, as shown in Figure 25-15.

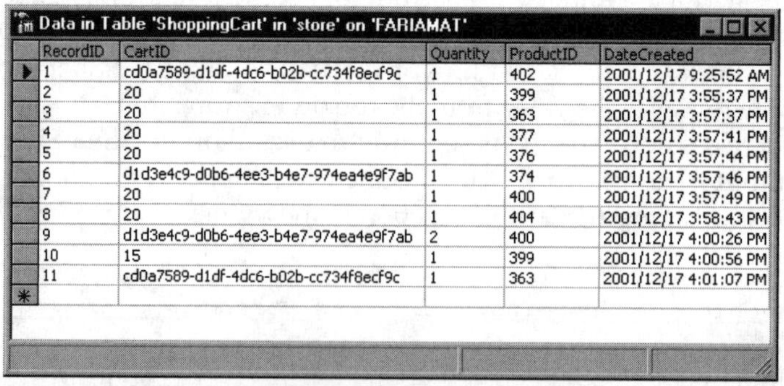

Data in Table 'ShoppingCart' in 'store' on 'FARIAMAT'

| RecordID | CartID | Quantity | ProductID | DateCreated |
|---|---|---|---|---|
| 1 | cd0a7589-d1df-4dc6-b02b-cc734f8ecf9c | 1 | 402 | 2001/12/17 9:25:52 AM |
| 2 | 20 | 1 | 399 | 2001/12/17 3:55:37 PM |
| 3 | 20 | 1 | 363 | 2001/12/17 3:57:37 PM |
| 4 | 20 | 1 | 377 | 2001/12/17 3:57:41 PM |
| 5 | 20 | 1 | 376 | 2001/12/17 3:57:44 PM |
| 6 | d1d3e4c9-d0b6-4ee3-b4e7-974ea4e9f7ab | 1 | 374 | 2001/12/17 3:57:46 PM |
| 7 | 20 | 1 | 400 | 2001/12/17 3:57:49 PM |
| 8 | 20 | 1 | 404 | 2001/12/17 3:58:43 PM |
| 9 | d1d3e4c9-d0b6-4ee3-b4e7-974ea4e9f7ab | 2 | 400 | 2001/12/17 4:00:26 PM |
| 10 | 15 | 1 | 399 | 2001/12/17 4:00:56 PM |
| 11 | cd0a7589-d1df-4dc6-b02b-cc734f8ecf9c | 1 | 363 | 2001/12/17 4:01:07 PM |

**Figure 25-15.** *ShoppingCart data*

## The ShoppingCart.aspx Pages

After the item has been added to the ShoppingCart table, the user is automatically forwarded to a new page, ShoppingCart.aspx, which provides a list of the currently selected items in a DataGrid control, as shown in Figure 25-16.

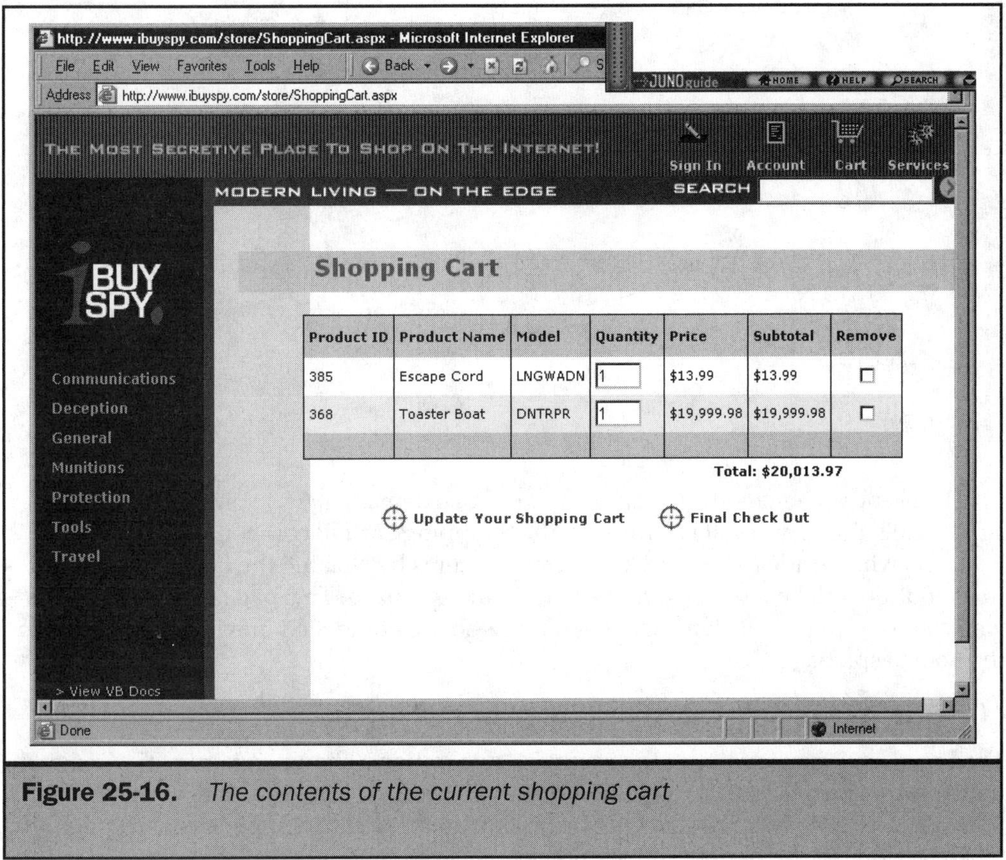


**Figure 25-16.** *The contents of the current shopping cart*

The first time the page loads, the code retrieves the user's shopping cart ID, looks up the corresponding items, and binds them to the DataGrid control using a custom subroutine called PopulateShoppingCartList.

```
Private Sub PopulateShoppingCartList()

    Dim cart As New IBuySpy.ShoppingCartDB()
```

```
    ' Obtain current user's shopping cart ID.
    Dim cartId As String = cart.GetShoppingCartId()

    ' If no items, hide details and display message.
    If cart.GetItemCount(cartId) = 0 Then
        DetailsPanel.Visible = False
        MyError.Text = "There are currently no items"
        MyError.Text &= "in your shopping cart."
    Else
        ' Databind Gridcontrol with Shopping Cart Items.
        MyList.DataSource = cart.GetItems(cartId)
        MyList.DataBind()

        ' Update Total Price label.
        lblTotal.Text = String.Format("{0:c}", _
                            cart.GetTotal(cartId))
    End If

End Sub
```

The user can then modify quantities or remove items. The ShoppingCart.aspx file simply calls the appropriate routines in the ShoppingCartDB component.

Users who decide to proceed and purchase items by clicking the Final Checkout ImageButton will be redirected to the Checkout.aspx page. This page is secured by the web.config settings, which means that users who are not logged in will be redirected to the Login.aspx page.

## The Login.aspx and Register.aspx Pages

The Login.aspx page provides the user with two options, shown in Figure 25-17: sign in with a recognized user ID and password combination, or register as a new user.

If the user chooses to register, the browser is redirected to the Register.aspx page, where various pieces of user information are collected and inserted in a record in the Customers database. This page uses input control validation to verify all values (as shown in Figure 25-18).

If the user chooses to log in, several steps are performed in sequence:

1. The input controls are validated to make sure reasonable values have been entered.
2. The CustomersDB.Login method is used to authenticate the user.
3. If successful, the user's shopping cart items (which were previously stored with a random GUID) are modified to use the corresponding customer ID. This change is performed through the ShoppingCartDB.MigrateCart method, which uses the ShoppingCartMigrate stored procedure.

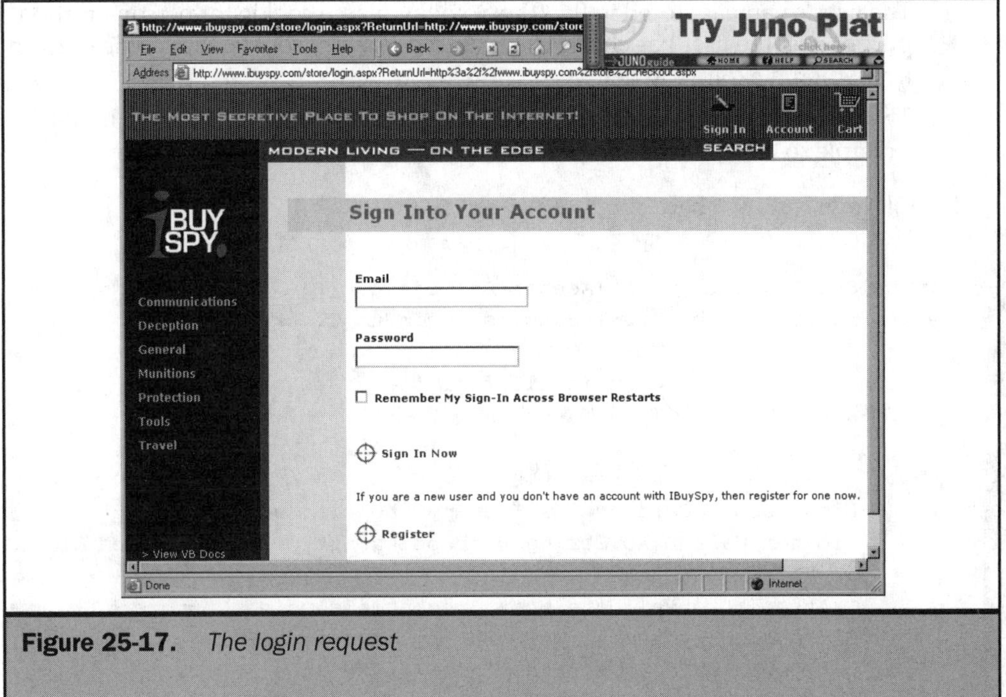


**Figure 25-17.** *The login request*

**Figure 25-18.** *Validating the Register.aspx page*

4. The user's name is stored in the IBuySpy_FullName cookie for personalization purposes. If the user has chosen to create a persistent cookie, the cookie is given a one-month expiration date.
5. The user is redirected back to the page that caused the security check. In our example so far, this would be the Checkout.aspx page.

The full code is shown here.

```
Private Sub LoginBtn_Click(sender As Object, _
  e As ImageClickEventArgs) Handles LoginBtn.Click

    ' Only attempt a login if all form fields on the page are valid.
    If Page.IsValid = True Then

        ' Save old ShoppingCartID.
        Dim shoppingCart As New IBuySpy.ShoppingCartDB()
        Dim tempCartID As String = shoppingCart.GetShoppingCartId()

        ' Attempt to Validate User Credentials using CustomersDB
        Dim accountSystem As New IBuySpy.CustomersDB()
        Dim customerId As String = _
          accountSystem.Login(email.Text, password.Text)

        If customerId <> "" Then
            ' Migrate existing shopping cart items.
            shoppingCart.MigrateCart(tempCartID, customerId)

            ' Lookup the customer's full account details.
            Dim customerDetails As IBuySpy.CustomerDetails
            customerDetails = accountSystem.GetCustomerDetails( _
                                  customerId)

            ' Store the user's fullname in a cookie
            ' for personalization purposes.
            Response.Cookies("IBuySpy_FullName").Value = _
              customerDetails.FullName

            ' Make the cookie persistent only if the user
            ' selects "persistent"
            ' login checkbox.
            If RememberLogin.Checked = True Then
```

```
                Response.Cookies("IBuySpy_FullName").Expires = _
                  DateTime.Now.AddMonths(1)
            End If

            ' Redirect browser back to originating page
            FormsAuthentication.RedirectFromLoginPage(customerId, _
              RememberLogin.Checked)

        Else
            Message.Text = "Login Failed!"
        End If

    End If

End Sub
```

## The Checkout.aspx Page

The final step is the Checkout.aspx page, which requires the user's final confirmation. Information is then shuffled from the ShoppingCart table to the Orders table, using the OrdersDB.PlaceOrder method, which relies on the OrdersAdd stored procedure to perform all the necessary database operations. The stored procedure also uses a transaction to ensure that the Orders and OrderDetail records are committed or canceled as a whole. This ensures that the IBuySpy code requires the least amount of database logic possible.

```
Private Sub SubmitBtn_Click(sender As Object, _
  e As ImageClickEventArgs) Handles SubmitBtn.Click

    Dim cart As New IBuySpy.ShoppingCartDB()

    Dim cartId As String = cart.GetShoppingCartId()
    Dim customerId As String = User.Identity.Name

    If (Not cartId Is Nothing) And (Not customerId Is Nothing) Then

        ' Place the order
        Dim ordersDatabase As New IBuySpy.OrdersDB()
        Dim orderId As Integer = _
          ordersDatabase.PlaceOrder(customerId, cartId)
```

```
            ' Update labels to reflect the fact that the order
            ' has taken place.
            Header.Text = "Check Out Complete!"
            Message.Text = "<b>Your Order Number Is: </b>"
            Message.Text &= orderId.ToString
            SubmitBtn.Visible = False

        End If

    End Sub
```

The page ends with a final confirmation message (see Figure 25-19).

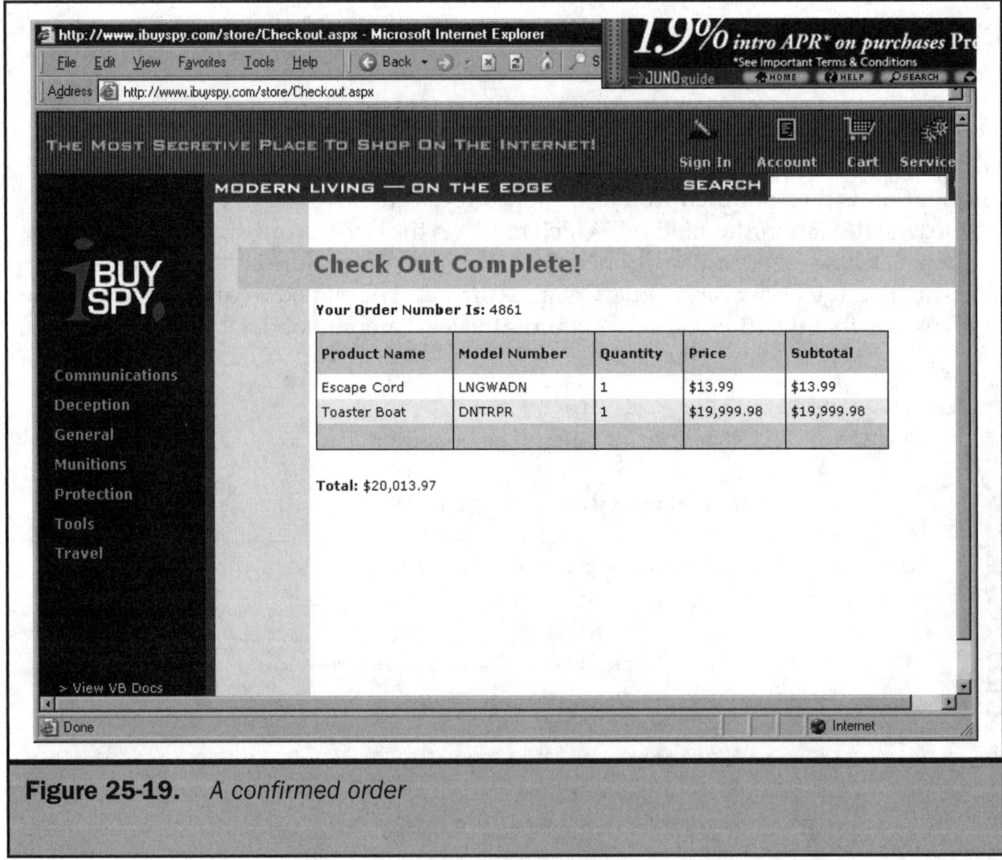


**Figure 25-19.** *A confirmed order*

### The IBuySpy Store Provides Other Features

Our discussion of the IBuySpy store walked through the process of selecting an item, creating an order, and registering the user. Several other topics, like searching for a specific item, retrieving information about currently ordered items, and adding user comments were not addressed at all. However, there's really nothing more to learn—the application framework follows the exact same pattern you've seen with orders. For example, user comments are added through the ReviewDB components, which relies on the ReviewsAdd and ReviewsList stored procedures. Reviews are themselves displayed in a templated DataList control, which is actually wrapped in a _ReviewList user control. Perhaps the most important aspect of the IBuySpy store case study is the way it demonstrates how a few simple guidelines can be used throughout a web site to make a predictable, well organized, and easily extensible framework.

## The IBuySpy Portal

A *portal* is a location on the web that groups together a cluster of different types of information, usually around a central theme. For example, you might visit a programming web site that provides code samples, news, and online discussions. Or you might visit a city-specific site that has information about local entertainment, the weather, and commuter traffic. The defining feature of a portal application is that this information is combined on a single page or a small group of pages. In other words, it provides "one-stop shopping" for a significant amount of information. Many portal sites also allow some level of user customization. The IBuySpy portal does not allow user-specific customization, but it does allow an administrator to choose the list of displayed modules, and even select where they appear on the page. In fact, the majority of the complexity of the IBuySpy portal results from the fact that almost every aspect of the portal is configurable and stored in a table in the database.

The IBuySpy portal module is intended to represent a company-specific site that could be hosted on an Intranet or on the web. For example, you could create a portal for a programming team that uses separate modules to display project deadlines, provide links to code resources, and even display information about upcoming social events.

In the last example we worked from the ground up, starting with the database foundation. This time we'll consider the user interface first, and gradually delve into the lower-level details.

## The User Interface

By default, IBuySpy portal presents five tabs. The first tab is shown in Figure 25-20.

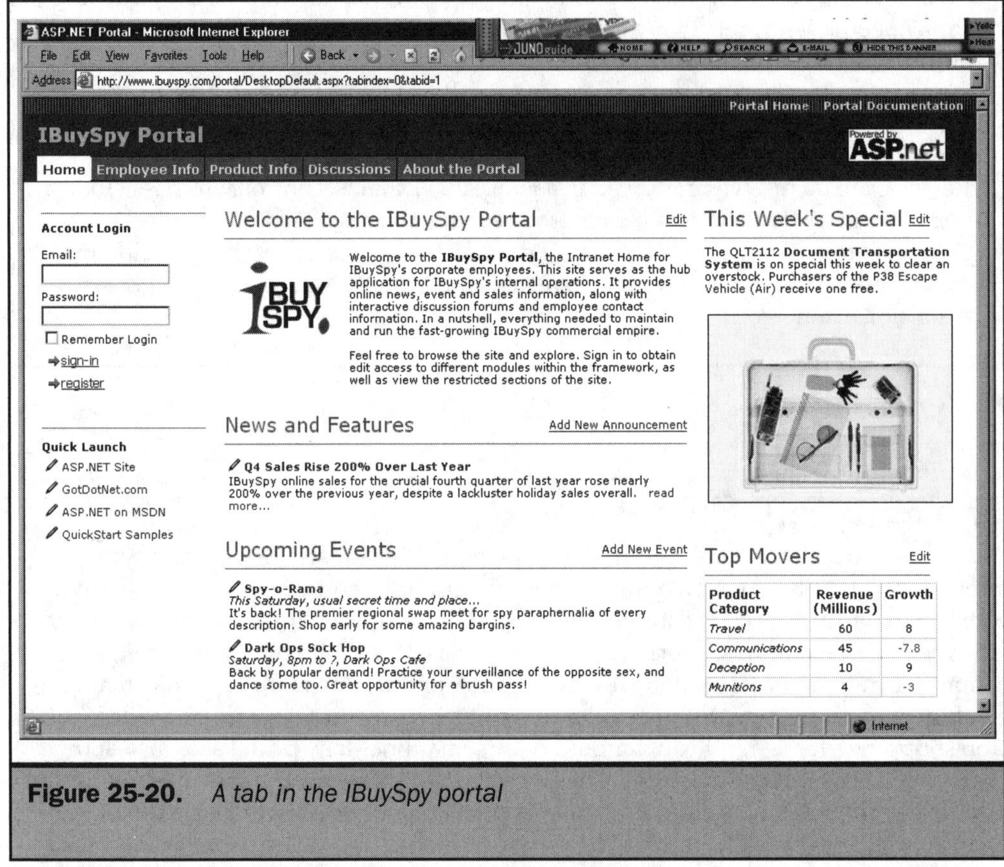


**Figure 25-20.** *A tab in the IBuySpy portal*

This tab is actually made up of seven distinct modules. Each module is contained in a separate control and completely independent from the other (see Figure 25-21).

Altogether, the IBuySpy portal provides ten different modules, which are all described in the documentation for the web site. Most of these modules provide Edit links that allow the user to configure or add to the content. A brief list is shown in Table 25-2.

In at least one way, the IBuySpy pages are probably unlike any ASP.NET web site you've worked with before. The entire interface is generated dynamically. Every module is supported by a single user control, which is supported by a separate component, which in turn draws information from a table in the database.

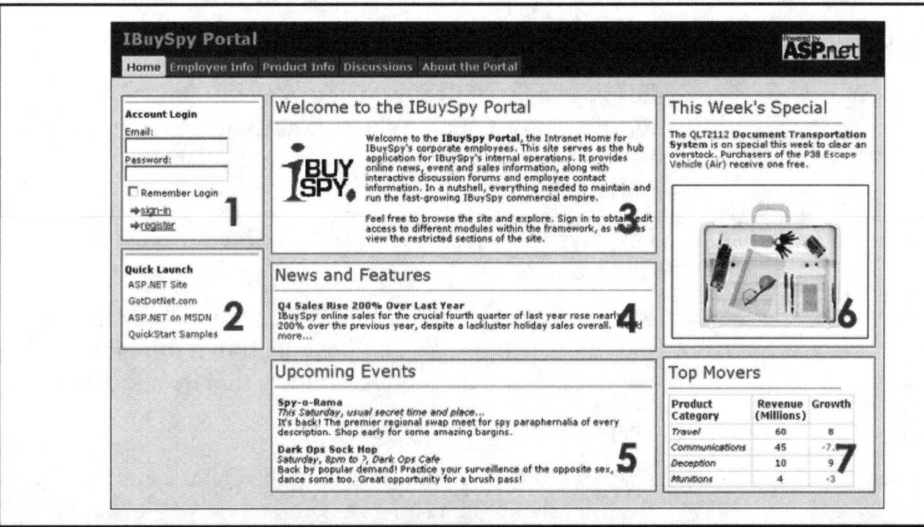


Figure 25-21. *The modules in a tab*

| **Module*** | **Description** |
|---|---|
| Announcements (4) | Displays a list of recent announcements, each of which includes a title, text and a "read more" link. Announcements can be set to automatically expire after a particular date. |
| Contacts | Displays information for a group of people, such as a project team. |
| Discussion | Displays a group of message threads on a specific topic. Includes a Read/Reply Message page, which allows authorized users to reply to existing messages or add a new message thread. |
| Documents | Displays a list of documents with links that allow the user to browse the document online or download it. The document itself can be linked by a URL or stored directly in the SQL database. |

*Number in Figure 25-12

**Table 25-2.** *The IBuySpy Modules*

| Module* | Description |
|---|---|
| Events (5) | Displays a list of upcoming events with time and location information. Like announcements, events can be set to automatically expire from the list after a particular date. |
| Html/Text (3 and 6) | Displays a block of HTML or text drawn from a database. |
| Image | Renders an image using an HTML <img> tag. The module sets the link to a filename drawn from the database, but it does not guarantee that the file exists. |
| Links | Displays a list of hyperlinks. |
| QuickLinks (2) | Displays a list of hyperlinks with the Quick Launch title. It's intended to be used as a compact list of global links that can be used for multiple different portal pages. |
| Sign-In (1) | Provides fields for entering user name and password information. This module is automatically inserted on the first tab if the user is not authenticated. |
| Xml/Xsl (7) | Displays the result of an XML/XSL transform. As with the Image control, only the link to XML and XSL file is stored in the database. |

*Number in Figure 25-12

**Table 25-2.** *The IBuySpy Modules (continued)*

The initial page for the application (DesktopDefault.aspx) loads the appropriate tabs and portal modules dynamically. The (abbreviated) code for this is shown next.

```
Private Sub Page_Init(sender As Object, e As EventArgs) _
  Handles MyBase.Init

    ' Obtain PortalSettings from Current Context.
    Dim _portalSettings As PortalSettings = _
      CType(HttpContext.Current.Items("PortalSettings"), _
```

```
      PortalSettings)

    ' Dynamically inject a signin login module into the top left
    ' corner of the home page if the client is not authenticated.
    If Request.IsAuthenticated = False And _
      _portalSettings.ActiveTab.TabIndex = 0 Then
        LeftPane.Controls.Add( _
          Page.LoadControl("~/DesktopModules/SignIn.ascx"))
        LeftPane.Visible = True
    End If

    If _portalSettings.ActiveTab.Modules.Count > 0 Then

        ' Loop through each entry in the configuration system
        ' for this tab.
        Dim _moduleSettings As ModuleSettings
        For Each _moduleSettings In _
          _portalSettings.ActiveTab.Modules

            Dim parent As Control
            parent = Page.FindControl(_moduleSettings.PaneName)

            ' Create the user control and dynamically
            ' inject it into the page.
            Dim portalModule As PortalModuleControl = _
              CType(Page.LoadControl(_moduleSettings.DesktopSrc), _
              PortalModuleControl)
            portalModule.PortalId = _portalSettings.PortalId
            portalModule.ModuleConfiguration = _moduleSettings
            parent.Controls.Add(portalModule)

            ' Dynamically inject separator break between
            ' portal modules.
            parent.Controls.Add(New LiteralControl("<" + "br" + ">"))
            parent.Visible = True

        Next _moduleSettings

    End If

End Sub
```

### Interesting Facts About this Code

- The foundation of this technique is the Page.LoadControl method, which retrieves a user control from the .ascx filename and turns it into an object. The user control can then be added to any container control, including a panel, table cell, or server-side <div> tag.
- The code in the IBuySpy portal does not make any assumptions about what panels are available on the page. Instead, it retrieves a list of container control names from the PortalSettings.ActiveTab.Modules collection, and uses the Page.FindControl method to locate the control with the indicated name. The PortalSettings class (provided in the Configuration component) retrieves the list of names from the database.
- The sign-in module is the only module that's hard-coded. You can see that it's retrieved from the DesktopModules/SignIn.ascx file and added to the control named LeftPane.

### The Portal Is Completely Customizable

There are several ways that you can configure the IBuySpy portal:

**Use the built-in administration tool.** Whenever you log in as a user with administrative privileges, an additional Admin tab will be added to the end of the tab row. This tab lets you choose modules and assign them to panels on each page.

**Modify the underlying data in the database.** You can perform this task directly using a database utility like SQL Server's Enterprise Manager, or you can click on the Edit link for the appropriate control when it is displayed on the page.

**Add your own controls.** All you need to do is develop a user control and add a record to the database that identifies its filename and title. Optionally, your user control can make use of additional database tables or a special component, like the default IBuySpy modules do.

## The Business Components

The IBuySpy portal follows a multi-tiered design that's similar to the IBuySpy store. The main difference is that each module is independent and uses its own user control, module, and data. The organization of layers is shown in Figure 25-22 for three of the modules.

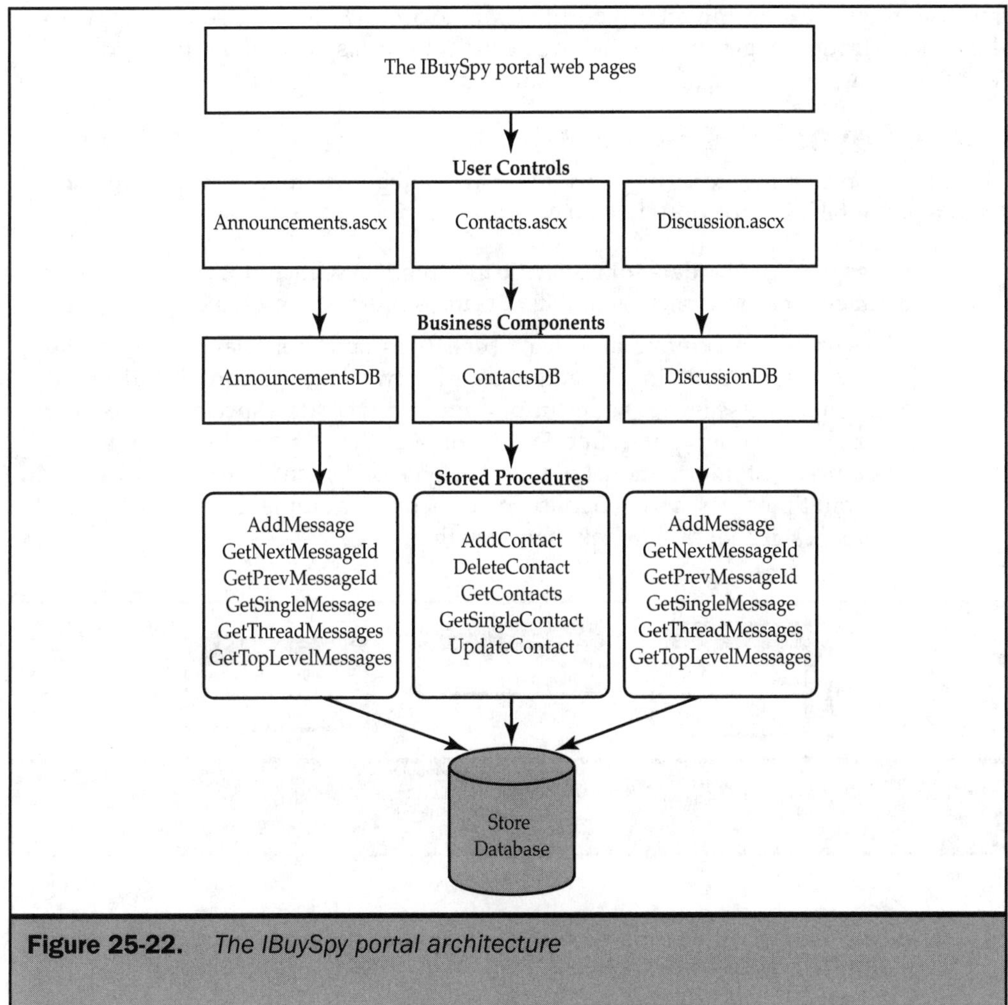


**Figure 25-22.** *The IBuySpy portal architecture*

This chapter won't delve into the methods exposed by each module, as there are far too many. The basic design is quite similar to the IBuySpy store. For example, the AnnouncementsDB component provides methods such as GetAnnouncements, GetSingleAnnouncement, DeleteAnnouncement, and AddAnnouncement. For a quick list of all the available methods, look at Visual Studio .NET's Class View window.

In addition, there are some components that are used as part of the portal framework. These are used to retrieve information such as the number of tabs to display and the modules to place on each one. These include Configuration.vb (where most of the dynamic layout information is retrieved) and Security.vb (where users are authenticated and user roles are determined). In addition, the AdminDB tool is used to support the administration pages, which include SecurityRoles.aspx, TabLayout.aspx, ModuleSettings.aspx, and ModuleDefinitions.aspx.

## The Data Layer

The IBuySpy portal site stores its information in a database named *portal*. There are three types of tables in the portal database:

- Tables that contain data for a specific module. These include Announcements, Contacts, Discussions, Documents, Events, HtmlText, and Links.
- Tables used for user information like Users, Roles, and UserRoles (see Figure 25-23). The Users table contains the actual user list, while Roles contains different configured access levels. For example, you could create a special role record called StaffPlanner that defines a type of user that can modify event and announcement information, but no other type of content. Because one user can have multiple roles, and one role can be used for multiple users, a third table (UserRoles) is required to link them together.

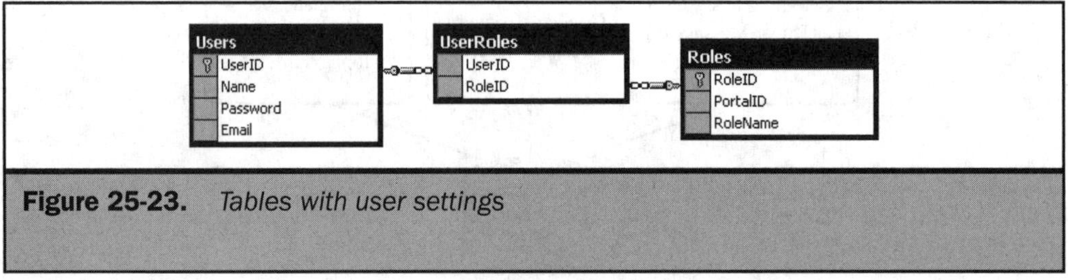


**Figure 25-23.** *Tables with user settings*

- Tables used to define the structure of the portal site, including the available modules (ModuleDefinitions) and tabs (Tabs). Figure 25-24 shows these tables.

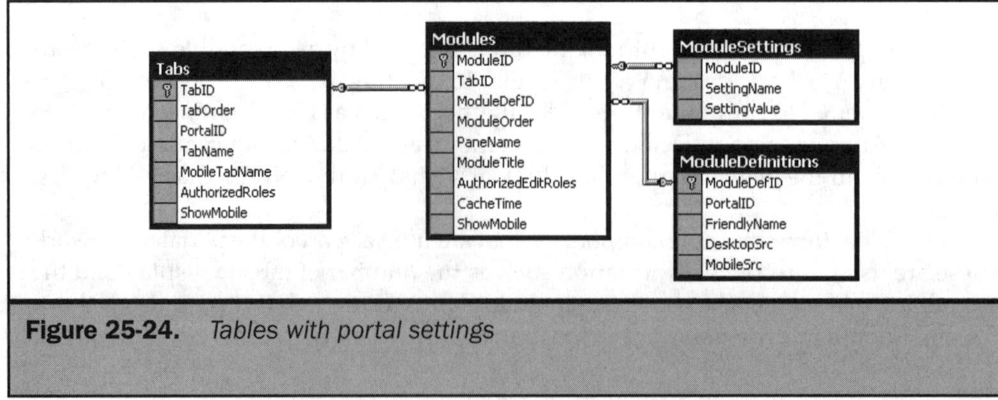


**Figure 25-24.** *Tables with portal settings*

The Modules, Tabs, ModuleSettings, and ModuleDefinitions tables are unique to the IBuySpy portal web site, and give a good insight into how it actually works. The principle is strikingly simple. First, the Tabs table (see Figure 25-25) provides a list of all the available tabs. Additional information specifies the tab title, the relative order, and a semicolon delimited list of user roles who are able to see this tab.

Data in Table 'Tabs' in 'portal' on 'FARIAMAT'

| TabID | TabOrder | PortalID | TabName | MobileTabName | AuthorizedRoles | ShowMobile |
|---|---|---|---|---|---|---|
| 0 | 0 | -1 | Unused Tab | Unused Tab | All Users; | 0 |
| 1 | 0 | 0 | Home | Home | All Users; | 1 |
| 2 | 1 | 0 | Employee Info | HR | All Users; | 1 |
| 3 | 2 | 0 | Product Info | Products | All Users; | 1 |
| 4 | 3 | 0 | Discussions | Discussions | All Users; | 0 |
| 5 | 4 | 0 | About the Portal | About | All Users; | 1 |
| 6 | 5 | 0 | Admin | Admin | Admins; | 0 |

**Figure 25-25.** *Data in the Tabs table*

The ModuleDefinitions table (see Figure 25-26) provides a list of available modules, their titles, and the location of the corresponding .ascx user control file. A second path is provided for a "mobile" version of the control, which would be used by the MobileDefault.aspx page when accessing the site from a browser on a mobile device such as a cell phone.

Data in Table 'ModuleDefinitions' in 'portal' on 'FARIAMAT'

| ModuleDefID | PortalID | FriendlyName | DesktopSrc | MobileSrc |
|---|---|---|---|---|
| 1 | 0 | Announcements | DesktopModules/Announcements.ascx | MobileModules/Announcements.ascx |
| 2 | 0 | Contacts | DesktopModules/Contacts.ascx | MobileModules/Contacts.ascx |
| 3 | 0 | Discussion | DesktopModules/Discussion.ascx | |
| 4 | 0 | Events | DesktopModules/Events.ascx | MobileModules/Events.ascx |
| 5 | 0 | Html Document | DesktopModules/HtmlModule.ascx | MobileModules/Text.ascx |
| 6 | 0 | Image | DesktopModules/ImageModule.ascx | |
| 7 | 0 | Links | DesktopModules/Links.ascx | MobileModules/Links.ascx |
| 8 | 0 | QuickLinks | DesktopModules/QuickLinks.ascx | MobileModules/Links.ascx |
| 9 | 0 | XML/XSL | DesktopModules/XmlModule.ascx | |
| 10 | 0 | Documents | DesktopModules/Document.ascx | |
| 11 | 0 | Module Types (Admin) | Admin/ModuleDefs.ascx | |
| 12 | 0 | Roles (Admin) | Admin/Roles.ascx | |
| 13 | 0 | Tabs (Admin) | Admin/Tabs.ascx | |
| 14 | 0 | Site Settings (Admin) | Admin/SiteSettings.ascx | |
| 15 | 0 | Manage Users (Admin) | Admin/Users.ascx | |

**Figure 25-26.** *Data in the ModuleDefinitions table*

Finally, the Modules tab links the ModuleDefinitions and Tabs tables together. It specifies the modules that will appear for each tab, and indicates the appropriate control name where the user control should be added.

The IBuySpy examples are important because they demonstrate where ASP.NET coding ends and application framework design begins. Both the portal and e-commerce store emphasize a component-based, multi-tiered design. Performance is guaranteed thanks to the careful use of stored procedures and output caching. (You'll note that the more advanced technique of data caching is bypassed entirely. This is partly for simplicity's sake—but data caching also isn't needed thanks to the clear, user-control-based designs.) Best of all, the code is more configurable, updateable, and understandable than anything you could find in traditional ASP design.

The Complete Reference

# Part VI

## ASP.NET Reference

# Chapter 26

## HTML Server Controls

HTML server controls were introduced in Chapter 6 as a simple way to start programming with ASP.NET's new event-driven web page model. While Chapter 6 is an ideal tutorial for getting started, this chapter provides a more detailed reference that describes the key properties and events for each HTML server control, along with sample control tag declarations.

This chapter *won't* teach you about the ASP.NET server control class hierarchy or how the classes relate to one another. Instead, this reference is designed to be as useful as possible "in the field"—in other words, while you are actually programming ASP.NET code. To get additional background information and ASP.NET insight, you should start with the tutorial chapters earlier in this book.

## HTML Controls

HTML controls are server controls that map directly to common HTML tags. They provide far fewer features than web controls, but they are more predictable, and easier to use for some migration tasks. HTML server controls give you the ability to manipulate portions of a web page in your code, but they also allow you to retain precise control over how the page will be rendered in the final HTML output sent to the client. You can create an HTML server control by adding a runat="server" attribute to most common HTML elements.

| Member | Description |
|---|---|
| Attributes | Provides a name/value collection of all the attributes in an HTML server control. Many attributes have corresponding control properties, but this collection allows you to use other attributes or add your own proprietary ones. |
| Style | Provides a name/value collection of all the cascading style sheet (CSS) properties that are applied to the control. |
| Visible | When False, the control will not be rendered in the final page output and will not be shown to the client. |
| Disabled | When True, the control will be read-only and will not accept user input. |
| TagName | A string that indicates the HTML tag name for the server control as a string (for example, "a" for the <a> tag). |

**Table 26-1.** *Common HTML Control Properties*

| Member | Description |
|---|---|
| InnerHtml* | Gets or sets the text found between the opening and closing tags of the control. Special characters are not converted to HTML entities, which means that you can use this property to apply formatting using nested tags such as <b>, <i>, and <h1>. |
| InnerText* | Gets or sets the text between the opening and closing tags of the specified HTML control. Special characters are automatically converted to HTML entities. For example, the less than character (<) is converted to <. |
| Name** | The unique identifier for an input control. |
| Value** | The user content for an input control (for example, the text entered in a text box). |
| Type** | A string representing the value of the type attribute for an input control (for example, "text" is returned for an HtmlInputText control). |

* Only provided for container controls that have both an opening and closing tag and inherit from HtmlContainerControl (includes HtmlTableCell, HtmlTable, HtmlTableRow, HtmlButton, HtmlForm, HtmlAnchor, HtmlGenericControl, HtmlSelect, and HtmlTextArea).

** Only provided for input controls (HtmlInputText, HtmlInputButton, HtmlInputCheckBox, HtmlInputImage, HtmlInputHidden, HtmlInputFile, and HtmlInputRadioButton), which inherit from HtmlInputControl.

**Table 26-1.** *Common HTML Control Properties (continued)*

## HtmlAnchor

HtmlAnchor represents the server-side equivalent of the HTML <a> tag. This tag creates a hyperlink to another page or a bookmark.

```
<a id="MyAnchor"
   href="http:\\www.prosetech.com"
   name="bookmarkname"
   target="_blank"
```

```
   title="My Site"
   runat="server" >
Click Here
</a>
```

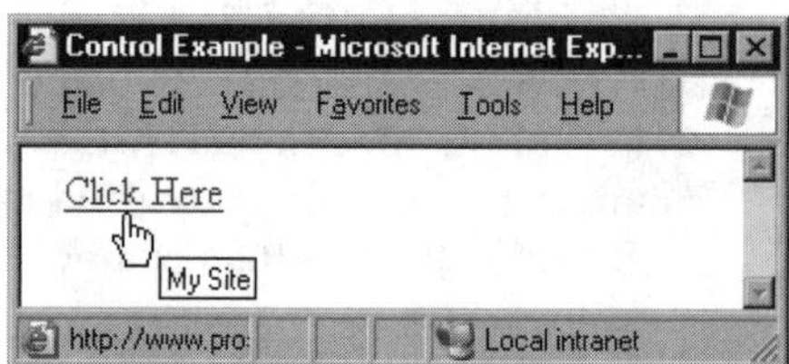


| Member | Description |
|---|---|
| HRef | The destination URL that the browser will go to when the hyperlink is clicked. |
| InnerText and InnerHtml | The content that the user must click to follow the link. You can use the InnerHtml property to add formatting tags to the text, or other HTML elements such as images and line breaks. |
| Name | The bookmark name, which can be used to identify a specific location in a page. You can then link to this location by adding #bookmarkname to the end of the page URL in a request. |
| Target | The target window or frame where the destination page will be opened. This can name a specific frame, or use a special constant such as _blank (for a new window), _parent (the containing frameset), _self (the current window), or _top (the top-level parent). |
| ServerClick event | Allows you to react to the link click programmatically. If you code an event handler for this event, you do not need to enter values for HRef and Target. |

**Table 26-2.** *HtmlAnchor Members*

## HtmlButton

HtmlButton represents the server-side equivalent of the <button> tag, which is supported in Internet Explorer 4.0 or higher. It creates a standard push button that can contain any HTML content, including images. In the following example, the button surface combines two pictures, some bolded text, and two horizontal lines:

```
<button id="MyButton"
        runat="server" type="button" >
   <img src="happy.gif" ><hr>
   <b>A Special Button</b><hr>
   <img src="happy.gif" >
</button>
```

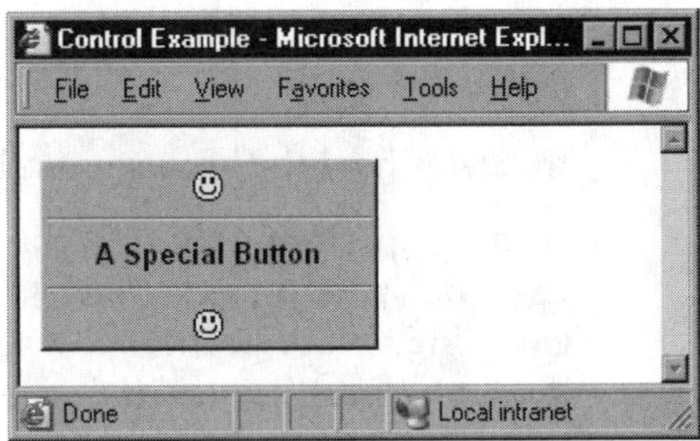


| Member | Description |
|---|---|
| CausesValidation | If set to True (the default), the page will automatically be validated using all the validation controls on the form when the button is clicked. Depending on the browser capabilities, an invalid page may not be posted back (see Chapter 9). |
| InnerText and InnerHtml | The content on the surface of the button. |
| ServerClick event | Occurs when the user clicks the button. |

**Table 26-3.** *HtmlButton Members*

## HtmlForm

HtmlForm represents the server-side equivalent of the <form> tag. All ASP.NET controls must be contained inside a server-side HtmlForm control for your code to be able to access them. However, you will rarely need to interact directly with the HtmlForm itself. In fact, by default, Visual Studio .NET does not even define a variable in code-behind classes for you to access the HtmlForm on a page.

```
<form id="MyForm"
      method="POST"
      runat="server" >
   [Other controls or content goes here.]
</form>
```

| Member | Description |
| --- | --- |
| Method | Indicates how the browser sends data to the server. |
| Enctype | A string specifying the encoding type the browser will use when posting data to the server. The standard encoding is "application/x-www-form-urlencoded" but "multipart/form-data" is required to allow file uploads on pages that use the HtmlInputFile control. |

**Table 26-4.** *HtmlForm Members*

## HtmlGenericControl

HtmlGenericControl represents HTML server controls that aren't represented by other dedicated classes, such as <div>, <span>, <body>, <font>, and so on.

```
<span | body | div | font | others
      id="MyControl"
      runat="server" >
   [Content goes here.]
</span | body | div | font | others>
```

| Member | Description |
|---|---|
| InnerText and InnerHtml | The text and HTML content contained between the opening and closing tags for the control. |
| TagName | Similar to the basic TagName property exposed by all HTML controls, but *not* read-only. This allows you to modify the actual tag programmatically (for example, changing a server-based <div> tag to a server-based <span> tag on postback). |

**Table 26-5.** *HtmlGenericControl Members*

## HtmlImage

HtmlImage represents the server-side equivalent of the HTML <img> tag, which displays a picture (typically a GIF, JPG, or PNG file).

```
<img id="MyImage"
     alt="The Monkey"
     align= "top"
     border="3"
     src="monkey.jpg"
     runat="server" >
```

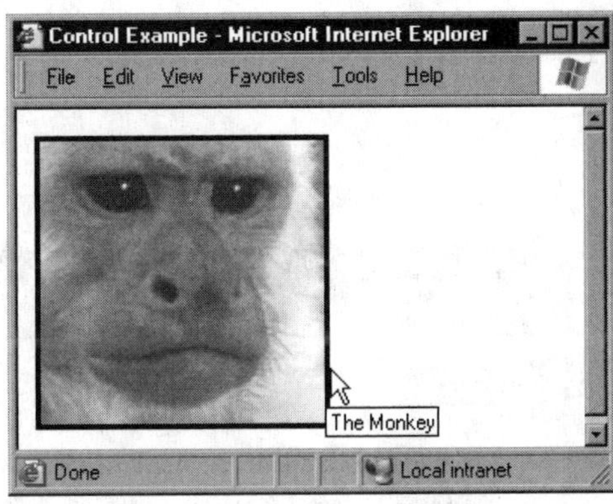

| Member | Description |
|---|---|
| Alt | The text that will be displayed in a browser that does not support pictures, and the pop-up ToolTip text shown in Internet Explorer when the user hovers over the picture with the mouse. |
| Align | The alignment of an image relative to the page (left, top, or right) or the contents of the page (top, middle, bottom). |
| Border | Sets the width of the border in pixels. |
| Height and Width | Sets the proportions of the image in pixels. To avoid distortion, it's usually easier not to specify these properties, and let the image automatically use its intrinsic size. |
| Src | The path and filename of the image that will be displayed. This can be an absolute or relative link. |

**Table 26-6.** *HtmlImage Members*

## HtmlInputButton

HtmlInputButton represents the server-side equivalent of the HTML <input type="button">, <input type="submit">, and <input type="reset"> tags.

```
<input type="button"
       id="MyButton"
       value="Click Me!"
       runat="server" >
```

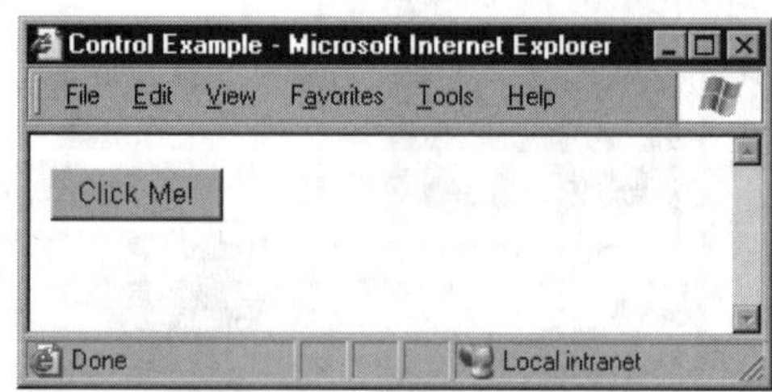

| Member | Description |
|---|---|
| CausesValidation | If set to True (the default), the page will automatically be validated using all the validation controls on the form when the button is clicked. Depending on the browser capabilities, an invalid page may not be posted back (see Chapter 9). |
| Type | Identifies the type of button tag (server, submit, or reset). |
| Value | Sets the button's caption. |
| ServerClick event | Occurs when the user clicks the button. |

**Table 26-7.** *HtmlInputButton Members*

## HtmlInputCheckBox

HtmlInputCheckBox represents the server-side equivalent of the HTML <input type="checkbox"> tag, which creates a checkbox that can be checked or unchecked. This control does not have any associated caption text. Instead, you need to add content next to the control tag.

```
<input type="checkbox"
       id="MyCheckBox"
       checked runat="server" >
  Keep Me Logged In
```

| Member | Description |
|---|---|
| Type | Returns "checkbox" for this type of input control. |
| Checked | Indicates True or False, depending on whether the control is checked. In the control tag, you do not specify True or False. Instead, include the word "checked" on its own to indicate that the initial state of the control is checked. |
| ServerChange event | Occurs when the checkbox state changes between checked and unchecked. Your event handler code cannot react to this event immediately. Instead, it will be triggered first with the next postback. For a checkbox that reacts instantaneously, use the CheckBox web control instead. |

**Table 26-8.** *HtmlInputCheckBox Members*

## HtmlInputFile

HtmlInputFile represents the server-side equivalent of the HTML <input type="file"> tag, which allows the user to upload a file. For a complete example of how to use this control, refer to Chapter 16.

```
<input type="file"
       id="MyFileUploader"
       accept="image/*"
       size="30"
       runat="server" >
```

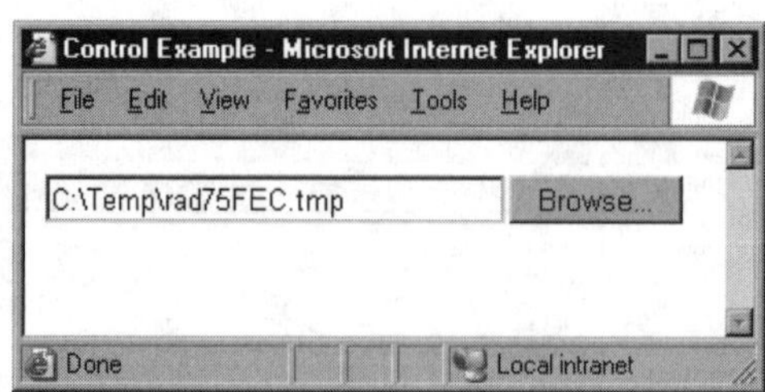

The browser provides the Browse button functionality automatically. However, to allow uploading you need to add a button control that triggers the start of the upload procedure. The event handler for this button simply attempts to read the HtmlInputFile.PostedFile property.

| Member | Description |
|---|---|
| Type | Returns "file" for this type of input control. |
| Accept | A comma-separated list of MIME encodings used to constrain the file types the user can select. MIME encodings take the format "application/type" where application represents a class of applications (such as video, image, or text), and type represents a unique MIME type (or asterisk for all). |
| Size | Sets the width of the file-path selection text box in character columns. |
| MaxLength | Sets the maximum number of characters that are allowed for the path. |
| PostedFile | Allows you to access the posted file as an HttpPostedFile object. Use the PostedFile.SaveAs method to save the file to a location on the server. If the user has not chosen a file, this property will be set to Nothing. |

**Table 26-9.** *HtmlInputFile Class*

## HtmlInputHidden

HtmlInputHidden represents the server-side equivalent of the HTML <input type="hidden"> tag, which allows you to store information between postbacks. In ASP.NET coding, it is generally easier to use the Page.ViewState collection instead to store any information you need to retain. This technique is described in Chapter 10.

```
<input type="hidden"
       id="MyHiddenInformation"
       value="[Some Hidden String Data]"
       runat="server"
```

| Member | Description |
|---|---|
| Type | Returns "hidden" for this type of input control. |
| Value | Contains the hidden information (as a single string). |

**Table 26-10.** *HtmlInputHidden Members*

## HtmlInputRadioButton

HtmlInputRadioButton represents the server-side equivalent of the HTML <input type="radio"> tag. Usually, you will add radio buttons in a group that allows only one item to be selected at a time. The following example shows two radio buttons in a group called GenderGroup. Note that this control does not have any associated caption text. Instead, you need to add content next to the control tag.

```
<input type=radio
       id="Option1"
       name="GenderGroup"
       runat="server" >
   Male<br>
<input type=radio
       id="Option2"
       name="GenderGroup"
       runat="server" >
   Female
```

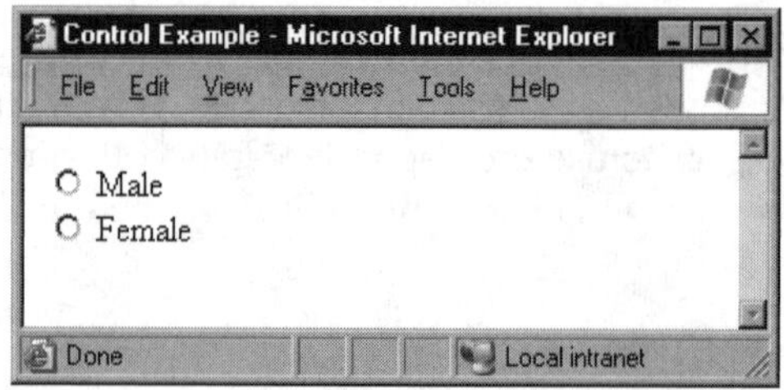

| Member | Description |
|---|---|
| Type | Returns "radio" for this type of input control. |
| Name | Identifies the radio button group. Only one radio button can be selected in a group. |
| Checked | Indicates True or False, depending on whether the radio button is selected. In the control tag, you can include the "checked" attribute on its own to indicate that the radio button is initially selected. |
| ServerChange event | Occurs when the radio button state changes between selected and unselected. Your event handler code cannot react to this event immediately. Instead, it will be triggered first with the next postback. For a radio button that reacts instantaneously, use the RadioButton web control instead. |

**Table 26-11.** *HtmlInputRadioButton Members*

## HtmlInputText

HtmlInputText represents the server-side equivalent of the HTML <input type="text"> tag, which allows single-line text box input.

```
<input type="text"
       id="MyText"
       maxlength="20"
       size="40"
       value="Matthew"
       runat="server">
```

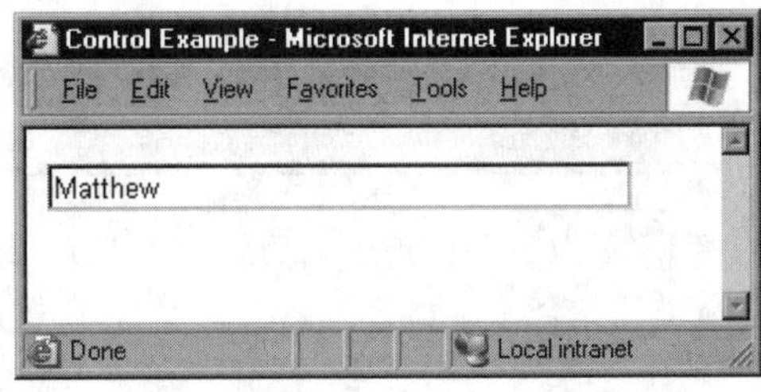

| Member | Description |
|---|---|
| Type | Can be the standard "text" or "password," which uses asterisks (*) to mask user input. |
| MaxLength | The maximum number of characters that the user can type into the text box. |
| Size | Sets the character width of the text box. |
| Value | Sets or returns the text in the text box. |
| ServerChange event | Occurs when the text in the text box is changed. Your event handler code cannot react to this event immediately. Instead, it will be triggered first with the next postback. For a text box that reacts instantaneously, use the TextBox web control instead. |

**Table 26-12.** *HtmlInputText Members*

## HtmlSelect

HtmlSelect represents the server-side equivalent of the HTML <select> tag, which is used to create a list of items. This can be a drop-down list that shows one item at a time or a multi-line list box. It can also be set to allow single or multiple selection.

```
<select id="MyList"
        size="3"
        runat="server" >
  <option value="1">Option 1</option>
  <option value="2">Option 2</option>
  <option value="3">Option 3</option>
  <option value="4">Option 4</option>
</select>
```

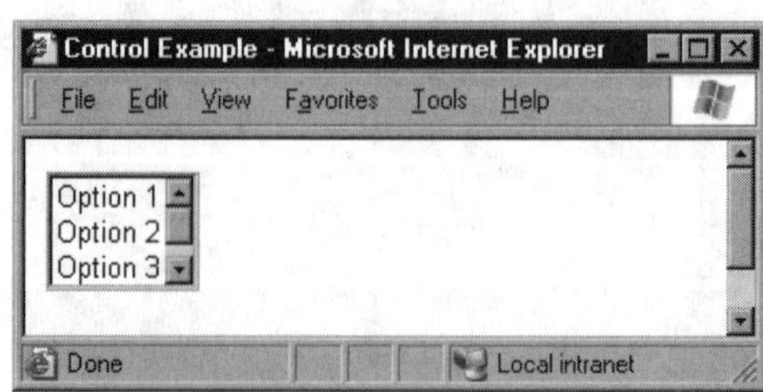

| Member | Description |
|---|---|
| DataSource, DataTextField, and DataValueField | Allows you to bind the list to any data source. If you are binding to a data source with more than one field, you can bind one field to the option item text, and another field to the hidden value attribute for each option item. |
| Size | The number of items that will be shown at once. When set to 1, the HtmlSelect control will become a drop-down list. |
| Multiple | When True, the user can select more than one list item at a time. To specify this in the control declaration, just include the attribute "multiple" on its own. A multiple-select list control will automatically be a list box instead of a drop-down list. |
| SelectedIndex | A zero-based index number that indicates or sets the currently selected item. |
| SelectedIndices | An array of selected index numbers that can be used when multiple item selection is enabled. |
| SelectedValue | Returns the text of the currently selected item. |
| Items | Provides a collection of System.Web.UI.WebControls .ListItem objects that represent all the items in the list. You can check each item's Selected property to see if it is currently selected. You can use the Text and Value items to retrieve or set the information in the option item's text or its value attribute. |
| ServerChange event | Occurs when the selection is changed. Your event handler code cannot react to this event immediately. Instead, it will be triggered first with the next postback. For a list that reacts instantaneously, use the ListBox or DropDownList web control instead. |

**Table 26-13.** *HtmlSelect Members*

## HtmlTable

HtmlTable represents the server-side equivalent of the HTML <table> tag, which is used to create a multi-column table. The basic format of an HtmlTable control tag is as follows:

```
<table id="programmaticID"
       align="left | center | right"
       bgcolor="bgcolor"
       border="borderwidth"
       bordercolor="bordercolor"
       cellpadding="spacing_within_cells"
       cellspacing="spacing_between_cells"
       height="tableheight"
       width="tablewidth"
       runat="server" >
   <tr>
      <td></td>
   </tr>

</table>
```

| Member | Description |
|---|---|
| Align | The alignment of a table relative to the page (left, top, or right) or the contents of the page (top, middle, bottom). |
| BgColor | The background color of all the cells in the table. |
| Border | The width of the border in pixels (the default of –1 means no border). |
| BorderColor | The color of the border as a color code or friendly name (such as "red"). |
| CellPadding | The space, in pixels, between the border of a cell and its contents. |

**Table 26-14.** *HtmlTable Members*

| Member | Description |
|---|---|
| CellSpacing | The space, in pixels, between cells in the table. |
| Height and Width | The height and width of the table in pixels. Alternatively, you can specify a percentage by appending a percent sign to the number in the control tag. Percentages are relative to the height or width of the browser window. |
| Rows | Provides a collection of HtmlTableRow objects that represent the individual <tr> elements in the table. You can use methods such as Add, Insert, and Remove to dynamically configure a table. |

**Table 26-14.** *HtmlTable Members (continued)*

The table is composed of HtmlTableRow and HtmlTableCell elements. You can interact with these elements individually to set row-specific or cell-specific properties (such as the text or the formatting).

| Member | Description |
|---|---|
| Align, BgColor, and BorderColor | These style properties have the same effect for individual rows as the corresponding HtmlTable properties have for the entire table. |
| Height | The height of a row in pixels, which may be constrained by the height of the table. |
| VAlign | The vertical alignment of a row, which can be middle, top, bottom, or baseline. |
| Cells | Provides a collection of HtmlTableCell objects that represent the individual <td> (table cell) and <th> (table header) elements in the table. You can use methods such as Add, Insert, and Remove to dynamically configure a table row. |

**Table 26-15.** *HtmlTableRow Members*

| Member | Description |
| --- | --- |
| Align, BgColor, and BorderColor | These style properties have the same effect for individual cells as the corresponding HtmlTable properties have for the entire table. |
| Height and Width | The height or width of a cell in pixels, which can be constrained by the height of the row. |
| InnerText and InnerHTML | The text or HTML content inside the table cell. |
| VAlign | The vertical alignment of a cell, which can be middle, top, bottom, or baseline. |
| NoWrap | If True, the text in the box will not wrap, but the column will be resized to fit. The default is False. |
| RowSpan and ColSpan | Specifies how many rows or columns a given cell should span. This setting, which allows one cell to occupy a larger area, is not supported by all browsers. |

**Table 26-16.** *HtmlTableCell Members*

A complete table can be created programmatically by adding HtmlTableCell and HtmlTableRow objects at runtime to the HtmlTableRow.Cells and HtmlTable.Rows collections, respectively. (An example of this technique is provided in Chapter 7 with the Table web control.) However, these dynamically created tables will not be persisted in viewstate automatically, and so must be manually recreated after each postback.

Another possibility is to create the table declaratively. Note that tags contained in the HtmlTable tag, such as <tr> and <td>, do not need the runat="server" tag, as this is assumed automatically.

```
<table id="MyTable" cellSpacing="1" cellPadding="1" width="300"
border="1"
       runat="server" >
  <tr>
    <td>Cell 1, 1</td>
    <td>Cell 1, 2</td>
    <td>Cell 1, 3</td></tr>
  <tr>
    <td>Cell 2, 1</td>
    <td>Cell 2, 2</td>
```

```
    <td>Cell 2, 3</td></tr>
  <tr>
    <td>Cell 3, 1</td>
    <td>Cell 3, 2</td>
    <td>Cell 3, 3</td></tr>
</table>
```

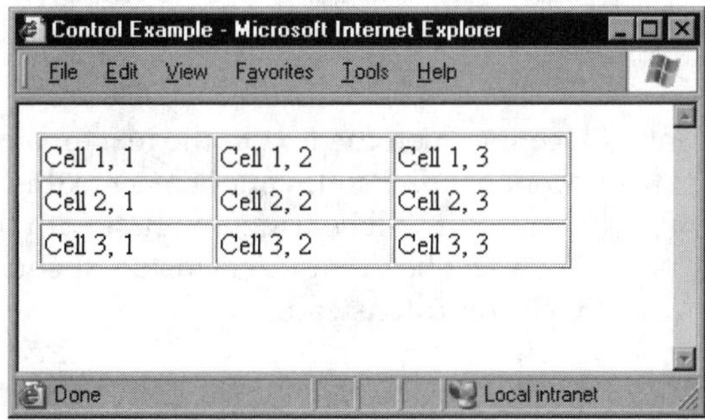

## HtmlTextArea

The HtmlTextArea class represents a multi-line text box and is the server-side equivalent of the HTML <textarea> tag.

```
<textarea id="MyText"
          cols="40"
          rows="5"
          runat="server" >
The Initial Text.
</textarea>
```

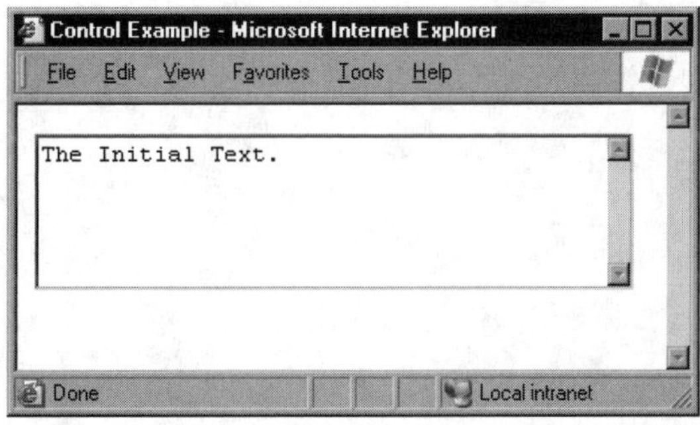

| Member | Description |
|---|---|
| Cols | The character width of the text area. The default is –1 (not set), in which case the browser will apply a default size. |
| Rows | The display height of the text area, in characters. The default is –1 (not set), in which case the browser will apply a default size. |
| Value | Can be used to get or set the text in the text area. You can insert initial text between opening and closing tags, as shown in the example. |
| ServerChange event | Occurs when the text in the text area is changed. Your event handler code cannot react to this event immediately. Instead, it will be triggered first with the next postback. For a text box that reacts instantaneously, use the TextBox web control instead. |

**Table 26-17.** *HtmlTextArea Class*

The Complete Reference

# Chapter 27

## Web Controls

ASP.NET server controls are introduced in Chapters 6, 7, and 9, and data controls are featured in Chapter 15. In these chapters, and throughout the book, you'll find numerous complete examples that show you how to use server controls in your web pages. When you are beginning your ASP.NET programming career, these tutorial chapters are the best place to start.

However, as you become more familiar with ASP.NET, it helps to have more detailed, concise information that shows each control at a glance. This chapter provides that service with a thorough reference that highlights the key points about each web control. The controls are organized by type, and each one is shown with a sample control tag declaration and a list of important members.

## Basic Web Controls

Some web controls duplicate the functionality of HTML server controls, and others are high-level objects that render themselves with dozens of lines of HTML code. When compared to HTML server controls as a whole, web controls provide a higher-level abstraction, more extensive functionality, and the ability to post back automatically and raise a much richer set of events. You'll also find that web controls are more consistent—mirroring their Windows equivalents with common properties such as Text, ForeColor, and BorderStyle.

| Member | Description |
| --- | --- |
| AccessKey | Specifies the keyboard shortcut as one letter. For example, if you set this to "Y", the ALT-Y keyboard combination will automatically change focus to this web control. This feature is only supported on Internet Explorer 4 and higher. |
| BackColor, BorderColor and ForeColor | Sets the colors used for the background, border, and foreground of the control. Usually, the foreground color is used for text. Colors can be set in the attribute tag using standard HTML color identifiers such as the name of a color (for example, "black" or "red") or an RGB value expressed in hexadecimal format (like #ffffff). You can also set the color in code by creating and assigning a System.Drawing.Color object. |

**Table 27-1.** *Common Web Server Control Properties*

| Member | Description |
|---|---|
| BorderWidth | Specifies the size of the control border in pixels. |
| BorderStyle | One of the values from the BorderStyle enumeration, such as Dashed, Dotted, Double, Groove, Ridge, Inset, Outset, Solid, or None. |
| Enabled | When set to False, the control will be visible, but will not be able to receive user input or focus. |
| Font | Specifies the font used to render any text in the control, as a special System.Drawing.Font object. In the control tag, you must specify the Font using the special object walker syntax, as described in Chapter 7. |
| Height and Width | Specifies the width and height of the control. By default, these numbers will be interpreted as pixel measurements, but you can specify otherwise, as described in Chapter 7. For some controls, these properties will be ignored when used with older browsers. |
| Style | Provides a name/value collection of all the cascading style sheet (CSS) properties that are applied to the control. This property is generally less used with web controls, in favor of higher-level properties (such as BackColor) that take precedence. |
| TabIndex | A number that allows you to control the TAB order. The control with a TabIndex of 0 has the focus when the page first loads. Pressing TAB moves the user to the control with the next lowest TabIndex, provided it is enabled. This property is only supported in Internet Explorer 4.0 and higher. |
| ToolTip | Displays a text message when the user hovers the mouse above the control. Many older browsers do not support this property. |
| Visible | When set to False, the control will be hidden and will not be rendered to the final HTML page that is sent to the client. |

**Table 27-1.** *Common Web Server Control Properties (continued)*

ASP.NET developers commonly ask what color names are valid to use in the .aspx control tag. To find the complete list, you can refer to the System.Drawing.KnownColor enumeration. You can also retrieve the named colors as Color objects through the properties of the System.Drawing.Color class. Following is a list of valid color names:

AliceBlue
AntiqueWhite
Aqua
Aquamarine
Azure
Beige
Bisque
Black
BlanchedAlmond
Blue
BlueViolet
Brown
BurlyWood
CadetBlue
Chartreuse
Chocolate
Coral
CornflowerBlue
Cornsilk
Crimson
Cyan
DarkBlue
DarkCyan
DarkGoldenrod
DarkGray
DarkGreen
DarkKhaki
DarkMagenta
DarkOliveGreen
DarkOrange
DarkOrchid
DarkRed
DarkSalmon
DarkSeaGreen
DarkSlateBlue
DarkSlateGray
DarkTurquoise
DarkViolet
DeepPink
DeepSkyBlue
DimGray
DodgerBlue
Firebrick
FloralWhite
ForestGreen
Fuchsia
Gainsboro
GhostWhite
Gold
Goldenrod
Gray
Green
GreenYellow
Honeydew
HotPink
IndianRed
Indigo
Ivory
Khaki
Lavender
LavenderBlush
LawnGreen
LemonChiffon
LightBlue
LightCoral
LightCyan
LightGoldenrodYellow
LightGray
LightGreen
LightPink
LightSalmon
LightSeaGreen
LightSkyBlue
LightSlateGray
LightSteelBlue
LightYellow
Lime
LimeGreen
Linen
Magenta
Maroon
MediumAquamarine
MediumBlue
MediumOrchid
MediumPurple
MediumSeaGreen
MediumSlateBlue

| | | |
|---|---|---|
| MediumSpringGreen | PaleVioletRed | SkyBlue |
| MediumTurquoise | PapayaWhip | SlateBlue |
| MediumVioletRed | PeachPuff | SlateGray |
| MidnightBlue | Peru | Snow |
| MintCream | Pink | SpringGreen |
| MistyRose | Plum | SteelBlue |
| Moccasin | PowderBlue | Tan |
| NavajoWhite | Purple | Teal |
| Navy | Red | Thistle |
| OldLace | RosyBrown | Tomato |
| Olive | RoyalBlue | Transparent |
| OliveDrab | SaddleBrown | Turquoise |
| Orange | Salmon | Violet |
| OrangeRed | SandyBrown | Wheat |
| Orchid | SeaGreen | White |
| PaleGoldenrod | SeaShell | WhiteSmoke |
| PaleGreen | Sienna | Yellow |
| PaleTurquoise | Silver | YellowGreen |

## Button

This control creates the familiar clickable push button on a web page. Clicking a button automatically posts back the page, and raises the appropriate Click event.

```
<asp:Button id="cmdClickMe"
     Text="Click Me"
     CausesValidation="True"
     runat="server"/>
```

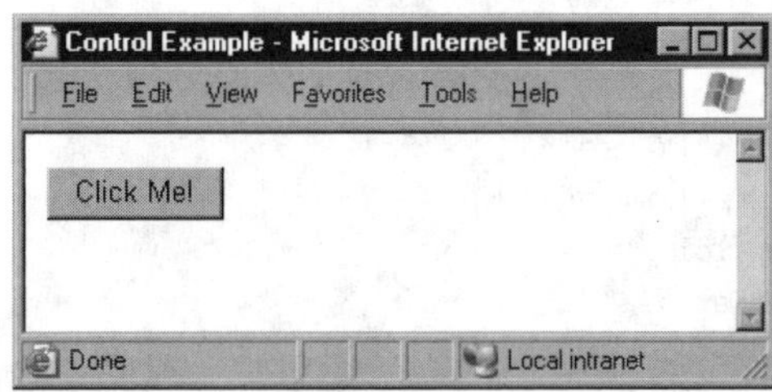

| Member | Description |
|---|---|
| Text | The button's caption. |
| CausesValidation | If set to True (the default), the page will automatically be validated using all the validation controls on the form when the button is clicked. Depending on the browser capabilities, an invalid page may not be posted back (see Chapter 9). |
| Click and Command events | Occur when the button is clicked. The only difference between the two is that the Command event receives extra information, namely the CommandName and CommandArgument properties. The examples in this book don't use the Command event (except in the case of templated data controls). Instead, they rely on .NET's ability to compare and identify control objects. |
| CommandName and CommandArgument | Extra information provided to the Command event, which can allow you to uniquely identify the button in the case that your event handler is receiving the events from multiple different button controls. The CommandName is a string meant to represent the action (such as "Sort) while CommandArgument stores any additional information (such as the field to sort by). |

**Table 27-2.** *Button Members*

## CheckBox

This control creates a checkbox that can be checked or unchecked, along with an associated label.

```
<asp:CheckBox id="chkSignUp"
     AutoPostBack="False"
     Text="Keep Me Logged In"
     TextAlign="Right"
     Checked="True"
     runat="server"/>
```

| Member | Description |
|---|---|
| AutoPostBack | Determines whether the page will be posted back when the checkbox state is changed. This allows your code to react to the CheckedChanged event immediately. |
| Text | The label that is displayed next to the checkbox. |
| TextAlign | The side of the checkbox where the text will be displayed. Can be Left or Right. |
| Checked | Indicates or sets the current state of the checkbox. |
| CheckedChanged event | Fires when the checkbox state changes (for example, when the user clicks to check or uncheck the checkbox). If AutoPostBack is False, this event will be "delayed" until the next postback. |

**Table 27-3.** *CheckBox Members*

## HyperLink

This control represents a link to another page, either as underlined hyperlink text or as an image. Unlike the anchor tag (and HtmlAnchor control), this control cannot be used to create a bookmark. The HyperLink class does not provide any type of Click event—for this type of functionality you need to use the LinkButton web control.

```
<asp:HyperLink id="lnkProseTech"
     NavigateUrl="http:\\www.prosetech.com "
     Text="Click Here"
     Target="_blank"
```

```
    ToolTip = "MySite"
    runat="server"/>
```

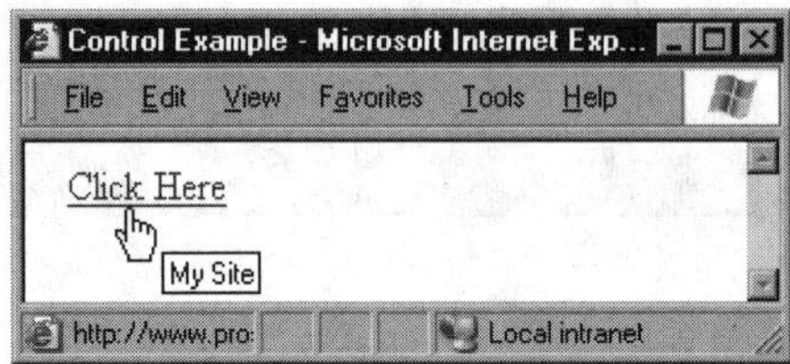


| Member | Description |
|---|---|
| NavigateUrl | The destination URL the browser will go to when the hyperlink is clicked. |
| Text | The text content that the user must click to follow the link. |
| ImageUrl | The image that the user must click to follow the link (as a relative or absolute filename). If both ImageUrl and Text are set, the image will take precedence and the text will not be shown, unless there is a problem finding and displaying the image. |
| Target | The target window or frame where the destination page will be opened. This can name a specific frame, or use a special constant such as _blank (for a new window), _parent (the containing frameset), _self (the current window) or _top (the top-level parent). |

**Table 27-4.** *HyperLink Members*

## Image

This control displays an image (typically a GIF, JPG, or PNG file).

```
<asp:Image id="imgMonkey" runat="server"
     ImageUrl="monkey.jpg"
     AlternateText="The Monkey"
     ImageAlign="top"
```

```
      BorderWidth="3"
      runat="server" />
```

| Member | Description |
|---|---|
| AlternateText | The text that will be displayed in a browser that does not support pictures, and the pop-up ToolTip text shown in Internet Explorer when the user hovers over the picture with the mouse. |
| ImageAlign | The alignment of an image relative to the page and its text (includes values such as Left, Right, Middle, Top, Bottom, and Texttop). |
| ImageUrl | The path and filename of the image that will be displayed. This can be an absolute or relative URL path. |

**Table 27-5.** *Image Members*

## ImageButton

This control is almost identical to the Image control, with one important difference—it raises a server-side Click event when the user clicks it.

```
<asp:ImageButton id="imgMonkey" runat="server"
      ImageUrl="monkey.jpg"
```

```
AlternateText="The Monkey"
ImageAlign="top"
BorderWidth="3"
runat="server" />
```

| Member | Description |
|---|---|
| AlternateText | The text that will be displayed in a browser that does not support pictures, and the pop-up ToolTip text shown in Internet Explorer when the user hovers over the picture with the mouse. |
| ImageAlign | The alignment of an image relative to the page and its text (includes values such as Left, Right, Middle, Top, Bottom, and Texttop). |
| ImageUrl | The path and filename of the image that will be displayed. This can be an absolute or relative URL path. |
| CausesValidation | If set to True (the default), the page will automatically be validated using all the validation controls on the form when the image is clicked. Depending on the browser capabilities, an invalid page may not be posted back (see Chapter 9). |
| Click and Command events | Occur when the image is clicked. The only difference between the two is that the Command event receives extra information, namely the CommandName and CommandArgument properties. |
| CommandName and CommandArgument | Extra information provided to the Command event, which can allow you to uniquely identify the image in the case that your event handler is receiving the events from multiple different controls. The CommandName is a string meant to represent the action (such as "Sort) while CommandArgument stores any additional information (such as the field to sort by). |

**Table 27-6.** *ImageButton Properties*

## Label

This control represents ordinary text on a web page. You can set the Text property as an attribute, as with any other control.

```
<asp:Label id="lblText"
     Text="This is the label text."
     runat="server"/>
```

You can also set the Text property by adding text between separate opening and closing tags.

```
<asp:Label id="lblText"
     runat="server">
  This is the label text.
</asp:Label>
```

This choice is provided by some other web controls, but it is most useful with the Label control, which may require a large amount of static text and embedded HTML elements.

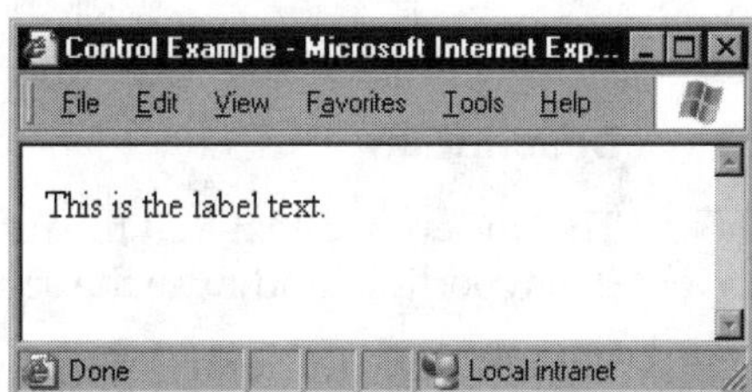


| Member | Description |
|---|---|
| Text | The text displayed in the label. You can embed HTML tags (such as <b> and <br>) along with the content to further format the text. |

**Table 27-7.** *Label Members*

## LinkButton

The LinkButton control is similar to the HyperLink control (in fact, the appearance is identical). The difference is that while the HyperLink control automatically navigates to the specified URL, the LinkButton control does not have any associated URL. Instead, it raises a server-side Click event. One reason you might want to use the LinkButton control is to replace a normal HyperLink with a hyperlink that forces the page to be validated before allowing the user to continue.

```
<asp:LinkButton id="lnkClickMe"
     Text="Click Here"
     Tooltip="My Site"
     CausesValidation="True"
     runat="server"/>
```

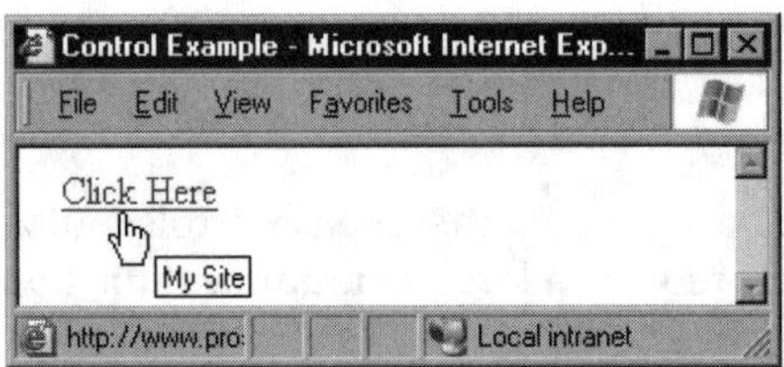


| Member | Description |
|---|---|
| Text | The underlined text that the user must click to activate the hyperlink (and raise the server-side Click event). |
| CausesValidation | If set to True (the default), the page will automatically be validated using all the validation controls on the form when the link is clicked. Depending on the browser capabilities, an invalid page may not be posted back (see Chapter 9). |
| Click and Command events | Occur when the link is clicked. The only difference between the two is that the Command event receives extra information, namely the CommandName and CommandArgument properties. |

**Table 27-8.** *LinkButton Properties*

| Member | Description |
|---|---|
| CommandName and CommandArgument | Extra information provided to the Command event, which can allow you to uniquely identify the link in the case that your event handler is receiving the events from multiple different controls. The CommandName is a string meant to represent the action (such as "Sort) while CommandArgument stores any additional information (such as the field to sort by). |

**Table 27-8.** *LinkButton Properties (continued)*

## Literal

A Literal control places plain text on a page without any HTML markup (unless you specify it). You can use a Literal control to provide the same functionality provided by the Label control. However, you cannot apply any formatting, styles, or fonts to a Literal control by using the standard WebControl properties.

```
<asp:Literal id="ltrText"
     Text="<i>This</i> is plain literal text."
     runat="server"/>
```

You can also set the Text property by adding text between separate opening and closing tags.

```
<asp:Literal id="ltrText"
     runat="server">
  <i>This</i> is plain literal text.
</asp:Label>
```

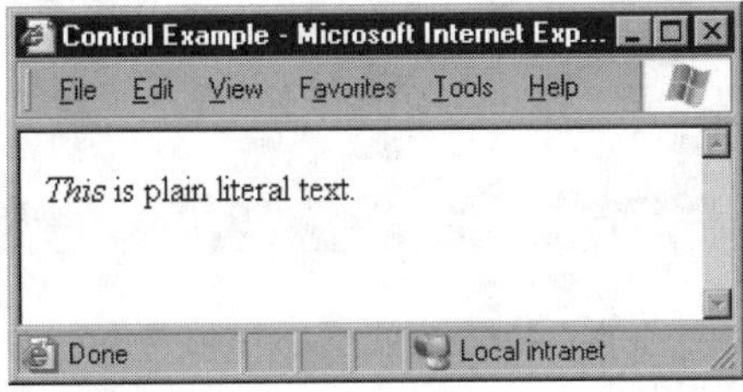

The System.Web.UI.WebControls.Literal class should not be confused with the System.Web.LiteralControl class, which is used by ASP.NET to represent static HTML content that does not need to be made available on the server side.

| Member | Description |
|---|---|
| Text | The text displayed on the page. You can embed HTML tags (such as <b> and <br>) along with the content to further format the text. |

**Table 27-9.** *Literal Members*

## Panel

The Panel control is used to group other controls. It can be used with or without a border. One of the most useful ways to use a Panel is to hide an entire group of controls, by setting the containing Panel's Visible property to False. This technique allows you to simulate a multi-page wizard in one page, by alternately hiding and showing different Panel controls. Panels are always made of both an opening and a closing tag.

```
<asp:Panel id="pnlControls"
     BackImageUrl="url"
     HorizontalAlign="Left"
     Wrap="True"
     runat="server">
  This is the first line....<br>
  This is the second line.
</asp:Panel>
```

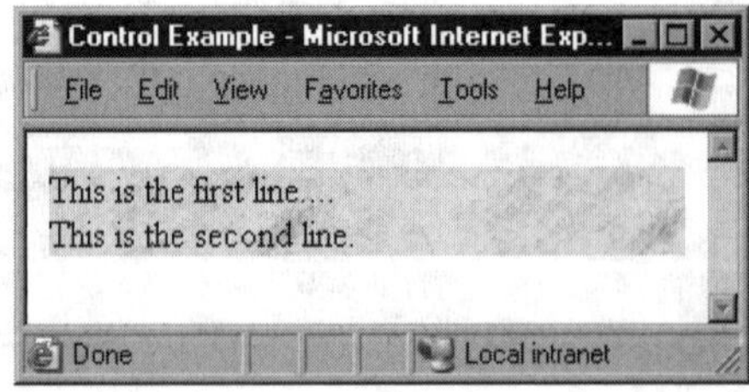

| Member | Description |
|---|---|
| BackImageUrl | This property sets an image that will be displayed behind the content in the Panel. If the image is smaller than the Panel, it will be tiled to fill in the Panel. |
| HorizontalAlign | Gets or sets the horizontal alignment of the contents within the panel. |
| Wrap | When set to True, the contents will be wrapped inside the Panel (depending on the Height and Width properties you have set for the Panel). Otherwise the Panel will be automatically sized to fit its contents. |

**Table 27-10.** *Panel Members*

## PlaceHolder

The PlaceHolder class can be used as a container for dynamically added controls. The PlaceHolder really has no useful properties of its own. However, you can place a control inside it by adding a control object to its Controls collection.

```
<asp:PlaceHolder id="Holder"
     runat="server"/>
```

## RadioButton

This control represents a radio button that, in conjunction with other radio buttons, allows a user to select exactly one choice from a group of options. Every RadioButton control has an associated label that you can use.

```
<asp:RadioButton id="optMale"
     AutoPostBack="False"
     Checked="True"
     GroupName="Gender"
     Text="Male"
```

```
        TextAlign="Right"
        runat="server"/>
<br>
<asp:RadioButton id="optFemale"
        AutoPostBack="False"
        GroupName="Gender"
        Text="Female"
        TextAlign="Right"
        runat="server"/>
```

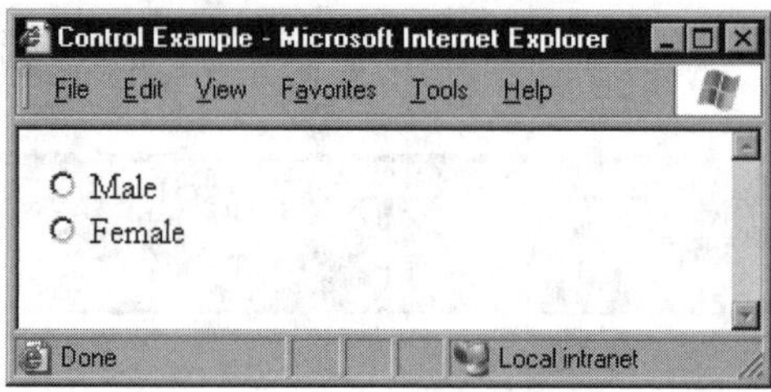


| Member | Description |
|---|---|
| AutoPostBack | Determines whether the page will be posted back when the radio button state is changed. This allows your code to react to the CheckedChanged event immediately. |
| GroupName | Identifies the radio button group. Only one radio button can be selected in a group. |
| Text | The label that is displayed next to the radio button. |
| TextAlign | The side of the radio button where the text will be displayed. Can be Left or Right. |
| Checked | Indicates or sets the current state of the radio button. When filled in, Checked is True. |
| CheckedChanged event | Fires when the radio button state changes (for example, when the user clicks on a different option in the same group). If AutoPostBack is False, this event will be "delayed" until the next postback. |

**Table 27-11.** *RadioButton Members*

## Table

This control represents a table with rows and columns. Tables are made up of TableRow controls, which in turn are made up of TableCell objects. The format is as follows:

```
<asp:Table id="programmaticID"
     BackImageUrl="url"
     CellPadding="cellpadding"
     CellSpacing="cellspacing"
     GridLines="None|Horizontal|Vertical|Both"
     HorizontalAlign="Center|Justify|Left|NotSet|Right"
     runat="server">

   <asp:TableRow>
      <asp:TableCell>
         Cell text
      </asp:TableCell>
   </asp:TableRow>

</asp:Table>
```

| Member | Description |
|---|---|
| BackImageUrl | This property sets an image that will be displayed "behind." The image will be tiled if it is smaller than the table. |
| CellPadding | The space, in pixels, between the border of a cell and its contents. |
| CellSpacing | The space, in pixels, between cells in the same table. |
| GridLines | Specifies the types of gridlines that will be shown in the table (None, Horizontal, Vertical, or Both). |
| HorizontalAlign | The alignment of the table with the rest of the page. |
| Rows | Provides a collection of TableRow objects that represent the individual rows in the table. You can use methods such as Add, Insert, and Remove to dynamically configure a table. |

**Table 27-12.** *Table Members*

The table is composed of TableRow and TableCell objects. You can interact with these elements individually to set row-specific or cell-specific properties (such as the text or the formatting). You can use the standard properties such as BorderStyle and BackColor with any of these objects to fine-tune the appearance of your table. Remember, however, any changes you make programmatically in code will *not* be persisted in the page's view state.

| Member | Description |
|---|---|
| HorizontalAlign | The horizontal alignment of a row, which can be Left, Center, Right, or Justify. |
| VerticalAlign | The vertical alignment of a row, which can be Middle, Top, Bottom, or Baseline. |
| Cells | Provides a collection of TableCell objects that represent the individual cells in the table. You can use methods such as Add, Insert, and Remove to dynamically configure a table row. |

**Table 27-13.** *TableRow Members*

| Member | Description |
|---|---|
| ColumnSpan and RowSpan | Specifies how many rows or columns a given cell should span. This setting, which allows one cell to occupy a larger area, is not supported by all browsers. |
| HorizontalAlign and VerticalAlign | The horizontal or vertical alignment of a single cell. These settings work the same as the corresponding TableRow properties. |
| Text | The actual text in the cell. |
| Wrap | If False, the text in the box will not wrap, but will extend the cell's border. The default is False. |

**Table 27-14.** *HtmlTableCell Members*

A complete table can be created programmatically by adding TableCell and TableRow objects at runtime to the TableRow.Cells and Table.Rows collections, respectively. (An example of this technique is provided in Chapter 7.) Another possibility is to create the table declaratively.

```
<asp:Table id="Table1" runat="server"
    CellPadding="10"
    GridLines="Both"
    HorizontalAlign="Center">
    <asp:TableRow>
       <asp:TableCell>
          Row 0, Col 0
       </asp:TableCell>
       <asp:TableCell>
          Row 0, Col 1
       </asp:TableCell>
    </asp:TableRow>
    <asp:TableRow>
       <asp:TableCell>
          Row 1, Col 0
       </asp:TableCell>
       <asp:TableCell>
          Row 1, Col 1
       </asp:TableCell>
    </asp:TableRow>
 </asp:Table>
```

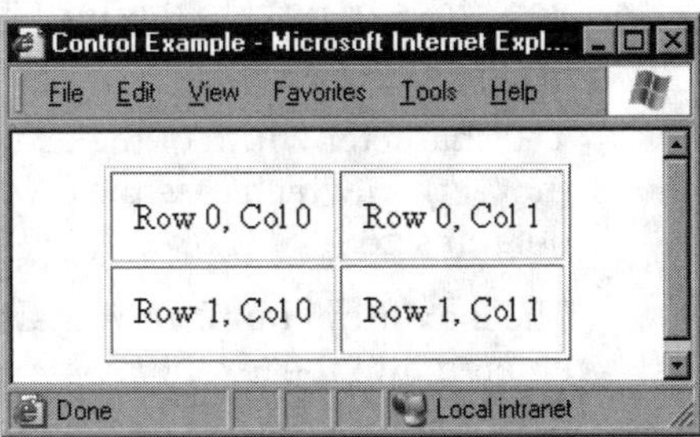


## TextBox

This control represents a text box where the user can enter information. Depending on the settings you specify, this control may be generated as an HTML <input type="text"> tag, a <textarea> tag, or an <input type="password"> tag.

```
<asp:TextBox id="txtEntry"
     AutoPostBack="False"
```

```
        Columns="30"
        MaxLength="100"
        Rows="2"
        Text="Sample Text"
        TextMode="Multiline"
        Wrap="True"
        runat="server"/>
```

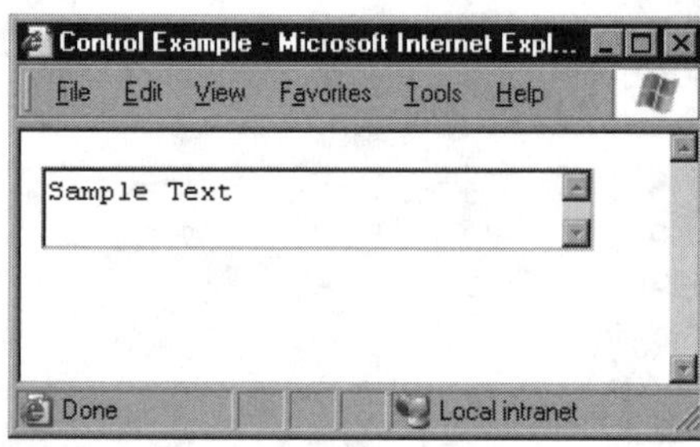


| Member | Description |
|---|---|
| AutoPostBack | Determines whether the page will be posted back when the text box is changed and focus changes to another control (for example, when the user presses the TAB key after making a modification). This allows your code to react to the TextChanged event immediately. |
| Columns | The character width of the text area. The default is -1 (not set), in which case the browser will apply a default size. |
| MaxLength | The maximum number of characters that can be entered into the text box. |
| Rows | The display height, in characters, of the text area. The default is -1 (not set), in which case the browser will apply a default size. |
| Text | Gets or sets the text. |

**Table 27-15.** *TextBox Members*

| Member | Description |
|---|---|
| TextMode | Specifies a value from the text mode enumeration, either SingleLine, MultiLine, or Password. |
| TextChanged event | Occurs when the text in the text area is changed and focus changes to another control. |
| Wrap | When set to True, the text will automatically wrap at the border. This setting is only applicable when TextMode is set to MultiLine. |

**Table 27-15.** *TextBox Members (continued)*

## List Controls

There are four basic list controls. Each of them inherits its basic functionality from the abstract ListControl class.

| Member | Description |
|---|---|
| AutoPostBack | Determines whether the page will be posted back when the list control selection is changed. This allows your code to react to the SelectedIndexChanged event immediately. |
| DataMember and DataSource | These properties allow the list control to be bound to a data source, as described in Chapter 14. The DataSource property identifies the data source that contains the information. If there is more than one table in the data source (as with a DataSet), DataMember identifies the table to use. |

**Table 27-16.** *ListControl Members*

| Member | Description |
| --- | --- |
| DataTextField, DataValueField, and DataTextFormattingString | DataTextField indicates the field that will be used to populate the visible portion of the list, and DataTextFormattingString specifies a format string that will be used to format it. DataValueField indicates the field that will be used to assign each item's value. The value is accessible through the ListItem class, but not visible to the user. |
| Items | Provides all the items in the list as a collection of ListItem objects. You can use the methods (such as Add, Remove, and Insert) to modify the class. These dynamic changes will be automatically persisted in the page's view state. |
| SelectedIndex | Gets or sets the integer index that identifies the selected item. The list is zero-based (so the first item has index 0) and -1 represents no selection. |
| SelectedItem | Retrieves the item that is currently selected, as a ListItem object. |
| DataBind() | This method fills the control with the data from the data source. This method is required to update the list control data and is often performed on postback. You can also call the Page.DataBind() method to bind all data-bound controls at once. |
| SelectedIndexChanged event | Fires when the selection in the list changes. If AutoPostBack is False, this event will be "delayed" until the next postback. |

**Table 27-16.** *ListControl Members (continued)*

The items of all web control lists are represented using the ListItem object.

| Member | Description |
| --- | --- |
| Text | Gets or sets the text that is displayed for this item in the list. |

**Table 27-17.** *ListItem Members*

| Member | Description |
|---|---|
| Value | Gets or sets the string value that is associated with this item (but not displayed). A typical use of the Value property is to store the unique database ID number for a row. |
| Selected | True if the item is currently selected. |

**Table 27-17.** *ListItem Members (continued)*

## DropDownList

This control represents a drop-down single-select list. To create a DropDownList, you can add entries in code using the Items collection, or you can nest ListItem tags inside the DropDownList tag, as shown next.

```
<asp:DropDownList id="lstItems"
                  AutoPostBack="False"
                  Width="100"
                  runat="server">
  <asp:ListItem value="1" selected="True" Text="Item 1"/>
  <asp:ListItem value="2" Text="Item 2"/>
  <asp:ListItem value="3" Text="Item 3"/>
</asp:DropDownList>
```

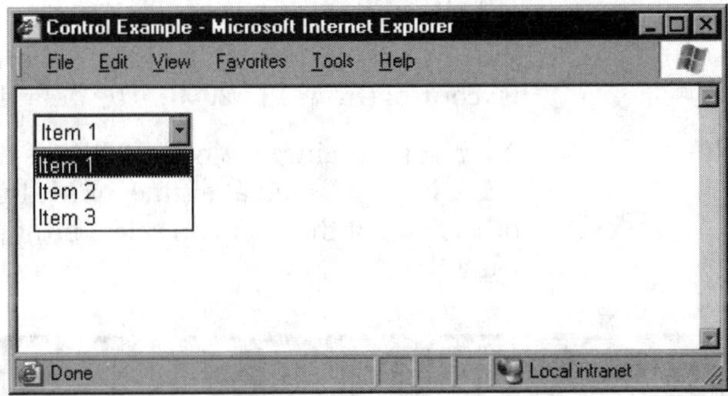


The DropDownList control does not add any new properties, methods, or events on top of the basic ListControl class.

## ListBox

This control displays a list of items. The ListBox control can allow single or multiple selection, and can be filled in the control tag or dynamically through code. ListBox item changes will be remembered across postbacks.

```
<asp:ListBox id="lstItems"
             AutoPostBack="False"
             Rows="3"
             SelectionMode="Single"
             Width="100"
             runat="server">
  <asp:ListItem value="1" selected="True" Text="Item 1"/>
  <asp:ListItem value="2" Text="Item 2"/>
  <asp:ListItem value="3" selected="True" Text="Item 3"/>
</asp:ListBox>
```

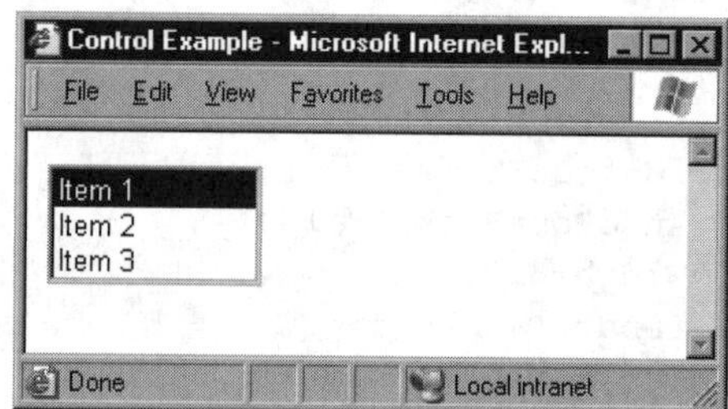


| Member | Description |
|---|---|
| Rows | The number of rows that will be visible at once in the list control (from 1 to 2000). The default value is 4. |
| SelectionMode | Can be either Single, which indicates that only one item can be selected at a time, or Multiple, which indicates that the user can select multiple items by using the CTRL key. |

**Table 27-18.** *ListBox Members*

## CheckBoxList

The CheckBoxList is a list of individual checkbox items grouped in a list, which can be checked or unchecked in any combination. The only difference between using a CheckBoxList control instead of multiple CheckBox controls is convenience, and more data binding options.

```
<asp:CheckBoxList id="lstItems"
                  CellPadding="5"
                  RepeatColumns="2"
                  RepeatDirection="Vertical"
                  RepeatLayout="Table"
                  TextAlign="Right"
                  AutoPostBack="False"
                  Width="200"
                  runat="server">
  <asp:ListItem value="1" selected="True" Text="Item 1"/>
  <asp:ListItem value="2" Text="Item 2"/>
  <asp:ListItem value="3" selected="True" Text="Item 3"/>
  <asp:ListItem value="3" Text="Item 4"/>
</asp:CheckBoxList>
```

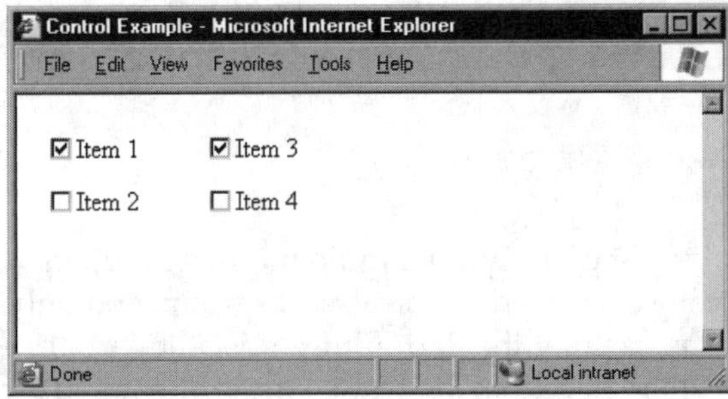


For more examples of how you can use different column ordering with the CheckBoxList, refer to Chapter 7.

| Member | Description |
|---|---|
| CellPadding | ASP.NET creates each checkbox in a separate cell of an invisible table. CellPadding is the space, in pixels, between the border of each cell and its contents. |

**Table 27-19.** *CheckBoxList Members*

| Member | Description |
|---|---|
| CellSpacing | The space, in pixels, between cells in the same table. |
| RepeatColumns | The number of columns that the checkbox list will use. |
| RepeatDirection | Defines how ASP.NET fills the checkbox grid. When set to Vertical, the items in the list are displayed in columns filled from top to bottom, then left to right, until all items are rendered. When set to Horizontal, the items in the list are displayed in rows filled left to right, then top to bottom, until all items are rendered. Remember, the number of columns is always set by the RepeatColumns property. |
| RepeatLayout | Specifies whether the checkboxes are displayed in an invisible table. This property can be either Table (the default) or Flow (in which case no table will be used). |
| TextAlign | Indicates whether text will be on the right or left of the checkbox. |

**Table 27-19.** *CheckBoxList Members (continued)*

## RadioButtonList

The RadioButtonList is a list of individual radio buttons grouped in a list. These radio buttons are automatically contained inside a single group, and only one can be selected at a time. Aside from the fact that the RadioButtonList allows one selection and the CheckBoxList allows multi-selection, the two controls offer an identical set of properties and events.

```
<asp:RadioButtonList id="lstItems"
                 CellPadding="5"
                 RepeatColumns="2"
                 RepeatDirection="Vertical"
                 RepeatLayout="Table"
                 TextAlign="Right"
                 AutoPostBack="False"
                 Width="200"
                 runat="server">
```

```
  <asp:ListItem value="1" Text="Item 1"/>
  <asp:ListItem value="2" Text="Item 2"/>
  <asp:ListItem value="3" selected="True" Text="Item 3"/>
  <asp:ListItem value="3" Text="Item 4"/>
</asp:RadioButtonList>
```

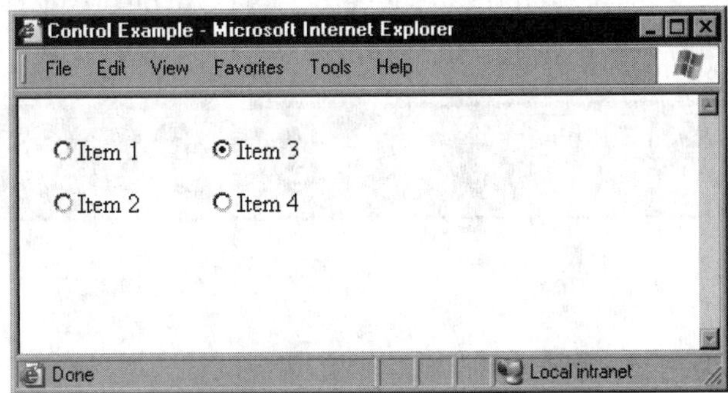


For more examples about how you can use different column ordering with the RadioButtonList, refer to Chapter 7.

| Member | Description |
|---|---|
| CellPadding | ASP.NET creates each radio button in a separate cell of an invisible table. CellPadding is the space, in pixels, between the border of each cell and its contents. |
| CellSpacing | The space, in pixels, between cells in the same table. |
| RepeatColumns | The number of columns that the list will use. |
| RepeatDirection | Defines how ASP.NET fills the radio button grid. When set to Vertical, the items in the list are displayed in columns filled from top to bottom, then left to right, until all items are rendered. When set to Horizontal, the items in the list are displayed in rows filled left to right, then top to bottom, until all items are rendered. Remember, the number of columns is always set by the RepeatColumns property. |

**Table 27-20.** *RadioButtonList Members*

| Member | Description |
|---|---|
| RepeatLayout | Specifies whether the radio buttons are displayed in an invisible table. This property can be either Table (the default) or Flow (in which case no table will be used). |
| TextAlign | Indicates whether text will be on the right or left of the radio button. |

**Table 27-20.** *RadioButtonList Members (continued)*

# Rich Controls

The designation "rich controls" is a loose one. Technically, there is no sharp distinction between the controls in this section—the AdRotator, Calendar, and Xml control—and those already explained in this chapter. Generally, however, these controls are separated because they represent a much higher level of abstraction. For example, there is no HTML tag that is at all similar to the Calendar control. Instead, ASP.NET generates dozens of lines of standard HTML code to create the Calendar's output with each postback. If you were to attempt to dynamically write this content to a web page on your own as needed, you would have an enormous, time-consuming task on your hands.

The AdRotator and Calendar controls were first introduced in Chapter 9, and this chapter includes complete examples that best demonstrate how they work in a web page.

## AdRotator

The AdRotator displays a randomly selected banner graphic on your page. Using the AdRotator control is a quick and easy way to ensure that a page rotates through a series of different graphics, without having to add this code yourself.

The AdRotator control uses a special XML file that lists all the different available images. This file uses the format shown here (only a single Ad element is shown).

```
<Advertisements>

  <Ad>
    <ImageUrl>prosetech.jpg</ImageUrl>
    <NavigateUrl>http://www.prosetech.com</NavigateUrl>
    <AlternateText>ProseTech Site</AlternateText>
```

```
    <Impressions>1</Impressions>
    <Keyword>Computer</Keyword>
  </Ad>

</Advertisements>
```

| Element | Description |
|---|---|
| ImageUrl | The image that will be displayed. This can be a relative link (a file in the current directory) or a fully qualified Internet URL. |
| NavigateUrl | The link that will be followed if the user clicks on the banner. |
| AlternateText | The text that will be displayed instead of the picture if it cannot be displayed. This text will also be used as a ToolTip in some newer browsers. |
| Impressions | A number that sets how often an advertisement will appear. This number is relative to the numbers specified for other ads. For example, a banner with the value 10 will be shown twice as often as the banner with the value 5. |
| Keyword | A keyword that identifies a group of advertisements. This can be used for filtering. For example, you could create ten advertisements, and give half of them the keyword "Retail" and the other half the keyword "Computer." The web page can then choose to filter the possible advertisements to include only one of these groups. |

**Table 27-21.** *Advertisement File Elements*

The AdRotator control provides a smaller set of properties. Its control tag is shown here.

```
<asp:AdRotator
     id="Ads"
```

```
        AdvertisementFile="MainAds.xml"
        KeyWordFilter="Computer"
        Target="_blank"
        runat="server"/>
```

| Member | Description |
|---|---|
| AdvertisementFile | The path to the XML advertisement file. This can be a relative or absolute path. |
| KeywordFilter | If you set the KeywordFilter, when ASP.NET randomly selects an image to display in the AdRotator control it will only consider those entries that have a matching keyword. |
| Target | The target window or frame where the destination page will be opened. This can name a specific frame, or use a special constant such as _blank (for a new window), _parent (the containing frameset), _self (the current window) or _top (the top-level parent). |
| AdCreated event | Occurs after the image is chosen but before the page is sent to the client. This event receives a special AdCreatedEventArgs object that describes the entry that was chosen (including its AlternateText, ImageUrl, and NavigateUrl). This allows you to synchronize other portions of your page to match. |

**Table 27-22.** *AdRotator Members*

## Calendar

The Calendar control displays the dates for a single month on a web page, and provides pager controls that allow the user to move from month to month. The Calendar control is the most sophisticated ASP.NET control (aside from the DataGrid), and provides a rich set of events and the ability to restrict or format any individual date.

In order to understand the Calendar control, you need to realize that it is ultimately rendered as an HTML table, with every date box in an individual cell. A template that shows all the Calendar tag options is shown below. As with many ASP.NET controls, all of these attributes are optional. You can create a default Calendar control on a page simply by specifying the tag <asp:Calendar id="MyCalendar" runat="server" />.

```
<asp:Calendar id="programmaticID"
     CellPadding="pixels"
     CellSpacing="pixels"
     DayNameFormat="FirstLetter|FirstTwoLetters|Full|Short"
     FirstDayOfWeek="Default|Monday|Tuesday|Wednesday|
                    Thursday|Friday|Saturday|Sunday"
     NextMonthText="HTML text"
     NextPrevFormat="ShortMonth|FullMonth|CustomText"
     PrevMonthText="HTML text"
     SelectedDate="date"
     SelectionMode="None|Day|DayWeek|DayWeekMonth"
     SelectMonthText="HTML text"
     SelectWeekText="HTML text"
     ShowDayHeader="True|False"
     ShowGridLines="True|False"
     ShowNextPrevMonth="True|False"
     ShowTitle="True|False"
     TitleFormat="Month|MonthYear"
     TodaysDate="date"
     VisibleDate="date"
     OnVisibleMonthChanged="OnVisibleMonthChangedMethod"
     runat="server">

   <TodayDayStyle />
   <DayHeaderStyle />
   <DayStyle />
   <NextPrevStyle />
   <OtherMonthDayStyle />
   <SelectedDayStyle />
   <SelectorStyle />
   <TitleStyle />
   <TodayDayStyle />
   <WeekendDayStyle />

</asp:Calendar>
```

| Member | Description |
|---|---|
| CellPadding | ASP.NET creates a date in a separate cell of an invisible table. CellPadding is the space, in pixels, between the border of each cell and its contents. |
| CellSpacing | The space, in pixels, between cells in the same table. |
| DayNameFormat | Determines how days are displayed in the calendar header. Valid values are Full (as in Sunday), FirstLetter (S), FirstTwoLetters (Su), and Short (Sun), which is the default. |
| FirstDayOfWeek | Determines which day is displayed in the first column of the calendar. The values are any day name from the FirstDayOfWeek enumeration (such as Sunday). |
| NextMonthText and PrevMonthText | Sets the text that the user clicks on to move to the next or previous month. These navigation links appear at the top of the calendar, and are the greater than (>) and less than (<) signs by default. This setting is only applied if NextPrevFormat is set to Custom. |
| NextPrevFormat | Sets the text that the user clicks on to move to the next or previous month. This can be FullMonth (for example, December), ShortMonth (Dec), or Custom, in which case the NextMonthText and PrevMonthText properties are used. Custom is the default. |
| SelectedDate and SelectedDates | Sets or gets the currently selected date as a DateTime object. You can specify this in the control tag in a format like this: "12:00:00 AM, 12/31/2002" (depending on your computer's regional settings). If you allow multiple date selection, the SelectedDates property will return a collection of DateTime objects, one for each selected date. You can use collection methods such as Add, Remove, and Clear to change the selection. |
| SelectionMode | Determines how many dates can be selected at once. The default is Day, which allows one date to be selected. Other options include DayWeek (a single date, or an entire week) or DayWeekMonth (a single date, entire week, or entire month). There is no way to allow the user to select multiple non-contiguous dates. |

**Table 27-23.** *Calendar Members*

| Member | Description |
|---|---|
| SelectMonthText and SelectWeekText | The text shown for the link that allows the user to select an entire month or week. These properties do not apply if the SelectionMode is Day. |
| ShowDayHeader, ShowGridLines, ShowNextPrevMonth, and ShowTitle | These Boolean properties allow you to configure whether various parts of the calendar are shown, including the day titles, gridlines between every day, the previous/next month navigation links, and the title section. Note that hiding the title section also hides the next and previous month navigation controls. |
| TitleFormat | Configures how the month is displayed in the title area. Valid values include Month and MonthYear (the default). |
| TodaysDate | Sets which day should be recognized as the current date, and formatted with the TodayDayStale. This defaults to the current day on the web server. |
| VisibleDate | Gets or sets the date that specifies what month will be displayed in the calendar. This allows you to change the calendar display without modifying the current date selection. |
| DayRender event | Occurs once for each day that is created and added to the currently visible month before the page is rendered. This event gives you the opportunity to apply special formatting, add content, or restriction selection for an individual date cell. For a complete example, refer to Chapter 7. |
| SelectionChanged event | Occurs when the user selects a day, a week, or an entire month by clicking the date selector controls. |
| VisibleMonthChanged event | Occurs when the user clicks on the next or previous event month navigation controls to move to another month. |

**Table 27-23.** *Calendar Members (continued)*

The Calendar also allows you to fine-tune its appearance by using nested style subtags. Each nested style tag specifies the formatting settings that it wants to override. These can include standard WebControl properties such as Font, BackColor, and

ForeColor, or some additional properties inherited from the TableItemStyle class, as described in Table 27-24. Note that more than one style may apply to a given cell.

```
<SelectedDayStyle
     Font="FontName"
     BackColor="HTML Color Name or Code"
     ForeColor="HTML Color Name or Code "
     HorizontalAlign="Center|Justify|Left|NotSet|Right"
     VerticalAlign="Bottom|Middle|Notset|Top"
     Wrap="True|False" />
```

| Member | Description |
|---|---|
| HorizontalAlign | Gets or sets the horizontal alignment of the contents within the date cell. |
| VerticalAlign | Gets or sets the vertical alignment of the contents within the date cell. |
| Wrap | Specifies whether the contents in the cell will wrap, or whether the cell will be automatically expanded to fit. This property is useful when adding custom content to a day cell. |

**Table 27-24.** *TableItemStyle Members*

| Member | Description |
|---|---|
| DayHeaderStyle | The style for the section of the calendar that displays the days of the week (as column headers). |
| DayStyle | The default style for the dates in the current month. |
| NextPrevStyle | The style for the navigation controls in the title section that move from month to month. |

**Table 27-25.** *Calendar Styles*

| Member | Description |
|---|---|
| OtherMonthDayStyle | The style for the dates that are not in the currently displayed month. These dates are used to "fill in" the calendar grid. For example, the first few cells in the topmost row may display the last few days from the previous month. |
| SelectedDayStyle | The style for the selected dates on the calendar. |
| SelectorStyle | The style for the week and month date selection controls. |
| TitleStyle | The style for the title section. |
| TodayDayStyle | The style for the date designated as today (represented by the TodaysDate property of the Calendar). |
| WeekendDayStyle | The style for dates that fall on the weekend. |

**Table 27-25.** *Calendar Styles (continued)*

A sample Calendar control tag is shown here.

```
<asp:Calendar id=Calendar
     NextMonthText="-->"
     PrevMonthText="<--"
     Width="200"
     Height="180"
     CellPadding="4"
     DayNameFormat="FirstLetter"
     Font-Size="8pt"
     Font-Names="Verdana"
     runat="server" >

    <DayHeaderStyle Font-Size="7pt" Font-Bold="True"
     BackColor="#CCCCCC" />
    <SelectedDayStyle Font-Bold="True" ForeColor="White"
     BackColor="#666666" />
```

```
    <TitleStyle Font-Bold="True" BorderColor="Black"
     BackColor="#999999" />
    <WeekendDayStyle BackColor="#FFFFCC" />

</asp:Calendar>
```

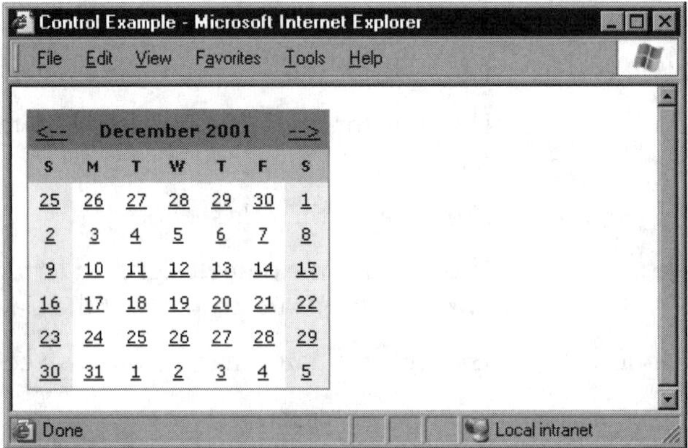


## Xml

The Xml control allows you to display an XML document on a web page. This control does not apply any special formatting, and by default it will just render all the embedded text in a continuous string with no spaces or line breaks. To add the appropriate formatting to the XML document, you need to specify an XSL transform to use with the control. The Xml control is shown in a full example in Chapter 17.

```
<asp:Xml id="xmlMyDoc"
     DocumentSource="MyDoc.xml"
     TransformSource="MyDoc.xsl"
     runat="server">
```

This example specifies an XML file by filename. Alternatively, you can specify XML content as a string (using the DocumentContent property) or by supplying an XmlDocument object (using the Document property). At least one of the XML document properties must be set. If more than one XML document property is set, the last property takes effect. The documents in the other properties are ignored.

| Member | Description |
|---|---|
| Document | The XML content to display as a System.Xml.XmlDocument object. |
| DocumentContent | The XML content to display as a string. |
| DocumentSource | The XML file to display. You can use a relative path (which is always relative to the location of the web page file) or an absolute path. |
| Transform | The XSL transform to apply to the content as a System.Xml.Xsl.XslTransform object. |
| TransformSource | The XSL transform file to apply to the content. You can use a relative or absolute path. |

**Table 27-26.** *Xml Members*

# Validation Controls

The validation controls were introduced in Chapter 9 as a powerful way to verify user input and display custom error messages. The validation controls come in five separate versions, each one tailored to perform a different type of validation. By default, when validation fails, the custom error message is displayed in the validation control. However, you can also display the combined error summaries in a separate ValidationSummary control. For more information about how validation controls work with the Page model, refer to Chapter 9.

All five validation controls inherit from the BaseValidator class, which defines some basic functionality, as described in Table 27-27. The BaseValidator class inherits the properties of the System.Web.UI.Label control, including formatting properties all web controls share, such as Font and ForeColor. You can also set the Enabled property to False to stop validation.

## CompareValidator

This control compares the value in one input control with the value in another. The type of comparison depends on the Operator property. For example, you can verify that two values are equal or that one is less than the other.

```
<asp:CompareValidator id="vldRetype"
    ErrorMessage="Your password does not match."
```

```
Operator="Equal"
Type="String"
ControlToCompare="txtPassword"
ControlToValidate="txtRetype"
runat="server" />
```

| Member | Description |
|---|---|
| ControlToValidate | Identifies the control that this validator will check. Each validator can verify the value in one input control. |
| Display | The Display property allows you to configure whether this error message will be added dynamically as needed (Dynamic), or whether an appropriate space will be reserved for the message (Static). Static is useful when the validator is in a table, and you don't want the width of the cell to collapse when no message is displayed. |
| EnableClientScript | If set to True, ASP.NET will add special JavaScript and DHTML code to allow client-side validation on browsers that support it. |
| ErrorMessage | If validation fails, the validator control will display this error message. |
| IsValid | After validation is performed, this returns True or False depending on whether it succeeded or failed. If you use automatic validation, you won't need to check this property manually. |
| PropertiesValid | Returns True if the control specified by ControlToValidate is a valid control. |
| RenderUplevel | Returns True if ASP.NET has determined that the client browser supports up-level rendering with JavaScript and DHTML code. You do not need to examine this property, as ASP.NET will automatically set the appropriate default for EnableClientScript. |

**Table 27-27.** *BaseValidator Members*

| Member | Description |
|---|---|
| ControlToCompare | The input control that contains the comparison value. |
| Operator | Specifies the type of comparison. By default, the operator is Equal, and validation succeeds as long as the two values are the same. Other possibilities are specified in the ValidationCompareOperator enumeration, and include GreaterThan (>), GreaterThanEqual (>=), LessThan (<), LessThanEqual (<=), NotEqual (<>), and DataTypeCheck (a comparison of data type only). |
| Type | The data type of the values that will be compared (such as String, Integer, Double, Date, or Currency). Before the comparison is made, ASP.NET attempts to convert both values to this data type, and throws an exception if it cannot. |
| ValueToCompare | The comparison value as a constant. You can set this instead of ControlToCompare. If both ValueToCompare and ControlToCompare are set, ControlToCompare takes precedence. |

**Table 27-28.** *CompareValidator Members*

## RangeValidator

This control checks whether a given value in an input control matches a set value or falls within a predefined range.

```
<asp:RangeValidator id="vldAge"
     ErrorMessage="The date is incorrect."
     Type="Date"
     MaximumValue="2001/12/01"
     MinimumValue="2002/12/30"
     ControlToValidate="txtDate"
     runat="server" />
```

| Member | Description |
|---|---|
| MaximumValue | The largest valid value for ControlToCompare. |
| MinimumValue | The smallest valid value for ControlToCompare. You can set MaximumValue and MinumumValue to the same number, date, or string to validate for a single value. |
| Type | The data type of the values that will be compared (such as String, Integer, Double, Date, or Currency). Before the comparison is made, ASP.NET attempts to convert both values to this data type, and throws an exception if it cannot. |

**Table 27-29.** *RangeValidatorMembers*

## RegularExpressionValidator

This control checks whether a user-entered value matches a specified regular expression. A quick introduction to regular expression syntax can be found in Chapter 9.

```
<asp:RegularExpressionValidator id="vldEmail"
     ErrorMessage="This email is missing the @ symbol."
     ValidationExpression=".+@.+"
     ControlToValidate="txtEmail"
     runat="server" />
```

| Member | Description |
|---|---|
| ValidationExpression | A string that contains the regular expression pattern ASP.NET will use for validation. |

**Table 27-30.** *RegularExpressionValidator*

## RequiredFieldValidator

This control checks whether a user has entered a value in a given control. This validator is often used in conjunction with other validation controls, because all other controls will automatically skip their validation if they find an empty value.

```
<asp:RequiredFieldValidator id="vldPassword"
     ErrorMessage="You must enter a password."
     ControlToValidate="txtPassword"
     runat="server" />
```

| Member | Description |
|---|---|
| InitialValue | This is the designated initial value of the associated input control. If the RequiredFieldValidator finds that the current value matches the initial value, validation will fail. Usually, InitialValue is set to an empty string, to ensure that a user has entered some content. |

**Table 27-31.** *RequiredFieldValidator Members*

## CustomValidator

This control allows you to use your own validation algorithm. You perform validation at the server side by responding to the ServerValidate event. In addition, you can specify a client-side validation function that will prevent the page from being posted back when an error is countered.

```
<asp:CustomValidator id="vldCode"
     ErrorMessage="Your entry did not match the secret code."
     ControlToValidate="txtCode"
     runat="server" />
```

| Member | Description |
|---|---|
| ClientValidationFunction | A string that contains the function name (typically written in JavaScript) that will be used for client-side validation. This property is not required (and in some cases, such as when you are using a "secret" algorithm, should not be used). Note that even if you do set this property, you must still add analogous ASP.NET code to the ServerValidate event to ensure that validation is performed even on down-level browsers, and even if the user spoofs your page. An example showing how you can write a ClientValidationFunction is shown in Chapter 9. |
| ServerValidate event | Your code responds to this event to perform the actual validation on the server-side. You receive a Server-ValidateEventArgs object that contains the user-entered value (Value) and allows you to specify whether validation succeeded (the Boolean property Valid). |

**Table 27-32.** *CustomValidator Members*

## ValidationSummary

This control displays a summary of all error messages for every validation control that failed to validate its content.

```
<asp:ValidationSummary id="vldSummary"
     DisplayMode="BulletList"
     HeaderText="Errors Found:"
     runat="server">
```

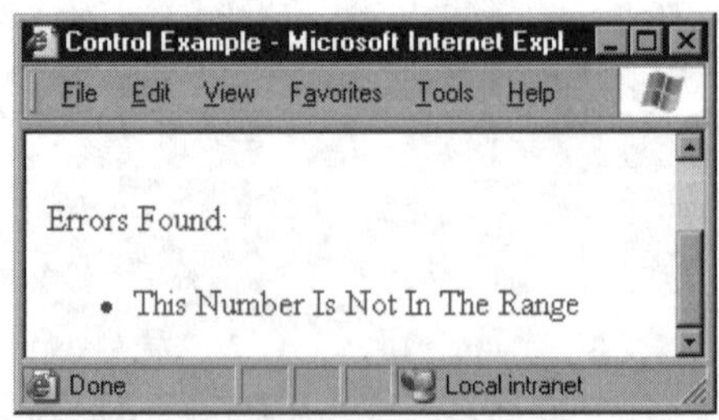

| Member | Description |
|---|---|
| DisplayMode | Sets the format for the validation summary text. This can be List, SingleParagraph, or BulletList (the default). |
| EnableClientScript | If set to True, ASP.NET uses additional client-side scripting code to ensure that the ValidationSummary control is updated dynamically as errors are entered or fixed. |
| HeaderText | Sets a title that appears at the top of the validation summary control. |
| ShowMessageBox | When set to True, the validation summary is shown in a message box window that appears as soon as validation fails. |
| ShowSummary | When set to True, the validation summary is shown inline in the page. |

**Table 27-33.** *ValidationSummary Members*

## Data Controls

The data controls are often considered ASP.NET's most sophisticated (and complex) controls. They include the DataGrid, DataList, and Repeater, all of which are designed to work with ASP.NET data binding. The basic principle is that you bind a data source such as an array, collection, or DataSet to the data control, and it generates a list with one entry for each item in the data source. All the data controls support templates, which allow you to fine-tune their appearance.

When starting out with these controls, it's absolutely necessary to have a good explanation that describes basics about templates and advanced control features such as sorting, paging, selection, and editing. For these examples, refer to Chapter 15.

The DataList and DataGrid inherit some basic functionality from the BaseDataList class. This includes support for data binding and some table-specific formatting properties. Note that the Repeater control does *not* inherit from BaseDataList, and so does not support these members.

| Member | Description |
|---|---|
| CellPadding | CellPadding is the space, in pixels, between the border of each cell and its contents. |
| CellSpacing | The space, in pixels, between cells in the same table. |
| DataMember and DataSource | These properties allow the control to be bound to a data source, as described in Chapters 14 and 15. The DataSource property identifies the data source that contains the information. If there is more than one table in the data source (as with a DataSet), DataMember identifies the table to use. |
| DataKeyField | Specifies a field from the data source that will automatically be used to assign a unique identifier to each row. This value will not be displayed, but is useful for accessing specific rows. |
| DataKeys | If the DataKeyField is set, the DataKeys collection automatically provides all the keys for the records in the data list. You cannot use this property to add or remove rows. Instead, you use this collection to look up the data key for a specific row by index number (usually in an event handler). |
| GridLines | Specifies the types of gridlines that will be shown in the table (None, Horizontal, Vertical, or Both). |
| HorizontalAlign | Gets or sets the horizontal alignment of the contents within the cell. |
| DataBind() | This method fills the control with the data from the data source. This method is required to update the data control display and is often performed on postback. You can also call the Page.DataBind() method to bind all data-bound controls at once. |
| SelectedIndexChanged event | Fires when the selection in the data control changes. |

**Table 27-34.** *BaseDataList Members*

## Repeater

Out of all the data controls, the Repeater is the most straightforward. Think of the Repeater as a no-frills way to repeat ASP.NET or HTML elements, once for each item in the data source. The Repeater has no support for additional features such as selection, editing, and sorting, and has no built-in layout. However, these characteristics also make the Repeater extremely flexible—unlike the DataList and DataGrid control, the Repeater does not place data inside any sort of table structure unless you explicitly add table tags. The Repeater is also the only control that allows the developers to split HTML tags across templates.

The format for the Repeater control tag is shown below. Note that the content for the Repeater control does not appear in the .aspx file. Instead, it is set at runtime through code, using data binding. That makes the Repeater control tag quite simple, with little more than the optional templates where you can specify formatting and HTML elements.

```
<asp:Repeater id="programmaticID"
     runat="server">

   <HeaderTemplate />
   <ItemTemplate />
   <AlternatingItemTemplate />
   <SeparatorTemplate />
   <FooterTemplate />

</asp:Repeater>
```

| Member | Description |
|---|---|
| DataMember and DataSource | These properties allow the control to be bound to a data source, as described in Chapters 14 and 15. The DataSource property identifies the data source that contains the information. If there is more than one table in the data source (as with a DataSet), DataMember identifies the table to use. |
| Items | Allows you to examine all the items in the Repeater control as a collection of RepeaterItem objects. Because the Repeater control is data-bound, you cannot directly modify the Items collection. |

**Table 27-35.** *Repeater Members*

| Member | Description |
|---|---|
| DataBind() | This method fills the control with the data from the data source. This method is required to update the Repeater control display and is often performed on postback. You can also call the Page.DataBind() method to bind all data-bound controls at once. |
| ItemCreated event | Occurs when an item is created and added to the Repeater control. The event arguments provide the relevant item as a RepeaterItem object. |
| ItemDataBound event | Occurs after an item is data-bound, but before it is rendered on the page. The event arguments provide the relevant item as a RepeaterItem object. |
| ItemCommand event | Occurs when any button is clicked in the Repeater control. (In order for a button to be present, you must have added it in one of the templates.) The event arguments provide the command name associated with the button (CommandName), a reference to the button (CommandSource), and the RepeaterItem where the button click occurred (Item). |

**Table 27-35.** *Repeater Members (continued)*

| Member | Description |
|---|---|
| DataItem | Provides the data associated with this item. |
| ItemIndex | Indicates the numeric (zero-based) index of the item in the Repeater control. |
| ItemType | Returns one of the ListItemType enumerated values identifying what template the item is in (such as Header, Footer, Item, and so on). |

**Table 27-36.** *RepeaterItem Members*

The formatting for the Repeater control is completely defined through templates. Every template can contain a mix of HTML elements, ASP.NET server controls, and data-binding expressions bracketed with <%# %> characters. You cannot set any attributes for the template tags. Many example templates are shown in Chapter 15.

| Member | Description |
|---|---|
| ItemTemplate | Defines the content and layout of the items in the list. This is the only required template. |
| AlternatingItemTemplate | If defined, this template is used for the format and layout of every second item. Every odd-numbered item uses the ItemTemplate. If not defined, every item uses ItemTemplate. |
| SeparatorTemplate | If defined, this is rendered between every item. |
| HeaderTemplate | If defined, this is rendered once at the beginning of the Repeater control as a heading. |
| FooterTemplate | If defined, this is rendered once at the end of the Repeater control as a footer. |

**Table 27-37.** *Repeater Templates*

A sample Repeater tag with three templates is shown below. It creates a table structure to hold data from a bound dataset (which must contain a field named au_fname). This example could be used with the Authors table from the pubs database installed with SQL Server.

```
<asp:Repeater id="repeatAuthor"
              runat="server">

    <HeaderTemplate>
       <h3>The Repeater:</h3>
       <table bgcolor="LightYellow" border="2">
    </HeaderTemplate>
    <ItemTemplate>
       <tr><td><%# Container.DataItem("au_fname") %></td></tr>
```

```
    </ItemTemplate>
    <FooterTemplate>
       </table>
    </FooterTemplate>

</asp:Repeater>
```

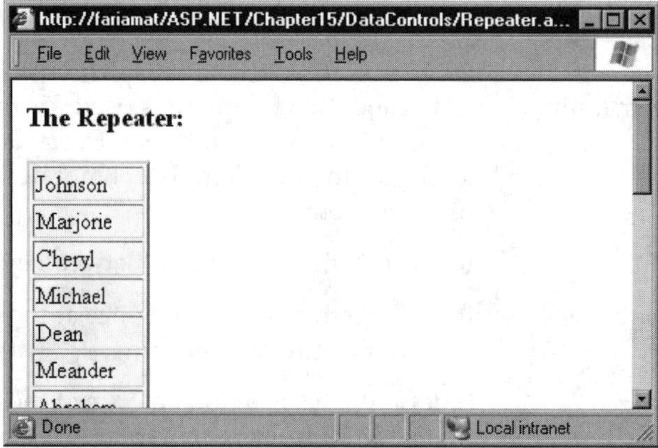


## DataList

The DataList displays data in a table with a single cell for each item. The DataList control provides built-in support for selection and editing. Unlike the DataGrid, the DataList does *not* support paging or sorting.

The format for the DataList tag is shown next. Note that the content for the DataList control does not appear in the .aspx file. Instead, it is set at runtime using data binding, as with all the data controls. Some of the properties shown in the control tag are inherited from the BaseDataList class, and are described in Table 27-34.

```
<asp:DataList id="programmaticID"
     CellPadding="pixels"
     CellSpacing="pixels"
     GridLines="None|Horizontal|Vertical|Both"
     RepeatColumns="ColumnCount"
     RepeatDirection="Vertical|Horizontal"
     RepeatLayout="Flow|Table"
     ShowFooter="True|False"
     ShowHeader="True|False"
     runat="server">

   <AlternatingItemStyle />
```

```
    <EditItemStyle />
    <FooterStyle />
    <HeaderStyle />
    <ItemStyle />
    <PagerStyle />
    <SelectedItemStyle />

    <HeaderTemplate />
    <ItemTemplate />
    <AlternatingItemTemplate />
    <EditItemTemplate />
    <SelectedItemTemplate />
    <SeparatorTemplate />
    <FooterTemplate />

</asp:DataList>
```

| Member | Description |
|---|---|
| EditItemIndex | Gets or sets the item in the DataList control that is currently being edited. To stop editing, set this value to -1. The index number is zero-based, so the first item is at index 0. |
| Items | Allows you to examine all the items in the DataList control as a collection of DataListItem objects. Because the DataList control is data-bound, you cannot directly modify the Items collection. |
| RepeatColumns | The number of columns that the DataList will use. (Each column contains all the information for a single item.) By default, only one column is used. |
| RepeatDirection | Defines how ASP.NET fills the DataList when you are using more than one column. When set to Vertical, the items are displayed in columns filled from top to bottom, then left to right, until all items are rendered. When set to Horizontal, the items in the list are displayed in rows filled left to right, then top to bottom, until all items are rendered. Remember, the number of columns is always set by the RepeatColumns property. |

**Table 27-38.** *DataList Members*

| Member | Description |
|---|---|
| RepeatLayout | Specifies whether the list items are displayed in an invisible table, with one cell for each item. This property can be either Table (the default) or Flow (in which case no table will be used). |
| SelectedIndex | Gets or sets the item in the DataList control that is currently selected. To clear the selection, set this value to -1. The index number is zero-based, so the first item is at index 0. |
| SelectedItem | Provides the currently selected item as DataListItem object. |
| ShowFooter | If set to True, the footer will be displayed at the bottom of the DataList, provided you have created a FooterTemplate. |
| ShowHeader | If set to True, the header will be displayed at the top of the DataList, provided you have created a HeaderTemplate. |
| EditCommand, CancelCommand, UpdateCommand, and DeleteCommand events | These commands occur when the user clicks the corresponding button. You must handle these events to perform the required data source updating, if required. Note also that the DataList does not have predefined editing controls. That means you need to add your own buttons for editing, and set their CommandName properties to Edit, Cancel, Update, or Delete. For more information, refer to Chapter 15. |
| ItemCreated event | Occurs when an item is created and added to the DataList control. The event arguments provide the relevant item as a DataListItem object. |
| ItemDataBound event | Occurs after an item is data-bound, but before it is rendered on the page. The event arguments provide the relevant item as a DataListItem object. |

**Table 27-38.** *DataList Members (continued)*

| Member | Description |
|---|---|
| ItemCommand event | Occurs when any button is clicked in the DataList control. (In order for a button to be present, you must have added it in one of the templates.) The event arguments provide the command name associated with the button (CommandName), a reference to the button (CommandSource), and the DataListItem where the button click occurred (Item). |

**Table 27-38.** *DataList Members (continued)*

| Member | Description |
|---|---|
| DataItem | Provides the data associated with this item. |
| ItemIndex | Indicates the numeric (zero-based) index of the item in the DataList control. |
| ItemType | Returns one of the ListItemType enumerated values identifying what template the item is in (such as Header, Footer, Item, SelectedItem, and so on). |

**Table 27-39.** *DataListItem Members*

Like the Repeater, you configure the content of the DataList using embedded template tags. You can also configure the appearance using style tags. Each nested style tag specifies the formatting settings that it wants to override. These can include standard WebControl properties such as Font, BackColor, and ForeColor, or some additional properties inherited from the TableItemStyle class, as described in Table 27-24. Note that more than one style may apply to a given item. For example, a selected item will be formatted with the normal ItemStyle, and then with the SelectedItemStyle.

| Member | Description |
|---|---|
| ItemTemplate and ItemStyle | Defines the content and layout of the items in the list. This is the only required template. |
| AlternatingItemTemplate and AlternatingItemStyle | If defined, this template is used for the format and layout of every second item. Every odd-numbered item uses the ItemTemplate (and ItemStyle). If not defined, every item uses ItemTemplate. |
| SeparatorTemplate and SeparatorStyle | If defined, this is rendered between every item. |
| HeaderTemplate and HeaderStyle | If defined, this is rendered once at the beginning of the DataList control as a heading. |
| FooterTemplate and FooterStyle | If defined, this is rendered once at the end of the DataList control as a footer. |
| SelectedItemTemplate and SelectedItemStyle | If defined, this template is used for the format of the selected item (as determined by the DataList.SelectedIndex). |
| EditItemTemplate and EditItemStyle | If defined, this template is used for the format of the item that is currently being edited (as determined by the DataList.EditItemIndex). |

**Table 27-40.** *DataList Templates and Styles*

A sample DataList tag with two templates and three styles is shown below. It binds to a data source which must contain a field named au_fname and au_lname. This example could be used with the Authors table from the pubs database installed with SQL Server.

```
<asp:DataList id="listAuthor"
     BorderColor="#DEBA84"
     CellSpacing="2"
     BackColor="#DEBA84"
     CellPadding="3"
    runat="server" >
```

```
    <HeaderStyle Font-Bold="True" ForeColor="White"
     BackColor="#A55129" />
    <ItemStyle Font-Size="Smaller" Font-Names="Verdana"
     ForeColor="#8C4510"
     BackColor="#FFF7E7" />
    <AlternatingItemStyle BackColor="#FFE0C0" />

    <HeaderTemplate>
        <h2>Author List</h2>
    </HeaderTemplate>
    <ItemTemplate>
        <b><%# Container.DataItem("au_fname") %>
        <%# Container.DataItem("au_lname") %></b>
    </ItemTemplate>

</asp:DataList>
```

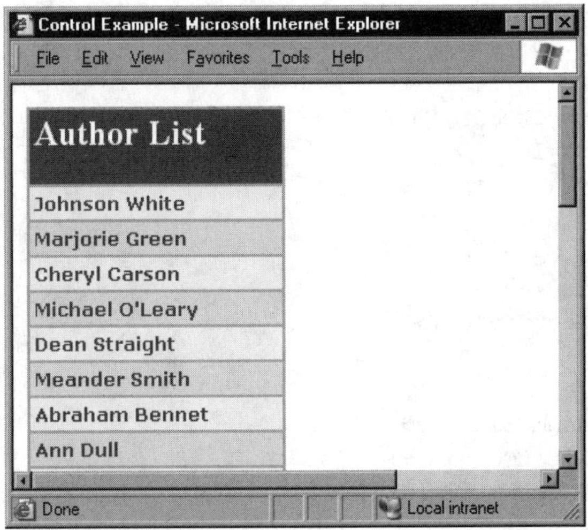


## DataGrid

The DataGrid displays data in a multi-column table with a single row for each item. The DataGrid control is the most feature-rich data control, and provides built-in support for selection, editing, paging, and sorting. It is also the only data control that can generate columns automatically without any templates, although you can insert nested Column tags for more precise control.

The format for the DataGrid tag is shown next. Note that the content for the DataGrid control does not appear in the .aspx file. Instead, it is set at runtime using data binding, as with all the data controls. Some of the properties shown in the control tag are inherited from the BaseDataList class, and are described in Table 27-34.

```
<asp:DataGrid id="programmaticID"
     AllowPaging="True|False"
     AllowSorting="True|False"
     AutoGenerateColumns="True|False"
     BackImageUrl="url"
     CellPadding="pixels"
     CellSpacing="pixels"
     GridLines="None|Horizontal|Vertical|Both"
     HorizontalAlign="Center|Justify|Left|NotSet|Right"
     PagedDataSource
     PageSize="ItemCount"
     ShowFooter="True|False"
     ShowHeader="True|False"
     runat="server" >

   <AlternatingItemStyle />
   <EditItemStyle />
   <FooterStyle />
   <HeaderStyle />
   <ItemStyle />
   <PagerStyle />
   <SelectedItemStyle />

   <Columns>
      <asp:BoundColumn />
      <asp:ButtonColumn />
      <asp:EditCommandColumn />
      <asp:HyperLinkColumn />
      <asp:TemplateColumn />
   </Columns>

</asp:DataGrid>
```

| Member | Description |
| --- | --- |
| AllowPaging | If set to True, a subset of the data will be displayed, along with the pager controls. The CurrentPageIndex and PageSize properties determine what data will be displayed. |
| AllowSorting | If set to True, the column headers will become hyperlinks. When the user clicks one of these hyperlinks, the SortCommand event will occur, and you will be provided with the SortExpression that has been defined for that column. You must then requery the database and rebind the DataGrid. |
| AutoGenerateColumns | If set to True, a new BoundColumn will be created for each field in the database when you bind the DataGrid. This will be in addition to any explicitly defined columns defined in the DataGrid tag. |
| BackImageUrl | The location of an image to display "behind" the DataGrid. |
| Columns | Provides a collection of DataGrid column objects. If the DataGrid columns are generated automatically (by setting the AutoGenerateColumns property to True) this collection will not contain them. |
| CurrentPageIndex | Gets or sets which page is currently being displayed, if AllowPaging is set to True. The first page has the index 0. |
| EditItemIndex | Gets or sets the item in the DataGrid control that is currently being edited. To stop editing, set this value to -1. The index number is zero-based, so the first item is at index 0. |
| Items | Allows you to examine all the items in the DataGrid control as a collection of DataGridItem objects. Because the DataGrid control is data-bound, you cannot directly modify the Items collection. |

**Table 27-41.** *DataGrid Members*

| Member | Description |
|---|---|
| PageCount | Returns the total number of pages if paging is enabled, based on the PageSize. |
| PageSize | Gets or sets the number of rows to provide on each page if AllowPaging is True. By default, this value is 10, so a DataSet with 100 rows will require 10 separate page views. |
| SelectedIndex | Gets or sets the item in the DataGrid control that is currently selected. To clear the selection, set this value to -1. The index number is zero-based, so the first item is at index 0. |
| SelectedItem | Provides the currently selected item as DataGridItem object. |
| ShowFooter | If set to True, the footer will be displayed at the bottom of the DataGrid. |
| ShowHeader | If set to True, the header (column titles) will be displayed at the top of the DataGrid. |
| EditCommand, CancelCommand, UpdateCommand, and DeleteCommand event | These commands occur when the user clicks the scorresponding button. You must handle these events to perform the required data source updating. To allow editing options, you need to have added the appropriate buttons or an EditCommandColumn. |
| ItemCreated event | Occurs when an item is created and added to the DataList control. The event arguments provide the relevant item as a DataListItem object. |
| ItemDataBound event | Occurs after an item is data-bound, but before it is rendered on the page. The event arguments provide the relevant item as a DataListItem object. |
| ItemCommand event | Occurs when any button is clicked in the DataList control. (In order for a button to be present, you must have added it in one of the templates.) The event arguments provide the command name associated with the button (CommandName), a reference to the button (CommandSource), and the DataListItem where the button click occurred (Item). |

**Table 27-41.** *DataGrid Members (continued)*

| Member | Description |
|---|---|
| PageIndexChanged event | Occurs when the user clicks one of the pager controls when paging is enabled. You will receive the NewPageIndex, and you must set the CurrentPageIndex to match and rebind the DataGrid. |
| SortCommand event | Occurs when the user clicks one of the column hyperlinks when sorting is enabled. You will receive the column's SortExpression, and you must requery the data source and rebind the DataGrid with the sorted results. |

**Table 27-41.** *DataGrid Members (continued)*

| Member | Description |
|---|---|
| DataItem | Provides the data associated with this item. |
| ItemIndex | Indicates the numeric (zero-based) index of the item in the DataGrid control. |
| ItemType | Returns one of the ListItemType enumerated values identifying what template the item is in (such as Header, Footer, Item, SelectedItem, and so on). |

**Table 27-42.** *DataGridItem Members*

You can configure the appearance of the DataGrid using style tags. Each nested style tag specifies the formatting settings that it wants to override. These can include standard WebControl properties such as Font, BackColor, and ForeColor, or some additional properties inherited from the TableItemStyle class, as described in Table 27-24. Note that more than one style may apply to a given item. For example, a selected item will be formatted with the normal ItemStyle and then with the SelectedItemStyle.

If AutoGenerateColumns is True, ASP.NET will automatically create a collection of rows, one for each field in the data source. This default behavior is useful for quick tests, but is often not suitable for a real application, because it forces you to use default column names, ordering, and sizes, and doesn't allow you the flexibility to add other controls or formatting inside a column.

To define your own columns, add a nested <Column> tag inside the <asp:DataGrid> tag. Then add each column control inside the <Column> tag in the order you want them to appear. You have five column choices, all of which inherit from the DataGridColumn class described in Table 27-44. Each type of column is described individually.

| Member | Description |
|---|---|
| ItemStyle | Defines the formatting for ordinary rows in the grid. |
| AlternatingItemStyle | If defined, this style is used for the format and layout of every second row. Every odd-numbered row uses the ItemStyle. If not defined, every item uses ItemStyle. |
| HeaderStyle | Defines the formatting for the header, where the column titles are displayed. |
| FooterStyle | Defines the formatting of the footer. |
| SelectedItemStyle | Defines the formatting of the selected item (as determined by the DataGrid.SelectedIndex). If you do not set this style, the user will not be able to distinguish which item is selected. |
| EditItemStyle | Defines the formatting of the item that is currently being edited (as determined by the DataGrid. EditItemIndex). |
| PagerStyle | Defines the formatting for the page selection links of the DataGrid control. This is only shown if you are using paging. |

**Table 27-43.** *DataGrid Styles*

| Member | Description |
|---|---|
| FooterText | A string that defines the text that will be shown in the footer region for this column. |
| HeaderImageUrl | The location of an image to display in the header region of the column. |

**Table 27-44.** *DataGridColumn Class*

| Member | Description |
|---|---|
| HeaderText | A string that defines the text that will be shown in the header region for this column. |
| SortExpression | The field that will be used for sorting. This field name will be passed to your code through the SortCommand event, at which point you can use it to create a new query. |
| Visible | Allows you to hide or show the column. |

**Table 27-44.** *DataGridColumn Class (continued)*

## BoundColumn

Each bound column represents a single field from the data source. The data is displayed in ordinary text. If you set the DataGrid to automatically generate its columns, it will create a single BoundColumn for each field in the data source.

```
<asp:BoundColumn
      DataField="DataSourceField"
      DataFormatString="FormatString"
      FooterText="FooterText"
      HeaderImageUrl="url"
      HeaderText="HeaderText"
      ReadOnly="True|False"
      SortExpression ="DataSourceFieldToSortBy"
      Visible="True|False" />
```

## ButtonColumn

This displays a column that contains a single button control. One common way to use this column is to add a View or a Details button that automatically navigates to a new window with more information about the selected item.

```
<asp:ButtonColumn
      ButtonType="LinkButton|PushButton"
      Command="CommandName"
      DataTextField="DataSourceField"
      DataTextFormatString="FormatString"
```

```
    FooterText="FooterText"
    HeaderImageUrl="url"
    HeaderText="HeaderText"
    Text="ButtonCaption"
    Visible="True|False"/>
```

| Member | Description |
|---|---|
| DataField | The name of the field in the data source that will be bound to the column. |
| DataFormatString | A string that specifies how the data from the field will be formatted. Format strings are particularly useful with numbers, dates, and currency values, and are described in Chapter 14. |
| ReadOnly | If False, the column will not be converted into a text box for editing, and the user will be able to modify the value. If the DataGrid does not contain any edit buttons, this setting will have no effect. The default is False. |

**Table 27-45.** *BoundColumn Members*

| Member | Description |
|---|---|
| ButtonType | Specifies LinkButton (which looks like a hyperlink) or CommandButton (which looks like a standard button control). The default is CommandButton. |
| CommandName | A string of text that represents the action that this button performs. Your code can examine the CommandName property, and use it to distinguish between buttons when one event handler handles several different commands. |

**Table 27-46.** *ButtonColumn Members*

| Member | Description |
|---|---|
| DataTextField | This optional property identifies the field in the data source that will be used as a caption for the button. |
| DataTextFormatString | A string that specifies how the data from the DataTextField will be formatted. Format strings are particularly useful with numbers, dates, and currency values, and are described in Chapter 14. |
| Text | Specifies the caption for the button. If you set this property, the button for every item in the grid will have the same text. You should set either Text or DataTextField, but not both. |

**Table 27-46.** *ButtonColumn Members (continued)*

## EditCommandColumn

This control displays a column with editing commands. Initially, this column will display a single button with a caption such as "Edit" next to every item. When the user clicks this button, you will handle the EditCommand event and place the appropriate row in edit mode. At that point, the edited row will display two buttons: a cancel button and an update button.

```
<asp:EditCommandColumn
     ButtonType="LinkButton|PushButton"
     CancelText="CancelButtonCaption"
     EditText="EditButtonCaption"
     FooterText="FooterText"
     HeaderImageUrl="url"
     HeaderText="HeaderText"
     UpdateText="UpdateButtonCaption"
     Visible="True|False"/>
```

| Member | Description |
|---|---|
| ButtonType | Specifies LinkButton (which looks like a hyperlink) or CommandButton (which looks like a standard button control). The default is CommandButton. |
| CancelText | Specifies the text that appears on the button that cancels editing. This is usually the word "Cancel," but you must set this property, or the cancel button will not be shown. |
| EditText | Specifies the text that appears on the button that initiates editing. This is usually the word "Edit," but you must set this property, or the edit button will not be shown. |
| UpdateText | Specifies the text that appears on the button that updates an edited row. This is usually the word "Update," but you must set this property, or the update button will not be shown. |

**Table 27-47.** *EditCommand Column*

## HyperLinkColumn

A hyperlink column allows you to create a hyperlink for each item in the grid. You can create a column that has the same text for every item (such as "View") by setting the Text property, or you can bind the hyperlink column to a field in the data source. You can also bind the URL to a field in the data source. Note that unlike the ButtonColumn, you cannot handle the hyperlink Click event. Instead, the NavigateUrl or DataNavigate-UrlField will be used automatically.

```
<asp:HyperLinkColumn
     DataNavigateUrlField="DataSourceField"
     DataNavigateUrlFormatString="FormatExpression"
     DataTextField="DataSourceField"
     DataTextFormatString="FormatExpression"
     FooterText="FooterText"
     HeaderImageUrl="url"
```

```
    HeaderText="HeaderText"
    NavigateUrl="url"
    Target="window"
    Text="HyperLinkText"
    Visible="True|False"/>
```

| Member | Description |
|---|---|
| DataNavigateUrlField | Identifies the field in the data source that will be used as the hyperlink destination. In other words, your data source must provide a field that specifies a web URL. Alternatively, you can set the NavigateUrl property with a constant value. |
| DataNavigateUrl-FormatString | Specifies a format string that will be applied to the DataNavigateUrlField. |
| DataTextField | Identifies the field in the data source that will be used for the text of the link. Alternatively, you can set the Text property with a constant value. |
| DataTextFormatString | Specifies a format string that will be applied to the DataTextFormatString. |
| NavigateUrl | The destination URL that the browser will go to when the hyperlink is clicked. If you use this property (instead of DataNavigateUrlField), every item will have the same destination URL. |
| Target | The target window or frame where the destination page will be opened. This can name a specific frame, or use a special constant such as _blank (for a new window), _parent (the containing frameset), _self (the current window) or _top (the top-level parent). |
| Text | The text content that the user must click to follow the link. If you use this property (instead of DataTextField), every item will have the same link text. |

**Table 27-48.** *HyperLinkColumn Members*

## TemplateColumn

The TemplateColumn is the most flexible type of column, as it allows you to specifically control the appearance of a control (for example, combining more than one field in a column) and the controls that are used to edit it. Using the template column is very similar to using the DataList control: you need to define a separate template for each part of the control. The template contains a mix of data binding expressions, HTML formatting, and ASP.NET controls.

Note that if you omit the <EditItemTemplate>, the column will be read-only.

```
<asp:TemplateColumn
     FooterText="FooterText"
     HeaderImageUrl="url"
     HeaderText="HeaderText"
     SortExpression="DataSourceFieldToSortBy"
     Visible="True|False">

        <ItemTemplate />
        <HeaderTemplate />
        <FooterTemplate />
        <EditItemTemplate />

</asp:TemplateColumn>
```

| Member | Description |
|---|---|
| ItemTemplate | Defines the content and layout of this column for each item in the grid. This is the only required template. |
| HeaderTemplate | Defines the content of the header portion of this column (the column title). When using this template, you won't set the HeaderText property. |
| FooterTemplate | Defines the content of the footer portion of this column. When using this template, you won't set the FooterText property. |
| EditItemTemplate | Defines the content and layout of the column in edit mode. This allows you to specify the controls that will be used by inserting ASP.NET control tags (as shown in Chapter 15). |

**Table 27-49.** *TemplateColumn Templates*

The Complete Reference

# Chapter 28

## Configuration Files

Chapter 5 introduced ASP.NET's new configuration system, which revolves around plain text XML files. This system is a great stride forward from ASP programming—it's easy, multi-layered, and supports dynamic updates. Making a modification requires little more than a few minutes with Notepad, and settings come into effect for all new client requests immediately after you make a change. The only ingredient ASP.NET configuration lacks is an attractive graphical tool for configuration—although you'll probably find that the simple text editor approach is refreshingly straightforward.

Chapter 5 provided an overview of ASP.NET's configuration system, and important settings for security, state management, and debugging are discussed throughout the book. This chapter is more of a reference and to use when you need one-stop-shopping for configuration file information. Every important web.config section is explained concisely and completely.

## Configuration Files

ASP.NET has two configuration files. The machine.config file is found in the framework configuration directory (typically C:\WINNT\Microsoft.NET\Framework\[version]\Config), and specifies settings that will be inherited by all the ASP.NET applications hosted by the current computer. This file includes far more information than the standard web.config file, including many options that you won't ever need to inspect or modify. In addition, each web application usually has its own web.config file, which specifies additional settings that override the machine.config defaults.

In fact, an application can use multiple web.config files to configure several layers of configuration. The rule is that only one web.config file can be used per directory, and every subdirectory inherits the settings from the web.config file of its parent (which, in turn, inherits the machine.config file settings). This multi-layered approach means that a web.config can be much shorter and omit unimportant details. web.config files only need to specify settings that are specific to the application.

More information about the technology behind ASP.NET's configuration files can be found in Chapter 5, along with information about how to add your own custom settings to represent global constants. This chapter focuses exclusively on the standard set of tags.

## Configuration File Sections

Both the machine.config and web.config files follow the same format. They use case-sensitive XML, a set of common tags, and camel casing (so section names always begin with a lowercase letter, and use capitals to denote each new word). If you don't want to set a particular setting in a web.config, you can leave out the related tag. However, the structure must always remain constant—if you need to use a subtag, you must also include the parent tag.

The first two levels of a configuration file look like this:

```
<configuration>
   <configSections />
   <system.diagnostics />
   <system.net />
   <system.runtime.remoting />
   <appSettings />
   <system.web />
</configuration>
```

The machine.config file uses <configSections> to specify the section handler classes that will process the configuration files, <system.diagnostics> to configure some low-level debugging options, <system.net> to specify a few network settings, and <system.remoting> to specify options for .NET remoting (a remote object framework used in controlled networks). These sections are never used in a web.config file, don't require any customization, and are not specific to ASP.NET applications. They aren't described in this chapter.

Out of the other two sections, <appSettings> is only used to create customized, application-specific constants, as described in Chapter 5. The following example adds a special global constant that can be used (with the help of the System.Configuration. ConfigurationSettings class) to retrieve the name of an XML file containing product information.

```
<appSettings>
   <add key="ProductCatalog" value="myXmlFileName.xml" />
</appSettings>
```

Using custom settings in this way allows you to create a central repository for application values that could change and shouldn't be embedded directly inside page code. It's similar to using an .ini file or the Windows registry, but it's easier to modify from another computer on the network, and it supports dynamic updates.

The other settings are all located under the <system.web> tag. These include various options that allow you to configure ASP.NET security, tracing, error handling, state management, and much more. Taken together, they represent the heart of ASP.NET configuration.

The following listing shows the hierarchy of <system.web> tags. The rest of the chapter will consider each of these sections, in alphabetical order. For best readability, this listing doesn't include any of the closing tags, except for the root <configuration> and <system.web> elements. It's meant to provide an at-a-glance overview.

```
<configuration>
   <system.web>
```

```
<authentication>
   <forms>
      <credentials>
   <passport>
<authorization>
   <allow>
   <deny>
<browserCaps>
   <result>
   <use>
   <filter>
      <case>
<compilation>
   <compilers>
      <compiler>
   <assemblies>
      <add>
      <remove>
      <clear>
<customErrors>
   <error>
<globalization>
<httpHandlers>
   <add>
   <remove>
   <clear>
<httpModules>
   <add>
   <remove>
   <clear>
<httpRuntime>
<identity>
<machineKey>
<pages>
<processModel>
<securityPolicy>
   <trustLevel>
<sessionState>
<trace>
<trust>
<webServices>
   <protocols>
      <add>
```

```
            <remove>
            <clear>
         <serviceDescriptionFormatExtensionTypes>
            <add>
            <remove>
            <clear>
         <soapExtensionTypes>
            <add>
         <soapExtensionReflectorTypes>
            <add>
         <soapExtensionImporterTypes>
            <add>
         <WsdlHelpGenerator>

   </system.web>
</configuration>
```

## <authentication>

This section allows you to configure the type of mechanism used to authenticate a user. Authentication is the process whereby your application verifies that a user is who he or she claims to be. These settings work in conjunction with the <authorization> section settings, which specify the permissions and restrictions for a specific user or user type, and the IIS security settings, which take effect before the request is processed by the ASP.NET application. The interactions between these different layers of security are a common source of confusion for new web developers, and are described in detail in Chapter 24.

```
<authentication mode="Windows|Forms|Passport|None">
   <forms name="name"
          loginUrl="url"
          protection="All|None|Encryption|Validation"
          timeout="30" path="/" >
      <credentials passwordFormat="Clear|SHA1|MD5">
         <user name="username" password="password" />
      </credentials>
   </forms>
   <passport redirectUrl="internal"/>
</authentication>
```

The <authentication> tag identifies the type of authorization. There are four supported options.

| Attribute Setting | Description |
|---|---|
| Mode="Windows" | Windows authentication is typically used in one of two ways. You can use it and configure IIS to allow anonymous access to all users. This option is similar to previous ASP applications, and not much different from setting the ASP.NET authentication mode to "None."<br><br>Alternatively, you can configure IIS to use Basic, Digest, or Integrated Windows authentication (NTLM/Kerberos), or certificates to authenticate each user. This system is typically best in an intranet (network) scenario with a limited set of known users, rather than a public web application. |
| Mode="Forms" | Forms authentication allows you to use a custom login page with your own authentication code. ASP.NET handles the underlying security management, automatically maintaining a cookie that tracks whether the user has been logged in, and automatically rerouting the user to your login page if the cookie is not present or is expired. |
| Mode="Passport" | Passport authentication uses Microsoft's Passport authentication service. It's similar to Forms authentication in that the user needs to sign in at a dedicated login page (although newer versions of Windows can perform this step automatically) and is tracked using a cookie. However, you do not handle any aspect of the login process. |
| Mode="None" | No authentication. All users are allowed, although you could secure specific pages with your own authentication code. |

**Table 28-1.** *<authentication> Attributes*

If you are using Forms authentication, the <forms> tag provides several additional customization options.

The <forms> tag also has a <credentials> subtag used to store the login information for users. You don't need to store user information here. For example, you could use database-based authentication in your custom login page, which would be better suited to handle a large number of users or track additional user information (such as credit card number or home address).

| Attribute Setting | Description |
|---|---|
| Name | The name of the HTTP cookie to use for authentication. (By default, the value of name is .ASPXAUTH.) If multiple applications are running on the same web server and each application requires a unique cookie, you must configure the cookie name in each application's Web.config file. Otherwise, you can use the default. |
| loginUrl | Your custom login page, where the user is redirected if no valid authentication cookie is found. The default value is default.aspx. |
| protection="All" | The application uses both data validation and encryption to protect the forms authentication cookie. This option uses the configured data validation algorithm and Triple-DES or DES for encryption. This is the default (and recommended) value. |
| protection="None" | Encryption and validation are disabled for the cookie. This is much less secure (but potentially faster) and is typically only used if you use authentication for simple personalization. |
| protection="Encryption" | The cookie will be encrypted using Triple-DES or DES, but data validation is not performed on the cookie. |
| protection="Validation" | Validation is used to verify that the contents of an encrypted cookie have not been altered in transit. |
| timeout | An integer that specifies the number of minutes before the cookie expires, if no page requests have been received. ASP.NET will refresh the cookie when it receives a request, as long as half of the cookie's lifetime has expired. The default value is 30. |
| Path | The path for cookies issued by the application. The default value (\) is recommended, because most browsers are case-sensitive and a path case-mismatch could restrict the cookie from being sent with the request. |

**Table 28-2.** *<forms> Attributes*

| Attribute Setting | Description |
|---|---|
| passwordFormat="Clear" | Passwords are not encrypted. |
| passwordFormat="MD5" | Passwords are encrypted using the MD5 hash algorithm. |
| passwordFormat="SHA1" | Passwords are encrypted using the SHA1 hash algorithm. |

**Table 28-3.** *<credentials> Attributes*

Add as many <user> attributes as you need, one for each separate login ID.

| Attribute Setting | Description |
|---|---|
| Name | The account's user name. |
| password | The account's password. |

**Table 28-4.** *<user> Attributes*

If you are using Passport authentication, you can configure the <passport> subtag of the <authentication> tag.

| Attribute Setting | Description |
|---|---|
| redirectUrl | The web page where the user is redirected to if the user requires authentication and has not signed on with Microsoft Passport. This could be a specially configured page on your site or the Passport site. |
| redirectUrl="internal" | Using the word "internal" indicates that you have the Passport service installed on your server, and allows ASP.NET to use it for user authentication automatically. If it has not been configured and the user is not already logged in, an error message will be shown. |

**Table 28-5.** *<passport> Attributes*

## <authorization>

The <authorization> group is a list of access rules that either allow or deny a particular type of user. At runtime, ASP.NET searches through the list of <authorization> elements from top to bottom, until it can match the currently authenticated user with a suitable access rule. If there is more than one match, ASP.NET examines them all, and gives precedence to the most specific rules. That means that a specific reference to a user takes precedence over any applicable role-based rule, and any rule that uses a wildcard. If it can't find any match, it will allow access to the requested resource, as the default authorization in the machine.config file is set to <allow users="*"/> (unless you modify it). ASP.NET will read this rule last, and assign it lowest precedence because it uses the * wildcard.

```
<authorization>
   <allow users="list of users"
          roles="list of roles"
          verbs="list of verbs" />
   <deny users="list of users"
         roles="list of roles"
         verbs="list of verbs" />
</authorization>
```

The asterisk (*) is a wildcard that means "all users." The question mark (?) is a wildcard that means "all anonymous users." Thus, a simple way to force users to log in with the specified authentication service is to add a single deny rule for anonymous users. To allow only a certain type of user, add an <allow> rule followed by <deny users="*" /> to deny all other users. There are also more complicated options to allow or deny certain users, which are discussed in Chapter 24 along with some specific examples.

| Attribute Setting | Description |
|---|---|
| users | A comma-separated list of user names that are allowed/denied access to the resource. |
| roles | A comma-separated list of roles that are allowed/denied access to the resource. |
| verbs | A comma-separated list of HTTP transmission methods that are allowed/denied access to the resource. Verbs registered to ASP.NET include GET, HEAD, POST, and DEBUG. |

**Table 28-6.** *<allow> and <deny> Attributes*

## <browserCaps>

This section replaces the browscap.ini file from traditional ASP programming. It specifies the set of default browser capabilities that will be assumed if ASP.NET cannot detect the client browser's capabilities. This is becoming a fairly unusual event, but can still occur for unknown or unsupported types of browsers. These default values will be returned by the HttpBrowserCapabilities class (which is exposed as the Request.Browser property of a web page).

```
<browserCaps>
   <result type="System.Web.HttpBrowserCapabilities, System.Web" />
   <use var="HTTP_USER_AGENT" />
        browser=Unknown
        version=0.0
        majorver=0
        minorver=0
        frames=false
        tables=false
    <filter>
        <case match="[regular expression]"
         with="[regular expression]" >
           browser=Unknown
           version=0.0
           majorver=0
           minorver=0
           frames=false
           tables=false
        </case>
    </filter>
</browserCaps>
```

The <use> subtag identifies the various default settings, which are fairly self-evident. The <result> subtag identifies the ASP.NET class where the resulting information will be stored and made available to your application, and should never need to be changed. In addition, you can use <filter> subtags as an advanced option to try and identify unknown browsers. Each <filter> subtag specifies a regular expression, which ASP.NET will use to interpret the browser's User-Agent string in order to try and "guess" what type of browser sent the request and apply additional settings. This option is tricky and rarely used.

## <compilation>

This section specifies the compile options for ASP.NET applications, and should be configured at the machine.config level, rather than in individual web.config files. These options are less important if you are using Visual Studio .NET, which can set its own command-line options for compilation according to the project settings. Typically, you won't modify this section yourself.

```
<compilation debug="true|false"
             defaultLanguage="language"
             explicit="true|false"
             strict="true|false"
             tempDirectory="directory for temporary files" >
   <compilers>
      <compiler language="language"
                extension="ext"
                type=".NET Type"
                warningLevel="number"
                compilerOptions="options" />
   </compilers>
   <assemblies>
      <add assembly="assembly" />
      <remove assembly="assembly"  />
      <clear />
   </assemblies>
</compilation>
```

The <compilation> tag specifies some basic compilation options. A few low-level settings have been omitted.

The <compilers> tag specifies the individual compilers used for each supported .NET language, what types of files they are responsible for, and what additional options are required. This section is configured at install time and shouldn't need to be changed. However, it's interesting to note that the language compiler is just another .NET class—meaning that the ASP.NET engine can easily handle other .NET-compatible languages, as long as they ship with suitable compiler classes.

In the case of Visual Basic, the Microsoft.VisualBasic.VBCodeProvider class is used.

```
<compiler language="vb;vbs;visualbasic;vbscript"
          extension=".vb"
          type="Microsoft.VisualBasic.VBCodeProvider,
                System, Version=1.0.3300.0,
                Culture=neutral, PublicKeyToken=b77a5c561934e089"/>
```

The <assemblies> tag references assemblies that will be required when compiling an ASP.NET page. You can also precompile your code-behind files, and reference additional assemblies at compilation time as command-line parameters, as explained in Chapter 5.

| Attribute Setting | Description |
|---|---|
| Debug | When set to True, debug symbols will be generated for testing your application in every compilation. The default is False, which is required for respectable performance. Visual Studio .NET, which allows you to test your application with a precompiled code-behind class, circumvents this setting. |
| DefaultLanguage | The default programming language, which is defined in an appropriate <compiler> subtag. The default is vb. |
| Explicit | Indicates the default setting of Option Explicit in Visual Basic. The default is True, which forces you to declare all variables before using them. |
| Strict | Indicates the setting of the Option Strict option for Visual Basic, which is False by default. You can override this in your code-behind files with the Option Strict statement and provide enhanced type safety. |
| TempDirectory | The directory used for temporary file storage during compilation. |

**Table 28-7.** *<compilation> Attributes*

## <customErrors>

This section (described in Chapter 11) allows you to configure how ASP.NET deals with errors. Depending on your settings, ASP.NET may report detailed error information, or it may redirect the user to a web page that contains a custom error message (and any other support information). Possible errors include unhandled application exceptions in your web page code and HTTP server errors. You can supplement these settings by configuring IIS error redirect settings, which will take effect for web server errors that aren't handled by ASP.NET (such as a user request for an .html page that does not exist).

```
<customErrors defaultRedirect="url"
              mode="On|Off|RemoteOnly">
   <error statusCode="statuscode"
          redirect="url"/>
</customErrors>
```

The <customErrors> tag configures the error mode and specifies the default behavior for unhandled exceptions.

| Attribute Setting | Description |
|---|---|
| defaultRedirect | Specifies the default web page that will be shown if an error occurs. If defaultRedirect is not specified, an ASP.NET-generated error page is shown instead. |
| mode="On" | Custom errors are enabled. If an error occurs, and no defaultRedirect page is specified, users will see a generic error page. |
| mode="Off" | Custom errors are disabled. If an error occurs, and no defaultRedirect page is specified, users will see a detailed error page with diagnostic information about the code where the problem occurred. |
| mode="RemoteOnly" | Custom errors are only shown to remote clients. If an error occurs when serving a local request, the rich error page is used. This option, which helps when debugging locally, is the default. |

**Table 28-8.** *<customErrors> Attributes*

You can also add as many <error> subtags as needed. Each <error> tag specifically identifies an HTTP server error, and a custom error page that will be used if it occurs.

| Attribute Setting | Description |
|---|---|
| statusCode | The HTTP error code that will cause redirection. |
| redirect | The custom error page that will be used for this HTTP error. |

**Table 28-9.** *<error> Attributes*

## <globalization>

The settings in this section allow you to configure culture and encoding options for multiple client languages. Strictly speaking, these settings do not need to be defined. Without them, the default machine.config file settings will be used, and any property that is not declared there will be set according to the server's regional settings (check the Regional and Language Options settings in the Control Panel).

```
<globalization requestEncoding="any valid encoding string"
               responseEncoding="any valid encoding string"
               fileEncoding="any valid encoding string"
               culture="any valid culture string"
               uiCulture="any valid culture string" />
```

Fine-tuning globalization settings is beyond the scope of this book. However, if you've programmed multi-lingual sites before, you'll already be familiar with the culture and encoding strings. The only difference is the location where you configure these settings.

## <httpHandlers>

This section allows you to map incoming URL requests to the specific classes that can handle them. These settings are similar to the file mapping in IIS, but they take effect later. When IIS receives a request, it first checks it against its list of registered file mappings (which is configured in IIS Manager). If the extension is mapped to aspnet_isapi.dll, IIS passes the request to ASP.NET, which then checks the file type against its list of recognized HttpHandlers.

```
<httpHandlers>
   <add verb="verb list"
        path="path/wildcard"
        type="type,assemblyname"
        validate="" />
   <remove verb="verb list"
           path="path/wildcard" />
   <clear />
</httpHandlers>
```

The machine.config configures several default HttpHandlers. A short list of some of the most important ones is shown here.

```
<httpHandlers>
   <add verb="*" path="trace.axd"
```

```
     type="System.Web.Handlers.TraceHandler"/>
    <add verb="*" path="*.aspx"
     type="System.Web.UI.PageHandlerFactory"/>
    <add verb="*" path="*.asmx"
     type="System.Web.Services.Protocols.WebServiceHandlerFactory,
     System.Web.Services, Version=1.0.3300.0, Culture=neutral,
     PublicKeyToken=b03f5f7f11d50a3a" validate="false"/>
    <add verb="*" path="*.config"
     type="System.Web.HttpForbiddenHandler"/>
    <add verb="*" path="*.vb"
     type="System.Web.HttpForbiddenHandler"/>
</httpHandlers>
```

As you can see, file types are mapped to .NET classes. (You won't actually see these classes in the class library reference, however, as they are marked private and hidden by default, because they can't be used in an application.) For example, all .aspx files are processed by the System.Web.UI.PageHandlerFactory, which transforms them into the familiar System.Web.UI.Page classes (a "factory" is object-oriented lingo for a class that produces other classes). Similarly, System.Web.Services.Protocols.WebServiceHandler-Factory handles Web Service requests, and various forbidden files, such as .config and .vb, are handled by the System.Web.HttpForbiddenHandler, which does little more than refuse the request.

If you want, you can create your own HttpHandler classes by implementing the System.Web.IHttpHandler interface, and use them to create simple CGI-like applications. Custom HttpHandlers are useful in some situations where you don't need ASP.NET's web page model—for example, if you just need a mechanism to let clients retrieve a dynamically modified binary file. However, for most programmers this effort isn't worthwhile and seems like a giant step backward to the old world of Internet programming.

| Attribute Setting | Description |
|---|---|
| verb | Either a comma-separated list of HTTP verbs (for example, "GET, PUT, POST") or an asterisk (*) to represent all. |
| path | Either a single URL path or a simple wildcard string (like "*.aspx"). |

**Table 28-10.** *<add> and <remove> Attributes*

| Attribute Setting | Description |
|---|---|
| type | A comma-separated combination of the class followed by the assembly. ASP.NET searches for the assembly DLL first in the application's private \bin directory and then in the system assembly cache. You can use unmanaged DLLs to replicate file mapping functionality like that in the IIS Manager settings, but it isn't recommended. |
| validate | If set to False, ASP.NET will not attempt to load the class until it receives a request for the registered file type, which can improve startup time (but may hide possible errors until later). |

**Table 28-10.** *<add> and <remove> Attributes (continued)*

## <httpModules>

This section allows you to configure HttpModules, special classes that will be automatically loaded and made available for each request. ASP.NET uses modules to provide support for security, caching, and session state management.

```
<httpModules>
   <add type="classname,assemblyname" name="modulename" />
   <remove name="modulename" />
   <clear />
</httpModules>
```

The machine.config file defines the basic set of HttpModules.

```
<httpModules>
   <add name="OutputCache"
        type="System.Web.Caching.OutputCacheModule"/>
   <add name="Session"
        type="System.Web.SessionState.SessionStateModule"/>
   <add name="WindowsAuthentication"
        type="System.Web.Security.WindowsAuthenticationModule"/>
   <add name="FormsAuthentication"
        type="System.Web.Security.FormsAuthenticationModule"/>
   <add name="PassportAuthentication"
```

```
        type="System.Web.Security.PassportAuthenticationModule"/>
    <add name="UrlAuthorization"
        type="System.Web.Security.UrlAuthorizationModule"/>
    <add name="FileAuthorization"
        type="System.Web.Security.FileAuthorizationModule"/>
</httpModules>
```

You can create your own modules by writing classes that implement the System.Web.IHttpModule interface. This could be a highly advanced technique to create a special security, caching, or authentication service that works at a lower level than a typical ASP.NET application.

| Attribute Setting | Description |
|---|---|
| name | Provides a "friendly name" for the module. This is the name that will be used for the event handlers in the global.asax file. |
| type | A comma-separated combination of the class, followed by the assembly. ASP.NET searches for the assembly DLL first in the application's private \bin directory and then in the system assembly cache. |

**Table 28-11.** *<add> or <remove> Attributes*

## <httpRuntime>

This section configures some miscellaneous HTTP runtime settings. These are similar to the ASP settings that are configured through IIS Manager (for example, they set the maximum number of requests and request timeout).

| Attribute Setting | Description |
|---|---|
| appRequestQueueLimit | Sets the maximum number of requests that ASP.NET will queue at a time. When the limit is reached, incoming requests will be rejected with a "503 – Server Too Busy" error. |

**Table 28-12.** *<httpRuntime> Attributes*

| Attribute Setting | Description |
|---|---|
| executionTimeout | Sets the maximum number of seconds that a request is allowed before ASP.NET shuts it down automatically. |
| maxRequestLength | Sets the maximum size for uploaded files. This is an important factor when using the HtmlInputFile control (as described in Chapter 16). You should not set this limit too high, however, or it will expose you to possible denial-of-service attacks. |
| minFreeLocalRequest-FreeThreads | The minimum number of free threads ASP.NET reserves (keeps available) for requests from the local computer. |
| minFreeThreads | ASP.NET will keep this many threads free for current requests that require additional threads to complete their processing. |
| useFullyQualified-RedirectUrl | Specifies if URL redirects are fully qualified (which is necessary for some mobile controls). Relative redirects are the default. |

**Table 28-12.** *<httpRuntime> Attributes (continued)*

## <identity>

You can use this section to specify a Windows user account under which your code will run. If you do *not* enable impersonation, ASP.NET code will automatically run under the local system process account, which tends to have full access to everything. Generally, impersonation is enabled so the programmer can avoid dealing with authentication and authorization issues in code. Instead, when impersonation is enabled, the operating system will permit or restrict access to certain resources (such as files) based on the authenticated IIS user account. Note that even when impersonation is enabled, the local system process account will still be used to compile the code and create the cached pages. Only the application code will execute under the impersonated account. However, as a bare minimum, an account requires read/write access to the "Temporary ASP.NET files" directory where the compiled ASP.NET files are stored, or it will not be able to run any pages.

You have two options with the <identity> section: configuring all users to run under a single specified user account or allowing each user to run under his or her specific account. Note that this is separate from the application's trust level, which effectively sets the maximum permissions that any user will have in an ASP.NET application.

```
<identity impersonate="true|false"
          userName="username"
          password="password"/>
```

| Attribute Setting | Description |
|---|---|
| impersonate | When True, ASP.NET will run under the identity provided by IIS. This could be a user-specific account or a generic anonymous user (typically IUSR_[servername] as in traditional ASP). When set to False, impersonation is not used, and the typical ASP.NET system account is used to execute requests. |
| username and password | When impersonate is set to True, you can override the IIS identity by specifying a user name and password. |

**Table 28-13.** *<identity> Attributes*

## <machineKey>

ASP.NET uses a machine-specific key to encode some data (such as the forms authentication cookie and viewstate data) so that it can only be accessed from the server that created it.

```
<machineKey validationKey="autogenerate|value"
            decryptionKey="autogenerate|value"
            validation="SHA1|MD5|3DES" />
```

In general, you can allow ASP.NET to automatically generate these key values. However, this will thwart multi-server scenarios (such as a web farm) where one server might handle a request at one moment and another server will handle it later. In this case, you must manually set the same keys on all web servers.

| Attribute Setting | Description |
|---|---|
| validationKey | Specifies the key used to validate data. Can be a hard-coded string of 40–128 hexadecimal characters (the longer the better) or the value AutoGenerate, which indicates that ASP.NET will create it automatically (the default). |

**Table 28-14.** *<machineKey> Attributes*

| Attribute Setting | Description |
|---|---|
| decryptionKey | Specifies the key used to encrypt data. Can be a hard-coded string of 40–128 hexadecimal characters (the longer the better) or the value AutoGenerate, which indicates that ASP.NET will create it automatically (the default). |
| validation="SHA1" | ASP.NET will use SHA1 encryption. |
| validation="MD5" | ASP.NET will use MD5 encryption. |
| validation="3DES" | ASP.NET will use Triple-DES (3DES) encryption. When 3DES is selected, forms authentication defaults to SHA1, and viewstate validation uses 3DES encryption. |

**Table 28-14.** *<machineKey> Attributes (continued)*

## <pages>

This section allows you to configure some miscellaneous settings that determine how pages are created and served.

```
<pages buffer="true|false"
       enableSessionState="true|false|ReadOnly"
       enableViewState="true|false"
       enableViewStateMac="true|false"
       autoEventWireup="true|false"
       smartNavigation="true|false"
       pageBaseType="typename, assembly"
       userControlBaseType="typename" />
```

| Attribute Setting | Description |
|---|---|
| buffer | When a response is buffered, transmission of the page to the client won't be initiated until the page is completely rendered. This is the default. |
| enableSessionState | Enables or disables session state. |

**Table 28-15.** *<pages> Attributes*

| Attribute Setting | Description |
|---|---|
| ReadOnly | If True, web pages can read, but not modify, session state variables. |
| enableViewState | Enables or disables viewstate, which allows controls to store their state across postbacks using a special hidden field. As a more flexible option, you can allow viewstate (the default) but disable viewstate use for specific controls on a specific web page. |
| pageBaseType | A code-behind class that web forms (.aspx pages) derive from automatically. By default, this is System.Web.UI.Page. |
| userControlBaseType | A code-behind class that user controls (.ascx files) derive from automatically. By default, this is System.Web.UI.UserControl. |
| autoEventWireup | When set to True, can connect web page events automatically (without the need for a Handles clause). This can also be configured using a page-level directive, as explained in Chapter 5. |

**Table 28-15.** *<pages> Attributes (continued)*

## <processModel>

This section stores a number of low-level settings that govern how the ASP.NET service works, and should be entered at the machine.config file level. Advanced users could use these settings to configure optimum performance for a specific hardware setup, but the default options are usually best.

```
<processModel enable="true|false"
              timeout="mins"
              idleTimeout="mins"
              shutdownTimeout="hrs:mins:secs"
              requestLimit="num"
              requestQueueLimit="Infinite|num"
              restartQueueLimit="Infinite|num"
              memoryLimit="percent"
```

```
cpuMask="num"
webGarden="true|false"
userName="username"
password="password"
logLevel="All|None|Errors"
clientConnectedCheck="HH:MM:SS"
comAuthenticationLevel="Default|None|Connect|Call|
                        Pkt|PktIntegrity|PktPrivacy"
comImpersonationLevel="Default|Anonymous|Identify|
                       Impersonate|Delegate"
maxWorkerThreads="num"
maxIoThreads="num" />
```

Most of these settings are beyond the scope of any ordinary web application. The most important or interesting ones are documented in Table 28-16.

| Attribute Setting | Description |
|---|---|
| enable | Determines whether ASP.NET should run in a separate worker process (True, the default) or in-process with IIS (False). When set to False, all other settings are ignored, and your web applications may be slightly faster (although if one crashes, they may all be affected). |
| timeout | Determines how long the process will run before it is recycled (a new process is created and the old one terminated). The default valus is Infinite, although you can specify a time in the format HH:MM:SS. |
| idleTimeout | Similar to the timeout setting, but takes effect when the ASP.NET worker process is idle. The default is Infinite. |
| shutDownTimeout | This sets the amount of time the ASP.NET worker process is given to try and shut down gracefully before it is assumed to be "locked up," and the process is terminated. By default, this value is only five seconds. |

**Table 28-16.** *<processModel> Attributes*

| Attribute Setting | Description |
|---|---|
| requestLimit | Provides another way to support ASP.NET worker process recycling. For example, if you notice that the performance of ASP.NET degrades after about 10,000 requests, you can set this value to 10000. After 10,000 requests, a new process will be started to handle the new requests and the old process will be terminated. |
| requestQueueLimit | This allows the ASP.NET process to be recycled if a certain number of queued requests is detected. This could detect that a thread is blocked or unable to service requests because of an error. The default is a fairly generous 5,000 queued requests. |
| memoryLimit | This provides automatic memory recycling if too much memory is used. The default value of 60 isn't a value in megabytes, but a percentage of the total system memory. Memory "leaks" are almost impossible with managed .NET code, but could still be a problem if you are using legacy COM components that don't properly clean up after themselves. |
| userName and Password | Can be used to specify the system account (and hence the security permissions and restrictions) that the ASP.NET worker process runs under. The default is the local system process account. |
| logLevel | Configures how ASP.NET logs events. The default is Errors, which only records information about errors that occur. All entries are written to the Windows event log, which was explained in Chapter 11. |
| clientConnectedCheck | Allows you to configure how often ASP.NET checks if the client is still connected. For example, during a long-running task the client might hit the Refresh button to start a new request, but leave the current request processing. ASP.NET can save some effort by detecting that these requests have been abandoned and then aborting the unnecessary work. By default, ASP.NET will check every five seconds. |

**Table 28-16.** *<processModel> Attributes (continued)*

## <securityPolicy>

This section maps named security levels to specific policy files. These definitions can then be used in other sections. For example, the <trust> section specifies the code access security level for your ASP.NET code by referring to one of the defined trust levels in the <securityPolicy> section.

```
<securityPolicy>
   <trustLevel name="value" policyFile="value" />
</securityPolicy>
```

By default the machine.config file defines four levels of authorization, named Full, High, Low, and None. Each option is mapped to a security policy file (except for Full).

```
<securityPolicy>
   <trustLevel name="Full" policyFile="internal"/>
   <trustLevel name="High" policyFile="web_hightrust.config"/>
   <trustLevel name="Low" policyFile="web_lowtrust.config"/>
   <trustLevel name="None" policyFile="web_notrust.config"/>
</securityPolicy>
```

These files provide an extensive set of options and are also found in the Config directory. You can create your own security configuration files and define your own <trustLevel> tags.

| Attribute Setting | Description |
|---|---|
| name | The name of the security level. |
| policyFile | The security policy file that contains the settings for this security level. |

**Table 28-17.** *<trustLevel> Attributes*

## <sessionState>

This section configures how session state information will be stored. There are typically two reasons for modifying the default values in this section—to provide a longer or shorter session timeout, or to configure a different session state management method in order to support a web farm setup.

```
<sessionState mode="Off|Inproc|StateServer|SQLServer"
              cookieless="true|false"
              timeout="number of minutes"
              stateConnectionString="tcpip=server:port"
              sqlConnectionString="sql connection string" />
```

Session state management is explored in Chapter 10, along with some common-sense advice about how to use it. Be aware that in order to enable a different type of session management, you may need to perform a few extra steps beyond just modifying the appropriate web.config file. These steps are described in Chapter 10.

| Attribute Setting | Description |
|---|---|
| mode="Off" | Session state is not enabled. |
| mode="Inproc" | Session state is stored on the web server in the same process as the ASP.NET worker threads. This provides the best performance by far and is the default setting. |
| mode="StateServer" | Session state is out-of-process and maintained by a dedicated service. This service can be hosted on any server, which allows multiple servers in a web farm to access the same session collection for a client. |
| mode="SQLServer" | Session state is stored in a temporary SQL Server database. This also allows multiple servers to access the same session state collection, and allows session state information to persist even after server restarts. |
| cookieless | When set to False (the default), a cookie is automatically used to track a client session. When True, munged URLs are used to encode the session ID in web links. |
| timeout | The number of minutes a session can be idle before it is abandoned (that is, the maximum amount of time that can be taken between client requests without losing session data). The default is 20 minutes. |

**Table 28-18.** *<sessionState> Attributes*

| Attribute Setting | Description |
|---|---|
| stateConnectionString | When StateServer mode is used, this attribute specifies the server name and port where session state is stored (such as "tcpip=127.0.0.1:42424"). |
| sqlConnectionString | When SQLServer mode is used, this attribute specifies the database connection string (such as "data source= 127.0.0.1;user id=sa"). |

**Table 28-18.** *<sessionState> Attributes (continued)*

## <trace>

This section configures tracing, which is useful when debugging and testing an application. When tracing is enabled, a long list of diagnostic information about a web page request is recorded.

```
<trace enabled="true|false"
       localOnly="true|false"
       pageOutput="true|false"
       requestLimit="integer"
       traceMode="SortByTime|SortByCategory" />
```

Tracing can be used in two ways: with output shown on every page or with output available through a special web page. Tracing is explored in Chapter 11.

| Attribute Setting | Description |
|---|---|
| enabled | Specifies whether tracing is enabled for an application. The default is False. |
| localOnly | True if tracing information is only available on the host web server (the default). When set to False, you can use remote tracing to debug or profile a deployed application. |

**Table 28-19.** *<trace> Attributes*

| Attribute Setting | Description |
|---|---|
| pageOutput | True if tracing output is appended to each page. False if tracing information is only available through the trace utility (which is accessed by requesting trace.axd). |
| requestLimit | The number of trace requests to store on the server at any one time. The default is 10. |
| traceMode= "SortByTime" | Trace information is displayed in the order it is processed. This is the default. |
| traceMode= "SortByCategory" | Trace information is displayed alphabetically by user-defined category. |

**Table 28-19.** *<trace> Attributes (continued)*

## <trust>

This section configures the code-access security level for a web application. This determines the trust level under which your code will run. For example, if you limit the trust level for your code, certain operations (such as deleting files or interacting with the system) may not be allowed.

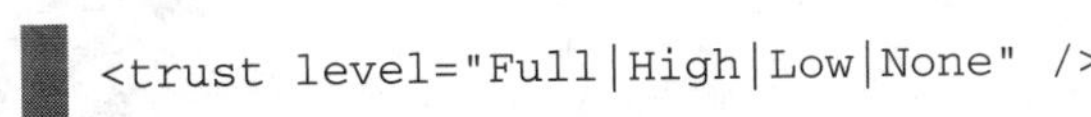

```
<trust level="Full|High|Low|None" />
```

By default, application code has Full trust level, and the operations of your code are not checked against any security policy settings.

| Attribute Setting | Description |
|---|---|
| level="Full" | The Full level is the only level that does not use any security policy file to apply limitations. |
| level= "High\|Low\|None" | These three options refer to the security levels defined in the <trustLevel> subtag in the <securityPolicy> section. For example, level="High" would apply the security restrictions from the "High" level policy file. |

**Table 28-20.** *<trust> Attributes*

## <webServices>

This section configures Web Service settings, such as the type of supported transmission protocols and the classes that provide various pieces of Web Service functionality. These settings are defined at the machine.config level and should not be modified.

The sole exception is the <WsdlHelpGenerator> subtag, which allows you to specify a custom page to use for the Internet Explorer Web Service test page.

```
<wsdlHelpGenerator href="DefaultWsdlHelpGenerator.aspx"/>
```

To create a custom version of this file, copy the standard DefaultWsdlHelpGenerator.aspx file (which is found in the Config directory along with the machine.config file), and modify the appropriate settings. For example, you could configure this page to use a special logo or header that represents your company by adding custom HTML or ASP.NET controls.

# Index

## Symbols



## A

## B



## C

## D

## E

## F

## G



## H

## I

## J



## K



## L

## P

## Q

## R

## S

## T

## V

## W

## X

## INTERNATIONAL CONTACT INFORMATION

**AUSTRALIA**
McGraw-Hill Book Company Australia Pty. Ltd.
TEL +61-2-9417-9899
FAX +61-2-9417-5687
http://www.mcgraw-hill.com.au
books-it_sydney@mcgraw-hill.com

**CANADA**
McGraw-Hill Ryerson Ltd.
TEL +905-430-5000
FAX +905-430-5020
http://www.mcgrawhill.ca

**GREECE, MIDDLE EAST, NORTHERN AFRICA**
McGraw-Hill Hellas
TEL +30-1-656-0990-3-4
FAX +30-1-654-5525

**MEXICO (Also serving Latin America)**
McGraw-Hill Interamericana Editores S.A. de C.V.
TEL +525-117-1583
FAX +525-117-1589
http://www.mcgraw-hill.com.mx
fernando_castellanos@mcgraw-hill.com

**SINGAPORE (Serving Asia)**
McGraw-Hill Book Company
TEL +65-863-1580
FAX +65-862-3354
http://www.mcgraw-hill.com.sg
mghasia@mcgraw-hill.com

**SOUTH AFRICA**
McGraw-Hill South Africa
TEL +27-11-622-7512
FAX +27-11-622-9045
robyn_swanepoel@mcgraw-hill.com

**UNITED KINGDOM & EUROPE (Excluding Southern Europe)**
McGraw-Hill Education Europe
TEL +44-1-628-502500
FAX +44-1-628-770224
http://www.mcgraw-hill.co.uk
computing_neurope@mcgraw-hill.com

**ALL OTHER INQUIRIES Contact:**
Osborne/McGraw-Hill
TEL +1-510-549-6600
FAX +1-510-883-7600
http://www.osborne.com
omg_international@mcgraw-hill.com